WHERE DO YOU WANT TO GO?

→ Do you want the best learning experience you've ever had?

→ Do you want to leave this course with practical, bankable skills?

→ Do you want all the advantages you'll need to enter professional life?

If the answer is yes to any of the above, then this new Second Edition of MANAGERIAL ACCOUNTING will take you there!

◆ WHY HOT AIR BALLOONS ON THE COVER?

The hot air balloons on the cover of the Second Edition represent an important idea—the quality of the journey is as important as the final destination.

◆ A FAST CAR CAN ACCELERATE FROM ZERO TO SIXTY IN TEN SECONDS...

... leaving you painfully pressed against your seat. MANAGERIAL ACCOUNTING by contrast starts your journey with a gentle lift, presenting the fundamental concepts of managerial accounting in an easy-to-understand fashion:

→ Carefully-paced and stepped-out explanations break the difficult or complicated processes down into manageable, understandable steps

→ MANAGERIAL ACCOUNTING sticks to the concepts you need, providing a series of examples and frequent illustrations

◆ ON A BUS OR TRAIN, YOU SIMPLY SIT THERE...

... while in a hot air balloon, passengers often actively participate in the flight. MANAGERIAL ACCOUNTING provides you with continual opportunities for hands-on learning:

◆ A New Interactive CD will show you clearly how to study, what to study, and why you study. It includes interactive Self-Tests, Key Terms Matching Activities, a Writing Handbook, an Accounting Cycle Tutorial, and Career Information.

◆ A New Companion Website includes problems from the text, Additional Demonstration Problems, Interactive Self- Study Questions, Exploring the Web Exercises and more

◆ THE VIEW OUT THE WINDOW OF A CAR, A PLANE, OR A TRAIN CAN BE PRETTY LIMITED...

... but the view from a hot air balloon is 360 degrees of breathtaking scenery! Weygandt, Kieso, and Kimmel believe that it is vital that you see managerial accounting's relevance to your future career.

→ The authors use financial information and accounting practices of real companies like Starbucks, Microsoft, Ben & Jerry's, and Intel.

→ As you become acquainted with the financial successes and failures of these familiar companies, you can begin to follow business news more closely, making your learning a dynamic, ongoing process.

→ Many of the companies used as examples are service based, reflecting the shift toward service industries. This shift is emphasized by the Business Insight–Service Company Perspective feature.

◆ PLUS, YOU GET ALL THE ROADSIDE ASSISTANCE YOU NEED!

The Interactive CD and the website mentioned above will give you a world of backup and assistance as you go through the course. In addition, a Student Owner's Manual begins the text. This walk-through of the text will help you understand how the text works and how to use the various built-in learning tools you'll encounter. Plus, a variety of other helpful tools are available to you:

→ Solving Managerial Accounting Problems Using Excel

→ Solutions to Excel Problems

→ Checklist of Key Figures

→ Study Guide

→ Working Papers

→ Excel Working Papers

www.wiley.com/college/weygandt

MANAGERIAL ACCOUNTING

Tools for Business Decision Making

2ND EDITION

JERRY J. WEYGANDT PhD, CPA

Arthur Andersen Alumni Professor of Accounting
University of Wisconsin
Madison, Wisconsin

DONALD E. KIESO PhD, CPA

KPMG Peat Marwick Emeritus Professor of Accounting
Northern Illinois University
DeKalb, Illinois

PAUL D. KIMMEL PhD, CPA

Associate Professor of Accounting
University of Wisconsin—Milwaukee
Milwaukee, Wisconsin

JOHN WILEY & SONS, INC.

Dedicated to
our former students and our colleagues, past and present
and to
our wives, Enid, Donna, and Merlynn

PUBLISHER	*Susan Elbe*
EXECUTIVE EDITOR	*Jay O'Callaghan*
SENIOR DEVELOPMENT EDITOR	*Nancy Perry*
ASSISTANT EDITOR	*Ed Brislin*
SENIOR MARKETING MANAGER	*Clancy Marshall*
PRODUCTION SERVICES MANAGER	*Jeanine Furino*
NEW MEDIA EDITOR	*David Kear*
PRODUCTION COORDINATOR	*Elm Street Publishing Services, Inc.*
SENIOR DESIGNER	*Kevin Murphy*
PHOTO EDITOR	*Sara Wight*
ILLUSTRATION EDITOR	*Anna Melhorn*
ART STUDIO	*Precision Graphics*
COVER PHOTO	*Ron Behrmann/International Stock*

This book was set in New Aster by TechBooks and printed and bound by Von Hoffmann Press.
The cover was printed by Von Hoffmann Press.

This book is printed on acid-free paper.

The specimen financial statements in Appendix A are reprinted with permission from
the Tootsie Roll Industries, Inc. 1998 Annual Report. © Tootsie Roll Industries, Inc. The
specimen financial statements in Appendix B are reprinted with permission from the
Hershey Foods Corporation 1998 Consolidated Financial Statements and Management's
Discussion and Analysis. © Hershey Foods Corporation.

Library of Congress Cataloging-in-Publication Data

Weygandt, Jerry J.
   Managerial accounting: tools for business decision making/Jerry J. Weygandt, Donald
E. Kieso, Paul D. Kimmel.—2nd ed.
      p. cm.
   Includes bibliographical references.
   ISBN 0-471-41365-8 (cloth: alk. paper)
   1. Managerial accounting. I. Kieso, Donald E. II. Kimmel, Paul D. III. Title.

HF5657.4.W49 2001
658.15'11—dc21

                          2001045558

ISBN 0-471-41365-8

Printed in the United States of America

10 9 8 7 6 5 4 3 2 1

Jerry J. Weygandt, PhD, CPA, is Arthur Andersen Alumni Professor of Accounting at the University of Wisconsin-Madison. He holds a Ph.D. in accounting from the University of Illinois. Articles by Professor Weygandt have appeared in the *Accounting Review, Journal of Accounting Research, Accounting Horizons, Journal of Accountancy,* and other academic and professional journals. These articles have examined such financial reporting issues as accounting for price-level adjustments, pensions, convertible securities, stock option contracts, and interim reports. Professor Weygandt is author of other accounting and financial reporting books and is a member of the American Accounting Association, the American Institute of Certified Public Accountants, and the Wisconsin Society of Certified Public Accountants. He has served on numerous committees of the American Accounting Association and as a member of the editorial board of the *Accounting Review;* he also has served as President and Secretary-Treasurer of the American Accounting Association. In addition, he has been actively involved with the American Institute of Certified Public Accountants and has been a member of the Accounting Standards Executive Committee (AcSEC) of that organization. He has served on the FASB task force that examined the reporting issues related to accounting for income taxes and is presently a trustee of the Financial Accounting Foundation. Professor Weygandt has received the Chancellor's Award for Excellence in Teaching and the Beta Gamma Sigma Dean's Teaching Award. He is on the board of directors of M & I Bank of Southern Wisconsin and the Dean Foundation. He is the recipient of the Wisconsin Institute of CPA's Outstanding Educator's Award and the Lifetime Achievement Award. In 2001 he received the American Accounting Association's Outstanding Accounting Educator Award.

Donald E. Kieso, PhD, CPA, received his bachelor's degree from Aurora University and his doctorate in accounting from the University of Illinois. He has served as chairman of the Department of Accountancy and is currently the KPMG Peat Marwick Emeritus Professor of Accounting at Northern Illinois University. He has public accounting experience with Price Waterhouse & Co. (San Francisco and Chicago) and Arthur Andersen & Co. (Chicago) and research experience with the Research Division of the American Institute of Certified Public Accountants (New York). He has done postdoctorate work as a Visiting Scholar at the University of California at Berkeley and is a recipient of NIU's Teaching Excellence Award and four Golden Apple Teaching Awards. Professor Kieso is the author of other accounting and business books and is a member of the American Accounting Association, the American Institute of Certified Public Accountants, and the Illinois CPA Society. He has served as a member of the Board of Directors of the Illinois CPA Society, the AACSB's Accounting Accreditation Committees, the State of Illinois Comptroller's Commission, as Secretary-Treasurer of the Federation of Schools of Accountancy, and as Secretary-Treasurer of the American Accounting Association. Professor Kieso is currently serving on the Board of Trustees and Executive Committee of Aurora University, as a member of the Board of Directors of Castle BancGroup Inc., and as Treasurer and Director of Valley West Community Hospital. He served as a charter member of the national Accounting Education Change Commission. He is the recipient of the Outstanding Accounting Educator Award from the Illinois CPA Society, the FSA's Joseph A. Silvoso Award of Merit, the NIU Foundation's Humanitarian Award for Service to Higher Education, the Distinguished Service Award from the Illinois CPA Society, and the Community Citizen of the Year Award from Rotary International.

Paul D. Kimmel, PhD, CPA, received his bachelor's degree from the University of Minnesota and his doctorate in accounting from the University of Wisconsin. He is an Associate Professor at the University of Wisconsin-Milwaukee, and has public accounting experience with Deloitte & Touche (Minneapolis). He was the recipient of the UWM School of Business Advisory Council Teaching Award, the Reggie Taite Excellence in Teaching Award, and a three-time winner of the Outstanding Teaching Assistant Award at the University of Wisconsin. He is also a recipient of the Elijah Watts Sells Award for Honorary Distinction for his results on the CPA exam. He is a member of the American Accounting Association and has published articles in *Accounting Review, Accounting Horizons, Advances in Management Accounting, Managerial Finance, Issues in Accounting Education, Journal of Accounting Education,* as well as other journals. His research interests include accounting for financial instruments and innovation in accounting education. He has published papers and given numerous talks on incorporating critical thinking into accounting education, and helped prepare a catalog of critical thinking resources for the Federated Schools of Accountancy.

PREFACE

In this Second Edition of *Managerial Accounting: Tools for Business Decision Making,* we strove to build on those things that made the First Edition a success in the classroom. Our goals are straightforward: We want this book to present the fundamental concepts of managerial accounting in an easy-to-understand fashion. We want to present only those concepts that students need to know. And we want students to leave the course confident that they will be able to apply the basic decision skills that they learned in this course when they enter the workforce. As a result, as you read through the list of changes to this edition and review the text, the common theme you will notice is that these changes were made to simplify and clarify our presentation of basic concepts or to strengthen the students' decision-making skills. We are very excited about this edition of the text. As in the First Edition, our efforts were driven by the following key beliefs:

"Less is more."

Our instructional objective is to provide students with an understanding of those concepts that are fundamental to the use of managerial accounting. Most students will forget procedural details within a short period of time. On the other hand, concepts, if well taught, should be remembered for a lifetime. Concepts are especially important in a world where the details are constantly changing.

"Don't just sit there— do something."

Students learn best when they are actively engaged. The overriding pedagogical objective of this book is to provide students with continual opportunities for active learning. One of the best tools for active learning is strategically placed questions. Our discussions are framed by questions, often beginning with rhetorical questions and ending with review questions. Even our selection of analytical devices, called *Decision Tools,* is referenced using key questions to emphasize the purpose of each. In addition, technology offers many opportunities to enhance the learning environment. Through the use of interactive activities on our CD-ROM, as well as our Web site at http://www.wiley.com/college/weygandt, we offer many opportunities for active learning.

"I'll believe it when I see it."

Students will be most willing to commit time and energy to a topic when they believe that it is relevant to their future careers. There is no better way to demonstrate relevance than to ground discussion in the real world. By using high-profile companies like Starbucks, Microsoft, Ben & Jerry's, and Intel to frame our discussion of accounting issues, we demonstrate the relevance of accounting while teaching students about companies with which they are familiar. In addition, because the economy has shifted toward service industries, many of the companies used as examples are service based. This shift is emphasized by our *Business Insight—Service Company Perspective* feature, as well as references to service companies such as American Express, Federal Express, and Union Pacific Railroad.

"You'll need to make a decision."

All business people must make decisions. Decision making involves critical evaluation and analysis of the information at hand, and this takes practice. We have integrated important analytical tools throughout the book. After each new decision tool is presented, we summarize the key features of that tool in a *Decision Toolkit.* At the end of each chapter, the *Using the Decision Toolkit* activity provides a comprehensive demonstration of an analysis of a real-world problem using the decision tools presented in the chapter. The *Broadening Your Perspective* homework activities require the student to employ these decision tools. Finally, an exciting new feature, *Cases for Management Decision Making,* provided at the end of the text, requires students to employ decision-making skills in rich, realistic business settings.

KEY FEATURES OF EACH CHAPTER

Chapter 1, Managerial Accounting
- Compares and contrasts managerial accounting with financial accounting.
- Identifies three broad functions of management.
- Defines three classes of manufacturing costs.
- Distinguishes between product costs and period costs.
- Presents costs of goods manufactured section of income statement.
- Presents overview of trends in managerial accounting including shift toward service industries, value chain management, enterprise resource planning, just-in-time inventory, and activity-based costing.

Chapter 2, Job Order Cost Accounting
- Provides overview of cost accounting systems.
- Illustrates flow of costs in a job order cost system.
- Presents use of job cost sheet.
- Demonstrates use of predetermined overhead rate.
- Illustrates basic entries for job order cost system.
- Provides simple presentation of overapplied and underapplied overhead.

Chapter 3, Process Cost Accounting
- Explains the difference between job order and process costing systems.
- Illustrates the flow of costs and end-of-period accounting procedures for process costing.
- Demonstrates computation of physical units of production, equivalent units of production, and unit costs.
- Shows how to assign costs to units of output and prepare a production cost report.

Chapter 4, Activity-Based Costing
- Explains the need for activity-based costing (ABC).
- Contrasts ABC to traditional costing systems.
- Identifies numerous activities, activity cost pools, and cost drivers.
- Discusses implications of value-added and non-value added activities.
- Illustrates use of ABC in service industries.
- Reviews the benefits and limitations of ABC.
- Illustrates use of just-in-time inventory systems.
- Appendix discusses the implications of activity hierarchies levels.

Chapter 5, Cost-Volume-Profit Relationships
- Distinguishes between variable and fixed costs, and explains relevant range and mixed costs.
- Identifies components and assumptions of CVP analysis.
- Discusses concept of contribution margin.
- Illustrates calculation of break-even point.
- Discusses margin of safety and target net income.
- Illustrates CVP income statement.
- Appendix presents variable and absorption costing.

Chapter 6, Budgetary Planning
- Discusses benefits of budgeting.
- Illustrates the process of assembling information for a master budget.
- Prepares budgeted income statement, balance sheet, and cash budget.
- Discusses use of budgets in merchandising, service, and not-for-profit enterprises.

Chapter 7, Budgetary Control and Responsibility Accounting
- Explains how budgets are used to control costs and operations.
- Contrasts static budgets and flexible budgets.
- Uses a case study to illustrate usefulness of flexible budgets.
- Illustrates responsibility reporting systems.
- Defines cost centers, profit centers, and investment centers.
- Illustrates the computation and use of return on investment and (in a chapter appendix) residual income.

Chapter 8, Performance Evaluation Through Standard Costs
- Differentiates between a standard and a budget.
- Discusses advantages of standard costs and methods of computing.
- Illustrates computation of direct materials variance, direct labor variance, and manufacturing overhead variance.
- Demonstrates analysis through comparison of actual with standard.
- Appendix illustrates the journal entries for a standard cost system.

Chapter 9, Incremental Analysis
- Presents the concept of incremental analysis through a simple example.
- Explains the concepts of relevant cost, opportunity cost, and sunk cost.
- Applies incremental analysis in the following decision settings:
  - Accept an order at a special price
  - Make or buy
  - Sell or process further, including discussion of joint costs
  - Retain or replace equipment
  - Eliminate an unprofitable segment
- Reviews sales mix issues, including how to allocate limited resources across multiple products and how to determine break-even points with more than one product.

Chapter 10, Capital Budgeting
- Discusses nature of capital budgeting decisions.
- Describes and illustrates four methods of evaluating capital expenditures:
  - Cash payback technique
  - Net present value method
  - Internal rate of return method
  - Annual rate of return technique
- Discusses the profitability index, post audits, and the implications of intangible benefits when making capital budgeting decisions.

Chapter 11, Pricing Decisions

- Demonstrates how to compute target cost when a product's price is determined by the market.
- Illustrates how to compute target selling price using cost-plus pricing.
- Demonstrates how to use time and materials pricing when services are provided.
- Discusses the objective of transfer pricing.
- Illustrates how to determine a transfer price using the cost-based, market-based, and negotiated approaches.
- Explains the issues involved when goods are transferred between countries with different tax rates.

Chapter 12, The Statement of Cash Flows

- Discusses the purpose and usefulness of the statement of cash flows.
- Discusses the implications of the product life-cycle for analysis of the statement of cash flows.
- Illustrates preparation of the statement of cash flows using a two-year progression of transactions. Year 1 is basic transactions, and year 2 involves more advanced transactions. The presentation is designed to allow the instructor to focus exclusively on either the indirect approach or the direct approach, or to cover both.
- Presents ratio analysis of the statement of cash flows using free cash flow, capital expenditure ratio, current cash debt coverage, cash debt coverage, and cash return on sales.

Chapter 13, Financial Analysis: The Big Picture

- Provides a comprehensive discussion of analytical tools and their interrelationships.
- Discusses the concept of earning power and the presentation of irregular items: discontinued operations, extraordinary items, and cumulative effect of change in accounting principle.
- Includes a basic discussion of comprehensive income.
- Illustrates horizontal and vertical analysis.
- Provides thorough analysis of the actual financial statements of Kellogg Company using ratio analysis.

NEW IN THIS EDITION

The First Edition of *Managerial Accounting* was very well received. In the spirit of continuous improvement, we have made many changes in this Second Edition. The changes can be categorized into three types: Cases for Management Decision Making, Interactive CD-ROM and Web site, and changes to the text chapters.

Cases for Management Decision Making

Consistent with our objective of developing decision-making skills, we have added a series of cases to this edition of the text. These cases provide opportunities to use the decision tools presented in the chapters in a realistic business situation. The cases can be used as a comprehensive capstone activity at the end of the course, or as a recurring activity during the course. These activities are intended to be richer and more challenging than a traditional problem but are still targeted at the introductory-level student.

Interactive CD-ROM and Web Site

Technology offers many opportunities to enrich the learning environment. With this edition of the text we have expanded the materials provided on our Web site, as well as developed an interactive CD-ROM. These materials include the following:

Learning Techniques resources are designed to improve student study skills.
- Learning Styles Quiz
- Interactive Study Skills Chart

Course Materials reinforce materials covered in the text or provide resources to develop communication skills.
- Interactive Self-Test
- Key Term Matching Activity
- Accounting Cycle Tutorial
- Interactive Problems and Demonstration Problems
- Writing Handbook
- Surviving the Group Project

Career Paths provides resources about careers in accounting.
- Why Accounting Is Important
- Careers in Accounting
- Professional Profiles

KEY CHANGES IN EACH CHAPTER

Chapter 1, Managerial Accounting

- New Feature Story on Compaq Computer
- Revised and streamlined presentation on management functions
- New Business Insight on auto manufacturing productivity
- New Business Insight on managing the delivery of bananas
- Revised coverage of service industry trends, significantly revised illustrations
- New section on value chain management
- Two new e-Business Insights on computerized business infrastructures and computer-integrated manufacturing
- Revised exercises and problems

Chapter 2, Job Order Cost Accounting

- Clarified rationale for predetermined overhead rates
- New e-Business Insight on GM's Web-based order system
- New Business Insight on the use of microcomputers by small manufacturers
- New Business Insight on overhead in service companies
- Revised exercises and problems

Chapter 3, Process Cost Accounting

- Added a six-page appendix discussing and illustrating the FIFO method of computing equivalent units (as contrasted to the weighted average method covered in the chapter)

Chapter 4, Activity-Based Costing

- Moved "Activity-Based Costing in Service Industries" section from appendix into body of the chapter
- Moved section on hierarchy of activity levels from the body of the chapter into an appendix
- Revised the infographic on activities and related cost drivers to tie it more conceptually to the illustrations, and expanded the text explanation of the related illustrations
- New Business Insight on General Mills's efforts to eliminate nonvalue-added activities
- Revised exercises and problems

Chapter 5, Cost-Volume-Profit Relationships

- Added new section on CVP income statement, including illustrations of the statement with and without net income
- Revised the section on use of the mathematical equation in breakeven analysis
- Simplified the presentation of detailed CVP income statement
- Revised the Decision Toolkit to include the contribution margin ratio
- New Business Insight on efficiency in woodworking
- New e-Business Insight on flightserve.com
- New e-Business Insight on Internet business "conversion rates"
- New Business Insight on the use of computer graphics in "what if analysis"
- Revised exercises and problems

Chapter 6, Budgetary Planning

- Simplified long-range planning discussion
- New e-Business Insight on improving planning and budgeting
- Revised exercises and problems

Chapter 7, Budgetary Control and Responsibility Accounting

- Added new chapter appendix on "Residual Income—Another Performance Measurement" and related homework material
- New e-Business insight on enterprise application systems (EAS)
- Revised exercises and problems

Chapter 8, Performance Evaluation Through Standard Costs

- Added a new Before You Go On (Review It/Do It) following direct materials variances section
- Moved the Standard Cost Accounting System section with journal entries into a chapter appendix
- New e-Business Insight on computerized standard cost systems
- Revised exercises and problems

Chapter 9, Incremental Analysis

- Added joint-product presentation with illustrations in sell-or-process-further section, plus related homework materials
- Revised exercises and problems

Chapter 10, Capital Budgeting

- Added several new marginal Helpful Hints
- New e-Business Insight on General Electric's e-business related capital expenditures
- Revised exercises and problems

Chapter 11, Pricing Decisions

- Entirely new chapter consisting of two major pricing-decision parts: I. External sales (customer pricing), and II. Internal sales (transfer pricing).
- A chapter appendix discusses the absorption cost and the contribution approaches
- All new homework material
- A Comprehensive Problem covering Chapters 1–11 is provided on the CD-Rom that accompanies the text, as well as on the book's Web site.

Chapter 12, The Statement of Cash Flows (formerly Chapter 11)

- New Feature Story—"Cash is Cash, and Everything Else is Accounting"
- New section on the corporate life cycle
- New section on the meaning of the term "cash flows"
- New Business Insight on the corporate life cycle of specific companies
- New infographic drawings
- New Business Insight comparing "net income" to "net cash from operations"
- Revised exercises and problems

Chapter 13, Financial Analysis: The Big Picture (formerly Chapter 12)

- New Feature Story on the day-trading New York cabby
- Updated Kellogg Company and Quaker Oats financial results used in analysis
- Expanded the explanation of comparative analysis
- New e-Business Insight on internal security analysis
- Revised exercises and problems

Appendix A, New Specimen Financial Statements: Tootsie Roll Industries, Inc.

Appendix B, New Comparative Specimen Financial Statements: Hershey Foods Corporation

Appendix C: Time Value of Money

Appendix D: Ethical Standards

Cases for Management Decision Making

- New selection of five cases to be used in conjunction with Chapters 2, 4, 5, 6, 9, 10, and 11.

PROVEN PEDAGOGICAL FRAMEWORK

In this book we have used many proven pedagogical tools to help students learn accounting concepts and apply them to decision making in the business world. This pedagogical framework emphasizes the *processes* students undergo as they learn.

Learning How to Use the Text

- The text begins with a **Student Owner's Manual,** which helps students understand the value of the text's learning aids and how to use them. After becoming familiar with the pedagogy, students can take a *Learning Styles Quiz* (p. xxiii) to help them identify how they learn best—visually, aurally, through reading and writing, kinesthetically, or through a combination of these styles. They then will find tips on in-class and at-home learning strategies, as well as help in identifying the text features that would be most useful to them based on their learning style.

- Additionally, Chapter 1 contains notes (printed in red) that explain each learning aid the first time it appears.

- **The Navigator** pulls all the learning aids together into a learning system. It is designed to guide students through each chapter and help them succeed in learning the material. The Navigator consists of (1) a checklist at the beginning of the chapter, which outlines text features and study aids students will need in order to master the topics, and (2) a series of check boxes that prompt students to use the learning aids and set priorities as they study. At the end of the chapter, students are reminded to return to The Navigator to check off their completed work. The Navigator from Chapter 2 is shown below.

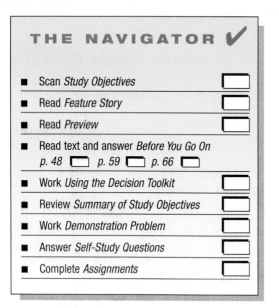

Understanding the Context

- **Study Objectives,** listed at the beginning of each chapter, form a learning framework throughout the text. Each objective is repeated in the margin at the appropriate place in the main body of the chapter and again in the **Summary of Study Objectives.** Also, end-of-chapter assignment materials are linked to the Study Objectives.

- A chapter-opening **Feature Story** presents a scenario that helps students picture how the chapter topic relates to the real world of accounting and business situations. It also serves as a recurrent example in the chapter. Each

story that focuses on a well-known company ends with the company's Web address to encourage students to go on-line for more information about these companies.

- A chapter **Preview** links the chapter-opening Feature Story to the major topics of the chapter. First, an introductory paragraph explains how the story relates to the topics to be discussed, and then a graphic outline of the chapter provides a "road map," useful for seeing the big picture as well as the connections between subtopics.

Learning the Material

- This book emphasizes the accounting experiences of **real companies and business situations throughout,** from chapter-opening Feature Stories to the chapter's last item of homework material. Details on these many features follow. In addition, every chapter uses accounting practices of real companies. Names of real companies are highlighted in red, and many of these real-world examples and illustrations are identified by a company logo.

- Continuing the real-world flavor of the book, **Business Insight** boxes in each chapter give students glimpses into how real companies make decisions using accounting information. The boxes, highlighted with striking photographs, focus on four different accounting perspectives—those of managers, international business, service companies, and e-business. The service company and e-business categories are new to this edition.

- Color **illustrations** support and reinforce the concepts of the text. **Infographics** help students visualize and apply accounting concepts to the real world. These infographics often portray important concepts in entertaining and memorable ways. When illustrations present financial statements or computations, numbers or categories are highlighted in colored type to draw students' attention to key information.

- **Before You Go On** sections occur at the end of each key topic and consists of two parts: *Review It* serves as a learning check within the chapter by asking students to stop and answer knowledge and comprehension questions about the material just covered. *Do It* is a brief demonstration problem that gives immediate practice using the material just covered. An **Action Plan** lists the steps necessary to complete the task, and a **Solution** is provided to help students understand the reasoning involved in reaching an answer. The *Do It* exercises are keyed to related homework exercises.

- **Helpful Hints** in the margins expand upon or help clarify concepts under discussion in the nearby text. This feature actually makes the book an Annotated *Student* Edition.

- **Key terms** and concepts are printed in blue where they are first explained in the text and are defined again in the end-of-chapter glossary. **Alternative Terminology** notes in the margins present synonymous terms that students may come across in subsequent accounting courses and in business.

- Each chapter presents **decision tools** that are useful for analyzing and solving the business problems discussed in that chapter. At the end of the text discussion relating to the decision tool, a **Decision Toolkit** summarizes the key features of that decision tool and reinforces its purpose.

- A **Using the Decision Toolkit** exercise, which follows the final Before You Go On section in the chapter, shows students how to use the decision tools presented in that chapter.

Putting It Together

At the end of each chapter, between the body of the text material and the homework materials, are several features useful for review and reference:

- A **Summary of Study Objectives** reviews the main points of the chapter; the **Decision Toolkit—A Summary** presents in one place the decision tools used throughout the chapter; and a **Glossary** of important terms gives definitions with page references to the text. A *CD icon* tells students that there is a Key Term Matching Activity on the *Managerial Accounting* CD-ROM that can help them master the material.
- Next, a **Demonstration Problem** gives students another opportunity to refer to a detailed solution to a representative problem before they do homework assignments. An **Action Plan** presented in the margin lists strategies to assist students in understanding the solution and help establish a logic for approaching similar problems. A *Web icon* tells students that there is an Interactive Demonstration Problem they can work on the book's Web site.

Developing Skills through Practice

Throughout the homework material, questions, exercises, and problems make use of the decision tools presented in the chapter.

- **Self-Study Questions** comprise a practice test to enable students to check their understanding of important concepts. These questions are keyed to the Study Objectives, so students can go back and review sections of the chapter in which they find they need further work. Answers appear on the last page of the chapter. A *Web* and a *CD icon* tell students that they can answer the Self-Study Questions in an interactive format on the text's CD-ROM or Web site. They can also take an additional Self-Test on the Web site to further help them master the material.
- **Questions** provide a full review of chapter content and help students prepare for class discussions and testing situations.
- **Brief Exercises** build students' confidence and test their basic skills. Each exercise focuses on a single *Study Objective.*
- Each of the **Exercises** focuses on one or more of the *Study Objectives.* These tend to take a little longer to complete and present more of a challenge to students than Brief Exercises. The Exercises help instructors and students make a manageable transition to more challenging problems. Certain exercises, marked with a ▭▭▭▭▷, help students practice business writing skills.

- **Problems** stress the application of the concepts presented in the chapter. Two sets of problems—A and B—have corresponding problems keyed to the same *Study Objectives*, thus giving instructors greater flexibility in assigning homework. Certain problems, marked with an icon ▭▭▭▭▷, help build business writing skills. The *Web icon* indicates that students can complete certain problems in an interactive format on the text's Web site.
- Each Brief Exercise, Exercise, and Problem has a **description of the concept** covered and is keyed to the Study Objectives.
- **Spreadsheet Exercises and Problems,** identified by an icon, can be solved using *Solving Managerial Accounting Problems Using Excel.*

Expanding and Applying Knowledge

Broadening Your Perspective is a unique section at the end of each chapter that offers a wealth of resources to help instructors and students pull together the learning for the chapter. This section offers problems and projects for those instructors who want to broaden the learning experience by bringing in more real-world decision making, analysis, and critical thinking activities. The elements of the **Broadening Your Perspective** section are as follows.

- **Group Decision Cases** help students build decision-making skills by analyzing accounting information in a less structured situation. These cases either require evaluation of a manager's decision, or lead to a decision among alternative courses of action. As group activities, these cases promote teamwork and help prepare students for the business world, where they will be working with teams of people.
- Like the decision cases, the **Managerial Analysis** assignments build analytical and decision-making skills in problematic situations encountered by business managers. They also require the application of business communication skills.
- The **Real-World Focus** problems ask students to apply techniques and concepts presented in the chapter to specific situations faced by actual companies.
- **Exploring the Web** exercises guide students to Web sites where they can find and analyze information related to the chapter topic. These sites can be reached directly or by linking through the text's Web site.
- **Communication Activities** give students practice in communicating to different audiences in varying modes—letters, reports, memos, explanations, and analyses. These are skills much in demand by employers.
- Since the ability to read and understand business publications is an asset used over the span of one's career, **Research Assignments** direct students to annual reports or articles published in the *Wall Street Journal* and other popular business periodicals for further study and analysis of key topics.
- **Ethics Cases** contain ethical dilemmas and ask students to analyze the situation, identify the stakeholders affected, describe the ethical issues involved, and decide on an appropriate course of action.

Cases for Management Decision Making, provided at the end of the text, require students to use the decision tools presented in the chapters in realistic business situations. The cases can be used as a comprehensive capstone activity at the end of the course, or as a recurring activity during the course. They are intended to be richer and more challenging than a traditional problem but are still targeted at an introductory level student.

ACTIVE TEACHING AND LEARNING SUPPLEMENTARY MATERIAL

The *Managerial Accounting* Web Site at http://www.wiley.com/college/weygandt

 A resource and learning tool, the Web site serves as a launching pad to numerous activities, resources, and related sites. On the Web site you will find an *Interactive Learning Styles Quiz,* an *Interactive Study Skills Chart, Interactive Self-Study Questions* and *Self-Tests,* and *Exploring the Web Exercises.* In addition, there are links to companies discussed in the text and items available for downloading such as *Power-Point presentations.* A link to the *Wiley Business Extra* site is also provided.

The Web site also contains an *Interactive Problem Set,* which allows students to work through additional demonstration problems and select homework problems found in the main text. It provides immediate feedback on a student's work and has a randomizing function, so students can work on multiple variations of the same problem.

Interactive CD-ROM

 The Interactive CD-ROM is designed to help students understand and apply managerial accounting concepts in both academic and real-world scenarios. In addition to an *Accounting Cycle Tutorial,* the CD-ROM contains an *Interactive Learning Styles Quiz,* an *Interactive Study Skills Chart, Interactive Self-Tests, Key Term Matching Activities,* a *Comprehensive Problem* covering Chapters 1-11, a *Writing Handbook,* and a *Surviving the Group Project* primer. The CD-ROM also addresses *Careers in Managerial Accounting* and provides *Professional Profiles,* audio interviews with accounting and other business professionals.

Instructor's Active-Teaching Aids

For the instructor, we have designed an extensive support package to help you maximize your teaching effectiveness, including print and technology tools. We offer useful supplements for instructors with various levels of experience and different instructional circumstances.

Instructor's Resource System on CD-ROM. Responding to the changing needs of instructors and to developments in distance learning and electronic classrooms, a CD-ROM supplement provides all the instructor support material in an electronic format that is easy to navigate and use. This CD-ROM contains print supplements, as well as the electronic ones, for use in the classroom, for printing out material, for uploading to your own Web site,

or for downloading and modifying. The CD-ROM gives you the flexibility to access and prepare instructional material based on your individual needs.

Solutions Manual. The Solutions Manual contains detailed solutions to all exercises and problems in the textbook and suggested answers to the questions and cases. Print is large and bold for easy readability in lecture settings, and instructors may duplicate any portion of the manual without paying a permissions fee. Each chapter includes an *assignment classification table* (identifies end-of-chapter items by study objectives), an *assignment characteristics table* (describes each problem and identifies difficulty level and estimated completion time), and a *Bloom's taxonomy table* (classifies end-of-chapter items by Bloom's taxonomy of learning objective and study objective). (Also available at http://www.wiley.com/college/weygandt.)

Solutions Transparencies. Packaged in an organizer box with chapter file folders, these transparencies feature detailed solutions to all exercises and problems in the textbook, and suggested answers to the cases. They feature large, bold type for better projection and easy readability in large classroom settings. Accuracy is assured—all solutions were extensively checked by the authors and reviewers.

Instructor's Manual. The Instructor's Manual is a comprehensive resource guide designed to assist professors in preparing lectures and assignments, and includes sample syllabi for preparing for the course. The print is set in a size large enough for easy reading or use as transparency masters.

Included for each chapter are an *assignment classification table;* an *assignment characteristics table;* a *list of study objectives* in extra-large, boldface print for transparencies; a *chapter review* of the significant topics and points contained in the chapter; *enhanced lecture outlines* with teaching tips and references to text material; *suggestions for integrating supplements* into the classroom; a *20-minute quiz* in the form of 10 true/false and 5 multiple-choice questions (with solutions); and illustrations, including diagrams, graphs, questions, and exercises, for use as classroom handouts. overhead transparencies, in-class quizzes, or demonstrations (solutions are provided). (Also available at http://www.wiley.com/college/weygandt.)

Teaching Transparencies. A number of illustrations are available in four-color format. We have selected these illustrations from the text and from original exhibits outside the text as well. Designed to support and clarify concepts in the text, the Teaching Transparencies will enhance lectures. Suggestions on how to integrate the Teaching Transparencies are included in the Instructor's Manual.

Examination Book and Test Bank. The Examination Book and Test Bank is a comprehensive testing package that allows instructors to tailor examinations according to study objectives, learning skills, and content. A main feature of this supplement is the revised Test Bank that, with the inclusion of 15 percent more multiple choice questions and two new exercises for each chapter, now totals over 800 examination questions and exercises accompanied by solutions. This revision of the Test Bank still includes the helpful *Summary of Questions by Objectives* and *Summary of Objectives by Questions,* tools effective in linking test items to study objectives. Each chapter also includes a chart indicating the placement of questions in Bloom's taxonomy. An estimated completion time for each question and exercise is also provided.

The Examination Book and Test Bank provides an achievement test and solutions bank for every two chapters in the textbook. Three comprehensive tests and a final exam are also provided. The tests, easy to photocopy and distribute to students, consist of problems and exercises as well as multiple-choice, matching, and true/false questions.

Computerized Test Bank. The Test Bank is also available for use with IBM and IBM true-compatibles running Windows 3.1 or higher. This Computerized Test Bank offers a number of valuable options that allow instructors to create multiple versions of the same test by scrambling questions; generate a large number of test questions randomly or manually; and modify and customize test questions by changing existing problems or adding your own. (Also available at http://www.wiley.com/college/weygandt.)

Test Preparation Service. Simply call Wiley's special number (1-800-541-5602) with the questions you want on an examination. Wiley will provide a customized master exam within 24 hours. If you prefer, random selection from a number of chapters is possible.

Checklist of Key Figures. A listing of key amounts for textbook problems, allowing students to verify the accuracy of their answers as they work through the assignments, is available at http://www.wiley.com/college/weygandt.

PowerPoint Presentation Material. This PowerPoint lecture aid contains a combination of key concepts, images, and problems from the textbook for use in the classroom. Designed according to the organization of the material in the textbook, this series of electronic transparencies can be used to reinforce managerial accounting principles visually and graphically. (Also available at http://www.wiley.com/college/weygandt.)

***Nightly Business Report* Video.** This video contains segments from the highly respected *Nightly Business Report* that have been selected for their applicability to managerial accounting and for their reinforcement of key concepts in the text. Each of the segments is approximately 3–5 minutes long and can be used to introduce topics to the students, enhance lecture material, and provide real-world context for related concepts. An Instructor's Manual with suggestions for integrating the material into the classroom accompanies the video.

Student Active-Learning Aids

Excel Working Papers. The Excel Working Papers CD-ROM compiles all the accounting forms you will need to successfully complete your study work for *Managerial Accounting* Second Edition. The templates on this CD-ROM can be found in the paperbound working papers and therefore include custom forms for all relevant end-of-chapter exercises, problems, and cases. The Excel Working Papers, however, provide you with the option of printing forms and completing them manually, or entering data electronically and then printing out a completed form. By entering data electronically, you can now paste homework to a new file and e-mail the worksheet to your instructor.

Working Papers. Working Papers are accounting forms for all end-of-chapter exercises, problems, and cases. A convenient resource for organizing and completing homework assignments, they demonstrate how to correctly set up solution formats and are directly tied to textbook assignments.

Student Study Guide. The Student Study Guide is a comprehensive review of accounting and a powerful tool for students to use in the classroom. Tied to study objectives, it guides students through chapter content and provides resources for use during lectures. **This is an excellent resource when preparing for exams.**

Each chapter of the Student Study Guide includes study objectives and a chapter review consisting of 20–30 key points; a demonstration problem linked to study objectives in the textbook; and additional opportunities for students to practice their knowledge and skills through true/false, multiple-choice, and matching questions related to key terms and exercises linked to study objectives. Solutions to the exercises explain the hows and whys so students get immediate feedback.

Business Extra Web Site at http://www.wiley.com/college/businessextra. To complement the On-Line Business Survival Guide in Accounting, the Business Extra Web site given professors and students instant access to a wealth of current articles dealing with all aspects of accounting. The articles are organized by topic, and discussion questions follow each article.

Solving Managerial Accounting Problems Using Excel. This workbook contains Excel templates that allow students to complete select end-of-chapter exercises and problems identified by a spreadsheet icon in the margin of the main text. A useful introduction to computers, this package details how students can work with preprogrammed spreadsheets and it instructs on how to design your own spreadsheet. The workbook and templates help students develop and hone their computer skills and effectively exposes them to Excel. Solutions are available at http://www.wiley.com/college/weygandt.

Our goal has been to make this book accurate, interesting, and educationally sound. Our hope is that this book provides a positive experience for both teacher and student.

Jerry J. Weygandt / Donald E. Kieso / Paul D. Kimmel
Madison, Wisconsin   DeKalb, Illinois   Milwaukee, Wisconsin

ACKNOWLEDGMENTS

During the course of producing the Second Edition of *Managerial Accounting*, the authors benefited greatly from the input of focus group participants, manuscript reviewers, First Edition users, ancillary authors, and proofers. The constructive suggestions and innovative ideas of the reviewers and the creativity and accuracy of the ancillary authors and checkers are greatly appreciated.

We are especially grateful to Chor Lau, California State University at Los Angeles, for his in-depth review and classroom use of our new chapter on pricing decisions.

REVIEWERS AND FOCUS GROUP PARTICIPANTS FOR *MANAGERIAL ACCOUNTING*, FIRST EDITION

Nancy Boyd, *Middle Tennessee State University*
Joan Cook, *Milwaukee Area Technical College*
Cecelia Fewox, *Trident Technical College*
Jeannie Folk, *College of DuPage*
Jane Grange, *Chicago State University*
Thomas Hofmeister, *Northwestern Business School*
Shirly Kleiner, *Johnson County Community College*

Robyn Lawrence, *University of Scranton*
Deanne Pannell, *Pellissippi State Technical College*
Jill Russell, *Camden County College*
Jerome Spallino, *Westmoreland County Community College*
Cynthia Tomes, *Des Moines Area Community College*
Chris Widmer, *Tidewater Community College*

REVIEWERS AND FOCUS GROUP PARTICIPANTS FOR *MANAGERIAL ACCOUNTING*, SECOND EDITION

Victoria Beard, *University of North Dakota*
Kelly A. Blacker, *Mercy College*
Ken Coubillion, *San Joaquin Delta College*
Linda Dening, *Jefferson Community College*
Denise M. English, *Boise State University*
Albert Fisher, *Community College of Southern Nevada*
George Gardner, *Bemidji State University*
Marc Giullian, *University of Louisiana at Lafayette*
John J. Goetz, *University of Texas at Arlington*
Kathy Horton, *College of DuPage*
Sharon Johnson, *Kansas City Community College*
David Karmon, *Central Michigan University*

J. Suzanne King, *University of Charleston*
Terry Kubichan, *Old Dominion University*
Chor Lau, *California State University at Los Angeles*
Melanie Mackey, *Ocean County College*
Jamie O'Brien, *South Dakota State University*
Shelly Ota, *Leeward Community College*
Kenneth R. Pelfrey, *Ohio State University*
Peter J. Poznanski, *Cleveland State University*
David Ravetch, *University of California at Los Angeles*
Paul J. Shinal, *Cayuga Community College*
Ellen Sweatt, *Georgia Perimeter College*
Michael F. van Breda, *Southern Methodist University*

ANCILLARY AUTHORS, CONTRIBUTORS, AND PROOFERS

John C. Borke, *University of Wisconsin at Platteville:* Solutions Manual proofer
Denise M. English, *Boise State University:* Excel Workbook author
Larry R. Falcetto, *Emporia Sate University:* Instructor's Manual, Check Figures, and Test Bank author, Solutions Manual proofer, and technical advisor
Jessica Frazier, *Eastern Kentucky University:* Test Bank co-author, Interactive Web Problems contributor, NBR video advisor, and Cases for Management Decision Making contributor
Mark Giullian, *University of Louisiana at Lafayette:* Interactive Web Self-tests and Questions contributor
Wayne Higley, *Buena Vista University:* Content proofer and technical advisor
Jack Kahn, *Nightly Business Report:* NBR video author

Douglas W. Kieso, *University of California at Irvine:* Study Guide author
David Koeppen, *Boise State University:* Excel Workbook author
Don Newell, *Delta Software: Managerial Accounting Second Edition* MicroTest compositor
Teresa Speck, *St. Mary's University:* Text and Solutions Manual proofer
Ellen Sweatt, *Georgia Perimeter College:* PowerPoint designer and author
Dick D. Wasson, *Southwestern College:* Excel Working Papers and Working Papers author and Solutions Manual proofer
Thomas Zeller, *Loyola University Chicago:* Cases for Management Decision Making contributor

We appreciate the exemplary support and professional commitment given us by our publisher Susan Elbe, senior development editor Nancy Perry, our senior marketing manager Clancy Marshall, vice-president of college production and manufacturing Ann Berlin, production services manager Jeanine Furino, photo editor Sara Wight, designer Kevin Murphy, illustration editor Anna Melhorn, our assistant editor Ed Brislin, our development editor Ann Torbert, our new media editor David Kear, and our word processor Mary Ann Benson. A note of gratitude to our production coordinators Martha Beyerlein and Jenny Wood at Elm Street Publishing Services.

We thank Tootsie Roll Industries, Inc. and Hershey Foods Corporation for permitting us the use of their Annual Reports for our specimen financial statements and accompanying notes.

Suggestions and comments from users are encouraged and appreciated. Please feel free to e-mail any one of us at account@wiley.com.

Jerry J. Weygandt / Donald E. Kieso / Paul D. Kimmel

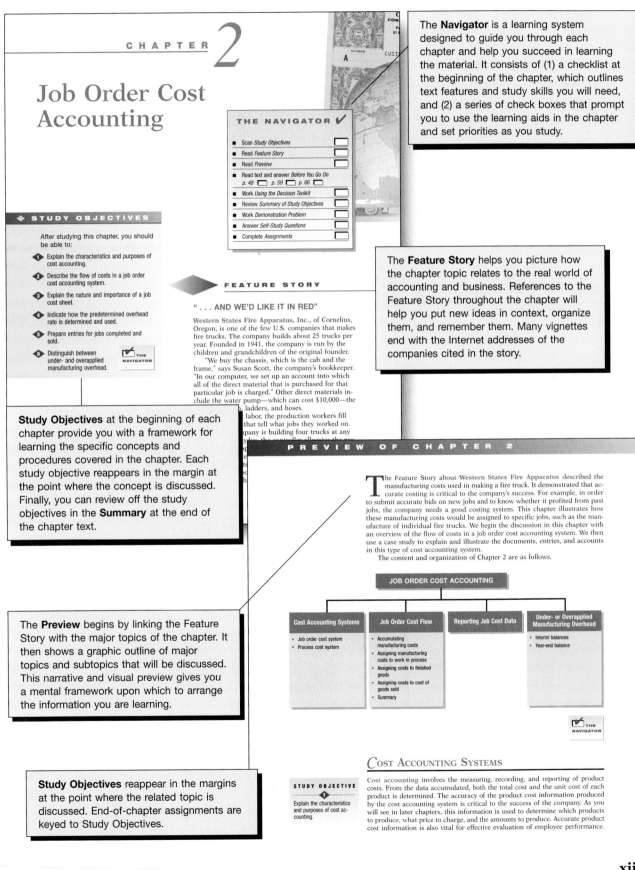

The **Navigator** is a learning system designed to guide you through each chapter and help you succeed in learning the material. It consists of (1) a checklist at the beginning of the chapter, which outlines text features and study skills you will need, and (2) a series of check boxes that prompt you to use the learning aids in the chapter and set priorities as you study.

The **Feature Story** helps you picture how the chapter topic relates to the real world of accounting and business. References to the Feature Story throughout the chapter will help you put new ideas in context, organize them, and remember them. Many vignettes end with the Internet addresses of the companies cited in the story.

Study Objectives at the beginning of each chapter provide you with a framework for learning the specific concepts and procedures covered in the chapter. Each study objective reappears in the margin at the point where the concept is discussed. Finally, you can review off the study objectives in the **Summary** at the end of the chapter text.

The **Preview** begins by linking the Feature Story with the major topics of the chapter. It then shows a graphic outline of major topics and subtopics that will be discussed. This narrative and visual preview gives you a mental framework upon which to arrange the information you are learning.

Study Objectives reappear in the margins at the point where the related topic is discussed. End-of-chapter assignments are keyed to Study Objectives.

CHAPTER 2

Job Order Cost Accounting

THE NAVIGATOR ✔

- Scan *Study Objectives* ☐
- Read *Feature Story* ☐
- Read *Preview* ☐
- Read text and answer *Before You Go On*
  p. 48 ☐   p. 59 ☐   p. 66 ☐
- Work *Using the Decision Toolkit* ☐
- Review *Summary of Study Objectives* ☐
- Work *Demonstration Problem* ☐
- Answer *Self-Study Questions* ☐
- Complete *Assignments* ☐

◆ STUDY OBJECTIVES

After studying this chapter, you should be able to:

1. Explain the characteristics and purposes of cost accounting.
2. Describe the flow of costs in a job order cost accounting system.
3. Explain the nature and importance of a job cost sheet.
4. Indicate how the predetermined overhead rate is determined and used.
5. Prepare entries for jobs completed and sold.
6. Distinguish between under- and overapplied manufacturing overhead.

FEATURE STORY

" . . . AND WE'D LIKE IT IN RED"

Western States Fire Apparatus, Inc., of Cornelius, Oregon, is one of the few U.S. companies that makes fire trucks. The company builds about 25 trucks per year. Founded in 1941, the company is run by the children and grandchildren of the original founder.

"We buy the chassis, which is the cab and the frame," says Susan Scott, the company's bookkeeper. "In our computer, we set up an account into which all of the direct material that is purchased for that particular job is charged." Other direct materials include the water pump—which can cost $10,000—the ladders, and hoses.

labor, the production workers fill that tell what jobs they worked on. pany is building four trucks at any

PREVIEW OF CHAPTER 2

The Feature Story about **Western States Fire Apparatus** described the manufacturing costs used in making a fire truck. It demonstrated that accurate costing is critical to the company's success. For example, in order to submit accurate bids on new jobs and to know whether it profited from past jobs, the company needs a good costing system. This chapter illustrates how these manufacturing costs would be assigned to specific jobs, such as the manufacture of individual fire trucks. We begin the discussion in this chapter with an overview of the flow of costs in a job order cost accounting system. We then use a case study to explain and illustrate the documents, entries, and accounts in this type of cost accounting system.

The content and organization of Chapter 2 are as follows.

JOB ORDER COST ACCOUNTING

Cost Accounting Systems	Job Order Cost Flow	Reporting Job Cost Data	Under- or Overapplied Manufacturing Overhead
• Job order cost system	• Accumulating manufacturing costs		• Interim balances
• Process cost system	• Assigning manufacturing costs to work in process		• Year-end balance
	• Assigning costs to finished goods		
	• Assigning costs to cost of goods sold		
	• Summary		

COST ACCOUNTING SYSTEMS

STUDY OBJECTIVE 1

Explain the characteristics and purposes of cost accounting.

Cost accounting involves the measuring, recording, and reporting of product costs. From the data accumulated, both the total cost and the unit cost of each product is determined. The accuracy of the product cost information produced by the cost accounting system is critical to the success of the company. As you will see in later chapters, this information is used to determine which products to produce, what price to charge, and the amounts to produce. Accurate product cost information is also vital for effective evaluation of employee performance.

Cost Accounting Systems   **47**

JOB ORDER COST SYSTEM

Under a job order cost system, costs are assigned to each **job** or to each **batch** of goods. An example of a job would be the manufacture of a mainframe computer by **IBM**, the production of a movie by **Disney**, or the making of a fire truck by **Western States**. An example of a batch would be the printing of 225 wedding invitations by a local print shop, or the printing of a weekly issue of *Fortune* magazine by a hi-tech printer such as **Quad Graphics**. Jobs or batches may be completed to fill a specific customer order or to replenish inventory.

An important feature of job order costing is that each job (or batch) has its own distinguishing characteristics. For example, each house is custom built, each consulting engagement by a CPA firm is unique, and each printing job is different. **The objective is to compute the cost per job.** At each point in the manufacturing of a product or the providing of a service, the job and its associated costs can be identified. A job order cost system measures costs for each completed job, rather than for set time periods. The recording of costs in a job order cost system is shown in Illustration 2-1.

> **Key terms** and concepts are printed in blue where they are first explained in the text. They are listed and defined again in the end-of-chapter **Glossary**.

Illustration 2-1   Job order cost system

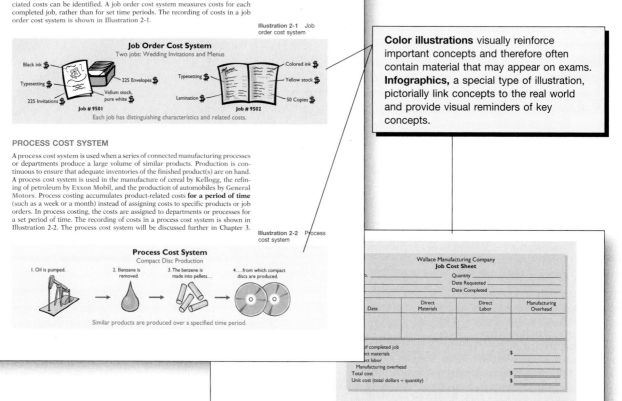

Job Order Cost System
Two jobs: Wedding Invitations and Menus

Job # 9501 — Black ink, Typesetting, 225 Invitations, 225 Envelopes, Vellum stock, pure white

Job # 9502 — Colored ink, Yellow stock, 50 Copies, Typesetting, Lamination

Each job has distinguishing characteristics and related costs.

> **Color illustrations** visually reinforce important concepts and therefore often contain material that may appear on exams. **Infographics,** a special type of illustration, pictorially link concepts to the real world and provide visual reminders of key concepts.

PROCESS COST SYSTEM

A process cost system is used when a series of connected manufacturing processes or departments produce a large volume of similar products. Production is continuous to ensure that adequate inventories of the finished product(s) are on hand. A process cost system is used in the manufacture of cereal by **Kellogg**, the refining of petroleum by **Exxon Mobil**, and the production of automobiles by **General Motors**. Process costing accumulates product-related costs **for a period of time** (such as a week or a month) instead of assigning costs to specific products or job orders. In process costing, the costs are assigned to departments or processes for a set period of time. The recording of costs in a process cost system is shown in Illustration 2-2. The process cost system will be discussed further in Chapter 3.

Illustration 2-2   Process cost system

Process Cost System
Compact Disc Production

1. Oil is pumped. → 2. Benzene is removed. → 3. The benzene is made into pellets... → 4. ...from which compact discs are produced.

Similar products are produced over a specified time period.

Wallace Manufacturing Company
Job Cost Sheet

Quantity _____
Date Requested _____
Date Completed _____

Date	Direct Materials	Direct Labor	Manufacturing Overhead

of completed job
ct materials
Direct labor
Manufacturing overhead
Total cost $ _____
Unit cost (total dollars ÷ quantity) $ _____

Postings to job cost sheets are made daily, directly from supporting documents. A separate job cost sheet is kept for each job. The job cost sheets constitute the subsidiary ledger for the Work in Process Inventory account. **Each entry to Work in Process Inventory must be accompanied by a corresponding posting to one or more job cost sheets.**

> **Business Insight** examples give you more glimpses into how real companies make decisions using accounting information. These high-interest boxes are classified by four different points of view—management perspectives, international perspectives, service company perspectives, and e-business insights.

e — BUSINESS INSIGHT

General Motors recently launched a new Internet-based ordering system intended to deliver custom vehicles in 15 to 20 days instead of the 55 to 60 days it previously took. Customers interested in a GM car can search online to see if any dealers have a car with the options they want. If not, the customer uses an online program to configure a car with the desired options and then places the order. While this online approach could potentially provide savings for automakers by reducing inventory costs, some people are skeptical. One auto analyst stated, "I don't think it's going to lead to a massive change in the way vehicles are built and sold in the next 10 years."

Source: Karen Lundegaard, "GM Tests Web-Based Ordering System, Seeking to Slash Custom-Delivery Time," *Wall Street Journal,* November 17, 2000.

> **Helpful Hints** in the margins are like having an instructor with you as you read. They further clarify concepts being discussed.

Helpful Hint Approvals are an important part of a materials requisition slip because they help to establish individual accountability over inventory.

Raw Materials Costs

Raw materials costs are assigned when the materials are issued by the storeroom. To achieve effective internal control over the issuance of materials, the storeroom worker should receive a written authorization before materials are released to production. Such authorization for issuing raw materials is made on a prenumbered materials requisition slip. This form is signed by an au-

One of the special types of *Business Insight* boxes, **Service Company Perspectives** highlight accounting practices in this growing segment of our economy.

BUSINESS INSIGHT
Service Company Perspective

Frequently when we think of service companies we think of specific, nonroutine tasks, such as rebuilding an automobile engine, providing consulting services on a business acquisition, or working on a major lawsuit. Clearly, such nonroutine situations would call for job order costing. However, many service companies specialize in performing repetitive, routine aspects of a particular business. For example, auto-care vendors such as **Jiffy Lube** focus on the routine aspects of car care. **H&R Block** focuses on the routine aspects of basic tax practice, and many large law firms focus on routine legal services, such as uncomplicated divorces. For service companies that perform routine, repetitive services, process costing provides a simple solution to their accounting needs. In fact, since in many instances there is little or no work in process at the end of the period, applying process costing in this setting can be even easier than for a manufacturer.

of $22,400 to Work in Process Inventory equals the sum of the overhead assigned to jobs: Job 101 $12,000 + Job 102 $7,200 + Job 103 $3,200.

At the end of each month, **the balance in Work in Process Inventory should equal the sum of the costs shown on the job cost sheets of unfinished jobs**. Assuming that all jobs are unfinished, proof of the agreement of the control and subsidiary accounts in Wallace Manufacturing is shown below.

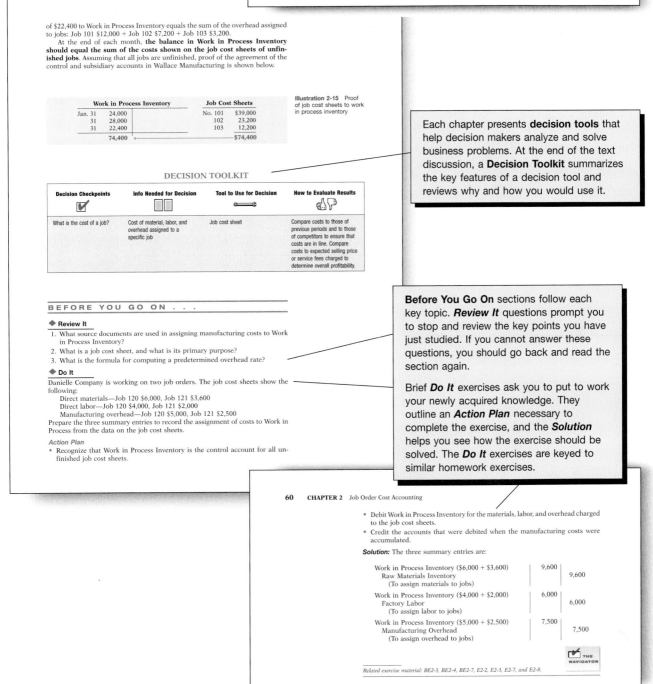

Work in Process Inventory		Job Cost Sheets	
Jan. 31	24,000	No. 101	$39,000
31	28,000	102	23,200
31	22,400	103	12,200
	74,400		$74,400

Illustration 2-15 Proof of job cost sheets to work in process inventory

DECISION TOOLKIT

Decision Checkpoints	Info Needed for Decision	Tool to Use for Decision	How to Evaluate Results
What is the cost of a job?	Cost of material, labor, and overhead assigned to a specific job	Job cost sheet	Compare costs to those of previous periods and to those of competitors to ensure that costs are in line. Compare costs to expected selling price or service fees charged to determine overall profitability.

Each chapter presents **decision tools** that help decision makers analyze and solve business problems. At the end of the text discussion, a **Decision Toolkit** summarizes the key features of a decision tool and reviews why and how you would use it.

BEFORE YOU GO ON . . .

◆ **Review It**

1. What source documents are used in assigning manufacturing costs to Work in Process Inventory?
2. What is a job cost sheet, and what is its primary purpose?
3. What is the formula for computing a predetermined overhead rate?

◆ **Do It**

Danielle Company is working on two job orders. The job cost sheets show the following:

   Direct materials—Job 120 $6,000, Job 121 $3,600
   Direct labor—Job 120 $4,000, Job 121 $2,000
   Manufacturing overhead—Job 120 $5,000, Job 121 $2,500

Prepare the three summary entries to record the assignment of costs to Work in Process from the data on the job cost sheets.

Action Plan
• Recognize that Work in Process Inventory is the control account for all unfinished job cost sheets.

Before You Go On sections follow each key topic. *Review It* questions prompt you to stop and review the key points you have just studied. If you cannot answer these questions, you should go back and read the section again.

Brief *Do It* exercises ask you to put to work your newly acquired knowledge. They outline an *Action Plan* necessary to complete the exercise, and the *Solution* helps you see how the exercise should be solved. The *Do It* exercises are keyed to similar homework exercises.

60   CHAPTER 2 Job Order Cost Accounting

• Debit Work in Process Inventory for the materials, labor, and overhead charged to the job cost sheets.
• Credit the accounts that were debited when the manufacturing costs were accumulated.

Solution: The three summary entries are:

Work in Process Inventory ($6,000 + $3,600)	9,600	
Raw Materials Inventory		9,600
(To assign materials to jobs)		
Work in Process Inventory ($4,000 + $2,000)	6,000	
Factory Labor		6,000
(To assign labor to jobs)		
Work in Process Inventory ($5,000 + $2,500)	7,500	
Manufacturing Overhead		7,500
(To assign overhead to jobs)		

Related exercise material: BE2-3, BE2-4, BE2-7, E2-2, E2-3, E2-7, and E2-8.

66   **CHAPTER 2**   Job Order Cost Accounting

BEFORE YOU GO ON . . .

◆ **Review It**

1. When are entries made to record the completion and sale of a job?
2. What costs are included in total manufacturing costs in the cost of goods manufactured schedule?
3. How is under- or overapplied manufacturing overhead reported in monthly financial statements?

THE NAVIGATOR

USING THE DECISION TOOLKIT

Martinez Building Products Company is one of the largest manufacturers and marketers of unique, custom-made residential garage doors in the U.S. as well as a major supplier of industrial and commercial doors, grills, and counter shutters for the new construction, repair, and remodel markets. Martinez has developed plans for continued expansion of a network of service operations that sell, install, and service manufactured fireplaces, garage doors, and related products.

Martinez uses a job cost system and applies overhead to production on the basis of direct labor cost. In computing a predetermined overhead rate for the year 2002, the company estimated manufacturing overhead to be $24 million and direct labor costs to be $20 million. In addition the following information is provided.

Actual costs incurred during 2002

Direct materials used	$30,000,000
Direct labor cost incurred	21,000,000

Manufacturing costs incurred during 2002

Insurance, factory	$ 500,000
Indirect labor	7,500,000
Maintenance	1,000,000
Rent on building	11,000,000
Depreciation on equipment	2,000,000

Instructions

Answer each of the following.

(a) Why is Martinez Building Products [...] system?
(b) On what basis does Martinez alloca[...] pute the predetermined overhead ra[...]
(c) Compute the amount of the under-[...]
(d) Martinez had balances in the beginn[...] finished goods accounts as follows.

	1/1
Work in process	$ 5,00
Finished goods	13,00

Determine the (1) cost of goods man[...] for Martinez during 2002. Assume t[...] head should be included in the cost [...]

A **Using the Decision Toolkit** exercise follows the final set of *Review It* questions in the chapter. It asks you to use business information and the decision tools presented in the chapter. You should think through the questions related to the decision before you study the printed *Solution*.

Summary of Study Objectives   **67**

(e) During 2002, Job G408 was started and completed. Its cost sheet showed a total cost of $100,000, and the company prices its product at 50% above its cost. What is the price to the customer if the company follows this pricing strategy?

Solution

(a) The company is using a job order system because each job (or batch) must have its own distinguishing characteristics. For example, each type of garage door would be different, and therefore a different cost per garage door should be assigned.

(b) The company allocates its overhead on the basis of direct labor cost. The predetermined overhead rate is 120%, computed as follows.

$$\$24,000,000 \div \$20,000,000 = 120\%$$

(c)		
Actual manufacturing overhead	$22,000,000	
Applied overhead cost ($21,000,000 × 120%)	25,200,000	
Overapplied overhead	$ 3,200,000	

(d) (1) Work in process, 1/1/02		$ 5,000,000
Direct materials used	$30,000,000	
Direct labor	21,000,000	
Manufacturing overhead applied	25,200,000	
Total manufacturing costs		76,200,000
Total cost of work in process		81,200,000
Less: Work in process, 12/31/02		4,000,000
Cost of goods manufactured		$77,200,000
(2) Finished goods inventory, 1/1/02	$13,000,000	
Cost of goods manufactured (see above)	77,200,000	
Cost of goods available for sale	90,200,000	
Finished goods inventory, 12/31/02	11,000,000	
Cost of goods sold (unadjusted)	79,200,000	
Less: Overapplied overhead	3,200,000	
Cost of goods sold	$76,000,000	

(e)	G408 cost	$ 100,000
	Markup percentage	× 50%
	Profit	$ 50,000

THE NAVIGATOR

Price to customer: $150,000 ($100,000 + $50,000)

The **Summary of Study Objectives** reviews the main points related to the Study Objectives. It provides you with another opportunity to review what you have learned as well as to see how the key topics within the chapter fit together.

SUMMARY OF STUDY OBJECTIVES

① *Explain the characteristics and purposes of cost accounting.* Cost accounting involves the procedures for measuring, recording, and reporting product costs. From the data accumulated, the total cost and the unit cost of each product is determined. The two basic types of cost accounting systems are job order cost and process cost.

② *Describe the flow of costs in a job order cost accounting system.* In job order cost accounting, manufacturing costs are first accumulated in three accounts: Raw Materials Inventory, Factory Labor, and Manufacturing Overhead. The accumulated costs are then assigned to Work in Process Inventory and eventually to Finished Goods Inventory and Cost of Goods Sold.

DECISION TOOLKIT—A SUMMARY

Decision Checkpoints	Info Needed for Decision	Tool to Use for Decision	How to Evaluate Results
What is the cost of a job?	Cost of material, labor, and overhead assigned to a specific job	Job cost sheet	Compare costs to those of previous periods and to those of competitors to ensure that costs are in line. Compare costs to expected selling price or service fees charged to determine overall profitability.
Has the company over- or underapplied overhead for the period?	Actual overhead costs and overhead applied	Manufacturing overhead account	If the account balance is a credit, overhead applied exceeded actual overhead costs. If the account balance is a debit, overhead applied was less than actual overhead costs.

> At the end of each chapter; the **Decision Toolkit—A Summary** reviews the contexts and techniques useful for decision making that were covered in the chapter.

GLOSSARY

Key Term Matching Activity

Cost accounting An area of accounting that involves measuring, recording, and reporting product costs. (p. 46)

Cost accounting system Manufacturing cost accounts that are fully integrated into the general ledger of a company. (p. 46)

Job cost sheet A form used to record the costs chargeable to a job and to determine the total and unit costs of the completed job. (p. 51)

Job order cost system A cost accounting system in which costs are assigned to each job or batch. (p. 47)

Materials requisition slip A document authorizing the issuance of raw materials from the storeroom to production. (p. 52)

Overapplied overhead A situation in which overhead assigned to work in process is greater than the overhead incurred. (p. 64)

Predetermined overhead rate A rate based on the relationship between estimated annual overhead costs and expected annual operating activity, expressed in terms of a common activity base. (p. 57)

Process cost system A system of accounting used by companies that manufacture relatively homogeneous products through a series of continuous processes or operations. (p. 47)

Summary entry A journal entry that summarizes the totals from multiple transactions. (p. 51)

Time ticket A document that indicates the employee, the hours worked, the account and job to be charged, and the total labor cost. (p. 55)

Underapplied overhead A situation in which overhead assigned to work in process is less than the overhead incurred. (p. 64)

> The **Glossary** defines all the **key terms** and **concepts** introduced in the chapter. Page references help you find any terms you need to study further. A **CD icon** tells you that there is a Key Term Matching Activity on the CD that can help you master the material.

> A **Demonstration Problem** is the final step before you begin homework. These sample problems provide you with an **Action Plan** in the margin that lists the strategies needed to approach and solve the problem. The **Solution** demonstrates both the form and content of complete answers. A **Web icon** tells you that there is an additional **Demonstration Problem** you can work on the book's Web site and self-grade using eGrade software.

DEMONSTRATION PROBLEM

During February, Cardella Manufacturing works on two jobs: A16 and B17. Summary data concerning these jobs are as follows.

eGrade Demonstration Problem

Manufacturing Costs Incurred

Purchased $54,000 of raw materials on account.
Factory labor $76,000, plus $4,000 employer payroll taxes.
Manufacturing overhead exclusive of indirect materials and indirect labor $59,800.

Assignment of Costs

Direct materials:	Job A16 $27,000, Job B17 $21,000
Indirect materials:	$3,000
Direct labor:	Job A16 $52,000, Job B17 $26,000
Indirect labor:	$2,000
Manufacturing overhead rate:	80% of direct labor costs.

Job A16 was completed and sold on account for $150,000. Job B17 was only partially completed.

Instructions

(a) Journalize the February transactions in the sequence followed in the chapter.
(b) What was the amount of under- or overapplied manufacturing overhead?

Solution to Demonstration Problem

(a)

1.

Feb. 28	Raw Materials Inventory	54,000	
	Accounts Payable		54,000
	(Purchase of raw materials on account)		

2.

28	Factory Labor	80,000	
	Factory Wages Payable		76,000
	Employer Payroll Taxes Payable		4,000
	(To record factory labor costs)		

3.

28	Manufacturing Overhead	59,800	
	Accounts Payable, Accumulated Depreciation, and Prepaid Insurance		59,800
	(To record overhead costs)		

4.

28	Work in Process Inventory	48,000	
	Manufacturing Overhead	3,000	
	Raw Materials Inventory		51,000
	(To assign raw materials to production)		

5.

28	Work in Process Inventory	78,000	
	Manufacturing Overhead	2,000	
	Factory Labor		80,000
	(To assign factory labor to production)		

6.

28	Work in Process Inventory	62,400	
	Manufacturing Overhead		62,400
	(To assign overhead to jobs— 80% × $78,000)		

Action Plan

- In accumulating costs, debit three accounts: Raw Materials Inventory, Factory Labor, and Manufacturing Overhead.
- When Work in Process Inventory is debited, credit one of the three accounts listed above.
- Debit Finished Goods Inventory for the cost of completed jobs. Debit Cost of Goods Sold for the cost of jobs sold.
- Overhead is underapplied when Manufacturing Overhead has a debit balance.

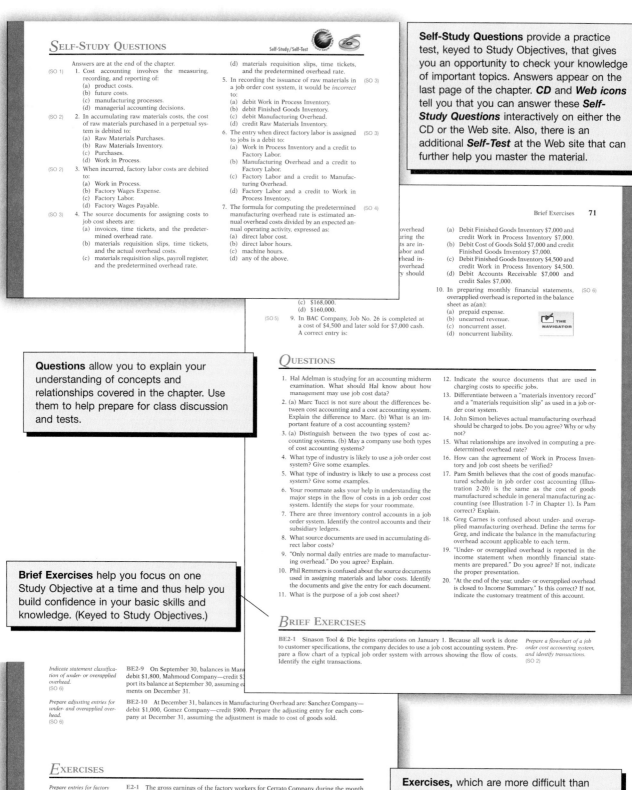

SELF-STUDY QUESTIONS

Self-Study/Self-Test

Answers are at the end of the chapter.

(SO 1)   1. Cost accounting involves the measuring, recording, and reporting of:
   (a) product costs.
   (b) future costs.
   (c) manufacturing processes.
   (d) managerial accounting decisions.

(SO 2)   2. In accumulating raw materials costs, the cost of raw materials purchased in a perpetual system is debited to:
   (a) Raw Materials Purchases.
   (b) Raw Materials Inventory.
   (c) Purchases.
   (d) Work in Process.

(SO 2)   3. When incurred, factory labor costs are debited to:
   (a) Work in Process.
   (b) Factory Wages Expense.
   (c) Factory Labor.
   (d) Factory Wages Payable.

(SO 3)   4. The source documents for assigning costs to job cost sheets are:
   (a) invoices, time tickets, and the predetermined overhead rate.
   (b) materials requisition slips, time tickets, and the actual overhead costs.
   (c) materials requisition slips, payroll register, and the predetermined overhead rate.

   (d) materials requisition slips, time tickets, and the predetermined overhead rate.

(SO 3)   5. In recording the issuance of raw materials in a job order cost system, it would be *incorrect* to:
   (a) debit Work in Process Inventory.
   (b) debit Finished Goods Inventory.
   (c) debit Manufacturing Overhead.
   (d) credit Raw Materials Inventory.

(SO 3)   6. The entry when direct factory labor is assigned to jobs is a debit to:
   (a) Work in Process Inventory and a credit to Factory Labor.
   (b) Manufacturing Overhead and a credit to Factory Labor.
   (c) Factory Labor and a credit to Manufacturing Overhead.
   (d) Factory Labor and a credit to Work in Process Inventory.

(SO 4)   7. The formula for computing the predetermined manufacturing overhead rate is estimated annual overhead costs divided by an expected annual operating activity, expressed as:
   (a) direct labor cost.
   (b) direct labor hours.
   (c) machine hours.
   (d) any of the above.

Self-Study Questions provide a practice test, keyed to Study Objectives, that gives you an opportunity to check your knowledge of important topics. Answers appear on the last page of the chapter. *CD* and *Web icons* tell you that you can answer these *Self-Study Questions* interactively on either the CD or the Web site. Also, there is an additional *Self-Test* at the Web site that can further help you master the material.

Brief Exercises   **71**

...overhead ...ring the ...ts are in... ...abor and ...rhead in... ...overhead ...y should

   (c) $168,000.
   (d) $160,000.

(SO 5)   9. In BAC Company, Job No. 26 is completed at a cost of $4,500 and later sold for $7,000 cash. A correct entry is:

   (a) Debit Finished Goods Inventory $7,000 and credit Work in Process Inventory $7,000.
   (b) Debit Cost of Goods Sold $7,000 and credit Finished Goods Inventory $7,000.
   (c) Debit Finished Goods Inventory $4,500 and credit Work in Process Inventory $4,500.
   (d) Debit Accounts Receivable $7,000 and credit Sales $7,000.

(SO 6)   10. In preparing monthly financial statements, overapplied overhead is reported in the balance sheet as a(an):
   (a) prepaid expense.
   (b) unearned revenue.
   (c) noncurrent asset.
   (d) noncurrent liability.

THE NAVIGATOR

Questions allow you to explain your understanding of concepts and relationships covered in the chapter. Use them to help prepare for class discussion and tests.

QUESTIONS

1. Hal Adelman is studying for an accounting midterm examination. What should Hal know about how management may use job cost data?

2. (a) Marc Tucci is not sure about the differences between cost accounting and a cost accounting system. Explain the difference to Marc. (b) What is an important feature of a cost accounting system?

3. (a) Distinguish between the two types of cost accounting systems. (b) May a company use both types of cost accounting systems?

4. What type of industry is likely to use a job order cost system? Give some examples.

5. What type of industry is likely to use a process cost system? Give some examples.

6. Your roommate asks your help in understanding the major steps in the flow of costs in a job order cost system. Identify the steps for your roommate.

7. There are three inventory control accounts in a job order system. Identify the control accounts and their subsidiary ledgers.

8. What source documents are used in accumulating direct labor costs?

9. "Only normal daily entries are made to manufacturing overhead." Do you agree? Explain.

10. Phil Remmers is confused about the source documents used in assigning materials and labor costs. Identify the documents and give the entry for each document.

11. What is the purpose of a job cost sheet?

12. Indicate the source documents that are used in charging costs to specific jobs.

13. Differentiate between a "materials inventory record" and a "materials requisition slip" as used in a job order cost system.

14. John Simon believes actual manufacturing overhead should be charged to jobs. Do you agree? Why or why not?

15. What relationships are involved in computing a predetermined overhead rate?

16. How can the agreement of Work in Process Inventory and job cost sheets be verified?

17. Pam Smith believes that the cost of goods manufactured schedule in job order cost accounting (Illustration 2-20) is the same as the cost of goods manufactured schedule in general manufacturing accounting (see Illustration 1-7 in Chapter 1). Is Pam correct? Explain.

18. Greg Carnes is confused about under- and overapplied manufacturing overhead. Define the terms for Greg, and indicate the balance in the manufacturing overhead account applicable to each term.

19. "Under- or overapplied overhead is reported in the income statement when monthly financial statements are prepared." Do you agree? If not, indicate the proper presentation.

20. "At the end of the year, under- or overapplied overhead is closed to Income Summary." Is this correct? If not, indicate the customary treatment of this account.

Brief Exercises help you focus on one Study Objective at a time and thus help you build confidence in your basic skills and knowledge. (Keyed to Study Objectives.)

BRIEF EXERCISES

BE2-1   Sinason Tool & Die begins operations on January 1. Because all work is done to customer specifications, the company decides to use a job cost accounting system. Prepare a flow chart of a typical job order system with arrows showing the flow of costs. Identify the eight transactions.

Prepare a flowchart of a job order cost accounting system, and identify transactions. (SO 2)

Indicate statement classification of under- or overapplied overhead. (SO 6)

BE2-9   On September 30, balances in Man... debit $1,800, Mahmoud Company—credit $... port its balance at September 30, assuming e... ments on December 31.

Prepare adjusting entries for under- and overapplied overhead. (SO 6)

BE2-10   At December 31, balances in Manufacturing Overhead are: Sanchez Company—debit $1,000, Gomez Company—credit $900. Prepare the adjusting entry for each company at December 31, assuming the adjustment is made to cost of goods sold.

EXERCISES

Prepare entries for factory labor. (SO 2)

E2-1   The gross earnings of the factory workers for Cerrato Company during the month of January are $90,000. The employer's payroll taxes for the factory payroll are $9,000. The fringe benefits to be paid by the employer on this payroll are $4,000. Of the total accumulated cost of factory labor, 85% is related to direct labor and 15% is attributable to indirect labor.

Instructions
(a) Prepare the entry to record the factory labor costs for the month of January.
(b) Prepare the entry to assign factory labor to production.

Prepare journal entries for manufacturing costs. (SO 2, 3, 4, 5)

E2-2   Alvarez Manufacturing uses a job order cost accounting system. On May 1, the company has a balance in Work in Process Inventory of $3,200 and two jobs in process: Job No. 429 $2,000, and Job No. 430 $1,200. During May, a summary of source documents reveals the following:

Exercises, which are more difficult than Brief Exercises, help you continue to build confidence in your ability to use the material learned in the chapter. (Keyed to Study Objectives.)

Certain exercises and problems, marked with a pencil icon ✏️➤, help you practice **business writing skills**, which are much in demand among employers.

Instructions
(a) ✏️➤ On the basis of the foregoing data answer the following questions.
  (1) What was the balance in Work in Process Inventory on January 1 if this was the only unfinished job?
  (2) If manufacturing overhead is applied on the basis of direct labor cost, what overhead rate was used in each year?
(b) Prepare summary entries at January 31 to record the current year's transactions pertaining to Job No. 92.

E2-4 Manufacturing cost data for Lopez Company, which uses a job order cost system, are presented below.

Analyze costs of manufacturing and determine missing amounts.
(SO 2, 5)

	Case A	Case B	Case C
Direct materials	$ (a)	$83,000	$ 63,150
Direct labor used	50,000	90,000	(h)
Manufacturing overhead applied	42,500	(d)	(i)
Total manufacturing costs	185,650	(e)	287,000
Work in process 1/1/02	(b)	15,500	18,000
Total cost of work in process	201,500	(f)	(j)
Work in process 12/31/02	(c)	11,800	(k)
Cost of goods manufactured	192,300	(g)	262,000

76 CHAPTER 2 Job Order Cost Accounting

Job 12 was completed in April. Job 10 was completed in May. Jobs 11 and 13 were completed in June. Each job was sold for 60% above its cost in the month following completion.

Instructions
(a) What is the balance in Work in Process Inventory at the end of each month?
(b) What is the balance in Finished Goods Inventory at the end of each month?
(c) What is the gross profit for May, June, and July?

PROBLEMS: SET A

Prepare entries in a job cost system and job cost sheets.
(SO 2, 3, 4, 5, 6)

P2-1A Don Tidrick Manufacturing uses a job order cost system and applies overhead to production on the basis of direct labor costs. On January 1, 2002, Job No. 50 was the only job in process. The costs incurred prior to January 1 on this job were as follows: direct materials $20,000, direct labor $12,000, and manufacturing overhead $21,000. As of January 1, Job No. 49 had been completed at a cost of $90,000 and was part of finished goods inventory. There was a $15,000 balance in the Raw Materials inventory account.

During the month of January, Don Tidrick Manufacturing began production on Jobs 51 and 52, and completed Jobs 50 and 51. Jobs 49 and 50 were sold on account during the month for $122,000 and $158,000, respectively. The following additional events occurred during the month.

1. Purchased additional raw materials of $90,000 on account.
2. Incurred factory labor costs of $63,000. Of this amount $13,000 related to employer payroll taxes.
3. Incurred manufacturing overhead costs as follows: indirect materials $14,000; indirect labor $15,000; depreciation expense $19,000, and various other manufacturing overhead costs on account $23,000.
4. Assigned direct materials and direct labor to jobs as follows.

Job No.	Direct Materials	Direct Labor
50	$10,000	$ 6,000
51	39,000	24,000
52	30,000	18,000

Instructions
(a) Calculate the predetermined overhead rate for 2002, assuming Don Tidrick Manufacturing estimates total manufacturing overhead costs of $1,050,000, direct labor costs of $700,000, and direct labor hours of 20,000 for the year.
(b) Open job cost sheets for Jobs 50, 51, and 52. Enter the January 1 balances on the job cost sheet for Job No. 50.
(c) Prepare the journal entries to record the ... bor costs incurred, and the manufacturi... of January.
(d) Prepare the journal entries to record the ... and manufacturing overhead costs to p... head costs, use the overhead rate calcula... as necessary.
(e) Total the job cost sheets for any job(s) co... nal entry (or entries) to record the com...
(f) Prepare the journal entry (or entries) ... month.
(g) What is the balance in the Finished Good... What does this balance consist of?
(h) What is the amount of over- or underap... this be reported on the financial statem...

Prepare entries in a job cost system and partial income statement.
(SO 2, 3, 4, 5, 6)

P2-2A For the year ended December 31, 20... contained the following data.

Compute predetermined overhead rate, apply overhead, and indicate statement presentation of under- or overapplied overhead.
(SO 4, 6)

eGrade Problem

Each **Problem** helps you pull together and apply several concepts from the chapter. Two sets of **Problems—A** and **B**—are keyed to the same Study Objectives and provide additional opportunities to apply concepts learned in the chapter. (Keyed to multiple Study Objectives.)

P2-4A Urbana Manufacturing Company uses a job order cost system in each of its three manufacturing departments. Manufacturing overhead is applied to jobs on the basis of direct labor cost in Department D, direct labor hours in Department E, and machine hours in Department K.

In establishing the predetermined overhead rates for 2003 the following estimates were made for the year.

	Department		
	D	E	K
Manufacturing overhead	$1,170,000	$1,500,000	$960,000
Direct labor costs	$1,500,000	$1,250,000	$450,000
Direct labor hours	100,000	120,000	40,000
Machine hours	400,000	500,000	120,000

During January, the job cost sheets showed the following costs and production data.

	Department		
	D	E	K
Direct materials used	$140,000	$126,000	$78,000
Direct labor costs	$120,000	$110,000	$37,500
Manufacturing overhead incurred	$98,000	$129,000	$80,000
Direct labor hours	8,000	11,000	3,500
Machine hours	34,000	45,000	10,400

Instructions
(a) Compute the predetermined overhead rate for each department.
(b) Compute the total manufacturing costs assigned to jobs in January in each department.
(c) Compute the under- or overapplied overhead for each department at January 31.
(d) Indicate the statement presentation of the under- or overapplied overhead at January 31.
(e) If the amount in (d) was the same at December 31, how would it be reported in the year-end financial statements?

Analyze manufacturing accounts and determine missing amounts.
(SO 2, 3, 4, 5, 6)

P2-5A Florida Boot Corporation's fiscal year ends on November 30. The following accounts are found in its job order cost accounting system for the first month of the new fiscal year.

Raw Materials Inventory

Dec. 1	Beginning balance	(a)	Dec. 31	Requisitions	14,850
31	Purchases	19,225			
Dec. 31	Ending balance	7,975			

Work in Process Inventory

Dec. 1	Beginning balance	(b)	Dec. 31	Jobs completed	(f)
31	Direct materials	(c)			
31	Direct labor	8,100			
31	Overhead	(d)			
Dec. 31	Ending balance	(e)			

A **Web icon** tells you that you can practice certain **Problems** interactively at the Web site.

Spreadsheet Problems, identified by an icon, can be solved using the spreadsheet software *Solving Managerial Accounting Problems Using Excel.*

3. On July 1, Job No. 4084, costing $135,000, was in the finished goods warehouse. On July 31, Job No. 4088, costing $143,000, was in finished goods.
4. Manufacturing overhead was applied at the rate of 130% of direct labor cost. Overhead was $3,000 underapplied in July.

Instructions
List the letters (a) through (n) and indicate the amount pertaining to each letter. Show computations.

The **Broadening Your Perspective** section helps you pull together various concepts covered in the chapter and apply them to real-world business situations.

◆ **BROADENING YOUR PERSPECTIVE**

GROUP DECISION CASE

BYP2-1   Du Page Products Company uses a job order cost system. For a number of months there has been an ongoing rift between the sales department and the production department concerning a special-order product, TC-1. TC-1 is a seasonal product that is manufactured in batches of 1,000 units. TC-1 is sold at cost plus a markup of 40% of cost.

The sales department is unhappy because fluctuating unit production costs significantly affect selling prices. Sales personnel complain that this has caused excessive customer complaints and the loss of considerable orders for TC-1.

The production department maintains that each job order must be fully costed on the basis of the costs incurred during the period in which the goods are produced. Production personnel maintain that the only real solution to the problem is for the sales department to increase sales in the slack periods.

Sandra Devona, president of the company, asks you as the company accountant to collect quarterly data for the past year on TC-1. From the cost accounting system, you accumulate the following production quantity and cost data.

| | Quarter | | | |
Costs	1	2	3	4
Direct materials	$100,000	$220,000	$ 80,000	$200,000
Direct labor	60,000	132,000	48,000	120,000
Manufacturing overhead	105,000	123,000	97,000	125,000
Total	$265,000	$475,000	$225,000	$445,000
Production in batches	5	11	4	10
Unit cost (per batch)	$ 53,000	$ 43,182	$ 56,250	$ 44,500

Instructions
With the class divided into groups, answer the following questions.
(a) What manufacturing cost element is responsible for the fluctuating unit costs? Why?
(b) What is your recommended solution to the problem of fluctuating unit costs?
(c) Restate the quarterly data on the basis of your recommended solution.

Group Decision Cases help you build decision-making skills by analyzing accounting information in a less structured situation. These cases require evaluation of a manager's decision, or they lead to a decision among alternative course of action. These group activities help you prepare for the business world, where you will work with teams of colleagues to solve problems.

Managerial Analysis assignments build analytical and decision-making skills in situations encountered by managers. They also will require you to apply and practice business communication skills.

MANAGERIAL ANALYSIS

BYP2-2   In the course of routine checking of all journal entries prior to preparing month-end reports, Sally Weber discovered several strange entries. She recalled that the president's son Jeff had come in to help out during an especially busy time and that he had recorded some journal entries. She was relieved that there were only a few of his entries, and even more relieved that he had included rather lengthy explanations. The entries Jeff made were:

1.

| Work in Process Inventory | 20,000 | |
| Cash | | 20,000 |

(This is for materials put into process. I don't find the record that we paid for these, so I'm crediting Cash, because I know we'll have to pay for them sooner or later.)

2.

| Manufacturing Overhead | 12,000 | |
| Cash | | 12,000 |

(This is for bonuses paid to salespeople. I know they're part of overhead, and I can't find an account called "Non-factory Overhead" or "Other Overhead" so I'm putting it in Manufacturing Overhead. I have the check stubs, so I know we paid these.)

3.

| Wages Expense | 120,000 | |
| Cash | | 120,000 |

(This is for the factory workers' wages. I have a note that payroll taxes are $8,000. I still think that's part of wages expense, and that we'll have to pay it all in cash sooner or later, so I credited Cash for the wages and the taxes.)

4.

| Work in Process Inventory | 3,000 | |
| Raw Materials Inventory | | 3,000 |

(This is for the glue used in the factory. I know we used this to make the products, even though we didn't use very much on any one of the products. I got it out of inventory, so I credited an inventory account.)

Instructions
(a) How should Jeff have recorded each of the four events?
(b) If the entry was not corrected, which financial statements (income statement or balance sheet) would be affected? What balances would be overstated or understated?

REAL-WORLD FOCUS

BYP2-3 Founded in 1970, Parlex Corporation is a world leader in the design and manufacture of flexible interconnect products. Utilizing proprietary and patented technologies, Parlex produces custom flexible interconnects including flexible circuits, polymer thick film, laminated cables, and value-added assemblies for sophisticated electronics used in automotive, telecommunications, computer, diversified electronics, and aerospace applications. In addition to manufacturing sites in Methuen, Massachusetts; Salem, New Hampshire; Cranston, Rhode Island; San Jose, California; Shanghai, China; Isle of Wight, UK; and Empalme, Mexico, Parlex has logistic support centers and strategic alliances throughout North America, Asia, and Europe.

Real-World Focus problems ask you to apply techniques and concepts presented in the chapter to specific situations faced by actual companies. These problems often have a global focus.

Communication Activity **85**

The following information was provided in the company's annual report.

PARLEX COMPANY
Notes to the Financial Statements

The Company's products are manufactured on a job order basis to customers' specifications. Customers submit requests for quotations on each job, and the Company prepares bids based on its own cost estimates. The Company attempts to reflect the impact of changing costs when establishing prices. However, during the past several years, the market conditions for flexible circuits and the resulting price sensitivity haven't always allowed this to transpire. Although still not satisfactory, the Company was able to reduce the cost of products sold as a percentage of sales to 85% this year versus 87% that was experienced in the two immediately preceding years. Management continues to focus on improving operational efficiency and further reducing costs.

Instructions
(a) Parlex management discusses the job order cost system employed by their company. What are several advantages of using the job order approach to costing?
(b) Contrast the products produced in a job order environment, like Parlex, to those produced when process cost systems are used.

EXPLORING THE WEB

BYP2-4 The Institute of Management Accountants sponsors a certification for management accountants, allowing them to obtain the title of Certified Management Accountant.

Address: www.imanet.org **(or go to www.wiley.com/college/weygandt)**

Steps:

1. Go to the site shown above.
2. Choose **Certification**.

Instructions
(a) What are the objectives of the certification program?
(b) What is the "experience requirement"?
(c) How many hours of continuing education are required, and what types of courses qualify?

Exploring the Web exercises guide you to Internet sites where you can find and analyze information related to the chapter topic. These sites can be reached directly or by linking through the text's Web site.

COMMUNICATION ACTIVITY

BYP2-5 You are the management accountant for Modine Manufacturing. Your company does custom carpentry work and uses a job order cost accounting system. Modine sends detailed job cost sheets to its customers, along with an invoice. The job cost sheets show the date materials were used, the dollar cost of materials, and the hours and cost of labor. A predetermined overhead application rate is used, and the total overhead applied is also listed.

Cindy Ross is a customer who recently had custom cabinets installed. Along with her check in payment for the work done, she included a letter. She thanked the company for including the detailed cost information but questioned why overhead was estimated. She stated that she would be interested in knowing exactly what costs were included in overhead, and she thought that other customers would, too.

Communication Activities help you build business communication skills by asking you to engage in real-world business situations using writing, speaking, or presentation skills.

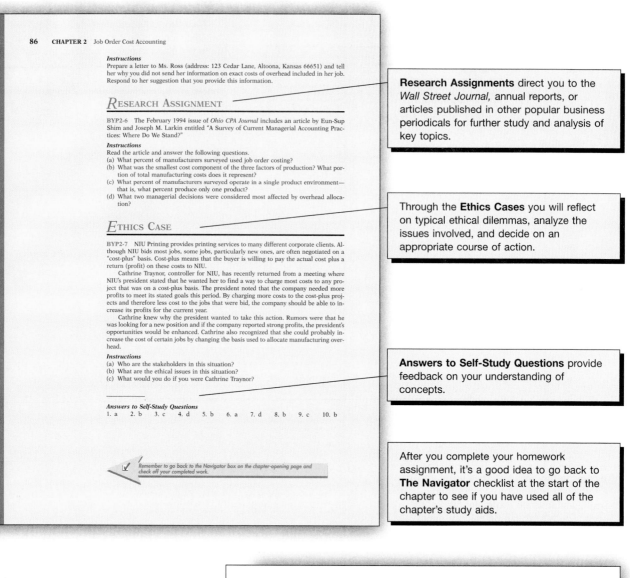

Research Assignments direct you to the *Wall Street Journal,* annual reports, or articles published in other popular business periodicals for further study and analysis of key topics.

Through the **Ethics Cases** you will reflect on typical ethical dilemmas, analyze the issues involved, and decide on an appropriate course of action.

Answers to Self-Study Questions provide feedback on your understanding of concepts.

After you complete your homework assignment, it's a good idea to go back to **The Navigator** checklist at the start of the chapter to see if you have used all of the chapter's study aids.

Cases for Management Decision Making, provided at the end of the text, ask you to use the decision tools presented in the chapters in realistic business situations. Your instructor can assign cases as a comprehensive capstone activity at the end of the course or as a recurring activity during the course.

CASE-1

CARD-MART SWIMS IN THE DOT-COM SEA: JOB ORDER COSTING

Developed by Thomas L. Zeller, Loyola University Chicago and Paul D. Kimmel, University of Wisconsin–Milwaukee

THE BUSINESS SITUATION

Card-Mart Inc. has operated for many years as a nationally recognized retailer of greeting cards and small gift items. It has 1,500 stores throughout the United States located in high-traffic malls.

During the late 1990s, as the stock price of many other companies soared, Card-Mart's stock price remained flat. As a result of a heated 1998 shareholders' meeting, the president of Card-Mart, William Green, came under pressure from shareholders to grow Card-Mart's stock value. As a consequence of this pressure, in 1999 Mr. Green called for a formal analysis of the company's options with regard to business opportunities.

HOW DO I LEARN BEST?

This questionnaire aims to find out something about your preferences for the way you work with information. You will have a preferred learning style and one part of that learning style is your preference for the intake and the output of ideas and information.

Circle the letter of the answer that best explains your preference. Circle more than one if a single answer does not match your perception. Leave blank any question that does not apply.

1. You are about to give directions to a person who is standing with you. She is staying in a hotel in town and wants to visit your house later. She has a rental car. Would you
   a. draw a map on paper?
   b. tell her the directions?
   c. write down the directions (without a map)?
   d. pick her up at the hotel in your car?

2. You are not sure whether a word should be spelled "dependent" or "dependant." Do you
   c. look it up in the dictionary?
   a. see the word in your mind and choose by the way it looks?
   b. sound it out in your mind?
   d. write both versions down on paper and choose one?

3. You have just received a copy of your itinerary for a world trip. This is of interest to a friend. Would you
   b. call her immediately and tell her about it?
   c. send her a copy of the printed itinerary?
   a. show her on a map of the world?
   d. share what you plan to do at each place you visit?

4. You are going to cook something as a special treat for your family. Do you
   d. cook something familiar without the need for instructions?
   a. thumb through the cookbook looking for ideas from the pictures?
   c. refer to a specific cookbook where there is a good recipe?

5. A group of tourists has been assigned to you to find out about wildlife reserves or parks. Would you
   d. drive them to a wildlife reserve or park?
   a. show them slides and photographs?
   c. give them pamphlets or a book on wildlife reserves or parks?
   b. give them a talk on wildlife reserves or parks?

6. You are about to purchase a new CD player. Other than price, what would most influence your decision?
   b. The salesperson telling you what you want to know.
   c. Reading the details about it.
   d. Playing with the controls and listening to it.
   a. Its fashionable and upscale appearance.

7. Recall a time in your life when you learned how to do something like playing a new board game. Try to avoid choosing a very physical skill, e.g., riding a bike. How did you learn best? By
   a. visual clues—pictures, diagrams, charts?
   c. written instructions?
   b. listening to somebody explaining it?
   d. doing it or trying it?

8. You have an eye problem. Would you prefer that the doctor
   b. tell you what is wrong?
   a. show you a diagram of what is wrong?
   d. use a model to show what is wrong?

9. You are about to learn to use a new program on a computer. Would you
   d. sit down at the keyboard and begin to experiment with the program's features?
   c. read the manual that comes with the program?
   b. call a friend and ask questions about it?

10. You are staying in a hotel and have a rental car. You would like to visit friends whose address/location you do not know. Would you like them to
    a. draw you a map on paper?
    b. tell you the directions?
    c. write down the directions (without a map)?
    d. pick you up at the hotel in their car?

11. Apart from price, what would most influence your decision to buy a particular book?
    d. You have used a copy before.
    b. A friend talking about it.
    c. Quickly reading parts of it.
    a. The appealing way it looks.

12. A new movie has arrived in town. What would most influence your decision to go (or not go)?
    b. You heard a radio review about it.
    c. You read a review about it.
    a. You saw a preview of it.

13. Do you prefer a lecturer or teacher who likes to use
    c. a textbook, handouts, readings?
    a. flow diagrams, charts, graphs?
    d. field trips, labs, practical sessions?
    b. discussion, guest speakers?

Count your choices:

a.	b.	c.	d.
V	A	R	K

Now match the letter or letters you have recorded most to the same letter or letters in the Learning Styles Chart. You may have more than one learning style preference—many people do. Next to each letter in the chart are suggestions that will refer you to different learning aids throughout this text.

LEARNING STYLES CHART

 **V** ISUAL

INTAKE: TO TAKE IN THE INFORMATION	TO MAKE A STUDY PACKAGE	TEXT FEATURES THAT MAY HELP YOU THE MOST	OUTPUT: TO DO WELL ON EXAMS
• Pay close attention to charts, drawings, and handouts your instructor uses. • Underline. • Use different colors. • Use symbols, flow charts, graphs, different arrangements on the page, white space.	Convert your lecture notes into "page pictures." To do this: • Use the "Intake" strategies. • Reconstruct images in different ways. • Redraw pages from memory. • Replace words with symbols and initials. • Look at your pages.	**The Navigator** **Feature Story** **Preview** **Infographics/Illustrations** **Photos** **Business Insights** **Decision Toolkits** **Key Terms in blue** **Words in bold** **Demonstration Problem/Action Plan** **Questions/Exercises/Problems** **Real-World Focus** **Exploring the Web**	• Recall your "page pictures." • Draw diagrams where appropriate. • Practice turning your visuals back into words.

 **A** URAL

INTAKE: TO TAKE IN THE INFORMATION	TO MAKE A STUDY PACKAGE	TEXT FEATURES THAT MAY HELP YOU THE MOST	OUTPUT: TO DO WELL ON EXAMS
• Attend lectures and tutorials. • Discuss topics with students and instructors. • Explain new ideas to other people. • Use a tape recorder. • Leave spaces in your lecture notes for later recall. • Describe overheads, pictures, and visuals to somebody who was not in class.	You may take poor notes because you prefer to listen. Therefore: • Expand your notes by talking with others and with information from your textbook. • Tape record summarized notes and listen. • Read summarized notes out loud. • Explain your notes to another "aural" person.	**Infographics/Illustrations** **Business Insights** **Review It/Do It/Action Plan** **Summary of Study Objectives** **Glossary** **Demonstration Problem/Action Plan** **Self-Study Questions** **Questions/Exercises/Problems** **Group Decision Case** **Managerial Analysis** **Exploring the Web** **Communication Activity** **Ethics Case**	• Talk with the instructor. • Spend time in quiet places recalling the ideas. • Practice writing answers to old exam questions. • Say your answers out loud.

R READING/WRITING

INTAKE: TO TAKE IN THE INFORMATION	TO MAKE A STUDY PACKAGE	TEXT FEATURES THAT MAY HELP YOU THE MOST	OUTPUT: TO DO WELL ON EXAMS
• Use lists and headings. • Use dictionaries, glossaries, and definitions. • Read handouts, textbooks, and supplementary library readings. • Use lecture notes.	• Write out words again and again. • Reread notes silently. • Rewrite ideas and principles into other words. • Turn charts, diagrams, and other illustrations into statements.	**The Navigator** **Feature Story** **Study Objectives** **Preview** **Review It/Do It/Action Plan** **Using the Decision Toolkit** **Summary of Study Objectives** **Glossary** **Self-Study Questions** **Questions/Exercises/Problems** **Writing Problems** **Group Decision Case** **Managerial Analysis** **Real-World Focus** **Communication Activity** **Ethics Case**	• Write exam answers. • Practice with multiple-choice questions. • Write paragraphs, beginnings and endings. • Write your lists in outline form. • Arrange your words into hierarchies and points.

K KINESTHETIC

INTAKE: TO TAKE IN THE INFORMATION	TO MAKE A STUDY PACKAGE	TEXT FEATURES THAT MAY HELP YOU THE MOST	OUTPUT: TO DO WELL ON EXAMS
• Use all your senses. • Go to labs, take field trips. • Listen to real-life examples. • Pay attention to applications. • Use hands-on approaches. • Use trial-and-error methods.	You may take poor notes because topics do not seem concrete or relevant. Therefore: • Put examples in your summaries. • Use case studies and applications to help with principles and abstract concepts. • Talk about your notes with another "kinesthetic" person. • Use pictures and photographs that illustrate an idea.	**The Navigator** **Feature Story** **Preview** **Infographics/Illustrations** **Decision Toolkits** **Review It/Do It/Action Plan** **Using the Decision Toolkit** **Summary of Study Objectives** **Demonstration Problem/ Action Plan** **Self-Study Questions** **Questions/Exercises/Problems** **Group Decision Case** **Managerial Analysis** **Real-World Focus** **Exploring the Web** **Communication Activity**	• Write practice answers. • Role-play the exam situation.

For all learning styles: Be sure to use the CD-ROM and Web site to enhance your understanding of the concepts and procedures of the text. In particular, use the **Accounting Cycle Tutorial, Interactive Demonstration Problems, Interactive Self-Study** and **Self-Tests,** and **Key Term Matching Activities.**

BRIEF CONTENTS

CONTENTS

CHAPTER 12   The Statement
of Cash Flows   478

CHAPTER 13   Financial
Analysis: The Big Picture   548

CHAPTER 1

Managerial Accounting

Study Objectives gives you a framework for learning the specific concepts covered in the chapter.

◆ STUDY OBJECTIVES

After studying this chapter, you should be able to:

1 Explain the distinguishing features of managerial accounting.

2 Identify the three broad functions of management.

3 Define the three classes of manufacturing costs.

4 Distinguish between product and period costs.

5 Explain the difference between a merchandising and a manufacturing income statement.

6 Indicate how cost of goods manufactured is determined.

7 Explain the difference between a merchandising and a manufacturing balance sheet.

THE NAVIGATOR

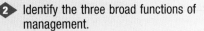

THE NAVIGATOR ✔

- Scan *Study Objectives* ☐
- Read *Feature Story* ☐
- Read *Preview* ☐
- Read text and answer *Before You Go On*
  p. 7 ☐   p. 9 ☐   p. 19 ☐
- Work *Using the Decision Toolkit* ☐
- Review *Summary of Study Objectives* ☐
- Work *Demonstration Problem* ☐
- Answer *Self-Study Questions* ☐
- Complete *Assignments* ☐

The **Navigator** is a learning system designed to prompt you to use the learning aids in the chapter and to help you set priorities as you study.

◆ FEATURE STORY

WHAT A DIFFERENCE A DAY MAKES

In January 1998 **Compaq Computer** had just become the largest seller of personal computers, and it was *Forbes* magazine's "company of the year." Its chief executive, Eckhard Pfeiffer, was riding high. But during the next two years Compaq lost $2 billion. The company was in chaos, and Mr. Pfeiffer was out of a job. What happened?

First, Dell happened. **Dell Computer** pioneered a new way of making and selling personal computers. Its customers "custom design" their computer over the Internet or phone. Dell reengineered its "supply chain": It coordinated its efforts with its suppliers and streamlined its order-taking and production process, and it can ship a computer within two days of taking an order. Personal computers lose 1 percent of their value every week they sit on a shelf. Thus, having virtually no inventory is a great advantage to Dell. Compaq tried to adopt Dell's approach, but with limited success.

The second shock to Compaq came when it acquired a company even larger than itself—**Digital**

Equipment. Digital was famous as much for its technical service as it was for its products. Mr. Pfeiffer believed that the purchase of Digital, with its huge and respected technical sales force, opened new opportunities for Compaq as a global service company. Now it could sell to and service high-end corporate customers. But combining the two companies proved to be hugely expensive and extremely complicated.

Managers are evaluated on the results of their decisions. In the long run, it may turn out that Mr. Pfeiffer had great strategic vision and made a good decision. But, in a world that wants results at "Internet speed," Compaq's board of directors wasn't willing to wait and see. Managers in today's rapidly changing global environment often must make decisions that determine their company's fate, and their own. This textbook discusses techniques used to assist managers in making these decisions.

THE NAVIGATOR

www.compaq.com
www.dell.com

The **Preview** describes the purpose of the chapter and outlines the major topics and subtopics you will find in it.

This book focuses on issues illustrated in the Feature Story about **Compaq Computer**. These include determining and controlling the costs of material, labor, and overhead and the relationship between costs and profits. In a previous financial accounting course, you learned about the form and content of **financial statements for external users** of financial information, such as stockholders and creditors. These financial statements represent the principal product of financial accounting. Managerial accounting focuses primarily on the preparation of **reports for internal users** of financial information, such as the managers and officers of a company. Managerial accounting provides tools for assisting management in making decisions and for evaluating the effectiveness of those decisions. The content and organization of this chapter are as follows.

MANAGERIAL ACCOUNTING

Managerial Accounting Basics	Managerial Cost Concepts	Manufacturing Costs in Financial Statements	Contemporary Developments in Managerial Accounting
• Comparing managerial and financial accounting • Ethical standards • Management functions	• Manufacturing costs • Product vs. period costs	• Income statement • Balance sheet • Cost concepts: A review	• Service industry trends • Value chain management

THE NAVIGATOR

MANAGERIAL ACCOUNTING BASICS

Essential terms and concepts are printed in blue where they first appear and are defined in the end-of-chapter Glossary.

Managerial accounting, also called management accounting, is a field of accounting that provides economic and financial information for managers and other internal users. The activities that are part of managerial accounting (and the chapters in which they are discussed) are as follows.

1. Explaining manufacturing and nonmanufacturing costs and how they are reported in the financial statements (Chapter 1).
2. Computing the cost of providing a service or manufacturing a product (Chapters 2, 3, and 4).
3. Determining the behavior of costs and expenses as activity levels change and analyzing cost–volume–profit relationships within a company (Chapter 5).
4. Assisting management in profit planning and formalizing these plans in the form of budgets (Chapter 6).
5. Providing a basis for controlling costs and expenses by comparing actual results with planned objectives and standard costs (Chapters 7 and 8).
6. Accumulating and presenting relevant data for management decision making (Chapters 9 and 10).
7. Determining prices for external and internal transactions (Chapter 11).

Managerial accounting applies to all types of businesses—service, merchandising, and manufacturing. It also applies to all forms of business organizations—proprietorships, partnerships, and corporations. Managerial accounting is needed in not-for-profit entities as well as in profit-oriented enterprises.

Not long ago, the managerial accountant was primarily engaged in cost accounting—collecting and reporting manufacturing costs to management. Today, the managerial accountant's responsibilities extend to **strategic cost management**—providing managers with data on the efficient use of company resources in both manufacturing and service industries.

COMPARING MANAGERIAL AND FINANCIAL ACCOUNTING

STUDY OBJECTIVE

1

Explain the distinguishing features of managerial accounting.

There are both similarities and differences between managerial and financial accounting. First, each field of accounting deals with the economic events of a business. Thus, their interests overlap. For example, determining the unit cost of manufacturing a product is part of managerial accounting. Reporting the total cost of goods manufactured and sold is part of financial accounting. In addition, both managerial and financial accounting require that a company's economic events be quantified and communicated to interested parties.

The principal differences between financial accounting and managerial accounting are summarized in Illustration 1-1. The diverse needs for economic data among interested parties are responsible for many of the differences.

Illustration 1-1 Differences between financial and managerial accounting

Financial Accounting		Managerial Accounting
• External users: stockholders, creditors, and regulators.	**Primary Users of Reports**	• Internal users: officers and managers.
• Financial statements. • Quarterly and annually.	**Types and Frequency of Reports**	• Internal reports. • As frequently as needed.
• General-purpose.	**Purpose of Reports**	• Special-purpose for specific decisions.
• Pertains to business as a whole. • Highly aggregated (condensed). • Limited to double-entry accounting and cost data. • Generally accepted accounting principles.	**Content of Reports**	• Pertains to subunits of the business. • Very detailed. • Extends beyond double-entry accounting to any relevant data. • Standard is relevance to decisions.
• Audit by CPA.	**Verification Process**	• No independent audits.

ETHICAL STANDARDS FOR MANAGERIAL ACCOUNTANTS

Managerial accountants have an ethical obligation to their companies and the public. To provide guidance for managerial accountants, the Institute of Management Accountants (IMA) has developed a code of ethical standards, entitled *Standards of Ethical Conduct for Practitioners of Management Accounting and Financial Management.* This code divides the managerial accountants' responsibilities into four areas: (1) competence, (2) confidentiality, (3) integrity, and (4) objectivity. The code states that management accountants should not commit acts in violation of these standards. Nor should they condone such acts by others within their organizations.

Helpful Hints clarify concepts being discussed.

Helpful Hint The IMA code of ethical standards is provided in Appendix D.

MANAGEMENT FUNCTIONS

Management's activities and responsibilities can be classified into three broad functions. They are:

1. Planning.
2. Directing and motivating.
3. Controlling.

In performing these functions, managers make decisions that have a significant impact on the organization.

Planning requires management to look ahead and to establish objectives. These objectives are often diverse: maximizing short-term profits and market share, maintaining a commitment to environmental protection, and contributing to social programs. A key objective of management is to add **value** to the business under its control. Value is usually measured by the trading price of the company's stock and by the potential selling price of the company.

Directing and **motivating** involves coordinating a company's diverse activities and human resources to produce a smooth-running operation. This function relates to implementing planned objectives and providing necessary incentives. For example, manufacturers such as **Campbell Soup Company**, **General Motors**, and **Compaq Computer** must coordinate purchasing, manufacturing, warehousing, and selling. Service corporations such as **American Airlines**, **Federal Express**, and **AT&T** must coordinate scheduling, sales, and acquisitions of equipment and supplies. Directing also involves selecting executives, appointing managers and supervisors, and hiring and training employees. Most companies prepare **organization charts** to show the interrelationship of activities and the delegation of authority and responsibility within the company.

The third management function, **controlling**, is the process of keeping the company's activities on track. In controlling operations, managers determine whether planned goals are being met. When there are deviations from targeted objectives, they must decide what changes are needed to get back on track.

How do managers achieve control? A smart manager in a small operation should make personal observations, ask good questions, and know how to evaluate the answers. But such a system in a large organization would be chaotic. Imagine the president of **Compaq Computer** attempting to determine whether planned objectives are being met without some record of what has happened

ℓ — BUSINESS INSIGHT

The trend toward more automated and computerized factories has changed the way managers and employees interact. For one thing, managers have fewer direct labor employees to supervise because fewer are needed on the line. Instead of standing in one spot all day, employees and managers have become more mobile, monitoring the computers that control production, and involving themselves in a variety of jobs.

Recently, two technology giants, **General Electric** and **Cisco Systems**, joined forces to build computerized infrastructures for manufacturers. Their goal is to improve productivity by making better use of data generated by factory-automation equipment. Ultimately their systems should provide a closer link between the factory and corporate offices. They believe the market for such systems will be $3 billion by 2003.

and what is expected to occur. Thus, a formal system of evaluation is typically used in large businesses. It would include such items as budgets, responsibility centers, and performance evaluation reports.

Decision making is not a separate management function. Rather, it is the outcome of the exercise of good judgment in planning, directing, motivating, and controlling.

You are now ready to study specific applications of managerial accounting. As you study the managerial chapters, you will encounter many new terms, concepts, and reports. At the same time, you will find some new uses and interpretations of a number of familiar financial accounting terms.

BEFORE YOU GO ON . . .

◆ Review It

1. Compare financial accounting and managerial accounting, identifying the principal differences.
2. Identify and discuss the three broad functions of management.

THE NAVIGATOR

Before You Go On . . . Review It questions at the end of major text sections offer an opportunity to stop and re-examine the key points you have studied.

MANAGERIAL COST CONCEPTS

To perform the three management functions effectively, management needs information. One very important type of information is related to costs. For example, questions such as the following should be asked.

1. What costs are involved in making a product or providing a service?
2. If production volume is decreased, will costs decrease?
3. What impact will automation have on total costs?
4. How can costs best be controlled?

To answer these questions, management needs reliable and relevant cost information. We now explain and illustrate the costs that management uses.

MANUFACTURING COSTS

Manufacturing consists of activities and processes that convert raw materials into finished goods. Contrast this type of operation with merchandising, which sells merchandise in the form in which it is purchased. Manufacturing costs are typically classified as shown in Illustration 1-2.

STUDY OBJECTIVE

3

Define the three classes of manufacturing costs.

Illustrations like this one convey information in pictorial form to help you visualize and apply the ideas as you study.

Illustration 1-2 Classifications of manufacturing costs

Manufacturing Costs

Direct Materials

Direct Labor

Manufacturing Overhead

Direct Materials

Direct Materials

To obtain the materials that will be converted into the finished product, the manufacturer purchases raw materials. **Raw materials** are the basic materials and parts used in the manufacturing process. For example, auto manufacturers such as **General Motors**, **Ford**, and **DaimlerChrysler** use steel, plastics, and tires as raw materials in making cars.

Raw materials that can be physically and directly associated with the finished product during the manufacturing process are called direct materials. Examples include flour in the baking of bread, syrup in the bottling of soft drinks, and steel in the making of automobiles. In the Feature Story, direct materials for **Compaq Computer** and **Dell Computer** include plastic, glass, hard drives, and processing chips.

But some raw materials cannot be easily associated with the finished product. These are considered indirect materials. Indirect materials (1) do not physically become part of the finished product, such as lubricants and polishing compounds, or (2) cannot be traced because their physical association with the finished product is too small in terms of cost, such as cotter pins and lock washers. Indirect materials are accounted for as part of **manufacturing overhead**.

Helpful Hint A manufacturer uses masking tape to protect certain sections of its product while other sections are painted. The tape is removed and thrown away when the paint is dry. Is the tape a direct or an indirect material? Answer: Indirect.

Direct Labor

Direct Labor

The work of factory employees that can be physically and directly associated with converting raw materials into finished goods is considered direct labor. Bottlers at **Coca-Cola**, bakers at **Sara Lee**, and typesetters at **TechBooks** are employees whose activities are usually classified as direct labor. In contrast, the wages of maintenance people, time-keepers, and supervisors are usually identified as indirect labor. Their efforts have no physical association with the finished product, or it is impractical to trace the costs to the goods produced. Like indirect materials, indirect labor is classified as **manufacturing overhead**.

BUSINESS INSIGHT
Management Perspective

Recently a closely watched study of productivity reported that a U.S. manufacturer, **Ford**, outperformed the North American plants of many of its Japanese rivals. It also reported that productivity at **General Motors** had improved the most of all auto makers. On a per car basis, GM spends $1,979 on labor and benefits. Ford spends $1,667, and **Nissan**, the most efficient of all North American operators, spends just $1,055. If GM were as efficient as Nissan it would reduce labor spending by $5.3 billion.

Source: Karen Lundegaard, "Ford Plant, GM Receive High Marks in Study of Auto Makers' Productivity." *Wall Street Journal*, June 16, 2000.

Manufacturing Overhead

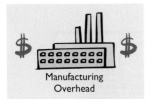
Manufacturing Overhead

Manufacturing overhead consists of costs that are indirectly associated with the manufacture of the finished product. These costs may also be manufacturing costs that cannot be classified as direct materials or direct labor. Manufacturing overhead includes indirect materials, indirect labor, depreciation on factory buildings and machines, and insurance, taxes, and maintenance on factory facilities.

One study found the following magnitudes of the three different product costs as a percentage of the total product cost: direct materials 54.4 percent, direct labor 12.9 percent, and manufacturing overhead 32.6 percent. Note that the direct labor component is the smallest. This component of product cost is dropping substantially because of automation. In some companies, direct labor has become as little as 5 percent of the total cost.

Allocating materials and labor costs to specific products is fairly straightforward. But dealing with overhead presents problems. How much of the purchasing agent's salary is attributable to the hundreds of products made in the same plant? What about the grease that keeps the machines humming, or the computers that make sure paychecks come out on time? Boiled down to its simplest form, the question becomes: Which products cause which costs? In subsequent chapters we show various methods of allocating overhead to products.

PRODUCT VERSUS PERIOD COSTS

Each of the manufacturing cost components (direct materials, direct labor, and manufacturing overhead) are product costs. As the term suggests, **product costs** are costs that are a necessary and integral part of producing the finished product. Product costs are recorded as inventory when incurred. Under the matching principle, these costs do not become expenses until the finished goods inventory is sold. The expense is cost of goods sold.

Period costs are costs that are matched with the revenue of a specific time period rather than included as part of the cost of a salable product. These are nonmanufacturing costs. Period costs include selling and administrative expenses. They are deducted from revenues in the period in which they are incurred.

The foregoing relationships and cost terms are summarized in Illustration 1-3. Our main concern in this chapter is with product costs.

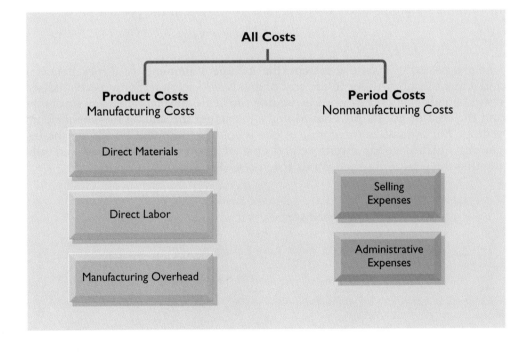

Alternative Terminology notes present synonymous terms used in practice.

Alternative Terminology Terms such as *factory overhead*, *indirect manufacturing costs*, and *burden* are sometimes used instead of manufacturing overhead.

STUDY OBJECTIVE
4
Distinguish between product and period costs.

Alternative Terminology Product costs are also called *inventoriable costs*.

Illustration 1-3 Product versus period costs

All Costs

Product Costs
Manufacturing Costs

Direct Materials

Direct Labor

Manufacturing Overhead

Period Costs
Nonmanufacturing Costs

Selling Expenses

Administrative Expenses

Helpful Hint An unethical manager may choose to inflate the company's earnings by absorbing period costs (such as selling and administrative expenses not pertaining to production) in the ending inventory balances.

BEFORE YOU GO ON . . .

◆ **Review It**

1. What are the major cost classifications involved in manufacturing a product?
2. What are product and period costs, and what is their relationship to the manufacturing process?

◆ Do It

A bicycle company has these costs: tires, salaries of employees who put tires on the wheels, factory building depreciation, wheel nuts, spokes, salary of factory manager, handle bars, and salaries of factory maintenance employees. Classify each cost as direct materials, direct labor, or overhead.

Action Plan
• Classify as direct materials any raw materials that can be physically and directly associated with the finished product.
• Classify as direct labor the work of factory employees that can be physically and directly associated with the finished product.
• Classify as manufacturing overhead any costs that are indirectly associated with the finished product.

Solution: Tires, spokes, and handle bars are direct materials. Salaries of employees who put tires on the wheels are direct labor. All of the other costs are manufacturing overhead.

Related exercise material: BE1-4, BE1-5, BE1-7, E1-1, and E1-2.

MANUFACTURING COSTS IN FINANCIAL STATEMENTS

The financial statements of a manufacturer are very similar to those of a merchandiser. The principal differences pertain to the cost of goods sold section in the income statement and the current assets section in the balance sheet.

INCOME STATEMENT

Under a periodic inventory system, the income statements of a merchandiser and a manufacturer differ in the cost of goods sold section. For a merchandiser, cost of goods sold is computed by adding the beginning merchandise inventory and the **cost of goods purchased** and subtracting the ending merchandise inventory. For a manufacturer, cost of goods sold is computed by adding the beginning finished goods inventory and **cost of goods manufactured** and subtracting the ending finished goods inventory. (See Illustration 1-4.)

Illustration 1-4 Cost of goods sold components

Helpful Hint A periodic inventory system is assumed here.

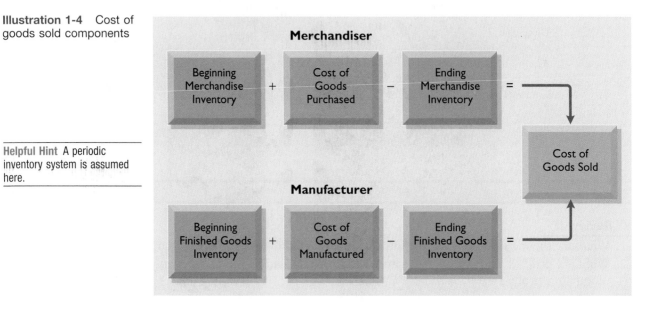

The cost of goods sold sections for merchandising and manufacturing companies in Illustration 1-5 show the different presentations. The other sections of an income statement are similar for merchandisers and manufacturers.

Illustration 1-5 Cost of goods sold sections of merchandising and manufacturing income statements

MERCHANDISING COMPANY Income Statement (partial) For the Year Ended December 31, 2002		MANUFACTURING COMPANY Income Statement (partial) For the Year Ended December 31, 2002	
Cost of goods sold		Cost of goods sold	
Merchandise inventory, January 1	$ 70,000	Finished goods inventory, January 1	$ 90,000
Cost of goods purchased	650,000	Cost of goods manufactured (see Illustration 1-7)	370,000
Cost of goods available for sale	720,000	Cost of goods available for sale	460,000
Merchandise inventory, December 31	400,000	Finished goods inventory, December 31	80,000
Cost of goods sold	$320,000	Cost of goods sold	$380,000

A number of accounts are involved in determining the cost of goods manufactured. To eliminate excessive detail, it is customary to show in the income statement only the total cost of goods manufactured. The details are presented in a Cost of Goods Manufactured Schedule. The form and content of this schedule are shown in Illustration 1-7 (page 12).

Determining the Cost of Goods Manufactured

An example may help show how the cost of goods manufactured is determined. Assume that **Compaq Computer** has a number of computers in various stages of production on January 1. In total, these partially completed units are called **beginning work in process inventory**. The costs assigned to beginning work in process inventory are based on the **manufacturing costs incurred in the prior period**.

The manufacturing costs incurred in the current year are used first to complete the work in process on January 1. They then are used to start the production of other computers. The sum of the direct materials costs, direct labor costs, and manufacturing overhead incurred in the current year is the **total manufacturing costs** for the current period.

We now have two cost amounts: (1) the cost of the beginning work in process and (2) the total manufacturing costs for the current period. The sum of these costs is the **total cost of work in process** for the year.

At the end of the year, some computers may be only partially completed. The costs of these units become the cost of the **ending work in process inventory**. To find the **cost of goods manufactured**, we subtract this cost from the total cost of work in process. The determination of the cost of goods manufactured is shown graphically in Illustration 1-6 on the next page.

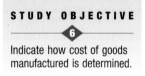

STUDY OBJECTIVE
6
Indicate how cost of goods manufactured is determined.

Helpful Hint Does the amount of "total manufacturing costs for the current year" include the amount of "beginning work in process inventory?" Answer: No.

Illustration 1-6   Cost of goods manufactured formula

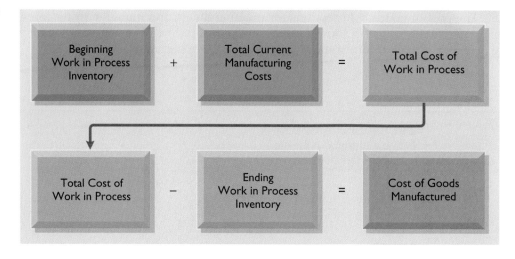

Cost of Goods Manufactured Schedule

An internal report shows each of the cost elements shown in Illustration 1-6. This report is called the **cost of goods manufactured schedule**. The schedule for Olsen Manufacturing Company (using assumed data) is shown in Illustration 1-7. Note that the schedule presents detailed data for direct materials and for manufacturing overhead.

Review Illustration 1-6 and then examine the cost of goods manufactured schedule in Illustration 1-7. You should be able to distinguish between "total manufacturing costs" and "cost of goods manufactured." The difference is the effect of the change in work in process during the period.

Illustration 1-7   Cost of goods manufactured schedule

Often, numbers or categories in the financial statements are highlighted in **red type** to draw your attention to key information.

OLSEN MANUFACTURING COMPANY Cost of Goods Manufactured Schedule For the Year Ended December 31, 2002			
Work in process, January 1			$ 18,400
Direct materials			
Raw materials inventory, January 1	$ 16,700		
Raw materials purchases	152,500		
Total raw materials available for use	169,200		
Less: Raw materials inventory, December 31	22,800		
Direct materials used		$146,400	
Direct labor		175,600	
Manufacturing overhead			
Indirect labor	14,300		
Factory repairs	12,600		
Factory utilities	10,100		
Factory depreciation	9,440		
Factory insurance	8,360		
Total manufacturing overhead		54,800	
Total manufacturing costs			376,800
Total cost of work in process			395,200
Less: Work in process, December 31			25,200
Cost of goods manufactured			$370,000

DECISION TOOLKIT

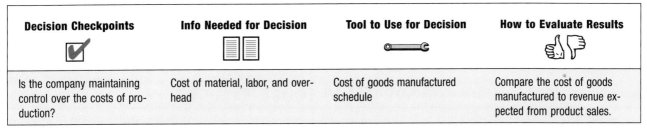

Decision Checkpoints	Info Needed for Decision	Tool to Use for Decision	How to Evaluate Results
Is the company maintaining control over the costs of production?	Cost of material, labor, and overhead	Cost of goods manufactured schedule	Compare the cost of goods manufactured to revenue expected from product sales.

BALANCE SHEET

The balance sheet for a merchandising company shows just one category of inventory. In contrast, the balance sheet for a manufacturer may have three inventory accounts. They are:

> Each chapter presents useful information about how decision makers analyze and solve business problems. **Decision Toolkits** summarize the key features of a decision tool and review why and how to use it.

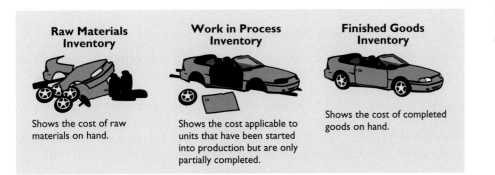

Raw Materials Inventory
Shows the cost of raw materials on hand.

Work in Process Inventory
Shows the cost applicable to units that have been started into production but are only partially completed.

Finished Goods Inventory
Shows the cost of completed goods on hand.

Illustration 1-8
Inventory accounts for a manufacturer

Finished Goods Inventory is to a manufacturer what Merchandise Inventory is to a merchandiser. It represents the goods that are available for sale.

The current assets sections presented in Illustration 1-9 contrast the presentations of inventories for merchandising and manufacturing companies. Manufacturing inventories are generally listed in the order of their liquidity—the order in which they are expected to be realized in cash. Thus, finished goods inventory is listed first. The remainder of the balance sheet is similar for the two types of companies.

STUDY OBJECTIVE

Explain the difference between a merchandising and a manufacturing balance sheet.

Illustration 1-9 Current assets sections of merchandising and manufacturing balance sheets

MERCHANDISING COMPANY Balance Sheet December 31, 2002			MANUFACTURING COMPANY Balance Sheet December 31, 2002		
Current assets			Current assets		
Cash		$100,000	Cash		$180,000
Receivables (net)		210,000	Receivables (net)		210,000
Merchandise inventory		400,000	Inventories		
Prepaid expenses		22,000	Finished goods	$80,000	
			Work in process	25,200	
Total current assets		$732,000	Raw materials	22,800	128,000
			Prepaid expenses		18,000
			Total current assets		$536,000

Each step in the accounting cycle for a merchandiser applies to a manufacturer. For example, prior to preparing financial statements, adjusting entries are required. The adjusting entries are essentially the same as those of a merchandiser. The closing entries are also similar for manufacturers and merchandisers. (For more detail, see Appendix 1A at the end of the chapter.)

DECISION TOOLKIT

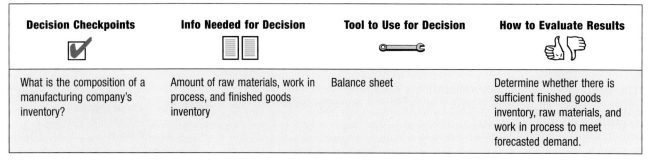

Decision Checkpoints	Info Needed for Decision	Tool to Use for Decision	How to Evaluate Results
What is the composition of a manufacturing company's inventory?	Amount of raw materials, work in process, and finished goods inventory	Balance sheet	Determine whether there is sufficient finished goods inventory, raw materials, and work in process to meet forecasted demand.

COST CONCEPTS—A REVIEW

You have learned a number of cost concepts in this chapter. Because many of these concepts are new, we believe an extended example will help illustrate how they are used. Assume that Northridge Company manufactures and sells pre-hung metal doors. Recently, it also has decided to start selling pre-hung wood doors.

An old warehouse that the company owns will be used to manufacture the new product. Northridge identifies the following costs associated with manufacturing and selling the pre-hung wood doors.

1. The material cost (wood) for each door is $10.
2. Labor costs required to construct a wood door are $8 per door.
3. Depreciation on the new equipment used to make the wood doors using the straight-line method is $25,000 per year.
4. Property taxes on the warehouse used to make the wood doors are $6,000 per year.
5. Advertising costs for the pre-hung wood doors total $2,500 per month or $30,000 per year.
6. Sales commissions related to pre-hung wood doors sold are $4 per door.
7. Salaries for employees who maintain the warehouse are $28,000.
8. The salary of the plant manager in charge of pre-hung wood doors is $70,000.
9. The cost of shipping pre-hung wood doors is $12 per door sold.

These manufacturing and selling costs can be assigned to the various categories shown in Illustration 1-10 on page 15.

Remember that total manufacturing costs are the sum of the **product costs**—direct materials, direct labor, and manufacturing overhead. If Northridge Company produces 10,000 pre-hung wood doors the first year, the total manufacturing costs would be $309,000 as shown in Illustration 1-11 on page 15.

Knowing the total manufacturing costs, Northridge can compute the manufacturing cost per unit, assuming 10,000 units: The cost to produce one pre-hung wood door is $30.90 ($309,000 ÷ 10,000 units).

The cost concepts discussed in this chapter will be used extensively in subsequent chapters. Study Illustration 1-10 carefully. If you do not understand any of these classifications, go back and reread the appropriate section in this chapter.

Illustration 1-10
Assignment of costs to
cost categories

Cost Item	Direct Materials	Direct Labor	Manufacturing Overhead	Period Costs
	Product Costs			
1. Material cost ($10) per door	X			
2. Labor costs ($8) per door		X		
3. Depreciation on new equipment ($25,000 per year)			X	
4. Property taxes ($6,000 per year)			X	
5. Advertising costs ($30,000 per year)				X
6. Sales commissions ($4 per door)				X
7. Maintenance salaries ($28,000 per year)			X	
8. Salary of plant manager ($70,000)			X	
9. Cost of shipping pre-hung doors ($12 per door)				X

Illustration 1-11 Computation of total manufacturing costs

Cost Number and Item	Manufacturing Cost
1. Material cost ($10 × 10,000)	$100,000
2. Labor cost ($8 × 10,000)	80,000
3. Depreciation on new equipment	25,000
4. Property taxes	6,000
7. Maintenance salaries	28,000
8. Salary of plant manager	70,000
Total manufacturing costs	**$309,000**

CONTEMPORARY DEVELOPMENTS IN MANAGERIAL ACCOUNTING

Since the 1970s, the competitive environment for U.S. businesses has changed significantly. For example, the airline, financial services, and telecommunications industries have been deregulated. Global competition has intensified, particularly in the automotive and electronics industries. Today, business managers demand from managerial accountants different and better information than they needed just a few years ago. Factors such as those discussed below will contribute to the expanding role of managerial accounting in the twenty-first century.

SERVICE INDUSTRY TRENDS

The Feature Story notes that at the peak of its success as a personal computer manufacturer, **Compaq** purchased **Digital Equipment**. Its management believes that the future of computing lies in providing computer services, rather than in manufacturing hardware. In fact, during the most recent decade, the U.S. economy in general shifted toward an emphasis on providing services, rather than goods. Today over 50 percent of U.S. workers are employed by service companies, and that percentage is projected to increase in coming years. Much of this chapter focused on manufacturers. But most of the techniques that you will learn in this course are equally applicable to service entities.

In some respects, the challenges for managerial accounting are greater in service companies than in manufacturing companies. Further complicating matters in recent years, many service industries have been deregulated (for example: trucking, airlines, telecommunications, and banking). In a deregulated environment the information provided by managerial accounting is even more important. Illustration 1-12 presents examples of questions faced by service-company managers.

Managers of service companies look to managerial accounting to answer these questions. In some instances the managerial accountant may need to develop new systems for measuring the cost of serving individual customers. In others, he or she may need new operating controls to improve the quality and efficiency of specific services. Many of the examples we present in subsequent chapters will be based on service companies.

Illustration 1-12 Service industries and companies and the managerial accounting questions they face

Industry/Company	Questions Faced by Service-Company Managers
Transportation (**American Airlines, Amtrak**)	Whether to buy new or used planes? Whether to service a new route?
Package delivery services (**FedEx, UPS**)	What fee structure to use? What mode of transportation to use?
Telecommunications (**AT&T, AOL Time Warner**)	What fee structure to use? Whether to service a new community? How many households will it take to break even? Whether to invest in a new satellite or lay new cable?
Professional services (attorneys, accountants, physicians)	How much to charge for particular services? How much office overhead to allocate to particular jobs? How efficient and productive are individual staff members?
Financial institutions (**Wells Fargo, Merrill Lynch**)	Which services to charge for, and which to provide for free? Whether to build a new branch office or to install a new ATM? Should fees vary depending on the size of the customers' accounts?
Health care (**Blue Cross-Blue Shield**, HMOs)	Whether to invest in new equipment? How much to charge for various services? How to measure the quality of services provided?

Service Company Perspective

At **South Central Bell (Telephone)**, management accountants have shed their scorekeeping image. A corporate reorganization plan challenged the accountants to "show their stuff." They took on the roles of interpreter, advisor, and partner. To do so, they had to understand what the accounting numbers mean, relate the numbers to business activity, and recommend alternative courses of action. In addition, they must evaluate these alternatives and make decisions to maximize business efficiency.

VALUE CHAIN MANAGEMENT

The **value chain** is the term that describes all activities associated with providing a product or service. The value chain includes activities such as research and development, ordering raw materials, manufacturing, marketing, delivery, and customer relations. Each of these activities should be designed and operated so that they add value to the product or service. A critical component of the value chain is the supply chain. The **supply chain** is all of the activities from receipt of an order to delivery of a product or service. A number of factors affect efforts to manage the value chain and supply chain.

Technological Change

Many companies now employ **enterprise resource planning (ERP)** software systems to manage their value chain. ERP systems provide a comprehensive, centralized, integrated source of information used to manage all major business processes, from purchasing to manufacturing to recording human resources. In large companies, an ERP system might replace as many as 200 individual software packages. For example, an ERP system can eliminate the need for individual software packages for personnel, inventory management, receivables, and payroll. Because the value chain extends beyond the walls of the company, ERP systems both collect and provide information from and to the company's major suppliers, customers, and business partners.

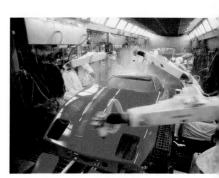

Through **computer-integrated manufacturing (CIM)**, many companies can now manufacture products that are untouched by human hands. An example is the use of robotic equipment in the steel and automobile industries. Automation significantly reduces direct labor costs in many cases. The worker simply monitors the manufacturing process by watching instrument panels.

Also, the widespread use of computers has greatly reduced the cost of accumulating, storing, and reporting managerial accounting information. Computers now make it possible to do more detailed costing of products, processes, and services than was possible under manual processing.

Technology is also affecting the value chain through business-to-business e-commerce on the Internet. The Internet has dramatically changed the way corporations do business with one another. It enables customers and suppliers to share information nearly instantaneously. In addition, it has changed the marketplace, often having the effect of cutting out the "middle man." Industries such as the automobile, airline, hotel, and electronics have made commitments

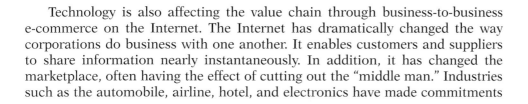

to purchase some or all of their supplies and raw materials in the huge business-to-business electronic marketplaces. For example, **Hilton Hotels** recently committed to purchase as much as $1.5 billion of bed sheets, pest control services, and other items from an Internet supplier, **PurchasePro.com**.

Just-in-Time Inventory Methods

Many companies have significantly lowered inventory levels and costs using **just-in-time (JIT) inventory** methods. Under a just-in-time method, goods are manufactured or purchased just in time for use. As noted in the Feature Story, **Dell Computer** is famous for having developed a system for making computers in response to individual customer requests. Even though each computer is custom-made to meet each customer's particular specifications, it takes Dell less than 48 hours to assemble the computer and put it on a truck. By integrating its information systems with those of its suppliers, Dell reduced its inventories to nearly zero. This is a huge advantage in an industry where products become obsolete nearly overnight.

Quality

JIT inventory systems require an increased emphasis on product quality. If products are produced only as they are needed, it is very costly for the company to have to stop production because of defects or machine breakdowns. Many companies have installed **total quality management (TQM)** systems to reduce defects in finished products. The goal is to achieve zero defects. These systems require timely data on defective products, rework costs, and the cost of honoring warranty contracts. Often this information is used to help redesign the product in a way that makes it less prone to defect. Or it may be used to reengineer the production process to reduce setup time and decrease the potential for error. TQM systems also provide information on nonfinancial measures such as customer satisfaction, number of service calls, and time to generate reports. Attention to these measures, which employees can control, leads to increased profitability.

BUSINESS INSIGHT
Management Perspective

When it comes to total quality management, few companies can compare with **Chiquita Brands International**. Grocery store customers are very picky about bananas—bad bananas are consistently the number one grocery store complaint. Because bananas often account for up to 3 percent of a grocery store's sales, Chiquita goes to great lengths to protect the popular fruit. While bananas are in transit from Central America, "black box" recording devices attached to shipping crates ensure that they are kept in an environment of 90 percent humidity and an unvarying 55-degree temperature. Upon arrival in the U.S., bananas are ripened in airtight warehouses that use carefully monitored levels of ethylene gas. Regular checks are made of each warehouse using ultrasonic detectors that can detect leaks the size of a pinhole. Says one grocery store executive, "No other item in the store has this type of attention and resources devoted to it."

Source: Devon Spurgeon, "When Grocers in U.S. Go Bananas Over Bad Fruit, They Call Laubenthal," *Wall Street Journal*, August 14, 2000, p. A1.

Focus on Activities

As discussed earlier, overhead costs have become an increasingly large component of product and service costs. By definition, overhead costs cannot be directly traced to individual products. But to determine each product's cost, overhead must be **allocated** to the various products. In order to obtain more accurate product costs, many companies now allocate overhead using **activity-based costing**

(ABC). Under ABC, overhead is allocated based on each product's use of activities in making the product. For example, the company can keep track of the cost of setting up machines for each batch of a production process. Then a particular product can be allocated part of the total set-up cost based on the number of set-ups that product required. Activity-based costing is beneficial because it results in more accurate product costing and in more careful scrutiny of all activities in the supply chain. For example, if a product's cost is high because it requires a high number of set-ups, management will be motivated to determine how to produce the product using the optimal number of machine set-ups.

BEFORE YOU GO ON . . .

◆ Review It

1. How does the content of an income statement for a merchandiser differ from that for a manufacturer?
2. How are the work in process inventories reported in the cost of goods manufactured schedule?
3. How does the content of the balance sheet for a merchandiser differ from that for a manufacturer?
4. Identify a number of factors that affect the management of a company's value chain.

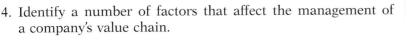

THE NAVIGATOR

*U*SING THE DECISION TOOLKIT

Giant Manufacturing Co. Ltd. specializes in manufacturing many different models of bicycles. Assume that a new model, the Jaguar, has been well accepted. As a result, the company has established a separate manufacturing facility to produce these bicycles. The company produces 1,000 bicycles per month. Giant's monthly manufacturing cost and other expenses data related to these bicycles are as follows.

1. Rent on manufacturing equipment (lease cost) $2,000/month
2. Insurance on manufacturing building $750/month
3. Raw materials (frames, tires, etc.) $80/bicycle
4. Utility costs for manufacturing facility $1,000/month
5. Supplies for general office $800/month
6. Wages for assembly line workers in manufacturing facility $30/bicycle
7. Depreciation on office equipment $650/month
8. Miscellaneous materials (lubricants, solders, etc.) $1.20/bicycle
9. Property taxes on manufacturing building $2,400/year
10. Manufacturing supervisor's salary $3,000/month
11. Advertising for bicycles $30,000/year
12. Sales commissions $10/bicycle
13. Depreciation on manufacturing building $1,500/month

*Using the Decision Toolkit exercises, which follow the final set of Review It questions in the chapter, ask you to use business information and the decision tools presented in the chapter. We encourage you to think through the questions related to the decision before you study the **Solution**.*

Instructions

(a) Prepare an answer sheet with the following column headings.

	Product Costs			
Cost Item	Direct Materials	Direct Labor	Manufacturing Overhead	Period Costs

Enter each cost item on your answer sheet, placing an "X" mark under the appropriate headings.

(b) Compute total manufacturing costs for the month.

Solution

(a)

Cost Item	Direct Materials	Direct Labor	Manufacturing Overhead	Period Costs
			Product Costs	
1. Rent on equipment ($2,000/month)			X	
2. Insurance on manufacturing building ($750/month)			X	
3. Raw materials ($80/bicycle)	X			
4. Manufacturing utilities ($1,000/month)			X	
5. Office supplies ($800/month)				X
6. Wages for workers ($30/bicycle)		X		
7. Depreciation on office equipment ($650/month)				X
8. Miscellaneous materials ($1.20/bicycle)			X	
9. Property taxes on building ($2,400/year)			X	
10. Manufacturing supervisor's salary ($3,000/month)			X	
11. Advertising cost ($30,000/year)				X
12. Sales commissions ($10/bicycle)				X
13. Depreciation on manufacturing building ($1,500/month)			X	

(b)

Cost Item	Manufacturing Cost
Rent on equipment	$ 2,000
Insurance	750
Raw materials ($80 × 1,000)	80,000
Manufacturing utilities	1,000
Labor ($30 × 1,000)	30,000
Miscellaneous materials ($1.20 × 1,000)	1,200
Property taxes ($2,400 ÷ 12)	200
Manufacturing supervisor's salary	3,000
Depreciation on building	1,500
Total manufacturing costs	$119,650

THE NAVIGATOR

SUMMARY OF STUDY OBJECTIVES

① *Explain the distinguishing features of managerial accounting.* The distinguishing features of managerial accounting are:

Primary users of reports—internal users, who are officers, department heads, managers, and supervisors in the company.

Type and frequency of reports—internal reports that are issued as frequently as the need arises.

Purpose of reports—to provide special-purpose information for a particular user for a specific decision.

Content of reports—pertains to subunits of the business and may be very detailed; may extend beyond double-entry accounting system; the reporting standard is relevance to the decision being made.

Verification of reports—no independent audits.

② *Identify the three broad functions of management.* The three functions are planning, directing and motivating, and controlling. Planning requires management to look ahead and to establish objectives. Directing and motivating involves coordinating the diverse activities and human resources of a company to produce a smooth-running operation. Controlling is the process of keeping the activities on track.

③ *Define the three classes of manufacturing costs.* Manufacturing costs are typically classified as either (1) direct materials, (2) direct labor, or (3) manufacturing overhead. Raw materials that can be physically and directly associated with the finished product during the manufacturing process are called direct materials. The work of factory employees that can be physically and directly associated with converting raw materials into finished goods is considered direct labor. Manufacturing overhead consists of costs that are indirectly associated with the manufacture of the finished product.

④ *Distinguish between product and period costs.* Product costs are costs that are a necessary and integral part of producing the finished product. Product costs are also called inventoriable costs. Under the matching principle, these costs do not become expenses until the inventory to which they attach is sold. Period costs are costs that are identified with a specific time period rather than with a salable product. These costs relate to nonmanufacturing costs and therefore are not inventoriable costs.

⑤ *Explain the difference between a merchandising and a manufacturing income statement.* The difference between a merchandising and a manufacturing income statement is in the cost of goods sold section. A manufacturing cost of goods sold section shows beginning and ending finished goods inventories and the cost of goods manufactured.

⑥ *Indicate how cost of goods manufactured is determined.* The cost of the beginning work in process is added to the total manufacturing costs for the current year to arrive at the total cost of work in process for the year. The ending work in process is then subtracted from the total cost of work in process to arrive at the cost of goods manufactured.

⑦ *Explain the difference between a merchandising and a manufacturing balance sheet.* The difference between a merchandising and a manufacturing balance sheet is in the current assets section. In the current assets section of a manufacturing company's balance sheet, three inventory accounts are presented: finished goods inventory, work in process inventory, and raw materials inventory.

DECISION TOOLKIT—A SUMMARY

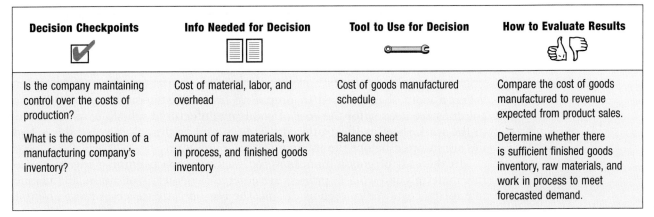

Decision Checkpoints	Info Needed for Decision	Tool to Use for Decision	How to Evaluate Results
Is the company maintaining control over the costs of production?	Cost of material, labor, and overhead	Cost of goods manufactured schedule	Compare the cost of goods manufactured to revenue expected from product sales.
What is the composition of a manufacturing company's inventory?	Amount of raw materials, work in process, and finished goods inventory	Balance sheet	Determine whether there is sufficient finished goods inventory, raw materials, and work in process to meet forecasted demand.

ACCOUNTING CYCLE FOR A MANUFACTURING COMPANY

STUDY OBJECTIVE

◆ 8 ◆

Prepare a work sheet and closing entries for a manufacturing company.

The accounting cycle for a manufacturing company is the same as for a merchandising company when a periodic inventory system is used. The journalizing and posting of transactions is the same, except for the additional manufacturing inventories and manufacturing cost accounts. Similarly, the preparation of a trial balance and the journalizing and posting of adjusting entries are the same. Some changes, however, occur in the use of a work sheet and in preparing closing entries.

To illustrate the changes in the work sheet, we will use the cost of goods manufactured schedule for Olsen Manufacturing presented in Illustration 1-7, along with other assumed data. For convenience, the cost of goods manufactured schedule is reproduced in Illustration 1A-1.

Illustration 1A-1 Cost of goods manufactured schedule

OLSEN MANUFACTURING COMPANY		
Cost of Goods Manufactured Schedule		
For the Year Ended December 31, 2002		
Work in process, January 1		$ 18,400
Direct materials		
Raw materials inventory, January 1	$ 16,700	
Raw materials purchases	152,500	
Total raw materials available for use	169,200	
Less: Raw materials inventory, December 31	22,800	
Direct materials used	$146,400	
Direct labor	175,600	
Manufacturing overhead		
Indirect labor	14,300	
Factory repairs	12,600	
Factory utilities	10,100	
Factory depreciation	9,440	
Factory insurance	8,360	
Total manufacturing overhead	54,800	
Total manufacturing costs		376,800
Total cost of work in process		395,200
Less: Work in process, December 31		25,200
Cost of goods manufactured		$370,000

WORK SHEET

When a work sheet is used in preparing financial statements, two additional columns are needed for the cost of goods manufactured schedule. As illustrated in the work sheet in Illustration 1A-2, debit and credit columns for this schedule are inserted before the income statement columns.

In the cost of goods manufactured columns, the beginning inventories of raw materials and work in process are entered as debits. In addition, all the manufacturing costs are entered as debits. The reason is that each of these amounts

Illustration 1A-2 Partial work sheet

OLSEN MANUFACTURING COMPANY Work Sheet (partial) For the Year Ended December 31, 2002	Adjusted Trial Balance		Cost of Goods Manufactured		Income Statement		Balance Sheet	
	Dr.	Cr.	Dr.	Cr.	Dr.	Cr.	Dr.	Cr.
Cash	42,500						42,500	
Accounts Receivable (Net)	71,900						71,900	
Finished Goods Inv.	24,600				24,600	19,500	19,500	
Work in Process Inv.	18,400		18,400	25,200			25,200	
Raw Materials Inv.	16,700		16,700	22,800			22,800	
Plant Assets	724,000						724,000	
Accumulated Depr.		278,400						278,400
Notes Payable		100,000						100,000
Accounts Payable		40,000						40,000
Income Taxes Payable		5,000						5,000
Common Stock		200,000						200,000
Retained Earnings		205,100						205,100
Sales		680,000				680,000		
Raw Materials Purchases	152,500		152,500					
Direct Labor	175,600		175,600					
Indirect Labor	14,300		14,300					
Factory Repairs	12,600		12,600					
Factory Utilities	10,100		10,100					
Factory Depreciation	9,440		9,440					
Factory Insurance	8,360		8,360					
Selling Expenses	114,900				114,900			
Administrative Exp.	92,600				92,600			
Income Tax Exp.	20,000				20,000			
Totals	1,508,500	1,508,500	418,000	48,000				
Cost of Goods Manufactured				370,000	370,000			
Totals			418,000	418,000	622,100	699,500	905,900	828,500
Net Income					77,400			77,400
Totals					699,500	699,500	905,900	905,900

increases cost of goods manufactured. Ending inventories for raw materials and work in process are entered as credits in the cost of goods manufactured columns because they have the opposite effect—they decrease cost of goods manufactured. The balancing amount for these columns is the cost of goods manufactured. Note that the amount ($370,000) agrees with the amount reported for cost of goods manufactured in Illustration 1A-1. This amount is also entered in the income statement debit column.

The income statement and balance sheet columns for a manufacturing company are basically the same as for a merchandising company. For example, the treatment of the finished goods inventories is identical with the treatment of merchandise inventory. That is, the beginning inventory is entered in the debit column, and the ending finished goods inventory is entered in the income statement credit column and in the balance sheet debit column.

As in the case of a merchandising company, financial statements can be prepared from the statement columns of the work sheet. In addition, the cost of goods manufactured schedule can also be prepared directly from the work sheet.

CLOSING ENTRIES

The closing entries for a manufacturing company are different than for a merchandising company. **A Manufacturing Summary account is used to close all accounts that appear in the cost of goods manufactured schedule.** The balance of the Manufacturing Summary account is the Cost of Goods Manufactured for the period. Manufacturing Summary is then closed to Income Summary. The closing entries can be prepared from the work sheet. As illustrated below, the closing entries for the manufacturing accounts are prepared first. The closing entries for Olsen Manufacturing are as follows.

Dec. 31	Work in Process Inventory (Dec. 31)	25,200	
	Raw Materials Inventory (Dec. 31)	22,800	
	Manufacturing Summary		**48,000**
	(To record ending raw materials and work in process inventories)		
31	**Manufacturing Summary**	**418,000**	
	Work in Process Inventory (Jan. 1)		18,400
	Raw Materials Inventory (Jan. 1)		16,700
	Raw Materials Purchases		152,500
	Direct Labor		175,600
	Indirect Labor		14,300
	Factory Repairs		12,600
	Factory Utilities		10,100
	Factory Depreciation		9,440
	Factory Insurance		8,360
	(To close beginning raw materials and work in process inventories and manufacturing cost accounts)		
31	Finished Goods Inventory (Dec. 31)	19,500	
	Sales	680,000	
	Income Summary		699,500
	(To record ending finished goods inventory and close sales account)		
31	Income Summary	622,100	
	Finished Goods Inventory (Jan. 1)		24,600
	Manufacturing Summary		**370,000**
	Selling Expenses		114,900
	Administrative Expenses		92,600
	Income Tax Expense		20,000
	(To close beginning finished goods inventory, manufacturing summary, and expense accounts)		
31	Income Summary	77,400	
	Retained Earnings		77,400
	(To close net income to retained earnings)		

After posting, the summary accounts will show the following.

Manufacturing Summary

Dec. 31	Close	418,000	Dec. 31	Close	48,000
			31	Close	370,000

Income Summary

Dec. 31	Close	622,100	Dec. 31	Close	699,500
31	Close	77,400			

Illustration 1A-3 Summary accounts for a manufacturing company, after posting

These data precisely track the closing entries. It also would be possible to post each account balance to the Manufacturing Summary account.

SUMMARY OF STUDY OBJECTIVE FOR APPENDIX 1A

8 *Prepare a work sheet and closing entries for a manufacturing company.* Two additional columns are needed in the work sheet for the cost of goods manufactured. In these columns, the beginning inventories of raw materials and work in process are entered as debits, and the ending inventories are entered as credits. All manufacturing costs are entered as debits. To close all of the accounts that appear in the cost of goods manufactured schedule, a Manufacturing Summary account is used.

GLOSSARY

 Key Term Matching Activity

Activity-based costing (ABC) A method of allocating overhead based on each product's use of activities in making the product. (p. 19)

Cost of goods manufactured Total cost of work in process less the cost of the ending work in process inventory. (p. 11)

Direct labor The work of factory employees that can be physically and directly associated with converting raw materials into finished goods. (p. 8)

Direct materials Raw materials that can be physically and directly associated with manufacturing the finished product. (p. 8)

Enterprise resource planning (ERP) system Software that provides a comprehensive, centralized, integrated source of information used to manage all major business processes. (p. 17)

Indirect labor Work of factory employees that has no physical association with the finished product, or for which it is impractical to trace the costs to the goods produced. (p. 8)

Indirect materials Raw materials that do not physically become part of the finished product or cannot be traced because their physical association with the finished product is too small. (p. 8)

Just-in-time (JIT) inventory Inventory system in which goods are manufactured or purchased just in time for use. (p. 18)

Managerial accounting A field of accounting that provides economic and financial information for managers and other internal users. (p. 4)

Manufacturing overhead Manufacturing costs that are indirectly associated with the manufacture of the finished product. (p. 8)

Period costs Costs that are matched with the revenue of a specific time period and charged to expense as incurred. (p. 9)

Product costs Costs that are a necessary and integral part of producing the finished product. (p. 9)

Supply chain All activities from receipt of an order to delivery of a product or service. (p. 17)

Total cost of work in process Cost of the beginning work in process plus total manufacturing costs for the current period. (p. 11)

Total manufacturing costs The sum of direct materials, direct labor, and manufacturing overhead incurred in the current period. (p. 11)

Total quality management (TQM) Systems implemented to reduce defects in finished products with the goal of achieving zero defects. (p. 18)

Value chain All activities associated with providing a product or service. (p. 17)

DEMONSTRATION PROBLEM

Demonstration Problems are a final review before you begin homework. **Action Plans** that appear in the margins give you tips about how to approach the problem, and the **Solution** provided demonstrates both the form and content of complete answers.

eGrade Demonstration Problem

Superior Manufacturing Company has the following cost and expense data for the year ending December 31, 2002.

Raw materials, 1/1/02	$ 30,000	Insurance, factory	$ 14,000
Raw materials, 12/31/02	20,000	Property taxes, factory building	6,000
Raw materials purchased	205,000	Sales (net)	1,500,000
Indirect materials	15,000	Delivery expenses	100,000
Work in process, 1/1/02	80,000	Sales commissions	150,000
Work in process, 12/31/02	50,000	Indirect labor	90,000
Finished goods, 1/1/02	110,000	Factory machinery rent	40,000
Finished goods, 12/31/02	120,000	Factory utilities	65,000
Direct labor	350,000	Depreciation, factory building	24,000
Factory manager's salary	35,000	Administrative expenses	300,000

Instructions

(a) Prepare a cost of goods manufactured schedule for Superior Company for 2002.

(b) Prepare an income statement for Superior Company for 2002.

(c) Assume that Superior Company's ledgers show the balances of the following current asset accounts: Cash $17,000, Accounts Receivable (net) $120,000, Prepaid Expenses $13,000, and Short-term Investments $26,000. Prepare the current assets section of the balance sheet for Superior Company as of December 31, 2002.

Solution to Demonstration Problem

Action Plan

- Start with beginning work in process as the first item in the cost of goods manufactured schedule.
- Sum direct materials used, direct labor, and total manufacturing overhead to determine total current manufacturing costs.
- Sum beginning work in process and total current manufacturing costs to determine total cost of work in process.
- Cost of goods manufactured is the total cost of work in process less ending work in process.
- In the cost of goods sold section of the income statement, show beginning and ending finished goods inventory and cost of goods manufactured.
- In the balance sheet, list manufacturing inventories in the order of their expected realization in cash, with finished goods first.

(a)

SUPERIOR MANUFACTURING COMPANY
Cost of Goods Manufactured Schedule
For the Year Ended December 31, 2002

Work in process, 1/1			$ 80,000
Direct materials			
Raw materials inventory, 1/1	$ 30,000		
Raw materials purchased	205,000		
Total raw materials available for use	235,000		
Less: Raw materials inventory, 12/31	20,000		
Direct materials used		$215,000	
Direct labor		350,000	
Manufacturing overhead			
Indirect labor	90,000		
Factory utilities	65,000		
Factory machinery rent	40,000		
Factory manager's salary	35,000		
Depreciation on building	24,000		
Indirect materials	15,000		
Factory insurance	14,000		
Property taxes	6,000		
Total manufacturing overhead		289,000	
Total manufacturing costs			854,000
Total cost of work in process			934,000
Less: Work in process, 12/31			50,000
Cost of goods manufactured			$884,000

(b)
SUPERIOR MANUFACTURING COMPANY
Income Statement
For the Year Ended December 31, 2002

Sales (net)		$1,500,000
Cost of goods sold		
Finished goods inventory, January 1	$110,000	
Cost of goods manufactured	884,000	
Cost of goods available for sale	994,000	
Less: Finished goods inventory, December 31	120,000	
Cost of goods sold		874,000
Gross profit		626,000
Operating expenses		
Administrative expenses	300,000	
Sales commissions	150,000	
Delivery expenses	100,000	
Total operating expenses		550,000
Net income		$ 76,000

(c)
SUPERIOR MANUFACTURING COMPANY
Balance Sheet (partial)
December 31, 2002

Current assets		
Cash		$ 17,000
Short-term investments		26,000
Accounts receivable (net)		120,000
Inventories		
Finished goods	$120,000	
Work in process	50,000	
Raw materials	20,000	190,000
Prepaid expenses		13,000
Total current assets		$366,000

THE
NAVIGATOR

This would be a good time to return to the Student Owner's Manual at the beginning of the book (or look at it for the first time if you skipped it before) to read about the various types of homework materials that appear at the ends of chapters. Knowing the purpose of different assignments will help you appreciate what each contributes to your accounting skills and competencies.

Note: All asterisked Questions, Exercises, and Problems relate to material in the appendix to the chapter.

SELF-STUDY QUESTIONS

Self-Study/Self-Test

Answers are at the end of the chapter.

(SO 1) 1. Managerial accounting:
  (a) is governed by generally accepted accounting principles.
  (b) places emphasis on special-purpose information.
  (c) pertains to the entity as a whole and is highly aggregated.
  (d) is limited to cost data.

(SO 1) 2. Which of the following is *not* one of the categories in *Standards of Ethical Conduct for Management Accountants*?

  (a) Confidentiality.   (c) Integrity.
  (b) Competence.   (d) Independence.

3. The management of an organization performs   (SO 2)
several broad functions. They are:
  (a) planning, directing and motivating, and selling.
  (b) planning, directing and motivating, and controlling.
  (c) planning, manufacturing, and controlling.
  (d) directing and motivating, manufacturing, and controlling.

(SO 3)   4. Direct materials are a:

	Product Cost	Manufacturing Overhead	Period Cost
(a)	Yes	Yes	No
(b)	Yes	No	No
(c)	Yes	Yes	Yes
(d)	No	No	No

(SO 4)   5. Indirect labor is a:
(a) nonmanufacturing cost.
(b) raw material cost.
(c) product cost.
(d) period cost.

(SO 3)   6. Which of the following costs would be included in manufacturing overhead of a computer manufacturer?
(a) The cost of the $3\frac{1}{2}$-inch disk drives.
(b) The wages earned by computer assemblers.
(c) The cost of the memory chips.
(d) Depreciation on testing equipment.

(SO 3)   7. Which of the following is *not* an element of manufacturing overhead?
(a) Sales manager's salary.
(b) Plant manager's salary.
(c) Factory repairman's wages.
(d) Product inspector's salary.

(SO 5)   8. For the year, Redder Company has cost of goods manufactured of $600,000, beginning finished goods inventory of $200,000, and ending finished goods inventory of $250,000. The cost of goods sold is:
(a) $450,000.
(b) $500,000.
(c) $550,000.
(d) $600,000.

(SO 6)   9. A cost of goods manufactured schedule shows beginning and ending inventories for:
(a) raw materials and work in process only.
(b) work in process only.
(c) raw materials only.
(d) raw materials, work in process, and finished goods.

(SO 7)   10. In a manufacturer's balance sheet, three inventories may be reported: (1) raw materials, (2) work in process, and (3) finished goods. Indicate in what sequence these inventories generally appear on a balance sheet.
(a) (1), (2), (3)
(b) (2), (3), (1)
(c) (3), (1), (2)
(d) (3), (2), (1)

QUESTIONS

1. (a) "Managerial accounting is a field of accounting that provides economic information for all interested parties." Do you agree? Explain.
   (b) Pat Gonzalez believes that managerial accounting serves only manufacturing firms. Is Pat correct? Explain.

2. Distinguish between managerial and financial accounting as to (a) primary users of reports, (b) types and frequency of reports, and (c) purpose of reports.

3. How does the content of reports and the verification of reports differ between managerial and financial accounting?

4. (a) Identify the four categories of ethical standards for management accountants.
   (b) Is the responsibility of the management accountant limited to only his or her own acts? Explain.

5. Karen Gish is studying for the next accounting midterm examination. Summarize for Karen what she should know about management functions.

6. "Decision making is management's most important function." Do you agree? Why or why not?

7. Sue Sablow is studying for her next accounting examination. Explain to Sue what she should know about the differences between the income statements for a manufacturing and for a merchandising company.

8. Bob Jackson is unclear as to the difference between the balance sheets of a merchandising company and a manufacturing company. Explain the difference to Bob.

9. How are manufacturing costs classified?

10. Gene Toni claims that the distinction between direct and indirect materials is based entirely on physical association with the product. Is Gene correct? Why?

11. Jane Diaz is confused about the differences between a product cost and a period cost. Explain the differences to Jane.

12. Identify the differences in the cost of goods sold section of an income statement between a merchandising company and a manufacturing company.

13. The determination of the cost of goods manufactured involves the following factors: (A) beginning work in process inventory, (B) total manufacturing costs, and (C) ending work in process inventory. Identify the meaning of x in the following formulas:
   (a) $A + B = x$
   (b) $A + B - C = x$

14. Sajjad Manufacturing has beginning raw materials inventory $12,000, ending raw materials inventory $18,000, and raw materials purchases $180,000. What is the cost of direct materials used?

15. Jam Manufacturing Inc. has beginning work in process $27,200, direct materials used $240,000, direct labor $200,000, total manufacturing overhead $150,000, and ending work in process $32,000. What are total manufacturing costs?

16. Using the data in Q15, what are (a) the total cost of work in process and (b) the cost of goods manufactured?

17. In what order should manufacturing inventories be listed in a balance sheet?

*18. How, if at all, does the accounting cycle differ between a manufacturing company and a merchandising company?

*19. What typical account balances are carried into the cost of goods manufactured columns of the manufacturing work sheet?

*20. Prepare the closing entries for (a) ending work in process and raw materials inventories and (b) manufacturing summary. Use XXXs for amounts.

BRIEF EXERCISES

BE1-1 Complete the following comparison table between managerial and financial accounting.

Distinguish between managerial and financial accounting.
(SO 1)

	Financial Accounting	Managerial Accounting
Primary users		
Type of reports		
Frequency of reports		
Purpose of reports		
Content of reports		
Verification		

BE1-2 The Institute of Management Accountants has promulgated ethical standards for managerial accountants. Identify the four specific standards.

Identify ethical standards.
(SO 1)

BE1-3 Listed below are the three functions of the management of an organization.

Identify the three management functions.
(SO 2)

1. Planning   2. Directing and motivating   3. Controlling

Identify which of the following statements best describes each of the above functions.

(a) ____ require(s) management to look ahead and to establish objectives. A key objective of management is to add value to the business.

(b) ____ involve(s) coordinating the diverse activities and human resources of a company to produce a smooth-running operation. This function relates to the implementation of planned objectives.

(c) ____ is the process of keeping the activities on track. Management must determine whether goals are being met and what changes are necessary when there are deviations.

BE1-4 Determine whether each of the following costs should be classified as direct materials (DM), direct labor (DL), or manufacturing overhead (MO).

Classify manufacturing costs.
(SO 3)

(a) ____Frames and tires used in manufacturing bicycles.
(b) ____Wages paid to production workers.
(c) ____Insurance on factory equipment and machinery.
(d) ____Depreciation on factory equipment.

BE1-5 Indicate whether each of the following costs of an automobile manufacturer would be classified as direct materials, direct labor, or manufacturing overhead.

Classify manufacturing costs.
(SO 3)

(a) ____Windshield.
(b) ____Engine.
(c) ____Wages of assembly line worker
(d) ____Depreciation of factory machinery.
(e) ____Factory machinery lubricants.
(f) ____Tires.
(g) ____Steering wheel.
(h) ____Salary of painting supervisor.

BE1-6 Identify whether each of the following costs should be classified as product costs or period costs.

Identify product and period costs.
(SO 4)

(a) ____Manufacturing overhead.
(b) ____Selling expenses.
(c) ____Administrative expenses.
(d) ____Advertising expenses.
(e) ____Direct labor.
(f) ____Direct material.

Classify manufacturing costs.
(SO 3, 4)

BE1-7   Presented below are Hyde Company's monthly manufacturing cost data related to its personal computer products.

(a) Utilities for manufacturing equipment $116,000
(b) Raw material (CPU, chips, etc.) $85,000
(c) Depreciation on manufacturing building $880,000
(d) Wages for production workers $191,000

Enter each cost item in the following table, placing an "X" under the appropriate headings.

	Product Costs		
	Direct Materials	**Direct Labor**	**Factory Overhead**
(a)			
(b)			
(c)			
(d)			

Compute total manufacturing costs and total cost of work in process.
(SO 6)

BE1-8   Buslik Manufacturing Company has the following data: direct labor $242,000, direct materials used $180,000, total manufacturing overhead $208,000, and beginning work in process $25,000. Compute (a) total manufacturing costs and (b) total cost of work in process.

Prepare current assets section.
(SO 7)

BE1-9   In alphabetical order below are current asset items for Ivy Company's balance sheet at December 31, 2002. Prepare the current assets section (including a complete heading).

Accounts receivable	$200,000
Cash	62,000
Finished goods	75,000
Prepaid expenses	38,000
Raw materials	68,000
Work in process	87,000

Determine missing amounts in computing total manufacturing costs.
(SO 6)

BE1-10   Presented below are incomplete 2002 manufacturing cost data for Hyun Corporation. Determine the missing amounts.

	Direct Materials Used	**Direct Labor Used**	**Factory Overhead**	**Total Manufacturing Costs**
(a)	$35,000	$61,000	$ 50,000	?
(b)	?	$75,000	$120,000	$296,000
(c)	$55,000	?	$111,000	$300,000

Determine missing amounts in computing cost of goods manufactured.
(SO 6)

BE1-11   Use the same data from BE1–10 above and the data below. Determine the missing amounts.

	Total Manufacturing Costs	**Work in Process (1/1)**	**Work in Process (12/31)**	**Cost of Goods Manufactured**
(a)	?	$120,000	$86,000	?
(b)	$296,000	?	$98,000	$321,000
(c)	$300,000	$463,000	?	$715,000

Identify work sheet columns for selected accounts.
(SO 8)

*****BE1-12**   A work sheet is used in preparing financial statements for Lawney Manufacturing Company. The following accounts are included in the adjusted trial balance: Finished Goods Inventory $28,000, Work in Process Inventory $21,600, Raw Materials Purchases $175,000, and Direct Labor $140,000. Indicate the work sheet column(s) to which each account should be extended.

EXERCISES

E1-1   Presented below is a list of costs and expenses usually incurred by Iguana Corporation, a manufacturer of furniture, in its factory.

Classify costs into three classes of manufacturing costs.
(SO 3)

1. Salaries for assembly line inspectors.
2. Insurance on factory machines.
3. Property taxes on the factory building.
4. Factory repairs.
5. Upholstery used in manufacturing furniture.
6. Wages paid to assembly line workers.
7. Factory machinery depreciation.
8. Glue, nails, paint, and other small parts used in production.
9. Factory supervisors' salaries.
10. Wood used in manufacturing furniture.

Instructions
Classify the above items into the following categories: (a) direct materials, (b) direct labor, and (c) manufacturing overhead.

E1-2   Honmura Company reports the following costs and expenses in May.

Determine the total amount of various types of costs.
(SO 3, 4)

Factory utilities	$ 8,500	Direct labor	$69,100
Depreciation on factory		Sales salaries	49,400
equipment	12,650	Property taxes on factory	
Depreciation on delivery trucks	3,500	building	2,500
Indirect factory labor	48,900	Repairs to office equipment	1,300
Indirect materials	89,800	Factory repairs	2,000
Direct materials used	137,600	Advertising	18,000
Factory manager's salary	8,000	Office supplies used	2,640

Instructions
From the information, determine the total amount of:
(a) Manufacturing overhead.
(b) Product costs.
(c) Period costs.

E1-3   Karpman Company is a manufacturer of personal computers. Various costs and expenses associated with its operations are as follows.

Classify various costs into different cost categories.
(SO 3, 4)

1. Property taxes on the factory building.
2. Production superintendents' salaries.
3. Memory boards and chips used in assembling computers.
4. Depreciation on the factory equipment.
5. Salaries for assembly line quality control inspectors.
6. Sales commissions paid to sell personal computers.
7. Electrical wiring in assembling computers.
8. Wages of workers assembling personal computers.
9. Soldering materials used on factory assembly lines.
10. Salaries for the night security guards for the factory building.

The company intends to classify these costs and expenses into the following categories:
(a) direct materials, (b) direct labor, (c) manufacturing overhead, and (d) period costs.

Instructions
List the items (1)–(10). For each item, indicate the cost category to which the item belongs.

*Determine missing amounts
in cost of goods
manufactured schedule.*
(SO 5, 6)

E1-4 The cost of goods manufactured schedule shows each of the cost elements. Complete the following schedule for Salazar Manufacturing Company.

SALAZAR MANUFACTURING COMPANY
Cost of Goods Manufactured Schedule
For the Year Ended December 31, 2002

Work in process (1/1)			$200,000
Direct materials			
Raw materials inventory (1/1)	$?		
Add: Raw materials purchases	158,000		
Less: Raw materials inventory (12/31)	7,500		
Direct materials used		$190,000	
Direct labor		?	
Manufacturing overhead			
Indirect labor	$ 18,000		
Factory depreciation	36,000		
Factory utilities	68,000		
Total overhead		122,000	
Total manufacturing costs			?
Total cost of work in process			?
Less: Work in process (12/31)			81,000
Cost of goods manufactured			$560,000

*Determine the missing
amount of different cost
items.*
(SO 6)

E1-5 Manufacturing cost data for Hermes Company are presented below.

	Case A	Case B	Case C
Direct materials used	(a)	$68,400	$130,000
Direct labor	$ 57,000	86,000	(g)
Manufacturing overhead	42,500	81,600	102,000
Total manufacturing costs	180,650	(d)	253,700
Work in process 1/1/02	(b)	16,500	(h)
Total cost of work in process	221,500	(e)	327,000
Work in process 12/31/02	(c)	9,000	70,000
Cost of goods manufactured	185,275	(f)	(i)

Instructions
Indicate the missing amount for each letter (a) through (i).

*Determine the missing
amount of different cost
items, and prepare a
condensed cost of goods
manufactured schedule.*
(SO 5, 6)

E1-6 Incomplete manufacturing cost data for Hollis Company for 2002 are presented as follows.

	Direct Materials Used	Direct Labor Used	Manufacturing Overhead	Total Manufacturing Costs	Work in Process 1/1	Work in Process 12/31	Cost of Goods Manufactured
(1)	$117,000	$140,000	$ 77,000	(a)	$30,000	(b)	$360,000
(2)	(c)	200,000	132,000	$440,000	(d)	$40,000	470,000
(3)	80,000	100,000	(e)	255,000	60,000	80,000	(f)
(4)	70,000	(g)	75,000	294,000	45,000	(h)	270,000

Instructions
(a) Indicate the missing amount for each letter.
(b) Prepare a condensed cost of goods manufactured schedule for situation (1) for the year ended December 31, 2002.

*Prepare a cost of goods
manufactured schedule and
a partial income statement.*
(SO 5, 6)

E1-7 Issey Corporation has the following cost records for June 2002.

Indirect factory labor	$ 4,500	Factory utilities	$ 400
Direct materials used	20,000	Depreciation, factory equipment	1,400
Work in process, 6/1/02	3,000	Direct labor	25,000
Work in process, 6/30/02	3,500	Maintenance, factory equipment	1,300
Finished goods, 6/1/02	5,000	Indirect materials	2,200
Finished goods, 6/30/02	7,500	Factory manager's salary	3,000

Instructions

(a) Prepare a cost of goods manufactured schedule for June 2002.
(b) Prepare an income statement through gross profit for June 2002 assuming net sales are $97,100.

E1-8 Hippo Manufacturing Company produces blankets. From its accounting records it prepares the following schedule and financial statements on a yearly basis.

Indicate in which schedule or financial statement(s) different cost items will appear.
(SO 5, 6, 7)

(a) Cost of goods manufactured schedule.
(b) Income statement.
(c) Balance sheet.

The following items are found in its ledger and accompanying data.

1. Direct labor
2. Raw materials inventory, 1/1
3. Work in process inventory, 12/31
4. Finished goods inventory, 1/1
5. Indirect labor
6. Depreciation on factory machinery
7. Work in process, 1/1
8. Finished goods inventory, 12/31

9. Factory maintenance salaries
10. Cost of goods manufactured
11. Depreciation on delivery equipment
12. Cost of goods available for sale
13. Direct materials used
14. Heat and electricity for factory
15. Repairs to roof of factory building
16. Cost of raw materials purchases

Instructions

List the items (1)–(16). For each item, indicate by using the appropriate letter or letters, the schedule and/or financial statement(s) in which the item will appear.

E1-9 An analysis of the accounts of Lanier Manufacturing reveals the following manufacturing cost data for the month ended June 30, 2002.

Prepare a cost of goods manufactured schedule, and present the ending inventories of the balance sheet.
(SO 5, 6, 7)

Inventories	Beginning	Ending
Raw materials	$9,000	$11,100
Work in process	5,000	8,000
Finished goods	8,000	6,000

Costs incurred:

Raw materials purchases $64,000, direct labor $50,000, manufacturing overhead $19,900. The specific overhead costs were: indirect labor $5,500, factory insurance $4,000, machinery depreciation $4,000, machinery repairs $1,800, factory utilities $3,100, miscellaneous factory costs $1,500.

Instructions

(a) Prepare the cost of goods manufactured schedule for the month ended June 30, 2002.
(b) Show the presentation of the ending inventories on the June 30, 2002, balance sheet.

E1-10 Jazz Motor Company manufactures automobiles. During September 2002 the company purchased 5,000 head lamps at a cost of $9 per lamp. Jazz withdrew 4,650 lamps from the warehouse during the month. Fifty of these lamps were used to replace the head lamps in autos used by traveling sales staff. The remaining 4,600 lamps were put in autos manufactured during the month.

Determine the amount of cost to appear in various accounts, and indicate in which financial statements these accounts would appear.
(SO 5, 6, 7)

Of the autos put into production during September 2002, 90% were completed and transferred to the company's storage lot. Of the cars completed during the month, 70% were sold by September 30.

Instructions

(a) Determine the cost of head lamps that would appear in each of the following accounts at September 30, 2002: Raw Materials, Work in Process, Finished Goods, Cost of Goods Sold, and Selling Expenses.
(b) ▭▭▭▸ Write a short memo to the chief accountant, indicating whether and where each of the accounts in **(a)** would appear on the income statement or on the balance sheet at September 30, 2002.

*E1-11 Data for Lanier Manufacturing are presented in Exercise 1-9.

Prepare a partial work sheet for a manufacturing firm.
(SO 8)

Instructions

Prepare a partial work sheet for Lanier Manufacturing.

PROBLEMS: SET A

Classify manufacturing costs into different categories and compute the unit cost.
(SO 3, 4)

eGrade
Problem

P1-1A   Snapper Company specializes in manufacturing a unique model of bicycle helmet. The model is well accepted by consumers, and the company has enough orders to keep the factory production at 10,000 helmets per month (80% of its full capacity). Snapper's monthly manufacturing cost and other expense data are as follows.

Rent on factory equipment	$ 6,000
Insurance on factory building	1,500
Raw materials (plastics, polystyrene, etc.)	70,000
Utility costs for factory	900
Supplies for general office	300
Wages for assembly line workers	46,000
Depreciation on office equipment	800
Miscellaneous materials (lubricants, solders, etc.)	1,100
Factory manager's salary	5,700
Property taxes on factory building	400
Advertising for helmets	11,000
Sales commissions	7,000
Depreciation on factory building	1,500

Instructions

(a) Prepare an answer sheet with the following column headings.

	Product Costs			
Cost Item	Direct Materials	Direct Labor	Manufacturing Overhead	Period Costs

Enter each cost item on your answer sheet, placing the dollar amount under the appropriate headings. Total the dollar amounts in each of the columns.

(b) Compute the cost to produce one helmet

Classify manufacturing costs into different categories and compute the unit cost.
(SO 3, 4)

P1-2A   Galex Company, a manufacturer of stereo systems, started its production in October 2002. For the preceding 3 years Galex had been a retailer of stereo systems. After a thorough survey of stereo system markets, Galex decided to turn its retail store into a stereo equipment factory.

Raw materials cost for a stereo system will total $70 per unit. Workers on the production lines are on average paid $10 per hour. A stereo system usually takes 5 hours to complete. In addition, the rent on the equipment used to assemble stereo systems amounts to $4,500 per month. Indirect materials cost $5 per system. A supervisor was hired to oversee production; her monthly salary is $2,700.

Janitorial costs were $1,300 monthly. Advertising costs for the stereo system will be $8,500 per month. The factory building depreciation expense is $7,200 per year. Property taxes on the factory building will be $6,000 per year.

Instructions

(a) Prepare an answer sheet with the following column headings.

	Product Costs			
Cost Item	Direct Materials	Direct Labor	Manufacturing Overhead	Period Costs

Assuming that Galex manufactures, on average, 1,300 stereo systems per month, enter each cost item on your answer sheet, placing the dollar amount per month under the appropriate headings. Total the dollar amounts in each of the columns.

(b) Compute the cost to produce one stereo system.

P1-3A   Incomplete manufacturing costs, expenses, and selling data for two different cases are as follows.

Indicate the missing amount of different cost items, and prepare a condensed cost of goods manufactured schedule, an income statement, and a partial balance sheet.
(SO 5, 6, 7)

	Case 1	Case 2
Direct Materials Used	$ 7,600	$ (g)
Direct Labor	6,000	8,000
Manufacturing Overhead	5,000	4,000
Total Manufacturing Costs	(a)	19,000
Beginning Work in Process Inventory	1,000	(h)
Ending Work in Process Inventory	(b)	3,000
Sales	24,500	(i)
Sales Discounts	2,500	1,400
Cost of Goods Manufactured	16,000	22,000
Beginning Finished Goods Inventory	(c)	3,300
Goods Available for Sale	18,000	(j)
Cost of Goods Sold	(d)	(k)
Ending Finished Goods Inventory	3,400	2,500
Gross Profit	(e)	7,000
Operating Expenses	2,500	(l)
Net Income	(f)	3,000

Instructions
(a) Indicate the missing amount for each letter.
(b) Prepare a condensed cost of goods manufactured schedule for Case 1.
(c) Prepare an income statement and the current assets section of the balance sheet for Case 1. Assume that in Case 1 the other items in the current assets section are as follows: Cash $4,000, Receivables (net) $15,000, Raw Materials $600, and Prepaid Expenses $400.

P1-4A   The following data were taken from the records of Gamma Manufacturing Company for the fiscal year ended June 30, 2002.

Prepare a cost of goods manufactured schedule, a partial income statement, and a partial balance sheet.
(SO 5, 6, 7)

Raw Materials Inventory 7/1/01	$ 48,000	Factory Insurance	$ 4,600
Raw Materials Inventory 6/30/02	39,600	Factory Machinery Depreciation	15,000
Finished Goods Inventory 7/1/01	96,000	Freight-in on Raw Materials Purchased	8,600
Finished Goods Inventory 6/30/02	95,900	Factory Utilities	24,600
Work in Process Inventory 7/1/01	19,800	Office Utilities Expense	8,650
Work in Process Inventory 6/30/02	17,600	Sales	547,000
Direct Labor	147,250	Sales Discounts	4,200
Indirect Labor	24,460	Plant Manager's Salary	29,000
Accounts Receivable	27,000	Factory Property Taxes	9,600
		Factory Repairs	1,400
		Raw Materials Purchases	89,800
		Cash	32,000

Instructions
(a) Prepare a cost of goods manufactured schedule.
(b) Prepare an income statement through gross profit.
(c) Prepare the current assets section of the balance sheet at June 30, 2002.

P1-5A   Istanbul Company is a manufacturer of computers. Its controller resigned in October 2002. An inexperienced assistant accountant has prepared the following income statement for the month of October 2002.

Prepare a cost of goods manufactured schedule and a correct income statement.
(SO 5, 6)

ISTANBUL COMPANY
Income Statement
For the Month Ended October 31, 2002

Sales (net)		$780,000
Less: Operating expenses		
Raw materials purchased	$260,000	
Direct labor cost	190,000	
Advertising expense	92,000	
Selling and administrative salaries	75,000	
Rent on factory facilities	60,000	
Depreciation on sales equipment	45,000	
Depreciation on factory equipment	35,000	
Indirect labor cost	25,000	
Utilities expense	12,000	
Insurance expense	8,000	802,000
Net loss		$(22,000)

Prior to October 2002 the company had been profitable every month. The company's president is concerned about the accuracy of the income statement. As his friend, you have been asked to review the income statement and make necessary corrections. After examining other manufacturing cost data, you have acquired additional information as follows.

1. Inventory balances at the beginning and end of October were:

	October 1	October 31
Raw materials	$18,000	$31,000
Work in process	16,000	14,000
Finished goods	30,000	48,000

2. Only 70% of the utilities expense and 60% of the insurance expense apply to factory operations. The remaining amounts should be charged to selling and administrative activities.

Instructions
(a) Prepare a schedule of cost of goods manufactured for October 2002.
(b) Prepare a correct income statement for October 2002.

Complete a work sheet; prepare a cost of goods manufactured schedule, an income statement, and a balance sheet; journalize and post the closing entries.
(SO 8)

*P1-6A   Everheart Manufacturing Company uses a simple manufacturing accounting system. At the end of its fiscal year on August 31, 2002, the adjusted trial balance contains the following accounts.

Debits			**Credits**	
Cash	$ 16,700		Accumulated Depreciation	$353,000
Accounts Receivable (net)	62,900		Notes Payable	45,000
Finished Goods Inventory	56,000		Accounts Payable	38,200
Work in Process Inventory	27,800		Income Taxes Payable	9,000
Raw Materials Inventory	37,200		Common Stock	352,000
Plant Assets	890,000		Retained Earnings	205,300
Raw Materials Purchases	236,500		Sales	996,000
Direct Labor	280,900			$1,998,500
Indirect Labor	27,400			
Factory Repairs	17,200			
Factory Depreciation	19,000			
Factory Manager's Salary	40,000			
Factory Insurance	11,000			
Factory Property Taxes	12,900			
Factory Utilities	13,300			
Selling Expenses	98,500			
Administrative Expenses	115,200			
Income Tax Expense	36,000			
	$1,998,500			

Physical inventory accounts on August 31, 2002, show the following inventory amounts: Finished Goods $54,600, Work in Process $23,400, and Raw Materials $46,500.

Instructions

(a) Enter the adjusted trial balance data on a work sheet in financial statement order and complete the work sheet.

(b) Prepare a cost of goods manufactured schedule for the year.

(c) Prepare an income statement for the year and a balance sheet at August 31, 2002.

(d) Journalize the closing entries.

(e) Post the closing entries to Manufacturing Summary and to Income Summary.

PROBLEMS: SET B

P1-1B   Kanjo Company specializes in manufacturing motorcycles. The company has enough orders to keep the factory production at 1,000 motorcycles per month. Kanjo's monthly manufacturing cost and other expense data are as follows.

Classify manufacturing costs into different categories and compute the unit cost.
(SO 3, 4)

Maintenance costs on factory building	$ 300
Factory manager's salary	5,000
Advertising for motorcycles	10,000
Sales commissions	5,000
Depreciation on factory building	700
Rent on factory equipment	5,000
Insurance on factory building	3,000
Raw materials (frames, tires, etc.)	20,000
Utility costs for factory	800
Supplies for general office	200
Wages for assembly line workers	40,000
Depreciation on office equipment	500
Miscellaneous materials (lubricants, solders, etc.)	1,000

Instructions

(a) Prepare an answer sheet with the following column headings.

	Product Costs			
Cost Item	Direct Materials	Direct Labor	Manufacturing Overhead	Period Costs

Enter each cost item on your answer sheet, placing the dollar amount under the appropriate headings. Total the dollar amounts in each of the columns.

(b) Compute the cost to produce one motorcycle.

P1-2B   Match Company, a manufacturer of tennis rackets, started production in November 2002. For the preceding 5 years Match had been a retailer of sports equipment. After a thorough survey of tennis racket markets, Match decided to turn its retail store into a tennis racket factory.

Classify manufacturing costs into different categories and compute the unit cost.
(SO 3, 4)

Raw materials cost for a tennis racket will total $20 per racket. Workers on the production lines are paid on average $13 per hour. A racket usually takes 2 hours to complete. In addition, the rent on the equipment used to produce rackets amounts to $1,000 per month. Indirect materials cost $3 per racket. A supervisor was hired to oversee production; her monthly salary is $3,500.

Janitorial costs are $1,200 monthly. Advertising costs for the rackets will be $6,000 per month. The factory building depreciation expense is $8,400 per year. Property taxes on the factory building will be $4,320 per year.

Instructions

(a) Prepare an answer sheet with the following column headings.

	Product Costs			
Cost Item	Direct Materials	Direct Labor	Manufacturing Overhead	Period Costs

Assuming that Match manufactures, on average, 2,000 tennis rackets per month, enter each cost item on your answer sheet, placing the dollar amount per month under the appropriate headings. Total the dollar amounts in each of the columns.

(b) Compute the cost to produce one racket.

P1-3B Incomplete manufacturing costs, expenses, and selling data for two different cases are as follows.

	Case 1	Case 2
Direct Materials Used	$ 8,300	$ (g)
Direct Labor	3,000	4,000
Manufacturing Overhead	4,000	5,000
Total Manufacturing Costs	(a)	22,000
Beginning Work in Process Inventory	1,000	(h)
Ending Work in Process Inventory	(b)	2,000
Sales	21,500	(i)
Sales Discounts	1,500	1,200
Cost of Goods Manufactured	12,800	21,000
Beginning Finished Goods Inventory	(c)	4,000
Goods Available for Sale	17,300	(j)
Cost of Goods Sold	(d)	(k)
Ending Finished Goods Inventory	1,200	2,500
Gross Profit	(e)	6,000
Operating Expenses	2,700	(l)
Net Income	(f)	2,800

Instructions
(a) Indicate the missing amount for each letter.
(b) Prepare a condensed cost of goods manufactured schedule for Case 1.
(c) Prepare an income statement and the current assets section of the balance sheet for Case 1. Assume that in Case 1 the other items in the current assets section are as follows: Cash $3,000, Receivables (net) $10,000, Raw Materials $700, and Prepaid Expenses $200.

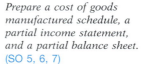

P1-4B The following data were taken from the records of Mauro Manufacturing Company for the year ended December 31, 2002.

Raw Materials Inventory 1/1/02	$ 45,000	Factory Insurance	$ 5,400
Raw Materials Inventory 12/31/02	44,200	Factory Machinery Depreciation	7,700
Finished Goods Inventory 1/1/02	85,000	Freight-in on Raw Materials Purchased	3,900
Finished Goods Inventory 12/31/02	77,800	Factory Utilities	15,900
Work in Process Inventory 1/1/02	9,500	Office Utilities Expense	8,600
Work in Process Inventory 12/31/02	8,000	Sales	475,000
		Sales Discounts	3,500
Direct Labor	145,100	Plant Manager's Salary	30,000
Indirect Labor	19,100	Factory Property Taxes	6,100
Accounts Receivable	27,000	Factory Repairs	800
		Raw Materials Purchases	64,600
		Cash	28,000

Instructions
(a) Prepare a cost of goods manufactured schedule.
(b) Prepare an income statement through gross profit.
(c) Prepare the current assets section of the balance sheet at December 31.

P1-5B Chelsea Company is a manufacturer of toys. Its controller, Marie Klinger, resigned in August 2002. An inexperienced assistant accountant has prepared the following income statement for the month of August 2002.

CHELSEA COMPANY
Income Statement
For the Month Ended August 31, 2002

Sales (net)		$670,000
Less: Operating expenses		
Raw materials purchased	$200,000	
Direct labor cost	150,000	
Advertising expense	75,000	
Selling and administrative salaries	70,000	
Rent on factory facilities	60,000	
Depreciation on sales equipment	55,000	
Depreciation on factory equipment	35,000	
Indirect labor cost	20,000	
Utilities expense	10,000	
Insurance expense	5,000	680,000
Net loss		$ (10,000)

Prior to August 2002 the company had been profitable every month. The company's president is concerned about the accuracy of the income statement. As her friend, you have been asked to review the income statement and make necessary corrections. After examining other manufacturing cost data, you have acquired additional information as follows.

1. Inventory balances at the beginning and end of August were:

	August 1	August 31
Raw materials	$19,500	$33,000
Work in process	25,000	21,000
Finished goods	40,000	62,000

2. Only 60% of the utilities expense and 70% of the insurance expense apply to factory operations; the remaining amounts should be charged to selling and administrative activities.

Instructions
(a) Prepare a cost of goods manufactured schedule for August 2002.
(b) Prepare a correct income statement for August 2002.

◆ **BROADENING YOUR PERSPECTIVE**

GROUP DECISION CASE

BYP 1-1   Intermix Manufacturing Company specializes in producing fashion outfits. On July 31, 2002, a tornado touched down at its factory and general office. The inventories in the warehouse and the factory were completely destroyed as was the general office nearby. Next morning, through a careful search of the disaster site, however, Ed Loder, the company's controller, and Susan Manning, the cost accountant, were able to recover a small part of manufacturing cost data for the current month.

"What a horrible experience," sighed Ed. "And the worst part is that we may not have enough records to use in filing an insurance claim."

"It was terrible," replied Susan. "However, I managed to recover some of the manufacturing cost data that I was working on yesterday afternoon. The data indicate that our direct labor cost in July totaled $250,000 and that we had purchased $345,000 of raw materials. Also, I recall that the amount of raw materials used for July was $350,000. But I'm not sure this information will help. The rest of our records are blown away."

"Well, not exactly," said Ed. "I was working on the year-to-date income statement when the tornado warning was announced. My recollection is that our sales in July were $1,250,000 and our gross profit ratio has been 40% of sales. Also, I can remember that our cost of goods available for sale was $790,000 for July."

"Maybe we can work something out from this information!" exclaimed Susan. "My experience tells me that our manufacturing overhead is usually 60% of direct labor."

"Hey, look what I just found," cried Susan. "It's a copy of this June's balance sheet, and it shows that our inventories as of June 30 are Finished goods $36,000, Work in process $22,000, and Raw materials $19,000."

"Super," yelled Ed. "Let's go work something out."

In order to file an insurance claim Intermix Company must determine the amount of its inventories as of July 31, 2002, the date of the tornado touchdown.

Instructions

With the class divided into groups, determine the amount of cost in the Raw Materials, Work in Process, and Finished Goods inventory accounts as of the date of the tornado touchdown.

MANAGERIAL ANALYSIS

BYP 1-2 Tennis, Anyone? is a fairly large manufacturing company located in the southern United States. The company manufactures tennis rackets, tennis balls, tennis clothing, and tennis shoes, all bearing the company's distinctive logo, a large green question mark on a white flocked tennis ball. The company's sales have been increasing over the past 10 years.

The tennis racket division has recently implemented several advanced manufacturing techniques. Robot arms hold the tennis rackets in place while glue dries, and machine vision systems check for defects. The engineering and design team uses computerized drafting and testing of new products. The following managers work in the tennis racket division.

Wayne Gryer, Sales Manager (supervises all sales representatives)
Tommye Stevens, technical specialist (supervises computer programmers)
Martie Lefever, cost accounting manager (supervises cost accountants)
Jack Marler, production supervisor (supervises all manufacturing employees)
Tina Roy, engineer (supervises all new-product design teams)

Instructions
(a) What are the primary information needs of each manager?
(b) Which, if any, financial accounting report(s) is each likely to use?
(c) Name one special-purpose management accounting report that could be designed for each manager. Include the name of the report, the information it would contain, and how frequently it should be issued.

REAL-WORLD FOCUS

BYP 1-3 Anchor Glass Container Corporation, the third largest manufacturer of glass containers in the U.S., supplies beverage and food producers and consumer products manufacturers nationwide. Parent company **Consumers Packaging Inc.** *(Toronto Stock Exchange:* CGC) is a leading international designer and manufacturer of glass containers.

The following management discussion appeared in a recent annual report of Anchor Glass.

ANCHOR GLASS CONTAINER CORPORATION Management Discussion

Cost of Products Sold Cost of products sold as a percentage of net sales was 89.3% in the current year compared to 87.6% in the prior year. The increase in cost of products sold as a percentage of net sales principally reflected the impact of operational problems during the second quarter of the current year at a major furnace at one of the Company's plants, higher downtime, and costs and expenses associated with an increased number of scheduled capital improvement projects, increases in labor, and certain other manufacturing costs (with no corresponding selling price increases in the current year). Reduced fixed costs from the closing of the Streator, Illinois, plant in June of the current year and productivity and efficiency gains partially offset these cost increases.

Instructions
What factors affect the costs of products sold at Anchor Glass Container Corporation?

*E*XPLORING THE *W*EB

BYP 1-4   The Institute of Management Accountants (IMA) is the largest organization of its kind in the world, dedicated to excellence in the practice of management accounting and financial management.

Address: **www.imanet.org** *(or go to www.wiley.com/college/weygandt)*

Instructions
At the IMA's home page, locate the answers to the following questions.
(a) How many members does the IMA have, and what are their job titles?
(b) What are some of the benefits of joining the IMA as a student?
(c) Use the chapter locator function to locate the IMA chapter nearest you, and find the name of the chapter president.

*C*OMMUNICATION *A*CTIVITY

BYP 1-5   Refer to Problem 1–5B and add the following requirement.
Prepare a letter to the president of the company, Ruth Chelsea, describing the changes you made. Explain clearly why net income is different after the changes. Keep the following points in mind as you compose your letter.

1. This is a letter to the president of a company, who is your friend. The style should be generally formal, but you may relax some requirements. For example, you may call the president by her first name.

2. Executives are very busy. Your letter should tell the president your main results first (for example, the amount of net income).

3. You should include brief explanations so that the president can understand the changes you made in the calculations.

RESEARCH ASSIGNMENT

BYP1-6 The December 1995 issue of *Management Accounting* includes an article by William L. Ferrara entitled "Cost/Management Accounting: The 21st Century Paradigm." The article contains a historical perspective on management accounting as well as a prediction of the future.

Instructions
Read the article and answer the following questions.
(a) What are the four eras into which management accounting is divided? (Identify the dates of each era. These are labeled paradigm A, B, C, and D in the article.)
(b) What is the costing/pricing formula shown in Table 1 for paradigm (model) D, the fourth era?
(c) What are the three "provocative new issues" created by the future model of management accounting (paradigm D)?

ETHICS CASE

BYP 1-7 Carlos Morales, controller for Tredway Industries, was reviewing production cost reports for the year. One amount in these reports continued to bother him—advertising. During the year, the company had instituted an expensive advertising campaign to sell some of its slower-moving products. It was still too early to tell whether the advertising campaign was successful.

There had been much internal debate as how to report advertising cost. The vice president of finance argued that advertising costs should be reported as a cost of production, just like direct materials and direct labor. He therefore recommended that this cost be identified as manufacturing overhead and reported as part of inventory costs until sold. Others disagreed. Morales believed that this cost should be reported as an expense of the current period, based on the conservatism principle. Others argued that it should be reported as Prepaid Advertising and reported as a current asset.

The president finally had to decide the issue. He argued that these costs should be reported as inventory. His arguments were practical ones. He noted that the company was experiencing financial difficulty and expensing this amount in the current period might jeopardize a planned bond offering. Also, by reporting the advertising costs as inventory rather than as prepaid advertising, less attention would be directed to it by the financial community.

Instructions
(a) Who are the stakeholders in this situation?
(b) What are the ethical issues involved in this situation?
(c) What would you do if you were Carlos Morales?

Answers to Self-Study Questions
1. b   2. d   3. b   4. b   5. c   6. d   7. a   8. c   9. a   10. d

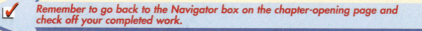
Remember to go back to the Navigator box on the chapter-opening page and check off your completed work.

2

Job Order Cost Accounting

THE NAVIGATOR ✔

- Scan *Study Objectives* ☐
- Read *Feature Story* ☐
- Read *Preview* ☐
- Read text and answer *Before You Go On*
  p. 48 ☐ p. 59 ☐ p. 66 ☐
- Work *Using the Decision Toolkit* ☐
- Review *Summary of Study Objectives* ☐
- Work *Demonstration Problem* ☐
- Answer *Self-Study Questions* ☐
- Complete *Assignments* ☐

◆ STUDY OBJECTIVES

After studying this chapter, you should be able to:

1. Explain the characteristics and purposes of cost accounting.

2. Describe the flow of costs in a job order cost accounting system.

3. Explain the nature and importance of a job cost sheet.

4. Indicate how the predetermined overhead rate is determined and used.

5. Prepare entries for jobs completed and sold.

6. Distinguish between under- and overapplied manufacturing overhead.

 THE NAVIGATOR

◆ FEATURE STORY

" . . . AND WE'D LIKE IT IN RED"

Western States Fire Apparatus, Inc., of Cornelius, Oregon, is one of the few U.S. companies that makes fire trucks. The company builds about 25 trucks per year. Founded in 1941, the company is run by the children and grandchildren of the original founder.

"We buy the chassis, which is the cab and the frame," says Susan Scott, the company's bookkeeper. "In our computer, we set up an account into which all of the direct material that is purchased for that particular job is charged." Other direct materials include the water pump—which can cost $10,000—the lights, the siren, ladders, and hoses.

As for direct labor, the production workers fill out time tickets that tell what jobs they worked on. Usually, the company is building four trucks at any one time. On payday, the controller allocates the payroll to the appropriate job record.

Indirect materials, such as nuts and bolts, wiring, lubricants, and abrasives, are allocated to each job in proportion to direct material dollars. Other costs, such as insurance and supervisors'

salaries, are allocated based on direct labor hours. "We need to allocate overhead in order to know what kind of price we have to charge when we submit our bids," she says.

Western gets orders through a "blind-bidding" process. That is, Western submits its bid without knowing the bid prices made by its competitors. "If we bid too low, we won't make a profit. If we bid too high, we don't get the job."

Regardless of the final price for the truck, the quality had better be first-rate. "The fire departments let you know if they don't like what you did, and you usually end up fixing it."

THE NAVIGATOR

The Feature Story about **Western States Fire Apparatus** described the manufacturing costs used in making a fire truck. It demonstrated that accurate costing is critical to the company's success. For example, in order to submit accurate bids on new jobs and to know whether it profited from past jobs, the company needs a good costing system. This chapter illustrates how these manufacturing costs would be assigned to specific jobs, such as the manufacture of individual fire trucks. We begin the discussion in this chapter with an overview of the flow of costs in a job order cost accounting system. We then use a case study to explain and illustrate the documents, entries, and accounts in this type of cost accounting system.

The content and organization of Chapter 2 are as follows.

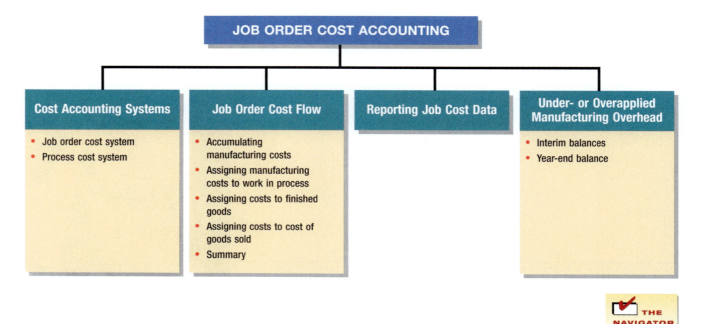

JOB ORDER COST ACCOUNTING			
Cost Accounting Systems	**Job Order Cost Flow**	**Reporting Job Cost Data**	**Under- or Overapplied Manufacturing Overhead**
• Job order cost system • Process cost system	• Accumulating manufacturing costs • Assigning manufacturing costs to work in process • Assigning costs to finished goods • Assigning costs to cost of goods sold • Summary		• Interim balances • Year-end balance

THE NAVIGATOR

COST ACCOUNTING SYSTEMS

STUDY OBJECTIVE

1

Explain the characteristics and purposes of cost accounting.

Cost accounting involves the measuring, recording, and reporting of product costs. From the data accumulated, both the total cost and the unit cost of each product is determined. The accuracy of the product cost information produced by the cost accounting system is critical to the success of the company. As you will see in later chapters, this information is used to determine which products to produce, what price to charge, and the amounts to produce. Accurate product cost information is also vital for effective evaluation of employee performance.

A **cost accounting system** consists of accounts for the various manufacturing costs. These accounts are fully integrated into the general ledger of a company. **An important feature of a cost accounting system is the use of a perpetual inventory system.** Such a system **provides immediate, up-to-date information on the cost of a product**. There are two basic types of cost accounting systems: (1) a job order cost system and (2) a process cost system. Although cost accounting systems differ widely from company to company, most are based on one of these two traditional product costing systems.

JOB ORDER COST SYSTEM

Under a job order cost system, costs are assigned to each **job** or to each **batch** of goods. An example of a job would be the manufacture of a mainframe computer by **IBM**, the production of a movie by **Disney**, or the making of a fire truck by **Western States**. An example of a batch would be the printing of 225 wedding invitations by a local print shop, or the printing of a weekly issue of *Fortune* magazine by a hi-tech printer such as **Quad Graphics**. Jobs or batches may be completed to fill a specific customer order or to replenish inventory.

An important feature of job order costing is that each job (or batch) has its own distinguishing characteristics. For example, each house is custom built, each consulting engagement by a CPA firm is unique, and each printing job is different. **The objective is to compute the cost per job.** At each point in the manufacturing of a product or the providing of a service, the job and its associated costs can be identified. A job order cost system measures costs for each completed job, rather than for set time periods. The recording of costs in a job order cost system is shown in Illustration 2-1.

Illustration 2-1 Job order cost system

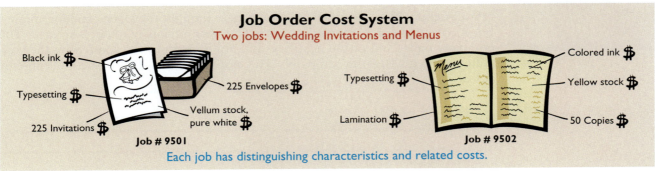

Job Order Cost System
Two jobs: Wedding Invitations and Menus

Black ink $ — Typesetting $ — 225 Invitations $ — 225 Envelopes $ — Vellum stock, pure white $

Job # 9501

Colored ink $ — Typesetting $ — Yellow stock $ — Lamination $ — 50 Copies $

Job # 9502

Each job has distinguishing characteristics and related costs.

PROCESS COST SYSTEM

A process cost system is used when a series of connected manufacturing processes or departments produce a large volume of similar products. Production is continuous to ensure that adequate inventories of the finished product(s) are on hand. A process cost system is used in the manufacture of cereal by **Kellogg**, the refining of petroleum by **Exxon Mobil**, and the production of automobiles by **General Motors**. Process costing accumulates product-related costs **for a period of time** (such as a week or a month) instead of assigning costs to specific products or job orders. In process costing, the costs are assigned to departments or processes for a set period of time. The recording of costs in a process cost system is shown in Illustration 2-2. The process cost system will be discussed further in Chapter 3.

Illustration 2-2 Process cost system

Process Cost System
Compact Disc Production

1. Oil is pumped.   2. Benzene is removed.   3. The benzene is made into pellets…   4. …from which compact discs are produced.

Similar products are produced over a specified time period.

A company may use both types of cost systems. For example, **General Motors** uses process cost accounting for its standard model cars, such as Saturns and Corvettes, and job order cost accounting for a custom-made limousine for the President of the United States. The objective of both systems is to provide unit cost information for product pricing, cost control, inventory valuation, and financial statement presentation. End-of-period inventory values are computed by using unit cost data.

BUSINESS INSIGHT
Management Perspective

Many companies suffer from poor cost accounting. As a result, they sometimes make products they ought not to be selling at all and buy others that they could more profitably make themselves. Also, inaccurate cost data lead companies to misallocate capital and frustrate efforts by plant managers to improve efficiency.

For example, consider the case of a diversified company in the business of rebuilding diesel locomotives. The managers thought they were making money, but a consulting firm found that costs had been seriously underestimated. The company bailed out of the business, and not a moment too soon. Says the consultant who advised the company: "The more contracts it won, the more money it lost."

BEFORE YOU GO ON . . .

◆ **Review It**

1. What is cost accounting?
2. What does a cost accounting system consist of?
3. How does a job order cost system differ from a process cost system?

THE NAVIGATOR

JOB ORDER COST FLOW

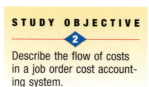

STUDY OBJECTIVE

2

Describe the flow of costs in a job order cost accounting system.

The flow of costs (direct materials, direct labor, and manufacturing overhead) in job order cost accounting parallels the physical flow of the materials as they are converted into finished goods. As shown in Illustration 2-3, manufacturing costs are assigned to the Work in Process Inventory account. When a job is completed, the cost of the job is transferred to Finished Goods Inventory. Later when the goods are sold, their cost is transferred to Cost of Goods Sold.

Illustration 2-3 provides a basic overview of the flow of costs in a manufacturing setting. A more detailed presentation of the flow of costs is shown in Illustration 2-4. It indicates that there are two major steps in the flow of costs: (1) *accumulating* the manufacturing costs incurred and (2) *assigning* the accumulated costs to the work done. As shown, manufacturing costs incurred are accumulated in entries 1–3 by debits to Raw Materials Inventory, Factory Labor, and Manufacturing Overhead. When these costs are incurred no attempt is made to associate the costs with specific jobs. The remaining entries (entries 4–8) assign manufacturing costs incurred. In the remainder of this chapter, pages 50–65, we will use a case study to explain how a job order system operates.

Illustration 2-3 Flow of costs in job order cost accounting

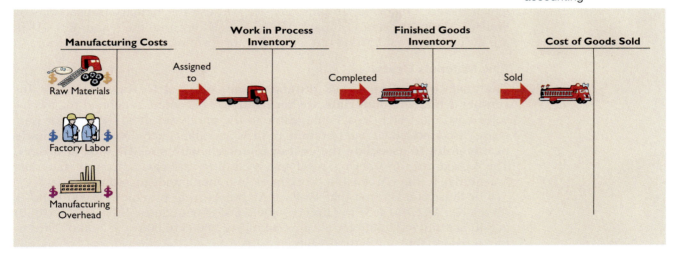

Illustration 2-4 Job order cost accounting system

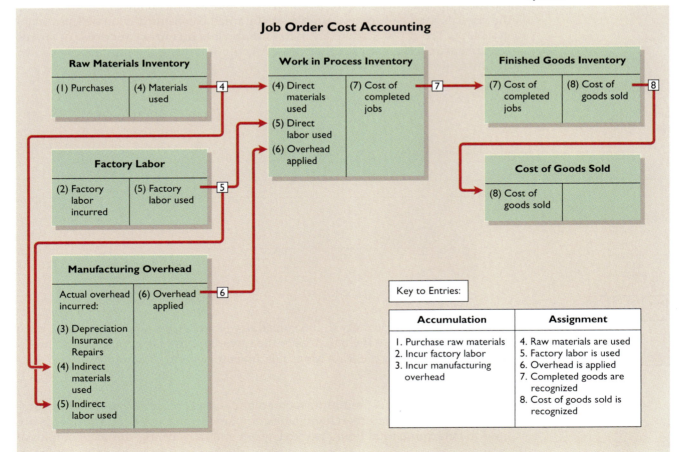

ACCUMULATING MANUFACTURING COSTS

In a job order cost system, manufacturing costs are recorded in the period in which they are incurred. To illustrate, we will use the January transactions of Wallace Manufacturing Company, which makes machine tools and dies. (Dies are devices used for cutting out, stamping, or forming metals and plastics.)

Raw Materials Costs

The costs of raw materials purchased are debited to Raw Materials Inventory when the materials are received. This account is debited for the invoice cost and freight costs chargeable to the purchaser. It is credited for purchase discounts taken and purchase returns and allowances. **No effort is made at this point to associate the cost of materials with specific jobs or orders.** The procedures for ordering, receiving, recording, and paying for raw materials are similar to the purchasing procedures of a merchandising company.

To illustrate, assume that Wallace Manufacturing purchases 2,000 handles (Stock No. AA2746) at $5 per unit ($10,000) and 800 modules (Stock No. AA2850) at $40 per unit ($32,000) for a total cost of $42,000 ($10,000 + $32,000). The entry to record this purchase on January 4 is:

			(1)		
Jan. 4	Raw Materials Inventory			42,000	
	Accounts Payable				42,000
	(Purchase of raw materials on account)				

Raw Materials Inventory is a control account. The subsidiary ledger consists of individual records for each item of raw materials. The records may take the form of accounts (or cards) that are manually or mechanically prepared. Or the records may be kept as data files maintained electronically on disks or magnetic tape. The records are referred to as **materials inventory records** (or **stores ledger cards**). The card for Stock No. AA2746 following the purchase is shown in Illustration 2-5.

Illustration 2-5 Materials inventory card

Item: Handles								Part No: AA2746		
	Receipts			Issues			Balance			
Date	Units	Cost	Total	Units	Cost	Total	Units	Cost	Total
1/4	2,000	$5	$10,000				2,000	$5	$10,000

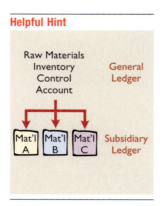

Helpful Hint

Raw Materials Inventory Control Account — General Ledger

Mat'l A   Mat'l B   Mat'l C — Subsidiary Ledger

Postings are made daily to the subsidiary ledger. After all postings have been completed, the sum of the balances in the raw materials subsidiary ledger should equal the balance in the Raw Materials Inventory control account.

Factory Labor Costs

The procedures for accumulating factory labor costs are similar to those for computing the payroll for a merchandising company. Time clocks and time cards are used to determine total hours worked; gross and net earnings for each employee are listed in a payroll register; and individual employee earnings records are maintained. To help ensure the accuracy of data, a company should follow the principles of internal control.

In a manufacturing company, the cost of factory labor consists of (1) gross earnings of factory workers, (2) employer payroll taxes on such earnings, and (3) fringe benefits (such as sick pay, pensions, and vacation pay) incurred by the employer. **Labor costs are debited to Factory Labor when they are incurred.**

To illustrate, assume that Wallace Manufacturing incurs $32,000 of factory labor costs. Of that amount, $27,000 relates to wages payable and $5,000 relates to payroll taxes payable in January. The entry is:

	(2)		
Jan. 31	Factory Labor	32,000	
	Factory Wages Payable		27,000
	Employer Payroll Taxes Payable		5,000
	(To record factory labor costs)		

Factory labor is subsequently assigned to work in process and manufacturing overhead, as explained later in the chapter.

Manufacturing Overhead Costs

A company may have many types of overhead costs. These costs may be recognized **daily**, as in the case of machinery repairs and the use of indirect materials and indirect labor. Or overhead costs may be recorded **periodically** through adjusting entries. Property taxes, depreciation, and insurance are recorded periodically, for example. Using assumed data, a summary entry for manufacturing overhead in Wallace Manufacturing Company is:

	(3)		
Jan. 31	Manufacturing Overhead	13,800	
	Utilities Payable		4,800
	Prepaid Insurance		2,000
	Accounts Payable (for repairs)		2,600
	Accumulated Depreciation		3,000
	Property Taxes Payable		1,400
	(To record overhead costs)		

Helpful Hint This is referred to as a **summary entry** because it summarizes the totals from multiple transactions.

Manufacturing Overhead is a control account. The subsidiary ledger consists of individual accounts for each type of cost, such as Factory Utilities, Factory Insurance, and Factory Repairs.

ASSIGNING MANUFACTURING COSTS TO WORK IN PROCESS

As shown in Illustration 2-4, assigning manufacturing costs to work in process results in the following entries: (1) **Debits** are made to Work in Process Inventory. (2) **Credits** are made to Raw Materials Inventory, Factory Labor, and Manufacturing Overhead. Journal entries to assign costs to work in process are usually made and posted **monthly**.

An essential accounting record in assigning costs to jobs is a **job cost sheet** shown in Illustration 2-6. A job cost sheet is a form used to record the costs chargeable to a specific job and to determine the total and unit costs of the completed job.

STUDY OBJECTIVE
3

Explain the nature and importance of a job cost sheet.

Illustration 2-6 Job cost sheet

Helpful Hint In today's electronic environment, job cost sheets are maintained as computer files.

Wallace Manufacturing Company
Job Cost Sheet

Job No. _____   Quantity _____

Item _____   Date Requested _____

For _____   Date Completed _____

Date	Direct Materials	Direct Labor	Manufacturing Overhead

Cost of completed job
  Direct materials $ _____
  Direct labor   _____
  Manufacturing overhead   _____
Total cost $ _____
Unit cost (total dollars ÷ quantity) $ _____

Postings to job cost sheets are made daily, directly from supporting documents.

A separate job cost sheet is kept for each job. The job cost sheets constitute the subsidiary ledger for the Work in Process Inventory account. **Each entry to Work in Process Inventory must be accompanied by a corresponding posting to one or more job cost sheets.**

e — BUSINESS INSIGHT

General Motors recently launched a new Internet-based ordering system intended to deliver custom vehicles in 15 to 20 days instead of the 55 to 60 days it previously took. Customers interested in a GM car can search online to see if any dealers have a car with the options they want. If not, the customer uses an online program to configure a car with the desired options and then places the order. While this online approach could potentially provide savings for automakers by reducing inventory costs, some people are skeptical. One auto analyst stated, "I don't think it's going to lead to a massive change in the way vehicles are built and sold in the next 10 years."

Source: Karen Lundegaard, "GM Tests Web-Based Ordering System, Seeking to Slash Custom-Delivery Time," *Wall Street Journal,* November 17, 2000.

Raw Materials Costs

Helpful Hint Approvals are an important part of a materials requisition slip because they help to establish individual accountability over inventory.

Raw materials costs are assigned when the materials are issued by the storeroom. To achieve effective internal control over the issuance of materials, the storeroom worker should receive a written authorization before materials are released to production. Such authorization for issuing raw materials is made on a prenumbered **materials requisition slip**. This form is signed by an authorized employee such as a department supervisor. The materials issued may be used directly on a job, or they may be considered indirect materials. As shown in Illustration 2-7, the requisition should indicate the quantity and type of materials withdrawn and the account to be charged. Direct materials will be charged to Work in Process Inventory, and indirect materials to Manufacturing Overhead.

Illustration 2-7   Materials requisition slip

Wallace Manufacturing Company
Materials Requisition Slip

Deliver to: Assembly Department   Req. No. R247
Charge to: Work in Process—Job No. 101   Date: 1/6/02

Quantity	Description	Stock No.	Cost per Unit	Total
200	Handles	AA2746	$5.00	$1,000

Requested by *Bruce Howart*   Received by *Herb Crowley*
Approved by *Kap Shin*   Costed by *Heather Remmers*

Helpful Hint The internal control principle of documentation includes prenumbering to enhance accountability.

The requisition is prepared in duplicate. A copy is retained in the storeroom as evidence of the materials released. The original is sent to accounting, where the cost per unit and total cost of the materials used are determined. Any of the inventory costing methods (FIFO, LIFO, or average cost) may be used in costing the requisitions. After the requisition slips have been costed, they are posted daily to the materials inventory records. Also, **requisitions for direct materials are posted daily to the individual job cost sheets**.

Periodically, the requisitions are sorted, totaled, and journalized. For example, if $24,000 of direct materials and $6,000 of indirect materials are used in Wallace Manufacturing in January, the entry is:

(4)

Jan. 31	Work in Process Inventory	24,000	
	Manufacturing Overhead	6,000	
	Raw Materials Inventory		30,000
	(To assign materials to jobs and overhead)		

The requisition slips show total direct materials costs of $12,000 for Job No. 101, $7,000 for Job No. 102, and $5,000 for Job No. 103. The posting of requisition slip R247 and other assumed postings to the job cost sheets for materials are shown in Illustration 2-8. After all postings have been completed, the sum of the direct materials columns of the job cost sheets should equal the direct materials debited to Work in Process Inventory.

Illustration 2-8 Job cost sheets—direct materials

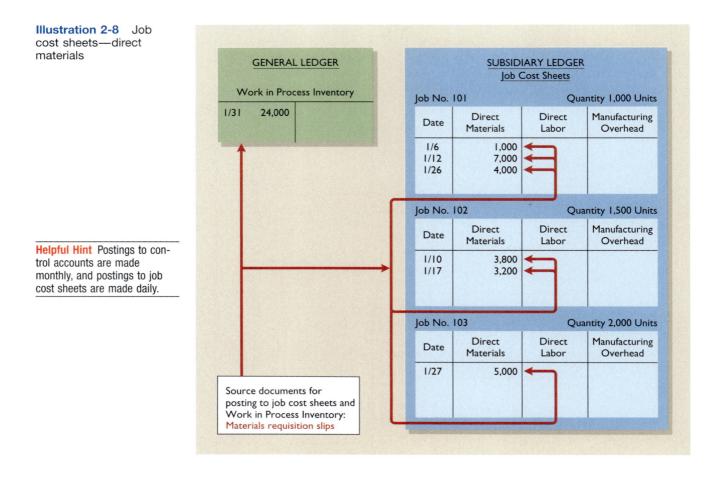

Helpful Hint Postings to control accounts are made monthly, and postings to job cost sheets are made daily.

The materials inventory record for Part No. AA2746 is shown in Illustration 2-9. It shows the posting of requisition slip R247 for 200 handles and an assumed requisition slip for 760 handles costing $3,800 on January 10 for Job 102.

Illustration 2-9 Materials inventory card following issuances

Item: Handles									Part No: AA2746
	Receipts			Issues			Balance		
Date	Units	Cost	Total	Units	Cost	Total	Units	Cost	Total
1/4	2,000	$5	$10,000				2,000	$5	$10,000
1/6				200	$5	$1,000	1,800	$5	9,000
1/10				760	$5	3,800	1,040	$5	5,200

Factory Labor Costs

Factory labor costs are assigned to jobs on the basis of time tickets prepared when the work is performed. The time ticket should indicate the employee, the hours worked, the account and job to be charged, and the total labor cost. In many companies these data are accumulated through the use of bar coding and scanning devices. When they start and end work, employees scan bar codes on their identification badges and bar codes associated with each job they work on. The account Work in Process Inventory is debited for direct labor, and Manufacturing Overhead is debited for indirect labor. When direct labor is involved, the job number must be indicated, as shown in Illustration 2-10. All time tickets should be approved by the employee's supervisor.

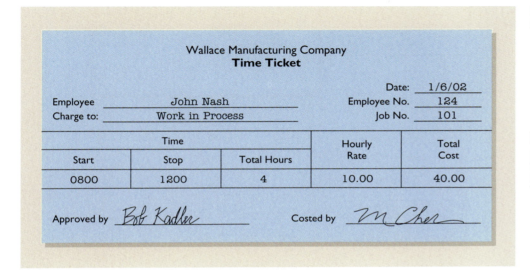

Illustration 2-10 Time ticket

Helpful Hint In some companies, different colored time tickets are used for direct and indirect labor.

The time tickets are later sent to the payroll department. There, the total time reported for an employee for a pay period is reconciled with total hours worked, as shown on the employee's time card. Then the employee's hourly wage rate is applied, and the total labor cost is computed. Finally, the time tickets are sorted, totaled, and journalized. For example, if the $32,000 total factory labor cost consists of $28,000 of direct labor and $4,000 of indirect labor, the entry is:

	(5)		
Jan. 31	Work in Process Inventory	28,000	
	Manufacturing Overhead	4,000	
	Factory Labor		32,000
	(To assign labor to jobs and overhead)		

As a result of this entry, Factory Labor is left with a zero balance, and gross earnings are assigned to the appropriate manufacturing accounts.

Let's assume that the labor costs chargeable to Wallace's three jobs are $15,000, $9,000, and $4,000. The Work in Process Inventory and job cost sheets after posting are shown in Illustration 2-11. As in the case of direct materials, the postings to the direct labor columns of the job cost sheets should equal the posting of direct labor to Work in Process Inventory.

Illustration 2-11 Job
cost sheets—direct labor

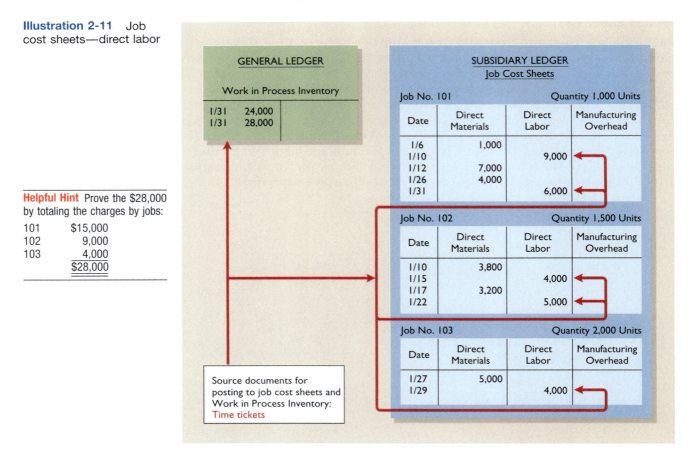

Helpful Hint Prove the $28,000
by totaling the charges by jobs:

101	$15,000
102	9,000
103	4,000
	$28,000

Manufacturing Overhead Costs

STUDY OBJECTIVE

4

Indicate how the predetermined overhead rate is determined and used.

We've seen that direct materials and direct labor can be applied to specific jobs. In contrast, manufacturing overhead relates to production operations **as a whole**. As a result, overhead costs cannot be assigned to specific jobs on the basis of actual costs incurred. Instead, manufacturing overhead is assigned to work in process and to specific jobs **on an estimated basis through the use of a predetermined overhead rate**.

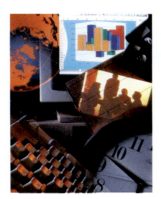

BUSINESS INSIGHT
Management Perspective

A job cost computer program provides summaries of material and labor costs by job. The program accumulates costs by jobs, provides data to accounts receivable for billings, assigns overhead costs, and provides up-to-date management reports. The reports generated by such systems are basically the same as those shown for Wallace Manufacturing. The major difference between manual and computerized systems is the time involved in converting data into information and in getting feedback (reports) to management.

The **predetermined overhead rate** is based on the relationship between estimated annual overhead costs and expected annual operating activity. This relationship is expressed in terms of a common **activity base**. The activity may be stated in terms of direct labor costs, direct labor hours, machine hours, or any other measure that will provide an equitable basis for applying overhead costs to jobs. The predetermined overhead rate is established at the beginning of the year. Small companies often will have a single, company-wide predetermined overhead rate. Large companies, however, often have rates that vary from department to department. The formula for a predetermined overhead rate is:

Illustration 2-12 Formula for predetermined overhead rate

We indicated earlier that overhead relates to production operations as a whole. In order to know what "the whole" is, the logical thing would be to wait until the end of the year's operations, when all costs for the period would be available. But as a practical matter, that wouldn't work: managers could not wait that long before having information about product costs of specific jobs completed during the year. Instead, using a predetermined overhead rate enables a cost to be determined for the job immediately. Illustration 2-13 indicates how manufacturing overhead is assigned to work in process.

Helpful Hint In contrast to overhead, actual costs for direct materials and direct labor are used to assign costs to Work in Process.

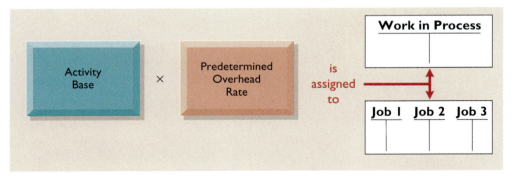

Illustration 2-13 Using predetermined overhead rates

Wallace Manufacturing uses direct labor cost as the activity base. Assuming that annual overhead costs are expected to be $280,000 and that $350,000 of direct labor costs are anticipated for the year, the overhead rate is 80 percent, computed as follows:

$$\$280,000 \div \$350,000 = 80\%$$

This means that for every dollar of direct labor, 80 cents of manufacturing overhead will be assigned to a job. The use of a predetermined overhead rate enables the company to determine the approximate total cost of each job **when the job is completed**.

Historically, direct labor costs or direct labor hours have often been used as the activity base. The reason was the relatively high correlation between direct labor and manufacturing overhead. In recent years, **there has been a trend toward use of machine hours as the activity base, due to increased reliance on automation in manufacturing operations**. Or, as mentioned in Chapter 1, activity-based costing has resulted in more accurate allocation of overhead costs based on the activities that give rise to the costs.

A company may use more than one activity base. For example, if a job order is manufactured in more than one factory department, each department may have its own overhead rate. In the Feature Story about fire trucks, two bases were used in assigning overhead to jobs: direct materials dollars for indirect materials, and direct labor hours for such costs as insurance and supervisors' salaries.

For Wallace Manufacturing, the total amount of manufacturing overhead is assigned to work in process. It then is **charged to jobs when direct labor costs are assigned**. Overhead applied for January is $22,400 ($28,000 × 80%). This application is recorded through the following entry.

	(6)		
Jan. 31	Work in Process Inventory	22,400	
	Manufacturing Overhead		22,400
	(To assign overhead to jobs)		

The overhead assigned to each job will be 80 percent of the direct labor cost of the job for the month. After posting, the Work in Process Inventory account and the job cost sheets will appear as shown in Illustration 2-14. Note that the debit

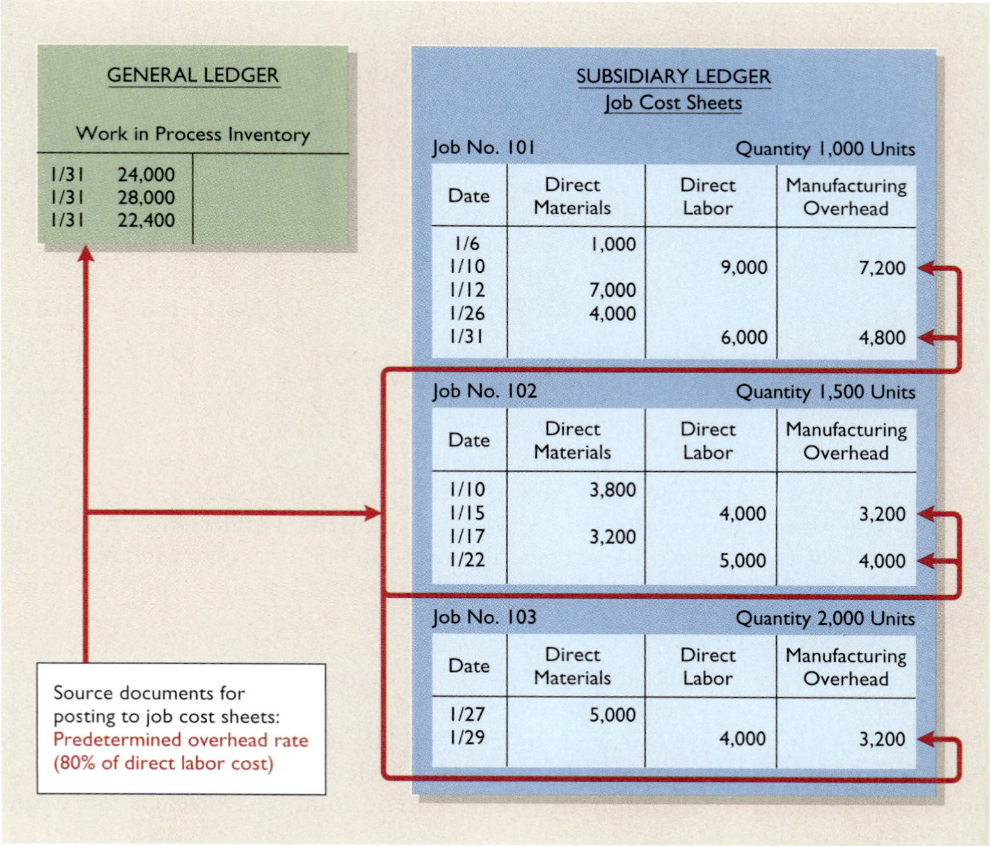

Illustration 2-14 Job cost sheets—manufacturing overhead applied

of $22,400 to Work in Process Inventory equals the sum of the overhead assigned to jobs: Job 101 $12,000 + Job 102 $7,200 + Job 103 $3,200.

At the end of each month, **the balance in Work in Process Inventory should equal the sum of the costs shown on the job cost sheets of unfinished jobs**. Assuming that all jobs are unfinished, proof of the agreement of the control and subsidiary accounts in Wallace Manufacturing is shown below.

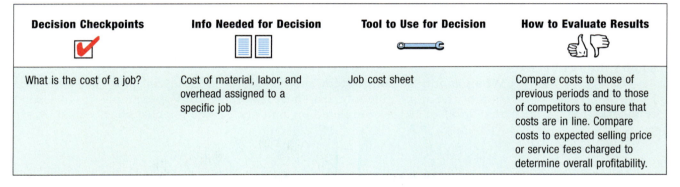

Work in Process Inventory		Job Cost Sheets	
Jan. 31	24,000	No. 101	$39,000
31	28,000	102	23,200
31	22,400	103	12,200
	74,400		**$74,400**

Illustration 2-15 Proof of job cost sheets to work in process inventory

DECISION TOOLKIT

Decision Checkpoints	Info Needed for Decision	Tool to Use for Decision	How to Evaluate Results
What is the cost of a job?	Cost of material, labor, and overhead assigned to a specific job	Job cost sheet	Compare costs to those of previous periods and to those of competitors to ensure that costs are in line. Compare costs to expected selling price or service fees charged to determine overall profitability.

BEFORE YOU GO ON . . .

◆ Review It

1. What source documents are used in assigning manufacturing costs to Work in Process Inventory?
2. What is a job cost sheet, and what is its primary purpose?
3. What is the formula for computing a predetermined overhead rate?

◆ Do It

Danielle Company is working on two job orders. The job cost sheets show the following:

Direct materials—Job 120 $6,000, Job 121 $3,600
Direct labor—Job 120 $4,000, Job 121 $2,000
Manufacturing overhead—Job 120 $5,000, Job 121 $2,500

Prepare the three summary entries to record the assignment of costs to Work in Process from the data on the job cost sheets.

Action Plan

• Recognize that Work in Process Inventory is the control account for all unfinished job cost sheets.

- Debit Work in Process Inventory for the materials, labor, and overhead charged to the job cost sheets.
- Credit the accounts that were debited when the manufacturing costs were accumulated.

Solution: The three summary entries are:

Work in Process Inventory ($6,000 + $3,600)	9,600	
Raw Materials Inventory		9,600
(To assign materials to jobs)		
Work in Process Inventory ($4,000 + $2,000)	6,000	
Factory Labor		6,000
(To assign labor to jobs)		
Work in Process Inventory ($5,000 + $2,500)	7,500	
Manufacturing Overhead		7,500
(To assign overhead to jobs)		

THE NAVIGATOR

Related exercise material: BE2-3, BE2-4, BE2-7, E2-2, E2-3, E2-7, and E2-8.

STUDY OBJECTIVE

5

Prepare entries for jobs completed and sold.

ASSIGNING COSTS TO FINISHED GOODS

When a job is completed, the costs are summarized and the lower portion of the applicable job cost sheet is completed. For example, if we assume that Job No. 101 is completed on January 31, the job cost sheet will show the following.

Illustration 2-16 Completed job cost sheet

Wallace Manufacturing Company
Job Cost Sheet

Job No.	101	Quantity	1,000
Item	Magnetic Sensors	Date Requested	February 5
For	Tanner Company	Date Completed	January 31

Date	Direct Materials	Direct Labor	Manufacturing Overhead
1/6	$ 1,000		
1/10		$ 9,000	$ 7,200
1/12	7,000		
1/26	4,000		
1/31		6,000	4,800
	$12,000	$15,000	$12,000

Cost of completed job		
Direct materials	$	12,000
Direct labor		15,000
Manufacturing overhead		12,000
Total cost	$	39,000
Unit cost ($39,000 ÷ 1,000)	$	39.00

When a job is finished, an entry is made to transfer its total cost to finished goods inventory. The entry for Wallace Manufacturing is:

	(7)		
Jan. 31	Finished Goods Inventory	39,000	
	Work in Process Inventory		39,000
	(To record completion of Job No. 101)		

Finished Goods Inventory is a control account. It controls individual finished goods records in a finished goods subsidiary ledger. Postings to the receipts columns are made directly from completed job cost sheets. The finished goods inventory record for Job No. 101 is shown in Illustration 2-17.

Illustration 2-17 Finished goods record

Item: Magnetic Sensors							Job No: 101		
	Receipts			Issues			Balance		
Date	Units	Cost	Total	Units	Cost	Total	Units	Cost	Total
1/31	1,000	$39	$39,000				1,000	$39	$39,000
1/31				1000	$39	$39,000			−0−

ASSIGNING COSTS TO COST OF GOODS SOLD

Cost of goods sold is recognized when each sale occurs. To illustrate the entries when a completed job is sold, assume that on January 31 Wallace Manufacturing sells on account Job 101, costing $39,000, for $50,000. The entries to record the sale and recognize cost of goods sold are:

	(8)		
Jan. 31	Accounts Receivable	50,000	
	Sales		50,000
	(To record sale of Job No. 101)		
31	Cost of Goods Sold	39,000	
	Finished Goods Inventory		39,000
	(To record cost of Job No. 101)		

The units sold, the cost per unit, and the total cost of goods sold for each job sold are recorded in the issues section of the finished goods record, as shown in Illustration 2-17 above.

SUMMARY OF JOB ORDER COST FLOWS

A completed flow chart for a job order cost accounting system is shown in Illustration 2-18. All postings are keyed to entries 1–8 in Wallace Manufacturing's accounts presented in the cost flow graphic in Illustration 2-4. Illustration 2-19 provides a summary of the flow of documents in a job order cost system.

Illustration 2-18   Flow of costs in a job order cost system

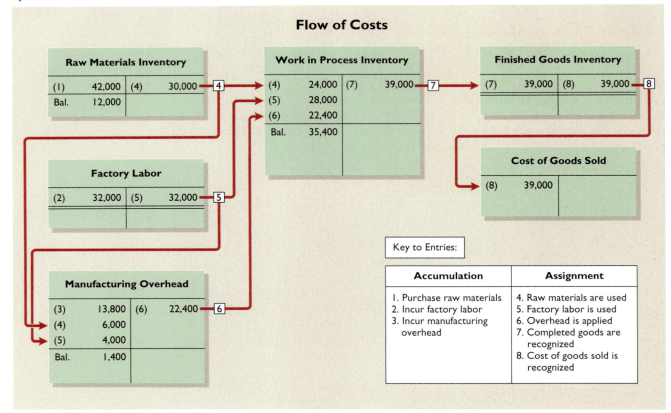

Flow of Costs

Raw Materials Inventory			
(1)	42,000	(4)	30,000
Bal.	12,000		

Work in Process Inventory			
(4)	24,000	(7)	39,000
(5)	28,000		
(6)	22,400		
Bal.	35,400		

Finished Goods Inventory			
(7)	39,000	(8)	39,000

Factory Labor			
(2)	32,000	(5)	32,000

Cost of Goods Sold		
(8)	39,000	

Manufacturing Overhead			
(3)	13,800	(6)	22,400
(4)	6,000		
(5)	4,000		
Bal.	1,400		

Key to Entries:

Accumulation	Assignment
1. Purchase raw materials	4. Raw materials are used
2. Incur factory labor	5. Factory labor is used
3. Incur manufacturing overhead	6. Overhead is applied
	7. Completed goods are recognized
	8. Cost of goods sold is recognized

Illustration 2-19   Flow of documents in a job order cost system

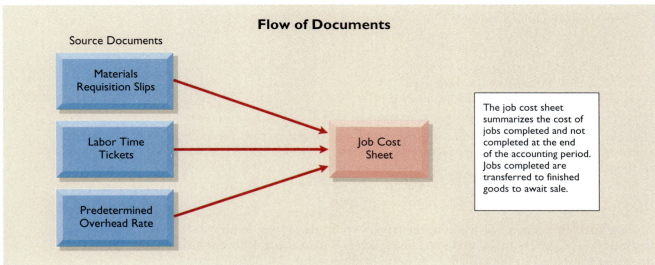

Flow of Documents

Source Documents

Materials Requisition Slips

Labor Time Tickets

Predetermined Overhead Rate

Job Cost Sheet

The job cost sheet summarizes the cost of jobs completed and not completed at the end of the accounting period. Jobs completed are transferred to finished goods to await sale.

Management Perspective

With the increased sophistication of microcomputers, small manufacturers can now use micros to perform (1) computer-aided manufacturing (CAM), (2) computer-aided testing (CAT), (3) computer-aided design (CAD), (4) electronic data interchange (EDI), and (5) materials requirement planning (MRP). For a small investment, manufacturers can now use software with capabilities only dreamed about a few years ago.

REPORTING JOB COST DATA

At the end of a period, financial statements are prepared that present aggregate data on all jobs manufactured and sold. The cost of goods manufactured schedule in job order costing is the same as in Chapter 1 with one exception: **Manufacturing overhead applied is shown, rather than actual overhead costs. This amount is added to direct materials and direct labor to determine total manufacturing costs.** The schedule is prepared directly from the Work in Process Inventory account. A condensed schedule for Wallace Manufacturing Company for January is as follows.

Helpful Hint Monthly financial statements are usually prepared for management use only.

WALLACE MANUFACTURING COMPANY Cost of Goods Manufactured Schedule For the Month Ended January 31, 2002		
Work in process, January 1		$ –0–
Direct materials used	$24,000	
Direct labor	28,000	
Manufacturing overhead applied	**22,400**	
Total manufacturing costs		74,400
Total cost of work in process		74,400
Less: Work in process, January 31		35,400
Cost of goods manufactured		$39,000

Illustration 2-20 Cost of goods manufactured schedule

Note that the cost of goods manufactured ($39,000) agrees with the amount transferred from Work in Process Inventory to Finished Goods Inventory in journal entry no. 7 in Illustration 2-18.

The income statement and balance sheet are the same as those illustrated in Chapter 1. For example, the partial income statement for Wallace Manufacturing for the month of January is shown in Illustration 2-21.

Illustration 2-21   Partial income statement

WALLACE MANUFACTURING COMPANY Income Statement (partial) For the Month Ending January 31, 2002		
Sales		$50,000
Cost of goods sold		
Finished goods inventory, January 1	$ –0–	
Cost of goods manufactured (See Illustration 2-20)	**39,000**	
Cost of goods available for sale	39,000	
Less: Finished goods inventory, January 31	–0–	
Cost of goods sold		39,000
Gross profit		$11,000

UNDER- OR OVERAPPLIED MANUFACTURING OVERHEAD

STUDY OBJECTIVE

6

Distinguish between under- and overapplied manufacturing overhead.

When Manufacturing Overhead has a **debit balance**, overhead is said to be underapplied. **Underapplied overhead** means that the overhead assigned to work in process is less than the overhead incurred. Conversely, when manufacturing overhead has a **credit balance**, overhead is overapplied. **Overapplied overhead** means that the overhead assigned to work in process is greater than the overhead incurred. These concepts are shown in Illustration 2-22.

Manufacturing Overhead	
Actual (Costs incurred)	Applied (Costs assigned)

Manufacturing Overhead

If actual is *greater* than applied, manufacturing overhead is underapplied.

If actual is *less* than applied, manufacturing overhead is overapplied.

Illustration 2-22   Under- and overapplied overhead

INTERIM BALANCES

The existence of under- or overapplied overhead at the end of a month is expected. It usually does not require corrective action by management. Monthly differences between actual and applied overhead will usually be offsetting over the course of the year.

When monthly financial statements are prepared, under- or overapplied overhead is reported on the balance sheet. **Underapplied overhead is shown as a prepaid expense in the current assets section. Overapplied overhead is reported as unearned revenue in the current liabilities section.**

YEAR-END BALANCE

At the end of the year, all manufacturing overhead transactions are complete. There is no further opportunity for offsetting events to occur. Accordingly, any balance in Manufacturing Overhead is eliminated by an adjusting entry. Usually, under- or overapplied overhead is considered to be an **adjustment to cost of**

goods sold. Thus, **underapplied overhead is debited to Cost of Goods Sold. Overapplied overhead is credited to Cost of Goods Sold.** To illustrate, assume that Wallace Manufacturing has a $2,500 credit balance in Manufacturing Overhead at December 31. The adjusting entry for the overapplied overhead is:

Dec. 31	Manufacturing Overhead	2,500	
	Cost of Goods Sold		2,500
	(To transfer overapplied overhead to		
	cost of goods sold)		

After this entry is posted, Manufacturing Overhead will have a zero balance. In preparing an income statement for the year, the amount reported for cost of goods sold will be the account balance **after the adjustment** for either under- or overapplied overhead.

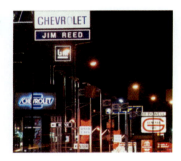

BUSINESS INSIGHT
Management Perspective

Overhead also applies in nonmanufacturing companies. The State of Michigan found that auto dealers were charging documentary and service fees ranging from $18 to $445 per automobile and inspection fees from $88 to $360. These fees often were charged auto buyers after a base sales price for the car had been negotiated. The Attorney General of the State of Michigan ruled that auto dealers cannot charge customers additional fees for routine overhead costs. The attorney general said: "Overhead is part of the sales price of a motor vehicle. Processing paper work, dealer incurred costs, and inspection fees to qualify cars for extended warranty plans are ordinary overhead expenses."

    Conceptually, it can be argued that under- or overapplied overhead at the end of the year should be allocated among ending work in process, finished goods, and cost of goods sold. However, most management accountants do not believe allocation is worth the cost and effort. The bulk of the under- or overapplied amount will be allocated to cost of goods sold anyway, because most of the jobs will be sold during the year.

DECISION TOOLKIT

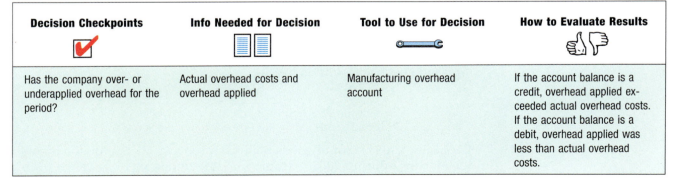

Decision Checkpoints	Info Needed for Decision	Tool to Use for Decision	How to Evaluate Results
Has the company over- or underapplied overhead for the period?	Actual overhead costs and overhead applied	Manufacturing overhead account	If the account balance is a credit, overhead applied exceeded actual overhead costs. If the account balance is a debit, overhead applied was less than actual overhead costs.

BEFORE YOU GO ON . . .

◆ **Review It**

1. When are entries made to record the completion and sale of a job?
2. What costs are included in total manufacturing costs in the cost of goods manufactured schedule?
3. How is under- or overapplied manufacturing overhead reported in monthly financial statements?

USING THE DECISION TOOLKIT

Martinez Building Products Company is one of the largest manufacturers and marketers of unique, custom-made residential garage doors in the U.S. as well as a major supplier of industrial and commercial doors, grills, and counter shutters for the new construction, repair, and remodel markets. Martinez has developed plans for continued expansion of a network of service operations that sell, install, and service manufactured fireplaces, garage doors, and related products.

Martinez uses a job cost system and applies overhead to production on the basis of direct labor cost. In computing a predetermined overhead rate for the year 2002, the company estimated manufacturing overhead to be $24 million and direct labor costs to be $20 million. In addition the following information is provided.

Actual costs incurred during 2002

Direct materials used	$30,000,000
Direct labor cost incurred	21,000,000

Manufacturing costs incurred during 2002

Insurance, factory	$ 500,000
Indirect labor	7,500,000
Maintenance	1,000,000
Rent on building	11,000,000
Depreciation on equipment	2,000,000

Instructions

Answer each of the following.

(a) Why is Martinez Building Products Company using a job order costing system?
(b) On what basis does Martinez allocate its manufacturing overhead? Compute the predetermined overhead rate for the current year.
(c) Compute the amount of the under- or overapplied overhead for 2002.
(d) Martinez had balances in the beginning and ending work in process and finished goods accounts as follows.

	1/1/02	12/31/02
Work in process	$ 5,000,000	$ 4,000,000
Finished goods	13,000,000	11,000,000

Determine the (1) cost of goods manufactured and (2) cost of goods sold for Martinez during 2002. Assume that any under- or overapplied overhead should be included in the cost of goods sold.

(e) During 2002, Job G408 was started and completed. Its cost sheet showed a total cost of $100,000, and the company prices its product at 50% above its cost. What is the price to the customer if the company follows this pricing strategy?

Solution

(a) The company is using a job order system because each job (or batch) must have its own distinguishing characteristics. For example, each type of garage door would be different, and therefore a different cost per garage door should be assigned.

(b) The company allocates its overhead on the basis of direct labor cost. The predetermined overhead rate is 120%, computed as follows.

$$\$24,000,000 \div \$20,000,000 = 120\%$$

(c)		
Actual manufacturing overhead	$22,000,000	
Applied overhead cost ($21,000,000 × 120%)	25,200,000	
Overapplied overhead	$ 3,200,000	

(d) (1)		
Work in process, 1/1/02		$ 5,000,000
Direct materials used	$30,000,000	
Direct labor	21,000,000	
Manufacturing overhead applied	25,200,000	
Total manufacturing costs		76,200,000
Total cost of work in process		81,200,000
Less: Work in process, 12/31/02		4,000,000
Cost of goods manufactured		$77,200,000
(2) Finished goods inventory, 1/1/02	$13,000,000	
Cost of goods manufactured (see above)	77,200,000	
Cost of goods available for sale	90,200,000	
Finished goods inventory, 12/31/02	11,000,000	
Cost of goods sold (unadjusted)	79,200,000	
Less: Overapplied overhead	3,200,000	
Cost of goods sold	$76,000,000	

(e)		
G408 cost	$ 100,000	
Markup percentage	× 50%	
Profit	$ 50,000	

Price to customer: $150,000 ($100,000 + $50,000)

SUMMARY OF STUDY OBJECTIVES

1 *Explain the characteristics and purposes of cost accounting.* Cost accounting involves the procedures for measuring, recording, and reporting product costs. From the data accumulated, the total cost and the unit cost of each product is determined. The two basic types of cost accounting systems are job order cost and process cost.

2 *Describe the flow of costs in a job order cost accounting system.* In job order cost accounting, manufacturing costs are first accumulated in three accounts: Raw Materials Inventory, Factory Labor, and Manufacturing Overhead. The accumulated costs are then assigned to Work in Process Inventory and eventually to Finished Goods Inventory and Cost of Goods Sold.

3 *Explain the nature and importance of a job cost sheet.* A job cost sheet is a form used to record the costs chargeable to a specific job and to determine the total and unit costs of the completed job. Job cost sheets constitute the subsidiary ledger for the Work in Process Inventory control account.

4 *Indicate how the predetermined overhead rate is determined and used.* The predetermined overhead rate is based on the relationship between estimated annual overhead costs and expected annual operating activity. This is expressed in terms of a common activity base, such as direct labor cost. The rate is used in assigning overhead costs to work in process and to specific jobs.

5 *Prepare entries for jobs completed and sold.* When jobs are completed, the cost is debited to Finished Goods Inventory and credited to Work in Process Inventory. When a job is sold the entries are: (a) Debit Cash or Accounts Receivable and credit Sales for the selling price. And (b) debit Cost of Goods Sold and credit Finished Goods Inventory for the cost of the goods.

6 *Distinguish between under- and overapplied manufacturing overhead.* Underapplied manufacturing overhead means that the overhead assigned to work in process is less than the overhead incurred. Overapplied overhead means that the overhead assigned to work in process is greater than the overhead incurred.

DECISION TOOLKIT—A SUMMARY

Decision Checkpoints	Info Needed for Decision	Tool to Use for Decision	How to Evaluate Results
What is the cost of a job?	Cost of material, labor, and overhead assigned to a specific job	Job cost sheet	Compare costs to those of previous periods and to those of competitors to ensure that costs are in line. Compare costs to expected selling price or service fees charged to determine overall profitability.
Has the company over- or underapplied overhead for the period?	Actual overhead costs and overhead applied	Manufacturing overhead account	If the account balance is a credit, overhead applied exceeded actual overhead costs. If the account balance is a debit, overhead applied was less than actual overhead costs.

GLOSSARY

Cost accounting An area of accounting that involves measuring, recording, and reporting product costs. (p. 46)

Cost accounting system Manufacturing cost accounts that are fully integrated into the general ledger of a company. (p. 46)

Job cost sheet A form used to record the costs chargeable to a job and to determine the total and unit costs of the completed job. (p. 51)

Job order cost system A cost accounting system in which costs are assigned to each job or batch. (p. 47)

Materials requisition slip A document authorizing the issuance of raw materials from the storeroom to production. (p. 52)

Overapplied overhead A situation in which overhead assigned to work in process is greater than the overhead incurred. (p. 64)

Predetermined overhead rate A rate based on the relationship between estimated annual overhead costs and expected annual operating activity, expressed in terms of a common activity base. (p. 57)

Process cost system A system of accounting used by companies that manufacture relatively homogeneous products through a series of continuous processes or operations. (p. 47)

Summary entry A journal entry that summarizes the totals from multiple transactions. (p. 51)

Time ticket A document that indicates the employee, the hours worked, the account and job to be charged, and the total labor cost. (p. 55)

Underapplied overhead A situation in which overhead assigned to work in process is less than the overhead incurred. (p. 64)

DEMONSTRATION PROBLEM

During February, Cardella Manufacturing works on two jobs: A16 and B17. Summary data concerning these jobs are as follows.

Manufacturing Costs Incurred

Purchased $54,000 of raw materials on account.
Factory labor $76,000, plus $4,000 employer payroll taxes.
Manufacturing overhead exclusive of indirect materials and indirect labor $59,800.

Assignment of Costs

Direct materials: Job A16 $27,000, Job B17 $21,000
Indirect materials: $3,000
Direct labor: Job A16 $52,000, Job B17 $26,000
Indirect labor: $2,000
Manufacturing overhead rate: 80% of direct labor costs.

Job A16 was completed and sold on account for $150,000. Job B17 was only partially completed.

Instructions

(a) Journalize the February transactions in the sequence followed in the chapter.
(b) What was the amount of under- or overapplied manufacturing overhead?

eGrade Demonstration Problem

Solution to Demonstration Problem

(a)

1.

Feb. 28	Raw Materials Inventory	54,000	
	Accounts Payable		54,000
	(Purchase of raw materials on account)		

2.

28	Factory Labor	80,000	
	Factory Wages Payable		76,000
	Employer Payroll Taxes Payable		4,000
	(To record factory labor costs)		

3.

28	Manufacturing Overhead	59,800	
	Accounts Payable, Accumulated		
	Depreciation, and Prepaid Insurance		59,800
	(To record overhead costs)		

4.

28	Work in Process Inventory	48,000	
	Manufacturing Overhead	3,000	
	Raw Materials Inventory		51,000
	(To assign raw materials to production)		

5.

28	Work in Process Inventory	78,000	
	Manufacturing Overhead	2,000	
	Factory Labor		80,000
	(To assign factory labor to production)		

6.

28	Work in Process Inventory	62,400	
	Manufacturing Overhead		62,400
	(To assign overhead to jobs—		
	80% × $78,000)		

Action Plan

- In accumulating costs, debit three accounts: Raw Materials Inventory, Factory Labor, and Manufacturing Overhead.
- When Work in Process Inventory is debited, credit one of the three accounts listed above.
- Debit Finished Goods Inventory for the cost of completed jobs. Debit Cost of Goods Sold for the cost of jobs sold.
- Overhead is underapplied when Manufacturing Overhead has a debit balance.

7.

Feb. 28	Finished Goods Inventory		120,600	
	Work in Process Inventory			120,600
	(To record completion of Job A16: direct materials $27,000, direct labor $52,000, and manufacturing overhead $41,600)			

8.

28	Accounts Receivable		150,000	
	Sales			150,000
	(To record sale of Job A16)			
28	Cost of Goods Sold		120,600	
	Finished Goods Inventory			120,600
	(To record cost of sale for Job A16)			

(b) Manufacturing Overhead has a debit balance of $2,400 as shown below.

Manufacturing Overhead

(3)	59,800	(6)	62,400
(4)	3,000		
(5)	2,000		
Bal.	2,400		

THE NAVIGATOR

Thus, manufacturing overhead is underapplied for the month.

SELF-STUDY QUESTIONS

Self-Study/Self-Test

Answers are at the end of the chapter.

(SO 1) 1. Cost accounting involves the measuring, recording, and reporting of:
   (a) product costs.
   (b) future costs.
   (c) manufacturing processes.
   (d) managerial accounting decisions.

(SO 2) 2. In accumulating raw materials costs, the cost of raw materials purchased in a perpetual system is debited to:
   (a) Raw Materials Purchases.
   (b) Raw Materials Inventory.
   (c) Purchases.
   (d) Work in Process.

(SO 2) 3. When incurred, factory labor costs are debited to:
   (a) Work in Process.
   (b) Factory Wages Expense.
   (c) Factory Labor.
   (d) Factory Wages Payable.

(SO 3) 4. The source documents for assigning costs to job cost sheets are:
   (a) invoices, time tickets, and the predetermined overhead rate.
   (b) materials requisition slips, time tickets, and the actual overhead costs.
   (c) materials requisition slips, payroll register, and the predetermined overhead rate.
   (d) materials requisition slips, time tickets, and the predetermined overhead rate.

(SO 3) 5. In recording the issuance of raw materials in a job order cost system, it would be *incorrect* to:
   (a) debit Work in Process Inventory.
   (b) debit Finished Goods Inventory.
   (c) debit Manufacturing Overhead.
   (d) credit Raw Materials Inventory.

(SO 3) 6. The entry when direct factory labor is assigned to jobs is a debit to:
   (a) Work in Process Inventory and a credit to Factory Labor.
   (b) Manufacturing Overhead and a credit to Factory Labor.
   (c) Factory Labor and a credit to Manufacturing Overhead.
   (d) Factory Labor and a credit to Work in Process Inventory.

(SO 4) 7. The formula for computing the predetermined manufacturing overhead rate is estimated annual overhead costs divided by an expected annual operating activity, expressed as:
   (a) direct labor cost.
   (b) direct labor hours.
   (c) machine hours.
   (d) any of the above.

(SO 4) 8. In Cleo Company, the predetermined overhead rate is 80% of direct labor cost. During the month, $210,000 of factory labor costs are incurred, of which $180,000 is direct labor and $30,000 is indirect labor. Actual overhead incurred was $200,000. The amount of overhead debited to Work in Process Inventory should be:
  (a) $120,000.
  (b) $144,000.
  (c) $168,000.
  (d) $160,000.

(SO 5) 9. In BAC Company, Job No. 26 is completed at a cost of $4,500 and later sold for $7,000 cash. A correct entry is:

(a) Debit Finished Goods Inventory $7,000 and credit Work in Process Inventory $7,000.
(b) Debit Cost of Goods Sold $7,000 and credit Finished Goods Inventory $7,000.
(c) Debit Finished Goods Inventory $4,500 and credit Work in Process Inventory $4,500.
(d) Debit Accounts Receivable $7,000 and credit Sales $7,000.

10. In preparing monthly financial statements, (SO 6) overapplied overhead is reported in the balance sheet as a(an):
  (a) prepaid expense.
  (b) unearned revenue.
  (c) noncurrent asset.
  (d) noncurrent liability.

QUESTIONS

1. Hal Adelman is studying for an accounting midterm examination. What should Hal know about how management may use job cost data?

2. (a) Marc Tucci is not sure about the differences between cost accounting and a cost accounting system. Explain the difference to Marc. (b) What is an important feature of a cost accounting system?

3. (a) Distinguish between the two types of cost accounting systems. (b) May a company use both types of cost accounting systems?

4. What type of industry is likely to use a job order cost system? Give some examples.

5. What type of industry is likely to use a process cost system? Give some examples.

6. Your roommate asks your help in understanding the major steps in the flow of costs in a job order cost system. Identify the steps for your roommate.

7. There are three inventory control accounts in a job order system. Identify the control accounts and their subsidiary ledgers.

8. What source documents are used in accumulating direct labor costs?

9. "Only normal daily entries are made to manufacturing overhead." Do you agree? Explain.

10. Phil Remmers is confused about the source documents used in assigning materials and labor costs. Identify the documents and give the entry for each document.

11. What is the purpose of a job cost sheet?

12. Indicate the source documents that are used in charging costs to specific jobs.

13. Differentiate between a "materials inventory record" and a "materials requisition slip" as used in a job order cost system.

14. John Simon believes actual manufacturing overhead should be charged to jobs. Do you agree? Why or why not?

15. What relationships are involved in computing a predetermined overhead rate?

16. How can the agreement of Work in Process Inventory and job cost sheets be verified?

17. Pam Smith believes that the cost of goods manufactured schedule in job order cost accounting (Illustration 2-20) is the same as the cost of goods manufactured schedule in general manufacturing accounting (see Illustration 1-7 in Chapter 1). Is Pam correct? Explain.

18. Greg Carnes is confused about under- and overapplied manufacturing overhead. Define the terms for Greg, and indicate the balance in the manufacturing overhead account applicable to each term.

19. "Under- or overapplied overhead is reported in the income statement when monthly financial statements are prepared." Do you agree? If not, indicate the proper presentation.

20. "At the end of the year, under- or overapplied overhead is closed to Income Summary." Is this correct? If not, indicate the customary treatment of this account.

BRIEF EXERCISES

BE2-1 Sinason Tool & Die begins operations on January 1. Because all work is done to customer specifications, the company decides to use a job cost accounting system. Prepare a flow chart of a typical job order system with arrows showing the flow of costs. Identify the eight transactions.

Prepare a flowchart of a job order cost accounting system, and identify transactions.
(SO 2)

Prepare entries in accumulating manufacturing costs.
(SO 2)

BE2-2   During the first month of operations, Sinason Tool & Die accumulated the following manufacturing costs: raw materials $3,000 on account, factory labor $4,000 of which $3,600 relates to factory wages payable and $400 relates to payroll taxes payable, and utilities payable $2,000. Prepare separate journal entries for each type of manufacturing cost.

Prepare entry for the assignment of raw materials costs.
(SO 2)

BE2-3   In January, Sinason Tool & Die requisitions raw materials for production as follows: Job 1 $900, Job 2 $1,200, Job 3 $200, and general factory use $600. Prepare a summary journal entry to record raw materials used.

Prepare entry for the assignment of factory labor costs.
(SO 2)

BE2-4   Factory labor data for Sinason Tool & Die is given in BE2-2. During January, time tickets show that the factory labor of $4,000 was used as follows: Job 1 $1,200, Job 2 $1,600, Job 3 $700, and general factory use $500. Prepare a summary journal entry to record factory labor used.

Prepare job cost sheets.
(SO 3)

BE2-5   Data pertaining to job cost sheets for Sinason Tool & Die are given in BE2-3 and BE2-4. Prepare the job cost sheets for each of the three jobs. (*Note:* You may omit the column for Manufacturing Overhead.)

Compute predetermined overhead rates.
(SO 4)

BE2-6   Carlos Company estimates that annual manufacturing overhead costs will be $400,000. Estimated annual operating activity bases are: direct labor cost $500,000, direct labor hours 50,000, and machine hours 100,000. Compute the predetermined overhead rate for each activity base.

Assign manufacturing overhead to production.
(SO 4)

BE2-7   During the first quarter, Carlos Company incurs the following direct labor costs: January $40,000, February $30,000, and March $50,000. For each month, prepare the entry to assign overhead to production using a predetermined rate of 80% of direct labor cost.

Prepare entries for completion and sale of completed jobs.
(SO 5)

BE2-8   In March, Santana Company completes Jobs 10 and 11. Job 10 cost $20,000 and Job 11 $32,000. On March 31, Job 10 is sold to the customer for $35,000 in cash. Journalize the entries for the completion of the two jobs and the sale of Job 10.

Indicate statement classification of under- or overapplied overhead.
(SO 6)

BE2-9   On September 30, balances in Manufacturing Overhead are: Wendy Company—debit $1,800, Mahmoud Company—credit $3,000. Indicate how each company should report its balance at September 30, assuming each company prepares annual financial statements on December 31.

Prepare adjusting entries for under- and overapplied overhead.
(SO 6)

BE2-10   At December 31, balances in Manufacturing Overhead are: Sanchez Company—debit $1,000, Gomez Company—credit $900. Prepare the adjusting entry for each company at December 31, assuming the adjustment is made to cost of goods sold.

EXERCISES

Prepare entries for factory labor.
(SO 2)

E2-1   The gross earnings of the factory workers for Cerrato Company during the month of January are $90,000. The employer's payroll taxes for the factory payroll are $9,000. The fringe benefits to be paid by the employer on this payroll are $4,000. Of the total accumulated cost of factory labor, 85% is related to direct labor and 15% is attributable to indirect labor.

Instructions
(a) Prepare the entry to record the factory labor costs for the month of January.
(b) Prepare the entry to assign factory labor to production.

Prepare journal entries for manufacturing costs.
(SO 2, 3, 4, 5)

E2-2   Alvarez Manufacturing uses a job order cost accounting system. On May 1, the company has a balance in Work in Process Inventory of $3,200 and two jobs in process: Job No. 429 $2,000, and Job No. 430 $1,200. During May, a summary of source documents reveals the following.

Job Number	Materials Requisition Slips	Labor Time Tickets
429	$2,500	$ 2,400
430	2,000	3,000
431	4,400	7,600
General use	800	1,200
	$9,700	$14,200

Alvarez Manufacturing applies manufacturing overhead to jobs at an overhead rate of 80% of direct labor cost. Job No. 429 is completed during the month.

Instructions
(a) Prepare summary journal entries to record the requisition slips, time tickets, the assignment of manufacturing overhead to jobs, and the completion of Job No. 429.
(b) Post the entries to Work in Process Inventory, and prove the agreement of the control account with the job cost sheets.

E2-3 A job order cost sheet for Stan Free Company is shown below.

Analyze a job cost sheet and prepare entries for manufacturing costs.
(SO 2, 3, 4, 5)

Job No. 92			For 2,000 Units
Date	Direct Materials	Direct Labor	Manufacturing Overhead
Beg. bal. Jan. 1	5,000	6,000	3,900
8	6,000		
12		8,000	6,000
25	2,000		
27		4,000	3,000
	13,000	18,000	12,900

Cost of completed job:
Direct materials	$13,000
Direct labor	18,000
Manufacturing overhead	12,900
Total cost	$43,900
Unit cost ($43,900 ÷ 2,000)	$21.95

Instructions
(a) On the basis of the foregoing data answer the following questions.
  (1) What was the balance in Work in Process Inventory on January 1 if this was the only unfinished job?
  (2) If manufacturing overhead is applied on the basis of direct labor cost, what overhead rate was used in each year?
(b) Prepare summary entries at January 31 to record the current year's transactions pertaining to Job No. 92.

E2-4 Manufacturing cost data for Lopez Company, which uses a job order cost system, are presented below.

Analyze costs of manufacturing and determine missing amounts.
(SO 2, 5)

	Case A	Case B	Case C
Direct materials	$ (a)	$83,000	$ 63,150
Direct labor used	50,000	90,000	(h)
Manufacturing overhead applied	42,500	(d)	(i)
Total manufacturing costs	185,650	(e)	287,000
Work in process 1/1/02	(b)	15,500	18,000
Total cost of work in process	201,500	(f)	(j)
Work in process 12/31/02	(c)	11,800	(k)
Cost of goods manufactured	192,300	(g)	262,000

Instructions
Indicate the missing amount for each letter. Assume that in all cases manufacturing overhead is applied on the basis of direct labor cost and the rate is the same.

Compute the manufacturing overhead rate and under- or overapplied overhead.
(SO 4, 6)

E2-5   Ramirez Company applies manufacturing overhead to jobs on the basis of machine hours used. Overhead costs are expected to total $275,000 for the year, and machine usage is estimated at 125,000 hours.

In January, $26,000 of overhead costs are incurred and 12,000 machine hours are used. For the remainder of the year, $274,000 of overhead costs are incurred and 118,000 machine hours are worked.

Instructions
(a) Compute the manufacturing overhead rate for the year.
(b) What is the amount of under- or overapplied overhead at January 31? How should this amount be reported in the financial statements prepared on January 31?
(c) What is the amount of under- or overapplied overhead at December 31?
(d) Assuming the under- or overapplied overhead for the year is not allocated to inventory accounts, prepare the adjusting entry to assign the amount to cost of goods sold.

Analyze job cost sheet and prepare entry for completed job.
(SO 2, 3, 4, 5)

E2-6   A job cost sheet of Serrano Company is given below.

Job Cost Sheet

JOB NO.   469   Quantity   2,000
ITEM   White Lion Cages   Date Requested   7/2
FOR   Tesla Company   Date Completed   7/31

Date	Direct Materials	Direct Labor	Manufacturing Overhead
7/10	825		
12	900		
15		440	572
22		380	494
24	1,600		
27	1,500		
31		540	702

Cost of completed job:
   Direct materials   _____
   Direct labor   _____
   Manufacturing overhead   _____
Total cost   _____
Unit cost   _____

Instructions
(a) Answer the following questions.
   (1) What are the source documents for direct materials, direct labor, and manufacturing overhead costs assigned to this job?
   (2) What is the predetermined manufacturing overhead rate?
   (3) What are the total cost and the unit cost of the completed job?
(b) Prepare the entry to record the completion of the job.

Prepare entries for manufacturing costs.
(SO 2, 4, 5)

E2-7   Tejada Corporation incurred the following transactions.

1. Purchased raw materials on account $46,300.
2. Raw materials of $36,000 were requisitioned to the factory. An analysis of the materials requisition slips indicated that $8,800 was classified as indirect materials.
3. Factory labor costs incurred were $64,900, of which $59,000 pertained to factory wages payable and $5,900 pertained to employer payroll taxes payable.

4. Time tickets indicated that $60,000 was direct labor and $4,900 was indirect labor.
5. Overhead costs incurred on account were $80,500.
6. Manufacturing overhead was applied at the rate of 150% of direct labor cost.
7. Goods costing $88,000 were completed and transferred to finished goods.
8. Finished goods costing $68,000 to manufacture were sold on account for $103,000.

Instructions
Journalize the transactions. (Omit explanations.)

E2-8 Barajas Printing Corp. uses a job order cost system. The following data summarize the operations related to the first quarter's production.

Prepare entries for manufacturing costs.
(SO 2, 3, 4, 5)

1. Materials purchased on account $172,000, and factory wages incurred $87,300.
2. Materials requisitioned and factory labor used by job:

Job Number	Materials	Factory Labor
A20	$ 32,240	$18,000
A21	42,920	26,000
A22	36,100	15,000
A23	39,270	25,000
General factory use	4,470	3,300
	$155,000	$87,300

3. Manufacturing overhead costs incurred on account $39,500.
4. Depreciation on machinery and equipment $14,550.
5. Manufacturing overhead rate is 75% of direct labor cost.
6. Jobs completed during the quarter: A20, A21, and A23.

Instructions
Prepare entries to record the operations summarized above. (Prepare a schedule showing the individual cost elements and total cost for each job in item 6.)

E2-9 At May 31, 2002, the accounts of Corrales Manufacturing Company show the following.

Prepare a cost of goods manufactured schedule and partial financial statements.
(SO 2, 5)

1. May 1 inventories—finished goods $12,600, work in process $14,700, and raw materials $8,200.
2. May 31 inventories—finished goods $10,500, work in process $17,900, and raw materials $7,100.
3. Debit postings to work in process were: direct materials $62,400, direct labor $32,000, and manufacturing overhead applied $64,000.
4. Sales totaled $200,000.

Instructions
(a) Prepare a condensed cost of goods manufactured schedule.
(b) Prepare an income statement for May through gross profit.
(c) Indicate the balance sheet presentation of the manufacturing inventories at May 31, 2002.

E2-10 Mendoza Company begins operations on April 1. Information from job cost sheets shows the following.

Compute work in process and finished goods from job cost sheets.
(SO 3, 5)

Job Number	**Manufacturing Costs Assigned**		
	April	May	June
10	$5,200	$4,400	
11	4,100	3,900	$3,000
12	1,200		
13		4,700	4,500
14		3,900	3,600

Job 12 was completed in April. Job 10 was completed in May. Jobs 11 and 13 were completed in June. Each job was sold for 60% above its cost in the month following completion.

Instructions
(a) What is the balance in Work in Process Inventory at the end of each month?
(b) What is the balance in Finished Goods Inventory at the end of each month?
(c) What is the gross profit for May, June, and July?

PROBLEMS: SET A

Prepare entries in a job cost system and job cost sheets.
(SO 2, 3, 4, 5, 6)

P2-1A Don Tidrick Manufacturing uses a job order cost system and applies overhead to production on the basis of direct labor costs. On January 1, 2002, Job No. 50 was the only job in process. The costs incurred prior to January 1 on this job were as follows: direct materials $20,000, direct labor $12,000, and manufacturing overhead $21,000. As of January 1, Job No. 49 had been completed at a cost of $90,000 and was part of finished goods inventory. There was a $15,000 balance in the Raw Materials inventory account.

During the month of January, Don Tidrick Manufacturing began production on Jobs 51 and 52, and completed Jobs 50 and 51. Jobs 49 and 50 were sold on account during the month for $122,000 and $158,000, respectively. The following additional events occurred during the month.

1. Purchased additional raw materials of $90,000 on account.
2. Incurred factory labor costs of $63,000. Of this amount $13,000 related to employer payroll taxes.
3. Incurred manufacturing overhead costs as follows: indirect materials $14,000; indirect labor $15,000; depreciation expense $19,000, and various other manufacturing overhead costs on account $23,000.
4. Assigned direct materials and direct labor to jobs as follows.

Job No.	Direct Materials	Direct Labor
50	$10,000	$ 6,000
51	39,000	24,000
52	30,000	18,000

Instructions
(a) Calculate the predetermined overhead rate for 2002, assuming Don Tidrick Manufacturing estimates total manufacturing overhead costs of $1,050,000, direct labor costs of $700,000, and direct labor hours of 20,000 for the year.
(b) Open job cost sheets for Jobs 50, 51, and 52. Enter the January 1 balances on the job cost sheet for Job No. 50.
(c) Prepare the journal entries to record the purchase of raw materials, the factory labor costs incurred, and the manufacturing overhead costs incurred during the month of January.
(d) Prepare the journal entries to record the assignment of direct materials, direct labor, and manufacturing overhead costs to production. In assigning manufacturing overhead costs, use the overhead rate calculated in (a). Post all costs to the job cost sheets as necessary.
(e) Total the job cost sheets for any job(s) completed during the month. Prepare the journal entry (or entries) to record the completion of any job(s) during the month.
(f) Prepare the journal entry (or entries) to record the sale of any job(s) during the month.
(g) What is the balance in the Finished Goods Inventory account at the end of the month? What does this balance consist of?
(h) What is the amount of over- or underapplied overhead for the month? How would this be reported on the financial statements for the month of January?

Prepare entries in a job cost system and partial income statement.
(SO 2, 3, 4, 5, 6)

P2-2A For the year ended December 31, 2002, the job cost sheets of Chicago Company contained the following data.

Job Number	Explanation	Direct Materials	Direct Labor	Manufacturing Overhead	Total Costs
7640	Balance 1/1	$25,000	$24,000	$28,800	$ 77,800
	Current year's costs	34,000	36,000	43,200	113,200
7641	Balance 1/1	11,000	18,000	21,600	50,600
	Current year's costs	40,000	48,000	57,600	145,600
7642	Current year's costs	48,000	55,000	66,000	169,000

Other data:

1. Raw materials inventory totaled $15,000 on January 1. During the year, $140,000 of raw materials were purchased on account.
2. Finished goods on January 1 consisted of Job No. 7638 for $87,000 and Job No. 7639 for $92,000.
3. Job No. 7640 and Job No. 7641 were completed during the year.
4. Jobs No. 7638, 7639, and 7641 were sold on account for $530,000.
5. Manufacturing overhead incurred on account totaled $115,000.
6. Other manufacturing overhead consisted of indirect materials $14,000, indirect labor $20,000, and depreciation on factory machinery $8,000.

Instructions
(a) Prove the agreement of Work in Process Inventory with job cost sheets pertaining to unfinished work. *Hint:* Use a single T account for Work in Process Inventory. Calculate each of the following, then post each to the T account: (1) beginning balance, (2) direct materials, (3) direct labor, (4) manufacturing overhead, and (5) completed jobs.
(b) Prepare the adjusting entry for manufacturing overhead, assuming the balance is allocated entirely to Cost of Goods Sold.
(c) Determine the gross profit to be reported for 2002.

P2-3A Peoria Inc. is a construction company specializing in custom patios. The patios are constructed of concrete, brick, fiberglass, and lumber, depending upon customer preference. On June 1, 2002, the general ledger for Peoria Inc. contains the following data.

Prepare entries in a job cost system and cost of goods manufactured schedule.
(SO 2, 3, 4, 5)

Raw Materials Inventory	$4,200	Manufacturing Overhead Applied	$32,640
Work in Process Inventory	$5,900	Manufacturing Overhead Incurred	$31,650

Subsidiary data for Work in Process Inventory on June 1 are as follows.

Job Cost Sheets

	Customer Job		
Cost Element	Rockford	Aurora	Moline
Direct materials	$ 600	$ 800	$ 900
Direct labor	320	540	580
Manufacturing overhead	480	810	870
	$1,400	$2,150	$2,350

A summary of materials requisition slips and time tickets for June shows the following.

Customer Job	Materials Requisition Slips	Time Tickets
Rockford	$ 800	$ 450
Elgin	2,000	800
Aurora	500	360
Moline	1,300	800
Rockford	300	250
	4,900	2,660
General use	1,500	1,200
	$6,400	$3,860

During June, raw materials purchased on account were $3,900, and all wages were paid. Additional overhead costs consisted of depreciation on equipment $700 and miscellaneous costs of $400 incurred on account. Overhead was charged to jobs at the same rate that was used in May. The patios for customers Rockford, Aurora, and Moline were completed during June and sold for a total of $18,900. Each customer paid in full.

Instructions
(a) Journalize the June transactions.
(b) Post the entries to Work in Process Inventory.
(c) Reconcile the balance in Work in Process Inventory with the costs of unfinished jobs.
(d) Prepare a cost of goods manufactured schedule for June.

Compute predetermined overhead rate, apply overhead, and indicate statement presentation of under- or overapplied overhead.
(SO 4, 6)

eGrade
Problem

P2-4A Urbana Manufacturing Company uses a job order cost system in each of its three manufacturing departments. Manufacturing overhead is applied to jobs on the basis of direct labor cost in Department D, direct labor hours in Department E, and machine hours in Department K.

In establishing the predetermined overhead rates for 2003 the following estimates were made for the year.

	Department		
	D	**E**	**K**
Manufacturing overhead	$1,170,000	$1,500,000	$960,000
Direct labor costs	$1,500,000	$1,250,000	$450,000
Direct labor hours	100,000	120,000	40,000
Machine hours	400,000	500,000	120,000

During January, the job cost sheets showed the following costs and production data.

	Department		
	D	**E**	**K**
Direct materials used	$140,000	$126,000	$78,000
Direct labor costs	$120,000	$110,000	$37,500
Manufacturing overhead incurred	$98,000	$129,000	$80,000
Direct labor hours	8,000	11,000	3,500
Machine hours	34,000	45,000	10,400

Instructions
(a) Compute the predetermined overhead rate for each department.
(b) Compute the total manufacturing costs assigned to jobs in January in each department.
(c) Compute the under- or overapplied overhead for each department at January 31.
(d) Indicate the statement presentation of the under- or overapplied overhead at January 31.
(e) If the amount in (d) was the same at December 31, how would it be reported in the year-end financial statements?

Analyze manufacturing accounts and determine missing amounts.
(SO 2, 3, 4, 5, 6)

P2-5A Florida Boot Corporation's fiscal year ends on November 30. The following accounts are found in its job order cost accounting system for the first month of the new fiscal year.

Raw Materials Inventory

Dec. 1	Beginning balance	(a)	Dec. 31	Requisitions	14,850
31	Purchases	19,225			
Dec. 31	Ending balance	7,975			

Work in Process Inventory

Dec. 1	Beginning balance	(b)	Dec. 31	Jobs completed	(f)
31	Direct materials	(c)			
31	Direct labor	8,100			
31	Overhead	(d)			
Dec. 31	Ending balance	(e)			

Finished Goods Inventory

Dec.	1	Beginning balance	(g)	Dec. 31	Cost of goods sold	(i)
	31	Completed jobs	(h)			
Dec. 31		Ending balance	(j)			

Factory Labor

| Dec. 31 | Factory wages | 10,800 | Dec. 31 | Wages assigned | (k) |

Manufacturing Overhead

Dec. 31	Indirect materials	1,900	Dec. 31	Overhead applied	(m)
31	Indirect labor	(l)			
31	Other overhead	1,245			

Other data:

1. On December 1, two jobs were in process: Job No. 154 and Job No. 155. These jobs had combined direct materials costs of $9,750 and direct labor costs of $12,000. Overhead was applied at a rate that was 75% of direct labor cost.
2. During December, Job Nos. 156, 157, and 158 were started. On December 31, Job No. 158 was unfinished. This job had charges for direct materials $3,800 and direct labor $4,400, plus manufacturing overhead. All jobs, except for Job No. 158, were completed in December.
3. On December 1, Job No. 153 was in the finished goods warehouse. It had a total cost of $5,000. On December 31, Job No. 157 was the only job finished that was not sold. It had a cost of $4,000.
4. Manufacturing overhead was $230 overapplied in December.

Instructions
List the letters (a) through (m) and indicate the amount pertaining to each letter.

PROBLEMS: SET B

P2-1B Han Wu Manufacturing uses a job order cost system and applies overhead to production on the basis of direct labor hours. On January 1, 2002, Job No. 25 was the only job in process. The costs incurred prior to January 1 on this job were as follows: direct materials $10,000; direct labor $6,000; and manufacturing overhead $10,500. Job No. 23 had been completed at a cost of $45,000 and was part of finished goods inventory. There was a $5,000 balance in the Raw Materials inventory account.

Prepare entries in a job cost system and job costs sheets.
(SO 2, 3, 4, 5, 6)

During the month of January, the company began production on Jobs 26 and 27, and completed Jobs 25 and 26. Jobs 23 and 25 were sold on account during the month for $67,000 and $74,000, respectively. The following additional events occurred during the month.

1. Purchased additional raw materials of $45,000 on account.
2. Incurred factory labor costs of $31,500. Of this amount $6,500 related to employer payroll taxes.
3. Incurred manufacturing overhead costs as follows: indirect materials $10,000; indirect labor $7,500; depreciation expense $12,000; and various other manufacturing overhead costs on account $15,000.
4. Assigned direct materials and direct labor to jobs as follows.

Job No.	Direct Materials	Direct Labor
25	$ 5,000	$ 3,000
26	20,000	12,000
27	15,000	9,000

5. The company uses direct labor hours as the activity base to assign overhead. Direct labor hours incurred on each job were as follows: Job No. 25, 200; Job No. 26, 800; and Job No. 27, 600.

Instructions

(a) Calculate the predetermined overhead rate for the year 2002, assuming Han Wu Manufacturing estimates total manufacturing overhead costs of $500,000, direct labor costs of $300,000, and direct labor hours of 20,000 for the year.

(b) Open job cost sheets for Jobs 25, 26, and 27. Enter the January 1 balances on the job cost sheet for Job No. 25.

(c) Prepare the journal entries to record the purchase of raw materials, the factory labor costs incurred, and the manufacturing overhead costs incurred during the month of January.

(d) Prepare the journal entries to record the assignment of direct materials, direct labor, and manufacturing overhead costs to production. In assigning manufacturing overhead costs, use the overhead rate calculated in (a). Post all costs to the job cost sheets as necessary.

(e) Total the job cost sheets for any job(s) completed during the month. Prepare the journal entry (or entries) to record the completion of any job(s) during the month.

(f) Prepare the journal entry (or entries) to record the sale of any job(s) during the month.

(g) What is the balance in the Work in Process Inventory account at the end of the month? What does this balance consist of?

(h) What is the amount of over- or underapplied overhead for the month? How would this be reported on the financial statements for the month of January?

Prepare entries in a job cost system and partial income statement.
(SO 2, 3, 4, 5, 6)

P2-2B For the year ended December 31, 2002, the job cost sheets of Ying Chen Company contained the following data.

Job Number	Explanation	Direct Materials	Direct Labor	Manufacturing Overhead	Total Costs
7650	Balance 1/1	$18,000	$20,000	$25,000	$ 63,000
	Current year's costs	22,000	30,000	37,500	89,500
7651	Balance 1/1	12,000	18,000	22,500	52,500
	Current year's costs	28,000	40,000	50,000	118,000
7652	Current year's costs	40,000	60,000	75,000	175,000

Other data:

1. Raw materials inventory totaled $20,000 on January 1. During the year, $100,000 of raw materials were purchased on account.

2. Finished goods on January 1 consisted of Job No. 7648 for $98,000 and Job No. 7649 for $62,000.

3. Job No. 7650 and Job No. 7651 were completed during the year.

4. Jobs No. 7648, 7649, and 7650 were sold on account for $390,000.

5. Manufacturing overhead incurred on account totaled $120,000.

6. Other manufacturing overhead consisted of indirect materials $12,000, indirect labor $18,000, and depreciation on factory machinery $19,500.

Instructions

(a) Prove the agreement of Work in Process Inventory with job cost sheets pertaining to unfinished work. *Hint:* Use a single T account for Work in Process Inventory. Calculate each of the following, then post each to the T account: (1) beginning balance, (2) direct materials, (3) direct labor, (4) manufacturing overhead, and (5) completed jobs.

(b) Prepare the adjusting entry for manufacturing overhead, assuming the balance is allocated entirely to cost of goods sold.

(c) Determine the gross profit to be reported for 2002.

P2-3B Richard E. Baker is a contractor specializing in custom-built jacuzzis. On May 1, 2002, his ledger contains the following data.

Prepare entries in a job cost system and cost of goods manufactured schedule.
(SO 2, 3, 4, 5)

Raw Materials Inventory	$30,000
Work in Process Inventory	12,400
Manufacturing Overhead	2,500 (dr.)

The Manufacturing Overhead account has debit totals of $12,500 and credit totals of $10,000. Subsidiary data for Work in Process Inventory on May 1 include:

Job Cost Sheets

Job by Customer	Direct Materials	Direct Labor	Manufacturing Overhead
Engstrom	$2,500	$2,000	$1,500
Hendricks	2,000	1,200	900
Keys	900	800	600
	$5,400	$4,000	$3,000

A summary of materials requisition slips and time tickets for the month of May reveals the following.

Job by Customer	Materials Requisition Slips	Time Tickets
Engstrom	$ 500	$ 400
Hendricks	600	1,000
Keys	2,300	1,300
Bennett	2,400	3,300
	5,800	6,000
General use	1,500	2,600
	$7,300	$8,600

During May, the following costs were incurred: (a) raw materials purchased on account $5,000, (b) labor paid $8,600, (c) manufacturing overhead paid $1,400. Overhead was charged to jobs on the basis of direct labor cost at the same rate as in the previous month.

The jacuzzis for customers Engstrom, Hendricks, and Keys were completed during May. Each jacuzzi was sold for $12,500 cash.

Instructions
(a) Prepare journal entries for the May transactions.
(b) Post the entries to Work in Process Inventory.
(c) Reconcile the balance in Work in Process Inventory with the costs of unfinished jobs.
(d) Prepare a cost of goods manufactured schedule for May.

P2-4B Hopkins Manufacturing uses a job order cost system in each of its three manufacturing departments. Manufacturing overhead is applied to jobs on the basis of direct labor cost in Department A, direct labor hours in Department B, and machine hours in Department C.

In establishing the predetermined overhead rates for 2002 the following estimates were made for the year.

Compute predetermined overhead rates, apply overhead, and indicate statement presentation of under- or overapplied overhead.
(SO 4, 6)

	Department		
	A	**B**	**C**
Manufacturing overhead	$900,000	$760,000	$780,000
Direct labor cost	$600,000	$400,000	$600,000
Direct labor hours	50,000	50,000	40,000
Machine hours	100,000	120,000	150,000

During January, the job cost sheets showed the following costs and production data.

	Department		
	A	**B**	**C**
Direct materials used	$92,000	$86,000	$64,000
Direct labor cost	$48,000	$35,000	$50,400
Manufacturing overhead incurred	$76,000	$54,000	$64,500
Direct labor hours	4,000	3,500	4,200
Machine hours	8,000	10,500	12,600

Instructions

(a) Compute the predetermined overhead rate for each department.
(b) Compute the total manufacturing costs assigned to jobs in January in each department.
(c) Compute the under- or overapplied overhead for each department at January 31.
(d) Indicate the statement presentation of the under- or overapplied overhead at January 31.
(e) If the amount in (d) was the same at December 31, how would it be reported in the year-end financial statements?

Analyze manufacturing cost accounts and determine missing amounts.
(SO 2, 3, 4, 5, 6)

P2-5B Devona Company's fiscal year ends on June 30. The following accounts are found in its job order cost accounting system for the first month of the new fiscal year.

Raw Materials Inventory

July	1	Beginning balance	19,000	July 31	Requisitions	(a)
	31	Purchases	90,400			
July	31	Ending balance	(b)			

Work in Process Inventory

July	1	Beginning balance	(c)	July 31	Jobs completed	(f)
	31	Direct materials	75,000			
	31	Direct labor	(d)			
	31	Overhead	(e)			
July	31	Ending balance	(g)			

Finished Goods Inventory

July	1	Beginning balance	(h)	July 31	Cost of goods sold	(j)
	31	Completed jobs	(i)			
July	31	Ending balance	(k)			

Factory Labor

July 31	Factory wages	(l)	July 31	Wages assigned	(m)

Manufacturing Overhead

July	31	Indirect materials	8,900	July 31	Overhead applied	91,000
	31	Indirect labor	16,000			
	31	Other overhead	(n)			

Other data:

1. On July 1, two jobs were in process: Job No. 4085 and Job No. 4086, with costs of $17,000 and $8,200, respectively.

2. During July, Job Nos. 4087, 4088, and 4089 were started. On July 31, only Job No. 4089 was unfinished. This job had charges for direct materials $2,000 and direct labor $1,500, plus manufacturing overhead.

3. On July 1, Job No. 4084, costing $135,000, was in the finished goods warehouse. On July 31, Job No. 4088, costing $143,000, was in finished goods.

4. Manufacturing overhead was applied at the rate of 130% of direct labor cost. Overhead was $3,000 underapplied in July.

Instructions

List the letters (a) through (n) and indicate the amount pertaining to each letter. Show computations.

BROADENING YOUR PERSPECTIVE

GROUP DECISION CASE

BYP2-1　Du Page Products Company uses a job order cost system. For a number of months there has been an ongoing rift between the sales department and the production department concerning a special-order product, TC-1. TC-1 is a seasonal product that is manufactured in batches of 1,000 units. TC-1 is sold at cost plus a markup of 40% of cost.

The sales department is unhappy because fluctuating unit production costs significantly affect selling prices. Sales personnel complain that this has caused excessive customer complaints and the loss of considerable orders for TC-1.

The production department maintains that each job order must be fully costed on the basis of the costs incurred during the period in which the goods are produced. Production personnel maintain that the only real solution to the problem is for the sales department to increase sales in the slack periods.

Sandra Devona, president of the company, asks you as the company accountant to collect quarterly data for the past year on TC-1. From the cost accounting system, you accumulate the following production quantity and cost data.

Costs	Quarter			
	1	2	3	4
Direct materials	$100,000	$220,000	$ 80,000	$200,000
Direct labor	60,000	132,000	48,000	120,000
Manufacturing overhead	105,000	123,000	97,000	125,000
Total	$265,000	$475,000	$225,000	$445,000
Production in batches	5	11	4	10
Unit cost (per batch)	$ 53,000	$ 43,182	$ 56,250	$ 44,500

Instructions

With the class divided into groups, answer the following questions.

(a) What manufacturing cost element is responsible for the fluctuating unit costs? Why?

(b) What is your recommended solution to the problem of fluctuating unit costs?

(c) Restate the quarterly data on the basis of your recommended solution.

MANAGERIAL ANALYSIS

BYP2-2 In the course of routine checking of all journal entries prior to preparing month-end reports, Sally Weber discovered several strange entries. She recalled that the president's son Jeff had come in to help out during an especially busy time and that he had recorded some journal entries. She was relieved that there were only a few of his entries, and even more relieved that he had included rather lengthy explanations. The entries Jeff made were:

1.

Work in Process Inventory	20,000	
Cash		20,000

(This is for materials put into process. I don't find the record that we paid for these, so I'm crediting Cash, because I know we'll have to pay for them sooner or later.)

2.

Manufacturing Overhead	12,000	
Cash		12,000

(This is for bonuses paid to salespeople. I know they're part of overhead, and I can't find an account called "Non-factory Overhead" or "Other Overhead" so I'm putting it in Manufacturing Overhead. I have the check stubs, so I know we paid these.)

3.

Wages Expense	120,000	
Cash		120,000

(This is for the factory workers' wages. I have a note that payroll taxes are $8,000. I still think that's part of wages expense, and that we'll have to pay it all in cash sooner or later, so I credited Cash for the wages and the taxes.)

4.

Work in Process Inventory	3,000	
Raw Materials Inventory		3,000

(This is for the glue used in the factory. I know we used this to make the products, even though we didn't use very much on any one of the products. I got it out of inventory, so I credited an inventory account.)

Instructions
(a) How should Jeff have recorded each of the four events?
(b) If the entry was not corrected, which financial statements (income statement or balance sheet) would be affected? What balances would be overstated or understated?

REAL-WORLD FOCUS

BYP2-3 Founded in 1970, **Parlex Corporation** is a world leader in the design and manufacture of flexible interconnect products. Utilizing proprietary and patented technologies, Parlex produces custom flexible interconnects including flexible circuits, polymer thick film, laminated cables, and value-added assemblies for sophisticated electronics used in automotive, telecommunications, computer, diversified electronics, and aerospace applications. In addition to manufacturing sites in Methuen, Massachusetts; Salem, New Hampshire; Cranston, Rhode Island; San Jose, California; Shanghai, China; Isle of Wight, UK; and Empalme, Mexico, Parlex has logistic support centers and strategic alliances throughout North America, Asia, and Europe.

The following information was provided in the company's annual report.

> ### PARLEX COMPANY
> ### Notes to the Financial Statements
>
> The Company's products are manufactured on a job order basis to customers' specifications. Customers submit requests for quotations on each job, and the Company prepares bids based on its own cost estimates. The Company attempts to reflect the impact of changing costs when establishing prices. However, during the past several years, the market conditions for flexible circuits and the resulting price sensitivity haven't always allowed this to transpire. Although still not satisfactory, the Company was able to reduce the cost of products sold as a percentage of sales to 85% this year versus 87% that was experienced in the two immediately preceding years. Management continues to focus on improving operational efficiency and further reducing costs.

Instructions
(a) Parlex management discusses the job order cost system employed by their company. What are several advantages of using the job order approach to costing?
(b) Contrast the products produced in a job order environment, like Parlex, to those produced when process cost systems are used.

EXPLORING THE WEB

BYP2-4   The Institute of Management Accountants sponsors a certification for management accountants, allowing them to obtain the title of Certified Management Accountant.

Address: **www.imanet.org** (*or go to www.wiley.com/college/weygandt*)

Steps:

1. Go to the site shown above.
2. Choose **Certification**.

Instructions
(a) What are the objectives of the certification program?
(b) What is the "experience requirement"?
(c) How many hours of continuing education are required, and what types of courses qualify?

COMMUNICATION ACTIVITY

BYP2-5   You are the management accountant for Modine Manufacturing. Your company does custom carpentry work and uses a job order cost accounting system. Modine sends detailed job cost sheets to its customers, along with an invoice. The job cost sheets show the date materials were used, the dollar cost of materials, and the hours and cost of labor. A predetermined overhead application rate is used, and the total overhead applied is also listed.

Cindy Ross is a customer who recently had custom cabinets installed. Along with her check in payment for the work done, she included a letter. She thanked the company for including the detailed cost information but questioned why overhead was estimated. She stated that she would be interested in knowing exactly what costs were included in overhead, and she thought that other customers would, too.

Instructions
Prepare a letter to Ms. Ross (address: 123 Cedar Lane, Altoona, Kansas 66651) and tell her why you did not send her information on exact costs of overhead included in her job. Respond to her suggestion that you provide this information.

RESEARCH ASSIGNMENT

BYP2-6 The February 1994 issue of *Ohio CPA Journal* includes an article by Eun-Sup Shim and Joseph M. Larkin entitled "A Survey of Current Managerial Accounting Practices: Where Do We Stand?"

Instructions
Read the article and answer the following questions.
(a) What percent of manufacturers surveyed used job order costing?
(b) What was the smallest cost component of the three factors of production? What portion of total manufacturing costs does it represent?
(c) What percent of manufacturers surveyed operate in a single product environment—that is, what percent produce only one product?
(d) What two managerial decisions were considered most affected by overhead allocation?

ETHICS CASE

BYP2-7 NIU Printing provides printing services to many different corporate clients. Although NIU bids most jobs, some jobs, particularly new ones, are often negotiated on a "cost-plus" basis. Cost-plus means that the buyer is willing to pay the actual cost plus a return (profit) on these costs to NIU.

Cathrine Traynor, controller for NIU, has recently returned from a meeting where NIU's president stated that he wanted her to find a way to charge most costs to any project that was on a cost-plus basis. The president noted that the company needed more profits to meet its stated goals this period. By charging more costs to the cost-plus projects and therefore less cost to the jobs that were bid, the company should be able to increase its profits for the current year.

Cathrine knew why the president wanted to take this action. Rumors were that he was looking for a new position and if the company reported strong profits, the president's opportunities would be enhanced. Cathrine also recognized that she could probably increase the cost of certain jobs by changing the basis used to allocate manufacturing overhead.

Instructions
(a) Who are the stakeholders in this situation?
(b) What are the ethical issues in this situation?
(c) What would you do if you were Cathrine Traynor?

Answers to Self-Study Questions
1. a   2. b   3. c   4. d   5. b   6. a   7. d   8. b   9. c   10. b

✓ **Remember to go back to the Navigator box on the chapter-opening page and check off your completed work.**

CHAPTER 3

Process Cost Accounting

THE NAVIGATOR ✔

- Scan *Study Objectives* ☐
- Read *Feature Story* ☐
- Read *Preview* ☐
- Read text and answer *Before You Go On*
  p. 96 ☐ p. 105 ☐ p. 106 ☐
- Work *Using the Decision Toolkit* ☐
- Review *Summary of Study Objectives* ☐
- Work *Demonstration Problem* ☐
- Answer *Self-Study Questions* ☐
- Complete *Assignments* ☐

◆ STUDY OBJECTIVES

After studying this chapter, you should be able to:

1. Understand who uses process cost systems.

2. Explain the similarities and differences between job order cost and process cost systems.

3. Explain the flow of costs in a process cost system.

4. Make the journal entries to assign manufacturing costs in a process cost system.

5. Compute equivalent units.

6. Explain the four steps necessary to prepare a production cost report.

7. Prepare a production cost report.

THE NAVIGATOR

◆ FEATURE STORY

BEN & JERRY'S TRACKS ITS MIX-UPS

At one time, one of the fastest growing companies in the nation was **Ben & Jerry's Homemade, Inc.**, based in Waterbury, Vermont. The ice cream company that started out of a garage in 1978 is now a public company.

Making ice cream is a process—a movement of product from a mixing department to a prepping department to a pint department. The mixing department is where the ice cream is created. The prep area is where extras such as cherries and walnuts are added to make plain ice cream into "Cherry Garcia." And the pint department is where the ice cream is actually put into containers. As the product is processed from one department to the next, the appropriate materials, labor, and overhead are added to it.

"The incoming ingredients from the shipping and receiving departments are stored in certain locations, either in a freezer or dry warehouse," says Beecher Eurich, staff accountant. "As ingredients get added, so do the costs associated with them." How much

ice cream is actually produced? Running the plant around the clock, 24,000 pints are produced per 8-hour shift, or 72,000 pints per day.

Using a process costing system, Eurich can tell you how much a certain batch of ice cream costs to make—its materials, labor, and overhead in each of the production departments. She generates reports for the production department heads, but makes sure not to overdo it. "You can get bogged down in numbers," says Eurich. "If you're generating a report that no one can use, then that's a waste of time." More likely, though, Ben & Jerry's production people want to know how efficient they are. Why? Many own stock in the company.

THE NAVIGATOR

www.benjerry.com

The cost accounting system used by companies such as **Ben & Jerry's** is called a **process cost accounting** system. In contrast to job order cost accounting, which focuses on the individual job, process cost accounting focuses on the processes involved in mass-producing products that are identical or very similar in nature. The primary objective of the chapter is to explain and illustrate process cost accounting.

The content and organization of this chapter are as follows.

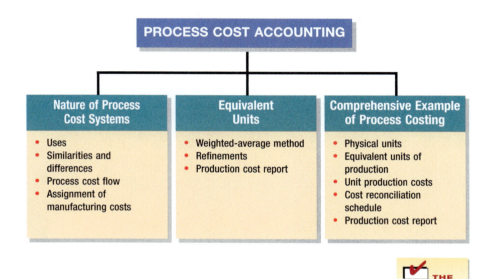

THE NAVIGATOR

THE NATURE OF PROCESS COST SYSTEMS

USES OF PROCESS COST SYSTEMS

STUDY OBJECTIVE

1

Understand who uses process cost systems.

Process cost systems are used to apply costs to similar products that are mass-produced in a continuous fashion. Ben & Jerry's uses a process cost system: Production of the ice cream, once it begins, continues until the ice cream emerges, and the processing is the same for the entire run—with precisely the same amount of materials, labor, and overhead. Each finished pint of ice cream is indistinguishable from another.

A company such as **USX** uses process costing in the manufacturing of steel. **Kellogg** and **General Mills** use process costing for cereal production; **Exxon-Mobil** uses process costing for its oil refining. And **Sherwin Williams** uses process costing for its paint products. At a bottling company like **Coca-Cola**, the manufacturing process begins with the blending of the beverages. Next the beverage is dispensed into bottles that are moved into position by automated machinery. The bottles are then capped, packaged, and forwarded to the finished goods warehouse. This process is shown in Illustration 3-1.

Illustration 3-1   Manufacturing processes

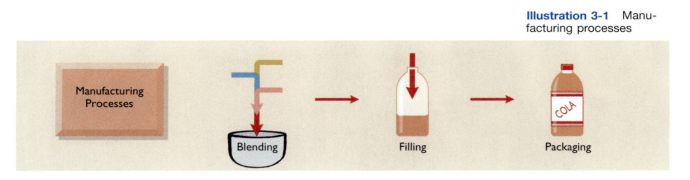

Illustration 3-1   Manufacturing processes

For Coca-Cola, as well as the other companies just mentioned, once the production begins, it continues until the finished product emerges, and each unit of finished product is like every other unit.

In comparison, costs in a job order cost system are assigned to a specific job. Examples are the construction of a customized home, the making of a motion picture, or the manufacturing of a specialized machine. Illustration 3-2 provides examples of companies that primarily use either a process cost system or a job order cost system.

Illustration 3-2   Process cost and job order cost companies and products

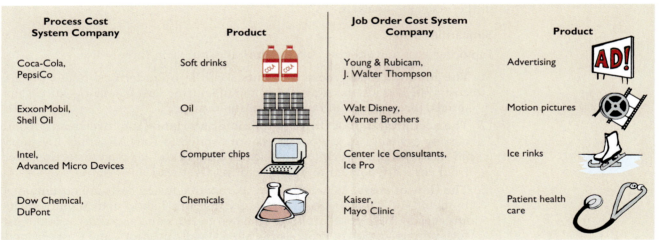

Process Cost System Company	Product	Job Order Cost System Company	Product
Coca-Cola, PepsiCo	Soft drinks	Young & Rubicam, J. Walter Thompson	Advertising
ExxonMobil, Shell Oil	Oil	Walt Disney, Warner Brothers	Motion pictures
Intel, Advanced Micro Devices	Computer chips	Center Ice Consultants, Ice Pro	Ice rinks
Dow Chemical, DuPont	Chemicals	Kaiser, Mayo Clinic	Patient health care

SIMILARITIES AND DIFFERENCES BETWEEN JOB ORDER COST AND PROCESS COST SYSTEMS

In a job order cost system, costs are assigned to each job. In a process cost system, costs are tracked through a series of connected manufacturing processes or departments, rather than by individual jobs. Thus, process cost systems are used when a large volume of uniform or relatively homogeneous products is produced. The basic flow of costs in these two systems is shown in Illustration 3-3.

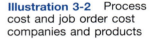

STUDY OBJECTIVE

2

Explain the similarities and differences between job order cost and process cost systems.

Illustration 3-3   Job
order cost and process
cost flow

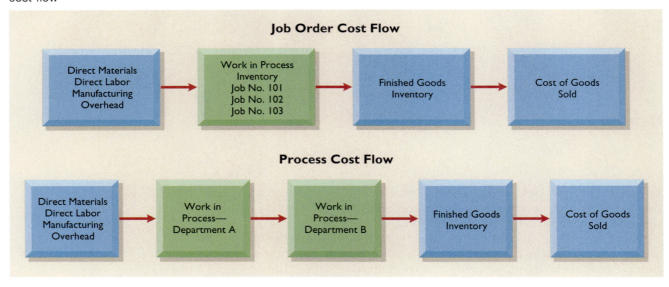

The basic similarities and differences between these two systems are highlighted in the following analysis.

Similarities

Job order cost and process cost systems are similar in three ways:

1. **The manufacturing cost elements.** Both a job order cost and a process cost system track the same three manufacturing cost elements—direct materials, direct labor, and manufacturing overhead.

2. **The accumulation of the costs of materials, labor, and overhead.** In both costing systems, all raw materials are debited to Raw Materials Inventory; all factory labor is debited to Factory Labor; and all manufacturing overhead costs are debited to Manufacturing Overhead.

3. **The flow of costs.** As noted above, all manufacturing costs are accumulated by debits to Raw Materials Inventory, Factory Labor, and Manufacturing Overhead. These costs are then assigned to the same accounts in both costing systems—Work in Process, Finished Goods Inventory, and Cost of Goods Sold. **The methods of assigning costs, however, differ significantly.** These differences are explained and illustrated later in the chapter.

Differences

The differences between a job order cost and a process cost system are as follows.

1. **The number of work in process accounts used.** In a job order cost system, only one work in process account is used. In a process cost system, multiple work in process accounts are used; separate accounts are maintained for each production department or manufacturing process.

2. **Documents used to track costs.** In a job order cost system, costs are charged to individual jobs and summarized in a job cost sheet. In a process cost system, costs are summarized in a production cost report for each department.

3. **The point at which costs are totaled.** In a job order cost system, total costs are determined when the job is completed. In a process cost system, total costs are determined at the end of a period of time, such as a month or year.

4. **Unit cost computations.** In a job order cost system, the unit cost is the total cost per job divided by the units produced. In a process cost system, the unit cost is total manufacturing costs for the period divided by the units produced during the period.

The major differences between a job order cost and a process cost system are summarized in Illustration 3-4.

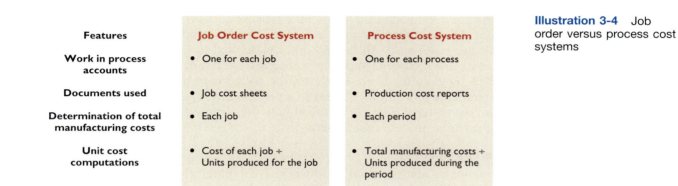

Features	Job Order Cost System	Process Cost System
Work in process accounts	• One for each job	• One for each process
Documents used	• Job cost sheets	• Production cost reports
Determination of total manufacturing costs	• Each job	• Each period
Unit cost computations	• Cost of each job ÷ Units produced for the job	• Total manufacturing costs ÷ Units produced during the period

Illustration 3-4   Job order versus process cost systems

PROCESS COST FLOW

Illustration 3-5 shows the flow of costs in the process cost system for Tyler Company. Tyler Company manufactures automatic can openers that are sold to retail outlets. Manufacturing consists of two processes: machining and assembly. In the Machining Department, the raw materials are shaped, honed, and drilled. In the Assembly Department, the parts are assembled and packaged.

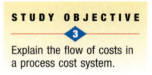

STUDY OBJECTIVE
3
Explain the flow of costs in a process cost system.

Illustration 3-5   Flow of costs in process cost system

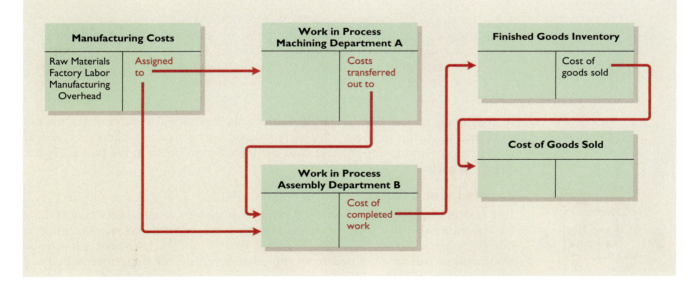

As the flow of costs indicates, materials, labor, and manufacturing overhead can be added in both the Machining and Assembly Departments. When the Machining Department finishes its work, the partially completed units are transferred to the Assembly Department. In the Assembly Department, the goods are finished and are then transferred to the finished goods inventory. Upon sale, the goods are removed from the finished goods inventory. Within each department, a similar set of activities is performed on each unit processed.

ASSIGNMENT OF MANUFACTURING COSTS— JOURNAL ENTRIES

STUDY OBJECTIVE
◆4◆
Make the journal entries to assign manufacturing costs in a process cost system.

As indicated earlier, the accumulation of the costs of materials, labor, and manufacturing overhead is the same in a process cost system as in a job order cost system. All raw materials are debited to Raw Materials Inventory when the materials are purchased. All factory labor is debited to Factory Labor when the labor costs are incurred. And overhead costs are debited to Manufacturing Overhead as they are incurred. However, the assignment of the three manufacturing cost elements to Work in Process in a process cost system is different from a job order cost system. Here we'll look at how these manufacturing cost elements are assigned in a process cost system.

Materials Costs

Materials

All raw materials issued for production are a materials cost to the producing department. Materials requisition slips may be used in a process cost system, but **fewer requisitions are generally required than in a job order cost system, because the materials are used for processes rather than for specific jobs.** Requisitions are issued less frequently in a process cost system because the requisitions are for larger quantities.

Materials are usually added to production at the beginning of the first process. However, in subsequent processes, other materials may be added at various points. For example, in the manufacture of **Hershey** candy bars, the chocolate and other ingredients are added at the beginning of the first process, and the wrappers and cartons are added at the end of the packaging process. At Tyler Company, materials are entered at the beginning of each process. The entry to record the materials used is:

Work in Process—Machining	XXXX	
Work in Process—Assembly	XXXX	
Raw Materials Inventory		XXXX
(To record materials used)		

At ice cream maker **Ben & Jerry's,** materials are added in three departments: milk and flavoring in the mixing department; extras such as cherries and walnuts in the prepping department; and cardboard containers in the pinting (packaging) department.

Factory Labor Costs

Factory Labor

In a process cost system, as in a job order cost system, time tickets may be used to determine the cost of labor assignable to production departments. Since labor costs are assigned to a process rather than a job, the labor cost chargeable to a process can be obtained from the payroll register or departmental payroll summaries.

All labor costs incurred within a producing department are a cost of processing the raw materials. Thus, labor costs for the Machining Department will include the wages of employees who shape, hone, and drill the raw materials. The entry to assign these costs for Tyler Company is:

Work in Process—Machining	XXXX	
Work in Process—Assembly	XXXX	
Factory Labor		XXXX
(To assign factory labor to production)		

Manufacturing Overhead Costs

The objective in assigning overhead in a process cost system is to allocate the overhead costs to the production departments on an objective and equitable basis. That basis is the activity that "drives" or causes the costs. A primary driver of overhead costs in continuous manufacturing operations is **machine time used**, not direct labor. Thus, **machine hours are widely used** in allocating manufacturing overhead costs. The entry to allocate overhead to the two processes is:

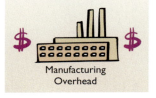

Manufacturing Overhead

Work in Process—Machining	XXXX	
Work in Process—Assembly	XXXX	
Manufacturing Overhead		XXXX
(To assign overhead to production)		

BUSINESS INSIGHT
Management Perspective

In one of **Caterpillar's** automated cost centers, work is fed into the cost center, processed by robotic machines, and transferred to the next cost center without human intervention. One person tends all of the machines and spends more time maintaining machines than operating them. In such cases, overhead rates based on direct labor hours may be misleading. Surprisingly, some companies continue to assign manufacturing overhead on the basis of direct labor despite the fact that there is no cause-and-effect relationship between labor and overhead.

Transfer to Next Department

At the end of the month, an entry is needed to record the cost of the goods transferred out of the department. In this case, the transfer is to the Assembly Department, and the following entry is made.

Work in Process—Assembly	XXXXX	
Work in Process—Machining		XXXXX
(To record transfer of units to the Assembly		
Department)		

Transfer to Finished Goods

The units completed in the Assembly Department are transferred to the finished goods warehouse. The entry for this transfer is as follows.

Finished Goods Inventory	XXXXX	
Work in Process—Assembly		XXXXX
(To record transfer of units to finished goods)		

Transfer to Cost of Goods Sold

When finished goods are sold, the entry to record the cost of goods sold is as follows.

Cost of Goods Sold	XXXXX	
Finished Goods Inventory		XXXXX
(To record cost of units sold)		

BEFORE YOU GO ON . . .

◆ Review It

1. What type of manufacturing companies might use a process cost accounting system?
2. What are the principal similarities and differences between a job order cost system and a process cost system?

◆ Do It

Ruth Company manufactures ZEBO through two processes: Blending and Bottling. In June, raw materials used were Blending $18,000 and Bottling $4,000; factory labor costs were Blending $12,000 and Bottling $5,000; manufacturing overhead costs were Blending $6,000 and Bottling $2,500. Units completed at a cost of $19,000 in the Blending Department are transferred to the Bottling Department. Units completed at a cost of $11,000 in the Bottling Department are transferred to Finished Goods. Journalize the assignment of these costs to the two processes and the transfer of units as appropriate.

Action Plan

- In process cost accounting, keep separate work in process accounts for each process.
- When the costs are assigned to production, debit the separate work in process accounts.
- Transfer cost of completed units to the next process or to Finished Goods.

Solution: The entries are:

Work in Process—Blending	18,000	
Work in Process—Bottling	4,000	
Raw Materials Inventory		22,000
(To record materials used)		
Work in Process—Blending	12,000	
Work in Process—Bottling	5,000	
Factory Labor		17,000
(To assign factory labor to production)		

Work in Process—Blending		6,000	
Work in Process—Bottling		2,500	
Manufacturing Overhead			8,500
(To assign overhead to production)			
Work in Process—Bottling		19,000	
Work in Process—Blending			19,000
(To record transfer of units to the Bottling			
Department)			
Finished Goods Inventory		11,000	
Work in Process—Bottling			11,000
(To record transfer of units to finished goods)			

THE NAVIGATOR

Related exercise material: BE3-1, BE3-2, BE3-3, E3-1, and E3-2.

EQUIVALENT UNITS

STUDY OBJECTIVE

5

Compute equivalent units.

Suppose you were asked to compute the cost of instruction at your college per full-time equivalent student. You are provided the following information.

Illustration 3-6 Information for full-time student example

Costs:	
Total cost of instruction	$900,000
Student population:	
Full-time students	900
Part-time students	1,000

Part-time students take 60 percent of the classes of a full-time student during the year. To compute the number of full-time equivalent students per year, you would make the following computation.

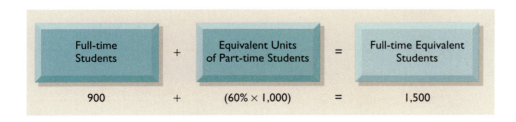

Illustration 3-7 Full-time equivalent unit computation

The cost of instruction per full-time equivalent student is therefore the total cost of instruction ($900,000) divided by the number of full-time equivalent students (1,500), which is $600 ($900,000 ÷ 1,500).

In a process cost system, the same idea, called equivalent units of production, is used. **Equivalent units of production** measure the work done during the period, expressed in fully completed units. This concept is used to determine the cost per unit of completed product.

WEIGHTED-AVERAGE METHOD

The formula to compute equivalent units of production is as follows.

Illustration 3-8 Equivalent units of production formula

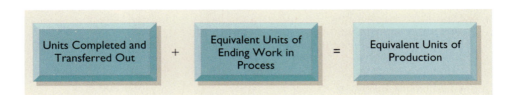

To better understand this concept of equivalent units, consider the following two examples.

> **Example 1:** The Blending Department's entire output during the period consists of ending work in process of 4,000 units which are 60 percent complete as to materials, labor, and overhead. The equivalent units of production for the Blending Department are therefore 2,400 units (4,000 × 60%).

> **Example 2:** The Packaging Department's output during the period consists of 10,000 units completed and transferred out, and 5,000 units in ending work in process which are 70 percent completed. The equivalent units of production are therefore 13,500 [10,000 + (5,000 × 70%)].

This method of computing equivalent units is referred to as the **weighted-average method**. It considers the degree of completion (weighting) of the units completed and transferred out and the ending work in process. It is the method most widely used in practice. A less-used method, called the FIFO method, is discussed in the appendix to this chapter.

REFINEMENTS ON THE WEIGHTED-AVERAGE METHOD

Kellogg Company has produced Eggo® Waffles since 1970. Three departments are used to produce these waffles: Mixing, Baking, and Freezing and Packaging. In the Mixing Department dry ingredients, including flour, salt, and baking powder, are mixed with liquid ingredients, including eggs and vegetable oil, to make waffle batter. Information related to the Mixing Department at the end of June is provided in Illustration 3-9.

Illustration 3-9 Information for Mixing Department

Mixing Department			
		Percentage Complete	
	Physical Units	Materials	Conversion Costs
Work in process, June 1	100,000	100%	70%
Started into production	800,000		
Total units	900,000		
Units transferred out	700,000		
Work in process, June 30	200,000	100%	60%
Total units	900,000		

Illustration 3-9 indicates that the beginning work in process is 100 percent complete as to materials cost and 70 percent complete as to conversion costs. **Conversion costs** **refers to the sum of labor costs and overhead costs.** In other words, both the dry and liquid ingredients (materials) are added at the beginning of the process to make Eggo® Waffles. The conversion costs (labor and overhead) related to the mixing of these ingredients were incurred uniformly and are 70 percent complete. The ending work in process is 100 percent complete as to materials cost and 60 percent complete as to conversion costs.

We then use the Mixing Department information to determine equivalent units. **In computing equivalent units, the beginning work in process is not part of the equivalent units of production formula.** The units transferred out to the Baking Department are fully complete as to both materials and conversion costs. The ending work in process is fully complete as to materials, but only 60 percent complete as to conversion costs. **Two equivalent unit computations are therefore necessary:** one for materials and the other for conversion costs. Illustration 3-10 shows these computations.

Helpful Hint Question: When are separate unit cost computations needed for materials and conversion costs? Answer: Whenever the two types of costs do not occur in the process at the same time.

	Equivalent Units	
	Materials	**Conversion Costs**
Units transferred out	700,000	700,000
Work in process, June 30		
200,000 × 100%	200,000	
200,000 × 60%		120,000
Total equivalent units	900,000	820,000

Illustration 3-10 Computation of equivalent units—Mixing Department

The earlier formula used to compute equivalent units of production can be refined to show the computations for materials and for conversion costs, as follows.

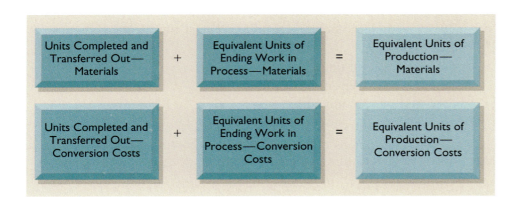

Illustration 3-11 Refined equivalent unit of production formula

PRODUCTION COST REPORT

As mentioned earlier, a production cost report is prepared for each department in a process cost system. A **production cost report** is the key document used by management to understand the activities in a department because it shows the production quantity and cost data related to that department. For example, in producing Eggo® Waffles, **Kellogg Company** would have three production cost reports: Mixing, Baking, and Freezing and Packaging. Illustration 3-12 shows the flow of costs to make an Eggo® Waffle and the related production cost reports for each department.

Illustration 3-12   Flow of costs in making Eggo® Waffles

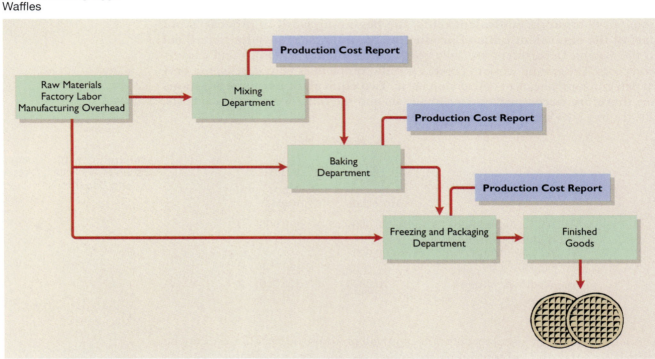

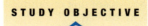

STUDY OBJECTIVE

6

Explain the four steps necessary to prepare a production cost report.

In order to be ready to complete a production cost report, the company must perform four steps:

1. Compute the physical unit flow.
2. Compute the equivalent units of production.
3. Compute unit production costs.
4. Prepare a cost reconciliation schedule.

As a whole, these four steps make up the process costing system. The next section explores these steps in an extended example.

COMPREHENSIVE EXAMPLE OF PROCESS COSTING

Assumed data for the Mixing Department at **Kellogg Company** for the month of June are shown in Illustration 3-13. We will use this information to complete a production cost report for the Mixing Department.

Mixing Department	
Units	
Work in process, June 1	100,000
Direct materials: 100% complete	
Conversion costs: 70% complete	
Units started into production during June	800,000
Units completed and transferred out to Baking Department	700,000
Work in process, June 30	200,000
Direct materials: 100% complete	
Conversion costs: 60% complete	
Costs	
Work in process, June 1	
Direct materials: 100% complete	$50,000
Conversion costs: 70% complete	35,000
Cost of work in process, June 1	$85,000
Costs incurred during production in June	
Direct materials	$400,000
Conversion costs	170,000
Costs incurred in June	$570,000

Illustration 3-13 Unit and cost data—Mixing Department

COMPUTE THE PHYSICAL UNIT FLOW (STEP 1)

Physical units are the actual units to be accounted for during a period, irrespective of any work performed. To keep track of these units, it is necessary to add the units started (or transferred) into production during the period to the units in process at the beginning of the period. This amount is referred to as the **total units to be accounted for**.

The total units then are accounted for by the output of the period. The output consists of units transferred out during the period and any units in process at the end of the period. This amount is referred to as the **total units accounted for**. Illustration 3-14 shows the flow of physical units for Kellogg Company for the month of June for the Mixing Department.

Mixing Department	
	Physical Units
Units to be accounted for	
Work in process, June 1	100,000
Started (transferred) into production	800,000
Total units	**900,000**
Units accounted for	
Completed and transferred out	700,000
Work in process, June 30	200,000
Total units	**900,000**

Illustration 3-14 Physical unit flow—Mixing Department

The records indicate that 900,000 units must be accounted for in the Mixing Department. Of this sum, 700,000 units were transferred to the Baking Department and 200,000 units were still in process.

COMPUTE EQUIVALENT UNITS OF PRODUCTION (STEP 2)

Helpful Hint Materials are not always added at the beginning of the process. For example, materials are sometimes added uniformly during the process.

Once the physical flow of the units is established, it is necessary to measure the Mixing Department's productivity in terms of equivalent units of production. In the Mixing Department, materials are added at the beginning of the process, and conversion costs are incurred uniformly during the process. Thus, two computations of equivalent units are required: one for materials and one for conversion costs. The equivalent unit computation is as follows.

Illustration 3-15 Computation of equivalent units—Mixing Department

	Equivalent Units	
	Materials	**Conversion Costs**
Units transferred out	700,000	700,000
Work in process, June 30		
200,000 × 100%	200,000	
200,000 × 60%		120,000
Total equivalent units	**900,000**	**820,000**

Remember that the beginning work in process is ignored in this computation.

COMPUTE UNIT PRODUCTION COSTS (STEP 3)

Armed with the knowledge of the equivalent units of production, we can now compute the unit production costs. **Unit production costs** are costs expressed in terms of equivalent units of production. When equivalent units of production are different for materials and conversion costs, three unit costs are computed: (1) materials, (2) conversion, and (3) total manufacturing.

The computation of total materials cost related to Eggo® Waffles is as follows.

Illustration 3-16 Materials cost computation

Work in process, June 1	
Direct materials cost	$ 50,000
Costs added to production during June	
Direct materials cost	400,000
Total materials cost	**$450,000**

The computation of unit materials cost is as follows.

Illustration 3-17 Unit materials cost computation

The computation of total conversion costs is shown in Illustration 3-18.

Work in process, June 1		
Conversion costs		$ 35,000
Costs added to production during June		
Conversion costs		170,000
Total conversion costs		**$205,000**

Illustration 3-18 Total conversion costs computation

The computation of unit conversion cost is as follows.

Illustration 3-19 Unit conversion cost computation

Total manufacturing cost per unit is therefore computed as follows.

Illustration 3-20 Total manufacturing cost per unit

PREPARE A COST RECONCILIATION SCHEDULE (STEP 4)

We are now ready to determine the cost of goods transferred out of the Mixing Department to the Baking Department and the costs in ending work in process. The total costs that were charged to the Mixing Department in June are as follows.

Costs to be accounted for	
Work in process, June 1	$ 85,000
Started into production	570,000
Total costs	**$655,000**

Illustration 3-21 Costs charged to Mixing Department

The total costs charged to the Mixing Department in June are therefore $655,000. A cost reconciliation schedule is then prepared to assign these costs to (1) units transferred out to the Baking Department and (2) ending work in process.

Illustration 3-22 Cost reconciliation schedule—Mixing Department

Mixing Department **Cost Reconciliation Schedule**		
Costs accounted for		
Transferred out (700,000 × $0.75)		$525,000
Work in process, June 30		
Materials (200,000 × $0.50)	$100,000	
Conversion costs (120,000 × $0.25)	30,000	130,000
Total costs		**$655,000**

The total manufacturing cost per unit, $0.75, is used in costing the units completed and transferred to the Baking Department. In contrast, the unit cost of materials and the unit cost of conversion are needed in costing units in process. The **cost reconciliation schedule** shows that the **total costs accounted for** (Illustration 3-22) equal the **total costs to be accounted for** (see Illustration 3-21).

PREPARING THE PRODUCTION COST REPORT

STUDY OBJECTIVE

7

Prepare a production cost report.

At this point, we are ready to prepare the production cost report for the Mixing Department. As indicated earlier, this report is an internal document for management that shows production quantity and cost data for a production department.

There are four steps in preparing a production cost report. They are: (1) Prepare a physical unit schedule. (2) Compute equivalent units. (3) Compute unit costs. (4) Prepare a cost reconciliation schedule. The production cost report for the Mixing Department is shown in Illustration 3-23. The four steps are identified in the report.

Illustration 3-23 Production cost report

Helpful Hint What are the two self-checks in the report? Answer: (1) Total physical units accounted for must equal the total units to be accounted for. (2) Total costs accounted for must equal the total costs to be accounted for.

Mixing Department
Production Cost Report
For the Month Ended June 30, 2002

| | | Equivalent Units | |
	Physical Units	Materials	Conversion Costs
QUANTITIES	Step 1	Step 2	
Units to be accounted for			
Work in process, June 1	100,000		
Started into production	800,000		
Total units	900,000		
Units accounted for			
Transferred out	700,000	700,000	700,000
Work in process, June 30	200,000	200,000	120,000 (200,000 × 60%)
Total units	900,000	900,000	820,000

| **COSTS** | | | Conversion | |
Unit costs Step 3		Materials	Costs	Total
Costs in June	(a)	$450,000	$205,000	$655,000
Equivalent units	(b)	900,000	820,000	
Unit costs [(a) ÷ (b)]		$0.50	$0.25	$0.75

Costs to be accounted for	
Work in process, June 1	$ 85,000
Started into production	570,000
Total costs	$655,000

Cost Reconciliation Schedule Step 4

Costs accounted for		
Transferred out (700,000 × $0.75)		$525,000
Work in process, June 30		
Materials (200,000 × $0.50)	$100,000	
Conversion costs (120,000 × $0.25)	30,000	130,000
Total costs		$655,000

Production cost reports provide a basis for evaluating the productivity of a department. In addition, the cost data can be used to assess whether unit costs and total costs are reasonable. By comparing the quantity and cost data with predetermined goals, top management can also judge whether current performance is meeting planned objectives.

Helpful Hint Because production cost reports are used as the basis for evaluating department productivity and efficiency, the units, costs, and computations reported therein should be independently accumulated and analyzed to prevent misstatements by department managers.

DECISION TOOLKIT

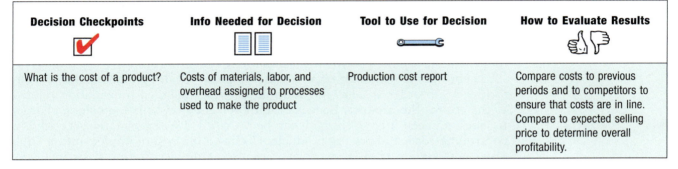

Decision Checkpoints	Info Needed for Decision	Tool to Use for Decision	How to Evaluate Results
What is the cost of a product?	Costs of materials, labor, and overhead assigned to processes used to make the product	Production cost report	Compare costs to previous periods and to competitors to ensure that costs are in line. Compare to expected selling price to determine overall profitability.

BEFORE YOU GO ON . . .

◆ Review It

1. How do physical units differ from equivalent units of production?
2. What are the formulas for computing unit costs of production?
3. How are costs assigned to units transferred out and in process?
4. What are the four steps in preparing a production cost report?

◆ Do It

In March, Rodayo Manufacturing had the following unit production costs: materials $6 and conversion costs $9. On March 1, it had zero work in process. During March, 12,000 units were transferred out, and 800 units that were 25 percent completed as to conversion costs and 100 percent complete as to materials were in ending work in process at March 31. Assign the costs to the units transferred out and in process.

Action Plan
• Assign the total manufacturing cost of $15 per unit to the 12,000 units transferred out.
• Assign the materials cost and conversion costs based on equivalent units of production to units in process.

Solution: The assignment of costs is as follows.

Costs accounted for		
Transferred out (12,000 × $15)		$180,000
Work in process, March 31		
Materials (800 × $6)	$4,800	
Conversion costs (200[a] × $9)	1,800	6,600
Total costs		$186,600

[a]800 × 25%

Related exercise material: BE3-4, BE3-5, BE3-6, BE3-7, BE3-8, E3-4, E3-6, E3-8, E3-9, and E3-10.

THE NAVIGATOR

FINAL COMMENTS

Companies often use a combination of a process cost and a job order cost system, called **operations costing**. Operations costing is similar to process costing in that standardized methods are used to manufacture the product. At the same time, the product may have some customized, individual features that require the use of a job order cost system. Consider, for example, the automobile manufacturer **Ford Motor Company**. Each vehicle at a given plant goes through the same assembly line, but different materials (such as seat coverings, paint, and tinted glass) may be used for different vehicles. Similarly, **Kellogg's** Pop-Tarts Toaster Pastries® go through numerous processes—mixing, filling, baking, frosting, and packaging. The pastry dough, though, comes in three flavors—plain, chocolate, and graham—and fillings include Smucker's® real fruit, chocolate fudge, vanilla creme, brown sugar cinnamon, and S'mores.

A cost–benefit tradeoff occurs as a company decides which costing system to use. A job order system, for example, provides detailed information related to the cost of the product. Because each job has its own distinguishing characteristics, an accurate cost per job can be provided. This information is useful in controlling costs and pricing products. However, the cost of implementing a job order cost system is often expensive because of the accounting costs involved.

On the other hand, for a company like **Intel**, which makes computer chips, is there a benefit in knowing whether the cost of the one hundredth chip produced is different from the one thousandth chip produced? Probably not. An average cost of the product will suffice for control and pricing purposes. In summary, when deciding to use one of these systems, or a combination system, a company must weigh the costs of implementing the system against the benefits from the additional information provided.

BUSINESS INSIGHT
Service Company Perspective

Frequently when we think of service companies we think of specific, nonroutine tasks, such as rebuilding an automobile engine, providing consulting services on a business acquisition, or working on a major lawsuit. Clearly, such nonroutine situations would call for job order costing. However, many service companies specialize in performing repetitive, routine aspects of a particular business. For example, auto-care vendors such as **Jiffy Lube** focus on the routine aspects of car care. **H&R Block** focuses on the routine aspects of basic tax practice, and many large law firms focus on routine legal services, such as uncomplicated divorces. For service companies that perform routine, repetitive services, process costing provides a simple solution to their accounting needs. In fact, since in many instances there is little or no work in process at the end of the period, applying process costing in this setting can be even easier than for a manufacturer.

BEFORE YOU GO ON . . .

◆ **Review It**

1. In what circumstances would a manufacturer use operations costing instead of process costing?
2. Describe the cost–benefit tradeoff in deciding what costing system to use.

DECISION TOOLKIT

Decision Checkpoints	Info Needed for Decision	Tool to Use for Decision	How to Evaluate Results
✔			
What costing method should be used?	Type of product produced	Cost of accounting system; benefits of additional information	The benefits of providing the additional information should exceed the costs of the accounting system needed to develop the information.

*U*SING THE DECISION TOOLKIT

Essence Company manufactures a high-end after-shave lotion, called Eternity, in 10-ounce shaped glass bottles. Because the market for after-shave lotion is highly competitive, the company is very concerned about keeping its costs under control. Eternity is manufactured through three processes: mixing, filling, and corking. Materials are added at the beginning of the process, and labor and overhead are incurred uniformly throughout each process. The company uses a weighted-average method to cost its product. A partially completed production cost report for the month of May for the Mixing Department is shown below.

ESSENCE COMPANY
Mixing Department
Production Cost Report
For the Month Ended May 31, 2002

		Equivalent Units	
	Physical Units	Materials	Conversion Costs
QUANTITIES	Step 1		Step 2
Units to be accounted for			
Work in process, May 1	1,000		
Started into production	2,000		
Total units	3,000		
Units accounted for			
Transferred out	2,200	?	?
Work in process, May 31	800	?	?
Total units	3,000	?	?

COSTS		Materials	Conversion Costs	Total
Unit costs Step 3				
Costs in May	(a)	?	?	?
Equivalent units	(b)	?	?	
Unit costs [(a) ÷ (b)]		?	?	?
Costs to be accounted for				
Work in process, May 1				$ 56,300
Started into production				119,320
Total costs				$175,620

Cost Reconciliation Schedule Step 4

Costs accounted for
  Transferred out   ?
  Work in process, May 31
    Materials   ?
    Conversion costs   ?   ?
Total costs   ?

Additional information:		
Work in process, May 1, 1000 units		
Materials cost, 1,000 units (100% complete)	$49,100	
Conversion costs, 1,000 units (70% complete)	7,200	$ 56,300
Materials cost for May, 2,000 units		$100,000
Conversion costs for May		$ 19,320

Work in process, May 31, 800 units, 100% complete as to materials and 50% complete as to conversion costs.

Instructions

(a) Prepare a production cost report for the Mixing Department for the month of May.

(b) Prepare the journal entry to record the transfer of goods from the Mixing Department to the Filling Department.

(c) Explain why Essence Company is using a process cost system to account for its costs.

Solution

(a) A completed production cost report for the Mixing Department is shown below. Computations to support the amounts reported follow the report.

ESSENCE COMPANY
Mixing Department
Production Cost Report
For the Month Ended May 31, 2002

	Physical Units	Equivalent Units	
		Materials	Conversion Costs
QUANTITIES	Step 1		Step 2
Units to be accounted for			
Work in process, May 1	1,000		
Started into production	2,000		
Total units	3,000		
Units accounted for			
Transferred out	2,200	2,200	2,200
Work in process, May 31	800	800	400 (800 × 50%)
Total units	3,000	3,000	2,600

COSTS		Materials	Conversion Costs	Total
Unit costs Step 3				
Costs in May	(a)	$149,100	$26,520	$175,620
Equivalent units	(b)	3,000	2,600	
Unit costs [(a) ÷ (b)]		$49.70	$10.20	$59.90

	Conversion Costs	Total
Costs to be accounted for		
Work in process, May 1		$ 56,300
Started into production		119,320
Total costs		$175,620

Cost Reconciliation Schedule | Step 4 |

	Conversion Costs	Total
Costs accounted for		
Transferred out (2,200 × $59.90)		$131,780
Work in process, May 31		
Materials (800 × $49.70)	$39,760	
Conversion costs (400 × $10.20)	4,080	43,840
Total costs		$175,620

Additional computations to support production cost report data:
   Materials cost—$49,100 + $100,000
   Conversion costs—$7,200 + $19,320

(b) Work in Process—Filling | 131,780 |
      Work in Process—Mixing | | 131,780

(c) Process cost systems are used to apply costs to similar products that are mass-produced in a continuous fashion. Essence Company uses a process cost system: production of the after-shave lotion, once it begins, continues until the after-shave lotion emerges. The processing is the same for the entire run—with precisely the same amount of materials, labor, and overhead. Each bottle of Eternity after-shave lotion is indistinguishable from another.

SUMMARY OF STUDY OBJECTIVES

① *Understand who uses process cost systems.* Process cost systems are used by companies that mass-produce similar products in a continuous fashion. Once production begins, it continues until the finished product emerges. Each unit of finished product is indistinguishable from every other unit.

② *Explain the similarities and differences between job order cost and process cost systems.* Job order cost systems are similar to process cost systems in three ways: (1) Both systems track the same cost elements—direct materials, direct labor, and manufacturing overhead. (2) Costs are accumulated in the same accounts—Raw Materials Inventory, Factory Labor, and Manufacturing Overhead. (3) Accumulated costs are assigned to the same accounts—Work in Process, Finished Goods Inventory, and Cost of Goods Sold. However, the method of assigning costs differs significantly.

There are four main differences between the two cost systems: (1) A process cost system uses separate accounts for each production department or manufacturing process, rather than only one work in process ac-

count used in a job order cost system. (2) In a process cost system, costs are summarized in a production cost report for each department; in a job cost system, costs are charged to individual jobs and summarized in a job cost sheet. (3) Costs are totaled at the end of a time period in a process cost system and at the completion of a job in a job cost system. (4) In a process cost system, unit cost is calculated as: Total manufacturing costs for the period ÷ Units produced during the period. Unit cost in a job cost system is: Total cost per job ÷ Units produced.

③ *Explain the flow of costs in a process cost system.* Manufacturing costs for raw materials, labor, and overhead are assigned to work in process accounts for various departments or manufacturing processes, and the costs of units completed in a department are transferred from one department to another as those units move through the manufacturing process. The costs of completed work are transferred to Finished Goods Inventory. When inventory is sold, costs are transferred to Cost of Goods Sold.

4 *Make the journal entries to assign manufacturing costs in a process cost system.* Entries to assign the costs of raw materials, labor, and overhead consist of a credit to Raw Materials Inventory, Factory Labor, and Manufacturing Overhead, and a debit to Work in Process for each of the departments doing the processing. Entries to record the cost of goods transferred to another department are a credit to Work in Process for the department whose work is finished and a debit to the department to which the goods are transferred. The entry to record units completed and transferred to the warehouse is a credit for the department whose work is finished and a debit to Finished Goods Inventory. Finally, the entry to record the sale of goods is a credit to Finished Goods Inventory and a debit to Cost of Goods Sold.

5 *Compute equivalent units.* Equivalent units of production measure work done during a period, expressed in fully completed units. This concept is used to deter-

mine the cost per unit of completed product. Equivalent units are the sum of units completed and transferred out plus equivalent units of ending work in process.

6 *Explain the four steps necessary to prepare a production cost report.* The four steps to complete a production cost report are: (1) Compute the physical unit flow—that is, the total units to be accounted for. (2) Compute the equivalent units of production. (3) Compute the unit production costs, expressed in terms of equivalent units of production. (4) Prepare a cost reconciliation schedule, which shows that the total costs accounted for equal the total costs to be accounted for.

7 *Prepare a production cost report.* The production cost report contains both quantity and cost data for a production department. There are four sections in the report: (1) number of physical units, (2) equivalent units determination, (3) unit costs, and (4) cost reconciliation schedule.

DECISION TOOLKIT—A SUMMARY

Decision Checkpoints	Info Needed for Decision	Tool to Use for Decision	How to Evaluate Results
What is the cost of a product?	Costs of materials, labor, and overhead assigned to processes used to make the product	Production cost report	Compare costs to previous periods and to competitors to ensure that costs are in line. Compare to expected selling price to determine overall profitability.
Which costing method should be used?	Type of product produced	Cost of accounting system; benefits of additional information	The benefits of providing the additional information should exceed the costs of the accounting system needed to develop the information.

APPENDIX 3A
FIFO METHOD

In Chapter 3, we demonstrated the weighted-average method of computing equivalent units. Some companies use a different method to compute equivalent units, which is referred to as the **first-in, first-out (FIFO) method**. The purpose of this appendix is to illustrate how the FIFO method is used in practice.

EQUIVALENT UNITS UNDER FIFO

Under the FIFO method, the computation of equivalent units is done on a first-in, first-out basis. Some companies favor the FIFO method because the FIFO cost assumption usually corresponds to the actual physical flow of the goods. Under the FIFO method, it is assumed therefore that the beginning work in process is completed before new work is started.

Using the FIFO method, equivalent units are the sum of the work performed to:

Helpful Hint The computation of unit production costs and the assignment of costs to units transferred out and in process also are done on the same basis.

1. Finish the units of beginning work in process inventory.
2. Complete the units started into production during the period (referred to as the **units started and completed**).
3. Start, but only partially complete, the units in ending work in process inventory.

Normally, in a process costing system, some units will always be in process at both the beginning and end of the period.

ILLUSTRATION

Illustration 3A-1 shows the physical flow of units for the Assembly Department of Shutters Inc. In addition, the illustration indicates the degree of completion of the work in process accounts in regard to conversion costs.

Assembly Department	
	Physical Units
Units to be accounted for	
Work in process, June 1 (40% complete)	500
Started (transferred) into production	8,000
Total units	**8,500**
Units accounted for	
Completed and transferred out	8,100
Work in process, June 30 (75% complete)	400
Total units	**8,500**

Illustration 3A-1 Physical unit flow—Assembly Department

In this case the units completed and transferred out (8,100) plus the units in ending work in process (400) equal the total units to be accounted for (8,500).

We then compute equivalent units using FIFO as follows.

1. The 500 units of beginning work in process were 40 percent complete. Thus, 300 equivalent units (60% × 500 units) were required to complete the beginning inventory.
2. The units started and completed during the current month are the units transferred out minus the units in beginning work in process. For the Assembly Department, units started and completed are 7,600 (8,100 − 500).
3. The 400 units of ending work in process were 75 percent complete. Thus, equivalent units were 300 (400 × 75%).

Thus, equivalent units for the Assembly Department are 8,200, computed as follows.

Illustration 3A-2 Computation of equivalent units—FIFO method

Assembly Department			
Production Data	Physical Units	Work Added This Period	Equivalent Units
Work in process, June 1	500	60%	300
Started and completed	7,600	100%	7,600
Work in process, June 30	400	75%	300
Total	8,500		8,200

COMPREHENSIVE EXAMPLE

To provide a complete illustration of the FIFO method, we will use the data for the Mixing Department at **Kellogg Company** for the month of June, as shown in Illustration 3A-3.

Illustration 3A-3 Unit and cost data—Mixing Department

Mixing Department	
Units	
Work in process, June 1	100,000
Direct materials: 100% complete	
Conversion costs: 70% complete	
Units started into production during June	800,000
Units completed and transferred out to Baking Department	700,000
Work in process, June 30	200,000
Direct materials: 100% complete	
Conversion costs: 60% complete	
Costs	
Work in process, June 1	
Direct materials: 100% complete	$50,000
Conversion costs: 70% complete	35,000
Cost of work in process, June 1	$85,000
Costs incurred during production in June	
Direct materials	$400,000
Conversion costs	170,000
Costs incurred in June	$570,000

COMPUTE THE PHYSICAL UNIT FLOW (STEP 1)

Illustration 3A-4 shows the physical flow of units for **Kellogg Company** for the month of June for the Mixing Department.

Mixing Department

	Physical Units
Units to be accounted for	
Work in process, June 1	100,000
Started (transferred) into production	800,000
Total units	900,000
Units accounted for	
Completed and transferred out	700,000
Work in process, June 30	200,000
Total units	900,000

Illustration 3A-4 Physical unit flow—Mixing Department

Under the FIFO method, the physical units schedule is often expanded to explain the transferred-out section. As a result, in this section the beginning work in process and the units started and completed are reported. These two items further explain the completed and transferred out section, as shown in Illustration 3A-5.

Mixing Department

	Physical Units
Units to be accounted for	
Work in process, June 1	100,000
Started (transferred) into production	800,000
Total units	900,000
Units accounted for	
Completed and transferred out	
Work in process, June 1	**100,000**
Started and completed	**600,000**
	700,000
Work in process, June 30	200,000
Total units	900,000

Illustration 3A-5 Physical unit flow (FIFO)—Mixing Department

The records indicate that 900,000 units must be accounted for in the Mixing Department. Of this sum, 700,000 units were transferred to the Baking Department and 200,000 units were still in process.

COMPUTE EQUIVALENT UNITS OF PRODUCTION (STEP 2)

As with the method presented in the chapter, once the physical flow of the units is established, it is necessary to determine equivalent units of production. In the Mixing Department, materials are added at the beginning of the process, and conversion costs are incurred uniformly during the process. Thus, two computations of equivalent units are required: one for materials and one for conversion costs.

Helpful Hint Materials are not always added at the beginning of the process. For example, materials are sometimes added uniformly during the process.

Equivalent Units for Materials

Since materials are entered at the beginning of the process, no additional materials costs are required to complete the beginning work in process. In addition, 100 percent of the materials costs has been incurred on the ending work in process. Thus, the computation of equivalent units for materials is as follows.

Illustration 3A-6 Computation of equivalent units—materials

Mixing Department			
Production Data	Physical Units	Materials Added This Period	Equivalent Units
Work in process, June 1	100,000	–0–	–0–
Started and finished	600,000	100%	600,000
Work in process, June 30	200,000	100%	200,000
Total	900,000		800,000

Equivalent Units for Conversion Costs

The 100,000 units of beginning work in process were 70 percent complete in terms of conversion costs. Thus, 30,000 equivalent units (30% × 100,000 units) of conversion costs were required to complete the beginning inventory. In addition, the 200,000 units of ending work in process were 60 percent complete in terms of conversion costs. Thus, the equivalent units for conversion costs is 750,000, computed as follows.

Illustration 3A-7 Computation of equivalent units—conversion costs

Mixing Department			
Production Data	Physical Units	Work Added This Period	Equivalent Units
Work in process, June 1	100,000	30%	30,000
Started and finished	600,000	100%	600,000
Work in process, June 30	200,000	60%	120,000
Total	900,000		750,000

COMPUTE UNIT PRODUCTION COSTS (STEP 3)

Armed with the knowledge of the equivalent units of production, we can now compute the unit production costs. Unit production costs are costs expressed in terms of equivalent units of production. When equivalent units of production are different for materials and conversion costs, three unit costs are computed: (1) materials, (2) conversion costs, and (3) total manufacturing.

Under the FIFO method, the unit costs of production are based entirely on the production costs incurred during the month. Thus, the costs in the beginning work in process are not relevant, because they were incurred on work done in the preceding month. As indicated from Illustration 3A-3, the costs incurred during production in June were:

Illustration 3A-8 Costs incurred during production in June

Direct materials	$400,000
Conversion costs	170,000
Total costs	$570,000

The computation of unit materials cost, unit conversion costs, and total unit cost related to Eggo® Waffles is as follows.

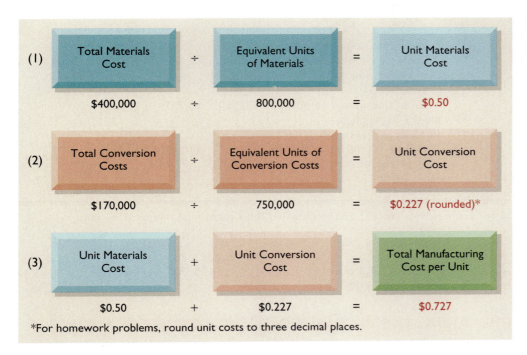

Illustration 3A-9 Unit cost formulas and computations—Mixing Department

*For homework problems, round unit costs to three decimal places.

As shown, the unit costs are $0.50 for materials, $0.227 for conversion costs, and $0.727 for total manufacturing costs.

PREPARE A COST RECONCILIATION SCHEDULE (STEP 4)

We are now ready to determine the cost of goods transferred out of the Mixing Department to the Baking Department and the costs in ending work in process. The total costs that were charged to the Mixing Department in June are as follows.

Costs to be accounted for	
Work in process, June 1	$ 85,000
Started into production	570,000
Total costs	$655,000

Illustration 3A-10
Costs charged to Mixing Department

The total costs charged to the Mixing Department in June are $655,000. A cost reconciliation is then prepared to assign these costs to (1) units transferred out to the Baking Department and (2) ending work in process. Under the FIFO method, the first goods to be completed during the period are the units in beginning work in process. Thus, the cost of the beginning work in process is always assigned to the goods transferred to finished goods (or the next department). The FIFO method also means that ending work in process will be assigned only production costs that are incurred in the current period. Illustration 3A-11 shows a cost reconciliation schedule for the Mixing Department.

Illustration 3A-11 Cost reconciliation report

Mixing Department Cost Reconciliation Schedule		
Costs accounted for		
Transferred out		
Work in process, June 1		$ 85,000
Costs to complete beginning work in process		
Conversion costs (30,000 × $0.227)		6,810
Total costs		91,810
Units started and completed (600,000 × $0.727)		435,950*
Total costs transferred out		527,760
Work in process, June 30		
Materials (200,000 × $0.50)	$100,000	
Conversion costs (120,000 × $0.227)	27,240	127,240
Total costs		**$655,000**

*Any rounding errors should be adjusted in the "Units started and completed" section.

As you can see, the total costs accounted for ($655,000) equal the total costs to be accounted for ($655,000).

PREPARING THE PRODUCTION COST REPORT

At this point, we are ready to prepare the production cost report for the Mixing Department. This report is an internal document for management that shows production quantity and cost data for a production department.

There are four steps in preparing a production cost report. They are: (1) Prepare a physical unit schedule. (2) Compute equivalent units. (3) Compute unit costs. (4) Prepare a cost reconciliation schedule. The production cost report for the Mixing Department is shown in Illustration 3A-12, with the four steps identified in the report.

Illustration 3A-12 Production cost report

Mixing Department Production Cost Report For the Month Ended June 30, 2002		Equivalent Units	
	Physical Units	Materials	Conversion Costs
QUANTITIES	Step 1		Step 2
Units to be accounted for			
Work in process, June 1	100,000		
Started into production	800,000		
Total units	900,000		
Units accounted for			
Completed and transferred out			
Work in process, June 1	100,000	–0–	30,000
Started and completed	600,000	600,000	600,000
Work in process, June 30	200,000	200,000	120,000
Total units	900,000	800,000	750,000

COSTS		Materials	Conversion Costs	Total
Unit costs $\boxed{\text{Step 3}}$				
Costs in June (excluding beginning work in process)	(a)	$400,000	$170,000	$570,000
Equivalent units	(b)	800,000	750,000	
Unit costs [(a) ÷ (b)]		$0.50	$0.227	$0.727
Costs to be accounted for				
Work in process, June 1				$ 85,000
Started into production				570,000
Total costs				$655,000

Cost Reconciliation Schedule $\boxed{\text{Step 4}}$

	Materials	
Costs accounted for		
Transferred out		
Work in process, June 1		$ 85,000
Costs to complete beginning work in process		
Conversion costs (30,000 × $0.227)		6,810
Total costs		91,810
Units started and completed (600,000 × $0.727)		435,950
Total costs transferred out		527,760
Work in process, June 30		
Materials (200,000 × $0.50)	$100,000	
Conversion costs (120,000 × $0.227)	27,240	127,240
Total costs		$655,000

As indicated earlier, production cost reports provide a basis for evaluating the productivity of a department. In addition, the cost data can be used to assess whether unit costs and total costs are reasonable. By comparing the quantity and cost data with predetermined goals, top management can also judge whether current performance is meeting planned objectives.

FIFO AND WEIGHTED-AVERAGE

The weighted-average method of computing equivalent units has **one major advantage:** It is simple to understand and apply. In cases where prices do not fluctuate significantly from period to period, the weighted-average method will be very similar to the FIFO method. In addition, companies that have been using just-in-time procedures effectively for inventory control purposes will have minimal inventory balances, and therefore differences between the weighted-average and the FIFO methods will not be material.

Conceptually, the FIFO method is superior to the weighted-average method because **current performance is measured** using only costs incurred in the current period. Managers are, therefore, not held responsible for costs from prior periods over which they may not have any control. In addition, the FIFO method **provides current cost information**, which can be used to establish **more accurate pricing strategies** for goods manufactured and sold in the current period.

SUMMARY OF STUDY OBJECTIVE FOR APPENDIX 3A

8 *Compute equivalent units using the FIFO method.* Equivalent units under the FIFO method are the sum of the work performed to: (1) Finish the units of beginning work in process inventory, if any; (2) complete the units started into production during the period; and (3) start, but only partially complete, the units in ending work in process inventory.

GLOSSARY

Key Term Matching Activity

Conversion costs   The sum of labor costs and overhead costs. (p. 99)

Cost reconciliation schedule   A schedule that shows that the total costs accounted for equal the total costs to be accounted for. (p. 104)

Equivalent units of production   A measure of the work done during the period, expressed in fully completed units. (p. 97)

Operations costing   A combination of a process cost and a job order cost system, in which products are manufactured primarily by standardized methods, with some customization. (p. 106)

Physical units   Actual units to be accounted for during a period, irrespective of any work performed. (p. 101)

Process cost system   An accounting system used to apply costs to similar products that are mass-produced in a continuous fashion. (p. 90)

Production cost report   An internal report for management that shows both production quantity and cost data for a production department. (p. 99)

Total units (costs) accounted for   The sum of the units (costs) transferred out during the period plus the units (costs) in process at the end of the period. (pp. 101, 104)

Total units (costs) to be accounted for   The sum of the units (costs) started (or transferred) into production during the period plus the units (costs) in process at the beginning of the period. (pp. 101, 104)

Unit production costs   Costs expressed in terms of equivalent units of production. (p. 102)

Weighted-average method   Method used to compute equivalent units of production which considers the degree of completion (weighting) of the units completed and transferred out and the ending work in process. (p. 98)

DEMONSTRATION PROBLEM

eGrade Demonstration Problem

Karlene Industries produces plastic ice cube trays in two processes: heating and stamping. All materials are added at the beginning of the Heating Department. Karlene uses the weighted-average method to compute equivalent units.

On November 1, 1,000 trays that were 70% complete were in process in the Heating Department. During November 12,000 trays were started into production. On November 30, 2,000 trays that were 60% complete were in process.

The following cost information for the Heating Department was also available.

Work in process, November 1		Costs incurred in November	
Materials	$640	Material	$3,000
Conversion costs	360	Labor	2,300
Cost of work in process, Nov. 1	$1,000	Overhead	4,050

Instructions

(a) Prepare a production cost report for the Heating Department for the month of November 2002, using the weighted-average method.
(b) Journalize the transfer of costs to the Stamping Department.

Solution to Demonstration Problem

(a)

KARLENE INDUSTRIES
Heating Department
Production Cost Report
For the Month Ended November 30, 2002

	Physical Units	Equivalent Units Materials	Conversion Costs
QUANTITIES	Step 1		Step 2
Units to be accounted for			
Work in process, November 1	1,000		
Started into production	12,000		
Total units	13,000		
Units accounted for			
Transferred out	11,000	11,000	11,000
Work in process, November 30	2,000	2,000	1,200
Total units	13,000	13,000	12,200

COSTS

Unit costs Step 3		Materials	Conversion Costs	Total
Costs in November	(a)	$3,640	$6,710	$10,350
Equivalent units	(b)	13,000	12,200	
Unit costs [(a) ÷ (b)]		$0.28	$0.55	$0.83
Costs to be accounted for				
Work in process, November 1				$ 1,000
Started into production				9,350
Total costs				$10,350

Cost Reconciliation Schedule Step 4

Costs accounted for			
Transferred out (11,000 × $0.83)			$ 9,130
Work in process, November 30			
Materials (2,000 × $0.28)		$560	
Conversion costs (1,200 × $0.55)		660	1,220
Total costs			$10,350

(b) Work in Process—Stamping		9,130	
Work in Process—Heating			9,130
(To record transfer of units to the Stamping Department)			

THE NAVIGATOR

Note: All asterisked Questions, Exercises, and Problems relate to material in the appendix to the chapter.

SELF-STUDY QUESTIONS

Self-Study/Self-Test

Answers are at the end of the chapter.

(SO 1)   1. Which of the following items is *not* a characteristic of a process cost system?

(a) Once production begins, it continues until the finished product emerges.

(b) The products produced are heterogeneous in nature.

(c) The focus is on continually producing homogeneous products.

(d) When the finished product emerges, all units have precisely the same amount of materials, labor, and overhead.

(SO 2) 2. Indicate which of the following statements is *not* correct.

(a) Both a job order and a process cost system track the same three manufacturing cost elements—direct materials, direct labor, and manufacturing overhead.

(b) In a job order cost system, only one work in process account is used, whereas in a process cost system, multiple work in process accounts are used.

(c) Manufacturing costs are accumulated the same way in a job order and in a process cost system.

(d) Manufacturing costs are assigned the same way in a job order and in a process cost system.

(SO 3) 3. In a process cost system, costs are assigned only:

(a) to one work in process account.

(b) to work in process and finished goods inventory.

(c) to work in process, finished goods, and cost of goods sold.

(d) to work in process accounts.

(SO 4) 4. In making the journal entry to assign raw materials costs:

(a) the debit is to Finished Goods Inventory.

(b) the debit is often to two or more work in process accounts.

(c) the credit is generally to two or more work in process accounts.

(d) the credit is to Finished Goods Inventory.

(SO 5) 5. The Mixing Department's output during the period consists of 20,000 units completed and transferred out, and 5,000 units in ending work in process 60% complete as to materials and conversion costs. Beginning inventory is 1,000 units, 40% complete as to materials and conversion costs. The equivalent units of production are:

(a) 22,600.   (c) 24,000.
(b) 23,000.   (d) 25,000.

(SO 6) 6. In the RYZ Company, there are zero units in beginning work in process, 7,000 units started into production, and 500 units in ending work in process 20% completed. The physical units to be accounted for are:

(a) 7,000.   (c) 7,600.
(b) 7,360.   (d) 7,340.

(SO 6) 7. Mora Company has 2,000 units in beginning work in process, 20% complete as to conversion costs, 23,000 units transferred out to finished goods, and 3,000 units in ending work in process 33⅓% complete as to conversion costs.

The beginning and ending inventory is fully complete as to materials costs. Equivalent units for materials and conversion costs are, respectively:

(a) 22,000, 24,000.
(b) 24,000, 26,000.
(c) 26,000, 24,000.
(d) 26,000, 26,000.

8. Fortner Company has no beginning work (SO 6)
in process; 9,000 units are transferred out and 3,000 units in ending work in process are one-third finished as to conversion costs and fully complete as to materials cost. If total materials cost is $60,000, the unit materials cost is:

(a) $5.00.
(b) $5.45 rounded.
(c) $6.00.
(d) No correct answer is given.

9. Largo Company has unit costs of $10 for ma- (SO 6)
terials and $30 for conversion costs. If there are 2,500 units in ending work in process, 40% complete as to conversion costs, and fully complete as to materials cost, the total cost assignable to the ending work in process inventory is:

(a) $45,000.
(b) $55,000.
(c) $75,000.
(d) $100,000.

10. A production cost report (SO 7)

(a) is an external report.

(b) shows costs charged to a department and costs accounted for.

(c) shows equivalent units of production but not physical units.

(d) contains six sections.

*11. Hollins Company uses the FIFO method to (SO 8)
compute equivalent units. It has 2,000 units in beginning work in process, 20% complete as to conversion costs, 25,000 units started and completed, and 3,000 units in ending work in process, 30% complete as to conversion costs. Equivalent units for materials and conversion costs are, respectively:

(a) 28,000 and 26,600.
(b) 28,000 and 27,500.
(c) 27,000 and 26,200.
(d) 27,000 and 29,600.

*12. KLM Company uses the FIFO method to com- (SO 8)
pute equivalent units. It has no beginning work in process; 9,000 units are started and completed and 3,000 units in ending work in process are one-third completed. If total materials cost is $60,000, the unit materials cost is:

(a) $5.00.
(b) $6.00.
(c) $6.67 (rounded).
(d) No correct answer given.

(SO 8) *13. Toney Company uses the FIFO method to compute equivalent units. It has unit costs of $10 for materials and $30 for conversion costs. If there are 2,500 units in ending work in process, 40% complete as to conversion costs, the total cost assignable to the ending work in process inventory is:
(a) $45,000.   (c) $75,000.
(b) $55,000.   (d) $100,000.

THE NAVIGATOR

QUESTIONS

1. Identify which costing system—job order or process cost—the following companies would use: (a) **Quaker Oats**, (b) **Ford Motor Company**, (c) **Kinko's Print Shop**, and (d) **Warner Bros. Motion Pictures**.

2. Contrast the primary focus of job order cost accounting and of process cost accounting.

3. What are the similarities between a job order and a process cost system?

4. Your roommate is confused about the features of process cost accounting. Identify and explain the distinctive features for your roommate.

5. Tina Turner believes there are no significant differences in the flow of costs between job order cost accounting and process cost accounting. Is Turner correct? Explain.

6. (a) What source documents are used in assigning (1) materials and (2) labor to production?
   (b) What criterion and basis are commonly used in allocating overhead to processes?

7. At Kun Company, overhead is assigned to production departments at the rate of $15 per machine hour. In July, machine hours were 3,000 in the Machining Department and 2,400 in the Assembly Department. Prepare the entry to assign overhead to production.

8. Kent Krause is uncertain about the steps used to prepare a production cost report. State the procedures that are required, in the sequence in which they are performed.

9. Alan Bruski is confused about computing physical units. Explain to Alan how physical units to be accounted for and physical units accounted for are determined.

10. What is meant by the term "equivalent units of production"?

11. How are equivalent units of production computed?

12. Sandy Company had zero units of beginning work in process. During the period, 9,000 units were completed, and there were 600 units of ending work in process. What were the units started into production?

13. Cesska Co. has zero units of beginning work in process. During the period 12,000 units were completed, and there were 600 units of ending work in process one-fifth complete as to conversion cost and 100% complete as to materials cost. What were the equivalent units of production for (a) materials and (b) conversion costs?

14. Hipp Co. started 3,000 units for the period. Its beginning inventory is 800 units one-fourth complete as to conversion costs and 100% complete as to materials costs. Its ending inventory is 400 units one-fifth complete as to conversion costs and 100% complete as to materials costs. How many units were transferred out this period?

15. Gruber Company transfers out 14,000 units and has 2,000 units of ending work in process that are 25% complete. Materials are entered at the beginning of the process and there is no beginning work in process. Assuming unit materials costs of $3 and unit conversion costs of $9, what are the costs to be assigned to units (a) transferred out and (b) in ending work in process?

16. (a) Jane Jelk believes the production cost report is an external report for stockholders. Is Jane correct? Explain.
    (b) Identify the sections in a production cost report.

17. What purposes are served by a production cost report?

18. At Apex Company, there are 800 units of ending work in process that are 100% complete as to materials and 40% complete as to conversion costs. If the unit cost of materials is $4 and the costs assigned to the 800 units is $6,600, what is the per-unit conversion cost?

19. What is the difference between operations costing and a process costing system?

20. How does a company decide whether to use a job order or a process cost system?

*21. Sielert Co. started and completed 2,000 units for the period. Its beginning inventory is 600 units one-fourth complete and its ending inventory is 400 units one-fifth complete. Sielert uses the FIFO method to compute equivalent units. How many units were transferred out this period?

*22. Osgood Company transfers out 12,000 units and has 2,000 units of ending work in process that are 25% complete. Materials are entered at the beginning of the process and there is no beginning work in process. Osgood uses the FIFO method to compute equivalent units. Assuming unit materials costs of $3 and unit conversion costs of $9, what are the costs to be assigned to units (a) transferred out and (b) in ending work in process?

BRIEF EXERCISES

*Journalize entries for accu-
mulating costs.*
(SO 4)

BE3-1   Table Manufacturing purchases $50,000 of raw materials on account, and it incurs $40,000 of factory labor costs. Journalize the two transactions on March 31 assuming the labor costs are not paid until April.

*Journalize the assignment of
materials and labor costs.*
(SO 4)

BE3-2   Data for Table Manufacturing are given in BE3-1. Supporting records show that (a) the Assembly Department used $24,000 of raw materials and $28,000 of the factory labor, and (b) the Finishing Department used the remainder. Journalize the assignment of the costs to the processing departments on March 31.

*Journalize the assignment of
overhead costs.*
(SO 4)

BE3-3   Factory labor data for Table Manufacturing are given in BE3-2. Manufacturing overhead is assigned to departments on the basis of 200% of labor costs. Journalize the assignment of overhead to the Assembly and Finishing Departments.

*Compute physical units of
production.*
(SO 6)

BE3-4   Burrand Manufacturing Company has the following production data for selected months.

			Ending Work in Process	
Month	**Beginning Work in Process**	**Units Transferred Out**	**Units**	**% Complete as to Conversion Cost**
January	–0–	30,000	5,000	40%
March	–0–	40,000	4,000	75
July	–0–	40,000	10,000	25

Compute the physical units for each month.

*Compute equivalent units of
production.*
(SO 5)

BE3-5   Using the data in BE3-4, compute equivalent units of production for materials and conversion costs, assuming materials are entered at the beginning of the process.

*Compute unit costs of
production.*
(SO 6)

BE3-6   In Caroline Company, total material costs are $48,000, and total conversion costs are $60,000. Equivalent units of production are materials 10,000 and conversion costs 12,000. Compute the unit costs for materials, conversion costs, and total manufacturing costs.

*Assign costs to units trans-
ferred out and in process.*
(SO 6)

BE3-7   Sota Company has the following production data for April: units transferred out 40,000, and ending work in process 5,000 units that are 100% complete for materials and 40% complete for conversion costs. If unit materials cost is $8 and unit conversion cost is $12, determine the costs to be assigned to the units transferred out and the units in ending work in process.

Compute unit costs.
(SO 6)

BE3-8   Production costs chargeable to the Finishing Department in June in Madlock Company are materials $9,000, labor $20,000, overhead $18,000. Equivalent units of production are materials 20,000 and conversion costs 19,000. Compute the unit costs for materials and conversion costs.

*Prepare cost reconciliation
schedule.*
(SO 6)

BE3-9   Data for Madlock Company are given in BE3-8. Production records indicate that 18,000 units were transferred out, and 2,000 units in ending work in process were 50% complete as to conversion cost and 100% complete as to materials. Prepare a cost reconciliation schedule.

*Compute equivalent units of
production.*
(SO 5)

BE3-10   The Smelting Department of Darlinda Manufacturing Company has the following production and cost data for November.
> Production: Beginning work in process 2,000 units that are 100% complete as to materials and 20% complete as to conversion costs; units transferred out 8,000 units; and ending work in process 2,000 units that are 100% complete as to materials and 40% complete as to conversion costs.

Compute the equivalent units of production for (a) materials and (b) conversion costs for the month of November.

*Assign costs to units trans-
ferred out and in process.*
(SO 6, 8)

***BE 3-11**   Motta Company has the following production data for April: units started and completed 40,000, and ending work in process 5,000 units that are 100% complete for materials and 40% complete for conversion costs. Motta uses the FIFO method to compute equivalent units. If unit materials cost is $8 and unit conversion cost is $12, determine the costs to be assigned to the units transferred out and the units in ending work in process. The total costs to be assigned are $864,000.

*BE 3-12   Using the data in BE3-11, prepare the cost section of the production cost report for Motta Company.

*BE 3-13   Production costs chargeable to the Finishing Department in June in Berger Company are materials $8,000, labor $20,000, overhead $18,000, and transferred-in costs $72,000. Equivalent units of production are materials 20,000 and conversion costs 19,000. Berger uses the FIFO method to compute equivalent units. Compute the unit costs for materials and conversion costs. Transferred-in costs are considered materials costs.

Prepare a partial production cost report.
(SO 7, 8)
Compute unit costs.
(SO 8)

EXERCISES

E3-1   Mary Lou Company manufactures pizza sauce through two production departments: Cooking and Canning. In each process, materials and conversion costs are incurred evenly throughout the process. For the month of April, the work in process accounts show the following debits.

Journalize transactions.
(SO 3, 4)

	Cooking	Canning
Beginning work in process	$ –0–	$ 4,000
Materials	15,000	6,000
Labor	8,500	7,000
Overhead	29,500	21,800
Costs transferred in		45,000

Instructions
Journalize the April transactions.

E3-2   Yellowknife Manufacturing Company has two production departments: Cutting and Assembly. July 1 inventories are Raw Materials $4,200, Work in Process—Cutting $2,900, Work in Process—Assembly $10,600, and Finished Goods $31,000. During July, the following transactions occurred.

Journalize transactions for two processes.
(SO 4)

1. Purchased $56,300 of raw materials on account.
2. Incurred $56,000 of factory labor. (Credit Wages Payable.)
3. Incurred $70,000 of manufacturing overhead; $36,000 was paid and the remainder is unpaid.
4. Requisitioned materials for Cutting $15,700 and Assembly $8,900.
5. Used factory labor for Cutting $29,000 and Assembly $27,000.
6. Applied overhead at the rate of $20 per machine hour. Machine hours were Cutting 1,640 and Assembly 1,720.
7. Transferred goods costing $77,600 from the Cutting Department to the Assembly Department.
8. Transferred goods costing $134,900 from Assembly to Finished Goods.
9. Sold goods costing $130,000 for $200,000 on account.

Instructions
Journalize the transactions. (Omit explanations.)

E3-3   In Kam Company, materials are entered at the beginning of each process. Work in process inventories, with the percentage of work done on conversion costs, and production data for its Sterilizing Department in selected months during 2002 are as follows.

Compute physical units and equivalent units of production.
(SO 5, 6)

	Beginning Work in Process				Ending Work in Process	
Month	Units	Conversion Cost %	Units Transferred Out		Units	Conversion Cost %
January	–0–	—	7,000		2,000	60
March	–0–	—	12,000		3,000	30
May	–0–	—	16,000		4,000	80
July	–0–	—	10,000		1,500	40

Instructions

(a) Compute the physical units for January and May.

(b) Compute the equivalent units of production for (1) materials and (2) conversion costs for each month.

Determine equivalent units, unit costs, and assignment of costs.
(SO 5, 6)

E3-4   The Cutting Department of Bjerg Manufacturing has the following production and cost data for July.

Production	Costs	
1. Transferred out 8,000 units.	Beginning work in process	$ –0–
2. Started 1,000 units that are 40% complete as to conversion costs and 100% complete as to materials at July 31.	Materials	45,000
	Labor	14,700
	Manufacturing overhead	18,900

Materials are entered at the beginning of the process. Conversion costs are incurred uniformly during the process.

Instructions

(a) Determine the equivalent units of production for (1) materials and (2) conversion costs.

(b) Compute unit costs and prepare a cost reconciliation schedule.

Prepare a production cost report.
(SO 5, 6, 7)

E3-5   The Sanding Department of Copa Furniture Company has the following production and manufacturing cost data for March 2002.

Production: 12,000 units finished and transferred out; 3,000 units started that are 100% complete as to materials and 30% complete as to conversion costs.

Manufacturing costs: Materials $33,000; labor $30,000; overhead $35,790.

Instructions

Prepare a production cost report.

Determine equivalent units, unit costs, and assignment of costs.
(SO 5, 6)

E3-6   The Blending Department of Battle Company has the following cost and production data for the month of April.

Work in process, April 1	
Direct materials: 100% complete	$100,000
Conversion costs: 20% complete	70,000
Cost of work in process, April 1	$170,000
Costs incurred during production in April	
Direct materials	$ 800,000
Conversion costs	350,000
Costs incurred in April	$1,150,000

Units transferred out totaled 8,000. Ending work in process was 1,000 units that are 100% complete as to materials and 40% complete as to conversion costs.

Instructions

(a) Compute the equivalent units of production for (1) materials and (2) conversion costs for the month of April.

(b) Compute the unit costs for the month.

(c) Determine the costs to be assigned to the units transferred out and in ending work in process.

E3-7   The ledger of Tombert Company has the following work in process account.

Answer questions on costs and production.
(SO 3, 5, 6)

Work in Process—Painting

5/1	Balance	3,590	5/31	Transferred out	?
5/31	Materials	6,060			
5/31	Labor	2,500			
5/31	Overhead	1,650			
5/31	Balance	?			

Production records show that there were 700 units in the beginning inventory, 30% complete, 1,100 units started, and 1,300 units transferred out. The beginning work in process had materials cost of $2,040 and conversion costs of $1,550. The units in ending inventory were 40% complete. Materials are entered at the beginning of the painting process.

Instructions
(a) How many units are in process at May 31?
(b) What is the unit materials cost for May?
(c) What is the unit conversion cost for May?
(d) What is the total cost of units transferred out in May?
(e) What is the cost of the May 31 inventory?

E3-8   The Polishing Department of Medina Manufacturing Company has the following production and manufacturing cost data for September. Materials are entered at the beginning of the process.

Compute equivalent units, unit costs, and costs assigned.
(SO 5, 6)

   Production: Beginning inventory 1,600 units that are 100% complete as to materials and 30% complete as to conversion costs; units started during the period are 12,000; ending inventory of 3,000 units 10% complete as to conversion costs.

   Manufacturing costs: Beginning inventory costs, comprised of $20,000 of materials and $43,180 of conversion costs; materials costs added in Polishing during the month, $177,200; labor and overhead applied in Polishing during the month, $100,080 and $257,860, respectively.

Instructions
(a) Compute the equivalent units of production for materials and conversion costs for the month of September.
(b) Compute the unit costs for materials and conversion costs for the month.
(c) Determine the costs to be assigned to the units transferred out and in process.

E3-9   Larry Lair has recently been promoted to production manager, and so he has just started to receive various managerial reports. One of the reports he has received is the production cost report that you prepared. It showed that his department had 1,000 equivalent units in ending inventory. His department has had a history of not keeping enough inventory on hand to meet demand. He has come to you, very angry, and wants to know why you credited him with only 1,000 units when he knows he had at least twice that many on hand.

Explain the production cost report.
(SO 7)

Instructions
Explain to him why his production cost report showed only 1,000 equivalent units in ending inventory. Write an informal memo. Be kind and explain very clearly why he is mistaken.

E3-10   The Welding Department of Tomlin Manufacturing Company has the following production and manufacturing cost data for February 2002. All materials are added at the beginning of the process.

Prepare a production cost report.
(SO 5, 6, 7)

Manufacturing Costs			Production Data	
Beginning work in process			Beginning work in process	15,000 units,
Materials	$18,000			1/10 complete
Conversion costs	14,175	$ 32,175	Units transferred out	49,000
Materials		180,000	Units started	60,000
Labor		35,100	Ending work in process	26,000,
Overhead		64,545		1/5 complete

Instructions

Prepare a production cost report for the Welding Department for the month of February.

Determine equivalent units, unit costs, and assignment of costs.
(SO 4, 5, 6, 8)

*E3-11 The Cutting Department of Cruz Manufacturing has the following production and cost data for July.

Production	Costs	
1. Started and completed 9,000 units.	Beginning work in process	$ –0–
2. Started 1,000 units that are 40%	Materials	45,000
completed at July 31.	Labor	14,000
	Manufacturing overhead	18,900

Materials are entered at the beginning of the process. Conversion costs are incurred uniformly during the process. Cruz Manufacturing uses the FIFO method to compute equivalent units.

Instructions

(a) Determine the equivalent units of production for (1) materials and (2) conversion costs.

(b) Compute unit costs and show the assignment of manufacturing costs to units transferred out and in work in process

Compute equivalent units, unit costs, and costs assigned.
(SO 4, 5, 6, 8)

*E3-12 The Smelting Department of Agler Manufacturing Company has the following production and cost data for November.

Production: Beginning work in process 2,000 units that are 100% complete as to materials and 20% complete as to conversion costs; units started and finished 9,000 units; and ending work in process 1,000 units that are 100% complete as to materials and 40% complete as to conversion costs.

Manufacturing costs: Work in process, November 1, $15,200; materials added $60,000; labor and overhead $121,000.

Agler uses the FIFO method to compute equivalent units.

Instructions

(a) Compute the equivalent units of production for (1) materials and (2) conversion costs for the month of November.

(b) Compute the unit costs for the month.

(c) Determine the costs to be assigned to the units transferred out and in process.

Answer questions on costs and production.
(SO 3, 4, 5, 6, 8)

*E3-13 The ledger of Grogan Company has the following work in process account.

Work in Process—Painting

5/1	Balance	3,680	5/31	Transferred out		?
5/31	Materials	6,600				
5/31	Labor	2,500				
5/31	Overhead	1,400				
5/31	Balance	?				

Production records show that there were 800 units in the beginning inventory, 30% complete, 1,100 units started, and 1,300 units transferred out. The units in ending inventory were 40% complete. Materials are entered at the beginning of the painting process. Grogan uses the FIFO method to compute equivalent units.

Instructions
Answer the following questions.
(a) How many units are in process at May 31?
(b) What is the unit materials cost for May?
(c) What is the unit conversion cost for May?
(d) What is the total cost of units started in April and completed in May?
(e) What is the total cost of units started and finished in May?
(f) What is the cost of the May 31 inventory?

E3-14 The Welding Department of Nagano Manufacturing Company has the following production and manufacturing cost data for February 2002. All materials are added at the beginning of the process. Nagano uses the FIFO method to compute equivalent units.

Prepare a production cost report for a second process. (SO 8)

Manufacturing Costs		Production Data	
Beginning work in process	$ 32,175	Beginning work in process	15,000 units,
Costs transferred in	135,000		1/10 complete
Materials	45,000	Units transferred out	49,000
Labor	35,100	Units transferred in	60,000
Overhead	70,300	Ending work in process	26,000,
			1/5 complete

Instructions
Prepare a production cost report for the Welding Department for the month of February. Transferred-in costs are considered materials costs.

PROBLEMS: SET A

P3-1A Vargas Company manufactures its product, Vitadrink, through two manufacturing processes: Mixing and Packaging. All materials are entered at the beginning of each process. On October 1, 2002, inventories consisted of Raw Materials $26,000, Work in Process—Mixing $0, Work in Process—Packaging $250,000, and Finished Goods $89,000. The beginning inventory for Packaging consisted of 10,000 units that were 50% complete as to conversion costs and fully complete as to materials. During October, 50,000 units were started into production in the Mixing Department and the following transactions were completed.

Journalize transactions. (SO 3, 4)

1. Purchased $400,000 of raw materials on account.
2. Issued raw materials for production: Mixing $210,000 and Packaging $45,000.
3. Incurred labor costs of $238,900.
4. Used factory labor: Mixing $182,500 and Packaging $56,400.
5. Incurred $790,000 of manufacturing overhead on account.
6. Applied manufacturing overhead on the basis of $25 per machine hour. Machine hours were 28,000 in Mixing and 7,000 in Packaging.
7. Transferred 45,000 units from Mixing to Packaging at a cost of $999,000.
8. Transferred 53,000 units from Packaging to Finished Goods at a cost of $1,455,000.
9. Sold goods costing $1,540,000 for $2,500,000 on account.

Instructions
Journalize the October transactions.

P3-2A Zion Company manufactures bowling balls through two processes: Molding and Packaging. In the Molding Department, the urethane, rubber, plastics, and other materials are molded into bowling balls. In the Packaging Department, the balls are placed in cartons and sent to the finished goods warehouse. All materials are entered at the beginning of each process. Labor and manufacturing overhead are incurred uniformly

Complete four steps necessary to prepare a production cost report. (SO 5, 6, 7)

throughout each process. Production and cost data for the Molding Department during June 2002 are presented below.

Production Data	June
Beginning work in process units	–0–
Units started into production	22,000
Ending work in process units	2,000
Percent complete—ending inventory	45%

Cost Data	
Materials	$286,000
Labor	114,000
Overhead	136,800
Total	$536,800

Instructions
(a) Prepare a schedule showing physical units of production.
(b) Determine the equivalent units of production for materials and conversion costs.
(c) Compute the unit costs of production.
(d) Determine the costs to be assigned to the units transferred and in process for June.
(e) Prepare a production cost report for the Molding Department for the month of June.

Complete four steps neces-
sary to prepare a production
cost report.
(SO 5, 6, 7)

P3-3A Stein Industries Inc. manufactures in separate processes furniture for homes. In each process, materials are entered at the beginning, and conversion costs are incurred uniformly. Production and cost data for the first process in making two products in two different manufacturing plants are as follows.

	Cutting Department	
	Plant 1	**Plant 2**
Production Data—July	**T12-Tables**	**C10-Chairs**
Work in process units, July 1	–0–	–0–
Units started into production	20,000	18,000
Work in process units, July 31	1,000	500
Work in process percent complete	60%	80%

Cost Data—July		
Work in process, July 1	$ –0–	$ –0–
Materials	380,000	288,000
Labor	190,000	118,100
Overhead	104,000	96,700
Total	$674,000	$502,800

Instructions
(a) For each plant:
    (1) Compute the physical units of production.
    (2) Compute equivalent units of production for materials and for conversion costs.
    (3) Determine the unit costs of production.
    (4) Show the assignment of costs of units transferred out and in process.
(b) Prepare the production cost report for Plant 1 for July 2002.

Assign costs and prepare
production cost report.
(SO 5, 6, 7)

P3-4A Elite Company has several processing departments. Costs charged to the Assembly Department for November 2002 totaled $2,129,000 as follows.

Work in process, November 1		
Materials	$69,000	
Conversion costs	48,150	$ 117,150
Materials added		1,405,000
Labor		225,920
Overhead		380,930

Production records show that 30,000 units were in beginning work in process 30% complete as to conversion costs, 640,000 units were started into production, and 25,000 units were in ending work in process 40% complete as to conversion costs. Materials are entered at the beginning of each process.

Instructions

(a) Determine the equivalent units of production and the unit costs for the Assembly Department.

(b) Determine the assignment of costs to goods transferred out and in process.

(c) Prepare a production cost report for the Assembly Department.

P3-5A Sprague Company manufactures basketballs. Materials are added at the beginning of the production process and conversion costs are incurred uniformly. Production and cost data for the month of July 2002 are as follows.

Determine equivalent units and unit costs and assign costs.
(SO 5, 6, 7)

Production Data—Basketballs	Units	Percent Complete
Work in process units, July 1	500	60%
Units started into production	1,600	
Work in process units, July 31	600	40%

Cost Data—Basketballs

Work in process, July 1		
Materials	$750	
Conversion costs	600	$1,350
Direct materials		2,400
Direct labor		1,580
Manufacturing overhead		1,300

Instructions

(a) Calculate the following.

(1) The equivalent units of production for materials and conversion.

(2) The unit costs of production for materials and conversion costs.

(3) The assignment of costs to units transferred out and in process at the end of the accounting period.

(b) Prepare a production cost report for the month of July for the basketballs.

P3-6A Taylor Processing Company uses a weighted-average process costing system and manufactures a single product—a premium rug shampoo and cleaner. The manufacturing activity for the month of October has just been completed. A partially completed production cost report for the month of October for the Mixing and Cooking Department is shown below.

Compute equivalent units and complete production cost report.
(SO 5, 7)

TAYLOR PROCESSING COMPANY
Mixing and Cooking Department
Production Cost Report
For the Month Ended October 31

QUANTITIES	Physical Units	Equivalent Units	
		Materials	Conversion Costs
Units to be accounted for			
Work in process, October 1 (all materials, 70% conversion costs)	20,000		
Started into production	160,000		
Total units	180,000		
Units accounted for			
Transferred out	140,000	?	?
Work in process, October 31 (50% materials, 25% conversion costs)	40,000	?	?
Total units accounted for	180,000	?	?

COSTS

Unit costs	Materials	Conversion Costs	Total
Costs in October	$240,000	$90,000	$330,000
Equivalent units	?	?	
Unit costs	$? +	$? =	$?

Costs to be accounted for			
Work in process, October 1			$ 30,000
Started into production			300,000
Total costs			$330,000

Cost Reconciliation Schedule

Costs accounted for		
Transferred out		$?
Work in process, October 31		
Materials	$?	
Conversion costs	?	?
Total costs		$?

Instructions

(a) Prepare a schedule that shows how the equivalent units were computed so that you can complete the "Quantities: Units accounted for" equivalent units section shown in the production cost report above, and compute October unit costs.

(b) Complete the "Cost Reconciliation Schedule" part of the production cost report above.

Determine equivalent units and unit costs, and prepare production cost report.
(SO 8)

eGrade Problem

*P3-7A Nicholas Company manufactures basketballs and soccer balls. For both products, materials are added at the beginning of the production process and conversion costs are incurred uniformly. Nicholas uses the FIFO method to compute equivalent units. Production and cost data for the month of July are as follows.

Production Data—Basketballs	Units	Percent Complete
Work in process units, July 1	500	60%
Units started into production	1,600	
Work in process units, July 31	600	40%

Cost Data—Basketballs	
Work in process, July 1	$1,125
Direct materials	1,600
Direct labor	1,160
Manufacturing overhead	1,000

Production Data—Soccer Balls	Units	Percent Complete
Work in process units, July 1	200	80%
Units started into production	2,000	
Work in process units, July 31	150	70%

Cost Data—Soccer Balls	
Work in process, July 1	$ 450
Direct materials	2,500
Direct labor	1,000
Manufacturing overhead	995

Instructions

(a) Calculate the following for both the basketballs and the soccer balls.
  (1) The equivalent units of production for materials and conversion.
  (2) The unit costs of production for materials and conversion costs.
  (3) The assignment of costs to units transferred out and in process at the end of the accounting period.
(b) Prepare a production cost report for the month of July for the basketballs only.

PROBLEMS: SET B

P3-1B Pepi Company manufactures a nutrient, Everlife, through two manufacturing processes: Blending and Packaging. All materials are entered at the beginning of each process. On August 1, 2002, inventories consisted of Raw Materials $5,000, Work in Process—Blending $0, Work in Process—Packaging $3,945, and Finished Goods $7,500. The beginning inventory for Packaging consisted of 500 units, two-fifths complete as to conversion costs and fully complete as to materials. During August, 9,000 units were started into production in Blending, and the following transactions were completed.

Journalize transactions.
(SO 3, 4)

1. Purchased $25,000 of raw materials on account.
2. Issued raw materials for production: Blending $16,930 and Packaging $7,140.
3. Incurred labor costs of $18,770.
4. Used factory labor: Blending $13,320 and Packaging $5,450.
5. Incurred $41,500 of manufacturing overhead on account.
6. Applied manufacturing overhead at the rate of $35 per machine hour. Machine hours were Blending 900 and Packaging 300.
7. Transferred 8,200 units from Blending to Packaging at a cost of $54,940.
8. Transferred 8,600 units from Packaging to Finished Goods at a cost of $74,490.
9. Sold goods costing $62,000 for $90,000 on account.

Instructions
Journalize the August transactions.

P3-2B Acquatic Corporation manufactures water skis through two processes: Molding and Packaging. In the Molding Department fiberglass is heated and shaped into the form of a ski. In the Packaging Department, the skis are placed in cartons and sent to the finished goods warehouse. Materials are entered at the beginning of both processes. Labor and manufacturing overhead are incurred uniformly throughout each process. Production and cost data for the Molding Department for January 2002 are presented below.

Complete four steps necessary to prepare a production cost report.
(SO 5, 6, 7)

Production Data	January
Beginning work in process units	–0–
Units started into production	42,500
Ending work in process units	2,500
Percent complete—ending inventory	40%

Cost Data	
Materials	$552,500
Labor	117,000
Overhead	170,000
Total	$839,500

Instructions
(a) Compute the physical units of production.
(b) Determine the equivalent units of production for materials and conversion costs.
(c) Compute the unit costs of production.
(d) Determine the costs to be assigned to the units transferred out and in process.
(e) Prepare a production cost report for the Molding Department for the month of January.

Complete four steps neces-
sary to prepare a production
cost report.
(SO 5, 6, 7)

P3-3B Freedo Corporation manufactures in separate processes refrigerators and freezers for homes. In each process, materials are entered at the beginning and conversion costs are incurred uniformly. Production and cost data for the first process in making two products in two different manufacturing plants are as follows.

	Stamping Department	
	Plant A	**Plant B**
Production Data—June	**R12 Refrigerators**	**F24 Freezers**
Work in process units, June 1	–0–	–0–
Units started into production	20,000	20,000
Work in process units, June 30	2,000	2,500
Work in process percent complete	75%	60%
Cost Data—June		
Work in process, June 1	$ –0–	$ –0–
Materials	840,000	700,000
Labor	223,500	251,000
Overhead	420,000	319,000
Total	$1,483,500	$1,270,000

Instructions
(a) For each plant:
  (1) Compute the physical units of production.
  (2) Compute equivalent units of production for materials and for conversion costs.
  (3) Determine the unit costs of production.
  (4) Show the assignment of costs to units transferred out and in process.
(b) Prepare the production cost report for Plant A for June 2002.

Assign costs and prepare pro-
duction cost report.
(SO 5, 6, 7)

P3-4B Wang Company has several processing departments. Costs charged to the Assembly Department for October 2002 totaled $1,347,200 as follows.

Work in process, October 1		
Materials	$29,000	
Conversion costs	26,200	$ 55,200
Materials added		1,071,000
Labor		90,000
Overhead		131,000

Production records show that 25,000 units were in beginning work in process 40% complete as to conversion cost, 415,000 units were started into production, and 35,000 units were in ending work in process 20% complete as to conversion costs. Materials are entered at the beginning of each process.

Instructions
(a) Determine the equivalent units of production and the unit costs for the Assembly Department.
(b) Determine the assignment of costs to goods transferred out and in process.
(c) Prepare a production cost report for the Assembly Department.

Determine equivalent units
and unit costs and assign
costs.
(SO 5, 6, 7)

P3-5B Clemente Company manufactures bicycles and tricycles. For both products, materials are added at the beginning of the production process, and conversion costs are incurred uniformly. Production and cost data for the month of May are as follows.

Production Data—Bicycles	**Units**	**Percent Complete**
Work in process units, May 1	500	80%
Units started in production	1,000	
Work in process units, May 31	600	9.5%

Cost Data—Bicycles

Work in process, May 1		
Materials	$10,000	
Conversion costs	9,280	$19,280
Direct materials		50,000
Direct labor		18,140
Manufacturing overhead		30,000

Instructions
(a) Calculate the following.
   (1) The equivalent units of production for materials and conversion.
   (2) The unit costs of production for materials and conversion costs.
   (3) The assignment of costs to units transferred out and in process at the end of the accounting period.
(b) Prepare a production cost report for the month of May for the bicycles.

P3-6B Magic Cleaner Company uses a weighted-average process costing system and manufactures a single product—an all-purpose liquid cleaner. The manufacturing activity for the month of March has just been completed. A partially completed production cost report for the month of March for the Mixing and Blending Department is shown below.

Compute equivalent units and complete production cost report.
(SO 5, 7)

MAGIC CLEANER COMPANY
Mixing and Blending Department
Production Cost Report
For the Month Ended March 31

QUANTITIES	Physical Units	Materials	Conversion Costs
Units to be accounted for			
Work in process, March 1 (40% materials, 20% conversion costs)	10,000		
Started into production	100,000		
Total units	110,000		
Units accounted for			
Transferred out	95,000	?	?
Work in process, March 31 (2/3 materials, 1/3 conversion costs)	15,000	?	?
Total units accounted for	110,000	?	?

COSTS	Materials	Conversion Costs	Total
Unit costs			
Costs in March	$170,100	$98,000	$268,100
Equivalent units	?	?	
Unit costs	$?	+ $?	= $?
Costs to be accounted for			
Work in process, March 1			$ 15,700
Started into production			252,400
Total costs			$268,100

Cost Reconciliation Schedule

Costs accounted for		
Transferred out		$?
Work in process, March 31		
Materials	$?	
Conversion costs	?	$?
Total costs		$?

Instructions

(a) Prepare a schedule that shows how the equivalent units were computed so that you can complete the "Quantities: Units accounted for" equivalent units section shown in the production cost report above, and compute March unit costs.

(b) Complete the "Cost Reconciliation Schedule" part of the production cost report above.

Determine equivalent units and unit costs and prepare production cost report.
(SO 8)

*P3-7B   Jessica Company manufactures bicycles and tricycles. For both products, materials are added at the beginning of the production process, and conversion costs are incurred uniformly. Jessica Company uses the FIFO method to compute equivalent units. Production and cost data for the month of May are as follows.

Production Data—Bicycles	Units	Percent Complete
Work in process units, May 1	200	80%
Units started into production	1,000	
Work in process units, May 31	300	30%

Cost Data—Bicycles	
Work in process, May 1	$19,280
Direct materials	50,000
Direct labor	18,140
Manufacturing overhead	30,000

Production Data—Tricycles	Units	Percent Complete
Work in process units, May 1	100	75%
Units started into production	800	
Work in process units, May 31	60	25%

Cost Data—Tricycles	
Work in process, May 1	$ 6,125
Direct materials	38,000
Direct labor	15,100
Manufacturing overhead	20,000

Instructions

(a) Calculate the following for both the bicycles and the tricycles.
   (1) The equivalent units of production for materials and conversion.
   (2) The unit costs of production for materials and conversion costs.
   (3) The assignment of costs to units transferred out and in process at the end of the accounting period.

(b) Prepare a production cost report for the month of May for the bicycles only.

GROUP DECISION CASE

BYP3-1 English Bay Beach Company manufactures suntan lotion, called Surtan, in 11-ounce plastic bottles. Surtan is sold in a competitive market. As a result, management is very cost-conscious. Surtan is manufactured through two processes: mixing and filling. Materials are entered at the beginning of each process, and labor and manufacturing overhead occur uniformly throughout each process. Unit costs are based on the cost per gallon of Surtan using the weighted-average costing approach.

On June 30, 2002, Sara Simmons, the chief accountant for the past 20 years, opted to take early retirement. Her replacement, Joe Jacobs, had extensive accounting experience with motels in the area but only limited contact with manufacturing accounting.

During July, Joe correctly accumulated the following production quantity and cost data for the Mixing Department.

> Production quantities: Work in process, July 1, 8,000 gallons 75% complete; started into production 100,000 gallons; work in process, July 31, 5,000 gallons 20% complete. Materials are added at the beginning of the process.
>
> Production costs: Beginning work in process $88,000, comprised of $21,000 of materials costs and $67,000 of conversion costs; incurred in July: materials $600,000, conversion costs $785,800.

Joe then prepared a production cost report on the basis of physical units started into production. His report showed a production cost of $14.738 per gallon of Surtan. The management of English Bay Beach was surprised at the high unit cost. The president comes to you, as Sara's top assistant, to review Joe's report and prepare a correct report if necessary.

Instructions
With the class divided into groups, answer the following questions.
(a) Show how Joe arrived at the unit cost of $14.738 per gallon of Surtan.
(b) What error(s) did Joe make in preparing his production cost report?
(c) Prepare a correct production cost report for July.

MANAGERIAL ANALYSIS

BYP3-2 Logan Furniture Company manufactures living room furniture through two departments: Framing and Upholstering. Materials are entered at the beginning of each process. For May, the following cost data are obtained from the two work in process accounts.

	Framing	**Upholstering**
Work in process, May 1	$ –0–	$?
Materials	420,000	?
Conversion costs	210,000	330,000
Costs transferred in	–0–	550,000
Costs transferred out	550,000	?
Work in process, May 31	80,000	?

Instructions
Answer the following questions.
(a) If 3,000 sofas were started into production on May 1 and 2,500 sofas were transferred to Upholstering, what was the unit cost of materials for May in the Framing Department?

(b) Using the data in (a) above, what was the per unit conversion cost of the sofas transferred to Upholstering?

(c) Continuing the assumptions in (a) above, what is the percentage of completion of the units in process at May 31 in the Framing Department?

REAL-WORLD FOCUS

BYP3-3   General Microwave Corp. is engaged primarily in the design, development, manufacture, and marketing of microwave, electronic, and fiber-optic test equipment, components, and subsystems. A substantial portion of the company's microwave product is sold to manufacturers and users of microwave systems and equipment for applications in the defense electronics industry.

General Microwave Corp. reports the following information in one of the notes to its financial statements.

GENERAL MICROWAVE CORPORATION
Notes to the Financial Statement

Work in process inventory reflects all accumulated production costs, which are comprised of direct production costs and overhead, reduced by amounts attributable to units delivered. Work in process inventory is reduced to its estimated net realizable value by a charge to cost of sales in the period [in which] excess costs are identified. Raw materials and finished goods inventories are reflected at the lower of cost or market.

Instructions

(a) What types of manufacturing costs are accumulated in the work in process inventory account?

(b) What types of information must General Microwave have to be able to compute equivalent units of production?

(c) How does General Microwave assign costs to the units transferred out of work in process that are completed?

EXPLORING THE WEB

BYP3-4   Search the Internet and find the Web sites of two manufacturers that you think are likely to use process costing. Are there any specifics included in their Web sites that confirm the use of process costing for each of these companies?

COMMUNICATION ACTIVITY

BYP3-5   Catherine Harper was a good friend of yours in high school and is from your home town. While you chose to major in accounting when you both went away to college, she majored in marketing and management. You have recently been promoted to accounting manager for the Snack Foods Division of Clark Enterprises, and your friend was promoted to regional sales manager for the same division of Clark. Catherine recently telephoned you. She explained that she was familiar with job cost sheets, which had been used by the Special Projects division where she had formerly worked. She was, however, very uncomfortable with the production cost reports prepared by your division. She faxed you a list of her particular questions. These included the following.

1. Since Clark occasionally prepares snack foods for special orders in the Snack Foods Division, why don't we track costs of the orders separately?
2. What is an equivalent unit?
3. Why am I getting four production cost reports? Isn't there only one Work in Process account?

Instructions

Prepare a memo to Catherine. Answer her questions, and include any additional information you think would be helpful. You may write informally, but be careful to use proper grammar and punctuation.

ETHICS CASE

BYP3-6   R. B. Robin Company manufactures a high-tech component that passes through two production processing departments, Molding and Assembly. Department managers are partially compensated on the basis of units of products completed and transferred out relative to units of product put into production. This was intended as encouragement to be efficient and to minimize waste.

Barb Crusmer is the department head in the Molding Department, and Wayne Terrago is her quality control inspector. During the month of June, Barb had three new employees who were not yet technically skilled. As a result, many of the units produced in June had minor molding defects. In order to maintain the department's normal high rate of completion, Barb told Wayne to pass through inspection and on to the Assembly Department all units that had defects nondetectable to the human eye. "Company and industry tolerances on this product are too high anyway," says Barb. "Less than 2% of the units we produce are subjected in the market to the stress tolerance we've designed into them. The odds of those 2% being any of this month's units are even less. Anyway, we're saving the company money."

Instructions
(a) Who are the potential stakeholders involved in this situation?
(b) What alternatives does Wayne have in this situation? What might the company do to prevent this situation from occurring?

Answers to Self-Study Questions
1. b   2. d   3. c   4. b   5. b   6. a   7. c   8. a   9. b   10. b
11. b   12. a   13. b

Remember to go back to the Navigator box on the chapter-opening page and check off your completed work.

CHAPTER 4

Activity-Based Costing

THE NAVIGATOR ✔

- ■ Scan *Study Objectives* ☐
- ■ Read *Feature Story* ☐
- ■ Read *Preview* ☐
- ■ Read text and answer *Before You Go On*
  p. 148 ☐ p. 156 ☐ p. 160 ☐
- ■ Work *Using the Decision Toolkit* ☐
- ■ Review *Summary of Study Objectives* ☐
- ■ Work *Demonstration Problem* ☐
- ■ Answer *Self-Study Questions* ☐
- ■ Complete *Assignments* ☐

◆ STUDY OBJECTIVES

After studying this chapter, you should be able to:

1 Recognize the difference between traditional costing and activity-based costing.

2 Identify the steps in the development of an activity-based costing system.

3 Know how companies identify the activity cost pools used in activity-based costing.

4 Know how companies identify and use the activity cost drivers in activity-based costing.

5 Understand the benefits and limitations of activity-based costing.

6 Differentiate between value-added and nonvalue-added activities.

7 Apply activity-based costing to service industries.

8 Explain just-in-time (JIT) processing.

THE NAVIGATOR

FEATURE STORY

THE ABCs OF DONUT MAKING— VIRTUAL-REALITY STYLE

Super Bakery, Inc., created in 1990 by former Pittsburgh Steelers' running back Franco Harris, is a nationwide supplier of mineral-, vitamin-, and protein-enriched donuts and other baked goods to the institutional food market, primarily school systems. Super Bakery is a *virtual corporation*, in which only the core, strategic functions of the business are performed inside the company. The remaining activities—selling, manufacturing, warehousing, and shipping—are outsourced to a network of external companies.

Super Bakery draws these cooperating companies together and organizes the work flow. The goal is to add maximum value to the company while making the minimum investment in permanent staff, fixed assets, and working capital. The results are notable: Super Bakery's sales have grown at an average rate of approximately 20 percent during most of its existence.

One of Super Bakery's challenges has been to control the cost of the outsourced activities. Management suspected a wide variation in the cost of serving customers in different parts of the country. Yet its traditional costing methods were spreading costs over the entire customer base. Each customer's order *appeared* to cost the same amount to complete. In actuality, orders with high profit margins were subsidizing orders with low profit margins. Super Bakery desired a system that would more accurately assign the costs of each order. With such a system, pricing could be improved.

The company looked at and eventually changed to a system that could identify the costs associated with the *activities* performed in the business—manufacturing, sales, warehousing, and shipping. The new activity-based costing system showed that the costs and profit margins on each sale vary significantly. Super Bakery is now able to track the profitability of each customer's account and the performance of outsourced activities. This donut maker, as a result, even knows the cost of the donut holes!

Source: Tom R.V. Davis and Bruce L. Darling, "ABC in a Virtual Corporation," *Management Accounting,* Oct. 1996, pp. 18–26.

As indicated in our Feature Story about **Super Bakery, Inc.,** the traditional costing systems described in earlier chapters are not the best answer for every company. Because Super Bakery suspected that the traditional system was masking significant differences in its real cost structure, it sought a new method of assigning costs. Similar searches by other companies for ways to improve operations and gather more accurate data for decision-making have resulted in the development of powerful new management tools, including **activity-based costing (ABC)** and **just-in-time (JIT) processing**. The primary objective of this chapter is to explain and illustrate activity-based costing. A brief overview of just-in-time processing is presented at the end of the chapter.

The content and organization of this chapter are as follows.

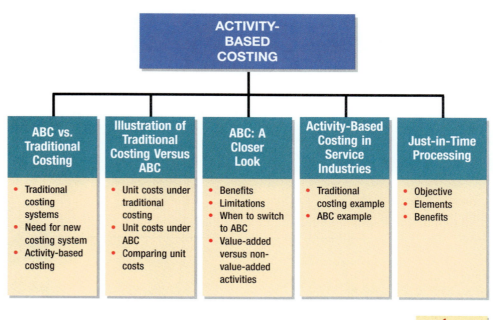

ACTIVITY-BASED COSTING VERSUS TRADITIONAL COSTING

TRADITIONAL COSTING SYSTEMS

STUDY OBJECTIVE
1
Recognize the difference between traditional costing and activity-based costing.

It is probably impossible to determine the **exact** cost of a product or service. However, in order to achieve improved management decisions, every effort to provide decision makers with the best possible cost estimates must be made. The best estimate of product cost occurs when the costs are traceable directly to the product produced or the service provided. Direct material and direct labor costs are the easiest to trace directly to the product through the use of material requisition forms and payroll time sheets. Overhead costs, on the other hand, are an indirect or common cost that generally cannot be easily or directly traced to individual products or services. Instead, we use estimates to assign overhead costs to products and services.

Often the most difficult part of computing accurate unit costs is determining the proper amount of **overhead cost** to assign to each product, service, or job. In our coverage of job order costing in Chapter 2 and of process costing in Chapter 3, we used a single or plantwide overhead rate throughout the year for the entire factory operation. That rate was called the **predetermined overhead rate.** For job order costing we assumed that **direct labor cost** was the relevant activity base for assigning all overhead costs to jobs. For process costing, we assumed that **machine hours** was the relevant activity base for assigning all overhead to the process or department.

Those assumptions made sense when overhead cost allocation systems were first developed. At that time, direct labor made up a large portion of total manufacturing cost. Therefore, it was widely accepted that there was a high correlation between direct labor and the incurrence of overhead cost. As a result, direct labor became the most popular basis for allocating overhead.

Even in today's increasingly automated environment, direct labor is often the appropriate basis for assigning overhead cost to products. It is appropriate to use direct labor when (a) direct labor constitutes a significant part of total product cost, and (b) a high correlation exists between direct labor and changes in the amount of overhead costs. A simplified (one-stage) traditional costing system relying on direct labor to assign overhead is displayed in Illustration 4-1.

THE NEED FOR A NEW COSTING SYSTEM

The last decade brought tremendous change to manufacturers and service providers. Advances in computerized systems, technological innovation, global competition, and automation have changed the manufacturing environment drastically. As a result, the amount of direct labor used in many industries has greatly decreased, and total overhead costs resulting from depreciation on expensive equipment and machinery, utilities, repairs, and maintenance have significantly increased. When the correlation between direct labor and overhead no longer exists, it is inappropriate to continue to use plantwide predetermined overhead rates based on direct labor. Companies that continue to use such overhead rates based on direct labor when this correlation does not exist experience significant product cost distortions.

Illustration 4-1 Traditional one-stage costing system

Recognizing these distortions, many companies now use machine hours as the basis on which to allocate overhead in an automated manufacturing environment. But even machine hours may not suffice as the only plantwide basis for allocating all overhead. If the manufacturing process is complex, then only multiple allocation bases can result in more accurate product-cost computations. In such situations, managers need to consider a new overhead cost allocation method that uses multiple bases. That method is **activity-based costing**.

ACTIVITY-BASED COSTING

Activities and Cost Drivers

Activity-based costing (ABC) allocates overhead to multiple activity cost pools, and it then assigns the activity cost pools to products by means of cost drivers. In activity-based costing, an **activity** is any event, action, transaction, or work sequence that incurs cost when producing a product or providing a service. A **cost driver** is any factor or activity that has a direct cause–effect relationship with the resources consumed.

ABC first allocates costs to activity cost pools and then to the products based on each product's use of those activities. The reasoning behind ABC cost allocation is simple: **Products consume activities; activities consume resources.**

ABC allocates overhead in a two-stage process. In the first stage, overhead costs are allocated to **activity cost pools**, rather than to departments. Each cost pool is a distinct type of activity (e.g., ordering materials, setting up machines, assembling, and inspecting). In the second stage, the overhead allocated to the activity cost pools is assigned to products using **cost drivers**. The cost drivers measure the number of individual activities undertaken or performed (e.g., number of purchase orders, number of setups, labor hours, or number of inspections) to produce products or provide services. Examples of activities and the possible cost drivers that measure them are shown in Illustration 4-2 for a company that manufactures two products—axles and steering wheels.

Illustration 4-2   Activities and related cost drivers

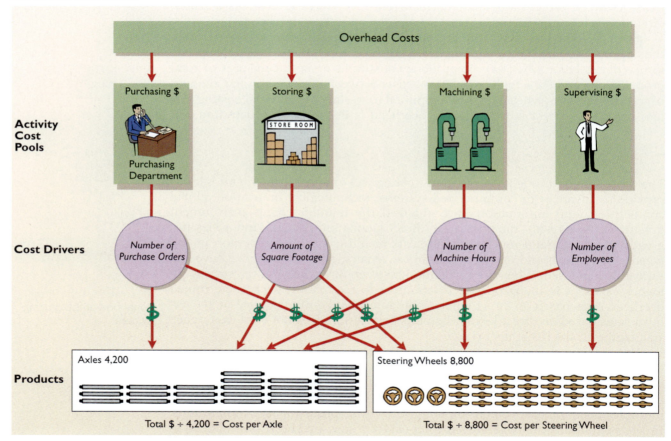

In the first step (as shown at the top of the illustration), the company's overhead costs are allocated to activity cost pools. In this simplified example, four activity cost pools have been identified: purchasing, storing, machining, and supervising. After the costs are allocated to the activity cost pools, costs are assigned to the individual products (either axles or steering wheels) based on each product's use of each activity as measured by the cost drivers. For example, if axles require more activity by the purchasing department, as measured by the number of required purchase orders, then more of the overhead cost from the purchasing pool will be allocated to the axles.

As you might imagine, not all products or services share equally in these activities. The more complex a product's manufacturing operation, the more activities and cost drivers it is likely to have. If there is little or no correlation between changes in the cost driver and consumption of the overhead cost, inaccurate product costs are inevitable.

The design of a more complex activity-based costing system with seven activity cost pools is graphically shown in Illustration 4-3 for Lift Jack Company. Lift Jack Company manufactures two automotive jacks—an automobile scissors jack and a truck hydraulic jack.

Illustration 4-3 ABC system design—Lift Jack Company

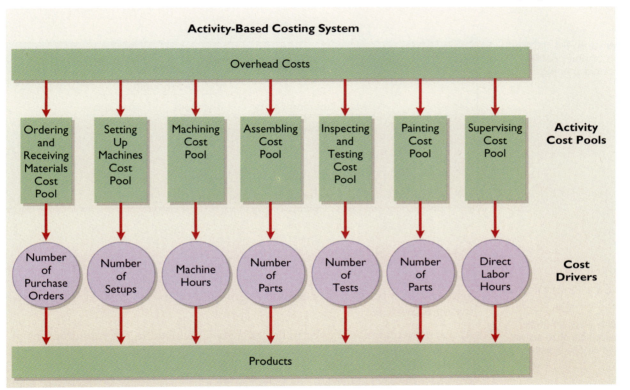

The Lift Jack Company illustration contains seven activity cost pools. In some companies the number of activities related to a cost pool can be substantial. For example, at **Clark-Hurth** (a division of **Clark Equipment Company**), a manufacturer of axles and transmissions, over 170 activities were identified; at **Compumotor** (a division of **Parker Hannifin**) over 80 activities were identified in just the procurement function of its Material Control Department.

Helpful Hint Computers alleviate the problems of huge numbers of activities and are delivering the potential of ABC to improve product costing.

ILLUSTRATION OF TRADITIONAL COSTING VERSUS ABC

In this section we present a simple case example that compares traditional costing and activity-based costing and illustrates how ABC eliminates the distortion that can occur in traditional overhead cost allocation.

UNIT COSTS UNDER TRADITIONAL COSTING

Atlas Company produces two automobile antitheft devices, The Boot and The Club. The Boot is a high-volume item totaling 25,000 units annually. The Club is a low-volume item totaling only 5,000 units per year. Each product requires one hour of direct labor for completion. Therefore, total annual direct labor hours are 30,000 (25,000 + 5,000). Expected annual manufacturing overhead costs are $900,000. Thus, the predetermined overhead rate is $30 ($900,000 ÷ 30,000) per direct labor hour.

The direct materials cost per unit is $40 for The Boot and $30 for The Club. The direct labor cost is $12 per unit for each product. The computation of the unit cost for The Boot and The Club under traditional costing is shown in Illustration 4-4.

Illustration 4-4 Computation of unit costs—traditional costing

ATLAS COMPANY

	Products	
Manufacturing Costs	The Boot	The Club
Direct materials	$40	$30
Direct labor	12	12
Overhead	30*	30*
Total unit cost	$82	$72

*Predetermined overhead rate times direct labor hours ($30 × 1 hr. = $30).

UNIT COSTS UNDER ABC

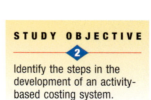

STUDY OBJECTIVE
2
Identify the steps in the development of an activity-based costing system.

Let's now calculate unit costs under ABC, in order to compare activity-based costing with a traditional costing system. Activity-based costing involves the following four steps.

1. Identify and classify the major activities involved in the manufacture of specific products, and allocate manufacturing overhead costs to the appropriate activity cost pools.
2. Identify the cost driver that has a strong correlation to the costs accumulated in the activity cost pool.
3. Compute the activity-based overhead rate per cost driver.
4. Assign manufacturing overhead costs for each activity cost pool to products, using the activity-based overhead rates (cost per driver).

Step 1—Identify and Classify Activities and Allocate Overhead to Cost Pools

STUDY OBJECTIVE
3
Know how companies identify the activity cost pools used in activity-based costing.

A well-designed activity-based costing system starts with an analysis of the activities performed to manufacture a product or provide a service. This analysis should identify all resource-consuming activities. It requires a detailed, step-by-step walk-through of each operation, documenting every activity undertaken to accomplish a task. Atlas Company identified three activity-cost pools: setting up machines, machining, and inspecting.

Next, overhead costs are assigned directly to the appropriate activity cost pool. For example, all overhead costs directly associated with Atlas Company's machine setups (such as salaries, supplies, and depreciation) would be assigned to the machine setup cost pool. These activity cost pools, along with the estimated overhead allocated to each activity cost pool, are shown in Illustration 4-5.

Illustration of Traditional Costing versus ABC

ATLAS COMPANY

Activity Cost Pools	Estimated Overhead
Setting up machines	$300,000
Machining	500,000
Inspecting	100,000
Total	$ 900,000

Illustration 4-5 Activity cost pools and estimated overhead

Step 2—Identify Cost Drivers

After costs are allocated to the activity cost pools, the cost drivers for each activity cost pool must be identified. The cost driver must accurately measure the actual consumption of the activity by the various products. To achieve accurate costing, a **high degree of correlation** must exist between the activity cost driver and the actual consumption of the overhead costs in the activity cost pool.

The cost drivers identified by Atlas and their total expected use per activity cost pool are shown in Illustration 4-6.

STUDY OBJECTIVE

4

Know how companies identify and use the activity cost drivers in activity-based costing.

ATLAS COMPANY

Activity Cost Pools	Cost Drivers	Expected Use of Cost Drivers per Activity
Setting up machines	Number of setups	1,500 setups
Machining	Machine hours	50,000 machine hours
Inspecting	Number of inspections	2,000 inspections

Illustration 4-6 Cost drivers and their expected use

Availability and ease of obtaining data relating to the activity cost driver is an important factor that must be considered in its selection.

Step 3—Compute Overhead Rates

Next, an **activity-based overhead rate** per cost driver is computed by dividing the estimated overhead per activity by the number of cost drivers expected to be used per activity. The formula for this computation is shown in Illustration 4-7.

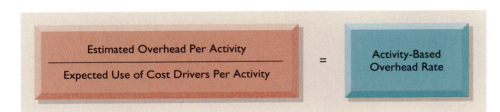

$$\frac{\text{Estimated Overhead Per Activity}}{\text{Expected Use of Cost Drivers Per Activity}} = \text{Activity-Based Overhead Rate}$$

Illustration 4-7 Formula for computing activity-based overhead rate

Atlas Company computes its activity-based overhead rates by using total estimated overhead per activity cost pool, shown in Illustration 4-5, and the total expected use of cost drivers per activity, shown in Illustration 4-6. The computations are presented in Illustration 4-8.

Illustration 4-8 Computation of activity-based overhead rates

	ATLAS COMPANY			
Activity Cost Pools	Estimated Overhead	÷ Expected Use of Cost Drivers per Activity	=	Activity-Based Overhead Rates
Setting up machines	$300,000	1,500 setups		$200 per setup
Machining	500,000	50,000 machine hours		$10 per machine hour
Inspecting	100,000	2,000 inspections		$50 per inspection
Total	$900,000			

Step 4—Assign Overhead Costs to Products under ABC

In assigning overhead costs, it is necessary to know the expected use of cost drivers **for each product**. Because of its low volume, The Club requires more setups and inspections than The Boot. The expected use of cost drivers per product for each of Atlas's products is shown in Illustration 4-9.

Illustration 4-9 Expected use of cost drivers per product

		ATLAS COMPANY	Expected Use of Cost Drivers per Product	
Activity Cost Pools	Cost Drivers	Expected Use of Cost Drivers per Activity	The Boot	The Club
Setting up machines	Number of setups	1,500 setups	500	1,000
Machining	Machine hours	50,000 machine hours	30,000	20,000
Inspecting	Number of inspections	2,000 inspections	500	1,500

To assign overhead costs to each product, the activity-based overhead rates per cost driver (Illustration 4-8) are multiplied by the number of cost drivers expected to be used per product (Illustration 4-9). The amount of overhead cost assigned to each product for Atlas Company is shown in Illustration 4-10.

Illustration 4-10 Assignment of activity cost pools to products

	ATLAS COMPANY					
	The Boot			The Club		
Activity Cost Pools	Expected Use of Cost Drivers per Product ×	Activity-Based Overhead Rates	Cost = Assigned	Expected Use of Cost Drivers per Product ×	Activity-Based Overhead Rates	Cost = Assigned
Setting up machines	500	$200	$100,000	1,000	$200	$200,000
Machining	30,000	$10	300,000	20,000	$10	200,000
Inspecting	500	$50	25,000	1,500	$50	75,000
Total assigned costs [(a)]			$425,000			$475,000
Units produced [(b)]			25,000			5,000
Overhead cost per unit [(a) ÷ (b)]			$17			$95

These data show that under ABC, overhead costs are shifted from the high-volume product (The Boot) to the low-volume product (The Club). This shift results in more accurate costing for two reasons:

1. Low-volume products often require more special handling, such as more machine setups and inspections, than high-volume products. This is true for Atlas Company. Thus, the low-volume product frequently is responsible for more overhead costs per unit than is a high-volume product.[1]
2. Assigning overhead using ABC will usually increase the cost per unit for low-volume products. Therefore, a traditional overhead allocation such as direct labor hours is usually a poor cost driver for assigning overhead costs to low-volume products.

COMPARING UNIT COSTS

A comparison of unit manufacturing costs under traditional costing and ABC shows the following significant differences.

Illustration 4-11 Comparison of unit product costs

ATLAS COMPANY

Manufacturing Costs	The Boot — Traditional Costing	The Boot — ABC	The Club — Traditional Costing	The Club — ABC
Direct materials	$40	$40	$30	$30
Direct labor	12	12	12	12
Overhead	30	17	30	95
Total cost per unit	$82	$69	$72	$137

Overstated $13   Understated $65

The comparison shows that unit costs under traditional costing are significantly distorted. The cost of producing The Boot is overstated $13 per unit ($82 − $69), and the cost of producing The Club is understated $65 per unit ($137 − $72). These differences are attributable entirely to how manufacturing overhead is assigned. A likely consequence of the differences in assigning overhead is that Atlas Company has been overpricing The Boot and possibly losing market share to competitors. Moreover, it has been sacrificing profitability by underpricing The Club.

---

[1]Robin Cooper and Robert S. Kaplan, "How Cost Accounting Distorts Product Costs," *Management Accounting* 69, No. 10 (April 1988), pp. 20–27.

International Perspective

Activity-based costing was pioneered in the United States: **John Deere Company** coined the term less than 25 years ago. Although ABC has been adopted by numerous well-known U.S. companies including **IBM**, **AT&T**, **Hewlett-Packard**, **Procter and Gamble**, **Tektronix**, **Hughes Aircraft**, **Caterpillar**, **American Express**, and **Compaq Computer**, its use outside the U.S. is limited. The cost of implementation may discourage some foreign companies.

In Japan, where activity-based costing is less used, companies prefer volume measures such as direct labor hours to assign overhead cost to products. Japanese managers are convinced that reducing direct labor is essential to continuous cost reduction. And, using direct labor as the basis for overhead allocation forces Japanese companies to watch direct labor more closely. Possibly, labor cost reduction is more of a priority than developing more accurate product costs.

BEFORE YOU GO ON . . .

◆ Review It

1. Historically, why has direct labor hours been the most popular basis for allocating overhead costs to products?
2. What changes have occurred in the industrial environment to diminish the appeal of traditional volume-based overhead allocation systems?
3. What four steps are involved in developing an ABC system?

◆ Do It

Lift Jack Company, as shown in Illustration 4-3, page 143, has seven activity cost pools and two products. It expects to produce 200,000 units of its automobile scissors jack, and 80,000 units of its truck hydraulic jack. Having identified its activity cost pools and the cost drivers for each cost pool, Lift Jack Company accumulated the following data relative to those activity cost pools and cost drivers.

LIFT JACK COMPANY

Activity Cost Pools	Cost Drivers	Estimated Overhead	Expected Use of Cost Drivers per Activity	Scissors Jacks	Hydraulic Jacks
	Annual Overhead Data			Expected Use of Cost Drivers per Product	
Ordering and receiving	Purchase orders	$ 200,000	2,500 orders	1,000	1,500
Machine setup	Setups	600,000	1,200 setups	500	700
Machining	Machine hours	2,000,000	800,000 hours	300,000	500,000
Assembling	Parts	1,800,000	3,000,000 parts	1,800,000	1,200,000
Inspecting and testing	Inspections	700,000	35,000 inspections	20,000	15,000
Painting	Parts	300,000	3,000,000 parts	1,800,000	1,200,000
Supervising	Labor hours	1,200,000	200,000 hours	130,000	70,000
		$6,800,000			

Using the above data, do the following: (a) Prepare a schedule showing the computations of the activity-based overhead rates per cost driver. (b) Prepare a schedule assigning each activity's overhead cost to the two products. (c) Compute the overhead cost per unit for each product. (d) Comment on the comparative overhead cost per unit.

Action Plan

* Determine the activity-based overhead rate by dividing the estimated overhead per activity by the expected use of cost drivers per activity.
* Assign the overhead of each activity cost pool to the individual products by multiplying the expected use of cost driver per product times the activity-based overhead rate.
* Determine overhead cost per unit by dividing the overhead assigned to each product by the number of units of that product.

Solution

(a) Computations of activity-based overhead rates per cost driver:

LIFT JACK COMPANY

Activity Cost Pools	Estimated Overhead	÷	Expected Use of Cost Drivers per Activity	=	Activity-Based Overhead Rates
Ordering and receiving	$ 200,000		2,500 purchase orders		$80 per order
Machine setup	600,000		1,200 setups		$500 per setup
Machining	2,000,000		800,000 machine hours		$2.50 per machine hour
Assembling	1,800,000		3,000,000 parts		$0.60 per part
Inspecting and testing	700,000		35,000 inspections		$20 per inspection
Painting	300,000		3,000,000 parts		$0.10 per part
Supervising	1,200,000		200,000 labor hours		$6 per labor hour
	$6,800,000				

(b) Assignment of each activity's overhead cost to products using ABC:

LIFT JACK COMPANY

Activity Cost Pools	Scissors Jacks Expected Use of Cost Drivers per Product ×	Scissors Jacks Activity-Based Overhead Rates	Scissors Jacks Cost = Assigned	Hydraulic Jacks Expected Use of Cost Drivers per Product ×	Hydraulic Jacks Activity-Based Overhead Rates	Hydraulic Jacks Cost = Assigned
Ordering and receiving	1,000	$80	$ 80,000	1,500	$80	$ 120,000
Machine setup	500	$500	250,000	700	$500	350,000
Machining	300,000	$2.50	750,000	500,000	$2.50	1,250,000
Assembling	1,800,000	$0.60	1,080,000	1,200,000	$0.60	720,000
Inspecting and testing	20,000	$20	400,000	15,000	$20	300,000
Painting	1,800,000	$0.10	180,000	1,200,000	$0.10	120,000
Supervising	130,000	$6	780,000	70,000	$6	420,000
Total assigned costs			$3,520,000			$3,280,000

(c)

	Scissors Jack	Hydraulic Jack
Total costs assigned	$3,520,000	$3,280,000
Total units produced	200,000	80,000
Overhead cost per unit	$17.60	$41.00

(d) These data show that the total overhead assigned to 80,000 hydraulic jacks is nearly as great as the overhead assigned to 200,000 scissors jacks. However, the overhead cost per hydraulic jack is $41.00. It is only $17.60 per scissors jack.

Related exercise material: BE4-1, BE4-2, BE4-3, BE4-4, BE4-5, E4-1, E4-2, E4-3, E4-4, E4-5, E4-6, E4-7, and E4-8.

ACTIVITY-BASED COSTING: A CLOSER LOOK

As the use of activity-based costing has grown, both its practical benefits and its limitations have now become apparent.

BENEFITS OF ABC

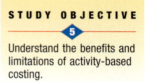

The primary benefit of ABC is **more accurate product costing**. Here's why:

1. **ABC leads to more cost pools** used to assign overhead costs to products. Instead of one plantwide pool (or even departmental pools) and a single cost driver, numerous activity cost pools with more relevant cost drivers are utilized. Costs are assigned more directly on the basis of the number of cost drivers used to produce each product.

2. **ABC leads to enhanced control over overhead costs.** Under ABC, many overhead costs can be traced directly to activities—some indirect costs can instead be identified as direct costs. Thus, managers have become more aware of their responsibility to control the activities that generate those costs.

3. **ABC leads to better management decisions.** More accurate product costing should contribute to setting selling prices that can help achieve desired product profitability levels. In addition, the more accurate cost data could be helpful in deciding whether to make or buy a product part or component, and sometimes even whether to eliminate a product.

In fact, the determination of what activities drive costs has led to some costs, which were previously accounted for as indirect costs, being accounted for as direct costs. This is because, under ABC, these costs are traceable to specific activities.

Activity-based costing does not change the amount of overhead costs. What it does do, in certain circumstances, is to allocate those overhead costs in a more accurate manner. Furthermore, if the score-keeping is more realistic, more accurate, and better understood, managers should be able to better understand cost behavior and overall profitability.

LIMITATIONS OF ABC

Although ABC systems often provide better product cost data than traditional volume-based systems, there are limitations:

1. **ABC can be expensive to use.** Many companies are discouraged from using ABC by the increased cost of identifying multiple activities and applying numerous cost drivers. Activity-based costing systems are more complex than traditional costing systems—sometimes significantly more complex. So companies must ask, is the cost of implementation greater than the benefits of greater accuracy? Sometimes it may be. For some companies there may be no need to consider ABC at all because their existing system is sufficient. If the costs of ABC outweigh the benefits, then the company should not implement ABC.

2. **Some arbitrary allocations continue.** Even though more overhead costs can be assigned directly to products through ABC's multiple activity cost pools, certain overhead costs remain to be allocated by means of some arbitrary volume-based cost driver such as labor or machine hours.

BUSINESS INSIGHT
Service Company Perspective

Although most publicized ABC applications are in manufacturing companies or large service firms, ABC can be applied in a very small service business. **Mahany Welding Supply**, a small family-run welding service business in Rochester, NY, applied ABC to determine the cost of servicing customers and to identify feasible cost reduction opportunities.

Application of ABC at Mahany Welding's operations provided information about the five employees who are involved in different activities of revenue generation—i.e., delivery of supplies (rural versus city), welding services, repairs, telephone sales, field or door-to-door sales, repeat business sales, and cold-call sales. Activity cost pools were assigned to the five revenue-producing employees using relevant cost drivers. ABC revealed annual net income (loss) by employee as follows: Employee #1, $65,431; Employee #2, $35,154; Employee #3, $13,731; Employee #4, ($10,957); Employee #5, ($46,180). This comparative information was an eye-opener to the owner of Mahany Welding—who was Employee #5!

Source: Michael Krupnicki and Thomas Tyson, "Using ABC to Determine the Cost of Servicing Customers," *Management Accounting*, December 31, 1997, pp. 40–46.

WHEN TO SWITCH TO ABC

Activity-based costing is a useful tool and under certain conditions is the appropriate costing system to use. How does a company know when to switch to ABC? The presence of one or more of the following factors would point to ABC as the superior costing system:

1. Product lines differ greatly in volume and manufacturing complexity.
2. Product lines are numerous, diverse, and require differing degrees of support services.
3. Overhead costs constitute a significant portion of total costs.
4. The manufacturing process or the number of products has changed significantly—for example, from labor-intensive to capital-intensive due to automation.
5. Production or marketing managers are ignoring data provided by the existing system and are instead using "bootleg" costing data or other alternative data when pricing or making other product decisions.

The redesign and installation of a new product-costing system is a significant decision that requires considerable cost and a major effort to accomplish. Therefore, financial managers need to be very cautious and deliberative when initiating changes in costing systems. A key factor in implementing a successful ABC system is the support of top management.

DECISION TOOLKIT

Decision Checkpoints	Info Needed for Decision	Tool to Use for Decision	How to Evaluate Results
✔			👍👎
When should we switch to ABC?	Knowledge of the products or product lines, the manufacturing process, overhead costs, and the needs of managers for accurate cost information	A detailed and accurate cost accounting system; cooperation between accountants and operating managers	Compare the results under both costing systems. If managers are better able to understand and control their operations using ABC, and the costs are not prohibitive, the switch would be beneficial.

VALUE-ADDED VERSUS NONVALUE-ADDED ACTIVITIES

STUDY OBJECTIVE

6

Differentiate between value-added and nonvalue-added activities.

Some companies that have experienced the benefits of activity-based costing have applied it to a broader range of management activities. **Activity-based management (ABM)** is an extension of ABC from a product costing system to a management function that focuses on reducing costs and improving processes and decision making. A refinement of activity-based costing used in ABM is the classification of activities as either value-added or nonvalue-added.

Value-added activities **increase the worth of a product or service** to customers; they involve resource usage and related costs that customers are willing to pay for. Value-added activities are the functions of actually manufacturing a product or performing a service—they increase the worth of the product or service. Examples of value-added activities in a manufacturing operation are engineering design, machining, assembly, painting, and packaging. Examples of value-added activities in a service company would be performing surgery, providing legal research for legal services, or delivering packages by a delivery service.

Nonvalue-added activities are production- or service-related activities that simply **add cost to, or increase the time spent on, a product or service without increasing its market value**. Examples of nonvalue-added activities in a manufacturing operation include the repair of machines; the storage of inventory; the moving of raw materials, assemblies, and finished product within the factory; building maintenance; inspections; and inventory control. Examples of nonvalue-added activities in service enterprises might include taking appointments, reception, bookkeeping, billing, traveling, ordering supplies, advertising, cleaning, and computer repair.

After activities are identified and classified in Step 1 of implementing ABC, it should be determined whether the activities are value-added or nonvalue-added. Illustration 4-12 shows an **activity flowchart**. Activity flowcharts are often used to help identify the activities that will be used in ABC costing. In the top part of this flowchart, activities are identified as value-added or nonvalue-added. The value-added activities are highlighted in red, while the nonvalue-added activities are highlighted in blue.

In the lower part of the flowchart there are two rows showing the number of days spent on each activity. The first row shows the number of days spent on each activity under the current manufacturing process. The second row shows the number of days spent on each activity under management's proposed reengineered manufacturing process. The proposed changes would reduce time spent on nonvalue-added activities by 17 days. This 17-day improvement would be due entirely to moving inventory more quickly through the nonvalue-added processes—that is, by reducing inventory time in moving, storage, and waiting.

Illustration 4-12 Flowchart showing value-added and nonvalue-added activities

HEARTLAND MANUFACTURING COMPANY
Activity Flowchart

Activities

NVA	NVA	NVA	NVA	VA		NVA	NVA	VA	NVA	NVA	NVA	VA
Receive and Inspect Materials	Move and Store Materials	Move Materials to Production and Wait	Set up Machines	Machining: Drill	Lathe	Inspect	Move and Wait	Assembly	Inspect and Test	Move to Storage	Store Finished Goods	Package and Ship
Current Days 1	12	2.5	1.5	2	1	0.2	6	2	0.3	0.5	14	1

◄──────────── Total Current Average Time = 44 days ────────────►

| Proposed Days 1 | 4 | 1.5 | 1.5 | 2 | 1 | 0.2 | 2 | 2 | 0.3 | 0.5 | 10 | 1 |

◄──────────── Total Proposed Average Time = **27** days ────────────►

Proposed reduction in nonvalue-added time = 17 days

VA = Value-added   NVA = Nonvalue-added

Not all activities labeled nonvalue-added are totally wasteful, nor can they be totally eliminated. For example, although inspection time is a nonvalue-added activity from a customer's perspective, few companies would eliminate their quality control functions. Similarly, moving and waiting time is nonvalue-added, but it would be impossible to completely eliminate. Nevertheless, when managers recognize the nonvalue-added characteristic of these activities, they are motivated to minimize them as much as possible. Attention to such matters is part of the growing practice of activity-based management which helps managers concentrate on **continuous improvement** of operations and activities.

BUSINESS INSIGHT
Management Perspective

Often the best way to improve a process is to learn from observing a different process. At the giant food producer **General Mills**, production line technicians were flown to North Carolina to observe first-hand how race-car pit crews operate. In a NASCAR car race, the value-added activity is driving toward the finish-line; any time spent in the pit is nonvalue-added. Every split second saved in the pit increases the chances of winning. From what the General Mills technicians learned at the car race, as well as other efforts, they were able to reduce set-up time from 5 hours to just 20 minutes.

ACTIVITY-BASED COSTING IN SERVICE INDUSTRIES

Although initially developed and implemented by manufacturing companies that produce products, activity-based costing has been widely adopted in service industries as well. ABC has been found to be a useful tool in such diverse industries as airlines, railroads, hotels, hospitals, banks, insurance companies, telephone companies, and financial services firms. The overall objective of installing ABC in service firms is no different than it is in a manufacturing company. That objective is to identify the key activities that generate costs and to keep track of how many of those activities are performed for each service provided (by job, service, contract, or customer).

The general approach to identifying activities, activity cost pools, and cost drivers is used by a service company in the same manner as a manufacturing company. Also, the labeling of activities as value-added and nonvalue-added and the attempt to reduce or eliminate nonvalue-added activities as much as possible is just as valid in service industries as in manufacturing operations. What sometimes makes implementation of activity-based costing difficult in service industries is that **a larger proportion of overhead costs are company-wide costs** that cannot be directly traced to specific services provided by the company.

To illustrate the application of activity-based costing to a service enterprise, contrasted to traditional costing, we use a public accounting firm. This illustration is equally applicable to a law firm, consulting firm, architect, or any service firm that performs numerous services for a client as part of a job.

TRADITIONAL COSTING EXAMPLE

Assume that the public accounting firm of Check and Doublecheck prepares the following condensed annual budget (see Illustration 4-13).

Illustration 4-13   Condensed annual budget of a service firm under traditional costing

CHECK AND DOUBLECHECK, CPAs
Annual Budget

Revenue		$2,000,000
Direct labor	$ 600,000	
Overhead (expected)	1,200,000	
Total costs		1,800,000
Operating income		$ 200,000

$$\frac{\text{Estimated overhead}}{\text{Direct labor cost}} = \text{Predetermined overhead rate}$$

$$\frac{\$1,200,000}{\$600,000} = 200\%$$

Under traditional costing direct labor is the professional service performed, and it is the basis for overhead application to each audit job. To determine the operating income earned on any job, Check and Doublecheck applies overhead at the rate of 200 percent of actual direct professional labor costs incurred. For example, assume that the firm of Check and Doublecheck records $70,000 of actual direct professional labor cost during its audit of Plano Molding Company, which was billed an audit fee of $260,000. Under traditional costing, using 200 percent as the rate for applying overhead to the job, applied overhead and operating income related to the Plano Molding Company audit would be computed as shown in Illustration 4-14.

CHECK AND DOUBLECHECK, CPAs Plano Molding Company Audit		
Revenue		$260,000
Less: Direct professional labor	$ 70,000	
Applied overhead (200% × $70,000)	140,000	210,000
Operating income		$ 50,000

Illustration 4-14 Overhead applied under traditional costing system

In this example, only one direct cost item and one overhead application rate are used under traditional costing.

ACTIVITY-BASED COSTING EXAMPLE

Under activity-based costing, Check and Doublecheck's estimated annual overhead costs of $1,200,000 are distributed to several activity cost pools. Activity-based overhead rates per cost driver are computed by dividing each activity overhead cost pool by the expected number of cost drivers used per activity. Illustration 4-15 shows an annual overhead budget using an ABC system.

Illustration 4-15 Condensed annual budget of a service firm under activity-based costing

CHECK AND DOUBLECHECK, CPAs Annual Overhead Budget				
Activity Cost Pools	Cost Drivers	Estimated Overhead ÷	Expected Use of Cost Drivers per Activity =	Activity-Based Overhead Rates
Secretarial support	Direct professional hours	$ 210,000	30,000	$7 per hour
Direct labor fringe benefits	Direct labor cost	240,000	$600,000	$0.40 per $1 labor cost
Printing and photocopying	Working paper pages	20,000	20,000	$1 per page
Computer support	CPU minutes	200,000	50,000	$4 per minute
Telephone and postage	None (Traced directly)	71,000	$71,000	Based on usage
Legal support	Hours used	129,000	860	$150 per hour
Insurance (professional liability, etc.)	Revenue billed	120,000	$2,000,000	$0.06 per $1 revenue
Recruiting and training	Direct professional hours	210,000	30,000	$7 per hour
		$1,200,000		

Note that some of the overhead costs can be directly assigned (see telephone and postage).

The assignment of the individual overhead activity rates to the actual number of activities used in the performance of the Plano Molding audit results in total overhead assigned of $165,100 as shown in Illustration 4-16.

Illustration 4-16 Assigning overhead in a service company

CHECK AND DOUBLECHECK, CPAs Plano Molding Company Audit				
Activity Cost Pools	Cost Drivers	Actual Use of Drivers	Activity-Based Overhead Rates	Costs Assigned
Secretarial support	Direct professional hours	3,800	$7.00	$ 26,600
Direct labor fringe benefits	Direct labor cost	$70,000	$0.40	28,000
Printing and photocopying	Working paper pages	1,800	$1.00	1,800
Computer support	CPU minutes	8,600	$4.00	34,400
Telephone and postage	None (Traced directly)			8,700
Legal support	Hours used	156	$150.00	23,400
Insurance (professional liability, etc.)	Revenue billed	$260,000	$0.06	15,600
Recruiting and training	Direct professional hours	3,800	$7.00	26,600
				$165,100

Under activity-based costing, overhead costs of $165,100 are assigned to the Plano Molding Company audit, as compared to $140,000 under traditional costing. A comparison of total costs and operating margins is shown in Illustration 4-17.

Illustration 4-17 Comparison of traditional costing with ABC in a service company

CHECK AND DOUBLECHECK, CPAs Plano Molding Company Audit				
	Traditional Costing		ABC	
Revenue		$260,000		$260,000
Expenses				
Direct professional labor	$ 70,000		$ 70,000	
Applied overhead	140,000		165,100	
Total expenses		210,000		235,100
Operating income		$ 50,000		$ 24,900
Profit margin		19.2%		9.6%

The comparison shows that the assignment of overhead costs under traditional costing is distorted. The total cost assigned to performing the audit of Plano Molding Company is greater under activity-based costing by $25,100, or 18 percent higher, and the profit margin is only half as great. Traditional costing gives the false impression of an operating profit of $50,000. This is more than double what it is at $24,900 using ABC.

BEFORE YOU GO ON . . .

◆ **Review It**

1. What are the benefits of activity-based costing?
2. What are the limitations of activity-based costing?

3. What factors would indicate ABC as the superior costing system?

4. What is the benefit of classifying activities as value-added and nonvalue-added?

5. What is the primary barrier to effectively implementing ABC in a service company environment?

DECISION TOOLKIT

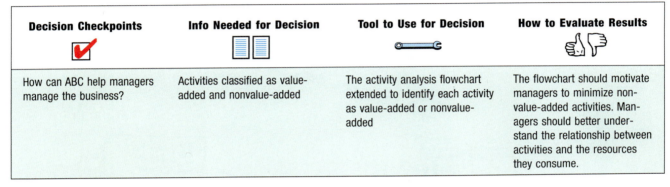

Decision Checkpoints	Info Needed for Decision	Tool to Use for Decision	How to Evaluate Results
How can ABC help managers manage the business?	Activities classified as value-added and nonvalue-added	The activity analysis flowchart extended to identify each activity as value-added or nonvalue-added	The flowchart should motivate managers to minimize non-value-added activities. Managers should better understand the relationship between activities and the resources they consume.

JUST-IN-TIME PROCESSING

STUDY OBJECTIVE

8

Explain just-in-time (JIT) processing.

The benefit of classifying activities as value-added and nonvalue-added is that managers know which activities to eliminate or minimize in order to reduce costs without affecting production efficiency or product quality. The activity analysis flowcharts shown in Illustration 4-12 revealed lots of inventory storage and waiting time at several places in the operation. These are nonvalue-added activities. One way to minimize inventory storage and waiting time is to implement a **just-in-time processing system**.

Traditionally, continuous process manufacturing has been based on a **just-in-case** philosophy: Inventories of raw materials are maintained **just in case** some items are of poor quality or a key supplier is shut down by a strike. Similarly, subassembly parts are manufactured and stored **just in case** they are needed later in the manufacturing process. Finished goods are completed and stored **just in case** unexpected and rush customer orders are received. This philosophy often results in a **push approach** in which raw materials and subassembly parts are pushed through each process. Traditional processing often results in the buildup of extensive manufacturing inventories.

Primarily in response to foreign competition, many U.S. firms have switched to **just-in-time (JIT) processing**. JIT manufacturing is dedicated to having the right amount of materials, products, or parts at the time they are needed. Under JIT processing, raw materials are received **just in time** for use in production, subassembly parts are completed **just in time** for use in finished goods, and finished goods are completed **just in time** to be sold. Illustration 4-18 shows the sequence of activities in just-in-time processing.

Helpful Hint JIT is easier said than done. JIT requires a total commitment by management and employees, a complete change in philosophy, and significant changes in the way production is organized. JIT takes time to implement.

Illustration 4-18 Just-in-time processing

OBJECTIVE OF JIT PROCESSING

A primary objective of JIT is to eliminate all manufacturing inventories. Inventories are considered to have an adverse effect on net income because they tie up funds and storage space that could be made available for more productive purposes. JIT strives to eliminate inventories by using a **demand-pull approach** in manufacturing. This approach begins with the customer placing an order with the company. This order, which indicates product demand, starts the process of pulling the product through the manufacturing process. A signal is sent via a computer to the next preceding work station indicating the exact materials (parts and subassemblies) needed for a time period, such as an eight-hour shift, to complete the production of a specified product. The preceding process, in turn, sends its signal to other preceding processes. The goal is a smooth continuous flow in the manufacturing process, with no buildup of inventories at any point.

ELEMENTS OF JIT PROCESSING

There are three important elements in JIT processing:

Helpful Hint Buyer leverage is important in finding dependable suppliers. Companies like GM and GE have more success than smaller companies.

1. A company must have dependable suppliers who are willing to deliver on short notice exact quantities of raw materials according to precise quality specifications. (This may even include multiple deliveries within the same day.) Suppliers must also be willing to deliver the raw materials at specified work stations rather than at a central receiving department. This type of purchasing requires constant and direct communication with suppliers, which is facilitated by an online computer linkage between the company and its suppliers.

2. A multiskilled work force must be developed. Under JIT, machines are often strategically grouped into work cells or centers and much of the work is automated. As a result, one worker may have the responsibility to operate and maintain several different types of machines.

3. A total quality control system must be established throughout the manufacturing operations. Total quality control means **no defects.** Since only required quantities are signaled by the demand-pull approach, any defects at a work station will shut down operations at subsequent work stations. Total quality control requires continuous monitoring by both employees and supervisors at each work station.

BUSINESS INSIGHT
Management Perspective

JIT first hit the USA in the early 1980s when it was adopted by automobile companies to help compete with foreign competition. It is now being successfully used in many companies, including **General Electric**, **Caterpillar**, and **Harley-Davidson**. The effects in most cases have been dramatic. For example, after using JIT for two years, a major division of Hewlett-Packard found that work-in-process inventories (in dollars) were down 82 percent, scrap/rework costs were down 30 percent, space utilization was down 40 percent, and labor efficiency improved 50 percent. As indicated, JIT not only reduces inventory but also enables a manufacturer to produce a better product faster and with less waste.

BENEFITS OF JIT PROCESSING

The major benefits of implementing JIT processing are:

1. Manufacturing inventories are significantly reduced or eliminated.
2. Product quality is enhanced.
3. Rework costs and inventory storage costs are reduced or eliminated.
4. Production cost savings are realized from the improved flow of goods through the processes.

Helpful Hint Without its emphasis on quality control, JIT would be impractical or even impossible. In JIT, quality is engineered into the production process.

One of the major accounting benefits of JIT is the elimination of separate raw materials and work-in-process inventory accounts. These accounts are replaced by one account called Raw and In-Process Inventory. All materials and conversion costs are charged to this account. Due to the reduction (or elimination) of in-process inventories, the computation of equivalent units of production is simplified.

DECISION TOOLKIT

Decision Checkpoints	Info Needed for Decision	Tool to Use for Decision	How to Evaluate Results
Can we benefit from installation and implementation of JIT processing?	Amounts of raw materials, work-in-process, and finished goods inventory; days that inventory is in storage or waiting to be processed or sold	Establish that we have dependable suppliers, a multiskilled work force, and a total quality control system.	JIT should reduce or nearly eliminate inventories, storage, and waiting time and should minimize waste and defects. Inventory should be pulled rather than pushed through each production process.

◆ **Review It**

1. What is the difference between the push approach and the demand-pull approach to handling inventories in a manufacturing operation?
2. What are the major benefits of implementing JIT?
3. What are the principal accounting effects of just-in-time processing?

*U*SING THE DECISION TOOLKIT

Precor Company manufactures a line of high-end exercise equipment of commercial quality. Assume that the chief accountant has proposed changing from a traditional costing system to an activity-based costing system. The financial vice-president is not convinced, so she requests that the next large order for equipment be costed under both systems for purposes of comparison and analysis. An order from Slim-Way Salons, Inc., for 150 low-impact treadmills is received and is identified as the order to be subjected to dual costing. The following cost data relate to the Slim-Way order.

Data relevant to both costing systems

Direct materials	$55,500
Direct labor hours	820
Direct labor rate per hour	$18.00

Data relevant to the traditional costing system

Predetermined overhead rate is 300% of direct labor cost.

Data relevant to the activity-based costing system

Activity Cost Pools	Cost Drivers	Activity-Based Overhead Rate	Expected Use of Cost Drivers per Treadmill
Engineering design	Engineering hours	$30 per hour	330
Machine setup	Setups	$200 per setup	22
Machining	Machine hours	$25 per hour	732
Assembly	Number of subassemblies	$8 per subassembly	1,450
Packaging and shipping	Packaging/shipping hours	$15 per hour	152
Building occupancy	Machine hours	$6 per hour	732

Instructions

Compute the total cost of the Slim-Way Salons, Inc. order under (a) the traditional costing system and (b) the activity-based costing system. (c) As a result of this comparison, which costing system is Precor likely to adopt? Why?

Solution

(a) Traditional costing system:

Direct materials	$ 55,500
Direct labor (820 × $18)	14,760
Overhead assigned ($14,760 × 300%)	44,280
Total costs assigned to Slim-Way order	$114,540
Number of low-impact treadmills	150
Cost per unit	$763.60

(b) Activity-based costing system:

Direct materials		$ 55,500
Direct labor (820 × $18)		14,760
Overhead activities costs:		
Engineering design (330 hours @ $30)	$ 9,900	
Machine setup (22 setups @ $200)	4,400	
Machining (732 machine hours @ $25)	18,300	
Assembly (1,450 subassemblies @ $8)	11,600	
Packaging and shipping (152 hours @ $15)	2,280	
Building occupancy (732 hours @ $6)	4,392	50,872
Total costs assigned to Slim-Way order		$121,132
Number of low-impact treadmills		150
Cost per unit		$807.55

(c) Precor Company will likely adopt ABC because of the difference in the cost per unit (which ABC found to be higher). More importantly, ABC provides greater insight into the sources and causes of the cost per unit. Managers are given greater insight into which activities to control in order to reduce costs. ABC will provide better product costing and greater profitability for the company.

SUMMARY OF STUDY OBJECTIVES

1 *Recognize the difference between traditional costing and activity-based costing.* A traditional costing system allocates overhead to products on the basis of predetermined plantwide or departmentwide volume of unit-based output rates such as direct labor or machine hours. An ABC system allocates overhead to identified activity cost pools, and costs are then assigned to products using related cost drivers that measure the activities (resources) consumed.

2 *Identify the steps in the development of an activity-based costing system.* The development of an activity-based costing system involves four steps: (1) Identify and classify the major activities that pertain to the manufacture of specific products, and allocate manufacturing overhead costs to the appropriate cost pools. (2) Identify the cost driver that has a strong correlation to the costs accumulated in the activity cost pool. (3) Compute the activity-based overhead rate per cost driver. (4) Assign overhead costs for each activity cost pool to products or services using the cost drivers.

3 *Know how companies identify the activity cost pools used in activity-based costing.* To identify activity cost pools, a company must perform an analysis of each operation or process, documenting and timing every task, action, or transaction.

4 *Know how companies identify and use the activity cost drivers in activity-based costing.* Cost drivers identified for assigning activity cost pools must (a) accurately measure the actual consumption of the activity by the various products, and (b) have related data easily available.

5 *Understand the benefits and limitations of activity-based costing.* What makes ABC a more accurate product costing system is: (1) the increased number of cost pools used to assign overhead, (2) the enhanced control over overhead costs, and (3) the better management decisions it makes possible. The limitations of ABC are: (1) the higher analysis and measurement costs that accompany multiple activity centers and cost drivers, and (2) the necessity still to allocate some costs arbitrarily.

6 *Differentiate between value-added and nonvalue-added activities.* Value-added activities increase the worth of a product or service. Nonvalue-added activities simply add cost to, or increase the time spent on, a product or service without increasing its market value. Awareness of these classifications encourages managers to reduce or eliminate the time spent on the nonvalue-added activities.

7 *Apply activity-based costing to service industries.* The overall objective of using ABC in service industries is no different than for manufacturing industries, that is, improved costing of services provided (by job, service, contract, or customer). The general approach to costing is the same: analyze operations, identify activities, accumulate overhead costs by activity cost pools, and identify and use cost drivers to assign the cost pools to the services.

8 *Explain just-in-time (JIT) processing.* JIT is a processing system that is dedicated to having on hand the right materials and products at the time they are needed, thereby reducing the amount of inventory and the time inventory is held. One of the principal accounting effects is that one account, Raw and In-Process Inventory, replaces both the raw materials and work-in-process inventory accounts.

THE NAVIGATOR

DECISION TOOLKIT—A SUMMARY

Decision Checkpoints	Info Needed for Decision	Tool to Use for Decision	How to Evaluate Results
When should we switch to ABC?	Knowledge of the products or product lines, the manufacturing process, overhead costs, and the needs of managers for accurate cost information	A detailed and accurate cost accounting system; cooperation between accountants and operating managers	Compare the results under both costing systems. If managers are better able to understand and control their operations using ABC, and the costs are not prohibitive, the switch would be beneficial.
How can ABC help managers manage the business?	Activities classified as value-added and nonvalue-added	The activity analysis flowchart extended to identify each activity as value-added or nonvalue-added	The flowchart should motivate managers to minimize non-value-added activities. Managers should better understand the relationship between activities and the resources they consume.
Can we benefit from installation and implementation of JIT processing?	Amounts of raw materials, work-in-process, and finished goods inventory; days that inventory is in storage or waiting to be processed or sold	Establish that we have dependable suppliers, a multiskilled work force, and a total quality control system.	JIT should reduce or nearly eliminate inventories, storage, and waiting time and should minimize waste and defects. Inventory should be pulled rather than pushed through each production process.

APPENDIX 4A

HIERARCHY OF ACTIVITY LEVELS

STUDY OBJECTIVE
9
Understand the value of a hierarchy of activity levels to activity-based costing.

As mentioned in the chapter, traditional costing systems are volume-driven—driven by unit-based cost drivers such as direct labor or machine hours. Some activity costs are strictly variable and are caused by the production or acquisition of a single unit of product or the performance of a single unit of service. However, the recognition that other activity costs are not driven by unit-based cost drivers has led to the development of a hierarchy of ABC activities, consisting of four levels. The four levels of activities are classified and defined as follows.

1. **Unit-level activities**. These are performed for each unit of production.
2. **Batch-level activities**. These are performed for each batch of products rather than each unit.

3. **Product-level activities**. These are performed in support of an entire product line, but are not always performed every time a new unit or batch of products is produced.

4. **Facility-level activities**. These are required to support or sustain an entire production process.

Greater accuracy in overhead cost allocation may be achieved by recognizing these four different levels of activities and, from them, developing specific activity cost pools and their related cost drivers. Illustration 4A-1 graphically displays this four-level activity hierarchy, along with the types of activities and examples of costs traceable to those activities at each level.

Illustration 4A-1 Hierarchy of activity levels

Four Levels	Types of Activities	Examples of Costs
Unit-Level Activities	Machine-related: Drilling, cutting, milling, trimming, pressing	Direct materials Depreciation of machines Power costs Machine maintenance
	Labor-related: Assembling, painting, sanding, sewing	Direct labor Fringe benefits Payroll taxes
Batch-Level Activities	Equipment setups Purchase ordering Inspection Material handling	Labor setup costs Purchasing clerical costs Quality control costs Material handling costs
Product-Level Activities	Product design Engineering changes Inventory management	Design costs Product engineering costs Inventory carrying costs
Facility-Level Activities	Plant management Personnel administration Training Security	Building depreciation Heating, air conditioning Property taxes Insurance

This hierarchy provides managers and accountants a structured way of thinking about the relationships between activities and the resources they consume. In contrast, traditional volume-based costing recognizes only unit-level costs. **Failure to recognize this hierarchy of activities is one of the reasons that volume-based cost allocation causes distortions in product costing.**

As indicated earlier, allocating all overhead costs by unit-based cost drivers can send false signals to managers: Dividing batch-, product-, or facility-level costs by the number of units produced gives the mistaken impression that these costs vary with the number of units. **The resources consumed by batch-, product-, and facility-level supporting activities do not vary at the unit level,** nor can they be controlled at the unit level. The number of activities performed at the batch level goes up as the number of batches rises—not as the number of units within the batches changes. Similarly, the number of product-level activities performed depends on the number of different products—not on how many units or batches are produced. Furthermore, facility-sustaining activity costs are not dependent upon the number of products, batches, or units produced. Batch-, product-, and facility-level costs can be controlled only by modifying batch-, product-, and facility-level activities.

B E F O R E   Y O U   G O   O N . . .

◆ Review It

1. How is the differentiation of activities into unit-level, batch-level, product-level, and facility-level important to managers?

◆ Do It

Morgan Toy Company manufactures six primary product lines in its Morganville plant. As a result of an activity analysis, the accounting department has identified eight activity cost pools. Each of the toy products is produced in large batches, with the whole plant devoted to one product at a time. Classify each of the following activities as either unit-level, batch-level, product-level, or facility-level: (a) engineering design, (b) machine setup, (c) inventory management, (d) plant cafeteria, (e) inspections after each setup, (f) polishing parts, (g) assembling parts, (h) health and safety.

Action Plan
• Recall that:
  Unit-level activities are performed for each individual unit of product.
  Batch-level activities are performed each time a batch of a product is produced.
  Product-level activities are performed to support an entire product line.
  Facility-level activities support the production process across the entire range of products.

Solution: (a) Product-level, (b) batch-level, (c) product-level, (d) facility-level, (e) batch-level, (f) unit-level, (g) unit-level, (h) facility-level.

Related exercise material: BE4-9, BE4-10, E4-12, and E4-13.

SUMMARY OF STUDY OBJECTIVE FOR APPENDIX 4A

9 *Understand the value of a hierarchy of activity levels to activity-based costing.* Activities may be classified as unit-level, batch-level, product-level, and facility-level. Unit-, batch-, product-, and facility-level overhead costs are controlled by modifying unit-, batch-, product-, and facility-level activities, respectively. Failure to recognize this hierarchy of levels can result in distorted product costing.

GLOSSARY

Key Term Matching Activity

Activity Any event, action, transaction, or work sequence that causes a cost to be incurred in producing a product or providing a service. (p. 141)

Activity-based costing (ABC) An overhead cost allocation system that allocates overhead to multiple activity cost pools and assigns the activity cost pools to products or services by means of cost drivers that represent the activities used. (p. 141)

Activity-based management (ABM) An extension of ABC from a product costing system to a management function that focuses on reducing costs and improving processes and decision making. (p. 152)

Activity cost pool The overhead cost allocated to a distinct type of activity or related activities. (p. 142).

Batch-level activities Activities performed for each batch of products. (p. 162)

Cost driver Any factor or activity that has a direct cause–effect relationship with the resources consumed. In ABC cost drivers are used to assign activity cost pools to products or services. (p. 141)

Facility-level activities Activities required to support or sustain an entire production process and not dependent on number of products, batches, or units produced. (p. 163)

Just-in-time (JIT) processing A processing system dedicated to having the right amount of materials, products, or parts arrive as they are needed, thereby reducing the amount of inventory. (p. 157)

Nonvalue-added activity An activity that adds cost to, or increases the time spent on, a product or service without increasing its market value. (p. 152)

Product-level activities Activities performed for and identifiable with an entire product line. (p. 163)

Unit-level activities Activities performed for each unit of production. (p. 162)

Value-added activity An activity that increases the worth of a product or service. (p. 152)

*D*EMONSTRATION *P*ROBLEM

Spreadwell Paint Company manufactures two high-quality base paints: an **oil-based** paint and a **latex** paint. Both paints are manufactured in neutral white color only. The white base paints are sold to franchised retail paint and decorating stores where pigments are added to tint (color) the paint as desired by the customer. The oil-based paint is made from, thinned, and cleaned with organic solvents (petroleum products) such as mineral spirits or turpentine. The latex paint is made from, thinned, and cleaned with water; synthetic resin particles are suspended in the water and dry and harden when exposed to the air. Both paints are housepaints. Spreadwell uses the same processing equipment to produce both paints in differing production runs. Between batches, the vats and other processing equipment must be washed and cleaned.

eGrade Demonstration
Problem

After analyzing the company's entire operations, Spreadwell's accountants and production managers have identified activity cost pools and accumulated annual budgeted overhead costs by pool as follows.

Activity Cost Pools	Estimated Overhead
Purchasing	$ 240,000
Processing (weighing and mixing, grinding, thinning and drying, straining)	1,400,000
Packaging (quarts, gallons, and 5-gallons)	580,000
Testing	240,000
Storage and inventory control	180,000
Washing and cleaning equipment	560,000
Total annual budgeted overhead	$3,200,000

Following further analysis, activity cost drivers were identified and their expected use by product and activity were scheduled as follows.

Activity Cost Pool	Cost Drivers	Expected Cost Drivers per Activity	Expected Use of Drivers per Product	
			Oil-based	Latex
Purchasing	Purchase orders	1,500 orders	800	700
Processing	Gallons processed	1,000,000 gals.	400,000	600,000
Packaging	Containers filled	400,000 containers	180,000	220,000
Testing	Number of tests	4,000 tests	2,100	1,900
Storing	Avg. gals. on hand	18,000 gals.	10,400	7,600
Washing	Number of batches	800 batches	350	450

Spreadwell has budgeted 400,000 gallons of oil-based paint and 600,000 gallons of latex paint for processing during the year.

Instructions

(a) Prepare a schedule showing the computations of the activity-based overhead rates.
(b) Prepare a schedule assigning each activity's overhead cost pool to each product.
(c) Compute the overhead cost per unit for each product.
(d) Classify each activity cost pool as value-added or nonvalue-added.

Solution to Demonstration Problem

(a) Computations of activity-based overhead rates:

SPREADWELL PAINT COMPANY

Activity Cost Pools	Estimated Overhead	÷	Expected Use of Cost Drivers	=	Activity-Based Overhead Rates
Purchasing	$ 240,000		1,500 orders		$160 per order
Processing	1,400,000		1,000,000 gallons		$1.40 per gallon
Packaging	580,000		400,000 containers		$1.45 per container
Testing	240,000		4,000 tests		$60 per test
Storing	180,000		18,000 gallons		$10 per gallon
Washing	560,000		800 batches		$700 per batch
	$3,200,000				

(b) Assignment of activity cost pools to products:

SPREADWELL PAINT COMPANY

Activity Cost Pools	Oil-Based Paint			Latex Paint		
	Expected Use of Drivers	Overhead Rates	Cost Assigned	Expected Use of Drivers	Overhead Rates	Cost Assigned
Purchasing	800	$160	$ 128,000	700	$160	$ 112,000
Processing	400,000	$1.40	560,000	600,000	$1.40	840,000
Packaging	180,000	$1.45	261,000	220,000	$1.45	319,000
Testing	2,100	$60	126,000	1,900	$60	114,000
Storing	10,400	$10	104,000	7,600	$10	76,000
Washing	350	$700	245,000	450	$700	315,000
Total overhead assigned			$1,424,000			$1,776,000

(c) Computation of overhead cost assigned per unit:

	Oil-Based Paint	Latex Paint
Total overhead cost assigned	$1,424,000	$1,776,000
Total gallons produced	400,000	600,000
Overhead cost per gallon	$3.56	$2.96

(d) Value-added activities: processing and packaging
Nonvalue-added activities: purchasing, testing, storing, and washing

Action Plan

- Identify the major activities that pertain to the manufacture of specific products and allocate manufacturing overhead costs to activity cost pools.
- Identify the cost drivers that accurately measure each activity's contribution to the finished product.
- Compute the activity-based overhead rates.
- Assign manufacturing overhead costs for each activity cost pool to products, using the activity-based overhead rates.

Note: All asterisked Questions, Exercises, and Problems relate to material in the appendix to the chapter.

SELF-STUDY QUESTIONS

Self-Study/Self-Test

Answers are at the end of the chapter.

(SO 1) 1. Activity-based costing (ABC):
   (a) can be used only in a process cost system.
   (b) focuses on units of production.
   (c) focuses on activities performed to produce a product.
   (d) uses only a single basis of allocation.

(SO 1) 2. Activity-based costing:
   (a) is the initial phase of converting to a just-in-time operating environment.
   (b) can be used only in a job order costing system.
   (c) is a two-stage overhead cost allocation system that identifies activity cost pools and cost drivers.
   (d) uses direct labor as its primary cost driver.

(SO 3) 3. Any activity that causes resources to be consumed is called a:
   (a) just-in-time activity.
   (b) facility-level activity.
   (c) cost driver.
   (d) nonvalue-added activity.

(SO 4) 4. The overhead rate for Machine Setups is $100 per setup. Products A and B have 80 and 60 setups, respectively. The overhead assigned to each product is:
   (a) Product A $8,000, Product B $8,000.
   (b) Product A $8,000, Product B $6,000.
   (c) Product A $6,000, Product B $6,000.
   (d) Product A $6,000, Product B $8,000.

(SO 4) 5. Donna Crawford Co. has identified an activity cost pool to which it has allocated estimated overhead of $1,920,000. It has determined the expected use of cost drivers per that activity to be 160,000 inspections. Widgets require 40,000 inspections, Gadgets 30,000 inspections, and Targets, 90,000 inspections. The overhead assigned to each product is:
   (a) Widgets $40,000, Gadgets $30,000, Targets $90,000.

   (b) Widgets $480,000, Gadgets $360,000, Targets $108,000.
   (c) Widgets $360,000, Gadgets $480,000, Targets $1,080,000.
   (d) Widgets $480,000, Gadgets $360,000, Targets $1,080,000.

(SO 6) 6. An activity that adds costs to the product but does not increase its market value is a:
   (a) value-added activity.
   (b) cost driver.
   (c) cost–benefit activity.
   (d) nonvalue-added activity.

(SO 6) 7. The following activity is value-added:
   (a) Storage of raw materials.
   (b) Moving parts from machine to machine.
   (c) Shaping a piece of metal on a lathe.
   (d) All of the above.

(SO 8) 8. Under just-in-time processing:
   (a) raw materials are received just in time for use in production.
   (b) subassembly parts are completed just in time for use in assembling finished goods.
   (c) finished goods are completed just in time to be sold.
   (d) All of the above.

(SO 8) 9. The primary objective of just-in-time processing is to:
   (a) accumulate overhead in activity cost pools.
   (b) eliminate or reduce all manufacturing inventories.
   (c) identify relevant activity cost drivers.
   (d) identify value-added activities.

(SO 9) *10. A relevant facility-level cost driver for heating costs is:
   (a) machine hours.
   (b) direct material.
   (c) floor space.
   (d) direct labor cost.

THE NAVIGATOR

QUESTIONS

1. Under what conditions is direct labor a valid basis for allocating overhead?

2. What has happened in recent industrial history to reduce the usefulness of direct labor as the primary basis for allocating overhead to products?

3. In an automated manufacturing environment, what basis of overhead allocation is frequently more relevant than direct labor hours?

4. What is generally true about overhead allocation to high-volume products versus low-volume products under a traditional costing system?

5. (a) What are the principal differences between activity-based costing (ABC) and traditional product costing?
   (b) What assumptions must be met for ABC costing to be useful?

6. What is the formula for computing activity-based overhead rates?

7. What steps are involved in developing an activity-based costing system?

8. Explain the preparation and use of an activity flow-chart in an ABC system.

9. What is an activity cost pool?

10. What is a cost driver?

11. What makes a cost driver accurate and appropriate?

12. What is the formula for assigning activity cost pools to products?

13. What are the benefits of activity-based costing?

14. What are the limitations of activity-based costing?

15. Under what conditions is ABC generally the superior overhead costing system?

16. What refinement has been made to enhance the efficiency and effectiveness of ABC for use in managing costs?

17. Of what benefit is classifying activities as value-added and nonvalue-added?

18. In what ways is the application of ABC to service industries the same as its application to manufacturing companies?

19. (a) Describe the philosophy and approach of just-in-time processing.
    (b) Identify the major elements of JIT processing.

*20. What is the relevance of the hierarchy of levels of activity to ABC?

BRIEF EXERCISES

Identify cost drivers.
(SO 4)

BE4-1   Mynex Co. identifies the following activities that pertain to manufacturing overhead: Materials Handling, Machine Setups, Factory Machine Maintenance, Factory Supervision, and Quality Control. For each activity, identify an appropriate cost driver.

Identify cost drivers.
(SO 4)

BE4-2   Multi-Products Company manufactures four products in a single production facility. The company uses activity-based costing. The following activities have been identified through the company's activity analysis: (a) inventory control, (b) machine setups, (c) employee training, (d) quality inspections, (e) material ordering, (f) drilling operations, and (g) building maintenance. For each activity, name a cost driver that might be used to assign overhead costs to products.

Compute activity-based overhead rates.
(SO 4)

BE4-3   Martinez Company identifies three activities in its manufacturing process: machine setups, machining, and inspections. Estimated annual overhead cost for each activity is $180,000, $325,000, and $70,000, respectively. The cost driver for each activity and the expected annual usage are: number of setups 2,000, machine hours 25,000, and number of inspections 1,750. Compute the overhead rate for each activity.

Compute activity-based overhead rates.
(SO 4)

BE4-4   Hats Galore, Inc. uses activity-based costing as the basis for information to set prices for its six lines of seasonal hats. Compute the activity-based overhead rates using the following budgeted data for each of the activity cost pools.

Activity Cost Pool	Estimated Overhead	Expected Use of Cost Drivers per Activity
Designing	$ 450,000	12,000 designer hours
Sizing and cutting	4,000,000	160,000 machine hours
Stitching and trimming	1,400,000	80,000 labor hours
Blocking and packing	336,000	32,000 finished units

Compute activity-based overhead rates.
(SO 4)

BE4-5   Electronic Parts, Inc., a manufacturer of woofers and chips for computers, employs activity-based costing. Compute activity-based overhead rates from the following budgeted data for each of the activity cost pools.

Activity Cost Pool	Estimated Overhead	Expected Use of Cost Drivers per Activity
Ordering and receiving	$ 90,000	12,000 orders
Annealing	96,000	32,000 pounds
Etching	447,000	60,000 machine hours
Soldering	1,298,000	440,000 labor hours
Packing and shipping	436,800	28,000 boxes

BE4-6 Norm Johnson Novelty Company identified the following activities in its production and support operations. Classify each of these activities as either value-added or nonvalue-added.

Classify activities as value-or nonvalue-added.
(SO 6)

(a) Purchasing.
(b) Receiving.
(c) Design engineering.
(d) Storing inventory.

(e) Cost accounting.
(f) Moving work-in-process.
(g) Inspecting and testing.
(h) Painting and packing.

BE4-7 Loggers Construction Company, a builder of log cabins on order for farm machinery storage, identifies the following six activities: (1) receiving and handling materials, (2) painting and maintaining scaffolding, (3) setting poles, (4) siding, (5) roofing, (6) inspecting. Classify each of their activities as value-added or nonvalue-added.

Classify activities as value-or nonvalue-added.
(SO 6)

BE4-8 Ayala and Ortiz is an architectural firm that is contemplating the installation of activity-based costing. The following activities are performed daily by staff architects. Classify these activities as value-added or nonvalue-added: (1) designing and drafting, 3 hours; (2) staff meetings, 1 hour; (3) on-site supervision, 2 hours; (4) lunch, 1 hour; (5) consultation with client on specifications, 1.5 hours; (6) entertaining a prospective client for dinner, 2 hours.

Classify service company activities as value- or nonvalue-added.
(SO 6, 7)

*BE4-9 Pete's Pix Center is a large film developing and processing center that serves 130 outlets in grocery stores, service stations, camera and photo shops, and drug stores in 16 nearby towns. The Center operates 24 hours a day, 6 days a week. Classify each of the following activity costs of the Center as either unit-level, batch-level, product-level, or facility-level.

Classify activities according to level.
(SO 9)

(a) Developing fluids.
(b) Photocopy paper.
(c) Depreciation of machinery.
(d) Setups for enlargements.
(e) Supervisor's salary.

(f) Ordering materials.
(g) Pickup and delivery.
(h) Commission to dealers.
(i) Insurance on building.
(j) Loading developing machines.

*BE4-10 Mechanic's Aids Company operates 20 injection molding machines in the production of tool boxes of four different sizes, named the Apprentice, the Handyman, the Journeyman, and the Professional. Classify each of the following costs as unit-level, batch-level, product-level, or facility-level.

Classify activities according to level.
(SO 9)

(a) First-shift supervisor's salary.
(b) Powdered raw plastic.
(c) Dies for casting plastic components.
(d) Depreciation on injection molding machines.
(e) Changing dies on machines.
(f) Moving components to assembly department.
(g) Engineering design.
(h) Employee health and medical insurance coverage.

*E*XERCISES

E4-1 Waring Corporation manufactures safes—large mobile safes, and large walk-in stationary bank safes. As part of its annual budgeting process, Waring is analyzing the profitability of its two products. Part of this analysis involves estimating the amount of overhead to be allocated to each product line. The following information relates to overhead.

Assign overhead using traditional costing and ABC.
(SO 1, 4)

	Mobile Safes	Walk-in Safes
Units planned for production	200	50
Material moves per product line	300	200
Purchase orders per product line	450	350
Direct labor hours per product line	700	1,700

Instructions

(a) The total estimated manufacturing overhead was $237,000. Under traditional costing (which assigns overhead on the basis of direct-labor hours), what amount of manufacturing overhead costs are assigned to (do not round):
  (1) One mobile safe?
  (2) One walk-in safe?

(b) The total estimated manufacturing overhead of $237,000 was comprised of $150,000 for material-handling costs and $87,000 for purchasing activity costs. Under activity-based costing (ABC):
  (1) What amount of material handling costs are assigned to:
    (a) One mobile safe?
    (b) One walk-in safe?
  (2) What amount of purchasing activity costs are assigned to:
    (a) One mobile safe?
    (b) One walk-in safe?

(c) Compare the amount of overhead allocated to one mobile safe and to one walk-in safe under the traditional costing approach versus under ABC.

Assign overhead using traditional costing and ABC; classify activities as value- or nonvalue-added and by level.
(SO 1, 4, 6)

E4-2 Lieberman Clothing Company manufactures its own designed and labeled sports attire and sells its products through catalog sales and retail outlets. While Lieberman has for years used activity-based costing in its manufacturing activities, it has always used traditional costing in assigning its selling costs to its product lines. Selling costs have traditionally been assigned to Lieberman's product lines at a rate of 60% of direct material costs. Its direct material costs for the month of March for Lieberman's "high intensity" line of attire are $400,000. The company has decided to extend activity-based costing to its selling costs. Data relating to the "high intensity" line of products for the month of March are as follows.

Activity Cost Pool	Cost Driver	Overhead Rates	Number of Cost Drivers Used per Activity
Sales commissions	Dollar sales	$0.05 per dollar sales	$930,000
Advertising—TV/Radio	Minutes	$300 per minute	250
Advertising—Newspaper	Column inches	$10 per column inch	3,000
Catalogs	Catalogs mailed	$2.50 per catalog	60,000
Cost of catalog sales	Catalog orders	$1 per catalog order	8,500
Credit and collection	Dollar sales	$0.03 per dollar sales	$930,000

Instructions

(a) Compute the selling costs to be assigned to the "high-intensity" line of attire for the month of March: (1) using the traditional product costing system (direct material cost is the cost driver), and (2) using activity-based costing.

(b) By what amount does the traditional product costing system undercost or overcost the "high-intensity" product line?

(c) Classify each of the activities as value-added or nonvalue-added.

Assign overhead using traditional costing and ABC; classify activities as value- or nonvalue-added and by level.
(SO 1, 4, 6)

E4-3 Nutrition Products, Inc., uses a traditional product costing system to assign overhead costs uniformly to all products. To meet Food and Drug Administration requirements and to assure its customers of safe, sanitary, and nutritious food, Nutrition engages in a high level of quality control. Nutrition assigns its quality-control overhead costs to all products at a rate of 18% of direct-labor costs. Its direct-labor cost for the month of June for its low-calorie dessert line is $55,000. In response to repeated requests from its financial vice president, Nutrition's management agrees to adopt activity-based costing. Data relating to the low-calorie dessert line for the month of June are as follows.

Activity Cost Pool	Cost Driver	Overhead Rate	Number of Cost Drivers Used per Activity
Inspections of material received	Number of pounds	$0.60 per pound	6,000 pounds
In-process inspections	Number of servings	$0.33 per serving	10,000 servings
FDA certification	Customer orders	$12.00 per order	400 orders

Instructions

(a) Compute the quality-control overhead cost to be assigned to the low-calorie dessert product line for the month of June: (1) using the traditional product costing system (direct labor cost is the cost driver), and (2) using activity-based costing.
(b) By what amount does the traditional product costing system undercost or overcost the low-calorie dessert line?
(c) Classify each of the activities as value-added or nonvalue-added.

E4-4   Quick Copies Company is a small printing and copying firm with three high-speed offset printing presses, five copiers (two color and three black and white), one collator, one cutting and folding machine, and one fax machine. To improve its pricing practices, owner-manager Morgan Hough is installing activity-based accounting. Additionally, Morgan employs five employees: two printers/designers, one receptionist/bookkeeper, one sales and copy-machine operator, and one janitor/delivery clerk. Morgan can operate any of the machines and, in addition to managing the entire operation, he performs the training, designing, selling, and marketing functions.

*Identify activity cost pools.
(SO 3)*

Instructions

As Quick Copies' independent accountant who prepares tax forms and quarterly financial statements, you have been asked to identify the activities that would be used to accumulate overhead costs for assignment to jobs and customers. Using your knowledge of a small printing and copying firm (and some imagination), identify at least twelve activity cost pools as the start of an activity-based costing system for Quick Copies Company.

E4-5   Gulino Corporation manufactures snowmobiles in its White Mountain, Wisconsin plant. The following costs are budgeted for the first quarter's operations.

*Identify activity cost pools and cost drivers.
(SO 3, 4)*

Direct factory labor-wages	$ 860,000
Raw material and purchased components	1,200,000
Engineering design	140,000
Engineering development	60,000
Depreciation, plant	210,000
Depreciation, machinery	520,000
Machine setup, wages	15,000
Machine setup, supplies	4,000
Inspections	16,000
Tests	4,000
Insurance, plant	110,000
Property taxes	29,000
Natural gas, heating	19,000
Electricity, plant lighting	21,000
Electricity, machinery	36,000
Custodial (machine maintenance) wages	17,000

Instructions

Classify the above costs of Gulino Corporation into activity cost pools using the following: engineering, machinery, machine setup, quality control, utilities, maintenance. Next, identify a cost driver that may be used to assign each cost pool to each line of snowmobiles.

E4-6   Tommy Colina's Rijo Vineyards in Mendocino, California produces three varieties of wine: Merlot, Viognier, and Pinot Noir. His winemaster, Richard Watson, has identified the following activities as cost pools for accumulating overhead and assigning it to products.

*Identify activity cost drivers.
(SO 4)*

1. Culling and replanting. Dead or overcrowded vines are culled, and new vines are planted or relocated. (Separate vineyards by variety.)
2. Trimming. At the end of the harvest the vines are cut and trimmed back in preparation for the next season.
3. Tying. The posts and wires are reset, and vines are tied to the wires for the dormant season.
4. Spraying. The vines are sprayed with chemicals for protection against insects and fungi.
5. Harvesting. The grapes are hand-picked, placed in carts, and transported to the crushers.

6. Stemming and crushing. Cartfuls of bunches of grapes of each variety are separately loaded into machines which remove stems and gently crush the grapes.

7. Pressing and filtering. The crushed grapes are transferred to presses which mechanically remove the juices and filter out bulk and impurities.

8. Fermentation. The grape juice, by variety, is fermented in either stainless-steel tanks or oak barrels.

9. Aging. The wines are aged in either stainless-steel tanks or oak barrels for one to three years depending on variety.

10. Bottling and corking. Bottles are machine-filled and corked.

11. Labeling and boxing. Each bottle is labeled, as is each nine-bottle case, with the name of the vintner, vintage, and variety.

12. Storing. Packaged and boxed bottles are stored awaiting shipment.

13. Shipping. The wine is shipped to distributors and private retailers.

14. Maintenance of buildings and equipment. Printing, repairs, replacements, and general maintenance are performed in the off-season.

15. Heating and air-conditioning of plant and offices.

Instructions
For each of Rijo's fifteen activity cost pools, identify a probable cost driver that might be used to assign overhead costs to its three wine varieties.

Identify activity cost drivers.
(SO 4)

E4-7 Andrea Boss, Inc. manufactures five models of kitchen appliances at its Vista plant. The company is installing activity-based costing and has identified the following activities performed at its Vista plant.

1. Designing new models.
2. Purchasing raw materials and parts.
3. Receiving and inspecting raw materials and parts.
4. Storing and managing inventory.
5. Interviewing and hiring new personnel.
6. Machine forming sheet steel into appliance parts.
7. Manually assembling parts into appliances.
8. Maintaining and repairing machinery and equipment.
9. Insuring all tangible fixed assets.
10. Supervising production.
11. Training all employees of the company.
12. Painting and packaging finished appliances.

Having analyzed its Vista plant operations for purposes of installing activity-based costing, Andrea Boss, Inc. identified its activity cost centers. It now needs to identify relevant activity cost drivers in order to assign overhead costs to its products.

Instructions
Using the activities listed above, identify for each activity one or more cost drivers that might be used to assign overhead to Andrea Boss's five products.

Compute overhead rates and
assign overhead using ABC.
(SO 4, 5)

E4-8 Fribourg Instrument, Inc. manufactures two products: missile range instruments and space pressure gauges. During April, 50 range instruments and 300 pressure gauges were produced, and overhead costs of $89,000 were incurred. An analysis of overhead costs reveals the following activities.

Activity	Cost Driver	Total Cost
1. Materials handling	Number of requisitions	$35,000
2. Machine setups	Number of setups	27,000
3. Quality inspections	Number of inspections	27,000

The cost driver volume for each product was as follows.

Cost Driver	Instruments	Gauges	Total
Number of requisitions	400	600	1,000
Number of setups	200	300	500
Number of inspections	200	400	600

Instructions
(a) Determine the overhead rate for each activity.
(b) Assign the manufacturing overhead costs for April to the two products using activity-based costing.
(c) ▭▬▭▷ Write a memorandum to the president of Fribourg Instrument explaining the benefits of activity-based costing.

E4-9 In an effort to expand the usefulness of its activity-based costing system, Tommy Colina's Rijo Vineyards decides to adopt activity-based management techniques. One of these ABM techniques is qualifying its activities as either value-added or nonvalue-added.

Classify activities as value-added or nonvalue-added.
(SO 6)

Instructions
Using Rijo's list of fifteen activity cost pools in Exercise 4-6, classify each of the activities as either value-added or nonvalue-added.

E4-10 Andrea Boss, Inc. is interested in using its activity-based costing system to improve its operating efficiency and its profit margins by applying activity-based management techniques. As part of this undertaking, you have been asked to classify its Vista plant activities as value-added or nonvalue-added.

Classify activities as value-added or nonvalue-added.
(SO 6)

Instructions
Using the list of activities identified in Exercise 4-7, classify each activity as either value-added or nonvalue-added.

E4-11 Cheatham and Howe is a law firm that is initiating an activity-based costing system. Jim Cheatham, the senior partner and strong supporter of ABC, has prepared the following list of activities performed by a typical attorney in a day at the firm.

Classify service company activities by level.
(SO 6, 7)

Activity	Hours
Writing contracts and letters	1.0
Attending staff meetings	0.5
Taking depositions	1.5
Doing research	1.0
Traveling to/from court	1.0
Contemplating legal strategy	1.0
Eating lunch	1.0
Litigating a case in court	2.5
Entertaining a prospective client	1.5

Instructions
Classify each of the activities listed by Jim Cheatham as value-added or nonvalue-added; be able to defend your classification. How much was value-added time and how much was nonvalue-added?

*E4-12 Having itemized its costs for the first quarter of next year's budget, Gulino Corporation desires to install an activity-based costing system. First it identified the activity cost pools in which to accumulate factory overhead; second, it identified the relevant cost drivers. (This was done in Exercise 4-5.)

Classify activities by level.
(SO 9)

Instructions
Using the activity cost pools identified in Exercise 4-5, classify each of those cost pools as either unit-level, batch-level, product-level, or facility-level.

*E4-13 Paul DiGiovanni & Sons, Inc. is a small manufacturing company in Balboa that uses activity-based costing. DiGiovanni & Sons accumulates overhead in the following activity cost pools.

Classify activities by level.
(SO 9)

1. Managing parts inventory.
2. Hiring personnel.
3. Purchasing.
4. Designing products.
5. Testing prototypes.
6. Setting up equipment.
7. Inspecting machined parts.
8. Training employees.
9. Machining.
10. Assembling.

Instructions

For each activity cost pool, indicate whether the activity cost pool would be unit-level, batch-level, product-level, or facility-level.

PROBLEMS: SET A

Assign overhead using traditional costing and ABC; compute unit costs; classify activities as value- or nonvalue-added.
(SO 1, 4, 6)

P4-1A Curly-Soo, Inc. manufactures hair curlers and blow-dryers. The handheld hair curler is Curly-Soo's high volume product (80,000 units annually). It is a "large barrel," 20-watt, triple-heat appliance designed to appeal to the teenage market segment with its glow-in-the-dark handle. The handheld blow-dryer is Curly-Soo's lower-volume product (40,000 units annually). It is a three-speed, 2,000 watt appliance with a "cool setting" and a removable filter. It also is designed for the teen market.

Both products require one hour of direct labor for completion. Therefore, total annual direct labor hours are 120,000, (80,000 + 40,000). Expected annual manufacturing overhead is $441,600. Thus, the predetermined overhead rate is $3.68 per direct labor hour. The direct materials cost per unit is $5.25 for the hair curler and $9.75 for the blow-dryer. The direct labor cost is $8.00 per unit for the hair curler and the blow-dryer.

Curly-Soo purchases most of the parts from suppliers and assembles the finished product at its Fargo, North Dakota plant. It recently adopted activity-based costing, which after this year-end will totally replace its traditional direct labor-based cost accounting system. Curly-Soo has identified the following six activity cost pools and related cost drivers and has assembled the following information.

Activity Cost Pool	Cost Driver	Estimated Overhead	Expected Use of Cost Drivers	Expected Use of Cost Drivers per Product	
				Curlers	Dryers
Purchasing	Orders	$ 57,500	500	170	330
Receiving	Pounds	42,000	168,000	70,000	98,000
Assembling	Parts	169,600	848,000	424,000	424,000
Testing	Tests	52,000	130,000	82,000	48,000
Finishing	Units	60,000	120,000	80,000	40,000
Packing and shipping	Cartons	60,500	12,100	8,040	4,060
		$441,600			

Instructions

(a) Under traditional product costing, compute the total unit cost of both products. Prepare a simple comparative schedule of the individual costs by product (similar to Illustration 4-4).

(b) Under ABC, prepare a schedule showing the computations of the activity-based overhead rates (per cost driver).

(c) Prepare a schedule assigning each activity's overhead cost pool to each product based on the use of cost drivers. (Include a computation of overhead cost per unit, rounding to the nearest cent.)

(d) Compute the total cost per unit for each product under ABC.

(e) Classify each of the activities as a value-added activity or a nonvalue-added activity.

(f) Comment on (1) the comparative overhead cost per unit for the two products under ABC, and (2) the comparative total costs per unit under traditional costing and ABC.

P4-2A Petty Plastics, Inc. manufactures two plastic thermos containers at its plastic molding facility in Elum, Washington. Its large container, called the Ice House, has a volume of 5 gallons, side carrying handles, a snap-down lid, and a side drain and plug. Its smaller container, called the Cool Chest, has a volume of 2 gallons, an over-the-top carrying handle which is part of a tilting lid, and a removable shelf. Both containers and their parts are made entirely of hard-molded plastic. The Ice House sells for $35 and the Cool Chest sells for $24. The production costs computed per unit under traditional costing for each model in 2002 were as follows.

Assign overhead to products using ABC and evaluate decision.
(SO 4)

eGrade
Problem

Traditional Costing	Ice House	Cool Chest
Direct materials	$ 9.50	$ 6.00
Direct labor ($10 per hour)	8.00	5.00
Manufacturing overhead ($17.20 per DLH)	13.76	8.60
Total per unit cost	$31.26	$19.60

In 2002, Petty Plastics manufactured 50,000 units of the Ice House and 20,000 units of the Cool Chest. The overhead rate of $17.20 per direct labor hour was determined by dividing total expected manufacturing overhead of $860,000 by the total direct labor hours (50,000) for the 2 models.

Under traditional costing, the gross profit on the two containers was: Ice House $3.74 or ($35 − $31.26), and Cool Chest $4.40 or ($24 − $19.60). The gross margin rates on cost are: Ice House 12% or ($3.74 ÷ $31.26), and Cool Chest 22% or ($4.40 ÷ $19.60). Because Petty can earn a gross margin rate on the Cool Chest that is nearly twice as great as that earned on the Ice House, with less investment in inventory and labor costs, its management is urging its sales staff to put its efforts into selling the Cool Chest over the Ice House.

Before finalizing its decision, management asks the controller Dinna Martinez to prepare a product costing analysis using activity-based costing (ABC). Martinez accumulates the following information about overhead for the year ended December 31, 2002.

Activity	Cost Driver	Estimated Total Expected Overhead	Cost Drivers	Activity-Based Overhead Rate
Purchasing	Number of orders	$180,000	4,500	$40 per order
Machine setups	Number of setups	200,000	800	$250 per setup
Extruding	Machine hours	320,000	80,000	$4 per machine hour
Quality control	Tests and inspections	160,000	8,000	$20 per test

The cost drivers used for each product were:

Cost Driver	Ice House	Cool Chest	Total
Purchase orders	2,500	2,000	4,500
Machine setups	500	300	800
Machine hours	60,000	20,000	80,000
Tests and inspections	5,000	3,000	8,000

Instructions
(a) Assign the total 2002 manufacturing overhead costs to the two products using activity-based costing (ABC).
(b) What was the cost per unit and gross profit of each model using ABC costing?
(c) ▭▭▭▭▷ Are management's future plans for the two models sound?

P4-3A Castro Cabinets Company designs and builds upscale kitchen cabinets for luxury homes. Many of the kitchen cabinet and counter arrangements are custom made, but occasionally the company does mass production on order. Its budgeted manufacturing overhead costs for the year 2003 are as follows.

Assign overhead costs using traditional costing and ABC; compare results.
(SO 1, 4)

Overhead Cost Pools	Amount
Purchasing	$ 114,400
Handling materials	164,320
Production (cutting, milling, finishing)	400,000
Setting up machines	174,480
Inspecting	184,800
Inventory control (raw materials and finished goods)	252,000
Utilities	360,000
Total budget overhead costs	$1,650,000

For the last 3 years, Castro Cabinets Company has been charging overhead to products on the basis of machine hours. For the year 2003, 100,000 machine hours are budgeted.

Maribel Castro, owner-manager of Castro, recently directed her accountant, John Kandy, to implement the activity-based costing system he has repeatedly proposed. At Maribel's request, John and the production foreman identify the following cost drivers and their usage for the previously budgeted overhead cost pools.

Overhead Cost Pools	Activity Cost Drivers	Total Drivers
Purchasing	Number of orders	650
Handling materials	Numbers of moves	8,000
Production (cutting, milling, finishing)	Direct labor hours	100,000
Setting up machines	Number of setups	1,200
Inspecting	Number of inspections	6,000
Inventory control (raw materials and finished goods)	Number of components	36,000
Utilities	Square feet occupied	90,000

Kelly Garber, sales manager, has received an order for 50 kitchen cabinet arrangements from Bitty Builders, a housing development contractor. At Kelly's request, John prepares cost estimates for producing components for 50 cabinet arrangements so Kelly can submit a contract price per kitchen arrangement to Bitty Builders. He accumulates the following data for the production of 50 kitchen cabinet arrangements.

Direct materials	$180,000
Direct labor	$200,000
Machine hours	15,000
Direct labor hours	12,000
Number of purchase orders	50
Number of material moves	800
Number of machine setups	100
Number of inspections	450
Number of components (cabinets and accessories)	3,000
Number of square feet occupied	8,000

Instructions

(a) Compute the predetermined overhead rate using traditional costing with machine hours as the basis. (Round to the nearest cent.)

(b) What is the manufacturing cost per complete kitchen arrangement under traditional costing?

(c) What is the manufacturing cost per kitchen arrangement under the proposed activity-based costing? (Prepare all of the necessary schedules.)

(d) [pencil icon] Which of the two costing systems is preferable in pricing decisions and why?

Assign overhead costs using traditional costing and ABC; compare results.
(SO 1, 4)

P4-4A   Frazzle Corporation produces two grades of wine from grapes that it buys from California growers. It produces and sells, in 1-gallon jugs, roughly 800,000 gallons per year of a low-cost, high-volume product called StarDew. It also produces and sells roughly 200,000 gallons per year of a low-volume, high-cost product called VineRose. VineRose is sold in 1-liter bottles; thus 200,000 gallons results in roughly 800,000 bottles. Based on recent data, the StarDew product has not been as profitable as VineRose. Management is considering dropping the inexpensive StarDew so it can focus more attention on the VineRose line product. VineRose already demands considerably more attention than StarDew.

Tom Edwards, president and founder of Frazzle, is skeptical about this idea. He points out that for many decades the company produced only the StarDew line, and that it was always quite profitable. It wasn't until the company started producing the more complicated VineRose wine that the profitability of StarDew declined. Prior to the introduction of VineRose the company had simple equipment, simple growing and production procedures, and virtually no need for quality control. Because VineRose is bottled in 1-liter bottles it requires considerably more time and effort, both to bottle and to label and box, than does StarDew. (There are roughly 4 liters in a gallon; thus the company must bottle and handle 4 bottles of VineRose to sell the same amount of wine as StarDew.) StarDew requires 1 month of aging; VineRose requires 1 year. StarDew requires cleaning and inspection of equipment every 5,000 gallons; VineRose requires such maintenance every 500 gallons.

Tom has asked the accounting department to prepare an analysis of the cost per gallon using the traditional costing approach and using activity-based costing. The following information was collected.

	StarDew	VineRose
Direct materials per gallon	$1.10	$2.40
Direct labor cost per gallon	$0.50	$1.00
Direct labor hours per gallon	0.075	0.15
Total direct labor hours	60,000	30,000

Activity Cost Pool	Cost Driver	Estimated Overhead	Expected Use of Cost Drivers	StarDew	VineRose
Grape processing	Cart of grapes	$ 180,000	10,000	8,000	2,000
Aging	Total months	416,000	10,400,000	800,000	9,600,000
Bottling and corking	Number of bottles	360,000	1,600,000	800,000	800,000
Labeling and boxing	Number of bottles	240,000	1,600,000	800,000	800,000
Maintain, and inspect equipment	Number of inspections	280,000	560	160	400
		$1,476,000			

Instructions
Answer each of the following questions. (Round all calculations to three decimal places.)
(a) Under traditional product costing using direct labor hours, compute the total manufacturing cost per **gallon** of both products.
(b) Under ABC, prepare a schedule showing the computation of the activity-based overhead rates (per cost driver).
(c) Prepare a schedule assigning each activity's overhead cost pool to each product, based on the use of cost drivers. Include a computation of overhead cost per unit.
(d) Compute the total manufacturing cost per gallon for both products under ABC.
(e) ▭▭▭▶ Write a memo to Tom Edwards discussing the implications of your analysis for the company's plans. In this memo provide a brief description of ABC, as well as an explanation of how the traditional approach can result in distortions.

Assign overhead costs to services using traditional costing and ABC; compute overhead rates and unit costs; compare results.
(SO 1, 4, 6, 7)

P4-5A Horses and Dogs Veterinary Clinic is a small-town partnership that offers two primary services, farm animal services and pet care services. Providing veterinary care to farm animals requires travel to the farm animal (house calls), while veterinary care to pets generally requires that the pet be brought into the clinic. As part of an investigation to determine the contribution that each of these two types of services makes to overall profit, one partner argues for allocating overhead using activity-based costing while the other partner argues for a more simple overhead cost allocation on the basis of direct labor hours. The partners agree to use next year's budgeted data, as prepared by their public accountant, for analysis and comparison purposes. The following overhead data are collected to develop the comparison.

Activity Cost Pool	Cost Driver	Estimated Overhead	Total Expected Cost Drivers	Expected Use of Drivers by Service	
				Farm Animals	Pets
Drug treatment	Treatments	$ 64,000	4,000	1,800	2,200
Surgery	Operations	65,000	800	200	600
Travel	Mileage	28,000	28,000	26,000	2,000
Consultation	Appointment/Calls	33,000	3,000	600	2,400
Accounting/office	Direct labor hours	30,000	5,000	2,000	3,000
Boarding and grooming	100% pets	40,000			
		$260,000			

Instructions

(a) Using traditional product costing as proposed by the one partner, compute the total overhead cost assigned to both services of Horses and Dogs Veterinary Clinic.

(b) (1) Using activity-based costing, prepare a schedule showing the computations of the activity-based overhead rates (per cost driver).

(2) Prepare a schedule assigning each activity's overhead cost pool to each service based on the use of the cost drivers.

(c) Classify each of the activities as a value-added activity or a nonvalue-added activity.

(d) ▭▭▭▷ Comment on the comparative overhead cost assigned to the two services under both traditional costing and ABC.

PROBLEMS: SET B

Assign overhead using traditional costing and ABC; compute unit costs; classify activities as value- or nonvalue-added.
(SO 1, 4, 6)

P4-1B Fire Safety Products, Inc. manufactures steel cylinders and nozzles for two models of fire extinguishers: (1) a home fire extinguisher and (2) a commercial fire extinguisher. The **home model** is a high-volume (54,000 units), half-gallon cylinder that holds $2\frac{1}{2}$ pounds of multipurpose dry chemical at 480 PSI. The **commercial model** is a low-volume (10,200 units), two-gallon cylinder that holds 10 pounds of multi-purpose dry chemical at 390 PSI. Both products require 1.5 hours of direct labor for completion. Therefore, total annual direct labor hours are 96,300 or [1.5 hrs. × (54,000 + 10,200)]. Expected annual manufacturing overhead is $1,492,780. Thus, the predetermined overhead rate is $15.50 or ($1,492,780 ÷ 96,300) per direct labor hour. The direct materials cost per unit is $18.50 for the home model and $26.50 for the commercial model. The direct labor cost is $19 per unit for both the home and the commercial models.

The company's managers identified six activity cost pools and related cost drivers and accumulated overhead by cost pool as follows.

Activity Cost Pool	Cost Driver	Estimated Overhead	Expected Use of Cost Drivers	Expected Use of Drivers by Product	
				Home	Commercial
Receiving	Pounds	$ 70,350	335,000	215,000	120,000
Forming	Machine hours	150,500	35,000	27,000	8,000
Assembling	Number of parts	381,600	212,000	162,000	50,000
Testing	Number of tests	51,000	25,500	15,500	10,000
Painting	Gallons	52,080	6,510	4,510	2,000
Packing and shipping	Pounds	787,250	335,000	215,000	120,000
		$1,492,780			

Instructions

(a) Under traditional product costing, compute the total unit cost of both products. Prepare a simple comparative schedule of the individual costs by product (similar to Illustration 4-4).

(b) Under ABC, prepare a schedule showing the computations of the activity-based overhead rates (per cost driver).

(c) Prepare a schedule assigning each activity's overhead cost pool to each product based on the use of cost drivers. (Include a computation of overhead cost per unit, rounding to the nearest cent.)

(d) Compute the total cost per unit for each product under ABC.

(e) Classify each of the activities as a value-added activity or a nonvalue-added activity.

(f) Comment on (1) the comparative overhead cost per unit for the two products under ABC, and (2) the comparative total costs per unit under traditional costing and ABC.

P4-2B   Jackson Electronics manufactures two large-screen television models: the Royale which sells for $1,600, and a new model, the Majestic, which sells for $1,300. The production cost computed per unit under traditional costing for each model in 2002 was as follows.

Assign overhead to products using ABC and evaluate decision.
(SO 4)

Traditional Costing	**Royale**	**Majestic**
Direct materials	$ 700	$420
Direct labor ($20 per hour)	120	100
Manufacturing overhead ($38 per DLH)	228	190
Total per unit cost	$1,048	$710

In 2002, Jackson manufactured 25,000 units of the Royale and 10,000 units of the Majestic. The overhead rate of $38 per direct labor hour was determined by dividing total expected manufacturing overhead of $7,600,000 by the total direct labor hours (200,000) for the two models.

Under traditional costing, the gross profit on the models was: Royale $552 or ($1,600 − $1,048), and Majestic $590 or ($1,300 − $710). Because of this difference, management is considering phasing out the Royale model and increasing the production of the Majestic model.

Before finalizing its decision, management asks Jackson's controller to prepare an analysis using activity-based costing (ABC). The controller accumulates the following information about overhead for the year ended December 31, 2002.

Activity	Cost Driver	Estimated Overhead	Expected Use of Cost Drivers	Activity-Based Overhead Rate
Purchasing	Number of orders	$1,200,000	40,000	$30
Machine setups	Number of setups	900,000	18,000	50
Machining	Machine hours	4,800,000	120,000	40
Quality control	Number of inspections	700,000	28,000	25

The cost drivers used for each product were:

Cost Driver	Royale	Majestic	Total
Purchase orders	15,000	25,000	40,000
Machine setups	6,000	12,000	18,000
Machine hours	75,000	45,000	120,000
Inspections	8,000	20,000	28,000

Instructions

(a) Assign the total 2002 manufacturing overhead costs to the two products using activity-based costing (ABC).

(b) What was the cost per unit and gross profit of each model using ABC costing?

(c) ▱▱▱▱▱▷ Are management's future plans for the two models sound? Explain.

Assign overhead costs using traditional costing and ABC; compare results.
(SO 1, 4)

P4-3B Customized Stairs Co. of Poway designs and builds factory-made premium wooden stairs for homes. The manufactured stair components (spindles, risers, hangers, hand rails) permit installation of stairs of varying lengths and widths. All are of white oak wood. Its budgeted manufacturing overhead costs for the year 2003 are as follows.

Overhead Cost Pools	Amount
Purchasing	$ 57,000
Handling materials	82,000
Production (cutting, milling, finishing)	200,000
Setting up machines	84,840
Inspecting	90,000
Inventory control (raw materials and finished goods)	126,000
Utilities	180,000
Total budget overhead costs	$819,840

For the last 4 years, Customized Stairs Co. has been charging overhead to products on the basis of machine hours. For the year 2003, 100,000 machine hours are budgeted.

Saida Fang, owner-manager of Customized Stairs Co., recently directed his accountant, Maria Barrila, to implement the activity-based costing system that she has repeatedly proposed. At Saida Fang's request, Maria and the production foreman identify the following cost drivers and their usage for the previously budgeted overhead cost pools.

Overhead Cost Pools	Activity Cost Drivers	Expected Use of Cost Drivers
Purchasing	Number of orders	600
Handling materials	Number of moves	8,000
Production (cutting, milling, finishing)	Direct labor hours	100,000
Setting up machines	Number of setups	1,200
Inspecting	Number of inspections	6,000
Inventory control (raw materials and finished goods)	Number of components	168,000
Utilities	Square feet occupied	90,000

Nick Duich, sales manager, has received an order for 280 stairs from Mall Builders, Inc., a large housing development contractor. At Nick's request, Maria prepares cost estimates for producing components for 280 stairs so Nick can submit a contract price per stair to Mall Builders. She accumulates the following data for the production of 280 stairways.

Direct materials	$103,600
Direct labor	$112,000
Machine hours	14,500
Direct labor hours	5,000
Number of purchase orders	60
Number of material moves	800
Number of machine setups	100
Number of inspections	450
Number of components	16,000
Number of square feet occupied	8,000

Instructions

(a) Compute the predetermined overhead rate using traditional costing with machine hours as the basis.

(b) What is the manufacturing cost per stairway under traditional costing?

(c) What is the manufacturing cost per stairway under the proposed activity-based costing? (Prepare all of the necessary schedules.)

(d) ▮▮▯▯▷ Which of the two costing systems is preferable in pricing decisions and why?

P4-4B Bastille Corporation produces two grades of wine from grapes that it buys from California growers. It produces and sells roughly 3,000,000 liters per year of a low-cost, high-volume product called CoolDay. It sells this in 600,000 5-liter jugs. Bastille also produces and sells roughly 300,000 liters per year of a low-volume, high-cost product called LiteMist. LiteMist is sold in 1-liter bottles. Based on recent data, the CoolDay product has not been as profitable as LiteMist. Management is considering dropping the inexpensive CoolDay line so it can focus more attention on the LiteMist product. The LiteMist product already demands considerably more attention than the CoolDay line.

Assign overhead costs using traditional costing and ABC; compare results.
(SO 1, 4)

Frank Summer, president and founder of Bastille, is skeptical about this idea. He points out that for many decades the company produced only the CoolDay line, and that it was always quite profitable. It wasn't until the company started producing the more complicated LiteMist wine that the profitability of CoolDay declined. Prior to the introduction of LiteMist, the company had simple equipment, simple growing and production procedures, and virtually no need for quality control. Because LiteMist is bottled in 1-liter bottles, it requires considerably more time and effort, both to bottle and to label and box than does CoolDay. The company must bottle and handle 5 times as many bottles of LiteMist to sell the same quantity as CoolDay. CoolDay requires 1 month of aging; LiteMist requires 1 year. CoolDay requires cleaning and inspection of equipment every 10,000 liters; LiteMist requires such maintenance every 600 liters.

Frank has asked the accounting department to prepare an analysis of the cost per liter using the traditional costing approach and using activity-based costing. The following information was collected.

	CoolDay	LiteMist
Direct materials per liter	$0.40	$1.20
Direct labor cost per liter	$0.25	$0.50
Direct labor hours per liter	0.04	0.09
Total direct labor hours	120,000	27,000

Activity Cost Pool	Cost Driver	Estimated Overhead	Expected Use of Cost Drivers	Expected Use of Cost Drivers per Product CoolDay	LiteMist
Grape processing	Cart of grapes	$ 145,200	6,600	6,000	600
Aging	Total months	396,000	6,600,000	3,000,000	3,600,000
Bottling and corking	Number of bottles	270,000	900,000	600,000	300,000
Labeling and boxing	Number of bottles	189,000	900,000	600,000	300,000
Maintain and inspect equipment	Number of inspections	240,000	800	300	500
		$1,240,200			

Instructions
Answer each of the following questions. (Round all calculations to three decimal places.)
(a) Under traditional product costing using direct labor hours, compute the total manufacturing cost per **liter** of both products.
(b) Under ABC, prepare a schedule showing the computation of the activity-based overhead rates (per cost driver).
(c) Prepare a schedule assigning each activity's overhead cost pool to each product, based on the use of cost drivers. Include a computation of overhead cost per liter.
(d) Compute the total manufacturing cost per liter for both products under ABC.
(e) ▮▮▯▯▷ Write a memo to Frank Summer discussing the implications of your analysis for the company's plans. In this memo provide a brief description of ABC, as well as an explanation of how the traditional approach can result in distortions.

Assign overhead costs to services using traditional costing and ABC; compute overhead rates and unit costs; compare results.
(SO 1, 4, 6, 7)

P4-5B Les and Moore is a public accounting firm that offers two primary services, auditing and tax return preparation. A controversy has developed between the partners of the two service lines as to who is contributing the greater amount to the bottom line. The area of contention is the assignment of overhead. The tax partners argue for assigning overhead on the basis of 40% of direct labor dollars, while the audit partners argue for implementing activity-based costing. The partners agree to use next year's budgeted data for purposes of analysis and comparison. The following overhead data are collected to develop the comparison.

Activity Cost Pool	Cost Driver	Estimated Overhead	Expected Use of Cost Drivers	Expected Use of Cost Drivers per Service	
				Audit	Tax
Employee training	Direct labor dollars	$209,000	$1,900,000	$1,000,000	$900,000
Typing and secretarial	Number of reports/ forms	76,200	2,500	600	1,900
Computing	Number of minutes	204,000	60,000	25,000	35,000
Facility rental	Number of employees	142,500	38	20	18
Travel	Per expense reports	128,300	Direct	86,800	41,500
		$760,000			

Instructions
(a) Using traditional product costing as proposed by the tax partners, compute the total overhead cost assigned to both services (audit and tax) of Les and Moore.
(b) (1) Using activity-based costing, prepare a schedule showing the computations of the activity-based overhead rates (per cost driver).
   (2) Prepare a schedule assigning each activity's overhead cost pool to each service based on the use of the cost drivers.
(c) Classify each of the activities as a value-added activity or a nonvalue-added activity.
(d) ▭▭▭▭▭▭▷ Comment on the comparative overhead cost per unit for the two products under both traditional costing and ABC.

◆ **BROADENING YOUR PERSPECTIVE**

GROUP DECISION CASE

BYP4-1 Valley West Hospital is a primary medical health care facility and trauma center that serves 11 small, rural midwestern communities within a 40-mile radius. The hospital offers all the medical/surgical services of a typical small hospital. It has a staff of 18 full-time doctors and 20 part-time visiting specialists. Valley West has a payroll of 150 employees consisting of technicians, nurses, therapists, managers, directors, administrators, dieticians, secretaries, data processors, and janitors.

Instructions
With the class divided into groups, discuss and answer the following.
(a) Using your (limited, moderate, or in-depth) knowledge of a hospital's operations, identify as many **activities** as you can that would serve as the basis for implementing an activity-based costing system.
(b) For each of the activities listed in (a), identify a **cost driver** that would serve as a valid measure of the resources consumed by the activity.

MANAGERIAL ANALYSIS

BYP4-2   Ideal Manufacturing Company of Sycamore, Illinois has supported a research and development (R&D) department that has for many years been the sole contributor to the company's new farm machinery products. The R&D activity is an overhead cost center that provides services only to in-house manufacturing departments (4 different product lines), all of which produce agricultural/farm/ranch related machinery products. The department has never sold its services outside, but because of its long history of success, larger manufacturers of agricultural products have approached Ideal to hire its R&D department for special projects. Because the costs of operating the R&D department have been spiraling uncontrollably, Ideal's management is considering entertaining these outside approaches to absorb the increasing costs. But, (1) management doesn't have any cost basis for charging R&D services to outsiders, and (2) it needs to gain control of its R&D costs. Management decides to implement an activity-based costing system in order to determine the charges for both outsiders and the in-house users of the department's services.

R&D activities fall into four pools with the following annual costs.

Market analysis	$1,050,000
Product design	2,280,000
Product development	3,600,000
Prototype testing	1,400,000

Activity analysis determines that the appropriate cost drivers and their usage for the four activities are:

Activity	Cost Drivers	Total Estimated Drivers
Market analysis	Hours of analysis	15,000 hours
Product design	Number of designs	2,500 designs
Product development	Number of products	90 products
Prototype testing	Number of tests	700 tests

Instructions
(a) Compute the activity-based overhead rate for each activity cost pool.
(b) How much cost would be charged to an in-house manufacturing department that consumed 1,800 hours of market analysis time, was provided 280 designs relating to 10 products, and requested 92 engineering tests?
(c) How much cost would serve as the basis for pricing an R&D bid with an outside company on a contract that would consume 800 hours of analysis time, require 178 designs relating to 3 products, and result in 70 engineering tests?
(d) What is the benefit to Ideal Manufacturing of applying activity-based costing to its R&D activity for both in-house and outside charging purposes?

REAL-WORLD FOCUS

BYP4-3   Hewlett-Packard is considered one of the best managed and most innovative companies in the world. It continually has shown an ability to adapt to global competitive challenges through technical innovation and continual reassessment of its management and control mechanisms. Most applications of activity-based costing by Hewlett-Packard have been successful.

But, over the period August 1988 to August 1989, the Colorado Springs Division of Hewlett-Packard designed an activity-based costing system with the goal of providing for better product costing and inventory valuation. It began implementation in November 1989 but halted the process in the summer of 1992. Since then, the Colorado Springs Division has made no further attempts to re-implement a more expansive ABC approach.

Instructions

The March 1997 issue of *Management Accounting* contains an article by Steven P. Landry, Larry M. Wood, and Tim M. Linquist about the Colorado Springs Division entitled "Can ABC Bring Mixed Results?" Read the article and answer the following questions.

(a) What went wrong at H-P's Colorado Springs Division in the design, development, and implementation of its activity-based costing system?

(b) What conclusions were drawn from H-P's Colorado Springs Division experience? What does successful ABC implementation require?

Exploring the Web

BYP4-4   **Cost Technology** describes itself as a "global consulting company specializing in profit management." The company helps manufacturing, service, and government organizations implement methods, such as activity-based costing and activity-based management, that will improve corporate profitability. The home page of Cost Technology includes information about the company, its markets, and products. The following exercise investigates the company's training programs.

Address: **http://costtechnology.com/training.htm**
         (**or go to www.wiley.com/college/weygandt**)

Instructions

This page refers to other pages that describe three different training courses. Read the descriptions of these courses to answer the following questions.

(a) List four types of employees that the company says would benefit from the course "Introduction of Activity-Based Management Solutions."

(b) What is target costing?

(c) What is the major cause of failure of many ABC implementations? Describe "Workforce Activity-Based Management."

Communication Activity

BYP4-5   In our Feature Story about **Super Bakery, Inc.,** we described a virtual corporation as one that consists of a core unit that is supported by a network of outsourced activities. A virtual corporation minimizes investment in human resources, fixed assets, and working capital. The application of ABC to Super Bakery, Inc. is described in an article entitled "ABC in a Virtual Corporation" by Tom Davis and Bruce Darling, in *Management Accounting*, October 1996.

Instructions

Assume you are the controller of a virtual corporation. Using the article as a basis for your communication, write a summary that answers the following questions.

(a) What unique strategies and tactics did Super Bakery's management implement that caused sales to take off and continue to grow at an average rate of 20%?

(b) Why did Super Bakery's management feel that it was necessary to install an ABC system?

(c) What is the main difference between Super Bakery's ABC system and other manufacturers' ABC systems?

Research Assignment

BYP4-6   The April 1998 issue of *Management Accounting* includes an article by Kip R. Krumwiede entitled "ABC: Why It's Tried and How It Succeeds."

Instructions

Read the article and answer the following questions.

(a) What is the adoption and implementation status of ABC according to the survey conducted in 1996 by the Cost Management Group of the Institute of Management Accountants?

(b) What did Krumwiede's survey attempt to determine?

(c) In Krumwiede's survey, what factors appeared to separate those companies that adopted ABC from those that did not adopt ABC?

(d) Identify at least five "Basic ABC Implementation Tips" recommended in the article.

*E*THICS *C*ASE

BYP4-7   Ernie Lobb, the cost accountant for Superior Mower Company, recently installed activity-based costing at its St. Louis lawn tractor (riding mower) plant where three models—the 8-horsepower Bladerunner, the 12-horsepower Quickcut, and the 18-horsepower Supercut—are manufactured. Ernie's new product costs for these three models show that the company's traditional costing system had been significantly undercosting the 18-horsepower Supercut. This was due primarily to the lower sales volume of the Supercut compared to the Bladerunner and the Quickcut.

Before completing his analysis and reporting these results to management, Ernie is approached by his friend Eddie Polyester, who is the production manager for the 18-horsepower Supercut model. Eddie has heard from one of Ernie's staff about the new product costs and is upset and worried for his job because the new costs show the Supercut to be losing, rather than making, money.

At first Eddie condemns the new cost system, whereupon Ernie explains the practice of activity-based costing and why it is more accurate than the company's present system. Even more worried now, Eddie begs Ernie, "Massage the figures just enough to save the line from being discontinued. You don't want me to lose my job do you? Anyway, nobody will know."

Ernie holds firm but agrees to recompute all his calculations for accuracy before submitting his costs to management.

Instructions

(a) Who are the stakeholders in this situation?

(b) What, if any, are the ethical considerations in this situation?

(c) What are Ernie's ethical obligations to the company? To his friend?

Answers to Self-Study Questions

1. c   2. c   3. c   4. b   5. d   6. d   7. c   8. d   9. b   *10. c

Remember to go back to the Navigator box on the chapter-opening page and check off your completed work.

CHAPTER 5

Cost-Volume-Profit Relationships

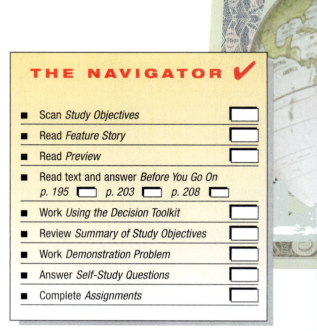

THE NAVIGATOR ✔

■ Scan *Study Objectives* ☐

■ Read *Feature Story* ☐

■ Read *Preview* ☐

■ Read text and answer *Before You Go On*
  p. 195 ☐   p. 203 ☐   p. 208 ☐

■ Work *Using the Decision Toolkit* ☐

■ Review *Summary of Study Objectives* ☐

■ Work *Demonstration Problem* ☐

■ Answer *Self-Study Questions* ☐

■ Complete *Assignments* ☐

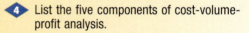

STUDY OBJECTIVES

After studying this chapter, you should be able to:

1. Distinguish between variable and fixed costs.

2. Explain the significance of the relevant range.

3. Explain the concept of mixed costs.

4. List the five components of cost-volume-profit analysis.

5. Indicate what contribution margin is and how it can be expressed.

6. Identify the three ways to determine the break-even point.

7. Define margin of safety, and give the formulas for computing it.

8. Give the formulas for determining sales required to earn target net income.

9. Describe the essential features of a cost-volume-profit income statement.

THE NAVIGATOR

FEATURE STORY

GROWING BY LEAPS AND LEOTARDS

When the last of her three children went off to school, Amy began looking for a job. At this same time, her daughter asked to take dance classes. The nearest dance studio was over 20 miles away, and Amy didn't know how she would balance a new job and drive her daughter to dance class. Suddenly it hit her—why not start her own dance studio?

Amy sketched out a business plan: A local church would rent its basement for $6 per hour. The size of the basement limited the number of students she could teach, but the rent was low. Insurance for a small studio was $50 per month. Initially she would teach classes only for young kids since that was all she felt qualified to do. She thought she could charge $2.50 for a one-hour class. There was room for 8 students per class. She wouldn't get rich—but at least it would be fun, and she didn't have much at risk.

Amy soon realized that the demand for dance classes far exceeded her capacity. She considered renting a bigger space that could serve 15 students per class. But her rent would also increase signifi-

cantly. Also, rather than paying rent by the hour, she would have to pay $600 per month, even during the summer months when demand for dance classes was low. She also would have to pay utilities—roughly $70 per month.

However, with a bigger space Amy could offer classes for teens and adults. Teens and adults would pay a higher fee—$5 per hour—though the number of students per class would have to be smaller, probably only 8 per class. She could hire a part-time instructor at about $18 per hour to teach advanced classes. Insurance costs could increase to $100 per month. In addition, she would need a part-time adminis-

trator at $100 per month to keep records. Amy also realized she could increase her income by selling dance supplies such as shoes, towels, and leotards.

Amy laid out a new business plan based on these estimates. If she failed, she stood to lose real money. Convinced she could make a go of it, she made the big plunge.

Her planning paid off: Within 10 years of starting her business in a church basement Amy had over 800 students, seven instructors, two administrators, and a facility with three separate studios.

THE NAVIGATOR

s the Feature Story indicates, to manage any size business you must understand how costs respond to changes in sales volume and the effect of costs and revenues on profits. A prerequisite to understanding cost-volume-profit (CVP) relationships is knowledge of how costs behave. In this chapter, we first explain the considerations involved in cost behavior analysis. Then we discuss and illustrate CVP analysis and variable costing.

The content and organization of Chapter 5 are as follows.

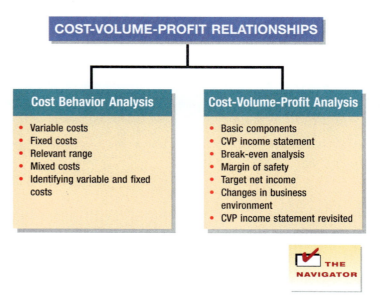

COST BEHAVIOR ANALYSIS

Cost behavior analysis is the study of how specific costs respond to changes in the level of business activity. As you might expect, some costs change, and others remain the same. For example, for an airline company such as **Southwest** or **United**, the longer the flight the higher the fuel costs. On the other hand, **Massachusetts General Hospital**'s employee costs to run the emergency room on any given night are relatively constant regardless of the number of patients serviced. A knowledge of cost behavior helps management plan operations and decide between alternative courses of action. Cost behavior analysis applies to all types of entities, as the Feature Story about Amy's dance studio indicates.

The starting point in cost behavior analysis is measuring the key business activities. Activity levels may be expressed in terms of sales dollars (in a retail company), miles driven (in a trucking company), room occupancy (in a hotel), or dance classes taught (by a dance studio). Many companies use more than one measurement base. A manufacturer, for example, may use direct labor hours or units of output for manufacturing costs and sales revenue or units sold for selling expenses.

For an activity level to be useful in cost behavior analysis, changes in the level or volume of activity should be correlated with changes in costs. The activity level selected is referred to as the activity (or volume) index. The **activity index** identifies the activity that causes changes in the behavior of costs.

With an appropriate activity index, it is possible to classify the behavior of costs in response to changes in activity levels into three categories: variable, fixed, or mixed.

VARIABLE COSTS

Variable costs are costs that vary **in total** directly and proportionately with changes in the activity level. If the level increases 10 percent, total variable costs will increase 10 percent. If the level of activity decreases by 25 percent, variable costs will decrease 25 percent. Examples of variable costs include direct materials and direct labor for a manufacturer; cost of goods sold, sales commissions, and freight-out for a merchandiser; and gasoline in airline and trucking companies. A variable cost may also be defined as a cost that **remains the same *per unit* at every level of activity**.

To illustrate the behavior of a variable cost, assume that Damon Company manufactures radios that contain a $10 digital clock. The activity index is the number of radios produced. As each radio is manufactured, the total cost of the clocks increases by $10. As shown in part (a) of Illustration 5-1, total cost of the clocks will be $20,000 if 2,000 radios are produced, and $100,000 when 10,000 radios are produced. We also can see that a variable cost remains the same per unit as the level of activity changes. As shown in part (b) of Illustration 5-1, the unit cost of $10 for the clocks is the same whether 2,000 or 10,000 radios are produced.

STUDY OBJECTIVE

1

Distinguish between variable and fixed costs.

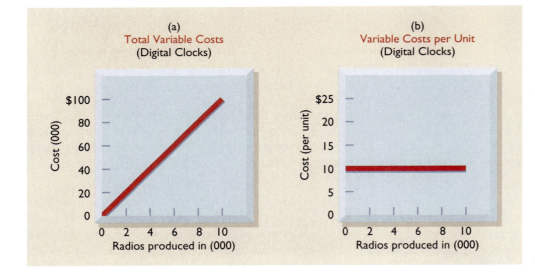

Illustration 5-1 Behavior of total and unit variable costs

Helpful Hint True or false: Variable cost per unit changes directly and proportionately with changes in activity. Answer: False. Per unit cost remains constant at all levels of activity.

Companies that rely heavily on labor to manufacture a product, such as **Nike** or **Reebok**, or to provide a service, such as **Hilton** or **Marriott**, are likely to have many variable costs. In contrast, companies that use a high proportion of machinery and equipment in producing revenue, such as **ATT** or **Duke Energy Co.**, may have few variable costs.

FIXED COSTS

Fixed costs are costs that **remain the same in total** regardless of changes in the activity level. Examples include property taxes, insurance, rent, supervisory salaries, and depreciation on buildings and equipment. Because total fixed costs remain constant as activity changes, it follows that **fixed costs *per unit* vary inversely with activity**: **As volume increases, unit cost declines, and vice versa**.

To illustrate the behavior of fixed costs, assume that Damon Company leases its productive facilities at a cost of $10,000 per month. Total fixed costs of the facilities will remain constant at every level of activity, as shown in part (a) of Illustration 5-2. But, on a per unit basis, the cost of rent will decline as activity increases, as shown in part (b) of Illustration 5-2. At 2,000 units, the unit cost is $5 ($10,000 ÷ 2,000). When 10,000 radios are produced, the unit cost is only $1 ($10,000 ÷ 10,000).

Illustration 5-2   Behavior of total and unit fixed costs

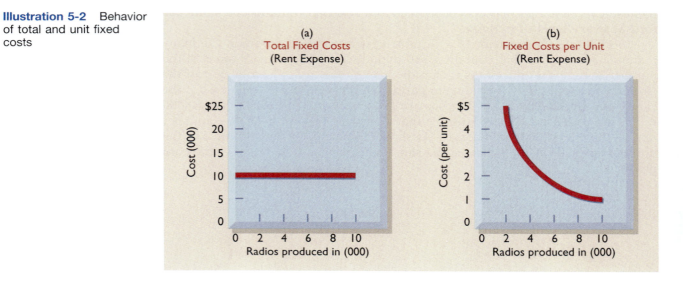

The trend for many manufacturers is to have more fixed costs and fewer variable costs. This trend is the result of increased use of automation and less use of employee labor. As a result, depreciation and lease charges (fixed costs) increase, whereas direct labor costs (variable costs) decrease.

B U S I N E S S   I N S I G H T

Management Perspective

When Thomas Moser quit teaching communications at Bates College 25 years ago, he turned to what he loved doing—furniture woodworking. Today he has over 120 employees. In a business where profit margins are seldom thicker than wood shavings, cost control is everything. Moser keeps no inventory; a 50 percent deposit buys the wood. Because computer-driven machines cut most of the standardized parts and joints, "we're free to be inefficient in assembly and finishing work, where the craft is most obviously expressed," says Moser. Direct labor costs are a manageable 30 percent of revenues. By keeping a tight lid on costs and running an efficient operation, Moser is free to spend most of his time doing what he enjoys most—designing furniture.

Source: Excerpts from "Out of the Woods," *Forbes*, April 5, 1999, p. 74.

RELEVANT RANGE

In Illustrations 5-1 and 5-2, straight lines were drawn throughout the entire activity index for total variable costs and total fixed costs. In essence, the assumption was made that the costs were **linear.** It is now necessary to ask: Is the straight-line relationship realistic? Does the linear assumption produce useful data for CVP analysis?

STUDY OBJECTIVE
2

Explain the significance of the relevant range.

In most business situations, a straight-line relationship **does not exist** for variable costs throughout the entire range of possible activity. At abnormally low levels of activity, it may be impossible to be cost efficient. Small-scale operations may not allow the company to obtain quantity discounts for raw materials or to use specialized labor. In contrast, at abnormally high levels of activity, labor costs may increase sharply because of overtime pay. Also at high activity levels, materials costs may jump significantly because of excess spoilage caused by worker fatigue. As a result, in the real world, the relationship between the behavior of a variable cost and changes in the activity level is often **curvilinear**, as shown in part (a) of Illustration 5-3.

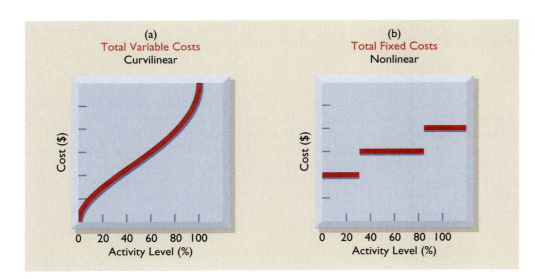

Illustration 5-3 Nonlinear behavior of variable and fixed costs

Total fixed costs also do not have a straight-line relationship over the entire range of activity. Some fixed costs will not change. But it is possible for management to change other fixed costs. For example, in the Feature Story the dance studio's rent was originally variable and then became fixed at a certain amount. It then increased to a new fixed amount when the size of the studio increased beyond a certain point. An example of the behavior of total fixed costs through all potential levels of activity is shown in part (b) of Illustration 5-3.

For most companies, operating at almost zero or at 100 percent capacity is the exception rather than the rule. Instead, companies often operate over a somewhat narrower range, such as 40–80 percent of capacity. The range over which a company expects to operate during a year is called the **relevant range** of the activity index. Within the relevant range, as shown in both diagrams in Illustration 5-4, a straight-line relationship generally exists for both variable and fixed costs.

Helpful Hint Fixed costs that may be changeable include research, such as new product development, and management training programs.

Alternative Terminology The relevant range is also called the *normal* or *practical range.*

Illustration 5-4 Linear behavior within relevant range

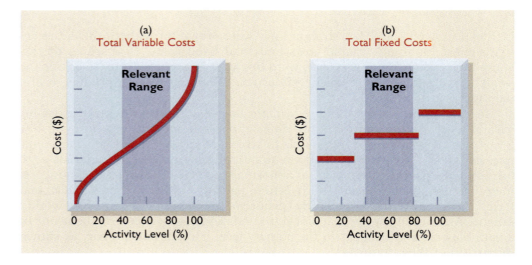

As you can see, although the straight-line relationship may not be completely realistic, **the linear assumption produces useful data for CVP analysis as long as the level of activity remains within the relevant range**.

MIXED COSTS

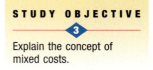

STUDY OBJECTIVE

3

Explain the concept of mixed costs.

Mixed costs are costs that contain both a variable element and a fixed element. Sometimes called **semivariable costs, mixed costs change in total but not proportionately with changes in the activity level**. The rental of a **U-Haul** truck is a good example of a mixed cost. Assume that local rental terms for a 17-foot truck, including insurance, are $50 per day plus 50 cents per mile. The per diem charge is a fixed cost with respect to miles driven, whereas the mileage charge is a variable cost. The graphic presentation of the rental cost for a one-day rental is as follows.

Illustration 5-5 Behavior of a mixed cost

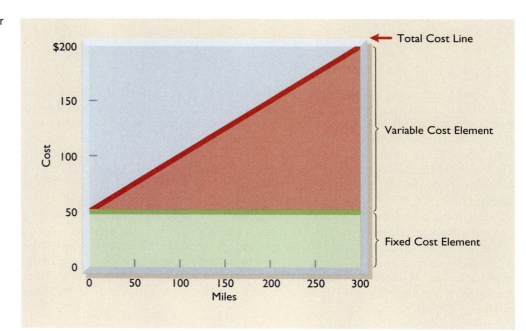

In this case, the fixed cost element is the cost of having the service available. The variable cost element is the cost of actually using the service. Another example of a mixed cost is utility costs (electric, telephone, and so on), where there is a flat service fee plus a usage charge.

For purposes of CVP analysis, **mixed costs must be classified into their fixed and variable elements**. How does management make the classification? One possibility is to determine the variable and fixed components each time a mixed cost is incurred. But because of time and cost constraints, this approach is rarely followed. Instead, the customary approach is to determine variable and fixed costs on an **aggregate basis at the end of a period of time**. The company does this by using its past experience with the behavior of the mixed cost at various levels of activity. Management may use any of several methods in making the determination. We will explain the **high-low method** here. Other methods are more appropriately explained in cost accounting courses.[1]

High-Low Method

The high-low method uses the total costs incurred at the high and low levels of activity. The difference in costs between the high and low levels represents variable costs, since only the variable cost element can change as activity levels change. The steps in computing fixed and variable costs under this method are as follows.

1. **Determine variable cost per unit from the following formula.**

Illustration 5-6 Formula for variable cost per unit using high-low method

To illustrate, assume that Metro Transit Company has the following maintenance costs and mileage data for its fleet of buses over a 4-month period.

Month	Miles Driven	Total Cost	Month	Miles Driven	Total Cost
January	20,000	$30,000	March	35,000	$49,000
February	40,000	48,000	April	50,000	63,000

Illustration 5-7 Assumed maintenance costs and mileage data

The high and low levels of activity are 50,000 miles in April and 20,000 miles in January. The maintenance costs at these two levels are $63,000 and $30,000, respectively. The difference in maintenance costs is $33,000 ($63,000 − $30,000) and the difference in miles is 30,000 (50,000 − 20,000). Therefore, for Metro Transit, variable cost per unit is $1.10, computed as follows.

$$\$33,000 \div 30,000 = \$1.10$$

2. **Determine the fixed cost by subtracting the total variable cost at either the high or the low activity level from the total cost at that activity level.**

---

[1]Other methods include the scatter diagram method and least squares regression analysis.

For Metro Transit, the computations are shown in Illustration 5-8.

Illustration 5-8 High-low method computation of fixed costs

	Activity Level	
	High	**Low**
Total cost	$63,000	$30,000
Less: Variable costs		
50,000 × $1.10	55,000	
20,000 × $1.10		22,000
Total fixed costs	**$ 8,000**	**$ 8,000**

Maintenance costs are therefore $8,000 per month plus $1.10 per mile. For example, at 45,000 miles, estimated maintenance costs would be $8,000 fixed and $49,500 variable (45,000 × $1.10).

The high-low method generally produces a reasonable estimate for analysis. However, it does not produce a precise measurement of the fixed and variable elements in a mixed cost because other activity levels are ignored in the computation.

IMPORTANCE OF IDENTIFYING VARIABLE AND FIXED COSTS

Why is it important to segregate costs into variable and fixed elements? The answer may become apparent if we look at the following four business decisions.

1. If **American Airlines** is to make a profit when it reduces all domestic fares by 30 percent, what reduction in costs or increase in passengers will be required? **Answer:** To make a profit when it cuts domestic fares by 30 percent, American Airlines will have to increase the number of passengers or cut its variable costs for those flights. Its fixed costs will not change.

2. If **Ford Motor Company** meets the United Auto Workers' demands for higher wages, what increase in sales revenue will be needed to maintain current profit levels? **Answer:** Higher wages to UAW members at Ford Motor Company will increase the variable costs of manufacturing automobiles. To maintain present profit levels, Ford will have to cut other variable costs or increase the price of its automobiles.

3. If **USX Corp.**'s program to modernize plant facilities reduces the work force by 50 percent, what will be the effect on the cost of producing one ton of steel? **Answer:** The modernizing of plant facilities at USX Corp. changes the proportion of fixed and variable costs of producing one ton of steel. Fixed costs increase because of higher depreciation charges, whereas variable costs decrease due to the reduction in the number of steelworkers.

4. What happens if **Kellogg Company** increases its advertising expenses but cannot increase prices because of competitive pressure? **Answer:** Sales volume must be increased to cover three items: (1) the increase in advertising, (2) the variable cost of the increased sales volume, and (3) the desired additional net income.

BEFORE YOU GO ON . . .

◆ **Review It**

1. What are the effects on (a) a variable cost and (b) a fixed cost due to a change in activity?
2. What is the relevant range, and how do costs behave within this range?
3. What are the steps in applying the high-low method to mixed costs?

◆ **Do It**

Helena Company reports the following total costs at two levels of production.

	10,000 units	20,000 units
Direct materials	$20,000	$40,000
Maintenance	8,000	10,000
Depreciation	4,000	4,000

Classify each cost as either variable, fixed, or mixed.

Action Plan

• Recall that a variable cost varies in total directly and proportionately with each change.
• Recall that a fixed cost remains the same in total with each change.
• Recall that a mixed cost changes in total but not proportionately with each change.

Solution: Direct materials is a variable cost. Maintenance is a mixed cost. Depreciation is a fixed cost.

Related exercise material: BE5-1, E5-1, and E5-2.

COST-VOLUME-PROFIT ANALYSIS

Cost-volume-profit (CVP) analysis is the study of the effects of changes in costs and volume on a company's profits. CVP analysis is important in profit planning. It also is a critical factor in such management decisions as setting selling prices, determining product mix, and maximizing use of production facilities.

STUDY OBJECTIVE
◆ 4
List the five components of cost-volume-profit analysis.

BASIC COMPONENTS

CVP analysis considers the interrelationships among the components shown in Illustration 5-9.

Illustration 5-9 Components of CVP analysis

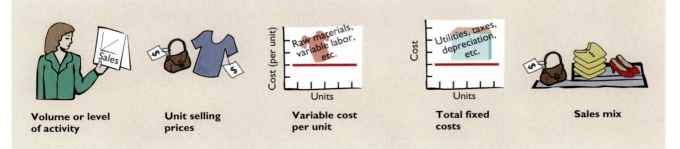

| Volume or level of activity | Unit selling prices | Variable cost per unit | Total fixed costs | Sales mix |

The following assumptions underlie each CVP analysis.

1. The behavior of both costs and revenues is linear throughout the relevant range of the activity index.
2. All costs can be classified with reasonable accuracy as either variable or fixed.
3. Changes in activity are the only factors that affect costs.
4. All units produced are sold.
5. When more than one type of product is sold, the sales mix will remain constant. That is, the percentage that each product represents of total sales will stay the same. Sales mix complicates CVP analysis because different products will have different cost relationships. In this chapter we assume a single product. Sales mix issues are addressed in Chapter 9.

When these five assumptions are not valid, the results of CVP analysis may be inaccurate.

CVP INCOME STATEMENT

STUDY OBJECTIVE
◆5◆

Indicate what contribution margin is and how it can be expressed.

Because CVP is so important for decision making, management often wants this information reported in a **CVP income statement** **format**. The CVP income statement classifies costs as variable and fixed and computes a contribution margin. **Contribution margin** is the amount of revenue remaining after deducting variable costs. It is often stated both as a total amount and on a per unit basis. We will use Vargo Video Company to illustrate a CVP income statement. Relevant data for the CD/DVD players made by this company are as follows.

Illustration 5-10
Assumed selling and cost data for Vargo Video

Unit selling price of CD/DVD	$500
Unit variable costs	$300
Total monthly fixed costs	$200,000
Units sold	1,600

The CVP income statement for Vargo Video therefore would be reported as follows.

Illustration 5-11 CVP income statement, with net income

VARGO VIDEO COMPANY
CVP Income Statement
For the Month Ended June 30, 2002

	Total	Per Unit
Sales (1,600 CD/DVDs)	$800,000	$500
Variable costs	480,000	300
Contribution margin	**320,000**	**$200**
Fixed costs	200,000	
Net income	**$120,000**	

A traditional income statement and a CVP income statement both report the same bottom-line net income of $120,000. However a traditional income statement does not classify costs as variable and fixed, and therefore a contribution margin would not be reported. In addition, both a total and a per unit amount are often shown on a CVP income statement to facilitate CVP analysis. In the applications of CVP analysis that follow, we will assume that the term "cost" includes all costs and expenses pertaining to production and sale of the product. That is, cost includes manufacturing costs plus selling and administrative expenses.

Contribution Margin Per Unit

From Vargo Video's CVP income statement, we can see that the contribution margin is $320,000, and the contribution margin per unit is $200 ($500 − $300). The formula for **contribution margin per unit** and the computation for Vargo Video are:

Illustration 5-12 Formula for contribution margin per unit

Contribution margin per unit indicates that for every CD/DVD sold, Vargo will have $200 to cover fixed costs and contribute to net income. Because Vargo Video has fixed costs of $200,000, it must sell 1,000 CD/DVDs ($200,000 ÷ $200) before it earns any net income. Vargo's CVP income statement, assuming a zero net income, would report the following.

Illustration 5-13 CVP income statement, with zero net income

VARGO VIDEO COMPANY CVP Income Statement For the Month Ended June 30, 2002		
	Total	Per Unit
Sales (1,000 CD/DVDs)	$500,000	$500
Variable costs	300,000	300
Contribution margin	**200,000**	**$200**
Fixed costs	200,000	
Net income	**$ –0–**	

It follows that for every CD/DVD sold above 1,000 units, net income is increased $200. For example, assume that Vargo sold one more CD/DVD, for a total of 1,001 CD/DVDs sold. In this case it would report net income of $200 as shown in Illustration 5-14.

Illustration 5-14   CVP income statement, with net income

VARGO VIDEO COMPANY CVP Income Statement For the Month Ended June 30, 2002		
	Total	Per Unit
Sales (1,001 CD/DVDs)	$500,500	$500
Variable costs	300,300	300
Contribution margin	**200,200**	**$200**
Fixed costs	200,000	
Net income	**$ 200**	

Contribution Margin Ratio

Some managers prefer to use a contribution margin ratio in CVP analysis. The **contribution margin ratio** is the contribution margin per unit divided by the unit selling price. For Vargo Video, the ratio is as follows.

Illustration 5-15   Formula for contribution margin ratio

The contribution margin ratio of 40 percent means that $0.40 of each sales dollar ($1 × 40%) is available to apply to fixed costs and to contribute to net income.

This expression of contribution margin is very helpful in determining the effect of changes in sales on net income. For example, net income will increase $40,000 (40% × $100,000) if sales increase $100,000. Thus, by using the contribution margin ratio, managers can quickly determine increases in net income from any change in sales. We can also see this effect through a CVP income statement. Assume that Vargo Video's current sales are $500,000 and it wants to know the effect of a $100,000 increase in sales. It could prepare a comparative CVP income statement analysis as follows.

Illustration 5-16   Comparative CVP income statements

VARGO VIDEO COMPANY CVP Income Statements For the Month Ended June 30, 2002				
	No Change		With Change	
	Total	Per Unit	Total	Per Unit
Sales	$500,000	$500	$600,000	$500
Variable costs	300,000	300	360,000	300
Contribution margin	**200,000**	**$200**	**240,000**	**$200**
Fixed costs	200,000		200,000	
Net income	**$ –0–**		**$ 40,000**	

Study these CVP income statements carefully. The concepts used in these statements will be used extensively in this and later chapters.

DECISION TOOLKIT

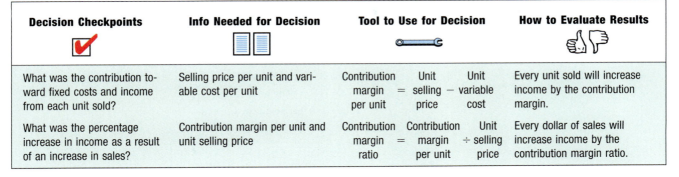

Decision Checkpoints	Info Needed for Decision	Tool to Use for Decision	How to Evaluate Results
What was the contribution toward fixed costs and income from each unit sold?	Selling price per unit and variable cost per unit	Contribution margin per unit = Unit selling price − Unit variable cost	Every unit sold will increase income by the contribution margin.
What was the percentage increase in income as a result of an increase in sales?	Contribution margin per unit and unit selling price	Contribution margin ratio = Contribution margin per unit ÷ Unit selling price	Every dollar of sales will increase income by the contribution margin ratio.

BREAK-EVEN ANALYSIS

STUDY OBJECTIVE

6

Identify the three ways to determine the break-even point.

A key relationship in CVP analysis is the level of activity at which total revenues equal total costs (both fixed and variable). This level of activity is called the **break-even point**. At this volume of sales, the company will realize no income and will suffer no loss. The process of finding the break-even point is called **break-even analysis**. Knowledge of the break-even point is useful to management when it decides whether to introduce new product lines, change sales prices on established products, or enter new market areas.

The break-even point can be:

1. Computed from a mathematical equation.
2. Computed by using contribution margin.
3. Derived from a cost-volume-profit (CVP) graph.

The break-even point can be expressed **either in sales units or sales dollars**.

Mathematical Equation

A common equation used for CVP analysis is shown in Illustration 5-17.

Illustration 5-17 Basic CVP equation

$$\text{Sales} = \text{Variable Costs} + \text{Fixed Costs} + \text{Net Income}$$

Identifying the break-even point is a special case of CVP analysis. Because at the break-even point net income is zero, **break-even occurs where total sales equal variable costs plus fixed costs.**

The break-even point **in units** can be computed directly from the equation by **using unit selling prices** and **unit variable costs**. The computation for Vargo Video is:

Illustration 5-18 Computation of break-even point in units

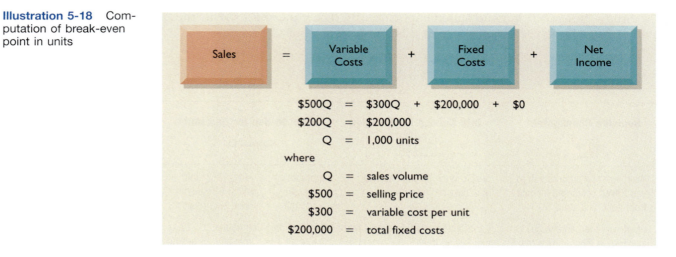

$$\$500Q = \$300Q + \$200,000 + \$0$$
$$\$200Q = \$200,000$$
$$Q = 1,000 \text{ units}$$

where

$$Q = \text{sales volume}$$
$$\$500 = \text{selling price}$$
$$\$300 = \text{variable cost per unit}$$
$$\$200,000 = \text{total fixed costs}$$

Thus, Vargo Video must sell 1,000 units to break even.

To find **sales dollars** required to break even, we multiply the units sold at the break-even point times the selling price per unit, as shown below.

$$1,000 \times \$500 = \$500,000 \text{ (break-even sales dollars)}$$

e — BUSINESS INSIGHT

The Internet is wringing inefficiencies out of nearly every industry. While commercial aircraft spend roughly 4,000 hours a year in the air, chartered aircraft spend only 500 hours flying. That means that they are sitting on the ground—not making any money—nearly 90 percent of the time. Enter **flightserve.com**. For about the same cost as a first-class ticket, flightserve.com matches up executives with charter flights in small "private jets." The executive gets a more comfortable ride and can avoid the hassle of big airports. Flightserve.com says that the average charter jet has eight seats. When all eight seats are full, the company has an 80 percent profit margin. It breaks even at an average of 3.3 full seats per flight.

Source: "Jet Set Go," *The Economist*, March 18, 2000, p. 68.

Contribution Margin Technique

We know that contribution margin equals total revenues less variable costs. It follows that at the break-even point, **contribution margin must equal total fixed costs**. On the basis of this relationship, we can compute the break-even point using either the contribution margin per unit or the contribution margin ratio.

When the contribution margin per unit is used, the formula to compute break-even point in units is as follows.

Illustration 5-19 Formula for break-even point in units using contribution margin

For Vargo Video, the contribution margin per unit is $200, as explained earlier. Thus, the break-even point in units is:

$$\$200,000 \div \$200 = 1,000 \text{ units}$$

When the contribution margin ratio is used, the formula to compute break-even point in dollars is:

Illustration 5-20 Formula for break-even point in dollars using contribution margin ratio

Fixed Costs ÷ Contribution Margin Ratio = Break-even Point in Dollars

We know that the contribution margin ratio for Vargo Video is 40 percent. Thus, the break-even point in dollars is:

$$\$200,000 \div 40\% = \$500,000$$

Graphic Presentation

An effective way to find the break-even point is to prepare a break-even graph. Because this graph also shows costs, volume, and profits, it is referred to as a **cost-volume-profit (CVP) graph**.

As shown in the CVP graph in Illustration 5-21, sales volume is recorded along the horizontal axis. This axis should extend to the maximum level of expected sales. Both total revenues (sales) and total costs (fixed plus variable) are recorded on the vertical axis.

The construction of the graph, using the data for Vargo Video, is as follows.

1. Plot the total-revenue line, starting at the zero activity level. For every CD/DVD sold, total revenue increases by $500. For example, at 200 units, sales are $100,000. At the upper level of activity (1,800 units), sales are $900,000. Note that the revenue line is assumed to be linear throughout the full range of activity.

2. Plot the total fixed cost using a horizontal line. For the CD/DVDs, this line is plotted at $200,000. The fixed cost is the same at every level of activity.

3. Plot the total cost line. This starts at the fixed-cost line at zero activity. It increases by the variable cost at each level of activity. For each CD/DVD, variable costs are $300. Thus, at 200 units, total variable cost is $60,000, and the total cost is $260,000. At 1,800 units total variable cost is $540,000, and total cost is $740,000. On the graph, the amount of the variable cost can be derived from the difference between the total cost and fixed cost lines at each level of activity.

4. Determine the break-even point from the intersection of the total cost line and the total revenue line. The break-even point in dollars is found by drawing a horizontal line from the break-even point to the vertical axis. The break-even point in units is found by drawing a vertical line from the break-even point to the horizontal axis. For the CD/DVDs, the break-even point is $500,000 of sales, or 1,000 units. At this sales level, Vargo Video will cover costs but make no profit.

The CVP graph also shows both the net income and net loss areas. Thus, the amount of income or loss at each level of sales can be derived from the total sales and total cost lines.

Illustration 5-21 CVP graph

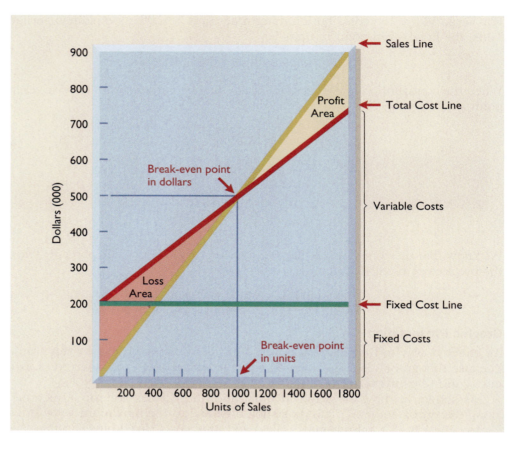

A CVP graph is useful because the effects of a change in any element in the CVP analysis can be quickly seen. For example, a 10 percent increase in selling price will change the location of the total revenue line. Likewise, the effects on total costs of wage increases can be quickly observed.

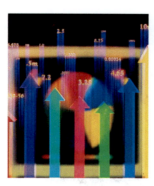

BUSINESS INSIGHT

Management Perspective

Computer graphics are a valuable companion to many computer software packages. Color graphs can be instantly changed to provide visual "what if" analysis.

Current technology allows for stunning graphs in a variety of different formats (pie charts, bar, stacked bar, two-dimensional, three-dimensional, etc.). In the appropriate situation, a graph can literally be worth a thousand words.

DECISION TOOLKIT

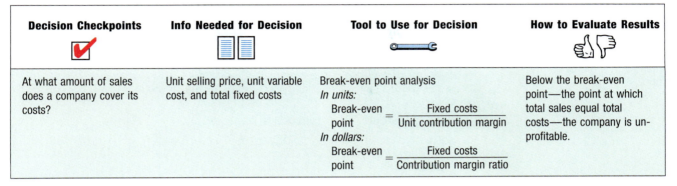

Decision Checkpoints	Info Needed for Decision	Tool to Use for Decision	How to Evaluate Results
At what amount of sales does a company cover its costs?	Unit selling price, unit variable cost, and total fixed costs	Break-even point analysis *In units:* $$\text{Break-even point} = \frac{\text{Fixed costs}}{\text{Unit contribution margin}}$$ *In dollars:* $$\text{Break-even point} = \frac{\text{Fixed costs}}{\text{Contribution margin ratio}}$$	Below the break-even point—the point at which total sales equal total costs—the company is unprofitable.

BEFORE YOU GO ON . . .

◆ Review It

1. What are the assumptions that underlie each CVP application?
2. What is contribution margin, and how can it be expressed?
3. How can the break-even point be determined?

◆ Do It

Lombardi Company has a unit selling price of $400, variable costs per unit of $240, and fixed costs of $160,000. Compute the break-even point in units using (a) a mathematical equation and (b) contribution margin per unit.

Action Plan

• Apply the formula: Sales = Variable costs + Fixed costs + Net income.
• Apply the formula: Fixed costs ÷ Contribution margin per unit = Break-even point in units.

Solution: (a) The formula is $400Q = $240Q + $160,000. The break-even point in units is 1,000 ($160,000 ÷ $160Q). (b) Contribution margin per unit is $160 ($400 − $240). The formula is $160,000 ÷ $160, and the break-even point in units is 1,000.

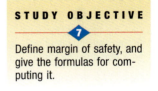
THE NAVIGATOR

Related exercise material: BE5-5, BE5-6, E5-3, E5-4, E5-5, E5-6, and E5-7.

MARGIN OF SAFETY

The margin of safety is another relationship that may be calculated in CVP analysis. **Margin of safety** is the difference between actual or expected sales and sales at the break-even point. This relationship measures the "cushion" that management has, allowing it to still break even if expected sales fail to materialize. The margin of safety may be expressed in dollars or as a ratio.

The formula for stating the **margin of safety in dollars** is as follows.

STUDY OBJECTIVE
◆7

Define margin of safety, and give the formulas for computing it.

Actual (Expected) Sales − Break-even Sales = Margin of Safety in Dollars

Illustration 5-22 Formula for margin of safety in dollars

Assuming that actual (expected) sales for Vargo Video are $750,000, the computation is:

$$\$750{,}000 - \$500{,}000 = \$250{,}000$$

The formula and computation for determining the **margin of safety ratio** are:

Illustration 5-23 Formula for margin of safety ratio

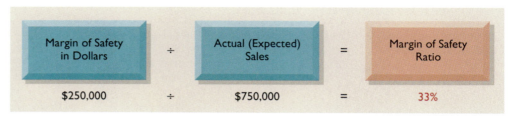

Margin of Safety in Dollars	÷	Actual (Expected) Sales	=	Margin of Safety Ratio
$250,000	÷	$750,000	=	33%

The higher the dollars or the percentage, the greater the margin of safety. The adequacy of the margin of safety should be evaluated by management in terms of such factors as the vulnerability of the product to competitive pressures and to downturns in the economy.

BUSINESS INSIGHT
Service Company Perspective

Computation of break-even and margin of safety is important for service companies as well. Consider how the promoter for the Rolling Stones' tour used the break-even point and margin of safety. For example, one outdoor show should bring 70,000 individuals for a gross of $2.45 million. The promoter guarantees $1.2 million to the Rolling Stones. In addition, 20 percent of gross, or approximately $500,000, goes to the stadium in which the performance is staged. Add another $400,000 for other expenses such as ticket takers, parking attendants, advertising, and so on. This leaves $350,000 to the promoter per show, if it sells out. At 75 percent, the promoter breaks about even. At 50 percent, the promoter loses hundreds of thousands of dollars. However, the promoter also shares in sales of T-shirts and memorabilia for which the promoter will net over $7 million during the tour. From a successful Rolling Stones' tour, the promoter could make $35 million!

TARGET NET INCOME

STUDY OBJECTIVE

8

Give the formulas for determining sales required to earn target net income.

Management usually sets an income objective for individual product lines. This objective is called **target net income**. It indicates the sales necessary to achieve a specified level of income. The sales necessary to achieve target net income can be determined from each of the approaches used to determine break-even sales.

Mathematical Equation

We know that at the break-even point no profit or loss results for the company. By instead adding an amount for target net income to the same basic equation, we obtain the following formula for determining required sales.

Illustration 5-24 Formula for required sales to meet target net income

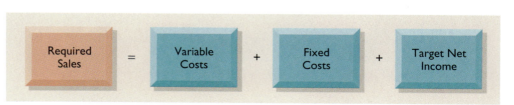

Required Sales	=	Variable Costs	+	Fixed Costs	+	Target Net Income

Required sales may be expressed in **either sales units or sales dollars**. Assuming that target net income is $120,000 for Vargo Video, the computation of required sales in units is as follows.

$$\$500Q = 300Q + \$200,000 + \$120,000$$
$$\$200Q = \$320,000$$
$$Q = \textbf{1,600}$$

where:

$$Q = \text{sales volume}$$
$$\$500 = \text{selling price}$$
$$\$300 = \text{variable costs per unit}$$
$$\$200,000 = \text{total fixed costs}$$
$$\$120,000 = \text{target net income}$$

Illustration 5-25 Computation of required sales

The sales dollars required to achieve the target net income is found by multiplying the units sold by the unit selling price [(1,600 × $500) = $800,000].

Contribution Margin Technique

As in the case of break-even sales, the sales required to meet a target net income can be computed in either units or dollars. The formula using the contribution margin per unit is as follows.

Illustration 5-26 Formula for required sales in units using contribution margin per unit

The computation for Vargo Video is as follows.

$$(\$200,000 + \$120,000) \div \$200 = 1,600 \text{ units}$$

The formula using the contribution margin ratio is as follows.

Illustration 5-27 Formula for required sales in dollars using contribution margin ratio

The computation for Vargo Video is as follows.

$$\$320,000 \div 40\% = \$800,000$$

Graphic Presentation

The CVP graph in Illustration 5-21 (on page 202) can also be used to find the sales required to meet target net income. In the profit area of the graph, the distance between the sales line and the total cost line at any point equals net income. Required sales are found by analyzing the differences between the two lines until the desired net income is found.

CVP AND CHANGES IN THE BUSINESS ENVIRONMENT

When the **IBM** personal computer (PC) was introduced, it sold for $2,500. Today the same type of computer sells for much less. Recently, when oil prices rose, the break-even point for airline companies such as **American**, **Southwest**, and **United** rose dramatically. Because of lower prices for imported steel, the demand for domestic steel dropped significantly. The point should be clear: Business conditions change rapidly, and management must respond intelligently to these changes. CVP analysis can help.

To illustrate how CVP analysis can be used in responding to change, we will look at three independent situations that might occur at Vargo Video. Each case is based on the original CD/DVD sales and cost data, which were:

Illustration 5-28 Original CD/DVD sales and cost data

Unit selling price	$500
Unit variable cost	$300
Total fixed costs	$200,000
Break-even sales	$500,000 or 1,000 units

Case I. A competitor is offering a 10% discount on the selling price of its CD/DVDs. Management must decide whether to offer a similar discount. **Question**: What effect will a 10 percent discount on selling price have on the break-even point for CD/DVDs? **Answer**: A 10 percent discount on selling price reduces the selling price per unit to $450 [$500 − ($500 × 10%)]. Variable costs per unit remain unchanged at $300. Thus, the contribution margin per unit is $150. Assuming no change in fixed costs, break-even sales are 1,333 units, computed as follows.

Illustration 5-29 Computation of break-even sales in units

Fixed Costs	÷	**Contribution Margin per Unit**	=	**Break-even Sales**
$200,000	÷	$150	=	**1,333 units (rounded)**

For Vargo Video, this change would require monthly sales to increase by 333 units, or $33\frac{1}{3}$ percent, in order to break even. In reaching a conclusion about offering a 10 percent discount to customers, management must determine how likely it is to achieve the increased sales. Also, management should estimate the possible loss of sales if the competitor's discount price is not matched.

Case II. To meet the threat of foreign competition, management invests in new robotic equipment that will lower the amount of direct labor required to make CD/DVDs. It is estimated that total fixed costs will increase 30 percent and that variable cost per unit will decrease 30 percent. **Question**: What effect will the new equipment have on the sales volume required to break even? **Answer**: Total fixed costs become $260,000 [$200,000 + (30% × $200,000)]. The variable cost per unit becomes $210 [$300 − (30% × $300)]. The new break-even point is approximately 900 units, computed as follows.

Illustration 5-30 Computation of break-even sales in units

Fixed Costs	÷	**Contribution Margin per Unit**	=	**Break-even Sales**
$260,000	÷	($500 − $210)	=	**900 units (rounded)**

These changes appear to be advantageous for Vargo Video. The break-even point is reduced by 10 percent, or 100 units.

Case III. Vargo's principal supplier of raw materials has just announced a price increase. The higher cost is expected to increase the variable cost of CD/DVDs by $25 per unit. Management would like to hold the line on the selling price of CD/DVDs. It plans a cost-cutting program that will save $17,500 in fixed costs per month. Vargo is currently realizing monthly net income of $80,000 on sales of 1,400 CD/DVDs. **Question**: What increase in units sold will be needed to maintain the same level of net income? **Answer**: The variable cost per unit increases to $325 ($300 + $25). Fixed costs are reduced to $182,500 ($200,000 − $17,500). Because of the change in variable cost, the contribution margin per unit becomes $175 ($500 − $325). The required number of units sold to achieve the target net income is computed as follows.

Fixed Costs + Target Net Income	÷	Contribution Margin per Unit	=	Required Sales in Units
($182,500 + $80,000)	÷	$175	=	1,500

Illustration 5-31 Computation of required sales

To achieve the required sales, 1,500 CD/DVDs will have to be sold, an increase of 100 units. If this does not seem to be a reasonable expectation, management will either have to make further cost reductions or accept less net income if the selling price remains unchanged.

e — BUSINESS INSIGHT

When analyzing an Internet business, the so-called "conversion rate" is closely watched. It is calculated by dividing the number of people who actually take action at an Internet site (e.g., buy something) by the total number of people who visit the site. Average conversion rates are from 3 to 5 percent. A rate below 2 percent is poor, while a rate above 10 percent is great.

Conversion rates have an obvious effect on break-even point. Suppose you spend $10,000 on your site, and you attract 5,000 visitors. If you get a 2 percent conversion rate (100 purchases), your site costs $100 per purchase ($10,000 ÷ 100). A 4 percent conversion rate gets you down to a cost of $50 per transaction, and an 8 percent conversion rate gets you down to $25. Studies have shown that conversion rates increase if the site has an easy-to-use interface, fast-performing screens, a convenient ordering process, and advertising that is both clever and clear.

Source: J. William Gurley, "The One Internet Metric That Really Counts," *Fortune*, March 6, 2000, p. 392.

DECISION TOOLKIT

Decision Checkpoints	Info Needed for Decision	Tool to Use for Decision	How to Evaluate Results
How can a company use CVP analysis to improve profitability?	Data on what effect a price change, a fixed-cost change, or a trade-off between fixed and variable costs, would have on volume and costs	Measurement of income at new volume levels	If profitability increases under proposed change, adopt change.

CVP INCOME STATEMENT REVISITED

At the beginning of the chapter we presented a simple CVP income statement. When companies prepare a CVP income statement, they provide more detail about specific variable and fixed-cost items.

To illustrate a more detailed CVP income statement, we will assume that Vargo Video reaches its target net income of $120,000 (see Illustration 5-25 on page 205). The following information is obtained on the $680,000 of costs that were incurred in June.

Illustration 5-32 Assumed cost and expense data

	Variable	Fixed	Total
Cost of goods sold	$400,000	$120,000	$520,000
Selling expenses	60,000	40,000	100,000
Administrative expenses	20,000	40,000	60,000
	$480,000	$200,000	$680,000

The detailed CVP income statement for Vargo is shown below.

Illustration 5-33 Detailed CVP income statement

VARGO VIDEO COMPANY
CVP Income Statement
For the Month Ended June 30, 2002

		Total	Per Unit
Sales		$ 800,000	$500
Variable expenses			
Cost of goods sold	$400,000		
Selling expenses	60,000		
Administrative expenses	20,000		
Total variable expenses		480,000	300
Contribution margin		**320,000**	**$200**
Fixed expenses			
Cost of goods sold	120,000		
Selling expenses	40,000		
Administrative expenses	40,000		
Total fixed expenses		200,000	
Net income		**$120,000**	

BEFORE YOU GO ON . . .

◆ Review It

1. What is the formula for computing the margin of safety (a) in dollars and (b) as a ratio?
2. What is the equation to compute target net income?

THE NAVIGATOR

USING THE DECISION TOOLKIT

B.T. Hernandez Company, maker of high-quality flashlights, has experienced steady growth over the last 6 years. However, increased competition has led Mr. Hernandez, the president, to believe that an aggressive campaign is needed next year to maintain the company's present growth. The company's accountant has presented Mr. Hernandez with the following data for the current year, 2002, for use in preparing next year's advertising campaign.

Cost Schedules

Variable costs	
Direct labor per flashlight	$ 8.00
Direct materials	4.00
Variable overhead	3.00
Variable cost per flashlight	$15.00
Fixed costs	
Manufacturing	$ 25,000
Selling	40,000
Administrative	70,000
Total fixed costs	$135,000
Selling price per flashlight	$25.00
Expected sales, 2002 (20,000 flashlights)	$500,000

Mr. Hernandez has set the sales target for the year 2003 at a level of $550,000 (22,000 flashlights).

Instructions

(Ignore any income tax considerations.)

(a) What is the projected operating income for 2002?

(b) What is the contribution margin per unit for 2002?

(c) What is the break-even point in units for 2002?

(d) Mr. Hernandez believes that to attain the sales target in the year 2003, the company must incur an additional selling expense of $10,000 for advertising in 2003, with all other costs remaining constant. What will be the break-even point in dollar sales for 2003 if the company spends the additional $10,000?

(e) If the company spends the additional $10,000 for advertising in 2003, what is the sales level in dollars required to equal 2002 operating income?

Solution

(a)

Expected sales	$500,000
Less:	
Variable cost (20,000 flashlights × $15)	300,000
Fixed costs	135,000
Projected operating income	$ 65,000

(b) $500,000 ÷ 20,000 = $25 selling price per flashlight

Selling price per flashlight	$25
Variable cost per flashlight	15
Contribution margin per unit	$10

(c) Fixed costs ÷ Contribution margin per unit = Break-even point in units
$135,000 ÷ $10 = 13,500 units

(d) Fixed costs ÷ Contribution margin ratio = Break-even point in dollars
$145,000 ÷ 40% = $362,500

Fixed costs (from 2002)	$135,000
Additional advertising expense	10,000
Fixed costs (2003)	$145,000

Contribution margin = Sales − Variable costs	
Expected sales	$550,000
Variable costs (22,000 × $15)	330,000
Contribution margin	$220,000

Contribution margin ratio = Contribution margin ÷ Sales
40% = $220,000 ÷ $550,000

(e) Required sales = (Fixed costs + Target net income) ÷ Contribution margin ratio

$525,000 = ($145,000 + $65,000) ÷ 40%

THE NAVIGATOR

SUMMARY OF STUDY OBJECTIVES

1 Distinguish between variable and fixed costs. Variable costs are costs that vary in total directly and proportionately with changes in the activity index. Fixed costs are costs that remain the same in total regardless of changes in the activity index.

2 Explain the significance of the relevant range. The relevant range is the range of activity in which a company expects to operate during a year. It is important in CVP analysis because the behavior of costs is linear throughout the relevant range.

3 Explain the concept of mixed costs. Mixed costs increase in total but not proportionately with changes in the activity level. For purposes of CVP analysis, mixed costs must be classified into their fixed and variable elements. One method that management may use is the high-low method.

4 List the five components of cost-volume-profit analysis. The five components of CVP analysis are (a) volume or level of activity, (b) unit selling prices, (c) variable cost per unit, (d) total fixed costs, and (e) sales mix.

5 Indicate what contribution margin is and how it can be expressed. Contribution margin is the amount of revenue remaining after deducting variable costs. It can be expressed as a per unit amount or as a ratio.

6 Identify the three ways to determine the break-even point. The break-even point can be (a) computed from a mathematical equation, (b) computed by using a contribution margin technique, and (c) derived from a CVP graph.

7 Define margin of safety, and give the formulas for computing it. Margin of safety is the difference between actual or expected sales and sales at the break-even point. The formulas for margin of safety are: Actual (expected) sales − Break-even sales = Margin of safety in dollars; Margin of safety in dollars ÷ Actual (expected) sales = Margin of safety ratio.

8 *Give the formulas for determining sales required to earn target net income.* One formula is: Required sales = Variable costs + Fixed costs + Target net income. Another formula is: Fixed costs + Target net income ÷ Contribution margin ratio = Required sales.

9 *Describe the essential features of a cost-volume-profit income statement.* The CVP income statement classifies costs and expenses as variable or fixed and reports contribution margin in the body of the statement.

DECISION TOOLKIT—A SUMMARY

Decision Checkpoints	Info Needed for Decision	Tool to Use for Decision	How to Evaluate Results
What was the contribution toward fixed costs and income from each unit sold?	Selling price per unit and variable cost per unit	$\text{Contribution margin} = \text{Unit selling price} - \text{Unit variable cost}$	Every unit sold will increase income by the contribution margin.
What was the percentage increase in income as a result of an increase in sales?	Contribution margin per unit and unit selling price	$\text{Contribution margin ratio} = \text{Contribution margin per unit} \div \text{Unit selling price}$	Every dollar of sales will increase income by the contribution margin ratio.
At what amount of sales does a company cover its costs?	Unit selling price, unit variable cost, and total fixed costs	Break-even point analysis *In units:* $\text{Break-even point} = \dfrac{\text{Fixed costs}}{\text{Unit contribution margin}}$ *In dollars:* $\text{Break-even point} = \dfrac{\text{Fixed costs}}{\text{Unit contribution ratio}}$	Below the break-even point—the point at which total sales equal total costs—the company is unprofitable.
How can a company use CVP analysis to improve profitability?	Data on what effect a price change, a fixed-cost change, or a trade-off between fixed and variable costs would have on volume and costs	Measurement of income at new volume levels	If profitability increases under proposed change, adopt change.

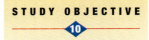

APPENDIX 5A

VARIABLE COSTING

In the earlier chapters, both variable and fixed manufacturing costs have been classified as product costs. In job order costing, for example, a job is assigned the costs of direct materials, direct labor, and both variable and fixed manufacturing overhead. This costing approach is referred to as **full** or **absorption costing**. It is so named because all manufacturing costs are charged to, or absorbed by, the product.

An alternative approach is to use variable costing. Under **variable costing** only direct materials, direct labor, and variable manufacturing overhead costs are considered product costs. Fixed manufacturing overhead costs are recognized as period costs (expenses) when incurred. The difference between absorption costing and variable costing is graphically shown as follows.

STUDY OBJECTIVE

10

Explain the difference between absorption costing and variable costing.

Illustration 5A-1 Difference between absorption costing and variable costing

Selling and administrative expenses are period costs under both absorption and variable costing.

To illustrate the computation of unit production cost under absorption and variable costing, assume that Premium Products Corporation manufactures a polyurethane sealant called Fix-it for car windshields. Relevant data for Fix-it in January 2002, the first month of production, are as follows.

Illustration 5A-2
Sealant sales and cost data for Premium Products Corporation

Selling price	$20 per unit.
Units	Produced 30,000; sold 20,000; beginning inventory zero.
Variable unit costs	Manufacturing $9 (direct materials $5, direct labor $3, and variable overhead $1). Selling and administrative expenses $2.
Fixed costs	Manufacturing overhead $120,000. Selling and administrative expenses $15,000.

The per unit production cost under each costing approach is:

Illustration 5A-3 Computation of per unit production cost

Type of Cost	Absorption Costing	Variable Costing
Direct materials	$ 5	$5
Direct labor	3	3
Variable manufacturing overhead	1	1
Fixed manufacturing overhead **($120,000 ÷ 30,000 units produced)**	4	0
Total unit cost	**$13**	**$9**

The total unit cost is $4 ($13 − $9) higher for absorption costing. This occurs because fixed manufacturing costs are a product cost under absorption costing. They are a period cost under variable costing and so are expensed, instead. Based on these data, each unit sold and each unit remaining in inventory is costed at $13 under absorption costing and at $9 under variable costing.

EFFECTS OF VARIABLE COSTING ON INCOME

The income statements under the two costing approaches are shown in Illustrations 5A-4 and 5A-5. The traditional income statement format is used with absorption costing. The cost-volume-profit format is used with variable costing. Computations are inserted parenthetically in the statements to facilitate your understanding of the amounts.

Income from operations under absorption costing shown in Illustration 5A-4 is $40,000 higher than under variable costing ($85,000 − $45,000) shown in Illustration 5A-5.

As highlighted in the two income statements, there is a $40,000 difference in the ending inventories ($130,000 under absorption costing versus $90,000 under variable costing). Under absorption costing, $40,000 of the fixed overhead costs (10,000 units × $4) has been deferred to a future period as a product cost. In contrast, under variable costing the entire fixed manufacturing costs are expensed when incurred.

Illustration 5A-4   Absorption costing income statement

PREMIUM PRODUCTS CORPORATION
Income Statement
For the Month Ended January 31, 2002
(Absorption Costing)

Sales (20,000 units × $20)		$400,000
Cost of goods sold		
Inventory, January 1	$ –0–	
Cost of goods manufactured (30,000 units × $13)	390,000	
Cost of goods available for sale	390,000	
Inventory, January 31 (10,000 units × $13)	**130,000**	
Cost of goods sold (20,000 units × $13)		260,000
Gross profit		140,000
Selling and administrative expenses		
(Variable 20,000 units × $2 + fixed $15,000)		55,000
Income from operations		**$ 85,000**

Helpful Hint This is the traditional statement that would result from job order and processing costing explained in Chapters 2 and 3.

Illustration 5A-5 Variable costing income statement

PREMIUM PRODUCTS CORPORATION
Income Statement
For the Month Ended January 31, 2002
(Variable Costing)

Sales (20,000 units × $20)		$400,000
Variable expenses		
Variable cost of goods sold		
Inventory, January 1	$ –0–	
Variable manufacturing costs (30,000 units × $9)	270,000	
Cost of goods available for sale	270,000	
Inventory, January 31 (10,000 units × $9)	**90,000**	
Variable cost of goods sold	180,000	
Variable selling and administrative expenses		
(20,000 units × $2)	40,000	
Total variable expenses		220,000
Contribution margin		180,000
Fixed expenses		
Manufacturing overhead	120,000	
Selling and administrative expenses	15,000	
Total fixed expenses		135,000
Income from operations		**$ 45,000**

Helpful Hint Note the difference in the computation of the ending inventory: $9 per unit here, $13 per unit above.

As shown, when units produced exceed units sold, income under absorption costing is higher. When units produced are less than units sold, income under absorption costing is lower. The reason is that the cost of the **ending inventory will be higher under absorption costing** than under variable costing. For example, if 30,000 units of Fix-it are sold in February and only 20,000 units are produced, income from operations will be $40,000 less under absorption costing because of the $40,000 difference in the ending inventories.

When units produced and sold are the same, income from operations will be equal under the two costing approaches. In this case, there is no increase in ending inventory. So fixed overhead costs of the current period are not deferred to future periods through the ending inventory.

The foregoing effects of the two costing approaches on income from operations may be summarized as follows.

Illustration 5A-6 Summary of income effects

RATIONALE FOR VARIABLE COSTING

The rationale for variable costing centers on the purpose of fixed manufacturing costs. That purpose is **to have productive facilities available for use**. These costs are incurred whether a company operates at zero or at 100 percent of capacity. Thus, proponents of variable costing argue that these costs should be expensed in the period in which they are incurred.

Supporters of absorption costing defend the assignment of fixed manufacturing overhead costs to inventory. They say that these costs are as much a cost of getting a product ready for sale as direct materials or direct labor. Accordingly, these costs should not be matched with revenues until the product is sold.

The use of variable costing is acceptable **only for internal use by management**. It cannot be used in determining product costs in financial statements prepared in accordance with generally accepted accounting principles because it understates inventory costs. To comply with the matching principle, a company must use absorption costing for its work in process and finished goods inventories. Similarly, absorption costing must be used for income tax purposes.

SUMMARY OF STUDY OBJECTIVE FOR APPENDIX 5A

10 *Explain the difference between absorption costing and variable costing.* Under absorption costing, fixed manufacturing costs are product costs. Under variable costing, fixed manufacturing costs are period costs.

GLOSSARY

Key Term Matching Activity

Absorption costing   A costing approach in which all manufacturing costs are charged to the product. (p. 211)

Activity index   The activity that causes changes in the behavior of costs. (p. 188)

Break-even point   The level of activity at which total revenues equal total costs. (p. 199)

Contribution margin (CM)   The amount of revenue remaining after deducting variable costs. (p. 196)

Contribution margin per unit   The amount of revenue remaining per unit after deducting variable costs; calculated as unit selling price minus unit variable cost. (p. 197)

Contribution margin ratio   The percentage of each dollar of sales that is available to contribute to net income; calculated as contribution margin per unit divided by unit selling price. (p. 198)

Cost behavior analysis   The study of how specific costs respond to changes in the level of business activity. (p. 188)

Cost-volume-profit (CVP) analysis   The study of the effects of changes in costs and volume on a company's profits. (p. 195)

Cost-volume-profit (CVP) graph   A graph showing the relationship between costs, volume, and profits. (p. 201)

Cost-volume-profit (CVP) income statement   A statement for internal use that classifies costs and expenses as fixed or variable and reports contribution margin in the body of the statement. (p. 196)

Fixed costs   Costs that remain the same in total regardless of changes in the activity level. (p. 189)

High-low method   A mathematical method that uses the total costs incurred at the high and low levels of activity. (p. 193)

Margin of safety   The difference between actual or expected sales and sales at the break-even point. (p. 203)

Mixed costs   Costs that contain both a variable and a fixed cost element and change in total but not proportionately with changes in the activity level. (p. 192)

Relevant range   The range of the activity index over which the company expects to operate during the year. (p. 191)

Target net income   The income objective for individual product lines. (p. 204)

Variable costing   A costing approach in which only variable manufacturing costs are product costs, and fixed manufacturing costs are period costs (expenses). (p. 211)

Variable costs   Costs that vary in total directly and proportionately with changes in the activity level. (p. 189)

DEMONSTRATION PROBLEM

Mabo Company makes calculators that sell for $20 each. For the coming year, management expects fixed costs to total $220,000 and variable costs to be $9 per unit.

Instructions

(a) Compute break-even point in units using the mathematical equation.
(b) Compute break-even point in dollars using the contribution margin (CM) ratio.
(c) Compute the margin of safety percentage assuming actual sales are $500,000.
(d) Compute the sales required in dollars to earn net income of $165,000.

eGrade Demonstration Problem

Solution to Demonstration Problem

(a) Sales = Variable costs + Fixed costs + Net income
$$\$20Q = \$9Q + \$220,000 + \$0$$
$$\$11Q = \$220,000$$
$$Q = 20,000 \text{ units}$$

(b) Contribution margin per unit = Unit selling price − Unit variable costs
$$\$11 = \$20 - \$9$$
Contribution margin ratio = Contribution margin per unit ÷ Unit selling price
$$55\% = \$11 \div \$20$$
Break-even point in dollars = Fixed cost ÷ Contribution margin ratio
$$= \$220,000 \div 55\%$$
$$= \$400,000$$

(c) $$\text{Margin of safety} = \frac{\text{Actual sales} - \text{Break-even sales}}{\text{Actual sales}}$$
$$= \frac{\$500,000 - \$400,000}{\$500,000}$$
$$= 20\%$$

(d) Required sales = Variable costs + Fixed costs + Net income
$$\$20Q = \$9Q + \$220,000 + \$165,000$$
$$\$11Q = \$385,000$$
$$Q = 35,000 \text{ units}$$
$$35,000 \text{ units} \times \$20 = \$700,000 \text{ required sales}$$

Action Plan

• Know the formulas.
• Recognize that variable costs change with sales volume; fixed costs do not.
• Avoid computational errors.
• Prove your answers.

THE NAVIGATOR

Note: All asterisked Questions, Exercises, and Problems relate to material contained in the appendix to the chapter.

SELF-STUDY QUESTIONS

Answers are at the end of the chapter.

(SO 1) 1. Variable costs are costs that:
    (a) vary in total directly and proportionately with changes in the activity level.
    (b) remain the same per unit at every activity level.
    (c) Neither of the above.
    (d) Both (a) and (b) above.

(SO 2) 2. The relevant range is:
    (a) the range of activity in which variable costs will be curvilinear.
    (b) the range of activity in which fixed costs will be curvilinear.
    (c) the range over which the company expects to operate during a year.
    (d) usually from zero to 100% of operating capacity.

(SO 3) 3. Mixed costs consist of a:
    (a) variable cost element and a fixed cost element.
    (b) fixed cost element and a controllable cost element.
    (c) relevant cost element and a controllable cost element.
    (d) variable cost element and a relevant cost element.

(SO 4) 4. One of the following is *not* involved in CVP analysis. That factor is:
    (a) sales mix.
    (b) unit selling prices.
    (c) fixed costs per unit.
    (d) volume or level of activity.

(SO 5) 5. Contribution margin:
    (a) is revenue remaining after deducting variable costs.

    (b) may be expressed as contribution margin per unit.
    (c) is selling price less cost of goods sold.
    (d) Both (a) and (b) above.

6. Gossen Company is planning to sell 200,000 (SO 6) pliers for $4 per unit. The contribution margin ratio is 25%. If Gossen will break even at this level of sales, what are the fixed costs?
    (a) $100,000.   (c) $200,000.
    (b) $160,000.   (d) $300,000.

7. Marshall Company had actual sales of (SO 7) $600,000 when break-even sales were $420,000. What is the margin of safety ratio?
    (a) 25%.   (c) $33\frac{1}{3}$%.
    (b) 30%.   (d) 45%.

8. The mathematical equation for computing (SO 8) required sales to obtain target net income is: Required sales =
    (a) Variable costs + Target net income.
    (b) Variable costs + Fixed costs + Target net income.
    (c) Fixed costs + Target net income.
    (d) No correct answer is given.

9. Cournot Company sells 100,000 wrenches for (SO 9) $12 a unit. Fixed costs are $300,000, and net income is $200,000. What should be reported as variable expenses in the CVP income statement?
    (a) $700,000.   (c) $500,000.
    (b) $900,000.   (d) $1,000,000.

*10. Under variable costing, fixed manufacturing (SO 10) costs are classified as:
    (a) period costs.
    (b) product costs.
    (c) both (a) and (b).
    (d) neither (a) nor (b).

QUESTIONS

1. (a) What is cost behavior analysis?
    (b) Why is cost behavior analysis important to management?

2. (a) Jenny Beason asks your help in understanding the term "activity index." Explain the meaning and importance of this term for Jenny.
    (b) State the two ways that variable costs may be defined.

3. Contrast the effects of changes in the activity level on total fixed costs and on unit fixed costs.

4. R.E. Leon claims that the relevant range concept is important only for variable costs.

    (a) Explain the relevant range concept.
    (b) Do you agree with R.E.'s claim? Explain.

5. "The relevant range is indispensable in cost behavior analysis." Is this true? Why or why not?

6. Bart Gomez is confused. He does not understand why rent on his apartment is a fixed cost and rent on a Hertz rental truck is a mixed cost. Explain the difference to Bart.

7. How should mixed costs be classified in CVP analysis? What approach is used to effect the appropriate classification?

8. At the high and low levels of activity during the month, direct labor hours are 90,000 and 40,000, respectively. The related costs are $175,000 and $100,000. What are the fixed and variable costs at any level of activity?

9. "Cost-volume-profit (CVP) analysis is based entirely on unit costs." Do you agree? Explain.

10. Patty Dye defines contribution margin as the amount of profit available to cover operating expenses. Is there any truth in this definition? Discuss.

11. Doolin Company's Speedo pocket calculator sells for $40. Variable costs per unit are estimated to be $24. What are the contribution margin per unit and the contribution margin ratio?

12. "Break-even analysis is of limited use to management because a company cannot survive by just breaking even." Do you agree? Explain.

13. Total fixed costs are $22,000 for Froelich Inc. It has a contribution margin per unit of $15, and a contribution margin ratio of 20%. Compute the break-even sales in dollars.

14. Linda Fearn asks your help in constructing a CVP graph. Explain to Linda (a) how the break-even point is plotted, and (b) how the level of activity and dollar sales at the break-even point are determined.

15. Define the term "margin of safety." If Hancock Company expects to sell 1,500 units of its product at $12 per unit, and break-even sales for the product are $12,000, what is the margin of safety ratio?

16. Jung Company's break-even sales are $600,000. Assuming fixed costs are $240,000, what sales volume is needed to achieve a target net income of $56,000?

17. The traditional income statement for Reeves Company shows sales $900,000, cost of goods sold $600,000, and operating expenses $200,000. Assuming all costs and expenses are 70% variable and 30% fixed, prepare a CVP income statement through contribution margin.

*18. Distinguish between absorption costing and variable costing.

*19. (a) What is the major rationale for the use of variable costing? (b) Discuss why variable costing may not be used for financial reporting purposes.

BRIEF EXERCISES

BE5-1 Monthly production costs in Obianwu Company for two levels of production are as follows.

Classify costs as variable, fixed, or mixed.
(SO 1, 3)

Cost	2,000 units	4,000 units
Indirect labor	$10,000	$20,000
Supervisory salaries	5,000	5,000
Maintenance	3,000	4,000

Indicate which costs are variable, fixed, and mixed, and give the reason for each answer.

BE5-2 For Lundy Company, the relevant range of production is 40–80% of capacity. At 40% of capacity, a variable cost is $2,000 and a fixed cost is $4,000. Diagram the behavior of each cost within the relevant range assuming the behavior is linear.

Diagram the behavior of costs within the relevant range.
(SO 2)

BE5-3 For Skole Company, a mixed cost is $40,000 plus $8 per direct labor hour. Diagram the behavior of the cost using increments of 1,000 hours up to 5,000 hours on the horizontal axis and increments of $20,000 up to $80,000 on the vertical axis.

Diagram the behavior of a mixed cost.
(SO 3)

BE5-4 Sass Company accumulates the following data concerning a mixed cost, using miles as the activity level.

Determine variable and fixed cost elements using the high-low method.
(SO 3)

	Miles Driven	Total Cost		Miles Driven	Total Cost
January	8,000	$14,100	March	8,500	$15,000
February	7,500	13,400	April	8,200	14,400

Compute the variable and fixed cost elements using the high-low method.

BE5-5 Determine the missing amounts.

Determine missing amounts for contribution margin.
(SO 5)

	Unit Selling Price	Unit Variable Costs	Contribution Margin per Unit	Contribution Margin Ratio
1.	$250	$160	(a)	(b)
2.	$500	(c)	$150	(d)
3.	(e)	(f)	$360	30%

Compute the break-even point.
(SO 6)

BE5-6 Low Company has a unit selling price of $400, variable costs per unit of $280, and fixed costs of $150,000. Compute the break-even point in units using (a) the mathematical equation and (b) contribution margin per unit.

Compute the margin of safety and the margin of safety ratio.
(SO 7)

BE5-7 For Koren Company actual sales are $1,200,000 and break-even sales are $900,000. Compute (a) the margin of safety in dollars and (b) the margin of safety ratio.

Compute sales for target net income.
(SO 8)

BE5-8 For Bianco Company, variable costs are 75% of sales, and fixed costs are $180,000. Management's net income goal is $60,000. Compute the required sales in dollars needed to achieve management's target net income of $60,000. (Use the contribution margin approach.)

Prepare CVP income statement.
(SO 9)

BE5-9 Friedman Manufacturing Inc. has sales of $1,800,000 for the first quarter of 2002. In making the sales, the company incurred the following costs and expenses.

	Variable	Fixed
Cost of goods sold	$760,000	$540,000
Selling expenses	95,000	60,000
Administrative expenses	79,000	66,000

Prepare a CVP income statement for the quarter ended March 31, 2002.

Compute net income under absorption and variable costing.
(SO 10)

*BE5-10 Gigliuto Company's fixed overhead costs are $4 per unit, and its variable overhead costs are $8 per unit. In the first month of operations, 50,000 units are produced, and 45,000 units are sold. Write a short memo to the chief financial officer explaining which costing approach will produce the higher income and what the difference will be.

EXERCISES

Define and classify variable, fixed, and mixed costs.
(SO 1, 3)

E5-1 Fox Company manufactures a single product. Annual production costs incurred in the manufacturing process are shown below for two levels of production.

	Costs Incurred			
Production in Units	**5,000**		**10,000**	
Production Costs	**Total Cost**	**Cost/ Unit**	**Total Cost**	**Cost/ Unit**
Direct materials	$8,250	$1.65	$16,500	$1.65
Direct labor	9,500	1.90	19,000	1.90
Utilities	1,400	0.28	2,300	0.23
Rent	4,000	0.80	4,000	0.40
Maintenance	800	0.16	1,100	0.11
Supervisory salaries	1,000	0.20	1,000	0.10

Instructions
(a) Define the terms variable costs, fixed costs, and mixed costs.
(b) Classify each cost above as either variable, fixed, or mixed.

Determine fixed and variable costs using the high-low method and prepare graph.
(SO 1, 3)

E5-2 The controller of Getty Industries has collected the following monthly expense data for use in analyzing the cost behavior of maintenance costs.

Month	Total Maintenance Costs	Total Machine Hours
January	$2,900	3,000
February	3,000	4,000
March	3,600	6,000
April	4,500	7,900
May	3,200	5,000
June	4,900	8,000

Instructions
(a) Determine the fixed and variable cost components using the high-low method.
(b) Prepare a graph showing the behavior of maintenance costs, and identify the fixed and variable cost elements. Use 2,000 unit increments and $1,000 cost increments.

E5-3 In the month of June, Andrea's Beauty Salon gave 2,500 haircuts, shampoos, and permanents at an average price of $30. During the month, fixed costs were $18,000 and variable costs were 70% of sales.

Compute contribution margin, break-even point, and margin of safety.
(SO 5, 6, 7)

Instructions
(a) Determine the contribution margin in dollars, per unit, and as a ratio.
(b) Using the contribution margin technique, compute the break-even point in dollars and in units.
(c) Compute the margin of safety in dollars and as a ratio.

E5-4 Ewing Company estimates that variable costs will be 50% of sales, and fixed costs will total $800,000. The selling price of the product is $4.

Prepare a CVP graph and compute break-even point and margin of safety.
(SO 6, 7)

Instructions
(a) Prepare a CVP graph, assuming maximum sales of $3,200,000. (*Note*: Use $400,000 increments for sales and costs and 100,000 increments for units.)
(b) Compute the break-even point in (1) units and (2) dollars.
(c) Compute the margin of safety in (1) dollars and (2) as a ratio, assuming actual sales are $2 million.

E5-5 In 2002, Donnin Company had a break-even point of $350,000 based on a selling price of $7 per unit and fixed costs of $140,000. In 2003, the selling price and the variable cost per unit did not change, but the break-even point increased to $455,000.

Compute variable cost per unit, contribution margin ratio, and increase in fixed costs.
(SO 5)

Instructions
(a) Compute the variable cost per unit and the contribution margin ratio for 2002.
(b) Compute the increase in fixed costs for 2003.

E5-6 Jain Company had $150,000 of net income in 2002 when the selling price per unit was $150, the variable costs per unit were $90, and the fixed costs were $750,000. Management expects per unit data and total fixed costs to remain the same in 2003. The president of Jain Company is under pressure from stockholders to increase net income by $60,000 in 2003.

Compute various components to derive target net income under different assumptions.
(SO 6, 8)

Instructions
(a) Compute the number of units sold in 2002.
(b) Compute the number of units that would have to be sold in 2003 to reach the stockholders' desired profit level.
(c) Assume that Jain Company sells the same number of units in 2003 as it did in 2002. What would the selling price have to be in order to reach the stockholders' desired profit level?

E5-7 Gomez Company reports the following operating results for the month of August: Sales $300,000 (units 5,000); variable costs $210,000; and fixed costs $80,000. Management is considering the following independent courses of action to increase net income.

Compute net income under different alternatives.
(SO 8)

1. Increase selling price by 10% with no change in total variable costs.
2. Reduce variable costs to 65% of sales.
3. Reduce fixed costs by $10,000.

Instructions
Compute the net income to be earned under each alternative. Which course of action will produce the highest net income?

E5-8 Halko Company had sales in 2002 of $1,500,000 on 60,000 units. Variable costs totaled $720,000, and fixed costs totaled $500,000.
  A new raw material is available that will decrease the variable costs per unit by 20% (or $2.40). However, to process the new raw material, fixed operating costs will increase by $50,000. Management feels that one-half of the decline in the variable costs per unit

Prepare a CVP income statement before and after changes in business environment.
(SO 9)

should be passed on to customers in the form of a sales price reduction. The marketing department expects that this sales price reduction will result in a 5% increase in the number of units sold.

Instructions

Prepare a CVP income statement for 2002, assuming the changes are made as described.

Compute total product cost and prepare an income statement using variable costing.
(SO 10)

*E5-9   Wu Equipment Company manufactures and distributes industrial air compressors. The following costs are available for the year ended December 31, 2002. The company has no beginning inventory. In 2002, 1,500 units were produced, but only 1,200 units were sold. The unit selling price was $4,500. Costs and expenses were:

Variable costs per unit	
Direct materials	$ 800
Direct labor	1,500
Variable manufacturing overhead	300
Variable selling and administrative expenses	70
Annual fixed costs and expenses	
Manufacturing overhead	$1,200,000
Selling and administrative expenses	100,000

Instructions

(a) Compute the manufacturing cost of one unit of product using variable costing.
(b) Prepare a 2002 income statement for Wu Company using variable costing.

PROBLEMS: SET A

Determine variable and fixed costs, compute break-even point, prepare a CVP graph, and determine net income.
(SO 1, 3, 5, 6)

P5-1A   Joe Vida owns the Peace Barber Shop. He employs five barbers and pays each a base rate of $1,200 per month. One of the barbers serves as the manager and receives an extra $600 per month. In addition to the base rate, each barber also receives a commission of $3.50 per haircut.

Other costs are as follows.

Advertising	$200 per month
Rent	$800 per month
Barber supplies	$0.30 per haircut
Utilities	$175 per month plus $0.20 per haircut
Magazines	$25 per month

Joe currently charges $10 per haircut.

Instructions

(a) Determine the variable cost per haircut and the total monthly fixed costs.
(b) Compute the break-even point in units and dollars.
(c) Prepare a CVP graph, assuming a maximum of 1,800 haircuts in a month. Use increments of 300 haircuts on the horizontal axis and $3,000 on the vertical axis.
(d) Determine net income, assuming 1,500 haircuts are given in a month.

Prepare a CVP income statement, compute break-even point, contribution margin ratio, margin of safety ratio, and sales for target net income.
(SO 5, 6, 7, 8, 9)

P5-2A   Tyson Company bottles and distributes NO-KAL, a diet soft drink. The beverage is sold for 40 cents per 16-ounce bottle to retailers, who charge customers 60 cents per bottle. At full (100%) plant capacity, management estimates the following revenues and costs.

Net sales	$1,800,000	Selling expenses—variable	$80,000
Direct materials	400,000	Selling expenses—fixed	65,000
Direct labor	280,000	Administrative expenses—	
Manufacturing overhead—		variable	20,000
variable	300,000	Administrative expenses—	
Manufacturing overhead—		fixed	52,000
fixed	283,000		

eGrade
Problem

Instructions

(a) Prepare a CVP income statement for 2002 based on management's estimates.
(b) Compute the break-even point in (1) units and (2) dollars.

(c) Compute the contribution margin ratio and the margin of safety ratio. (Round to full percents.)

(d) Determine the sales required to earn net income of $150,000.

P5-3A   Cruz Manufacturing's sales slumped badly in 2002. For the first time in its history, it operated at a loss. The company's income statement showed the following results from selling 600,000 units of product: Net sales $2,400,000; total costs and expenses $2,600,000; and net loss $200,000. Costs and expenses consisted of the following.

Compute break-even point under alternative courses of action.
(SO 5, 6)

	Total	Variable	Fixed
Cost of goods sold	$2,100,000	$1,440,000	$ 660,000
Selling expenses	300,000	72,000	228,000
Administrative expenses	200,000	48,000	152,000
	$2,600,000	$1,560,000	$1,040,000

Management is considering the following independent alternatives for 2003.

1. Increase unit selling price 25% with no change in costs, expenses, and sales volume.

2. Change the compensation of salespersons from fixed annual salaries totaling $210,000 to total salaries of $70,000 plus a 4% commission on net sales.

3. Purchase new automated equipment that will change the proportion between variable and fixed cost of goods sold to 60% variable and 40% fixed.

Instructions

(a) Compute the break-even point in dollars for 2002.

(b) Compute the break-even point in dollars under each of the alternative courses of action. (Round to nearest full percent.) Which course of action do you recommend?

P5-4A   Lois Baiser is the advertising manager for Value Shoe Store. She is currently working on a major promotional campaign. Her ideas include the installation of a new lighting system and increased display space that will add $44,000 in fixed costs to the $280,000 currently spent. In addition, Lois is proposing that a 5% price decrease ($40 to $38) will produce a 20% increase in sales volume (20,000 to 24,000). Variable costs will remain at $20 per pair of shoes. Management is impressed with Lois's ideas but concerned about the effects that these changes will have on the break-even point and the margin of safety.

Compute break-even point and margin of safety ratio, and prepare a CVP income statement before and after changes in business environment.
(SO 6, 7, 9)

Instructions

(a) Compute the current break-even point in units, and compare it to the break-even point in units if Lois's ideas are used.

(b) Compute the margin of safety ratio for current operations and after Lois's changes are introduced. (Round to nearest full percent.)

(c) Prepare a CVP income statement for current operations and after Lois's changes are introduced. Would you make the changes suggested?

*P5-5A   AFN produces plastic that is used for injection molding applications such as gears for small motors. In 2002, the first year of operations, AFN produced 4,000 tons of plastic and sold 3,000 tons. In 2003, the production and sales results were exactly reversed. In each year, selling price per ton was $2,000, variable manufacturing costs were 15% of the sales price of units produced, variable selling expenses were 10% of the selling price of units sold, fixed manufacturing costs were $2,400,000, and fixed administrative expenses were $600,000.

Prepare income statements under absorption and variable costing.
(SO 10)

Instructions

(a) Prepare comparative income statements for each year using variable costing.

(b) Prepare comparative income statements for each year using absorption costing.

(c) Reconcile the differences each year in income from operations under the two costing approaches.

(d) Comment on the effects of production and sales on net income under the two costing approaches.

PROBLEMS: SET B

Determine variable and fixed costs, compute break-even point, prepare a CVP graph, and determine net income.
(SO 1, 3, 5, 6)

P5-1B   The College Barber Shop employs four barbers. One barber, who also serves as the manager, is paid a salary of $2,000 per month. The other barbers are paid $1,400 per month. In addition, each barber is paid a commission of $4 per haircut. Other monthly costs are: store rent $800 plus 60 cents per haircut, depreciation on equipment $500, barber supplies 40 cents per haircut, utilities $300, and advertising $200. The price of a haircut is $10.

Instructions
(a) Determine the variable cost per haircut and the total monthly fixed costs.
(b) Compute the break-even point in units and dollars.
(c) Prepare a CVP graph, assuming a maximum of 1,800 haircuts in a month. Use increments of 300 haircuts on the horizontal axis and $3,000 increments on the vertical axis.
(d) Determine the net income, assuming 1,800 haircuts are given in a month.

Prepare a CVP income statement, compute break-even point, contribution margin ratio, margin of safety ratio, and sales for target net income.
(SO 5, 6, 7, 8, 9)

P5-2B   Corbin Company bottles and distributes LO-KAL, a fruit drink. The beverage is sold for 50 cents per 16-ounce bottle to retailers, who charge customers 70 cents per bottle. At full (100%) plant capacity, management estimates the following revenues and costs.

Net sales	$2,000,000	Selling expenses—variable	$ 90,000
Direct materials	360,000	Selling expenses—fixed	150,000
Direct labor	650,000	Administrative expenses—	
Manufacturing overhead—		variable	30,000
variable	270,000	Administrative expenses—	
Manufacturing overhead—		fixed	70,000
fixed	260,000		

Instructions
(a) Prepare a CVP income statement for 2002 based on management's estimates.
(b) Compute the break-even point in (1) units and (2) dollars.
(c) Compute the contribution margin ratio and the margin of safety ratio.
(d) Determine the sales required to earn net income of $240,000.

Compute break-even point under alternative courses of action.
(SO 5, 6)

P5-3B   Griffey Manufacturing had a bad year in 2002. For the first time in its history it operated at a loss. The company's income statement showed the following results from selling 60,000 units of product: Net sales $1,500,000; total costs and expenses $1,740,000; and net loss $240,000. Costs and expenses consisted of the following.

	Total	Variable	Fixed
Cost of goods sold	$1,200,000	$780,000	$420,000
Selling expenses	420,000	75,000	345,000
Administrative expenses	120,000	45,000	75,000
	$1,740,000	$900,000	$840,000

Management is considering the following independent alternatives for 2003.

1. Increase unit selling price 20% with no change in costs, expenses, and sales volume.
2. Change the compensation of salespersons from fixed annual salaries totaling $200,000 to total salaries of $40,000 plus a 5% commission on net sales.
3. Purchase new high-tech factory machinery that will change the proportion between variable and fixed cost of goods sold to 50:50.

Instructions
(a) Compute the break-even point in dollars for 2002.
(b) Compute the break-even point in dollars under each of the alternative courses of action. Which course of action do you recommend?

P5-4B   Barb Tsai is the advertising manager for Thrifty Shoe Store. She is currently working on a major promotional campaign. Her ideas include the installation of a new lighting system and increased display space that will add $35,000 in fixed costs to the

$225,000 currently spent. In addition, Barb is proposing that a $6\frac{2}{3}\%$ price decrease (from $30 to $28) will produce an increase in sales volume from 17,000 to 22,000 units. Variable costs will remain at $15 per pair of shoes. Management is impressed with Barb's ideas but concerned about the effects that these changes will have on the break-even point and the margin of safety.

Compute break-even point and margin of safety ratio, and prepare a CVP income statement before and after changes in business environment.
(SO 6, 7, 9)

Instructions

(a) Compute the current break-even point in units, and compare it to the break-even point in units if Barb's ideas are used.

(b) Compute the margin of safety ratio for current operations and after Barb's changes are introduced. (Round to nearest full percent.)

(c) Prepare a CVP income statement for current operations and after Barb's changes are introduced. Would you make the changes suggested?

*P5-5B   Zaki Metal Company produces the steel wire that goes into the production of paper clips. In 2002, the first year of operations, Zaki produced 40,000 miles of wire and sold 30,000 miles. In 2003, the production and sales results were exactly reversed. In each year, selling price per mile was $80, variable manufacturing costs were 25% of the sales price, variable selling expenses were $6.00 per mile sold, fixed manufacturing costs were $1,200,000, and fixed administrative expenses were $200,000.

Prepare income statements under absorption and variable costing.
(SO 10)

Instructions

(a) Prepare comparative income statements for each year using variable costing.

(b) Prepare comparative income statements for each year using absorption costing.

(c) Reconcile the differences each year in income from operations under the two costing approaches.

(d) Comment on the effects of production and sales on net income under the two costing approaches.

◆ BROADENING YOUR PERSPECTIVE

GROUP DECISION CASE

BYP5-1   Cedeno Company has decided to introduce a new product. The new product can be manufactured by either a capital-intensive method or a labor-intensive method. The manufacturing method will not affect the quality of the product. The estimated manufacturing costs by the two methods are as follows.

	Capital-Intensive	Labor-Intensive
Direct materials	$5 per unit	$5.50 per unit
Direct labor	$6 per unit	$7.20 per unit
Variable overhead	$3 per unit	$4.80 per unit
Fixed manufacturing costs	$2,440,000	$1,390,000

Cedeno's market research department has recommended an introductory unit sales price of $30. The incremental selling expenses are estimated to be $500,000 annually plus $2 for each unit sold, regardless of manufacturing method.

Instructions

With the class divided into groups, answer the following.

(a) Calculate the estimated break-even point in annual unit sales of the new product if Cedeno Company uses the:
  (1) capital-intensive manufacturing method.
  (2) labor-intensive manufacturing method.

(b) Determine the annual unit sales volume at which Cedeno Company would be indifferent between the two manufacturing methods.

(c) Explain the circumstance under which Cedeno should employ each of the two manufacturing methods.

(CMA adapted)

MANAGERIAL ANALYSIS

BYP5-2 The condensed income statement for the Rivera and Santos partnership for 2002 is as follows.

RIVERA AND SANTOS COMPANY
Income Statement
For the Year Ended December 31, 2002

Sales (200,000 units)		$1,200,000
Cost of goods sold		800,000
Gross profit		400,000
Operating expenses		
Selling	$320,000	
Administrative	160,000	480,000
Net loss		($80,000)

A cost behavior analysis indicates that 75% of the cost of goods sold are variable, 50% of the selling expenses are variable, and 25% of the administrative expenses are variable.

Instructions

(Round to nearest unit, dollar, and percentage, where necessary. Use the CVP income statement format in computing profits.)

(a) Compute the break-even point in total sales dollars and in units for 2002.

(b) Rivera has proposed a plan to get the partnership "out of the red" and improve its profitability. She feels that the quality of the product could be substantially improved by spending $0.55 more per unit on better raw materials. The selling price per unit could be increased to only $6.50 because of competitive pressures. Rivera estimates that sales volume will increase by 30%. What effect would Rivera's plan have on the profits and the break-even point in dollars of the partnership?

(c) Santos was a marketing major in college. He believes that sales volume can be increased only by intensive advertising and promotional campaigns. He therefore proposed the following plan as an alternative to Rivera's. (1) Increase variable selling expenses to $0.85 per unit, (2) lower the selling price per unit by $0.20, and (3) increase fixed selling expenses by $20,000. Santos quoted an old marketing research report that said that sales volume would increase by 50% if these changes were made. What effect would Santos's plan have on the profits and the break-even point in dollars of the partnership?

(d) Which plan should be accepted? Explain your answer.

REAL-WORLD FOCUS

BYP5-3 The **Coca-Cola Company** hardly needs an introduction. A line taken from the cover of a recent annual report says it all: If you measured time in servings of Coca-Cola, "a billion Coca-Cola's ago was yesterday morning." On average, every U.S. citizen drinks 363 8-ounce servings of Coca-Cola products each year. Coca-Cola's primary line of business is the making and selling of syrup to bottlers. These bottlers then sell the finished bottles and cans of Coca-Cola to the consumer.

In the annual report of Coca-Cola, the following information was provided.

> **THE COCA-COLA COMPANY**
> **Management Discussion**
>
> Our gross margin declined to 61 percent in 1995 from 62 percent in 1994, primarily due to costs for materials such as sweeteners and packaging.
>
> The increases [in selling expenses] in 1996 and 1995 were primarily due to higher marketing expenditures in support of our Company's volume growth.
>
> We measure our sales volume in two ways: (1) gallon shipments of concentrates and syrups and (2) unit cases of finished product (bottles and cans of Coke sold by bottlers).

Instructions
Answer the following questions.
(a) Are sweeteners and packaging a variable cost or a fixed cost? What is the impact on the contribution margin of an increase in the per unit cost of sweeteners or packaging? What are the implications for profitability?
(b) In your opinion, are marketing expenditures a fixed cost, variable cost, or mixed cost to The Coca-Cola Company? Give justification for your answer.
(c) Which of the two measures cited for measuring volume represents the activity index as defined in this chapter? Why might Coca-Cola use two different measures?

EXPLORING THE WEB

BYP5-4   Ganong Bros. Ltd., located in St. Stephen, New Brunswick, is Canada's oldest independent candy company. Its products are distributed worldwide. In 1885, Ganong invented the popular "chicken bone," a cinnamon flavored, pink, hard candy jacket over a chocolate center. The home page of Ganong, listed below, includes information about the company and its products.

Address: **www.pcsolutions.nb.ca/ganong/times.htm**
          (or go to www.wiley.com/college/weygandt)

Instructions
Read the description of "chicken bones," and answer the following.
(a) Describe the steps in making "chicken bones."
(b) Identify at least two variable and two fixed costs that are likely to affect the production of "chicken bones."

COMMUNICATION ACTIVITY

BYP5-5   Your roommate asks your help on the following questions about CVP analysis formulas.
(a) How can the mathematical equation for break-even sales show both sales units and sales dollars?
(b) How do the formulas differ for contribution margin per unit and contribution margin ratio?
(c) How can contribution margin be used to determine break-even sales in units and in dollars?

Instructions
Write a memo to your roommate stating the relevant formulas and answering each question.

RESEARCH ASSIGNMENT

BYP5-6   The February 1998 issue of *Management Accounting* includes an article by Bonnie Stivers, Teresa Covin, Nancy Green Hall, and Steven Smalt entitled "How Nonfinancial Performance Measures Are Used."

Instructions

Read the article and answer the following questions.

(a) The article is based on a study and survey. What is the objective of this study? Describe the specific nature of the survey that was conducted.

(b) What were the five categories of nonfinancial performance measures identified and surveyed in this study?

(c) What factors were identified, as a result of the survey, to be the most important nonfinancial measures?

(d) What are the "three red flags" (conclusions) that the study results highlight?

ETHICS CASE

BYP5-7   Donny Blake is an accountant for Swenson Company. Early this year Donny made a highly favorable projection of sales and profits over the next 3 years for Swenson's hot-selling computer PLEX. As a result of the projections Donny presented to senior management, they decided to expand production in this area. This decision led to dislocations of some plant personnel who were reassigned to one of the company's newer plants in another state. However, no one was fired, and in fact the company expanded its work force slightly.

Unfortunately Donny rechecked his computations on the projections a few months later and found that he had made an error that would have reduced his projections substantially. Luckily, sales of PLEX have exceeded projections so far, and management is satisfied with its decision. Donny, however, is not sure what to do. Should he confess his honest mistake and jeopardize his possible promotion? He suspects that no one will catch the error because sales of PLEX have exceeded his projections, and it appears that profits will materialize close to his projections.

Instructions

(a) Who are the stakeholders in this situation?

(b) Identify the ethical issues involved in this situation.

(c) What are the possible alternative actions for Donny? What would you do in Donny's position?

Answers to Self-Study Questions

1. d   2. c   3. a   4. c   5. d   6. c   7. b   8. b   9. a   10. a

✓ *Remember to go back to the Navigator box on the chapter-opening page and check off your completed work.*

CHAPTER 6

Budgetary Planning

THE NAVIGATOR ✔

- Scan *Study Objectives* ☐
- Read *Feature Story* ☐
- Read *Preview* ☐
- Read text and answer *Before You Go On*
  p. 235 ☐ p. 246 ☐ p. 249 ☐
- Work *Using the Decision Toolkit* ☐
- Review *Summary of Study Objectives* ☐
- Work *Demonstration Problem* ☐
- Answer *Self-Study Questions* ☐
- Complete *Assignments* ☐

◆ STUDY OBJECTIVES

After studying this chapter, you should be able to:

1. Indicate the benefits of budgeting.

2. State the essentials of effective budgeting.

3. Identify the budgets that comprise the master budget.

4. Describe the sources for preparing the budgeted income statement.

5. Explain the principal sections of a cash budget.

6. Indicate the applicability of budgeting in nonmanufacturing companies.

THE NAVIGATOR

◆ FEATURE STORY

THE NEXT AMAZON.COM? WELL, ALMOST

The bursting of the dot-com bubble resulted in countless stories of dot-com failures. Many of these ventures were half-baked, get-rich-quick schemes, rarely based on sound business practices. Initially they saw money flowing in faster than they knew what to do with—which was precisely the problem. Without proper planning and budgeting, much of the money went to waste. In some cases, failure was actually brought on by rapid, uncontrolled growth.

One such example was the Web site **www. Positively-You.com**, an online discount bookseller. One of the co-founders, Lyle Bowline, had never run a business. However, his experience as an assistant director of an entrepreneurial center had provided him with knowledge about the do's and don'ts of small business. To minimize costs, he started the company off small and simple. He invested $5,000 in computer equipment and ran the business out of his basement. In the early months, even though sales were only about $2,000 a month, the company actually made a profit because it kept its costs low (a feat few other dot-coms could boast of).

Things changed dramatically when the company received national publicity in the financial press. Suddenly the company's sales increased to $50,000 a month—fully 25 times the previous level. The "simple" little business suddenly needed a business plan, a strategic plan, and a budget. It needed to rent office space and to hire employees. Initially, members of a local book club donated time to help meet the sudden demand. But quickly the number of paid employees ballooned. The sudden growth necessitated detailed planning and budgeting. The need for a proper budget was accentuated by the fact that the company's gross profit was only 16 cents on each dollar of goods sold. This meant that after paying for its inventory, the company had only 16 cents of every dollar to cover its remaining operating costs.

Unfortunately, the company never got things under control. Within a few months, sales had plummeted to $12,000 per month. At this level of sales the company could not meet the mountain of monthly expenses that it had accumulated in trying to grow. Ironically, the company's sudden success, and the turmoil it created, appears to have been what eventually caused the company to fail.

THE NAVIGATOR

As the Feature Story about the **Positively-You.com** indicates, budgeting is critical to financial well-being. As a student, you budget your study time and your money. Families budget income and expenses. Governmental agencies budget revenues and expenditures. Business enterprises use budgets in planning and controlling their operations.

Our primary focus in this chapter is budgeting—specifically, how budgeting is used as a **planning tool** by management. Through budgeting, it should be possible for management to maintain enough cash to pay creditors, to have sufficient raw materials to meet production requirements, and to have adequate finished goods to meet expected sales.

The content and organization of Chapter 6 are as follows.

BUDGETARY PLANNING			
Budgeting Basics	**Preparing the Operating Budgets**	**Preparing the Financial Budgets**	**Budgeting in Non-manufacturing Companies**
• Budgets and accounting • Benefits • Essentials of effective budgeting • Length of budget period • Budgeting process • Budgeting and human behavior • Budgeting and long-range planning • The master budget	• Sales • Production • Direct materials • Direct labor • Manufacturing overhead • Selling and administrative expense • Budgeted income statement	• Cash • Budgeted balance sheet	• Merchandisers • Service • Not-for-profit

THE NAVIGATOR

BUDGETING BASICS

One of management's major responsibilities is planning. As explained in Chapter 1, **planning** is the process of establishing enterprise-wide objectives. A successful organization makes both long-term and short-term plans. These plans set forth the objectives of the company and the proposed way of accomplishing them.

A **budget** is a formal written statement of management's plans for a specified future time period, expressed in financial terms. It normally represents the primary method of communicating agreed-upon objectives throughout the organization. Once adopted, a budget becomes an important basis for evaluating performance. It promotes efficiency and serves as a deterrent to waste and inefficiency. We consider the role of budgeting as a **control device** in Chapter 7.

BUDGETING AND ACCOUNTING

Accounting information makes major contributions to the budgeting process. From the accounting records, historical data on revenues, costs, and expenses can be obtained. These data are helpful in formulating future budget goals.

Normally, accountants have the responsibility for expressing management's budgeting goals in financial terms. In this role, they translate management's plans and communicate the budget to all areas of responsibility. Accountants also prepare periodic budget reports that provide the basis for measuring performance and comparing actual results with planned objectives. The budget itself, and the administration of the budget, however, are entirely management responsibilities.

THE BENEFITS OF BUDGETING

The primary benefits of budgeting are:

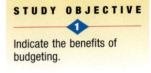

1. It requires all levels of management to **plan ahead** and to formalize their goals on a recurring basis.
2. It provides **definite objectives** for evaluating performance at each level of responsibility.
3. It creates an **early warning system** for potential problems. With early warning, management has time to make changes before things get out of hand.
4. It facilitates the **coordination of activities** within the business. It does this by correlating the goals of each segment with overall company objectives. Thus, production and sales promotion can be integrated with expected sales.
5. It results in greater **management awareness** of the entity's overall operations and the impact on operations of external factors, such as economic trends.
6. It **motivates personnel** throughout the organization to meet planned objectives.

A budget is an aid to management; it is not a substitute for management. A budget cannot operate or enforce itself. The benefits of budgeting will be realized only when budgets are carefully prepared and properly administered by management.

ESSENTIALS OF EFFECTIVE BUDGETING

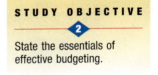

Effective budgeting depends on a **sound organizational structure**. In such a structure, authority and responsibility for all phases of operations are clearly defined. Budgets based on **research and analysis** should result in realistic goals that will contribute to the growth and profitability of a company. And, the effectiveness of a budget program is directly related to its **acceptance by all levels of management**.

Once the budget has been adopted, it should be an important tool for evaluating performance. Variations between actual and expected results should be systematically and periodically reviewed to determine their cause(s). However, individuals should not be held responsible for variations that are beyond their control.

LENGTH OF THE BUDGET PERIOD

The budget period is not necessarily one year in length. **A budget may be prepared for any period of time**. Various factors influence the length of the budget period. These factors include the type of budget, the nature of the organization, the need for periodic appraisal, and prevailing business conditions. For example, cash may be budgeted monthly, whereas a plant expansion budget may cover a ten-year period.

The budget period should be long enough to provide an attainable goal under normal business conditions. Ideally, the time period should minimize the impact of seasonal or cyclical fluctuations. On the other hand, the budget period should not be so long that reliable estimates are impossible.

The **most common budget period is one year**. The annual budget, in turn, is often supplemented by monthly and quarterly budgets. Many companies use **continuous twelve-month budgets**. These budgets drop the month just ended and add a future month. One advantage of continuous budgeting is that it keeps management planning a full year ahead.

THE BUDGETING PROCESS

The development of the budget for the coming year generally starts several months before the end of the current year. The budgeting process usually begins with the collection of data from each organizational unit of the company. Past performance is often the starting point from which future budget goals are formulated.

The budget is developed within the framework of a **sales forecast**. This forecast shows potential sales for the industry and the company's expected share of such sales. Sales forecasting involves a consideration of various factors: (1) general economic conditions, (2) industry trends, (3) market research studies, (4) anticipated advertising and promotion, (5) previous market share, (6) changes in prices, and (7) technological developments. The input of sales personnel and top management are essential to the sales forecast.

In small companies like **Positively-You.com**, the budgeting process is often informal. In larger companies, responsibility for coordinating the preparation of the budget is assigned to a **budget committee**. The committee ordinarily includes the president, treasurer, chief accountant (controller), and management personnel from each of the major areas of the company, such as sales, production, and research. The budget committee serves as a review board where managers can defend their budget goals and requests. Differences are reviewed, modified if necessary, and reconciled. The budget is then put in its final form by the budget committee, approved, and distributed.

BUSINESS INSIGHT
Management Perspective

A recent study by Willard & Shullman Group Ltd. found that fewer than 14 percent of businesses with fewer than 500 employees do an annual budget or have a written business plan. In all, nearly 60 percent of these businesses have no plans on paper at all. For many small businesses the basic assumption is that, "As long as I sell as much as I can, and keep my employees paid, I'm doing OK." A few small business owners even say that they see no need for budgeting and planning. Most small business owners, though, say that they understand that budgeting and planning is critical for survival and growth. But given the long hours that they already work addressing day-to-day challenges, they also say that they are "just too busy to plan for the future."

BUDGETING AND HUMAN BEHAVIOR

A budget can have a significant impact on human behavior. It may inspire a manager to higher levels of performance. Or, it may discourage additional effort and pull down the morale of a manager. Why do these diverse effects occur? The answer is found in how the budget is developed and administered.

In **developing the budget**, each level of management should be invited to participate. The overall goal is to reach agreement on a budget that the manager considers fair and achievable. When this objective is met, the budget will have a positive effect on the manager. In contrast, if the manager views the budget as being unfair and unrealistic, he or she may feel discouraged and uncommitted to the budget goals. The risk of having unrealistic budgets is generally greater when the budget is developed from top management down to lower management than vice versa. Illustration 6-1 graphically displays the appropriate flow of budget data from bottom to top in an organization.

Illustration 6-1   Flow of budget data from lower levels of management to top levels

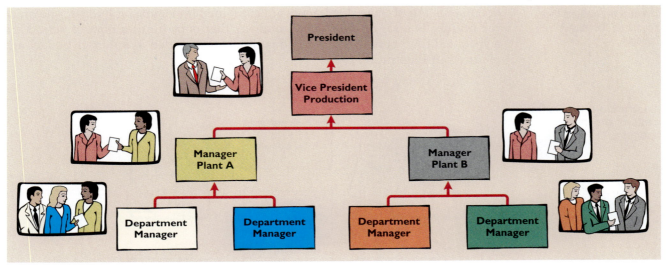

Administering the budget relates to how the budget is used by top management. As explained earlier, the budget should have the complete support of top management. The budget also should be an important basis for evaluating performance. The effect of an evaluation will be positive when top management tempers criticism with advice and assistance. In contrast, a manager is likely to respond negatively if the budget is used exclusively to assess blame.

A budget may be used improperly as a pressure device to force improved performance. Or, it can be used as a positive aid in achieving projected goals. In sum, a budget can become a manager's friend or a foe.

Helpful Hint Unrealistic budgets can lead to unethical employee behavior such as cutting corners on the job or distorting internal financial reports.

BUDGETING AND LONG-RANGE PLANNING

In business, you may hear talk about the need for long-range planning. Budgeting and long-range planning are not the same. One important difference is the **time period involved**. The maximum length of a budget is usually one year, and budgets are often prepared for shorter periods of time, such as a month or a quarter. In contrast, long-range planning usually encompasses a period of at least five years.

A second significant difference is in **emphasis**. Budgeting focuses on achieving specific short-term goals, such as meeting annual profit objectives. **Long-range planning**, on the other hand, identifies long-term goals, selects strategies to achieve those goals, and develops policies and plans to implement the strategies. In long-range planning, management also considers anticipated trends in the economic and political environment and how the company should cope with them.

Helpful Hint In comparing a budget with a long-range plan: (1) Which has more detail? (2) Which is done for a longer period of time? (3) Which is more concerned with short-term goals?
Answer: (1) Budget. (2) Long-range plan. (3) Budget.

The final difference between budgeting and long-range planning pertains to the **amount of detail presented**. Budgets, as you will see in this chapter, can be very detailed. Long-range plans contain considerably less detail. The data in long-range plans are intended more for a review of progress toward long-term goals than as a basis of control for achieving specific results. The primary objective of long-range planning is to develop the best strategy to maximize the company's performance over an extended future period.

THE MASTER BUDGET

The term "budget" is actually a shorthand term to describe a variety of budget documents. All of these documents are combined into a master budget. The **master budget** is a set of interrelated budgets that constitutes a plan of action for a specified time period. The individual budgets included in a master budget are pictured in Illustration 6-2.

Illustration 6-2 Components of the master budget

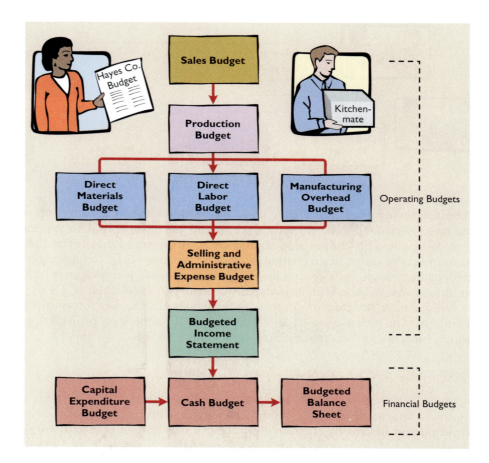

As the illustration shows, the master budget contains two classes of budgets. **Operating budgets** are the individual budgets that result in the preparation of the budgeted income statement. These budgets establish goals for the company's sales and production personnel. In contrast, **financial budgets** are the capital expenditure budget, the cash budget, and the budgeted balance sheet. These budgets focus primarily on the cash resources needed to fund expected operations and planned capital expenditures.

The master budget is prepared in the sequence shown in Illustration 6-2. The operating budgets are developed first, beginning with the sales budget. Then the financial budgets are prepared. We will explain and illustrate each budget shown in Illustration 6-2 except the capital expenditure budget. This budget is discussed under the topic Capital Budgeting in Chapter 10.

BEFORE YOU GO ON . . .

◆ **Review It**

1. What are the benefits of budgeting?
2. What are the factors essential to effective budgeting?
3. How does the budget process work?
4. How does budgeting differ from long-range planning?
5. What is a master budget?

PREPARING THE OPERATING BUDGETS

A case study of Hayes Company will be used in preparing the operating budgets. Hayes manufactures and sells a single product, Kitchen-mate. The budgets will be prepared by quarters for the year ending December 31, 2002. Hayes Company begins its annual budgeting process on September 1, 2001, and it completes the budget for 2002 by December 1, 2001.

SALES BUDGET

As shown in the master budget in Illustration 6-2, **the sales budget is the first budget prepared**. Each of the other budgets depends on the sales budget. The sales budget is derived from the sales forecast. It represents management's best estimate of sales revenue for the budget period. An inaccurate sales budget may adversely affect net income. For example, an overly optimistic sales budget may result in excessive inventories that may have to be sold at reduced prices. In contrast, an unduly conservative budget may result in loss of sales revenue due to inventory shortages.

The sales budget is prepared by multiplying the expected unit sales volume for each product by its anticipated unit selling price. For Hayes Company, sales volume is expected to be 3,000 units in the first quarter, with 500-unit increments in each succeeding quarter. Based on a sales price of $60 per unit, the sales budget for the year, by quarters, is shown in Illustration 6-3.

Helpful Hint For a retail or manufacturing company, what is the starting point in preparing the master budget, and why? Answer: Preparation of the sales budget is the starting point for the master budget. It sets the level of activity for other functions such as production and purchasing.

Illustration 6-3 Sales budget

HAYES COMPANY
Sales Budget
For the Year Ending December 31, 2002

	Quarter				
	1	2	3	4	Year
Expected unit sales	3,000	3,500	4,000	4,500	15,000
Unit selling price	× $60	× $60	× $60	× $60	× $60
Total sales	$180,000	$210,000	$240,000	$270,000	$900,000

Some companies classify the anticipated sales revenue as cash or credit sales and by geographical regions, territories, or salespersons.

PRODUCTION BUDGET

The **production budget** shows the units that must be produced to meet anticipated sales. Production requirements are determined from the following formula.[1]

Illustration 6-4 Production requirements formula

A realistic estimate of ending inventory is essential in scheduling production requirements. Excessive inventories in one quarter may lead to cutbacks in production and employee layoffs in a subsequent quarter. On the other hand, inadequate inventories may result either in added costs for overtime work or in lost sales. Hayes Company believes it can meet future sales requirements by maintaining an ending inventory equal to 20 percent of the next quarter's budgeted sales volume. For example, the ending finished goods inventory for the first quarter is 700 units (20% × anticipated second-quarter sales of 3,500 units). The production budget is shown in Illustration 6-5.

Illustration 6-5 Production budget

HAYES COMPANY
Production Budget
For the Year Ending December 31, 2002

| | \multicolumn{5}{c}{Quarter} | | | | |
	1	2	3	4	Year
Expected unit sales (Illustration 6-3)	3,000	3,500	4,000	4,500	
Add: Desired ending finished goods units[a]	700	800	900	1,000[b]	
Total required units	3,700	4,300	4,900	5,500	
Less: Beginning finished goods units	600[c]	700	800	900	
Required production units	**3,100**	**3,600**	**4,100**	**4,600**	**15,400**

[a]20% of next quarter's sales
[b]Expected 2003 first-quarter sales, 5,000 units × 20%
[c]20% of estimated first-quarter 2002 sales units

---

[1]This formula ignores any work in process inventories, which are assumed to be nonexistent in Hayes Company.

The production budget, in turn, provides the basis for determining the budgeted costs for each manufacturing cost element, as explained in the following pages.

BUSINESS INSIGHT

Management Perspective

Wrong move, wrong time, poor planning. When **Fruit of the Loom Inc.** saw underwear and apparel sales slowing, it cut back production sharply. Too sharply, in fact: almost overnight, demand soared. Caught with its shorts down, the company hired back thousands of workers and frantically increased production. The mistimed production cuts contributed to a 43 percent fall in first-quarter profits. For the year, Fruit stood to lose $200 million in sales, and analysts expected an 11 percent drop in profits for the year.

DIRECT MATERIALS BUDGET

The **direct materials budget** shows both the quantity and cost of direct materials to be purchased. The quantities of direct materials are derived from the following formula.

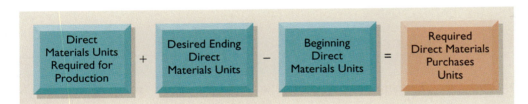

Illustration 6-6   Formula for direct materials quantities

The budgeted cost of direct materials to be purchased is then computed by multiplying the required units of direct materials by the anticipated cost per unit.

The desired ending inventory is again a key component in the budgeting process. For example, inadequate inventories could result in temporary shutdowns of production. Because of its close proximity to suppliers, Hayes Company has found that an ending inventory of raw materials equal to 10 percent of the next quarter's production requirements is sufficient. The manufacture of each Kitchen-mate requires 2 pounds of raw materials, and the expected cost per pound is $4. The direct materials budget is shown in Illustration 6-7.

Illustration 6-7   Direct materials budget

			Quarter		
	1	2	3	4	Year
HAYES COMPANY					
Direct Materials Budget					
For the Year Ending December 31, 2002					

	1	2	3	4	Year
Units to be produced (Illustration 6-5)	3,100	3,600	4,100	4,600	
Direct materials per unit	× 2	× 2	× 2	× 2	
Total pounds needed for production	6,200	7,200	8,200	9,200	
Add: Desired ending direct materials (pounds)[a]	720	820	920	1,020[b]	
Total materials required	6,920	8,020	9,120	10,220	
Less: Beginning direct materials (pounds)	620[c]	720	820	920	
Direct materials purchases	6,300	7,300	8,300	9,300	
Cost per pound	× $4	× $4	× $4	× $4	
Total cost of direct materials purchases	**$25,200**	**$29,200**	**$33,200**	**$37,200**	**$124,800**

[a]10% of next quarter's production requirements
[b]Estimated 2003 first-quarter pounds needed for production, 10,200 × 10%
[c]10% of estimated first-quarter pounds needed for production

BUSINESS INSIGHT

Management Perspective

The successful manufacturers of the twenty-first century will be fully computerized. A crucial step on the way is material requirements planning (MRP) systems. Early MRP systems accepted a sales forecast and computed how much materials, inventory, people, and machinery a company needed to manufacture the product. Current MRP systems link the company's manufacturing resource planning with its financial management. This new capability creates a powerful system of control over the entire business planning and operating process. With MRP, management can make decisions on facts rather than on "hunches" and "instinct."

DIRECT LABOR BUDGET

Like the direct materials budget, the **direct labor budget** contains the quantity (hours) and cost of direct labor necessary to meet production requirements. Direct labor hours are determined from the production budget. At Hayes Company, two hours of direct labor are required to produce each unit of finished goods. The anticipated hourly wage rate is $10. These data are shown in Illustration 6-8. The direct labor budget is critical in maintaining a labor force that can meet the expected levels of production.

Illustration 6-8 Direct labor budget

HAYES COMPANY
Direct Labor Budget
For the Year Ending December 31, 2002

	Quarter				
	1	2	3	4	Year
Units to be produced (Illustration 6-5)	3,100	3,600	4,100	4,600	
Direct labor time (hours) per unit	× 2	× 2	× 2	× 2	
Total required direct labor hours	6,200	7,200	8,200	9,200	
Direct labor cost per hour	× $10	× $10	× $10	× $10	
Total direct labor cost	**$62,000**	**$72,000**	**$82,000**	**$92,000**	**$308,000**

MANUFACTURING OVERHEAD BUDGET

The **manufacturing overhead budget** shows the expected manufacturing overhead costs for the budget period. As shown in Illustration 6-9, **this budget distinguishes between variable and fixed overhead costs.** Hayes Company expects variable costs to fluctuate with production volume on the basis of the following rates per direct labor hour: indirect materials $1.00, indirect labor $1.40, utilities $0.40, and maintenance $0.20. Thus, for 6,200 direct labor hours, budgeted indirect materials are $6,200 (6,200 × $1), and budgeted indirect labor is $8,680 (6,200 × $1.40). Hayes also recognizes that some maintenance is fixed. The amounts reported for fixed costs are assumed.

At Hayes Company, overhead is applied to production on the basis of direct labor hours. Thus, as shown in Illustration 6-9, the annual rate is $8 per hour ($246,400 ÷ 30,800).

Illustration 6-9 Manufacturing overhead budget

HAYES COMPANY
Manufacturing Overhead Budget
For the Year Ending December 31, 2002

	Quarter				
	1	2	3	4	Year
Variable costs					
Indirect materials	$ 6,200	$ 7,200	$ 8,200	$ 9,200	$ 30,800
Indirect labor	8,680	10,080	11,480	12,880	43,120
Utilities	2,480	2,880	3,280	3,680	12,320
Maintenance	1,240	1,440	1,640	1,840	6,160
Total variable	18,600	21,600	24,600	27,600	92,400
Fixed costs					
Supervisory salaries	20,000	20,000	20,000	20,000	80,000
Depreciation	3,800	3,800	3,800	3,800	15,200
Property taxes and insurance	9,000	9,000	9,000	9,000	36,000
Maintenance	5,700	5,700	5,700	5,700	22,800
Total fixed	38,500	38,500	38,500	38,500	154,000
Total manufacturing overhead	**$57,100**	**$60,100**	**$63,100**	**$66,100**	**$246,400**
Direct labor hours	6,200	7,200	8,200	9,200	30,800
Manufacturing overhead rate per direct labor hour ($246,400 ÷ 30,800)					**$8.00**

SELLING AND ADMINISTRATIVE EXPENSE BUDGET

Hayes Company combines its operating expenses into one budget, the **selling and administrative expense budget**. This budget projects anticipated selling and administrative expenses for the budget period. In this budget, as in the preceding one, expenses are classified as either variable or fixed. In this case, the variable expense rates per unit of sales are sales commissions $3.00 and freight-out $1.00. Variable expenses per quarter are based on the unit sales from the sales budget (Illustration 6-3). For example, sales in the first quarter are expected to be 3,000 units. Thus, Sales Commissions Expense is $9,000 (3,000 × $3), and Freight-out is $3,000 (3,000 × $1). Fixed expenses are based on assumed data. The selling and administrative expense budget is shown in Illustration 6-10.

Illustration 6-10 Selling and administrative expense budget

HAYES COMPANY
Selling and Administrative Expense Budget
For the Year Ending December 31, 2002

	Quarter				
	1	2	3	4	Year
Variable expenses					
Sales commissions	$ 9,000	$10,500	$12,000	$13,500	$ 45,000
Freight-out	3,000	3,500	4,000	4,500	15,000
Total variable	12,000	14,000	16,000	18,000	60,000
Fixed expenses					
Advertising	5,000	5,000	5,000	5,000	20,000
Sales salaries	15,000	15,000	15,000	15,000	60,000
Office salaries	7,500	7,500	7,500	7,500	30,000
Depreciation	1,000	1,000	1,000	1,000	4,000
Property taxes and insurance	1,500	1,500	1,500	1,500	6,000
Total fixed	30,000	30,000	30,000	30,000	120,000
Total selling and administrative expenses	**$42,000**	**$44,000**	**$46,000**	**$48,000**	**$180,000**

e – BUSINESS INSIGHT

Good budgeting depends on good information. And good information is what e-business is all about. As manufacturers, suppliers, and customers become electronically linked, each benefits by being better informed. **Dell Computer** not only is directly linked to **Solectron**, one of its main suppliers, but also to **Texas Instruments**, one of the main suppliers of parts to Solectron. This linking takes a lot of guesswork out of planning and budgeting for all three companies.

To further improve planning and budgeting, Dell hopes that some day everyone in its industry will anonymously provide their up-to-the-minute production and sales information at a central, electronic exchange. A centralized database such as this would provide valuable information about the supply and demand of computer goods in the marketplace. This information might dramatically improve sales projections, leading to significant improvements in the budgeting process.

Source: "E-Management," *The Economist*, November 11, 2000.

BUDGETED INCOME STATEMENT

The **budgeted income statement** is the important end-product of the operating budgets. This budget indicates the expected profitability of operations for the budget period. The budgeted income statement provides the basis for evaluating company performance.

As you would expect, this budget is prepared from the various operating budgets. For example, to find the cost of goods sold, it is first necessary to determine the total unit cost of producing one Kitchen-mate, as follows.

STUDY OBJECTIVE

4

Describe the sources for preparing the budgeted income statement.

Cost Element	Illustration	Quantity	Unit Cost	Total
Direct materials	6-7	2 pounds	$ 4.00	$ 8.00
Direct labor	6-8	2 hours	$10.00	20.00
Manufacturing overhead	6-9	2 hours	$ 8.00	16.00
Total unit cost				**$44.00**

Cost of One Kitchen-mate

Illustration 6-11 Computation of total unit cost

Cost of goods sold can then be determined by multiplying the units sold by the unit cost. For Hayes Company, budgeted cost of goods sold is $660,000 (15,000 × $44). All data for the statement are obtained from the individual operating budgets except the following: (1) interest expense is expected to be $100, and (2) income taxes are estimated to be $12,000. The budgeted income statement is shown in Illustration 6-12.

Illustration 6-12 Budgeted income statement

HAYES COMPANY
Budgeted Income Statement
For the Year Ending December 31, 2002

Sales (Illustration 6-3)	$900,000
Cost of goods sold (15,000 × $44)	660,000
Gross profit	240,000
Selling and administrative expenses (Illustration 6-10)	180,000
Income from operations	60,000
Interest expense	100
Income before income taxes	59,900
Income tax expense	12,000
Net income	$ 47,900

DECISION TOOLKIT

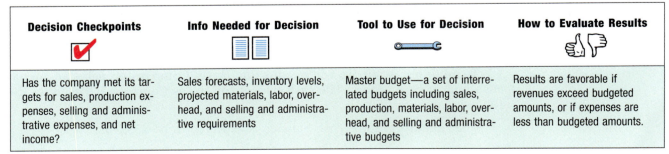

Decision Checkpoints	Info Needed for Decision	Tool to Use for Decision	How to Evaluate Results
Has the company met its targets for sales, production expenses, selling and administrative expenses, and net income?	Sales forecasts, inventory levels, projected materials, labor, overhead, and selling and administrative requirements	Master budget—a set of interrelated budgets including sales, production, materials, labor, overhead, and selling and administrative budgets	Results are favorable if revenues exceed budgeted amounts, or if expenses are less than budgeted amounts.

PREPARING THE FINANCIAL BUDGETS

As shown in Illustration 6-2, the financial budgets consist of the capital expenditure budget, the cash budget, and the budgeted balance sheet. The capital expenditure budget is discussed in Chapter 10; the other budgets are explained in the following sections.

CASH BUDGET

STUDY OBJECTIVE

5

Explain the principal sections of a cash budget.

The **cash budget** shows anticipated cash flows. Because cash is so vital, this budget is considered to be the most important output in preparing financial budgets. The cash budget contains three sections (cash receipts, cash disbursements, and financing) and the beginning and ending cash balances, as shown in Illustration 6-13.

Illustration 6-13 Basic form of a cash budget

ANY COMPANY
Cash Budget

Beginning cash balance	$X,XXX
Add: Cash receipts (Itemized)	X,XXX
Total available cash	X,XXX
Less: Cash disbursements (Itemized)	X,XXX
Excess (deficiency) of available cash over cash disbursements	X,XXX
Financing	X,XXX
Ending cash balance	$X,XXX

Helpful Hint Why is the cash budget prepared after the other budgets are prepared? Answer: Because the information generated by the other budgets dictates the need for inflows and outflows of cash.

The **cash receipts section** includes expected receipts from the company's principal source(s) of revenue. These are usually cash sales and collections from customers on credit sales. This section also shows anticipated receipts of interest and dividends, and proceeds from planned sales of investments, plant assets, and the company's capital stock.

The **cash disbursements section** shows expected cash payments. Such payments include direct materials, direct labor, manufacturing overhead, and selling and administrative expenses. This section also includes projected payments for income taxes, dividends, investments, and plant assets.

The **financing section** shows expected borrowings and the repayment of the borrowed funds plus interest. This section is needed when there is a cash deficiency or when the cash balance is below management's minimum required balance.

Data in the cash budget must be prepared in sequence. The ending cash balance of one period becomes the beginning cash balance for the next period. Data for preparing the cash budget are obtained from other budgets and from information provided by management. In practice, cash budgets are often prepared for the year on a monthly basis.

To minimize detail, we will assume that Hayes Company prepares an annual cash budget by quarters. The cash budget for Hayes Company is based on the following assumptions.

1. The January 1, 2002, cash balance is expected to be $38,000.

2. Sales (Illustration 6-3): 60 percent are collected in the quarter sold and 40 percent are collected in the following quarter. Accounts receivable of $60,000 at December 31, 2001, are expected to be collected in full in the first quarter of 2002.

3. Short-term investments are expected to be sold for $2,000 cash in the first quarter.

4. Direct materials (Illustration 6-7): 50 percent are paid in the quarter purchased and 50 percent are paid in the following quarter. Accounts payable of $10,600 at December 31, 2001, are expected to be paid in full in the first quarter of 2002.

5. Direct labor (Illustration 6-8): 100 percent is paid in the quarter incurred.

6. Manufacturing overhead (Illustration 6-9) and selling and administrative expenses (Illustration 6-10): All items except depreciation are paid in the quarter incurred.

7. Management plans to purchase a truck in the second quarter for $10,000 cash.

8. Hayes makes equal quarterly payments of its estimated annual income taxes.

9. Loans are repaid in the earliest quarter in which there is sufficient cash (i.e., when the cash on hand exceeds the $15,000 minimum required balance).

In preparing the cash budget, it is useful to prepare schedules for collections from customers (assumption No. 2, above) and cash payments for direct materials (assumption No. 4, above). The schedules are shown in Illustrations 6-14 and 6-15.

Schedule of Expected Collections from Customers

	Quarter			
	1	2	3	4
Accounts receivable, 12/31/01	$ 60,000			
First quarter ($180,000)	108,000	$ 72,000		
Second quarter ($210,000)		126,000	$ 84,000	
Third quarter ($240,000)			144,000	$ 96,000
Fourth quarter ($270,000)				162,000
Total collections	$168,000	$198,000	$228,000	$258,000

Illustration 6-14 Collections from customers

Schedule of Expected Payments for Direct Materials

	Quarter			
	1	2	3	4
Accounts payable, 12/31/01	$10,600			
First quarter ($25,200)	12,600	$12,600		
Second quarter ($29,200)		14,600	$14,600	
Third quarter ($33,200)			16,600	$16,600
Fourth quarter ($37,200)				18,600
Total payments	$23,200	$27,200	$31,200	$35,200

Illustration 6-15 Payments for direct materials

The cash budget for Hayes Company is shown in Illustration 6-16. The budget indicates that $3,000 of financing will be needed in the second quarter to maintain a minimum cash balance of $15,000. Since there is an excess of available cash over disbursements of $22,500 at the end of the third quarter, the borrowing, plus $100 interest, is repaid in this quarter.

Illustration 6-16 Cash budget

	Assumption	Quarter			
		1	2	3	4
Beginning cash balance	1	$ 38,000	$ 25,500	$ 15,000	$ 19,400
Add: Receipts					
Collections from customers	2	168,000	198,000	228,000	258,000
Sale of securities	3	2,000	0	0	0
Total receipts		170,000	198,000	228,000	258,000
Total available cash		208,000	223,500	243,000	277,400
Less: Disbursements					
Direct materials	4	23,200	27,200	31,200	35,200
Direct labor	5	62,000	72,000	82,000	92,000
Manufacturing overhead	6	53,300[1]	56,300	59,300	62,300
Selling and administrative expenses	6	41,000[2]	43,000	45,000	47,000
Purchase of truck	7	0	10,000	0	0
Income tax expense	8	3,000	3,000	3,000	3,000
Total disbursements		182,500	211,500	220,500	239,500
Excess (deficiency) of available cash over disbursements		25,500	12,000	22,500	37,900
Financing					
Borrowings		0	**3,000**	0	0
Repayments—plus $100 interest	9	0	0	**3,100**	0
Ending cash balance		$ 25,500	$ 15,000	$ 19,400	$ 37,900

HAYES COMPANY
Cash Budget
For the Year Ending December 31, 2002

[1]$57,100 − $3,800 depreciation
[2]$42,000 − $1,000 depreciation

BUSINESS INSIGHT
Management Perspective

Douglas Roberson, president of **Atlantic Network**, woke up one morning to find that his company was out of cash. At that point, Roberson realized that managing cash flow is different from simply accumulating sales. He says: "If you don't do serious projections about how much cash you will need to handle sales—and how long it will take to collect on invoices— you can end up out of business no matter how fast you are growing." In fact, Roberson says, fast growth makes cash flow problems worse because the company can be spending cash on supplies and payroll at an accelerated pace while waiting 45 days or longer to collect receivables.

A cash budget contributes to more effective cash management. It can show managers when additional financing will be necessary well before the actual need arises. And, it can indicate when excess cash will be available for investments or other purposes.

DECISION TOOLKIT

Decision Checkpoints	Info Needed for Decision	Tool to Use for Decision	How to Evaluate Results
Is the company going to need to borrow funds in the coming quarter?	Beginning cash balance, cash receipts, cash disbursements, and desired cash balance	Cash budget	The company will need to borrow money if the cash budget indicates a projected cash deficiency of available cash over cash disbursements for the quarter.

BUDGETED BALANCE SHEET

The **budgeted balance sheet** is a projection of financial position at the end of the budget period. This budget is developed from the budgeted balance sheet for the preceding year and the budgets for the current year. Pertinent data from the budgeted balance sheet at December 31, 2001, are as follows.

Buildings and equipment	$182,000	Common stock	$225,000
Accumulated depreciation	$ 28,800	Retained earnings	$ 46,480

The budgeted balance sheet at December 31, 2002, is shown below.

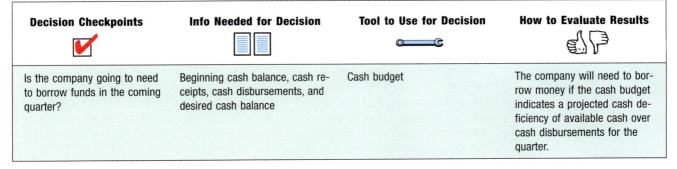

HAYES COMPANY
Budgeted Balance Sheet
December 31, 2002

Assets

Cash		$ 37,900
Accounts receivable		108,000
Finished goods inventory		44,000
Raw materials inventory		4,080
Buildings and equipment	$192,000	
Less: Accumulated depreciation	48,000	144,000
Total assets		$337,980

Liabilities and Stockholders' Equity

Accounts payable	$ 18,600
Common stock	225,000
Retained earnings	94,380
Total liabilities and stockholders' equity	$337,980

Illustration 6-17 Budgeted balance sheet

The computations and sources of the amounts are explained below.

Cash: Ending cash balance $37,900, shown in the cash budget (Illustration 6-16).

Accounts receivable: 40 percent of fourth-quarter sales $270,000, shown in the schedule of expected collections from customers (Illustration 6-14).

Finished goods inventory: Desired ending inventory 1,000 units, shown in the production budget (Illustration 6-5) times the total unit cost $44 (shown in Illustration 6-11).

Raw materials inventory: Desired ending inventory 1,020 pounds, times the cost per pound $4, shown in the direct materials budget (Illustration 6-7).

Buildings and equipment: December 31, 2001, balance $182,000, plus purchase of truck for $10,000.

Accumulated depreciation: December 31, 2001, balance $28,800, plus $15,200 depreciation shown in manufacturing overhead budget (Illustration 6-9) and $4,000 depreciation shown in selling and administrative expense budget (Illustration 6-10).

Accounts payable: 50 percent of fourth-quarter purchases $37,200, shown in schedule of expected payments for direct materials (Illustration 6-15).

Common stock: Unchanged from the beginning of the year.

Retained earnings: December 31, 2001, balance $46,480, plus net income $47,900, shown in budgeted income statement (Illustration 6-12).

BUSINESS INSIGHT
Management Perspective

After the budgeting data are entered into the computer, the various budgets (sales, cash, etc.) can be prepared, as well as the budgeted financial statements. Management can also manipulate the budgets in "what if" (sensitivity) analyses based on different hypothetical assumptions. For example, suppose that sales were budgeted to be 10 percent higher in the coming quarter. What impact would the change have on the rest of the budgeting process and the financing needs of the business? The computer can quickly "play out" the impact of the various assumptions on the budgets. Armed with these analyses, management can make more informed decisions about the impact of various projects. They also can anticipate future problems and business opportunities. Budgeting is one of the top uses of electronic spreadsheets. Template versions of every one of the Hayes Company budgets shown in this chapter could easily be prepared.

BEFORE YOU GO ON . . .

◆ **Review It**

1. What are the two classifications of the individual budgets in the master budget?
2. What is the sequence for preparing the budgets that comprise the operating budgets?
3. Identify some of the source documents that would be used in preparing each of the operating budgets.

4. What are the three principal sections of the cash budget?

◆ Do It

In Martian Company, management wants to maintain a minimum monthly cash balance of $15,000. At the beginning of March, the cash balance is $16,500, expected cash receipts for March are $210,000, and cash disbursements are expected to be $220,000. How much cash, if any, must be borrowed to maintain the desired minimum monthly balance?

Action Plan

• Write down the basic form of the cash budget, starting with the beginning cash balance, adding cash receipts for the period, deducting cash disbursements, and identifying the needed financing to achieve the desired minimum ending cash balance.

• Insert the data given into the outlined form of the cash budget.

Solution

MARTIAN COMPANY
Cash Budget
For the Month Ending March 31, 2002

Beginning cash balance	$ 16,500
Add: Cash receipts for March	210,000
Total available cash	226,500
Less: Cash disbursements for March	220,000
Excess of available cash over cash disbursements	6,500
Financing	8,500
Ending cash balance	$ 15,000

To maintain the desired minimum cash balance of $15,000, Martian Company must borrow $8,500 of cash.

Related exercise material: BE6-9 and E6-9.

BUDGETING IN NONMANUFACTURING COMPANIES

Budgeting is not limited to manufacturers. Budgets may also be used by merchandisers, service enterprises, and not-for-profit organizations.

STUDY OBJECTIVE
6
Indicate the applicability of budgeting in nonmanufacturing companies.

MERCHANDISERS

As in manufacturing operations, the sales budget for a merchandiser is both the starting point and the key factor in the development of the master budget. The major differences between the master budgets of a merchandiser and a manufacturer are these: (1) A merchandiser **uses a merchandise purchases budget instead of a production budget.** (2) A merchandiser **does not use the manufacturing budgets (direct materials, direct labor, and manufacturing overhead)**. The merchandise purchases budget shows the estimated cost of goods to be purchased to meet expected sales. The formula for determining budgeted merchandise purchases is:

Illustration 6-18 Merchandise purchases formula

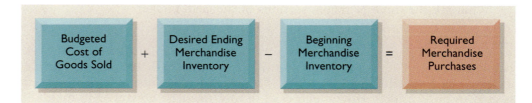

To illustrate, assume that the budget committee of Lima Company is preparing the merchandise purchases budget for July. It estimates that budgeted sales will be $300,000 in July and $320,000 in August. Cost of goods sold is expected to be 70 percent of sales. The company's desired ending inventory is 30 percent of the following month's cost of goods sold. Required merchandise purchases for July are $214,200, computed as follows.

Illustration 6-19 Computation of required merchandise purchases

Budgeted cost of goods sold (budgeted sales for July of $300,000 × 70%)	$ 210,000
Desired ending merchandise inventory (budgeted sales for August of $320,000 × 70% × 30%)	67,200
Total	277,200
Less: Beginning merchandise inventory (budgeted sales for July of $300,000 × 70% × 30%)	63,000
Required merchandise purchases for July	**$214,200**

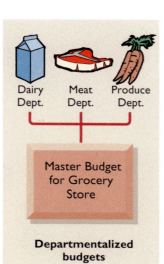

Departmentalized budgets

When a merchandiser is departmentalized, separate budgets are prepared for each department. For example, a grocery store may start by preparing sales budgets and purchases budgets for each of its major departments, such as meats, dairy, and produce. These budgets are then combined into a master budget for the store. When a retailer has branch stores, separate master budgets are prepared for each store. Then these budgets are incorporated into master budgets for the company as a whole.

SERVICE ENTERPRISES

In a service enterprise, such as a public accounting firm, a law office, or a medical practice, the critical factor in budgeting is **coordinating professional staff needs with anticipated services**. If a firm is overstaffed, several problems may result: (1) Labor costs will be disproportionately high. (2) Profits will be lower because of the additional salaries. (3) Staff turnover may increase because of lack of challenging work. In contrast, if an enterprise is understaffed, revenue may be lost because existing and prospective client needs for service cannot be met. Also, professional staff may seek other jobs because of excessive work loads.

Budget data for service revenue may be obtained from **expected output** or **expected input**. When output is used, it is necessary to determine the expected billings of clients for services rendered. In a public accounting firm, for example, output would be the sum of its billings in auditing, tax, and consulting services. When input data are used, each professional staff member is required to project his or her billable time. Billing rates are then applied to billable time to produce expected service revenue.

BUSINESS INSIGHT
Service Company Perspective

Lucy Carter, managing partner of a small CPA firm in Nashville, uses formal budgets as the principal tool for keeping cash flow on an even keel throughout the year. The firm budgets annually for both revenues and expenses on a month-by-month basis. For example, the revenue budget is derived from chargeable-hour goals set by the staff. The firm sets a threshold of 1,800 hours for each staff member and 1,700 hours for each manager. Each month the budget is compared with the financial statements, and adjustments are made if necessary.

NOT-FOR-PROFIT ORGANIZATIONS

Budgeting is just as important for not-for-profit organizations as for profit-oriented enterprises. The budget process, however, is significantly different. In most cases not-for-profit entities budget **on the basis of cash flows (expenditures and receipts), rather than on a revenue and expense basis**. Further, the starting point in the process is usually expenditures, not receipts. For the not-for-profit entity, management's task generally is to find the receipts needed to support the planned expenditures. The activity index is also likely to be significantly different. For example, in a not-for-profit entity, such as a university, budgeted faculty positions may be based on full-time equivalent students or credit hours expected to be taught in a department.

For some governmental units, the budget must be approved by voters. In other cases, such as state governments and the federal government, legislative approval is required. After the budget is adopted, it must be strictly followed. Overspending is often illegal. In governmental budgets, authorizations tend to be on a line-by-line basis. That is, the budget for a municipality may have a specified authorization for police and fire protection, garbage collection, street paving, and so on. The line-item authorization of governmental budgets significantly limits the amount of discretion management can exercise. The city manager often cannot use savings from one line item, such as street paving, to cover increased spending in another line item, such as snow removal.

BEFORE YOU GO ON . . .

◆ **Review It**

1. What is the formula for computing required merchandise purchases?
2. How does budgeting in service and not-for-profit organizations differ from budgeting for manufacturers and merchandisers?

THE NAVIGATOR

USING THE DECISION TOOLKIT

The **University of Wisconsin** and its subunits must prepare budgets. One unique subunit of the University of Wisconsin is **Babcock Ice Cream**, a functioning producer of dairy products (and famous, at least on campus, for its delicious ice cream).

Assume that Babcock Ice Cream prepares monthly cash budgets. Relevant data from assumed operating budgets for 2002 are:

	January	February
Sales	$460,000	$412,000
Direct materials purchases	185,000	210,000
Direct labor	70,000	85,000
Manufacturing overhead	50,000	65,000
Selling and administrative expenses	85,000	95,000

Babcock sells 50% of its ice cream in its shops on campus, as well as selling to local stores. Collections from local stores are expected to be 50% in the month of sale, and 50% in the month following sale. Sixty percent (60%) of direct materials purchases are paid in cash in the month of purchase, and the balance due is paid in the month following the purchase. All other items above are paid in the month incurred. (Depreciation has been excluded from manufacturing overhead and selling and administrative expenses.)

Other data:

(1) Sales: November 2001, $370,000; December 2001, $320,000
(2) Purchases of direct materials: December 2001, $175,000
(3) Other receipts: January—Donation received, $2,000
            February—Sale of used equipment, $4,000
(4) Other disbursements: February—Purchased equipment, $10,000
(5) Repaid debt: January, $30,000

The company's cash balance on January 1, 2002, is expected to be $50,000. The company wants to maintain a minimum cash balance of $45,000.

Instructions

(a) Prepare schedules for (1) expected collections from customers and (2) expected payments for direct materials purchases.
(b) Prepare a cash budget for January and February in columnar form.

Solution

(a) (1)   **Expected Collections from Customers**

	January	February
December ($320,000)	$ 80,000	$ 0
January ($460,000)	345,000	115,000
February ($412,000)	0	309,000
Totals	$425,000	$424,000

(2)   **Expected Payments for Direct Materials**

	January	February
December ($175,000)	$ 70,000	$ 0
January ($185,000)	111,000	74,000
February ($210,000)	0	126,000
Totals	$181,000	$200,000

(b)

BABCOCK ICE CREAM
Cash Budget
For the Two Months Ending February 28, 2002

	January	February
Beginning cash balance	$ 50,000	$ 61,000
Add: Receipts		
Collections from customers	425,000	424,000
Donations received	2,000	0
Sale of used equipment	0	4,000
Total receipts	427,000	428,000
Total available cash	477,000	489,000
Less: Disbursements		
Direct materials	181,000	200,000
Direct labor	70,000	85,000
Manufacturing overhead	50,000	65,000
Selling and administrative expenses	85,000	95,000
Purchase of equipment	0	10,000
Total disbursements	386,000	455,000
Excess (deficiency) of available cash over		
disbursements	91,000	34,000
Financing		
Borrowings	0	11,000
Repayments	30,000	0
Ending cash balance	$ 61,000	$ 45,000

Summary of Study Objectives

❶ Indicate the benefits of budgeting. The primary advantages of budgeting are that it (a) requires management to plan ahead, (b) provides definite objectives for evaluating performance, (c) creates an early warning system for potential problems, (d) facilitates coordination of activities, (e) results in greater management awareness, and (f) motivates personnel to meet planned objectives.

❷ State the essentials of effective budgeting. The essentials of effective budgeting are (a) sound organizational structure, (b) research and analysis, and (c) acceptance by all levels of management.

❸ Identify the budgets that comprise the master budget. The master budget consists of the following budgets: (a) sales, (b) production, (c) direct materials, (d) direct labor, (e) manufacturing overhead, (f) selling and administrative expense, (g) budgeted income statement, (h) capital expenditure budget, (i) cash budget, and (j) budgeted balance sheet.

❹ Describe the sources for preparing the budgeted income statement. The budgeted income statement is prepared from (a) the sales budget, (b) the budgets for direct materials, direct labor, and manufacturing overhead, and (c) the selling and administrative expense budget.

❺ Explain the principal sections of a cash budget. The cash budget has three sections (receipts, disbursements, and financing) and the beginning and ending cash balances.

❻ Indicate the applicability of budgeting in nonmanufacturing companies. Budgeting may be used by merchandisers for development of a master budget. In service enterprises budgeting is a critical factor in coordinating staff needs with anticipated services. In not-for-profit organizations, the starting point in budgeting is usually expenditures, not receipts.

DECISION TOOLKIT—A SUMMARY

Decision Checkpoints	Info Needed for Decision	Tool to Use for Decision	How to Evaluate Results
Has the company met its targets for sales, production expenses, selling and administrative expenses, and net income?	Sales forecasts, inventory levels, projected materials, labor, overhead, and selling and administrative requirements	Master budget—a set of interrelated budgets including sales, production, materials, labor, overhead, and selling and administrative budgets	Results are favorable if revenues exceed budgeted amounts, or if expenses are less than budgeted amounts.
Is the company going to need to borrow funds in the coming quarter?	Beginning cash balance, cash receipts, cash disbursements, and desired cash balance	Cash budget	The company will need to borrow money if the cash budget indicates a projected cash deficiency of available cash over cash disbursements for the quarter.

GLOSSARY

Key Term Matching Activity

Budget A formal written statement of management's plans for a specified future time period, expressed in financial terms. (p. 230)

Budget committee A group responsible for coordinating the preparation of the budget. (p. 232)

Budgeted balance sheet A projection of financial position at the end of the budget period. (p. 245)

Budgeted income statement An estimate of the expected profitability of operations for the budget period. (p. 241)

Cash budget A projection of anticipated cash flows. (p. 242)

Direct labor budget A projection of the quantity and cost of direct labor to be incurred to meet production requirements. (p. 238)

Direct materials budget An estimate of the quantity and cost of direct materials to be purchased. (p. 237)

Financial budgets Individual budgets that indicate the cash resources needed for expected operations and planned capital expenditures. (p. 234)

Long-range planning A formalized process of selecting strategies to achieve long-term goals and devel-

oping policies and plans to implement the strategies. (p. 233)

Manufacturing overhead budget An estimate of expected manufacturing overhead costs for the budget period. (p. 239)

Master budget A set of interrelated budgets that constitutes a plan of action for a specific time period. (p. 234)

Merchandise purchases budget The estimated cost of goods to be purchased by a merchandiser to meet expected sales. (p. 247)

Operating budgets Individual budgets that result in a budgeted income statement. (p. 234)

Production budget A projection of the units that must be produced to meet anticipated sales. (p. 236)

Sales budget An estimate of expected sales for the budget period. (p. 235)

Sales forecast The projection of potential sales for the industry and the company's expected share of such sales. (p. 232)

Selling and administrative expense budget A projection of anticipated selling and administrative expenses for the budget period. (p. 240)

DEMONSTRATION PROBLEM

eGrade Demonstration Problem

Soroco Company is preparing its master budget for 2002. Relevant data pertaining to its sales and production budgets are as follows:

Sales: Sales for the year are expected to total 1,200,000 units. Quarterly sales are 20%, 25%, 30%, and 25% respectively. The sales price is expected to be $50 per unit for the first three quarters and $55 per unit beginning in the fourth quarter. Sales in the first quarter of 2003 are expected to be 10% higher than the budgeted sales volume for the first quarter of 2002.

Production: Management desires to maintain ending finished goods inventories at 25% of the next quarter's budgeted sales volume.

Instructions

Prepare the sales budget and production budget by quarters for 2002.

Solution to Demonstration Problem

SOROCO COMPANY
Sales Budget
For the Year Ending December 31, 2002

			Quarter		
	1	2	3	4	Year
Expected unit sales	240,000	300,000	360,000	300,000	1,200,000
Unit selling price	× $50	× $50	× $50	× $55	—
	$12,000,000	$15,000,000	$18,000,000	$16,500,000	$61,500,000

SOROCO COMPANY
Production Budget
For the Year Ending December 31, 2002

		Quarter			
	1	2	3	4	Year
Expected unit sales	240,000	300,000	360,000	300,000	
Add: Desired ending finished goods units	75,000	90,000	75,000	66,000[1]	
Total required units	315,000	390,000	435,000	366,000	
Less: Beginning finished goods units	60,000[2]	75,000	90,000	75,000	
Units to be produced	255,000	315,000	345,000	291,000	1,206,000

[1]Estimated first-quarter 2003 sales volume 240,000 + (240,000 × 10%) = 264,000; 264,000 × 25%.
[2]25% of estimated first-quarter 2002 sales units.

Action Plan
- Know the form and content of the sales budget.
- Prepare the sales budget first as the basis for the other budgets.
- Determine the units that must be produced to meet anticipated sales.
- Know how to compute the beginning and ending finished goods units.

SELF-STUDY QUESTIONS

Self-Study/Self-Test

Answers are at the end of the chapter.

(SO 1) 1. The benefits of budgeting include *all but one* of the following:
(a) Management can plan ahead.
(b) An early warning system is provided for potential problems.
(c) It enables disciplinary action to be taken at every level of responsibility.
(d) The coordination of activities is facilitated.

(SO 2) 2. The essentials of effective budgeting do *not* include:
(a) top-down budgeting.
(b) management acceptance.
(c) research and analysis.
(d) sound organizational structure.

3. Compared to budgeting, long-range planning (SO 2) generally has the:
(a) same amount of detail.
(b) longer time period.
(c) same emphasis.
(d) same time period.

4. A sales budget is: (SO 3)
(a) derived from the production budget.
(b) management's best estimate of sales revenue for the year.
(c) not the starting point for the master budget.
(d) prepared only for credit sales.

5. The formula for the production budget is budgeted sales in units plus: (SO 3)

(a) desired ending merchandise inventory less beginning merchandise inventory.
(b) beginning finished goods units less desired ending finished goods units.
(c) desired ending direct materials units less beginning direct materials units.
(d) desired ending finished goods units less beginning finished goods units.

(SO 3) 6. Direct materials inventories are kept in pounds in Byrd Company, and the total pounds of direct materials needed for production is 9,500. If the beginning inventory is 1,000 pounds and the desired ending inventory is 2,200 pounds, the total pounds to be purchased is:
(a) 9,400.
(b) 9,500.
(c) 9,700.
(d) 10,700.

(SO 3) 7. The formula for computing the direct labor cost budget is to multiply the direct labor cost per hour by the:
(a) total required direct labor hours.
(b) physical units to be produced.
(c) equivalent units to be produced.
(d) No correct answer is given.

8. Each of the following budgets is used in preparing the budgeted income statement *except* the: (SO 4)
(a) sales budget.
(b) selling and administrative budget.
(c) capital expenditure budget.
(d) direct labor budget.

9. Expected direct materials purchases in Read (SO 5) Company are $70,000 in the first quarter and $90,000 in the second quarter. Forty percent of the purchases are paid in cash as incurred, and the balance is paid in the following quarter. The budgeted cash payments for purchases in the second quarter are:
(a) $96,000.
(b) $90,000.
(c) $78,000.
(d) $72,000.

10. The budget for a merchandiser differs from a (SO 6) budget for a manufacturer because:
(a) a merchandise purchases budget replaces the production budget.
(b) the manufacturing budgets are not applicable.
(c) None of the above.
(d) Both (a) and (b) above.

QUESTIONS

1. (a) What is a budget?
   (b) How does a budget contribute to good management?

2. Valerie Flynn and Ken Leask are discussing the benefits of budgeting. They ask you to identify the primary advantages of budgeting. Comply with their request.

3. Lorraine Scott asks your help in understanding the essentials of effective budgeting. Identify the essentials for Lorraine.

4. (a) "Accounting plays a relatively unimportant role in budgeting." Do you agree? Explain.
   (b) What responsibilities does management have in budgeting?

5. What criteria are helpful in determining the length of the budget period? What is the most common budget period?

6. Mary Miller maintains that the only difference between budgeting and long-range planning is time. Do you agree? Why or why not?

7. Distinguish between a master budget and a sales budget.

8. What budget is the starting point in preparing the master budget? What may result if this budget is inaccurate?

9. "The production budget shows both unit production data and unit cost data." Is this true? Explain.

10. Wheaton Company has 8,000 beginning finished goods units. Budgeted sales units are 160,000. If management desires 20,000 ending finished goods units, what are the required units of production?

11. In preparing the direct materials budget for Dukane Company, management concludes that required purchases are 54,000 units. If 50,000 direct materials units are required in production and there are 7,000 units of beginning direct materials, what is the desired units of ending direct materials?

12. The production budget of Hinsdale Company calls for 90,000 units to be produced. If it takes 30 minutes to make one unit and the direct labor rate is $14 per hour, what is the total budgeted direct labor cost?

13. Villanova Company's manufacturing overhead budget shows total variable costs of $168,000 and total fixed costs of $147,000. Total production in units is expected to be 160,000. It takes 15 minutes to make one unit, and the direct labor rate is $15 per hour. Express the manufacturing overhead rate as (a) a percentage of direct labor cost, and (b) an amount per direct labor hour.

14. Westphal Company's variable selling and administrative expenses are 15% of net sales. Fixed expenses are $60,000 per quarter. The sales budget shows expected sales of $200,000 and $250,000 in the first and second quarters, respectively. What are the total budgeted selling and administrative expenses for each quarter?

15. For Advent Company, the budgeted cost for one unit of product is direct materials $10, direct labor $20, and manufacturing overhead 80% of direct labor cost. If 25,000 units are expected to be sold at $77 each, what is the budgeted gross profit?

16. Indicate the supporting schedules used in preparing a budgeted income statement through gross profit for a manufacturer.

17. Identify the three sections of a cash budget. What balances are also shown in this budget?

18. Andrew Manion Company has credit sales of $500,000 in January. Past experience suggests that 45% is collected in the month of sale, 50% in the month following the sale, and 4% in the second month following the sale. Compute the cash collections from January sales in January, February, and March.

19. What is the formula for determining required merchandise purchases for a merchandiser?

20. How may expected revenues in a service enterprise be computed?

BRIEF EXERCISES

BE6-1 Sharon Livingston Manufacturing Company uses the following budgets: Balance Sheet, Capital Expenditure, Cash, Direct Labor, Direct Materials, Income Statement, Manufacturing Overhead, Production, Sales, and Selling and Administrative. Prepare a diagram of the interrelationships of the budgets in the master budget. Indicate whether each budget is an operating or a financial budget.

Prepare a diagram of a master budget.
(SO 3)

BE6-2 Emil Company estimates that unit sales will be 10,000 in quarter 1; 12,000 in quarter 2; 14,000 in quarter 3; and 15,000 in quarter 4. Using a sales price of $70 per unit, prepare the sales budget by quarters and for the year ending December 31, 2002.

Prepare a sales budget.
(SO 3)

BE6-3 Sales budget data for Emil Company are given in BE6-2. Management desires to have an ending finished goods inventory equal to 30% of the next quarter's expected unit sales. Prepare a production budget by quarters for the first 6 months of 2002.

Prepare a production budget for 2 quarters.
(SO 3)

BE6-4 Korenewych Company has 1,200 pounds of raw materials in its December 31, 2002, ending inventory. Required production for January and February are 4,000 and 5,000 units, respectively. Two pounds of raw materials are needed for each unit, and the estimated cost per pound is $6. Management desires an ending inventory equal to 15% of next month's materials requirements. Prepare the direct materials budget for January.

Prepare a direct materials budget for 1 month.
(SO 3)

BE6-5 For Shawn Green Company, units to be produced are 5,000 in quarter 1 and 6,000 in quarter 2. It takes 1.8 hours to make a finished unit, and the expected hourly wage rate is $12 per hour. Prepare a direct labor budget by quarters and for the 6 months ending June 30, 2002.

Prepare a direct labor budget for 2 quarters.
(SO 3)

BE6-6 For John Dunham Inc. variable manufacturing overhead costs are expected to be $20,000 in the first quarter of 2002, with $3,000 increments in each of the remaining three quarters. Fixed overhead costs are estimated to be $35,000 in each quarter. Prepare the manufacturing overhead budget by quarters and for the year.

Prepare a manufacturing overhead budget.
(SO 3)

BE6-7 Chudzick Company classifies its selling and administrative expense budget into variable and fixed components. Variable expenses are expected to be $25,000 in the first quarter, and $5,000 increments are expected in the remaining quarters of 2002. Fixed expenses are expected to be $40,000 in each quarter. Prepare the selling and administrative expense budget by quarters and for 2002.

Prepare a selling and administrative expense budget.
(SO 3)

BE6-8 Bitterman Company has completed all of its operating budgets. The sales budget for the year shows 50,000 units and total sales of $2,000,000. The total unit cost of making one unit of sales is $28. Selling and administrative expenses are expected to be $300,000. Income taxes are estimated to be $50,000. Prepare a budgeted income statement for the year ending December 31, 2002.

Prepare a budgeted income statement for the year.
(SO 4)

BE6-9 Jorie Aloisio Industries expects credit sales for January, February, and March to be $200,000, $275,000, and $310,000, respectively. It is expected that 70% of the sales will be collected in the month of sale, and 30% will be collected in the following month. Compute cash collections from customers for each month.

Prepare data for a cash budget.
(SO 5)

Determine required merchandise purchases for 1 month.
(SO 6)

BE6-10 Maggie Sharrer Wholesalers is preparing its merchandise purchases budget. Budgeted sales are $400,000 for April and $450,000 for May. Cost of goods sold is expected to be 75% of sales. The company's desired ending inventory is 20% of the following month's cost of goods sold. Compute the required purchases for April.

EXERCISES

Prepare a sales budget for 2 quarters.
(SO 3)

E6-1 L. Quick Electronics Inc. produces and sells two models of pocket calculators, XQ-103 and XQ-104. The calculators sell for $12 and $20, respectively. Because of the intense competition Quick faces, management budgets sales semiannually. Its projections for the first 2 quarters of 2002 are as follows.

	Unit Sales	
Product	**Quarter 1**	**Quarter 2**
XQ-103	30,000	27,000
XQ-104	12,000	13,000

No changes in selling prices are anticipated.

Instructions
Prepare a sales budget for the 2 quarters ending June 30, 2002. List the products and show for each quarter and for the 6 months, units, selling price, and total sales by product and in total.

Prepare quarterly production budgets.
(SO 3)

E6-2 S. Stahl Company produces and sells two types of automobile batteries, the heavy-duty HD-240 and the long-life LL-250. The 2002 sales budget for the two products is as follows.

Quarter	HD-240	LL-250
1	5,000	10,000
2	7,000	18,000
3	8,000	20,000
4	10,000	35,000

The January 1, 2002, inventory of HD-240 and LL-250 units is 3,500 and 6,000, respectively. Management desires an ending inventory each quarter equal to 60% of the next quarter's sales. Sales in the first quarter of 2003 are expected to be 30% higher than sales in the same quarter in 2002.

Instructions
Prepare separate quarterly production budgets for each product by quarters for 2002.

Prepare a direct materials budget.
(SO 3)

E6-3 Gosh-by-Golly Industries has adopted the following production budget for the first 4 months of 2003.

Month	Units	Month	Units
January	10,000	March	6,000
February	8,000	April	4,000

Each unit requires 5 pounds of raw materials costing $1.50 per pound. On December 31, 2002, the ending raw materials inventory was 25,000 pounds. Management wants to have a raw materials inventory at the end of each month equal to 50% of next month's production requirements.

Instructions
Prepare a direct materials budget by months for the first quarter.

E6-4   The W. Sublette Company budget committee has reached agreement on the following data for the 6 months ending June 30, 2003.

Prepare production and direct materials budgets by quarters for 6 months.
(SO 3)

Sales units: First quarter 5,000; second quarter 8,000
Ending raw materials inventory: 40% of the next quarter's production requirements
Ending finished goods inventory: 20% of the next quarter's expected sales units

The ending raw materials and finished goods inventories at December 31, 2002, follow the same percentage relationships to production and sales that occur in 2003. Three pounds of raw materials are required to make each unit of finished goods. Raw materials purchased are expected to cost $4 per pound. Sales of 7,000 units and required production of 7,250 units are expected in the third quarter of 2003.

Instructions
(a) Prepare a production budget by quarters for the 6 months.
(b) Prepare a direct materials budget by quarters for the 6 months.

E6-5   Twyla, Inc., is preparing its direct labor budget for 2002 from the following production budget based on a calendar year.

Prepare a direct labor budget.
(SO 3)

Quarter	Units	Quarter	Units
1	20,000	3	35,000
2	25,000	4	30,000

Each unit requires 1.5 hours of direct labor.

Instructions
Prepare a direct labor budget by quarter and for 2002. Wage rates are expected to be $14 for the first 2 quarters and $16 for quarters 3 and 4.

E6-6   Vincent Nathan Company is preparing its manufacturing overhead budget for 2002. Relevant data consist of the following.

Prepare a manufacturing overhead budget for the year.
(SO 3)

Units to be produced (by quarters):   10,000, 12,000, 14,000, 16,000.

Direct labor: Time is 1.5 hours per unit.

Variable overhead costs per direct labor hour: Indirect materials $0.70; indirect labor $1.20; and maintenance $0.30.

Fixed overhead costs per quarter: Supervisory salaries $35,000; depreciation $12,000; and maintenance $9,000.

Instructions
Prepare the manufacturing overhead budget by quarter and for the year in total.

E6-7   Marcum Company combines its operating expenses for budget purposes in a selling and administrative expense budget. For the first 6 months of 2002, the following data are available.

Prepare a selling and administrative expense budget for 2 quarters.
(SO 3)

1. Sales: 15,000 units quarter 1; 18,000 units quarter 2.

2. Variable costs per dollar of sales: Sales commissions 5%, delivery expense 2%, and advertising 3%.

3. Fixed costs per quarter: Sales salaries $10,000, office salaries $6,000, depreciation $4,200, insurance $1,500, utilities $800, and repairs expense $600.

4. Unit selling price: $20.

Instructions
Prepare a selling and administrative expense budget by quarters and for the first 6 months of 2002.

E6-8   Longhead Company has accumulated the following budget data for the year 2002.

Prepare a budgeted income statement for the year.
(SO 3, 4)

1. Sales: 30,000 units, unit selling price $80.

2. Cost of one unit of finished goods: Direct materials 3 pounds at $5 per pound, direct labor 3 hours at $12 per hour, and manufacturing overhead $6 per direct labor hour.

3. Inventories (raw materials only): Beginning, 10,000 pounds; ending, 15,000 pounds.
4. Raw materials cost: $5 per pound.
5. Selling and administrative expenses: $150,000.
6. Income taxes: 30% of income before income taxes.

Instructions
Prepare a budgeted income statement for 2002. Show the computation of cost of goods sold.

Prepare a cash budget for 2 months.
(SO 5)

E6-9 Campagna Company expects to have a cash balance of $46,000 on January 1, 2002. Relevant monthly budget data for the first 2 months of 2002 are as follows.

Collections from customers: January $80,000, February $150,000.

Payments to suppliers: January $40,000, February $75,000.

Direct labor: January $30,000, February $45,000. Wages are paid in the month they are incurred.

Manufacturing overhead: January $21,000, February $30,000. These costs include depreciation of $1,000 per month. All other overhead costs are paid as incurred.

Selling and administrative expenses: January $15,000, February $20,000. These costs are exclusive of depreciation. They are paid as incurred.

Sales of marketable securities in January are expected to realize $10,000 in cash. Campagna Company has a line of credit at a local bank that enables it to borrow up to $25,000. The company wants to maintain a minimum monthly cash balance of $20,000.

Instructions
Prepare a cash budget for January and February.

Prepare a purchases budget and budgeted income statement for a merchandiser.
(SO 6)

E6-10 In May 2002, the budget committee of Sherrick Stores assembles the following data in preparation of budgeted merchandise purchases for the month of June.

1. Expected sales: June $500,000, July $600,000.
2. Cost of goods sold is expected to be 65% of sales.
3. Desired ending merchandise inventory is 40% of the following (next) month's cost of goods sold.
4. The beginning inventory at June 1 will be the desired amount.

Instructions
(a) Compute the budgeted merchandise purchases for June.
(b) Prepare the budgeted income statement for June through gross profit on sales.

PROBLEMS: SET A

Prepare budgeted income statement and supporting budgets.
(SO 3, 4)

P6-1A Oakbrook Farm Supply Company manufactures and sells a pesticide called Snare. The following data are available for preparing budgets for Snare for the first 2 quarters of 2003.

1. Sales: Quarter 1, 35,000 bags; quarter 2, 50,000 bags. Selling price is $60 per bag.
2. Direct materials: Each bag of Snare requires 5 pounds of Gumm at a cost of $3 per pound and 8 pounds of Tarr at $1.50 per pound.
3. Desired inventory levels:

Type of Inventory	January 1	April 1	July 1
Snare (bags)	8,000	12,000	18,000
Gumm (pounds)	9,000	10,000	13,000
Tarr (pounds)	14,000	20,000	25,000

4. Direct labor: Direct labor time is 15 minutes per bag at an hourly rate of $12 per hour.
5. Selling and administrative expenses are expected to be 8% of sales plus $175,000 per quarter.
6. Income taxes are expected to be 30% of income from operations.

Your assistant has prepared two budgets: (1) The manufacturing overhead budget shows expected costs to be 150% of direct labor cost. (2) The direct materials budget for Tarr shows the cost of Tarr to be $477,000 in quarter 1 and $679,500 in quarter 2.

Instructions
Prepare the budgeted income statement for the first 6 months and all required supporting budgets by quarters and in total. (*Note:* Use variable and fixed in the selling and administrative expense budget.)

P6-2A   Joe Dunham Inc. is preparing its annual budgets for the year ending December 31, 2003. Accounting assistants furnish the following data.

Prepare sales, production, direct materials, direct labor, and income statement budgets.
(SO 3, 4)

	Product JB 50	Product JB 60
Sales budget:		
Anticipated volume in units	480,000	180,000
Unit selling price	$20.00	$25.00
Production budget:		
Desired ending finished goods units	25,000	15,000
Beginning finished goods units	30,000	10,000
Direct materials budget:		
Direct materials per unit (pounds)	2	3
Desired ending direct materials pounds	30,000	15,000
Beginning direct materials pounds	40,000	10,000
Cost per pound	$3.00	$4.00
Direct labor budget:		
Direct labor hours per unit	0.4	0.6
Direct labor rate per hour	$11.00	$11.00
Budgeted income statement:		
Total unit cost	$12.00	$20.00

An accounting assistant has prepared the detailed manufacturing overhead budget and the selling and administrative expense budget. The latter shows selling expenses of $660,000 for product JB 50 and $360,000 for product JB 60, and administrative expenses of $420,000 for product JB 50 and $340,000 for product JB 60. Income taxes are expected to be 30%.

Instructions
Prepare the following budgets for the year. Show data for each product. Quarterly budgets should not be prepared.
(a) Sales
(b) Production
(c) Direct materials
(d) Direct labor
(e) Income statement (*Note:* Income taxes are not allocated to the products.)

P6-3A   Hindu Industries had sales in 2002 of $6,300,000 and gross profit of $1,500,000. Management is considering two alternative budget plans to increase its gross profit in 2003.

Prepare sales and production budgets and compute cost per unit under two plans.
(SO 3, 4)

Plan A would increase the selling price per unit from $9.00 to $9.40. Sales volume would decrease by 5% from its 2002 level. Plan B would decrease the selling price per unit by $0.50. The marketing department expects that the sales volume would increase by 150,000 units.

At the end of 2002, Hindu has 30,000 units of inventory on hand. If Plan A is accepted, the 2003 ending inventory should be equal to 4% of the 2003 sales. If Plan B is accepted, the ending inventory should be equal to 40,000 units. Each unit produced will cost $1.60 in direct labor, $2.00 in direct materials, and $0.90 in variable overhead. The fixed overhead for 2003 should be $1,800,000.

Instructions
(a) Prepare a sales budget for 2003 under each plan.
(b) Prepare a production budget for 2003 under each plan.
(c) Compute the production cost per unit under each plan. Why is the cost per unit different for each of the two plans? (Round to two decimals.)
(d) Which plan should be accepted? (*Hint:* Compute the gross profit under each plan.)

Prepare cash budget for 2 months.
(SO 5)

eGrade Problem

P6-4A   Yaeger Company prepares monthly cash budgets. Relevant data from operating budgets for 2003 are:

	January	February
Sales	$360,000	$400,000
Direct materials purchases	125,000	130,000
Direct labor	90,000	100,000
Manufacturing overhead	70,000	75,000
Selling and administrative expenses	79,000	86,000

All sales are on account. Collections are expected to be 50% in the month of sale, 30% in the first month following the sale, and 20% in the second month following the sale. Sixty percent (60%) of direct materials purchases are paid in cash in the month of purchase, and the balance due is paid in the month following the purchase. All other items above are paid in the month incurred except for selling and administrative expenses that include $1,000 of depreciation per month.

    Other data:

1. Credit sales: November 2002, $260,000; December 2002, $300,000.
2. Purchases of direct materials: December 2002, $100,000.
3. Other receipts: January—Collection of December 31, 2002, notes receivable $15,000; February—Proceeds from sale of securities $6,000.
4. Other disbursements: February—Withdrawal of $5,000 cash for personal use of owner, Dewey Yaeger.

The company's cash balance on January 1, 2003, is expected to be $70,000. The company wants to maintain a minimum cash balance of $50,000.

Instructions
(a) Prepare schedules for (1) expected collections from customers and (2) expected payments for direct materials purchases.
(b) Prepare a cash budget for January and February in columnar form.

Prepare purchases and income statement budgets for a merchandiser.
(SO 6)

P6-5A   The budget committee of Henning Company collects the following data for its San Miguel Store in preparing budgeted income statements for May and June 2003.

1. Sales for May are expected to be $600,000. Sales in June and July are expected to be 10% higher than the preceding month.
2. Cost of goods sold is expected to be 70% of sales.
3. Company policy is to maintain ending merchandise inventory at 25% of the following month's cost of goods sold.
4. Operating expenses are estimated to be:

Sales salaries	$25,000 per month
Advertising	5% of monthly sales
Delivery expense	3% of monthly sales
Sales commissions	4% of monthly sales
Rent expense	$5,000 per month
Depreciation	$800 per month
Utilities	$600 per month
Insurance	$500 per month

5. Income taxes are estimated to be 30% of income from operations.

Instructions

(a) Prepare the merchandise purchases budget for each month in columnar form.
(b) Prepare budgeted income statements for each month in columnar form. Show in the statements the details of cost of goods sold.

P6-6A   East Asian Industries' balance sheet at December 31, 2002, is presented below.

Prepare budgeted income statement and balance sheet. (SO 3, 4)

EAST ASIAN INDUSTRIES
Balance Sheet
December 31, 2002

Assets

Current assets		
Cash		$ 7,500
Accounts receivable		82,500
Finished goods inventory (2,000 units)		30,000
Total current assets		120,000
Property, plant, and equipment		
Equipment	$40,000	
Less: Accumulated depreciation	10,000	30,000
Total assets		$150,000

Liabilities and Stockholders' Equity

Liabilities		
Notes payable		$ 25,000
Accounts payable		45,000
Total liabilities		70,000
Stockholders' equity		
Common stock	$50,000	
Retained earnings	30,000	
Total stockholders' equity		80,000
Total liabilities and stockholders' equity		$150,000

Additional information accumulated for the budgeting process is as follows.
Budgeted data for the year 2003 include the following.

	4th Quarter of 2003	Year 2003 Total
Sales budget (8,000 units at $35)	$80,000	$280,000
Direct materials used	17,000	72,400
Direct labor	8,500	38,600
Manufacturing overhead applied	10,000	42,000
Selling and administrative expenses	18,000	76,000

   To meet sales requirements and to have 2,500 units of finished goods on hand at December 31, 2003, the production budget shows 8,500 required units of output. The total unit cost of production is expected to be $18. East Asian Industries uses the first-in, first-out (FIFO) inventory costing method. Total depreciation for the year is $4,000. Interest expense is expected to be $3,500 for the year. Income taxes are expected to be 30% of income before income taxes.
   All sales and purchases are on account. It is expected that 60% of quarterly sales are collected in cash within the quarter and the remainder is collected in the following quarter. Direct materials purchased from suppliers are paid 50% in the quarter incurred and the remainder in the following quarter. Purchases in the fourth quarter were the same as the materials used. In 2003, the company expects to purchase additional equipment cost-

ing $24,000. It expects to pay $8,000 on notes payable plus all interest due and payable to December 31 (included in interest expense $3,500, above). Accounts payable at December 31, 2003, includes amounts due suppliers (see above) plus other accounts payable of $7,500. In 2003, the company expects to declare and pay a $5,000 cash dividend. Unpaid income taxes at December 31 will be $5,000. The company's cash budget shows an expected cash balance of $29,750 at December 31, 2003.

Instructions
Prepare a budgeted income statement for 2003 and a budgeted balance sheet at December 31, 2003. In preparing the income statement, you will need to compute cost of goods manufactured and finished goods inventory (December 31, 2003).

PROBLEMS: SET B

Prepare a budgeted income statement and supporting budgets.
(SO 3, 4)

P6-1B Alcorn Farm Supply Company manufactures and sells a fertilizer called Basic II. The following data are available for preparing budgets for Basic II for the first 2 quarters of 2002.

1. Sales: Quarter 1, 50,000 bags; quarter 2, 70,000 bags. Selling price is $60 per bag.
2. Direct materials: Each bag of Basic II requires 5 pounds of Crup at a cost of $3 per pound and 10 pounds of Dert at $1.50 per pound.
3. Desired inventory levels:

Type of Inventory	January 1	April 1	July 1
Basic II (bags)	10,000	15,000	20,000
Crup (pounds)	9,000	12,000	15,000
Dert (pounds)	15,000	20,000	25,000

4. Direct labor: Direct labor time is 15 minutes per bag at an hourly rate of $10 per hour.
5. Selling and administrative expenses are expected to be 10% of sales plus $150,000 per quarter.
6. Income taxes are expected to be 30% of income from operations.

Your assistant has prepared two budgets: (1) The manufacturing overhead budget shows expected costs to be 100% of direct labor cost. (2) The direct materials budget for Dert which shows the cost of Dert to be $832,500 in quarter 1 and $132,500 in quarter 2.

Instructions
Prepare the budgeted income statement for the first 6 months of 2002 and all required supporting budgets by quarters and in total. (*Note:* Use variable and fixed in the selling and administrative expense budget.)

Prepare sales, production, direct materials, direct labor, and income statement budgets.
(SO 3, 4)

P6-2B Borealis Inc. is preparing its annual budgets for the year ending December 31, 2002. Accounting assistants furnish the following data.

	Product LN 35	Product LN 40
Sales budget:		
Anticipated volume in units	300,000	150,000
Unit selling price	$20.00	$30.00
Production budget:		
Desired ending finished goods units	30,000	25,000
Beginning finished goods units	20,000	15,000
Direct materials budget:		
Direct materials per unit (pounds)	2	3
Desired ending direct materials pounds	50,000	20,000
Beginning direct materials pounds	40,000	10,000
Cost per pound	$2.00	$3.00

	LN 35	**LN 40**
Direct labor budget:		
Direct labor hours per unit	0.5	0.75
Direct labor rate per hour	$9.00	$9.00
Budgeted income statement:		
Total unit cost	$10.00	$20.00

An accounting assistant has prepared the detailed manufacturing overhead budget and the selling and administrative expense budget. The latter shows selling expenses of $460,000 for product LN 35 and $440,000 for product LN 40, and administrative expenses of $420,000 for product LN 35 and $380,000 for product LN 40. Income taxes are expected to be 30%.

Instructions
Prepare the following budgets for the year. Show data for each product. Quarterly budgets should not be prepared.
(a) Sales
(b) Production
(c) Direct materials
(d) Direct labor
(e) Income statement (*Note:* Income taxes are not allocated to the products.)

P6-3B David Chambers Industries has sales in 2002 of $5,250,000 (656,250 units) and gross profit of $1,587,500. Management is considering two alternative budget plans to increase its gross profit in 2003.

Prepare sales and production budgets and compute cost per unit under two plans.
(SO 3, 4)

Plan A would increase the selling price per unit from $8.00 to $8.60. Sales volume would decrease by 10% from its 2002 level. Plan B would decrease the selling price per unit by 5%. The marketing department expects that the sales volume would increase by 100,000 units.

At the end of 2002, Chambers has 75,000 units on hand. If Plan A is accepted, the 2003 ending inventory should be equal to 87,500 units. If Plan B is accepted, the ending inventory should be equal to 100,000 units. Each unit produced will cost $2.00 in direct materials, $1.50 in direct labor, and $0.50 in variable overhead. The fixed overhead for 2003 should be $965,000.

Instructions
(a) Prepare a sales budget for 2003 under (1) Plan A and (2) Plan B.
(b) Prepare a production budget for 2003 under (1) Plan A and (2) Plan B.
(c) Compute the cost per unit under (1) Plan A and (2) Plan B. Explain why the cost per unit is different for each of the two plans. (Round to two decimals.)
(d) Which plan should be accepted? (*Hint:* Compute the gross profit under each plan.)

P6-4B Flypaper Company prepares monthly cash budgets. Relevant data from operating budgets for 2003 are:

Prepare cash budget for 2 months.
(SO 5)

	January	**February**
Sales	$350,000	$400,000
Direct materials purchases	95,000	110,000
Direct labor	100,000	115,000
Manufacturing overhead	60,000	75,000
Selling and administrative expenses	75,000	85,000

All sales are on account. Collections are expected to be 60% in the month of sale, 30% in the first month following the sale, and 10% in the second month following the sale. Thirty percent (30%) of direct materials purchases are paid in cash in the month of purchase, and the balance due is paid in the month following the purchase. All other items above are paid in the month incurred. Depreciation has been excluded from manufacturing overhead and selling and administrative expenses.
   Other data:

1. Credit sales: November 2002, $200,000; December 2002, $280,000.
2. Purchases of direct materials: December 2002, $90,000.

3. Other receipts: January—Collection of December 31, 2002, interest receivable $3,000; February—Proceeds from sale of securities $5,000.
4. Other disbursements: February—payment of $20,000 for land.

The company's cash balance on January 1, 2003, is expected to be $60,000. The company wants to maintain a minimum cash balance of $50,000.

Instructions
(a) Prepare schedules for (1) expected collections from customers and (2) expected payments for direct materials purchases.
(b) Prepare a cash budget for January and February in columnar form.

Prepare purchases and income statement budgets for a merchandiser.
(SO 6)

P6-5B The budget committee of Oriental Company collects the following data for its Westwood Store in preparing budgeted income statements for July and August 2002.

1. Expected sales: July $400,000, August $450,000, September $500,000.
2. Cost of goods sold is expected to be 75% of sales.
3. Company policy is to maintain ending merchandise inventory at 30% of the following month's cost of goods sold.
4. Operating expenses are estimated to be:

Sales salaries	$20,000 per month
Advertising	4% of monthly sales
Delivery expense	2% of monthly sales
Sales commissions	3% of monthly sales
Rent expense	$3,000 per month
Depreciation	$700 per month
Utilities	$500 per month
Insurance	$300 per month

5. Income taxes are estimated to be 30% of income from operations.

Instructions
(a) Prepare the merchandise purchases budget for each month in columnar form.
(b) Prepare budgeted income statements for each month in columnar form. Show the details of cost of goods sold in the statements.

◆ BROADENING YOUR PERSPECTIVE

GROUP DECISION CASE

BYP6-1 Castle Corporation operates on a calendar-year basis. It begins the annual budgeting process in late August when the president establishes targets for the total dollar sales and net income before taxes for the next year.

The sales target is given first to the marketing department. The marketing manager formulates a sales budget by product line in both units and dollars. From this budget, sales quotas by product line in units and dollars are established for each of the corporation's sales districts. The marketing manager also estimates the cost of the marketing activities required to support the target sales volume and prepares a tentative marketing expense budget.

The executive vice president uses the sales and profit targets, the sales budget by product line, and the tentative marketing expense budget to determine the dollar amounts that can be devoted to manufacturing and corporate office expense. The executive vice president prepares the budget for corporate expenses. She then forwards to the production department the product-line sales budget in units and the total dollar amount that can be devoted to manufacturing.

The production manager meets with the factory managers to develop a manufacturing plan that will produce the required units when needed within the cost constraints set by the executive vice president. The budgeting process usually comes to a halt at this point because the production department does not consider the financial resources allocated to be adequate.

When this standstill occurs, the vice president of finance, the executive vice president, the marketing manager, and the production manager meet together to determine the final budgets for each of the areas. This normally results in a modest increase in the total amount available for manufacturing costs and cuts in the marketing expense and corporate office expense budgets. The total sales and net income figures proposed by the president are seldom changed. Although the participants are seldom pleased with the compromise, these budgets are final. Each executive then develops a new detailed budget for the operations in his or her area.

None of the areas has achieved its budget in recent years. Sales often run below the target. When budgeted sales are not achieved, each area is expected to cut costs so that the president's profit target can be met. However, the profit target is seldom met because costs are not cut enough. In fact, costs often run above the original budget in all functional areas (marketing, production, and corporate office).

The president is disturbed that Castle has not been able to meet the sales and profit targets. He hired a consultant with considerable experience with companies in Castle's industry. The consultant reviewed the budgets for the past 4 years. He concluded that the product-line sales budgets were reasonable and that the cost and expense budgets were adequate for the budgeted sales and production levels.

Instructions
With the class divided into groups, answer the following.
(a) Discuss how the budgeting process employed by Castle Corporation contributes to the failure to achieve the president's sales and profit targets.
(b) Suggest how Castle Corporation's budgeting process could be revised to correct the problems.
(c) Should the functional areas be expected to cut their costs when sales volume falls below budget? Explain your answer. (CMA adapted.)

Managerial Analysis

BYP6-2 Thebeau & Lewis Inc. manufactures ergonomic devices for computer users. Some of their more popular products include glare screens (for computer monitors), keyboard stands with wrist rests, and carousels that allow easy access to floppy disks. Over the past 5 years, they experienced rapid growth, with sales of all products increasing 20% to 50% each year.

Last year, some of the primary manufacturers of computers began introducing new products with some of the ergonomic designs, such as glare screens and wrist rests, already built in. As a result, sales of Thebeau & Lewis's accessory devices have declined somewhat. The company believes that the disk carousels will probably continue to show growth, but that the other products will probably continue to decline. When the next year's budget was prepared, increases were built in to research and development so that replacement products could be developed or the company could expand into some other product line. Some product lines being considered are general-purpose ergonomic devices including back supports, foot rests, and sloped writing pads.

The most recent results have shown that sales decreased more than was expected for the glare screens. As a result, the company may have a shortage of funds. Top management has therefore asked that all expenses be reduced 10% to compensate for these reduced sales. Summary budget information is as follows.

Raw materials	$240,000
Direct labor	110,000
Insurance	50,000
Depreciation	90,000
Machine repairs	30,000
Sales salaries	50,000
Office salaries	80,000
Factory salaries (indirect labor)	50,000
Total	$700,000

Instructions

Using the information above, answer the following questions.

(a) What are the implications of reducing each of the costs? For example, if the company reduces raw materials costs, it may have to do so by purchasing lower-quality materials. This may affect sales in the long run.

(b) Based on your analysis in (a), what do you think is the best way to obtain the $70,000 in cost savings requested? Be specific. Are there any costs that cannot or should not be reduced? Why?

*R*EAL-WORLD FOCUS

BYP6-3   Network Computing Devices Inc. was founded in 1988 in Mountain View, Calif. The company develops hardware and software thin-client computing products. (Thin clients are computers that do not have a hard drive but, rather, are served from a central computer through a network.) Presented below is a discussion by management in an annual report.

NCD

NETWORK COMPUTING DEVICES, INC.
Management Discussion

The Company's operating results have varied significantly, particularly on a quarterly basis, as a result of a number of factors, including general economic conditions affecting industry demand for computer products, the timing and market acceptance of new product introductions by the Company and its competitors, the timing of significant orders from large customers, periodic changes in product pricing and discounting due to competitive factors, and the availability of key components, such as video monitors and electronic subassemblies, some of which require substantial order lead times. The Company's operating results may fluctuate in the future as a result of these and other factors, including the Company's success in developing and introducing new products, its product and customer mix, and the level of competition which it experiences. The Company operates with a small backlog. Sales and operating results, therefore, generally depend on the volume and timing of orders received, which are difficult to forecast. The Company has experienced slowness in orders from some customers during the first quarter of each calendar year due to budgeting cycles common in the computer industry. In addition, sales in Europe typically are adversely affected in the third calendar quarter as many European customers reduce their business activities during the month of August.

Due to the Company's rapid growth rate and the effect of new product introductions on quarterly revenues, these seasonal trends have not materially impacted the Company's results of operations to date. However, as the Company's product lines mature and its rate of revenue growth declines, these seasonal factors may become more evident. Additionally, the Company's international sales are denominated in U.S. dollars, and an increase or decrease in the value of the U.S. dollar relative to foreign currencies could make the Company's products less or more competitive in those markets.

Instructions

(a) Identify the factors that affect the budgeting process at Network Computing Devices Inc.

(b) Explain the additional budgeting concerns created by the international operations of the company.

EXPLORING THE WEB

BYP6-4 The opportunities for business consulting in the areas of corporate planning, budgeting, and strategy are almost limitless as new, more powerful software continues to be developed. This exercise takes you to the Web site of **CP Corporate Planning**, a European consulting firm.

Address: www.corporate-planning.com/home/fse_home.html
            (or go to www.wiley.com/college/weygandt)

Steps:
Go to the site above.

Instructions
Choose three case studies, and in each case identify the problem the company faced and how the situation was resolved.

COMMUNICATION ACTIVITY

BYP6-5 In order to better serve their rural patients, Drs. Jim and Jeff Howell (brothers) began giving safety seminars. Especially popular were their "emergency-preparedness" talks given to farmers. Many people asked whether the "kit" of materials the doctors recommended for common farm emergencies was commercially available.

After checking with several suppliers, the doctors realized that no other company offered the supplies they recommended in their seminars, packaged in the way they described. Their wives, Marie and Pam, agreed to make a test package by ordering supplies from various medical supply companies and assembling them into a "kit" that could be sold at the seminars. When these kits proved a runaway success, the sisters-in-law decided to market them. At the advice of their accountant, they organized this venture as a separate company, called Life Protection Products (LPP), with Marie Howell as CEO and Pam Howell as Secretary-Treasurer.

LPP soon started receiving requests for the kits from all over the country, as word spread about their availability. Even without advertising, LPP was able to sell its full inventory every month. However, the company was becoming financially strained. Marie and Pam had about $100,000 in savings, and they invested about half that amount initially. They believed that this venture would allow them to make money. However, at the present time, only about $30,000 of the cash remains, and the company is constantly short of cash.

Marie Howell has come to you for advice. She does not understand why the company is having cash flow problems. She and Pam have not even been withdrawing salaries. However, they have rented a local building and have hired two more full-time workers to help them cope with the increasing demand. They do not think they could handle the demand without this additional help.

Marie is also worried that the cash problems mean that the company may not be able to support itself. She has prepared the cash budget shown on the next page. All seminar customers pay for their products in full at the time of purchase. In addition, several large companies have ordered the kits for use by employees who work in remote sites. They have requested credit terms and have been allowed to pay in the month following the sale. These large purchasers amount to about 25% of the sales at the present time. LPP purchases the materials for the kits about 2 months ahead of time. Marie and Pam are considering slowing the growth of the company by simply purchasing less materials, which will mean selling fewer kits.

The workers are paid in cash weekly. Marie and Pam need about $15,000 cash on hand at the beginning of the month to pay for purchases of raw materials. Right now they have been using cash from their savings, but as noted, only $30,000 is left.

The cash budget that Marie Howell has given you is shown below.

LIFE PROTECTION PRODUCTS
Cash Budget
For the Quarter Ending June 30, 2003

	April	May	June
Cash balance, beginning	$15,000	$15,000	$15,000
Cash received			
From prior month sales	5,000	7,500	12,500
From current sales	15,000	22,500	37,500
Total cash on hand	35,000	45,000	65,000
Cash payments			
To employees	3,000	3,000	3,000
For products	25,000	35,000	45,000
Miscellaneous expenses	5,000	6,000	7,000
Postage	1,000	1,000	1,000
Total cash payments	34,000	45,000	56,000
Cash balance	$ 1,000	$ 0	$ 9,000
Borrow from savings	$14,000	$15,000	$ 1,000
Borrow from bank?	$ 0	$ 0	$ 7,000

Instructions
Write a response to Marie Howell. Explain why LPP is short of cash. Will this company be able to support itself? Explain your answer. Make any recommendations you deem appropriate.

RESEARCH ASSIGNMENT

BYP6-6 The April 2000 issue of the *Journal of Accountancy* contains an article by Lawrence B. Macgregor Serven entitled "The Planning Peril."

Instructions
Read the article and answer the following questions.
(a) Describe the three reasons why revamping the planning process can be perilous.
(b) What four recommendations does the author provide to improve the chances of success of efforts to revamp the planning and budgeting process?
(c) Review the sample survey. Identify what you believe are the three most important questions in this survey, and explain why you think they are important.

ETHICS CASE

BYP6-7 You are an accountant in the budgetary, projections, and special projects department of American Bare Conductor, Inc., a large manufacturing company. The president, Robert Boey, asks you on very short notice to prepare some sales and income projections covering the next 2 years of the company's much heralded new product lines. He wants these projections for a series of speeches he is making while on a 2-week trip to eight East Coast brokerage firms. The president hopes to bolster American Bare's stock sales and price.

You work 23 hours in 2 days to compile the projections, hand deliver them to the president, and are swiftly but graciously thanked as he departs. A week later you find time to go over some of your computations and discover a miscalculation that makes the projections grossly overstated. You quickly inquire about the president's itinerary and learn that he has made half of his speeches and has half yet to make. You are in a quandary as to what to do.

Instructions
(a) What are the consequences of telling the president of your gross miscalculations?
(b) What are the consequences of *not* telling the president of your gross miscalculations?
(c) What are the ethical considerations to you and the president in this situation?

Answers to Self-Study Questions
1. c   2. a   3. b   4. b   5. d   6. d   7. a   8. c   9. c   10. d

Remember to go back to the Navigator box on the chapter-opening page and check off your completed work.

7

Budgetary Control and Responsibility Accounting

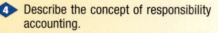

THE NAVIGATOR ✔

- ■ Scan *Study Objectives* ☐
- ■ Read *Feature Story* ☐
- ■ Read *Preview* ☐
- ■ Read text and answer *Before You Go On*
  p. 282 ☐   p. 290 ☐   p. 295 ☐
- ■ Work *Using the Decision Toolkit* ✔
- ■ Review *Summary of Study Objectives* ☐
- ■ Work *Demonstration Problem* ☐
- ■ Answer *Self-Study Questions* ☐
- ■ Complete *Assignments* ☐

 STUDY OBJECTIVES

After studying this chapter, you should be able to:

1 Describe the concept of budgetary control.

2 Evaluate the usefulness of static budget reports.

3 Explain the development of flexible budgets and the usefulness of flexible budget reports.

4 Describe the concept of responsibility accounting.

5 Indicate the features of responsibility reports for cost centers.

6 Identify the content of responsibility reports for profit centers.

7 Explain the basis and formula used in evaluating performance in investment centers.

THE NAVIGATOR

◆ **FEATURE STORY**

TRYING TO AVOID AN ELECTRIC SHOCK

Budgets are critical to evaluating an organization's success. They are based on management's expectations of what is most likely to happen in the future. In order to be useful, they must be accurate. But what if management's expectations are wrong? Estimates are never exactly correct, and sometimes, especially in volatile industries, estimates can be "off by a mile."

In recent years the electric utility industry has become very volatile. Deregulation, volatile prices for natural gas, coal, and oil, changes in environmental regulations, and economic swings have all contributed to large changes in the profitability of electric utility companies. This means that for planning and budgeting purposes, utilites must plan and budget based on multiple "what if" scenarios that take into account factors beyond management's control. For example, in recent years, **Duke Energy Corporation**, headquartered in Charlotte, North Carolina, built budgeting and planning models based on three

different scenarios of what the future might hold. One scenario assumes that the U.S. economy will slow considerably. A second scenario assumes that the company will experience "pricing pressure" as the market for energy becomes more efficient as a result of more energy being traded in Internet auctions. A third scenario assumes a continuation of the current environment of rapid growth, changing regulation, and large swings in the prices for the fuels the company uses to create energy.

Compounding this budgeting challenge is the fact that changes in many indirect costs can also significantly affect the company. For example, even a tiny change in market interest rates has a huge effect on the company because it has massive amounts of outstanding debt. And finally, as a result of the California energy crisis, there is mounting pressure for government intervention and regulation. This pressure has resulted in setting "rate caps" that limit the amount that utilities and energy companies can charge, thus lowering profits. The bottom line is that for budgeting and planning purposes, utility companies must remain alert and flexible.

THE NAVIGATOR

In contrast to Chapter 6, we now consider how budgets are used by management to control operations. In the Feature Story on **Duke Energy**, we saw that budgeting must take into account factors beyond management's control. This chapter focuses on two aspects of management control: (1) budgetary control and (2) responsibility accounting.

The content and organization of Chapter 7 are as follows.

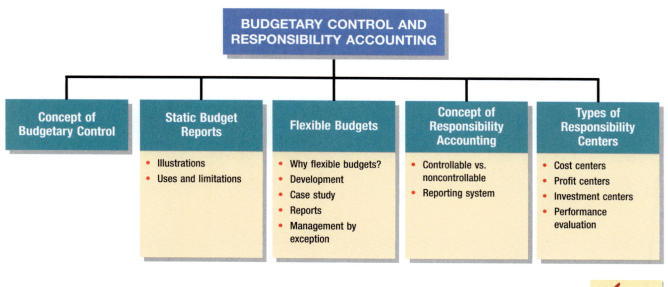

CONCEPT OF BUDGETARY CONTROL

STUDY OBJECTIVE
1

Describe the concept of budgetary control.

One of management's major functions is to control company operations. Control consists of the steps taken by management to see that planned objectives are met. We now ask: How do budgets contribute to control of operations?

The use of budgets in controlling operations is known as **budgetary control**. Such control takes place by means of **budget reports** that compare actual results with planned objectives. The use of budget reports is based on the belief that planned objectives lose much of their potential value without some monitoring of progress along the way. Just as your professors give midterm exams to evaluate your progress, so top management requires periodic reports on the progress of department managers toward their planned objectives.

Budget reports provide management with feedback on operations. The feedback for a crucial objective, such as having enough cash on hand to pay bills, may be made daily. For other objectives, such as meeting budgeted annual sales and operating expenses, monthly budget reports may suffice. Budget reports can be prepared as frequently as needed. From these reports, management analyzes any differences between actual and planned results and determines their causes. Management then may take corrective action, or it may decide to modify future plans.

Budgetary control involves the following activities.

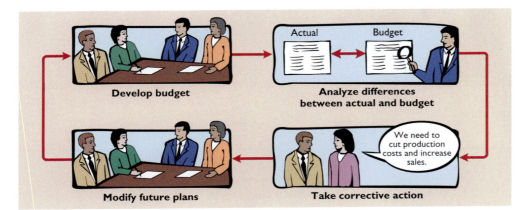

Illustration 7-1 Budgetary control

Budgetary control works best when a company has a formalized reporting system. The system should do the following: (1) Identify the name of the budget report, such as the sales budget or the manufacturing overhead budget. (2) State the frequency of the report, such as weekly or monthly. (3) Specify the purpose of the report. And (4) indicate the primary recipient(s) of the report. The following schedule illustrates a partial budgetary control system for a manufacturing company. Note the frequency of the reports and their emphasis on control. For example, there is a daily report on scrap and a weekly report on labor.

Illustration 7-2 Budgetary control reporting system

Name of Report	Frequency	Purpose	Primary Recipient(s)
Sales	Weekly	Determine whether sales goals are being met	Top management and sales manager
Labor	Weekly	Control direct and indirect labor costs	Vice president of production and production department managers
Scrap	Daily	Determine efficient use of materials	Production manager
Departmental overhead costs	Monthly	Control overhead costs	Department manager
Selling expenses	Monthly	Control selling expenses	Sales manager
Income statement	Monthly and quarterly	Determine whether income objectives are being met	Top management

STATIC BUDGET REPORTS

You learned in Chapter 6 that the master budget formalizes management's planned objectives for the coming year. When used in budgetary control, each budget included in the master budget is considered to be static. A **static budget** is a projection of budget data **at one level of activity**. Data for different levels of activity are not considered. As a result, actual results are always compared with budget data at the activity level that was used in developing the master budget.

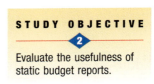

STUDY OBJECTIVE
2
Evaluate the usefulness of static budget reports.

ILLUSTRATIONS

To illustrate the role of a static budget in budgetary control, we will use selected data prepared for Hayes Company in Chapter 6. Budget and actual sales data for the Kitchen-mate product in the first and second quarters of 2002 are as follows.

Illustration 7-3 Budget and actual sales data

Sales	First Quarter	Second Quarter	Total
Budgeted	$180,000	$210,000	$390,000
Actual	179,000	199,500	378,500
Difference	$ 1,000	$ 10,500	$ 11,500

The sales budget report for Hayes Company's first quarter is shown below. The right-most column reports the difference between the budgeted and actual amounts.

Illustration 7-4 Sales budget report—first quarter

Alternative Terminology The difference between budget and actual is sometimes called a *budget variance.*

HAYES COMPANY
Sales Budget Report
For the Quarter Ended March 31, 2002

Product Line	Budget	Actual	Difference Favorable F Unfavorable U
Kitchen-mate[a]	$180,000	$179,000	**$1,000 U**

[a]In practice, each product line would be included in the report.

The report shows that sales are $1,000 under budget—an unfavorable result. This difference is less than 1 percent of budgeted sales ($1,000 ÷ $180,000 = .0056). Top management's reaction to unfavorable differences is often influenced by the materiality (significance) of the difference. Since the difference of $1,000 is immaterial in this case, we will assume that Hayes Company management takes no specific corrective action.

The budget report for the second quarter is presented in Illustration 7-5. It contains one new feature: cumulative year-to-date information. This report indicates that sales for the second quarter were $10,500 below budget. This is 5 percent of budgeted sales ($10,500 ÷ $210,000). Top management may now conclude that the difference between budgeted and actual sales requires investigation.

Illustration 7-5 Sales budget report—second quarter

HAYES COMPANY
Sales Budget Report
For the Quarter Ended June 30, 2002

	Second Quarter			Year-to-Date		
Product Line	Budget	Actual	Difference Favorable F Unfavorable U	Budget	Actual	Difference Favorable F Unfavorable U
Kitchen-mate	$210,000	$199,500	**$10,500 U**	$390,000	$378,500	**$11,500 U**

Management's analysis should start by asking the sales manager the cause(s) of the shortfall. The need for corrective action should be considered. For example, management may decide to spur sales by offering sales incentives to customers or by increasing the advertising of Kitchen-mates. Or, if management concludes that a downturn in the economy is responsible for the lower sales, it may modify planned sales and profit goals for the remainder of the year.

USES AND LIMITATIONS

From these examples, you can see that a master sales budget is useful in evaluating the performance of a sales manager. It is now necessary to ask: Is the master budget appropriate for evaluating a manager's performance in controlling costs? Recall that in a static budget, data are not modified or adjusted, regardless of changes in activity. It follows, then, that a static budget is appropriate in evaluating a manager's effectiveness in controlling costs when:

1. The actual level of activity closely approximates the master budget activity level, and/or
2. The behavior of the costs in response to changes in activity is fixed.

A static budget report is, therefore, appropriate for **fixed manufacturing costs** and for **fixed selling and administrative expenses**. But, as you will see shortly, static budget reports may not be a proper basis for evaluating a manager's performance in controlling variable costs.

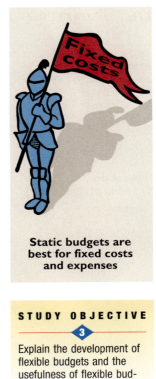

Static budgets are best for fixed costs and expenses

FLEXIBLE BUDGETS

STUDY OBJECTIVE

3

Explain the development of flexible budgets and the usefulness of flexible budget reports.

In contrast to a static budget, which is based on one level of activity, a **flexible budget** projects budget data for various levels of activity. In essence, **the flexible budget is a series of static budgets at different levels of activity**. The flexible budget recognizes that the budgetary process is more useful if it is adaptable to changed operating conditions.

Flexible budgets can be prepared for each of the types of budgets included in the master budget. For example, **Marriott Hotels** can budget revenues and net income on the basis of 60 percent, 80 percent, and 100 percent of room occupancy. Similarly, **American Van Lines** can budget its operating expenses on the basis of various levels of truck miles driven. Likewise, in the Feature Story, **Duke Energy** can budget revenue and net income on the basis of estimated billions of kwh (kilowatt hours) of residential, commercial, and industrial electricity generated. In the following pages, we will illustrate a flexible budget for manufacturing overhead.

WHY FLEXIBLE BUDGETS?

Assume that you are the manager in charge of manufacturing overhead in the Forging Department of Barton Steel. In preparing the manufacturing overhead budget for 2002, you prepare the following static budget based on a production volume of 10,000 units of steel ingots.

Flexible budgets are static budgets at different activity levels

Illustration 7-6 Static overhead budget

BARTON STEEL
Manufacturing Overhead Budget (Static)
Forging Department
For the Year Ended December 31, 2002

Budgeted production in units (steel ingots)	10,000
Budgeted costs	
Indirect materials	$ 250,000
Indirect labor	260,000
Utilities	190,000
Depreciation	280,000
Property taxes	70,000
Supervision	50,000
	$1,100,000

Helpful Hint The static budget is the master budget of Chapter 6.

Helpful Hint Which of the following is likely to be of little use when costs are variable—the static budget or the flexible budget? Answer: The static budget.

Fortunately for the company, the demand for steel ingots has increased, and 12,000 units are produced and sold during the year, rather than 10,000. You are elated: Increased sales means increased profitability, which should mean a bonus or a raise for you and the employees in your department. Unfortunately, a comparison of Forging Department actual and budgeted costs has put you on the spot. The budget report is shown below.

Illustration 7-7   Static overhead budget report

BARTON STEEL
Manufacturing Overhead Budget Report (Static)
Forging Department
For the Year Ended December 31, 2002

	Budget	Actual	Difference Favorable F Unfavorable U
Production in units	10,000	12,000	
Costs			
Indirect materials	$ 250,000	$ 295,000	$ 45,000 U
Indirect labor	260,000	312,000	52,000 U
Utilities	190,000	225,000	35,000 U
Depreciation	280,000	280,000	–0–
Property taxes	70,000	70,000	–0–
Supervision	50,000	50,000	–0–
	$1,100,000	$1,232,000	$132,000 U

Helpful Hint A static budget will not work if a company has substantial variable costs.

This comparison uses budget data based on the original activity level (10,000 steel ingots). It indicates that the Forging Department is significantly **over budget** for three of the six overhead costs. And, there is a total unfavorable difference of $132,000, which is 12 percent over budget ($132,000 ÷ $1,100,000). Your supervisor is very unhappy! Instead of sharing in the company's success, you may find yourself looking for another job. What went wrong?

When you calm down and carefully examine the manufacturing overhead budget, you identify the problem: The budget data are not relevant! At the time the budget was developed, the company anticipated that only 10,000 units of steel ingots would be produced, **not** 12,000 ingots. Comparing actual with budgeted variable costs is meaningless. As production increases, the budget allowances for variable costs should increase both directly and proportionately. The variable costs in this example are indirect materials, indirect labor, and utilities.

Analyzing the budget data for these costs at 10,000 units, you arrive at the following per unit results.

Illustration 7-8   Variable costs per unit

Item	Total Cost	Per Unit
Indirect materials	$250,000	$25
Indirect labor	260,000	26
Utilities	190,000	19
	$700,000	$70

You then can calculate the budgeted variable costs at 12,000 units as follows.

Illustration 7-9 Budgeted variable costs, 12,000 units

Item	Computation	Total
Indirect materials	$25 × 12,000	$300,000
Indirect labor	26 × 12,000	312,000
Utilities	19 × 12,000	228,000
		$840,000

Because fixed costs do not change in total as activity changes, the budgeted amounts for these costs remain the same. The budget report based on the flexible budget for **12,000 units** of production is shown in Illustration 7-10. (Compare this with Illustration 7-7.)

Illustration 7-10 Flexible overhead budget report

BARTON STEEL
Manufacturing Overhead Budget Report (Flexible)
Forging Department
For the Year Ended December 31, 2002

	Budget	Actual	Difference Favorable F Unfavorable U
Production in units	12,000	12,000	
Variable costs			
Indirect materials	$ 300,000	$ 295,000	$5,000 F
Indirect labor	312,000	312,000	–0–
Utilities	228,000	225,000	3,000 F
Total variable	840,000	832,000	8,000 F
Fixed costs			
Depreciation	280,000	280,000	–0–
Property taxes	70,000	70,000	–0–
Supervision	50,000	50,000	–0–
Total fixed	400,000	400,000	–0–
Total costs	$1,240,000	$1,232,000	$8,000 F

This report indicates that the Forging Department is below budget—a favorable difference. Instead of worrying about being fired, you may be in line for a bonus or a raise after all! As this analysis shows, the only appropriate comparison is between actual costs at 12,000 units of production and budgeted costs at 12,000 units. Flexible budget reports provide this comparison.

DEVELOPING THE FLEXIBLE BUDGET

The flexible budget uses the master budget as its basis. To develop the flexible budget, management should take the following steps.

1. Identify the activity index and the relevant range of activity.
2. Identify the variable costs, and determine the budgeted variable cost per unit of activity for each cost.

3. Identify the fixed costs, and determine the budgeted amount for each cost.
4. Prepare the budget for selected increments of activity within the relevant range.

The activity index chosen should be one that significantly influences the costs that are being budgeted. For manufacturing overhead costs, for example, the activity index is usually the same as the index used in developing the predetermined overhead rate—that is, direct labor hours or machine hours. For selling and administrative expenses, the activity index usually is sales or net sales.

The choice of the increment of activity is largely a matter of judgment. For example, if the relevant range is 8,000 to 12,000 direct labor hours, increments of 1,000 hours may be selected. The flexible budget is then prepared for each increment within the relevant range.

DECISION TOOLKIT

Decision Checkpoints	Info Needed for Decision	Tool to Use for Decision	How to Evaluate Results
Are the increased costs resulting from increased production reasonable?	Variable costs projected at different levels of production	Flexible budget	After taking into account different production levels, results are favorable if expenses are less than budgeted amounts.

FLEXIBLE BUDGET—A CASE STUDY

To illustrate the flexible budget, we will use Fox Manufacturing Company. Fox's management wants to use a **flexible budget for monthly comparisons** of actual and budgeted manufacturing overhead costs of the Finishing Department. The master budget for the year ending December 31, 2002, shows expected annual operating capacity of 120,000 direct labor hours and the following overhead costs.

Illustration 7-11 Master budget data

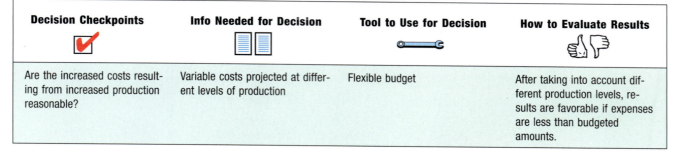

Variable Costs		Fixed Costs	
Indirect materials	$180,000	Depreciation	$180,000
Indirect labor	240,000	Supervision	120,000
Utilities	60,000	Property taxes	60,000
Total	$480,000	Total	$360,000

The four steps for developing the flexible budget are applied as follows.

STEP 1. **Identify the activity index and the relevant range of activity.** The activity index is direct labor hours. Management concludes that the relevant range is 8,000–12,000 direct labor hours per month.

STEP 2. **Identify the variable costs, and determine the budgeted variable cost per unit of activity for each cost.** There are three variable costs. The variable cost per unit is found by dividing each total budgeted cost by the direct labor hours used in preparing the master budget (120,000 hours). For Fox Manufacturing, the computations are:

Illustration 7-12 Computation of variable costs per direct labor hour

Variable Cost	Computation	Variable Cost per Direct Labor Hour
Indirect materials	$180,000 ÷ 120,000	$1.50
Indirect labor	$240,000 ÷ 120,000	2.00
Utilities	$ 60,000 ÷ 120,000	0.50
Total		$4.00

STEP 3.   **Identify the fixed costs, and determine the budgeted amount for each cost.** There are three fixed costs. Since Fox desires **monthly budget data,** the budgeted amount is found by dividing each annual budgeted cost by 12. For Fox Manufacturing, the monthly budgeted fixed costs are: depreciation $15,000, supervision $10,000, and property taxes $5,000.

STEP 4.   **Prepare the budget for selected increments of activity within the relevant range.** Management decides to prepare the budget in increments of 1,000 direct labor hours.

The flexible budget is shown in Illustration 7-13.

Illustration 7-13 Flexible monthly overhead budget

FOX MANUFACTURING COMPANY
Flexible Monthly Manufacturing Overhead Budget
Finishing Department
For the Year 2002

Activity level					
Direct labor hours	8,000	9,000	10,000	11,000	12,000
Variable costs					
Indirect materials	$12,000	$13,500	$15,000	$16,500	$18,000
Indirect labor	16,000	18,000	20,000	22,000	24,000
Utilities	4,000	4,500	5,000	5,500	6,000
Total variable	32,000	36,000	40,000	44,000	48,000
Fixed costs					
Depreciation	15,000	15,000	15,000	15,000	15,000
Supervision	10,000	10,000	10,000	10,000	10,000
Property taxes	5,000	5,000	5,000	5,000	5,000
Total fixed	30,000	30,000	30,000	30,000	30,000
Total costs	$62,000	$66,000	$70,000	$74,000	$78,000

From the budget, the following formula may be used to determine total budgeted costs at any level of activity.

Illustration 7-14 Formula for total budgeted costs

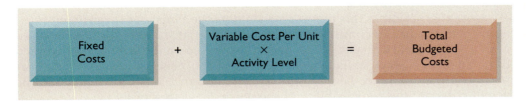

Fixed Costs + Variable Cost Per Unit × Activity Level = Total Budgeted Costs

Helpful Hint Using the data given for the Fox Manufacturing Company, what amount of total costs would be budgeted for 10,600 direct labor hours?
Answer:

Fixed	$30,000
Variable (10,600 × $4)	42,400
Total	$72,400

For Fox Manufacturing, fixed costs are $30,000, and total variable cost per unit is $4.00. Thus, at 9,000 direct labor hours, total budgeted costs are $66,000 [$30,000 + ($4.00 × 9,000)]. Similarly, at 8,622 direct labor hours, total budgeted costs are $64,488 [$30,000 + ($4.00 × 8,622)].

Total budgeted costs can also be shown graphically, as in Illustration 7-15. In the graph, the activity index is shown on the horizontal axis, and costs are indicated on the vertical axis. The graph highlights two activity levels (10,000 and 12,000). As shown, total budgeted costs at these activity levels are $70,000 [$30,000 + ($4.00 × 10,000)] and $78,000 [$30,000 + ($4.00 × 12,000)], respectively.

Illustration 7-15
Graphic flexible budget data highlighting 10,000 and 12,000 activity levels

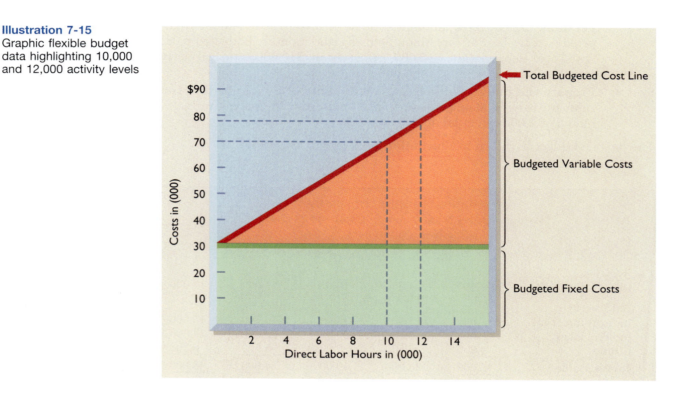

FLEXIBLE BUDGET REPORTS

Helpful Hint An assembly department is a production department, and a maintenance department is a service department, as explained on page 287.

Flexible budget reports are another type of internal report. The flexible budget report consists of two sections: (1) production data for a selected activity index, such as direct labor hours, and (2) cost data for variable and fixed costs. The report provides a basis for evaluating a manager's performance in two areas: production control and cost control. Flexible budget reports are widely used in production and service departments.

A budget report for the Finishing Department of Fox Company for the month of January is shown in Illustration 7-16 (on page 281). In this month, 9,000 hours were worked. The budget data are therefore based on the flexible budget for 9,000 hours in Illustration 7-13. The actual cost data are assumed.

How appropriate is this report in evaluating the Finishing Department manager's performance in controlling overhead costs? The report clearly provides a reliable basis. Both actual and budget costs are based on the activity level worked during January. Since variable costs generally are incurred directly by the department, the difference between the budget allowance for those hours and the actual costs are the responsibility of the department manager.

FOX MANUFACTURING COMPANY
Flexible Manufacturing Overhead Budget Report
Finishing Department
For the Month Ended January 31, 2002

	Budget at 9,000 DLH	Actual Costs 9,000 DLH	Difference Favorable F Unfavorable U
Direct labor hours (DLH)			
Variable costs			
Indirect materials	$13,500	$14,000	$ 500 U
Indirect labor	18,000	17,000	1,000 F
Utilities	4,500	4,600	100 U
Total variable	36,000	35,600	400 F
Fixed costs			
Depreciation	15,000	15,000	–0–
Supervision	10,000	10,000	–0–
Property taxes	5,000	5,000	–0–
Total fixed	30,000	30,000	–0–
Total costs	$66,000	$65,600	$ 400 F

Illustration 7-16 Flexible overhead budget report

Helpful Hint Note that this flexible budget is based on a single cost driver. A more accurate budget often can be developed using the activity-based costing concepts explained in Chapter 4.

In subsequent months, other flexible budget reports will be prepared. For each month, the budget data are based on the actual activity level attained. In February that level may be 11,000 direct labor hours, in July 10,000, and so on.

MANAGEMENT BY EXCEPTION

Management by exception means that top management's review of a budget report is focused either entirely or primarily on differences between actual results and planned objectives. This approach enables top management to focus on problem areas. Management by exception does not mean that top management will investigate every difference. For this approach to be effective, there must be guidelines for identifying an exception. The usual criteria are materiality and controllability.

Materiality

Without quantitative guidelines, management would have to investigate every budget difference regardless of the amount. Materiality is usually expressed as a percentage difference from budget. For example, management may set the percentage difference at 5 percent for important items and 10 percent for other items. All differences either over or under budget by the specified percentage will be investigated. Costs over budget warrant investigation to determine why they were not controlled. Likewise, costs under budget merit investigation to determine whether costs critical to profitability are being curtailed. For example, if maintenance costs are budgeted at $80,000 but only $40,000 is spent, major unexpected breakdowns in productive facilities may occur in the future.

Alternatively, a company may specify a single percentage difference from budget for all items and supplement this guideline with a minimum dollar limit. For example, the exception criteria may be stated at 5 percent of budget or more than $10,000.

Controllability of the Item

Exception guidelines are more restrictive for controllable items than for items that are not controllable by the manager. In fact, there may be no guidelines for noncontrollable items. For example, a large unfavorable difference between actual and budgeted property tax expense may not be flagged for investigation because the only possible causes are an unexpected increase in the tax rate or in the assessed value of the property. An investigation into the difference will be useless: the manager cannot control either cause.

BEFORE YOU GO ON . . .

◆ Review It

1. What is the meaning of budgetary control?
2. When is a static budget appropriate for evaluating a manager's effectiveness in controlling costs?
3. What is a flexible budget?
4. How is a flexible budget developed?
5. What are the criteria used in management by exception?

◆ Do It

Your roommate asks your help in understanding how total budgeted costs are computed at any level of activity. Compute total budgeted costs at 30,000 direct labor hours, assuming that in the flexible budget graph, the fixed cost line and the total budgeted cost line intersect the vertical axis at $36,000 and that the total budget cost line is $186,000 at an activity level of 50,000 direct labor hours.

Action Plan

- Apply the formula: Fixed costs + Variable costs (Total variable costs per unit × Activity level) = Total budgeted costs.

Solution: Using the graph, fixed costs are $36,000, and variable costs are $3 per direct labor hour [($186,000 − $36,000) ÷ 50,000]. Thus, at 30,000 direct labor hours, total budgeted costs are $126,000 [$36,000 + ($3 × 30,000)].

Related exercise material: BE7-3, BE7-4, BE7-5, E7-1, E7-2, E7-3, E7-4, E7-5, E7-6, and E7-7.

---

*T*HE CONCEPT OF RESPONSIBILITY ACCOUNTING

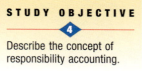
STUDY OBJECTIVE
4
Describe the concept of responsibility accounting.

Like budgeting, responsibility accounting is an important part of management accounting. **Responsibility accounting** involves accumulating and reporting costs (and revenues, where relevant) on the basis of the manager who has the authority to make the day-to-day decisions about the items. Under responsibility accounting, a manager's performance is evaluated on matters directly under that manager's control. Responsibility accounting can be used at every level of management in which the following conditions exist.

1. Costs and revenues can be directly associated with the specific level of management responsibility.

2. The costs and revenues are controllable at the level of responsibility with which they are associated.
3. Budget data can be developed for evaluating the manager's effectiveness in controlling the costs and revenues.

Levels of responsibility for controlling costs are depicted in Illustration 7-17.

Illustration 7-17 Responsibility for controllable costs at varying levels of management

Under responsibility accounting, any individual who has control and is accountable for a specified set of activities can be recognized as a responsibility center. Thus, responsibility accounting may extend from the lowest level of control to the top strata of management. Once responsibility has been established, the effectiveness of the individual's performance is first measured and reported for the specified activity. It is then reported upward throughout the organization.

Responsibility accounting is especially valuable in a decentralized company. **Decentralization** means that the control of operations is delegated to many managers throughout the organization. The term **segment** is sometimes used to identify an area of responsibility in decentralized operations. Under responsibility accounting, segment reports are prepared periodically such as monthly, quarterly, and annually, to evaluate managers' performance.

Responsibility accounting is an essential part of any effective system of budgetary control. The reporting of costs and revenues under responsibility accounting differs from budgeting in two respects.

1. A distinction is made between controllable and noncontrollable items.
2. Performance reports either emphasize or include only items controllable by the individual manager.

Responsibility accounting applies to both profit and not-for-profit entities. The former seek to maximize net income. The latter wish to minimize the cost of providing services.

Helpful Hint All companies use responsibility accounting. Without some form of responsibility accounting, there would be chaos in discharging management's control function.

CONTROLLABLE VERSUS NONCONTROLLABLE REVENUES AND COSTS

All costs and revenues are controllable at some level of responsibility within a company. This truth underscores the adage by the CEO of any organization that "the buck stops here." Under responsibility accounting, the critical issue is **whether the cost or revenue is controllable at the level of responsibility with which it is associated.**

A cost is considered to be **controllable** at a given level of managerial responsibility if the manager has the power to incur it within a given period of time. From this criterion, it follows that:

1. All costs are controllable by top management because of the broad range of its authority.
2. Fewer costs are controllable as one moves down to each lower level of managerial responsibility because of the manager's decreasing authority.

Helpful Hint Are there more or fewer controllable costs as you move to higher levels of management? Answer: More.

In general, **costs incurred directly by a level of responsibility are controllable at that level**. In contrast, costs incurred indirectly and allocated to a responsibility level are considered to be **noncontrollable** at that level.

Helpful Hint The longer the time span, the more likely that the cost becomes controllable.

RESPONSIBILITY REPORTING SYSTEM

A **responsibility reporting system** involves the preparation of a report for each level of responsibility in the company's organization chart. To illustrate such a system, we will use the partial organization chart and production departments of Francis Chair Company in Illustration 7-18.

The responsibility reporting system begins with the lowest level of responsibility for controlling costs and moves upward to each higher level. The connections between levels are detailed in Illustration 7-19 (on page 286). A brief description of the four reports for Francis Chair Company is as follows.

1. **Report D** is typical of reports that go to managers at the lowest level of responsibility shown in the organization chart—department managers. Similar reports are prepared for the managers of the Fabricating, Assembling, and Enameling Departments.
2. **Report C** is an example of reports that are sent to plant managers. It shows the costs of the Chicago plant that are controllable at the second level of re-

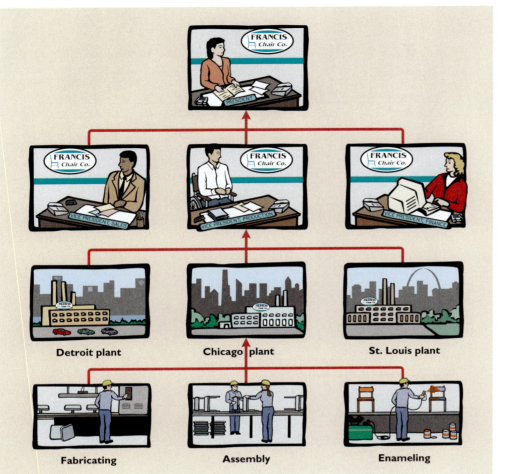

Illustration 7-18 Partial organization chart

Report A
President sees summary data of vice presidents.

Report B
Vice president sees summary of controllable costs in his/her functional area.

Report C
Plant manager sees summary of controllable costs for each department in the plant.

Report D
Department manager sees controllable costs of his/her department.

sponsibility. In addition, Report C shows summary data for each department that is controlled by the plant manager. Similar reports are prepared for the Detroit and St. Louis plant managers.

3. **Report B** illustrates the reports at the third level of responsibility. It shows the controllable costs of the vice president of production and summary data on the three assembly plants for which this officer is responsible.

4. **Report A** is typical of the reports that go to the top level of responsibility—the president. This report shows the controllable costs and expenses of this office and summary data on the vice presidents that are accountable to the president.

A responsibility reporting system permits management by exception at each level of responsibility. And, each higher level of responsibility can obtain the detailed report for each lower level of responsibility. For example, the vice president of production in the Francis Chair Company may request the Chicago plant manager's report because this plant is $5,300 over budget.

This type of reporting system also permits comparative evaluations. In Illustration 7-19, the Chicago plant manager can easily rank the department managers' effectiveness in controlling manufacturing costs. Comparative rankings provide further incentive for a manager to control costs. For example, the Detroit plant manager will want to continue to be No. 1 in the report to the vice president of production. The Chicago plant manager will not want to remain No. 3 in future reporting periods.

Illustration 7-19 Responsibility reporting system

Report A
President sees summary data of vice presidents.

Report B
Vice president sees summary of controllable costs in his/her functional area.

Report C
Plant manager sees summary of controllable costs for each department in the plant.

Report D
Department manager sees controllable costs of his/her department.

REPORT A

To President   Month: January

Controllable Costs:	Budget	Actual	Fav/Unfav
President	$ 150,000	$ 151,500	$ 1,500 U
Vice Presidents:			
Sales	185,000	187,000	2,000 U
Production	1,179,000	1,186,300	7,300 U
Finance	100,000	101,000	1,000 U
Total	$1,614,000	$1,625,800	$11,800 U

REPORT B

To Vice President Production   Month: January

Controllable Costs:	Budget	Actual	Fav/Unfav
V P Production	$ 125,000	$ 126,000	$ 1,000 U
Assembly Plants:			
Detroit	420,000	418,000	2,000 F
Chicago	304,000	309,300	5,300 U
St. Louis	330,000	333,000	3,000 U
Total	$1,179,000	$1,186,300	$ 7,300 U

REPORT C

To Plant Manager-Chicago   Month: January

Controllable Costs:	Budget	Actual	Fav/Unfav
Chicago Plant	$110,000	$113,000	$ 3,000 U
Departments:			
Fabricating	84,000	85,300	1,300 U
Enameling	62,000	64,000	2,000 U
Assembly	48,000	47,000	1,000 F
Total	$304,000	$309,300	$ 5,300 U

REPORT D

To Fabricating Department Manager   Month: January

Controllable Costs:	Budget	Actual	Fav/Unfav
Direct Materials	$ 20,000	$ 20,500	$ 500 U
Direct Labor	40,000	41,000	1,000 U
Overhead	24,000	23,800	200 F
Total	$ 84,000	$ 85,300	$ 1,300 U

e — BUSINESS INSIGHT

In Chapter 1 we discussed enterprise resource planning (ERP) software packages that collect all information regarding the results of the supply chain. A recent innovation is to attach enterprise application systems (EAS) to ERP systems. EAS systems are budgeting and planning tools. By attaching an EAS system called Hyperion Pillar to its ERP system, **Fujitsu Computer Products of America** found that it could more easily compare its budgeted amounts to its actual results. It also reduced its typical time spent on planning and budgeting from 6 to 8 weeks down to 10 to 15 days. Finally, the new system has enabled the company to respond quickly to new developments. For example, in 1999, the software forewarned the company of a potential oversupply problem, and provided recommendations for changes in staffing and capital needs.

Source: Russ Banham, "Better Budgets," *Journal of Accountancy*, February 2000, p. 37.

TYPES OF RESPONSIBILITY CENTERS

There are three basic types of responsibility centers: cost centers, profit centers, and investment centers. These centers indicate the degree of responsibility the manager has for the performance of the center.

A **cost center** incurs costs (and expenses) but does not directly generate revenues. Managers of cost centers have the authority to incur costs. They are evaluated on their ability to control costs. **Cost centers are usually either production departments or service departments.** The former participate directly in making the product. The latter provide only support services. In a **Ford Motor Company** automobile plant, the welding, painting, and assembling departments are production departments; the maintenance, cafeteria, and human resources departments are service departments. All of them are cost centers.

A **profit center** incurs costs (and expenses) and also generates revenues. Managers of profit centers are judged on the profitability of their centers. Examples of profit centers include the individual departments of a retail store, such as clothing, furniture, and automotive products, and branch offices of banks.

Like a profit center, an **investment center** incurs costs (and expenses) and generates revenues. In addition, an investment center has control over the investment funds available for use. Managers of investment centers are evaluated on both the profitability of the center and the rate of return earned on the funds invested. Investment centers are often associated with subsidiary companies. For example, **General Mills**'s product lines include cereals, helper dinner mixes, fruit snacks, popcorn, and yogurt. And, our Feature Story utility, **Duke Energy**, has operating divisions such as electric utility, energy, trading, and natural gas. The manager of the investment center (product line) is able to control or significantly influence investment decisions pertaining to such matters as plant expansion and entry into new market areas. These three types of responsibility centers are depicted in Illustration 7-20.

The evaluation of a manager's performance in each type of responsibility center is explained in the remainder of this chapter.

Helpful Hint (1) Is the jewelry department of **Marshall Field's** department store a profit center or a cost center? (2) Is the props department of a movie studio a profit center or a cost center? Answers: (1) Profit center. (2) Cost center.

Illustration 7-20 Types of responsibility centers

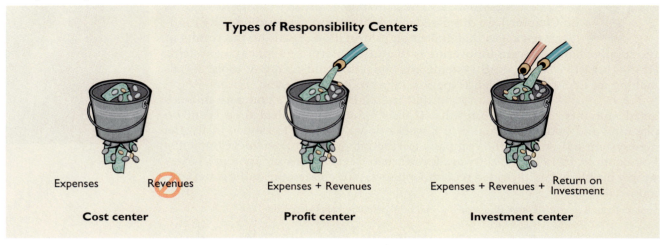

RESPONSIBILITY ACCOUNTING FOR COST CENTERS

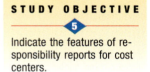

STUDY OBJECTIVE

5

Indicate the features of responsibility reports for cost centers.

The evaluation of a manager's performance for cost centers is based on his or her ability to meet budgeted goals for controllable costs. **Responsibility reports for cost centers compare actual controllable costs with flexible budget data.**

A responsibility report is illustrated in Illustration 7-21. The report is adapted from the budget report for Fox Manufacturing Company in Illustration 7-16 on page 281. It assumes that the Finishing Department manager is able to control all manufacturing overhead costs except depreciation, property taxes, and his own monthly salary of $6,000. The remaining $4,000 of supervision costs are assumed to apply to other supervisory personnel within the Finishing Department, whose salaries are controllable by the manager.

Illustration 7-21 Responsibility report for a cost center

FOX MANUFACTURING COMPANY
Finishing Department
Responsibility Report
For the Month Ended January 31, 2002

Controllable Cost	Budget	Actual	Difference Favorable F Unfavorable U
Indirect materials	$13,500	$14,000	$ 500 U
Indirect labor	18,000	17,000	1,000 F
Utilities	4,500	4,600	100 U
Supervision	**4,000**	**4,000**	**–0–**
	$40,000	$39,600	$ 400 F

Only controllable costs are included in the report, and no distinction is made between variable and fixed costs. The responsibility report continues the concept of management by exception. In this case, top management may request an explanation of the $1,000 favorable difference in indirect labor and/or the $500 unfavorable difference in indirect materials.

RESPONSIBILITY ACCOUNTING FOR PROFIT CENTERS

To evaluate the performance of a manager of a profit center, detailed information is needed about both controllable revenues and controllable costs. The operating revenues earned by a profit center, such as sales, are controllable by the manager. All variable costs (and expenses) incurred by the center are also controllable by the manager because they vary with sales. However, to determine the controllability of fixed costs, it is necessary to distinguish between direct and indirect fixed costs.

STUDY OBJECTIVE

6

Identify the content of responsibility reports for profit centers.

Direct and Indirect Fixed Costs

A profit center may have both direct and indirect fixed costs. **Direct fixed costs** are costs that relate specifically to one center and are incurred for the sole benefit of that center. Examples of such costs include the salaries established by the profit center manager for supervisory personnel and the cost of a timekeeping department for the center's employees. Since these fixed costs can be traced directly to a center, they are also called **traceable costs**. **Most direct fixed costs are controllable by the profit center manager.**

In contrast, **indirect fixed costs** pertain to a company's overall operating activities and are incurred for the benefit of more than one profit center. Indirect fixed costs are allocated to profit centers on some type of equitable basis. For example, property taxes on a building occupied by more than one center may be allocated on the basis of square feet of floor space used by each center. Or, the costs of a company's human resources department may be allocated to profit centers on the basis of the number of employees in each center. Because these fixed costs apply to more than one center, they are also called **common costs**. **Most indirect fixed costs are not controllable by the profit center manager.**

Responsibility Report

The responsibility report for a profit center shows budgeted and actual **controllable revenues and costs**. The report is prepared using the cost-volume-profit income statement explained in Chapter 5. In the report:

1. Controllable fixed costs are deducted from contribution margin.
2. The excess of contribution margin over controllable fixed costs is identified as **controllable margin**.
3. Noncontrollable fixed costs are not reported.

The responsibility report for the manager of the Marine Division, a profit center of Mantle Manufacturing Company, is shown in Illustration 7-22. For the year, the Marine Division also had $60,000 of indirect fixed costs that were not controllable by the profit center manager.

Controllable margin is considered to be the best measure of the manager's performance **in controlling revenues and costs**. This report shows that the manager's performance was below budgeted expectations by approximately 10 percent ($36,000 ÷ $360,000). Top management would likely investigate the causes of this unfavorable result. Note that the report does not show the Marine Division's noncontrollable fixed costs of $60,000. These costs would be included in a report on the profitability of the profit center.

Responsibility reports for profit centers may also be prepared monthly. In addition, they may include cumulative year-to-date results.

Helpful Hint Responsibility reports are helpful tools for evaluating managerial performance. Too much emphasis on profits or investments, however, can be harmful because it ignores other important performance issues such as quality and social responsibility.

Illustration 7-22 Responsibility report for profit center

MANTLE MANUFACTURING COMPANY
Marine Division
Responsibility Report
For the Year Ended January 31, 2002

	Budget	Actual	Difference Favorable F Unfavorable U
Sales	$1,200,000	$1,150,000	$ 50,000 U
Variable costs			
Cost of goods sold	500,000	490,000	10,000 F
Selling and administrative	160,000	156,000	4,000 F
Total	660,000	646,000	14,000 F
Contribution margin	540,000	504,000	36,000 U
Controllable fixed costs			
Cost of goods sold	100,000	100,000	–0–
Selling and administrative	80,000	80,000	–0–
Total	180,000	180,000	–0–
Controllable margin	**$ 360,000**	**$ 324,000**	**$36,000 U**

Helpful Hint Recognize that we are emphasizing financial measures of performance. These days companies are also making an effort to stress nonfinancial performance measures such as product quality, labor productivity, market growth, materials' yield, manufacturing flexibility, and technological capability.

DECISION TOOLKIT

Decision Checkpoints	Info Needed for Decision	Tool to Use for Decision	How to Evaluate Results
Have the individual managers been held accountable for the costs and revenues under their control?	Relevant costs and revenues, where the individual manager has authority to make day-to-day decisions about the items	Responsibility reports focused on cost centers, profit centers, and investment centers as appropriate	Compare budget to actual costs and revenues for controllable items.

BEFORE YOU GO ON . . .

◆ Review It

1. What conditions are essential for responsibility accounting?
2. What is involved in a responsibility reporting system?
3. What is the primary objective of a responsibility report for a cost center?
4. How does contribution margin differ from controllable margin in a responsibility report for a profit center?

◆ Do It

Midwest Division operates as a profit center. It reports the following actual results for the year: Sales $1,700,000, variable costs $800,000, controllable fixed costs $400,000, noncontrollable fixed costs $200,000. Annual budgeted amounts were $1,500,000, $700,000, $400,000, and $200,000, respectively. Prepare a responsibility report for the Midwest Division for December 31, 2002.

Action Plan

- Deduct variable costs from sales to show contribution margin.
- Deduct controllable fixed costs from the contribution margin to show controllable margin.
- Do not report noncontrollable fixed costs.

Solution

MIDWEST DIVISION
Responsibility Report
For the Year Ended December 31, 2002

	Budget	Actual	Difference Favorable F Unfavorable U
Sales	$1,500,000	$1,700,000	$200,000 F
Variable costs	700,000	800,000	100,000 U
Contribution margin	800,000	900,000	100,000 F
Controllable fixed costs	400,000	400,000	–0–
Controllable margin	$ 400,000	$ 500,000	$100,000 F

☑ **THE NAVIGATOR**

Related exercise material: BE7-7 and E7-9.

RESPONSIBILITY ACCOUNTING FOR INVESTMENT CENTERS

As explained earlier, an investment center manager can control or significantly influence the investment funds available for use. Thus, the primary basis for evaluating the performance of a manager of an investment center is **return on investment (ROI)**. The return on investment is considered to be superior to any other performance measurement because it shows the **effectiveness of the manager in utilizing the assets at his or her disposal**.

STUDY OBJECTIVE

◆ **7**

Explain the basis and formula used in evaluating performance in investment centers.

Return on Investment (ROI)

The formula for computing ROI for an investment center, together with assumed illustrative data, is shown in Illustration 7-23. Both factors in the formula are controllable by the investment center manager. Operating assets consist of current assets and plant assets used in operations by the center and controlled by the manager. Nonoperating assets such as idle plant assets and land held for future use are excluded. Average operating assets are usually based on the cost or book value of the assets at the beginning and end of the year.

Illustration 7-23 ROI formula

Controllable Margin	÷	Average Operating Assets	=	Return on Investment (ROI)
$1,000,000	÷	$5,000,000	=	20%

Responsibility Report

The scope of the investment center manager's responsibility significantly affects the content of the performance report. Since an investment center is an independent entity for operating purposes, **all fixed costs are controllable by its manager**. For example, the manager is responsible for depreciation on investment center assets. Therefore, more fixed costs are identified as controllable in the performance report for an investment center manager than in a performance report for a profit center manager. The report also shows budgeted and actual ROI below controllable margin.

To illustrate this responsibility report, we will now assume that the Marine Division of Mantle Manufacturing Company is an investment center. It has budgeted and actual average operating assets of $2,000,000. We now will assume that the manager can control the $60,000 of fixed costs that were not controllable when the division was a profit center. The responsibility report is shown in Illustration 7-24.

Illustration 7-24 Responsibility report for investment center

MANTLE MANUFACTURING COMPANY Marine Division Responsibility Report For the Year Ended December 31, 2002			
			Difference
	Budget	Actual	Favorable F Unfavorable U
Sales	$1,200,000	$1,150,000	$50,000 U
Variable costs			
Cost of goods sold	500,000	490,000	10,000 F
Selling and administrative	160,000	156,000	4,000 F
Total	660,000	646,000	14,000 F
Contribution margin	540,000	504,000	36,000 U
Controllable fixed costs			
Cost of goods sold	100,000	100,000	–0–
Selling and administrative	80,000	80,000	–0–
Other fixed costs	**60,000**	**60,000**	**–0–**
Total	240,000	240,000	–0–
Controllable margin	**$ 300,000**	**$ 264,000**	**$36,000 U**
Return on investment	**15%**	**13.2%**	**1.8% U**
	(a)	(b)	(c)

(a) $\dfrac{\$300,000}{\$2,000,000}$ (b) $\dfrac{\$264,000}{\$2,000,000}$ (c) $\dfrac{\$36,000}{\$2,000,000}$

The report shows that the manager's performance based on ROI was 12 percent (1.8% ÷ 15%) below budget expectations. Top management would likely want an explanation of the reasons for this unfavorable result.

Judgmental Factors in ROI

The return on investment approach includes two judgmental factors:

1. **Valuation of operating assets.** Operating assets may be valued at acquisition cost, book value, appraised value, or market value. The first two bases are readily available from the accounting records.

2. **Margin (income) measure.** This measure may be controllable margin, income from operations, or net income.

Each of the alternative values for operating assets can provide a reliable basis for evaluating a manager's performance as long as it is consistently applied between reporting periods. However, the use of income measures other than controllable margin will not result in a valid basis for evaluating the performance of an investment center manager.[1]

Improving ROI

The manager of an investment center can improve ROI in two ways: (1) increase controllable margin, and/or (2) reduce average operating assets. To illustrate, we will use the following assumed data for the Marine Division of Mantle Manufacturing.

Sales	$2,000,000
Variable cost	1,100,000
Contribution margin (45%)	900,000
Controllable fixed costs	300,000
Controllable margin (a)	$ 600,000
Average operating assets (b)	$5,000,000
Return on investment (a) ÷ (b)	**12%**

Illustration 7-25
Assumed data for Marine Division

Increasing Controllable Margin. Controllable margin can be increased by increasing sales or by reducing variable and controllable fixed costs as follows.

1. **Increase sales 10 percent.** Sales will increase $200,000 ($2,000,000 × .10). Assuming no change in the contribution margin percentage of 45 percent, contribution margin will increase $90,000 ($200,000 × .45). Controllable margin will increase by the same amount because controllable fixed costs will not change. Thus, controllable margin becomes $690,000 ($600,000 + $90,000). The new ROI is 13.8 percent, computed as follows.

$$\text{ROI} = \frac{\text{Controllable margin}}{\text{Average operating assets}} = \frac{\$690,000}{\$5,000,000} = \textbf{13.8\%}$$

Illustration 7-26 ROI computation—increase in sales

An increase in sales benefits both the investment center and the company if it results in new business. It would not benefit the company if the increase was achieved at the expense of other investment centers.

2. **Decrease variable and fixed costs 10 percent.** Total costs will decrease $140,000 [($1,100,000 + $300,000) × .10]. This reduction will result in a corresponding increase in controllable margin. Thus, controllable margin becomes $740,000 ($600,000 + $140,000). The new ROI is 14.8 percent, computed as follows.

$$\text{ROI} = \frac{\text{Controllable margin}}{\text{Average operating assets}} = \frac{\$740,000}{\$5,000,000} = \textbf{14.8\%}$$

Illustration 7-27 ROI computation—decrease in costs

[1]Although the ROI approach is often used in evaluating investment performance, it has some disadvantages. The appendix to this chapter illustrates a second method for evaluation referred to as the residual income approach.

This course of action is clearly beneficial when waste and inefficiencies are eliminated. But, a reduction in vital costs such as required maintenance and inspections is not likely to be acceptable to top management.

Reducing Average Operating Assets. Assume that average operating assets are reduced 10 percent or $500,000 ($5,000,000 × .10). Average operating assets become $4,500,000 ($5,000,000 − $500,000). Since controllable margin remains unchanged at $600,000, the new ROI is 13.3 percent, computed as follows.

Illustration 7-28 ROI computation—decrease in operating assets

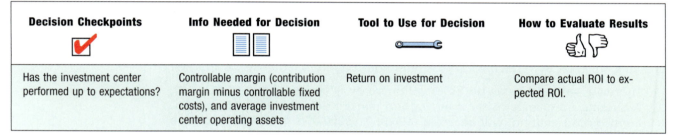

$$\text{ROI} = \frac{\text{Controllable margin}}{\text{Average operating assets}} = \frac{\$600,000}{\$4,500,000} = \textbf{13.3\%}$$

Reductions in operating assets may or may not be prudent. It is beneficial to eliminate overinvestment in inventories and to dispose of excessive plant assets. However, it is unwise to reduce inventories below expected needs or to dispose of essential plant assets.

DECISION TOOLKIT

Decision Checkpoints	Info Needed for Decision	Tool to Use for Decision	How to Evaluate Results
Has the investment center performed up to expectations?	Controllable margin (contribution margin minus controllable fixed costs), and average investment center operating assets	Return on investment	Compare actual ROI to expected ROI.

PRINCIPLES OF PERFORMANCE EVALUATION

Performance evaluation is at the center of responsibility accounting. **Performance evaluation** is a management function that compares actual results with budget goals. Performance evaluation involves both behavioral and reporting principles.

Behavioral Principles

The human factor is critical in evaluating performance. Behavioral principles include the following.

1. **Managers of responsibility centers should have direct input into the process of establishing budget goals of their area of responsibility.** Without such input, managers may view the goals as unrealistic or arbitrarily set by top management. Such views adversely affect the managers' motivation to meet the targeted objectives.

2. **The evaluation of performance should be based entirely on matters that are controllable by the manager being evaluated.** Criticism of a manager on matters outside his or her control reduces the effectiveness of the evaluation process. It leads to negative reactions by a manager and to doubts about the fairness of the company's evaluation policies.

3. **Top management should support the evaluation process.** As explained earlier, the evaluation process begins at the lowest level of responsibility and extends upward to the highest level of management. Managers quickly lose

faith in the process when top management ignores, overrules, or bypasses established procedures for evaluating a manager's performance.

4. **The evaluation process must allow managers to respond to their evaluations.** Evaluation is not a one-way street. Managers should have the opportunity to defend their performance. Evaluation without feedback is both impersonal and ineffective.

5. **The evaluation should identify both good and poor performance.** Praise for good performance is a powerful motivating factor for a manager. This is especially true when a manager's compensation includes rewards for meeting budget goals.

Reporting Principles of Performance Evaluation

Performance evaluation under responsibility accounting should be based on certain reporting principles. These principles pertain primarily to the internal reports that provide the basis for evaluating performance. Performance reports should:

1. Contain only data that are controllable by the manager of the responsibility center.
2. Provide accurate and reliable budget data to measure performance.
3. Highlight significant differences between actual results and budget goals.
4. Be tailor-made for the intended evaluation.
5. Be prepared at reasonable intervals.

BEFORE YOU GO ON . . .

◆ Review It

1. What is the formula for computing return on investment (ROI)?
2. Identify three actions a manager may take to improve ROI.

THE NAVIGATOR

*U*SING THE DECISION TOOLKIT

The manufacturing overhead budget for Reebles Company contains the following items.

Variable expenses	
Indirect materials	$25,000
Indirect labor	12,000
Maintenance expenses	10,000
Manufacturing supplies	6,000
Total variable	$53,000
Fixed expenses	
Supervision	$17,000
Inspection costs	1,000
Insurance expenses	2,000
Depreciation	15,000
Total fixed	$35,000

The budget was based on an estimated 2,000 units being produced. During November, 1,500 units were produced, and the following costs incurred.

Variable expenses		
Indirect materials	$25,200	
Indirect labor	13,500	
Maintenance expenses	8,200	
Manufacturing supplies	5,100	
Total variable	$52,000	
Fixed expenses		
Supervision	$19,300	
Inspection costs	1,200	
Insurance expenses	2,200	
Depreciation	14,700	
Total fixed	$37,400	

Instructions

(a) Determine which items would be controllable by Ed Lopat, the production manager. (Assume "supervision" excludes Lopat's own salary.)

(b) How much should have been spent during the month for the manufacture of the 1,500 units?

(c) Prepare a flexible manufacturing overhead budget report for Mr. Lopat.

(d) Prepare a responsibility report. Include only the costs that would have been controllable by Mr. Lopat. In an attached memo, describe clearly for Mr. Lopat the areas in which his performance needs to be improved.

Solution

(a) Ed Lopat should be able to control all the variable expenses and the fixed expenses of supervision and inspection. Insurance and depreciation ordinarily are not the responsibility of the department manager.

(b) The total variable cost per unit is $26.50 ($53,000 ÷ 2,000). The total budgeted cost during the month to manufacture 1,500 units is variable costs $39,750 (1,500 × $26.50) plus fixed costs ($35,000), for a total of $74,750 ($39,750 + $35,000).

(c)

REEBLES COMPANY
Production Department
Manufacturing Overhead Budget Report (Flexible)
For the Month Ended November 30, 2002

	Budget at 1,500 units	Actual at 1,500 units	Difference Favorable F Unfavorable U
Variable costs			
Indirect materials	$18,750	$25,200	$ 6,450 U
Indirect labor	9,000	13,500	4,500 U
Maintenance	7,500	8,200	700 U
Manufacturing supplies	4,500	5,100	600 U
Total variable	39,750	52,000	12,250 U
Fixed costs			
Supervision	17,000	19,300	2,300 U
Inspection	1,000	1,200	200 U
Insurance	2,000	2,200	200 U
Depreciation	15,000	14,700	300 F
Total fixed	35,000	37,400	2,400 U
Total costs	$74,750	$89,400	$14,650 U

(d) Because a production department is a cost center, the responsibility report should include only the costs that are controllable by the production manager. In this type of report, no distinction is made between variable and fixed costs. Budget data in the report should be based on the units actually produced.

REEBLES COMPANY
Production Department
Manufacturing Overhead Responsibility Report
For the Month Ended November 30, 2002

Controllable Cost	Budget	Actual	Difference Favorable F Unfavorable U
Indirect materials	$18,750	$25,200	$ 6,450 U
Indirect labor	9,000	13,500	4,500 U
Maintenance	7,500	8,200	700 U
Manufacturing supplies	4,500	5,100	600 U
Supervision	17,000	19,300	2,300 U
Inspection	1,000	1,200	200 U
Total	$57,750	$72,500	$14,750 U

To: Mr. Ed Lopat, Production Manager

From: _____, Vice-President of Production

Subject: Performance Evaluation for the Month of November
Your performance in controlling costs that are your responsibility was very disappointing in the month of November. As indicated in the accompanying responsibility report, total costs were $14,750 over budget. On a percentage basis, costs were 26% over budget. As you can see, actual costs were over budget for every cost item. In three instances, costs were significantly over budget (indirect materials 34%, indirect labor 50%, and supervision 14%).

Ed, it is imperative that you get costs under control in your department as soon as possible.

I think we need to talk about ways to implement more effective cost control measures. I would like to meet with you in my office at 9 a.m. on Wednesday to discuss possible alternatives.

SUMMARY OF STUDY OBJECTIVES

1 *Describe the concept of budgetary control.* Budgetary control consists of (a) preparing periodic budget reports that compare actual results with planned objectives, (b) analyzing the differences to determine their causes, (c) taking appropriate corrective action, and (d) modifying future plans, if necessary.

2 *Evaluate the usefulness of static budget reports.* Static budget reports are useful in evaluating the progress toward planned sales and profit goals. They are also appropriate in assessing a manager's effectiveness in controlling fixed costs and expenses when (a) actual activity closely ap-

proximates the master budget activity level, and/or (b) the behavior of the costs in response to changes in activity is fixed.

3 *Explain the development of flexible budgets and the usefulness of flexible budget reports.* To develop the flexible budget it is necessary to:
(a) Identify the activity index and the relevant range of activity.
(b) Identify the variable costs, and determine the budgeted variable cost per unit of activity for each cost.
(c) Identify the fixed costs, and determine the budgeted amount for each cost.

(d) Prepare the budget for selected increments of activity within the relevant range.

Flexible budget reports permit an evaluation of a manager's performance in controlling production and costs.

4 *Describe the concept of responsibility accounting.* Responsibility accounting involves accumulating and reporting revenues and costs on the basis of the individual manager who has the authority to make the day-to-day decisions about the items. The evaluation of a manager's performance is based on the matters directly under the manager's control. In responsibility accounting, it is necessary to distinguish between controllable and noncontrollable fixed costs and to identify three types of responsibility centers: cost, profit, and investment.

5 *Indicate the features of responsibility reports for cost centers.* Responsibility reports for cost centers compare actual costs with flexible budget data. The reports show only controllable costs, and no distinction is made between variable and fixed costs.

6 *Identify the content of responsibility reports for profit centers.* Responsibility reports show contribution margin, controllable fixed costs, and controllable margin for each profit center.

7 *Explain the basis and formula used in evaluating performance in investment centers.* The primary basis for evaluating performance in investment centers is return on investment (ROI). The formula for computing ROI for investment centers is: Controllable margin ÷ Average operating assets.

DECISION TOOLKIT—A SUMMARY

Decision Checkpoints	Info Needed for Decision	Tool to Use for Decision	How to Evaluate Results
Are the increased costs resulting from increased production reasonable?	Variable costs projected at different levels of production	Flexible budget	After taking into account different production levels, results are favorable if expenses are less than budgeted amounts.
Have the individual managers been held accountable for the costs and revenues under their control?	Relevant costs and revenues, where the individual manager has authority to make day-to-day decisions about the items	Responsibility reports focused on cost centers, profit centers, and investment centers as appropriate	Compare budget to actual costs and revenues for controllable items.
Has the investment center performed up to expectations?	Controllable margin (contribution margin minus controllable fixed costs), and average investment center operating assets	Return on investment	Compare actual ROI to expected ROI.

A P P E N D I X   7 A

RESIDUAL INCOME—ANOTHER PERFORMANCE MEASUREMENT

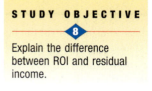

Although most companies use ROI in evaluating their investment performance, ROI has a significant disadvantage. To illustrate, let's look at the Marine Division of Mantle Manufacturing Company. It has an ROI of 20 percent computed as follows.

Illustration 7A-1 ROI formula

The Marine Division is considering producing a new product, a GPS satellite tracker (hereafter referred to as Tracker), for its boats. To produce Tracker, operating assets will have to increase $2,000,000. Tracker is expected to generate an additional $260,000 of controllable margin. A comparison of how Tracker will affect ROI is shown in Illustration 7A-2.

	Without Tracker	Tracker	With Tracker
Controllable margin (a)	$1,000,000	$ 260,000	$1,260,000
Average operating assets (b)	$5,000,000	$2,000,000	$7,000,000
Return on investment [(a) ÷ (b)]	20%	13%	18%

Illustration 7A-2   ROI comparison

The investment in Tracker reduces ROI from 20 percent to 18 percent.

Let's suppose that you are the manager of the Marine Division and must make the decision to produce or not produce Tracker. If you were evaluated using ROI, you probably would not produce Tracker because your ROI would drop from 20 percent to 18 percent. The problem with this ROI analysis is that it ignores an important variable, the minimum rate of return on a company's operating assets. The **minimum rate of return** is the rate at which the Marine Division can cover its costs and earn a profit. Assuming that the Marine Division has a minimum rate of return of 10 percent, it should invest in Tracker because its ROI of 13 percent is greater than 10 percent.

RESIDUAL INCOME COMPARED TO ROI

To evaluate performance using the minimum rate of return, companies use the residual income approach. **Residual income** is the income that remains after subtracting from the controllable margin the minimum rate of return on a company's average operating assets. The residual income for Tracker would be computed as follows.

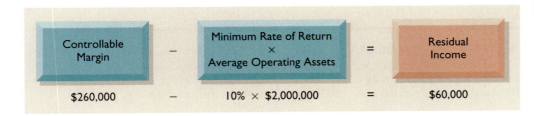

Illustration 7A-3   Residual income formula

As shown, the residual income related to the Tracker investment is $60,000. Illustration 7A-4 indicates how residual income changes as the additional investment is made.

	Without Tracker	Tracker	With Tracker
Controllable margin (a)	$1,000,000	$260,000	$1,260,000
Average operating assets × 10% (b)	500,000	200,000	700,000
Residual income [(a) − (b)]	$ 500,000	$ 60,000	$ 560,000

Illustration 7A-4   Residual income comparison

This example illustrates how performance evaluation based on ROI can be misleading and can even cause managers to reject projects that would actually increase income for the company. As a result, many companies such as **Coca-Cola**, **Briggs and Stratton**, **Eli Lilly**, and **Siemens AG** use residual income (or a variant often referred to as economic value added) to evaluate investment alternatives and measure company performance.

RESIDUAL INCOME WEAKNESS

The goal of residual income is to maximize the total amount of residual income. This goal, however, ignores the fact that one division might use substantially fewer assets to attain the same level of residual income as another division. For example, we know that to produce Tracker, the Marine Division of Mantle Manufacturing used $2,000,000 of average operating assets to generate $260,000 of controllable margin. Now let's say a different division produced a product called SeaDog, which used $4,000,000 to generate $460,000 of controllable margin, as shown in Illustration 7A-5.

Illustration 7A-5 Comparison of two products

	Tracker	SeaDog
Controllable margin (a)	$260,000	$460,000
Average operating assets × 10% (b)	200,000	400,000
Residual income [(a) − (b)]	$ 60,000	$ 60,000

If the performance of these two investments were evaluated using residual income, they would be considered equal: Both products have the same total residual income. This ignores, however, the fact that SeaDog required **twice** as many operating assets to achieve the same level of residual income.

SUMMARY OF STUDY OBJECTIVE FOR APPENDIX 7A

8 *Explain the difference between ROI and residual income.* ROI is controllable margin divided by average operating assets. Residual income is the income that remains after subtracting the minimum rate of return on a company's average operating assets. ROI sometimes provides misleading results because profitable investments are often rejected when the investment reduces ROI but increases overall profitability.

GLOSSARY

Key Term Matching Activity

Budgetary control The use of budgets to control operations. (p. 272)

Controllable costs Costs that a manager has the authority to incur within a given period of time. (p. 284)

Controllable margin Contribution margin less controllable fixed costs. (p. 289)

Cost center A responsibility center that incurs costs but does not directly generate revenues. (p. 287)

Decentralization Control of operations is delegated to many managers throughout the organization. (p. 283)

Direct fixed costs Costs that relate specifically to a responsibility center and are incurred for the sole benefit of the center. (p. 289)

Flexible budget A projection of budget data for various levels of activity. (p. 275)

Indirect fixed costs Costs that are incurred for the benefit of more than one profit center. (p. 289)

Investment center A responsibility center that incurs costs, generates revenues, and has control over the investment funds available for use. (p. 287)

Management by exception The review of budget reports by top management focused entirely or primarily on differences between actual results and planned objectives. (p. 281)

Noncontrollable costs Costs incurred indirectly and allocated to a responsibility center that are not controllable at that level. (p. 284)

Profit center A responsibility center that incurs costs and also generates revenues. (p. 287)

Residual income The income that remains after subtracting from the controllable margin the minimum rate of return on a company's operating assets. (p. 299)

Responsibility accounting A part of management accounting that involves accumulating and reporting revenues and costs on the basis of the manager who has the authority to make the day-to-day decisions about the items. (p. 282)

Responsibility reporting system The preparation of reports for each level of responsibility in the company's organization chart. (p. 284)

Return on investment (ROI) A measure of management's effectiveness in utilizing assets at its disposal in an investment center. (p. 291)

Segment An area of responsibility in decentralized operations. (p. 283)

Static budget A projection of budget data at one level of activity. (p. 273)

DEMONSTRATION PROBLEM

Glenda Company uses a flexible budget for manufacturing overhead based on direct labor hours. For 2002 the master overhead budget for the Packaging Department at normal capacity of 300,000 direct labor hours was as follows.

Variable Costs		Fixed Costs	
Indirect labor	$360,000	Supervision	$ 60,000
Supplies and lubricants	150,000	Depreciation	24,000
Maintenance	210,000	Property taxes	18,000
Utilities	120,000	Insurance	12,000
	$840,000		$114,000

During July, 24,000 direct labor hours were worked. The company incurred the following variable costs in July: indirect labor $30,200, supplies and lubricants $11,600, maintenance $17,500, and utilities $9,200. Actual fixed overhead costs were the same as monthly budgeted fixed costs.

Instructions

Prepare a flexible budget report for the Packaging Department for July.

eGrade Demonstration
Problem

Solution to Demonstration Problem

GLENDA COMPANY
Manufacturing Overhead Budget Report (Flexible)
Packaging Department
For the Month Ended July 31, 2002

	Budget	Actual Costs	Difference Favorable F Unfavorable U
Direct labor hours (DLH)	24,000 DLH	24,000 DLH	
Variable costs			
Indirect labor	$28,800	$30,200	$1,400 U
Supplies and lubricants	12,000	11,600	400 F
Maintenance	16,800	17,500	700 U
Utilities	9,600	9,200	400 F
Total variable	67,200	68,500	1,300 U

Action Plan

- Use budget data for actual direct labor hours worked.
- Classify each cost as variable or fixed.
- Determine the difference between budgeted and actual costs.
- Identify the difference as favorable or unfavorable.
- Determine the difference in total variable costs, total fixed costs, and total costs.

	Budget 24,000 DLH	Actual Costs 24,000 DLH	Difference Favorable F Unfavorable U
Direct labor hours (DLH)			
Fixed costs			
Supervision	$ 5,000	$ 5,000	–0–
Depreciation	2,000	2,000	–0–
Property taxes	1,500	1,500	–0–
Insurance	1,000	1,000	–0–
Total fixed	9,500	9,500	–0–
Total costs	$76,700	$78,000	$1,300 U

THE NAVIGATOR

Note: All asterisked Questions, Exercises, and Problems relate to the material contained in the appendix to the chapter.

SELF-STUDY QUESTIONS

Self-Study/Self-Test

Answers are at the end of the chapter.

(SO 1) 1. Budgetary control involves all but one of the following:
  (a) modifying future plans.
  (b) analyzing differences.
  (c) using static budgets.
  (d) determining differences between actual and planned results.

(SO 2) 2. A static budget is useful in controlling costs when cost behavior is:
  (a) mixed.   (c) variable.
  (b) fixed.   (d) linear.

(SO 3) 3. At zero direct labor hours in a flexible budget graph, the total budgeted cost line intersects the vertical axis at $30,000. At 10,000 direct labor hours, a horizontal line drawn from the total budgeted cost line intersects the vertical axis at $90,000. Fixed and variable costs may be expressed as:
  (a) $30,000 fixed plus $6 per direct labor hour variable.
  (b) $30,000 fixed plus $9 per direct labor hour variable.
  (c) $60,000 fixed plus $3 per direct labor hour variable.
  (d) $60,000 fixed plus $6 per direct labor hour variable.

(SO 3) 4. At 9,000 direct labor hours, the flexible budget for indirect materials is $27,000. If $28,000 of indirect materials costs are incurred at 9,200 direct labor hours, the flexible budget report should show the following difference for indirect materials:
  (a) $1,000 unfavorable.
  (b) $1,000 favorable.

  (c) $400 favorable.
  (d) $400 unfavorable.

(SO 4) 5. Under responsibility accounting, the evaluation of a manager's performance is based on matters that the manager:
  (a) directly controls.
  (b) directly and indirectly controls.
  (c) indirectly controls.
  (d) has shared responsibility for with another manager.

(SO 4) 6. Responsibility centers include:
  (a) cost centers.
  (b) profit centers.
  (c) investment centers.
  (d) all of the above.

(SO 5) 7. Responsibility reports for cost centers:
  (a) distinguish between fixed and variable costs.
  (b) use static budget data.
  (c) include both controllable and noncontrollable costs.
  (d) include only controllable costs.

(SO 6) 8. In a responsibility report for a profit center, controllable fixed costs are deducted from contribution margin to show:
  (a) profit center margin.
  (b) controllable margin.
  (c) net income.
  (d) income from operations.

(SO 7) 9. In the formula for return on investment (ROI), the factors for controllable margin and operating assets are, respectively:
  (a) controllable margin percentage and total operating assets.

(b) controllable margin dollars and average operating assets.

(c) controllable margin dollars and total assets.

(d) controllable margin percentage and average operating assets.

(SO 7) 10. A manager of an investment center can improve ROI by:

(a) increasing average operating assets.

(b) reducing sales.

(c) increasing variable costs.

(d) reducing variable and/or controllable fixed costs.

*11. In the formula for residual income, the factors (SO 8) for computing residual income are:

(a) contribution margin, controllable margin, and average total assets.

(b) controllable margin, average total assets, and ROI.

(c) controllable margin, average total assets, and minimum rate of return.

(d) controllable margin, ROI, and minimum rate of return.

THE NAVIGATOR

QUESTIONS

1. (a) What is budgetary control?

(b) Tony Crespino is describing budgetary control. What steps should be included in Tony's description?

2. The following purposes are part of a budgetary reporting system: (a) Determine efficient use of materials. (b) Control overhead costs. (c) Determine whether income objectives are being met. For each purpose, indicate the name of the report, the frequency of the report, and the primary recipient(s) of the report.

3. How may a budget report for the second quarter differ from a budget report for the first quarter?

4. Don Cox questions the usefulness of a master sales budget in evaluating sales performance. Is there justification for Don's concern? Explain.

5. Under what circumstances may a static budget be an appropriate basis for evaluating a manager's effectiveness in controlling costs?

6. "A flexible budget is really a series of static budgets." Is this true? Why?

7. The static manufacturing overhead budget based on 40,000 direct labor hours shows budgeted indirect labor costs of $56,000. During March, the department incurs $66,000 of indirect labor while working 45,000 direct labor hours. Is this a favorable or unfavorable performance? Why?

8. A static overhead budget based on 40,000 direct labor hours shows Factory Insurance $6,500 as a fixed cost. At the 50,000 direct labor hours worked in March, factory insurance costs were $6,200. Is this a favorable or unfavorable performance? Why?

9. Kate Coulter is confused about how a flexible budget is prepared. Identify the steps for Kate.

10. Alou Company has prepared a graph of flexible budget data. At zero direct labor hours, the total budgeted cost line intersects the vertical axis at $25,000. At 10,000 direct labor hours, the line drawn from the total budgeted cost line intersects the vertical axis at $85,000. How may the fixed and variable costs be expressed?

11. The flexible budget formula is fixed costs $40,000 plus variable costs of $2 per direct labor hour. What is the total budgeted cost at (a) 9,000 hours and (b) 12,345 hours?

12. What is management by exception? What criteria may be used in identifying exceptions?

13. What is responsibility accounting? Explain the purpose of responsibility accounting.

14. Ann Wilkins is studying for an accounting examination. Describe for Ann what conditions are necessary for responsibility accounting to be used effectively.

15. Distinguish between controllable and noncontrollable costs.

16. How do responsibility reports differ from budget reports?

17. What is the relationship, if any, between a responsibility reporting system and a company's organization chart?

18. Distinguish among the three types of responsibility centers.

19. (a) What costs are included in a performance report for a cost center? (b) In the report, are variable and fixed costs identified?

20. How do direct fixed costs differ from indirect fixed costs? Are both types of fixed costs controllable?

21. Lori Quan is confused about controllable margin reported in an income statement for a profit center. How is this margin computed, and what is its primary purpose?

22. What is the primary basis for evaluating the performance of the manager of an investment center? Indicate the formula for this basis.

23. Explain the ways that ROI can be improved.

24. Indicate two behavioral principles that pertain to (a) the manager being evaluated and (b) top management.

*25. What is a major disadvantage of using ROI to evaluate investment and company performance?

*26. What is residual income, and what is one of its major weaknesses?

BRIEF EXERCISES

Prepare static budget report.
(SO 2)

BE7-1 For the quarter ended March 31, 2002, Russo Company accumulates the following sales data for its product, Garden-Tools: $315,000 budget; $302,000 actual. Prepare a static budget report for the quarter.

Prepare static budget report for 2 quarters.
(SO 2)

BE7-2 Data for Russo Company are given in BE7-1. In the second quarter, budgeted sales were $380,000, and actual sales were $389,000. Prepare a static budget report for the second quarter and for the year to date.

Show usefulness of flexible budgets in evaluating performance.
(SO 3)

BE7-3 In Maltz Company, direct labor is $20 per hour. The company expects to operate at 10,000 direct labor hours each month. In January 2002, direct labor totaling $207,000 is incurred in working 10,400 hours. Prepare (a) a static budget report and (b) a flexible budget report. Evaluate the usefulness of each report.

Prepare a flexible budget for variable costs.
(SO 3)

BE7-4 Gomez Company expects to produce 1,200,000 units of Product XX in 2002. Monthly production is expected to range from 80,000 to 120,000 units. Budgeted variable manufacturing costs per unit are: direct materials $5, direct labor $6, and overhead $9. Prepare a flexible manufacturing budget for the relevant range value using 20,000 unit increments.

Prepare flexible budget report.
(SO 3)

BE7-5 Data for Gomez Company are given in BE7-4. In March 2002, the company incurs the following costs in producing 100,000 units: direct materials $520,000, direct labor $590,000, and variable overhead $915,000. Prepare a flexible budget report for March. Were costs controlled?

Prepare a responsibility report for a cost center.
(SO 5)

BE7-6 In the Assembly Department of Rado Company, budgeted and actual manufacturing overhead costs for the month of April 2002 were as follows.

	Budget	**Actual**
Indirect materials	$15,000	$14,500
Indirect labor	20,000	20,800
Utilities	10,000	10,750
Supervision	5,000	5,000

All costs are controllable by the department manager. Prepare a responsibility report for April for the cost center.

Prepare a responsibility report for a profit center.
(SO 6)

BE7-7 Savage Manufacturing Company accumulates the following summary data for the year ending December 31, 2002, for its Water Division which it operates as a profit center: sales—$2,000,000 budget, $2,080,000 actual; variable costs—$1,000,000 budget, $1,050,000 actual; and controllable fixed costs—$300,000 budget, $307,000 actual. Prepare a responsibility report for the Water Division.

Prepare a responsibility report for an investment center.
(SO 7)

BE7-8 For the year ending December 31, 2002, Stoker Company accumulates the following data for the Plastics Division which it operates as an investment center: contribution margin—$700,000 budget, $715,000 actual; controllable fixed costs—$300,000 budget, $295,000 actual. Average operating assets for the year were $1,600,000. Prepare a responsibility report for the Plastics Division beginning with contribution margin.

Compute return on investment using the ROI formula.
(SO 7)

BE7-9 For its three investment centers, Chow Company accumulates the following data.

	I	**II**	**III**
Sales	$2,000,000	$3,000,000	$ 4,000,000
Controllable margin	1,200,000	2,400,000	3,200,000
Average operating assets	6,000,000	8,000,000	10,000,000

Compute the return on investment (ROI) for each center.

Compute return on investment under changed conditions.
(SO 7)

BE7-10 Data for the investment centers for Chow Company are given in BE7-9. The centers expect the following changes in the next year: (I) increase sales 10%; (II) decrease costs $200,000; (III) decrease average operating assets $400,000. Compute the expected return on investment (ROI) for each center. Assume center I has a contribution margin percentage of 80%.

*BE7-11   Napstem, Inc. reports the following financial information.

Compute ROI and residual income.
(SO 8)

Average operating assets	$2,400,000
Controllable margin	$ 600,000
Minimum rate of return	9%

Compute the return on investment and the residual income.

*BE7-12   Presented below is information related to the Pulp Division of Wood Products, Inc.

Compute ROI and residual income.
(SO 8)

Contribution margin	$1,000,000
Controllable margin	$ 800,000
Average operating assets	$4,000,000
Minimum rate of return	15%

Compute the Pulp Division's return on investment and residual income.

EXERCISES

E7-1   Voss Company uses a flexible budget for manufacturing overhead based on direct labor hours. Variable manufacturing overhead costs per direct labor hour are as follows.

Prepare flexible manufacturing overhead budget.
(SO 3)

Indirect labor	$1.00
Indirect materials	0.50
Utilities	0.30

Fixed overhead costs per month are: Supervision $4,000, Depreciation $1,500, and Property Taxes $800. The company believes it will normally operate in a range of 7,000–10,000 direct labor hours per month.

Instructions
Prepare a monthly flexible manufacturing overhead budget for 2002 for the expected range of activity, using increments of 1,000 direct labor hours.

E7-2   Using the information in E7-1, assume that in July 2002, Voss Company incurs the following manufacturing overhead costs.

Prepare flexible budget reports for manufacturing overhead costs, and comment on findings.
(SO 3)

Variable Costs		**Fixed Costs**	
Indirect labor	$8,700	Supervision	$4,000
Indirect materials	4,300	Depreciation	1,500
Utilities	2,500	Property taxes	800

Instructions
(a) Prepare a flexible budget performance report, assuming that the company worked 9,000 direct labor hours during the month. The company expected to work 9,000 direct labor hours.
(b) Prepare a flexible budget performance report, assuming that the company worked 8,500 direct labor hours during the month. The company expected to work 8,500 direct labor hours.
(c)   Comment on your findings.

E7-3   Samano Company uses flexible budgets to control its selling expenses. Monthly sales are expected to range from $170,000 to $200,000. Variable costs and their percentage relationship to sales are: Sales Commissions 5%, Advertising 4%, Traveling 3%, and Delivery 2%. Fixed selling expenses will consist of Sales Salaries $30,000, Depreciation on Delivery Equipment $7,000, and Insurance on Delivery Equipment $1,000.

Prepare flexible selling expense budget.
(SO 3)

Instructions
Prepare a monthly flexible budget for each $10,000 increment of sales within the relevant range for the year ending December 31, 2002.

E7-4   The actual selling expenses incurred in March 2002 by Samano Company are as follows.

Prepare flexible budget reports for selling expenses.
(SO 3)

	Variable Expenses		**Fixed Expenses**	
Sales commissions	$9,200		Sales salaries	$30,000
Advertising	7,000		Depreciation	7,000
Travel	5,100		Insurance	1,000
Delivery	3,500			

Instructions

(a) Prepare a flexible budget performance report for March using the budget data in E7-3, assuming that March sales were $170,000. Expected and actual sales are the same.

(b) Prepare a flexible budget performance report, assuming that March sales were $180,000. Expected sales and actual sales are the same.

(c) ▭▭▶ Comment on the importance of using flexible budgets in evaluating the performance of the sales manager.

Prepare flexible budget and responsibility report for manufacturing overhead.
(SO 3, 5)

E7-5   Sanchez Company's manufacturing overhead budget for the first quarter of 2002 contained the following data.

	Variable Costs			**Fixed Costs**	
Indirect materials	$12,000		Supervisory salaries	$30,000	
Indirect labor	10,000		Depreciation	7,000	
Utilities	8,000		Property taxes and insurance	8,000	
Maintenance	5,000		Maintenance	5,000	

Actual variable costs were: indirect materials $14,200, indirect labor $9,600, utilities $8,700, and maintenance $4,200. Actual fixed costs equaled budgeted costs except for property taxes and insurance, which were $8,300.

All costs are considered controllable by the production department manager except for depreciation, and property taxes and insurance.

Instructions

(a) Prepare a flexible overhead budget report for the first quarter.
(b) Prepare a responsibility report for the first quarter.

Prepare flexible budget report, and answer question.
(SO 2, 3)

E7-6   As sales manager, Todd Keyser was given the following static budget report for selling expenses in the Clothing Department of Pace Company for the month of October.

PACE COMPANY
Clothing Department
Budget Report
For the Month Ended October 31, 2002

	Budget	Actual	Difference Favorable F Unfavorable U
Sales in units	8,000	10,000	2,000 F
Variable costs			
Sales commissions	$ 2,000	$ 2,500	$ 500 U
Advertising expense	800	850	50 U
Travel expense	4,400	4,900	500 U
Free samples given out	1,000	1,300	300 U
Total variable	8,200	9,550	1,350 U
Fixed costs			
Rent	1,500	1,500	–0–
Sales salaries	1,200	1,200	–0–
Office salaries	800	800	–0–
Depreciation—autos (sales staff)	500	500	–0–
Total fixed	4,000	4,000	–0–
Total costs	$12,200	$13,550	$1,350 U

As a result of this budget report, Todd was called into the president's office and congratulated on his fine sales performance. He was reprimanded, however, for allowing his costs to get out of control. Todd knew something was wrong with the performance report that he had been given. However, he was not sure what to do, and comes to you for advice.

Instructions
(a) Prepare a budget report based on flexible budget data to help Todd.
(b) Should Todd have been reprimanded? Explain.

E7-7 Lockwood Company has two production departments, Fabricating and Assembling. At a department managers' meeting, the controller uses flexible budget graphs to explain total budgeted costs. Separate graphs based on direct labor hours are used for each department. The graphs show the following.

State total budgeted cost formulas, and prepare flexible budget graph.
(SO 3)

1. At zero direct labor hours, the total budgeted cost line and the fixed cost line intersect the vertical axis at $50,000 in the Fabricating Department and $45,000 in the Assembling Department.
2. At normal capacity of 50,000 direct labor hours, the line drawn from the total budgeted cost line intersects the vertical axis at $160,000 in the Fabricating Department, and $110,000 in the Assembling Department.

Instructions
(a) State the total budgeted cost formula for each department.
(b) Compute the total budgeted cost for each department, assuming actual direct labor hours worked were 53,000 and 47,000, in the Fabricating and Assembling Departments, respectively.
(c) Prepare the flexible budget graph for the Fabricating Department, assuming the maximum direct labor hours in the relevant range is 100,000. Use increments of 10,000 direct labor hours on the horizontal axis and increments of $50,000 on the vertical axis.

E7-8 Loebs Company's organization chart includes the president; the vice president of production; three assembly plants—Dallas, Atlanta, and Tucson; and two departments within each plant—Machining and Finishing. Budget and actual manufacturing cost data for July 2002 are as follows.

Prepare reports in a responsibility reporting system.
(SO 4)

Finishing Department—Dallas: Direct materials $41,000 actual, $46,000 budget; direct labor $83,000 actual, $82,000 budget; manufacturing overhead $51,000 actual, $49,200 budget.

Machining Department—Dallas: Total manufacturing costs $218,000 actual, $214,000 budget.

Atlanta Plant: Total manufacturing costs $426,000 actual, $421,000 budget.

Tucson Plant: Total manufacturing costs $494,000 actual, $499,000 budget.

The Dallas plant manager's office costs were $95,000 actual and $92,000 budget. The vice president of production's office costs were $132,000 actual and $130,000 budget. Office costs are not allocated to departments and plants.

Instructions
Using the format on page 286, prepare the reports in a responsibility system for:
(a) The Finishing Department—Dallas.
(b) The plant manager—Dallas.
(c) The vice president of production.

E7-9 Haven Manufacturing Inc. has three divisions which are operated as profit centers. Operating data for the divisions listed alphabetically are as follows.

Compute missing amounts in responsibility reports for three profit centers, and prepare a report.
(SO 6)

Operating Data	Women's Shoes	Men's Shoes	Children's Shoes
Contribution margin	$270,000	(3)	$160,000
Controllable fixed costs	100,000	(4)	(5)
Controllable margin	(1)	$ 90,000	96,000
Sales	600,000	450,000	(6)
Variable costs	(2)	310,000	250,000

Instructions

(a) Compute the missing amounts. Show computations.

(b) Prepare a responsibility report for the Women's Shoe Division assuming (1) the data are for the month ended June 30, 2002, and (2) all data equal budget except variable costs which are $10,000 over budget.

Compute ROI for current year and for possible future changes.
(SO 7)

E7-10   The Hackcraft Division of Nunez Company reported the following data for the current year.

Sales	$3,000,000
Variable costs	1,800,000
Controllable fixed costs	600,000
Average operating assets	6,000,000

Top management is unhappy with the investment center's return on investment (ROI). It asks the manager of the Hackcraft Division to submit plans to improve ROI in the next year. The manager believes it is feasible to consider the following independent courses of action.

1. Increase sales by $320,000 with no change in the contribution margin percentage.
2. Reduce variable costs by $100,000.
3. Reduce average operating assets by 5%.

Instructions

(a) Compute the return on investment (ROI) for the current year.

(b) Using the ROI formula, compute the ROI under each of the proposed courses of action. (Round to one decimal.)

Compare ROI and residual income.
(SO 8)

*E7-11   Presented below is selected information for three regional divisions of Sako Company.

	Divisions		
	West	**East**	**South**
Contribution margin	$ 200,000	$ 600,000	$ 300,000
Controllable margin	$ 140,000	$ 400,000	$ 225,000
Average operating assets	$1,000,000	$2,000,000	$1,500,000
Minimum rate of return	13%	18%	10%

Instructions

(a) Compute the return on investment for each division.

(b) Compute the residual income for each division.

(c) Assume that each division has an investment opportunity that would provide a rate of return of 19%.

(1) If ROI is used to measure performance, which division or divisions will probably make the additional investment?

(2) If residual income is used to measure performance, which division or divisions will probably make the additional investment?

Fill in information related to ROI and residual income.
(SO 8)

*E7-12   Presented below is selected financial information for two divisions of Ashahi Brewery. You are to supply the missing information.

	Lager	**Lite Lager**
Contribution margin	$600,000	$ 200,000
Controllable margin	200,000	?
Average operating assets	?	$1,000,000
Minimum rate of return	?	13%
Return on investment	20%	?
Residual income	$ 90,000	$ 200,000

PROBLEMS: SET A

P7-1A   Tick Company estimates that 360,000 direct labor hours will be worked during the coming year, 2002, in the Packaging Department. On this basis, the following budgeted manufacturing overhead cost data are computed for the year.

Prepare flexible budget and budget report for manufacturing overhead.
(SO 3)

eGrade Problem

Fixed Overhead Costs		Variable Overhead Costs	
Supervision	$ 90,000	Indirect labor	$144,000
Depreciation	60,000	Indirect materials	90,000
Insurance	27,000	Repairs	54,000
Rent	36,000	Utilities	108,000
Property taxes	18,000	Lubricants	18,000
	$231,000		$414,000

It is estimated that direct labor hours worked each month will range from 27,000 to 36,000 hours.

During October, 27,000 direct labor hours were worked and the following overhead costs were incurred.

Fixed overhead costs: Supervision $7,500, Depreciation $5,000, Insurance $2,225, Rent $3,000, and Property taxes $1,500.

Variable overhead costs: Indirect labor $11,760, Indirect materials, $6,400, Repairs $4,000, Utilities $8,550, and Lubricants $1,640.

Instructions
(a) Prepare a monthly flexible manufacturing overhead budget for each increment of 3,000 direct labor hours over the relevant range for the year ending December 31, 2002.
(b) Prepare a flexible budget report for October, when 27,500 direct labor hours were expected.
(c) ▭▬▬▬▷ Comment on management's efficiency in controlling manufacturing overhead costs in October.

P7-2A   Wahlen Company manufactures tablecloths. Sales have grown rapidly over the past 2 years. As a result, the president has installed a budgetary control system for 2002. The following data were used in developing the master manufacturing overhead budget for the Ironing Department, which is based on an activity index of direct labor hours.

Prepare flexible budget, budget report, and graph for manufacturing overhead.
(SO 3)

Variable Costs	Rate per Direct Labor Hour	Annual Fixed Costs	
Indirect labor	$0.40	Supervision	$30,000
Indirect materials	0.50	Depreciation	18,000
Factory utilities	0.30	Insurance	12,000
Factory repairs	0.20	Rent	24,000

The master overhead budget was prepared on the expectation that 480,000 direct labor hours will be worked during the year. In June, 42,000 direct labor hours were worked and 42,000 were expected. At that level of activity, actual costs were as follows.

Variable—per direct labor hour: Indirect labor $0.43, Indirect materials $0.50, Factory utilities $0.32, and Factory repairs $0.24.

Fixed: same as budgeted.

Instructions
(a) Prepare a monthly flexible manufacturing overhead budget for the year ending December 31, 2002, assuming production levels range from 35,000 to 50,000 direct labor hours. Use increments of 5,000 direct labor hours.
(b) Prepare a budget performance report for June comparing actual results with budget data based on the flexible budget.
(c) Were costs effectively controlled? Explain.

(d) State the formula for computing the total budgeted costs for Wahlen Company.
(e) Prepare the flexible budget graph, showing total budgeted costs at 35,000 and 45,000 direct labor hours. Use increments of 5,000 direct labor hours on the horizontal axis and increments of $10,000 on the vertical axis.

State total budgeted cost formula, and prepare flexible budget reports for 2 time periods.
(SO 2, 3)

P7-3A   Nigh Company uses budgets in controlling costs. The August 2002 budget report for the company's Assembling Department is as follows.

NIGH COMPANY
Budget Report
Assembling Department
For the Month Ended August 31, 2002

Manufacturing Costs	Budget	Actual	Difference Favorable F Unfavorable U
Variable costs			
Direct materials	$ 48,000	$ 47,000	$1,000 F
Direct labor	78,000	74,100	3,900 F
Indirect materials	24,000	24,200	200 U
Indirect labor	18,000	17,500	500 F
Utilities	15,000	14,900	100 F
Maintenance	9,000	9,200	200 U
Total variable	192,000	186,900	5,100 F
Fixed costs			
Rent	10,000	10,000	–0–
Supervision	17,000	17,000	–0–
Depreciation	7,000	7,000	–0–
Total fixed	34,000	34,000	–0–
Total costs	$226,000	$220,900	$5,100 F

The budget data in the report are based on the master budget for the year, which assumed that 720,000 units would be produced. The Assembling Department manager is pleased with the report and expects a raise, or at least praise for a job well done. The company president, however, is unhappy with the results for August, because only 58,000 units were produced. (*Hint:* The budget amounts above are one-twelfth of the master budget.)

Instructions
(a) State the total monthly budgeted cost formula.
(b) Prepare a budget report for August using flexible budget data. Why does this report provide a better basis for evaluating performance than the report based on static budget data? Assume 62,000 units were expected to be produced.
(c) In September, 64,000 units were produced when 65,000 were expected. Prepare the budget report using flexible budget data, assuming (1) each variable cost was 10% higher than its actual cost in August, and (2) fixed costs were the same in September as in August.

Prepare responsibility report for a profit center.
(SO 6)

P7-4A   Lococo Manufacturing Inc. operates the Patio Furniture Division as a profit center. Operating data for this division for the year ended December 31, 2002, are as follows.

	Budget	**Difference from Budget**
Sales	$2,500,000	$50,000 F
Cost of goods sold		
Variable	1,300,000	43,000 F
Controllable fixed	200,000	5,000 U
Selling and administrative		
Variable	220,000	7,000 U
Controllable fixed	50,000	2,000 U
Noncontrollable fixed costs	70,000	4,000 U

In addition, Lococo Manufacturing incurs $180,000 of indirect fixed costs that were budgeted at $175,000. Twenty percent (20%) of these costs are allocated to the Patio Furniture Division.

Instructions
(a) Prepare a responsibility report for the Patio Furniture Division for the year.
(b) ▭▬▬▭▷ Comment on the manager's performance in controlling revenues and costs.
(c) Identify any costs excluded from the responsibility report and explain why they were excluded.

P7-5A Kurian Manufacturing Company manufactures a variety of tools and industrial equipment. The company operates through three divisions. Each division is an investment center. Operating data for the Home Division for the year ended December 31, 2002, and relevant budget data are as follows.

Prepare responsibility report for an investment center, and compute ROI.
(SO 7)

	Actual	Comparison with Budget
Sales	$1,500,000	$100,000 favorable
Variable cost of goods sold	700,000	$100,000 unfavorable
Variable selling and administrative expenses	125,000	$ 25,000 unfavorable
Controllable fixed cost of goods sold	170,000	On target
Controllable fixed selling and administrative expenses	100,000	On target

Average operating assets for the year for the Home Division were $2,000,000 which was also the budgeted amount.

Instructions
(a) Prepare a responsibility report (in thousands of dollars) for the Home Division.
(b) Evaluate the manager's performance. Which items will likely be investigated by top management?
(c) Compute the expected ROI in 2003 for the Home Division, assuming the following changes.
   (1) Variable cost of goods sold is decreased by 6%.
   (2) Average operating assets are decreased by 10%.
   (3) Sales are increased by $200,000, and this increase is expected to increase contribution margin by $90,000.

P7-6A Tilg Company uses a responsibility reporting system. It has divisions in Denver, Seattle, and San Diego. Each division has three production departments: Cutting, Shaping, and Finishing. The responsibility for each department rests with a manager who reports to the division production manager. Each division manager reports to the vice president of production. There are also vice presidents for marketing and finance. All vice presidents report to the president.

In January 2002, controllable actual and budget manufacturing overhead cost data for the departments and divisions were as follows.

Prepare reports for cost centers under responsibility accounting, and comment on performance of managers.
(SO 4)

Manufacturing Overhead	Actual	Budget
Individual costs—Cutting Department—Seattle		
Indirect labor	$ 73,000	$ 70,000
Indirect materials	46,700	46,000
Maintenance	20,500	18,000
Utilities	20,100	17,000
Supervision	31,000	30,000
	$ 191,300	$ 181,000
Total costs		
Shaping Department—Seattle	$ 158,000	$ 148,000
Finishing Department—Seattle	210,000	208,000
Denver division	676,000	673,000
San Diego division	722,000	715,000
	$1,766,000	$1,744,000

Additional overhead costs were incurred as follows: Seattle division production manager—actual costs $52,500, budget $51,000; vice president of production—actual costs $65,000, budget $64,000; president—actual costs $76,400, budget $74,200. These expenses are not allocated.

The vice presidents who report to the president, other than the vice president of production, had the following expenses.

Vice president	Actual	Budget
Marketing	$133,600	$130,000
Finance	$107,000	$105,000

Instructions

(a) Using the format on page 286, prepare the following responsibility reports.
  (1) Manufacturing overhead—Cutting Department manager—Seattle division.
  (2) Manufacturing overhead—Seattle division manager.
  (3) Manufacturing overhead—vice president of production.
  (4) Manufacturing overhead and expenses—president.
(b) Comment on the comparative performances of:
  (1) Department managers in the Seattle division.
  (2) Division managers.
  (3) Vice presidents.

Compare ROI and residual income.
(SO 8)

*P7-7A Sawtell Industries has manufactured prefabricated houses for over 20 years. The houses are constructed in sections to be assembled on customers' lots. Sawtell expanded into the precut housing market when it acquired Baron Company, one of its suppliers. In this market, various types of lumber are precut into the appropriate lengths, banded into packages, and shipped to customers' lots for assembly. Sawtell designated the Baron Division as an investment center.

Sawtell uses return on investment (ROI) as a performance measure with investment defined as average operating assets. Management bonuses are based in part on ROI. All investments are expected to earn a minimum rate of return of 15%. Baron's ROI has ranged from 19.3% to 22.1% since it was acquired. Baron had an investment opportunity in 2002 that had an estimated ROI of 18%. Baron's management decided against the investment because it believed the investment would decrease the division's overall ROI.

Selected financial information for Baron are presented below. The division's average operating assets were $12,300,000 for the year 2002.

BARON DIVISION
Selected Financial Information
For the Year Ended December 31, 2002

Sales	$24,000,000
Contribution margin	8,200,000
Controllable margin	2,460,000

Instructions

(a) Calculate the following performance measures for 2002 for the Baron Division.
  (1) Return on investment (ROI).
  (2) Residual income.
(b) ▭▭▭▭▷ Would the management of Baron Division have been more likely to accept the investment opportunity it had in 2002 if residual income were used as a performance measure instead of ROI? Explain your answer.   (CMA, adapted)

PROBLEMS: SET B

Prepare flexible budget and budget report for manufacturing overhead.
(SO 3)

P7-1B Greish Company estimates that 240,000 direct labor hours will be worked during 2002 in the Assembly Department. On this basis, the following budgeted manufacturing overhead data are computed.

Variable Overhead Costs		Fixed Overhead Costs	
Indirect labor	$ 72,000	Supervision	$ 72,000
Indirect materials	48,000	Depreciation	36,000
Repairs	24,000	Insurance	9,600
Utilities	19,200	Rent	7,200
Lubricants	9,600	Property taxes	6,000
	$172,800		$130,800

It is estimated that direct labor hours worked each month will range from 18,000 to 24,000 hours.

During January, 20,000 direct labor hours were worked and the following overhead costs were incurred.

Variable Overhead Costs		Fixed Overhead Costs	
Indirect labor	$ 6,200	Supervision	$ 6,000
Indirect materials	3,600	Depreciation	3,000
Repairs	1,600	Insurance	800
Utilities	1,250	Rent	700
Lubricants	830	Property taxes	500
	$13,480		$11,000

Instructions
(a) Prepare a monthly flexible manufacturing overhead budget for each increment of 2,000 direct labor hours over the relevant range for the year ending December 31, 2002.
(b) Prepare a manufacturing overhead budget report for January, assuming 20,500 direct labor hours were expected.
(c) ✏️ Comment on management's efficiency in controlling manufacturing overhead costs in January.

P7-2B Juds Manufacturing Company produces one product, Kebo. Because of wide fluctuations in demand for Kebo, the Assembly Department experiences significant variations in monthly production levels.

Prepare flexible budget, budget report, and graph for manufacturing overhead. (SO 3)

The annual master manufacturing overhead budget is based on 300,000 direct labor hours. In July 27,500 labor hours were worked, and 27,500 hours were expected to be worked. The master manufacturing overhead budget for the year and the actual overhead costs incurred in July are as follows.

Overhead Costs	Master Budget (annual)	Actual in July
Variable		
Indirect labor	$ 360,000	$32,000
Indirect materials	210,000	17,000
Utilities	90,000	8,100
Maintenance	60,000	5,400
Fixed		
Supervision	192,000	16,000
Depreciation	120,000	10,000
Insurance and taxes	60,000	5,000
Total	$1,092,000	$93,500

Instructions
(a) Prepare a monthly flexible overhead budget for the year ending December 31, 2002, assuming monthly production levels range from 22,500 to 30,000 direct labor hours. Use increments of 2,500 direct labor hours.
(b) Prepare a budget performance report for the month of July 2002 comparing actual results with budget data based on the flexible budget.
(c) ✏️ Were costs effectively controlled? Explain.
(d) State the formula for computing the total monthly budgeted costs in Juds Company.

(e) Prepare the flexible budget graph showing total budgeted costs at 25,000 and 27,500 direct labor hours. Use increments of 5,000 on the horizontal axis and increments of $10,000 on the vertical axis.

State total budgeted cost formula, and prepare flexible budget reports for 2 time periods.
(SO 2, 3)

P7-3B Lorch Company uses budgets in controlling costs. The May 2002 budget report for the company's Packaging Department is as follows.

LORCH COMPANY
Budget Report
Packaging Department
For the Month Ended May 31, 2002

Manufacturing Costs	Budget	Actual	Difference Favorable F Unfavorable U
Variable costs			
Direct materials	$ 30,000	$ 32,000	$2,000 U
Direct labor	50,000	53,000	3,000 U
Indirect materials	15,000	15,200	200 U
Indirect labor	12,500	13,000	500 U
Utilities	7,500	7,100	400 F
Maintenance	5,000	5,200	200 U
Total variable	120,000	125,500	5,500 U
Fixed costs			
Rent	9,000	9,000	–0–
Supervision	9,000	9,000	–0–
Depreciation	5,000	5,000	–0–
Total fixed	23,000	23,000	–0–
Total costs	$143,000	$148,500	$5,500 U

The budget amounts in the report were on the master budget for the year, which assumed that 600,000 units would be produced. (*Hint:* The budget amounts above are one-twelfth of the master budget for the year.)

The company president was displeased with the department manager's performance. The department manager, who thought he had done a good job, could not understand the unfavorable results. In May, 55,000 units were produced.

Instructions
(a) State the total budgeted cost formula.
(b) Prepare a budget report for May using flexible budget data. Why does this report provide a better basis for evaluating performance than the report based on static budget data? Assume 57,000 units were expected to be produced in the Packaging Department.
(c) In June, 40,000 units were produced when 39,000 were expected. Prepare the budget report using flexible budget data, assuming (1) each variable cost was 20% less in June than its actual cost in May, and (2) fixed costs were the same in the month of June as in May.

Prepare responsibility report for a profit center.
(SO 6)

P7-4B Peters Manufacturing Inc. operates the Home Appliance Division as a profit center. Operating data for this division for the year ended December 31, 2002, are as follows.

	Budget	**Difference from Budget**
Sales	$2,400,000	$100,000 U
Cost of goods sold		
Variable	1,200,000	57,000 U
Controllable fixed	200,000	10,000 F
Selling and administrative		
Variable	240,000	8,000 F
Controllable fixed	60,000	6,000 U
Noncontrollable fixed costs	50,000	2,000 U

In addition, Peters Manufacturing incurs $150,000 of indirect fixed costs that were budgeted at $155,000. Twenty percent (20%) of these costs are allocated to the Home Appliance Division. None of these costs are controllable by the division manager.

Instructions
(a) Prepare a responsibility report for the Home Appliance Division (a profit center) for the year.
(b) ▭▬▬▶ Comment on the manager's performance in controlling revenues and costs.
(c) Identify any costs excluded from the responsibility report and explain why they were excluded.

P7-5B Ridder Manufacturing Company manufactures a variety of garden and lawn equipment. The company operates through three divisions. Each division is an investment center. Operating data for the Lawnmower Division for the year ended December 31, 2002, and relevant budget data are as follows.

Prepare responsibility report for an investment center, and compute ROI.
(SO 7)

	Actual	Comparison with Budget
Sales	$2,800,000	$200,000 unfavorable
Variable cost of goods sold	1,400,000	$150,000 unfavorable
Variable selling and administrative expenses	300,000	$ 50,000 favorable
Controllable fixed cost of goods sold	270,000	On target
Controllable fixed selling and administrative expenses	130,000	On target

Average operating assets for the year for the Lawnmower Division were $4,000,000 which was also the budgeted amount.

Instructions
(a) Prepare a responsibility report (in thousands of dollars) for the Lawnmower Division.
(b) Evaluate the manager's performance. Which items will likely be investigated by top management?
(c) Compute the expected ROI in 2003 for the Lawnmower Division, assuming the following changes.
  (1) Variable cost of goods sold is decreased by 15%.
  (2) Average operating assets are decreased by 20%.
  (3) Sales are increased by $500,000 and this increase is expected to increase contribution margin by $200,000.

◆ **BROADENING YOUR PERSPECTIVE**

GROUP DECISION CASE

BYP7-1 Green Pastures is a 400-acre farm on the outskirts of the Kentucky Bluegrass, specializing in the boarding of broodmares and their foals. A recent economic downturn in the thoroughbred industry has led to a decline in breeding activities, and it has made the boarding business extremely competitive. To meet the competition, Green Pastures planned in 2002 to entertain clients, advertise more extensively, and absorb expenses formerly paid by clients such as veterinary and blacksmith fees.

The budget report for 2002 is presented on the next page. As shown, the static income statement budget for the year is based on an expected 21,900 boarding days at $25 per mare. The variable expenses per mare per day were budgeted: Feed $5, Veterinary fees $3, Blacksmith fees $0.30, and Supplies $0.40. All other budgeted expenses were either semifixed or fixed.

During the year, management decided not to replace a worker who quit in March, but it did issue a new advertising brochure and did more entertaining of clients.[2]

GREEN PASTURES
Static Budget Income Statement
Year Ended December 31, 2002

	Actual	Master Budget	Difference
Number of mares	52	60	8*
Number of boarding days	18,980	21,900	2,920*
Sales	$379,600	$547,500	$167,900*
Less variable expenses:			
Feed	104,390	109,500	5,110
Veterinary fees	58,838	65,700	6,862
Blacksmith fees	6,074	6,570	496
Supplies	7,402	8,760	1,358
Total variable expenses	176,704	190,530	13,826
Contribution margin	202,896	356,970	154,074*
Less fixed expenses:			
Depreciation	40,000	40,000	–0–
Insurance	11,000	11,000	–0–
Utilities	12,000	14,000	2,000
Repairs and maintenance	10,000	11,000	1,000
Labor	88,000	96,000	8,000
Advertisement	12,000	8,000	4,000*
Entertainment	7,000	5,000	2,000*
Total fixed expense	180,000	185,000	5,000
Net income	$ 22,896	$171,970	$149,074*

*Unfavorable.

Instructions
With the class divided into groups, answer the following.
(a) Based on the static budget report:
  (1) What was the primary cause(s) of the loss in net income?
  (2) Did management do a good, average, or poor job of controlling expenses?
  (3) Were management's decisions to stay competitive sound?
(b) Prepare a flexible budget report for the year.
(c) Based on the flexible budget report, answer the three questions in part (a) above.
(d) What course of action do you recommend for the management of Green Pastures?

MANAGERIAL ANALYSIS

BYP7-2 Lakenvelder Dutch manufactures expensive watch cases sold as souvenirs. Three of its sales departments are: Retail Sales, Wholesale Sales, and Outlet Sales. The Retail Sales Department is a profit center. The Wholesale Sales Department is a cost center. Its managers merely take orders from customers who purchase through the company's wholesale catalog. The Outlet Sales Department is an investment center, because each manager is given full responsibility for an outlet store location. The manager can hire and discharge employees, purchase, maintain, and sell equipment, and in general is fairly independent of company control.

---

[2]Data for this case are based on Hans Sprohge and John Talbott, "New Applications for Variance Analysis," *Journal of Accountancy* (AICPA, New York), April 1989, pp. 137–141.

Rena Worthington is a manager in the Retail Sales Department. Winston Hillhouse manages the Wholesale Sales Department. Oscar Hadley manages the Golden Gate Club outlet store in San Francisco. The following are the budget responsibility reports for each of the three departments.

Budget

	Retail Sales	Wholesale Sales	Outlet Sales
Sales	$ 750,000	$ 400,000	$200,000
Variable costs			
Cost of goods sold	150,000	100,000	25,000
Advertising	100,000	30,000	5,000
Sales salaries	75,000	15,000	3,000
Printing	10,000	20,000	5,000
Travel	20,000	30,000	2,000
Fixed costs			
Rent	50,000	30,000	10,000
Insurance	5,000	2,000	1,000
Depreciation	75,000	100,000	40,000
Investment in assets	$1,000,000	$1,200,000	$800,000

Actual Results

	Retail Sales	Wholesale Sales	Outlet Sales
Sales	$ 750,000	$ 400,000	$200,000
Variable costs			
Cost of goods sold	195,000	120,000	26,250
Advertising	100,000	30,000	5,000
Sales salaries	75,000	15,000	3,000
Printing	10,000	20,000	5,000
Travel	15,000	20,000	1,500
Fixed costs			
Rent	40,000	50,000	12,000
Insurance	5,000	2,000	1,000
Depreciation	80,000	90,000	60,000
Investment in assets	$1,000,000	$1,200,000	$800,000

Instructions
(a) Determine which of the items should be included in the responsibility report for each of the three managers.
(b) Compare the budgeted measures with the actual results. Decide which results should be called to the attention of each manager.

REAL-WORLD FOCUS

BYP7-3 Computer Associates International, Inc., delivers the software that manages e-business. CA's world-class solutions address all aspects of e-business process management, information management, and infrastructure management. Founded in 1976, CA serves organizations in more than 100 countries, including 99 percent of the *Fortune* 500 companies.

Presented on the next page is information from the company's annual report.

COMPUTER ASSOCIATES INTERNATIONAL
Management Discussion

The Company has experienced a pattern of business whereby revenue for its third and fourth fiscal quarters reflects an increase over first- and second-quarter revenue. The Company attributes this increase to clients' increased spending at the end of their calendar year budgetary periods and the culmination of its annual sales plan. Since the Company's costs do not increase proportionately with the third- and fourth-quarters' increase in revenue, the higher revenue in these quarters results in greater profit margins and income. Fourth-quarter profitability is traditionally affected by significant new hirings, training, and education expenditures for the succeeding year.

Instructions
(a) Why don't the company's costs increase proportionately as the revenues increase in the third and fourth quarters?
(b) What type of budgeting seems appropriate for the Computer Associates situation?

*E*XPLORING THE *W*EB

BYP7-4 Genelle and Doug have recorded the story of their wedding planning. They are on a strict budget and need help in preparing what they call "a somewhat flexible budget."

Address: **www.wednet.com/inspire/wedstory/story1.htm**
(or go to www.wiley.com/college/weygandt)

Steps:

1. Go to Genelle and Doug's Web site, and read about their trials and tribulations in planning a wedding.
2. Review the **Planning and Budgeting** section in "Part 1" of their story. They mention that this is a "somewhat flexible budget" for 250 guests, totalling $7,150. They would like to reduce their total costs to $7,000, if at all possible.

Instructions
Recast Genelle and Doug's budget into a truly flexible budget so that they can see the effects on their total costs of reducing the number of invited guests to 225 or 200.

*C*OMMUNICATION *A*CTIVITY

BYP7-5 The manufacturing overhead budget for Carthage Corporation contains the following items.

Variable factory expenses		Fixed factory expenses	
Indirect materials	$ 75,000	Supervision	$ 51,000
Indirect labor	36,000	Inspection costs	3,000
Maintenance expenses	30,000	Insurance expenses	6,000
Manufacturing supplies	18,000	Depreciation	45,000
Total variable	$159,000	Total fixed	$105,000

The budget was based on an estimated 6,000 units being produced. During the past month, 4,500 units were produced, and the following costs incurred.

Variable factory expenses		Fixed factory expenses	
Indirect materials	$75,600	Supervision	$57,900
Indirect labor	40,500	Inspection costs	3,600
Maintenance expenses	24,600	Insurance expenses	6,600
Manufacturing supplies	15,300	Depreciation	44,100
Total variable	$156,000	Total fixed	$112,200

Instructions
(a) Determine which items would be controllable by B. Sherrick, the production manager.
(b) How much should have been spent to manufacture 4,500 units?
(c) Prepare a flexible manufacturing overhead budget report for Ms. Sherrick.
(d) Prepare a responsibility report. Include only the costs that would have been controllable by Ms. Sherrick. In an attached memo, describe clearly for Ms. Sherrick the areas in which her performance needs to be improved.

RESEARCH ASSIGNMENT

BYP7-6   The February 2000 issue of the *Journal of Accountancy* contains an article by Russ Banham entitled "Better Budgets."

Instructions
Read the article and answer the following questions.
(a) Why have some companies decided not to do major overhauls of their budgeting systems after some initial investigations into the possibility? What percentage of companies that attempt overhauls give up before finishing?
(b) What is the "new planning paradigm"?
(c) What does the author argue is the "final link" necessary for successful budgeting and planning?

ETHICS CASE

BYP7-7   In order to meet competition and achieve its profit goals, NP Corporation has chosen the decentralized form of organization. Each manager of a decentralized investment center is measured on the basis of profit contribution, market penetration, and return on investment. Failure to meet the objectives established by corporate management for these measures has not been acceptable and usually has resulted in demotion or dismissal of an investment center manager.

An anonymous survey of managers in the company revealed that the managers feel the pressure to compromise their personal ethical standards to achieve the corporate objectives. For example, at certain plant locations there was pressure to reduce quality control to a level which could not assure that all unsafe products would be rejected. Also, sales personnel were encouraged to use questionable sales tactics, including gifts and other incentives to purchasing agents, to obtain orders.

The chief executive officer is disturbed by the survey findings. In his opinion such behavior cannot be condoned by the company.

Instructions
(a) Who are the stakeholders (the affected parties) in the situation?
(b) Identify the ethical implications, conflicts, or dilemmas in the above situation.
(c) What might the company do to reduce the pressures on managers and decrease the ethical conflicts?   (CMA adapted)

Answers to Self-Study Questions
1. c   2. b   3. a   4. d   5. a   6. d   7. d   8. b   9. b
10. d   *11. c

Remember to go back to the Navigator box on the chapter-opening page and check off your completed work.

CHAPTER 8

Performance Evaluation Through Standard Costs

THE NAVIGATOR ✔

- Scan *Study Objectives* ☐
- Read *Feature Story* ☐
- Read *Preview* ☐
- Read text and answer *Before You Go On*
  p. 327 ☐ p. 332 ☐ p. 341 ☐
- Work *Using the Decision Toolkit* ☐
- Review *Summary of Study Objectives* ☐
- Work *Demonstration Problem* ☐
- Answer *Self-Study Questions* ☐
- Complete *Assignments* ☐

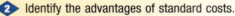

STUDY OBJECTIVES

After studying this chapter, you should be able to:

1. Distinguish between a standard and a budget.

2. Identify the advantages of standard costs.

3. Describe how standards are set.

4. State the formulas for determining direct materials and direct labor variances.

5. State the formulas for determining manufacturing overhead variances.

6. Discuss the reporting of variances.

7. Prepare an income statement for management under a standard costing system.

THE NAVIGATOR

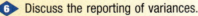
FEATURE STORY

HIGHLIGHTING PERFORMANCE EFFICIENCY

There's a very good chance that the highlighter you're holding in your hand was made by **Sanford**, a maker of permanent markers and other writing instruments. Sanford, headquartered in Illinois, annually sells hundreds of millions of dollars' worth of ACCENT highlighters, fine-point pens, Sharpie permanent markers, Expo dry-erase markers for overhead projectors, and other writing instruments.

Since Sanford makes literally billions of writing utensils per year, the company must keep tight control over manufacturing costs. A very important part of Sanford's manufacturing process is determining how much direct materials, labor, and overhead should cost. These costs are then compared to actual costs to assess performance efficiency. Raw materials for Sanford's markers include a barrel, plug, cap, ink reservoir, and a nib (tip). These parts are assembled by machine to produce thousands of units per hour. A major component of manufacturing overhead is machine maintenance—some fixed, some variable.

"Labor costs are associated with material handling and equipment maintenance functions. Although the assembly process is highly automated, labor is still required to move raw materials to the machine and to package the finished product. In addition, highly skilled technicians are required to service and maintain each piece of equipment," says Mike Orr, vice president, operations.

Labor rates are predictable because the hourly workers are covered by a union contract. The story is the same with the fringe benefits and some supervisory salaries. Even volume levels are fairly predictable—demand for the product is high—so fixed overhead is efficiently absorbed. Raw material standard costs are based on the previous year's actual prices plus any anticipated inflation. Lately, though, inflation has been so low that the company is considering any price increase in raw material to be unfavorable because its standards will remain unchanged.

www.sanfordcorp.com

Standards are a fact of life. You met the admission standards for the school you are attending. The vehicle that you drive had to meet certain governmental emissions standards. The hamburgers and salads you eat in a restaurant have to meet certain health and nutritional standards before they can be sold. And, as described in our Feature Story, **Sanford Corp.** develops standards for the costs of its materials, labor, and overhead which it compares with its actual costs. The reason for standards in these cases is very simple: They help to ensure that overall product quality is high. Without standards, quality control is lost.

In this chapter we continue the study of controlling costs. You will learn how to develop standard costs that permit the evaluation of performance.

The content and organization of Chapter 8 are as follows.

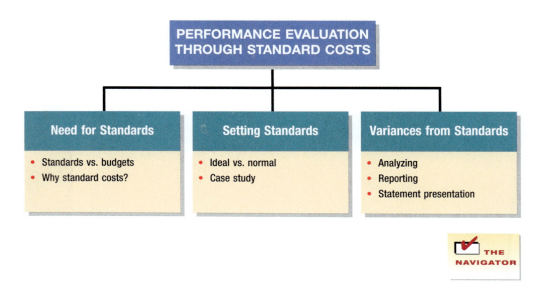

THE NEED FOR STANDARDS

Standards are common in business. Those imposed by government agencies are often called **regulations**. They include the Fair Labor Standards Act, the Equal Employment Opportunity Act, and a multitude of environmental standards. Standards established internally by a company may extend to personnel matters, such as employee absenteeism and ethical codes of conduct, quality control standards for products, and standard costs for goods and services. In managerial accounting, **standard costs** are predetermined unit costs, which are used as measures of performance.

We will focus on manufacturing operations in the remainder of this chapter. But you should also recognize that standard costs also apply to many types of service businesses as well. For example, a fast-food restaurant such as **McDonald's** knows the price it should pay for pickles, beef, buns, and other ingredients. It also knows how much time it should take an employee to flip hamburgers. If too much is paid for pickles or too much time is taken to prepare Big Macs, the deviations are noticed and corrective action is taken. Standard costs also may be used in not-for-profit enterprises such as universities, charitable organizations, and governmental agencies.

DISTINGUISHING BETWEEN STANDARDS AND BUDGETS

In concept, **standards** and **budgets** are essentially the same. Both are predetermined costs, and both contribute to management planning and control. There is a difference, however, in the way the terms are expressed. A standard is a **unit** amount. A budget is a **total** amount. Thus, it is customary to state that the standard cost of direct labor for a unit of product is $10. If 5,000 units of the product are produced, the $50,000 of direct labor is the **budgeted** labor cost. A standard is the budgeted cost per unit of product. A standard is therefore concerned with each individual cost component that makes up the entire budget.

There are important accounting differences between budgets and standards. Except in the application of manufacturing overhead to jobs and processes, budget data are not journalized in cost accounting systems. In contrast, as will be illustrated in the appendix to this chapter, standard costs may be incorporated into cost accounting systems. Also, a company may report its inventories at standard cost in its financial statements, but it would not report inventories at budgeted costs.

STUDY OBJECTIVE
1
Distinguish between a standard and a budget.

WHY STANDARD COSTS?

Standard costs offer a number of advantages to an organization, as shown in Illustration 8-1. These advantages will be realized only when standard costs are carefully established and prudently used. Using standards solely as a means of placing blame can have a negative effect on managers and employees. In an effort to minimize this effect, many companies offer wage incentives to those who meet their standards.

STUDY OBJECTIVE
2
Identify the advantages of standard costs.

Illustration 8-1 Advantages of standard costs

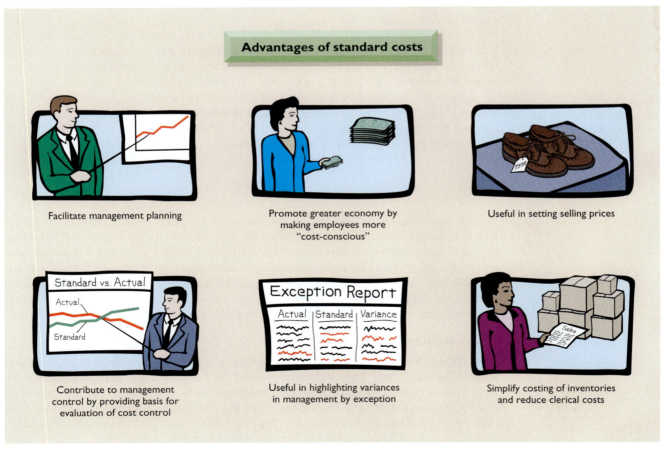

Advantages of standard costs

Facilitate management planning

Promote greater economy by making employees more "cost-conscious"

Useful in setting selling prices

Contribute to management control by providing basis for evaluation of cost control

Useful in highlighting variances in management by exception

Simplify costing of inventories and reduce clerical costs

SETTING STANDARD COSTS—
A DIFFICULT TASK

The setting of standard costs to produce a unit of product is a difficult task. It requires input from all persons who have responsibility for costs and quantities. To determine the standard cost of direct materials, management may have to consult purchasing agents, product managers, quality control engineers, and production supervisors. In setting the cost standard for direct labor, pay rate data are obtained from the payroll department, and the labor time requirements may be determined by industrial engineers. The managerial accountant provides important input to management into the standards-setting process by accumulating historical cost data and by knowing how costs respond to changes in activity levels.

To be effective in controlling costs, standard costs need to be current at all times. Thus, standards should be under continuous review. They should be changed whenever it is determined that the existing standard is not a good measure of performance. Circumstances that may warrant revision of a standard include changed wage rates resulting from a new union contract, a change in product specifications, or the implementation of a new manufacturing method.

IDEAL VERSUS NORMAL STANDARDS

Standards may be set at one of two levels: ideal or normal. **Ideal standards** represent optimum levels of performance under perfect operating conditions. **Normal standards** represent efficient levels of performance that are attainable under expected operating conditions.

Some managers believe ideal standards will stimulate workers to ever-increasing improvement. However, most managers believe that ideal standards lower the morale of the entire workforce because they are so difficult, if not impossible, to meet. Very few companies use ideal standards.

Most companies that use standards set them at a normal level. Properly set, normal standards should be **rigorous but attainable**. Normal standards allow for rest periods, machine breakdowns, and other "normal" contingencies in the production process. It will be assumed in the remainder of this chapter that standard costs are set at a normal level.

Helpful Hint When standards are set too high, employees sometimes feel pressure to consider unethical practices to meet these standards.

A CASE STUDY

To establish the standard cost of producing a product, it is necessary to establish standards for each manufacturing cost element—direct materials, direct labor, and manufacturing overhead. The standard for each element is derived from the standard price to be paid and the standard quantity to be used. To illustrate, we will look at a case study of how standard costs are set. In this extended example, we will assume that Xonic, Inc. wishes to use standard costs to measure performance in filling an order for 1,000 gallons of Weed-O, a liquid weed killer.

Direct Materials

The **direct materials price standard** is the cost per unit of direct materials that should be incurred. This standard should be based on the purchasing department's best estimate of the **cost of raw materials**. This is frequently based on current purchase prices. The price standard should also include an amount for related costs such as receiving, storing, and handling. The materials price standard per pound of material for Xonic's weed killer is:

Illustration 8-2   Setting direct materials price standard

Item	Price
Purchase price, net of discounts	$2.70
Freight	0.20
Receiving and handling	0.10
Standard direct materials price per pound	**$3.00**

The **direct materials quantity standard** is the quantity of direct materials that should be used per unit of finished goods. This standard is expressed as a physical measure, such as pounds, barrels, or board feet. In setting the standard, management should consider both the quality and quantity of materials required to manufacture the product. The standard should include allowances for unavoidable waste and normal spoilage. The standard quantity per unit for Xonic, Inc. is as follows.

Illustration 8-3   Setting direct materials quantity standard

Item	Quantity (Pounds)
Required materials	3.5
Allowance for waste	0.4
Allowance for spoilage	0.1
Standard direct materials quantity per unit	**4.0**

The standard direct materials cost per unit is the standard direct materials price times the standard direct materials quantity. For Xonic, Inc., the standard direct materials cost per gallon of Weed-O is $12.00 ($3.00 × 4.0 pounds).

Direct Labor

The **direct labor price standard** is the rate per hour that should be incurred for direct labor. This standard is based on current wage rates, adjusted for anticipated changes such as cost of living adjustments (COLAs). The price standard also generally includes employer payroll taxes and fringe benefits, such as paid holidays and vacations. For Xonic, Inc., the direct labor price standard is as follows.

Alternative Terminology The direct labor price standard is also called the *direct labor rate standard.*

Illustration 8-4   Setting direct labor price standard

Item	Price
Hourly wage rate	$ 7.50
COLA	0.25
Payroll taxes	0.75
Fringe benefits	1.50
Standard direct labor rate per hour	**$10.00**

The **direct labor quantity standard** is the time that should be required to make one unit of the product. This standard is especially critical in labor-intensive companies. Allowances should be made in this standard for rest periods, cleanup, machine setup, and machine downtime. For Xonic, Inc., the direct labor quantity standard is as follows.

Alternative Terminology The direct labor quantity standard is also called the *direct labor efficiency standard.*

Illustration 8-5 Setting direct labor quantity standard

Item	Quantity (Hours)
Actual production time	1.5
Rest periods and cleanup	0.2
Setup and downtime	0.3
Standard direct labor hours per unit	**2.0**

The standard direct labor cost per unit is the standard direct labor rate times the standard direct labor hours. For Xonic, Inc., the standard direct labor cost per gallon of Weed-O is $20 ($10.00 × 2.0 hours).

Manufacturing Overhead

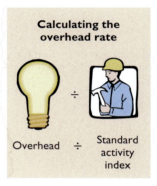

Calculating the overhead rate

Overhead ÷ Standard activity index

For manufacturing overhead, a **standard predetermined overhead rate** is used in setting the standard. This overhead rate is determined by dividing budgeted overhead costs by an expected standard activity index. For example, the index may be standard direct labor hours or standard machine hours.

As discussed in Chapter 4, many companies employ activity-based costing (ABC) to allocate overhead costs. Because ABC uses multiple activity indices to allocate overhead costs, it results in a better correlation between activities and costs incurred. As a result, the use of ABC can significantly improve the usefulness of a standard costing system for management decision making.

Xonic, Inc. uses standard direct labor hours as the activity index. The company expects to produce 13,200 gallons of Weed-O during the year at normal capacity. Since it takes 2 direct labor hours for each gallon, total standard direct labor hours are 26,400 (13,200 × 2). At this level of activity, overhead costs are expected to be $132,000. Of that amount, $79,200 are variable and $52,800 are fixed. The standard predetermined overhead rates are computed as shown in Illustration 8-6.

Illustration 8-6 Computing predetermined overhead rates

Budgeted Overhead Costs	Amount	÷ Standard Direct Labor Hours	= Overhead Rate per Direct Labor Hour
Variable	$ 79,200	26,400	**$3.00**
Fixed	52,800	26,400	**2.00**
Total	$132,000	26,400	**$5.00**

The standard manufacturing overhead rate per unit is the predetermined overhead rate times the activity index quantity standard. For Xonic, Inc., which uses direct labor hours as its activity index, the standard manufacturing overhead rate per gallon of Weed-O is $10 ($5 × 2 hours).

Total Standard Cost per Unit

Now that the standard quantity and price have been established per unit of product, the total standard cost can be determined. The total standard cost per unit is the sum of the standard costs of direct materials, direct labor, and manufacturing overhead. For Xonic, Inc., the total standard cost per gallon of Weed-O is $42, as shown on the following standard cost card.

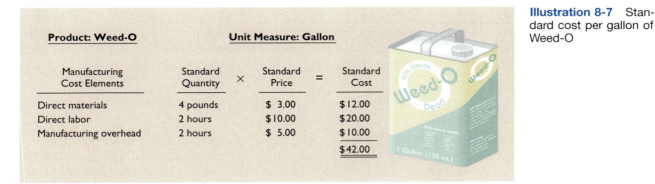

Product: Weed-O		Unit Measure: Gallon		
Manufacturing Cost Elements	Standard Quantity	× Standard Price	=	Standard Cost
Direct materials	4 pounds	$ 3.00		$12.00
Direct labor	2 hours	$10.00		$20.00
Manufacturing overhead	2 hours	$ 5.00		$10.00
				$42.00

Illustration 8-7 Standard cost per gallon of Weed-O

A standard cost card is prepared for each product. This card provides the basis for determining variances from standards.

BUSINESS INSIGHT
Management Perspective

Setting standards can be difficult. Consider **Susan's Chili Factory**, which manufactures and sells chili. The cost of manufacturing Susan's chili consists of the costs of raw materials, labor to convert the basic ingredients to chili, and overhead. We will use materials cost as an example. Three standards need to be developed: (1) What should be the formula (mix) of ingredients for one gallon of chili? (2) What should be the normal wastage (or shrinkage) for the individual ingredients? (3) What should be the standard cost for the individual ingredients that go into the chili?

Susan's Chili Factory also illustrates how standard costs can be used by management in controlling costs. Suppose that summer droughts have reduced crop yields. As a result, prices have doubled for beans, onions, and peppers. In this case, actual costs will be significantly higher than standard costs, which will cause management to evaluate the situation. Management might decide to increase the price charged for a gallon of chili. It might reexamine the product mix to see if other types of ingredients can be used. Or it might curtail production until ingredients can be purchased at or near standard costs. Similarly, assume that poor maintenance caused the onion-dicing blades to become dull. As a result, usage of onions to make a gallon of chili tripled. Because this deviation is quickly highlighted through standard costs, corrective action can be promptly taken.

Source: Adapted from David R. Beran, "Cost Reduction Through Control Reporting," *Management Accounting,* April 1982, pp. 29–33.

BEFORE YOU GO ON . . .

◆ Review It

1. How do standards differ from budgets?
2. What are the advantages of standard costs to an organization?
3. Distinguish between normal standards and ideal standards. Which standard is more widely used? Why?

◆ Do It

The management of Arapahoe Company has decided to use standard costs. Management asks you to explain the components used in setting the standard cost per unit for direct materials, direct labor, and manufacturing overhead.

Action Plan
- Differentiate between the two components of each standard: price and quantity.

Solution: The standard direct materials cost per unit is the standard direct materials price times the standard direct materials quantity. The standard direct labor cost per unit is the standard direct labor rate times the standard direct labor hours. The standard manufacturing overhead rate per unit is the standard predetermined overhead rate times the activity index quantity standard.

Related exercise material: BE8-2, BE8-3, and E8-1.

VARIANCES FROM STANDARDS

Alternative Terminology In business, the term *variance* is also used to indicate differences between total budgeted and total actual costs.

One of the major management uses of standard costs is to identify variances from standards. **Variances** are the differences between total actual costs and total standard costs. To illustrate, we will assume that in producing 1,000 gallons of Weed-O in the month of June, Xonic, Inc. incurred the following costs.

Illustration 8-8 Actual production costs

Direct materials	$13,020
Direct labor	20,580
Variable overhead	6,500
Fixed overhead	4,400
Total actual costs	$44,500

Total standard costs are determined by multiplying the units produced by the standard cost per unit. The total standard cost of Weed-O is $42,000 (1,000 gallons × $42). Thus, the total variance is $2,500, as shown below.

Illustration 8-9 Computation of total variance

Actual costs	$44,500
Standard costs	42,000
Total variance	**$ 2,500**

Note that the variance is expressed in total dollars and not on a per unit basis.

When actual costs exceed standard costs, the variance is **unfavorable**. The $2,500 variance in June for Weed-O is unfavorable. An unfavorable variance has a negative connotation. It suggests that too much was paid for one or more of the manufacturing cost elements or that the elements were used inefficiently.

If actual costs are less than standard costs, the variance is **favorable**. A favorable variance has a positive connotation. It suggests efficiencies in incurring manufacturing costs and in using direct materials, direct labor, and manufacturing overhead. However, be careful: A favorable variance could be obtained by using inferior materials. In printing wedding invitations, for example, a favorable variance could result from using an inferior grade of paper. Or, a favorable variance might be achieved in installing tires on an automobile assembly line by tightening only half of the lug bolts. The point should be obvious: A variance is not favorable if quality control standards have been sacrificed.

ANALYZING VARIANCES

To interpret properly the significance of a variance, you must analyze it to determine the underlying factors. Analyzing variances begins by determining the cost elements that comprise the variance. **For each manufacturing cost element, a total dollar variance is computed. Then this variance is analyzed into a price variance and a quantity variance.** The relationships are shown graphically as follows.

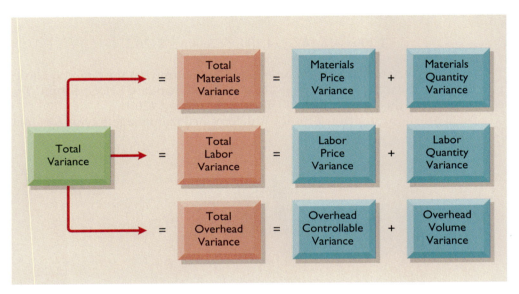

Illustration 8-10 Variance relationships

Each of the variances is explained below.

Direct Materials Variances

In completing the order for 1,000 gallons of Weed-O, Xonic used 4,200 pounds of direct materials. These were purchased at a cost of $3.10 per unit. The **total materials variance** is computed from the following formula.

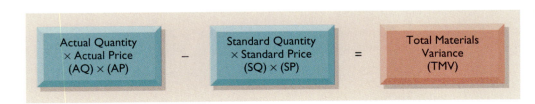

Illustration 8-11 Formula for total materials variance

For Xonic, Inc., the total materials variance is $1,020 ($13,020 − $12,000) unfavorable as shown below.

$$(4{,}200 \times \$3.10) - (4{,}000 \times \$3.00) = \$1{,}020 \ \text{U}$$

Next, the total variance is analyzed to determine the amount attributable to price (costs) and to quantity (use). The **materials price variance** is computed from the following formula.[1]

Illustration 8-12 Formula for materials price variance

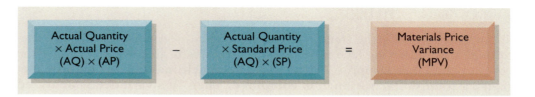

For Xonic, Inc., the materials price variance is $420 ($13,020 − $12,600) unfavorable as shown below.

$$(4,200 \times \$3.10) - (4,200 \times \$3.00) = \$420 \text{ U}$$

Helpful Hint The alternative formula is:

$$\boxed{AQ} \times \boxed{AP - SP} = \boxed{MPV}$$

The price variance can also be computed by multiplying the actual quantity purchased by the difference between the actual and standard price per unit. The computation in this case is $4,200 \times (\$3.10 - \$3.00) = \$420$ U.

The **materials quantity variance** is determined from the following formula.

Illustration 8-13 Formula for materials quantity variance

For Xonic, Inc., the materials quantity variance is $600 ($12,600 − $12,000) unfavorable, as shown below.

$$(4,200 \times \$3.00) - (4,000 \times \$3.00) = \$600 \text{ U}$$

Helpful Hint The alternative formula is:

$$\boxed{SP} \times \boxed{AQ - SQ} = \boxed{MQV}$$

This variance can also be computed by applying the standard price to the difference between actual and standard quantities used. The computation in this example is $3.00 \times (4,200 - 4,000) = \$600$ U.

The total materials variance of $1,020(U), therefore, consists of the following.

Illustration 8-14 Summary of materials variances

Materials price variance	$ 420 U
Materials quantity variance	600 U
Total materials variance	**$1,020 U**

A matrix is sometimes used to analyze a variance. **When the matrix is used, the formulas for each cost element are computed first and then the vari-**

---

[1]We will assume that all materials purchased during the period are used in production and that no units remain in inventory at the end of the period.

ances. The completed matrix for the direct materials variance for Xonic, Inc. is shown in Illustration 8-15. The matrix provides a convenient structure for determining each variance.

Illustration 8-15 Matrix for direct materials variances

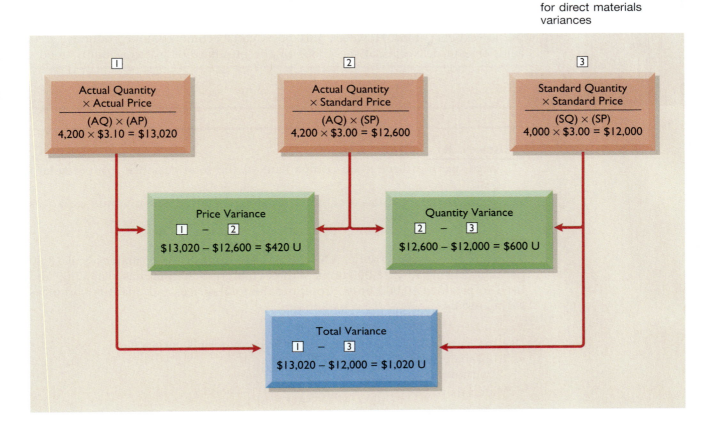

Causes of Materials Variances. What are the causes of a variance? The causes may relate to both internal and external factors. **The investigation of a materials price variance usually begins in the purchasing department.** Many factors affect the price paid for raw materials. These include the delivery method used, availability of quantity and cash discounts, and the quality of the materials requested. To the extent that these factors have been considered in setting the price standard, the purchasing department should be responsible for any variances.

However, a variance may be beyond the control of the purchasing department. Sometimes, for example, prices may rise faster than expected. Moreover, actions by groups over which the company has no control, such as the OPEC nations' oil price increases, may cause an unfavorable variance. There are also times when a production department may be responsible for the price variance. This may occur when a rush order forces the company to pay a higher price for the materials.

The starting point for determining the cause(s) of an unfavorable **materials quantity variance** is in the **production department**. If the variances are due to inexperienced workers, faulty machinery, or carelessness, the production department would be responsible. However, if the materials obtained by the purchasing department were of inferior quality, then the purchasing department should be responsible.

"What caused materials price variances?"

Purchasing Dept.

"What caused materials quantity variances?"

Production Dept.

BUSINESS INSIGHT

Management Perspective

If purchase price variances are used as a basis for measuring performance, purchasing departments often will continually search for the lowest-cost item. However, this basis can become counterproductive if it leads to late deliveries of the goods or the purchase of inferior-quality goods.

BEFORE YOU GO ON . . .

◆ Review It

1. What are the three main components of the total variance from standard cost?
2. What are the formulas for computing the total, price, and quantity variances for direct materials?

◆ Do It

The standard cost of Product XX includes two units of direct materials at $8.00 per unit. During July, 22,000 units of direct materials are purchased at $7.50 and used to produce 10,000 units. Compute the total, price, and quantity variances for materials.

Action Plan

Use the formulas for computing each of the materials variances:

- Total materials variance $= (AQ \times AP) - (SQ \times SP)$
- Materials price variance $= (AQ \times AP) - (AQ \times SP)$
- Materials quantity variance $= (AQ \times SP) - (SQ \times SP)$

Solution: Substituting amounts into the formulas, the variances are:

Total materials variance $= (22{,}000 \times \$7.50) - (20{,}000 \times \$8.00) = \$5{,}000$ unfavorable.

Materials price variance $= (22{,}000 \times \$7.50) - (22{,}000 \times \$8.00) = \$11{,}000$ favorable.

Materials quantity variance $= (22{,}000 \times \$8.00) - (20{,}000 \times \$8.00) = \$16{,}000$ unfavorable.

Related exercise material: BE8-4, BE8-5, BE8-6, BE8-7, BE8-8, E8-2, E8-3, E8-4, E8-6, E8-7, E8-8, E8-9, and E8-12.

DECISION TOOLKIT

Decision Checkpoints	Info Needed for Decision	Tool to Use for Decision	How to Evaluate Results
Has management accomplished its price and quantity objectives regarding materials?	Actual cost and standard cost of materials	Materials price and materials quantity variances	Positive (favorable) variances suggest that price and quantity objectives have been met.

Direct Labor Variances

The process of determining direct labor variances is the same as for determining the direct materials variances. In completing the Weed-O order, Xonic, Inc. incurred 2,100 direct labor hours at an average hourly rate of $9.80. The standard hours allowed for the units produced were 2,000 hours (1,000 units × 2 hours). The standard labor rate was $10 per hour. The **total labor variance** is obtained from the following formula.

Illustration 8-16 Formula for total labor variance

The total labor variance is $580 ($20,580 − $20,000) unfavorable, as shown below.

$$(2{,}100 \times \$9.80) - (2{,}000 \times \$10.00) = \$580 \text{ U}$$

The formula for the **labor price variance** is:

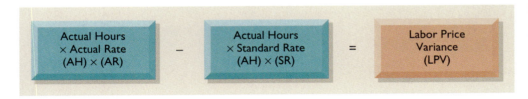

Illustration 8-17 Formula for labor price variance

For Xonic, Inc., the labor price variance is $420 ($20,580 − $21,000) favorable as shown below.

$$(2{,}100 \times \$9.80) - (2{,}100 \times \$10.00) = \$420 \text{ F}$$

This variance can also be computed by multiplying actual hours worked by the difference between the actual pay rate and the standard pay rate. The computation in this example is 2,100 × ($10.00 − $9.80) = $420 F.

The **labor quantity variance** is derived from the following formula.

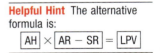

Helpful Hint The alternative formula is:

$$AH \times \boxed{AR - SR} = \boxed{LPV}$$

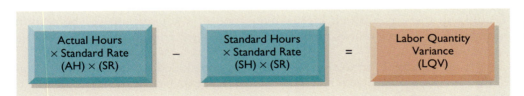

Illustration 8-18 Formula for labor quantity variance

For Xonic, Inc., the labor quantity variance is $1,000 ($21,000 − $20,000) unfavorable:

$$(2{,}100 \times \$10.00) - (2{,}000 \times \$10.00) = \$1{,}000 \text{ U}$$

The same result can be obtained by multiplying the standard rate by the difference between actual hours worked and standard hours allowed. In this case the computation is $10.00 × (2,100 − 2,000) = $1,000 U.

Helpful Hint The alternative formula is:

$$SR \times \boxed{AH - SH} = \boxed{LQV}$$

The total direct labor variance of $580 U, therefore, consists of:

Illustration 8-19 Summary of labor variances

Labor price variance	$ 420 F
Labor quantity variance	1,000 U
Total direct labor variance	**$ 580 U**

These results can also be obtained from the matrix in Illustration 8-20.

Illustration 8-20 Matrix for direct labor variances

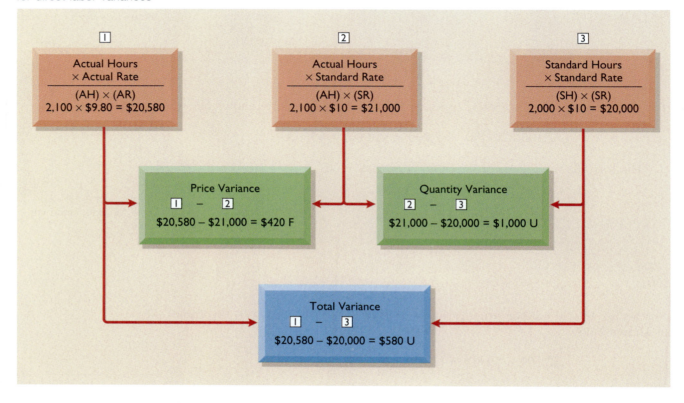

Causes of Labor Variances. **Labor price variances** usually result from two factors: (1) paying workers **higher wages than expected**, and (2) **misallocation of workers**. In companies where pay rates are determined by union contracts, labor price variances should be infrequent. When workers are not unionized, there is a much higher likelihood of such variances. The responsibility for these variances rests with the manager who authorized the wage increase.

"What caused labor price variances?"

Personnel decisions

Misallocation of the workforce refers to using skilled workers in place of unskilled workers and vice versa. The use of an inexperienced worker instead of an experienced one will result in a favorable price variance because of the lower pay rate of the unskilled worker. An unfavorable price variance would result if a skilled worker were substituted for an inexperienced one. The production department generally is responsible for labor price variances resulting from misallocation of the workforce.

Labor quantity variances relate to the **efficiency of workers**. The cause of a quantity variance generally can be traced to the production department. The causes of an unfavorable variance may be poor training, worker fatigue, faulty machinery, or carelessness. These causes are the responsibility of the **production department**. However, if the excess time is due to inferior materials, the responsibility falls outside the production department.

"What caused labor quantity variances?"

Production Dept.

Service Company Perspective

At **United Parcel Service (UPS)** performance standards are set by industrial engineers for many tasks performed by UPS employees. For example, a UPS driver is expected to walk at a pace of three feet per second when going to a customer's door and knock rather than take the time to look for a doorbell. UPS executives attribute the company's success to its ability to manage and hold labor accountable.

Manufacturing Overhead Variances

The computation of the manufacturing overhead variances is conceptually the same as the computation of the materials and labor variances. However, the task is more challenging for manufacturing overhead because both variable and fixed overhead costs must be considered.

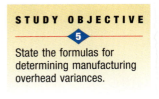

STUDY OBJECTIVE

5

State the formulas for determining manufacturing overhead variances.

Total Overhead Variance.   The **total overhead variance** is the difference between actual overhead costs and overhead costs applied to work done. As indicated earlier, manufacturing overhead costs incurred by Xonic were $10,900, as follows.

Variable overhead	$ 6,500
Fixed overhead	4,400
Total actual overhead	**$10,900**

Illustration 8-21   Actual overhead costs

With standard costs, manufacturing overhead costs are applied to work in process on the basis of the **standard hours allowed** for the work done. **Standard hours allowed** are the hours that should have been worked for the units produced. For the Weed-O order, the standard hours allowed are 2,000. The predetermined overhead rate is $5 per direct labor hour. Thus, overhead applied is $10,000 (2,000 × $5). Note that actual hours of direct labor (2,100) are not used in applying manufacturing overhead.

The formula for the total overhead variance is:

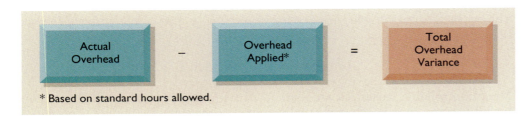

$$\boxed{\text{Actual Overhead}} - \boxed{\text{Overhead Applied*}} = \boxed{\text{Total Overhead Variance}}$$

* Based on standard hours allowed.

Illustration 8-22   Formula for total overhead variance

Thus, for Xonic, Inc., the total overhead variance is $900 unfavorable as shown below.

$$\$10,900 - \$10,000 = \$900 \text{ U}$$

The overhead variance is generally analyzed through a price variance and a quantity variance. The name usually given to the price variance is the **overhead controllable variance**, whereas the quantity variance is referred to as the **overhead volume variance**.

Overhead Controllable Variance. The **overhead controllable variance** shows whether overhead costs were effectively controlled. To compute this variance, actual overhead costs incurred are compared with budgeted costs for the **standard hours allowed**. The budgeted costs are determined from the flexible manufacturing overhead budget. The budget for Xonic, Inc. is as follows.

Illustration 8-23 Flexible budget using standard direct labor hours

XONIC, INC.				
Flexible Manufacturing Overhead Budget				
Activity Index				
Standard direct labor hours	1,800	**2,000**	2,200	2,400
Costs				
Variable costs				
Indirect materials	$1,800	**$ 2,000**	$ 2,200	$ 2,400
Indirect labor	2,700	**3,000**	3,300	3,600
Utilities	900	**1,000**	1,100	1,200
Total variable	5,400	**6,000**	6,600	7,200
Fixed costs				
Supervision	3,000	**3,000**	3,000	3,000
Depreciation	1,400	**1,400**	1,400	1,400
Total fixed	4,400	**4,400**	4,400	4,400
Total costs	$9,800	**$10,400**	$11,000	$11,600

As shown, the budgeted costs for 2,000 standard hours are $10,400 ($6,000 variable and $4,400 fixed).[2]

The formula for the overhead controllable variance is:

Illustration 8-24 Formula for overhead controllable variance

* Based on standard hours allowed.

The overhead controllable variance for Xonic, Inc. is $500 unfavorable as shown below.

$$\$10,900 - \$10,400 = \$500 \text{ U}$$

Most controllable variances are associated with variable costs, which are controllable costs. Fixed costs are usually known at the time the budget is prepared. At Xonic, Inc., the variance is accounted for by comparing the actual variable overhead costs ($6,500) with the budgeted variable costs ($6,000).

Management can compare actual and budgeted overhead for each manufacturing overhead cost that contributes to the controllable variance. In addition, cost and quantity variances can be developed for each overhead cost, such as indirect materials and indirect labor.

---

[2]The flexible budget formula is: fixed costs $4,400 plus variable costs $3 per hour. Thus, total budgeted costs are $4,400 + ($3 × 2,000), or $10,400.

Overhead Volume Variance. The overhead volume variance indicates whether plant facilities were efficiently used. The formula for computing the volume variance is as follows.

* Based on standard hours allowed.

Illustration 8-25 Formula for overhead volume variance

Both the factors in this formula have been explained above. The overhead budgeted is the same as the amount used in computing the controllable variance, or $10,400 in our example. Overhead applied of $10,000 is the amount used in determining the total overhead variance. For Xonic Inc. the overhead volume variance is $400 unfavorable as shown below.

$$\$10,400 - \$10,000 = \$400 \ U$$

We can analyze the volume variance in even more detail. As shown in the flexible manufacturing overhead budget, the budgeted overhead of $10,400 consists of $6,000 variable and $4,400 fixed. As shown in Illustration 8-6 (page 326), the predetermined overhead rate of $5 consists of $3 variable and $2 fixed. The detailed analysis, therefore, is:

Illustration 8-26 Detailed analysis of overhead volume variance

Overhead budgeted		
Variable costs	$6,000	
Fixed costs	**4,400**	$10,400
Overhead applied		
Variable costs (2,000 × $3)	6,000	
Fixed costs (2,000 × $2)	**4,000**	10,000
Overhead volume variance—unfavorable		$ 400

This analysis indicates that **the overhead volume variance relates solely to fixed costs** (fixed costs budgeted $4,400 − fixed costs applied $4,000). Thus, **the volume variance measures the amount that fixed overhead costs are under- or overapplied**.

We have already established that total fixed costs remain the same at every level of activity within the relevant range. A predetermined overhead rate based on normal capacity is used in applying overhead. **It follows that if the standard hours allowed are less than the standard hours at normal capacity, fixed overhead costs will be underapplied.** In contrast, **if production exceeds normal capacity, fixed overhead costs will be overapplied**.

An alternative formula for computing the overhead volume variance is shown in Illustration 8-27.

Illustration 8-27 Alternative formula for overhead volume variance

In Xonic, Inc. normal capacity is 26,400 hours for the year, or 2,200 hours for a month (26,400 ÷ 12). The fixed overhead rate is $2 per hour. Thus, the volume variance is $400 unfavorable as shown below.

$$\$2 \times (2{,}200 - 2{,}000) = \$400 \text{ U}$$

The total overhead variance of $900 unfavorable for Xonic, Inc., therefore, consists of the following.

Illustration 8-28 Summary of overhead variances

Overhead controllable variance	$ 500 U
Overhead volume variance	400 U
Total overhead variance	**$900 U**

Illustration 8-29 Matrix for manufacturing overhead variances

The results can also be obtained from the matrix in Illustration 8-29.

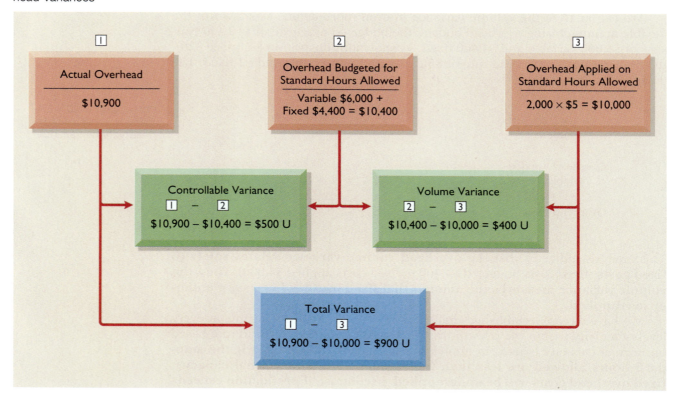

In computing the overhead variances, it is important to remember the following.

1. Standard hours allowed are used in each of the variances.
2. Budgeted costs for the controllable variance are derived from the flexible budget.
3. The controllable variance generally pertains to variable costs.
4. The volume variance pertains solely to fixed costs.

Causes of Manufacturing Overhead Variances. Since the **controllable variance** relates to variable manufacturing costs, the responsibility for the variance rests with the **production department**. The cause of an unfavorable variance may be: (1) **higher than expected use** of indirect materials, indirect labor, and factory supplies, or (2) **increases in indirect manufacturing costs**, such as fuel and maintenance costs.

The **overhead volume variance** is the responsibility of the **production department** if the cause is inefficient use of direct labor or machine breakdowns. When the cause is a **lack of sales orders**, the responsibility rests **outside** the production department.

"What caused manufacturing overhead variances?"

Controllable Variance — Overhead Volume Variance

Production Dept. — **Production or Sales Dept.**

DECISION TOOLKIT

Decision Checkpoints	Info Needed for Decision	Tool to Use for Decision	How to Evaluate Results
Has management accomplished its price and quantity objectives regarding overhead?	Actual cost and standard cost of overhead	Overhead controllable variance and overhead volume variance	Positive (favorable) variances suggest that price and quantity objectives have been met.

REPORTING VARIANCES

All variances should be reported to appropriate levels of management as soon as possible. The sooner management is informed, the sooner problems can be evaluated and corrective actions taken if necessary.

The form, content, and frequency of variance reports vary considerably among companies. One approach is to prepare a weekly report for each department that has primary responsibility for cost control. Under this approach, materials price variances are reported to the purchasing department, and all other variances are reported to the production department that did the work. The following report for Xonic, Inc., with the materials for the Weed-O order listed first, illustrates this approach.

STUDY OBJECTIVE
6
Discuss the reporting of variances.

Illustration 8-30
Materials price variance report

XONIC, INC.
Variance Report—Purchasing Department
For Week Ended June 8, 2002

Type of Materials	Quantity Purchased	Actual Price	Standard Price	Price Variance	Explanation
× 100	4,200 lbs.	$3.10	$3.00	$420 U	Rush order
× 142	1,200 units	2.75	2.80	60 F	Quantity discount
A 85	600 doz.	5.20	5.10	60 U	Regular supplier on strike
Total price variance				**$420 U**	

The explanation column is completed after consultation with the purchasing department manager.

Variance reports facilitate the principle of "management by exception" explained in Chapter 7. For example, the vice president of purchasing can use the report shown above to evaluate the effectiveness of the purchasing department manager. Or, the vice president of production can use production department variance reports to determine how well each production manager is controlling costs. In using variance reports, top management normally looks for **significant variances**. These may be judged on the basis of some quantitative measure, such as more than 10 percent of the standard or more than $1,000.

e – BUSINESS INSIGHT

Computerized standard cost systems represent one of the most complex accounting systems to develop and maintain. The standard cost system must be fully integrated into the general ledger. It must allow for the creation and timely maintenance of the database of standard usage and costs for every product. It must perform variance computations. And it must also produce variance reports by product, department, or employee. With the increased use of automation and robotics, the computerized standard cost system may even be tied directly into these systems to gather variance information.

STATEMENT PRESENTATION OF VARIANCES

STUDY OBJECTIVE

7

Prepare an income statement for management under a standard costing system.

In income statements **prepared for management** under a standard cost accounting system, **cost of goods sold is stated at standard cost and the variances are separately disclosed**, as shown in Illustration 8-31. The statement shown is based entirely on the production and sale of Weed-O. It assumes selling and administrative costs of $3,000. Observe that each variance is shown, as well as the total net variance. In this example, variations from standard costs reduced net income by $2,500.

Illustration 8-31
Variances in income statement for management

XONIC, INC. Income Statement For the Month Ended June 30, 2002		
Sales		$60,000
Cost of goods sold (at standard)		42,000
Gross profit (at standard)		18,000
Variances		
Materials price	$ 420	
Materials quantity	600	
Labor price	(420)	
Labor quantity	1,000	
Overhead controllable	500	
Overhead volume	400	
Total variance unfavorable		2,500
Gross profit (actual)		15,500
Selling and administrative expenses		3,000
Net income		$12,500

In financial statements prepared for stockholders and other external users, standard costs may be used. The costing of inventories at standard costs is in accordance with generally accepted accounting principles when there are no significant differences between actual costs and standard costs. **Hewlett-Packard** and **Jostens, Inc.**, for example, report their inventories at standard costs. However, if there are significant differences between actual and standard costs, inventories and cost of goods sold must be reported at actual costs.

It is also possible to show the variances in an income statement prepared in the contribution margin format. To do so, it is necessary to analyze the overhead variances into variable and fixed components. This type of analysis is explained in cost accounting textbooks.

BEFORE YOU GO ON . . .

◆ **Review It**

1. What are the formulas for computing the total, price, and quantity variances for direct labor?
2. What are the formulas for computing the total, controllable, and volume variances for manufacturing overhead?
3. How are standard costs and variances reported in income statements prepared for management?

*U*SING THE *D*ECISION *T*OOLKIT

Assume that during the past month **Sanford** produced 10,000 cartons of Liquid ACCENT® highlighters. Liquid ACCENT® offers a translucent barrel and cap with a visible ink supply for see-through color. The special fluorescent ink is fade- and water-resistant. Each carton contains 100 boxes of markers, and each box contains five markers. The markers come in boxes of one of five fluorescent colors — orange, blue, yellow, green, and pink — and in a five-color set.

Assume the following additional facts: The standard cost for one carton of 500 markers is as follows.

Manufacturing Cost Elements	Standard		
	Quantity	× Price =	Cost
Direct materials			
Tips (boxes of 500)	500	× $ 0.03 =	$ 15.00
Translucent barrels and caps (boxes of 500)	500	× $ 0.09 =	45.00
Fluorescent ink (100 oz. containers)	100 oz.	× $ 0.32 =	32.00
Total direct materials			92.00
Direct labor	0.25 hours	× $ 9.00 =	2.25
Overhead	0.25 hours	× $48.00 =	12.00
			$106.25

During the month, the following transactions occurred in manufacturing the 10,000 cartons of highlighters.

1. Purchased 10,000 boxes of tips for $148,000 ($14.80 per 500 tips); purchased 10,200 boxes of translucent barrels and caps for $453,900 ($44.50 per 500 barrels and caps); and purchased 9,900 containers of fluorescent ink for $328,185 ($33.15 per 100 ounces).
2. All materials purchased during the period were used to make markers during the period.
3. 2,300 direct labor hours were worked at a total labor cost of $20,240 (an average hourly rate of $8.80).
4. Variable manufacturing overhead incurred was $34,600, and fixed overhead incurred was $84,000.

The manufacturing overhead rate of $48.00 is based on a normal capacity of 2,600 direct labor hours. The total budget at this capacity is $83,980 fixed and $40,820 variable.

Instructions

Determine whether Sanford met its price and quantity objectives relative to materials, labor, and overhead.

Solution

To determine whether Sanford met its price and quantity objectives, compute the total variance and the variances for each of the manufacturing cost elements.

Total Variance

Actual cost incurred:		
Direct materials		
Tips	$148,000	
Translucent barrels and caps	453,900	
Fluorescent ink	328,185	
Total direct materials		$ 930,085
Direct labor		20,240
Overhead		118,600
Total actual costs		1,068,925
Standard cost (10,000 × $106.25)		1,062,500
Total variance		$ 6,425 U

Direct Materials Variances

Total	=	$930,085	−	$920,000 (10,000 × $92)	=	$10,085 U
Price (Tips)	=	$148,000 (10,000 × $14.80)	−	$150,000 (10,000 × $15.00)	=	$ 2,000 F
Price (Barrels and caps)	=	$453,900 (10,200 × $44.50)	−	$459,000 (10,200 × $45.00)	=	$ 5,100 F
Price (Ink)	=	$328,185 (9,900 × $33.15)	−	$316,800 (9,900 × $32.00)	=	$11,385 U
Quantity (Tips)	=	$150,000 (10,000 × $15.00)	−	$150,000 (10,000 × $15.00)	=	$ 0
Quantity (Barrels and caps)	=	$459,000 (10,200 × $45.00)	−	$450,000 (10,000 × $45.00)	=	$ 9,000 U
Quantity (Ink)	=	$316,800 (9,900 × $32.00)	−	$320,000 (10,000 × $32.00)	=	$ 3,200 F

Direct Labor Variances

Total	=	$20,240 (2,300 × $8.80)	−	$22,500 (2,500 × $9.00)	=	$ 2,260 F
Price	=	$20,240 (2,300 × $8.80)	−	$20,700 (2,300 × $9.00)	=	$ 460 F
Quantity	=	$20,700 (2,300 × $9.00)	−	$22,500 (2,500 × $9.00)	=	$ 1,800 F

Overhead Variances

Total	=	$118,600	−	$120,000	= $ 1,400 F
		($84,000 + $34,600)		(2,500 × $48)	
Controllable	=	$118,600	−	$123,230	= $ 4,630 F
		($84,000 + $34,600)		[(2,500 × $15.70) + $83,980]	
Volume	=	$123,230	−	$120,000	= $ 3,230 U
		[(2,500 × $15.70) + $83,980] − (2,500 × $48)			

Sanford's total variance was an unfavorable $6,425. The unfavorable materials variance outweighed the favorable labor and overhead variances. The primary determinants were an unfavorable price variance for ink and an unfavorable quantity variance for barrels and caps.

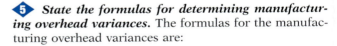
THE NAVIGATOR

SUMMARY OF STUDY OBJECTIVES

1 *Distinguish between a standard and a budget.* Both standards and budgets are predetermined costs. The primary difference is that a standard is a unit amount, whereas a budget is a total amount. A standard may be regarded as the budgeted cost per unit of product.

2 *Identify the advantages of standard costs.* Standard costs offer a number of advantages. They (a) facilitate management planning, (b) promote greater economy and efficiency, (c) are useful in setting selling prices, (d) contribute to management control, (e) permit "management by exception," and (f) simplify the costing of inventories and reduce clerical costs.

3 *Describe how standards are set.* The direct materials price standard should be based on the delivered cost of raw materials plus an allowance for receiving and handling. The direct materials quantity standard should establish the required quantity plus an allowance for waste and spoilage.

The direct labor price standard should be based on current wage rates and anticipated adjustments such as COLAs. It also generally includes payroll taxes and fringe benefits. Direct labor quantity standards should be based on required production time plus an allowance for rest periods, cleanup, machine setup, and machine downtime.

For manufacturing overhead, a standard predetermined overhead rate is used. It is based on an expected standard activity index such as standard direct labor hours or standard direct labor cost.

4 *State the formulas for determining direct materials and direct labor variances.* The formulas for the direct materials variances are:

$$\left(\begin{array}{c}\text{Actual quantity} \\ \times \text{ Actual price}\end{array}\right) - \left(\begin{array}{c}\text{Standard quantity} \\ \times \text{ Standard price}\end{array}\right) = \begin{array}{l}\text{Total} \\ \text{materials} \\ \text{variance}\end{array}$$

$$\left(\begin{array}{c}\text{Actual quantity} \\ \times \text{ Actual price}\end{array}\right) - \left(\begin{array}{c}\text{Actual quantity} \\ \times \text{ Standard price}\end{array}\right) = \begin{array}{l}\text{Materials} \\ \text{price} \\ \text{variance}\end{array}$$

$$\left(\begin{array}{c}\text{Actual quantity} \\ \times \text{ Standard price}\end{array}\right) - \left(\begin{array}{c}\text{Standard quantity} \\ \times \text{ Standard price}\end{array}\right) = \begin{array}{l}\text{Materials} \\ \text{quantity} \\ \text{variance}\end{array}$$

The formulas for the direct labor variances are:

$$\left(\begin{array}{c}\text{Actual hours} \\ \times \text{ Actual rate}\end{array}\right) - \left(\begin{array}{c}\text{Standard hours} \\ \times \text{ Standard rate}\end{array}\right) = \begin{array}{l}\text{Total} \\ \text{labor} \\ \text{variance}\end{array}$$

$$\left(\begin{array}{c}\text{Actual hours} \\ \times \text{ Actual rate}\end{array}\right) - \left(\begin{array}{c}\text{Actual hours} \\ \times \text{ Standard rate}\end{array}\right) = \begin{array}{l}\text{Labor} \\ \text{price} \\ \text{variance}\end{array}$$

$$\left(\begin{array}{c}\text{Actual hours} \\ \times \text{ Standard rate}\end{array}\right) - \left(\begin{array}{c}\text{Standard hours} \\ \times \text{ Standard rate}\end{array}\right) = \begin{array}{l}\text{Labor} \\ \text{quantity} \\ \text{variance}\end{array}$$

5 *State the formulas for determining manufacturing overhead variances.* The formulas for the manufacturing overhead variances are:

$$\begin{array}{l}\text{Actual} \\ \text{overhead}\end{array} - \begin{array}{l}\text{Overhead} \\ \text{applied}\end{array} = \begin{array}{l}\text{Total overhead} \\ \text{variance}\end{array}$$

$$\begin{array}{l}\text{Actual} \\ \text{overhead}\end{array} - \begin{array}{l}\text{Overhead} \\ \text{budgeted}\end{array} = \begin{array}{l}\text{Overhead controllable variance}\end{array}$$

$$\begin{array}{l}\text{Overhead} \\ \text{budgeted}\end{array} - \begin{array}{l}\text{Overhead} \\ \text{applied}\end{array} = \begin{array}{l}\text{Overhead volume} \\ \text{variance}\end{array}$$

6 ***Discuss the reporting of variances.*** Variances are reported to management in variance reports. The reports facilitate management by exception by highlighting significant differences.

7 ***Prepare an income statement for management under a standard costing system.*** Under a stan-

dard costing system, an income statement prepared for management will report cost of goods sold at standard cost and then disclose each variance separately.

THE NAVIGATOR

DECISION TOOLKIT—A SUMMARY

Decision Checkpoints	Info Needed for Decision	Tool to Use for Decision	How to Evaluate Results
Has management accomplished its price and quantity objectives regarding materials?	Actual cost and standard cost of materials	Materials price and materials quantity variances	Positive (favorable) variances suggest that price and quantity objectives have been met.
Has management accomplished its price and quantity objectives regarding labor?	Actual cost and standard cost of labor	Labor price and labor quantity variances	Positive (favorable) variances suggest that price and quantity objectives have been met.
Has management accomplished its price and quantity objectives regarding overhead?	Actual cost and standard cost of overhead	Overhead controllable variance and overhead volume variance	Positive (favorable) variances suggest that price and quantity objectives have been met.

APPENDIX 8A

STANDARD COST ACCOUNTING SYSTEM

STUDY OBJECTIVE
8
Identify the features of a standard cost accounting system.

A **standard cost accounting system** is a double-entry system of accounting. In this system, standard costs are used in making entries, and variances are formally recognized in the accounts. A standard cost system may be used with either job order or process costing. At this point, we will explain and illustrate a **standard cost**, **job order cost accounting system**. The system is based on two important assumptions: (1) Variances from standards are recognized at the earliest opportunity. (2) The Work in Process account is maintained exclusively on the basis of standard costs. In practice, there are many variations among standard cost systems. The system described here should prepare you for systems you see in the "real world."

JOURNAL ENTRIES

We will use the transactions of Xonic, Inc. to illustrate the journal entries. Note as you study the entries that the major difference between the entries here and those for the job order cost accounting system in Chapter 2 is the **variance accounts**.

1. Purchase raw materials on account for $13,020 when the standard cost is $12,600.

Raw Materials Inventory	12,600	
Materials Price Variance	420	
Accounts Payable		13,020
(To record purchase of materials)		

The inventory account is debited for actual quantities at standard cost. This enables the perpetual materials records to show actual quantities. The price variance, which is unfavorable, is debited to Materials Price Variance.

2. Incur direct labor costs of $20,580 when the standard labor cost is $21,000.

Factory Labor	21,000	
Labor Price Variance		420
Wages Payable		20,580
(To record direct labor costs)		

Like the raw materials inventory account, Factory Labor is debited for actual hours worked at the standard hourly rate of pay. In this case, the labor variance is favorable. Thus, Labor Price Variance is credited.

3. Incur actual manufacturing overhead costs of $10,900.

Manufacturing Overhead	10,900	
Accounts Payable/Cash/Acc. Depreciation		10,900
(To record overhead incurred)		

The controllable overhead variance is not recorded at this time. It depends on standard hours applied to work in process. This amount is not known at the time overhead is incurred.

4. Issue raw materials for production at a cost of $12,600 when the standard cost is $12,000.

Work in Process Inventory	12,000	
Materials Quantity Variance	600	
Raw Materials Inventory		12,600
(To record issuance of raw materials)		

Work in Process Inventory is debited for standard materials quantities used at standard prices. The variance account is debited because the variance is unfavorable. Raw Materials Inventory is credited for actual quantities at standard prices.

5. Assign factory labor to production at a cost of $21,000 when standard cost is $20,000.

Work in Process Inventory	20,000	
Labor Quantity Variance	1,000	
Factory Labor		21,000
(To assign factory labor to jobs)		

Work in Process Inventory is debited for standard labor hours at standard rates. The unfavorable variance is debited to Labor Quantity Variance. The credit to Factory Labor produces a zero balance in this account.

6. Applying manufacturing overhead to production $10,000.

Work in Process Inventory	10,000	
Manufacturing Overhead		10,000
(To assign overhead to jobs)		

Work in Process Inventory is debited for standard hours allowed multiplied by the standard overhead rate.

7. Transfer completed work to finished goods $42,000.

Finished Goods Inventory	42,000	
Work in Process Inventory		42,000
(To record transfer of completed work to finished goods)		

In this example, both inventory accounts are at standard cost.

8. The 1,000 gallons of Weed-O are sold for $60,000.

Accounts Receivable	60,000	
Cost of Goods Sold	42,000	
Sales		60,000
Finished Goods Inventory		42,000
(To record sale of finished goods and the cost of goods sold)		

Cost of Goods Sold is debited at standard cost. Gross profit, in turn, is the difference between sales and the standard cost of goods sold.

9. Recognize unfavorable overhead variances: controllable, $500; volume, $400.

Overhead Controllable Variance	500	
Overhead Volume Variance	400	
Manufacturing Overhead		900
(To recognize overhead variances)		

Prior to this entry, a debit balance of $900 existed in Manufacturing Overhead. This entry therefore produces a zero balance in the Manufacturing Overhead account. The information needed for this entry is often not available until the end of the accounting period.

*L*EDGER ACCOUNTS

The cost accounts for Xonic, Inc., after posting the entries, are shown in Illustration 8A-1. Note that six variance accounts are included in the ledger. The remaining accounts are the same as those illustrated for a job order cost system in Chapter 2, in which only actual costs were used.

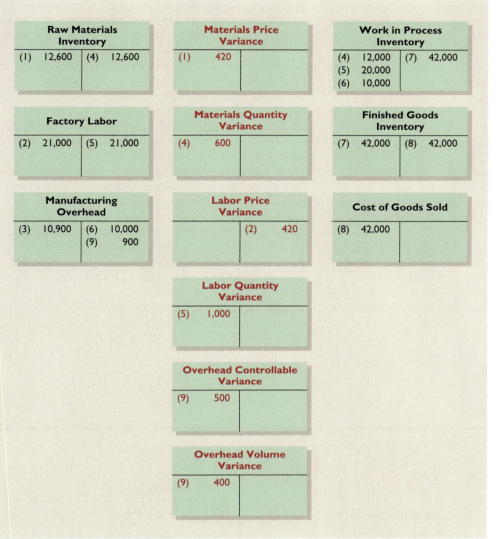

Illustration 8A-1 Cost accounts with variances

Helpful Hint All debit balances in variance accounts indicate unfavorable variances; all credit balances indicate favorable variances.

Raw Materials Inventory			
(1)	12,600	(4)	12,600

Materials Price Variance			
(1)	420		

Work in Process Inventory			
(4)	12,000	(7)	42,000
(5)	20,000		
(6)	10,000		

Factory Labor			
(2)	21,000	(5)	21,000

Materials Quantity Variance			
(4)	600		

Finished Goods Inventory			
(7)	42,000	(8)	42,000

Manufacturing Overhead			
(3)	10,900	(6)	10,000
		(9)	900

Labor Price Variance			
		(2)	420

Cost of Goods Sold			
(8)	42,000		

Labor Quantity Variance			
(5)	1,000		

Overhead Controllable Variance			
(9)	500		

Overhead Volume Variance			
(9)	400		

Summary of Study Objective for Appendix 8A

8 *Identify the features of a standard cost accounting system.* In a standard cost accounting system, standard costs are journalized and posted, and separate variance accounts are maintained in the ledger. When differences between actual costs and standard costs do not differ significantly, inventories may be reported at standard costs.

Glossary

Key Term Matching Activity

Direct labor price standard The rate per hour that should be incurred for direct labor. (p. 325)

Direct labor quantity standard The time that should be required to make one unit of product. (p. 325)

Direct materials price standard The cost per unit of direct materials that should be incurred. (p. 324)

Direct materials quantity standard The quantity of direct materials that should be used per unit of finished goods. (p. 325)

Ideal standards Standards based on the optimum level of performance under perfect operating conditions. (p. 324)

Labor price variance The difference between the actual hours times the actual rate and the actual hours times the standard rate for labor. (p. 333)

Labor quantity variance The difference between actual hours times the standard rate and standard hours times the standard rate for labor. (p. 333)

Materials price variance The difference between the actual quantity times the actual price and the actual quantity times the standard price for materials. (p. 330)

Materials quantity variance The difference between the actual quantity times the standard price and the standard quantity times the standard price for materials. (p. 330)

Normal standards Standards based on an efficient level of performance that are attainable under expected operating conditions. (p. 324)

Overhead controllable variance The difference between actual overhead incurred and overhead budgeted for the standard hours allowed. (p. 336)

Overhead volume variance The difference between overhead budgeted for the standard hours allowed and the overhead applied. (p. 337)

Standard cost accounting system A double-entry system of accounting in which standard costs are used in making entries and variances are recognized in the accounts. (p. 344)

Standard costs Predetermined unit costs which are used as measures of performance. (p. 322)

Standard hours allowed The hours that should have been worked for the units produced. (p. 335)

Standard predetermined overhead rate An overhead rate determined by dividing budgeted overhead costs by an expected standard activity index. (p. 326)

Total labor variance The difference between actual hours times the actual rate and standard hours times the standard rate for labor. (p. 333)

Total materials variance The difference between the actual quantity times the actual price and the standard quantity times the standard price of materials. (p. 329)

Total overhead variance The difference between actual overhead costs and overhead costs applied to work done. (p. 335)

Variances The difference between total actual costs and total standard costs. (p. 328)

DEMONSTRATION PROBLEM

eGrade Demonstration Problem

Manlow Company makes a cologne called Allure. The standard cost for one bottle of Allure is as follows.

Manufacturing Cost Elements	Quantity	×	Price	=	Cost
			Standard		
Direct materials	6 oz.	×	$ 0.90	=	$ 5.40
Direct labor	0.5 hrs.	×	$12.00	=	6.00
Manufacturing overhead	0.5 hrs.	×	$ 4.80	=	2.40
					$13.80

During the month, the following transactions occurred in manufacturing 10,000 bottles of Allure.

1. 58,000 ounces of materials were purchased at $1.00 per ounce.
2. All the materials purchased were used to produce the 10,000 bottles of Allure.
3. 4,900 direct labor hours were worked at a total labor cost of $56,350.
4. Variable manufacturing overhead incurred was $15,000 and fixed overhead incurred was $10,400.

The manufacturing overhead rate of $4.80 is based on a normal capacity of 5,200 direct labor hours. The total budget at this capacity is $10,400 fixed and $14,560 variable.

Instructions

Compute the total variance and the variances for each of the manufacturing cost elements.

Solution to Demonstration Problem

Total Variance

Actual costs incurred		
Direct materials	$ 58,000	
Direct labor	56,350	
Manufacturing overhead	25,400	
	139,750	
Standard cost (10,000 × $13.80)	138,000	
Total variance	$ 1,750 (U)	

Direct Materials Variances

Total	=	$58,000	−	$54,000	=	$4,000 U
		(58,000 × $1.00)		(60,000 × $0.90)		
Price	=	$58,000	−	$52,200	=	$5,800 U
		(58,000 × $1.00)		(58,000 × $0.90)		
Quantity	=	$52,200	−	$54,000	=	$1,800 F
		(58,000 × $0.90)		(60,000 × $0.90)		

Direct Labor Variances

Total	=	$56,350	−	$60,000	=	$3,650 F
		(4,900 × $11.50)		(5,000 × $12.00)		
Price	=	$56,350	−	$58,800	=	$2,450 F
		(4,900 × $11.50)		(4,900 × $12.00)		
Quantity	=	$58,800	−	$60,000	=	$1,200 F
		(4,900 × $12.00)		(5,000 × $12.00)		

Overhead Variances

Total	=	$25,400	−	$24,000	=	$1,400 U
		($15,000 + $10,400)		(5,000 × $4.80)		
Controllable	=	$25,400	−	$24,400	=	$1,000 U
		($15,000 + $10,400)		($14,000 + $10,400)		
Volume	=	$24,400	−	$24,000	=	$ 400 U
		($14,000 + $10,400)		(5,000 × $4.80)		

Action Plan

- Check to make sure the total variance and the sum of the individual variances are equal.
- Find the price variance first, then the quantity variance.
- Base budgeted overhead costs on flexible budget data.
- Base overhead applied on standard hours allowed.
- Ignore actual hours worked in computing overhead variances.
- Relate the overhead volume variance solely to fixed costs.

Note: All asterisked Questions, Exercises, and Problems relate to material in the appendix to the chapter.

SELF-STUDY QUESTIONS

Self-Study/Self-Test

Answers are at the end of the chapter.

(SO 1) 1. Standards differ from budgets in that:
- (a) budgets but not standards may be used in valuing inventories.
- (b) budgets but not standards may be journalized and posted.
- (c) budgets are a total amount and standards are a unit amount.
- (d) only budgets contribute to management planning and control.

(SO 2) 2. The advantages of standard costs include all of the following *except:*

- (a) management by exception may be used.
- (b) management planning is facilitated.
- (c) they may simplify the costing of inventories.
- (d) management must use a static budget.

3. The setting of standards is: (SO 3)
- (a) a managerial accounting decision.
- (b) a management decision.
- (c) a worker decision.
- (d) preferably set at the ideal level of performance.

4. Each of the following formulas is correct   (SO 4)
except:

(a) Labor price variance = (Actual hours × Actual rate) − (Actual hours × Standard rate).

(b) Overhead controllable variance = Actual overhead − Overhead budgeted.

(c) Materials price variance = (Actual quantity × Actual cost) − (Standard quantity × Standard cost).

(d) Overhead volume variance = Overhead budgeted − Overhead applied.

(SO 4) 5. In producing product AA, 6,300 pounds of direct materials were used at a cost of $1.10 per pound. The standard was 6,000 pounds at $1 per pound. The direct materials quantity variance is:
  (a) $330 unfavorable.
  (b) $300 unfavorable.
  (c) $600 unfavorable.
  (d) $630 unfavorable.

(SO 4) 6. In producing product ZZ, 14,800 direct labor hours were used at a rate of $8.20 per hour. The standard was 15,000 hours at $8.00 per hour. Based on these data, the direct labor:
  (a) quantity variance is $1,600 favorable.
  (b) quantity variance is $1,600 unfavorable.
  (c) price variance is $2,960 favorable.
  (d) price variance is $3,000 unfavorable.

(SO 5) 7. Which of the following is *correct* about overhead variances?
  (a) The controllable variance generally pertains to fixed overhead costs.

(b) The volume variance pertains solely to variable overhead costs.

(c) Standard hours actually worked are used in each variance.

(d) Budgeted overhead costs are based on the flexible overhead budget.

8. The formula for computing the total overhead variance is: (SO 5)
  (a) actual overhead less overhead applied.
  (b) overhead budgeted less overhead applied.
  (c) actual overhead less overhead budgeted.
  (d) No correct answer given.

9. Which of the following is *incorrect* about variance reports? (SO 6)
  (a) They facilitate "management by exception."
  (b) They should only be sent to the top level of management.
  (c) They should be prepared as soon as possible.
  (d) They may vary in form, content, and frequency among companies.

*10. Which of the following is *incorrect* about a standard cost accounting system? (SO 8)
  (a) It is applicable to job order costing.
  (b) It is applicable to process costing.
  (c) It is a single-entry system.
  (d) It keeps separate accounts for each variance.

THE NAVIGATOR

QUESTIONS

1. (a) "Standard costs are the expected total cost of completing a job." Is this correct? Explain.
   (b) "A standard imposed by a governmental agency is known as a regulation." Do you agree? Explain.

2. (a) Explain the similarities and differences between standards and budgets.
   (b) Contrast the accounting for standards and budgets.

3. Standard costs facilitate management planning. What are the other advantages of standard costs?

4. Contrast the roles of the management accountant and management in setting standard costs.

5. Distinguish between an ideal standard and a normal standard.

6. What factors should be considered in setting (a) the materials price standard and (b) the materials quantity standard?

7. "The objective in setting the direct labor quantity standard is to determine the aggregate time required to make one unit of product." Do you agree? What allowances should be made in setting this standard?

8. How is the predetermined overhead rate determined when standard costs are used?

9. What is the difference between a favorable cost variance and an unfavorable cost variance?

10. In each of the following formulas, supply the words that should be inserted for each number in parentheses.
   (a) (Actual quantity × (1)) − (Standard quantity × (2)) = Total materials variance
   (b) ((3) × Actual price) − (Actual quantity × (4)) = Materials price variance
   (c) (Actual quantity × (5)) − ((6) × Standard price) = Materials quantity variance

11. In the direct labor variance matrix, there are three factors: (1) Actual hours × Actual rate, (2) Actual hours × Standard rate, and (3) Standard hours × Standard rate. Using the numbers, indicate the formulas for each of the direct labor variances.

12. Dant Company's standard predetermined overhead rate is $6.00 per direct labor hour. For the month of June, 26,000 actual hours were worked, and 27,500 standard hours were allowed. Normal capacity hours were 28,000. How much overhead was applied?

13. If the $6.00 per hour overhead rate in question 12 consists of $4.00 variable, and actual overhead costs were $163,000, what is the overhead controllable variance for June? Is the variance favorable or unfavorable?

14. Using the data in questions 12 and 13, what is the overhead volume variance for June? Is the variance favorable or unfavorable?

15. What is the purpose of computing the overhead volume variance? What is the basic formula for this variance?

16. Ellen Landis does not understand why the overhead volume variance indicates that fixed overhead costs are under- or overapplied. Clarify this matter for Ellen.

17. Stan LaRue is attempting to outline the important points about overhead variances on a class examination. List four points that Stan should include in his outline.

18. How often should variances be reported to management? What principle may be used with variance reports?

19. What circumstances may cause the purchasing department to be responsible for both an unfavorable materials price variance and an unfavorable materials quantity variance?

20. (a) How are variances reported in income statements prepared for management? (b) May standard costs be used in preparing financial statements for stockholders? Explain.

*21. (a) Explain the basic features of a standard cost accounting system. (b) What type of balance will exist in the variance account when (1) the materials price variance is unfavorable and (2) the labor quantity variance is favorable?

BRIEF EXERCISES

BE8-1   Tumbo Company uses both standards and budgets. For the year, estimated production of Product X is 500,000 units. Total estimated costs for materials and labor are $1,200,000 and $1,600,000. Compute the estimates for (a) a standard cost and (b) a budgeted cost.

Distinguish between a standard and a budget.
(SO 1)

BE8-2   Nurmi Company accumulates the following data concerning raw materials in making one gallon of finished product: (1) Price—net purchase price $3.50, freight-in $0.20, and receiving and handling $0.10. (2) Quantity—required materials 2.6 pounds, allowance for waste and spoilage 0.4 pounds. Compute the following.
(a) Standard direct materials price per gallon.
(b) Standard direct materials quantity per gallon.
(c) Total standard material cost per gallon.

Set direct materials standard.
(SO 3)

BE8-3   Labor data for making one gallon of finished product in Nurmi Company are as follows: (1) Price—hourly wage rate $10.00, payroll taxes $0.80, and fringe benefits $1.20. (2) Quantity—actual production time 1.6 hours, rest periods and clean up 0.25 hours, and setup and downtime 0.15 hours. Compute the following.
(a) Standard direct labor rate per hour.
(b) Standard direct labor hours per gallon.
(c) Standard labor cost per gallon.

Set direct labor standard.
(SO 3)

BE8-4   Nadia Company's standard materials cost per unit of output is $8 (2 pounds × $4.00). During July, the company purchases and uses 3,300 pounds of materials costing $13,365 in making 1,500 units of finished product. Compute the total, price, and quantity materials variances.

Compute direct materials variances.
(SO 4)

BE8-5   Kimiko Company's standard labor cost per unit of output is $18 (2 hours × $9.00 per hour). During August, the company incurs 1,850 hours of direct labor at an hourly cost of $9.60 per hour in making 1,000 units of finished product. Compute the total, price, and quantity labor variances.

Compute direct labor variances.
(SO 4)

BE8-6   In October, Hilo Company reports 21,000 actual direct labor hours, and it incurs $98,000 of manufacturing overhead costs. Standard hours allowed for the work done is 20,000 hours. The predetermined overhead rate is $5.00 per direct labor hour. Compute the total manufacturing overhead variance.

Compute total manufacturing overhead variance.
(SO 5)

BE8-7   Some overhead data for Hilo Company are given in BE8-6. In addition, the flexible manufacturing overhead budget shows that budgeted costs are $4.00 variable per direct labor hour and $25,000 fixed. Compute the manufacturing overhead controllable variance.

Compute the manufacturing overhead controllable variance.
(SO 5)

Compute overhead volume variance.
(SO 5)

BE8-8   Using the data in BE8-6 and BE8-7, compute the manufacturing overhead volume variance.

Journalize materials variances.
(SO 8)

*BE8-9   Journalize the following transactions for Nashua Manufacturing.
(a) Purchased 6,000 units of raw materials on account for $11,700. The standard cost was $12,000.
(b) Issued 5,600 units of raw materials for production. The standard units were 5,800.

Journalize labor variances.
(SO 8)

*BE8-10   Journalize the following transactions for Harlem Manufacturing.
(a) Incurred direct labor costs of $24,000 for 3,000 hours. The standard labor cost was $24,300.
(b) Assigned 3,000 direct labor hours costing $24,000 to production. Standard hours were 3,100.

EXERCISES

Compute standard materials costs.
(SO 3)

E8-1   Robin Ritz manufactures and sells homemade wine, and he wants to develop a standard cost per gallon. The following are required for production of a 50-gallon batch.

 3,000 ounces of grape concentrate at $0.05 per ounce
 54 pounds of granulated sugar at $0.30 per pound
 70 lemons at $0.60 each
 50 yeast tablets at $0.25 each
 50 nutrient tablets at $0.20 each
 2,500 ounces of water at $0.0043 per ounce

Robin estimates that 4% of the grape concentrate is wasted, 10% of the sugar is lost, and 20% of the lemons cannot be used.

Instructions
Compute the standard cost of the ingredients for one gallon of wine. (Carry computations to three decimal places.)

Compute materials price and quantity variances.
(SO 4)

E8-2   The standard cost of Product B manufactured by Lopez Company includes three units of direct materials at $5.00 per unit. During June, 30,000 units of direct materials are purchased at a cost of $4.80 per unit, and 27,200 units of direct materials are used to produce 9,000 units of Product B.

Instructions
(a) Compute the materials price and quantity variances.
(b) Repeat (a), assuming the purchase price is $5.10 and the quantity used is 26,400 units.

Compute labor price and quantity variances.
(SO 4)

E8-3   Napier Company's standard labor cost of producing one unit of Product DD is 3.9 hours at the rate of $12.00 per hour. During August, 40,800 hours of labor are incurred at a cost of $12.10 per hour to produce 10,000 units of Product DD.

Instructions
(a) Compute the labor price and quantity variances.
(b) Repeat (a), assuming the standard is 4.2 hours of direct labor at $12.20 per hour.

Compute materials and labor variances.
(SO 4)

E8-4   Kayjay Inc., which produces a single product, has prepared the following standard cost sheet for one unit of the product.

Direct materials (8 pounds at $2.50 per pound)	$20.00
Direct labor (3 hours at $12.00 per hour)	$36.00

During the month of April, the company manufactures 250 units and incurs the following actual costs.

Direct materials (1,900 pounds—purchased and used)	$5,035
Direct labor (700 hours)	$8,050

Instructions
Compute the total, price, and quantity variances for materials and labor.

E8-5 The following direct materials and direct labor data pertain to the operations of Juan Manufacturing Company for the month of August.

Costs		Quantities	
Actual labor rate	$13.00 per hour	Actual hours incurred and used	4,200 hours
Actual materials price	$128.00 per ton	Actual quantity of materials purchased and used	1,230 tons
Standard labor rate	$12.00 per hour	Standard hours used	4,300 hours
Standard materials price	$130.00 per ton	Standard quantity of materials used	1,200 tons

Instructions
(a) Compute the total, price, and quantity variances for materials and labor.
(b) ▭▭▭▭▷ Provide two possible explanations for each of the unfavorable variances calculated above, and suggest where responsibility for the unfavorable result might be placed.

E8-6 The following information was taken from the annual manufacturing overhead cost budget of SooTech Company.

Variable manufacturing overhead costs	$33,000
Fixed manufacturing overhead costs	$19,800
Normal production level in hours	16,500
Normal production level in units	4,125

During the year, 4,000 units were produced, 16,100 hours were worked, and the actual manufacturing overhead was $54,000. Actual fixed manufacturing overhead costs equaled budgeted fixed manufacturing overhead costs. Overhead is applied on the basis of direct labor hours.

Instructions
(a) Compute the total, fixed, and variable predetermined manufacturing overhead rates.
(b) Compute the total, controllable, and volume overhead variances.
(c) ▭▭▭▭▷ Briefly interpret the overhead controllable and volume variances computed in (b).

E8-7 Manufacturing overhead data for the production of Product H by Fierello Company are as follows.

Overhead incurred for 51,000 actual direct labor hours worked	$213,000
Overhead rate (variable $3.00; fixed $1.00) at normal capacity of 54,000 direct labor hours	$4.00
Standard hours allowed for work done	51,000

Instructions
(a) Compute the total, controllable, and volume overhead variances.
*(b) Journalize the incurrence of the overhead costs and the application of overhead to the job, assuming a standard cost accounting system is used.
*(c) Prepare the adjusting entry for the overhead variances.

E8-8 During March 2002, Tenza Tool & Die Company worked on four jobs. A review of direct labor costs reveals the following summary data.

Job Number	Actual Hours	Actual Costs	Standard Hours	Standard Costs	Total Variance
A257	220	$ 4,400	226	$4,520	$ 120 F
A258	450	10,350	430	8,600	1,750 U
A259	300	6,150	300	6,000	150 U
A260	116	2,088	110	2,200	112 F
Total variance					$1,668 U

Analysis reveals that Job A257 was a repeat job. Job A258 was a rush order that required overtime work at premium rates of pay. Job A259 required a more experienced replacement worker on one shift. Work on Job A260 was done for one day by a new trainee when a regular worker was absent.

Instructions
Prepare a report for the plant supervisor on direct labor cost variances for March. The report should have columns for (1) Job No., (2) Actual Hours, (3) Standard Hours, (4) Labor Quantity Variance, (5) Actual Rate, (6) Standard Rate, (7) Labor Price Variance, and (8) Explanations.

Prepare income statement for management.
(SO 7)

E8-9 Alvarez Company uses a standard cost accounting system. During January, the company reported the following manufacturing variances account balances.

Materials price variance	$1,250 debit	Labor quantity variance	$ 725 debit
Materials quantity variance	700 credit	Overhead controllable	200 credit
Labor price variance	525 debit	Overhead volume	1,000 debit

In addition, 6,000 units of product were sold at $8.00 per unit. Each unit sold had a standard cost of $5.00. Selling and administrative expenses were $9,000 for the month.

Instructions
Prepare an income statement for management for the month ending January 31, 2002.

Journalize entries for materials and labor variances.
(SO 8)

*E8-10 Data for Kayjay Inc. are given in E8-4.

Instructions
Journalize the entries to record the materials and labor variances.

Journalize entries in a standard cost accounting system.
(SO 8)

*E8-11 DeSoto Company installed a standard cost system on January 1. Selected transactions for the month of January are as follows.

1. Purchased 18,000 units of raw materials on account at a cost of $4.50 per unit. Standard cost was $4.00 per unit.
2. Issued 18,000 units of raw materials for jobs that required 17,600 standard units of raw materials.
3. Incurred 15,200 actual hours of direct labor at an actual rate of $4.80 per hour. The standard rate is $5.00 per hour. (Credit Wages Payable)
4. Performed 15,200 hours of direct labor on jobs when standard hours were 15,400.
5. Applied overhead to jobs at the rate of 100% of direct labor cost for standard hours allowed.

Instructions
Journalize the January transactions.

Answer questions concerning missing entries and balances.
(SO 4, 5, 8)

*E8-12 Amand Company uses a standard cost accounting system. Some of the ledger accounts have been destroyed in a fire. The controller asks your help in reconstructing some missing entries and balances. (*Note:* Assume that the amount of raw materials purchased was equal to the amount used.)

Instructions
Answer the following questions.
(a) Materials Price Variance shows a $3,000 favorable balance. Accounts Payable shows $126,000 of raw materials purchases. What was the amount debited to Raw Materials Inventory for raw materials purchased?
(b) Materials Quantity Variance shows a $3,000 unfavorable balance. Raw Materials Inventory shows a zero balance. What was the amount debited to Work in Process Inventory for direct materials used?
(c) Labor Price Variance shows a $1,500 unfavorable balance. Factory Labor shows a debit of $152,000 for wages incurred. What was the amount credited to Wages Payable?
(d) Factory Labor shows a credit of $152,000 for direct labor used. Labor Quantity Variance shows a $900 unfavorable balance. What was the amount debited to Work in Process for direct labor used?

(e) Overhead applied to Work in Process totaled $165,000. If the total overhead variance was $1,300 unfavorable, what was the amount of overhead costs debited to Manufacturing Overhead?

(f) Overhead Controllable Variance shows a debit balance of $1,500. What was the amount and type of balance (debit or credit) in Overhead Volume Variance?

PROBLEMS: SET A

P8-1A   Moore Corporation manufactures a single product. The standard cost per unit of product is shown below.

Compute variances.
(SO 4, 5)

Direct materials—1 pound plastic at $7.00 per pound	$ 7.00
Direct labor—1.5 hours at $12.00 per hour	18.00
Variable manufacturing overhead	11.25
Fixed manufacturing overhead	3.75
Total standard cost per unit	$40.00

The predetermined manufacturing overhead rate is $10 per direct labor hour ($15.00 ÷ 1.5). This rate was computed from a master manufacturing overhead budget based on normal production of 90,000 direct labor hours (60,000 units) for the year. The master budget showed total variable costs of $675,000 and total fixed costs of $225,000. Actual costs for October in producing 5,000 units were as follows.

Direct materials (5,100 pounds)	$ 36,720
Direct labor (7,000 hours)	86,100
Variable overhead	56,170
Fixed overhead	19,680
Total manufacturing costs	$198,670

The purchasing department normally buys the quantities of raw materials that are expected to be used in production each month. Raw materials inventories, therefore, can be ignored.

Instructions
Compute all of the materials, labor, and overhead variances.

P8-2A   Ellison Manufacturing Corporation accumulates the following data relative to jobs started and finished during the month of June 2002.

Compute variances, and
prepare income statement.
(SO 4, 5, 7)

Costs and Production Data	Actual	Standard
Raw materials purchases, 10,500 units	$23,100	$21,000
Raw materials units used	10,500	10,000
Direct labor payroll	$122,100	$120,000
Direct labor hours worked	14,800	15,000
Manufacturing overhead incurred	$182,500	
Manufacturing overhead applied		$184,500
Machine hours expected to be used at normal capacity		42,500
Budgeted fixed overhead for June		$46,750
Variable overhead rate per hour		$3.00

Overhead is applied on the basis of standard machine hours. Three hours of machine time are required for each direct labor hour. The jobs were sold for $400,000. Selling and administrative expenses were $40,000.

Instructions
(a) Compute all of the variances for direct materials, direct labor, and manufacturing overhead.

(b) Prepare an income statement for management. Ignore income taxes.

Compute variances, and identify significant variances.
(SO 4, 5, 6)

eGrade Problem

P8-3A Novall Clothiers is a small company that manufactures tall-men's suits. The company has used a standard cost accounting system. In May 2003, 11,300 suits were produced.

The following standard and actual cost data applied to the month of May when normal capacity was 14,000 direct labor hours.

Cost Element	Standard (per unit)	Actual
Direct materials	8 yards at $4.50 per yard	$375,150 for 91,500 yards ($4.10 per yard)
Direct labor	1.2 hours at $13.00 per hour	$204,450 for 14,500 hours ($14.10 per hour)
Overhead	1.2 hours at $6.00 per hour (fixed $3.50; variable $2.50)	$49,000 fixed overhead $36,000 variable overhead

Overhead is applied on the basis of direct labor hours. At normal capacity, budgeted fixed overhead costs were $49,000, and budgeted variable overhead was $35,000.

Instructions
(a) Compute the total, price, and quantity variances for (1) materials and (2) labor, and the total, controllable, and volume variances for manufacturing overhead.
(b) ▭▭▭▭▭▶ Which of the materials and labor variances should be investigated if management considers a variance of more than 7% from standard to be significant?

Answer questions about variances.
(SO 4, 5)

P8-4A Calpine Manufacturing Company uses a standard cost accounting system. In 2002, 32,000 units were produced. Each unit took several pounds of direct materials and $1\frac{1}{4}$ standard hours of direct labor at a standard hourly rate of $12.00. Normal capacity was 50,000 direct labor hours. During the year, 133,000 pounds of raw materials were purchased at $0.92 per pound. All pounds purchased were used during the year.

Instructions
(a) If the materials price variance was $3,990 favorable, what was the standard materials price per pound?
(b) If the materials quantity variance was $1,710 unfavorable, what was the standard materials quantity per unit?
(c) What were the standard hours allowed for the units produced?
(d) If the labor quantity variance was $7,200 unfavorable, what were the actual direct labor hours worked?
(e) If the labor price variance was $6,000 favorable, what was the actual rate per hour?
(f) If total budgeted manufacturing overhead was $340,000 at normal capacity, what was the predetermined overhead rate?
(g) What was the standard cost per unit of product?
(h) How much overhead was applied to production during the year?
(i) If the fixed overhead rate was $2.00, what was the overhead volume variance?
(j) If the overhead controllable variance is $3,000 unfavorable, what were the total variable overhead costs incurred?
(k) Using one or more answers above, what were the total costs assigned to work in process?

Journalize and post standard cost entries, and prepare income statement.
(SO 4, 5, 8)

***P8-5A** Walton Corporation uses standard costs with its job order cost accounting system. In January, an order (Job No. 12) for 2,000 units of Product B was received. The standard cost of one unit of Product B is as follows.

Direct materials	3 pounds at $1.00 per pound	$ 3.00
Direct labor	1 hour at $8.00 per hour	8.00
Overhead	2 hours (variable $4.00 per machine hour; fixed $2.25 per machine hour)	12.50
Standard cost per unit		$23.50

Normal capacity for the month was 4,200 machine hours. During January, the following transactions applicable to Job No. 12 occurred.

1. Purchased 6,250 pounds of raw materials on account at $1.06 per pound.
2. Requisitioned 6,250 pounds of raw materials for Job No. 12.

3. Incurred 2,200 hours of direct labor at a rate of $7.80 per hour.
4. Worked 2,200 hours of direct labor on Job No. 12.
5. Incurred manufacturing overhead on account $25,800.
6. Applied overhead to Job No. 12 on basis of standard machine hours used.
7. Completed Job No. 12.
8. Billed customer for Job No. 12 at a selling price of $70,000.
9. Incurred selling and administrative expenses on account $2,000.

Instructions
(a) Journalize the transactions.
(b) Post to the job order cost accounts.
(c) Prepare the entry to recognize the overhead variances.
(d) Prepare the January 2003 income statement for management.

PROBLEMS: SET B

P8-1B Flesch Corporation manufactures a single product. The standard cost per unit of product is as follows.

Compute variances.
(SO 4, 5)

Direct materials—2 pounds of plastic at $5.00 per pound	$10.00
Direct labor—2 hours at $12.00 per hour	24.00
Variable manufacturing overhead	12.00
Fixed manufacturing overhead	6.00
Total standard cost per unit	$52.00

The master manufacturing overhead budget for the year based on normal productive capacity of 180,000 direct labor hours (90,000 units) shows total variable costs of $1,080,000 and total fixed costs of $540,000. Overhead is applied on the basis of direct labor hours. Actual costs for November in producing 7,700 units were as follows.

Direct materials (15,000 pounds)	$ 72,000
Direct labor (14,900 hours)	183,270
Variable overhead	88,990
Fixed overhead	44,000
Total manufacturing costs	$388,260

The purchasing department normally buys the quantities of raw materials that are expected to be used in production each month. Raw materials inventories, therefore, can be ignored.

Instructions
Compute all of the materials, labor, and overhead variances.

P8-2B Onasis Manufacturing Company uses a standard cost accounting system. In July 2002, it accumulates the following data relative to jobs started and finished.

Compute variances, and
prepare income statement.
(SO 4, 5, 7)

Cost and Production Data	Actual	Standard
Raw materials		
Units purchased	17,500	
Units used	17,500	18,000
Unit cost	$3.40	$3.00
Direct labor		
Hours worked	2,900	3,000
Hourly rate	$11.80	$12.00
Manufacturing overhead		
Incurred	$87,500	
Applied		$97,500

Manufacturing overhead was applied on the basis of direct labor hours. Normal capacity for the month was 2,800 direct labor hours. At normal capacity, budgeted overhead costs were: variable $56,000 and fixed $35,000.

Jobs finished during the month were sold for $240,000. Selling and administrative expenses were $25,000.

Instructions
(a) Compute all of the variances for direct materials, direct labor, and manufacturing overhead.
(b) Prepare an income statement for management. Ignore income taxes.

Compute variances, and identify significant variances.
(SO 4, 5, 7)

P8-3B   True-Value Clothiers manufactures women's business suits. The company uses a standard cost accounting system. In March 2002, 12,000 suits were made. The following standard and actual cost data applied to the month of March when normal capacity was 15,000 direct labor hours.

Cost Element	Standard (per unit)	Actual
Direct materials	5 yards at $7.00 per yard	$424,800 for 59,000 yards ($7.20 per yard)
Direct labor	1.0 hour at $12.00 per hour	$127,680 for 11,400 hours ($11.20 per hour)
Overhead	1.0 hour at $9.30 per hour (fixed $6.30; variable $3.00)	$90,000 fixed overhead $42,000 variable overhead

Overhead is applied on the basis of direct labor hours. At normal capacity, budgeted fixed overhead costs were $94,500, and budgeted variable overhead costs were $45,000.

Instructions
(a) Compute the total, price, and quantity variances for (1) materials and (2) labor, and compute the total, controllable, and volume variances for manufacturing overhead.
(b)   ▭▬▬▶ Which of the materials and labor variances should be investigated if management considers a variance of more than 6% from standard to be significant?

Answer questions about variances.
(SO 4, 5)

P8-4B   Oaks Manufacturing Company uses a standard cost accounting system. In 2002, 36,000 units were produced. Each unit took several pounds of direct materials and $1\frac{1}{4}$ standard hours of direct labor at a standard hourly rate of $12.00. Normal capacity was 42,000 direct labor hours. During the year, 132,000 pounds of raw materials were purchased at $0.90 per pound. All pounds purchased were used during the year.

Instructions
(a) If the materials price variance was $6,600 unfavorable, what was the standard materials price per pound?
(b) If the materials quantity variance was $2,550 favorable, what was the standard materials quantity per unit?
(c) What were the standard hours allowed for the units produced?
(d) If the labor quantity variance was $8,400 unfavorable, what were the actual direct labor hours worked?
(e) If the labor price variance was $9,140 favorable, what was the actual rate per hour?
(f) If total budgeted manufacturing overhead was $319,200 at normal capacity, what was the predetermined overhead rate?
(g) What was the standard cost per unit of product?
(h) How much overhead was applied to production during the year?
(i) If the fixed overhead rate was $2.50, what was the overhead volume variance?
(j) If the overhead controllable variance was $3,000 favorable, what were the total variable overhead costs incurred?
(k) Using selected answers above, what were the total costs assigned to work in process?

Journalize and post standard cost entries, and prepare income statement.
(SO 4, 5, 8)

*P8-5B   Pomona Manufacturing Company uses standard costs with its job order cost accounting system. In January, an order (Job 84) was received for 4,000 units of Product D. The standard cost of 1 unit of Product D is as follows.

Direct materials—1.4 pounds at $4.00 per pound	$ 5.60
Direct labor—1 hour at $9.00 per hour	9.00
Overhead—1 hour (variable $7.40; fixed $10.00)	17.40
Standard cost per unit	$32.00

Overhead is applied on the basis of direct labor hours. Normal capacity for the month of January was 4,500 direct labor hours. During January, the following transactions applicable to Job No. 84 occurred.

1. Purchased 6,200 pounds of raw materials on account at $3.50 per pound.
2. Requisitioned 6,200 pounds of raw materials for production.
3. Incurred 3,900 hours of direct labor at $9.25 per hour.
4. Worked 3,900 hours of direct labor on Job No. 84.
5. Incurred $73,650 of manufacturing overhead on account.
6. Applied overhead to Job No. 84 on the basis of direct labor hours.
7. Transferred Job No. 84 to finished goods.
8. Billed customer for Job No. 84 at a selling price of $250,000.
9. Incurred selling and administrative expenses on account $61,000.

Instructions
(a) Journalize the transactions.
(b) Post to the job order cost accounts.
(c) Prepare the entry to recognize the overhead variances.
(d) Prepare the income statement for management for January 2002.

◆ BROADENING YOUR PERSPECTIVE

GROUP DECISION CASE

BYP8-1   Gates Professionals, a management consulting firm, specializes in strategic planning for financial institutions. Bob Menard and Alice Chavez, partners in the firm, are assembling a new strategic planning model for use by clients. The model is designed for use on most microcomputers and replaces a rather lengthy manual model currently marketed by the firm. To market the new model Bob and Alice will need to provide clients with an estimate of the number of labor hours and computer time needed to operate the model. The model is currently being test marketed at five small financial institutions. These financial institutions are listed below, along with the number of combined computer/labor hours used by each institution to run the model one time.

Financial Institutions	Computer/Labor Hours Required
Midland National	25
First State	45
Financial Federal	40
Pacific America	30
Lakeview National	30
Total	170
Average	34

Any company that purchases the new model will need to purchase user manuals to access and operate the system. Also required are specialized computer forms that are sold only by Gates Professionals. User manuals will be sold to clients in cases of 20, at a cost of $400 per case. One manual must be used each time the model is run because each manual includes a nonreusable computer accessed password for operating the system. The specialized computer forms are sold in packages of 250, at a cost of $75 per package. One application of the model requires the use of 50 forms. This amount includes two forms that are generally wasted in each application due to printer alignment errors. The overall cost of the strategic planning model to user clients is $12,000. Most clients will use the model four times annually.

Gates Professionals must provide its clients with estimates of ongoing costs incurred in operating the new strategic planning model. They would like to provide this information in the form of standard costs.

Instructions
With the class divided into groups, answer the following.
(a) What factors should be considered in setting a standard for computer/labor hours?
(b) What alternatives for setting a standard for computer/labor hours might be used?
(c) What standard for computer/labor hours would you select? Justify your answer.
(d) Determine the standard materials cost associated with the user manuals and computer forms for each application of the strategic planning model.

MANAGERIAL ANALYSIS

BYP8-2 Mo Vaugh and Associates is a medium-sized company located near a large metropolitan area in the Midwest. The company manufactures cabinets of mahogany, oak, and other fine woods for use in expensive homes, restaurants, and hotels. Although some of the work is custom, many of the cabinets are a standard size.

One such non-custom model is called Luxury Base Frame. Standard production is 1,000 units. Each unit has a direct labor hour standard of 5 hours. Overhead is applied to production based on standard direct labor hours. During the most recent month, only 900 units were produced; 4,500 direct labor hours were allowed for standard production, but only 4,000 hours were used. Standard and actual overhead costs were as follows.

	Standard (1,000 units)	Actual (900 units)
Indirect materials	$ 12,000	$ 12,300
Indirect labor	43,000	51,000
(Fixed) Manufacturing supervisors salaries	22,000	22,000
(Fixed) Manufacturing office employees salaries	13,000	11,500
(Fixed) Engineering costs	27,000	25,000
Computer costs	10,000	10,000
Electricity	2,500	2,500
(Fixed) Manufacturing building depreciation	8,000	8,000
(Fixed) Machinery depreciation	3,000	3,000
(Fixed) Trucks and forklift depreciation	1,500	1,500
Small tools	700	1,400
(Fixed) Insurance	500	500
(Fixed) Property taxes	300	300
Total	$143,500	$149,000

Instructions
(a) Determine the overhead application rate.
(b) Determine how much overhead was applied to production.
(c) Calculate the controllable overhead variance and the overhead volume variance.
(d) Decide which overhead variances should be investigated.
(e) Discuss causes of the overhead variances. What can management do to improve its performance next month?

REAL-WORLD FOCUS

BYP8-3 Glassmaster Co. was incorporated in 1946 as Koolvent Metal Awning Company. Its current name was adopted in 1982 to reflect the more general nature of its products. The company is organized as two divisions and one subsidiary. One division focuses on the manufacture of filaments such as fishing line and sewing thread; the other division manufactures antennas and specialty fiberglass products. Its subsidiary manufactures flexible steel wire controls and molded control panels.

The annual report of Glassmaster provides the following information.

GLASSMASTER COMPANY
Management Discussion

Gross profit margins for the year improved to 20.9% of sales compared to last year's 18.5%. All operations reported improved margins due in large part to improved operating efficiencies as a result of cost reduction measures implemented during the second and third quarters of the fiscal year and increased manufacturing throughout due to higher unit volume sales. Contributing to the improved margins was a favorable materials price variance due to competitive pricing by suppliers as a result of soft demand for petrochemical-based products. This favorable variance is temporary and will begin to reverse itself as stronger worldwide demand for commodity products improves in tandem with the economy. Partially offsetting these positive effects on profit margins were competitive pressures on sales prices of certain product lines. The company responded with pricing strategies designed to maintain and/or increase market share.

Instructions
(a) Is it apparent from the information whether Glassmaster utilizes standard costs?
(b) Do you think the price variance experienced should lead to changes in standard costs for the next fiscal year?

EXPLORING THE WEB

BYP8-4 Computer manufacturer **Hewlett-Packard's** Web site provides information about Hewlett-Packard's 25,000 electronic products and services, its worldwide operations, and its financial picture.

Address: www.hp.com/ (or go to www.wiley.com/college/weygandt)

Steps:

1. Choose **HP Financials**.
2. Choose the current **Annual Report**.
3. Review the Summary of Significant Accounting Policies in the Notes to the Financial Statements.

Instructions
(a) At what cost does Hewlett-Packard report its inventories?
(b) What inventory costing method does standard cost approximate for Hewlett-Packard?
(c) Has the lower-of-cost-or-market rule been applied to the Hewlett-Packard inventories?
(d) Why do you suppose that Hewlett-Packard accounts for and reports its inventories at standard cost?

COMMUNICATION ACTIVITY

BYP8-5 The setting of standards is critical to the effective use of standards in evaluating performance.

Instructions
Explain the following in a memo to your instructor.
(a) The comparative advantages and disadvantages of ideal versus normal standards.
(b) The factors that should be included in setting the price and quantity standards for direct materials, direct labor, and manufacturing overhead.

RESEARCH ASSIGNMENT

BYP8-6 The December 1996 issue of *Accounting Horizons* contains an article by Carol B. Cheatham and Leo R. Cheatham entitled "Redesigning Cost Systems: Is Standard Costing Obsolete?"

Instructions
Read the article and answer the following questions.
(a) For what percent of U.S. manufacturing firms are standard cost systems still the cost system of choice?
(b) What are the major criticisms of standard cost systems?
(c) How does a standard cost system relate to activity-based costing (ABC)? And, how might activity-based costing (ABC) be used to enhance a company's costing system when standard costing is the primary system?
(d) What do the authors conclude from their study of standard cost systems?

ETHICS CASE

BYP8-7 At Lofton Manufacturing Company, production workers in the Painting Department are paid on the basis of productivity. The labor time standard for a unit of production is established through periodic time studies conducted by the Fisher Management Department. In a time study, the actual time required to complete a specific task by a worker is observed. Allowances are then made for preparation time, rest periods, and clean-up time. Dion Young is one of several veterans in the Painting Department.

Dion is informed by Fisher Management that he will be used in the time study for the painting of a new product. The findings will be the basis for establishing the labor time standard for the next 6 months. During the test, Dion deliberately slows his normal work pace in an effort to obtain a labor time standard that will be easy to meet. Because it is a new product, the Fisher Management representative who conducted the test is unaware that Dion did not give the test his best effort.

Instructions
(a) Who was benefited and who was harmed by Dion's actions?
(b) Was Dion ethical in the way he performed the time study test?
(c) What measure(s) might the company take to obtain valid data for setting the labor time standard?

Answers to Self-Study Questions
1. c   2. d   3. b   4. c   5. b   6. a   7. d   8. a   9. b   10. c

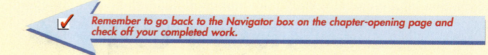
✓ *Remember to go back to the Navigator box on the chapter-opening page and check off your completed work.*

CHAPTER 9

Incremental Analysis

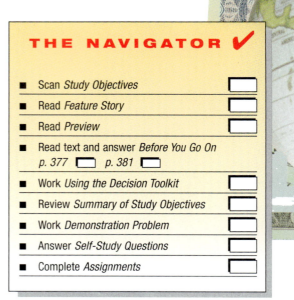

THE NAVIGATOR ✔

- Scan *Study Objectives* ☐
- Read *Feature Story* ☐
- Read *Preview* ☐
- Read text and answer *Before You Go On*
  p. 377 ☐   p. 381 ☐
- Work *Using the Decision Toolkit* ☐
- Review *Summary of Study Objectives* ☐
- Work *Demonstration Problem* ☐
- Answer *Self-Study Questions* ☐
- Complete *Assignments* ☐

◆ STUDY OBJECTIVES

After studying this chapter, you should be able to:

1. Identify the steps in management's decision-making process.

2. Describe the concept of incremental analysis.

3. Identify the relevant costs in accepting an order at a special price.

4. Identify the relevant costs in a make-or-buy decision.

5. Give the decision rule for whether to sell or process materials further.

6. Identify the factors to be considered in retaining or replacing equipment.

7. Explain the relevant factors in deciding whether to eliminate an unprofitable segment.

8. Explain the term "sales mix" and its effects in determining break-even sales.

9. Determine sales mix when a company has limited resources.

THE NAVIGATOR

◆ FEATURE STORY

MAKE IT OR BUY IT?

When is a manufacturer not a manufacturer? When it outsources. An extension of the classic "make or buy" decision, outsourcing involves hiring other companies to make all or part of a product or to perform services. Who is outsourcing? **Nike**, **General Motors**, **Sara Lee**, and **Hewlett-Packard**, to name a few. Even a recent trade journal article for small cabinet makers outlined the pros and cons of building cabinet doors and drawers internally, or outsourcing them to other shops.

Gibson Greetings, Inc., one of the country's largest sellers of greeting cards, has experienced both the pros and cons of outsourcing. In April one year it announced it would outsource the manufacturing of all of its cards and gift wrap. Gibson's stock price shot up quickly because investors believed the strategy could save the company $10 million a year, primarily by reducing manufacturing costs. But later in the same year Gibson got a taste of the negative side of outsourcing: When one of its suppliers was unable to meet its production schedule, about $20 million of

Christmas cards went to stores a month later than scheduled.

Outsourcing is often a point of dispute in labor negotiations. Although many of the jobs lost to outsourcing go overseas, that is not always the case. In fact, a recent trend is to hire out work to vendors located close to the company. This reduces shipping costs and can improve coordination of efforts.

One company that has benefited from local outsourcing is **Solectron Corporation** in Silicon Valley. It makes things like cell phones, printers, and computers for high-tech companies in the region. To the surprise of many, it has kept 5,600 people employed in California, rather than watching those jobs go overseas. What is its secret? It produces high-quality products efficiently. Solectron has to be efficient because it operates on a very thin profit margin—that is, it makes a tiny amount of money on each part—but it makes millions and millions of parts. It has proved the logic of outsourcing as a management decision, both for the companies for whom it makes parts and for its owners and employees.

THE NAVIGATOR

An important purpose of management accounting is to provide managers with relevant information for decision making. Companies of all sorts must make product decisions. **Philip Morris** decided to cut prices to raise market share. **Oral-B Laboratories** opted to produce a new, higher priced ($5) toothbrush. **General Motors** discontinued making the Buick Riviera and announced the closure of its Oldsmobile Division. **Quaker Oats** decided to sell a line of beverages, at a price more than one billion dollars less than it paid for that product line only a few years before. Ski manufacturers like **Dynastar** had to decide whether to use their limited resources to make snowboards instead of downhill skis.

This chapter explains management's decision-making process and a decision-making approach called incremental analysis. The use of incremental analysis is demonstrated in a variety of situations.

The content and organization of this chapter are as follows.

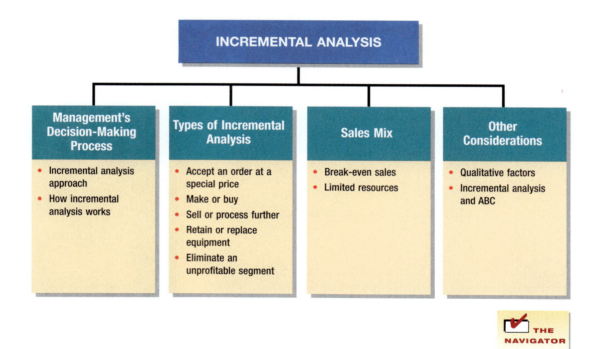

INCREMENTAL ANALYSIS

Management's Decision-Making Process	Types of Incremental Analysis	Sales Mix	Other Considerations
• Incremental analysis approach • How incremental analysis works	• Accept an order at a special price • Make or buy • Sell or process further • Retain or replace equipment • Eliminate an unprofitable segment	• Break-even sales • Limited resources	• Qualitative factors • Incremental analysis and ABC

THE NAVIGATOR

MANAGEMENT'S DECISION-MAKING PROCESS

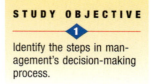

STUDY OBJECTIVE

◆ 1 ◆

Identify the steps in management's decision-making process.

Making decisions is an important management function. Management's decision-making process does not always follow a set pattern, because decisions vary significantly in their scope, urgency, and importance. It is possible, though, to identify some steps that are frequently involved in the process. These steps are shown in Illustration 9-1.

Accounting's contribution to the decision-making process occurs primarily in Steps 2 and 4. In Step 2, for each possible course of action, relevant revenue and cost data are provided. These show the expected overall effect on net income. In Step 4, internal reports are prepared that review the actual impact of the decision.

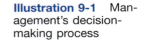

Illustration 9-1 Management's decision-making process

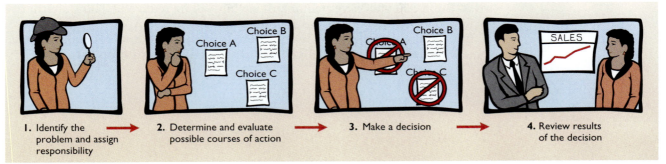

1. Identify the problem and assign responsibility → 2. Determine and evaluate possible courses of action → 3. Make a decision → 4. Review results of the decision

In making business decisions, management ordinarily considers both financial and nonfinancial information. **Financial** information is related to revenues and costs and their effect on the company's overall profitability. **Nonfinancial** information relates to such factors as the effect of the decision on employee turnover, the environment, or the overall image of the company in the community. Although nonfinancial information can be as important as the financial information, we will focus primarily on financial information that is relevant to the decision.

INCREMENTAL ANALYSIS APPROACH

Decisions involve a choice among alternative courses of action. Suppose that you were deciding whether to purchase or lease a computer for use in doing your accounting homework. The financial data relate to the cost of leasing versus the cost of purchasing. For example, leasing would involve periodic lease payments; purchasing would require "up-front" payment of the purchase price. In other words, the financial data relevant to the decision are the data that would vary in the future among the possible alternatives. The process used to identify the financial data that change under alternative courses of action is called **incremental analysis**. In some cases, you will find that when you use incremental analysis, both costs **and** revenues will vary. In other cases, only costs **or** revenues will vary.

Just as your decision to buy or lease a PC will affect your future, similar decisions, on a larger scale, will affect a company's future. Incremental analysis identifies the probable effects of those decisions on future earnings. Such analysis inevitably involves estimates and uncertainty. Gathering data for incremental analyses may involve market analysts, engineers, and accountants. In quantifying the data, the accountant is expected to produce the most reliable information available at the time the decision must be made.

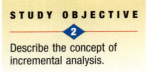

STUDY OBJECTIVE
2
Describe the concept of incremental analysis.

Alternative Terminology
Incremental analysis is also called *differential analysis* because the analysis focuses on differences.

HOW INCREMENTAL ANALYSIS WORKS

The basic approach in incremental analysis is illustrated in the following example.

Illustration 9-2 Basic approach in incremental analysis

	Alternative A	Alternative B	Net Income Increase (Decrease)
Revenues	$125,000	$110,000	$(15,000)
Costs	100,000	80,000	20,000
Net income	$ 25,000	$ 30,000	$ 5,000

In this example, alternative B is being compared with alternative A. The net income column shows the differences between the alternatives. In this case, incremental revenue will be $15,000 less under alternative B than under alternative A. But a $20,000 incremental cost saving will be realized.[1] Thus, alternative B will produce $5,000 more net income than alternative A.

In the following pages you will encounter three important cost concepts used in incremental analysis, as defined and discussed in Illustration 9-3.

Illustration 9-3 Key cost concepts in incremental analysis

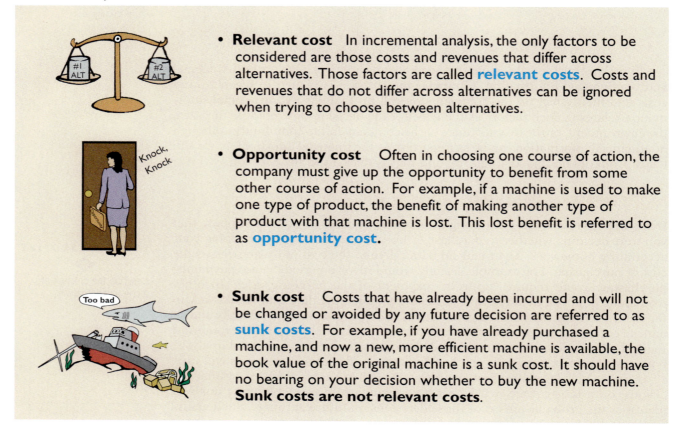

- **Relevant cost**   In incremental analysis, the only factors to be considered are those costs and revenues that differ across alternatives. Those factors are called **relevant costs**. Costs and revenues that do not differ across alternatives can be ignored when trying to choose between alternatives.

- **Opportunity cost**   Often in choosing one course of action, the company must give up the opportunity to benefit from some other course of action. For example, if a machine is used to make one type of product, the benefit of making another type of product with that machine is lost. This lost benefit is referred to as **opportunity cost**.

- **Sunk cost**   Costs that have already been incurred and will not be changed or avoided by any future decision are referred to as **sunk costs**. For example, if you have already purchased a machine, and now a new, more efficient machine is available, the book value of the original machine is a sunk cost. It should have no bearing on your decision whether to buy the new machine. **Sunk costs are not relevant costs.**

Incremental analysis sometimes involves changes that at first glance might seem contrary to your intuition. For example, sometimes variable costs **do not** change under the alternative courses of action. Also, sometimes fixed costs **do** change. For example, direct labor, normally a variable cost, is not an incremental cost in deciding between two new factory machines if each asset requires the same amount of direct labor. In contrast, rent expense, normally a fixed cost, is an incremental cost in a decision whether to continue occupancy of a building or to purchase or lease a new building.

---

[1]Although income taxes are sometimes important in incremental analysis, they are ignored in the chapter for simplicity's sake.

TYPES OF INCREMENTAL ANALYSIS

A number of different types of decisions involve incremental analysis. The more common types of decisions are whether to:

1. Accept an order at a special price.
2. Make or buy component parts or finished products.
3. Sell products or process them further.
4. Retain or replace equipment.
5. Eliminate an unprofitable business segment.

We will consider each of these types of incremental analysis in the following pages.

ACCEPT AN ORDER AT A SPECIAL PRICE

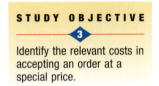

STUDY OBJECTIVE

3

Identify the relevant costs in accepting an order at a special price.

Sometimes a company may have an opportunity to obtain additional business if it is willing to make a major price concession to a specific customer. To illustrate, assume that Sunbelt Company produces 100,000 automatic blenders per month, which is 80 percent of plant capacity. Variable manufacturing costs are $8 per unit. Fixed manufacturing costs are $400,000, or $4 per unit. The blenders are normally sold directly to retailers at $20 each. Sunbelt has an offer from Mexico Co. (a foreign wholesaler) to purchase an additional 2,000 blenders at $11 per unit. Acceptance of the offer would not affect normal sales of the product, and the additional units can be manufactured without increasing plant capacity. What should management do?

If management makes its decision on the basis of the total cost per unit of $12 ($8 + $4), the order would be rejected, because costs ($12) would exceed revenues ($11) by $1 per unit. However, since the units can be produced within existing plant capacity, the special order **will not increase fixed costs**. Let's identify the relevant data for the decision. First, the variable manufacturing costs will increase $16,000, ($8 × 2,000). Second, the expected revenue will increase $22,000, ($11 × 2,000). Thus, as shown in Illustration 9-4, Sunbelt will increase its net income by $6,000 by accepting this special order.

Helpful Hint This is a good example of different costs for different purposes. In the long run all costs are relevant, but for this decision only costs that change are relevant.

	Reject Order	Accept Order	Net Income Increase (Decrease)
Revenues	$-0-	$22,000	**$22,000**
Costs	-0-	16,000	**(16,000)**
Net income	$-0-	$ 6,000	**$ 6,000**

Illustration 9-4 Incremental analysis—accepting an order at a special price

Two points should be emphasized: First, it is assumed that sales of the product in other markets **would not be affected by this special order**. If other sales were affected, then Sunbelt would have to consider the lost sales in making the decision. Second, if Sunbelt is operating **at full capacity**, it is likely that the special order would be rejected. Under such circumstances, the company would have to expand plant capacity. In that case, the special order would have to absorb these additional fixed manufacturing costs, as well as the variable manufacturing costs.

MAKE OR BUY

STUDY OBJECTIVE

4

Identify the relevant costs in a make-or-buy decision.

When a manufacturer assembles component parts in producing a finished product, management must decide whether to make or buy the components. The decision to buy parts or services is often referred to as outsourcing. For example, as discussed in the *Feature Story*, a company such as **General Motors Corporation** may either make or buy the batteries, tires, and radios used in its cars. Similarly, **Hewlett-Packard Corporation** may make or buy the electronic circuitry, cases, and printer heads for its printers. The decision to make or buy components should be made on the basis of incremental analysis.

To illustrate the analysis, assume that Baron Company incurs the following annual costs in producing 25,000 ignition switches for motor scooters.

Illustration 9-5 Annual product cost data

Direct materials	$ 50,000
Direct labor	75,000
Variable manufacturing overhead	40,000
Fixed manufacturing overhead	60,000
Total manufacturing costs	$225,000
Total cost per unit ($225,000 ÷ 25,000)	**$9.00**

Or, instead of making its own switches, Baron Company might purchase the ignition switches from Ignition, Inc. at a price of $8 per unit. The question again is, "What should management do?"

At first glance, it appears that management should purchase the ignition switches for $8, rather than make them at a cost of $9. However, a review of operations indicates that if the ignition switches are purchased from Ignition, Inc., *all* of Baron's variable costs but only $10,000 of its fixed manufacturing costs will be eliminated. Thus, $50,000 of the fixed manufacturing costs will remain if the ignition switches are purchased. The relevant costs for incremental analysis, therefore, are as follows.

Illustration 9-6 Incremental analysis—make or buy

	Make	Buy	Net Income Increase (Decrease)
Direct materials	$ 50,000	$ –0–	$ 50,000
Direct labor	75,000	–0–	75,000
Variable manufacturing costs	40,000	–0–	40,000
Fixed manufacturing costs	60,000	50,000	10,000
Purchase price (25,000 × $8)	–0–	200,000	(200,000)
Total annual cost	$225,000	$250,000	$ (25,000)

Helpful Hint In the make-or-buy decision it is important for management to take into account the social impact of the choice. For instance, buying may be the most economically feasible solution, but such action could result in the closure of a manufacturing plant that employs many good workers.

This analysis indicates that Baron Company will incur $25,000 of additional cost by buying the ignition switches. Therefore, Baron should continue to make the ignition switches, even though the total manufacturing cost is $1 higher than the purchase price. The reason is that if the company purchases the ignition switches, it will still have fixed costs of $50,000 to absorb.

Opportunity Cost

The foregoing make-or-buy analysis is complete only if it is assumed that the productive capacity used to make the ignition switches cannot be converted to another purpose. If there is an opportunity to use this productive capacity in some other manner, then this opportunity cost must be considered. As indicated earlier, **opportunity cost** is the potential benefit that may be obtained by following an alternative course of action.

To illustrate, assume that through buying the switches, Baron Company can use the released productive capacity to generate additional income of $28,000 from producing a different product. This lost income is an additional cost of continuing to make the switches in the make-or-buy decision. This opportunity cost therefore is added to the "Make" column, for comparison. As shown, it is now advantageous to buy the ignition switches.

	Make	Buy	Net Income Increase (Decrease)
Total annual cost	$225,000*	$250,000*	$(25,000)
Opportunity cost	**28,000**	–0–	**28,000**
Total cost	$253,000	$250,000	$ 3,000

*From Illustration 9-6.

Illustration 9-7   Incremental analysis—make or buy, with opportunity cost

The qualitative factors in this decision include the possible loss of jobs for employees who produce the ignition switches. In addition, management must assess how long the supplier will be able to satisfy the company's quality control standards at the quoted price per unit.

BUSINESS INSIGHT
Management Perspective

In the bicycle industry, nearly all bikes of quality are made with **Shimano** parts. This dominance by a single supplier has made bikes a sort of commodity. That is, if all bikes are made from the same parts, then what does it matter what brand of bike you buy? As a consequence, the majority of profits go to Shimano, with bike manufacturers that use Shimano parts having to accept an increasingly small profit margin.

To break this trend, and increase its profit margins, **Cannondale Corporation** has decided to take the approach that "we manufacture the whole bicycle, not just take a frame and put somebody's parts on it." Similar steps are being taken by **Trek Bicycle Corporation** and **Specialized Bicycle Components Inc.** These companies recognize that they are taking a risk. In order to compete with Shimano, they will have to dramatically step up their research and development efforts and significantly increase their efficiency in the manufacture of parts. This will be difficult given Shimano's huge volume advantage.

Source: Ross Kerber, "Bike Maker Faces a Tactical Shift," *Wall Street Journal*, October 12, 1998, p. B1.

SELL OR PROCESS FURTHER

Many manufacturers have the option of selling products at a given point in the production cycle or continuing to process with the expectation of selling them at a later point at a higher price. For example, a bicycle manufacturer such as **Schwinn** could sell its 10-speed bicycles to retailers either unassembled or assembled. A furniture manufacturer such as **Ethan Allen** could sell its dining room sets to furniture stores either unfinished or finished. The sell-or-process-further

STUDY OBJECTIVE
◆
5

Give the decision rule for whether to sell or process materials further.

decision should be made on the basis of incremental analysis. The basic decision rule is: **Process further as long as the incremental revenue from such processing exceeds the incremental processing costs.**

Single-Product Case

Assume, for example, that Woodmasters Inc. makes tables. The cost to manufacture an unfinished table is $35, computed as follows.

Illustration 9-8 Per unit cost of unfinished table

Direct material	$15
Direct labor	10
Variable manufacturing overhead	6
Fixed manufacturing overhead	4
Manufacturing cost per unit	**$35**

The selling price per unfinished unit is $50. Woodmasters currently has unused productive capacity that is expected to continue indefinitely. What are the relevant costs? Management concludes that some of this capacity may be used to finish the tables and sell them at $60 per unit. For a finished table, direct materials will increase $2 and direct labor costs will increase $4. Variable manufacturing overhead costs will increase by $2.40 (60% of direct labor). No increase is anticipated in fixed manufacturing overhead. The incremental analysis on a per unit basis is as follows.

Illustration 9-9 Incremental analysis—sell or process further

	Sell	Process Further	Net Income Increase (Decrease)
Sales per unit	$50.00	$60.00	$10.00
Cost per unit			
Direct materials	15.00	17.00	(2.00)
Direct labor	10.00	14.00	(4.00)
Variable manufacturing overhead	6.00	8.40	(2.40)
Fixed manufacturing overhead	4.00	4.00	–0–
Total	35.00	43.40	(8.40)
Net income per unit	$15.00	$16.60	$ 1.60

Helpful Hint Current net income is known. Net income from processing further is an estimate. In making its decision, management could add a "risk" factor for the estimate.

It would be advantageous for Woodmaster to process the tables further. The incremental revenue of $10.00 from the additional processing is $1.60 higher than the incremental processing costs of $8.40.

Multiple-Product Case

Sell-or-process-further decisions are particularly applicable to production processes that produce multiple products simultaneously. In many industries, a number of end-products are produced from a single raw material and a common production process. These multiple end-products are commonly referred to as **joint products**. For example, in the meat-packing industry, a single sheep produces meat, internal organs, hides, wool, bones, and fat. In the petroleum industry, crude oil is refined to produce gasoline, lubricating oil, kerosene, paraffin, and ethylene.

Illustration 9-10 presents a joint product situation for Marais Creamery involving a decision **to sell or process further cream and skim milk**. Cream and skim milk are products that result from the processing of raw milk.

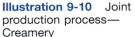

Illustration 9-10   Joint production process— Creamery

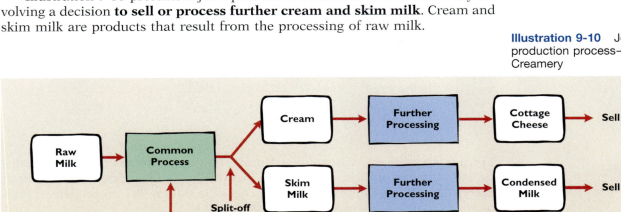

Marais incurs many costs prior to the manufacture of the cream and skim milk. All costs incurred prior to the point at which the two products are separately identifiable (the split-off point) are called **joint costs**. For purposes of determining the cost of each product, joint product costs must be allocated to the individual products. This is frequently done based on the relative sales value of the joint products. While this allocation is important for determination of product cost, it is irrelevant for any sell-or-process-further decisions. The reason is that these joint product costs are **sunk costs**. That is, they have already been incurred, and they cannot be changed or avoided by any subsequent decision.

The daily cost and revenue data for Marais Creamery are shown in Illustration 9-11.

Illustration 9-11   Cost and revenue data per day

Costs (per day)	
Joint cost allocated to cream	$ 9,000
Joint cost allocated to skim milk	5,000
Processing cream into cottage cheese	10,000
Processing skim milk into condensed milk	8,000
Expected Revenues from Products (per day)	
Cream	$19,000
Skim milk	11,000
Cottage cheese	27,000
Condensed milk	26,000

From this information we can determine whether the company should simply sell the cream and skim milk, or process them further into cottage cheese and condensed milk. Illustration 9-12 provides the analysis necessary to determine whether to sell the cream or process it further into cottage cheese.

Illustration 9-12 Analysis of whether to sell cream or process cottage cheese

	Sell	Process Further	Net Income Increase (Decrease)
Sales per day	$19,000	$27,000	$ 8,000
Cost per day			
Processing cream into			
cottage cheese	–0–	10,000	(10,000)
	$19,000	$17,000	**($2,000)**

From this analysis we can see that Marais should not process the cream further because it will sustain an incremental loss of $2,000. Illustration 9-13, however, shows that Marais Company should process the skim milk into condensed milk, as it will increase net income by $7,000.

Illustration 9-13 Analysis of whether to sell skim milk or process condensed milk

	Sell	Process Further	Net Income Increase (Decrease)
Sales per day	$11,000	$26,000	$15,000
Cost per day			
Processing skim milk			
into condensed milk	–0–	8,000	(8,000)
	$11,000	$18,000	**$7,000**

Note that the amount of joint costs allocated to each product ($9,000 to the cream and $5,000 to the skim milk) is irrelevant in deciding whether to sell or process further. Why? The joint costs remain the same whether or not further processing is performed.

RETAIN OR REPLACE EQUIPMENT

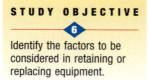

STUDY OBJECTIVE

6

Identify the factors to be considered in retaining or replacing equipment.

Management often has to decide whether to continue using an asset or replace it. To illustrate, assume that Jeffcoat Company has a factory machine with a book value of $40,000 and a remaining useful life of 4 years. It is considering replacing this machine with a new machine. A new machine is available that costs $120,000. It is expected to have zero salvage value at the end of its 4-year useful life. If the new machine is acquired, variable manufacturing costs are expected to decrease from $160,000 to $125,000 annually, and the old unit will be scrapped. The incremental analysis for the **4-year period** is as follows.

Illustration 9-14 Incremental analysis—retain or replace equipment

	Retain Equipment	Replace Equipment	Net Income Increase (Decrease)
Variable manufacturing costs	$640,000[a]	$500,000[b]	**$140,000**
New machine cost		120,000	**(120,000)**
Total	$640,000	$620,000	**$ 20,000**

[a](4 years × $160,000)
[b](4 years × $125,000)

In this case, it would be to the company's advantage to replace the equipment. The lower variable manufacturing costs due to replacement more than offset the cost of the new equipment.

One other point should be mentioned regarding Jeffcoat's decision: **The book value of the old machine does not affect the decision.** Book value is a **sunk cost,** which is a cost that cannot be changed by any present or future decision. Sunk costs **are not relevant in incremental analysis**. In this example, if the asset is retained, book value will be depreciated over its remaining useful life. Or, if the new unit is acquired, book value will be recognized as a loss of the current period. Thus, the effect of book value on current and future earnings is the same regardless of the replacement decision. **Any trade-in allowance or cash disposal value of the existing asset, however, is relevant** to the decision, because this value will not be realized if the asset is continued in use.

ELIMINATE AN UNPROFITABLE SEGMENT

Management sometimes must decide whether to eliminate an unprofitable business segment. Again, the key is to **focus on the relevant costs—the data that change under the alternative courses of action**. To illustrate, assume that Martina Company manufactures tennis racquets in three models: Pro, Master, and Champ. Pro and Master are profitable lines. Champ (highlighted in color in the table below) operates at a loss. Condensed income statement data are as follows.

STUDY OBJECTIVE

7

Explain the relevant factors in deciding whether to eliminate an unprofitable segment.

	Pro	Master	Champ	Total
Sales	$800,000	$300,000	**$100,000**	$1,200,000
Variable expenses	520,000	210,000	**90,000**	820,000
Contribution margin	280,000	90,000	**10,000**	380,000
Fixed expenses	80,000	50,000	**30,000**	160,000
Net income	$200,000	$ 40,000	**$ (20,000)**	$ 220,000

Illustration 9-15 Segment income data

Helpful Hint A decision to discontinue a segment based solely on the bottom line—net loss—is inappropriate.

It might be expected that total net income will increase by $20,000, to $240,000, if the unprofitable Champ line of racquets is eliminated. However, **net income may actually decrease if the Champ line is discontinued**. The reason is that the fixed expenses allocated to the Champ racquets will have to be absorbed by the other products. To illustrate, assume that the $30,000 of fixed costs applicable to the unprofitable segment are allocated $\frac{2}{3}$ to the Pro model and $\frac{1}{3}$ to the Master model if the Champ model is eliminated. Fixed expenses will increase to $100,000 ($80,000 + $20,000) in the Pro line and to $60,000 ($50,000 + $10,000) in the Master line. The revised income statement is:

	Pro	Master	Total
Sales	$800,000	$300,000	$1,100,000
Variable expenses	520,000	210,000	730,000
Contribution margin	280,000	90,000	370,000
Fixed expenses	**100,000**	**60,000**	160,000
Net income	$180,000	$ 30,000	**$ 210,000**

Illustration 9-16 Income data after eliminating unprofitable product line

Total net income has decreased $10,000 ($220,000 − $210,000). This result is also obtained in the following incremental analysis of the Champ racquets.

Illustration 9-17 Incremental analysis—eliminating an unprofitable segment

	Continue	Eliminate	Net Income Increase (Decrease)
Sales	$100,000	$ –0–	$(100,000)
Variable expenses	90,000	–0–	90,000
Contribution margin	10,000	–0–	(10,000)
Fixed expenses	30,000	30,000	–0–
Net income	$ (20,000)	$(30,000)	$ (10,000)

The loss in net income is attributable to the Champ line's contribution margin ($10,000) that will not be realized if the segment is discontinued.

In deciding on the future status of an unprofitable segment, management should consider the effect of elimination on related product lines. It may be possible for continuing product lines to obtain some or all of the sales lost by the discontinued product line. In some businesses, services or products may be linked—for example, free checking accounts at a bank, or coffee at a donut shop. In addition, management should consider the effect of eliminating the product line on employees who may have to be discharged or retrained.

BUSINESS INSIGHT

Management Perspective

In 1994 **Quaker Oats** paid $1.7 billion for one of America's hottest new beverage companies. While some observers thought that Quaker Oats had overpaid, Quaker's management believed it was an exciting purchase because it would make a great strategic partner for Quaker Oats' famous sport drink—Gatorade.

But for a variety of reasons, the acquisition didn't work out. One of the reasons was that at about the same time, several other major beverage manufacturers decided to begin producing and selling competing fruit and tea drinks. Worse yet, the processing methods used by these other manufacturers appeared to allow them to produce their drinks much more inexpensively.

Only a few years after purchasing the beverage company, Quaker Oats sold it and took a $1.4 billion loss. Management stated that by selling this division, the company could reduce its debt burden and focus its remaining assets on its cereal brands and Gatorade.

DECISION TOOLKIT

Decision Checkpoints	Info Needed for Decision	Tool to Use for Decision	How to Evaluate Results
Which alternative should the company choose?	All relevant costs and opportunity costs	Compare relevant cost of each alternative.	Choose the alternative that maximizes net income.

BEFORE YOU GO ON . . .

◆ **Review It**

1. Give three examples of how incremental analysis might be used.
2. What is the decision rule in deciding to sell or process products further?
3. How may the elimination of an unprofitable segment decrease the overall net income of a company?

◆ **Do It**

Cobb Company incurs a cost of $28 per unit, of which $18 is variable, to make a product that normally sells for $42. A foreign wholesaler offers to buy 5,000 units at $25 each. Cobb will incur shipping costs of $1 per unit. Compute the increase or decrease in net income Cobb will realize by accepting the special order, assuming Cobb has excess operating capacity.

Action Plan

• Identify all revenues that will change as a result of accepting the order.
• Identify all costs that will change as a result of accepting the order, and net this amount against the change in revenues.

Solution

	Reject	Accept	Net Income Increase (Decrease)
Revenues	$–0–	$125,000	$125,000
Costs	–0–	95,000*	(95,000)
Net income	$–0–	$ 30,000	$ 30,000

*(5,000 × $18) + (5,000 × $1)

Given the result of the analysis, Cobb Company should accept the special order.

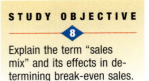

Related exercise material: BE9-2, BE9-3, and E9-1.

SALES MIX

Most companies sell more than one product. **Sales mix** is the relative combination in which a company's products are sold. For example, if 2 units of Product A are sold for 1 unit of Product B, the sales mix of the products is 2:1. Sales mix affects management's decision making process in a number of ways. In this section we discuss how sales mix affects break-even analysis and how restrictions on a company's resources can affect the decision on optimal sales mix.

STUDY OBJECTIVE
8
Explain the term "sales mix" and its effects in determining break-even sales.

BREAK-EVEN SALES

Break-even sales can be computed for a mix of two or more products by determining the **weighted average unit contribution margin of all the products**. To illustrate, we will assume that Vargo Video sells both VCRs and television sets (TVs) at the following per unit data.

Illustration 9-18 Per unit data—sales mix

Unit Data	VCRs	TVs
Selling price	$500	$800
Variable costs	300	400
Contribution margin	$200	$400
Sales mix	3	1

The total contribution margin for the sales mix of 3 VCRs to 1 TV is $1,000, which is computed as follows.

$$[(\$200 \times 3) + (\$400 \times 1)] = \$1,000$$

The weighted average unit contribution margin is calculated as total contribution margin divided by the number of units in the sales mix. For Vargo Video, the weighted average unit contribution margin is $250, computed as follows.

$$\$1,000 \div 4 \text{ units} = \$250$$

We then use the weighted average unit contribution margin to compute the break-even point in unit sales as follows.

Illustration 9-19
Break-even formula— sales mix

Helpful Hint What are break-even sales in units if the sales mix is reversed?
Answer: Total contribution margin = $1,400 ($200 + $1,200). Weighted average unit contrib. margin = $350 ($1,400 ÷ 4). Break-even units = 571 (rounded).

The computation of break-even sales in units for Vargo Video, assuming $200,000 of fixed costs, is as follows.

$$\$200,000 \div \$250 = 800 \text{ units}$$

Note that with the sales mix of 3 to 1, three-fourths of the units sold will be VCRs and one-fourth will be TVs. Therefore, in order to break even, Vargo Video must sell 600 VCRs ($\frac{3}{4} \times 800$) and 200 TVs ($\frac{1}{4} \times 800$). This can be verified by the following.

Illustration 9-20
Break-even proof—sales mix

Product	Unit Sales	×	Unit CM	=	Total CM
VCRs	600	×	$200	=	$ 120,000
TVs	200	×	400	=	80,000
	800				**$200,000**

Helpful Hint Continue the preceding Helpful Hint: How many VCRs and TVs must be sold?
Answer:
VCRs 143 (571 × ¼)
TVs 428 (571 × ¾)

Management should continually review the company's sales mix. At any level of units sold, **net income will be greater if more high contribution margin units are sold than low contribution margin units**. For Vargo Video, the television sets produce the higher contribution margin. Consequently, if 300 TVs and 500 VCRs are sold, net income would be higher than in the current sales mix, even though total units sold has not changed.

An analysis of these relationships shows that a shift from low-margin sales to high-margin sales may increase net income, even though there is a decline in total units sold. Likewise, a shift from high- to low-margin sales may result in a decrease in net income, even though there is an increase in total units sold.

DECISION TOOLKIT

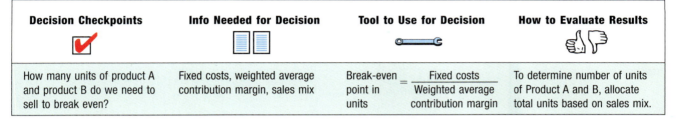

Decision Checkpoints	Info Needed for Decision	Tool to Use for Decision	How to Evaluate Results
How many units of product A and product B do we need to sell to break even?	Fixed costs, weighted average contribution margin, sales mix	Break-even point in units $=\dfrac{\text{Fixed costs}}{\text{Weighted average contribution margin}}$	To determine number of units of Product A and B, allocate total units based on sales mix.

LIMITED RESOURCES

In our break-even analysis we assumed a certain sales mix. But as the conclusion to that discussion noted, management must constantly evaluate its sales mix to determine whether it is optimal. One factor that affects the sales mix decision is the relative resources that each product uses.

Everyone's resources are limited. For a company, the limited resource may be floor space in a retail department store, or raw materials, direct labor hours, or machine capacity in a manufacturing company. When a company has limited resources, management must decide which products to make and sell in order to maximize net income.

To illustrate, assume that Collins Company manufactures deluxe and standard pen and pencil sets. The limiting resource is machine capacity, which is 3,600 hours per month. Relevant data consist of the following.

STUDY OBJECTIVE
9
Determine sales mix when a company has limited resources.

	Deluxe Sets	Standard Sets
Contribution margin per unit	$8	$6
Machine hours required per unit	0.4	0.2

Illustration 9-21 Contribution margin and machine hours

The deluxe sets may appear to be more profitable since they have a higher contribution margin ($8) than the standard sets ($6). However, note that the standard sets take fewer machine hours to produce than the deluxe sets. Therefore, it is necessary to find the **contribution margin per unit of limited resource**, in this case, contribution margin per machine hour. This is obtained by dividing the contribution margin per unit of each product by the number of units of the limited resource required for each product, as shown in Illustration 9-22.

Helpful Hint CM alone is not enough to make this decision. The key factor is CM per limited resource.

	Deluxe Sets	Standard Sets
Contribution margin per unit (a)	$8	$6
Machine hours required (b)	0.4	0.2
Contribution margin per unit of limited resource [(a) ÷ (b)]	**$20**	**$30**

Illustration 9-22 Contribution margin per unit of limited resource

The computation shows that the standard sets have a higher contribution margin per unit of limited resource. This would suggest that, given sufficient demand for standard sets, the company should shift the sales mix to standard sets or increase machine capacity.

If Collins Company is able to increase machine capacity from 3,600 hours to 4,200 hours, the additional 600 hours could be used to produce either the standard or deluxe pen and pencil sets. The total contribution margin under each alternative is found by multiplying the machine hours by the contribution margin per unit of limited resource, as shown below.

Illustration 9-23 Incremental analysis—computation of total contribution margin

	Produce Deluxe Sets	Produce Standard Sets
Machine hours (a)	600	600
Contribution margin per unit of limited resource (b)	$20	$30
Contribution margin [(a) × (b)]	**$12,000**	**$18,000**

From this analysis, we can see that to maximize net income, all of the increased capacity should be used to make and sell the standard sets.

BUSINESS INSIGHT

Management Perspective

When fragrance sales recently went flat, retailers turned up the heat on fragrance manufacturers. The amount of floor space devoted to fragrances was reduced, leaving fragrance manufacturers fighting each other for a smaller space. The retailer doesn't just choose the fragrance with the highest contribution margin. Instead, it chooses the fragrance with the highest contribution margin per square foot. In this game, a product with a lower contribution margin, but a higher turnover, could well be the winner.

DECISION TOOLKIT

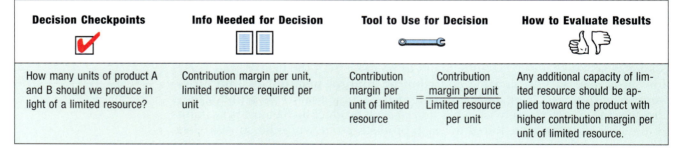

Decision Checkpoints	Info Needed for Decision	Tool to Use for Decision	How to Evaluate Results
How many units of product A and B should we produce in light of a limited resource?	Contribution margin per unit, limited resource required per unit	Contribution margin per unit of limited resource = Contribution margin per unit / Limited resource per unit	Any additional capacity of limited resource should be applied toward the product with higher contribution margin per unit of limited resource.

OTHER CONSIDERATIONS IN DECISION MAKING

QUALITATIVE FACTORS

In this chapter we have focused primarily on the quantitative factors that affect a decision—those attributes that can be easily expressed in terms of numbers or dollars. However, many of the decisions involving incremental analysis have important qualitative features; though not easily measured, they should not be ignored.

Consider, for example, the potential effects of the make-or-buy decision *or* of the decision to eliminate a line of business on existing employees and the community in which the plant is located. The cost savings that may be obtained from outsourcing or from eliminating a plant should be weighed against these qualitative attributes. One such would be the cost of lost morale that might result. Al "Chainsaw" Dunlap was a so-called "turnaround" artist who went into many companies, identified inefficiencies (using incremental analysis techniques), and tried to correct these problems to improve corporate profitability. Along the way he laid off thousands of employees at numerous companies. At his most recent position as head of **Sunbeam**, it was Al Dunlap who eventually lost his job because his Draconian approach failed to improve Sunbeam's profitability. It was widely reported that Sunbeam's employees openly rejoiced for days after his departure. Clearly, qualitative factors can matter.

RELATIONSHIP OF INCREMENTAL ANALYSIS AND ACTIVITY-BASED COSTING

In Chapter 4 we noted that many companies have shifted to activity-based costing to allocate overhead costs to products. The primary reason for using activity-based costing is that it results in a more accurate allocation of overhead. That is, activity-based costing better associates the actual increase in overhead costs that results from the manufacture of each product. The concepts presented in this chapter are completely consistent with the use of activity-based costing. In fact, activity-based costing will result in better identification of relevant costs and, therefore, better incremental analysis.

BUSINESS INSIGHT
Management Perspective

The existence of excess plant capacity is frequently the incentive for management to add new products. Adding one new product may not add much incremental cost. But continuing to add products will at some point create new constraints, perhaps requiring additional investments in people, equipment, and facilities.

The effects of product and product line proliferation are generally understood. But the effect on incremental overhead costs of *changes in servicing customers* is less understood. For example, if a company newly offers its customers the option of product delivery by case or by pallet, the new service may appear to be simple and low in cost. But, if the manufacturing process must be realigned to package in two different forms; if two sets of inventory records must be maintained; and if warehousing, handling, and shipping require two different arrangements or sets of equipment, the additional costs of this new option could be as high as a whole new product. If the customer service option were adopted for all products, the product line could effectively be doubled—but so might many overhead costs.

Source: Elizabeth Haas Edersheim and Joan Wilson, "Complexity at Consumer Goods Companies: Naming and Taming the Beast," *Journal of Cost Management.*

BEFORE YOU GO ON . . .

◆ **Review It**

1. State the formula for computing break-even sales in units when a company sells more than one product.

2. Explain how a company that shifts its sales mix might actually increase its net income even though the total number of units it sells declines.
3. What is the critical factor in allocating limited resources to various product lines?

USING THE DECISION TOOLKIT

Suppose **Hewlett-Packard Company** must decide whether to make or buy some of its components from **Solectron Corp**. The cost of producing 50,000 electrical connectors for its printers is $110,000, broken down as follows.

Direct materials	$60,000	Variable overhead	$12,000
Direct labor	30,000	Fixed overhead	8,000

Instead of making the electrical connectors at an average cost per unit of $2.20 ($110,000 ÷ 50,000), the company has an opportunity to buy the connectors at $2.15 per unit. If the connectors are purchased, all variable costs and one-half of the fixed costs will be eliminated.

Instructions

(a) Prepare an incremental analysis showing whether the company should make or buy the electrical connectors.

(b) Will your answer be different if the released productive capacity resulting from the purchase of the connectors will generate additional income of $25,000?

Solution

(a)

	Make	Buy	Net Income Increase (Decrease)
Direct materials	$ 60,000	$ –0–	$ 60,000
Direct labor	30,000	–0–	30,000
Variable manufacturing costs	12,000	–0–	12,000
Fixed manufacturing costs	8,000	4,000	4,000
Purchase price	–0–	107,500	(107,500)
Total cost	$110,000	$111,500	$ (1,500)

This analysis indicates that Hewlett-Packard will incur $1,500 of additional costs if it buys the electrical connectors. H-P therefore would choose to make the connectors.

(b)

	Make	Buy	Net Income Increase (Decrease)
Total cost	$110,000	$111,500	$(1,500)
Opportunity cost	25,000	–0–	25,000
Total cost	$135,000	$111,500	$23,500

Yes, the answer is different. The analysis shows that if additional capacity is released, net income will be increased by $23,500 if the electrical connectors are purchased. In this case, H-P would choose to purchase the connectors.

SUMMARY OF STUDY OBJECTIVES

1 *Identify the steps in management's decision-making process.* Management's decision-making process consists of (a) identifying the problem and assigning responsibility for the decision, (b) determining and evaluating possible courses of action, (c) making the decision, and (d) reviewing the results of the decision.

2 *Describe the concept of incremental analysis.* Incremental analysis is the process that is used to identify financial data that change under alternative courses of action. These data are relevant to the decision because they will vary in the future among the possible alternatives.

3 *Identify the relevant costs in accepting an order at a special price.* The relevant information in accepting an order at a special price is the difference between the variable manufacturing costs to produce the special order and expected revenues.

4 *Identify the relevant costs in a make-or-buy decision.* In a make-or-buy decision, the relevant costs are (a) the variable manufacturing costs that will be saved, (b) the purchase price, and (c) opportunity costs.

5 *Give the decision rule for whether to sell or process materials further.* The decision rule for whether to sell or process materials further is: Process further as long as the incremental revenue from processing exceeds the incremental processing costs.

6 *Identify the factors to be considered in retaining or replacing equipment.* The factors to be considered in determining whether equipment should be retained or replaced are the effects on variable costs and the cost of the new equipment. Also, any disposal value of the existing asset must be considered.

7 *Explain the relevant factors in deciding whether to eliminate an unprofitable segment.* In deciding whether to eliminate an unprofitable segment, it is necessary to determine the contribution margin, if any, produced by the segment and the disposition of the segment's fixed expenses.

8 *Explain the term "sales mix" and its effects in determining break-even sales.* Sales mix is the relative combination in which a company's products are sold. Break-even sales are determined by using the weighted average unit contribution margin of all the products.

9 *Determine sales mix when a company has limited resources.* When a company has limited resources, it is necessary to find the contribution margin per unit of limited resource. This amount is then multiplied by the units of limited resource to determine which product maximizes net income.

DECISION TOOLKIT—A SUMMARY

Decision Checkpoints	Info Needed for Decision	Tool to Use for Decision	How to Evaluate Results
Which alternative should the company choose?	All relevant costs and opportunity costs	Compare the relevant cost of each alternative.	Choose the alternative that maximizes net income.
How many units of product A and product B do we need to sell to break even?	Fixed costs, weighted average contribution margin, sales mix	$\text{Break-even point in units} = \dfrac{\text{Fixed costs}}{\text{Weighted average contribution margin}}$	To determine number of units of Product A and B, allocate total units based on sales mix.
How many units of product A and B should we produce in light of a limited resource?	Contribution margin per unit, limited resource required per unit	$\text{Contribution margin per unit of limited resource} = \dfrac{\text{Contribution margin per unit}}{\text{Limited resource per unit}}$	Any additional capacity of limited resource should be applied toward the product with higher contribution margin per unit of limited resource.

GLOSSARY

 Key Term Matching Activity

Incremental analysis The process of identifying the financial data that change under alternative courses of action. (p. 367)

Joint costs For joint products, all costs incurred prior to the point at which the two products are separately identifiable. (p. 373)

Joint products Multiple end-products produced from a single raw material and a common process. (p. 372)

Opportunity cost The potential benefit that may be obtained from following an alternative course of action. (p. 368)

Relevant costs Those costs and revenues that differ across alternatives. (p. 368)

Sales mix The relative combination in which a company's products are sold. (p. 377)

Sunk cost A cost that cannot be changed by any present or future decision. (p. 368)

DEMONSTRATION PROBLEM

eGrade Demonstration Problem

Carolina Corporation manufactures and sells three different types of high-quality sealed ball bearings. The bearings vary in terms of their quality specifications—primarily in terms of their smoothness and roundness. They are referred to as Fine, Extra-Fine, and Super-Fine bearings. Machine time is limited. More machine time is required to manufacture the Extra-Fine and Super-Fine bearings. Additional information is provided below.

	Product		
	Fine	**Extra-Fine**	**Super-Fine**
Selling price	$6.00	$10.00	$16.00
Variable costs and expenses	4.00	6.50	11.00
Contribution margin	$2.00	$ 3.50	$ 5.00
Machine hours required	0.02	0.04	0.08
Units sold	100,000	40,000	10,000
Sales mix	10	4	1

Total fixed costs: $234,000

Instructions

Answer each of the following questions.

1. What is the weighted average unit contribution margin?
2. What is the break-even point using the current sales mix?
3. Ignoring the machine time constraint, what strategy would appear optimal?
4. What is the contribution margin per unit of limited resource for each type of bearing?
5. If additional machine time could be obtained, how should the additional capacity be used?

Action Plan

- To compute the break-even point for a given sales mix, divide total fixed costs by the weighted average unit contribution margin.
- To determine how best to use a limited resource, calculate the contribution margin per unit of limited resource for each product type.

Solution to Demonstration Problem

1. The weighted average unit contribution margin is determined by dividing the total contribution margin for this sales mix by the number of units:

   Total contribution margin = (10 × $2) + (4 × $3.50) + (1 × $5) = $39

   Weighted average unit contribution margin is computed as:

   $$\frac{\text{Total contribution margin}}{\text{Number of units}} = \frac{\$39}{10 + 4 + 1} = \$2.60 \text{ per unit}$$

2. The break-even point given this sales mix is computed as:

   $$\frac{\text{Fixed costs}}{\text{Weighted average unit contribution margin}} = \frac{\$234,000}{\$2.60} = 90,000 \text{ units}$$

3. The Super-Fine bearings have the highest contribution margin per unit. Thus, ignoring any manufacturing constraints, it would appear that the company should shift toward production of more Super-Fine units.

4. The contribution margin per unit of limited resource is calculated as:

	Fine	**Extra-Fine**	**Super-Fine**
$\dfrac{\text{Contribution margin per unit}}{\text{Limited resource consumed per unit}}$	$\dfrac{\$2}{.02} = \$100$	$\dfrac{\$3.5}{.04} = \$87.50$	$\dfrac{\$5}{.08} = \$62.50$

5. The Fine bearings have the highest contribution margin per limited resource, even though they have the lowest contribution margin per unit. Given the resource constraint, any additional capacity should be used to make Fine bearings.

SELF-STUDY QUESTIONS

Answers are at the end of the chapter.

(SO 1)   1. Three of the steps in management's decision making process are (1) review results of decision, (2) determine and evaluate possible courses of action, and (3) make the decision. The steps are prepared in the following order:
   (a) (1), (2), (3).
   (b) (3), (2), (1).
   (c) (2), (1), (3).
   (d) (2), (3), (1).

(SO 2)   2. Incremental analysis is the process of identifying the financial data that:
   (a) do not change under alternative courses of action.
   (b) change under alternative courses of action.
   (c) are mixed under alternative courses of action.
   (d) No correct answer is given.

(SO 3)   3. It costs a company $14 of variable costs and $6 of fixed costs to produce product A that sells for $30. A foreign buyer offers to purchase 3,000 units at $18 each. If the special offer is accepted and produced with unused capacity, net income will:
   (a) decrease $6,000.
   (b) increase $6,000.
   (c) increase $12,000.
   (d) increase $9,000.

(SO 4)   4. In a make-or-buy decision, relevant costs are:
   (a) manufacturing costs that will be saved.
   (b) the purchase price of the units.
   (c) opportunity costs.
   (d) all of the above.

(SO 5)   5. The decision rule in a sell-or-process-further decision is: process further as long as the incremental revenue from processing exceeds:
   (a) incremental processing costs.
   (b) variable processing costs.
   (c) fixed processing costs.
   (d) No correct answer is given.

(SO 6)   6. In a decision to retain or replace equipment, the book value of the old equipment is a (an):
   (a) opportunity cost.
   (b) sunk cost.
   (c) incremental cost.
   (d) marginal cost.

(SO 7)   7. If an unprofitable segment is eliminated:
   (a) net income will always increase.
   (b) variable expenses of the eliminated segment will have to be absorbed by other segments.
   (c) fixed expenses allocated to the eliminated segment will have to be absorbed by other segments.
   (d) net income will always decrease.

(SO 8)   8. Keynes Company sells both radios and cassette players at the following per unit data:

Unit Data	Radios	Cassette Players
Selling price	$40	$70
Variable costs	35	50
Contribution margin	$ 5	$20
Sales mix	2	1

What is the number of radios and cassette players that Keynes must sell in order to break even if fixed costs are $45,000?

	Radios	Cassette Players
(a)	1,000	500
(b)	1,500	750
(c)	2,000	1,000
(d)	3,000	1,500

(SO 9)   9. If the contribution margin per unit is $15 and it takes 3.0 machine hours to produce the unit, the contribution margin per unit of limited resource is:
   (a) $25.
   (b) $5.
   (c) $4.
   (d) No correct answer is given.

QUESTIONS

1. What steps are frequently involved in management's decision-making process?

2. Your roommate, Bill Blair, contends that accounting contributes to most of the steps in management's decision-making process. Is your roommate correct? Explain.

3. "Incremental analysis involves the accumulation of information concerning a single course of action." Do you agree? Why?

4. Judy Segura asks your help concerning the relevance of variable and fixed costs in incremental analysis. Help Judy with her problem.

5. What data are relevant in deciding whether to accept an order at a special price?

6. Kai Wei Company has an opportunity to buy parts at $7 each that currently cost $10 to make. What manufacturing costs are relevant to this make-or-buy decision?

7. Define the term "opportunity cost." How may this cost be relevant in a make-or-buy decision?

8. What is the decision rule in deciding whether to sell a product or process it further?

9. What are joint products? What accounting issue results from the production process that creates joint products?

10. How are allocated joint costs treated when making a sell-or-process-further decision?

11. Your roommate, Cassie Helbrecht, is confused about sunk costs. Explain to your roommate the meaning of sunk costs and their relevance to a decision to retain or replace equipment.

12. Juanita Perez Inc. has one product line that is unprofitable. What circumstances may cause overall company net income to be lower if the unprofitable product line is eliminated?

13. The sales mix of Cambridge Company's two products is 5:2. What does 5:2 mean? What effect, if any, does a company's sales mix have on CVP analysis?

14. Ansara Company sells two products, X and Y. Their unit contribution margins are $52 and $70, respectively, and their sales mix is 2:1. What is the weighted average unit contribution margin?

15. How is the contribution margin per unit of limited resources computed?

BRIEF EXERCISES

Identify the steps in management's decision-making process.
(SO 1)

BE9-1 The steps in management's decision-making process are listed in random order below. Indicate the order in which the steps should be executed.

____ Make decision
____ Identify the problem and assign responsibility

____ Review results of decision
____ Determine and evaluate possible courses of action

Determine incremental changes.
(SO 2)

BE9-2 Amy Company is considering two alternatives. Alternative A will have sales of $160,000 and costs of $100,000. Alternative B will have sales of $180,000 and costs of $125,000. Compare Alternative A to Alternative B showing incremental revenues, costs, and net income.

Determine whether to accept a special order.
(SO 3)

BE9-3 In Melbourne Company it costs $30 per unit ($20 variable and $10 fixed) to make a product that normally sells for $45. A foreign wholesaler offers to buy 3,000 units at $25 each. Melbourne will incur special shipping costs of $1 per unit. Assuming that Melbourne has excess operating capacity, indicate the net income (loss) Melbourne would realize by accepting the special order.

Determine whether to make or buy a part.
(SO 4)

BE9-4 Zurich Manufacturing incurs unit costs of $8.50 ($5.50 variable and $3 fixed) in making a sub-assembly part for its finished product. A supplier offers to make 10,000 of the assembly part at $5 per unit. If the offer is accepted, Zurich will save all variable costs but no fixed costs. Prepare an analysis showing the total cost saving, if any, Zurich will realize by buying the part.

Determine whether to sell or process further.
(SO 5)

BE9-5 Abrogena Inc. makes unfinished bookcases that it sells for $60. Production costs are $35 variable and $10 fixed. Because it has unused capacity, Abrogena is considering finishing the bookcases and selling them for $70. Variable finishing costs are expected to be $5 per unit with no increase in fixed costs. Prepare an analysis on a per unit basis showing whether Abrogena should sell unfinished or finished bookcases.

BE9-6 Each day, Justin Corporation processes 1 ton of a secret raw material into two resulting products, AB1 and XY1. When it processes 1 ton of the raw material the company incurs joint processing costs of $60,000. It allocates $20,000 of these costs to AB1 and $40,000 of these costs to XY1. The resulting AB1 can be sold for $80,000. Alternatively, it can be processed further to make AB2 at an additional processing cost of $50,000, and sold for $150,000. Each day's batch of XY1 can be sold for $90,000. Alternatively, it can be processed further to create XY2, at an additional processing cost of $60,000, and sold for $130,000. Discuss what products Justin Corporation should make.

Determine whether to sell or process further, joint products.
(SO 5)

BE9-7 Wright Company has a factory machine with a book value of $90,000 and a remaining useful life of 4 years. A new machine is available at a cost of $250,000. This machine will have a 4-year useful life with no salvage value. The new machine will lower annual variable manufacturing costs from $600,000 to $450,000. Prepare an analysis showing whether the old machine should be retained or replaced.

Determine whether to retain or replace equipment.
(SO 6)

BE9-8 Alesch, Inc., manufactures golf clubs in three models. For the year, the Big Bart line has a net loss of $10,000 from sales $200,000, variable expenses $180,000, and fixed expenses $30,000. If the Big Bart line is eliminated, $15,000 of fixed costs will remain. Prepare an analysis showing whether the Big Bart line should be eliminated.

Determine whether to eliminate an unprofitable segment.
(SO 7)

BE9-9 Wigdor Company sells three units of AA to one unit of BB; the two products have contribution margins of $100 and $180, respectively. Fixed costs are $300,000. Compute the unit sales at the break-even point. How many units of each product must be sold?

Compute break-even sales units for two products.
(SO 8)

BE9-10 In Astorga Company, data concerning two products are: Contribution margin per unit—Product A $10, Product B $12; machine hours required for one unit—Product A 2.5, Product B 4. Compute the contribution margin per unit of limited resource for each product.

Show allocation of limited resources.
(SO 9)

EXERCISES

E9-1 Wallway Company manufactures toasters. For the first 8 months of 2002, the company reported the following operating results while operating at 75% of plant capacity:

Make incremental analysis for special order.
(SO 3)

Sales (437,500 units)	$4,375,000
Cost of goods sold	2,500,000
Gross profit	1,875,000
Operating expenses	875,000
Net income	$1,000,000

Cost of goods sold was 70% variable and 30% fixed; operating expenses were also 70% variable and 30% fixed.

In September, Wallway Company receives a special order for 15,000 toasters at $6.00 each from Colina Company of Mexico City. Acceptance of the order would result in $3,000 of shipping costs but no increase in fixed operating expenses.

Instructions
(a) Prepare an incremental analysis for the special order.
(b) Should Wallway Company accept the special order? Why or why not?

E9-2 Baer Inc. has been manufacturing its own shades for its table lamps. The company is currently operating at 100% of capacity, and variable manufacturing overhead is charged to production at the rate of 50% of direct labor cost. The direct materials and direct labor cost per unit to make the lamp shades are $5.00 and $7.00, respectively. Normal production is 30,000 table lamps per year.

A supplier offers to make the lamp shades at a price of $16 per unit. If Baer Inc. accepts the supplier's offer, all variable manufacturing costs will be eliminated, but the $45,000 of fixed manufacturing overhead currently being charged to the lamp shades will have to be absorbed by other products.

Make incremental analysis for make-or-buy decision.
(SO 4)

Instructions

(a) Prepare the incremental analysis for the decision to make or buy the lamp shades.

(b) ✏️▭ Should Baer Inc. buy the lamp shades?

(c) ✏️▭ Would your answer be different in (b) if the productive capacity released by not making the lamp shades could be used to produce income of $35,000?

Make incremental analysis for further processing of materials.
(SO 5)

E9-3   Andrea Valencia recently opened her own basketweaving studio. She sells finished baskets in addition to the raw materials needed by customers to weave baskets of their own. Andrea has put together a variety of raw material kits, each including materials at various stages of completion. Unfortunately, owing to space limitations, Andrea is unable to carry all varieties of kits originally assembled and must choose between two basic packages.

The basic introductory kit includes undyed, uncut reeds (with dye included) for weaving one basket. This basic package costs Andrea $12 and sells for $25. The second kit, called Stage 2, includes cut reeds that have already been dyed. With this kit the customer need only soak the reeds and weave the basket. Andrea is able to produce the second kit by using the basic materials included in the first kit and adding one hour of her own time, which she values at $18 per hour. Because she is more efficient at cutting and dying reeds than her average customer, Andrea is able to make two kits of the dyed reeds, in one hour, from one kit of undyed reeds. The kit of dyed and cut reeds sells for $30.

Instructions

Determine whether Andrea's basketweaving shop should carry the basic introductory kit with undyed and uncut reeds or the Stage 2 kit with reeds already dyed and cut. Prepare an incremental analysis to support your answer.

Determine whether to sell or process further, joint products.
(SO 5)

E9-4   Florescent Minerals processes materials extracted from mines. The most common raw material that it processes results in three joint products: Sarco, Barco, and Larco. Each of these products can be sold as is, or it can be processed further and sold for a higher price. The company incurs joint costs of $180,000 to process one batch of the raw material that produces the three joint products. The following cost and selling price information is available for one batch of each product.

	Selling Price at Split-off Point	Allocated Joint Costs	Cost to Process Further	Selling Price of Processed Product
Sarco	$200,000	$40,000	$ 70,000	$300,000
Barco	300,000	60,000	120,000	400,000
Larco	400,000	80,000	250,000	800,000

Instructions

Determine whether each of the three joint products should be sold as is, or processed further.

Make incremental analysis for retaining or replacing equipment.
(SO 6)

E9-5   Barrila Enterprises uses a word processing computer to handle its sales invoices. Lately, business has been so good that it takes an extra 3 hours per night, plus every third Saturday, to keep up with the volume of sales invoices. Management is considering updating its computer with a faster model that would eliminate all of the overtime processing.

	Current Machine	New Machine
Original purchase cost	$15,000	$25,000
Accumulated depreciation	$ 6,000	—
Estimated operating costs	$20,000	$15,000
Useful life	5 years	5 years

If sold now, the current machine would have a salvage value of $5,000. If operated for the remainder of its useful life, the current machine would have zero salvage value. The new machine is expected to have zero salvage value after five years.

Instructions

Should the current machine be replaced? (Ignore the time value of money.)

E9-6   Michelle Tracy, a recent graduate of Rolling's accounting program, evaluated the operating performance of Poway Company's six divisions. Michelle made the following presentation to Poway's Board of Directors and suggested the Erie Division be eliminated. "If the Erie Division is eliminated," she said, "our total profits would increase by $15,500."

Make incremental analysis concerning elimination of division.
(SO 7)

	The Other Five Divisions	Erie Division	Total
Sales	$1,664,200	$ 99,000	$1,763,200
Cost of goods sold	978,520	76,500	1,055,020
Gross profit	685,680	22,500	708,180
Operating expenses	527,940	38,000	565,940
Net income	$ 157,740	$(15,500)	$ 142,240

In the Erie Division, cost of goods sold is $60,000 variable and $16,500 fixed, and operating expenses are $15,000 variable and $23,000 fixed. None of the Erie Division's fixed costs will be eliminated if the division is discontinued.

Instructions
▭▭▭▷ Is Michelle right about eliminating the Erie Division? Prepare a schedule to support your answer.

E9-7   The following information is selected from the records of Burnside Company, which produces and sells two products.

Compute sales mix, weighted average unit contribution margin, and break-even point.
(SO 8)

	Product A	Product B
Selling price per unit	$ 11.00	$ 18.00
Units sold	80,000	40,000
Variable manufacturing cost per unit	$ 4.00	$ 8.00

Fixed manufacturing overhead costs are $248,000, and fixed selling and administrative expenses are $94,000.

Instructions
(a) Compute the sales mix for Burnside Company.
(b) Calculate the weighted average unit contribution margin.
(c) Compute the break-even point in units, assuming the sales mix computed in part (a).

E9-8   The Kitchen Appliance Center sells three models of Super Clean dishwashers. Selling price and variable cost data for the models are as follows.

Compute and prove the break-even point in units with sales mix.
(SO 8)

	Economy	Standard	Deluxe
Unit selling price	$500	$650	$800
Unit variable costs	$400	$500	$600
Expected sales volume (units)	500	300	200

Instructions
(a) Compute the break-even point in units, assuming total fixed costs are $229,500.
(b) Prove the correctness of your answer.

E9-9   Spencer Company manufactures and sells three products. Relevant per unit data concerning each product are given below.

Compute contribution margin and determine the product to be manufactured.
(SO 9)

	Product		
	A	B	C
Selling price	$8	$ 12	$14
Variable costs and expenses	$3	$8.50	$12
Machine hours to produce	2	1	2

Instructions
(a) Compute the contribution margin per unit of the limited resource (machine hour) for each product.

(b) Assuming 1,500 additional machine hours are available, which product should be manufactured?

(c) Prepare an analysis showing the total contribution margin if the additional hours are (1) divided equally among the products, and (2) allocated entirely to the product identified in (b) above.

PROBLEMS: SET A

Make incremental analysis for special order and identify nonfinancial factors in the decision.
(SO 3)

P9-1A Schaeffer Company is currently producing 18,000 units per month, which is 75% of its production capacity. Variable manufacturing costs are currently $12.10 per unit, and fixed manufacturing costs are $63,000 per month. Schaeffer pays a 9% sales commission to its sales people, has $30,000 in fixed administrative expenses per month, and is averaging $396,000 in sales per month.

A special order received from a foreign company would enable Schaeffer Company to operate at 100% capacity. The foreign company offered to pay 75% of Schaeffer's current selling price per unit. If the order is accepted, Schaeffer will have to spend an extra $2.00 per unit to package the product for overseas shipping. Also, Schaeffer Company would need to lease a new stamping machine to imprint the foreign company's logo on the product, at a monthly cost of $3,600. The special order would require a sales commission of $3,000.

Instructions

(a) Compute the number of units involved in the special order and the foreign company's offered price per unit.

(b) What is the manufacturing cost of producing one unit of Schaeffer's product for regular customers?

(c) Prepare an incremental analysis of the special order. Should management accept the order?

(d) What is the lowest price that Schaeffer could accept for the special order to earn net income of $1.20 per unit?

(e) ✏️➤ What nonfinancial factors should management consider in making its decision?

Make incremental analysis related to make or buy, consider opportunity cost, and identify nonfinancial factors.
(SO 4)

P9-2A The management of Conger Manufacturing Company has asked for your assistance in deciding whether to continue manufacturing a part or to buy it from an outside supplier. The part, called Tropica, is a component of Conger's finished product.

An analysis of the accounting records and the production data revealed the following information for the year ending December 31, 2002.

1. The Machinery Department produced 35,000 units of Tropica.

2. Each Tropica unit requires 10 minutes to produce. Three people in the Machinery Department work full time (2,000 hours per year) producing Tropica. Each person is paid $12.00 per hour.

3. The cost of materials per Tropica unit is $2.00.

4. Manufacturing costs directly applicable to the production of Tropica are: indirect labor, $7,500; utilities, $1,500; depreciation, $1,800; property taxes and insurance, $1,000. All of the costs will be eliminated if Tropica is purchased.

5. The lowest price for a Tropica from an outside supplier is $4 per unit. Freight charges will be $0.40 per unit, and a part-time receiving clerk at $8,500 per year will be required.

6. If Tropica is purchased, the excess space will be used to store Conger's finished product. Currently, Conger rents storage space at approximately $0.80 per unit stored per year. Approximately 4,500 units per year are stored in the rented space.

Instructions

(a) Prepare an incremental analysis for the make or buy decision. Should Conger make or buy the part? Why?

(b) Prepare an incremental analysis, assuming the released facilities can be used to produce $10,000 of net income in addition to the savings on the rental of storage space. What decision should now be made?

(c) ▭▬▬▷ What nonfinancial factors should be considered in the decision?

P9-3A Sano Manufacturing Company has four operating divisions. During the first quarter of 2002, the company reported total income from operations of $61,000 and the following results for the divisions.

Compute contribution margin and prepare incremental analysis concerning elimination of divisions.
(SO 7)

	Division			
	Denver	**Helena**	**Portland**	**Seattle**
Sales	$530,000	$730,000	$920,000	$450,000
Cost of goods sold	450,000	480,000	576,000	390,000
Selling and administrative expenses	100,000	207,000	246,000	120,000
Income (loss) from operations	$ (20,000)	$ 43,000	$ 98,000	$ (60,000)

Analysis reveals the following percentages of variable costs in each division.

	Denver	**Helena**	**Portland**	**Seattle**
Cost of goods sold	90%	80%	90%	95%
Selling and administrative expenses	60	60	70	80

Discontinuance of any division would save 60% of the fixed costs and expenses for that division.

Top management is deeply concerned about the unprofitable divisions (Denver and Seattle). The consensus is that one or both of the divisions should be eliminated.

Instructions

(a) Compute the contribution margin for the two unprofitable divisions.

(b) Prepare an incremental analysis concerning the possible elimination of (1) the Denver Division and (2) the Seattle Division. What course of action do you recommend for each division?

(c) Prepare a columnar condensed income statement using the CVP format for Sano Manufacturing Company, assuming (1) the Seattle Division is eliminated, and (2) the unavoidable fixed costs and expenses of the Seattle Division are allocated 30% to Helena, 50% to Portland, and 20% to Denver.

(d) Compare the total income from operations with the Denver Division ($61,000) to total income from operations without this division.

P9-4A Costa Electronics manufactures two models of cameras, Superfast and Ultrafast. Unit data for each model are as follows.

Compute contribution margin, break-even point, and sales to meet target net income.
(SO 8)

	Superfast	**Ultrafast**
Selling price	$400	$500
Variable costs and expenses		
Direct materials	80	91
Direct labor	60	101
Manufacturing overhead	54	67
Selling	40	56
Administrative	46	60
Total variable	$280	$375

Monthly fixed costs are: manufacturing overhead $55,000; selling expenses $40,000; and administrative expenses $25,000.

Instructions

(a) Compute the contribution margin for each model.

(b) Compute the break-even point in dollars for each model using the contribution margin, assuming fixed costs are divided equally between the products.

(c) Compute the sales necessary to make net income of $30,000 on Superfast and $40,000 on Ultrafast. Each model incurs 50% of the fixed costs.

eGrade
Problem

PROBLEMS: SET B

Make incremental analysis for special order and identify nonfinancial factors in the decision.
(SO 3)

P9-1B Top Sports Inc. manufactures basketballs for the National Basketball Association (NBA). For the first 6 months of 2002, the company reported the following operating results while operating at 90% of plant capacity.

	Amount	Per Unit
Sales	$4,500,000	$50.00
Cost of goods sold	3,600,000	40.00
Selling and administrative expenses	450,000	5.00
Net income	$ 450,000	$ 5.00

Fixed costs for the period were: cost of goods sold $1,080,000, and selling and administrative expenses $225,000.

In July, normally a slack manufacturing month, Top Sports receives a special order for 10,000 basketballs at $34 each from the Italian Basketball Association (IBA). Acceptance of the order would increase variable selling and administrative expenses $0.50 per unit because of shipping costs but would not increase fixed costs and expenses.

Instructions
(a) Prepare an incremental analysis for the special order.
(b) Should Top Sports Inc. accept the special order?
(c) What is the minimum selling price on the special order to produce net income of $4 per ball?
(d) ▭▱▱▱▱▱▱▷ What nonfinancial factors should management consider in making its decision?

Make incremental analysis related to make or buy; consider opportunity cost and identify nonfinancial factors.
(SO 4)

P9-2B The management of Caesar Manufacturing Company is trying to decide whether to continue manufacturing a part or to buy it from an outside supplier. The part, called WISCO, is a component of the company's finished product.

The following information was collected from the accounting records and production data for the year ending December 31, 2002.

1. 7,000 units of WISCO were produced in the Machining Department.
2. Variable manufacturing costs applicable to the production of each WISCO unit were: direct materials $4.50, direct labor $4.30, indirect labor $0.50, utilities $0.40.
3. Fixed manufacturing costs applicable to the production of WISCO were:

Cost Item	Direct	Allocated
Depreciation	$1,600	$ 900
Property taxes	500	200
Insurance	900	600
	$3,000	$1,700

All variable manufacturing and direct fixed costs will be eliminated if WISCO is purchased. Allocated costs will have to be absorbed by other production departments.
4. The lowest quotation for 7,000 WISCO units from a supplier is $70,000.
5. If WISCO units are purchased, freight and inspection costs would be $0.30 per unit, and receiving costs totaling $750 per year would be incurred by the Machining Department.

Instructions
(a) Prepare an incremental analysis for WISCO. Your analysis should have columns for (1) Make WISCO, (2) Buy WISCO, and (3) Net Income Increase/Decrease.
(b) Based on your analysis, what decision should management make?
(c) Would the decision be different if Caesar Company has the opportunity to produce $4,000 of net income with the facilities currently being used to manufacture WISCO? Show computations.

(d) ▰▰▰▰▷ What nonfinancial factors should management consider in making its decision?

P9-3B Simpson Manufacturing Company has four operating divisions. During the first quarter of 2002, the company reported aggregate income from operations of $120,000 and the following divisional results.

Compute contribution margin and prepare incremental analysis concerning elimination of divisions.
(SO 7)

	Division			
	I	**II**	**III**	**IV**
Sales	$490,000	$410,000	$200,000	$300,000
Cost of goods sold	300,000	250,000	195,000	280,000
Selling and administrative expenses	60,000	80,000	65,000	50,000
Income (loss) from operations	$130,000	$ 80,000	$ (60,000)	$ (30,000)

Analysis reveals the following percentages of variable costs in each division.

	I	**II**	**III**	**IV**
Cost of goods sold	70%	80%	90%	75%
Selling and administrative expenses	40	50	70	60

Discontinuance of any division would save 50% of the fixed costs and expenses for that division.

Top management is very concerned about the unprofitable divisions (III and IV). Consensus is that one or both of the divisions should be discontinued.

Instructions
(a) Compute the contribution margin for Divisions III and IV.
(b) Prepare an incremental analysis concerning the possible discontinuance of (1) Division III and (2) Division IV. What course of action do you recommend for each division?
(c) Prepare a columnar condensed income statement for Simpson Manufacturing, assuming Division III is eliminated. Use the CVP format. Division III's unavoidable fixed costs are allocated equally to the continuing divisions.
(d) Reconcile the total income from operations ($120,000) with the total income from operations without Division IV.

P9-4B Juan Castorena Company manufactures two models of televisions, Superclear and Ultraclear. Unit data for each model are as follows.

Compute contribution margin, break-even point, and sales to meet target net income.
(SO 8)

	Superclear	**Ultraclear**
Selling price	$420	$630
Variable costs and expenses		
Direct materials	90	125
Direct labor	50	90
Manufacturing overhead	60	100
Selling	32	70
Administrative	20	56
Total variable	$252	$441

Monthly fixed costs are: manufacturing overhead $80,000; selling expenses $54,000; and administrative expenses $34,000.

Instructions
(a) Compute the contribution margin for each model.
(b) Compute the break-even point in dollars for each model using the contribution margin, assuming fixed costs are divided equally between the products.
(c) Compute the sales necessary to make net income of $36,000 on Superclear and $48,000 on Ultraclear. Each model incurs 50% of all fixed costs.

GROUP DECISION CASE

BYP9-1 Saldajeno Company is considering the purchase of a new machine. The invoice price of the machine is $125,000, freight charges are estimated to be $4,000, and installation costs are expected to be $6,000. Salvage value of the new equipment is expected to be zero after a useful life of 4 years. Existing equipment could be retained and used for an additional 4 years if the new machine is not purchased. At that time, the salvage value of the equipment would be zero. If the new machine is purchased now, the existing machine would have to be scrapped. Saldajeno's accountant, Shaida Fang, has accumulated the following data regarding annual sales and expenses with and without the new machine.

1. Without the new machine, Saldajeno can sell 12,000 units of product annually at a per unit selling price of $100. If the new unit is purchased, the number of units produced and sold would increase by 20%, and the selling price would remain the same.
2. The new machine is faster than the old machine, and it is more efficient in its usage of materials. With the old machine the gross profit rate will be 25% of sales, whereas the rate will be 30% of sales with the new machine.
3. Annual selling expenses are $180,000 with the current equipment. Because the new equipment would produce a greater number of units to be sold, annual selling expenses are expected to increase by 10% if it is purchased.
4. Annual administrative expenses are expected to be $100,000 with the old machine, and $113,000 with the new machine.
5. The current book value of the existing machine is $36,000. Saldajeno uses straight-line depreciation.

Instructions

With the class divided into groups, prepare an incremental analysis for the 4 years showing whether Saldajeno should keep the existing machine or buy the new machine. (Ignore income tax effects.)

MANAGERIAL ANALYSIS

BYP9-2 Electronix Plus manufactures private-label small electronic products, such as alarm clocks, calculators, kitchen timers, stopwatches, and automatic pencil sharpeners. Some of the products are sold as sets, and others are sold individually. Products are studied as to their sales potential, and then cost estimates are made. The Engineering Department develops production plans, and then production begins. The company has generally had very successful product introduction. Only two products introduced by the company have been discontinued.

One of the products currently sold is a multi-alarm alarm clock. The clock has four alarms that can be programmed to sound at various times and for varying lengths of time. The company has experienced a great deal of difficulty in making the circuit boards for the clocks. The production process has never operated smoothly. The product is unprofitable at the present time, primarily because of warranty repairs and product recalls. Two models of the clocks were recalled, for example, because they sometimes caused an electric shock when the alarms were being shut off. The Engineering Department is attempting to revise the manufacturing process, but the revision will take another 6 months at least.

The clocks were very popular when they were introduced, and since they are private-label, the company has not suffered much from the recalls. Presently, the company has a very large order for several items from Kmart Stores. The order includes 5,000 of the multi-alarm clocks. When the company suggested that Kmart purchase the clocks from another manufacturer, Kmart threatened to rescind the entire order unless the clocks were included.

The company has therefore investigated the possibility of having another company make the clocks for them. The clocks were bid for the Kmart order based on an estimated $6.65 cost to manufacture:

Circuit board, 1 each @ $2.00	$2.00
Plastic case, 1 each @ $0.75	0.75
Alarms, 4 @ $0.10 each	0.40
Labor, 15 minutes @ $12/hour	3.00
Overhead, $2.00 per labor hour	0.50

Electronix Plus could purchase clocks to fill the Kmart order for $11 from Silver Star, a Korean manufacturer with a very good quality record. Silver Star has offered to reduce the price to $7.50 after Electronix Plus has been a customer for 6 months, placing an order of at least 1,000 units per month. If Electronix Plus becomes a "preferred customer" by purchasing 15,000 units per year, the price would be reduced still further to $4.50.

Alpha Products, a local manufacturer, has also offered to make clocks for Electronix Plus. They have offered to sell 5,000 clocks for $4 each. However, Alpha Products has been in business for only 6 months. They have experienced significant turnover in their labor force, and the local press has reported that the owners may face tax evasion charges soon. The owner of Alpha Products is an electronic engineer, however, and the quality of the clocks is likely to be good.

If Electronix Plus decides to purchase the clocks from either Silver Star or Alpha, all the costs to manufacture could be avoided, except a total of $5,000 in overhead costs for machine depreciation. The machinery is fairly new, and has no alternate use.

Instructions

(a) What is the difference in profit under each of the alternatives if the clocks are to be sold for $14.50 each to Kmart?

(b) What are the most important nonfinancial factors that Electronix Plus should consider when making this decision?

(c) What do you think Electronix Plus should do in regard to the Kmart order? What should it do in regard to continuing to manufacture the multi-alarm alarm clocks? Be prepared to defend your answer.

*R*EAL-WORLD FOCUS

BYP9-3   Founded in 1983, the **Beverly Hills Fan Company** is located in Woodland Hills, California. With 23 employees and sales of less than $10 million, the company is relatively small. Management feels that there is potential for growth in the upscale market for ceiling fans and lighting. They are particularly optimistic about growth in Mexican and Canadian markets.

Presented below is information from the president's letter in the company's annual report.

BEVERLY HILLS FAN COMPANY
President's Letter

An aggressive product development program was initiated during the past year resulting in new ceiling fan models planned for introduction in 1993. Award winning industrial designer Ron Rezek created several new fan models for the Beverly Hills Fan and L.A. Fan lines, including a new Showroom Collection, designed specifically for the architectural and designer markets. Each of these models has received critical acclaim, and order commitments for 1993 have been outstanding. Additionally, our Custom Color and special order fans continued to enjoy increasing popularity and sales gains as more and more customers desire fans that match their specific interior decors. Currently, Beverly Hills Fan Company offers a product line of over 100 models of contemporary, traditional, and transitional ceiling fans.

Instructions

(a) What points did the company management need to consider before deciding to offer the special-order fans to customers?

(b) How would incremental analysis be employed to assist in this decision?

EXPLORING THE WEB

BYP9-4   Many companies today choose to outsource even key elements of product design and development. **PEPdesigns** is a leading supplier of outsourced engineering and manufacturing product development for the telecommunications, networking, Internet appliance, and industrial markets. It has expertise in providing networking and DSL product development solutions.

Address: **www.pepinc.com** *(or go to www.wiley.com/college/weygandt)*

Instructions

Go to the Web page of PEPdesigns at the address shown above, and answer the following questions.

(a) What are the types of engineering services that PEPdesigns says it can provide for its clients?

(b) Name some clients that PEPdesigns has served.

(c) Who are some of the companies that PEPdesigns partners with to provide its services?

COMMUNICATION ACTIVITY

BYP9-5   Harvey Mudd is a production manager at a metal fabricating plant. Last night he read an article about a new piece of equipment that would dramatically reduce his division's costs. Harvey was very excited about the prospect, and the first thing he did this morning was to bring the article to his supervisor, Nathan Peas, the plant manager. The following conversation occurred:

Harvey: Nathan, I thought you would like to see this article on the new PDD1130; they've made some fantastic changes that could save us millions of dollars.

Nathan: I appreciate your interest Harvey, but I actually have been aware of the new machine for two months. The problem is that we just bought a new machine last year. We spent $2 million on that machine, and it was supposed to last us 12 years. If we replace it now we would have to write its book value off of the books for a huge loss. If I go to top management now and say that I want a new machine, they will fire me. I think we should use our existing machine for a couple of years, and then when it becomes obvious that we have to have a new machine, I will make the proposal.

Instructions

Harvey just completed a course in managerial accounting, and he believes that Nathan is making a big mistake. Write a memo from Harvey to Nathan explaining Nathan's decision-making error.

RESEARCH ASSIGNMENT

BYP9-6   The April 1998 issue of *Management Accounting* includes an article by Julie Hertenstein and Marjorie Platt entitled "Why Product Development Teams Need Management Accountants."

Instructions

Read the article and answer the following questions.

(a) What percentage of a product's cost are determined at the design stage?

(b) Why do the authors say that management accountants can provide a broader perspective on costs than purchasing managers?

(c) What are some of the roles and responsibilities that management accountants can have on a design team?

(d) What are some nonfinancial measures used to evaluate industrial design performance?

ETHICS CASE

BYP9-7   Harold Dean became Chief Executive Officer of Wriston Manufacturing two years ago. At the time, the company was reporting lagging profits, and Harold was brought in to "stir things up." The company has three divisions, electronics, fiber optics, and plumbing supplies. Harold has no interest in plumbing supplies, and one of the first things he did was to put pressure on his accountants to reallocate some of the company's fixed costs away from the other two divisions to the plumbing division. This had the effect of causing the plumbing division to report losses during the last two years; in the past it had always reported low, but acceptable, net income. Harold felt that this reallocation would shine a favorable light on him in front of the board of directors because it meant that the electronics and fiber optics divisions would look like they were improving. Given that these are "businesses of the future," he believed that the stock market would react favorably to these increases, while not penalizing the poor results of the plumbing division. Without this shift in the allocation of fixed costs, the profits of the electronics and fiber optics divisions would not have improved. But now the board of directors has suggested that the plumbing division be closed because it is reporting losses. This would mean that nearly 500 employees, many of whom have worked for Wriston their whole lives, would lose their jobs.

Instructions
(a) If a division is reporting losses, does that necessarily mean that it should be closed?
(b) Was the reallocation of fixed costs across divisions unethical?
(c) What should Harold do?

Answers to Self-Study Questions
1. d   2. b   3. c   4. d   5. a   6. b   7. c   8. d   9. b

Remember to go back to the Navigator box on the chapter-opening page and check off your completed work.

CHAPTER 10

Capital Budgeting

THE NAVIGATOR ✔

- Scan *Study Objectives*
- Read *Feature Story*
- Read *Preview*
- Read text and answer *Before You Go On*
  p. 407 [ ]   p. 417 [ ]
- Work *Using the Decision Toolkit*
- Review *Summary of Study Objectives*
- Work *Demonstration Problem*
- Answer *Self-Study Questions*
- Complete *Assignments*

◆ STUDY OBJECTIVES

After studying this chapter, you should be able to:

1. Discuss the capital budgeting evaluation process, and explain what inputs are used in capital budgeting.

2. Describe the cash payback technique.

3. Explain the net present value method.

4. Identify the challenges presented by intangible benefits in capital budgeting.

5. Describe the profitability index.

6. Indicate the benefits of performing a post-audit.

7. Explain the internal rate of return method.

8. Describe the annual rate of return method.

THE NAVIGATOR

◆ FEATURE STORY

SOUP IS GOOD FOOD

When you hear the word *Campbell's,* what is the first thing that comes to mind? Soup. Campbell's *is* soup. It sells 38 percent of all the soup—including home-made—consumed in the United States.

But can a company survive on soup alone? In an effort to expand its operations and to lessen its reliance on soup, **Campbell Soup Company** in 1990 began searching for an additional line of business. Campbell's management believed it saw an opportunity in convenient meals that were low in fat, nutritionally rich, and had therapeutic value for heart patients and diabetics. This venture would require a huge investment—but the rewards were potentially tremendous.

The initial investment required building food labs, hiring nutritional scientists, researching prototype products, constructing new production facilities, and marketing the new products. Management predicted that with an initial investment of roughly $55 million, the company might generate sales of $200 million per year.

By 1994 the company had created 24 meals, and an extensive field-study revealed considerable health benefits from the products. Unfortunately, initial sales of the new product line, called Intelligent Quisine, were less than stellar. In 1997 a consulting firm was hired to evaluate whether the project should be continued. Product development of the new line was costing $20 million per year—a sum that some managers felt could be better spent developing new products in other divisions, or expanding overseas operations. In 1998 the project was discontinued.

Campbell's was not giving up on growth, but simply had decided to refocus its efforts on soup. The company's annual report stated management's philosophy: "Soup will be our growth engine." Campbell's is now selling off many of its non-soup businesses, and in a recent year introduced 20 new soup products.

THE NAVIGATOR

Source: Vanessa O'Connell, "Food for Thought: How Campbell Saw a Breakthrough Menu Turn into Leftovers," *Wall Street Journal,* October 6, 1998.

www.campbellsoup.com

Companies like **Campbell Soup** must constantly determine how to invest their resources. Other examples: Hollywood studios recently built 25 new sound stage projects to allow for additional filming in future years. **Starwood Hotels and Resorts Worldwide, Inc.** committed a total of $1 billion to renovate its existing hotel properties, while, at roughly the same time, the hotel industry canceled about $2 billion worth of *new* construction. And **Union Pacific Resources Group Inc.** announced that it would cut its capital budget by 19 percent in order to use the funds to reduce its outstanding debt.

The process of making such capital expenditure decisions is referred to as **capital budgeting**. Capital budgeting involves choosing among various capital projects to find the one(s) that will maximize a company's return on its financial investment. The purpose of this chapter is to discuss the various techniques used to make effective capital budgeting decisions.

The content and organization of this chapter are as follows.

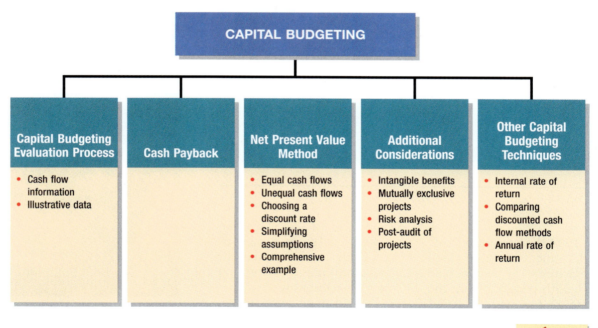

CAPITAL BUDGETING

Capital Budgeting Evaluation Process	Cash Payback	Net Present Value Method	Additional Considerations	Other Capital Budgeting Techniques
• Cash flow information • Illustrative data		• Equal cash flows • Unequal cash flows • Choosing a discount rate • Simplifying assumptions • Comprehensive example	• Intangible benefits • Mutually exclusive projects • Risk analysis • Post-audit of projects	• Internal rate of return • Comparing discounted cash flow methods • Annual rate of return

THE NAVIGATOR

*T*HE CAPITAL BUDGETING EVALUATION PROCESS

STUDY OBJECTIVE

1

Discuss the capital budgeting evaluation process, and explain what inputs are used in capital budgeting.

Many companies follow a carefully prescribed process in capital budgeting. At least once a year, proposals for projects are requested from each department. The proposals are screened by a capital budgeting committee, which submits its findings to the officers of the company. The officers, in turn, select the projects they believe to be most worthy of funding. They submit this list of projects to the board of directors. Ultimately, the directors approve the capital expenditure budget for the year. This process is shown in Illustration 10-1.

1. Project proposals are requested from departments, plants, and authorized personnel.

2. Proposals are screened by a capital budget committee.

3. Officers determine which projects are worthy of funding.

4. Board of directors approves capital budget.

Illustration 10-1
Corporate capital budget authorization process

The involvement of top management and the board of directors in the process demonstrates the importance of capital budgeting decisions. These decisions often have a significant impact on a company's future profitability. In fact, poor capital budgeting decisions can cost a lot of money, as the **Campbell Soup** story demonstrated. Such decisions have even led to the bankruptcy of some companies.

BUSINESS INSIGHT
Management Perspective

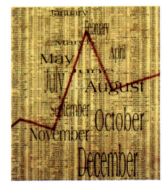

Monitoring capital expenditure amounts is one way to learn about a company's growth potential. Few companies can grow if they don't make significant capital investments. Here is a list of well-known companies and their amounts and types of capital expenditures in the year 2000.

Company Name	Amount	Type of Expenditure
Campbell Soup Company	$200 million	Acquisitions and plant expansions.
Barrick Gold Corporation	$550 million	Land acquisition and mine expansion.
Dell Computer Corporation	$397 million	Manufacturing and office facilities.
Sears, Roebuck and Co.	$1,400 million	Thirty new full-line stores and 100 specialty stores.
NIKE, Inc.	$466 million	Warehouse locations, management information systems, and world headquarters expansion.

CASH FLOW INFORMATION

In this chapter we will look at several methods that help companies make effective capital budgeting decisions. Most of these methods employ **cash flow numbers**, rather than accrual accounting revenues and expenses. Remember from your financial accounting course that accrual accounting records *revenues* and *expenses,* rather than cash inflows and cash outflows. In fact, revenues and expenses measured during a period often differ significantly from their cash flow counterparts. Accrual accounting has advantages over cash accounting in many contexts. **But for purposes of capital budgeting, estimated cash inflows and**

outflows are the preferred inputs. Ultimately, the value of all financial investments is determined by the value of cash flows received and paid.

Some typical cash outflows and inflows related to equipment purchase and replacement are listed in Illustration 10-2.

Illustration 10-2 Typical cash flows relating to capital budgeting decisions

Cash Outflows

Initial investment
Repairs and maintenance
Increased operating costs
Overhaul of equipment

Cash Inflows

Sale of old equipment
Increased cash received from customers
Reduced cash outflows related to operating costs
Salvage value of equipment when project is complete

These cash flows are the inputs that are considered relevant in capital budgeting decisions.

The capital budgeting decision, under any technique, depends in part on a variety of considerations:

- *The availability of funds:* Does the company have unlimited funds, or will it have to ration capital investments?
- *Relationships among proposed projects:* Are proposed projects independent of each other, or does the acceptance or rejection of one depend on the acceptance or rejection of another?
- *The company's basic decision-making approach:* Does the company want to produce an accept-reject decision, or a ranking of desirability among possible projects?
- *The risk associated with a particular project:* How certain are the projected returns? The certainty of estimates varies with such issues as market considerations or the length of time before returns are expected.

ILLUSTRATIVE DATA

For our initial discussion of quantitative techniques, we will use a continuing example, which will enable us to easily compare the results of the various techniques. Assume that Stewart Soup Company is considering an investment of $130,000 in new equipment. The new equipment is expected to last 10 years. It will have a zero salvage value at the end of its useful life. The annual cash inflows are $200,000, and the annual net cash outflows are $176,000. These data are summarized in Illustration 10-3.

Illustration 10-3 Investment information for Stewart Soup example

Initial investment	$130,000
Estimated useful life	10 years
Estimated salvage value	–0–
Estimated annual cash flows	
Cash inflows from customers	$200,000
Cash outflows for operating costs	176,000
Net annual cash inflow	$ 24,000

In the following two sections we will examine two popular techniques: cash payback and the net present value method.

CASH PAYBACK

The **cash payback technique** identifies the time period required to recover the cost of the capital investment from the annual cash inflow produced by the investment. The formula for computing the cash payback period is:

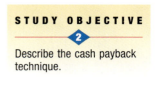

Illustration 10-4 Cash payback formula

Net annual cash inflow is approximated by taking net income and adding back depreciation expense. Depreciation expense is added back because depreciation on the capital expenditure does not involve an annual outflow of cash. Accordingly, the depreciation deducted in determining net income must be added back to determine annual cash inflows. The cash payback period in the Stewart Soup example is 5.42 years, computed as follows.

Helpful Hint Annual cash inflow can also be approximated by "Net cash provided by operating activities" from the statement of cash flows.

$$\$130,000 \div \$24,000 = 5.42 \text{ years}$$

The evaluation of the payback period is often related to the expected useful life of the asset. For example, assume that at Stewart Soup a project is unacceptable if the payback period is longer than 60 percent of the asset's expected useful life. The 5.42-year payback period in this case is a bit over 50 percent of the project's expected useful life. Thus, the project is acceptable.

It follows that when the payback technique is used to decide among acceptable alternative projects, **the shorter the payback period, the more attractive the investment**. This is true for two reasons: (1) The earlier the investment is recovered, the sooner the cash funds can be used for other purposes. (2) The risk of loss from obsolescence and changed economic conditions is less in a shorter payback period.

The cash payback technique may be useful as an initial screening tool. It also may be the most critical factor in the capital budgeting decision for a company that desires a fast turnaround of its investment because of a weak cash position. It also is relatively easy to compute and understand.

However, cash payback should not ordinarily be the only basis for the capital budgeting decision because it ignores the expected profitability of the project. To illustrate, assume that Projects A and B have the same payback period, but Project A's useful life is double the useful life of Project B. Project A's earning power, therefore, is twice as long as Project B's. A further disadvantage of this technique is that it ignores the time value of money.

NET PRESENT VALUE METHOD

Recognition of the time value of money can make a significant difference in the long-term impact of the capital budgeting decision. For example, cash flows that occur early in the life of an investment will be worth more than those that occur later—because of the time value of money. Therefore it is useful to recognize the timing of cash flows when evaluating projects.

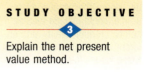

Capital budgeting techniques that take into account both the time value of money and the estimated total cash flows from an investment are called **discounted cash flow techniques**. They are generally recognized as the most informative and best conceptual approaches to making capital budgeting decisions. The expected total cash inflow calculated in discounted cash flow techniques consists of the sum of the annual cash inflows plus the estimated liquidation proceeds (salvage value) when the asset is sold at the end of its useful life.

The primary capital budgeting method that uses discounted cash flow techniques is called **net present value**. A second method, discussed later in the chapter, is the **internal rate of return**. At this point, before you read on, **we recommend that you examine Appendix C** to review time value of money concepts, upon which these methods are based.

Under the **net present value (NPV) method**, cash inflows are discounted to their present value and then compared with the capital outlay required by the investment. The difference between these two amounts is referred to as **net present value (NPV)**. The interest rate to be used in discounting the future cash inflows is the required minimum rate of return.

The decision rule is this: **A proposal is acceptable when net present value is zero or positive**. At either of those values, the rate of return on the investment equals or exceeds the required rate of return. When net present value is negative, the project is unacceptable. Illustration 10-5 shows the net present value decision criteria.

Illustration 10-5 Net present value decision criteria

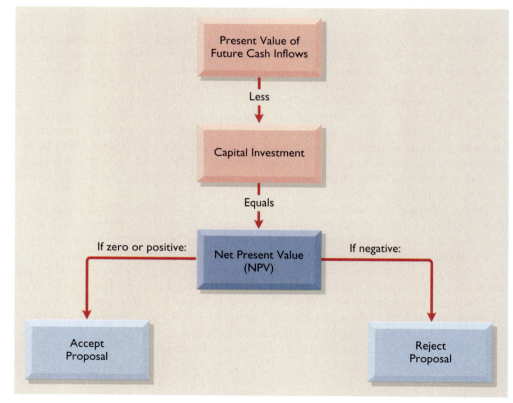

Helpful Hint Discounted future cash flows may not take into account all of the important considerations needed to make an informed capital budgeting decision. Other issues, for example, could include worker safety, product quality, and environmental impact. We look at these issues later.

When making a selection among acceptable proposals, **the higher the positive net present value, the more attractive the investment**. The application of this method to two cases is described in the next two sections. In each case, we will assume that the investment has no salvage value at the end of its useful life.

EQUAL ANNUAL CASH FLOWS

Stewart's annual cash inflows are $24,000. If we assume this amount **is uniform over the asset's useful life**, the present value of the annual cash flows can be computed by using the present value of an annuity of 1 for 10 periods (from Table 4, Appendix C). Assuming a discount rate of 12 percent, the present value of cash flows is computed as follows (rounded to the nearest dollar).

	Present Value at 12%
Discount factor for 10 periods	5.65022
Present value of cash flows:	
$24,000 × 5.65022	**$135,605**

Illustration 10-6 Computation of present value of equal annual cash flows

The analysis of the proposal by the net present value method is as follows.

	12%
Present value of cash flows	$135,605
Capital investment	130,000
Net present value	**$ 5,605**

Illustration 10-7 Computation of net present value—equal annual cash flows proposal

The proposed capital expenditure is acceptable at a required rate of return of 12 percent because the net present value is positive.

UNEQUAL ANNUAL CASH FLOWS

When annual cash flows are unequal, we cannot use annuity tables to calculate their present value. Instead, tables showing the **present value of a single future amount must be applied to each annual cash flow**. To illustrate, assume that the Stewart management expects the same aggregate annual cash flows ($240,000) but a declining market demand for the new product over the life of the equipment. The present value of the annual cash flows is calculated as follows, using Table 3 in Appendix C.

Helpful Hint The ABC Co. expects equal cash flows over an asset's 5-year useful life. What discount factor should be used in determining present values if management wants (1) a 12% return or (2) a 15% return? Answer: Using Table 4, the factors are (1) 3.60478 and (2) 3.35216.

Year	Assumed Annual Cash Flows	Discount Factor 12%	Present Value 12%
	(1)	(2)	(1) × (2)
1	$ 34,000	.89286	$ 30,357
2	30,000	.79719	23,916
3	27,000	.71178	19,218
4	25,000	.63552	15,888
5	24,000	.56743	13,618
6	22,000	.50663	11,146
7	21,000	.45235	9,499
8	20,000	.40388	8,078
9	19,000	.36061	6,852
10	18,000	.32197	5,795
	$240,000		**$144,367**

Illustration 10-8 Computation of present value of unequal annual cash flows

Therefore, the analysis of the proposal by the net present value method is as follows.

	12%
Present value of cash flows	$144,367
Capital investment	130,000
Net present value	**$ 14,367**

In this example, the present value of the cash flows is greater than the $130,000 capital investment. Thus, the project is acceptable at a 12 percent required rate of return. The difference between the present values using the 12 percent rate under equal cash flows ($135,605) and unequal cash flows ($144,367) is due to the pattern of the flows. Since more money is received sooner under this particular uneven cash flow scenario, its present value is greater.

CHOOSING A DISCOUNT RATE

Now that you understand how the net present value method is applied, it is logical to ask a related question: How is a discount rate determined in real capital budgeting decisions? In most instances a company uses a discount rate equal to its **cost of capital**—that is, the rate that it must pay to obtain funds from creditors and stockholders.

Helpful Hint Cost of capital is the rate that management expects to pay on all borrowed and equity funds. It does not relate to the cost of funding a *specific* project.

The cost of capital is a weighted average of the rates paid on borrowed funds as well as on funds provided by investors in the company's common stock and preferred stock. If a project is believed to be of higher risk than the company's usual line of business, the discount rate should be increased. That is, the discount rate has two elements, a cost of capital element and a risk element. Often companies assume the risk element is equal to zero.

Using an incorrect discount rate can lead to incorrect capital budgeting decisions. Consider again the Stewart Soup example in Illustration 10-7, where we used a discount rate of 12 percent. Suppose that this discount rate does not take into account the fact that this project is riskier than most of the company's investments. A more appropriate discount rate, given the risk, might be 15 percent. Illustration 10-10 compares the net present values at the two rates. At the higher, more appropriate discount rate of 15 percent, the net present value is negative, and the company should reject the project.

	Present Values at Different Discount Rates	
	12%	15%
Discount factor for 10 periods	5.65022	5.01877
Present value of cash flows:		
$24,000 × 5.65022	$135,605	
$24,000 × 5.01877		$120,450
Capital investment	130,000	130,000
Positive (negative) net present value	$ 5,605	$ (9,550)

The discount rate is often referred to by alternative names, including the **hurdle rate**, the **required rate of return**, and the **cutoff rate**. Determination of the cost of capital varies somewhat depending on whether the entity is a for-profit or not-for-profit enterprise. Calculation of the cost of capital is discussed more fully in advanced accounting and finance courses.

SIMPLIFYING ASSUMPTIONS

In our examples of the net present value method, we have made a number of simplifying assumptions:

- *All cash flows come at the end of each year.* In reality, cash flows will come at uneven intervals throughout the year. However, it is far simpler to assume that all cash flows come at the end (or in some cases the beginning) of the year. In fact, this assumption is frequently made in practice.
- *All cash flows are immediately reinvested in another project that has a similar return.* In most capital budgeting situations, cash flows are received during each year of a project's life. In order to determine the return on the investment, some assumption must be made about how the cash flows are reinvested in the year that they are received. It is customary to assume that cash flows received are reinvested in some other project of similar return until the end of the project's life.
- *All cash flows can be predicted with certainty.* The outcomes of business investments are full of uncertainty, as the **Campbell Soup** *Feature Story* shows. There is no way of knowing how popular a new product will be, how long a new machine will last, or what competitors' reactions might be to changes in your product. But, in order to make investment decisions, analysts must estimate future outcomes. In this chapter we have assumed that future amounts are known with certainty.[1] In reality, little is known with certainty. More advanced capital budgeting techniques deal with uncertainty by considering the probability that various outcomes will occur.

BEFORE YOU GO ON . . .

◆ **Review It**

1. What is the cash payback technique? What are its strengths and weaknesses?
2. What is the net present value decision rule to determine whether a project is acceptable?
3. What are common assumptions made in capital budgeting decisions?

◆ **Do It**

Watertown Paper Corporation is considering adding another machine for the manufacture of corrugated cardboard. The machine would cost $800,000. It would have an estimated life of 7 years and a salvage value of $40,000. It is estimated that annual cash inflows would increase by $400,000 and that annual cash outflows would increase by $190,000. Management believes a discount rate of 9 percent is appropriate. Using the net present value technique, should the project be accepted?

Action Plan
- Use the NPV technique to calculate the difference between the present value of future cash flows and the initial investment.
- Accept the project if the net present value is positive.

---

[1]One exception is a brief discussion of sensitivity analysis later in the chapter.

Solution

Estimated annual cash inflows		$400,000
Estimated annual cash outflows		190,000
Net annual cash inflow		$210,000

	Cash Flows	×	9% Discount Factor	=	Present Value
Present value of net annual cash flows	$210,000	×	5.03295[a]	=	$1,056,920
Present value of salvage value	$ 40,000	×	.54703[b]	=	21,881
Present value of cash flows					1,078,801
Capital investment					800,000
Net present value					$ 278,801

[a]Table 4, Appendix C.
[b]Table 3, Appendix C.

Since the net present value is positive, the project is acceptable.

THE NAVIGATOR

Related exercise material: BE10-3, BE10-4, BE10-5, E10-1, E10-2, and E10-3.

COMPREHENSIVE EXAMPLE

Best Taste Foods is considering investing in new equipment to produce fat-free snack foods. Management believes that although demand for fat-free foods has leveled off, fat-free foods are here to stay. The following estimated cost flows, cost of capital, and cash flows were determined in consultation with the marketing, production, and finance departments.

Illustration 10-11 Investment information for Best Taste Foods example

Initial investment	$1,000,000
Cost of equipment overhaul in 5 years	$ 200,000
Salvage value of equipment in 10 years	$ 20,000
Cost of capital	15%
Estimated annual cash flows	
Cash inflows received from sales	$500,000
Cash outflows for cost of goods sold	$200,000
Maintenance costs	$ 30,000
Other direct operating costs	$ 40,000

Remember that we are using cash flows in our analysis, not accrual revenues and expenses. Thus, for example, the direct operating costs would not include depreciation expense, since depreciation expense does not use cash. Illustration 10-12 presents the computation of the net annual cash inflows of this project.

Illustration 10-12 Computation of net annual cash inflow

Cash inflows received from sales	$ 500,000
Cash outflows for cost of goods sold	(200,000)
Maintenance costs	(30,000)
Other direct operating costs	(40,000)
Net annual cash inflow	**$230,000**

The computation of the net present value for this proposed investment is shown in Illustration 10-13.

Illustration 10-13 Computation of net present value for Best Taste Foods investment

Event	Time Period	Cash Flow	×	15% Discount Factor	=	Present Value
Equipment purchase	0	$1,000,000		1.00000		$(1,000,000)
Equipment overhaul	5	200,000		.49718		(99,436)
Net annual cash inflow	1–10	230,000		5.01877		1,154,317
Salvage value	10	20,000		.24719		4,944
Net present value						**$ 59,825**

Because the net present value of the project is positive, the project should be accepted.

DECISION TOOLKIT

Decision Checkpoints	Info Needed for Decision	Tool to Use for Decision	How to Evaluate Results
Should the company invest in a proposed project?	Cash flow estimates, discount rate	Net present value = Present value of future cash flows less capital investment	The investment is financially acceptable if net present value is positive.

ADDITIONAL CONSIDERATIONS

Now that you understand how the net present value method works, we can add some "additional wrinkles." Specifically, these are: the impact of intangible benefits, a way to compare mutually exclusive projects, refinements that take risk into account, and the need to conduct post-audits of investment projects.

INTANGIBLE BENEFITS

The NPV evaluation techniques employed thus far rely on tangible costs and benefits that can be relatively easily quantified. Some investment projects, especially high-tech projects, fail to make it through initial capital budget screens because only the project's "tangible" benefits are considered. But by ignoring intangible benefits, such as increased quality or safety or employee loyalty, capital budgeting techniques might incorrectly eliminate projects that could be financially beneficial to the company.

STUDY OBJECTIVE 4

Identify the challenges presented by intangible benefits in capital budgeting.

To avoid rejecting projects that actually should be accepted, two possible approaches are suggested:

1. Calculate net present value ignoring intangible benefits. Then, if the NPV is negative, ask whether the intangible benefits are worth at least the amount of the negative NPV.
2. Project rough, conservative estimates of the value of the intangible benefits, and incorporate these values into the NPV calculation.

Example

Assume that Berg Company is considering the purchase of a new mechanical robot to be used for soldering electrical connections. The estimates related to this proposed purchase are shown in Illustration 10-14.

Illustration 10-14 Investment information for Berg Company example

			12% Discount		Present
Initial investment	$200,000				
Annual cash inflows	$ 50,000				
Annual cash outflows	20,000				
Net annual cash inflow	**$ 30,000**				
Estimated life of equipment	10 years				
Discount rate	12%				
	Cash Flows	×	**Factor**	=	**Value**
Present value of cash flows	$30,000	×	5.65022	=	$ 169,507
Initial investment					200,000
Net present value					**$(30,493)**

Based on the negative net present value of $30,493, the proposed project is not acceptable. This calculation, however, ignores important information. First, the company's engineers believe that purchasing this machine will dramatically improve the electrical connections in the company's products. As a result, future warranty costs will be reduced. Also, the company believes that higher quality will translate into higher future sales. Finally, the new machine will be much safer than the previous one.

This new information can be incorporated into the capital budgeting decision in the two ways listed earlier. First, one might simply ask whether the reduced warranty costs, increased sales, and improved safety benefits have an estimated total present value to the company of at least $30,493. If yes, then the project is acceptable.

Alternatively, an estimate of the annual cash flows of these benefits can be made. In our initial calculation, each of these benefits was assumed to have a value of zero. It seems likely that their actual values are much higher than zero. Given the difficulty of estimating these benefits, however, conservative values should be assigned to them. If, after using conservative estimates, the net present value is positive, the project should be accepted.

To illustrate, assume that Berg estimates a sales increase of $10,000 annually as a result of an increase in perceived quality. Berg also estimates that cost outflows would be reduced by $5,000 as a result of lower warranty claims, reduced injury claims, and missed work. Consideration of the intangible benefits results in the following revised NPV calculation.

Illustration 10-15 Revised investment information for Berg Company example, including intangible benefits

			12% Discount		Present
Initial investment	$200,000				
Annual cash inflows (revised)	$ 60,000				
Annual cash outflows (revised)	15,000				
Net annual cash inflow	**$ 45,000**				
Estimated life of equipment	10 years				
Discount rate	12%				
	Cash Flows	×	**Factor**	=	**Value**
Present value of cash flows	$45,000	×	5.65022	=	$254,260
Initial investment					200,000
Net present value					**$ 54,260**

Using these conservative estimates of the value of the additional benefits, it appears that Berg should accept the project.

MUTUALLY EXCLUSIVE PROJECTS

In theory, all projects with positive NPVs should be accepted. However, companies rarely are able to adopt all positive-NPV proposals. First, proposals often are **mutually exclusive**. This means that if the company adopts one proposal, it would be impossible also to adopt the other proposal. For example, a company may be considering the purchase of a new packaging machine and is looking at various brands and models. Only one packaging machine is needed. Once the company has determined which brand and model to purchase, the others will not be purchased—even though they may also have positive net present values.

Even in instances where projects are not mutually exclusive, managers often must choose between various positive-NPV projects because of limited resources. For example, the company might have ideas for two new lines of business, each of which has a projected positive NPV. However, both of these proposals require skilled personnel, and the company determines that it will not be able to find enough skilled personnel to staff both projects. Management will have to choose the project it thinks is a better option.

When choosing between alternative proposals, it is tempting simply to choose the project with the higher NPV. Consider the following example of two mutually exclusive projects. Each is assumed to have a 10-year life and a 12 percent discount rate.

	Project A	Project B
Initial investment	$40,000	$90,000
Net annual cash inflow	10,000	19,000
Salvage value	5,000	10,000
Net present value	18,112	20,574

Illustration 10-16 Investment information for mutually exclusive projects

Project B has the higher NPV, and so it would seem that the company should adopt B. Note, however, that Project B also requires more than twice the original investment of Project A. In choosing between the two projects, the company should also include in its calculations the amount of the original investment.

One relatively simple method of comparing alternative projects is the **profitability index**. This method takes into account both the size of the original investment and the discounted cash flows. The profitability index is calculated by dividing the present value of cash flows that occur after the initial investment by the initial investment.

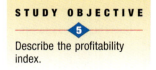

STUDY OBJECTIVE

5

Describe the profitability index.

Illustration 10-17 Formula for profitability index

The profitability index allows comparison of the relative desirability of projects that require differing initial investments. Note that any project with a positive NPV will have a profitability index above 1. Applying the profitability index to the preceding example, we get the following present values.

Illustration 10-18 Revised investment information for mutually exclusive projects

	Project A	Project B
Initial investment	$40,000	$ 90,000
Net annual cash inflow	10,000	19,000
Present value of cash flows		
($10,000 × 5.65022) + ($5,000 × .32197)	58,112	
($19,000 × 5.65022) + ($10,000 × .32197)		110,574

The profitability index for the two projects is calculated below.

Illustration 10-19 Calculation of profitability index

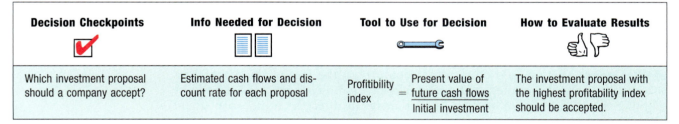

$$\text{Profitability Index} = \frac{\text{Present Value of Cash Flows}}{\text{Initial Investment}}$$

Project A

$$\frac{\$58,112}{\$40,000} = 1.45$$

Project B

$$\frac{\$110,574}{\$90,000} = 1.23$$

In this case the profitability index of Project A exceeds that of Project B. Thus, Project A is more desirable. Again, if these were not mutually exclusive projects, and if resources were not limited, then the company should invest in both projects, since both have positive NPVs. Additional considerations related to preference decisions are discussed in more advanced courses.

DECISION TOOLKIT

Decision Checkpoints	Info Needed for Decision	Tool to Use for Decision	How to Evaluate Results
✔	📄📄	⚒	👍👎
Which investment proposal should a company accept?	Estimated cash flows and discount rate for each proposal	$\text{Profitibility index} = \dfrac{\text{Present value of future cash flows}}{\text{Initial investment}}$	The investment proposal with the highest profitability index should be accepted.

RISK ANALYSIS

A simplifying assumption made by many financial analysts is that projected results are known with certainty. In reality, projected results are only estimates based upon the forecaster's belief as to the most probable outcome. One approach for dealing with such uncertainty is **sensitivity analysis**. Sensitivity analysis uses a number of outcome estimates to get a sense of the variability among potential returns. An example of sensitivity analysis was presented in Illustration 10-10, where we illustrated the impact on NPV of different discount rate assumptions. A higher-risk project would be evaluated using a higher discount rate.

Similarly, to take into account that more distant cash flows are often more uncertain, a higher discount rate can be used to discount more distant cash flows. Other techniques to address uncertainty are discussed in advanced courses.

POST-AUDIT OF INVESTMENT PROJECTS

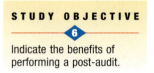

Any well-run organization should perform an evaluation, called a **post-audit**, of its investment projects after their completion. A post-audit is a thorough evaluation of how well a project's actual performance matches the original projections. An example of a post-audit is seen in the *Feature Story* about **Campbell Soup**. The original decision to invest in the Intelligent Quisine line was made based on management's best estimates of future cash flows. During the development phase of the project an outside consulting firm was hired to evaluate the project's potential for success. Because actual results during the initial years were far below the estimated results, and because the future also did not look promising, the project was terminated.

Performing a post-audit is important for a variety of reasons. First, if managers know that their estimates will be compared to actual results they will be more likely to submit reasonable and accurate data when they make investment proposals. This clearly is better for the company than for managers to submit overly optimistic estimates in an effort to get pet projects approved. Second, as seen with Campbell Soup, a post-audit provides a formal mechanism by which the company can determine whether existing projects should be supported or terminated. Third, post-audits improve future investment proposals because, by evaluating past successes and failures, managers improve their estimation techniques.

A post-audit involves the same evaluation techniques that were used in making the original capital budgeting decision—for example, use of the NPV method. The difference is that, in the post-audit, actual figures are inserted where known, and estimation of future amounts is revised based on new information. The managers responsible for the estimates used in the original proposal must explain the reasons for any significant differences between their estimates and actual results.

Post-audits are not foolproof. In the case of Campbell Soup, some observers suggested that the company was too quick to abandon the project. Industry analysts suggested that with more time and more advertising expenditures, the company might have enjoyed a success.

BUSINESS INSIGHT
Management Perspective

Inaccurate trend forecasting and market positioning are more detrimental to a budget than using the wrong discount rate. **Ampex** patented the VCR, but failed to see its market potential. **Westinghouse** made the same mistake with flat-screen video display. More often, companies adopt projects or businesses only to discontinue them in response to market changes. **Texas Instruments** announced it would stop manufacturing computer chips, after investing to become one of the world's leading suppliers. The company has dropped out of some twelve business lines in recent years.

Source: World Research Advisory Inc.; London; August 1998; page 4.

OTHER CAPITAL BUDGETING TECHNIQUES

Some companies use capital budgeting techniques other than, or in addition to, the cash payback and net present value methods. In this section we will briefly discuss these other approaches.

INTERNAL RATE OF RETURN METHOD

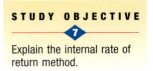

STUDY OBJECTIVE

7

Explain the internal rate of return method.

The **internal rate of return method** differs from the net present value method in that it finds the **interest yield of the potential investment**. The **internal rate of return** is the rate that will cause the present value of the proposed capital expenditure to equal the present value of the expected annual cash inflows (that is, NPV equals zero). Note that because it recognizes the time value of money, the internal rate of return method is, like the NPV method, a discounted cash flow technique.

Suppose that Tampa Company is considering a new project with an 8-year estimated life, an initial cost of $249,000, and a net annual cash inflow of $45,000. When the net annual cash inflow is assumed to be equal each year, determining the internal rate of return involves two steps.

Step 1. Compute the internal rate of return factor. The formula for this factor is:

Illustration 10-20   Formula for internal rate of return factor

The computation of the internal rate of return factor for Tampa Company, assuming an equal net annual cash inflow, is:

$$\$249,000 \div \$45,000 = 5.5333^2$$

Step 2. Use the factor and the present value of an annuity of 1 table to find the internal rate of return. Table 4 of Appendix C is used in this step. The internal rate of return is found by locating the discount factor in the table that is closest to the internal rate of return factor for the time period covered by the net annual cash inflow.

For Tampa, the net annual cash inflow is expected to continue for 8 years. Thus, it is necessary to read across the period-8 row in Table 4 to find the discount factor that is closest in value to the internal rate of return factor. Row 8 is reproduced below for your convenience.

TABLE 4   Present Value of an Annuity of 1

(*n*) Periods	5%	6%	8%	9%	10%	11%	12%	15%
8	6.46321	6.20979	5.74664	5.53482	5.33493	5.14612	4.96764	4.48732

---

[2] When the net annual cash inflow is equal, the internal rate of return factor is the same as the cash payback period.

In this case, the closest discount factor to 5.53333 is 5.53482. The factor represents an interest rate of approximately 9 percent. The rate of return can be further determined by interpolation, but since we are using estimated annual cash inflows, such precision is seldom required.

It is important to note that **steps 1 and 2 assume that net annual cash inflows will be equal.** If they are not assumed to be equal, then the internal rate of return must be calculated differently. This alternative is based on the fact that the internal rate of return is the discount rate that will result in a net present value of zero. To determine this rate, one must experiment with various discount rates to arrive at the rate that results in a zero net present value.

Once we know the internal rate of return, we compare it to management's required minimum rate of return. The decision rule is: **Accept the project when the internal rate of return is equal to or greater than the required rate of return. Reject the project when the internal rate of return is less than the required rate.** These relationships are shown graphically in Illustration 10-21. Assuming the minimum required rate of return is 8 percent for Tampa Company, the project is acceptable because the 9 percent internal rate of return is greater than the required rate.

Alternative Terminology The minimum required rate of return is sometimes referred to as the *hurdle rate* or the *cutoff rate*.

Illustration 10-21 Internal rate of return decision criteria

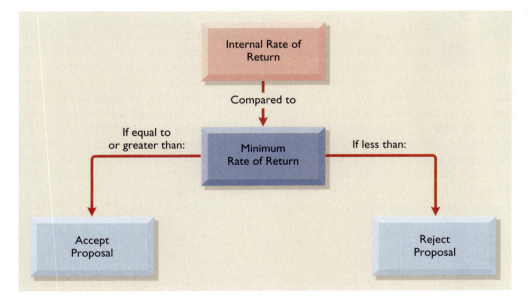

The internal rate of return method is widely used in practice. Most managers find the internal rate of return easy to interpret.

DECISION TOOLKIT

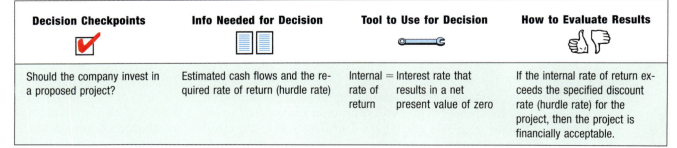

Decision Checkpoints	Info Needed for Decision	Tool to Use for Decision	How to Evaluate Results
Should the company invest in a proposed project?	Estimated cash flows and the required rate of return (hurdle rate)	Internal rate of return = Interest rate that results in a net present value of zero	If the internal rate of return exceeds the specified discount rate (hurdle rate) for the project, then the project is financially acceptable.

COMPARING DISCOUNTED CASH FLOW METHODS

A comparison of the two discounted cash flow methods—net present value and internal rate of return—is presented in Illustration 10-22. When properly used, either method will provide management with relevant quantitative data for making capital budgeting decisions.

Illustration 10-22 Comparison of discounted cash flow methods

	Net Present Value	**Internal Rate of Return**
1. Objective	Compute net present value (a dollar amount).	Compute internal rate of return (a percentage).
2. Decision rule	If net present value is zero or positive, accept the proposal. If net present value is negative, reject the proposal.	If internal rate of return is equal to or greater than the minimum required rate of return, accept the proposal. If internal rate of return is less than the minimum rate, reject the proposal.

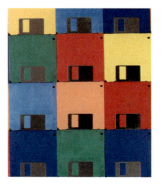

e — BUSINESS INSIGHT

One reason that e-business is changing the face of business so quickly is that the cost of the necessary hardware and software has fallen so rapidly. For example, an executive at **General Electric (GE)** reports that the company developed software for its own electronic-auction site for only $15,000. In discussing e-business related capital expenditures, a GE executive in Europe noted, "the incremental investment required is extraordinarily small compared with our overall investment. A $300 million investment for a company making $4 billion to $5 billion is [just a few] weeks of cash flow." He added that the cash payback period on these projects is a few months, rather than years. Thus, GE experienced almost "instant" productivity gains.

Source: "E-Management: Inside the Machine," *The Economist*, November 11, 2000.

ANNUAL RATE OF RETURN METHOD

The final capital budgeting technique we will look at is the **annual rate of return method**, which is based directly on accrual accounting data. It indicates **the profitability of a capital expenditure** by dividing expected annual net income by the average investment. The formula for computing annual rate of return is shown in Illustration 10-23.

Illustration 10-23 Annual rate of return formula

Expected Annual Net Income ÷ Average Investment = Annual Rate of Return

Assume that Reno Company is considering an investment of $130,000 in new equipment. The new equipment is expected to last 5 years and have zero salvage value at the end of its useful life. The straight-line method of depreciation is used for accounting purposes. The expected annual revenues and costs of the new product that will be produced from the investment are:

Sales		$200,000
Less: Costs and expenses		
Manufacturing costs (exclusive of depreciation)	$132,000	
Depreciation expense ($130,000 ÷ 5)	26,000	
Selling and administrative expenses	22,000	180,000
Income before income taxes		20,000
Income tax expense		7,000
Net income		$ 13,000

Illustration 10-24 Estimated annual net income from Reno Company's capital expenditure

Reno's expected annual net income is $13,000. Average investment is derived from the following formula.

$$\text{Average investment} = \frac{\text{Original investment} + \text{Value at end of useful life}}{2}$$

Illustration 10-25 Formula for computing average investment

The value at the end of useful life is equal to the asset's salvage value, if any. For Reno, average investment is $65,000 [($130,000 + $0) ÷ 2]. The expected annual rate of return for Reno's investment in new equipment is therefore 20 percent, computed as follows.

$$\$13,000 \div \$65,000 = 20\%$$

Management then compares the annual rate of return with its required minimum rate of return for investments of similar risk. The minimum rate of return is generally based on the company's cost of capital. The decision rule is: **A project is acceptable if its rate of return is greater than management's minimum rate of return. It is unacceptable when the reverse is true.** When the rate of return technique is used in deciding among several acceptable projects, **the higher the rate of return for a given risk, the more attractive the investment**.

The principal advantages of this method are the simplicity of its calculation and management's familiarity with the accounting terms used in the computation. A major limitation of the annual rate of return method is that it does not consider the time value of money. For example, no consideration is given as to whether cash inflows will occur early or late in the life of the investment. As explained in Appendix C, recognition of the time value of money can make a significant difference between the future value and the discounted present value of an investment. A second disadvantage is that this method relies on accrual accounting numbers rather than expected cash flows.

Helpful Hint A capital budgeting decision based on only one technique may be misleading. It is often wise to analyze an investment from a number of different perspectives.

BEFORE YOU GO ON . . .

◆ Review It

1. When is a proposal acceptable under (a) the net present value method and (b) the internal rate of return method?

2. How does the internal rate of return method differ from the net present value method?

3. What is the formula for and the decision rule in using the annual rate of return method? What are the drawbacks to the annual rate of return method?

*U*SING THE DECISION TOOLKIT

Campbell Soup is considering expanding its international presence. It sells 38 percent of the soup consumed in the United States, but only 2 percent of soup worldwide. Thus the company believes that it has great potential for international sales. Recently, 20 percent of Campbell's sales were in foreign markets (and nearly all of that was in Europe). Its goal is to have 30 percent of its sales be in foreign markets. In order to accomplish this goal, the company will have to invest heavily.

In recent years Campbell has spent between $300 and $400 million on capital expenditures. Suppose that Campbell is interested in expanding its South American presence by building a new production facility. After considering tax, marketing, labor, transportation, and political issues, Campbell has determined that the most desirable location is either in Buenos Aires or Rio de Janeiro. The following estimates have been provided (all amounts are stated in U.S. dollars).

	Buenos Aires	Rio de Janeiro
Initial investment	$2,500,000	$1,400,000
Estimated useful life	20 years	20 years
Annual revenues (accrual)	$ 500,000	$ 380,000
Annual expenses (accrual)	$ 200,000	$ 180,000
Annual cash inflows	$ 550,000	$ 430,000
Annual cash outflows	$ 222,250	$ 206,350
Estimated salvage value	$ 500,000	$0
Discount rate	9%	9%

Instructions

Evaluate each of these mutually exclusive proposals employing (1) cash payback, (2) net present value, (3) the profitability index, (4) the internal rate of return, and (5) annual rate of return. Discuss the implications of your findings.

Solution

	Buenos Aires	Rio de Janeiro
(1) Cash payback	$\dfrac{\$2,500,000}{\$327,750} = 7.63$ years	$\dfrac{\$1,400,000}{\$223,650} = 6.26$ years

(2) Net present value

Present value of cash flows

	Buenos Aires		Rio de Janeiro
$327,750 × 9.12855 =	$2,991,882		$223,650 × 9.12855 = $2,041,600
$500,000 × 0.17843 =	89,215		
	3,081,097		
Less: Initial investment	2,500,000		1,400,000
Net present value	$ 581,097		$ 641,600

(3) Profitability index

$$\frac{\$3,081,097}{\$2,500,000} = 1.23 \qquad \frac{\$2,041,600}{\$1,400,000} = 1.46$$

(4) Internal rate of return: The internal rate of return can be approximated by experimenting with different discount rates to see which one comes the closest to resulting in a net present value of zero. Doing this, we find that Buenos Aires has an internal rate of return of approximately 12%, while the internal rate of return of the Rio de Janeiro location is approximately 15% as shown below. Rio, therefore, is preferable.

Internal rate of return

Cash Flows	×	12% Discount Factor	=	Present Value	Cash Flows	×	15% Discount Factor	=	Present Value
$327,750 ×		7.46944	=	$2,448,109	$223,650 ×		6.25933	=	$1,399,899
$500,000 ×		0.10367	=	51,835					
				$2,499,944					
Less: Capital investment				2,500,000					1,400,000
Net present value				$ (56)					$ (101)

(5) Annual rate of return

Average investment

$$\frac{(\$2,500,000 + \$500,000)}{2} = \$1,500,000 \qquad \frac{(\$1,400,000 + \$0)}{2} = \$700,000$$

Annual rate of return
$$\frac{\$300,000}{\$1,500,000} = .20 = 20\% \qquad \frac{\$200,000}{\$700,000} = .286 = 28.6\%$$

Implications: Although the annual rate of return is higher for Rio de Janeiro, this method has the disadvantage of ignoring time value of money, as well as using accrual numbers rather than cash flows. The cash payback of Rio de Janeiro is also higher, but this method also ignores the time value of money. Thus, while these two methods can be used for a quick assessment, neither should be relied upon as the sole evaluation tool.

From the net present value calculation it would appear that the two projects are nearly identical in their acceptability. However, the profitability index indicates that the Rio de Janeiro investment is far more desirable because it generates its cash flows with a much smaller initial investment. A similar result is found by using the internal rate of return. Overall, assuming that the company will invest in only one project, it would appear that the Rio de Janeiro project should be chosen.

SUMMARY OF STUDY OBJECTIVES

1 *Discuss the capital budgeting evaluation process, and explain what inputs are used in capital budgeting.* Project proposals are gathered from each department and submitted to a capital budget committee, which screens the proposals and recommends worthy projects. Company officers decide which projects to fund, and the board of directors approves the capital budget. In capital budgeting, estimated cash inflows and outflows, rather than accrual-accounting numbers, are the preferred inputs.

2 *Describe the cash payback technique.* The cash payback technique identifies the time period to recover the cost of the investment. The formula is: Cost of capital expenditure divided by estimated net annual cash inflow equals cash payback period. The shorter the payback period, the more attractive the investment.

3 *Explain the net present value method.* Under the net present value method, the present value of future cash inflows is compared with the capital investment to determine net present value. The decision rule is: Accept the project if net present value is zero or positive. Reject the project if net present value is negative.

4 *Identify the challenges presented by intangible benefits in capital budgeting.* Intangible benefits are difficult to quantify, and thus are often ignored in capital budgeting decisions. This can result in incorrectly rejecting some projects. One method for considering intangible benefits is to calculate the NPV, ignoring intangible benefits; if the resulting NPV is below zero, evaluate whether the benefits are worth at least the amount of the negative net present value. Alternatively, intangible benefits can be incorporated into the NPV calculation, using conservative estimates of their value.

5 *Describe the profitability index.* The profitability index is a tool for comparing the relative merits of two alternative capital investment opportunities. It is computed by dividing the present value of future cash flows by the initial investment. The higher the index, the more desirable the project.

6 *Indicate the benefits of performing a post-audit.* A post-audit is an evaluation of a capital investment's actual performance. Post-audits create an incentive for managers to make accurate estimates. Post-audits also are useful for determining whether a project should be continued, expanded, or terminated. Finally, post-audits provide feedback that is useful for improving estimation techniques.

7 *Explain the internal rate of return method.* The objective of the internal rate of return method is to find the interest yield of the potential investment, which is expressed as a percentage rate. The decision rule is: Accept the project when the internal rate of return is equal to or greater than the required rate of return. Reject the project when the internal rate of return is less than the required rate.

8 *Describe the annual rate of return method.* The annual rate of return uses accounting data to indicate the profitability of a capital investment. It is obtained by dividing the expected annual net income by the amount of the average investment. The higher the rate of return, the more attractive the investment.

DECISION TOOLKIT—A SUMMARY

Decision Checkpoints	Info Needed for Decision	Tool to Use for Decision	How to Evaluate Results
Should the company invest in a proposed project?	Cash flow estimates, discount rate	Net present value = Present value of future cash flows less capital investment	The investment is financially acceptable if net present value is positive.
Which investment proposal should a company accept?	Estimated cash flows and discount rate for each proposal	Profitability index = Present value of future cash flows / Initial investment	The investment proposal with the highest profitability index should be accepted.
Should the company invest in a proposed project?	Estimated cash flows and the required rate of return (hurdle rate)	Internal rate of return = Interest rate that results in a net present value of zero	If the internal rate of return exceeds the specified discount rate (hurdle rate) for the project, then the project is financially acceptable.

GLOSSARY

Key Term Matching Activity

Annual rate of return method   The determination of the profitability of a capital expenditure, computed by dividing expected annual net income by the average investment. (p. 416)

Capital budgeting   The process of making capital expenditure decisions in business. (p. 400)

Cash payback technique   A capital budgeting technique that identifies the time period required to recover the cost of a capital investment from the annual cash inflow produced by the investment. (p. 403)

Cost of capital   The average rate of return that the firm must pay to obtain borrowed and equity funds. (p. 406)

Discounted cash flow technique   A capital budgeting technique that considers both the estimated total cash inflows from the investment and the time value of money. (p. 404)

Internal rate of return   The rate that will cause the present value of the proposed capital expenditure to equal the present value of the expected annual cash inflows. (p. 414)

Internal rate of return method A method used in capital budgeting that results in finding the interest yield of the potential investment. (p. 414)

Net present value The difference that results when the original capital outlay is subtracted from the discounted cash inflows. (p. 404)

Net present value method A method used in capital budgeting in which cash inflows are discounted to their present value and then compared to the capital outlay required by the investment. (p. 404)

Post-audit A thorough evaluation of how well a project's actual performance matches the projections made when the project was proposed. (p. 413)

Profitability index A method of comparing alternative projects that takes into account both the size of the investment and its discounted future cash flows. It is computed by dividing the present value of net future cash flows by the initial investment. (p. 411)

DEMONSTRATION PROBLEM

Sierra Company is considering a long-term capital investment project called ZIP. ZIP will require an investment of $120,000, and it will have a useful life of 4 years. Annual net income is expected to be $9,000 a year. Depreciation is computed by the straight-line method with no salvage value. The company's cost of capital is 12 percent. (*Hint:* Assume cash flows can be computed by adding back depreciation expense.)

eGrade Demonstration Problem

Instructions

(Round all computations to two decimal places.)
(a) Compute the cash payback period for the project. (Round to two decimals.)
(b) Compute the net present value for the project. (Round to nearest dollar.)
(c) Compute the annual rate of return for the project.
(d) Should the project be accepted? Why?

Solution to Demonstration Problem

(a) $120,000 ÷ $39,000, ($9,000 + $30,000), = 3.08 years
(b)

	Present Value at 12%
Discount factor for 4 periods	3.03735
Present value of cash flows:	
$39,000 × 3.03735	$118,457
Capital investment	120,000
Negative net present value	$ (1,543)

(c) $9,000 ÷ $60,000, ($120,000 ÷ 2), = 15%
(d) The annual rate of return of 15% is good. However, the cash payback period is 77% of the project's useful life, and net present value is negative. The recommendation is to reject the project.

THE NAVIGATOR

Action Plan
- Calculate the time it will take to pay back the investment: cost of the investment divided by annual cash inflows.
- When calculating NPV, remember that annual cash inflow equals annual net income plus annual depreciation expense.
- Be careful to use the correct discount factor in using the net present value method.
- Calculate the annual rate of return: expected annual net income divided by average investment.

SELF-STUDY QUESTIONS

Self-Study/Self-Test

Answers are at the end of the chapter.

(SO 1) 1. Which of the following is *not* an example of a capital budgeting decision?
(a) Decision to build a new plant.
(b) Decision to renovate an existing facility.
(c) Decision to buy a piece of machinery.
(d) All of these are capital budgeting decisions.

2. What is the order of involvement of the following parties in the capital budgeting authorization process? (SO 1)
(a) Plant managers, officers, capital budget committee, board of directors.
(b) Board of directors, plant managers, officers, capital budget committee.

(c) Plant managers, capital budget committee, officers, board of directors.

(d) Officers, plant managers, capital budget committee, board of directors.

(SO 2) 3. What is a weakness of the cash payback approach?
(a) It uses accrual-based accounting numbers.
(b) It ignores the time value of money.
(c) It ignores the useful life of alternative projects.
(d) Both (b) and (c) are true.

(SO 3) 4. Which is a true statement regarding using a higher discount rate to calculate the net present value of a project?
(a) It will make it less likely that the project will be accepted.
(b) It will make it more likely that the project will be accepted.
(c) It is appropriate to use a higher rate if the project is perceived as being less risky than other projects being considered.
(d) It is appropriate to use a higher rate if the project will have a short useful life relative to other projects being considered.

(SO 3) 5. A positive net present value means that the:
(a) project's rate of return is less than the cut-off rate.
(b) project's rate of return exceeds the required rate of return.
(c) project's rate of return equals the required rate of return.
(d) project is unacceptable.

(SO 3) 6. Which of the following is *not* an alternative name for the discount rate?
(a) Hurdle rate.
(b) Required rate of return.
(c) Cutoff rate.

(d) All of these are alternative names for the discount rate.

(SO 4) 7. If a project has intangible benefits whose value is hard to estimate, the best thing to do is:
(a) ignore these benefits, since any estimate of their value will most likely be wrong.
(b) include a conservative estimate of their value.
(c) ignore their value in your initial net present value calculation, but then estimate whether their potential value is worth at least the amount of the net present value deficiency.
(d) either (b) or (c) is correct.

(SO 6) 8. A post-audit of an investment project should be performed:
(a) on all significant capital expenditure projects.
(b) on all projects that management feels might be financial failures.
(c) on randomly selected projects.
(d) only on projects that enjoy tremendous success.

(SO 7) 9. A project should be accepted if its internal rate of return exceeds:
(a) zero.
(b) the rate of return on a government bond.
(c) the company's required rate of return.
(d) the rate the company pays on borrowed funds.

(SO 8) 10. Which of the following is *incorrect* about the annual rate of return technique?
(a) The calculation is simple.
(b) The accounting terms used are familiar to management.
(c) The timing of the cash in-flows is not considered.
(d) The time value of money is considered.

QUESTIONS

1. Describe the process a company may use in screening and approving the capital expenditure budget.

2. What are the advantages and disadvantages of the cash payback technique?

3. Petra Varnak claims the formula for the cash payback technique is the same as the formula for the annual rate of return technique. Is Petra correct? What is the formula for the cash payback technique?

4. Two types of present value tables may be used with the discounted cash flow technique. Identify the tables and the circumstance(s) when each table should be used.

5. What is the decision rule under the net present value method?

6. Discuss the factors that determine the appropriate discount rate to use when calculating the net present value.

7. What simplifying assumptions were made in the chapter regarding calculation of net present value?

8. What are some examples of potential intangible benefits of investment proposals? Why do these intangible benefits complicate the capital budget evaluation process? What might happen if intangible benefits are ignored in a capital budget decision?

9. What steps can be taken to incorporate intangible benefits into the capital budget evaluation process?

10. What advantages does the profitability index provide over direct comparison of net present value when comparing two projects?

11. What is a post-audit? What are the potential benefits of a post-audit?

12. Identify the steps required in using the internal rate of return method.

13. Harold Stine Company uses the internal rate of return method. What is the decision rule for this method?

14. What are the strengths of the annual rate of return approach? What are its weaknesses?

15. Your classmate, Joe Livingston, is confused about the factors that are included in the annual rate of return technique. What is the formula for this technique?

16. Sara Kay is trying to understand the term "cost of capital." Define the term and indicate its relevance to the decision rule under the annual rate of return technique.

BRIEF EXERCISES

Compute the cash payback period for a capital investment.
(SO 2)

BE10-1 Russell Company is considering purchasing new equipment for $450,000. It is expected that the equipment will produce annual net income of $15,000 over its 10-year useful life. Annual depreciation will be $45,000. Compute the payback period.

Compute net present value of an investment.
(SO 3)

BE10-2 Gruner Company accumulates the following data concerning a proposed capital investment: cash cost $280,000, annual cash inflow $50,000, present value factor of cash inflows for 10 years 5.65 (rounded). Determine the net present value, and indicate whether the investment should be made.

Compute net present value of an investment.
(SO 3)

BE10-3 Travis Corporation, an amusement park, is considering a capital investment in a new exhibit. The exhibit would cost $140,000 and have an estimated useful life of 5 years. It will be sold for $75,000 at that time. (Amusement parks need to rotate exhibits to keep people interested.) It will be expected to increase net annual cash inflows by $25,000. The company's borrowing rate is 8%. Its cost of capital is 10%. Calculate the net present value of this project to the company.

Compute net present value of an investment.
(SO 3)

BE10-4 Shandling Bottling Corporation is considering the purchase of a new bottling machine. The machine would cost $200,000 and has an estimated useful life of 8 years with zero salvage value. Management estimates that the new bottling machine will provide net annual cash inflows of $33,000. Management also believes that the new bottling machine will save the company money because it is expected to be more reliable than other machines, and thus will reduce downtime. How much would the reduction in downtime have to be worth in order for the project to be acceptable? Assume a discount rate of 9%. (*Hint:* Calculate the net present value.)

Compute net present value and profitability index.
(SO 3, 5)

BE10-5 Bierko Company is considering two different, mutually exclusive capital expenditure proposals. Project A will cost $395,000, has an expected useful life of 10 years, a salvage value of zero, and is expected to increase net cash inflows by $70,000. Project B will cost $220,000, has an expected useful life of 10 years, a salvage value of zero, and is expected to increase cash flows by $40,000. A discount rate of 9% is appropriate for both projects. Compute the net present value and profitability index of each project. Which project should be accepted?

Perform a post-audit.
(SO 6)

BE10-6 Swayze Company is performing a post-audit of a project completed one year ago. The initial estimates were that the project would cost $250,000, would have a useful life of 9 years, zero salvage value, and would result in net cash inflows of $45,000 per year. Now that the investment has been in operation for 1 year, revised figures indicate that it actually cost $260,000, will have a useful life of 11 years, and will produce net cash inflows of $37,000 per year. Evaluate the success of the project. Assume a discount rate of 10%.

Calculate internal rate of return.
(SO 7)

BE10-7 Selleck Company is evaluating the purchase of a rebuilt spot-welding machine to be used in the manufacture of a new product. The machine will cost $180,000, has an estimated useful life of 8 years, a salvage value of zero, and will increase net annual cash inflow by $33,740. What is its approximate internal rate of return?

Calculate internal rate of return.
(SO 7)

BE10-8 Marlowe Corporation is considering investing in a new facility. The estimated cost of the facility is $1,931,000. It will be used for 12 years, then sold for $600,000. The facility will generate annual cash inflows of $400,000 and will need new annual cash outflows of $160,000. The company has a hurdle rate of 7%. Calculate the internal rate of return on this project, and discuss whether the project should be accepted.

Compute annual rate of return.
(SO 8)

BE10-9   Caan Oil Company is considering investing in a new oil well. It is expected that the oil well will increase annual revenues by $120,000 and will increase annual expenses by $80,000 including depreciation. The oil well will cost $490,000 and will have a $10,000 salvage value at the end of its 10-year useful life. Calculate the annual rate of return.

EXERCISES

Compute cash payback and net present value.
(SO 2, 3)

E10-1   Padong Corporation is considering purchasing a new delivery truck. The truck has many advantages over the company's current truck (not the least of which is that it runs). The new truck would cost $56,000. Because of the increased capacity, reduced maintenance costs, and increased fuel economy, the new truck is expected to generate cost savings of $8,000. At the end of 8 years the company will sell the truck for an estimated $30,000. Traditionally the company has used a rule of thumb that a proposal should not be accepted unless it has a payback period that is less than 50% of the asset's estimated useful life. Kevin McCarthy, a new manager, has suggested that the company should not rely solely on the payback approach, but should also employ the net present value method when evaluating new projects. The company's cost of capital is 8%.

Instructions
(a) Compute the cash payback period and net present value of the proposed investment.
(b) Does the project meet the company's cash payback criteria? Does it meet the net present value criteria for acceptance? Discuss your results.

Compute cash payback period and net present value.
(SO 2, 3)

E10-2   Danny Sutton Manufacturing Company is considering three new projects, each requiring an equipment investment of $24,000. Each project will last for 3 years and produce the following cash inflows.

Year	AA	BB	CC
1	$15,000	$ 9,500	$13,000
2	9,000	9,500	11,000
3	7,500	9,500	9,000
Total	$31,500	$28,500	$33,000

The equipment's salvage value is zero, and Sutton uses straight-line depreciation. Sutton will not accept any project with a payback period over 2 years. Sutton's minimum required rate of return is 15%.

Instructions
(a) Compute each project's payback period, indicating the most desirable project and the least desirable project using this method. (Round to two decimals and use average annual cash flows in your computations.)
(b) Compute the net present value of each project. Does your evaluation change? (Round to nearest dollar.)

Compute net present value and profitability index.
(SO 3, 5)

E10-3   TekCare Corp. is considering purchasing one of two new diagnostic machines. Either machine would make it possible for the company to bid on jobs that it currently isn't equipped to do. Estimates regarding each machine are provided below.

	Machine A	Machine B
Original cost	$75,000	$190,000
Estimated life	8 years	8 years
Salvage value	–0–	–0–
Estimated annual cash inflows	$20,000	$40,000
Estimated annual cash outflows	$ 5,000	$10,000

Instructions
Calculate the net present value and profitability index of each machine. Assume a 9% discount rate. Which machine should be purchased?

E10-4 Baldwin Corporation is involved in the business of injection molding of plastics. It is considering the purchase of a new computer-aided design and manufacturing machine for $481,000. The company believes that with this new machine it will improve productivity and increase quality, resulting in an annual increase in net cash flows of $75,000 for the next 10 years. Management requires a 10% rate of return on all new investments.

Determine internal rate of return.
(SO 7)

Instructions
Calculate the internal rate of return on this new machine. Should the investment be accepted?

E10-5 Novak Company is considering three capital expenditure projects. Relevant data for the projects are as follows.

Determine internal rate of return.
(SO 7)

Project	Investment	Annual Income	Life of Project
22A	$240,000	$14,000	6 years
23A	270,000	24,400	9 years
24A	280,000	19,000	7 years

Annual income is constant over the life of the project. Each project is expected to have zero salvage value at the end of the project. Novak Company uses the straight-line method of depreciation.

Instructions
(a) Determine the internal rate of return for each project. Round the internal rate of return factor to three decimals.
(b) If Novak Company's minimum required rate of return is 11%, which projects are acceptable?

E10-6 Hair Fare is considering opening a new hair salon in Pompador, California. The cost of building a new salon is $250,000. A new salon will normally generate annual revenues of $70,000, with annual expenses (including depreciation) of $40,000. At the end of 15 years the salon will have a salvage value of $50,000.

Calculate annual rate of return.
(SO 8)

Instructions
Calculate the annual rate of return on the project.

E10-7 Wamser Service Center just purchased an automobile hoist for $39,000. The hoist has an 8-year life and an estimated salvage value of $3,000. Installation costs and freight charges were $3,300 and $700, respectively. Wamser uses straight-line depreciation.

Compute cash payback period and annual rate of return.
(SO 2, 8)

The new hoist will be used to replace mufflers and tires on automobiles. Wamser estimates that the new hoist will enable his mechanics to replace four extra mufflers per week. Each muffler sells for $70 installed. The cost of a muffler is $30, and the labor cost to install a muffler is $10.

Instructions
(a) Compute the payback period for the new hoist.
(b) Compute the annual rate of return for the new hoist. (Round to one decimal.)

E10-8 Bosworth Company is considering a capital investment of $168,000 in additional productive facilities. The new machinery is expected to have a useful life of 6 years with no salvage value. Depreciation is by the straight-line method. During the life of the investment, annual net income and cash inflows are expected to be $20,000 and $48,000 respectively. Bosworth has a 15% cost of capital rate which is the minimum acceptable rate of return on the investment.

Compute annual rate of return, cash payback period, and net present value.
(SO 2, 3, 8)

Instructions
(Round to two decimals.)
(a) Compute (1) the cash payback period and (2) the annual rate of return on the proposed capital expenditure.
(b) Using the discounted cash flow technique, compute the net present value.

PROBLEMS: SET A

P10-1A   The partnership of Malle and Stine is considering three long-term capital investment proposals. Relevant data on each project are as follows.

	Project		
	Brown	**Red**	**Yellow**
Capital investment	$200,000	$260,000	$300,000
Annual net income:			
Year 1	28,000	24,000	37,000
2	18,000	24,000	29,000
3	14,000	24,000	28,000
4	11,000	24,000	26,000
5	9,000	24,000	24,000
Total	$ 80,000	$120,000	$144,000

Salvage value is expected to be zero at the end of each project. Depreciation is computed by the straight-line method. The company's minimum rate of return is the company's cost of capital which is 11%. (Use average annual cash flows in your computations.)

Instructions
(a) Compute the cash payback period for each project. (Round to two decimals.)
(b) Compute the net present value for each project. (Round to nearest dollar.)
(c) Compute the average annual rate of return for each project. (Round to two decimals.)
(d) Rank the projects on each of the foregoing bases. What project do you recommend?

P10-2A   Sarah Kay is managing director of the City Day Care Center. City is currently set up as a full-time child care facility for children between the ages of 12 months and 6 years. Sarah Kay is trying to determine whether the center should expand its facilities to incorporate a newborn care room for infants between the ages of 6 weeks and 12 months. The necessary space already exists. An investment of $20,000 would be needed, however, to purchase cribs, high chairs, etc. The equipment purchased for the room would have a 5-year useful life with zero salvage value.

The newborn nursery would be staffed to handle 11 infants on a full-time basis. The parents of each infant would be charged $100 weekly, and the facility would operate 52 weeks of the year. Staffing the nursery would require two full-time specialists and five part-time assistants at an annual cost of $45,000. Food, diapers, and other miscellaneous supplies are expected to total $6,200 annually.

Instructions
(a) Determine (1) annual net income and (2) cash inflow for the new nursery.
(b) Compute (1) the cash payback period for the new nursery and (2) the annual rate of return. (Round to two decimals.)
(c) Compute the net present value of incorporating a newborn care room. (Round to the nearest dollar.) City's cost of capital is 12%.
(d) ▭▭▭▶ What should Sarah Kay conclude from these computations?

P10-3A   Fresh Water Testing is considering investing in a new testing device. It has two options: Option A would have an initial lower cost but would require a significant expenditure for rebuilding after 4 years. Option B would require no rebuilding expenditure, but its maintenance costs would be higher. Since the option B machine is of initial higher quality, it is expected to have a salvage value at the end of its useful life. The following estimates were provided.

	Option A	**Option B**
Initial cost	$ 90,000	$170,000
Annual cash inflows	$180,000	$140,000
Annual cash outflows	$160,000	$108,000
Cost to rebuild (end of year 4)	$ 24,500	$ 0
Salvage value	$ 0	$ 27,500
Estimated useful life	8 years	8 years

The company's cost of capital is 9%.

Instructions
(a) Compute the (1) net present value, (2) profitability index, and (3) internal rate of return for each option.
(b) Which option should be accepted? (*Hint:* To solve for internal rate of return, experiment with alternative discount rates to arrive at a net present value of zero.)

P10-4A The Chula Vista Sanitation Company is considering the purchase of a garbage truck. The $70,000 price tag for a new truck would represent a major expenditure for the company. Vu Duong, owner of the company, has compiled the following estimates in trying to determine whether the garbage truck should be purchased.

Compute net present value considering intangible benefits.
(SO 3, 4)

eGrade Problem

Initial cost	$70,000
Estimated useful life	10 years
Annual net cash flows	$10,000
Overhaul costs (end of year 5)	$ 7,000
Salvage value	$25,000

One of the company's employees is trying to convince Vu that the truck has other merits that haven't been considered in the initial estimates. First, the new truck will be more efficient, with lower maintenance and operating costs. Second, the new truck will be safer. Third, the new truck has the ability to handle recycled materials at the same time as trash, thus offering a new revenue source. Estimates of the minimum value of these benefits are the following.

Annual savings from reduced operating costs	$400
Annual savings from reduced maintenance costs	800
Additional annual net cash savings from reduced employee absence	500
Additional annual net cash inflows from recycling	300

The company's cost of capital is 10%.

Instructions
(a) Calculate the net present value, ignoring the additional benefits. Should the truck be purchased?
(b) Calculate the net present value, incorporating the additional benefits. Should the truck be purchased?
(c) Suppose management has been overly optimistic in the assessment of the value of the additional benefits. At a minimum, how much would the additional benefits have to be worth in order for the project to be accepted?

P10-5A Wang Corp. is thinking about opening an ice hockey camp in Idaho. In order to start the camp the company would need to purchase land, and build two ice rinks and a dormitory-type sleeping and dining facility to house 200 players. Each year the camp would be run for 8 sessions of 1 week each. The company would hire college hockey players as coaches. The camp attendees would be male and female hockey players age 12–18. Property values in Idaho have enjoyed a steady increase in recent years. Wang Corp. expects that after using the facility for 15 years, the rinks will have to be dismantled, but the land and buildings will be worth more than they were originally purchased for. The following amounts have been estimated.

Compute net present value and internal rate of return with sensitivity analysis.
(SO 3, 7)

Cost of land	$ 200,000
Cost to build dorm and dining hall	$ 500,000
Annual cash inflows assuming 200 players and 8 weeks	$ 920,000
Annual cash outflows	$ 740,000
Estimated useful life	15 years
Salvage value	$1,200,000
Discount rate	11%

Instructions
(a) Calculate the net present value of the project.
(b) To gauge the sensitivity of the project to these estimates, assume that if only 170 campers attend each week, revenues will be $700,000 and expenses will be

$670,000. What is the net present value using these alternative estimates? Discuss your findings.

(c) Assuming the original facts, what is the net present value if the project is actually riskier than first assumed, and a 15% discount rate is more appropriate?

(d) Assume that during the first 6 years the annual net cash flows each year were only $47,000. At the end of the sixth year the company is running low on cash, so management decides to sell the property for $1,000,000. What was the actual internal rate of return on the project? Explain how this return was possible given that the camp did not appear to be successful.

PROBLEMS: SET B

Compute rate of return, cash payback, and net present value.
(SO 2, 3, 8)

P10-1B The Bell and Howell partnership is considering three long-term capital investment proposals. Each investment has a useful life of 5 years. Relevant data on each project are as follows.

	Project Tic	Project Tac	Project Toe
Capital investment	$130,000	$150,000	$180,000
Annual net income:			
Year 1	11,000	17,000	24,000
2	11,000	16,000	20,000
3	11,000	15,000	19,000
4	11,000	11,000	16,000
5	11,000	8,000	11,000
Total	$ 55,000	$ 67,000	$ 90,000

Depreciation is computed by the straight-line method with no salvage value. The company's cost of capital is 15%. (Use average annual cash flows in your computations.)

Instructions
(a) Compute the cash payback period for each project. (Round to two decimals.)
(b) Compute the net present value for each project. (Round to nearest dollar.)
(c) Compute the annual rate of return for each project. (Round to two decimals.)
(d) Rank the projects on each of the foregoing bases. Which project do you recommend?

Compute annual rate of return, cash payback, and net present value.
(SO 2, 3, 8)

P10-2B Jason Parker is an accounting major at a midwestern state university located approximately 60 miles from a major city. Many of the students attending the university are from the metropolitan area and visit their homes regularly on the weekends. Jason, an entrepreneur at heart, realizes that few good commuting alternatives are available for students doing weekend travel. He believes that a weekend commuting service could be organized and run profitably from several suburban and downtown shopping mall locations. Jason has gathered the following investment information.

1. Five used vans would cost a total of $72,000 to purchase and would have a 3-year useful life with negligible salvage value. Jason plans to use straight-line depreciation.
2. Ten drivers would have to be employed at a total payroll expense of $50,000.
3. Other annual out-of-pocket expenses associated with running the commuter service would include Gasoline $14,000, Maintenance $4,300, Repairs $5,000, Insurance $4,200, Advertising $2,500.
4. Jason has visited several financial institutions to discuss funding for his new venture. The best interest rate he has been able to negotiate is 12%. Use this rate for cost of capital.
5. Jason expects each van to make ten round trips weekly and carry an average of six students each trip. The service is expected to operate 30 weeks each year, and each student will be charged $12.00 for a round-trip ticket.

Instructions
(a) Determine the annual (1) net income and (2) cash inflow for the commuter service.
(b) Compute (1) the cash payback period and (2) the annual rate of return. (Round to two decimals.)

(c) Compute the net present value of the commuter service. (Round to the nearest dollar.)
(d) ▭▭▭▭▭▭▭➤ What should Jason conclude from these computations?

P10-3B White Cliff Clinic is considering investing in new heart monitoring equipment. It has two options: Option A would have an initial lower cost but would require a significant expenditure for rebuilding after 4 years. Option B would require no rebuilding expenditure, but its maintenance costs would be higher. Since the option B machine is of initial higher quality, it is expected to have a salvage value at the end of its useful life. The following estimates were made of the cash flows.

Compute net present value, profitability index, and internal rate of return.
(SO 3, 5, 7)

	Option A	Option B
Initial cost	$170,000	$227,000
Annual cash inflows	$ 75,000	$ 80,000
Annual cash outflows	$ 34,400	$ 30,000
Cost to rebuild (end of year 4)	$ 50,000	$ 0
Salvage value	$ 0	$ 10,000
Estimated useful life	8 years	8 years

The company's cost of capital is 11%.

Instructions
(a) Compute the (1) net present value, (2) profitability index, and (3) internal rate of return for each option.
(b) Which option should be accepted? (*Hint:* To solve for internal rate of return, experiment with alternative discount rates to arrive at a net present value of zero.)

P10-4B Santana Auto Care is considering the purchase of a new tow truck. The garage doesn't currently have a tow truck, and the $50,000 price tag for a new truck would represent a major expenditure for the garage. Sally Roe, owner of the garage, has compiled the following estimates in trying to determine whether the tow truck should be purchased.

Compute net present value considering intangible benefits.
(SO 3, 4)

Initial cost	$50,000
Estimated useful life	8 years
Annual cash inflows from towing	$ 7,000
Overhaul costs (end of year 4)	$ 5,000
Salvage value	$15,000

Sally's good friend, Don Kline, stopped by. He is trying to convince Sally that the tow truck will have other benefits that Sally hasn't even considered. First, he says, cars that need towing need to be fixed. Thus, when Sally tows them to her facility her repair revenues will increase. Second, he notes that the tow truck could have a plow mounted on it, thus saving Sally the cost of plowing her parking lot. (Don will give her a used plow blade for free if Sally will plow Don's driveway.) Third, he notes that the truck will generate goodwill; that is, people who are rescued by Sally and her tow truck will feel grateful and might be more inclined to used her service station in the future, or buy gas there. Fourth, the tow truck will have "Santana Auto Care" on its doors, hood, and back tailgate—a form of free advertising wherever the tow truck goes.

Don estimates that, at a minimum, these benefits would be worth the following.

Additional annual net cash inflows from repair work	$3,000
Annual savings from plowing	500
Additional annual net cash inflows from customer "goodwill"	1,000
Additional annual net cash inflows resulting from free advertising	500

The company's cost of capital is 9%.

Instructions
(a) Calculate the net present value, ignoring the additional benefits described by Don. Should the tow truck be purchased?
(b) Calculate the net present value, incorporating the additional benefits suggested by Don. Should the tow truck be purchased?

(c) Suppose Don has been overly optimistic in his assessment of the value of the additional benefits (perhaps because he wants his driveway plowed). At a minimum, how much would the additional benefits have to be worth in order for the project to be accepted?

Compute net present value and internal rate of return with sensitivity analysis.
(SO 3, 7)

P10-5B Lafluer Corp. is thinking about opening a soccer camp in southern California. In order to start the camp, the company would need to purchase land, and build four soccer fields and a dormitory-type sleeping and dining facility to house 150 soccer players. Each year the camp would be run for 8 sessions of 1 week each. The company would hire college soccer players as coaches. The camp attendees would be male and female soccer players age 12–18. Property values in southern California have enjoyed a steady increase in value. It is expected that after using the facility for 20 years, Lafluer can sell the property for more than it was originally purchased for. The following amounts have been estimated.

Cost of land	$ 300,000
Cost to build dorm and dining facility	$ 500,000
Annual cash inflows assuming 150 players and 8 weeks	$ 950,000
Annual cash outflows	$ 860,000
Estimated useful life	20 years
Salvage value	$1,500,000
Discount rate	8%

Instructions
(a) Calculate the net present value of the project.
(b) To gauge the sensitivity of the project to these estimates, assume that if only 130 campers attend each week, revenues will be $800,000 and expenses will be $780,000. What is the net present value using these alternative estimates? Discuss your findings.
(c) Assuming the original facts, what is the net present value if the project is actually riskier than first assumed, and a 11% discount rate is more appropriate?
(d) Assume that during the first 5 years the annual net cash flows each year were only $25,200. At the end of the fifth year the company is running low on cash, so management decides to sell the property for $1,250,000. What was the actual internal rate of return on the project? Explain how this return was possible given that the camp did not appear to be successful.

◆ **BROADENING YOUR PERSPECTIVE**

GROUP DECISION CASE

BYP10-1 Bolus Company is considering the purchase of a new machine. The invoice price of the machine is $112,000, freight charges are estimated to be $3,000, and installation costs are expected to be $5,000. Salvage value of the new equipment is expected to be zero after a useful life of 4 years. Existing equipment could be retained and used for an additional 4 years if the new machine is not purchased. At that time, the salvage value of the equipment would be zero. If the new machine is purchased now, the existing machine would have to be scrapped. Bolus' accountant, Yvette Lopez, has accumulated the following data regarding annual sales and expenses with and without the new machine.

1. Without the new machine, Bolus can sell 10,000 units of product annually at a per unit selling price of $100. If the new unit is purchased, the number of units produced and sold would increase by 20%, and the selling price would remain the same.

2. The new machine is faster than the old machine, and it is more efficient in its usage of materials. With the old machine the gross profit rate will be 28.5% of sales, whereas the rate will be 30% of sales with the new machine.

3. Annual selling expenses are $170,000 with the current equipment. Because the new equipment would produce a greater number of units to be sold, annual selling expenses are expected to increase by 10% if it is purchased.

4. Annual administrative expenses are expected to be $100,000 with the old machine, and $110,000 with the new machine.

5. The current book value of the existing machine is $30,000. Bolus uses straight-line depreciation.

6. Bolus' management wants a minimum rate of return of 15% on its investment and a payback period of no more than 3 years.

Instructions
With the class divided into groups, answer the following (ignore income tax effects).
(a) Calculate the annual rate of return for the new machine. (Round to two decimals.)
(b) Compute the payback period for the new machine. (Round to two decimals.)
(c) Compute the net present value of the new machine. (Round to the nearest dollar.)
(d) On the basis of the foregoing data, would you recommend that Bolus buy the machine? Why?

MANAGERIAL ANALYSIS

BYP10-2 Hawk Skateboards is considering building a new plant. Robert Optimist, the company's marketing manager, is an enthusiastic supporter of the new plant. Roberta Wunderland, the company's chief financial officer, is not so sure that the plant is a good idea. Currently the company purchases its skateboards from foreign manufacturers. The following figures were estimated regarding the construction of a new plant.

Cost of plant	$4,000,000
Annual cash inflows	4,000,000
Annual cash outflows	3,600,000
Estimated useful life	15 years
Salvage value	$2,000,000
Discount rate	11%

Robert Optimist believes that these figures understate the true potential value of the plant. He suggests that by manufacturing its own skateboards the company will benefit from a "buy American" patriotism that he believes is common among skateboarders. He also notes that the firm has had numerous quality problems with the skateboards manufactured by its suppliers. He suggests that the inconsistent quality has resulted in lost sales, increased warranty claims, and some costly lawsuits. Overall, he believes sales will be $200,000 higher each year than projected above, and that the savings from lower warranty costs and legal costs will be $100,000 per year. He also believes that the project is not as risky as assumed above, and that an 8% discount rate is more reasonable.

Instructions
Answer each of the following questions.
(a) Compute the net present value of the project based on the original projections.
(b) Compute the net present value incorporating Robert's estimates of the value of the intangible benefits, but still using the 11% discount rate.
(c) Compute the net present value using the original estimates, but employing the 8% discount rate that Robert suggests is more appropriate.
(d) Comment on your findings.

REAL-WORLD FOCUS

BYP10-3   Tecumseh Products Company has its headquarters in Tecumseh, Michigan. It describes itself as "a global multinational corporation producing mechanical and electrical components essential to industries creating end-products for health, comfort, and convenience."

The following was excerpted from the management discussion and analysis section of the company's 1997 annual report.

TECUMSEH PRODUCTS COMPANY
Management Discussion and Analysis

The company has invested approximately $50 million in a scroll compressor manufacturing facility in Tecumseh, Michigan. After experiencing setbacks in developing a commercially acceptable scroll compressor, the Company is currently testing a new generation of scroll product. The Company is unable to predict when, or if, it will offer a scroll compressor for commercial sale, but it does anticipate that reaching volume production will require a significant additional investment. Given such additional investment and current market conditions, management is currently reviewing its options with respect to scroll product improvement, cost reductions, joint ventures and alternative new products.

Instructions

Discuss issues the company should consider and techniques the company should employ to determine whether to continue pursuing this project.

EXPLORING THE WEB

BYP10-4   Campbell Soup Company is an international provider of soup products. Management is very interested in continuing to grow the company in its core business, while "spinning off" those businesses that are not part of its core operation.

Address: **www.campbellsoups.com**
            (or go to www.wiley.com/college/weygandt)

Steps:

1. Go to the home page of Campbell Soup Company at the address shown above.
2. Choose the current annual report.

Instructions

Review the financial statements and management's discussion and analysis, and answer the following questions.

(a) What was the total amount of capital expenditures in the current year, and how does this amount compare with the previous year? If next year's projected expenditures are presented, provide this amount also.
(b) What interest rate did the company pay on new borrowings in the current year?
(c) Assume that this year's capital expenditures are expected to increase cash flows by $35 million. What is the expected internal rate of return (IRR) for these capital expenditures? (Assume a 10-year period for the cash flows.)

COMMUNICATION ACTIVITY

BYP10-5   Refer back to Exercise 10-7 to address the following.

Instructions
Prepare a memo to Mary Ann Griffin, your supervisor. Show your calculations from E10-7, (a) and (b). In one or two paragraphs, discuss important nonfinancial considerations. Make any assumptions you believe to be necessary. Make a recommendation based on your analysis.

RESEARCH ASSIGNMENT

BYP10-6   The April 21, 1997, issue of *Forbes* includes an article by Toni Mack entitled "The Tiger Is on the Prowl."

Instructions
Read the article and answer the following questions.
(a) What have been the relative capital spending practices of **Royal Dutch Shell** versus **Mobil Corp.** versus **Exxon**?
(b) What has been "the religion" (business objective) of Exxon's headquarters since 1983?
(c) What was Exxon's capital budget in 1994 and 1995? What is Exxon's capital budget expected to swell to in 2 or 3 years?
(d) Did Exxon's capital spending strategy pay off during the past 15 years?

ETHICS CASE

BYP10-7   Bristle Brush Company operates in a state where corporate taxes and workers' compensation insurance rates have recently doubled. Bristle's president has just assigned you the task of preparing an economic analysis and making a recommendation relative to moving the company's entire operation to Missouri. The president is slightly in favor of such a move because Missouri is his boyhood home and he also owns a fishing lodge there.

You have just completed building your dream house, moved in, and sodded the lawn. Your children are all doing well in school and sports and, along with your spouse, want no part of a move to Missouri. If the company does move, so will you because the town is a one-industry community and you and your spouse will have to move to have employment. Moving when everyone else does will cause you to take a big loss on the sale of your house. The same hardships will be suffered by your coworkers, and the town will be devastated.

In compiling the costs of moving versus not moving, you have latitude in the assumptions you make, the estimates you compute, and the discount rates and time periods you project. You are in a position to influence the decision singlehandedly.

Instructions
(a) Who are the stakeholders in this situation?
(b) What are the ethical issues in this situation?
(c) What would you do in this situation?

Answers to Self-Study Questions
1. d   2. c   3. d   4. a   5. b   6. d   7. d   8. a   9. c   10. d

Remember to go back to the Navigator box on the chapter-opening page and check off your completed work.

CHAPTER 11

Pricing Decisions

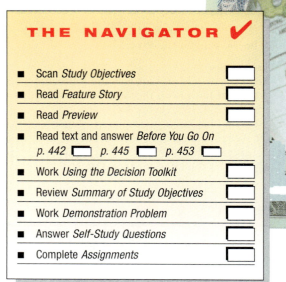

THE NAVIGATOR ✔

- ■ Scan *Study Objectives*   ☐
- ■ Read *Feature Story*   ☐
- ■ Read *Preview*   ☐
- ■ Read text and answer *Before You Go On*
  p. 442 ☐   p. 445 ☐   p. 453 ☐
- ■ Work *Using the Decision Toolkit*   ☐
- ■ Review *Summary of Study Objectives*   ☐
- ■ Work *Demonstration Problem*   ☐
- ■ Answer *Self-Study Questions*   ☐
- ■ Complete *Assignments*   ☐

◆ STUDY OBJECTIVES

After studying this chapter, you should be able to:

1. Compute a target cost when a product price is determined by the market.

2. Compute a target selling price using cost-plus pricing.

3. Use time and material pricing to determine the cost of services provided.

4. Determine a transfer price using the negotiated, cost-based, and market-based approaches.

5. Explain the issues that arise when transferring goods between divisions located in countries with different tax rates.

THE NAVIGATOR

◆ FEATURE STORY

"I'LL CALL YOUR BLUFF, AND RAISE YOU 43 PERCENT"

If you own a PC, then there is a roughly 85 percent chance that the microprocessor chip that runs your machine was made by **Intel**. That's because for as long as most people can remember, Intel has had at least an 85 percent share of the market for PC computer chips. It isn't that nobody else makes computer chips; it's just that the competition can't seem to get a foothold.

Intel's primary competition comes from a scrappy company called **Advanced Micro Devices (AMD)**. Recently, Intel made a couple of missteps that caused it to lose a few points of market share to AMD. First, Intel had two product recalls on its chips. Then it had problems meeting demand. In the meantime, AMD was boasting that it had a chip that was more powerful than Intel's, and that it had plenty of supply to meet demand. The result was that Intel's market share fell—to 82 percent.

To those familiar with Intel, its response was easily predicted. It cut prices by up to 26 percent. One

434

analyst noted, "When Intel screws up, they can't send flowers, so they cut prices." Said another analyst, "Intel has drawn a line in the sand at 85 percent market share, and they will use price to regain that share."

AMD had little choice but to respond with price cuts of its own. It cut prices by up to 46 percent on some of its chips. In the past, price wars have typically hurt AMD worse since Intel's massive volume allows it to produce chips at a lower cost. In 1999 Intel's gross profit rate was 59.7 percent, while AMD's was only 31.2 percent. An all-out price war, however, would leave both companies battered and bruised. The stock price of both companies fell on the news of the price cuts.

THE NAVIGATOR

Source: Molly Williams, "Intel Cuts Prices, Prompts AMD to Answer the Call," *Wall Street Journal*, October 17, 2000.

As the opening story about **Intel** and **AMD** indicates, few management decisions are more important than setting prices. Intel, for example, must sell computer chips at a price that is high enough to cover its costs and ensure a reasonable profit. But if the prices are too high, the chips will not sell. In this chapter, two types of pricing situations are examined. The first part of the chapter addresses pricing for goods sold or services provided to external parties. The second part of the chapter addresses pricing decisions faced when goods are sold to other divisions within the same company.

The content and organization of the chapter are as follows.

PRICING DECISIONS

External Sales
- Pricing in a competitive market
- Cost-plus pricing
- Time and material pricing

Internal Sales
- Negotiated transfer prices
- Cost-based transfer prices
- Market-based transfer prices
- Effect of outsourcing on transfer pricing
- Transfers between divisions in different countries

THE NAVIGATOR

SECTION 1

EXTERNAL SALES

Establishing the price for any good or service is affected by many factors. Take the pharmaceutical industry as an example. Its approach to profitability has been to spend heavily on research and development in an effort to find and patent a few new drugs, price them high, and market them aggressively. Due to the AIDS crisis in Africa, the drug industry has been under considerable pressure recently to lower prices on drugs used to treat AIDS. For example, **Merck Co.** lowered the price of its AIDS drug Crixivan to $600 per patient in these countries. This compares with the $6,016 it typically charges in the United States.[1] As a consequence, individuals in the United States are questioning whether prices in the U.S. market are too high. The drug companies counter that to take the financial risks to develop these products, they need to set the prices high. Illustration 11-1 indicates the many factors that can affect pricing decisions.

---

[1]"AIDS Gaffes in Africa Come Back to Haunt Drug Industry at Home," *Wall Street Journal*, April 23, 2001, p. 1.

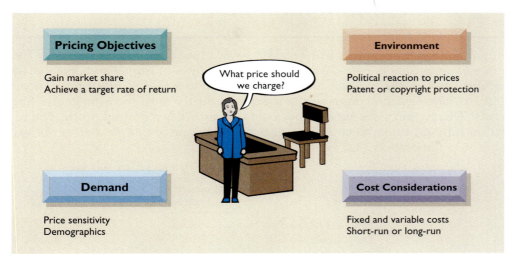

Illustration 11-1 Pricing factors

In the long run a company must price its product to cover its costs and earn a reasonable profit. But to price its product appropriately, it must have a good understanding of market forces at work. In most cases, a company does not set the prices. Instead the price is set by the competitive market (the laws of supply and demand). For example, a company such as **Shell Oil** or **Exxon Mobil** cannot set the price of gasoline by itself. These companies are called **price takers** because the price of gasoline is set by market forces (the supply of oil and the demand by customers). This is the case for any product that is not easily differentiated from competing products, such as farm products (corn or wheat) or minerals (coal or sand).

In other situations the company sets the prices. This would be the case where the product is specially made for a customer, as in a one-of-a-kind product such as a designer dress by **Zoran** or **Armani**. This also occurs when there are few or no other producers capable of manufacturing a similar item. An example would be a company that has a patent or copyright on a unique process, such as the case of computer chips by **Intel**. However, it is also the case when a company can effectively differentiate its product or service from others. Even in a competitive market like coffee, **Starbucks** has been able to differentiate its product and charge a premium for a cup of java.

 —BUSINESS INSIGHT

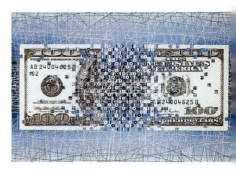

How has e-business affected pricing? The answer isn't simple, because of two conflicting forces. On the one hand, the Internet allows customers to easily compare prices, thus driving prices down. In fact, many companies feared that the Internet would squeeze all profits out of their businesses. However, e-business has also allowed many businesses to more effectively target their customers and differentiate their products, thus allowing them to avoid severe price competition by striving to create customer-focused "markets of one." E-business technology conveniently provides up-to-date information about "buying behaviors and the level of real-time local demand. Also, e-businesses are able to customize offerings by rebundling related services and products—often from a number of different companies—into attractive 'baskets'."

Source: M. V. Deise et al., *Executive's Guide to E-Business: From Tactics to Strategy*, New York: John Wiley & Sons, Inc., 2000, p. 195.

PRICING IN A COMPETITIVE MARKET

Automobile manufacturers like **Ford** or **Toyota** face a competitive market. The price of an automobile is affected greatly by the laws of supply and demand, so no company in this industry can affect the price to a significant degree. Therefore, to earn a profit, companies in the auto industry must focus on controlling costs. This requires setting a **target cost** that provides a desired profit. The relationship and importance of a target cost to the price and desired profit are shown in Illustration 11-2.

Illustration 11-2 Target cost as related to price and profit

	Competitive Market Pricing
Price set by market	$XXX
Less: Desired profit	XX
Target cost	$ XX

If **General Motors**, for example, can produce its automobiles for the target cost (or less), it will meet its profit goal. If it cannot achieve its target cost, it will fail to produce the desired profit (and will most likely "get hammered" by stockholders and the market). In a competitive market, a company chooses the segment of the market it wants to compete in—that is, find its market niche. For example, it may choose between selling luxury goods or economy goods in order to focus its efforts on one segment or the other.

Once the company has identified its segment of the market, it does market research to determine the target price. This target price is the price that the company believes would place it in the optimal position for its target audience. Once the company has determined this target price, it can determine its target cost by setting a desired profit. The difference between the target price and the desired profit is the target cost of the product. (This computation is shown in Illustration 11-2.) After the company determines the target cost, a team of employees with expertise in a variety of areas (production and operations, marketing, and finance) is assembled. The team's task is to design and develop a product that can meet quality specifications while not exceeding the target cost. The target cost includes all product and period costs necessary to make and market the product or service.

DECISION TOOLKIT

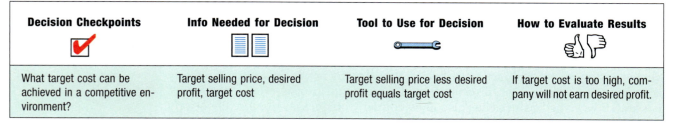

Decision Checkpoints	Info Needed for Decision	Tool to Use for Decision	How to Evaluate Results
What target cost can be achieved in a competitive environment?	Target selling price, desired profit, target cost	Target selling price less desired profit equals target cost	If target cost is too high, company will not earn desired profit.

COST-PLUS PRICING

As discussed, in a competitive, common-product environment the market price is already set, and the company instead must set a target cost. But, in a lesser competitive or noncompetitive environment, the company may be faced with the task of setting its own price. When the price is set by the company, price is com-

monly a function of the cost of the product or service. That is, the typical approach is to use **cost-plus pricing**. This approach involves establishing a cost base and adding to this cost base a **markup** to determine a **target selling price**. The size of the markup (the "plus") depends on the desired operating income or return on investment (ROI) for the product line, product, or service. The cost-plus pricing formula is expressed as follows.

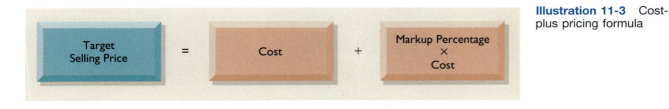

Illustration 11-3   Cost-plus pricing formula

To illustrate, assume that Cleanmore Products, Inc. is in the process of setting a selling price on its new top-of-the-line, 3-horsepower, 16-gallon, variable-speed wet/dry shop vacuum. The per unit variable cost estimates for the new shop vacuum are as follows.

	Per Unit
Direct materials	$ 23
Direct labor	17
Variable manufacturing overhead	12
Variable selling and administrative expenses	8
Variable cost per unit	$60

Illustration 11-4   Variable costs per unit

In addition, Cleanmore has the following fixed costs per unit at a budgeted sales volume of 10,000 units.

	Total Costs	÷	Budgeted Volume	=	Cost Per Unit
Fixed manufacturing overhead	$280,000	÷	10,000	=	$ 28
Fixed selling and administrative expenses	240,000	÷	10,000	=	24
Fixed cost per unit					$52

Illustration 11-5   Fixed cost per unit, 10,000 units

Cleanmore has decided to price its new shop vacuum to earn a 20 percent return on its investment (ROI) of $1,000,000. Therefore, Cleanmore expects to receive income of $200,000 (20% × $1,000,000) on its investment. On a per unit basis, the desired ROI is $20 ($200,000 ÷ 10,000). Given the per unit costs shown above, we then compute the sales price to be $132, as follows.

	Per Unit
Variable cost	$ 60
Fixed cost	52
Total cost	112
Desired ROI	20
Selling price per unit	$132

Illustration 11-6   Computation of selling price, 10,000 units

In most cases, companies like Cleanmore will use a percentage markup on cost to determine the selling price. The formula to compute the markup percentage to achieve a desired ROI of $20 per unit is as follows.

Illustration 11-7 Computation of markup percentage

Markup Percentage	=	Desired ROI Per Unit / Total Unit Cost
17.86%	=	$20 / $112

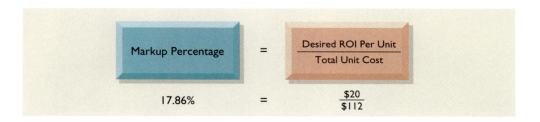

Using a 17.86 percent markup on cost, Cleanmore Products would compute the target selling price as follows.

Illustration 11-8 Computation of selling price—markup approach

Total Unit Cost	+	(Total Unit Cost	×	Markup Percentage)	=	Target Selling Price Per Unit
$112	+	($112	×	17.86%)	=	$132

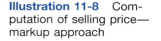

As indicated, Cleanmore should set the price for its wet/dry vacuum at $132 per unit.

LIMITATIONS OF COST-PLUS PRICING

The cost-plus pricing approach has a major advantage: It is simple to compute. However, the cost model does not give consideration to the demand side. That is, will customers pay the price Cleanmore computed for its vacuums? In addition, sales volume plays a large role in determining per unit costs. The lower the sales volume, for example, the higher the price Cleanmore must charge to meet its desired ROI. To illustrate, if the budgeted sales volume was 8,000 instead of 10,000, Cleanmore's variable cost per unit would remain the same. However, the fixed cost per unit would change as follows.

Illustration 11-9 Fixed cost per unit, 8,000 units

	Total Costs	÷	Budgeted Volume	=	Cost Per Unit
Fixed manufacturing overhead	$280,000	÷	8,000	=	$35
Fixed selling and administrative expenses	240,000	÷	8,000	=	30
Fixed cost per unit					$65

As indicated in Illustration 11-5, fixed costs per unit for 10,000 units were $52. However, at a lower sales volume of 8,000 units, fixed costs per unit increase to $65. Cleanmore's desired 20% ROI now results in a $25 ROI per unit [(20% × 1,000,000) ÷ 8,000]. The selling price can be computed as follows.

	Per Unit
Variable cost	$ 60
Fixed cost	65
Total cost	125
Desired ROI	25
Selling price per unit	**$150**

Illustration 11-10 Computation of selling price, 8,000 units

As shown, the lower the budgeted volume, the higher the per unit price. The reason: Fixed costs and ROI are spread over fewer units, and therefore the fixed cost and ROI per unit increase. In this case, at 8,000 units, Cleanmore would have to mark up its total unit costs 20 percent to earn a desired ROI of $25 per unit, as shown below.

$$20\% = \frac{\$25 \text{ (desired ROI)}}{\$125 \text{ (total unit cost)}}$$

The target selling price would then be $150, as indicated earlier:

$$\$125 + (\$125 \times 20\%) = \$150$$

The opposite effect will occur if budgeted volume is higher (say, at 12,000 units) because fixed costs and ROI can be spread over more units. As a result, the cost-plus model of pricing will work only when Cleanmore sells the quantity it budgeted. If actual volume is much less than budgeted volume, Cleanmore may sustain losses unless it can raise its prices.

BUSINESS INSIGHT

Management Perspective

Did you ever wonder what is the real cost of a high-buck meal? The answer might make you lose your appetite. On average, most restaurants shoot for a 300 percent markup above the cost of the basic ingredients. The actual markup differs across food items because a 300 percent markup on some items (such as expensive seafood or choice cuts of meat) would result in prices that no diner would be willing to pay. As a consequence, to achieve an average 300 percent markup, some items are marked up much more than 300 percent. For example, pasta and vegetables typically are marked up 500 percent, mussels 650 percent, and salmon 900 percent.

To be fair, focusing on the cost of a restaurant meal's raw ingredients is like "calculating the value of a Picasso based on the cost of the paint." The price of your meal has to cover the labor necessary to prepare and deliver the meal, the facility the meal is served in, and overhead, plus a profit.

Source: Eileen Daspin, "What Do Restaurants Really Pay for Meals?" *Wall Street Journal*, March 10, 2000.

DECISION TOOLKIT

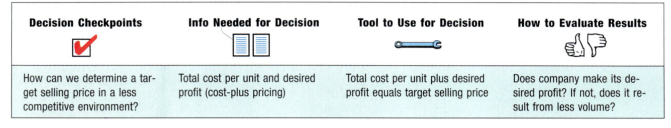

Decision Checkpoints	Info Needed for Decision	Tool to Use for Decision	How to Evaluate Results
How can we determine a target selling price in a less competitive environment?	Total cost per unit and desired profit (cost-plus pricing)	Total cost per unit plus desired profit equals target selling price	Does company make its desired profit? If not, does it result from less volume?

BEFORE YOU GO ON . . .

◆ **Review It**

1. What is a target cost, and how is it used by management?
2. What is the general formula for determining the target selling price with cost-plus pricing?
3. How is the per unit return on investment determined?

◆ **Do It**

Air Corporation produces air purifiers. The following per unit cost information is available: direct materials $16; direct labor $18; variable manufacturing overhead $11; fixed manufacturing overhead $10; variable selling and administrative expenses $6; and fixed selling and administrative expenses $10. Using a 45 percent markup percentage on total per unit cost, compute the target selling price.

Action Plan

• Calculate the total cost per unit.
• Multiply the total cost per unit by the markup percentage, then add this amount to the total cost per unit to determine the target selling price.

Solution

Direct materials	$16
Direct labor	18
Variable manufacturing overhead	11
Fixed manufacturing overhead	10
Variable selling and administrative expenses	6
Fixed selling and administrative expenses	10
Total unit cost	$71

$$\text{Total unit cost} + \left(\text{Total unit cost} \times \text{Markup percentage} \right) = \text{Target selling price}$$
$$\$71 + (\$71 \times 45\%) = \$102.95$$

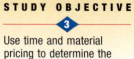

THE NAVIGATOR

TIME AND MATERIAL PRICING

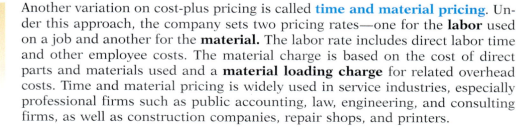

STUDY OBJECTIVE
3

Use time and material pricing to determine the cost of services provided.

Another variation on cost-plus pricing is called **time and material pricing**. Under this approach, the company sets two pricing rates—one for the **labor** used on a job and another for the **material.** The labor rate includes direct labor time and other employee costs. The material charge is based on the cost of direct parts and materials used and a **material loading charge** for related overhead costs. Time and material pricing is widely used in service industries, especially professional firms such as public accounting, law, engineering, and consulting firms, as well as construction companies, repair shops, and printers.

To illustrate a time and material pricing situation, assume the following data for Lake Holiday Marina, a boat and motor repair shop.

Illustration 11-11   Total annual budgeted time and material costs

LAKE HOLIDAY MARINA Budgeted Costs for the Year 2002		
	Time Charges	Material Charges
Mechanics' wages and benefits	$103,500	–
Parts manager's salary and benefits	–	$11,500
Office employee's salary and benefits	20,700	2,300
Other overhead (supplies, depreciation, property taxes, advertising, utilities)	26,800	14,400
Total budgeted costs	$151,000	$28,200

Using time and material pricing involves three steps: (1) calculate the per hour labor charge, (2) calculate the charge for obtaining and holding materials, and (3) calculate the charges for a particular job.

Step 1: Calculate the Labor Charge.   The first step for time and material pricing is to determine a charge for labor time. The charge for labor time is expressed as a rate per hour of labor. This rate includes: (1) the direct labor cost of the employee, including hourly rate or salary and fringe benefits; (2) selling, administrative, and similar overhead costs; and (3) an allowance for a desired profit or ROI per hour of employee time. In some industries, such as auto, boat, and farm equipment repair shops, the same hourly labor rate is charged regardless of which employee performs the work. In other industries, the rate charged is according to classification or level of the employee. In a public accounting firm, for example, the services of an assistant, senior, manager, or partner would be charged at different rates, as would those of a paralegal, associate, or partner in a law firm.

Computation of the hourly charges for Lake Holiday Marina during 2002 is shown in Illustration 11-12. The marina budgets 5,000 hours of repair time in 2002, and it desires a profit margin of $8 per hour of labor.

Illustration 11-12   Computation of hourly time-charge rate

Per Hour	Total Cost	÷	Total Hours	=	Per Hour Charge
Hourly labor rate for repairs					
Mechanics' wages and benefits	$103,500	÷	5,000	=	$ 20.70
Overhead costs					
Office employee's salary and benefits	20,700	÷	5,000	=	4.14
Other overhead	26,800	÷	5,000	=	5.36
Total hourly cost	$151,000	÷	5,000	=	30.20
Profit margin					8.00
Rate charged per hour of labor					**$38.20**

This rate of $38.20 is multiplied by the number of hours of labor used on any particular job to determine the labor charge for that job.

Step 2: Calculate the Material Loading Charge.   The charge for materials typically includes the invoice price of any materials used on the job plus a material loading charge. The **material loading charge** covers the costs of purchasing, receiving, handling, and storing materials, plus any desired profit margin on the materials themselves. The material loading charge is expressed as a **percentage** of the total estimated costs of parts and materials for the year. To determine this percentage, the company does the following: (1) It estimates its total annual costs for purchasing, receiving, handling, and storing materials. (2) It divides this amount by the total estimated cost of parts and materials. And (3) it adds a desired profit margin on the materials themselves.

Computation of the material loading charge used by Lake Holiday Marina during 2002 is shown in Illustration 11-13. The marina estimates that the total invoice cost of parts and materials used in 2002 will be $120,000. The marina desires a 20 percent profit margin on the invoice cost of parts and materials.

Illustration 11-13 Computation of material loading charge

	Material Charges	÷	Total Invoice Cost, Parts and Materials	=	Material Loading Charge
Overhead costs					
Parts manager's salary and benefits	$11,500				
Office employee's salary	2,300				
	13,800	÷	$120,000	=	11.50%
Other overhead	14,400	÷	$120,000	=	12.00%
	$28,200	÷	$120,000	=	23.50%
Profit margin					20.00%
Material loading charge					**43.50%**

The material loading charge on any particular job is 43.50 percent multiplied by the cost of materials used on the job. For example, if $100 of parts were used, the additional material loading charge would be $43.50.

Step 3: Calculate Charges for a Particular Job. The charges for any particular job are the sum of (1) the labor charge, (2) the charge for the materials, and (3) the material loading charge. For example, suppose that Lake Holiday Marina prepares a price quotation to estimate the cost to refurbish a used 28-foot pontoon boat. Lake Holiday Marina estimates the job will require 50 hours of labor and $3,600 in parts and materials. The marina's price quotation is shown in Illustration 11-14.

Illustration 11-14 Price quotation for time and material

LAKE HOLIDAY MARINA
Time and Material Price Quotation

Job: Marianne Perino, repair of 28-foot pontoon boat

Labor charges: 50 hours @ $38.20		$1,910
Material charges		
Cost of parts and materials	$3,600	
Material loading charge (43.5% × $3,600)	1,566	5,166
Total price of labor and material		$7,076

Included in the $7,076 price quotation for the boat repair and refurbishment are charges for labor costs, overhead costs, materials costs, materials handling and storage costs, and a profit margin on both labor and parts. Lake Holiday Marina used labor hours as a basis for computing the time rate. Other companies, such as machine shops, plastic molding shops, and printers, might use machine hours.

DECISION TOOLKIT

Decision Checkpoints	Info Needed for Decision	Tool to Use for Decision	How to Evaluate Results
How do we set prices when it is difficult to estimate total cost per unit?	Two pricing rates needed: one for labor use and another for materials	Compute labor rate charge and material rate charge. In each of these calculations, add a profit margin.	Is the company profitable under this pricing approach? Are employees earning reasonable wages?

BEFORE YOU GO ON . . .

◆ Review It

1. What is time and material pricing? Where is it often used?
2. What is a material loading charge?

◆ Do It

Presented below are data for Harmon Electrical Repair Shop for next year.

Repair-technician's wages	$130,000
Fringe benefits	30,000
Overhead	20,000

The desired profit margin per labor hour is $10. The material loading charge is 40 percent of invoice cost. It is estimated that 8,000 labor hours will be worked next year. If Harmon repairs a TV that takes 4 hours to repair and uses parts of $50, compute the bill for this job.

Action Plan

- Calculate the labor charge.
- Calculate the material loading charge.
- Compute the bill for specific repair.

Solution

	Total Cost	÷	Total Hours	=	Per Hour Charge
Repair-technician's wages	$130,000	÷	8,000	=	$16.25
Fringe benefits	30,000	÷	8,000	=	3.75
Overhead	20,000	÷	8,000	=	2.50
	$180,000	÷	8,000	=	22.50
Profit margin					10.00
Rate charged per hour of labor					$32.50
Materials cost					$50
Materials loading cost ($50 × 40%)					20
Total materials cost					$70
Cost of TV repair					
Labor costs ($32.50 × 4)					$130
Materials cost					70
Total repair cost					$200

THE NAVIGATOR

INTERNAL SALES

In today's global economy, growth is vital to survival. Frequently growth is "vertical," meaning the company expands in the direction of either its suppliers or its customers. For example, a manufacturer of bicycles, like **Trek**, may acquire a chain of bicycle shops. A movie production company like **Walt Disney** or **AOL Time Warner** might acquire a movie theater chain or a cable television company.

Divisions within vertically integrated companies normally transfer goods or services to other divisions within the same company, as well as make sales to customers outside the company. When goods are transferred internally, the price used to record the transfer between the two divisions is the **transfer price**. Illustration 11-15 highlights these transactions for Aerobic Bicycle Company. Aerobic Bicycle has a Bicycle Assembly Division and a Bicycle Component Division.

Illustration 11-15 Transfer pricing illustration

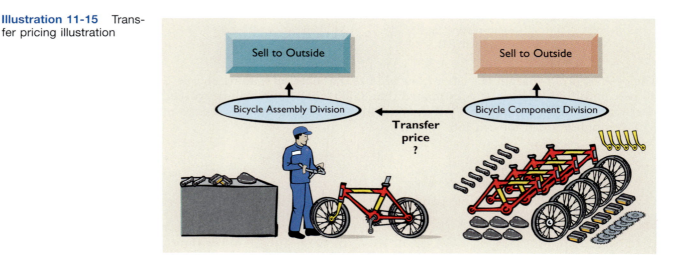

The pricing issues presented by transfer pricing are similar to those related to outside pricing issues. The objective is to maximize the return to the whole company. In addition, in the transfer pricing situation, it is important that divisional performance should not decline because of internal transfers. As a result, setting a transfer price is complicated because of competing interests among divisions within the company. For example, setting the transfer price high will benefit the Bicycle Component Division (the selling division), but will hurt the Bicycle Assembly Division (the purchasing division).

There are three possible approaches for determining a transfer price:

STUDY OBJECTIVE

4

Determine a transfer price using the negotiated, cost-based, and market-based approaches.

1. Negotiated transfer prices.
2. Cost-based transfer prices.
3. Market-based transfer prices.

Conceptually, a negotiated transfer price should work best, but due to practical considerations, the other two methods are often used.

NEGOTIATED TRANSFER PRICES

The **negotiated transfer price** is determined through agreement of division managers. To illustrate the negotiated transfer pricing approach, we will examine Alberta Boot Company. Until recently Alberta focused exclusively on making rubber soles for work boots and hiking boots. These rubber soles were sold to boot manufacturers. However, last year the company decided to take advantage of its strong reputation by expanding into the business of making hiking boots. As a consequence of this expansion, the company is now structured as two independent divisions, the Boot Division and the Sole Division. The manager of each division is compensated based on achievement of profitability targets for his or her division.

The Sole Division continues to make rubber soles for both hiking boots and work boots and to sell these soles to other boot manufacturers. The Boot Division manufactures leather uppers for hiking boots and attaches these uppers to rubber soles. During its first year the Boot Division purchased its rubber soles from outside suppliers so as not to disrupt the operations of the Sole Division. However, top management now wants the Sole Division to provide at least some of the soles used by the Boot Division. The following data are available for each division when the Boot Division purchases soles from an outside supplier.

Boot Division		Sole Division	
Selling price of hiking boots	$90	Selling price of sole	$18
Variable cost of manufacturing boot (not including sole)	35	Variable cost per sole	11
Cost of sole purchased from outside suppliers	17	**Contribution margin**	
Contribution margin per unit	**$38**	**per unit**	**$ 7**
Total contribution margin per unit	**$45** ($38 + $7)		

Illustration 11-16 Basic information for Alberta Boot Company

This information indicates that the Boot Division has a contribution margin per unit of $38 and the Sole Division $7. The total contribution margin per unit is $45 ($38 + $7). Now let's ask the question, "What would be a fair transfer price if the Sole Division sold 10,000 soles to the Boot Division?"

NO EXCESS CAPACITY

As indicated in Illustration 11-16, the Sole Division charges $18 and derives a contribution margin of $7 per sole. The Sole Division has no excess capacity and produces and sells 80,000 units (soles) to outside customers. Therefore, from the perspective of the Sole Division, it must receive from the Boot Division a payment that will at least cover its variable cost per sole **plus** its lost contribution margin per sole (often referred to as **opportunity cost**). Otherwise, it makes no sense for the Sole Division to sell its soles to the Boot Division. The minimum transfer price that would be acceptable to the Sole Division is $18, as shown below.

Illustration 11-17 Minimum transfer price—no excess capacity

From the perspective of the Boot Division (the buyer), the most it will pay is what the sole would cost from an outside supplier. In this case, therefore, the Boot Division would pay no more than $17. As shown in Illustration 11-18, an acceptable transfer price is not available in this situation.

Illustration 11-18 Transfer price negotiations—no deal

EXCESS CAPACITY

What happens if the Sole Division **has excess capacity?** In other words, assume the Sole Division can produce 80,000 soles but can sell only 70,000 soles in the open market. In this situation, the Sole Division does not lose its contribution margin of $7 per unit and, therefore, the minimum price it would now accept is $11, as shown below.

Illustration 11-19 Minimum transfer price formula—excess capacity

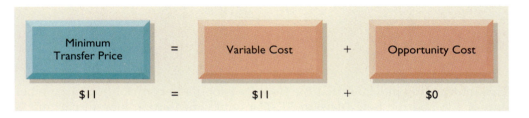

In this case, the Boot Division and the Sole Division should negotiate a transfer price within the range of $11 to $17, as shown in Illustration 11-20.

Illustration 11-20 Transfer pricing negotiations—deal

Given **excess capacity**, and therefore zero opportunity cost to the Sole Division, it would be in the company's best interest for the goods to be purchased internally as long as the Sole Division's variable cost is less than the outside price

of $17. The Sole Division will receive a positive contribution margin from any transfer price above its variable cost of $11. The Boot Division will benefit from any price below $17. At any transfer price above $17 the Boot Division will go to an outside supplier, a solution that would be undesirable to both divisions, as well as to the company as a whole.

VARIABLE COSTS

In the minimum transfer price formula, **variable cost is defined as the variable cost of units sold *internally***. In some instances the variable cost of units sold internally will differ from the variable cost of units sold externally. For example, variable selling expenses often are reduced when units are sold internally. In this case, the variable cost of units sold internally will be lower than that of units sold externally. Alternatively, the variable cost of units sold internally could be higher if the internal division requests a special order that requires more expensive materials or additional labor.

SPECIAL ORDER

Suppose that the Boot Division would like to make 5,000 new high-margin, heavy-duty boots. The Sole Division is at full capacity. The sole required for this boot will be made of a denser rubber and an intricate lug design. Alberta Boot Company is not aware of any supplier that currently makes such a sole, nor do they feel that any other supplier can meet the quality expectations. As a consequence, there is no available market price to use as the transfer price. We can, however, still employ the formula for the minimum transfer price to assist in arriving at a reasonable solution. After evaluating the special sole, the Sole Division determines that its variable cost would be $19 per sole. We also know that the Sole Division's opportunity cost at full capacity is the $7 ($18 − $11) per sole that it earns producing the standard sole and selling it to an outside customer. Therefore, the minimum transfer price that the Sole Division would be willing to accept would be:

Illustration 11-21 Minimum transfer price formula—special order

The transfer price of $26 provides the Sole Division with enough revenue to cover its increased variable cost and its opportunity cost (contribution margin on its standard sole).

SUMMARY OF NEGOTIATED TRANSFER PRICING APPROACH

Using the negotiated transfer pricing approach, a minimum transfer price is established by the selling division, and a maximum transfer price is established by the purchasing division. If used appropriately, this system provides a sound basis for establishing a transfer price because both divisions are better off if the proper decision rules are used by both. However, negotiated transfer pricing often is not always used because:

• Market price information is sometimes not easily obtainable.

- A lack of trust between the two negotiating divisions may lead to a breakdown in the negotiations.
- Negotiations often lead to different pricing strategies from division to division which is cumbersome and sometimes costly to implement.

Many companies, therefore, often use more objective and simple systems based on cost or market information to develop transfer prices.

COST-BASED TRANSFER PRICES

One method of determining transfer prices is to base the transfer price on the costs incurred by the division producing the goods or services. If a **cost-based transfer price** is used, the transfer price may be based on variable costs alone, or on variable costs plus fixed costs. A markup may be added to these cost numbers.

Unfortunately, under a cost-based approach, divisions sometimes use improper transfer prices. This leads to a loss of profitability for the company and unfair evaluations of division performance. To illustrate, assume that Alberta Boot requires the division to use a transfer price based on the variable cost of the sole. With no excess capacity, here is what happens to the contribution margin per unit of the two divisions.

Illustration 11-22 Cost-based transfer price—10,000 units

Boot Division		Sole Division	
Selling price of hiking boots	$90	Selling price of sole	$11
Variable cost of manufacturing boot (not including sole)	35	Variable cost per sole	11
		Contribution margin	
Cost of sole purchased from Sole Division	11	**per unit**	**$ 0**
Contribution margin per unit	**$44**		
Total contribution margin per unit	**$44** ($44 + $0)		

This cost-based transfer system is a bad deal for the Sole Division, as it reports no profit on the transfer of 10,000 soles to the Boot Division. The Boot Division, on the other hand, is delighted, as its contribution margin per unit increases from $38 to $44, or $6 per boot. Overall, Alberta Boot Company loses $10,000 (10,000 units × $1) because the Sole Division lost a contribution margin per unit of $7 and the Boot Division gained only a $6 contribution margin per unit. Illustration 11-23 illustrates this deficiency.

Illustration 11-23 Cost-based transfer price results—no excess capacity

The overall results change if the Sole Division **has excess capacity**. In this case, the Sole Division continues to report a zero profit on these 10,000 units but does not lose the $7 per unit (because it had excess capacity). The Boot Division gains $6. So overall, the company is better off by $60,000 (10,000 × $6). However, with a cost-based system, the Sole Division continues to report a zero profit on these 10,000 units.

From this analysis, we can see that a cost-based system does not reflect the division's true profitability. What's more, it does not even provide adequate incentive for the Sole Division to control costs. Whatever the division's costs are, these costs are passed on to the next division. One way that some companies attempt to overcome this problem is to base the transfer price on **standard costs**, rather than actual cost. Notwithstanding these disadvantages, the cost system is simple to understand and easy to use because the information is already available in the accounting system. In addition, market information is sometimes not available, so the only alternative is some type of cost-based system. As a result, it is the most popular method used by companies to establish transfer prices.

MARKET-BASED TRANSFER PRICES

The **market-based transfer price** is based on existing market prices of competing goods or services. A market-based system is often considered the best approach because it is objective and generally provides the proper economic incentives. For example, if the Sole Division can charge the market price, it is indifferent as to whether soles are sold to outside customers or internally to the Boot Division—it does not lose any contribution margin. Similarly, the Boot Division pays a price for the good or service that is at or reasonably close to market.

When the Sole Division has no excess capacity, the market-based system works reasonably well. The Sole Division receives market price and the Boot Division pays market price. If the Sole Division has excess capacity, however, the market-based system can lead to actions that are not in the best interest of the company. For example, the minimum transfer price that the Sole Division should receive is its variable cost plus opportunity cost. Given that the Sole Division has excess capacity, its opportunity cost is zero. However, under the market-based system, the Sole Division transfers the goods at the market price of $18, for a contribution margin per unit of $7. The Boot Division manager then has to accept the $18 sole price. The Boot Division must recognize, however, that this price is not the cost of the sole, given that the Sole Division had excess capacity. As a result, the Boot Division may overprice its boots in the market if it uses the market price of the sole plus a markup in setting the price of the boot. This action can lead to losses for Alberta overall.

As indicated earlier, in many cases, there simply is not a well-defined market for the good or service being transferred. As a result, a reasonable market value cannot be developed, and therefore companies resort to a cost-based system.

EFFECT OF OUTSOURCING ON TRANSFER PRICING

An increasing number of companies rely on **outsourcing**. Outsourcing involves contracting with an external party to provide a good or service, rather than performing the work internally. Some companies have taken outsourcing to the extreme by outsourcing all of their production. These so-called **virtual companies** have well-established brand names, but they don't manufacture any of their own products. As companies increasingly rely on outsourcing, it means that fewer components are transferred internally between divisions.

*T*RANSFERS *B*ETWEEN *D*IVISIONS IN *D*IFFERENT *C*OUNTRIES

As more companies "globalize" their operations, an increasing number of transfers are between divisions that are located in different countries. For example, one estimate suggests that 60 percent of trade between countries is simply transfers between divisions. Differences in tax rates across countries can complicate the determination of the appropriate transfer price.

Companies must pay income tax in the country where income is generated. In order to maximize income and minimize income tax, many companies prefer to report more income in countries with low tax rates, and less income in countries with high tax rates. This is accomplished by adjusting the transfer prices they use on internal transfers between divisions located in different countries. The division in the low-tax-rate country is allocated more contribution margin, and the division in the high-tax-rate country is allocated less.

To illustrate, suppose that Alberta's Boot Division is located in a country with a corporate tax rate of 10 percent, and the Sole Division is located in a country with a tax rate of 30 percent. Illustration 11-24 demonstrates the after-tax contribution margin to the company as a whole assuming first, that the soles are transferred at a transfer price of $18, and second, that the soles are transferred at a transfer price of $11.

Illustration 11-24 After-tax contribution margin per unit under alternative transfer prices

$18 Transfer Price

Boot Division		Sole Division	
Selling price of hiking boots	$90.00	Selling price of sole	$18.00
Variable cost of manufacturing boot (not including sole)	35.00	Variable cost per sole	11.00
Cost of sole purchased internally	18.00		
Before-tax contribution margin	37.00	Before-tax contribution margin	7.00
Tax at 10%	3.70	Tax at 30%	2.10
After-tax contribution margin	$33.30	After-tax contribution margin	$ 4.90

Before-tax total contribution margin to company = $37 + $7 = **$44**
After-tax total contribution margin to company = $33.30 + $4.90 = **$38.20**

$11 Transfer Price

Boot Division		Sole Division	
Selling price of hiking boots	$90.00	Selling price of sole	$11.00
Variable cost of manufacturing boot (not including sole)	35.00	Variable cost per sole	11.00
Cost of sole purchased internally	11.00		
Before-tax contribution margin	44.00	Before-tax contribution margin	0.00
Tax at 10%	4.40	Tax at 30%	0.00
After-tax contribution margin	$39.60	After-tax contribution margin	$ 0.00

Before-tax total contribution margin to company = $44 + $0 = **$44**
After-tax total contribution margin to company = $39.60 + $0 = **$39.60**

Note that the before-tax total contribution margin to Alberta Boot Company is $44 regardless of whether the transfer price is $18 or $11. However, the after-tax total contribution margin to Alberta Boot Company is $38.20 using the $18 transfer price, and $39.60 using the $11 transfer price. The reason: When the $11 transfer price is used, more of the contribution margin is attributed to the division that is in the country with the lower tax rate.

As this analysis shows, Alberta Boot Company would be better off using the $11 transfer price. However, this presents some concerns. First, the Sole Division manager won't be happy with an $11 transfer price. This price may lead to unfair evaluations of the Sole Division's manager. Second, the company must ask whether it is legal and ethical to use an $11 transfer price when the market price clearly is higher than that. Additional consideration of international transfer pricing is presented in advanced accounting texts.

BUSINESS INSIGHT
International Perspective

International transfer pricing issues create a huge headache for the Internal Revenue Service. Some estimates suggest that the United States loses over $25 billion in underpaid taxes due to transfer price abuses. Occasionally violators are caught. **Toyota**, for example, reportedly paid a $1 billion dollar settlement. But enforcement is complicated and time-consuming, and many foreign firms are reluctant to give access to their records. U.S. companies have also been accused of abuse. It has been noted that at one time U.S. giant **Westinghouse** booked over 25 percent of its profit in the tiny island of Puerto Rico. At the time, the corporate tax rate there was zero. The rules require that the transfer price be based on the current market price that a nonrelated party would pay for the goods. But often this is difficult to determine.

DECISION TOOLKIT

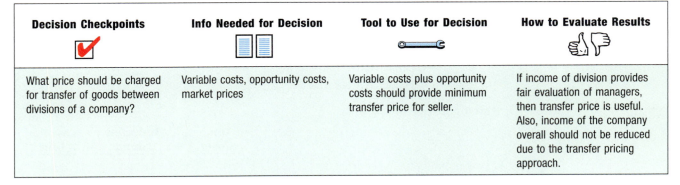

Decision Checkpoints	Info Needed for Decision	Tool to Use for Decision	How to Evaluate Results
What price should be charged for transfer of goods between divisions of a company?	Variable costs, opportunity costs, market prices	Variable costs plus opportunity costs should provide minimum transfer price for seller.	If income of division provides fair evaluation of managers, then transfer price is useful. Also, income of the company overall should not be reduced due to the transfer pricing approach.

BEFORE YOU GO ON . . .

◆ **Review It**

1. What are the objectives of transfer pricing?
2. What are the three approaches to transfer pricing? What are the advantages and disadvantages of each?
3. How do some companies reduce their tax payments through their choice of transfer price?

USING THE DECISION TOOLKIT

Cedarburg Lumber specializes in building "high-end" playhouses for kids. It builds the components in its factory, then ships the parts to the customer's home. It has contracted with carpenters across the country to do the final assembly. Each year it comes out with a new model. This year's model looks like a miniature castle, complete with spires and drawbridge. The following cost estimates for this new product have been provided by the accounting department for a budgeted volume of 1,000 units.

	Per Unit	Total
Direct materials	$ 840	
Direct labor	$1,600	
Variable manufacturing overhead	$ 400	
Fixed manufacturing overhead		$540,000
Variable selling and administrative expenses	$ 510	
Fixed selling and administrative expenses		$320,000

Cedarburg Lumber uses cost-plus pricing to set its selling price. Management also directs that the target price be set to provide a 25% return on investment (ROI) on invested assets of $4,200,000.

Instructions

(a) Compute the markup percentage and target selling price on this new playhouse.
(b) Assuming that the volume is 1,500 units instead of 1,000 units, compute the markup percentage and target selling price that will allow Cedarburg Lumber to earn its desired ROI of 25%.

Solution

(a)
Variable cost per unit

	Per Unit
Direct materials	$ 840
Direct labor	1,600
Variable manufacturing overhead	400
Variable selling and administrative expenses	510
Variable cost per unit	$3,350

Fixed cost per unit

	Total Costs	÷	Budgeted Volume	=	Cost Per Unit
Fixed manufacturing overhead	$540,000	÷	1,000	=	$540
Fixed selling and administrative expenses	320,000	÷	1,000	=	320
Fixed cost per unit	$860,000				$860

Computation of selling price (1,000 units)

Variable cost per unit	$3,350
Fixed cost per unit	860
Total unit cost	4,210
Desired ROI per unit*	1,050
Selling price	$5,260

*($4,200,000 × .25) ÷ 1,000

The markup percentage is:

$$\frac{\text{Desired ROI per unit}}{\text{Total unit cost}} = \frac{\$1,050}{\$4,210} = 24.9\%$$

(b) If the company produces 1,500 units, its selling price and markup percentage would be:

Computation of selling price (1,500 units)

Variable cost per unit	$3,350
Fixed cost per unit ($860,000 ÷ 1,500)	573
Total unit cost	3,923
Desired ROI per unit*	700
Selling price	$4,623

*($4,200,000 × .25) ÷ 1,500

The markup percentage would be:

$$\frac{\text{Desired ROI per unit}}{\text{Total unit cost}} = \frac{\$700}{\$3,923} = 17.8\%$$

SUMMARY OF STUDY OBJECTIVES

1 Compute a target cost when a product price is determined by the market. To compute a target cost, the company determines its target selling price. Once the target selling price is set, it determines its target cost by setting a desired profit. The difference between the target price and desired profit is the target cost of the product.

2 Compute a target selling price using cost-plus pricing. Cost-plus pricing involves establishing a cost base and adding to this cost base a markup to determine a target selling price. The cost-plus pricing formula is expressed as follows: Target selling price = Cost + (Markup percentage × Cost).

3 Use time and material pricing to determine the cost of services provided. Under time and material pricing, two pricing rates are set—one for the labor used on a job and another for the material. The labor rate includes direct labor time and other employee costs. The material charge is based on the cost of direct parts and materials used and a material loading charge for related overhead costs.

4 Determine a transfer price using the negotiated, cost-based, and market-based approaches. The negotiated price is determined through agreement of division managers. A cost-based transfer price may be based on full cost, variable cost, or some modification including a markup. The cost-based approach often leads to poor performance evaluations and purchasing decisions. The advantage of the cost-based system is its simplicity. Under a cost-based approach, the transfer price may be based on variable cost alone or on variable cost plus fixed costs. A markup may be added to these numbers. A market-based transfer price is based on existing competing market prices and services. A market-based system is often considered the best approach because it is objective and generally provides the proper economic incentives.

5 Explain the issues that arise when transferring goods between divisions located in countries with different tax rates. Companies must pay income tax in the country where income is generated. In order to maximize income and minimize income tax, many companies prefer to report more income in countries with low tax rates, and less income in countries with high tax rates. This is accomplished by adjusting the transfer prices they use on internal transfers between divisions located in different countries.

DECISION TOOLKIT—A SUMMARY

Decision Checkpoints ✔	Info Needed for Decision	Tool to Use for Decision	How to Evaluate Results 👍👎
What target cost can be achieved in a competitive environment?	Target selling price, desired profit, target cost	Target selling price less desired profit equals target cost	If target cost is too high, company will not earn desired profit.
How can we determine a target selling price in a less competitive environment?	Total cost per unit and desired profit (cost-plus pricing)	Total cost per unit plus desired profit equals target selling price	Does company make its desired profit? If not, does it result from less volume?
How do we set prices when it is difficult to estimate total cost per unit?	Two pricing rates needed: one for labor use and another for materials	Compute labor rate charge and materials rate charge. In each of these calculations, add a profit margin.	Is the company profitable under this pricing approach? Are employees earning reasonable wages?
What price should be charged for transfer of goods between divisions of a company?	Variable costs, opportunity costs, market prices	Variable costs plus opportunity costs should provide minimum transfer price for seller.	If income of division provides fair evaluation of managers, then transfer price is useful. Also, income of the company overall should not be reduced due to the transfer pricing approach.

APPENDIX 11A

OTHER COST APPROACHES TO PRICING

In calculating the target price of $132 for Cleanmore's shop vacuum in the chapter, we calculated the cost base by **including all costs incurred (full cost approach)**. Using total cost as the basis of the markup makes sense conceptually because in the long run the price must cover all costs and provide a reasonable profit. However, total cost is difficult to determine in practice. This is because period costs (selling and administrative expenses) are difficult to trace to a specific product. Activity-based-costing can be used to overcome this difficulty to some extent.

In practice, two other cost approaches are used: (1) the absorption cost approach, and (2) the contribution (variable cost) approach. The absorption cost approach is far more popular than the contribution approach.[2] We will illustrate both of them, though, because both have merit.

ABSORPTION COST APPROACH

The absorption cost approach is consistent with generally accepted accounting principles (GAAP) because it defines the cost base as the manufacturing cost. **Both variable and fixed selling and administrative costs are excluded from this cost base.** Thus, selling and administrative costs plus the target ROI must be provided for through the markup.

---

[2]For a discussion of cost-plus pricing, see Eunsup Skim and Ephraim F. Sudit, "How Manufacturers Price Products," *Management Accounting*, February 1995, pp. 37–39; and V. Govindarajan and R.N. Anthony, "How Firms Use Cost Data in Pricing Decisions," *Management Accounting* 65, no. 1, pp. 30–36.

The **first step** in the absorption cost approach is to compute the unit **manufacturing cost**. For Cleanmore Products, Inc., this amounts to $80 per unit at a volume of 10,000 units, as shown in Illustration 11A-1.

	Per Unit
Direct materials	$23
Direct labor	17
Variable manufacturing overhead	12
Fixed manufacturing overhead ($280,000 ÷ 10,000)	28
Total unit manufacturing cost (absorption cost)	$80

Illustration 11A-1
Computation of unit manufacturing cost

In addition, Cleanmore provided the following information regarding selling and administrative expenses per unit and desired ROI per unit.

Variable selling and administrative expenses	$ 8
Fixed selling and administrative expenses ($240,000 ÷ 10,000)	24
Desired ROI per unit	20

Illustration 11A-2 Other information

The **second step** in the absorption cost approach is to compute the markup percentage using the formula in Illustration 11A-3. Note that when manufacturing cost per unit is used as the cost base to compute the markup percentage, the **percentage must cover the desired ROI and also the selling and administrative expenses**.

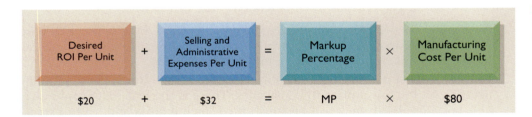

Illustration 11A-3
Markup percentage—absorption approach

Solving we find:

$$MP = (\$20 + \$32) \div \$80 = 65\%$$

The **third** and final **step** is to set the target selling price. Using a markup percentage of 65 percent and the absorption approach, we compute the target selling price as shown in Illustration 11A-4.

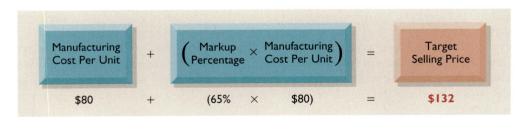

Illustration 11A-4
Computation of target price—absorption approach

Using a target price of $132 will produce the desired 20 percent return on investment for Cleanmore Products on its 3-horsepower, wet/dry shop vacuum at a volume level of 10,000 units, as proved in Illustration 11A-5.

Illustration 11A-5 Proof of 20% ROI—absorption approach

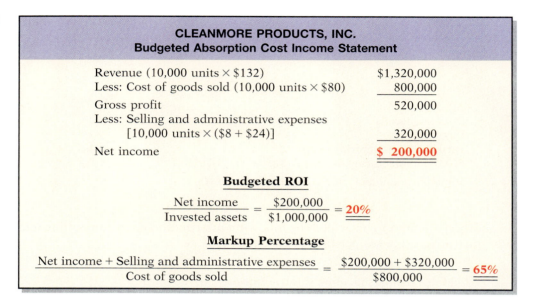

CLEANMORE PRODUCTS, INC.
Budgeted Absorption Cost Income Statement

Revenue (10,000 units × $132)	$1,320,000
Less: Cost of goods sold (10,000 units × $80)	800,000
Gross profit	520,000
Less: Selling and administrative expenses	
[10,000 units × ($8 + $24)]	320,000
Net income	$ 200,000

Budgeted ROI

$$\frac{\text{Net income}}{\text{Invested assets}} = \frac{\$200,000}{\$1,000,000} = \mathbf{20\%}$$

Markup Percentage

$$\frac{\text{Net income} + \text{Selling and administrative expenses}}{\text{Cost of goods sold}} = \frac{\$200,000 + \$320,000}{\$800,000} = \mathbf{65\%}$$

Because of the fixed cost element, if more than 10,000 units are sold, the ROI will be greater than 20 percent. And, if fewer than 10,000 units are sold, the ROI will be less than 20 percent. The markup percentage is also verified by adding $200,000 (the net income) and $320,000 (selling and administrative expenses) and then dividing by $800,000 (the cost of goods sold or the cost base).

Most companies that use cost-plus pricing use either absorption cost or full cost as the basis. The reasons for this tendency are as follows.

1. Absorption cost information is most readily provided by a company's cost accounting system. Because absorption cost data already exists in general ledger accounts, it is cost effective to use it for pricing.
2. Basing the cost-plus formula on only variable costs could encourage managers to set too low a price to boost sales. There is the fear that if only variable costs are used, they will be substituted for full costs and lead to suicidal price cutting.
3. Absorption cost or full cost provides the most defensible base for justifying prices to all interested parties—managers, customers, and government.

CONTRIBUTION (VARIABLE COST) APPROACH

Under the **contribution approach**, the cost base consists of all of the **variable costs** associated with a product, including variable selling and administrative costs. **Because fixed costs are not included in the base, the markup must provide for fixed costs (manufacturing, and selling and administrative) and the target ROI.** The contribution approach is more useful for making short-run decisions because it considers variable cost and fixed cost behavior patterns separately.

The **first step** in the contribution approach to cost-plus pricing is to compute the unit variable cost. For Cleanmore Products, Inc., this amounts to $60 per unit as shown in Illustration 11A-6.

	Per Unit
Direct materials	$23
Direct labor	17
Variable manufacturing overhead	12
Variable selling and administrative expense	8
Total unit variable cost	$60

Illustration 11A-6
Computation of unit variable cost

The **second step** in the contribution approach is to compute the markup percentage. The formula for the markup percentage is shown in Illustration 11A-7. For Cleanmore, fixed costs include fixed manufacturing overhead of $28 per unit ($280,000 ÷ 10,000) and fixed selling and administrative expenses of $24 per unit ($240,000 ÷ 10,000).

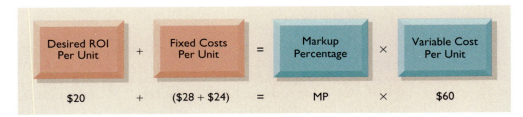

Illustration 11A-7
Computation of markup percentage—contribution approach

Solving we find:

$$MP = \frac{\$20 + (\$28 + \$24)}{\$60} = 120\%$$

The **third step** is to set the target selling price. Using a markup percentage of 120 percent and the contribution approach, the selling price is computed in Illustration 11A-8.

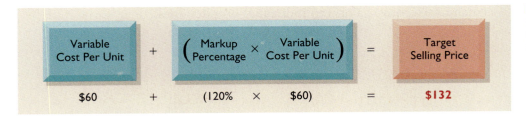

Illustration 11A-8
Computation of target price—contribution approach

Using a target price of $132 will produce the desired 20 percent return on investment for Cleanmore Products on its 3-horse power, wet/dry shop vacuum at a volume level of 10,000 units, as proved in Illustration 11A-9.

Illustration 11A-9 Proof of 20% ROI—contribution approach

CLEANMORE PRODUCTS, INC.
Budgeted Contribution Basis Income Statement

Revenue (10,000 units × $132)		$1,320,000
Less: Variable costs (10,000 units × $60)		600,000
Contribution margin		720,000
Less: Fixed costs		
Manufacturing (10,000 × $28)	$280,000	
Selling and administrative (10,000 × $24)	240,000	520,000
Net income		**$ 200,000**

Budgeted ROI

$$\frac{\text{Net income}}{\text{Invested assets}} = \frac{\$200,000}{\$1,000,000} = \textbf{20\%}$$

Markup Percentage

$$\frac{\text{Net income} + \text{Fixed costs}}{\text{Variable costs}} = \frac{\$200,000 + \$520,000}{\$600,000} = \textbf{120\%}$$

Under any of the three approaches we have looked at (total cost, absorption cost, and contribution), the desired ROI will be attained only if the budgeted sales volume for the period is attained. None of these approaches guarantees a profit or a desired ROI. Achieving a desired ROI is the result of many factors, some of which are beyond the company's control, such as market conditions, political and legal issues, customers' tastes, and competitive actions.

Because absorption cost includes allocated fixed costs, it does not make clear how the company's total costs will change as volume changes. To avoid blurring the effects of cost behavior on operating income, some managers therefore prefer the contribution approach. The specific reasons for using the contribution approach, even though the basic accounting data are less accessible, are as follows.

1. The contribution approach, being based on variable cost, is more consistent with cost-volume-profit analysis used by managers to measure the profit implications of changes in price and volume.
2. The contribution approach provides the type of data managers need for pricing special orders. It shows the incremental cost of accepting one more order.
3. The contribution approach avoids arbitrary allocation of common fixed costs (such as executive salary) to individual product lines.

SUMMARY OF STUDY OBJECTIVE FOR APPENDIX 11A

6 Determine prices using the absorption cost approach and the contribution (variable cost) approach. The absorption cost approach uses manufacturing cost as the cost base and provides for selling and administrative costs plus the target ROI through the markup. The target selling price is computed as: Manufacturing cost per unit + (Markup percentage × Manufacturing cost per unit). The contribution (variable cost) approach uses all of the variable costs, including selling and administrative costs, as the cost base and provides for fixed costs and target ROI through the markup. The target selling price is computed as: Variable cost per unit + (Markup percentage × Variable cost per unit).

GLOSSARY

Absorption cost approach An approach to pricing that defines the cost base as the manufacturing cost; it excludes both variable and fixed selling and administrative costs. (p. 456)

Contribution approach An approach to pricing that defines the cost base as all variable costs; it excludes both fixed manufacturing and fixed selling and administrative costs. (p. 458)

Cost-based transfer price A transfer price that uses as its foundation the costs incurred by the division producing the goods. (p. 450)

Cost-plus pricing A process whereby a product's selling price is determined by adding a markup to a cost base. (p. 439)

Market-based transfer price A transfer price that is based on existing market prices of competing products. (p. 451)

Markup The percentage applied to a product's cost to determine the product's selling price. (p. 439)

Material loading charge A charge added to cover the cost of purchasing, receiving, handling, and storing ma-

terials, plus any desired profit margin on the materials themselves. (p. 443)

Negotiated transfer price A transfer price that is determined by the agreement of the division managers when no external market price is available. (p. 447)

Outsourcing Contracting with an external party to provide a good or service, rather than performing the work internally. (p. 451)

Target cost The cost that will provide the desired profit on a product when the seller does not have control over the product's price. (p. 438)

Target selling price The selling price that will provide the desired profit on a product when the seller has the ability to determine the product's price. (p. 439)

Time and material pricing An approach to cost-plus pricing in which the company uses two pricing rates, one for the labor used on a job and another for the material. (p. 442)

Transfer price The price used to record the transfer between two divisions of a company. (p. 446)

DEMONSTRATION PROBLEM

Revco Electronics is a division of International Motors, an automobile manufacturer. Revco produces car radio/CD players. Revco sells its products to International Motors, as well as to other car manufacturers and electronics distributors. The following information is available regarding Revco's car radio/CD player.

Selling price of car radio/CD player to external customers	$49
Variable cost per unit	$28
Capacity	200,000 units

eGrade Demonstration Problem

Instructions

Determine whether the goods should be transferred internally or purchased externally and what the appropriate transfer price should be under each of the following **independent** situations.

(a) Revco Electronics is operating at full capacity. There is a saving of $4 per unit for variable cost if the car radio is made for internal sale. International Motors can purchase a comparable car radio from an outside supplier for $47.

(b) Revco Electronics has sufficient existing capacity to meet the needs of International Motors. International Motors can purchase a comparable car radio from an outside supplier for $47.

(c) International Motors wants to purchase a special-order car radio/CD player that also includes a tape deck. It needs 15,000 units. Revco Electronics has determined that the additional variable cost would be $12 per unit. Revco Electronics has no spare capacity. It will have to forgo sales of 15,000 units to external parties in order to provide this special order.

Solution

(a) Revco Electronics' opportunity cost (its lost contribution margin) would be $21 ($49 − $28). Using the formula for minimum transfer price, we determine:

Action Plan

- Determine whether company is at full capacity or not.
- Find the minimum transfer price, using formulas.
- Compare maximum price the buyer would pay to the minimum price for the seller.
- Determine if a deal can be made.

$$\text{Minimum transfer price} = \text{Variable cost} + \text{Opportunity cost}$$
$$\$45 \qquad = (\$28 - \$4) + \qquad \$21$$

Since this minimum transfer price is less than the $47 it would cost if International Motors purchases from an external party, internal transfer should take place. Revco Electronics and International Motors should negotiate a transfer price between $45 and $47.

(b) Since Revco Electronics has available capacity, its opportunity cost (its lost contribution margin) would be $0. Using the formula for minimum transfer price, we determine the following.

$$\text{Minimum transfer price} = \text{Variable cost} + \text{Opportunity cost}$$
$$\$28 \qquad = \qquad \$28 + \qquad \$0$$

Since International Motors can purchase the unit for $47 from an external party, the most it would be willing to pay would be $47. It is in the best interest of the company as a whole, as well as the two divisions, for a transfer to take place. The two divisions must reach a negotiated transfer price between $28 and $47 that recognizes the costs and benefits to each party and is acceptable to both.

(c) Revco Electronics' opportunity cost (its lost contribution margin per unit) would be $21 ($49 − $28). Its variable cost would be $40 ($28 + $12). Using the formula for minimum transfer price, we determine the following.

$$\text{Minimum transfer price} = \text{Variable cost} + \text{Opportunity cost}$$
$$\$61 \qquad = \qquad \$40 + \qquad \$21$$

Note that in this case Revco Electronics has no available capacity. Its management may decide that it does not want to provide this special order because to do so will require that it cut off the supply of the standard unit to some of its existing customers. This may anger those customers and result in the loss of customers.

Note: All asterisked Questions, Exercises, and Problems relate to material in the appendix to the chapter.

SELF-STUDY QUESTIONS

Self-Study / Self-Test

Answers are at the end of the chapter.

(SO 2) 1. Cost-plus pricing means that:
   (a) Selling price = Variable cost + (Markup percentage + Variable cost).
   (b) Selling price = Cost + (Markup percentage × Cost).
   (c) Selling price = Manufacturing cost + (Markup percentage + Manufacturing cost).
   (d) Selling price = Fixed cost + (Markup percentage × Fixed cost).

(SO 1) 2. Target cost related to price and profit means that:
   (a) cost and desired profit must be determined before selling price.
   (b) cost and selling price must be determined before desired profit.
   (c) price and desired profit must be determined before costs.
   (d) costs that can be achieved only if the company is at full capacity.

(SO 1) 3. Martinez Toys has examined the market for toy train locomotives. It believes there is a market niche in which it can sell locomotives at $80 apiece. It estimates that 10,000 of these locomotives could be sold annually. Variable costs to make a locomotive are expected to be $25. Martinez anticipates a profit of $15 per locomotive. The target cost for the locomotive is:
   (a) $80.   (c) $40.
   (b) $65.   (d) $25.

(SO 2) 4. Sprague Company is considering developing a new product. The company has gathered the following information on this product.

Expected total unit cost	$25
Estimated investment for new product	$500,000
Desired ROI	10%
Expected number of units to be produced and sold	1,000

The desired markup percentage and selling price given this information is:
   (a) markup percentage 10%; selling price $55.
   (b) markup percentage 200%; selling price $75.

(c) markup percentage 10%; selling price $50.

(d) markup percentage 100%; selling price $55.

(SO 2) 5. The following information is provided for Shaq Co. for the new product it recently introduced.

Total unit cost	$30
Desired ROI per unit	$10
Target selling price	$40

What would be Shaq Co.'s percentage markup on cost?

(a) 125%. (c) 33 $\frac{1}{3}$%.

(b) 75%.   (d) 25%.

(SO 3) 6. Jiminez's Electrical Repair has decided to price its work on a time and materials basis. It estimates the following costs for the year related to labor.

Technician wages and benefits	$100,000
Office employee's salary and benefits	$ 40,000
Other overhead	$ 80,000

Jiminez desires a profit margin of $10 per labor hour and budgets 5,000 hours of repair time for the year. The office employee salaries, benefits, and other overhead costs should be divided evenly between time charges and materials charges. Jiminez's labor charge per hour would be:

(a) $42.   (c) $32.

(b) $34.   (d) $30.

(SO 4) 7. The Plastics Division of Martin Company manufactures plastic molds and then sells them to customers for $70 per unit. Its variable cost is $30 per unit, and its fixed cost per unit is $10. Management would like the Plastics Division to transfer 10,000 of these molds to another division within the company at a price of $40.

The Plastics Division is operating at full capacity. What is the minimum transfer price that the Plastics Division should accept?

(a) $10.   (c) $40.

(b) $30.   (d) $70.

(SO 4) 8. Assume the same information as question 7, except that the Plastics Division has available capacity of 10,000 units for plastic moldings. What is the minimum transfer price that the Plastics Division should accept?

(a) $10.   (c) $40.

(b) $30.   (d) $70.

(SO 6) *9. AST Electrical provides the following cost information related to its production of electronic circuit boards.

	Per Unit
Variable manufacturing cost	$40
Fixed manufacturing cost	$30
Variable selling and administrative expenses	$ 8
Fixed selling and administrative expenses	$12
Desired ROI per unit	$15

What is its markup percentage assuming that AST Electrical uses the absorption cost approach?

(a) 16.67%.   (c) 54.28%.

(b) 50%.   (d) 118.75%.

(SO 6) *10. Assume the same information as question 9 and determine AST Electrical's markup percentage using the contribution approach.

(a) 16.67%.   (c) 54.28%.

(b) 50%.   (d) 118.75%.

QUESTIONS

1. What are the two types of pricing environments for sales to external parties?

2. In what situation does a company place the greatest focus on its target cost? How is the target cost determined?

3. What is the basic formula to determine the target selling price in cost-plus pricing?

4. Waterville Corporation produces a filter that has a per unit cost of $15. The company would like a 30% markup percentage. Using cost-plus pricing, determine the per unit selling price.

5. What is the basic formula for the markup percentage?

6. What are some of the factors that affect a company's target ROI?

7. Stillsville Corporation manufactures an electronic switch for dishwashers. The cost base per unit, ex-

cluding selling and administrative expenses, is $60. The per unit cost of selling and administrative expenses is $20. The company's desired ROI per unit is $5. Calculate its markup percentage on total unit cost.

8. Ramirez manufactures a standard cabinet for a DVD player. The variable cost per unit is $15. The fixed cost per unit is $10. The desired ROI per unit is $5. Compute the markup percentage on total unit cost and the target selling price for the DVD player.

9. When is time and material pricing most often used? Describe the process of time and material pricing.

10. What is the material loading charge? How is it expressed?

11. What is a transfer price? Why is determining a fair transfer price important to division managers?

12. When setting a transfer price, what objective(s) should the company have in mind?)

13. What are the three approaches for determining transfer prices?

14. If a company uses the cost-based approach to transfer pricing, should it use actual cost or standard cost? Explain your answer.

15. Describe the cost-based approach to transfer pricing. What is the strength of this approach? What are the weaknesses of this approach?

16. What is the general formula for determining the minimum transfer price that the selling division should be willing to accept?

17. When determining the minimum transfer price, what is meant by the "opportunity cost"?

18. In what circumstances will a negotiated transfer price be used instead of a market-based price?

19. Explain how transfer pricing between divisions located in different countries is used to reduce tax payments, and discuss the propriety of this approach.

*20. What costs are excluded from the cost base when the absorption cost approach is used to determine the markup percentage?

*21. Walter Corporation manufactures a fiber optic connector. The variable cost per unit is $16. The fixed cost per unit is $9. The company's desired ROI per unit is $3. Compute the markup percentage using the contribution approach.

*B*RIEF *E*XERCISES

Compute target cost.
(SO 1)

BE11-1   Marcus Company manufactures computer hard drives. The market for hard drives is very competitive. The current market price for a computer hard drive is $45. Marcus would like a profit of $12 per drive. How can Marcus Company accomplish this objective?

Use cost-plus pricing to determine selling price.
(SO 2)

BE11-2   Nien Corporation produces snowboards. The following per unit cost information is available: direct materials $12; direct labor $8; variable manufacturing overhead $6; fixed manufacturing overhead $14; variable selling and administrative expenses $4; and fixed selling and administrative expenses $12. Using a 35% markup percentage on total per unit cost, compute the target selling price.

Compute ROI per unit.
(SO 2)

BE11-3   Timo Corporation produces high-performance rotors. It expects to produce 50,000 rotors in the coming year. It has invested $10,000,000 to produce rotors. The company has a required return on investment of 15%. What is its ROI per unit?

Compute markup percentage.
(SO 2)

BE11-4   Michener Corporation produces microwave units. The following per unit cost information is available: direct materials $36; direct labor $24; variable manufacturing overhead $18; fixed manufacturing overhead $42; variable selling and administrative expenses $12; and fixed selling and administrative expenses $28. Its desired ROI per unit is $30. Compute its markup percentage using a total cost approach.

Compute ROI and markup percentage.
(SO 2)

BE11-5   During the current year Harry's Corporation expects to produce 10,000 units and has budgeted the following: net income $300,000; variable costs $1,200,000; and fixed costs $100,000. It has invested assets of $1,500,000. What was the company's budgeted ROI? What was its budgeted markup percentage using a total cost approach?

Use time and material pricing to determine bill.
(SO 3)

BE11-6   Mary's Small Engine Repair charges $45 per hour of labor. It has a material loading charge of 60%. On a recent job replacing the engine of a riding lawnmower, Mary worked 10.5 hours and used parts with a cost of $700. Calculate Mary's total bill.

Determine minimum transfer price.
(SO 5)

BE11-7   The Heating Division of ITA International produces a heating element that it sells to its customers for $41 per unit. Its variable cost per unit is $19, and its fixed cost per unit is $8. Top management of ITA International would like the Heating Division to transfer 15,000 heating units to another division within the company at a price of $27. The Heating Division is operating at full capacity. What is the minimum transfer price that the Heating Division should accept?

Determine minimum transfer price with excess capacity.
(SO 5)

BE11-8   Use the data from BE11-7, but assume that the Heating Division has sufficient excess capacity to provide the 15,000 heating units to the other division. What is the minimum transfer price that the Heating Division should accept?

Determine minimum transfer price for special order.
(SO 5)

BE11-9   Use the data from BE11-7, but assume that the units being requested are special high-performance units, and that the division's variable cost would be $26 per unit. What is the minimum transfer price that the Heating Division should accept?

*BE11-10   Using the data in BE11-4, compute the markup percentage using the absorption cost approach.

Compute markup percentage using absorption cost approach. (SO 6)

*BE11-11   Using the data in BE11-4, compute the markup percentage using the contribution approach.

Compute markup percentage using contribution approach. (SO 6)

EXERCISES

E11-1   Vinegar Corporation makes a commercial-grade cooking griddle. The following information is available for Vinegar Corporation's anticipated annual volume of 30,000 units.

Use cost-plus pricing to determine selling price. (SO 2)

	Per Unit	Total
Direct materials	$17	
Direct labor	$ 8	
Variable manufacturing overhead	$11	
Fixed manufacturing overhead		$330,000
Variable selling and administrative expenses	$ 4	
Fixed selling and administrative expenses		$150,000

The company uses a 50% markup percentage on total cost.

Instructions
(a) Compute the total cost per unit.
(b) Compute the target selling price.

E11-2   Frost Corporation makes a mechanical stuffed alligator that sings the Martian national anthem. The following information is available for Frost Corporation's anticipated annual volume of 500,000 units.

Use cost-plus pricing to determine various amounts. (SO 2)

	Per Unit	Total
Direct materials	$ 7	
Direct labor	$ 9	
Variable manufacturing overhead	$12	
Fixed manufacturing overhead		$3,300,000
Variable selling and administrative expenses	$14	
Fixed selling and administrative expenses		$1,500,000

The company has a desired ROI of 25%. It has invested assets of $28,000,000.

Instructions
(a) Compute the total cost per unit.
(b) Compute the desired ROI per unit.
(c) Compute the markup percentage using total cost per unit.
(d) Compute the target selling price.

E11-3   Engles Corporation produces industrial robots for high-precision manufacturing. The following information is given for Engles Corporation.

Use cost-plus pricing to determine various amounts. (SO 2, 3)

	Per Unit	Total
Direct materials	$380	
Direct labor	$290	
Variable manufacturing overhead	$ 72	
Fixed manufacturing overhead		$1,500,000
Variable selling and administrative expenses	$ 55	
Fixed selling and administrative expenses		$ 327,000

The company has a desired ROI of 18%. It has invested assets of $49,600,000. It anticipates production of 3,000 units per year.

Instructions
(a) Compute the cost per unit of the fixed manufacturing overhead and the fixed selling and administrative expenses.
(b) Compute the desired ROI per unit.
(c) Compute the target selling price.

Use time and material pricing to determine bill.
(SO 3)

E11-4 Dobbs Remanufacturing rebuilds spot welders for manufacturers. The following budgeted cost data for 2003 is available for Dobbs.

	Time Charges	Material Charges
Technicians' wages and benefits	$228,000	–
Parts manager's salary and benefits	–	$42,500
Office employee's salary and benefits	30,400	8,000
Other overhead	15,200	22,000
Total budgeted costs	$273,600	$72,500

The company desires a $35 profit margin per hour of labor and a 25% profit margin on parts. It has budgeted for 7,600 hours of repair time in the coming year, and estimates that the total invoice cost of parts and materials in 2003 will be $400,000.

Instructions
(a) Compute the rate charged per hour of labor.
(b) Compute the material loading charge. (Round to three decimal places.)
(c) Lindy Corporation has requested an estimate to rebuild its spot welder. Dobbs estimates that it would require 40 hours of labor and $2,500 of parts. Compute the total estimated bill.

Use time and material pricing to determine bill.
(SO 3)

E11-5 Jack's Custom Electronics (JCE) sells and installs complete security, computer, audio, and video systems for homes. On newly constructed homes it provides bids using time and material pricing. The following budgeted cost data are available.

	Time Charges	Material Charges
Technicians' wages and benefits	$150,000	–
Parts manager's salary and benefits	–	$32,500
Office employee's salary and benefits	28,000	12,000
Other overhead	12,000	42,000
Total budgeted costs	$190,000	$86,500

The company has budgeted for 6,000 hours of technician time during the coming year. It desires a $36 profit margin per hour of labor and a 100% profit on parts. It estimates the total invoice cost of parts and materials in 2003 will be $700,000.

Instructions
(a) Compute the rate charged per hour of labor. (Round to 2 decimal places.)
(b) Compute the material loading charge. (Round to 2 decimal places.)
(c) JCE has just received a request for a bid from R.J. Builders on a $1,200,000 new home. The company estimates that it would require 80 hours of labor and $40,000 of parts. Compute the total estimated bill.

Determine minimum transfer price.
(SO 4)

E11-6 LoudPlay Corporation manufactures car stereos. It is a division of RustBucket Motors, which manufactures vehicles. LoudPlay sells car stereos to RustBucket, as well as to other vehicle manufacturers and retail stores. The following information is available for LoudPlay's standard unit: variable cost per unit $35; fixed cost per unit $25; and selling price to outside customer $85. RustBucket currently purchases a standard unit from an outside supplier for $80. Because of quality concerns and to ensure a reliable supply, the top management of RustBucket has ordered LoudPlay to provide 200,000 units per year at a transfer price of $35 per unit. LoudPlay is already operating at full capacity. LoudPlay can avoid $3 per unit of variable selling costs by selling the unit internally.

Instructions
Answer each of the following questions.

(a) What is the minimum transfer price that LoudPlay should accept?
(b) What is the potential loss to the corporation as a whole resulting from this forced transfer?
(c) How should this situation be resolved?

E11-7 The Faucet Division of Kendra Plumbing Corporation has recently been approached by the Bathtub Division with a proposal. The Bathtub Division would like to make a special "ivory" tub with gold-plated fixtures for the company's 50-year anniversary. It would make only 5,000 of these units. It would like the Faucet Division to make the fixtures and provide them to the Bathtub Division at a transfer price of $160. The estimated variable cost per unit would be $135. However, by selling internally the Faucet Division would save $5 per unit on variable selling expenses. The Faucet Division is currently operating at full capacity. Its standard unit sells for $50 per unit and has variable costs of $27.

Compute minimum transfer price.
(SO 4)

Instructions
Compute the minimum transfer price that the Faucet Division should be willing to accept, and discuss whether it should accept this offer.

*E11-8 Information for Frost Corporation is given in E11-2.

Compute total cost per unit, ROI, and markup percentages.
(SO 1,2,6)

Instructions
Using the information given in E11-2, answer the following.
(a) Compute the total cost per unit.
(b) Compute the desired ROI per unit.
(c) Using the absorption cost approach, compute the markup percentage.
(d) Using the contribution approach, compute the markup percentage.

*E11-9 Summer Corporation produces outdoor portable fireplace units. The following per unit cost information is available: direct materials $24; direct labor $26; variable manufacturing overhead $16; fixed manufacturing overhead $20; variable selling and administrative expenses $9; and fixed selling and administrative expenses $14. The company's ROI per unit is $20.

Compute markup percentage using the absorption cost and contribution approaches.
(SO 6)

Instructions
Compute Summer Corporation's markup percentage using (1) the absorption cost approach and (2) the contribution approach.

*E11-10 Information for Engles Corporation is given in E11-3.

Compute various amounts using the absorption cost and contribution approaches.
(SO 6)

Instructions
Using the information given in E11-3, answer the following.
(a) Compute the cost per unit of the fixed manufacturing overhead and the fixed selling and administrative expenses.
(b) Compute the desired ROI per unit.
(c) Compute the markup percentage and target selling price using the absorption cost approach. (Round to 3 decimal places.)
(d) Compute the markup percentage and target selling price using the contribution approach. (Round to 3 decimal places.)

PROBLEMS: SET A

P11-1A Alameda Corporation needs to set a target price for its newly designed product E2-D2. The following data relate to this new product.

Use cost-plus pricing to determine various amounts.
(SO 2)

	Per Unit	Total
Direct materials	$18	
Direct labor	$30	
Variable manufacturing overhead	$ 9	
Fixed manufacturing overhead		$1,350,000
Variable selling and administrative expenses	$ 3	
Fixed selling and administrative expenses		$1,080,000

eGrade Problem

These costs are based on a budgeted volume of 90,000 units produced and sold each year. Alameda uses cost-plus pricing methods to set its target selling price. The markup on total unit cost is 20%.

Instructions
(a) Compute total variable cost per unit, total fixed cost per unit, and total cost per unit for E2-D2.
(b) Compute the desired ROI per unit for E2-D2.
(c) Compute the target selling price for E2-D2.
(d) Compute variable cost per unit, fixed cost per unit, and total cost per unit assuming that 80,000 E2-D2s are sold during the year. (Round to two decimal places.)

Use cost-plus pricing to determine various amounts.
(SO 2)

P11-2A Morgan Electronics Inc. is in the process of setting a selling price on a new CDL component it has just developed. The following cost estimates for this component have been provided by the accounting department for a budgeted volume of 50,000 units.

	Per Unit	Total
Direct materials	$36	
Direct labor	$24	
Variable manufacturing overhead	$18	
Fixed manufacturing overhead		$440,000
Variable selling and administrative expenses	$12	
Fixed selling and administrative expenses		$360,000

Morgan's management uses cost-plus pricing to set its selling price. Management also directs that the target price be set to provide a 30% return on investment (ROI) on invested assets of $1,400,000.

Instructions
(a) Compute the markup percentage and target selling price on this new CDL component.
(b) Assuming that the volume is 40,000 units, compute the markup percentage and target selling price that will allow Morgan Electronics to earn its desired ROI of 30%.

Use time and material pricing to determine bill.
(SO 3)

P11-3A Bud's Auto Body Shop has budgeted the following time and material for 2002.

BUD'S AUTO BODY SHOP
Budgeted Costs for the Year 2002

	Time Charges	Material Charges
Shop employees' wages and benefits	$108,000	–
Parts manager's salary and benefits	–	$ 23,600
Office employee's salary and benefits	21,000	12,000
Invoice cost of parts used	–	200,000
Overhead (supplies, depreciation, advertising, utilities)	24,600	15,000
Total budgeted costs	$153,600	$250,600

Bud's budgets 6,000 hours of repair time in 2002. It will bill a profit of $7 per labor hour along with a 40% profit markup on the invoice cost of parts.

On January 10, 2002, Bud's is asked to submit a price estimate for the repair of a 1999 Chevrolet Blazer that was damaged in a head-on collision. Bud's estimates that this repair will consume 61 hours of labor and $4,200 in parts and materials.

Instructions
(a) Compute the labor rate for Bud's Auto Body Shop for the year 2002.
(b) Compute the material loading charge rate for Bud's Auto Body Shop for the year 2002. (Round to 3 decimal places.)
(c) Prepare a time and material price quotation for the repair of the 1999 Blazer.

Determine minimum transfer price with no excess capacity and with excess capacity.
(SO 4)

P11-4A High Flying Sounds is a record company with a number of record labels. Each record label has contracts with a number of recording artists. It also owns a recording studio called Definite Loud Noise. The record labels and the recording studio operate as separate profit centers. The studio earns revenue by recording artists under contract with the labels owned by High Flying Sounds, as well as artists under contract with other companies. The studio bills out at $1,100 per hour, and a typical CD requires 80 hours of studio time. A manager from Big Bang, one of the High Flying Sounds' record labels, has approached the manager of the recording studio offering to pay $800 per hour for an 80-hour session. The record label pays outside studios $1,000 per hour. The recording studio's variable cost per hour is $500.

Instructions
Determine whether the recording should be done internally or hired externally, and the appropriate transfer price, under each of the following situations.
(a) Assume that the recording studio is booked solid for the next 3 years, and it would have to cancel an obligation with an outside customer in order to meet the needs of the internal division.
(b) Assume that the recording studio has available capacity.
(c) The top management of High Flying Sounds believes that the recording studio should always do the recording for the company's artists. On a number of occasions it has forced the recording studio to cancel jobs with outside customers in order to meet the needs of its own labels. Discuss the pros and cons of this approach.
(d) Calculate the change in contribution margin to each division, and to the company as a whole, if top management forces the recording studio to accept the $800 transfer price when it has no available capacity.

P11-5A Watertown Pump Company makes irrigation pump systems. The company is divided into a number of autonomous divisions that can either sell to internal units or sell externally. All divisions are located in buildings on the same piece of property. The Pump Division has offered the Washer Division $4 per unit to supply it with the washers for 50,000 units. It has been purchasing these washers for $4.25 per unit from outside suppliers. The Washer Divison receives $4.50 per unit for sales made to outside customers on this type of washer. The variable cost of units sold externally by the Washer Division is $3.00. It estimates that it will save 60 cents per unit of selling expenses on units sold internally to the Pump Division. The Washer Division has no excess capacity.

Determine minimum transfer price with no excess capacity.
(SO 4)

Instructions
(a) Calculate the minimum transfer price that the Washer Division should accept. Discuss whether it is in the Washer Division's best interest to accept the offer.
(b) Suppose that the Washer Division decides to reject the offer. What are the financial implications for each division, and the company as a whole, of the decision to reject the offer?

P11-6A Big Boy Engines is a division of Gas Guzzler Lawn Equipment Company. Big Boy makes engines for lawn mowers, snow blowers, and other types of lawn and garden equipment. It sells its engines to the Lawn Mower Division and the Snow Blower Division of the company, as well as to other lawn equipment companies. It was recently approached by the manager of the Lawn Mower Division with a request to make a special, high-performance engine for a lawn mower designed to mow heavy brush. The Lawn Mower Division has requested that Big Boy produce 8,000 units of this special engine. The following facts are available regarding the Big Boy Engine Division.

Determine minimum transfer price under different situations.
(SO 4)

Selling price of standard lawn mower engine	$86
Variable cost of standard lawn mower engine	$55
Additional variable cost of special engine	$40

Instructions
For each of the following independent situations, calculate the minimum transfer price, and discuss whether the internal transfer should take place or whether the Lawn Mower Division should purchase its goods externally.
(a) The Lawn Mower Division has offered to pay the Big Boy Engine Division $110 per engine. Big Boy Engine has no available capacity. Big Boy Engine would have to forgo sales of 8,000 units to existing customers in order to meet the request of the Lawn Mower Division.
(b) The Lawn Mower Division has offered to pay the Big Boy Engine Division $170 per engine. Big Boy has no available capacity. Big Boy Engine would have to forgo sales of 12,000 units to existing customers in order to meet the request of the Lawn Mower Division.
(c) The Lawn Mower division has offered to pay the Big Boy Engine Division $110 per engine. Big Boy Engine Division has available capacity.

Compute the target price using the absorption cost and contribution approaches.
(SO 6)

*P11-7A   Alameda Corporation needs to set a target price for its newly designed product E2-D2. The following data (the same as for Alameda in P11-1A) relate to this new product.

	Per Unit	Total
Direct materials	$18	
Direct labor	$30	
Variable manufacturing overhead	$ 9	
Fixed manufacturing overhead		$1,350,000
Variable selling and administrative expenses	$ 3	
Fixed selling and administrative expenses		$1,080,000

The above costs are based on a budgeted volume of 90,000 units produced and sold each year. Alameda uses cost-plus pricing methods to set its target selling price. Because some managers prefer to work with the absorption cost approach and other managers prefer the contribution approach, the accounting department provides information under both approaches using a markup of 50% on unit manufacturing cost and a markup of 80% on variable cost.

Instructions
(a) Compute the target price for one unit of E2-D2 using the absorption cost approach.
(b) Compute the target price for one unit of E2-D2 using the contribution approach.

Compute various amounts using the absorption cost and contribution approaches.
(SO 6)

*P11-8A   Carolina Furniture Inc. is in the process of setting a target price on its newly designed leather recliner sofa. Cost data relating to the sofa at a budgeted volume of 2,500 units are as follows.

	Per Unit	Total
Direct materials	$120	
Direct labor	$ 80	
Variable manufacturing overhead	$ 40	
Fixed manufacturing overhead		$150,000
Variable selling and administrative expenses	$ 20	
Fixed selling and administrative expenses		$100,000

Carolina Furniture uses cost-plus pricing methods that are designed to provide the company with a 40% ROI on its stuffed furniture line. A total of $600,000 in assets are committed to production of the new leather recliner sofa.

Instructions
(a) Compute the markup percentage under the absorption cost approach that will allow Carolina Furniture to realize its desired ROI.
(b) Compute the target price of the sofa under the absorption cost approach, and show proof that the desired ROI is realized.
(c) Compute the markup percentage under the contribution approach that will allow Carolina Furniture to realize its desired ROI.
(d) Compute the target price of the sofa under the contribution approach, and show proof that the desired ROI is realized.
(e) Since both the absorption cost approach and the contribution approach produce the same target price and provide the same desired ROI, why do both methods exist? Isn't one method clearly superior to the other?

Problems: Set B

Use cost-plus pricing to determine various amounts.
(SO 2)

P11-1B   Bonita Corporation needs to set a target price for its newly designed product M14–M16. The following data relate to this new product.

	Per Unit	Total
Direct materials	$20	
Direct labor	$40	
Variable manufacturing overhead	$10	
Fixed manufacturing overhead		$1,400,000
Variable selling and administrative expenses	$ 5	
Fixed selling and administrative expenses		$1,000,000

These costs are based on a budgeted volume of 80,000 units produced and sold each year. Bonita uses cost-plus pricing methods to set its target selling price. The markup on total unit cost is 25%.

Instructions
(a) Compute the total variable cost per unit, total fixed cost per unit, and total cost per unit for M14–M16.
(b) Compute the desired ROI per unit for M14–M16.
(c) Compute the target selling price for M14–M16.
(d) Compute variable cost per unit, fixed cost per unit, and total cost per unit assuming that 60,000 M14–M16s are sold during the year.

P11-2B Migami Computer Parts Inc. is in the process of setting a selling price on a new component it has just designed and developed. The following cost estimates for this new component have been provided by the accounting department for a budgeted volume of 40,000 units.

Use cost-plus pricing to determine various amounts.
(SO 2)

	Per Unit	Total
Direct materials	$50	
Direct labor	$25	
Variable manufacturing overhead	$20	
Fixed manufacturing overhead		$500,000
Variable selling and administrative expenses	$15	
Fixed selling and administrative expenses		$400,000

Migami Computer Parts management requests that the total cost per unit be used in cost-plus pricing its products. On this particular product, management also directs that the target price be set to provide a 20% return on investment (ROI) on invested assets of $1,200,000.

Instructions
(Round all calculations to two decimal places.)
(a) Compute the markup percentage and target selling price that will allow Migami Computer Parts to earn its desired ROI of 20% on this new component.
(b) Assuming that the volume is 25,000 units, compute the markup percentage and target selling price that will allow Migami Computer Parts to earn its desired ROI of 20% on this new component.

P11-3B Ernie's Electronic Repair Shop has budgeted the following time and material for 2002.

Use time and material pricing to determine bill.
(SO 3)

ERNIE'S ELECTRONIC REPAIR SHOP
Budgeted Costs for the Year 2002

	Time Charges	Material Charges
Shop employees' wages and benefits	$105,000	–
Parts manager's salary and benefits	–	$ 25,400
Office employee's salary and benefits	20,000	10,600
Invoice cost of parts used	–	100,000
Overhead (supplies, depreciation, advertising, utilities)	24,000	18,000
Total budgeted costs	$149,000	$154,000

Ernie's budgets 5,000 hours of repair time in 2002 and will bill a profit of $5 per labor hour along with a 30% profit markup on the invoice cost of parts.

On January 5, 2002 Ernie's is asked to submit a price estimate to fix a 72″ big-screen TV. Ernie's estimates that this job will consume 24 hours of labor and $500 in parts and materials.

Instructions
(a) Compute the labor rate for Ernie's Electronic Repair Shop for the year 2002.
(b) Compute the material loading charge rate for Ernie's Electronic Repair Shop for the year 2002.
(c) Prepare a time and material price quotation for fixing the big-screen TV.

Determine minimum transfer price with no excess capacity and with excess capacity.
(SO 4)

P11-4B   World of Words is a publishing company with a number of different book lines. Each line has contracts with a number of different authors. The company also owns a printing operation called Pronto Press. The book lines and the printing operation each operate as a separate profit center. The printing operation earns revenue by printing books by authors under contract with the book lines owned by World of Words, as well as authors under contract with other companies. The printing operation bills out at $0.01 per page, and a typical book requires 500 pages of print. A manager from Business Books, one of the World of Words' book lines, has approached the manager of the printing operation offering to pay $0.007 per page for 1,000 copies of a 500-page book. The book line pays outside printers $0.009 per page. The printing operation's variable cost per page is $0.005.

Instructions
Determine whether the printing should be done internally or externally, and the appropriate transfer price, under each of the following situations.
(a) Assume that the printing operation is booked solid for the next two years, and it would have to cancel an obligation with an outside customer in order to meet the needs of the internal division.
(b) Assume that the printing operation has available capacity.
(c) The top management of World of Words believes that the printing operation should always do the printing for the company's authors. On a number of occasions it has forced the printing operation to cancel jobs with outside customers in order to meet the needs of its own lines. Discuss the pros and cons of this approach.
(d) Calculate the change in contribution margin to each division, and to the company as a whole, if top management forces the printing operation to accept the $0.007 per page transfer price when it has no available capacity.

Determine minimum transfer price with no excess capacity.
(SO 4)

P11-5B   The Electronics Manufacturing Company makes various electronic products. The company is divided into a number of autonomous divisions that can either sell to internal units or sell externally. All divisions are located in buildings on the same piece of property. The Board Division has offered the Chip Division $20 per unit to supply it with chips for 40,000 boards. It has been purchasing these chips for $21.25 per unit from outside suppliers. The Chip Division receives $22.50 per unit for sales made to outside customers on this type of chip. The variable cost of chips sold externally by the Chip Division is $15. It estimates that it will save $3 per chip of selling expenses on units sold internally to the Board Division. The Chip Division has no excess capacity.

Instructions
(a) Calculate the minimum transfer price that the Chip Division should accept. Discuss whether it is in the Chip Division's best interest to accept the offer.
(b) Suppose that the Chip Division decides to reject the offer. What are the financial implications for each division, and for the company as a whole, of this decision?

Determine minimum transfer price under different situations.
(SO 4)

P11-6B   Communication Manufacturing (CM) is a division of Universal Communications, Inc. CM produces pagers and other personal communication devices. These devices are sold to other Universal divisions, as well as to other communication companies. CM was recently approached by the manager of the Personal Communications Division regarding a request to make a special pager designed to receive signals from anywhere in the world. The Personal Communications Division has requested that CM produce 10,000 units of this special pager. The following facts are available regarding the Communication Manufacturing Division.

Selling price of standard pager	$90
Variable cost of standard pager	50
Additional variable cost of special pager	35

Instructions
For each of the following independent situations, calculate the minimum transfer price, and discuss whether the internal transfer should take place or whether the Personal Communications Division should purchase the pager externally.
(a) The Personal Communications Division has offered to pay the CM Division $105 per pager. The CM Division has no available capacity. The CM Division would have to forgo sales of 10,000 pagers to existing customers in order to meet the request of the Personal Communications Division.

(b) The Personal Communications Division has offered to pay the CM Division $160 per pager. The CM Division has no available capacity. The CM Division would have to forgo sales of 15,000 pagers to existing customers in order to meet the request of the Personal Communications Division.

(c) The Personal Communications Division has offered to pay the CM Division $105 per pager. The CM Division has available capacity.

*P11-7B Mak-A-Buck Corporation needs to set a target price for its newly designed product AlwaysReady. The following data relate to this new product.

Compute the target price using the absorption cost and contribution approaches.
(SO 6)

	Per Unit	Total
Direct materials	$20	
Direct labor	$40	
Variable manufacturing overhead	$10	
Fixed manufacturing overhead		$1,400,000
Variable selling and administrative expenses	$5	
Fixed selling and administrative expenses		$1,120,000

The costs above are based on a budgeted volume of 80,000 units produced and sold each year. Mak-A-Buck uses cost-plus pricing methods to set its target selling price. Because some managers prefer the absorption cost approach and others prefer the contribution approach, the accounting department provides information under both approaches using a markup of 50% on unit manufacturing cost and a markup of 75% on variable cost.

Instructions
(a) Compute the target price for one unit of AlwaysReady using the absorption cost approach.
(b) Compute the target price for one unit of AlwaysReady using the contribution approach.

*P11-8B Wisconsin Windows Inc. is in the process of setting a target price on its newly designed tinted window. Cost data relating to the window at a budgeted volume of 3,000 units are as follows.

Compute various amounts using the absorption cost and contribution approaches.
(SO 6)

	Per Unit	Total
Direct materials	$100	
Direct labor	$ 70	
Variable manufacturing overhead	$ 30	
Fixed manufacturing overhead		$120,000
Variable selling and administrative expenses	$ 10	
Fixed selling and administrative expenses		$ 90,000

Wisconsin Windows uses cost-plus pricing methods that are designed to provide the company with a 30% ROI on its tinted window line. A total of $500,000 in assets is committed to production of the new tinted window.

Instructions
(a) Compute the markup percentage under the absorption cost approach that will allow Wisconsin Windows to realize its desired ROI.
(b) Compute the target price of the sofa under the absorption cost approach, and show proof that the desired ROI is realized.
(c) Compute the markup percentage under the contribution approach that will allow Wisconsin Windows to realize its desired ROI. (Round to 3 decimal places.)
(d) Compute the target price of the sofa under the contribution approach, and show proof that the desired ROI is realized.
(e) Since both the absorption approach and the contribution approach produce the same target price and provide the same desired ROI, why do both methods exist? Isn't one method clearly superior to the other?

COMPREHENSIVE PROBLEM: CHAPTERS 1–11

A Comprehensive Problem covering Chapters 1 through 11 is available on the CD that accompanies this text and also on the book's Web site.

GROUP DECISION CASE

BYP11-1   Harvey Manufacturing has multiple divisions that make a wide variety of products. Recently the Bearing Division and the Wheel Division got into an argument over a transfer price. The Wheel Division needed bearings for garden tractor wheels. It normally buys its bearings from an outside supplier for $22 per set. The company's top management recently initiated a campaign to persuade the different divisions to buy their materials from within the company whenever possible. As a result, Sam Stone, the purchasing manager for the Wheel Division, received a letter from the vice president of Purchasing, ordering him to contact the Bearing Division to discuss buying bearings from this division.

To comply with this request, Sam from the Wheel Division called Terry Tompkin of the Bearing Division, and asked the price for 15,000 bearings. Terry responded that the bearings normally sell for $32 per set. However, Terry noted that the Bearing Division would save $3 on marketing costs by selling internally, and would pass this cost savings on to the Wheel Division. He further commented that they were at full capacity, and therefore would not be able to provide any bearings presently. In the future, if they had available capacity, they would be happy to provide bearings.

Sam responded indignantly, "Thanks but no thanks." He said, "We can get all the bearings we need from Milken Manufacturing for $22 per set." Terry snorted back, "Milken makes junk. It costs us $21 per set just to make our bearings. Our bearings can withstand heat of 2,000 degrees centigrade, and are good to within .00001 centimeters. If you guys are happy buying junk, then go ahead and buy from Milken."

Two weeks later, Sam's boss from the central office stopped in to find out whether he had placed an order with the Bearing Division. Sam responded that he would sooner buy his bearings from his worst enemy than from the Bearing Division.

Instructions
With the class divided into groups, prepare answers to the following questions.
(a) Why might the company's top management want the divisions to start doing more business with one another?
(b) Under what conditions should a buying division be forced to buy from an internal supplier? Under what conditions should a selling division be forced to sell to an internal division, rather than to an outside customer?
(c) The Vice President of Purchasing thinks that this problem should be resolved by forcing the Bearing Division to sell to the Wheel Division at its cost of $21. Is this a good solution for the Wheel Division? Is this a good solution for the Bearing Division? Is this a good solution for the company?
(d) Provide at least two other possible solutions to this problem. Discuss the merits and drawbacks of each.

MANAGERIAL ANALYSIS

BYP11-2   Construction on the Stellar Full-Service Car Wash is nearing completion. The owner is Les Vin, a retired accounting professor. The car wash is strategically located on a busy street that separates an affluent suburban community from a middle-class community. It has two state-of-the-art stalls. Each stall can provide anything from a basic two-stage wash and rinse to a five-stage luxurious bath. It is all "touch-less," that is, there are no brushes to potentially damage the car. Outside each stall there is also a 400 horse-power vacuum. Les likes to joke that these vacuums are so strong that they will pull the carpet right out of your car if you aren't careful.

Les has some important decisions to make before he can open the car wash. First, he knows that there is one drive-through car wash only a 10-minute drive away. It is attached to a gas station; it charges $5 for a basic wash, and $4 if you also buy at least 8 gallons of gas. It is a "brush"-type wash with rotating brush heads. There is also a self-serve "stand outside your car and spray until you are soaked" car wash a 15-minute drive away from Les's location. He went over and tried this out. He went through $3 in quarters to get the equivalent of a basic wash. He knows that both of these locations always have long lines, which is one reason why he decided to build a new car wash.

Les is planning to offer three levels of wash service—Basic, Deluxe, and Premium. The Basic is all automated; it requires no direct intervention by employees. The Deluxe is all automated except that at the end an employee will wipe down the car and will put a window treatment on the windshield that reduces glare and allows rainwater to run off more quickly. The Premium level is a "pampered" service. This will include all the services of the Deluxe, plus a special wax after the machine wax, and an employee will vacuum the car, wipe down the entire interior, and wash the inside of the windows. To provide the Premium service, Les will have to hire a couple of "car wash specialists" to do the additional pampering.

Les has pulled together the following estimates, based on data he received from the local Chamber of Commerce and information from a trade association.

	Per Unit	Total
Direct materials per Basic wash	$0.25	
Direct materials per Deluxe wash	0.85	
Direct materials per Premium wash	1.05	
Direct labor per Basic wash	na	
Direct labor per Deluxe wash	0.40	
Direct labor per Premium wash	2.50	
Variable overhead per Basic wash	0.10	
Variable overhead per Deluxe and Premium washes	0.20	
Fixed overhead		$112,500
Variable selling and administrative expenses all washes	0.10	
Fixed selling and administrative expenses		121,500

The total estimated number of washes of any type is 45,000. Les has invested assets of $281,250. He would like a return on investment (ROI) of 28%.

Instructions

Answer each of the following questions.

(a) Identify the issues that Les must consider in deciding on the price of each level of service of his car wash. Also discuss what issues he should consider in deciding on what levels of service to provide.

(b) Les estimates that of the total 45,000 washes, 20,000 will be Basic, 20,000 will be Deluxe, and 5,000 will be Premium. Calculate the selling price, using cost-plus pricing, that Les should use for each type of wash to achieve his desired ROI of 28%.

(c) During the first year, instead of selling 45,000 washes, Les sold 43,000 washes. He was quite accurate in his estimate of first-year sales, but he was way off on the types of washes that he sold. He sold 3,000 Basic, 31,000 Deluxe, and 9,000 Premium. His actual total fixed expenses were as he expected, and his variable cost per unit was as estimated. Calculate Les's actual net income and his actual ROI.

(d) Les is using a traditional approach to allocate overhead. As a consequence, he is allocating overhead equally to all three types of washes, even though the Basic wash is considerably less complicated and uses very little of the technical capabilities of the machinery. What should Les do to determine more accurate costs per unit? How will this affect his pricing and, consequently, his sales?

REAL-WORLD FOCUS

BYP11-3   Merck & Co., Inc. is a global, research-driven pharmaceutical company that discovers, develops, manufactures, and markets a broad range of human and animal health products. The following are excerpts from the financial review section of the company's annual report.

MERCK & CO., INC.
Financial Review Section (partial)

In the United States, the Company has been working with private and governmental employers to slow the increase of health care costs.

Outside of the United States, in difficult environments encumbered by government cost containment actions, the Company has worked with payers to help them allocate scarce resources to optimize health care outcomes, limiting potentially detrimental effects of government actions on sales growth.

Several products face expiration of product patents in the near term.

The Company, along with other pharmaceutical manufacturers, received a notice from the Federal Trade Commission (FTC) that it was conducting an investigation into pricing practices.

Instructions
Answer each of the following questions.
(a) In light of the above excerpts from Merck's annual report, discuss some unique pricing issues faced by companies that operate in the pharmaceutical industry.
(b) What are some reasons why identical drugs sold by the same company often are sold for dramatically different prices in different countries? And how can the same drug used for both humans and animals cost significantly different prices?
(c) Suppose that Merck has just developed a revolutionary new drug for the treatment of arthritis. Discuss the steps it would go through in setting a price. Include a discussion of the information it would need to gather, and the issues it would need to consider.

EXPLORING THE WEB

BYP11-4 Shopping "robots" have become very popular on the Web. These are sites that will find the price of a specified product that is listed by retailers on the Web ("e-tailers"). This allows the customer to search for the lowest possible price.

Address: www.dealtime.com *(or go to www.wiley.com/college/weygandt)*

Steps:

1. Go to the Web page of DealTime.
2. Under the heading "**Electronics**," click on **DVD players**.
3. Choose one of the models under the heading "**Top Picks**."

Instructions
(a) Write down the name of the retailer and the price of the two lowest-priced units and the two highest-priced units.
(b) As a consumer, what concerns might you have in clicking on the "buy" button?
(c) Why might a consumer want to purchase a unit from a retailer that isn't offering the lowest price?
(d) What implications does the existence of these sites have for retailers?

COMMUNICATION ACTIVITY

BYP11-5 Ann Osborne recently graduated from college with a degree in landscape architecture. Her father runs a tree, shrub, and perennial-flower nursery, and her brother has a business delivering topsoil, mulch, and compost. Ann has decided that she would like to start a landscape business. She believes that she can generate a nice profit for herself, while providing an opportunity for both her brother and father's businesses to grow.

One potential problem that Ann is concerned about is that her father and brother tend to charge the highest prices for their products of any local suppliers. She is hoping that she can demonstrate that it would be in her interest, as well as theirs, for them to sell to her at a discounted price.

Instructions

Write a memo to Ann explaining what information she must gather, and what issues she must consider in working out an arrangement with her father and brother. In your memo, discuss how this situation differs from a "standard" transfer pricing problem, but also, how it has many of the characteristics of a transfer pricing problem.

RESEARCH ASSIGNMENT

BYP11-6   The April 17, 2001, issue of the *Wall Street Journal* includes an article by James Bandler and Mark Maremont entitled "How Xerox's Plan to Reduce Taxes While Boosting Earnings Backfired."

Instructions

Read the article and answer the following questions.
(a) What was "Project Global"? What were its goals, and how were they to be accomplished?
(b) What actually happened to Xerox's effective tax rate, and why?
(c) Have any other well-known companies made similar moves? What other motivations might there be to moving operations to a different country, other than just tax reduction?

ETHICS CASE

BYP11-7   Giant Airlines operates out of three main "hub" airports in the United States. Recently Mosquito Airlines began operating a flight from Reno, Nevada, into Giant's Metropolis hub for $190. Giant Airlines offers a price of $425 for the same route. The management of Giant is not happy about Mosquito invading its turf. In fact, Giant has driven off nearly every other competing airline from its hub, so that today 90% of flights into and out of Metropolis are Giant Airline flights. Mosquito is able to offer a lower fare because its pilots are paid less, it uses older planes, and it has lower overhead costs. Mosquito has been in business for only 6 months, and it services only two other cities. It expects the Metropolis route to be its most profitable.

Giant estimates that it would have to charge $210 just to break even on this flight. It estimates that Mosquito can break even at a price of $160. Within one day of Mosquito's entry into the market, Giant dropped its price to $140, whereupon Mosquito matched its price. They both maintained this fare for a period of 9 months, until Mosquito went out of business. As soon as Mosquito went out of business, Giant raised its fare back to $425.

Instructions

Answer each of the following questions.
(a) Who are the stakeholders in this case?
(b) What are some of the reasons why Mosquito's breakeven point is lower than that of Giant?
(c) What are the likely reasons why Giant was able to offer this price for this period of time, while Mosquito couldn't?
(d) What are some of the possible courses of action available to Mosquito in this situation?
(e) Do you think that this kind of pricing activity is ethical? What are the implications for the stakeholders in this situation?

Answers to Self-Study Questions
1. b   2. c   3. b   4. b   5. c   6. a   7. d   8. b   9. b   10. d

Remember to go back to the Navigator box on the chapter-opening page and check off your completed work.

The Statement of Cash Flows

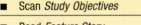

THE NAVIGATOR ✔

- Scan *Study Objectives* ☐
- Read *Feature Story* ☐
- Read *Preview* ☐
- Read text and answer *Before You Go On*
  p. 488 ☐   p. 499 ☐   p. 512 ☐
  p. 521 ☐
- Work *Using the Decision Toolkit* ☐
- Review *Summary of Study Objectives* ☐
- Work *Demonstration Problem* ☐
- Answer *Self-Study Questions* ☐
- Complete *Assignments* ☐

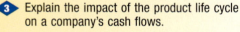

◆ STUDY OBJECTIVES

After studying this chapter, you should be able to:

1 Indicate the primary purpose of the statement of cash flows.

2 Distinguish among operating, investing, and financing activities.

3 Explain the impact of the product life cycle on a company's cash flows.

4 Prepare a statement of cash flows using the indirect method.

5 Prepare a statement of cash flows using the direct method.

6 Use the statement of cash flows to evaluate a company.

THE NAVIGATOR

◆ FEATURE STORY

"CASH IS CASH, AND EVERYTHING ELSE IS ACCOUNTING"

For Gerald Biby, vice president and chief financial officer of **Kilian Community College** in Sioux Falls, South Dakota, the statement of cash flows was the difference between being able to refinance a mortgage and being turned down by six local banks. "We recently wanted to refinance a $125,000 mortgage on a piece of property that we own," he says. "It was the statement of cash flows that finally showed our lender that we had the cash flow to service the debt."

As he explains, the traditional statement of cash flows for a not-for-profit, educational institution shows revenues and all expenditures, even the capital expenditures. According to this format, which the banks focused on initially, Kilian Community College was just breaking even. "In the business world, if we had spent $250,000 on a computer system, then we would have put that on a depreciation schedule. But in the non-profit arena, it's typical that the entire $250,000 is written off as an expense against the general fund." The statement of cash

flows showed the bankers that one of the uses of funds was really the purchase of computer equipment that had several years of life.

The college's statement of cash flows has over 30 classifications including tuition, fees, bookstore revenues, and so on. The school has 250 students, charges $70 a credit hour (12 hours is a full-time schedule), and has five terms each year.

The bankers granted the refinancing when they saw that the college's sources of funds exceeded the loan repayments, including principal and interest, by a ratio of 3-to-1. Not only did the school get the loan, but it did so at a favorable rate. "We were able to cut the mortgage rate by 2 percentage points."

THE NAVIGATOR

As the story about **Kilian Community College** indicates, the balance sheet, income statement, and retained earnings statement do not always show the whole picture of the financial condition of a company or institution. In fact, looking at the three traditional financial statements of some well-known companies, a thoughtful investor might have questions like the following: How did **Eastman Kodak** finance cash dividends of $649 million in a year in which it earned only $17 million? How could **Delta Airlines** purchase new planes costing $900 million in a year in which it reported a net loss of $86 million? How did the companies that spent a fantastic $3.4 trillion on merger deals in a recent year finance those deals? Answers to these and similar questions can be found in this chapter, which presents the **statement of cash flows**.

The content and organization of Chapter 12 are as follows.

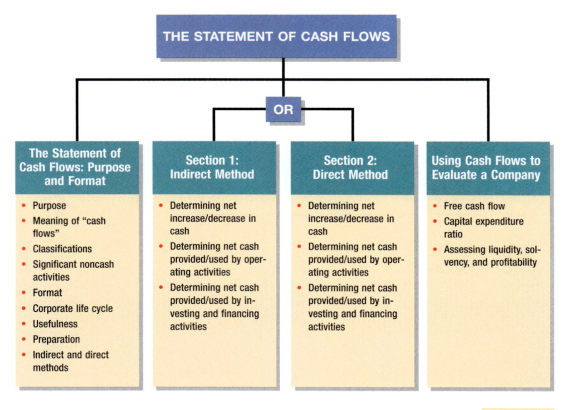

THE STATEMENT OF CASH FLOWS

OR

The Statement of Cash Flows: Purpose and Format	Section 1: Indirect Method	Section 2: Direct Method	Using Cash Flows to Evaluate a Company
• Purpose • Meaning of "cash flows" • Classifications • Significant noncash activities • Format • Corporate life cycle • Usefulness • Preparation • Indirect and direct methods	• Determining net increase/decrease in cash • Determining net cash provided/used by operating activities • Determining net cash provided/used by investing and financing activities	• Determining net increase/decrease in cash • Determining net cash provided/used by operating activities • Determining net cash provided/used by investing and financing activities	• Free cash flow • Capital expenditure ratio • Assessing liquidity, solvency, and profitability

THE NAVIGATOR

*T*HE STATEMENT OF CASH FLOWS: PURPOSE AND FORMAT

The three basic financial statements we've studied so far present only fragmentary information about a company's cash flows (cash receipts and cash payments). For example, **comparative balance sheets** show the increase in property, plant, and equipment during the year. But they do not show how the additions were financed or paid for. The **income statement** shows net income. But it does not indicate the amount of cash generated by operating activities. Similarly, the **retained earnings statement** shows cash dividends declared but not the cash dividends paid during the year. None of these statements presents a detailed summary of the net change in cash as a result of operating, investing, and financing activities during the period.

PURPOSE OF THE STATEMENT OF CASH FLOWS

The primary purpose of the statement of cash flows is to provide information about a company's cash receipts and cash payments during a period. It also provides information about its operating, investing, and financing activities. The statement of cash flows reports the cash receipts, cash payments, and net change in cash resulting from operating, investing, and financing activities during a period. It does so in a format that reconciles the beginning and ending cash balances.

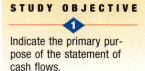

Reporting the causes of changes in cash helps investors, creditors, and other interested parties understand what is happening to a company's most liquid resource—its cash. As the Feature Story about **Kilian Community College** demonstrates, a statement of cash flows helps us understand what is happening. It provides answers to the following simple, but important, questions about an enterprise.

1. Where did the cash come from during the period?
2. What was the cash used for during the period?
3. What was the change in the cash balance during the period?

MEANING OF "CASH FLOWS"

The statement of cash flows is generally prepared using **"cash and cash equivalents"** as its basis. Cash equivalents are short-term, highly liquid investments that are both:

1. Readily convertible to known amounts of cash, and
2. So near their maturity that their market value is relatively insensitive to changes in interest rates.

Generally, only investments with original maturities of three months or less qualify under this definition. Examples of cash equivalents are Treasury bills, commercial paper (short-term corporate notes), and money market funds. All typically are purchased with cash that is in excess of immediate needs.

Note that since cash and cash equivalents are viewed as the same, transfers between cash and cash equivalents are not treated as cash receipts and cash payments. That is, such transfers are not reported in the statement of cash flows. When the term "cash" is used in this chapter, it includes cash equivalents.

CLASSIFICATION OF CASH FLOWS

The statement of cash flows classifies cash receipts and cash payments as operating, investing, and financing activities. Transactions and other events characteristic of each kind of activity are described in the list below.

1. **Operating activities** include the cash effects of transactions that create revenues and expenses. They thus enter into the determination of net income.

2. **Investing activities** include (a) acquiring and disposing of investments and productive long-lived assets, and (b) lending money and collecting the loans.
3. **Financing activities** include (a) obtaining cash from issuing debt and repaying the amounts borrowed, and (b) obtaining cash from stockholders and providing them with a return on their investment.

The category of operating activities is very important. As noted above, it shows the cash provided by company operations. This source of cash is the best measure of a company's ability to generate sufficient cash to continue as a going concern.

Illustration 12-1 below lists typical cash receipts and cash payments within each of the three classifications. **Study the list carefully.** It will prove very useful in solving homework exercises and problems.

Illustration 12-1 Typical receipts and payments classified by business activity and shown in the statement of cash flows

Operating activities

Helpful Hint Operating activities generally relate to changes in current assets and current liabilities. Investing activities generally relate to changes in noncurrent assets. Financing activities relate to changes in long-term liabilities and stockholders' equity accounts.

Investing activities

Financing activities

Types of Cash Inflows and Outflows

Operating activities
Cash inflows:
From sale of goods or services.
From returns on loans (interest received) and on equity securities (dividends received).
Cash outflows:
To suppliers for inventory.
To employees for services.
To government for taxes.
To lenders for interest.
To others for expenses.

Investing activities
Cash inflows:
From sale of property, plant, and equipment.
From sale of debt or equity securities of other entities.
From collection of principal on loans to other entities.
Cash outflows:
To purchase property, plant, and equipment.
To purchase debt or equity securities of other entities.
To make loans to other entities.

Financing activities
Cash inflows:
From sale of equity securities (company's own stock).
From issuance of debt (bonds and notes).
Cash outflows:
To stockholders as dividends.
To redeem long-term debt or reacquire capital stock.

As you can see, some cash flows related to investing or financing activities are classified as operating activities. For example, receipts of investment revenue (interest and dividends) are classified as operating activities. So are payments of interest to lenders. Why are these considered operating activities? **Because these items are reported in the income statement, where results of operations are shown.**

Note the following general guidelines: (1) Operating activities involve income determination (income statement) items. (2) Investing activities involve cash flows resulting from changes in investments and long-term asset items. (3) Financing activities involve cash flows resulting from changes in long-term liability and stockholders' equity items.

SIGNIFICANT NONCASH ACTIVITIES

Not all of a company's significant activities involve cash. Examples of significant noncash activities are:

1. Issuance of common stock to purchase assets.
2. Conversion of bonds into common stock.
3. Issuance of debt to purchase assets.
4. Exchanges of plant assets.

Significant financing and investing activities that do not affect cash are not reported in the body of the statement of cash flows. However, these activities are reported in either a **separate schedule** at the bottom of the statement of cash flows or in a **separate note or supplementary schedule** to the financial statements.

The reporting of these noncash activities in a separate schedule satisfies the **full disclosure principle**. In solving homework assignments you should present significant noncash investing and financing activities in a separate schedule at the bottom of the statement of cash flows. (See lower section of Illustration 12-2, at the top of page 484 for an example.)

Helpful Hint Do not include noncash investing and financing activities in the body of the statement of cash flows. Report this information in a separate schedule.

BUSINESS INSIGHT
Management Perspective

Net income is not the same as net cash provided by operating activities. The differences are illustrated by the following results from recent annual reports for the same fiscal year (all data are in millions of dollars).

Company	Net Income	Net Cash from Operations
Kmart Corporation	$ 518	$1,237
Wal-Mart Stores, Inc.	4,430	7,580
Gap Inc.	1,127	1,478
J.C. Penney Company, Inc.	594	1,058
Sears, Roebuck & Co.	1,048	3,090
The May Department Stores Company	849	1,505

Note the disparity among the companies that engaged in similar types of retail merchandising.

FORMAT OF THE STATEMENT OF CASH FLOWS

The general format of the statement of cash flows is the three activities discussed previously—operating, investing, and financing—plus the significant noncash investing and financing activities. A widely used form of the statement of cash flows is shown in Illustration 12-2.

Illustration 12-2 Format of statement of cash flows

COMPANY NAME
Statement of Cash Flows
Period Covered

Cash flows from operating activities		
(List of individual items)	XX	
Net cash provided (used) by operating activities		XXX
Cash flows from investing activities		
(List of individual inflows and outflows)	XX	
Net cash provided (used) by investing activities		XXX
Cash flows from financing activities		
(List of individual inflows and outflows)	XX	
Net cash provided (used) by financing activities		XXX
Net increase (decrease) in cash		XXX
Cash at beginning of period		XXX
Cash at end of period		XXX
Noncash investing and financing activities		
(List of individual noncash transactions)		XXX

As illustrated, the cash flows from operating activities section always appears first. It is followed by the investing activities and the financing activities sections.

Note also that **the individual inflows and outflows from investing and financing activities are reported separately**. Thus, cash outflow for the purchase of property, plant, and equipment is reported separately from the cash inflow from the sale of property, plant, and equipment. Similarly, the cash inflow from the issuance of debt securities is reported separately from the cash outflow for the retirement of debt. If a company did not report the inflows and outflows separately, it would obscure the investing and financing activities of the enterprise. This would make it more difficult to assess future cash flows.

The reported operating, investing, and financing activities result in either net cash **provided or used** by each activity. The amounts of net cash provided or used by each activity then are totaled. The result is the net increase (decrease) in cash for the period. This amount is then added to or subtracted from the beginning-of-period cash balance. This gives the end-of-period cash balance. Finally, any significant noncash investing and financing activities are reported in a separate schedule, usually at the bottom of the statement.

THE CORPORATE LIFE CYCLE

STUDY OBJECTIVE

3

Explain the impact of the product life cycle on a company's cash flows.

All products go through a series of phases called the **product life cycle**. The phases (in order of their occurrence) are often referred to as the **introductory phase, growth phase, maturity phase,** and **decline phase**. The introductory phase occurs when the company is purchasing fixed assets and beginning to produce and sell. In the growth phase, the company is striving to expand its production and sales. In the maturity phase, sales and production level off. And during the decline phase, sales of the product fall due to a weakening in consumer demand.

If a company had only one product and that product was, for example, nearing the end of its salable life, we would say that the company was in the decline phase. Companies generally have more than one product, however, and not all of a company's products are in the same phase of the product life cycle at the same time. We can still characterize a company as being in one of the four phases because the majority of its products are in a particular phase.

Illustration 12-3 shows that the product life cycle affects a company's cash flows. In the **introductory phase**, we expect that the company will be spending considerable amounts to purchase productive assets, but it will not be generating much (if any) cash from operations. To support its asset purchases it may have to issue stock or debt. Thus, we expect cash from operations to be negative, cash from investing to be negative, and cash from financing to be positive.

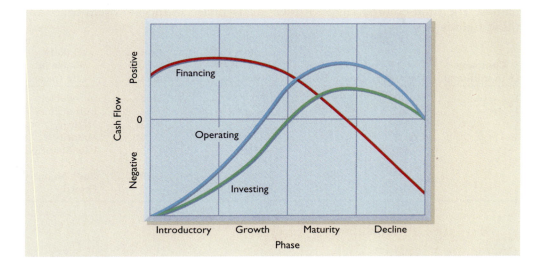

Illustration 12-3 Impact of product life cycle on cash flows

During the **growth phase**, we expect to see the company start to generate small amounts of cash from operations. Cash from operations continues to be less than net income during this phase, though, because inventory must be purchased for future projected sales. Since those sales are projected to be increasing, the size of inventory purchases must increase. Thus, less inventory will be expensed on an accrual basis than purchased on a cash basis in the growth phase. Also, collections on accounts receivable will lag behind sales. Because sales are growing, accrual sales during the period will exceed cash collections during that period. Cash needed for asset acquisitions will continue to exceed cash provided by operations, requiring that the company make up the deficiency by issuing new stock or debt. Thus, the company continues to show negative cash from investing and positive cash from financing in the growth phase.

During the **maturity phase**, cash from operations and net income are approximately the same. Cash generated from operations exceeds investing needs. Thus, in the maturity phase the company can actually start to retire debt or buy back stock.

Finally, during the **decline phase**, cash from operations decreases. Cash from investing might actually become positive as the company sells off excess assets. Cash from financing may be negative as the company buys back stock and retires debt.

Consider **Microsoft**: During its early years it had significant product development costs with little revenue. Microsoft was lucky in that its agreement with **IBM** to provide the operating system for IBM PCs gave it an early steady source of cash to support growth. One way it conserved cash was to pay employees with stock options rather than cash. Today Microsoft could best be characterized as being between the growth and maturity phases. It continues to spend considerable amounts on research and development and investment in new assets. For the last four years, however, its cash from operations has exceeded its net income. Cash from operations also exceeds cash used for investing, and common stock repurchased exceeds common stock issued. For Microsoft, as for any large company, the challenge is to maintain its growth. In the software industry, where products become obsolete very quickly, the challenge is particularly great.

Management Perspective

Listed here are the net income, and cash from operations, investing, and financing during a recent year for some well-known companies. The final column suggests their likely phase in the life cycle based on these figures.

Company ($ in millions)	Net Income	Cash Provided by Operations	Cash Provided (Used) by Investing	Cash Provided (Used) by Financing	Likely Phase in Life Cycle
Netscape	$ (3)	$ 15	$ (140)	$ 168	Introductory
Iomega	8.5	(27)	(43)	54	Introductory
Caterpillar	1,136	2,190	(1,749)	(208)	Maturity
Boeing	2,128	5,942	(7,628)	(658)	Maturity
Kellogg	490	1,041	(309)	(759)	Late Maturity
Southwest Airlines	183	456	(729)	415	Early Maturity
Starbucks	42	137	(211)	180	Growth

USEFULNESS OF THE STATEMENT OF CASH FLOWS

Many investors believe that "Cash is cash and everything else is accounting." That is, they feel that cash flow is less susceptible to management manipulation than traditional accounting measures such as net income. Though we would discourage reliance on cash flows to the exclusion of accrual accounting, comparing cash from operations to net income can reveal important information about the "quality" of reported net income. Such a comparison can reveal the extent to which net income provides a good measure of actual performance.

The information in a statement of cash flows should help investors, creditors, and others assess the following aspects of a company's financial position.

1. **The company's ability to generate future cash flows.** By examining relationships between items in the statement of cash flows, investors and others can make predictions of the amounts, timing, and uncertainty of future cash flows better than they can from accrual basis data.

2. **The company's ability to pay dividends and meet obligations.** If a company does not have adequate cash, employees cannot be paid, debts settled, or dividends paid. Employees, creditors, and stockholders should be particularly interested in this statement, because it alone shows the flows of cash in a business.

3. **The reasons for the difference between net income and net cash provided (used) by operating activities.** Net income provides information on the success or failure of a company. However, some are critical of accrual basis net income because it requires many estimates. As a result, the reliability of the number is often challenged. Such is not the case with cash. Many readers of the statement of cash flows want to know the reasons for the difference between net income and net cash provided by operating activities. Then they can assess for themselves the reliability of the income number.

4. **The cash investing and financing transactions during the period.** By examining a company's investing and financing transactions, a financial statement reader can better understand why assets and liabilities changed during the period.

In summary, the information in the statement of cash flows is useful in answering the following questions.

Helpful Hint Income from operations and cash flow from operating activities are different. Income from operations is based on accrual accounting; cash flow from operating activities is prepared on a cash basis.

How did cash increase when there was a net loss for the period?

How were the proceeds of the bond issue used?

How was the expansion in the plant and equipment financed?

Why were dividends not increased?

How was the retirement of debt accomplished?

How much money was borrowed during the year?

Is cash flow greater or less than net income?

PREPARING THE STATEMENT OF CASH FLOWS

The statement of cash flows is prepared differently from the three other basic financial statements. First, it is not prepared from an adjusted trial balance. The statement requires detailed information concerning the changes in account balances that occurred between two periods of time. An adjusted trial balance will not provide the necessary data. Second, the statement of cash flows deals with cash receipts and payments. As a result, **the accrual concept is not used in the preparation of a statement of cash flows**.

The information to prepare this statement usually comes from three sources:

- **Comparative balance sheets.** Information in the comparative balance sheets indicates the amount of the changes in assets, liabilities, and stockholders' equities from the beginning to the end of the period.
- **Current income statement.** Information in this statement helps determine the amount of cash provided or used by operations during the period.
- **Additional information.** Such information includes transaction data that are needed to determine how cash was provided or used during the period.

Preparing the statement of cash flows from these data sources involves three major steps, explained in Illustration 12-4.

Illustration 12-4 Three major steps in preparing the statement of cash flows

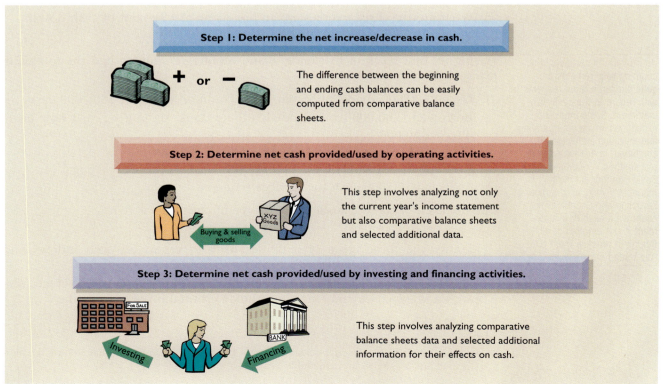

Step 1: Determine the net increase/decrease in cash.

The difference between the beginning and ending cash balances can be easily computed from comparative balance sheets.

Step 2: Determine net cash provided/used by operating activities.

This step involves analyzing not only the current year's income statement but also comparative balance sheets and selected additional data.

Step 3: Determine net cash provided/used by investing and financing activities.

This step involves analyzing comparative balance sheets data and selected additional information for their effects on cash.

INDIRECT AND DIRECT METHODS

In order to perform step 2, **the operating activities section must be converted from an accrual basis to a cash basis**. This conversion may be done by either of two methods: (1) the indirect method or (2) the direct method. **Both methods arrive at the same total amount** for "Net cash provided by operating activities." They differ in disclosing the items that comprise the total amount.

The indirect method is used by almost 99% of companies in practice, as shown in the nearby chart.[1] Companies favor the indirect method for two reasons: (1) It is easier to prepare, and (2) it focuses on the differences between net income and net cash flow from operating activities.

A minority of companies favor the direct method. This method shows operating cash receipts and payments, and so it is more consistent with the objective of a statement of cash flows. The FASB has expressed a preference for the direct method, but allows the use of either method. When the direct method is used, the net cash flow from operating activities as computed using the indirect method must also be reported in a separate schedule.

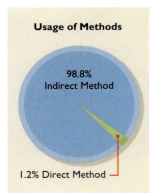

Usage of Methods

98.8% Indirect Method

1.2% Direct Method

BEFORE YOU GO ON . . .

◆ **Review It**

1. What is the primary purpose of a statement of cash flows?
2. What are the major classifications of cash flows on the statement of cash flows?
3. What are the phases of the product life cycle, and how do they affect the statement of cash flows?
4. Why is the statement of cash flows useful? What key information does it convey?
5. What are the three major steps in preparing a statement of cash flows?

◆ **Do It**

During its first week of existence, Plano Molding Company had the following transactions.

1. Issued 100,000 shares of $5 par value common stock for $800,000 cash.
2. Borrowed $200,000 from Sandwich State Bank, signing a 5-year note bearing 8% interest.
3. Purchased two semi-trailer trucks for $170,000 cash.
4. Paid employees $12,000 for salaries and wages.
5. Collected $20,000 cash for services rendered.

Classify each of these transactions by type of cash flow activity.

Action Plan

• Identify the three types of activities used to report all cash inflows and outflows.
• Report as operating activities the cash effects of transactions that create revenues and expenses and enter into the determination of net income.

Helpful Hint International accounting requirements are quite similar in most respects with regard to the cash flow statement. Some interesting exceptions: In Japan, operating and investing activities are combined. In Australia, the direct method is mandatory. In Spain, the indirect method is mandatory. Also, in a number of European and Scandinavian countries a cash flow statement is not required at all, although in practice most publicly traded firms provide one.

---

[1] *Accounting Trends and Techniques—2000* survey of 600 companies indicated that 593 use the indirect method and 7 use the direct method.

- Report as investing activities transactions that (a) acquire and dispose of investments and productive long-lived assets, and (b) lend money and collect loans.
- Report as financing activities transactions that (a) obtain cash from issuing debt and repay the amounts borrowed, and (b) obtain cash from stockholders and pay them dividends.

Solution
1. Financing activity.
2. Financing activity.
3. Investing activity.
4. Operating activity.
5. Operating activity.

Related exercise material: BE12-3, BE12-5, E12-1, and E12-2.

On the following pages, in two separate sections, we describe the use of the two methods. Section 1 illustrates the indirect method. Section 2 illustrates the direct method. These sections are independent of each other. *Only one or the other* needs to be covered in order to understand and prepare the statement of cash flows. When you have finished the section assigned by your instructor, turn to the concluding topic on page 515—"Using Cash Flows to Evaluate a Company."

SECTION 1

STATEMENT OF CASH FLOWS— INDIRECT METHOD

To explain and illustrate the indirect method, we will use the transactions of the Computer Services Company for two years, 2002 and 2003, to prepare annual statements of cash flows. We will show basic transactions in the first year, with additional transactions added in the second year.

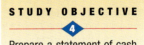

STUDY OBJECTIVE

4

Prepare a statement of cash flows using the indirect method.

*F*IRST YEAR OF OPERATIONS—2002

Computer Services Company started on January 1, 2002. At that time it issued 50,000 shares of $1 par value common stock for $50,000 cash. The company rented its office space and furniture and performed consulting services throughout the first year. The comparative balance sheets at the beginning and end of 2002, showing changes in each account, appear in Illustration 12-5. The income statement and additional information for Computer Services Company are shown in Illustration 12-6.

COMPUTER SERVICES COMPANY
Comparative Balance Sheets

Assets	Dec. 31, 2002	Jan. 1, 2002	Change Increase/Decrease
Cash	$34,000	$-0-	$34,000 Increase
Accounts receivable	30,000	-0-	30,000 Increase
Equipment	10,000	-0-	10,000 Increase
Total	$74,000	$-0-	
Liabilities and Stockholders' Equity			
Accounts payable	$ 4,000	$-0-	$ 4,000 Increase
Common stock	50,000	-0-	50,000 Increase
Retained earnings	20,000	-0-	20,000 Increase
Total	$74,000	$-0-	

COMPUTER SERVICES COMPANY
Income Statement
For the Year Ended December 31, 2002

Revenues	$85,000
Operating expenses	40,000
Income before income taxes	45,000
Income tax expense	10,000
Net income	$35,000

Additional information:
1. A dividend of $15,000 was declared and paid during the year.
2. The equipment was purchased at the end of 2002. No depreciation was taken in 2002.

STEP 1: DETERMINE THE NET INCREASE/ DECREASE IN CASH

To prepare a statement of cash flows, the first step is to **determine the net increase or decrease in cash**. This is a simple computation. For example, Computer Services Company had no cash on hand at the beginning of 2002. It had $34,000 on hand at the end of 2002. Thus, the change in cash for 2002 was an increase of $34,000.

STEP 2: DETERMINE NET CASH PROVIDED/USED BY OPERATING ACTIVITIES

To determine net cash provided by operating activities under the indirect method, **net income is adjusted for items that did not affect cash**. A useful starting point is to understand **why** net income must be converted. Under generally accepted accounting principles, most companies use the accrual basis of accounting. As you have learned, this basis requires that revenue be recorded when earned and that expenses be recorded when incurred. Earned revenues may include credit sales that have not been collected in cash. Expenses incurred may not have been paid in cash. Thus, under the accrual basis of accounting, net income is not the same as net cash provided by operating activities. Therefore, under the indirect method, net income must be adjusted to convert certain items to the cash basis.

The **indirect method** (or reconciliation method) starts with net income and converts it to net cash provided by operating activities. In other words, **the indirect method adjusts net income for items that affected reported net income but did not affect cash**. Illustration 12-7 shows this adjustment. That is, noncash charges in the income statement are added back to net income. Likewise, noncash credits are deducted. The result is net cash provided by operating activities.

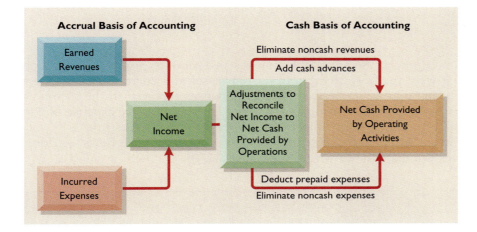

Illustration 12-7   Net income versus net cash provided by operating activities

A useful starting point in identifying the adjustments to net income is the current asset and current liability accounts other than cash. Those accounts—receivables, payables, prepayments, and inventories—should be analyzed for their effects on cash.

Increase in Accounts Receivable

When accounts receivable increase during the year, revenues on an accrual basis are higher than revenues on a cash basis. In other words, operations of the period led to revenues, **but not all of these revenues resulted in an increase in cash**. Some of the revenues resulted in an increase in accounts receivable.

Illustration 12-8 shows that Computer Services Company had $85,000 in revenues, but it collected only $55,000 in cash. To convert net income to net cash provided by operating activities, the increase of $30,000 in accounts receivable must be deducted from net income.

Illustration 12-8   Analysis of accounts receivable

Accounts Receivable			
1/1/02 Balance	–0–	**Receipts from customers**	**55,000**
Revenues	**85,000**		
12/31/02 Balance	30,000		

Increase in Accounts Payable

In the first year, operating expenses incurred on account were credited to Accounts Payable. When accounts payable increase during the year, operating expenses on an accrual basis are higher than they are on a cash basis. For

Computer Services, operating expenses reported in the income statement were $40,000. But, since Accounts Payable increased $4,000, only $36,000 ($40,000 − $4,000) of the expenses were paid in cash. To adjust net income to net cash provided by operating activities, the increase of $4,000 in accounts payable must be added to net income. A T-account analysis indicates that payments to creditors are less than operating expenses.

Illustration 12-9   Analysis of accounts payable

Accounts Payable			
Payments to creditors	**36,000**	1/1/02 Balance	–0–
		Operating expenses	**40,000**
		12/31/02 Balance	4,000

For Computer Services, the changes in accounts receivable and accounts payable were the only changes in current asset and current liability accounts. This means that any other revenues or expenses reported in the income statement were received or paid in cash. Thus, the income tax expense of $10,000 was paid in cash, and no adjustment of net income is necessary.

The operating activities section of the statement of cash flows for Computer Services Company is shown in Illustration 12-10.

Illustration 12-10   Presentation of net cash provided by operating activities, 2002—indirect method

COMPUTER SERVICES COMPANY Statement of Cash Flows—Indirect Method (partial) For the Year Ended December 31, 2002		
Cash flows from operating activities		
Net income		$35,000
Adjustments to reconcile net income to net cash provided by operating activities:		
Increase in accounts receivable	$(30,000)	
Increase in accounts payable	4,000	(26,000)
Net cash provided by operating activities		**$ 9,000**

STEP 3: DETERMINE NET CASH PROVIDED/USED BY INVESTING AND FINANCING ACTIVITIES

The third and final step in preparing the statement of cash flows begins with a study of the balance sheet. We look at it to determine changes in noncurrent accounts. The change in each noncurrent account is then analyzed to determine the effect, if any, the change had on cash.

In Computer Services Company, the three noncurrent accounts are Equipment, Common Stock, and Retained Earnings. All three have increased during the year. What caused these increases? No transaction data are given in the balance sheet for the increases in Equipment of $10,000 and Common Stock of $50,000. In solving your homework, you should assume that **any unexplained differences in noncurrent accounts involve cash**. Thus, the increase in Equipment is assumed to be a purchase of equipment for $10,000 cash. This purchase of equipment is reported as a cash outflow in the investing activities section of the statement of cash flows. The increase in Common Stock is assumed to result from the issuance of common stock for $50,000 cash. The issuance of common stock is reported as an inflow of cash in the financing activities section.

What caused the net increase of $20,000 in the Retained Earnings account? First, net income increased retained earnings by $35,000. Second, the additional information provided below the income statement in Illustration 12-6 indicates that a cash dividend of $15,000 was declared and paid.

This analysis can also be made directly from the Retained Earnings account in the ledger of Computer Services Company, as shown in Illustration 12-11.

Illustration 12-11   Analysis of retained earnings

Retained Earnings			
12/31/02 Cash dividend	**15,000**	1/1/02 Balance	–0–
		12/31/02 Net income	**35,000**
		12/31/02 Balance	20,000

The $20,000 increase in Retained Earnings in 2002 is a **net** change. When a net change in a noncurrent balance sheet account has occurred during the year, it generally is necessary to report the individual items that cause the net change. Therefore, the $35,000 increase due to net income is reported in the operating activities section. The cash dividend paid is reported in the financing activities section.

STATEMENT OF CASH FLOWS—2002

We now can prepare the statement of cash flows. The statement starts with the operating activities, followed by the investing activities, and then the financing activities. The 2002 statement of cash flows for Computer Services is shown in Illustration 12-12.

Computer Services' statement of cash flows for 2002 shows the following: Operating activities **provided** $9,000 cash. Investing activities **used** $10,000 cash. Financing activities **provided** $35,000 cash. The increase in cash of $34,000 reported in the statement of cash flows agrees with the increase of $34,000 shown as the change in the cash account in the comparative balance sheets.

Illustration 12-12   Statement of cash flows, 2002—indirect method

COMPUTER SERVICES COMPANY Statement of Cash Flows—Indirect Method For the Year Ended December 31, 2002		
Cash flows from operating activities		
Net income		$35,000
Adjustments to reconcile net income to net cash provided by operating activities:		
Increase in accounts receivable	$(30,000)	
Increase in accounts payable	4,000	(26,000)
Net cash provided by operating activities		9,000
Cash flows from investing activities		
Purchase of equipment	(10,000)	
Net cash used by investing activities		(10,000)
Cash flows from financing activities		
Issuance of common stock	50,000	
Payment of cash dividends	(15,000)	
Net cash provided by financing activities		35,000
Net increase in cash		34,000
Cash at beginning of period		–0–
Cash at end of period		$34,000

SECOND YEAR OF OPERATIONS—2003

Illustrations 12-13 and 12-14 present information related to the second year of operations for Computer Services Company.

Illustration 12-13 Comparative balance sheets, 2003, with increases and decreases

COMPUTER SERVICES COMPANY
Comparative Balance Sheets
December 31

Assets	2003	2002	Change Increase/Decrease
Cash	$ 56,000	$34,000	$ 22,000 Increase
Accounts receivable	20,000	30,000	10,000 Decrease
Prepaid expenses	4,000	–0–	4,000 Increase
Land	130,000	–0–	130,000 Increase
Building	160,000	–0–	160,000 Increase
Accumulated depreciation— building	(11,000)	–0–	11,000 Increase
Equipment	27,000	10,000	17,000 Increase
Accumulated depreciation— equipment	(3,000)	–0–	3,000 Increase
Total	$383,000	$74,000	
Liabilities and Stockholders' Equity			
Accounts payable	$ 59,000	$ 4,000	$ 55,000 Increase
Bonds payable	130,000	–0–	130,000 Increase
Common stock	50,000	50,000	–0–
Retained earnings	144,000	20,000	124,000 Increase
Total	$383,000	$74,000	

Illustration 12-14
Income statement and additional information, 2003

COMPUTER SERVICES COMPANY
Income Statement
For the Year Ended December 31, 2003

Revenues		$507,000
Operating expenses (excluding depreciation)	$261,000	
Depreciation expense	15,000	
Loss on sale of equipment	3,000	279,000
Income from operations		228,000
Income tax expense		89,000
Net income		$139,000

Additional information:
1. In 2003, the company declared and paid a $15,000 cash dividend.
2. The company obtained land through the issuance of $130,000 of long-term bonds.
3. A building costing $160,000 was purchased for cash. Equipment costing $25,000 was also purchased for cash.
4. During 2003, the company sold equipment with a book value of $7,000 (cost $8,000, less accumulated depreciation $1,000) for $4,000 cash.

STEP 1: DETERMINE THE NET INCREASE/
DECREASE IN CASH

To prepare a statement of cash flows from this information, the first step is to **determine the net increase or decrease in cash**. As indicated from the information presented, cash increased $22,000 ($56,000 − $34,000).

STEP 2: DETERMINE NET CASH PROVIDED/USED
BY OPERATING ACTIVITIES

As in step 2 in 2002, net income on an accrual basis must be adjusted to arrive at net cash provided/used by operating activities. Explanations for the adjustments to net income for Computer Services in 2003 follow.

Decrease in Accounts Receivable

Accounts receivable decreases during the period because cash receipts are higher than revenues reported on the accrual basis. To adjust net income to net cash provided by operating activities, the decrease of $10,000 in accounts receivable must be added to net income.

Increase in Prepaid Expenses

Prepaid expenses increase during a period because cash paid for expenses is higher than expenses reported on the accrual basis. Cash payments have been made in the current period, but expenses (as charges to the income statement) have been deferred to future periods. To adjust net income to net cash provided by operating activities, the $4,000 increase in prepaid expenses must be deducted from net income. An increase in prepaid expenses results in a decrease in cash during the period.

Increase in Accounts Payable

Like the increase in 2002, the 2003 increase of $55,000 in accounts payable must be added to net income to convert to net cash provided by operating activities.

Depreciation Expense

During 2003, the company reported depreciation expense of $15,000. Of this amount, $11,000 related to the building and $4,000 to the equipment. These two amounts were determined by analyzing the accumulated depreciation accounts in the balance sheets.

Increase in Accumulated Depreciation—Building.   The Accumulated Depreciation—Building account increased $11,000. This change represents the depreciation expense on the building for the year. **Depreciation expense is a noncash charge. So it is added back to net income** in order to arrive at net cash provided by operating activities.

Increase in Accumulated Depreciation—Equipment.   The Accumulated Depreciation—Equipment account increased $3,000. But this change does not represent depreciation expense for the year. The additional information at the bottom of the income statement indicates why not: This account was decreased (debited) $1,000 as a result of the sale of some equipment. Thus depreciation expense for 2003 was $4,000 ($3,000 + $1,000). That amount is added to net income to determine net cash provided by operating activities. The T-account below provides information about the changes that occurred in this account in 2003.

Helpful Hint Decrease in accounts receivable indicates that cash collections were greater than sales.
Increase in accounts receivable indicates that sales were greater than cash collections.
Increase in prepaid expenses indicates that the amount paid for the prepayments exceeded the amount that was recorded as an expense.
Decrease in prepaid expenses indicates that the amount recorded as an expense exceeded the amount of cash paid for the prepayments.
Increase in accounts payable indicates that expenses incurred exceed the cash paid for expenses that period.

Illustration 12-15 Analysis of accumulated depreciation—equipment

Accumulated Depreciation—Equipment			
Accumulated depreciation on equipment sold	1,000	1/1/03 Balance	–0–
		Depreciation expense	**4,000**
		12/31/03 Balance	3,000

Depreciation expense on the building ($11,000) plus depreciation expense on the equipment ($4,000) equals the depreciation expense of $15,000 reported in the income statement.

Other charges to expense that do not require the use of cash, such as the amortization of intangible assets and depletion expense, are treated in the same way as depreciation. Depreciation and similar noncash charges are frequently listed in the statement of cash flows as the first adjustments to net income.

Loss on Sale of Equipment

In the income statement, Computer Services Company reported a $3,000 loss on the sale of equipment (book value $7,000, less cash proceeds $4,000). The loss reduced net income but **did not reduce cash**. So the loss is **added to net income** in determining net cash provided by operating activities.[2]

As a result of the previous adjustments, net cash provided by operating activities is $218,000, as computed in Illustration 12-16.

Illustration 12-16 Presentation of net cash provided by operating activities, 2003—indirect method

COMPUTER SERVICES COMPANY		
Statement of Cash Flows—Indirect Method (partial)		
For the Year Ended December 31, 2003		
Cash flows from operating activities		
Net income		$139,000
Adjustments to reconcile net income to net cash provided by operating activities:		
Depreciation expense	$15,000	
Loss on sale of equipment	3,000	
Decrease in accounts receivable	10,000	
Increase in prepaid expenses	(4,000)	
Increase in accounts payable	55,000	79,000
Net cash provided by operating activities		$218,000

STEP 3: DETERMINE NET CASH PROVIDED/USED BY INVESTING AND FINANCING ACTIVITIES

The next step involves analyzing the remaining changes in balance sheet accounts to determine net cash provided (used) by investing and financing activities.

---

[2]If a gain on sale occurs, a different situation results. To allow a gain to flow through to net cash provided by operating activities would be double-counting the gain—once in net income and again in the investing activities section as part of the cash proceeds from sale. As a result, a gain is deducted from net income in reporting net cash provided by operating activities.

Increase in Land

As indicated from the change in the Land account and the additional information, land of $130,000 was purchased through the issuance of long-term bonds. The issuance of bonds payable for land has no effect on cash. But it is a significant noncash investing and financing activity that requires disclosure in a separate schedule.

Increase in Building

As the additional data indicate, an office building was acquired for $160,000 cash. This is a cash outflow reported in the investing section.

Increase in Equipment

The Equipment account increased $17,000. The additional information explains that this was a net increase that resulted from two transactions: (1) a purchase of equipment of $25,000 and (2) the sale for $4,000 of equipment costing $8,000. These transactions are classified as investing activities. Each transaction should be reported separately. Thus the purchase of equipment should be reported as an outflow of cash for $25,000. The sale should be reported as an inflow of cash for $4,000. The T-account below shows the reasons for the change in this account during the year.

Illustration 12-17
Analysis of equipment

Equipment			
1/1/03 Balance	10,000	Cost of equipment sold	8,000
Purchase of equipment	**25,000**		
12/31/03 Balance	27,000		

The following entry shows the details of the equipment sale transaction.

Cash	4,000	
Accumulated Depreciation	1,000	
Loss on Sale of Equipment	3,000	
Equipment		8,000

Increase in Bonds Payable

The Bonds Payable account increased $130,000. As indicated in the additional information, land was acquired from the issuance of these bonds. This noncash transaction is reported in a separate schedule at the bottom of the statement.

Increase in Retained Earnings

Retained earnings increased $124,000 during the year. This increase can be explained by two factors: (1) Net income of $139,000 increased retained earnings. (2) Dividends of $15,000 decreased retained earnings. Net income is adjusted to net cash provided by operating activities in the operating activities section. Payment of the dividends is a **cash outflow that is reported as a financing activity**.

Helpful Hint When stocks or bonds are issued for cash, the actual proceeds will appear in the statement of cash flows as a financing inflow (rather than the par value of the stocks or face value of bonds).

Helpful Hint It is the **payment** of dividends, not the declaration, that appears in the cash flow statement.

STATEMENT OF CASH FLOWS—2003

Combining the previous items, we obtain a statement of cash flows for 2003 for Computer Services Company as presented in Illustration 12-18.

Illustration 12-18 Statement of cash flows, 2003—indirect method

COMPUTER SERVICES COMPANY
Statement of Cash Flows—Indirect Method
For the Year Ended December 31, 2003

Cash flows from operating activities		
Net income		$139,000
Adjustments to reconcile net income to net cash		
provided by operating activities:		
Depreciation expense	$ 15,000	
Loss on sale of equipment	3,000	
Decrease in accounts receivable	10,000	
Increase in prepaid expenses	(4,000)	
Increase in accounts payable	55,000	79,000
Net cash provided by operating activities		218,000
Cash flows from investing activities		
Purchase of building	(160,000)	
Purchase of equipment	(25,000)	
Sale of equipment	4,000	
Net cash used by investing activities		(181,000)
Cash flows from financing activities		
Payment of cash dividends	(15,000)	
Net cash used by financing activities		(15,000)
Net increase in cash		22,000
Cash at beginning of period		34,000
Cash at end of period		$ 56,000
Noncash investing and financing activities		
Issuance of bonds payable to purchase land		$130,000

Helpful Hint Note that in the investing and financing activities sections, positive numbers indicate cash inflows (receipts), and negative numbers indicate cash outflows (payments).

SUMMARY OF CONVERSION TO NET CASH PROVIDED BY OPERATING ACTIVITIES— INDIRECT METHOD

As shown in the previous illustrations, the statement of cash flows prepared by the indirect method starts with net income. It then adds (or deducts) items not affecting cash, to arrive at net cash provided by operating activities. The additions and deductions consist of (1) changes in specific current assets and current liabilities and (2) noncash charges reported in the income statement. A summary of the adjustments for current assets and current liabilities is provided in Illustration 12-19.

Illustration 12-19 Adjustments for current assets and current liabilities

Current Assets and Current Liabilities	Adjustments to Convert Net Income to Net Cash Provided by Operating Activities	
	Add to Net Income a(n):	Deduct from Net Income a(n):
Accounts receivable	Decrease	Increase
Inventory	Decrease	Increase
Prepaid expenses	Decrease	Increase
Accounts payable	Increase	Decrease
Accrued expenses payable	Increase	Decrease

Helpful Hint
1. An increase in a current asset is deducted from net income.
2. A decrease in a current asset is added to net income.
3. An increase in a current liability is added to net income.
4. A decrease in a current liability is deducted from net income.

Adjustments for the noncash charges reported in the income statement are made as shown in Illustration 12-20.

Illustration 12-20 Adjustments for noncash charges

Noncash Charges	Adjustments to Convert Net Income to Net Cash Provided by Operating Activities
Depreciation expense	Add
Patent amortization expense	Add
Depletion expense	Add
Loss on sale of asset	Add

BEFORE YOU GO ON . . .

◆ Review It

1. What is the format of the operating activities section of the statement of cash flows using the indirect method?
2. Where is depreciation expense shown on a statement of cash flows using the indirect method?
3. Where are significant noncash investing and financing activities shown in a statement of cash flows? Give some examples.

◆ Do It

Presented below is information related to Reynolds Company. Use it to prepare a statement of cash flows using the indirect method.

REYNOLDS COMPANY
Comparative Balance Sheets
December 31

Assets	2003	2002	Change Increase/Decrease
Cash	$ 54,000	$ 37,000	$ 17,000 Increase
Accounts receivable	68,000	26,000	42,000 Increase
Inventories	54,000	–0–	54,000 Increase
Prepaid expenses	4,000	6,000	2,000 Decrease
Land	45,000	70,000	25,000 Decrease
Buildings	200,000	200,000	–0–
Accumulated depreciation—buildings	(21,000)	(11,000)	10,000 Increase
Equipment	193,000	68,000	125,000 Increase
Accumulated depreciation—equipment	(28,000)	(10,000)	18,000 Increase
Total	$569,000	$386,000	
Liabilities and Stockholders' Equity			
Accounts payable	$ 23,000	$ 40,000	$ 17,000 Decrease
Accrued expenses payable	10,000	–0–	10,000 Increase
Bonds payable	110,000	150,000	40,000 Decrease
Common stock ($1 par)	220,000	60,000	160,000 Increase
Retained earnings	206,000	136,000	70,000 Increase
Total	$569,000	$386,000	

REYNOLDS COMPANY
Income Statement
For the Year Ended December 31, 2003

Revenues		$890,000
Cost of goods sold	$465,000	
Operating expenses	221,000	
Interest expense	12,000	
Loss on sale of equipment	2,000	700,000
Income from operations		190,000
Income tax expense		65,000
Net income		$125,000

Additional information:
1. Operating expenses include depreciation expense of $33,000 and charges from pre-paid expenses of $2,000.
2. Land was sold at its book value for cash.
3. Cash dividends of $55,000 were declared and paid in 2003.
4. Interest expense of $12,000 was paid in cash.
5. Equipment with a cost of $166,000 was purchased for cash. Equipment with a cost of $41,000 and a book value of $36,000 was sold for $34,000 cash.
6. Bonds of $10,000 were redeemed at their book value for cash. Bonds of $30,000 were converted into common stock.
7. Common stock ($1 par) of $130,000 was issued for cash.
8. Accounts payable pertain to merchandise suppliers.

Action Plan
- Determine the net increase/decrease in cash.
- Determine net cash provided/used by operating activities by adjusting net income for items that did not affect cash.
- Determine net cash provided/used by investing activities.
- Determine net cash provided/used by financing activities.

Solution

REYNOLDS COMPANY Statement of Cash Flows—Indirect Method For the Year Ended December 31, 2003		
Cash flows from operating activities		
Net income		$125,000
Adjustments to reconcile net income to net cash		
provided by operating activities:		
Depreciation expense	$ 33,000	
Increase in accounts receivable	(42,000)	
Increase in inventories	(54,000)	
Decrease in prepaid expenses	2,000	
Decrease in accounts payable	(17,000)	
Increase in accrued expenses payable	10,000	
Loss on sale of equipment	2,000	(66,000)
Net cash provided by operating activities		59,000
Cash flows from investing activities		
Sale of land	25,000	
Sale of equipment	34,000	
Purchase of equipment	(166,000)	
Net cash used by investing activities		(107,000)
Cash flows from financing activities		
Redemption of bonds	(10,000)	
Sale of common stock	130,000	
Payment of dividends	(55,000)	
Net cash provided by financing activities		65,000
Net increase in cash		17,000
Cash at beginning of period		37,000
Cash at end of period		$ 54,000
Noncash investing and financing activities		
Conversion of bonds into common stock		$ 30,000

Helpful Hint
1. Determine net cash provided/used by operating activities, recognizing that operating activities generally relate to changes in current assets and current liabilities.
2. Determine net cash provided/used by investing activities, recognizing that investing activities generally relate to changes in noncurrent assets.
3. Determine net cash provided/used by financing activities, recognizing that financing activities generally relate to changes in long-term liabilities and stockholders' equity accounts.

Related exercise material: BE12-1, BE12-2, BE12-4, E12-4, E12-5, and E12-6.

Note: This concludes Section 1 on preparation of the statement of cash flows using the indirect method. Unless your instructor assigns Section 2, you should turn to the concluding section of the chapter, "Using Cash Flows to Evaluate a Company," on page 515.

STATEMENT OF CASH FLOWS— DIRECT METHOD

STUDY OBJECTIVE

5

Prepare a statement of cash flows using the direct method.

To explain and illustrate the direct method, we will use the transactions of Juarez Company for two years, 2002 and 2003, to prepare annual statements of cash flows. We will show basic transactions in the first year, with additional transactions added in the second year.

FIRST YEAR OF OPERATIONS—2002

Juarez Company began business on January 1, 2002. At that time it issued 300,000 shares of $1 par value common stock for $300,000 cash. The company rented office and sales space along with equipment. The comparative balance sheets at the beginning and end of 2002, showing changes in each account, appear in Illustration 12-21. The income statement and additional information for Juarez Company are shown in Illustration 12-22.

Illustration 12-21 Comparative balance sheets, 2002, with increases and decreases

JUAREZ COMPANY
Comparative Balance Sheets

Assets	Dec. 31, 2002	Jan. 1, 2002	Change Increase/Decrease
Cash	$159,000	$-0-	$159,000 Increase
Accounts receivable	15,000	-0-	15,000 Increase
Inventory	160,000	-0-	160,000 Increase
Prepaid expenses	8,000	-0-	8,000 Increase
Land	80,000	-0-	80,000 Increase
Total	$422,000	$-0-	

Liabilities and Stockholders' Equity

Accounts payable	$ 60,000	$-0-	$ 60,000 Increase
Accrued expenses payable	20,000	-0-	20,000 Increase
Common stock	300,000	-0-	300,000 Increase
Retained earnings	42,000	-0-	42,000 Increase
Total	$422,000	$-0-	

Illustration 12-22 Income statement and additional information, 2002

JUAREZ COMPANY
Income Statement
For the Year Ended December 31, 2002

Revenues	$780,000
Cost of goods sold	450,000
Gross profit	330,000
Operating expenses	170,000
Income before income taxes	160,000
Income tax expense	48,000
Net income	$112,000

Additional information:
1. Dividends of $70,000 were declared and paid in cash.
2. The accounts payable increase resulted from the purchase of merchandise.

The three steps cited in Illustration 12-4 on page 487 for preparing the statement of cash flows are used in the direct method.

STEP 1: DETERMINE THE NET INCREASE/
DECREASE IN CASH

The comparative balance sheets for Juarez Company show a zero cash balance at January 1, 2002, and a cash balance of $159,000 at December 31, 2002. Thus, the change in cash for 2002 was a net increase of $159,000.

STEP 2: DETERMINE NET CASH PROVIDED/USED
BY OPERATING ACTIVITIES

Under the **direct method**, net cash provided by operating activities is computed by **adjusting each item in the income statement** from the accrual basis to the cash basis. To simplify and condense the operating activities section, **only major classes of operating cash receipts and cash payments are reported**. For these major classes, the difference between cash receipts and cash payments is the net cash provided by operating activities. These relationships are as shown in Illustration 12-23.

Illustration 12-23   Major classes of cash receipts and payments

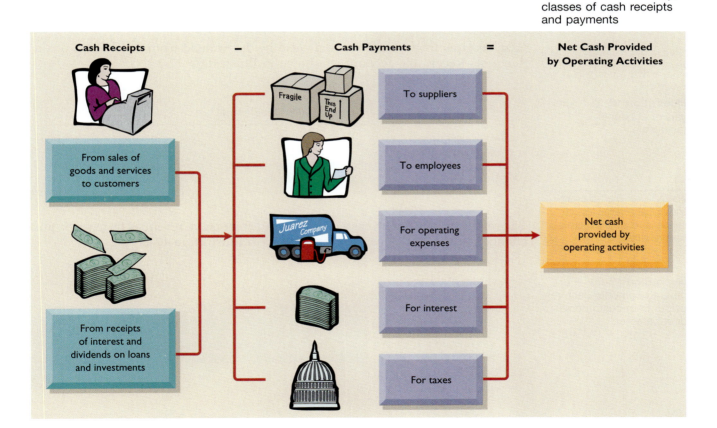

An efficient way to apply the direct method is to analyze the items reported in the income statement in the order in which they are listed. Cash receipts and cash payments related to these revenues and expenses are then determined. The direct method adjustments for Juarez Company in 2002 to determine net cash provided by operating activities are presented on the following pages.

Cash Receipts from Customers

The income statement for Juarez Company reported revenues from customers of $780,000. How much of that was cash receipts? To answer that, it is necessary to consider the change in accounts receivable during the year. When accounts receivable increase during the year, revenues on an accrual basis are higher than cash receipts from customers. Operations led to revenues, but not all of these revenues resulted in cash receipts. To determine the amount of cash receipts, the increase in accounts receivable is deducted from sales revenues. On the other hand, there may be a decrease in accounts receivable. That would occur if cash receipts from customers exceeded sales revenues. In that case, the decrease in accounts receivable is added to sales revenues.

For Juarez Company, accounts receivable increased $15,000. Thus, cash receipts from customers were $765,000, computed as follows.

Illustration 12-24   Computation of cash receipts from customers

Revenues from sales	$ 780,000
Deduct: Increase in accounts receivable	15,000
Cash receipts from customers	**$765,000**

Cash receipts from customers may also be determined from an analysis of the Accounts Receivable account, as shown in Illustration 12-25.

Illustration 12-25   Analysis of accounts receivable

Accounts Receivable			
1/1/02 Balance	–0–	**Receipts from customers**	**765,000**
Revenues from sales	780,000		
12/31/02 Balance	15,000		

The relationships among cash receipts from customers, revenues from sales, and changes in accounts receivable are shown in Illustration 12-26.

Illustration 12-26   Formula to compute cash receipts from customers—direct method

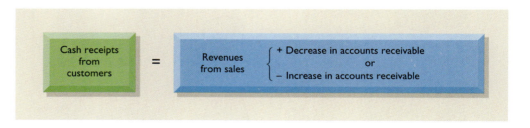

Cash Payments to Suppliers

Juarez Company reported cost of goods sold of $450,000 on its income statement. How much of that was cash payments to suppliers? To answer that, it is first necessary to find purchases for the year. To find purchases, cost of goods sold is adjusted for the change in inventory. When inventory increases during the year, purchases for the year have exceeded cost of goods sold. As a result, to determine the amount of purchases, the increase in inventory is added to cost of goods sold.

In 2002, Juarez Company's inventory increased $160,000. Purchases are computed as follows.

Cost of goods sold	$ 450,000
Add: Increase in inventory	160,000
Purchases	**$610,000**

Illustration 12-27 Computation of purchases

After purchases are computed, cash payments to suppliers can be determined. This is done by adjusting purchases for the change in accounts payable. When accounts payable increase during the year, purchases on an accrual basis are higher than they are on a cash basis. As a result, to determine cash payments to suppliers, an increase in accounts payable is deducted from purchases. On the other hand, there may be a decrease in accounts payable. That would occur if cash payments to suppliers exceed purchases. In that case, the decrease in accounts payable is added to purchases.

For Juarez Company, cash payments to suppliers were $550,000, computed as follows.

Purchases	$ 610,000
Deduct: Increase in accounts payable	60,000
Cash payments to suppliers	**$550,000**

Illustration 12-28 Computation of cash payments to suppliers

Cash payments to suppliers may also be determined from an analysis of the Accounts Payable account as shown in Illustration 12-29.

Accounts Payable			
Payments to suppliers 550,000	1/1/02 Balance		–0–
	Purchases		610,000
	12/31/02 Balance		60,000

Illustration 12-29 Analysis of accounts payable

Helpful Hint The T-account shows that purchases less increase in accounts payable equals payments to suppliers.

The relationships among cash payments to suppliers, cost of goods sold, changes in inventory, and changes in accounts payable are shown in the following formula.

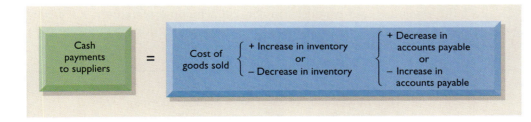

Illustration 12-30 Formula to compute cash payments to suppliers—direct method

Cash Payments for Operating Expenses

Operating expenses of $170,000 were reported on Juarez's income statement. How much of that amount was cash paid for operating expenses? To answer that, we need to adjust this amount for any changes in prepaid expenses and accrued expenses payable. For example, when prepaid expenses increased $8,000 during the year, cash paid for operating expenses was $8,000 higher than operating expenses reported on the income statement. To convert operating expenses

Helpful Hint Decrease in accounts receivable indicates that cash collections were greater than sales. **Increase in accounts receivable** indicates that sales were greater than cash collections.

Increase in prepaid expenses indicates that the amount paid for the prepayments exceeded the amount that was recorded as an expense.
Decrease in prepaid expenses indicates that the amount recorded as an expense exceeded the amount of cash paid for the prepayments.
Increase in accounts payable indicates that expenses incurred exceed the cash paid for expenses that period.

to cash payments for operating expenses, the increase must be added to operating expenses. On the other hand, if prepaid expenses decrease during the year, the decrease must be deducted from operating expenses.

Operating expenses must also be adjusted for changes in accrued expenses payable. When accrued expenses payable increase during the year, operating expenses on an accrual basis are higher than they are on a cash basis. As a result, to determine cash payments for operating expenses, an increase in accrued expenses payable is deducted from operating expenses. On the other hand, a decrease in accrued expenses payable is added to operating expenses because cash payments exceed operating expenses.

Juarez Company's cash payments for operating expenses were $158,000, computed as follows.

Illustration 12-31 Computation of cash payments for operating expenses

Operating expenses	$ 170,000
Add: Increase in prepaid expenses	8,000
Deduct: Increase in accrued expenses payable	(20,000)
Cash payments for operating expenses	**$158,000**

The relationships among cash payments for operating expenses, changes in prepaid expenses, and changes in accrued expenses payable are shown in the following formula.

Illustration 12-32 Formula to compute cash payments for operating expenses—direct method

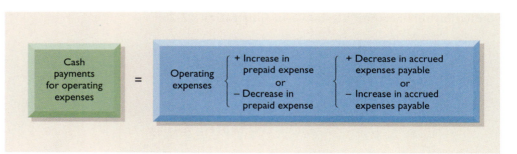

Cash Payments for Income Taxes

The income statement for Juarez shows income tax expense of $48,000. This amount equals the cash paid. The comparative balance sheets indicated no income taxes payable at either the beginning or end of the year.

All of the revenues and expenses in the 2002 income statement have now been adjusted to a cash basis. The operating activities section of the statement of cash flows is as follows.

Illustration 12-33 Operating activities section—direct method

JUAREZ COMPANY
Statement of Cash Flows—Direct Method (partial)
For the Year Ended December 31, 2002

Cash flows from operating activities		
Cash receipts from customers		$765,000
Cash payments		
To suppliers	$550,000	
For operating expenses	158,000	
For income taxes	48,000	756,000
Net cash provided by operating activities		**$ 9,000**

STEP 3: DETERMINE NET CASH PROVIDED/USED BY INVESTING AND FINANCING ACTIVITIES

Preparing the investing and financing activities sections of the statement of cash flows begins by determining the changes in noncurrent accounts reported in the comparative balance sheets. The change in each account is then analyzed to determine the effect, if any, the change had on cash.

Helpful Hint This is the same procedure used under the indirect method. The investing and financing activities are measured and reported the same under both methods.

Increase in Land

No additional information is given for the increase in land. In such case, you should assume that the increase affected cash. In solving homework problems, you should assume that **any unexplained differences in noncurrent accounts involve cash**. The purchase of land is an investing activity. Thus, an outflow of cash of $80,000 for the purchase of land should be reported in the investing activities section.

Increase in Common Stock

As indicated earlier, 300,000 shares of $1 par value stock were sold for $300,000 cash. The issuance of common stock is a financing activity. Thus, a cash inflow of $300,000 from the issuance of common stock is reported in the financing activities section.

Increase in Retained Earnings

What caused the net increase of $42,000 in the Retained Earnings account? First, net income increased retained earnings by $112,000. Second, the additional information section indicates that a cash dividend of $70,000 was declared and paid. The adjustment of revenues and expenses to arrive at net cash provided by operations was done in step 2 above. The cash dividend paid is reported as an outflow of cash in the financing activities section.

Helpful Hint It is the **payment** of dividends, not the declaration, that appears on the cash flow statement.

   This analysis can also be made directly from the Retained Earnings account in the ledger of Juarez Company as shown in Illustration 12-34.

Illustration 12-34 Analysis of retained earnings

Retained Earnings			
12/31/02 Cash dividend	70,000	1/1/02 Balance	–0–
		12/31/02 Net income	112,000
		12/31/02 Balance	42,000

The $42,000 increase in Retained Earnings in 2002 is a net change. When a net change in a noncurrent balance sheet account has occurred during the year, it generally is necessary to report the individual items that cause the net change.

STATEMENT OF CASH FLOWS—2002

We can now prepare the statement of cash flows. The operating activities section is reported first, followed by the investing and financing activities sections. The statement of cash flows for Juarez Company for 2002 is shown in Illustration 12-35.

   The statement of cash flows shows the following: Operating activities **provided** $9,000 of the net increase in cash. Investing activities **used** $80,000 of cash. Financing activities **provided** $230,000 of cash. The $159,000 net increase in cash for the year agrees with the increase in cash of $159,000 reported in the comparative balance sheets.

JUAREZ COMPANY
Statement of Cash Flows—Direct Method
For the Year Ended December 31, 2002

Cash flows from operating activities		
Cash receipts from customers		$765,000
Cash payments		
To suppliers	$550,000	
For operating expenses	158,000	
For income taxes	48,000	756,000
Net cash provided by operating activities		9,000
Cash flows from investing activities		
Purchase of land	(80,000)	
Net cash used by investing activities		(80,000)
Cash flows from financing activities		
Issuance of common stock	300,000	
Payment of cash dividend	(70,000)	
Net cash provided by financing activities		230,000
Net increase in cash		159,000
Cash at beginning of period		–0–
Cash at end of period		$159,000

Helpful Hint Note that in the investing and financing activities sections, positive numbers indicate cash inflows (receipts), and negative numbers indicate cash outflows (payments).

SECOND YEAR OF OPERATIONS—2003

Illustrations 12-36 and 12-37 present information related to the second year of operations for Juarez Company.

JUAREZ COMPANY
Comparative Balance Sheets
December 31

Assets	2003	2002	Change Increase/Decrease
Cash	$191,000	$159,000	$ 32,000 Increase
Accounts receivable	12,000	15,000	3,000 Decrease
Inventory	130,000	160,000	30,000 Decrease
Prepaid expenses	6,000	8,000	2,000 Decrease
Land	180,000	80,000	100,000 Increase
Equipment	160,000	–0–	160,000 Increase
Accumulated depreciation—equipment	(16,000)	–0–	16,000 Increase
Total	$663,000	$422,000	

Liabilities and Stockholders' Equity			
Accounts payable	$ 52,000	$ 60,000	$ 8,000 Decrease
Accrued expenses payable	15,000	20,000	5,000 Decrease
Income taxes payable	12,000	–0–	12,000 Increase
Bonds payable	90,000	–0–	90,000 Increase
Common stock	400,000	300,000	100,000 Increase
Retained earnings	94,000	42,000	52,000 Increase
Total	$663,000	$422,000	

JUAREZ COMPANY
Income Statement
For the Year Ended December 31, 2003

Revenues		$975,000
Cost of goods sold	$660,000	
Operating expenses (excluding depreciation)	176,000	
Depreciation expense	18,000	
Loss on sale of store equipment	1,000	855,000
Income before income taxes		120,000
Income tax expense		36,000
Net income		$ 84,000

Additional information:
1. In 2003, the company declared and paid a $32,000 cash dividend.
2. Bonds were issued at face value for $90,000 in cash.
3. Equipment costing $180,000 was purchased for cash.
4. Equipment costing $20,000 was sold for $17,000 cash when the book value of the equipment was $18,000.
5. Common stock of $100,000 was issued to acquire land.

Illustration 12-37 Income statement and additional information, 2003

STEP 1: DETERMINE THE NET INCREASE/ DECREASE IN CASH

The comparative balance sheets show a beginning cash balance of $159,000 and an ending cash balance of $191,000. Thus, there was a net increase in cash in 2003 of $32,000.

STEP 2: DETERMINE NET CASH PROVIDED/USED BY OPERATING ACTIVITIES

Cash Receipts from Customers

Revenues from sales were $975,000. Since accounts receivable decreased $3,000, cash receipts from customers were greater than sales revenues. Cash receipts from customers were $978,000, computed as follows.

Revenues from sales	$ 975,000
Add: Decrease in accounts receivable	3,000
Cash receipts from customers	**$978,000**

Illustration 12-38 Computation of cash receipts from customers

Cash Payments to Suppliers

The conversion of cost of goods sold to purchases and purchases to cash payments to suppliers is similar to the computations made in 2002. For 2003, purchases are computed using cost of goods sold of $660,000 from the income statement and the decrease in inventory of $30,000 from the comparative balance sheets. Purchases are then adjusted by the decrease in accounts payable of $8,000. Cash payments to suppliers were $638,000, computed as follows.

Illustration 12-39
Computation of cash payments to suppliers

Cost of goods sold	$ 660,000
Deduct: Decrease in inventory	30,000
Purchases	630,000
Add: Decrease in accounts payable	8,000
Cash payments to suppliers	**$638,000**

Cash Payments for Operating Expenses

Operating expenses (exclusive of depreciation expense) for 2003 were reported at $176,000. This amount is then adjusted for changes in prepaid expenses and accrued expenses payable to determine cash payments for operating expenses.

As shown in the comparative balance sheets, prepaid expenses decreased $2,000 during the year. This means that $2,000 was allocated to operating expenses (thereby increasing operating expenses), but cash payments did not increase by that $2,000. To determine cash payments for operating expenses, the decrease in prepaid expenses is deducted from operating expenses.

Accrued operating expenses decreased $5,000 during the period. As a result, cash payments were higher by $5,000 than the amount reported for operating expenses. The decrease in accrued expenses payable is added to operating expenses. Cash payments for operating expenses were $179,000, computed as follows.

Illustration 12-40
Computation of cash payments for operating expenses

Operating expenses, exclusive of depreciation	$176,000
Deduct: Decrease in prepaid expenses	(2,000)
Add: Decrease in accrued expenses payable	5,000
Cash payments for operating expenses	**$179,000**

Depreciation Expense and Loss on Sale of Equipment

Operating expenses are shown exclusive of depreciation. Depreciation expense in 2003 was $18,000. Depreciation expense is not shown on a statement of cash flows because it is a noncash charge. If the amount for operating expenses includes depreciation expense, operating expenses must be reduced by the amount of depreciation to determine cash payments for operating expenses.

The loss on sale of equipment of $1,000 is also a noncash charge. The loss on sale of equipment reduces net income, but it does not reduce cash. Thus, the loss on sale of equipment is not reported on a statement of cash flows.

Other charges to expense that do not require the use of cash, such as the amortization of intangible assets and depletion expense, are treated in the same manner as depreciation.

Cash Payments for Income Taxes

Income tax expense reported on the income statement was $36,000. Income taxes payable, however, increased $12,000. This increase means that $12,000 of the income taxes have not been paid. As a result, income taxes paid were less than income taxes reported in the income statement. Cash payments for income taxes were, therefore, $24,000 as shown below.

Illustration 12-41
Computation of cash payments for income taxes

Income tax expense	$ 36,000
Deduct: Increase in income taxes payable	12,000
Cash payments for income taxes	**$24,000**

The relationships among cash payments for income taxes, income tax expense, and changes in income taxes payable are shown in the following formula.

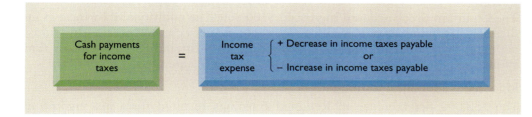

Illustration 12-42 Formula to compute cash payments for income taxes—direct method

STEP 3: DETERMINE NET CASH PROVIDED/USED BY INVESTING AND FINANCING ACTIVITIES

Increase in Land

Land increased $100,000. The additional information section indicates that common stock was issued to purchase the land. The issuance of common stock for land has no effect on cash. But it is a **significant noncash investing and financing transaction**. This transaction requires disclosure in a separate schedule at the bottom of the statement of cash flows.

Increase in Equipment

The comparative balance sheets show that equipment increased $160,000 in 2003. The additional information in Illustration 12-37 indicates that the increase resulted from two investing transactions: (1) Equipment costing $180,000 was purchased for cash. And (2) equipment costing $20,000 was sold for $17,000 cash when its book value was $18,000. The relevant data for the statement of cash flows is the cash paid for the purchase and the cash proceeds from the sale. For Juarez Company, the investing activities section will show the following: The $180,000 purchase of equipment as an outflow of cash, and the $17,000 sale of equipment also as an inflow of cash. The two amounts **should not be netted**. **Both individual outflows and inflows of cash should be shown.**

The analysis of the changes in equipment should include the related Accumulated Depreciation account. These two accounts for Juarez Company are shown in Illustration 12-43.

Equipment

1/1/03 Balance	–0–	Cost of equipment sold	20,000
Cash purchase	**180,000**		
12/31/03 Balance	160,000		

Accumulated Depreciation—Equipment

Sale of equipment	2,000	1/1/03 Balance	–0–
		Depreciation expense	18,000
		12/31/03 Balance	16,000

Illustration 12-43 Analysis of equipment and related accumulated depreciation

Increase in Bonds Payable

Bonds Payable increased $90,000. The additional information in Illustration 12-37 indicated that bonds with a face value of $90,000 were issued for $90,000 cash. The issuance of bonds is a financing activity. For Juarez Company, there is an inflow of cash of $90,000 from the issuance of bonds.

Increase in Common Stock

The Common Stock account increased $100,000. The additional information indicated that land was acquired from the issuance of common stock. This transaction is a **significant noncash investing and financing transaction** that should be reported separately at the bottom of the statement.

Increase in Retained Earnings

The $52,000 net increase in Retained Earnings resulted from net income of $84,000 and the declaration and payment of a cash dividend of $32,000. **Net income is not reported in the statement of cash flows under the direct method.** Cash dividends paid of $32,000 are reported in the financing activities section as an outflow of cash.

STATEMENT OF CASH FLOWS—2003

The statement of cash flows for Juarez Company is shown in Illustration 12-44.

Illustration 12-44 Statement of cash flows, 2003—direct method

JUAREZ COMPANY Statement of Cash Flows—Direct Method For the Year Ended December 31, 2003		
Cash flows from operating activities		
Cash receipts from customers		$978,000
Cash payments		
To suppliers	$638,000	
For operating expenses	179,000	
For income taxes	24,000	841,000
Net cash provided by operating activities		137,000
Cash flows from investing activities		
Purchase of equipment	(180,000)	
Sale of equipment	17,000	
Net cash used by investing activities		(163,000)
Cash flows from financing activities		
Issuance of bonds payable	90,000	
Payment of cash dividends	(32,000)	
Net cash provided by financing activities		58,000
Net increase in cash		32,000
Cash at beginning of period		159,000
Cash at end of period		$191,000
Noncash investing and financing activities		
Issuance of common stock to purchase land		$100,000

BEFORE YOU GO ON . . .

◆ Review It

1. What is the format of the operating activities section of the statement of cash flows using the direct method?
2. Where is depreciation expense shown on a statement of cash flows using the direct method?
3. Where are significant noncash investing and financing activities shown on a statement of cash flows? Give some examples.

◆ **Do It**

Presented below is information related to Reynolds Company. Use it to prepare a statement of cash flows using the direct method.

			Change
Assets	2003	2002	Increase/Decrease
REYNOLDS COMPANY **Comparative Balance Sheets** **December 31**			
Cash	$ 54,000	$ 37,000	$ 17,000 Increase
Accounts receivable	68,000	26,000	42,000 Increase
Inventories	54,000	–0–	54,000 Increase
Prepaid expenses	4,000	6,000	2,000 Decrease
Land	45,000	70,000	25,000 Decrease
Buildings	200,000	200,000	–0–
Accumulated depreciation—buildings	(21,000)	(11,000)	10,000 Increase
Equipment	193,000	68,000	125,000 Increase
Accumulated depreciation—equipment	(28,000)	(10,000)	18,000 Increase
Totals	$569,000	$386,000	
Liabilities and Stockholders' Equity			
Accounts payable	$ 23,000	$ 40,000	$ 17,000 Decrease
Accrued expenses payable	10,000	–0–	10,000 Increase
Bonds payable	110,000	150,000	40,000 Decrease
Common stock ($1 par)	220,000	60,000	160,000 Increase
Retained earnings	206,000	136,000	70,000 Increase
Totals	$569,000	$386,000	

REYNOLDS COMPANY
Income Statement
For the Year Ended December 31, 2003

Revenues		$890,000
Cost of goods sold	$465,000	
Operating expenses	221,000	
Interest expense	12,000	
Loss on sale of equipment	2,000	700,000
Income from operations		190,000
Income tax expense		65,000
Net income		$125,000

Additional information:
1. Operating expenses include depreciation expense of $33,000 and charges from prepaid expenses of $2,000.
2. Land was sold at its book value for cash.
3. Cash dividends of $55,000 were declared and paid in 2003.
4. Interest expense of $12,000 was paid in cash.
5. Equipment with a cost of $166,000 was purchased for cash. Equipment with a cost of $41,000 and a book value of $36,000 was sold for $34,000 cash.
6. Bonds of $10,000 were redeemed at their book value for cash. Bonds of $30,000 were converted into common stock.
7. Common stock ($1 par) of $130,000 was issued for cash.
8. Accounts payable pertain to merchandise suppliers.

Action Plan

- Determine the net increase/decrease in cash.
- Determine net cash provided/used by operating activities by adjusting each item in the income statement from the accrual basis to the cash basis.
- Determine net cash provided/used by investing activities.
- Determine net cash provided/used by financing activities.

Solution

Helpful Hint

1. Determine net cash provided/used by operating activities, recognizing that each item in the income statement must be adjusted to the cash basis.
2. Determine net cash provided/used by investing activities, recognizing that investing activities generally relate to changes in noncurrent assets.
3. Determine net cash provided/used by financing activities, recognizing that financing activities generally relate to changes in long-term liabilities and stockholders' equity accounts.

REYNOLDS COMPANY
Statement of Cash Flows—Direct Method
For the Year Ended December 31, 2003

Cash flows from operating activities		
Cash receipts from customers		$848,000ᵃ
Cash payments		
To suppliers	$536,000ᵇ	
For operating expenses	176,000ᶜ	
For interest expense	12,000	
For income taxes	65,000	789,000
Net cash provided by operating activities		59,000
Cash flows from investing activities		
Sale of land	25,000	
Sale of equipment	34,000	
Purchase of equipment	(166,000)	
Net cash used by investing activities		(107,000)
Cash flows from financing activities		
Redemption of bonds	(10,000)	
Sale of common stock	130,000	
Payment of dividends	(55,000)	
Net cash provided by financing activities		65,000
Net increase in cash		17,000
Cash at beginning of period		37,000
Cash at end of period		$ 54,000
Noncash investing and financing activities		
Conversion of bonds into common stock		$ 30,000

Computations:
ᵃ$848,000 = $890,000 − $42,000
ᵇ$536,000 = $465,000 + $54,000 + $17,000
ᶜ$176,000 = $221,000 − $33,000 − $2,000 − $10,000
Technically, an additional schedule reconciling net income to net cash provided by operating activities should be presented as part of the statement of cash flows when using the direct method.

Related exercise material: BE12-7, BE12-8, BE12-9, BE12-10, E12-7, E12-8, E12-9, E12-10, and E12-11.

Note: This concludes Section 2 on preparation of the statement of cash flows using the direct method. You should now proceed to the next—and concluding—section of the chapter, "Using Cash Flows to Evaluate a Company."

*U*SING *C*ASH *F*LOWS TO *E*VALUATE A *C*OMPANY

Traditionally, the ratios most commonly used by investors and creditors have been based on accrual accounting. In previous chapters we introduced cash-based ratios that are gaining increased acceptance among analysts. In this section we review those measures and introduce additional ones.

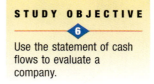

STUDY OBJECTIVE
6
Use the statement of cash flows to evaluate a company.

FREE CASH FLOW

In the statement of cash flows, cash provided by operating activities is intended to indicate the cash-generating capability of the company. Analysts have noted, however, that **cash provided by operating activities fails to take into account that a company must invest in new fixed assets** just to maintain its current level of operations, and it must at least **maintain dividends at current levels** to satisfy investors. **Free cash flow** is the term used to describe the cash remaining from operations after adjustment for capital expenditures and dividends.

Consider the following example: Suppose that MPC produced and sold 10,000 personal computers this year. It reported cash provided by operating activities of $100,000. In order to maintain production at 10,000 computers, MPC invested $15,000 in equipment. It chose to pay $5,000 in dividends. Its free cash flow was $80,000 ($100,000 − $15,000 − $5,000). The company could use this $80,000 either to purchase new assets to expand the business or to pay an $80,000 dividend and continue to produce 10,000 computers. In practice, free cash flow is often calculated with the formula in Illustration 12-45. Alternative definitions also exist.

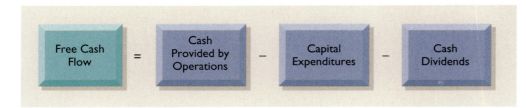

Illustration 12-45 Free cash flow

Illustration 12-46 provides basic information excerpted from the 2000 statement of cash flows of **Microsoft Corporation**.

Illustration 12-46
Microsoft cash flow information ($ in millions)

MICROSOFT CORPORATION Statement of Cash Flows (partial) 2000		
Net cash from operations		$ 13,961
Net cash flows from investing		
Additions to property and equipment	$ (879)	
Purchases of investments	(43,158)	
Maturities and sales of investments	32,110	
Net cash used for investing		$(11,927)
Cash paid for dividends on preferred stock		$(13)

Microsoft's free cash flow is calculated as shown in Illustration 12-47.

Illustration 12-47 Calculation of Microsoft's free cash flow ($ in millions)

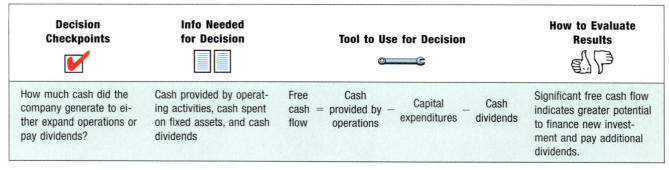

Net cash provided by operations	$13,961
Less: Expenditures on property and equipment	879
Preferred dividends paid	13
Free cash flow	**$13,069**

This is a tremendous amount of cash generated in a single year. It is available for the acquisition of new assets, the retirement of stock or debt, or the payment of dividends. It should also be noted that this amount far exceeds Microsoft's 2000 net income of $9,421 million. This lends additional credibility to Microsoft's income number as an indicator of potential future performance. If anything, Microsoft's net income might understate its actual performance.

Oracle Corporation is the world's largest seller of database software and information management services. Like Microsoft, its success depends on continuing to improve its existing products while developing new products to keep pace with rapid changes in technology. Oracle's free cash flow for 2000 was $2,660 million. This is impressive, but significantly less than Microsoft's amazing ability to generate cash.

DECISION TOOLKIT

Decision Checkpoints	Info Needed for Decision	Tool to Use for Decision	How to Evaluate Results
How much cash did the company generate to either expand operations or pay dividends?	Cash provided by operating activities, cash spent on fixed assets, and cash dividends	Free cash flow = Cash provided by operations − Capital expenditures − Cash dividends	Significant free cash flow indicates greater potential to finance new investment and pay additional dividends.

BUSINESS INSIGHT

Management Perspective

Managers in some industries have long suggested that accrual-based income measures understate the true long-term potential of their companies because of what they suggest are excessive depreciation charges. For example, cable companies frequently suggested that, once they had installed a cable, it would require minimal maintenance and would guarantee the company returns for a long time to come. As a consequence, cable companies, which reported strong operating cash flows but low net income, had high stock prices because investors focused more on their cash flows from operations than on their net income. A recent *Wall Street Journal* article suggested, however, that investors have grown impatient with the cable companies and have lost faith in cash flow from operations as an indicator of cable company performance. As it turns out, cable companies have had to make many expensive upgrades to previously installed cable systems. Today, after cable stock prices have fallen dramatically, cable industry analysts emphasize that either free cash flows or net income is a better indicator of a cable TV company's long-term potential than cash provided by operating activities.

Source: Susan Pulliam and Mark Robichaux, "Heard on the Street: Cash Flow Stops Propping Cable Stock," *Wall Street Journal,* January 9, 1997, p. C1.

CAPITAL EXPENDITURE RATIO

Capital expenditures are purchases of fixed assets. In addition to free cash flows, another indicator of a company's ability to generate sufficient cash to finance new fixed assets is the **capital expenditure ratio**. It is calculated as cash provided by operating activities divided by capital expenditures. This measure is similar to free cash flow, except that free cash flow reveals the *total* amount of cash available for discretionary use by management. In contrast, the capital expenditure ratio provides a *relative measure* of available discretionary cash by comparing cash provided by operations to cash used for the purchase of productive assets. Amounts spent on capital expenditures are listed in the investing activities section of the statement of cash flows. Using the Microsoft information in Illustration 12-46, we can calculate its capital expenditure ratio as shown in Illustration 12-48.

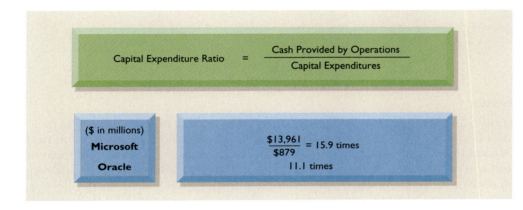

Illustration 12-48 Capital expenditure ratio for Microsoft

Microsoft's ratio of 15.9 times suggests that it could have purchased 15.9 times as much property, plant, and equipment as it did *without obtaining any additional outside financing.* In comparison, Oracle's capital expenditure ratio for 2000 was 11.1 times. This provides additional evidence of Microsoft's superior cash-generating capability. This ratio varies across industries depending on the capital intensity of the industry. That is, we would expect a manufacturing company to have a lower ratio (because by necessity it has higher capital expenditures) than a software company, which spends less of its money on fixed assets and more of its money on "intellectual" capital. This difference is evident in the Using the Decision Toolkit exercise at the end of this chapter where we evaluate two computer chip manufacturers.

DECISION TOOLKIT

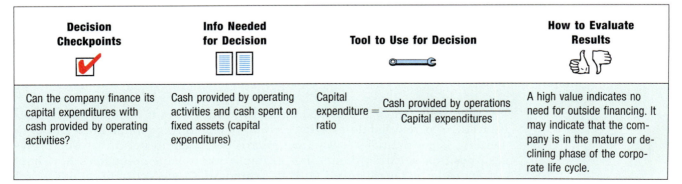

Decision Checkpoints	Info Needed for Decision	Tool to Use for Decision	How to Evaluate Results
Can the company finance its capital expenditures with cash provided by operating activities?	Cash provided by operating activities and cash spent on fixed assets (capital expenditures)	$\text{Capital expenditure ratio} = \dfrac{\text{Cash provided by operations}}{\text{Capital expenditures}}$	A high value indicates no need for outside financing. It may indicate that the company is in the mature or declining phase of the corporate life cycle.

ASSESSING LIQUIDITY, SOLVENCY, AND PROFITABILITY USING CASH FLOWS

Financial ratios may be used to analyze a company's liquidity, solvency, and profitability. Many of these ratios use accrual-based numbers from the income statement and balance sheet. In this section we focus on ratios that are *cash-based* rather than accrual-based. That is, instead of using numbers from the income statement, these ratios use numbers from the statement of cash flows.

As discussed earlier, many analysts are critical of accrual-based numbers because they feel that the adjustment process allows too much management discretion. These analysts like to supplement accrual-based analysis with measures that use the cash flow statement. One disadvantage of these measures is that, unlike the more commonly employed accrual-based measures, there are no readily available industry averages for comparison. In the following discussion we use cash flow–based ratios to analyze Microsoft. In addition to the cash flow information provided in Illustration 12-46, we need the following information related to Microsoft.

($ in millions)	1999	2000
Current liabilities	$ 8,802	$ 9,755
Total liabilities	10,187	10,782
Sales	19,747	22,956

Liquidity

Liquidity is the ability of a business to meet its immediate obligations. One measure of liquidity is the *current ratio:* current assets divided by current liabilities. A disadvantage of the current ratio is that it uses year-end balances of current asset and current liability accounts, and these year-end balances may not be representative of the company's position during most of the year.

A ratio that partially corrects this problem is the **current cash debt coverage ratio**: cash provided by operating activities divided by average current liabilities. Because cash provided by operating activities involves the entire year rather than a balance at one point in time, it is often considered a better representation of liquidity on the average day. The ratio is calculated as shown in Illustration 12-49, with the ratio computed for Microsoft Corporation and comparative numbers given for Oracle. We have also provided each company's current ratio for comparative purposes.

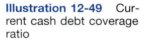**Illustration 12-49** Current cash debt coverage ratio

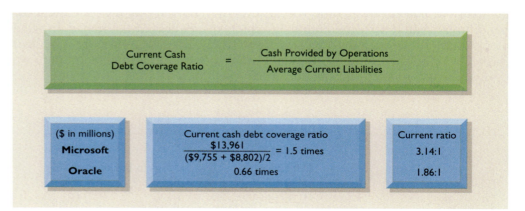

Microsoft's net cash provided by operating activities is one and a half times its average current liabilities. Oracle's ratio of 0.66 times, though not a cause for concern, is substantially lower than Microsoft's. Keep in mind that Microsoft's cash position is extraordinary. For example, many large companies now have current ratios in the range of 1.0. By this standard, Oracle's current ratio of 1.86:1 is respectable, but Microsoft's current ratio of 3.14:1 is very strong.

DECISION TOOLKIT

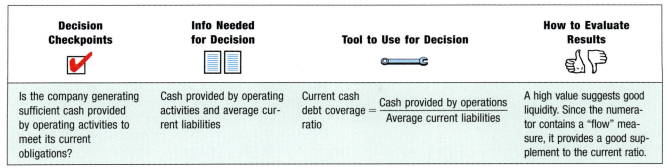

Decision Checkpoints	Info Needed for Decision	Tool to Use for Decision	How to Evaluate Results
Is the company generating sufficient cash provided by operating activities to meet its current obligations?	Cash provided by operating activities and average current liabilities	Current cash debt coverage ratio = $\dfrac{\text{Cash provided by operations}}{\text{Average current liabilities}}$	A high value suggests good liquidity. Since the numerator contains a "flow" measure, it provides a good supplement to the current ratio.

Solvency

Solvency is the ability of a company to survive over the long term. A measure of solvency that uses cash figures is the **cash debt coverage ratio**: the ratio of cash provided by operating activities to total debt as represented by average total liabilities. This ratio indicates a company's ability to repay its liabilities from cash generated from operations—that is, without having to liquidate productive assets such as property, plant, and equipment. The cash debt coverage ratios for Microsoft and Oracle for 2000 are given in Illustration 12-50. The debt to total assets ratios for each company are also provided for comparative purposes.

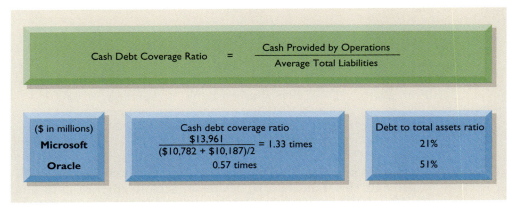

Illustration 12-50   Cash debt coverage ratio

$$\text{Cash Debt Coverage Ratio} \;=\; \frac{\text{Cash Provided by Operations}}{\text{Average Total Liabilities}}$$

($ in millions)	Cash debt coverage ratio	Debt to total assets ratio
Microsoft	$\dfrac{\$13,961}{(\$10,782 + \$10,187)/2} = 1.33$ times	21%
Oracle	0.57 times	51%

Microsoft has very low long-term obligations. Thus, its cash debt coverage ratio is nearly identical to its current cash debt coverage ratio. Obviously, Microsoft is very solvent. Oracle has some long-term debt, but like Microsoft its cash debt coverage ratio suggests that its long-term financial health is strong. Neither the cash nor accrual measures suggest any cause for concern for either company.

DECISION TOOLKIT

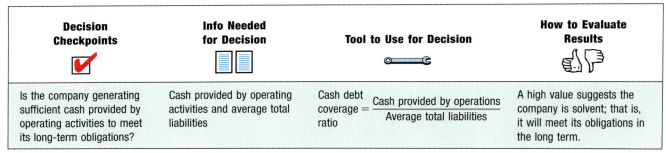

Decision Checkpoints	Info Needed for Decision	Tool to Use for Decision	How to Evaluate Results
Is the company generating sufficient cash provided by operating activities to meet its long-term obligations?	Cash provided by operating activities and average total liabilities	Cash debt coverage ratio = $\dfrac{\text{Cash provided by operations}}{\text{Average total liabilities}}$	A high value suggests the company is solvent; that is, it will meet its obligations in the long term.

Profitability

Profitability refers to a company's ability to generate a reasonable return. Earlier chapters introduced accrual-based ratios that measure profitability, such as gross profit rate, profit margin, and return on assets. In measures of profitability the potential differences between cash accounting and accrual accounting are most pronounced. Although some differences are expected because of the difference in the timing of revenue and expense recognition under cash versus accrual accounting, significant differences should be investigated. A cash-based measure of performance is the cash return on sales ratio.

The **cash return on sales ratio** is cash provided by operating activities divided by net sales. This ratio indicates the company's ability to turn sales into dollars. A low cash return on sales ratio should be investigated because it might indicate that the company is recognizing sales that are not really sales—that is, sales it will never collect. The cash return on sales ratios for Microsoft and Oracle for 2000 are presented in Illustration 12-51. The profit margin ratio is also presented for comparison.

Illustration 12-51 Cash return on sales ratio

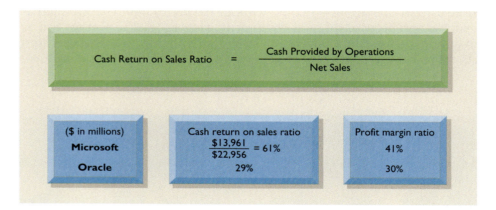

Oracle's cash return on sales ratio of 29 percent is substantially less than Microsoft's of 61 percent. This indicates that Microsoft is more efficient in turning sales into cash. Microsoft's cash return on sales ratio exceeds its profit margin, while Oracle's does not. This is the result of timing differences between cash-basis and accrual-basis accounting. It suggests that Microsoft employs conservative accounting practices that result in lower reported net income.

DECISION TOOLKIT

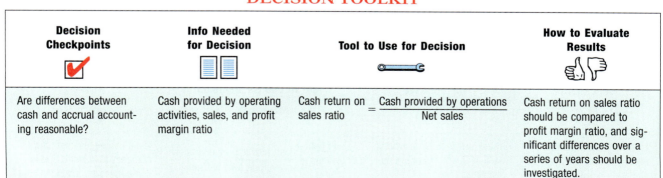

Decision Checkpoints	Info Needed for Decision	Tool to Use for Decision	How to Evaluate Results
Are differences between cash and accrual accounting reasonable?	Cash provided by operating activities, sales, and profit margin ratio	Cash return on sales ratio = $\dfrac{\text{Cash provided by operations}}{\text{Net sales}}$	Cash return on sales ratio should be compared to profit margin ratio, and significant differences over a series of years should be investigated.

BUSINESS INSIGHT

Management Perspective

A recent *Wall Street Journal* article noted that while **Microsoft's** cash position is enviable, it does present some challenges: management can't find enough ways to spend the cash. For example, unlike computer chip manufacturer **Intel Corporation** (another huge generator of cash), Microsoft has few manufacturing costs, so it does not spend huge sums on new plant and equipment. Microsoft's management would like to purchase other major software companies, but the federal government won't let it, for fear that it will reduce competition. (For example, the Justice Department blocked Microsoft's proposed purchase of software maker **Intuit**.) Instead, Microsoft is constrained to purchasing small software makers. Ironically, even this does not use much of its cash because, first of all, the companies are small, and second, the owners of these small companies prefer to be paid with Microsoft stock rather than cash.

Microsoft's huge holdings of liquid assets could eventually hurt its stock performance. Liquid assets typically provide about a 5 percent return, whereas Microsoft investors are accustomed to 30 percent returns. If Microsoft's performance starts to decline because it can't find enough good investment projects, it should distribute cash to its common stockholders in the form of dividends. One big problem: Bill Gates owns roughly 20 percent of Microsoft, and the last thing he wants to do is pay personal income tax on billions of dollars of dividend income. In the early years Microsoft did not pay dividends because it wanted to conserve cash. Today it is drowning in cash but still doesn't pay a dividend on its common stock.

Source: David Bank, "Microsoft's Problem Is What Many Firms Just Wish They Had," *Wall Street Journal*, January 17, 1997, p. A9.

BEFORE YOU GO ON . . .

◆ **Review It**

1. What is the difference between cash from operations and free cash flow?
2. What does it mean if a company has negative free cash flow?
3. Why might an analyst want to supplement accrual-based ratios with cash-based ratios? What are some cash-based ratios?

USING THE DECISION TOOLKIT

Intel Corporation is the leading producer of computer chips for personal computers. It makes the hugely successful Pentium chip. Its primary competitor is **AMD** (formerly Advanced Micro Devices). The two are vicious competitors, with frequent lawsuits filed between them. Financial statement data for Intel are provided on the next page.

Instructions

Calculate the following cash-based measures for Intel, and compare them with those provided on page 523 for AMD.

1. Free cash flow.
2. Capital expenditure ratio.
3. Current cash debt coverage ratio.
4. Cash debt coverage ratio.
5. Cash return on sales ratio.

INTEL CORPORATION
Balance Sheet
December 31, 2000 and 1999
(in millions)

	2000	1999
Assets		
Current assets	$21,150	$17,819
Noncurrent assets	26,795	26,030
Total assets	$47,945	$43,849
Liabilities and Stockholders' Equity		
Current liabilities	$ 8,650	$ 7,099
Long-term liabilities	1,973	4,215
Total liabilities	10,623	11,314
Stockholders' equity	37,322	32,535
Total liabilities and stockholders' equity	$47,945	$43,849

INTEL CORPORATION
Income Statement
For the Years Ended December 31, 2000 and 1999
(in millions)

	2000	1999
Net revenues	$33,726	$29,389
Expenses	23,191	22,075
Net income	$10,535	$ 7,314

INTEL CORPORATION
Statement of Cash Flows
For the Years Ended December 31, 2000 and 1999
(in millions)

	2000	1999
Net cash provided by operating activities	$ 12,827	$12,134
Net cash used for investing activities (see note 1)	(10,035)	(6,249)
Net cash used for financing activities	(3,511)	(4,228)
Net increase (decrease) in cash and cash equivalents	$ (719)	$ 1,657

Note 1. Cash spent on property, plant, and equipment in 2000 was $6,674. Cash paid for dividends was $470.

Here are the comparative data for AMD:

1. Free cash flow $400 million
2. Capital expenditure ratio   1.5 times
3. Current cash debt coverage ratio 1.13 times
4. Cash debt coverage ratio   0.48 times
5. Cash return on sales ratio   26%

Solution

1. Intel's free cash flow is $5,683 million ($12,827 − $6,674 − $470), and AMD's is $400 million. This gives Intel an advantage in the ability to move quickly to invest in new projects.
2. Intel's capital expenditure ratio is 1.92 times ($12,827 ÷ $6,674), and AMD's is 1.5 times. This is a useful supplement to the free cash flow measure. It provides further evidence of Intel's superior cash-generating ability. Note that these values are well below those of Oracle and Microsoft. Manufacturing computer chips is very capital intensive, so we would expect these measures to be lower than those for software producers.
3. The current cash debt coverage ratio for Intel is calculated as:

$$\frac{\$12,827}{(\$7,099 + \$8,650)/2} = 1.63 \text{ times}$$

   Compared to AMD's value of 1.13 times, Intel appears to be more liquid.
4. The cash debt coverage ratio for Intel is calculated as:

$$\frac{\$12,827}{(\$10,623 + \$11,314)/2} = 1.17 \text{ times}$$

   Compared to AMD's value of 0.48 times, Intel appears to be significantly more solvent.
5. The cash return on sales ratio for Intel is calculated as:

$$\frac{\$12,827}{\$33,726} = 38\%$$

AMD's cash return on sales ratio is 26%. Thus, Intel was more successful in its ability to generate cash from sales.

THE NAVIGATOR

SUMMARY OF STUDY OBJECTIVES

1 *Indicate the primary purpose of the statement of cash flows.* The primary purpose of the statement of cash flows is to provide information about the cash receipts and cash payments during a period. A secondary objective is to provide information about the operating, investing, and financing activities during the period.

2 *Distinguish among operating, investing, and financing activities.* Operating activities include the cash effects of transactions that enter into the determination of net income. Investing activities involve cash flows resulting from changes in investments and long-term asset items. Financing activities involve cash flows resulting from changes in long-term liability and stockholders' equity items.

3 *Explain the impact of the product life cycle on a company's cash flows.* During the introductory stage, cash provided by operating activities and cash from investing are negative, whereas cash from financing is positive. During the growth stage, cash provided by operating activities becomes positive. During the maturity stage, cash provided by operating activities exceeds investing needs, so the company begins to retire debt.

During the decline stage, cash provided by operating activities is reduced, cash from investing becomes positive, and cash from financing becomes more negative.

4 *Prepare a statement of cash flows using the indirect method.* The preparation of a statement of cash flows involves three major steps: (1) Determine the net increase or decrease in cash. (2) Determine net cash provided (used) by operating activities. (3) Determine net cash flows provided (used) by investing and financing activities. Under the indirect method, accrual basis net income is adjusted to net cash provided by operating activities.

5 *Prepare a statement of cash flows using the direct method.* The preparation of the statement of cash flows involves three major steps: (1) Determine the net increase or decrease in cash. (2) Determine net cash provided (used) by operating activities. (3) Determine net cash flows provided (used) by investing and financing activities. To determine net cash provided by operating activities, the direct method reports cash receipts less cash payments.

6 *Use the statement of cash flows to evaluate a company.* A number of measures can be derived by using information from the statement of cash flows as well as the other required financial statements. Free cash flow indicates the amount of cash a company generated during the current year that is available for the payment of dividends or for expansion. The capital expenditure ratio, cash provided by operating activities divided by capital expenditures, complements free cash flow by giving a relative indicator of the sufficiency of cash from operations to fund capital expenditures. Liquidity can be measured with the current cash debt coverage ratio (cash provided by operating activities divided by average current liabilities), solvency by the cash debt coverage ratio (cash provided by operating activities divided by average total liabilities), and profitability by the cash return on sales ratio (cash provided by operating activities divided by net sales).

DECISION TOOLKIT—A SUMMARY

Decision Checkpoints	Info Needed for Decision	Tool to Use for Decision	How to Evaluate Results
How much cash did the company generate to either expand operations or pay dividends?	Cash provided by operating activities, cash spent on fixed assets, and cash dividends	$$\text{Free cash flow} = \text{Cash provided by operations} - \text{Capital expenditures} - \text{Cash dividends}$$	Significant free cash flow indicates greater potential to finance new investment and pay additional dividends.
Can the company finance its capital expenditures with cash provided by operating activities?	Cash provided by operating activities and cash spent on fixed assets (capital expenditures)	$$\text{Capital expenditure ratio} = \frac{\text{Cash provided by operations}}{\text{Capital expenditures}}$$	A high value indicates no need for outside financing. It may indicate that the company is in the mature or declining phase of the corporate life cycle.
Is the company generating sufficient cash provided by operating activities to meet its current obligations?	Cash provided by operating activities and average current liabilities	$$\text{Current cash debt coverage ratio} = \frac{\text{Cash provided by operations}}{\text{Average current liabilities}}$$	A high value suggests good liquidity. Since the numerator contains a "flow" measure, it provides a good supplement to the current ratio.
Is the company generating sufficient cash provided by operating activities to meet its long-term obligations?	Cash provided by operating activities and average total liabilities	$$\text{Cash debt coverage ratio} = \frac{\text{Cash provided by operations}}{\text{Average total liabilities}}$$	A high value suggests the company is solvent; that is, it will meet its obligations in the long term.
Are differences between cash and accrual accounting reasonable?	Cash provided by operating activities, sales, and profit margin ratio	$$\text{Cash return on sales ratio} = \frac{\text{Cash provided by operations}}{\text{Net sales}}$$	Cash return on sales ratio should be compared to profit margin ratio, and significant differences over a series of years should be investigated.

GLOSSARY

Capital expenditure ratio A cash-based ratio that indicates the extent to which cash provided by operating activities was sufficient to fund capital expenditure (fixed asset) purchases during the year. (p. 517)

Cash debt coverage ratio A cash-basis measure of solvency; computed as net cash provided by operating activities divided by average total liabilities. (p. 519)

Cash return on sales ratio A cash-basis measure of profitability; computed as net cash provided by operating activities divided by net sales. Also called *cash flow margin*. (p. 520)

Current cash debt coverage ratio A cash-basis measure of liquidity; computed as net cash provided by operating activities divided by average current liabilities. (p. 518)

Direct method A method of determining the net cash provided by operating activities by adjusting each item in the income statement from the accrual basis to the cash basis. (p. 503)

Financing activities Cash flow activities that include (a) obtaining cash from issuing debt and repaying the amounts borrowed and (b) obtaining cash from stock-holders and providing them with a return on their investment. (p. 482)

Free cash flow Cash provided by operating activities adjusted for capital expenditures and dividends paid. (p. 515)

Indirect method A method of preparing a statement of cash flows in which net income is adjusted for items that did not affect cash, to determine net cash provided by operating activities. (p. 491)

Investing activities Cash flow activities that include (a) acquiring and disposing of investments and productive long-lived assets and (b) lending money and collecting on those loans. (p. 482)

Operating activities Cash flow activities that include the cash effects of transactions that create revenues and expenses and thus enter into the determination of net income. (p. 481)

Statement of cash flows A financial statement that provides information about the cash receipts and cash payments of an entity during a period, classified as operating, investing, and financing activities, in a format that reconciles the beginning and ending cash balances. (p. 481)

DEMONSTRATION PROBLEM

The income statement for John Kosinski Manufacturing Company contains the following condensed information.

eGrade Demonstration Problem

JOHN KOSINSKI MANUFACTURING COMPANY
Income Statement
For the Year Ended December 31, 2002

Revenues		$6,583,000
Operating expenses, excluding depreciation	$4,920,000	
Depreciation expense	880,000	5,800,000
Income before income taxes		783,000
Income tax expense		353,000
Net income		$ 430,000

Included in operating expenses is a $24,000 loss resulting from the sale of machinery for $270,000 cash. Machinery was purchased at a cost of $750,000. The following balances are reported on Kosinski's comparative balance sheets at December 31.

	2002	2001
Cash	$672,000	$130,000
Accounts receivable	775,000	610,000
Inventories	834,000	867,000
Accounts payable	521,000	501,000

Income tax expense of $353,000 represents the amount paid in 2002. Dividends declared and paid in 2002 totaled $200,000.

Instructions

(a) Prepare the statement of cash flows using the indirect method.
(b) Prepare the statement of cash flows using the direct method.

Solution to Demonstration Problem

(a)
JOHN KOSINSKI MANUFACTURING COMPANY
Statement of Cash Flows—Indirect Method
For the Year Ended December 31, 2002

Cash flows from operating activities		
Net income		$ 430,000
Adjustments to reconcile net income to net cash provided by operating activities:		
Depreciation expense	$880,000	
Loss on sale of machinery	24,000	
Increase in accounts receivable	(165,000)	
Decrease in inventories	33,000	
Increase in accounts payable	20,000	792,000
Net cash provided by operating activities		1,222,000
Cash flows from investing activities		
Sale of machinery	270,000	
Purchase of machinery	(750,000)	
Net cash used by investing activities		(480,000)
Cash flows from financing activities		
Payment of cash dividends	(200,000)	
Net cash used by financing activities		(200,000)
Net increase in cash		542,000
Cash at beginning of period		130,000
Cash at end of period		$ 672,000

(b)
JOHN KOSINSKI MANUFACTURING COMPANY
Statement of Cash Flows—Direct Method
For the Year Ended December 31, 2002

Cash flows from operating activities		
Cash collections from customers		$6,418,000*
Cash payments		
For operating expenses	$4,843,000**	
For income taxes	353,000	5,196,000
Net cash provided by operating activities		1,222,000
Cash flows from investing activities		
Sale of machinery	270,000	
Purchase of machinery	(750,000)	
Net cash used by investing activities		(480,000)
Cash flows from financing activities		
Payment of cash dividends	(200,000)	
Net cash used by financing activities		(200,000)
Net increase in cash		542,000
Cash at beginning of period		130,000
Cash at end of period		$ 672,000

Direct Method Computation

*Computation of cash collections from customers:

Revenues per the income statement		$6,583,000
Deduct: Increase in accounts receivable		(165,000)
Cash collections from customers		$6,418,000

**Computation of cash payments for operating expenses:

Operating expenses per the income statement	$4,920,000
Deduct: Loss from sale of machinery	(24,000)
Deduct: Decrease in inventories	(33,000)
Deduct: Increase in accounts payable	(20,000)
Cash payments for operating expenses	$4,843,000

THE NAVIGATOR

SELF-STUDY QUESTIONS

Self-Study/Self-Test

Answers are at the end of the chapter.

(SO 1) 1. Which of the following is *incorrect* about the statement of cash flows?
(a) It is a fourth basic financial statement.
(b) It provides information about cash receipts and cash payments of an entity during a period.
(c) It reconciles the ending cash account balance to the balance per the bank statement.
(d) It provides information about the operating, investing, and financing activities of the business.

(SO 2) 2. The statement of cash flows classifies cash receipts and cash payments by the following activities:
(a) operating and nonoperating.
(b) investing, financing, and operating.
(c) financing, operating, and nonoperating.
(d) investing, financing, and nonoperating.

(SO 2) 3. An example of a cash flow from an operating activity is:
(a) payment of cash to lenders for interest.
(b) receipt of cash from the sale of capital stock.
(c) payment of cash dividends to the company's stockholders.
(d) None of the above.

(SO 2) 4. An example of a cash flow from an investing activity is:
(a) receipt of cash from the issuance of bonds payable.
(b) payment of cash to repurchase outstanding capital stock.
(c) receipt of cash from the sale of equipment.
(d) payment of cash to suppliers for inventory.

(SO 2) 5. Cash dividends paid to stockholders are classified on the statement of cash flows as:
(a) operating activities.
(b) investing activities.
(c) a combination of the above.
(d) financing activities.

(SO 2) 6. An example of a cash flow from a financing activity is:
(a) receipt of cash from sale of land.
(b) issuance of debt for cash.
(c) purchase of equipment for cash.
(d) None of the above.

(SO 2) 7. Which of the following about the statement of cash flows is *incorrect*?
(a) The direct method may be used to report cash provided by operations.
(b) The statement shows the cash provided (used) for three categories of activity.
(c) The operating section is the last section of the statement.
(d) The indirect method may be used to report cash provided by operations.

(SO 3) 8. During the introductory phase of a company's life cycle, one would normally expect to see:
(a) negative cash from operations, negative cash from investing, and positive cash from financing.
(b) negative cash from operations, positive cash from investing, and positive cash from financing.
(c) positive cash from operations, negative cash from investing, and negative cash from financing.
(d) positive cash from operations, negative cash from investing, and positive cash from financing.

Questions 9 and 10 apply only to the indirect method.

(SO 4) 9. Net income is $132,000. During the year, accounts payable increased $10,000, inventory decreased $6,000, and accounts receivable increased $12,000. Under the indirect method, net cash provided by operations is:
(a) $102,000.
(b) $112,000.
(c) $124,000.
(d) $136,000.

(SO 4) 10. Noncash charges that are added back to net income in determining cash provided by operations under the indirect method do *not* include:
(a) depreciation expense.
(b) an increase in inventory.
(c) amortization expense.
(d) loss on sale of equipment.

Questions 11 and 12 apply only to the direct method.

(SO 5) 11. The beginning balance in accounts receivable is $44,000. The ending balance is $42,000. Sales during the period are $129,000. Cash receipts from customers are:
(a) $127,000.
(b) $129,000.
(c) $131,000.
(d) $141,000.

(SO 6) 12. Which of the following items is reported on a cash flow statement prepared by the direct method?
(a) Loss on sale of building.
(b) Increase in accounts receivable.

(c) Depreciation expense.
(d) Cash payments to suppliers.

13. The statement of cash flows should *not* be used (SO 6) to evaluate an entity's ability to:
(a) earn net income.
(b) generate future cash flows.
(c) pay dividends.
(d) meet obligations.

14. Free cash flow provides an indication of a com- (SO 6) pany's ability to:
(a) generate net income.
(b) generate cash to pay dividends.
(c) generate cash to invest in new capital expenditures.
(d) both (b) and (c).

15. Which one of the following ratios provides a (SO 6) useful comparison to the profit margin ratio?
(a) Capital expenditure ratio.
(b) Cash return on sales ratio.
(c) Cash debt coverage ratio.
(d) Current cash debt coverage ratio.

THE NAVIGATOR

QUESTIONS

1. (a) What is the statement of cash flows? (b) Alice Weiseman maintains that the statement of cash flows is an optional financial statement. Do you agree? Explain.

2. What questions about cash are answered by the statement of cash flows?

3. What are "cash equivalents"? How do cash equivalents affect the statement of cash flows?

4. Distinguish among the three types of activities reported in the statement of cash flows.

5. What are the major inflows of cash in a statement of cash flows? What are the major outflows of cash?

6. Why is it important to disclose certain noncash transactions? How should they be disclosed?

7. Wilma Flintstone and Barny Rublestone were discussing the presentation format of the statement of cash flows of Rock Candy Co. At the bottom of Rock Candy's statement of cash flows was a separate section entitled "Noncash investing and financing activities." Give three examples of significant noncash transactions that would be reported in this section.

8. Why is it necessary to use comparative balance sheets, a current income statement, and certain transaction data in preparing a statement of cash flows?

9. Contrast the advantages and disadvantages of the direct and indirect methods. Are both methods acceptable? Which method is preferred by the FASB? Which method is more popular?

10. When the total cash inflows exceed the total cash outflows in the statement of cash flows, how and where is this excess identified?

11. Describe the indirect method for determining net cash provided by operating activities.

12. Why is it necessary to convert accrual-based net income to cash-basis income when preparing a statement of cash flows?

13. The president of Styx Company is puzzled. During the year, the company experienced a net loss of $800,000, yet its cash increased $300,000 during the same period. Explain to the president how this situation could occur.

14. Identify five items that are adjustments to reconcile net income to net cash provided by operating activities under the indirect method.

15. Why and how is depreciation expense reported in a statement prepared using the indirect method?

16. Why is the statement of cash flows useful?

17. During 2002, Joe Pesci Company converted $1,600,000 of its total $2,000,000 of bonds payable into common stock. Indicate how the transaction would be reported on a statement of cash flows, if at all.

18. Describe the direct method for determining net cash provided by operating activities.

19. Give the formulas under the direct method for computing (a) cash receipts from customers and (b) cash payments to suppliers.

20. Kim Bassinger Inc. reported sales of $2 million for 2002. Accounts receivable decreased $200,000 and accounts payable increased $325,000. Compute cash receipts from customers, assuming that the receivable and payable transactions related to operations.

21. Why is depreciation expense not reported in the direct-method cash flow from operating activities section?

22. Give an example of one accrual-based ratio and one cash-based ratio to measure these characteristics of a company: (a) liquidity, (b) solvency, and (c) profitability.

*B*RIEF *E*XERCISES

BE12-1 Titanic Co. reported net income of $2.5 million in 2002. Depreciation for the year was $260,000, accounts receivable decreased $350,000, and accounts payable decreased $310,000. Compute net cash provided by operating activities using the indirect approach.

Compute cash provided by operating activities—indirect method.
(SO 4)

BE12-2 The net income for Robin Williams Co. for 2002 was $250,000. For 2002, depreciation on plant assets was $60,000, and the company incurred a loss on sale of plant assets of $10,000. Compute net cash provided by operating activities under the indirect method.

Compute cash provided by operating activities—indirect method.
(SO 4)

BE12-3 Each of the following items must be considered in preparing a statement of cash flows for Rudy Boesch Co. for the year ended December 31, 2002. For each item, state how it should be shown in the statement of cash flows for 2002.
(a) Issued bonds for $200,000 cash.
(b) Purchased equipment for $180,000 cash.
(c) Sold land costing $20,000 for $20,000 cash.
(d) Declared and paid a $50,000 cash dividend.

Indicate statement presentation of selected transactions.
(SO 2)

BE12-4 The comparative balance sheets for Survivor Company show the following changes in noncash current asset accounts: accounts receivable decrease $75,000, prepaid expenses increase $12,000, and inventories increase $30,000. Compute net cash provided by operating activities using the indirect method, assuming that net income is $220,000.

Compute net cash provided by operating activities using indirect method.
(SO 4)

BE12-5 Classify the following items as an operating, investing, or financing activity. Assume all items involve cash unless there is information to the contrary.
(a) Purchase of equipment.
(b) Sale of building.
(c) Redemption of bonds.
(d) Depreciation.
(e) Payment of dividends.
(f) Issuance of capital stock.

Classify items by activities.
(SO 2)

BE12-6 Answer the following questions.
(a) Why is cash from operations likely to be lower than reported net income during the growth phase?
(b) Why is cash from investing often positive during the late maturity phase and during the decline phase?

Answer questions related to phases of the product life cycle.
(SO 3)

BE12-7 Columbia Sportswear Company had accounts receivable of $118,709,000 at January 1, 2000, and $129,539,000 at December 31, 2000. Sales revenues were $614,825,000 for the year 2000. What is the amount of cash receipts from customers in 2000?

Compute receipts from customers—direct method.
(SO 5)

BE12-8 Wal-Mart Stores, Inc. reported income taxes of $3,692,000,000 on its 2001 income statement and income taxes payable of $1,129,000,000 at January 31, 2000, and $841,000,000 at January 31, 2001. What amount of cash payments were made for income taxes during fiscal 2001? (Ignore deferred taxes.)

Compute cash payments for income taxes—direct method.
(SO 5)

BE12-9 Excel Corporation reports operating expenses of $90,000 excluding depreciation expense of $15,000 for 2002. During the year prepaid expenses decreased $6,600 and accrued expenses payable increased $4,400. Compute the cash payments for operating expenses in 2002.

Compute cash payments for operating expenses—direct method.
(SO 5)

Compute cash payments for operating expenses using direct method.
(SO 5)

BE12-10 DiCaprio Company reports operating expenses of $270,000 excluding depreciation expense of $45,000 for 2002. During the year prepaid expenses decreased $19,800, and accrued expenses payable increased $13,200. Compute the cash payments for operating expenses in 2002.

Determine cash received in sale of equipment.
(SO 4, 5)

BE12-11 The T accounts for Equipment and the related Accumulated Depreciation for Sharon Stone Company at the end of 2002 are as follows.

Equipment			
Beg. bal.	80,000	Disposals	22,000
Acquisitions	41,600		
End. bal.	99,600		

Accumulated Depreciation			
Disposals	5,500	Beg. bal.	44,500
		Depr.	12,000
		End. bal.	51,000

Sharon Stone Company's income statement reported a loss on the sale of equipment of $4,900. What amount was reported on the statement of cash flows as "cash flow from sale of equipment"?

Identify financing activity transactions.
(SO 2)

BE12-12 The following T account is a summary of the cash account of Amy Company.

Cash (Summary Form)

Balance, 1/1/02	8,000		
Receipts from customers	364,000	Payments for goods	200,000
Dividends on stock investments	6,000	Payments for operating expenses	140,000
Proceeds from sale of equipment	36,000	Interest paid	10,000
Proceeds from issuance of bonds payable	200,000	Taxes paid	8,000
		Dividends paid	45,000
Balance, 12/31/02	211,000		

For Amy Company what amount of net cash provided (used) by financing activities should be reported in the statement of cash flows?

Calculate cash-based ratios.
(SO 6)

BE12-13 During 1998 **Cypress Semiconductor Corporation** reported cash provided by operations of $99,907,000, cash used in investing of $60,338,000, and cash used in financing of $57,522,000. In addition, cash spent for fixed assets during the period was $82,205,000. Average current liabilities were $96,331,000, and average total liabilities were $289,996,000. No dividends were paid. Calculate the following values.
(a) Free cash flow.
(b) Capital expenditure ratio.
(c) Current cash debt coverage ratio.

EXERCISES

Classify transactions by type of activity.
(SO 2)

E12-1 Barbara Eden Corporation had the following transactions during 2002.

1. Issued $50,000 par value common stock for cash.
2. Collected $16,000 of accounts receivable.
3. Declared and paid a cash dividend of $25,000.
4. Sold a long-term investment with a cost of $15,000 for $15,000 cash.
5. Issued $200,000 par value common stock upon conversion of bonds having a face value of $200,000.
6. Paid $18,000 on accounts payable.
7. Purchased a machine for $30,000, giving a long-term note in exchange.

Instructions
Analyze the transactions on the previous page and indicate whether each transaction resulted in a cash flow from (a) operating activities, (b) investing activities, (c) financing activities, or (d) noncash investing and financing activities.

Classify transactions by type of activity. (SO 2)

E12-2 An analysis of comparative balance sheets, the current year's income statement, and the general ledger accounts of Oprah Winfrey Corp. uncovered the following items. Assume all items involve cash unless there is information to the contrary.

1. Issuance of capital stock.
2. Amortization of patent.
3. Issuance of bonds for land.
4. Payment of interest on notes payable.
5. Conversion of bonds into common stock.
6. Sale of land at a loss.
7. Receipt of dividends on investment in stock.
8. Purchase of land.
9. Payment of dividends.
10. Sale of building at book value.
11. Exchange of land for patent.
12. Depreciation.
13. Redemption of bonds.
14. Receipt of interest on notes receivable.

Instructions
Indicate how the above items should be classified in the statement of cash flows using the following four major classifications: operating activity (indirect method), investing activity, financing activity, and significant noncash investing and financing activity.

Identify phases of product life cycle. (SO 3)

E12-3 The information in the table below is from the statement of cash flows for a company at four different points in time (A, B, C, and D). Negative values are presented in parentheses.

| | Point in Time | | | |
	A	B	C	D
Cash provided by operations	($ 60,000)	$30,000	$100,000	($ 10,000)
Cash provided by investing	(100,000)	25,000	30,000	(40,000)
Cash provided by financing	70,000	(110,000)	(50,000)	120,000
Net income	(40,000)	10,000	100,000	(5,000)

Instructions
For each point in time, state whether the company is most likely characterized as being in the introductory phase, growth phase, maturity phase, or decline phase. In each case explain your choice.

Prepare the operating activities section—indirect method. (SO 4)

E12-4 Porky Company reported net income of $195,000 for 2002. Porky also reported depreciation expense of $35,000, and a loss of $5,000 on the sale of equipment. The comparative balance sheets show an increase in accounts receivable of $15,000 for the year, an $8,000 increase in accounts payable, and a decrease in prepaid expenses $4,000.

Instructions
Prepare the operating activities section of the statement of cash flows for 2002 using the indirect method.

Prepare the operating activities section—indirect method. (SO 4)

E12-5 The current sections of Depeche Mode Co. balance sheets at December 31, 2001 and 2002, are presented as follows.

DEPECHE MODE CO.
Comparative Balance Sheets (partial)
December 31

	2002	2001
Current assets		
Cash	$105,000	$ 99,000
Accounts receivable	110,000	89,000
Inventory	171,000	186,000
Prepaid expenses	27,000	32,000
Total current assets	$413,000	$406,000
Current liabilities		
Accrued expenses payable	$ 15,000	$ 5,000
Accounts payable	85,000	92,000
Total current liabilities	$100,000	$ 97,000

Depeche Mode's net income for 2002 was $163,000. Depreciation expense was $30,000.

Instructions
Prepare the net cash provided by operating activities section of Depeche Mode's statement of cash flows for the year ended December 31, 2002, using the indirect method.

Prepare a partial statement of cash flows—indirect method. (SO 4)

E12-6 Presented below are three accounts that appear in the general ledger of Wesley Snipes Co. during 2002.

Equipment

Date		Debit	Credit	Balance
Jan. 1	Balance			160,000
July 31	Purchase of equipment	70,000		230,000
Sept. 2	Cost of equipment constructed	53,000		283,000
Nov. 10	Cost of equipment sold		45,000	238,000

Accumulated Depreciation—Equipment

Date		Debit	Credit	Balance
Jan. 1	Balance			71,000
Nov. 10	Accumulated depreciation on equipment sold	30,000		41,000
Dec. 31	Depreciation for year		24,000	65,000

Retained Earnings

Date		Debit	Credit	Balance
Jan. 1	Balance			105,000
Aug. 23	Dividends (cash)	14,000		91,000
Dec. 31	Net income		57,000	148,000

Instructions
From the postings in the accounts above, indicate how the information is reported on a statement of cash flows by preparing a partial statement of cash flows using the indirect method. The loss on sale of equipment was $4,000.

E12-7 Comparative balance sheets for Eddie Murphy Company are presented below.

Prepare a statement of cash flows—indirect method, and analyze the statement using ratios.
(SO 4, 6)

EDDIE MURPHY COMPANY
Comparative Balance Sheets
December 31

Assets	2002	2001
Cash	$ 63,000	$ 22,000
Accounts receivable	85,000	76,000
Inventories	180,000	189,000
Land	75,000	100,000
Equipment	260,000	200,000
Accumulated depreciation	(66,000)	(42,000)
Total	$597,000	$545,000

Liabilities and Stockholders' Equity	2002	2001
Accounts payable	$ 34,000	$ 47,000
Bonds payable	150,000	200,000
Common stock ($1 par)	214,000	164,000
Retained earnings	199,000	134,000
Total	$597,000	$545,000

Additional information:

1. Net income for 2002 was $125,000.
2. Cash dividends of $60,000 were declared and paid.
3. Bonds payable amounting to $50,000 were redeemed for cash $50,000.
4. Common stock was issued for $50,000 cash.
5. Depreciation expense was $24,000.
6. Sales for the year were $978,000.

Instructions
(a) Prepare a statement of cash flows for 2002 using the indirect method.
(b) Compute the following cash-basis ratios.
    (1) Current cash debt coverage ratio.
    (2) Cash return on sales ratio.
    (3) Cash debt coverage ratio.

E12-8 Satchmo Company has just completed its first year of operations on December 31, 2002. Its initial income statement showed that Satchmo had revenues of $137,000 and operating expenses of $88,000. Accounts receivable at year-end were $42,000. Accounts payable at year-end were $33,000. Assume that accounts payable related to operating expenses. Ignore income taxes.

Compute cash provided by operating activities—direct method.
(SO 5)

Instructions
Compute net cash provided by operating activities using the direct method.

E12-9 The income statement for Mel Gibson Company shows cost of goods sold $325,000 and operating expenses (exclusive of depreciation) $250,000. The comparative balance sheets for the year show that inventory increased $6,000, prepaid expenses decreased $6,000, accounts payable (merchandise suppliers) decreased $8,000, and accrued expenses payable increased $4,000.

Compute cash payments—direct method.
(SO 5)

Instructions
Using the direct method, compute (a) cash payments to suppliers and (b) cash payments for operating expenses.

E12-10 The 2002 accounting records of Winona Ryder Co. reveal the following transactions and events.

Compute cash flow from operating activities—direct method.
(SO 2, 5)

Payment of interest	$ 6,000	Collection of accounts receivable	$180,000
Cash sales	38,000	Payment of salaries and wages	65,000
Receipt of dividend revenue	14,000	Depreciation expense	18,000
Payment of income taxes	15,000	Proceeds from sale of aircraft	812,000

Net income	$38,000	Purchase of equipment for cash	$22,000
Payment of accounts payable		Loss on sale of aircraft	3,000
for merchandise	90,000	Payment of dividends	14,000
Payment for land	74,000	Payment of operating expenses	20,000

Instructions
Prepare the cash flows from operating activities section using the direct method. (Not all of the above items will be used.)

Calculate cash flows—direct method.
(SO 5)

E12-11   The following information is taken from the 2002 general ledger of Richard Gere Company.

Rent	Rent expense	$ 33,000
	Prepaid rent, January 1	7,900
	Prepaid rent, December 31	3,000
Salaries	Salaries expense	$ 54,000
	Salaries payable, January 1	5,000
	Salaries payable, December 31	8,000
Sales	Revenue from sales	$180,000
	Accounts receivable, January 1	12,000
	Accounts receivable, December 31	7,000

Instructions
In each of the above cases, compute the amount that should be reported in the operating activities section of the statement of cash flows using the direct method.

Compare two companies by using cash-based ratios.
(SO 6)

E12-12   Presented here is 1998 information for **PepsiCo, Inc.** and **The Coca-Cola Company**:

($ in millions)	PepsiCo	Coca-Cola
Cash provided by operations	$ 3,211	$ 3,433
Average current liabilities	6,085	6,175
Average total liabilities	14,712	10,175
Net income	1,993	3,533
Sales	22,348	18,813

Instructions
Using the cash-based ratios presented in this chapter, compare the (a) liquidity, (b) solvency, and (c) profitability of the two companies.

PROBLEMS: SET A

Prepare the operating activities section—indirect method.
(SO 4)

P12-1A   The income statement of Rebecca Sherrick Company is shown below.

REBECCA SHERRICK COMPANY
Income Statement
For the Year Ended December 31, 2002

Sales		$7,100,000
Cost of goods sold		
Beginning inventory	$1,700,000	
Purchases	5,430,000	
Goods available for sale	7,130,000	
Ending inventory	1,920,000	
Cost of goods sold		5,210,000
Gross profit		1,890,000
Operating expenses		
Selling expenses	380,000	
Administrative expense	525,000	
Depreciation expense	75,000	
Amortization expense	30,000	1,010,000
Net income		$ 880,000

Additional information:

1. Accounts receivable increased $490,000 during the year.
2. Prepaid expenses increased $170,000 during the year.
3. Accounts payable to merchandise suppliers increased $40,000 during the year.
4. Accrued expenses payable decreased $180,000 during the year.

Instructions
Prepare the operating activities section of the statement of cash flows for the year ended December 31, 2002, for Rebecca Sherrick Company using the indirect method.

P12-2A   Data for Rebecca Sherrick Company are presented in P12-1A.

Prepare the operating activities section—direct method.
(SO 5)

Instructions
Prepare the operating activities section of the statement of cash flows using the direct method.

P12-3A   The income statement of Dreamworks International Co. for the year ended December 31, 2002, reported the following condensed information.

Prepare the operating activities section—direct method.
(SO 5)

Revenue from fees	$470,000
Operating expenses	280,000
Income from operations	190,000
Income tax expense	47,000
Net income	$143,000

Dreamworks' balance sheet contained the following comparative data at December 31.

	2002	2001
Accounts receivable	$55,000	$40,000
Accounts payable	32,000	41,000
Income taxes payable	6,000	4,000

Dreamworks has no depreciable assets. (Accounts payable pertains to operating expenses.)

Instructions
Prepare the operating activities section of the statement of cash flows using the direct method.

P12-4A   Data for Dreamworks International Co. are presented in P12-3A.

Prepare the operating activities section—indirect method.
(SO 4)

Instructions
Prepare the operating activities section of the statement of cash flows using the indirect method.

P12-5A   The financial statements of Jim Carrey Company appear below.

Prepare a statement of cash flows — indirect method, and analyze the statement using ratios.
(SO 4, 6)

JIM CARREY COMPANY
Comparative Balance Sheets
December 31

Assets		2002		2001
Cash		$ 24,000		$ 13,000
Accounts receivable		20,000		14,000
Merchandise inventory		38,000		35,000
Property, plant, and equipment	$70,000		$78,000	
Less: Accumulated depreciation	(30,000)	40,000	(24,000)	54,000
Total		$122,000		$116,000

eGrade
Problem

Liabilities and Stockholders' Equity	2002	2001
Accounts payable	$ 26,000	$ 33,000
Income taxes payable	15,000	20,000
Bonds payable	20,000	10,000
Common stock	25,000	25,000
Retained earnings	36,000	28,000
Total	$122,000	$116,000

JIM CARREY COMPANY
Income Statement
For the Year Ended December 31, 2002

Sales		$240,000
Cost of goods sold		180,000
Gross profit		60,000
Selling expenses	$24,000	
Administrative expenses	10,000	34,000
Income from operations		26,000
Interest expense		2,000
Income before income taxes		24,000
Income tax expense		7,000
Net income		$ 17,000

Additional information:

1. Dividends of $9,000 were declared and paid.
2. During the year equipment was sold for $10,000 cash. This equipment cost $15,000 originally and had a book value of $10,000 at the time of sale.
3. All depreciation expense, $11,000, is in the selling expense category.
4. All sales and purchases are on account.
5. Additional equipment was purchased for $7,000 cash.

Instructions
(a) Prepare a statement of cash flows using the indirect method.
(b) Compute the following cash-basis ratios.
    (1) Current cash debt coverage ratio.
    (2) Cash return on sales ratio.
    (3) Cash debt coverage ratio.
    (4) Free cash flow.

Prepare a statement of cash flows—direct method, and analyze the statement using ratios.
(SO 5, 6)

P12-6A Data for the Jim Carrey Company are presented in P12-5A. Further analysis reveals the following.

1. Accounts payable pertains to merchandise creditors.
2. All operating expenses except for depreciation are paid in cash.

Instructions
(a) Prepare a statement of cash flows using the direct method.
(b) Compute the following cash-basis ratios.
    (1) Current cash debt coverage ratio.
    (2) Cash return on sales ratio.
    (3) Cash debt coverage ratio.
    (4) Free cash flow.

Prepare a statement of cash flows—indirect method.
(SO 4)

P12-7A Condensed financial data of Tom Cruise Company appear on the next page.

TOM CRUISE COMPANY
Comparative Balance Sheets
December 31

Assets	2002	2001
Cash	$ 92,700	$ 47,250
Accounts receivable	90,800	57,000
Inventories	121,900	102,650
Investments	84,500	87,000
Plant assets	250,000	205,000
Accumulated depreciation	(49,500)	(40,000)
	$590,400	$458,900

Liabilities and Stockholders' Equity		
Accounts payable	$ 57,700	$ 48,280
Accrued expenses payable	12,100	18,830
Bonds payable	100,000	70,000
Common stock	250,000	200,000
Retained earnings	170,600	121,790
	$590,400	$458,900

TOM CRUISE COMPANY
Income Statement Data
For the Year Ended December 31, 2002

Sales		$297,500
Gain on sale of plant assets		8,750
		306,250
Less:		
Cost of goods sold	$99,460	
Operating expenses (excluding depreciation expense)	14,670	
Depreciation expense	49,700	
Income taxes	7,270	
Interest expense	2,940	174,040
Net income		$132,210

Additional information:

1. New plant assets costing $92,000 were purchased for cash during the year.
2. Investments were sold at cost.
3. Plant assets costing $47,000 were sold for $15,550, resulting in a gain of $8,750.
4. A cash dividend of $83,400 was declared and paid during the year.

Instructions
Prepare a statement of cash flows using the indirect method.

P12-8A Data for Tom Cruise Company are presented in P12-7A. Further analysis reveals that accounts payable pertains to merchandise creditors.

Prepare a statement of cash flows—direct method.
(SO 5)

Instructions
Prepare a statement of cash flows for Tom Cruise Company using the direct method.

P12-9A Presented on page 538 are the comparative balance sheets for Nicolas Cage Company at December 31.

Prepare a statement of cash flows—indirect method, and analyze the statement using ratios.
(SO 4, 6)

NICOLAS CAGE COMPANY
Comparative Balance Sheets
December 31

Assets	2002	2001
Cash	$ 45,000	$ 57,000
Accounts receivable	72,000	64,000
Inventory	132,000	140,000
Prepaid expenses	12,140	16,540
Land	125,000	150,000
Equipment	200,000	175,000
Accumulated depreciation—equipment	(60,000)	(42,000)
Building	250,000	250,000
Accumulated depreciation—building	(75,000)	(50,000)
	$701,140	$760,540

Liabilities and Stockholders' Equity		
Accounts payable	$ 38,000	$ 45,000
Bonds payable	235,000	265,000
Common stock, $1 par	280,000	250,000
Retained earnings	148,140	200,540
	$701,140	$760,540

Additional information:

1. Operating expenses include depreciation expense of $70,000 and charges from prepaid expenses of $4,400.
2. Land was sold for cash at cost.
3. Cash dividends of $79,290 were paid.
4. Net income for 2002 was $26,890.
5. Equipment was purchased for $65,000 cash. In addition, equipment costing $40,000 with a book value of $13,000 was sold for $14,000 cash.
6. Bonds were converted at face value by issuing 30,000 shares of $1 par value common stock.
7. Net sales in 2002 were $367,000.

Instructions
(a) Prepare a statement of cash flows for 2002 using the indirect method.
(b) Compute the following cash-basis ratios for 2002.
    (1) Current cash debt coverage ratio.
    (2) Cash return on sales ratio.
    (3) Cash debt coverage ratio.
    (4) Free cash flow.

PROBLEMS: SET B

P12-1B   The income statement of Barbra Streisand Company is shown below.

Prepare the operating activities section—indirect method.
(SO 4)

BARBRA STREISAND COMPANY
Income Statement
For the Year Ended November 30, 2002

Sales		$6,900,000
Cost of goods sold		
Beginning inventory	$2,000,000	
Purchases	4,300,000	
Goods available for sale	6,300,000	
Ending inventory	1,600,000	
Total cost of goods sold		4,700,000
Gross profit		2,200,000
Operating expenses		
Selling expenses	450,000	
Administrative expenses	700,000	1,150,000
Net income		$1,050,000

Additional information:

1. Accounts receivable decreased $280,000 during the year.
2. Prepaid expenses increased $150,000 during the year.
3. Accounts payable to suppliers of merchandise decreased $200,000 during the year.
4. Accrued expenses payable decreased $100,000 during the year.
5. Administrative expenses include depreciation expense of $70,000.

Instructions
Prepare the operating activities section of the statement of cash flows for the year ended November 30, 2002, for Barbra Streisand Company using the indirect method.

P12-2B   Data for Barbra Streisand Company are presented in P12-1B.

Prepare the operating activities section—direct method.
(SO 5)

Instructions
Prepare the operating activities section of the statement of cash flows using the direct method.

P12-3B   George Clooney Company's income statement for the year ended December 31, 2002, contained the following condensed information.

Prepare the operating activities section—direct method.
(SO 5)

Revenue from fees		$900,000
Operating expenses (excluding depreciation)	$624,000	
Depreciation expense	60,000	
Loss on sale of equipment	26,000	710,000
Income before income taxes		190,000
Income tax expense		40,000
Net income		$150,000

Clooney's balance sheet contained the following comparative data at December 31.

	2002	2001
Accounts receivable	$47,000	$57,000
Accounts payable	41,000	36,000
Income taxes payable	4,000	9,000

(Accounts payable pertains to operating expenses.)

Prepare the operating activities section—indirect method.
(SO 4)

Prepare a statement of cash flows—indirect method, and analyze the statement using ratios.
(SO 4, 6)

Instructions
Prepare the operating activities section of the statement of cash flows using the direct method.

P12-4B Data for George Clooney Company are presented in P12-3B.

Instructions
Prepare the operating activities section of the statement of cash flows for George Clooney Company using the indirect method.

P12-5B The financial statements of Frank B. Robinson Company appear below.

FRANK B. ROBINSON COMPANY
Comparative Balance Sheets
December 31

Assets	2002	2001
Cash	$ 29,000	$ 13,000
Accounts receivable	28,000	14,000
Merchandise inventory	25,000	35,000
Property, plant, and equipment	60,000	78,000
Accumulated depreciation	(20,000)	(24,000)
Total	$122,000	$116,000

Liabilities and Stockholders' Equity		
Accounts payable	$ 27,000	$ 23,000
Income taxes payable	5,000	8,000
Bonds payable	27,000	33,000
Common stock	18,000	14,000
Retained earnings	45,000	38,000
Total	$122,000	$116,000

FRANK B. ROBINSON COMPANY
Income Statement
For the Year Ended December 31, 2002

Sales		$220,000
Cost of goods sold		180,000
Gross profit		40,000
Selling expenses	$14,000	
Administrative expenses	10,000	24,000
Income from operations		16,000
Interest expense		2,000
Income before income taxes		14,000
Income tax expense		4,000
Net income		$ 10,000

Additional information:

1. Dividends declared and paid were $3,000.
2. During the year equipment was sold for $8,500 cash. This equipment cost $18,000 originally and had a book value of $8,500 at the time of sale.
3. All depreciation expense is in the selling expense category.
4. All sales and purchases are on account.

Instructions
(a) Prepare a statement of cash flows using the indirect method.
(b) Compute the following cash-basis ratios.
    (1) Current cash debt coverage ratio.

(2) Cash return on sales ratio.
(3) Cash debt coverage ratio.
(4) Free cash flow.

P12-6B Data for the Frank B. Robinson Company are presented in P12-5B. Further analysis reveals the following.

1. Accounts payable pertain to merchandise suppliers.
2. All operating expenses except for depreciation were paid in cash.

Prepare a statement of cash flows—direct method, and analyze the statement using ratios.
(SO 5, 6)

Instructions
(a) Prepare a statement of cash flows for Frank B. Robinson Company using the direct method.
(b) Compute the following cash-basis ratios.
    (1) Current cash debt coverage ratio.
    (2) Cash return on sales ratio.
    (3) Cash debt coverage ratio.
    (4) Free cash flow.

P12-7B The financial statements of Bruce Willis Company appear below.

Prepare a statement of cash flows—indirect method.
(SO 4)

BRUCE WILLIS COMPANY
Comparative Balance Sheets
December 31

Assets	2002	2001
Cash	$ 23,000	$ 11,000
Accounts receivable	24,000	33,000
Merchandise inventory	20,000	29,000
Prepaid expenses	15,000	13,000
Land	40,000	40,000
Property, plant, and equipment	210,000	225,000
Less: Accumulated depreciation	(55,000)	(67,500)
Total	$277,000	$283,500

Liabilities and Stockholders' Equity		
Accounts payable	$ 9,000	$ 18,500
Accrued expenses payable	9,500	7,500
Interest payable	1,000	1,500
Income taxes payable	3,000	2,000
Bonds payable	50,000	80,000
Common stock	125,000	105,000
Retained earnings	79,500	69,000
Total	$277,000	$283,500

BRUCE WILLIS COMPANY
Income Statement
For the Year Ended December 31, 2002

Revenues		
Sales	$600,000	
Gain on sale of plant assets	2,500	$602,500
Less: Expenses		
Cost of goods sold	500,000	
Operating expenses (excluding depreciation)	60,000	
Depreciation expense	7,500	
Interest expense	5,000	
Income tax expense	9,000	581,500
Net income		$ 21,000

Additional information:

1. Plant assets were sold at a sales price of $37,500.
2. Additional equipment was purchased at a cost of $40,000.
3. Dividends of $10,500 were paid.
4. All sales and purchases were on account.
5. Bonds were redeemed at face value.
6. Additional shares of stock were issued for cash.

Instructions
Prepare a statement of cash flows for Bruce Willis Company for the year ended December 31, 2002, using the indirect method.

Prepare a statement of cash flows—direct method.
(SO 5)

P12-8B   Data for Bruce Willis Company is presented in P12-7B. Further analysis reveals the following.

1. Accounts payable relates to merchandise creditors.
2. All operating expenses, except depreciation expense, were paid in cash.

Instructions
Prepare a statement of cash flows for Bruce Willis Company for the year ended December 31, 2002, using the direct method.

Prepare a statement of cash flows—indirect method, and analyze the statement using ratios.
(SO 4, 6)

P12-9B   Presented below are the comparative balance sheets for Dennis Weigle Company as of December 31.

DENNIS WEIGLE COMPANY
Comparative Balance Sheets
December 31

Assets	2002	2001
Cash	$ 39,000	$ 45,000
Accounts receivable	49,500	52,000
Inventory	151,450	142,000
Prepaid expenses	16,780	21,000
Land	100,000	130,000
Equipment	228,000	155,000
Accumulated depreciation—equipment	(45,000)	(35,000)
Building	200,000	200,000
Accumulated depreciation—building	(60,000)	(40,000)
	$679,730	$670,000

Liabilities and Stockholders' Equity		
Accounts payable	$ 38,730	$ 40,000
Bonds payable	250,000	300,000
Common stock, $1 par	200,000	150,000
Retained earnings	191,000	180,000
	$679,730	$670,000

Additional information:

1. Operating expenses include depreciation expense of $42,000.
2. Land was sold for cash at book value.
3. Cash dividends of $27,000 were paid.
4. Net income for 2002 was $38,000.
5. Equipment was purchased for $95,000 cash. In addition, equipment costing $22,000 with a book value of $10,000 was sold for $8,100 cash.
6. Bonds were converted at face value by issuing 50,000 shares of $1 par value common stock.
7. Net sales for 2002 totaled $420,000.

Instructions
(a) Prepare a statement of cash flows for the year ended December 31, 2002, using the indirect method.
(b) Compute the following cash-basis ratios for 2002.
   (1) Current cash debt coverage ratio.
   (2) Cash return on sales ratio.
   (3) Cash debt coverage ratio.
   (4) Free cash flow.

◆ **B R O A D E N I N G   Y O U R   P E R S P E C T I V E**

*F*INANCIAL REPORTING AND ANALYSIS

FINANCIAL REPORTING PROBLEM: *Tootsie Roll Industries, Inc.*

BYP12-1 The financial statements of **Tootsie Roll Industries** are presented in Appendix A.

Instructions
Answer the following questions.
(a) What was the amount of net cash provided by operating activities for 1998? For 1997? What were the primary causes of any significant changes in cash from operations between 1997 and 1998?
(b) What was the amount of increase or decrease in cash and cash equivalents for the year ended December 31, 1998?
(c) Which method of computing net cash provided by operating activities does Tootsie Roll use?
(d) From your analysis of the 1998 statement of cash flows, was the change in accounts receivable a decrease or an increase? Was the change in inventories a decrease or an increase? Was the change in accounts payable a decrease or an increase?
(e) What was the total net cash used for investing activities for 1998?
(f) What was the amount of interest paid in 1998? What was the amount of income taxes paid in 1998?

COMPARATIVE ANALYSIS PROBLEM: *Tootsie Roll vs. Hershey Foods*

BYP12-2   The financial statements of **Hershey Foods** are presented in Appendix B, following the financial statements for **Tootsie Roll Industries** in Appendix A.

Instructions
(a) Based on the information in these financial statements, compute the following 1998 ratios for each company.
   (1) Current cash debt coverage.
   (2) Cash return on sales.
   (3) Cash debt coverage.
   (4) Free cash flow.
(b) What conclusions concerning the management of cash can be drawn from these data?

*I*NTERPRETING FINANCIAL STATEMENTS

BYP12-3   The incredible growth of **Amazon.com** has put fear into the hearts of traditional retailers. Amazon.com's stock price has soared to amazing levels. However, it is often pointed out in the financial press that the company has never reported a profit. The following financial information is taken from the 1998 financial statements of Amazon.com.

($ in thousands)	1998	1997
Current assets	$424,254	$137,709
Total assets	648,460	149,844
Current liabilities	161,575	44,551
Total liabilities	509,715	121,253
Cash provided by operations	31,035	687
Capital expenditures	28,333	7,603
Dividends paid	0	0
Net loss	(124,546)	(31,020)
Sales	609,996	147,787

Instructions

(a) Calculate the current ratio and current cash debt coverage ratio for Amazon.com for 1998, and discuss its liquidity.

(b) Calculate the cash debt coverage ratio and the debt to total assets ratio for Amazon.com for 1998, and discuss its solvency.

(c) Calculate free cash flow and the capital expenditure ratio for Amazon.com for 1998, and discuss its ability to finance expansion from internally generated cash. Thus far Amazon.com has avoided purchasing large warehouses; instead, it has used those of others. It is possible, however, that in order to increase customer satisfaction the company may have to build its own warehouses. If this happens, how might your impression of its ability to finance expansion change?

(d) Discuss any potential implications of the change in Amazon.com's cash provided by operations, and its net loss from 1997 to 1998.

(e) Based on your findings in parts (a) through (d), can you conclude whether or not Amazon.com's amazing stock price is justified?

GROUP DECISION CASE

BYP12-4 Greg Rhoda and Debra Sondgeroth are examining the following statement of cash flows for K.K. Bean Trading Company for the year ended January 31, 2002.

K.K. BEAN TRADING COMPANY
Statement of Cash Flows
For the Year Ended January 31, 2002

Sources of cash	
From sales of merchandise	$370,000
From sale of capital stock	420,000
From sale of investment (purchased below)	80,000
From depreciation	55,000
From issuance of note for truck	20,000
From interest on investments	6,000
Total sources of cash	951,000
Uses of cash	
For purchase of fixtures and equipment	340,000
For merchandise purchased for resale	258,000
For operating expenses (including depreciation)	160,000
For purchase of investment	75,000
For purchase of truck by issuance of note	20,000
For purchase of treasury stock	10,000
For interest on note payable	3,000
Total uses of cash	866,000
Net increase in cash	$ 85,000

Greg claims that K.K. Bean's statement of cash flows is an excellent portrayal of a superb first year with cash increasing $85,000. Debra replies that it was not a superb first year—but, rather, that the year was an operating failure, that the statement is presented incorrectly, and that $85,000 is not the actual increase in cash. The cash balance at the beginning of the year was $140,000.

Instructions

With the class divided into groups, answer the following.

(a) With whom do you agree, Greg or Debra? Explain your position.

(b) Using the data provided, prepare a statement of cash flows in proper form using the indirect method. The only noncash items in the income statement are depreciation and the gain from the sale of the investment.

REAL-WORLD FOCUS

BYP12-5   The statement of cash flows has become a commonly provided financial statement by companies throughout the world. It is interesting to note, however, that its format does vary across countries. The following statement of cash flows is from the 1998 financial statements of French building materials manufacturer **Saint-Gobain Group**.

SAINT-GOBAIN GROUP Consolidated Statements of Cash Flows		
(in millions of euro)	1998	1997
Cash flow from operating activities		
Net operating income	1,096	920
Profit on sale of non-current assets	(394)	(307)
Depreciation and amortization (note 14)	1,136	1,037
Dividends from associated companies	74	43
Sources from operations	**1,912**	**1,693**
(Increase) decrease in stocks	(174)	(41)
(Increase) decrease in trade accounts receivable	(59)	(241)
Increase (decrease) in trade accounts payable	79	79
Changes in income taxes payable and deferred taxes	14	3
Change in provisions	(48)	4
Cash provided by operating activities	**1,724**	**1,497**
Cash flow from investing activities		
Acquisition of fixed assets	(1,288)	(1,353)
Investments in consolidated companies (note 2)	(1,349)	(850)
Investments in unconsolidated companies	(382)	(244)
Total expenditure on fixed assets and investments	**(3,019)**	**(2,447)**
Cash (debt) acquired (note 2)	(19)	(17)
Acquisition of treasury stock	(344)	(3)
Disposal of fixed and intangible assets	25	55
Disposal of investments	1,107	814
(Cash) debt disposed of (note 2)	3	(125)
(Increase) decrease in deferred charges and other intangible assets	(68)	(48)
(Increase) decrease in deposits, long term receivables	9	31
(Increase) decrease in receivables related to investing activities	(124)	37
Cash used for investing activities	**(2,430)**	**(1,703)**
Cash flow from financing activities		
Issue of share capital	105	265
Minority interests in share capital increases of subsidiaries	4	4
(Decrease) increase in long term debt	132	541
Dividends paid	(248)	(221)

(in millions of euro)	1998	1997
Dividends paid to minority shareholders of consolidated subsidiaries	(44)	(82)
Cash provided by (used for) financing activities	**(51)**	**507**
Net effect of exchange rate fluctuations on cash and cash equivalents	(9)	(39)
Increase (decrease) in cash and cash equivalents (net)	**(766)**	**262**
Net cash and cash equivalents at the beginning of the year	(92)	(354)
Net cash and cash equivalents at the end of the year	**(858)**	**(92)**

Instructions
(a) What similarities to U.S. cash flow statements do you notice in terms of general format, as well as terminology?
(b) What differences do you notice in terms of general format, as well as terminology?
(c) Using the data provided in the statement of cash flows, compute (1) free cash flow and (2) capital expenditure ratio. Does the difference in the format of the statement or the terminology complicate your efforts to calculate these measures?

EXPLORING THE WEB

BYP12-6   *Purpose:* Locate SEC filing in Edgar Database.

Address: **www.sec.gov/index.html** *(or go to www.wiley.com/college/weygandt)*

Steps:

1. From the SEC homepage, choose **Edgar Database**.
2. Choose **Search the Edgar Database**.
3. Choose **Current Event Analysis**.
4. Select a company from the Edgar Daily Report.

Instructions
Answer the following questions.
(a) What form type did you retrieve?
(b) What is the company's name?
(c) What is the Standard Industrial Classification?
(d) What period does this report cover?
(e) In what state or jurisidiction is the organization?

BYP12-7   *Purpose:* Use the Internet to view SEC filings.

Address: **www.yahoo.com** *(or go to www.wiley.com/college/weygandt)*

Steps:

1. From the Yahoo homepage, choose **Stock Quotes**.
2. Enter a company's stock symbol or use "Symbol Lookup."
3. Choose **Get Quotes**.
4. Choose **SEC filings** (this will take you to Yahoo-Edgar Online).

Instructions
Answer the following questions.
(a) What company did you select?
(b) What is its stock symbol?
(c) What other recent SEC filings are available for your viewing?
(d) Which filing is the most recent? What is the date?

COMMUNICATION ACTIVITY

BYP12-8   Arnold Byte, the owner-president of Computer Services Company, is unfamiliar with the statement of cash flows that you, as his accountant, prepared. He asks for further explanation.

Instructions
Write him a brief memo explaining the form and content of the statement of cash flows as shown in Illustration 12-12.

RESEARCH ASSIGNMENT

BYP12-9   The March 21, 1997, issue of the *Wall Street Journal* contains an article by Greg Ip entitled "Cash Flow Rise Could Be Prop to Stock Prices."

Instructions
Read the article and answer the following questions.
(a) How is "free cash flow" defined in the article?
(b) What was the recent trend in free cash flow relative to earnings in the 1990s?
(c) How are stock prices related to companies' cash flows?
(d) Are there any negatives related to large free cash flows?

ETHICS CASE

BYP12-10   Puebla Corporation is a medium-sized wholesaler of automotive parts. It has ten stockholders who have been paid a total of $1 million in cash dividends for 8 consecutive years. The board of directors' policy requires that in order for this dividend to be declared, net cash provided by operating activities as reported in Puebla's current year's statement of cash flows must exceed $1 million. President and CEO Phil Monat's job is secure so long as he produces annual operating cash flows to support the usual dividend.

At the end of the current year, controller Rick Rodgers presents president Monat with some disappointing news: The net cash provided by operating activities is calculated by the indirect method to be only $970,000. The president says to Rick, "We must get that amount above $1 million. Isn't there some way to increase operating cash flow by another $30,000?" Rick answers, "These figures were prepared by my assistant. I'll go back to my office and see what I can do." The president replies, "I know you won't let me down, Rick."

Upon close scrutiny of the statement of cash flows, Rick concludes that he can get the operating cash flows above $1 million by reclassifying a $60,000, 2-year note payable listed in the financing activities section as "Proceeds from bank loan—$60,000." He will report the note instead as "Increase in payables—$60,000" and treat it as an adjustment of net income in the operating activities section. He returns to the president, saying, "You can tell the board to declare their usual dividend. Our net cash flow provided by operating activities is $1,030,000." "Good man, Rick! I knew I could count on you," exults the president.

Instructions
(a) Who are the stakeholders in this situation?
(b) Was there anything unethical about the president's actions? Was there anything unethical about the controller's actions?
(c) Are the board members or anyone else likely to discover the misclassification?

Answers to Self-Study Questions
1. c   2. b   3. a   4. c   5. d   6. b   7. c   8. a   9. d
10. b   11. c   12. d   13. a   14. d   15. b

✔ *Remember to go back to the Navigator box on the chapter-opening page and check off your completed work.*

CHAPTER 13

Financial Analysis: The Big Picture

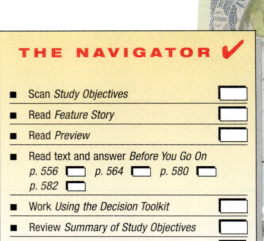

THE NAVIGATOR ✔

- Scan *Study Objectives* ☐
- Read *Feature Story* ☐
- Read *Preview* ☐
- Read text and answer *Before You Go On*
  p. 556 ☐   p. 564 ☐   p. 580 ☐
  p. 582 ☐
- Work *Using the Decision Toolkit* ☐
- Review *Summary of Study Objectives* ☐
- Work *Demonstration Problem* ☐
- Answer *Self-Study Questions* ☐
- Complete *Assignments* ☐

◆ **STUDY OBJECTIVES**

After studying this chapter, you should be able to:

1 Understand the concept of earning power and indicate how irregular items are presented.

2 Discuss the need for comparative analysis and identify the tools of financial statement analysis.

3 Explain and apply horizontal analysis.

4 Describe and apply vertical analysis.

5 Identify and compute ratios, and describe their purpose and use in analyzing a company's liquidity, solvency, and profitability.

6 Discuss the limitations of financial statement analysis.

THE NAVIGATOR

◆ **FEATURE STORY**

"FOLLOW THAT STOCK!"

If you thought cab drivers with cell phones were scary, how about a cab driver with a trading desk in the front seat?

When a stoplight turns red or traffic backs up, New York City cabby Carlos Rubino morphs into a day trader, scanning real-time quotes of his favorite stocks as they spew across a PalmPilot mounted next to his steering wheel. "It's kind of stressful," he says. "But I like it."

Itching to know how a particular stock is doing? Mr. Rubino is happy to look up quotes for passengers. Yahoo!, Amazon.com, and America Online are the most requested ones. He even lets customers use his Hitachi Traveler laptop to send urgent e-mails from the back seat. Aware of a new local law prohibiting cabbies from using cell phones while they're driving, Mr. Rubino extends that rule to his trading. "I stop the cab at the side of the road if I have to make a trade," he says. "Safety first."

Originally from São Paulo, Brazil, Mr. Rubino has been driving his cab since 1987, and started

trading stocks a few years ago. His curiosity grew as he began to educate himself by reading business publications. The Wall Street brokers he picks up are usually impressed with his knowledge, he says. But the feeling generally isn't mutual. Some of them "don't know much," he says. "They buy what people tell them to buy—they're like a toll collector."

Mr. Rubino is an enigma to his fellow cab drivers. A lot of his colleagues say they want to trade too. "But cab drivers are a little cheap," he says. "The [real-time] quotes cost $100 a month.

The wireless Internet access is $54 a month."

Will he give up his brokerage firm on wheels for a stationary job? Not likely. Though he claims a 70 percent return on his investments in recent months, he says he makes $1,300 and up a week driving his cab—more than he does trading. Besides, he adds, "Why go somewhere and have a boss?"

THE NAVIGATOR

Source: Excerpted from Barbara Boydston, "With this Cab, People Jump in and Shout, "Follow that Stock!", *Wall Street Journal,* August 18, 1999, p. C1.

A n important lesson can be learned from the Feature Story: Experience is the best teacher. By now you have learned a significant amount about financial reporting by U.S. corporations. Using some of the decision tools presented in this book, you can perform a rudimentary analysis on any U.S. company and draw basic conclusions about its financial health. Although it would not be wise for you to bet your life savings on a company's stock relying solely on your current level of knowledge, we strongly encourage you to practice your new skills wherever possible. Only with practice will you improve your ability to interpret financial numbers.

Before unleashing you on the world of high finance, we will present a few more important concepts and techniques. We also provide you with one last comprehensive review of corporate financial statements. We use nearly all of the decision tools presented in this text to analyze a single company—**Kellogg Company**, the world's leading producer of ready-to-eat cereal products.

The content and organization of this chapter are as follows.

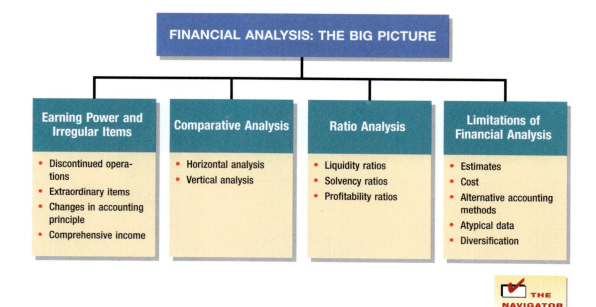

FINANCIAL ANALYSIS: THE BIG PICTURE

Earning Power and Irregular Items	Comparative Analysis	Ratio Analysis	Limitations of Financial Analysis
• Discontinued operations • Extraordinary items • Changes in accounting principle • Comprehensive income	• Horizontal analysis • Vertical analysis	• Liquidity ratios • Solvency ratios • Profitability ratios	• Estimates • Cost • Alternative accounting methods • Atypical data • Diversification

THE NAVIGATOR

EARNING POWER AND IRREGULAR ITEMS

STUDY OBJECTIVE

1

Understand the concept of earning power and indicate how irregular items are presented.

Ultimately, the value of a company is a function of its future cash flows. When analysts use this year's net income to estimate future cash flows, they must make sure that this year's net income does not include irregular revenues, expenses, gains, or losses. Net income adjusted for irregular items is referred to as **earning power**. **Earning power is the most likely level of income to be obtained in the future.** Earning power differs from actual net income by the amount of irregular revenues, expenses, gains, and losses included in this year's net income.

Users are interested in earning power because it helps them derive an estimate of future earnings without the "noise" of irregular items. For example, suppose Rye Corporation reports that this year's net income is $500,000, but included in that amount is a once-in-a-lifetime gain of $400,000. In estimating next year's net income for Rye Corporation, we would likely ignore this $400,000 gain and estimate that next year's net income will be in the neighborhood of $100,000. That is, based on this year's results, the company's earning power is roughly $100,000. Identifying irregular items is important if you are going to use reported earnings to estimate a company's value.

As an aid in determining earning power (or regular income), irregular items are identified by type on the income statement. Three types of irregular items are reported:

1. Discontinued operations
2. Extraordinary items
3. Changes in accounting principle

All these irregular items are reported net of income taxes. That is, the applicable income tax expense or tax savings is shown for income before income taxes and for each of the listed irregular items. The general concept is "Let the tax follow income or loss."

DISCONTINUED OPERATIONS

To downsize its operations, **General Dynamics Corp.** sold its missile business to **Hughes Aircraft Co.** for $450 million. In its income statement, General Dynamics was required to report the sale in a separate section entitled "Discontinued operations." **Discontinued operations** refer to the disposal of a significant segment of a business, such as the elimination of a major class of customers or an entire activity. Thus, the decision by **Singer Co.** to end its manufacture and sale of computers and the decision to close all overseas offices and terminate all foreign sales were both reported as discontinued operations. The phasing out of a model or part of a line of business, however, is *not* considered to be a disposal of a segment.

When the disposal of a significant segment occurs, the income statement should report both income from continuing operations and income (or loss) from discontinued operations. **The income (loss) from discontinued operations consists of the income (loss) from operations and the gain (loss) on disposal of the segment.** To illustrate, assume that Rozek Inc. has revenues of $2.5 million and expenses of $1.7 million from continuing operations in 2002. The company therefore has income before income taxes of $800,000. During 2002 the company discontinued and sold its unprofitable chemical division. The loss in 2002 from chemical operations (net of $60,000 taxes) was $140,000, and the loss on disposal of the chemical division (net of $30,000 taxes) was $70,000. Assuming a 30 percent tax rate on income before income taxes, we show the income statement presentation in Illustration 13-1.

Illustration 13-1 Statement presentation of discontinued operations

ROZEK INC. Income Statement (partial) For the Year Ended December 31, 2002		
Income before income taxes		$800,000
Income tax expense		240,000
Income from continuing operations		560,000
Discontinued operations		
Loss from operations of chemical division, **net of $60,000 income tax saving**	$140,000	
Loss from disposal of chemical division, net of **$30,000 income tax saving**	70,000	(210,000)
Net income		$350,000

Note that the caption "Income from continuing operations" is used, and the section "Discontinued operations" is added. **Within the new section, both the operating loss and the loss on disposal are reported net of applicable income taxes.** This presentation clearly indicates the separate effects of continuing operations and discontinued operations on net income. (In 2000 Kellogg Company did not report any discontinued operations.)

DECISION TOOLKIT

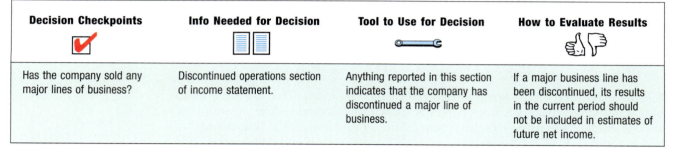

Decision Checkpoints	Info Needed for Decision	Tool to Use for Decision	How to Evaluate Results
Has the company sold any major lines of business?	Discontinued operations section of income statement.	Anything reported in this section indicates that the company has discontinued a major line of business.	If a major business line has been discontinued, its results in the current period should not be included in estimates of future net income.

EXTRAORDINARY ITEMS

Extraordinary items are events and transactions that meet two conditions: They are **unusual in nature** and **infrequent in occurrence.** To be considered *unusual*, the item should be abnormal and only incidentally related to the customary activities of the entity. To be regarded as *infrequent*, the event or transaction should not be reasonably expected to recur in the foreseeable future. Both criteria must be evaluated in terms of the environment in which the entity operates. Thus, **Weyerhaeuser Co.** reported the $36 million in damages to its timberland caused by the eruption of Mount St. Helens as an extraordinary item because the event was both unusual and infrequent. In contrast, Florida Citrus Company does not report frost damage to its citrus crop as an extraordinary item because frost damage is not viewed as infrequent.

Helpful Hint Ordinary gains and losses are reported at pretax amounts in arriving at income before income taxes.

Extraordinary items are reported net of taxes in a separate section of the income statement immediately below discontinued operations. To illustrate, assume that in 2002 a revolutionary foreign government expropriated property held as an investment by Rozek Inc. If the loss is $70,000 before applicable income taxes of $21,000, the income statement presentation will show a deduction of $49,000, as in Illustration 13-2.

Illustration 13-2 Statement presentation of extraordinary items

ROZEK INC. Income Statement (partial) For the Year Ended December 31, 2002		
Income before income taxes		$800,000
Income tax expense		240,000
Income from continuing operations		560,000
Discontinued operations		
Loss from operations of chemical division, net of $60,000 income tax saving	$140,000	
Loss from disposal of chemical division, net of $30,000 income tax saving	70,000	(210,000)
Income before extraordinary item		350,000
Extraordinary item		
Expropriation of investment, net of $21,000 income tax saving		**(49,000)**
Net income		$301,000

As illustrated, the caption "Income before extraordinary item" is added immediately before the listing of extraordinary items. This presentation clearly indicates the effect of the extraordinary item on net income. If there were no discontinued operations, the third line of the income statement in Illustration 13-2 would be "Income before extraordinary item."

If a transaction or event meets one, but not both, of the criteria for an extraordinary item, it should be reported in a separate line item in the upper half of the income statement, rather than being reported in the bottom half as an extraordinary item. Usually these items are reported under either "Other revenues and gains" or "Other expenses and losses" at their gross amount (not net of tax). This is true, for example, of gains (losses) resulting from the sale of property, plant, and equipment. Illustration 13-3 shows the appropriate classification of extraordinary and ordinary items.

Illustration 13-3   Classification of extraordinary and ordinary items

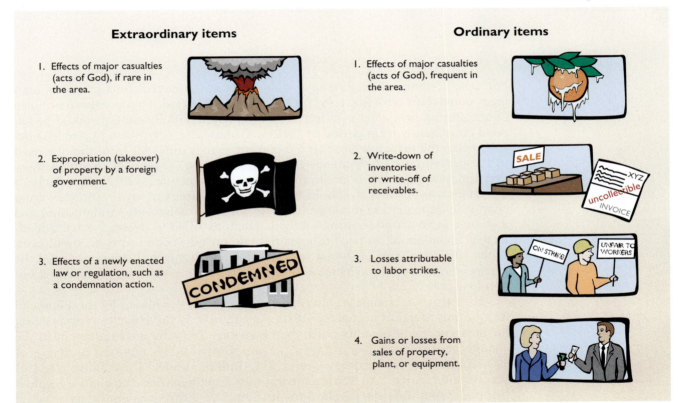

Kellogg Company, for example, did not report any extraordinary items in its 1999 or 2000 income statements. It did, however, incur significant charges as the result of "restructuring" efforts to reduce costs. These restructuring charges did not meet the criteria required for extraordinary item classification. Instead, Kellogg reported them as "Restructuring charges"—of $244.6 million in 1999 and $86.5 million in 2000—in the upper half (income from operations section) of its income statement. The title "nonrecurring" suggests that the charges occur infrequently. In analyzing Kellogg's results, we must decide whether to use its income as reported, or instead to assume that these charges are, in fact, not representative of the company's future earning power. If we assume they are not representative of Kellogg's earning power, we would add them back to net income (after consideration of their tax impact) to estimate next year's income. Further investigation reveals that Kellogg has had "nonrecurring charges" in every year except one since 1993. We therefore conclude that these charges are not "infrequent." As a consequence, we use net income as it was reported by the company for all subsequent analysis.

DECISION TOOLKIT

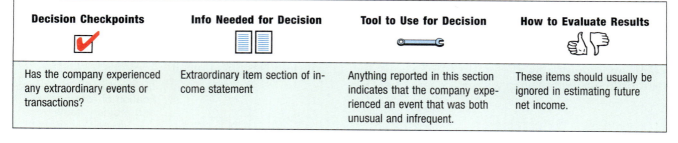

Decision Checkpoints	Info Needed for Decision	Tool to Use for Decision	How to Evaluate Results
Has the company experienced any extraordinary events or transactions?	Extraordinary item section of income statement	Anything reported in this section indicates that the company experienced an event that was both unusual and infrequent.	These items should usually be ignored in estimating future net income.

CHANGES IN ACCOUNTING PRINCIPLE

For ease of comparison, financial statements are expected to be prepared on a basis **consistent** with that used for the preceding period. That is, where a choice of accounting principles is available, the principle initially chosen should be applied consistently from period to period. A change in accounting principle occurs when the principle used in the current year is different from the one used in the preceding year. A change is permitted, when (1) management can show that the new principle is preferable to the old principle, and (2) the effects of the change are clearly disclosed in the income statement. Two examples are a change in depreciation methods (such as declining-balance to straight-line) and a change in inventory costing methods (such as FIFO to average cost). The effect of a change in an accounting principle on net income can be significant. When **U.S. West**, one of the six regional Bell telephone companies, changed the depreciation method for its telecommunications equipment, it posted a $3.2 billion loss (net of tax).

Sometimes a change in accounting principle is mandated by the Financial Accounting Standards Board (FASB). An example is the change in accounting for postretirement benefits other than pensions. In its income statement in the change period, **Owens-Corning Fiberglas Corporation** reported a charge of $227 million, net of income taxes of $117 million, under "Cumulative effect of accounting change." An accompanying note explained that the charge resulted from adopting the new standard for its domestic postretirement plans.

A change in an accounting principle affects reporting in two ways:

1. The new principle should be used in reporting the results of operations of the current year.
2. The cumulative effect of the change on all prior-year income statements should be disclosed net of applicable taxes in a special section immediately preceding Net Income.

To illustrate, we will assume that at the beginning of 2002, Rozek Inc. changes from the straight-line method to the declining-balance method for equipment that was purchased on January 1, 1999. The cumulative effect on prior-year income statements (statements for 1999–2001) is to increase depreciation expense and decrease income before income taxes by $24,000. If there is a 30 percent tax rate, the net-of-tax effect of the change is $16,800 ($24,000 × 70%). The income statement presentation is shown in Illustration 13-4.

ROZEK INC. Income Statement (partial) For the Year Ended December 31, 2002		
Income before income taxes		$800,000
Income tax expense		240,000
Income from continuing operations		560,000
Discontinued operations		
Loss from operations of chemical division, net of $60,000 income tax saving	$140,000	
Loss from disposal of chemical division, net of $30,000 income tax saving	70,000	(210,000)
Income before extraordinary item and cumulative effect of change in accounting principle		350,000
Extraordinary item		
Expropriation of investment, net of $21,000 income tax saving		(49,000)
Cumulative effect of change in accounting principle		
Effect on prior years of change in depreciation **method, net of $7,200 income tax saving**		**(16,800)**
Net income		$284,200

Illustration 13-4 Statement presentation of a change in accounting principle

The income statement for Rozek will also show depreciation expense for the current year. The amount is based on the new depreciation method. In this case the caption "Income before extraordinary item and cumulative effect of change in accounting principle" is inserted immediately following the section on discontinued operations. This presentation clearly indicates the cumulative effect of the change on prior years' income. If a company has neither discontinued operations nor extraordinary items, the caption "Income before cumulative effect of change in accounting principle" is used in place of "Income from continuing operations." A complete income statement showing all material items not typical of regular operations is presented in the Demonstration Problem on page 588.

In 1997 Kellogg reported an $18 million reduction in net income due to the cumulative effect of a change in the way it accounted for business process reengineering costs. In analyzing a company, we suggest eliminating any effect from a change in accounting principle (that is, using the amount of income before the change in accounting principle). So, in our subsequent analysis of Kellogg, we will eliminate this $18 million item.

In summary, in evaluating a company, it generally makes sense to eliminate all irregular items in estimating future earning power. In some cases you must decide whether certain information reported in the top half of the income statement should be ignored for analysis purposes, such as Kellogg's "nonrecurring" items.

DECISION TOOLKIT

Decision Checkpoints	Info Needed for Decision	Tool to Use for Decision	How to Evaluate Results
Has the company changed any of its accounting policies?	Cumulative effect of change in accounting principle section of income statement	Anything reported in this section indicates that the company has changed an accounting policy during the current year.	The cumulative effect should be ignored in estimating the future net income.

COMPREHENSIVE INCOME

Most revenues, expenses, gains, and losses recognized during the period are included in income. However, over time, specific exceptions to this general practice have developed so that certain items now bypass income and are reported directly in stockholders' equity. For example, unrealized gains and losses on available-for-sale securities are not included in income, but rather are reported in the balance sheet as adjustments to stockholders' equity.

Why are these gains and losses on available-for-sale securities excluded from net income? Disclosing them separately does two things: (1) It reduces the volatility of net income due to fluctuations in fair value. (2) It informs the financial statement user of the gain or loss that would be incurred if the securities were sold at fair value.

Many analysts have expressed concern that the number of items that bypass the income statement has increased significantly. They feel that this has reduced the usefulness of the income statement. To address this concern, the FASB now requires that, in addition to reporting net income, a company must also report comprehensive income. **Comprehensive income** includes all changes in stockholders' equity during a period except those resulting from investments by stockholders and distributions to stockholders. A number of alternative formats for reporting comprehensive income are allowed. The income statement of **Tootsie Roll Industries** in Appendix A provides an example of one format. These formats are discussed in advanced accounting courses.

BEFORE YOU GO ON . . .

◆ **Review It**

1. What is earning power?
2. What are irregular items, and what effect might they have on the estimation of future earnings and future cash flows?

COMPARATIVE ANALYSIS

Any item reported in a financial statement has significance: Its inclusion indicates that the item exists at a given time and in a certain quantity. For example, when **Kellogg Company** reports $136.4 million of cash on its balance sheet, we know that the company had that amount of cash on the balance sheet date. But we do not know whether the amount represents an increase over prior years, or whether it is adequate in relation to the company's need for cash. To obtain such information, it is necessary to compare the amount of cash with other financial statement data.

Comparisons can be made on a number of different bases. Three are illustrated in this chapter:

Intracompany

2002 ↔ 2003

1. **Intracompany basis.**   This basis compares an item or financial relationship **within a company** in the current year with the same item or relationship in one or more prior years. For example, Kellogg can compare its cash balance at the end of the current year with last year's balance to find the amount of the increase or decrease. Likewise, Kellogg can compare the percentage of cash to current assets at the end of the current year

with the percentage in one or more prior years. Intracompany comparisons are useful in detecting changes in financial relationships and significant trends.

2. **Intercompany basis.**   This basis compares an item or financial relationship of one company with the same item or relationship in **one or more competing companies**. The comparisons are made on the basis of the published financial statements of the individual companies. For example, Kellogg's total sales for the year can be compared with the total sales of its competitors in the breakfast cereal area, such as **Quaker Oats** and **General Mills**. Intercompany comparisons are useful in determining a company's competitive position.

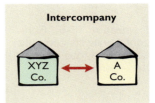

3. **Industry averages.**   This basis compares an item or financial relationship of a company with **industry averages** (or **norms**). For example, Kellogg's financial data can be compared with the averages for its industry compiled by financial ratings organizations such as **Dun & Bradstreet**, **Moody's**, and **Standard & Poor's**, or with information provided on the Internet by organizations such as **Yahoo**! on its financial site. Comparisons with industry averages provide information about a company's relative position within the industry.

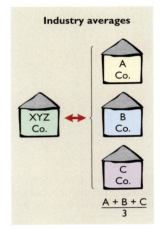

Three basic tools are used in financial statement analysis to highlight the significance of financial statement data:

- **Horizontal analysis** evaluates a series of financial statement data over a period of time.
- **Vertical analysis** evaluates financial statement data by expressing each item in a financial statement as a percent of a base amount.
- **Ratio analysis** expresses the relationship among selected items of financial statement data.

Horizontal analysis is used primarily in intracompany comparisons. Two features in published financial statements facilitate this type of comparison: First, each of the basic financial statements is presented on a comparative basis for a minimum of two years. Second, a summary of selected financial data is presented for a series of five to ten years or more. Vertical analysis is used in both intra- and intercompany comparisons. Ratio analysis is used in all three types of comparisons. In the following sections, we will explain and illustrate each of the three types of analysis.

HORIZONTAL ANALYSIS

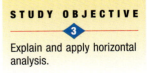

STUDY OBJECTIVE
3
Explain and apply horizontal analysis.

Horizontal analysis, also called **trend analysis**, is a technique for evaluating a series of financial statement data over a period of time. Its purpose is to determine the increase or decrease that has taken place. This change may be expressed as either an amount or a percentage. For example, here are recent net sales figures (in millions) for Kellogg Company:

2000	1999	1998	1997	1996
$6,954.7	$6,984.2	$6,762.1	$6,830.1	$6,676.6

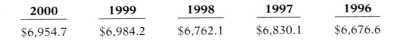

Alternative Terminology
Horizontal analysis is also often called **trend analysis**.

If we assume that 1996 is the base year, we can measure all percentage increases or decreases relative to this base-period amount with the formula shown in Illustration 13-5.

Illustration 13-5 Horizontal analysis computation of changes since base period

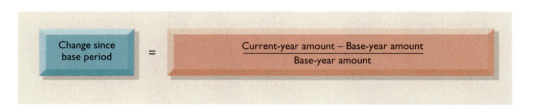

For example, we can determine that net sales for Kellogg Company increased approximately 2.3 percent [($6,830.1 − $6,676.6) ÷ $6,676.6] from 1996 to 1997. Similarly, we can also determine that net sales increased by 4.2 percent [($6,954.7 − $6,676.6) ÷ $6,676.6] from 1996 to 2000.

Alternatively, we can express current-year sales as a percentage of the base period. To do so, we would divide the current-year amount by the base-year amount, as shown in Illustration 13-6.

Illustration 13-6 Horizontal analysis computation of current year in relation to base year

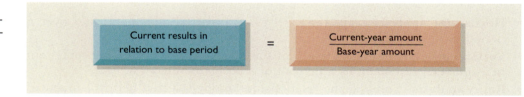

Current-period sales expressed as a percentage of the base period for each of the five years, using 1996 as the base period, are shown in Illustration 13-7.

Illustration 13-7 Horizontal analysis of net sales

KELLOGG COMPANY				
Net Sales (in millions)				
Base Period 1996				
2000	1999	1998	1997	1996
$6,954.7	$6,984.2	$6,762.1	$6,830.1	$6,676.6
104.2%	104.6%	101.3%	102.3%	100%

Balance Sheet

To further illustrate horizontal analysis, we use the financial statements of Kellogg Company. A horizontal analysis of its two-year condensed balance sheets for 2000 and 1999, showing dollar and percentage changes, is presented in Illustration 13-8.

Illustration 13-8 Horizontal analysis of a balance sheet

KELLOGG COMPANY, INC.
Condensed Balance Sheets
December 31
(in millions)

	2000	1999	Increase (Decrease) during 2000 Amount	Percent
Assets				
Current assets	$1,606.8	$1,569.2	$ 37.6	2.4
Property assets (net)	2,526.9	2,640.9	(114.0)	(4.3)
Other assets	762.6	598.6	164.0	27.4
Total assets	$4,896.3	$4,808.7	$ 87.6	1.8
Liabilities and Stockholders' Equity				
Current liabilities	$2,492.6	$1,587.8	$904.8	57.0
Long-term liabilities	1,506.2	2,407.7	(901.5)	(37.4)
Total liabilities	3,998.8	3,995.5	3.3	0.0
Stockholders' equity				
Common stock	205.8	208.3	(2.5)	(1.2)
Retained earnings and other	1,065.7	985.8	79.9	8.1
Treasury stock (cost)	(374.0)	(380.9)	(6.9)	(1.8)
Total stockholders' equity	897.5	813.2	84.3	10.4
Total liabilities and stockholders' equity	$4,896.3	$4,808.7	$ 87.6	1.8

Helpful Hint It is difficult to comprehend the significance of a change when only the dollar amount of change is examined. When the change is expressed in percentage form, it is easier to grasp the true magnitude of the change.

The comparative balance sheets show that a number of changes occurred in Kellogg's financial position from 1999 to 2000. In the assets section, current assets increased $37.6 million, or 2.4 percent ($37.6 ÷ $1,569.2), and property assets (net) decreased $114 million, or 4.3 percent. In the liabilities section, current liabilities increased $904.8 million, or 57.0 percent, while long-term liabilities decreased $901.5 million, or 37.4 percent. In the stockholders' equity section, retained earnings increased $79.9 million, or 8.1 percent. This suggests that the company expanded its asset base during 2000 and financed this expansion primarily by retaining income in the business. The 57 percent ($904.8 million) increase in current liabilities was nearly offset by the 37.4 percent ($901.5 million) decrease in long-term liabilities. The company increased its stockholders' equity 10.4 percent by retaining income.

Income Statement

Presented in Illustration 13-9 is a horizontal analysis of the two-year comparative income statements of Kellogg Company for 2000 and 1999 in a condensed format.

Illustration 13-9 Horizontal analysis of an income statement

KELLOGG COMPANY, INC. Condensed Income Statements For the Years Ended December 31 (in millions)				
			Increase (Decrease) during 2000	
	2000	1999	Amount	Percent
Net sales	$6,954.7	$6,984.2	$ (29.5)	**(0.4)**
Cost of goods sold	3,327.0	3,325.2	1.8	**0.0**
Gross profit	3,627.7	3,659.0	(31.3)	**(0.9)**
Selling and administrative expenses	2,551.4	2,585.6	(34.2)	**(1.3)**
Nonrecurring charges	86.5	244.6	(158.1)	**(64.6)**
Income from operations	989.8	828.8	161.0	**19.4**
Interest expense	137.5	118.8	18.7	**15.7**
Other income (expense), net	15.4	(173.3)	188.7	**–**
Income before income taxes	867.7	536.7	331.0	**61.7**
Income tax expense	280.0	198.4	81.6	**41.1**
Net income	$ 587.7	$ 338.3	$249.4	**73.7**

Horizontal analysis of the income statements shows the following changes: Net sales decreased $29.5 million, or 0.4 percent ($29.5 ÷ $6,984.2). Cost of goods sold increased $1.8 million, or 0.0 percent ($1.8 ÷ $3,325.2). Selling and administrative expenses decreased $34.3 million, or 1.3 percent ($34.2 ÷ $2,585.6). Overall, gross profit decreased 0.1 percent and net income increased 73.7 percent. The increase in net income can be attributed to the change in nonrecurring charges and other income (expenses).

The measurement of changes from period to period in percentages is relatively straightforward and quite useful. But complications can occur in making the computations. If an item has no value in a base year or preceding year and a value in the next year, no percentage change can be computed. And if a negative amount appears in the base or preceding period and a positive amount exists the following year, no percentage change can be computed.

DECISION TOOLKIT

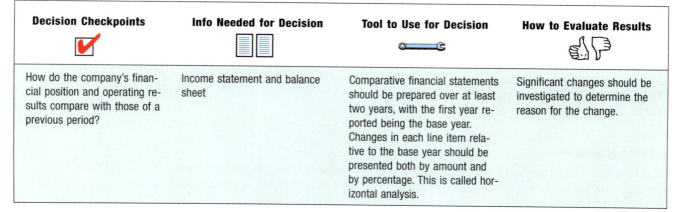

Decision Checkpoints	Info Needed for Decision	Tool to Use for Decision	How to Evaluate Results
How do the company's financial position and operating results compare with those of a previous period?	Income statement and balance sheet	Comparative financial statements should be prepared over at least two years, with the first year reported being the base year. Changes in each line item relative to the base year should be presented both by amount and by percentage. This is called horizontal analysis.	Significant changes should be investigated to determine the reason for the change.

VERTICAL ANALYSIS

Vertical analysis, also called **common-size analysis**, is a technique for evaluating financial statement data that expresses each item in a financial statement as a percent of a base amount. For example, on a balance sheet we might say that current assets are 22 percent of total assets (total assets being the base amount). Or on an income statement we might say that selling expenses are 16 percent of net sales (net sales being the base amount).

STUDY OBJECTIVE

4

Describe and apply vertical analysis.

Balance Sheet

Presented in Illustration 13-10 are the comparative balance sheets of Kellogg for 2000 and 1999, analyzed vertically. The base for the asset items is **total assets**. The base for the liability and stockholders' equity items is **total liabilities and stockholders' equity**.

Alternative Terminology
Vertical analysis is sometimes referred to as **common-size analysis**.

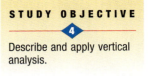

Illustration 13-10 Vertical analysis of a balance sheet

KELLOGG COMPANY, INC. Condensed Balance Sheets December 31 (in millions)				
	2000		**1999**	
Assets	Amount	Percent*	Amount	Percent*
Current assets	$1,606.8	32.8	$1,569.2	32.6
Property assets (net)	2,526.9	51.6	2,640.9	54.9
Other assets	762.6	15.6	598.6	12.5
Total assets	$4,896.3	100.0	$4,808.7	100.0
Liabilities and Stockholders' Equity				
Current liabilities	$2,492.6	50.9	$1,587.8	33.0
Long-term liabilities	1,506.2	30.8	2,407.7	50.1
Total liabilities	3,998.8	81.7	3,995.5	83.1
Stockholders' equity				
Common stock	205.8	4.2	208.3	4.3
Retained earnings and other	1,065.7	21.7	985.8	20.5
Treasury stock (cost)	(374.0)	(7.6)	(380.9)	(7.9)
Total stockholders' equity	897.5	18.3	813.2	16.9
Total liabilities and stockholders' equity	$4,896.3	100.0	$4,808.7	100.0

*Numbers have been rounded to total 100 percent.

Vertical analysis shows the **relative size** of each category on the balance sheet. It also can show the **percentage change** in the individual asset, liability, and stockholders' equity items. In this case, for example, we can see that even though current assets increased $37.6 million from 1999 to 2000, they remained virtually the same as a percent of total assets. Property assets (net) decreased from 54.9 percent to 51.6 percent of total assets. Also, total stockholders' equity increased from 16.9 percent to 18.3 percent of total liabilities and stockholders' equity. This switch to a lower percentage of debt financing has two causes: First, total liabilities decreased, going from 83.1 percent to 81.7 percent of total liabilities and stockholders' equity. Second, treasury stock decreased by $6.9 million, going from 7.9 percent to 7.6 percent of total liabilities and stockholders' equity.

Income Statement

Vertical analysis of Kellogg's comparative income statements is shown in Illustration 13-11. We see that cost of goods sold **as a percentage of net sales** increased from 47.6 percent to 47.8 percent, and selling and administrative expenses decreased from 37.0 percent to 36.7 percent. Net income as a percent of net sales increased from 4.9 percent to 8.5 percent. Kellogg's increase in net income as a percentage of sales is due primarily to the change in nonrecurring charges and other income (expense).

Illustration 13-11
Vertical analysis of an income statement

Kellogg's

KELLOGG COMPANY, INC.
Condensed Income Statements
For the Years Ended December 31
(in millions)

	2000		1999	
	Amount	Percent*	Amount	Percent*
Net sales	$6,954.7	100.0	$6,984.2	100.0
Cost of goods sold	3,327.0	47.8	3,325.2	47.6
Gross profit	3,627.7	52.2	3,659.0	52.4
Selling and administrative expenses	2,551.4	36.7	2,585.6	37.0
Nonrecurring charges	86.5	1.3	244.6	3.5
Income from operations	989.8	14.2	828.8	11.9
Interest expense	137.5	2.0	118.8	1.7
Other income (expense), net	15.4	0.2	(173.3)	2.5
Income before income taxes	867.7	12.5	536.7	7.7
Income tax expense	280.0	4.0	198.4	2.8
Net income	$ 587.7	8.5	$ 338.3	4.9

*Numbers have been rounded to total 100 percent.

An associated benefit of vertical analysis is that it enables you to compare companies of different sizes. For example, one of Kellogg's main competitors is **The Quaker Oats Company**. Using vertical analysis, we can more meaningfully compare the condensed income statements of Kellogg and Quaker Oats, as shown in Illustration 13-12.

CONDENSED INCOME STATEMENTS For the Year Ended December 31, 2000 (in millions)				
	Kellogg Company, Inc.		The Quaker Oats Company	
	Amount	Percent*	Amount	Percent*
Net sales	$6,954.7	100.0	$5,041.0	100.0
Cost of goods sold	3,327.0	47.8	2,288.3	45.4
Gross profit	3,627.7	52.2	2,752.7	54.6
Selling and administrative expenses	2,551.4	36.7	1,968.8	39.1
Nonrecurring charges	86.5	1.3	182.5	3.6
Income from operations	989.8	14.2	601.4	11.9
Other expenses and revenues (including income taxes)	402.1	5.8	240.8	4.8
Net income	$ 587.7	8.5	$ 360.6	7.1

*Numbers have been rounded to total 100 percent.

Illustration 13-12 Inter-company comparison by vertical analysis

Kellogg's net sales are 38 percent greater than the net sales of Quaker Oats. But vertical analysis eliminates the impact of this difference in size. Kellogg's income from operations as a percentage of net sales is 14.2 percent, compared to 11.9 percent for Quaker Oats. This difference can be attributed both to Kellogg's lower selling and administrative expense percentage (36.7 percent vs. 39.1 percent) and to Kellogg's lower nonrecurring charges. Kellogg's other expenses were 5.8 percent of net sales compared to only 4.8 percent for Quaker Oats. However, these items are usually not very predictable over time. Kellogg's gross profit rate of 52.2 percent was lower than Quaker's 54.6 percent.

DECISION TOOLKIT

Decision Checkpoints	Info Needed for Decision	Tool to Use for Decision	How to Evaluate Results
How do the relationships between items in this year's financial statements compare with those of last year or those of competitors?	Income statement and balance sheet	Each line item on the income statement should be presented as a percentage of net sales, and each line item on the balance sheet should be presented as a percentage of total assets or total liabilities and stockholders' equity. These percentages should be investigated for differences either across years in the same company or in the same year across different companies. This is called vertical analysis.	Any differences either across years or between companies should be investigated to determine the cause.

BEFORE YOU GO ON . . .

◆ **Review It**

1. What different bases can be used to compare financial information?
2. What is horizontal analysis?
3. What is vertical analysis?

◆ **Do It**

Summary financial information for Rosepatch Company is as follows.

	December 31, 2002	December 31, 2001
Current assets	$234,000	$180,000
Plant assets (net)	756,000	420,000
Total assets	$990,000	$600,000

Compute the amount and percentage changes in 2002 using horizontal analysis, assuming 2001 is the base year.

Action Plan

• Find the percentage change by dividing the amount of the increase by the 2001 amount (base year).

Solution

	Increase in 2002	
	Amount	**Percent**
Current assets	$ 54,000	30% [($234,000 − $180,000) ÷ $180,000]
Plant assets (net)	336,000	80% [($756,000 − $420,000) ÷ $420,000]
Total assets	$390,000	65% [($990,000 − $600,000) ÷ $600,000]

Related exercise material: BE13-1, BE13-3, BE13-4, BE13-6, E13-1, E13-3, and E13-4.

THE NAVIGATOR

*R*ATIO ANALYSIS

STUDY OBJECTIVE
5

Identify and compute ratios, and describe their purpose and use in analyzing a company's liquidity, solvency, and profitability.

Investors and financial analysts frequently use ratios to evaluate the financial health and performance of a company. In this section we provide comprehensive coverage of financial ratios, discuss some important relationships among the ratios, and focus on their interpretation.

The financial information in Illustrations 13-13 through 13-16 (pages 565 and 566) was used to calculate Kellogg's 2000 ratios. You can use these data to review the computations.

Illustration 13-13
Kellogg Company's
balance sheets

KELLOGG COMPANY, INC.
Balance Sheets
December 31
(in millions)

	2000	1999
Assets		
Current assets		
Cash and short-term investments	$ 204.4	$ 150.6
Accounts receivable (net)	685.3	678.5
Inventories	443.8	503.8
Prepaid expenses and other current assets	273.3	236.3
Total current assets	1,606.8	1,569.2
Property assets (net)	2,526.9	2,640.9
Intangibles and other assets	762.6	598.6
Total assets	$4,896.3	$4,808.7
Liabilities and Stockholders' Equity		
Current liabilities	$2,492.6	$1,587.8
Long-term liabilities	1,506.2	2,407.7
Stockholders' equity—common	897.5	813.2
Total liabilities and stockholders' equity	$4,896.3	$4,808.7

Illustration 13-14
Kellogg Company's
income statements

KELLOGG COMPANY, INC.
Condensed Income Statements
For the Years Ended December 31
(in millions)

	2000	1999
Net sales	$6,954.7	$6,984.2
Cost of goods sold	3,327.0	3,325.2
Gross profit	3,627.7	3,659.0
Selling and administrative expenses	2,551.4	2,585.6
Nonrecurring charges	86.5	244.6
Income from operations	989.8	828.8
Interest expense	137.5	118.8
Other income (expense), net	15.4	(173.3)
Income before income taxes	867.7	536.7
Income tax expense	280.0	198.4
Net income	$ 587.7	$ 338.3

Illustration 13-15
Kellogg Company's
statements of cash flows

KELLOGG COMPANY, INC.
Condensed Statements of Cash Flows
For the Years Ended December 31
(in millions)

	2000	1999
Cash flows from operating activities		
Cash receipts from operating activities	$6,947.9	$6,998.7
Cash payments for operating activities	6,067.0	6,203.5
Net cash provided by operating activities	880.9	795.2
Cash flows from investing activities		
Purchases of property, plant, and equipment	(230.9)	(266.2)
Other investing activities	(148.4)	22.0
Net cash used in investing activities	(379.3)	(244.2)
Cash flows from financing activities		
Issuance of common stock	4.5	12.9
Issuance of debt	294.0	292.1
Reductions of debt	(336.4)	(443.9)
Reductions of common stock	(0.0)	(0.0)
Payment of dividends	(403.9)	(388.7)
Net cash used in financing activities	(441.8)	(527.6)
Other	(6.0)	(9.2)
Increase (decrease) in cash and cash equivalents	53.8	14.2
Cash and cash equivalents at beginning of year	150.6	136.4
Cash and cash equivalents at end of year	$ 204.4	$ 150.6

Illustration 13-16
Additional information for
Kellogg Company

Additional information

	2000	1999
Average number of shares (millions)	405.3	407.6
Stock price at year-end	26\frac{1}{4}$	33\frac{5}{8}$

For analysis of the primary financial statements, ratios can be classified into three types:

1. **Liquidity ratios**: Measures of the short-term ability of the enterprise to pay its maturing obligations and to meet unexpected needs for cash.
2. **Solvency ratios**: Measures of the ability of the enterprise to survive over a long period of time.
3. **Profitability ratios**: Measures of the income or operating success of an enterprise for a given period of time.

Ratios can provide clues to underlying conditions that may not be apparent from individual financial statement components. But a single ratio by itself is not very meaningful. Accordingly, in this discussion of ratios we use the following types of comparisons.

1. **Intracompany comparisons** covering two years for Kellogg Company (using comparative financial information from Illustrations 13-10 and 13-11).
2. **Intercompany comparisons** using The Quaker Oats Company as one of Kellogg's principal competitors.

3. **Industry average comparisons** based on **Robert Morris Associates'** median ratios for manufacturers of flour and other grain mill products and comparisons with other sources. For some of the ratios that we use, industry comparisons are not available. (These are denoted "na.")

LIQUIDITY RATIOS

Liquidity ratios measure the short-term ability of the enterprise to pay its maturing obligations and to meet unexpected needs for cash. Short-term creditors such as bankers and suppliers are particularly interested in assessing liquidity. The ratios that can be used to determine the enterprise's short-term debt-paying ability are the current ratio, the acid-test ratio, the current cash debt coverage ratio, the receivables turnover ratio, the average collection period, the inventory turnover ratio, and average days in inventory.

1. **Current ratio.** The current ratio expresses the relationship of current assets to current liabilities. The ratio is computed by dividing current assets by current liabilities. It is widely used for evaluating a company's liquidity and short-term debt-paying ability. The 2000 and 1999 current ratios for Kellogg and comparative data are shown in Illustration 13-17.

Illustration 13-17 Current ratio

Ratio	Formula	Indicates:	Kellogg 2000	Kellogg 1999	Quaker Oats 2000	Industry 2000
Current ratio	Current assets / Current liabilities	Short-term debt-paying ability	0.64	0.99	1.18	1.30

What does the ratio actually tell us? Kellogg's 2000 current ratio of 0.64 means that for every dollar of current liabilities, Kellogg has $0.64 of current assets. We sometimes state such ratios as 0.64:1 to reinforce this interpretation. Kellogg's current ratio—and therefore its liquidity—decreased significantly in 2000. It is well below the industry average and also below that of Quaker Oats.

The current ratio is only one measure of liquidity. It does not take into account the composition of the current assets. For example, a satisfactory current ratio could conceal the fact that a portion of current assets may be tied up in slow-moving inventory. A dollar of cash would be more readily available to pay the bills than a dollar's worth of slow-moving inventory. These weaknesses are addressed by the next ratio.

BUSINESS INSIGHT
Management Perspective

The apparent simplicity of the current ratio can have real-world limitations. An addition of equal amounts to both the numerator and the denominator causes the ratio to decrease. Assume, for example, that a company has $2,000,000 of current assets and $1,000,000 of current liabilities. Its current ratio is 2:1. If it purchases $1,000,000 of inventory on account, it will have $3,000,000 of current assets and $2,000,000 of current liabilities. Its current ratio decreases to 1.5:1. If, instead, the company pays off $500,000 of its current liabilities, it will have $1,500,000 of current assets and $500,000 of current liabilities, and its current ratio increases to 3:1. Any trend analysis should be done with care, because this ratio is susceptible to quick changes and is easily influenced by management.

2. **Acid-test ratio.** The **acid-test (quick) ratio** is a measure of a company's immediate short-term liquidity. It is computed by dividing the sum of cash, short-term investments, and net receivables by current liabilities. Thus, it is an important complement to the current ratio. Note that it does not include inventory or prepaid expenses.

Cash, short-term investments, and receivables (net) are much more liquid than inventory and prepaid expenses. The inventory may not be readily salable, and the prepaid expenses may not be transferable to others. The acid-test ratio for Kellogg is shown in Illustration 13-18.

Illustration 13-18 Acid-test ratio

Ratio	Formula	Indicates:	Kellogg 2000	Kellogg 1999	Quaker Oats 2000	Industry 2000
Acid-test or quick ratio	$\text{Cash} + \dfrac{\text{Short-term investments} + \text{Net receivables}}{\text{Current liabilities}}$	Immediate short-term liquidity	0.36	0.52	0.75	0.66

The 2000 and 1999 acid-test ratios for Kellogg again suggest low liquidity. Is Kellogg's 2000 acid-test ratio of 0.36:1 adequate? Like its current ratio, its acid-test ratio decreased significantly in 2000. When compared with the industry average of 0.66:1 and Quaker Oats' 0.75:1, Kellogg's acid-test ratio seems to require additional investigation.

3. **Current cash debt coverage ratio.** A disadvantage of the current and acid-test ratios is that they use year-end balances of the current asset and current liability accounts. These balances may not represent the company's current position during most of the year. A ratio that partially corrects for this problem is the **current cash debt coverage ratio**. It is calculated by dividing cash provided by operating activities by average current liabilities. Because it uses cash provided by operating activities rather than a balance at one point in time, it may provide a better representation of a company's liquidity. Kellogg's current cash debt coverage ratio is shown in Illustration 13-19.

Illustration 13-19 Current cash debt coverage ratio

Ratio	Formula	Indicates:	Kellogg 2000	Kellogg 1999	Quaker Oats 2000	Industry 2000
Current cash debt coverage ratio	$\dfrac{\text{Cash provided by operating activities}}{\text{Average current liabilities}}$	Short-term debt-paying ability (cash basis)	0.43	0.48	0.58	na

Like the current ratio, this ratio decreased in 2000 for Kellogg. Is the coverage adequate? Probably so. Even though Kellogg's operating cash flow coverage of average current liabilities is less than Quaker Oats', it exceeds a commonly accepted threshold of 0.40. No industry comparison is available.

4. **Receivables turnover ratio.** Liquidity may be measured by how quickly certain assets can be converted to cash. How liquid, for example, are the

receivables? The ratio used to assess the liquidity of the receivables is the **receivables turnover ratio**. It measures the number of times, on average, receivables are collected during the period. The receivables turnover ratio is computed by dividing net credit sales (net sales less cash sales) by average net receivables during the year. Unless seasonal factors are significant, average net receivables can be computed from the beginning and ending balances of the net receivables. The receivables turnover ratio for Kellogg is shown in Illustration 13-20.

Illustration 13-20 Receivables turnover ratio

Ratio	Formula	Indicates:	Kellogg 2000	Kellogg 1999	Quaker Oats 2000	Industry 2000
Receivables turnover ratio	Net credit sales / Average net receivables	Liquidity of receivables	10.2	10.2	18.3	11.7

We have assumed that all Kellogg's sales are credit sales. The receivables turnover ratio for Kellogg remained the same in 2000. However, the turnover of 10.2 times is below the industry median of 11.7, and well below that of 18.3 times for Quaker Oats.

BUSINESS INSIGHT
Management Perspective

In some cases, the receivables turnover ratio may be misleading. Some companies, especially large retail chains, issue their own credit cards. They encourage customers to use these cards, and they may even slow their collections in order to earn a healthy return on the outstanding receivables at interest rates of 18 percent to 22 percent. In general, however, the faster the turnover, the greater the reliance that can be placed on the current and acid-test ratios for assessing liquidity.

5. **Average collection period.** A popular variant of the receivables turnover ratio is to convert it to an **average collection period** in terms of days. This is done by dividing the receivables turnover ratio into 365 days. The average collection period for Kellogg is shown in Illustration 13-21.

Illustration 13-21 Average collection period

Ratio	Formula	Indicates:	Kellogg 2000	Kellogg 1999	Quaker Oats 2000	Industry 2000
Average collection period	365 days / Receivables turnover ratio	Liquidity of receivables and collection success	35.8	35.8	19.9	31.2

Kellogg's 2000 receivables turnover of 10.2 times is divided into 365 days to obtain approximately 35.8 days. This means that receivables are collected on average every 35.8 days, or about every 5 weeks. Analysts frequently use the average collection period to assess the effectiveness of a company's credit and collection policies. The general rule is that the collection period should not greatly exceed the credit term period (the time allowed for payment).

It is interesting to note that Quaker Oats' average collection period is significantly shorter than those of Kellogg and the industry. This difference may be due to more aggressive collection practices. Or, more likely, it may be due to a difference in credit terms granted. Quaker Oats might grant more generous discounts for early payment than others in the industry.

6. **Inventory turnover ratio.** The **inventory turnover ratio** measures the number of times on average the inventory is sold during the period. Its purpose is to measure the liquidity of the inventory. The inventory turnover ratio is computed by dividing the cost of goods sold by the average inventory during the period. Unless seasonal factors are significant, average inventory can be computed from the beginning and ending inventory balances. Kellogg's inventory turnover ratio is shown in Illustration 13-22.

Illustration 13-22 Inventory turnover ratio

Ratio	Formula	Indicates:	Kellogg 2000	Kellogg 1999	Quaker Oats 2000	Industry 2000
Inventory turnover ratio	Cost of goods sold / Average inventory	Liquidity of inventory	7.0	7.0	8.3	6.9

Kellogg's inventory turnover ratio remained the same in 2000. The turnover ratio of 7.0 times is slightly higher than the industry average of 6.9 but lower than Quaker Oats' 8.3. Generally, the faster the inventory turnover, the less cash is tied up in inventory and the less the chance of inventory becoming obsolete. Of course, a downside of high inventory turnover is that the company can run out of inventory when it is needed.

7. **Days in inventory.** A variant of the inventory turnover ratio is the **days in inventory**, which measures the average number of days it takes to sell the inventory. The days in inventory for Kellogg is shown in Illustration 13-23.

Illustration 13-23 Days in inventory

Ratio	Formula	Indicates:	Kellogg 2000	Kellogg 1999	Quaker Oats 2000	Industry 2000
Days in inventory	365 days / Inventory turnover ratio	Liquidity of inventory and inventory management	52.1	52.1	44.0	52.9

Kellogg's 2000 inventory turnover ratio of 7.0 divided into 365 is approximately 52.1 days. An average selling time of 52.1 days is faster than the industry average but slower than that of Quaker Oats. Some of this difference might be explained by differences in product lines across the two companies, although in many ways the types of products of these two companies are quite similar.

Management Perspective

Inventory turnover ratios vary considerably among industries. For example, grocery store chains have a turnover of 10 times and an average selling period of 37 days. In contrast, jewelry stores have an average turnover of 1.3 times and an average selling period of 281 days. Within a company there may even be significant differences in inventory turnover among different types of products. Thus, in a grocery store the turnover of perishable items such as produce, meats, and dairy products is faster than the turnover of soaps and detergents.

To conclude, nearly all of these liquidity measures suggest that Kellogg's liquidity declined during 2000. However, its liquidity appears acceptable when compared both to that of Quaker Oats and to the industry as a whole.

SOLVENCY RATIOS

Solvency ratios measure the ability of the enterprise to survive over a long period of time. Long-term creditors and stockholders are particularly interested in a company's ability to pay interest as it comes due and to repay the face value of debt at maturity. The debt to total assets ratio, the times interest earned ratio, and the cash debt coverage ratio provide information about debt-paying ability. In addition, as discussed in Chapter 12, free cash flow provides information about the company's solvency and its ability to pay additional dividends or invest in new projects.

8. **Debt to total assets ratio.** The **debt to total assets ratio** measures the percentage of the total assets provided by creditors. It is computed by dividing total debt (both current and long-term liabilities) by total assets. This ratio indicates the company's degree of financial leverage. It also provides some indication of the company's ability to withstand losses without impairing the interests of creditors. The higher the percentage of debt to total assets, the greater the risk that the company may be unable to meet its maturing obligations. The lower the ratio, the more equity "buffer" is available to creditors if the company becomes insolvent. Thus, from the creditors' point of view, a low ratio of debt to total assets is desirable. Kellogg's debt to total assets ratio is shown in Illustration 13-24.

Illustration 13-24 Debt to total assets ratio

Ratio	Formula	Indicates:	Kellogg 2000	Kellogg 1999	Quaker Oats 2000	Industry 2000
Debt to total assets ratio	Total liabilities ÷ Total assets	Percentage of total assets provided by creditors	0.82	0.83	0.60	0.73

Kellogg's 2000 ratio of 0.82 means that creditors have provided financing sufficient to cover 82 percent of the company's total assets. Alternatively, it says that Kellogg would have to liquidate 82 percent of its assets at their book value in order to pay off all of its debts. Kellogg's 82 percent is above the industry average of 73 percent and above the 60 percent ratio of Quaker Oats. Kellogg's solvency improved slightly during the year.

The adequacy of this ratio is often judged in light of the company's earnings. Generally, companies with relatively stable earnings, such as public utilities, have higher debt to total assets ratios than cyclical companies with widely fluctuating earnings, such as many high-tech companies.

Another ratio with a similar meaning is the **debt to equity ratio**. It shows the relative use of borrowed funds (total liabilities) compared with resources invested by the owners. This ratio can be computed in several ways. Debt may be defined to include only the noncurrent portion of liabilities. Also, intangible assets may be excluded from stockholders' equity (resulting in tangible net worth). If debt and assets are defined as above (all liabilities and all assets), then when the debt to total assets ratio equals 50 percent, the debt to equity ratio is 1:1. When making comparisons using this ratio, take care to make sure you are comparing "apples to apples."

9. **Times interest earned ratio.**   The **times interest earned ratio** (also called **interest coverage**) indicates the company's ability to meet interest payments as they come due. It is computed by dividing income before interest expense and income taxes by interest expense. This ratio uses income before interest expense and income taxes because this amount represents what is available to cover interest. Kellogg's times interest earned ratio is shown in Illustration 13-25.

Illustration 13-25   Times interest earned ratio

Ratio	Formula	Indicates:	Kellogg 2000	Kellogg 1999	Quaker Oats 2000	Industry 2000
Times interest earned ratio	$\dfrac{\text{Net income} + \text{Interest expense} + \text{Tax expense}}{\text{Interest expense}}$	Ability to meet interest payments as they come due	7.3	5.5	13.2	8.72

For Kellogg the 2000 coverage was 7.3. This measure indicates that income before interest and taxes was 7.3 times the amount needed for interest expense. This is below both the rate for Quaker Oats and the average rate for the industry. However, although the debt to assets ratio suggests that Kellogg relies heavily on debt financing, the times interest earned ratio suggests that the company can easily service its debt.

10. **Cash debt coverage ratio.**   The ratio of cash provided by operating activities to average total liabilities is the **cash debt coverage ratio**. As discussed in Chapter 12, this measure is a cash-basis measure of solvency. This ratio indicates a company's ability to repay its liabilities from cash generated from operating activities without having to liquidate assets. Illustration 13-26 shows Kellogg's cash debt coverage ratio.

Illustration 13-26   Cash debt coverage ratio

Ratio	Formula	Indicates:	Kellogg 2000	Kellogg 1999	Quaker Oats 2000	Industry 2000
Cash debt coverage ratio	$\dfrac{\text{Cash provided by operating activities}}{\text{Average total liabilities}}$	Long-term debt-paying ability (cash basis)	0.22	0.19	0.37	na

An industry average for this measure is not available. Kellogg's 0.22 is less than Quaker Oats' 0.37, and it did increase from 0.19 in 1999. One way of interpreting this ratio is to say that net cash generated from one year of operations would be sufficient to pay off 22 percent of Kellogg's total liabilities. If 22 percent of this year's liabilities were retired each year, it would take approximately five years to retire all of its debt. It would take Quaker Oats approximately 2.7 years to do so. A general rule of thumb is that a measure above 0.20 is acceptable.

e – BUSINESS INSIGHT

Today, investors have access to information provided by corporate managers that used to be available only to professional analysts. Corporate managers have always made themselves available to security analysts for questions at the end of every quarter. Now, because of a combination of new corporate disclosure requirements by the Securities and Exchange Commission and technologies that make communication to large numbers of people possible at a very low price, the average investor can listen in on these discussions. For example, one individual investor, Matthew Johnson, a **Nortel Networks** local area network engineer in Belfast, Northern Ireland, "stayed up past midnight to listen to **Apple Computer's** recent Internet conference call. Hearing the company's news 'from the dog's mouth,' he says 'gave me better information' than hunting through chat-rooms."

Source: Jeff D. Opdyke, "Individuals Pick Up on Conference Calls," *Wall Street Journal*, November 20, 2000.

11. **Free cash flow.**   One indication of a company's solvency, as well as of its ability to pay dividends or expand operations, is the amount of excess cash it generated after investing to maintain its current productive capacity and paying dividends. As discussed in Chapter 12, this amount is referred to as **free cash flow**. For example, if you generate $100,000 of cash from operating activities but you spend $30,000 to maintain and replace your productive facilities at their current levels and pay $10,000 in dividends, you have $60,000 to use either to expand operations or to pay additional dividends.

Kellogg's free cash flow is shown in Illustration 13-27.

Illustration 13-27   Free cash flow

Ratio	Formula			Indicates:	Kellogg 2000	Kellogg 1999	Quaker Oats 2000	Industry 2000
Free cash flow	Cash provided by operating activities	− Capital expenditures	− Cash dividends	Cash available for paying dividends or expanding operations	$246.1 (in millions)	$140.3	$83.4 (in millions)	na

Kellogg's free cash flow increased considerably from 1999 to 2000. Both Kellogg and Quaker Oats have used a large portion of free cash flow in recent years to repurchase their own stock.

PROFITABILITY RATIOS

Profitability ratios measure the income or operating success of an enterprise for a given period of time. Income, or the lack of it, affects the company's ability to obtain debt and equity financing. It also affects the company's liquidity position, and its ability to grow. As a consequence, both creditors and investors are interested in evaluating profitability. Profitability is frequently used as the ultimate test of management's operating effectiveness.

The relationships among the numerous measures of profitability are very important. Understanding them can help management determine where to focus its efforts to improve profitability. Illustration 13-28 diagrams these relationships. Our discussion of Kellogg's profitability is structured around this diagram.

Illustration 13-28 Relationships among profitability measures

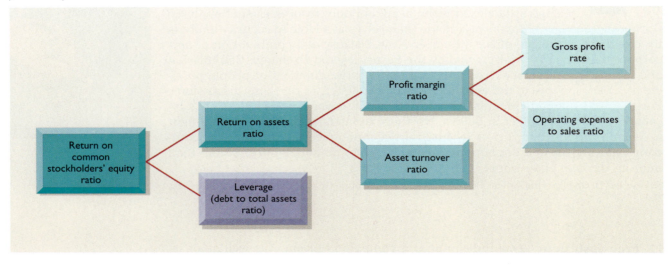

12. **Return on common stockholders' equity ratio.**   A widely used measure of profitability from the common stockholder's viewpoint is the **return on common stockholders' equity ratio**. This ratio shows how many dollars of net income were earned for each dollar invested by the owners. It is computed by dividing net income minus any preferred stock dividends—that is, income available to common stockholders—by average common stockholders' equity. The return on common stockholders' equity for Kellogg is shown in Illustration 13-29.

Illustration 13-29 Return on common stockholders' equity ratio

			Kellogg		Quaker Oats	Industry
Ratio	**Formula**	**Indicates:**	**2000**	**1999**	**2000**	**2000**
Return on common stockholders' equity ratio	$\dfrac{\text{Net income} - \text{Preferred stock dividends}}{\text{Average common stockholders' equity}}$	Profitability of common stockholders' investment	0.69	0.40	1.20	0.27

Kellogg's 2000 rate of return on common stockholders' equity is unusually high at 69 percent, considering an industry average of 27 percent. Quaker Oats' return of 120 percent is extraordinary. In the subsequent sections we investigate the causes of these high returns.

13. **Return on assets ratio.** The return on common stockholders' equity ratio is affected by two factors: the return on assets ratio and the degree of leverage. The **return on assets ratio** measures the overall profitability of assets in terms of the income earned on each dollar invested in assets. It is computed by dividing net income by average total assets. Kellogg's return on assets ratio is shown in Illustration 13-30.

Illustration 13-30 Return on assets ratio

Ratio	Formula	Indicates:	Kellogg 2000	Kellogg 1999	Quaker Oats 2000	Industry 2000
Return on assets ratio	Net income / Average total assets	Overall profitability of assets	0.12	0.07	0.15	0.08

Kellogg had a 12 percent return on assets in 2000 and 7 percent in 1999. This rate is lower than that of Quaker Oats, but exceeds the industry average in 2000.

Note that Kellogg's rate of return on stockholders' equity (69 percent) is substantially higher than its rate of return on assets (12 percent). The reason is that Kellogg has made effective use of **leverage**. **Leveraging** or **trading on the equity** at a gain means that the company has borrowed money at a lower rate of interest than the rate of return it earns on the assets it purchased with the borrowed funds. Leverage enables management to use money supplied by nonowners to increase the return to owners.

A comparison of the rate of return on assets with the rate of interest paid for borrowed money indicates the profitability of trading on the equity. If you borrow money at 8 percent and your rate of return on assets is 11 percent, you are trading on the equity at a gain. Note, however, that trading on the equity is a two-way street. For example, if you borrow money at 11 percent and earn only 8 percent on it, you are trading on the equity at a loss.

Kellogg earns more on its borrowed funds than it has to pay in interest. The notes to Kellogg's financial statements disclose that it pays interest rates of between 5 percent and 8 percent on outstanding debts. Yet, as noted above, it earns 12 percent on each dollar invested in assets. Thus, the return to stockholders exceeds the return on the assets because of the positive benefit of leverage. Recall from our earlier discussion that Kellogg's percentage of debt financing as measured by the ratio of debt to total assets (or debt to equity) remained high in 2000. It appears that Kellogg's high return on stockholders' equity is largely a function of its significant use of leverage.

14. **Profit margin ratio.** The return on assets ratio is affected by two factors, the first of which is the profit margin ratio. The **profit margin ratio**, or **rate of return on sales**, is a measure of the percentage of each dollar of sales that results in net income. It is computed by dividing net income by net sales for the period. Kellogg's profit margin ratio is shown in Illustration 13-31.

Illustration 13-31 Profit margin ratio

Ratio	Formula	Indicates:	Kellogg 2000	Kellogg 1999	Quaker Oats 2000	Industry 2000
Profit margin ratio	Net income / Net sales	Net income generated by each dollar of sales	0.08	0.05	0.07	0.06

Kellogg experienced a rise in its profit margin ratio from 1999 to 2000 of 5 percent to 8 percent. Its profit margin ratio in 2000 exceeds the industry average of 6 percent and Quaker Oats' 7 percent.

High-volume (high inventory turnover) enterprises such as grocery stores and pharmacy chains generally have low profit margins. In contrast, low-volume enterprises such as jewelry stores and airplane manufacturers generally have high profit margins.

15. **Asset turnover ratio.**   The other factor that affects the return on assets ratio is the asset turnover ratio. The **asset turnover ratio** measures how efficiently a company uses its assets to generate sales. It is determined by dividing net sales by average total assets for the period. The resulting number shows the dollars of sales produced by each dollar invested in assets. Illustration 13-32 shows the asset turnover ratio for Kellogg.

Illustration 13-32   Asset turnover ratio

Ratio	Formula	Indicates:	Kellogg 2000	Kellogg 1999	Quaker Oats 2000	Industry 2000
Asset turnover ratio	$\dfrac{\text{Net sales}}{\text{Average total assets}}$	How efficiently assets are used to generate sales	1.43	1.42	2.08	1.49

The asset turnover ratio shows that in 2000 Kellogg generated sales of $1.43 for each dollar it had invested in assets. The ratio increased a bit from 1999 to 2000. Kellogg's asset turnover ratio is below the industry average of 1.49 times and well below Quaker Oats' ratio of 2.08.

Asset turnover ratios vary considerably among industries. The average asset turnover for utility companies is 0.45, for example, while the grocery store industry has an average asset turnover of 3.49.

In summary, Kellogg's return on assets ratio rose from 7 percent in 1999 to 12 percent in 2000. Underlying this rise was an increased profitability on each dollar of sales, as measured by the profit margin ratio, and a rise in the sales-generating efficiency of its assets, as measured by the asset turnover ratio. The combined effects of profit margin and asset turnover on return on assets for Kellogg can be analyzed as shown in Illustration 13-33.

Illustration 13-33   Composition of return on assets ratio

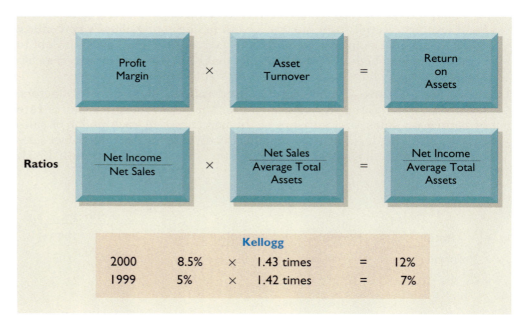

16. **Gross profit rate.** Two factors strongly influence the profit margin ratio. One is the gross profit rate. The **gross profit rate** is determined by dividing gross profit (net sales less cost of goods sold) by net sales. This rate indicates a company's ability to maintain an adequate selling price above its cost of goods sold.

As an industry becomes more competitive, the gross profit rate declines. For example, in the early years of the personal computer industry, gross profit rates were quite high. Today, because of increased competition and a belief that most brands of personal computers are similar in quality, gross profit rates have become thin. Gross profit rates should be closely monitored over time.

Illustration 13-34 shows Kellogg's gross profit rate.

Illustration 13-34 Gross profit rate

Ratio	Formula	Indicates:	Kellogg 2000	Kellogg 1999	Quaker Oats 2000	Industry 2000
Gross profit rate	Gross profit / Net sales	Margin between selling price and cost of goods sold	0.52	0.52	0.54	0.40

Kellogg's gross profit rate was unchanged from 1999 to 2000 in the face of cuts in the selling price of cereal by many of its competitors. Discussion in the financial press has often noted that Kellogg is somewhat slow to respond to price cuts but eventually also drops its prices.

17. **Operating expenses to sales ratio.** This is the other factor that directly affects the profit margin ratio. Management can influence a company's profitability by maintaining adequate prices, cutting expenses, or both. The **operating expenses to sales ratio** measures the costs incurred to support each dollar of sales. It is computed by dividing operating expenses (selling and administrative expenses) by net sales. The operating expenses to sales ratio for Kellogg is shown in Illustration 13-35.

Illustration 13-35 Operating expenses to sales ratio

Ratio	Formula	Indicates:	Kellogg 2000	Kellogg 1999	Quaker Oats 2000	Industry 2000
Operating expenses to sales ratio	Operating expenses / Net sales	The costs incurred to support each dollar of sales	0.37	0.37	0.39	na

In recent years the financial press has frequently carried stories about the cereal industry's efforts to "restructure" operations and cut expenses. This is necessary because cereal sales have leveled off, and so the only way to increase net income is to cut costs. Kellogg's operating expenses to sales ratio actually did not change during this two-year period, remaining at 37 percent, in spite of the incurrence of restructuring charges in 1998, 1999, and 2000.

18. **Cash return on sales ratio.** The profit margin ratio discussed earlier is an accrual-based ratio using net income as a numerator. The cash-basis counterpart to that ratio is the **cash return on sales ratio**. It uses cash provided by operating activities as the numerator and net sales as the denominator. The difference between these two ratios relates to differences between

accrual accounting and cash-basis accounting, that is, differences in the timing of revenue and expense recognition. The cash return on sales ratio for Kellogg is shown in Illustration 13-36.

Illustration 13-36 Cash return on sales ratio

Ratio	Formula	Indicates:	Kellogg 2000	Kellogg 1999	Quaker Oats 2000	Industry 2000
Cash return on sales ratio	Cash provided by operating activities / Net sales	Net cash flow generated by each dollar of sales	0.13	0.11	0.10	na

19. **Earnings per share (EPS).** Stockholders usually think in terms of the number of shares they own or plan to buy or sell. Expressing net income earned on a per share basis provides a useful perspective for determining profitability. **Earnings per share** is a measure of the net income earned on each share of common stock. It is computed by dividing net income by the average number of common shares outstanding during the year.

When we use "net income per share" or "earnings per share," it refers to the amount of net income applicable to each share of *common stock*. Therefore, when we compute earnings per share, if there are preferred dividends declared for the period, they must be deducted from net income to arrive at income available to the common stockholders.

Kellogg's earnings per share is shown in Illustration 13-37.

Illustration 13-37 Earnings per share

Ratio	Formula	Indicates:	Kellogg 2000	Kellogg 1999	Quaker Oats 2000	Industry 2000
Earnings per share (EPS)	Net income − Preferred stock dividends / Average common shares outstanding	Net income earned on each share of common stock	$1.45	$0.83	$2.61	na

Note that no industry average is presented in Illustration 13-37. Industry data for earnings per share are not reported, and in fact the Kellogg and Quaker Oats ratios should not be compared. Such comparisons are not meaningful because of the wide variations in the number of shares of outstanding stock among companies. Kellogg's earnings per share increased 62 cents per share in 2000. This represents a 75 percent increase over the 1999 EPS of $0.83.

20. **Price-earnings ratio.** The **price-earnings ratio** is an oft-quoted measure of the ratio of the market price of each share of common stock to the earnings per share. The price-earnings (P-E) ratio is a reflection of investors' assessments of a company's future earnings. It is computed by dividing the market price per share of the stock by earnings per share. Kellogg's price-earnings ratio is shown in Illustration 13-38.

Illustration 13-38 Price-earnings ratio

Ratio	Formula	Indicates:	Kellogg 2000	Kellogg 1999	Quaker Oats 2000	Industry 2000
Price-earnings ratio	Stock price per share / Earnings per share	Relationship between market price per share and earnings per share	18.1	40.5	37.3	25.5

At the end of 2000 and 1999 the market price of Kellogg's stock was $26\frac{1}{4}$ and $33\frac{5}{8}$, respectively. Quaker Oats' stock was selling for $97\frac{3}{8}$ at the end of 2000.

In 2000 each share of Kellogg's stock sold for 18.1 times the amount that was earned on each share. Kellogg's price-earnings ratio is lower than the industry average of 25.5 times and lower than its previous year's ratio of 40.5, and also lower than Quaker Oats' ratio of 37.3. This higher P-E ratio suggests that the market is more optimistic about Quaker Oats than about Kellogg and the other companies in the industry. However, it might also signal that Quaker Oats' stock is overpriced. The average price-earnings ratio for the stocks that constituted the Standard and Poor's Composite 500 Company Index at December 31, 2000, was 25 times.

21. **Payout ratio.** The **payout ratio** measures the percentage of earnings distributed in the form of cash dividends. It is computed by dividing cash dividends declared on common stock by net income. Companies that have high growth rates are characterized by low payout ratios because they reinvest most of their net income in the business. The payout ratio for Kellogg is shown in Illustration 13-39.

Illustration 13-39 Payout ratio

Ratio	Formula	Indicates:	Kellogg 2000	Kellogg 1999	Quaker Oats 2000	Industry 2000
Payout ratio	Cash dividends declared on common stock / Net income	Percentage of earnings distributed in the form of cash dividends	0.69	1.15	0.43	0.30

The 2000 and 1999 payout ratios for Kellogg are comparatively high in relation to Quakers Oats' 0.43 and the industry average of 0.30.

Management has some control over the amount of dividends paid each year. Companies are generally reluctant to reduce a dividend below the amount paid in a previous year. Therefore, the payout ratio will actually increase if a company's net income declines but the company keeps its total dividend payment the same. Of course, unless the company returns to its previous level of profitability, maintaining this higher dividend payout ratio is probably not possible over the long run.

Before drawing any conclusions regarding Kellogg's dividend payout ratio, we should calculate this ratio over a longer period of time to evaluate any trends. We also should try to find out whether management's philosophy regarding dividends has changed recently. Analysis shows that over the 10-year period 1990–2000 earnings per share have grown 2 percent per year, while dividends per share have grown 9 percent per year. Unless earnings growth improves, this rapid dividend growth is not sustainable over the long term.

BUSINESS INSIGHT
Management Perspective

Generally, companies with stable earnings have high payout ratios. For example, a utility such as **Potomac Electric Company** had an 86 percent payout ratio over a recent five-year period. **Kansas City Power and Light** had a 93 percent payout ratio over the same period. Conversely, companies that are expanding rapidly, such as **Toys 'R' Us** and **Microsoft**, have never paid a cash dividend.

In terms of the types of financial information available and the ratios used by various industries, what we can cover in this textbook gives you only the "Titanic approach": You are seeing only the tip of the iceberg compared to the vast databases and types of ratio analysis that are available on computers. The availability of information is not a problem. The real trick is to be discriminating enough to perform relevant analysis and select pertinent comparative data.

BEFORE YOU GO ON . . .

◆ Review It

1. What are liquidity ratios? Explain the current ratio, acid-test ratio, receivables turnover ratio, inventory turnover ratio, and current cash debt coverage ratio.
2. What are solvency ratios? Explain the debt to total assets ratio, the times interest earned ratio, the cash debt coverage ratio, and free cash flow.
3. What are profitability ratios? Explain the return on common stockholders' equity ratio, return on assets ratio, profit margin ratio, asset turnover ratio, gross profit rate, operating expenses to sales ratio, cash return on sales, earnings per share, price-earnings ratio, and payout ratio.

LIMITATIONS OF FINANCIAL ANALYSIS

Significant business decisions are frequently made using one or more of the analytical tools presented in this chapter: horizontal, vertical, and ratio analysis. But, you should be aware of some of the limitations of these tools and of the financial statements on which they are based.

ESTIMATES

Financial statements contain numerous estimates. Estimates are used, for example, in determining the allowance for uncollectible receivables, periodic depreciation, the costs of warranties, and contingent losses. To the extent that these estimates are inaccurate, the financial ratios and percentages are also inaccurate.

COST

Traditional financial statements are based on cost. They are not adjusted for price-level changes. Comparisons of unadjusted financial data from different periods may be rendered invalid by significant inflation or deflation. For example, a five-year comparison of Kellogg's revenues shows a growth of 5 percent. But if, for example, the general price level also increased by 5 percent, the company's real growth would be zero. Also, some assets such as property, plant, and equipment might be many years old. The historical cost at which they are shown on the balance sheet might be significantly lower than what they could currently be sold for.

ALTERNATIVE ACCOUNTING METHODS

Companies vary in the generally accepted accounting principles they use. Such variations may hamper comparability. For example, one company may use the FIFO method of inventory costing; another company in the same industry may use LIFO. If inventory is a significant asset to both companies, it is unlikely that their current ratios are comparable. For example, if **General Motors Corporation** had used FIFO instead of LIFO in valuing its inventories, its inventories would have been 26 percent higher, which significantly affects the current ratio (and other ratios as well).

In addition to differences in inventory costing methods, differences also exist in reporting such items as depreciation, depletion, and amortization. These differences in accounting methods might be detectable from reading the notes to the financial statements. But adjusting the financial data to compensate for the different methods is difficult, if not impossible in some cases.

ATYPICAL DATA

Fiscal year-end data may not be typical of a company's financial condition during the year. Companies frequently establish a fiscal year-end that coincides with the low point in operating activity or inventory levels. Therefore, certain account balances (cash, receivables, payables, and inventories) may not be representative of the balances in the accounts during the year.

DIVERSIFICATION

Diversification in U.S. industry also limits the usefulness of financial analysis. Many companies today are so diversified that they cannot be classified by a single industry. Others appear to be comparable but are not.

For example, you might think that **PepsiCo, Inc.** and **The Coca-Cola Company** would be comparable as soft drink industry competitors. But are they comparable? Until recently, PepsiCo, in addition to producing Pepsi-Cola, owned **Pizza Hut**, **Kentucky Fried Chicken**, **Taco Bell**, and **Frito-Lay**. Coca-Cola, in addition to producing Coke, owns **Hi-C** (fruit drinks), **Minute Maid** (frozen juice concentrate), and **Columbia Pictures** (motion pictures, TV shows, and commercials). Or, we might want to compare Kellogg to **Post Cereals**, another of its competitors. But since Post is owned by **Philip Morris**, and Philip Morris generates most of its profits from cigarette sales, and a lot of the rest of its profits from nongrain-related products, comparisons are difficult. As a consequence, deciding what industry a company is in is actually one of the main challenges to effective evaluation of its results.

When companies have significant operations in different lines of business, they are required to report additional disclosures in a segmental data note to their financial statements. Segmental data include total sales, total identifiable assets, operating profit, depreciation expense, and capital expenditures by business segment. Many analysts say that the segmental information is the most important data in the financial statements. Without it, comparison of diversified companies is very difficult.

DECISION TOOLKIT

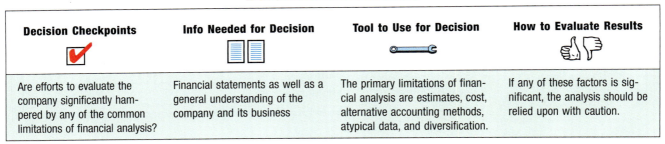

Decision Checkpoints	Info Needed for Decision	Tool to Use for Decision	How to Evaluate Results
Are efforts to evaluate the company significantly hampered by any of the common limitations of financial analysis?	Financial statements as well as a general understanding of the company and its business	The primary limitations of financial analysis are estimates, cost, alternative accounting methods, atypical data, and diversification.	If any of these factors is significant, the analysis should be relied upon with caution.

BEFORE YOU GO ON . . .

◆ **Review It**

1. What are some limitations of financial analysis?
2. Give examples of alternative accounting methods that hamper comparability.
3. In what way does diversification limit the usefulness of financial statement analysis?
4. What are the required disclosures in segmental data notes?

---

*U*SING THE *D*ECISION *T*OOLKIT

In analyzing a company, you should always investigate an extended period of time in order to determine whether the condition and performance of the company are changing. The condensed financial statements of Kellogg Company for 1998 and 1997 are presented here:

KELLOGG COMPANY, INC.
Balance Sheets
December 31
(in millions)

	1998	1997
Assets		
Current assets		
Cash and short-term investments	$ 136.4	$ 173.2
Accounts receivable (net)	693.0	587.5
Inventories	451.4	434.3
Prepaid expenses and other current assets	215.7	272.7
Total current assets	1,496.5	1,467.7
Property assets (net)	2,888.8	2,773.3
Intangibles and other assets	666.2	636.6
Total assets	$5,051.5	$4,877.6
Liabilities and Stockholders' Equity		
Current liabilities	$1,718.5	$1,657.3
Long-term liabilities	2,443.2	2,222.8
Stockholders' equity—common	889.8	997.5
Total liabilities and stockholders' equity	$5,051.5	$4,877.6

KELLOGG COMPANY, INC.
Condensed Income Statements
For the Years Ended December 31
(in millions)

	1998	1997
Net sales	$6,762.1	$6,830.1
Cost of goods sold	3,282.6	3,270.1
Gross profit	3,479.5	3,560.0
Selling and administrative expenses	2,513.9	2,366.8
Nonrecurring charges	70.5	184.1
Income from operations	895.1	1,009.1
Interest expense	119.5	108.3
Other income (expense), net	6.9	3.7
Income before income taxes	782.5	904.5
Income tax expense	279.9	340.5
Net income	$ 502.6	$ 564.0

Instructions

Compute the following ratios for Kellogg for 1998 and 1997, and comment on each relative to the amounts reported in the chapter.
1. Liquidity:
   (a) Current ratio.
   (b) Inventory turnover ratio. (Inventory on December 31, 1996, was $424.9 million.)
2. Solvency:
   (a) Debt to total assets ratio.
   (b) Times interest earned ratio.
3. Profitability:
   (a) Return on common stockholders' equity ratio. (Equity on December 31, 1996, was $1,282.4 million.)
   (b) Return on assets ratio. (Assets on December 31, 1996, were $5,050.0 million.)
   (c) Profit margin ratio.

Solution

1. Liquidity
   (a) Current ratio:

   1998: $\frac{\$1,496.5}{\$1,718.5} = 0.87:1$

   1997: $\frac{\$1,467.7}{\$1,657.3} = 0.89:1$

   (b) Inventory turnover ratio:

   1998: $\frac{\$3,282.6}{(\$451.4 + \$434.3)/2} = 7.4$ times

$$1997: \quad \frac{\$3,270.1}{(\$434.3 + \$424.9)/2} = 7.6 \text{ times}$$

In the chapter we noted that Kellogg's liquidity as measured by the current ratio declined sharply in 2000. We see that between 1997 and 1998 the current ratio declined slightly. Countering this decline in the current ratio, however, is the fact that the inventory turnover ratio has stayed consistently high since 1997. The faster inventory turns over (is sold), the more liquid it is. That is, the company can accept a lower current ratio if it can turn over its inventory (and receivables) more quickly.

2. Solvency

  (a) Debt to total assets ratio:

$$1998: \quad \frac{\$4,161.7}{\$5,051.5} = 82\%$$

$$1997: \quad \frac{\$3,880.1}{\$4,877.6} = 80\%$$

  (b) Times interest earned ratio:

$$1998: \quad \frac{\$502.6 + \$279.9 + \$119.5}{\$119.5} = 7.5 \text{ times}$$

$$1997: \quad \frac{\$564.0 + \$340.5 + \$108.3}{\$108.3} = 9.4 \text{ times}$$

Kellogg's solvency as measured by the debt to total assets ratio declined in 1999 and 2000 relative to its level in 1997 and 1998. We can also see from the 1997 and 1998 measures that the times interest earned ratio has also declined during this period, but remains relatively high. This consistently high times interest earned measure gives us confidence that Kellogg can meet its debt payments when due.

3. Profitability

  (a) Return on common stockholders' equity ratio:

$$1998: \quad \frac{\$502.6}{(\$889.8 + \$997.5)/2} = 53\%$$

$$1997: \quad \frac{\$564.0}{(\$997.5 + \$1,282.4)/2} = 49\%$$

  (b) Return on assets ratio:

$$1998: \quad \frac{\$502.6}{(\$5,051.5 + \$4,877.6)/2} = 10\%$$

$$1997: \quad \frac{\$564.0}{(\$4,877.6 + \$5,050.0)/2} = 11\%$$

  (c) Profit margin ratio:

$$1998: \quad \frac{\$502.6}{\$6,762.1} = 7\%$$

$$1997: \quad \frac{\$564.0}{\$6,830.1} = 8\%$$

We noted in the chapter that Kellogg's return on common stockholders' equity ratio was unusually high. We suggested that in 2000 Kellogg reached this high measure by increasing its leverage—that is, by trading on the equity. Note that its return on common stockholders' equity ratio was not nearly as high in 1997 and 1998. Its profit margin ratio and return on assets have been relatively unchanged during this period. By increasing its leverage, Kellogg has been able to increase its return on common stockholders' equity ratio. But, higher leverage means higher risk. That is, with higher leverage, if the company's sales turn sour, its profitability could really be hurt.

SUMMARY OF STUDY OBJECTIVES

1 *Understand the concept of earning power and indicate how irregular items are presented.* Earning power refers to a company's ability to sustain its profits from operations. Irregular items—discontinued operations, extraordinary items, and changes in accounting principles—are presented on the income statement net of tax below "Income from continuing operations" to highlight their unusual nature.

2 *Discuss the need for comparative analysis and identify the tools of financial statement analysis.* Comparative analysis is performed to evaluate a company's short-term liquidity, profitability, and long-term solvency. Comparisons can detect changes in financial relationships and significant trends. They also can provide insight into a company's competitive position and its relative position in its industry. Financial statements may be analyzed horizontally, vertically, and with ratios.

3 *Explain and apply horizontal analysis.* Horizontal analysis is a technique for evaluating a series of data over a period of time to determine the increase or decrease that has taken place. The change may be expressed as either an amount or a percentage.

4 *Describe and apply vertical analysis.* Vertical analysis is a technique that expresses each item in a financial statement as a percentage of a relevant total or a base amount.

5 *Identify and compute ratios, and describe their purpose and use in analyzing a company's liquidity, solvency, and profitability.* Financial ratios are provided in Illustrations 13-17 through 13-23 (liquidity), Illustrations 13-24 through 13-27 (solvency), and Illustrations 13-28 through 13-39 (profitability).

6 *Discuss the limitations of financial statement analysis.* The usefulness of analytical tools is limited by the use of estimates, the cost basis, the application of alternative accounting methods, atypical data at year-end, and the diversification of companies.

DECISION TOOLKIT—A SUMMARY

Decision Checkpoints	Info Needed for Decision	Tool to Use for Decision	How to Evaluate Results
Has the company sold any major lines of business?	Discontinued operations section of income statement	Anything reported in this section indicates that the company has discontinued a major line of business.	If a major business line has been discontinued, its results in the current period should not be included in estimates of future net income.
Has the company experienced any extraordinary events or transactions?	Extraordinary item section of income statement	Anything reported in this section indicates that the company experienced an event that was both unusual and infrequent.	These items should usually be ignored in estimating future net income.
Has the company changed any of its accounting policies?	Cumulative effect of change in accounting principle section of income statement	Anything reported in this section indicates that the company has changed an accounting policy during the current year.	The cumulative effect should be ignored in estimating the future net income.
How do the company's financial position and operating results compare with those of a previous period?	Income statement and balance sheet	Comparative financial statements should be prepared over at least two years, with the first year reported being the base year. Changes in each line item relative to the base year should be presented both by amount and by percentage. This is called horizontal analysis.	Significant changes should be investigated to determine the reason for the change.
How do the relationships between items in this year's financial statements compare with those of last year or those of competitors?	Income statement and balance sheet	Each line item on the income statement should be presented as a percentage of net sales, and each line item on the balance sheet should be presented as a percentage of total assets or total liabilities and stockholders' equity. These percentages should be investigated for differences either across years in the same company or in the same year across different companies. This is called vertical analysis.	Any differences either across years or between companies should be investigated to determine the cause.
Are efforts to evaluate the company significantly hampered by any of the common limitations of financial analysis?	Financial statements as well as a general understanding of the company and its business	The primary limitations of financial analysis are estimates, cost, alternative accounting methods, atypical data, and diversification.	If any of these factors is significant, the analysis should be relied upon with caution.

GLOSSARY

Key Term Matching Activity

Acid-test (quick) ratio   A measure of a company's immediate short-term liquidity; computed as the sum of cash, short-term investments, and net receivables divided by current liabilities. (p. 568)

Asset turnover ratio   A measure of how efficiently a company uses its assets to generate sales; computed as net sales divided by average total assets. (p. 576)

Average collection period   The average number of days that receivables are outstanding; computed as receivables turnover divided into 365 days. (p. 569)

Cash debt coverage ratio   A cash-basis measure used to evaluate solvency; computed as cash from operating activities divided by average total liabilities. (p. 572)

Cash return on sales ratio   The cash-basis measure of net income generated by each dollar of sales; computed as net cash from operating activities divided by net sales. (p. 577)

Change in accounting principle   Use of an accounting principle in the current year different from the one used in the preceding year. (p. 554)

Comprehensive income   Includes all changes in stockholders' equity during a period except those resulting from investments by stockholders and distributions to stockholders. (p. 556)

Current cash debt coverage ratio   A cash-basis measure of short-term debt-paying ability; computed as cash provided by operating activities divided by average current liabilities. (p. 568)

Current ratio   A measure used to evaluate a company's liquidity and short-term debt-paying ability; calculated as current assets divided by current liabilities. (p. 567)

Days in inventory   A measure of the average number of days it takes to sell the inventory; computed as inventory turnover divided into 365 days. (p. 570)

Debt to total assets ratio   A measure of the percentage of total assets provided by creditors; computed as total debt divided by total assets. (p. 571)

Discontinued operations   The disposal of a significant segment of a business. (p. 551)

Earnings per share   The net income earned by each share of common stock; computed as net income divided by the average common shares outstanding. (p. 578)

Extraordinary items   Events and transactions that meet two conditions: (1) unusual in nature and (2) infrequent in occurrence. (p. 552)

Free cash flow   The amount of cash from operations after adjusting for capital expenditures and cash dividends paid. (p. 573)

Gross profit rate   An indicator of a company's ability to maintain an adequate selling price of goods above their cost; computed as gross profit divided by net sales. (p. 577)

Horizontal analysis   A technique for evaluating a series of financial statement data over a period of time to determine the increase (decrease) that has taken place, expressed as either an amount or a percentage. (p. 557)

Inventory turnover ratio   A measure of the liquidity of inventory; computed as cost of goods sold divided by average inventory. (p. 570)

Leveraging   Borrowing money at a lower rate of interest than can be earned by using the borrowed money; also referred to as trading on the equity. (p. 575)

Liquidity ratios   Measures of the short-term ability of the enterprise to pay its maturing obligations and to meet unexpected needs for cash. (p. 566)

Operating expenses to sales ratio   A measure of the costs incurred to support each dollar of sales; computed as operating expenses divided by net sales. (p. 577)

Payout ratio   A measure of the percentage of earnings distributed in the form of cash dividends; calculated as cash dividends divided by net income. (p. 579)

Price-earnings (P-E) ratio   A comparison of the market price of each share of common stock to the earnings per share; computed as the market price of the stock divided by earnings per share. (p. 578)

Profit margin ratio   A measure of the net income generated by each dollar of sales; computed as net income divided by net sales. (p. 575)

Profitability ratios   Measures of the income or operating success of an enterprise for a given period of time. (p. 566)

Quick ratio   Another name for the acid-test ratio. (p. 568)

Receivables turnover ratio   A measure of the liquidity of receivables; computed as net credit sales divided by average net receivables. (p. 569)

Return on assets ratio   An overall measure of profitability; calculated as net income divided by average total assets. (p. 575)

Return on common stockholders' equity ratio   A measure of the dollars of net income earned for each dollar invested by the owners; computed as income available to common stockholders divided by average common stockholders' equity. (p. 574)

Segmental data   A required note disclosure for diversified companies in which the company reports sales, operating profit, identifiable assets, depreciation expense, and capital expenditures by major business segment. (p. 581)

Solvency ratios   Measures of the ability of the enterprise to survive over a long period of time. (p. 566)

Times interest earned ratio   A measure of a company's ability to meet interest payments as they come due; calculated as income before interest expense and income taxes divided by interest expense. (p. 572)

Trading on the equity   See Leveraging. (p. 575)

Vertical analysis   A technique for evaluating financial statement data that expresses each item in a financial statement as a percent of a base amount. (p. 561)

DEMONSTRATION PROBLEM

The events and transactions of Dever Corporation for the year ending December 31, 2002, resulted in the following data.

Cost of goods sold	$2,600,000
Net sales	4,400,000
Other expenses and losses	9,600
Other revenues and gains	5,600
Selling and administrative expenses	1,100,000
Income from operations of plastics division	70,000
Gain on sale of plastics division	500,000
Loss from tornado disaster (extraordinary loss)	600,000
Cumulative effect of changing from straight-line depreciation to double-declining-balance (increase in depreciation expense)	300,000

Analysis reveals:
1. All items are before the applicable income tax rate of 30%.
2. The plastics division was sold on July 1.
3. All operating data for the plastics division have been segregated.

Instructions

Prepare an income statement for the year, excluding the presentation of earnings per share.

Action Plan

- Remember that material items not typical of operations are reported in separate sections net of taxes.
- Associate income taxes with the item that affects the taxes.
- Remember that a corporation income statement has income tax expense when there is income before income tax.
- Use the same data presented in determining income before income taxes for unincorporated companies.

Solution to Demonstration Problem

DEVER CORPORATION
Income Statement
For the Year Ended December 31, 2002

Net sales		$4,400,000
Cost of goods sold		2,600,000
Gross profit		1,800,000
Selling and administrative expenses		1,100,000
Income from operations		700,000
Other revenues and gains	$ 5,600	
Other expenses and losses	9,600	4,000
Income before income taxes		696,000
Income tax expense ($696,000 × 30%)		208,800
Income from continuing operations		487,200
Discontinued operations		
Income from operations of plastics division,		
net of $21,000 income taxes ($70,000 × 30%)	49,000	
Gain on sale of plastics division, net of $150,000		
income taxes ($500,000 × 30%)	350,000	399,000
Income before extraordinary item and cumulative		
effect of change in accounting principle		886,200
Extraordinary item		
Tornado loss, net of income tax saving $180,000		
($600,000 × 30%)		(420,000)
Cumulative effect of change in accounting principle		
Effect on prior years of change in depreciation method,		
net of $90,000 income tax saving ($300,000 × 30%)		(210,000)
Net income		$ 256,200

SELF-STUDY QUESTIONS

Answers are at the end of the chapter.

(SO 1) 1. In reporting discontinued operations, the income statement should show in a special section:
  (a) gains and losses on the disposal of the discontinued segment.
  (b) gains and losses from operations of the discontinued segment.
  (c) Neither (a) nor (b).
  (d) Both (a) and (b).

(SO 1) 2. The Chicago Corporation has income before taxes of $400,000 and an extraordinary loss of $100,000. If the income tax rate is 25% on all items, the income statement should show income before extraordinary items, and extraordinary items, respectively, of:
  (a) $325,000 and $100,000.
  (b) $325,000 and $75,000.
  (c) $300,000 and $100,000.
  (d) $300,000 and $75,000.

(SO 2) 3. Comparisons of data within a company are an example of the following comparative basis:
  (a) industry averages.   (c) intercompany.
  (b) intracompany.   (d) Both (b) and (c).

(SO 3) 4. In horizontal analysis, each item is expressed as a percentage of the:
  (a) net income amount.
  (b) stockholders' equity amount.
  (c) total assets amount.
  (d) base-year amount.

(SO 3) 5. Earlville Corporation reported net sales of $300,000, $330,000, and $360,000 in the years 2000, 2001, and 2002, respectively. If 2000 is the base year, what is the trend percentage for 2002?
  (a) 77%.   (c) 120%.
  (b) 108%.   (d) 130%.

(SO 4) 6. The following schedule is a display of what type of analysis?

	Amount	Percent
Current assets	$200,000	25%
Property, plant, and equipment	600,000	75%
Total assets	$800,000	

  (a) Horizontal analysis.
  (b) Differential analysis.
  (c) Vertical analysis.
  (d) Ratio analysis.

(SO 4) 7. In vertical analysis, the base amount for depreciation expense is generally:
  (a) net sales.
  (b) depreciation expense in a previous year.
  (c) gross profit.
  (d) fixed assets.

(SO 5) 8. Which measure is an evaluation of a company's ability to pay current liabilities?
  (a) Acid-test ratio.   (c) Both (a) and (b).
  (b) Current ratio.   (d) None of the above.

(SO 5) 9. Which measure is useful in evaluating the efficiency in managing inventories?
  (a) Inventory turnover ratio.
  (b) Days in inventory.
  (c) Both (a) and (b).
  (d) None of the above.

(SO 5) 10. Which of these is *not* a liquidity ratio?
  (a) Current ratio.
  (b) Asset turnover ratio.
  (c) Inventory turnover ratio.
  (d) Receivables turnover ratio.

(SO 5) 11. Oswego Corporation reported net income $24,000; net sales $400,000; and average assets $600,000 for 2002. What is the 2002 profit margin?
  (a) 6%.
  (b) 12%.
  (c) 40%.
  (d) 200%.

(SO 6) 12. Which of the following is generally *not* considered to be a limitation of financial analysis?
  (a) Use of ratio analysis.
  (b) Use of estimates.
  (c) Use of cost.
  (d) Use of alternative accounting methods.

QUESTIONS

1. Your roommate, Alyssa Mandula, asks you to explain earning power. What relationship does this concept have to the treatment of irregular items on the income statement?

2. Indicate which of the following items would be reported as an extraordinary item on Alex Beeler Food Corporation's income statement.

  (a) Loss from damages caused by a volcano eruption.
  (b) Loss from the sale of short-term investments.
  (c) Loss attributable to a labor strike.
  (d) Loss caused when the Food and Drug Administration prohibited the manufacture and sale of a product line.

(e) Loss of inventory from flood damage because a warehouse is located in a flood plain that floods every 5 to 10 years.

(f) Loss on the write-down of outdated inventory.

(g) Loss from a foreign government's expropriation of a production facility.

(h) Loss from damage to a warehouse in southern California from a minor earthquake.

3. Kelly Berryman Inc. reported 2000 earnings per share of $3.26 and had no extraordinary items. In 2001 earnings per share on income before extraordinary items was $2.99, and earnings per share on net income was $3.49. Do you consider this trend to be favorable? Why or why not?

4. Alia Khan Robotics Inc. has been in operation for 3 years. All of its manufacturing equipment, which has a useful life of 10 to 12 years, has been depreciated on a straight-line basis. During the fourth year, Khan Robotics changes to an accelerated depreciation method for all of its equipment.
(a) Will Khan Robotics post a gain or a loss on this change?
(b) How will this change be reported?

5. (a) Josh Ayers believes that the analysis of financial statements is directed at two characteristics of a company: liquidity and profitability. Is Josh correct? Explain.
(b) Are short-term creditors, long-term creditors, and stockholders interested in primarily the same characteristics of a company? Explain.

6. (a) Distinguish among the following bases of comparison: intracompany, industry averages, and intercompany.
(b) Give the principal value of using each of the three bases of comparison.

7. Two popular methods of financial statement analysis are horizontal analysis and vertical analysis. Explain the difference between these two methods.

8. (a) If Nick Flach Company had net income of $540,000 in 2001 and it experienced a 24.5% increase in net income for 2002, what is its net income for 2002?
(b) If six cents of every dollar of Flach's revenue is net income in 2001, what is the dollar amount of 2001 revenue?

9. Name the major ratios useful in assessing (a) liquidity and (b) solvency.

10. Jon Alden is puzzled. His company had a profit margin of 10% in 2002. He feels that this is an indication that the company is doing well. Anna Weis, his accountant, says that more information is needed to determine the company's financial well-being. Who is correct? Why?

11. What does each type of ratio measure?
(a) Liquidity ratios.
(b) Solvency ratios.
(c) Profitability ratios.

12. What is the difference between the current ratio and the acid-test ratio?

13. Brian Tanaka Company, a retail store, has a receivables turnover ratio of 4.5 times. The industry average is 12.5 times. Does Tanaka have a collection problem with its receivables?

14. Which ratios should be used to help answer each of these questions?
(a) How efficient is a company in using its assets to produce sales?
(b) How near to sale is the inventory on hand?
(c) How many dollars of net income were earned for each dollar invested by the owners?
(d) How able is a company to meet interest charges as they fall due?

15. In May 2001 the price-earnings ratio of **General Motors** was 15, and the price-earnings ratio of **Microsoft** was 40. Which company did the stock market favor? Explain.

16. What is the formula for computing the payout ratio? Do you expect this ratio to be high or low for a growth company?

17. Holding all other factors constant, indicate whether each of the following changes generally signals good or bad news about a company:
(a) Increase in profit margin ratio.
(b) Decrease in inventory turnover ratio.
(c) Increase in current ratio.
(d) Decrease in earnings per share.
(e) Increase in price-earnings ratio.
(f) Increase in debt to total assets ratio.
(g) Decrease in times interest earned ratio.

18. The return on assets for Ray St. John Corporation is 7.6%. During the same year St. John's return on common stockholders' equity is 12.8%. What is the explanation for the difference in the two rates?

19. Which two ratios do you think should be of greatest interest in each of the following cases?
(a) A pension fund considering the purchase of 20-year bonds.
(b) A bank contemplating a short-term loan.
(c) A common stockholder.

20. (a) What is meant by trading on the equity?
(b) How would you determine the profitability of trading on the equity?

21. Jenna Greenlee Inc. has net income of $270,000, average shares of common stock outstanding of 50,000 and preferred dividends for the period of $40,000. What is Greenlee's earnings per share of common stock? Tegan Hunter, the president of Jenna Greenlee Inc., believes that the computed EPS of the company is high. Comment.

22. Identify and briefly explain five limitations of financial analysis.

23. Explain how the choice of one of the following accounting methods over the other raises or lowers a

company's net income during a period of continuing inflation.

(a) Use of FIFO instead of LIFO for inventory costing.

(b) Use of a 6-year life for machinery instead of a 9-year life.

(c) Use of straight-line depreciation instead of accelerated declining-balance depreciation.

BRIEF EXERCISES*

BE13-1   On June 30 Georgia Keen Corporation discontinued its operations in Mexico. During the year, the operating loss was $400,000 before taxes. On September 1 Keen disposed of the Mexico facility at a pretax loss of $150,000. The applicable tax rate is 30%. Show the discontinued operations section of Keen's income statement.

Prepare a discontinued operations section of an income statement.
(SO 1)

BE13-2   An inexperienced accountant for Luke Nayak Corporation showed the following in Nayak's 2002 income statement: income before income taxes $300,000; income tax expense $72,000; extraordinary loss from flood (before taxes) $60,000; and net income $168,000. The extraordinary loss and taxable income are both subject to a 30% tax rate. Prepare a corrected income statement beginning with "Income before income taxes."

Prepare a corrected income statement with an extraordinary item.
(SO 1)

BE13-3   On January 1, 2002, Elora Karim Inc. changed from the straight-line method of depreciation to the declining-balance method. The cumulative effect of the change was to increase the prior years' depreciation by $40,000 and 2002 depreciation by $8,000. Show the change in accounting principle section of the 2002 income statement, assuming the tax rate is 30%.

Prepare a change in accounting principles section of an income statement.
(SO 1)

BE13-4   Using these data from the comparative balance sheets of Morgan Sondgeroth Company, perform horizontal analysis.

Prepare horizontal analysis.
(SO 3)

	December 31, 2002	**December 31, 2001**
Accounts receivable	$ 600,000	$ 400,000
Inventory	780,000	600,000
Total assets	3,220,000	2,800,00

BE13-5   Using the data presented in BE13-4 for Morgan Sondgeroth Company, perform vertical analysis.

Prepare vertical analysis.
(SO 4)

BE13-6   Net income was $500,000 in 2000, $420,000 in 2001, and $504,000 in 2002. What is the percentage of change from (a) 2000 to 2001 and (b) 2001 to 2002? Is the change an increase or a decrease?

Calculate percentage of change.
(SO 3)

BE13-7   If Forest Hanold Company had net income of $672,300 in 2002 and it experienced a 25% increase in net income over 2001, what was its 2001 net income?

Calculate net income.
(SO 3)

BE13-8   Vertical analysis (common-size) percentages for Stroyan Company's sales, cost of goods sold, and expenses are listed here.

Calculate change in net income.
(SO 4)

Vertical Analysis	**2002**	**2001**	**2000**
Sales	100.0%	100.0%	100.0%
Cost of goods sold	59.2	62.4	64.5
Expenses	25.0	26.6	29.5

Did Stroyan's net income as a percent of sales increase, decrease, or remain unchanged over the 3-year period? Provide numerical support for your answer.

BE13-9   Horizontal analysis (trend analysis) percentages for Tyler Scott Company's sales, cost of goods sold, and expenses are listed here.

Calculate change in net income.
(SO 3)

---

*Follow the rounding procedures used in the chapter.

Horizontal Analysis	2002	2001	2000
Sales	96.2%	106.8%	100.0%
Cost of goods sold	102.0	97.0	100.0
Expenses	110.6	95.4	100.0

✏️➤ Explain whether Scott's net income increased, decreased, or remained unchanged over the 3-year period.

Calculate liquidity ratios.
(SO 5)

BE13-10   These selected condensed data are taken from a recent balance sheet of **Bob Evans Farms**.

Cash	$ 8,241,000
Short-term investments	1,947,000
Accounts receivable	12,545,000
Inventories	14,814,000
Other current assets	5,371,000
Total current assets	$42,918,000
Total current liabilities	$44,844,000

What are the (a) current ratio and (b) acid-test ratio?

Evaluate collection of accounts receivable.
(SO 5)

BE13-11   The following data are taken from the financial statements of Mallory Rodriguez Company.

	2002	2001
Accounts receivable (net), end of year	$ 560,000	$ 540,000
Net sales on account	5,500,000	4,100,000
Terms for all sales are 1/10, n/45.		

Compute for each year (a) the receivables turnover ratio and (b) the average collection period. What conclusions about the management of accounts receivable can be drawn from these data? At the end of 2000, accounts receivable (net) was $490,000.

Evaluate management of inventory.
(SO 5)

BE13-12   The following data were taken from the income statements of Alejandro Montesdeoca Company.

	2002	2001
Sales revenue	$6,420,000	$6,240,000
Beginning inventory	980,000	837,000
Purchases	4,640,000	4,661,000
Ending inventory	1,020,000	980,000

✏️➤ Compute for each year (a) the inventory turnover ratio and (b) days in inventory. What conclusions concerning the management of the inventory can be drawn from these data?

Calculate profitability ratios.
(SO 5)

BE13-13   Staples, Inc. is one of the largest suppliers of office products in the United States. It had net income of $59.7 million and net revenue of $10,673.7 million in fiscal 2001. Its total assets were $3,846.1 million at the beginning of the year and $3,989.4 million at the end of the year. What is Staples, Inc.'s (a) asset turnover ratio and (b) profit margin ratio?

Calculate profitability ratios.
(SO 5)

BE13-14   Janie McMahon Products Company has stockholders' equity of $200,000 and net income of $50,000. It has a payout ratio of 20% and a rate of return on assets of 16%. How much did McMahon Products pay in cash dividends, and what were its average assets?

Calculate cash-basis liquidity, profitability, and solvency ratios.
(SO 5)

BE13-15   Selected data taken from the fiscal 2001 financial statements of trading card company **Topps Company, Inc.** are as follows (in thousands).

Net sales for fiscal 2001	$439,300
Current liabilities, March 4, 2000	62,500
Current liabilities, March 3, 2001	72,700
Net cash provided by operating activities	104,400
Total liabilities, March 4, 2000	74,100
Total liabilities, March 3, 2001	83,700

Compute these ratios at March 3, 2001: (a) current cash debt coverage ratio, (b) cash return on sales ratio, and (c) cash debt coverage ratio.

*E*XERCISES*

E13-1   Dylan Karraker Company has income from continuing operations of $240,000 for the year ended December 31, 2002. It also has the following items (before considering income taxes): (1) an extraordinary fire loss of $60,000, (2) a gain of $40,000 from the discontinuance of a division, which includes a $110,000 gain from the operation of the division and a $70,000 loss on its disposal, and (3) a cumulative change in accounting principle that resulted in an increase in the prior year's depreciation of $30,000. Assume all items are subject to income taxes at a 30% tax rate.

Prepare irregular items portion of an income statement.
(SO 1)

Instructions
Prepare Dylan Karraker Company's income statement for 2002, beginning with "Income from continuing operations."

E13-2   The *Wall Street Journal* routinely publishes summaries of corporate quarterly and annual earnings reports in a feature called the "Earnings Digest." A typical "digest" report takes the following form.

Evaluate the effects of unusual or irregular items.
(SO 1, 5, 6)

ENERGY ENTERPRISES (A)

	Quarter ending July 31	
	2002	2001
Revenues	$2,049,000,000	$1,754,000,000
Net income	97,000,000	(a) 68,750,000
EPS: Net income	1.31	0.93

	9 months ending July 31	
	2002	2001
Revenues	$5,578,500,000	$5,065,300,000
Extraordinary item	(b) 1,900,000	
Net income	102,700,000	(a) 33,250,000
EPS: Net income	1.39	0.45

(a) Includes a net charge of $26,000,000 from loss on the sale of electrical equipment
(b) Extraordinary gain on Middle East property expropriation

The letter in parentheses following the company name indicates the exchange on which Energy Enterprises' stock is traded—in this case, the American Stock Exchange.

Instructions
Answer the following questions.
(a) How was the loss on the electrical equipment reported on the income statement? Was it reported in the third quarter of 2001? How can you tell?
(b) Why did the *Wall Street Journal* list the extraordinary item separately?
(c) What is the extraordinary item? Was it included in income for the third quarter? How can you tell?

---

*Follow the rounding procedures used in the chapter.

(d) Did Energy Enterprises have an operating loss in any quarter of 2001? Of 2002? How do you know?

(e) Approximately how many shares of stock were outstanding in 2002? Did the number of outstanding shares change from July 31, 2001, to July 31, 2002?

(f) As an investor, what numbers should you use to determine Energy Enterprises' profit margin ratio? Calculate the 9-month profit margin ratio for 2001 and 2002 that you consider most useful. Explain your decision.

Prepare horizontal analysis.
(SO 3)

E13-3 Here is financial information for Merchandise Inc.

	December 31, 2002	December 31, 2001
Current assets	$120,000	$100,000
Plant assets (net)	400,000	330,000
Current liabilities	91,000	70,000
Long-term liabilities	144,000	95,000
Common stock, $1 par	150,000	115,000
Retained earnings	135,000	150,000

Instructions

Prepare a schedule showing a horizontal analysis for 2002, using 2001 as the base year.

Prepare vertical analysis.
(SO 4)

E13-4 Operating data for Fleetwood Corporation are presented here.

	2002	2001
Sales	$800,000	$600,000
Cost of goods sold	472,000	390,000
Selling expenses	120,000	72,000
Administrative expenses	80,000	54,000
Income tax expense	38,400	25,200
Net income	89,600	58,800

Instructions

Prepare a schedule showing a vertical analysis for 2002 and 2001.

Prepare horizontal and vertical analyses.
(SO 3, 4)

E13-5 The comparative balance sheets of **Philip Morris Companies, Inc.,** are presented here.

PHILIP MORRIS COMPANIES, INC.
Comparative Balance Sheets
December 31
($ in millions)

	1998	1997
Assets		
Current assets	$20,230	$17,440
Property, plant, and equipment (net)	12,335	11,621
Other assets	27,355	26,886
Total assets	$59,920	$55,947
Liabilities and Stockholders' Equity		
Current liabilities	$16,379	$15,071
Long-term liabilities	27,344	25,956
Stockholders' equity	16,197	14,920
Total liabilities and stockholders' equity	$59,920	$55,947

Instructions

(a) Prepare a horizontal analysis of the balance sheet data for Philip Morris, using 1997 as a base.

(b) Prepare a vertical analysis of the balance sheet data for Philip Morris for 1998.

E13-6 Here are the comparative income statements of Olympic Corporation.

OLYMPIC CORPORATION
Comparative Income Statements
For the Years Ended December 31

	2002	2001
Net sales	$550,000	$550,000
Cost of goods sold	440,000	450,000
Gross profit	$110,000	$100,000
Operating expenses	57,200	54,000
Net income	$ 52,800	$ 46,000

Instructions
(a) Prepare a horizontal analysis of the income statement data for Olympic Corporation, using 2001 as a base.
(b) Prepare a vertical analysis of the income statement data for Olympic Corporation for both years.

E13-7 Nordstrom, Inc., operates department stores in numerous states. Selected financial statement data (in millions) for 1998 are presented here.

	End of Year	Beginning of Year
Cash and cash equivalents	$ 241.4	$ 24.8
Receivables (net)	587.1	664.4
Merchandise inventory	750.3	826.0
Other current assets	101.6	79.7
Total current assets	$1,680.4	$1,594.9
Total current liabilities	$ 768.5	$ 942.6

For the year, net credit sales were $5,135.0 million, cost of goods sold was $3,164.8 million, and cash from operating activities was $600.8 million.

Instructions
Compute the current ratio, acid-test ratio, current cash debt coverage ratio, receivables turnover ratio, average collection period, inventory turnover ratio, and days in inventory at the end of the current year.

E13-8 Eugene Incorporated had the following transactions involving current assets and current liabilities during February 2002.

Feb. 3	Collected accounts receivable of $15,000.
7	Purchased equipment for $25,000 cash.
11	Paid $3,000 for a 3-year insurance policy.
14	Paid accounts payable of $14,000.
18	Declared cash dividends, $6,000.

Additional information:

1. As of February 1, 2002, current assets were $140,000, and current liabilities were $50,000.
2. As of February 1, 2002, current assets included $15,000 of inventory and $5,000 of prepaid expenses.

Instructions
(a) Compute the current ratio as of the beginning of the month and after each transaction.
(b) Compute the acid-test ratio as of the beginning of the month and after each transaction.

Compute selected ratios.
(SO 5)

E13-9 Gladys Jeske Company has these comparative balance sheet data.

GLADYS JESKE COMPANY
Balance Sheets
December 31

	2002	2001
Cash	$ 20,000	$ 30,000
Receivables (net)	65,000	60,000
Inventories	60,000	50,000
Plant assets (net)	200,000	180,000
	$345,000	$320,000
Accounts payable	$ 50,000	$ 60,000
Mortgage payable (15%)	100,000	100,000
Common stock, $10 par	140,000	120,000
Retained earnings	55,000	40,000
	$345,000	$320,000

Additional information for 2002:

1. Net income was $25,000.
2. Sales on account were $420,000. Sales returns and allowances amounted to $20,000.
3. Cost of goods sold was $198,000.
4. Net cash provided by operating activities was $44,000.

Instructions
Compute the following ratios at December 31, 2002.
(a) Current.
(b) Acid-test.
(c) Receivables turnover.
(d) Average collection period.
(e) Inventory turnover.
(f) Days in inventory.
(g) Cash return on sales.
(h) Cash debt coverage.
(i) Current cash debt coverage.

Compute selected ratios.
(SO 5)

E13-10 Selected comparative statement data for the giant bookseller **Barnes & Noble** are presented here. All balance sheet data are as of December 31 (in millions).

	1998	1997
Net sales	$3,005.6	$2,796.9
Cost of goods sold	2,142.7	2,019.3
Interest expense	25.4	38.1
Net income	92.4	53.2
Accounts receivable	57.5	43.9
Inventory	945.1	852.1
Total assets	1,807.6	1,591.2
Total common stockholders' equity	678.8	531.8
Cash provided by operating activities	181.1	169.2

Instructions
Compute the following ratios for 1998.
(a) Profit margin.
(b) Asset turnover.
(c) Return on assets.
(d) Return on common stockholders' equity.
(e) Cash return on sales.
(f) Gross profit rate.

E13-11   Here is the income statement for Ernie Basler, Inc.

Compute selected ratios.
(SO 5)

ERNIE BASLER, INC.
Income Statement
For the Year Ended December 31, 2002

Sales	$400,000
Cost of goods sold	230,000
Gross profit	170,000
Expenses (including $20,000 interest and $24,000 income taxes)	100,000
Net income	$ 70,000

Additional information:

1. Common stock outstanding January 1, 2002, was 30,000 shares. On July 1, 2002, 10,000 more shares were issued.
2. The market price of Ernie Basler, Inc., stock was $15 in 2002.
3. Cash dividends of $21,000 were paid, $5,000 of which were to preferred stockholders.
4. Cash provided by operating activities was $98,000.

Instructions
Compute the following measures for 2002.
(a) Earnings per share.
(b) Price-earnings ratio.
(c) Payout ratio.
(d) Times interest earned ratio.
(e) Cash return on sales ratio.

E13-12   Easi Corporation experienced a fire on December 31, 2002, in which its financial records were partially destroyed. It has been able to salvage some of the records and has ascertained the following balances.

Compute amounts from ratios.
(SO 5)

	December 31, 2002	December 31, 2001
Cash	$ 30,000	$ 10,000
Receivables (net)	72,500	126,000
Inventory	200,000	180,000
Accounts payable	50,000	10,000
Notes payable	30,000	20,000
Common stock, $100 par	400,000	400,000
Retained earnings	113,500	101,000

Additional information:

1. The inventory turnover is 3.6 times.
2. The return on common stockholders' equity is 22%. The company had no additional paid-in capital.
3. The receivables turnover is 9.4 times.
4. The return on assets is 16%.
5. Total assets at December 31, 2001, were $605,000.

Instructions
Compute the following for Easi Corporation.
(a) Cost of goods sold for 2002.
(b) Net sales for 2002.
(c) Net income for 2002.
(d) Total assets at December 31, 2002.

PROBLEMS: SET A*

Prepare vertical analysis and comment on profitability.
(SO 4, 5)

P13-1A Here are comparative statement data for Catchem Company and Eatum Company, two competitors. All balance sheet data are as of December 31, 2002, and December 31, 2001.

	Catchem Company		Eatum Company	
	2002	**2001**	**2002**	**2001**
Net sales	$1,849,035		$539,038	
Cost of goods sold	1,080,490		238,006	
Operating expenses	302,275		79,000	
Interest expense	6,800		1,252	
Income tax expense	51,030		6,650	
Current assets	325,975	$312,410	83,336	$ 79,467
Plant assets (net)	521,310	500,000	139,728	125,812
Current liabilities	66,325	75,815	35,348	30,281
Long-term liabilities	108,500	90,000	29,620	25,000
Common stock, $10 par	500,000	500,000	120,000	120,000
Retained earnings	172,460	146,595	38,096	29,998

Instructions

(a) Prepare a vertical analysis of the 2002 income statement data for Catchem Company and Eatum Company.

(b) ▭▭▭▭▷ Comment on the relative profitability of the companies by computing the 2002 return on assets and the return on common stockholders' equity ratios for both companies.

Compute ratios from balance sheet and income statement.
(SO 5)

eGrade
Problem

P13-2A The comparative statements of Harry Connick, Jr., Company are presented here.

HARRY CONNICK, JR., COMPANY
Income Statements
For the Years Ended December 31

	2002	2001
Net sales	$1,918,500	$1,750,500
Cost of goods sold	1,005,500	996,000
Gross profit	913,000	754,500
Selling and administrative expenses	506,000	479,000
Income from operations	407,000	275,500
Other expenses and losses		
Interest expense	28,000	19,000
Income before income taxes	379,000	256,500
Income tax expense	86,700	77,000
Net income	$ 292,300	$ 179,500

---

*Follow the rounding procedures used in the chapter.

HARRY CONNICK, JR., COMPANY
Balance Sheets
December 31

	2002	2001
Assets		
Current assets		
Cash	$ 60,100	$ 64,200
Short-term investments	54,000	50,000
Accounts receivable (net)	107,800	102,800
Inventory	143,000	115,500
Total current assets	364,900	332,500
Plant assets (net)	625,300	520,300
Total assets	$990,200	$852,800
Liabilities and Stockholders' Equity		
Current liabilities		
Accounts payable	$170,000	$145,400
Income taxes payable	43,500	42,000
Total current liabilities	213,500	187,400
Bonds payable	210,000	200,000
Total liabilities	423,500	387,400
Stockholders' equity		
Common stock ($5 par)	280,000	300,000
Retained earnings	286,700	165,400
Total stockholders' equity	566,700	465,400
Total liabilities and stockholders' equity	$990,200	$852,800

On July 1, 2002, 4,000 shares were repurchased and canceled. All sales were on account. Net cash provided by operating activities for 2002 was $280,000.

Instructions
Compute the following ratios for 2002.

(a) Earnings per share.
(b) Return on common stockholders' equity.
(c) Return on assets.
(d) Current ratio.
(e) Acid-test.
(f) Receivables turnover.
(g) Average collection period.
(h) Inventory turnover.

(i) Days in inventory.
(j) Times interest earned.
(k) Asset turnover.
(l) Debt to total assets.
(m) Current cash debt coverage.
(n) Cash return on sales.
(o) Cash debt coverage.

P13-3A Condensed balance sheet and income statement data for Midnight Oil Corporation are presented here.

Perform ratio analysis.
(SO 5)

MIDNIGHT OIL CORPORATION
Balance Sheets
December 31

	2002	2001	2000
Cash	$ 25,000	$ 20,000	$ 18,000
Receivables (net)	50,000	45,000	48,000
Other current assets	90,000	85,000	64,000
Investments	55,000	70,000	45,000
Plant and equipment (net)	500,000	370,000	258,000
	$720,000	$590,000	$433,000

	2002	2001	2000
Current liabilities	$ 75,000	$ 80,000	$ 30,000
Long-term debt	160,000	85,000	20,000
Common stock, $10 par	340,000	300,000	300,000
Retained earnings	145,000	125,000	83,000
	$720,000	$590,000	$433,000

MIDNIGHT OIL CORPORATION
Income Statements
For the Years Ended December 31

	2002	2001
Sales	$640,000	$500,000
Less: Sales returns and allowances	40,000	50,000
Net sales	600,000	450,000
Cost of goods sold	420,000	300,000
Gross profit	180,000	150,000
Operating expenses (including income taxes)	126,000	88,000
Net income	$ 54,000	$ 62,000

Additional information:

1. The market price of Midnight Oil's common stock was $4.00, $6.00, and $7.95 for 2000, 2001, and 2002, respectively.
2. You must compute dividends paid. All dividends were paid in cash.
3. On July 1, 2002, 4,000 shares of common stock were issued.

Instructions
(a) Compute the following ratios for 2001 and 2002.
    (1) Profit margin.   (5) Price-earnings.
    (2) Gross profit.   (6) Payout.
    (3) Asset turnover.   (7) Debt to total assets.
    (4) Earnings per share.
(b) ✏️▶ Based on the ratios calculated, discuss briefly the improvement or lack thereof in the financial position and operating results from 2001 to 2002 of Midnight Oil Corporation.

Compute ratios; comment on overall liquidity and profitability.
(SO 5)

P13-4A This financial information is for Semisonic Company.

SEMISONIC COMPANY
Balance Sheets
December 31

	2002	2001
Assets		
Cash	$ 70,000	$ 65,000
Short-term investments	45,000	40,000
Receivables (net)	94,000	90,000
Inventories	230,000	125,000
Prepaid expenses	25,000	23,000
Land	130,000	130,000
Building and equipment (net)	290,000	175,000
Total assets	$884,000	$648,000

	2002	2001
Liabilities and Stockholders' Equity		
Notes payable	$200,000	$100,000
Accounts payable	45,000	42,000
Accrued liabilities	40,000	40,000
Bonds payable, due 2004	250,000	150,000
Common stock, $10 par	200,000	200,000
Retained earnings	149,000	116,000
Total liabilities and stockholders' equity	$884,000	$648,000

SEMISONIC COMPANY
Income Statements
For the Years Ended December 31

	2002	2001
Sales	$850,000	$790,000
Cost of goods sold	620,000	575,000
Gross profit	230,000	215,000
Operating expenses	194,000	180,000
Net income	$ 36,000	$ 35,000

Additional information:

1. Inventory at the beginning of 2001 was $115,000.
2. Receivables at the beginning of 2001 were $88,000.
3. Total assets at the beginning of 2001 were $630,000.
4. No common stock transactions occurred during 2001 or 2002.
5. All sales were on account.

Instructions

(a) Indicate, by using ratios, the change in liquidity and profitability of Semisonic Company from 2001 to 2002. [*Note:* Not all profitability ratios can be computed nor can cash-basis ratios be computed.]

(b) Given below are three independent situations and a ratio that may be affected. For each situation, compute the affected ratio (1) as of December 31, 2002, and (2) as of December 31, 2003, after giving effect to the situation. Net income for 2003 was $40,000. Total assets on December 31, 2003, were $900,000.

Situation	Ratio
1. 18,000 shares of common stock were sold at par on July 1, 2003.	Return on common stockholders' equity
2. All of the notes payable were paid in 2003.	Debt to total assets
3. The market price of common stock was $9 and $12.80 on December 31, 2002 and 2003, respectively.	Price-earnings

P13-5A   Selected financial data of **Kmart** and **Wal-Mart** for 1998 are presented here (in millions).

Compute selected ratios, and compare liquidity, profitability, and solvency for two companies.
(SO 5)

	Kmart Corporation	Wal-Mart Stores, Inc.
Income Statement Data for Year		
Net sales	$33,674	$137,634
Cost of goods sold	26,319	108,725
Selling and administrative expenses	6,245	22,363
Interest expense	343	797
Other income (expense)	(19)	1,421
Income tax expense	230	2,740
Net income	$ 518	$ 4,430
Balance Sheet Data (End of Year)		
Current assets	$ 7,830	$ 21,132
Noncurrent assets	6,336	28,864
Total assets	$14,166	$ 49,996
Current liabilities	$ 3,691	$ 16,762
Long-term debt	4,496	12,122
Total stockholders' equity	5,979	21,112
Total liabilities and stockholders' equity	$14,166	$ 49,996
Beginning-of-Year Balances		
Total assets	$13,558	$ 45,384
Total stockholders' equity	5,434	18,503
Current liabilities	3,274	14,460
Total liabilities	8,124	26,881
Other Data		
Average net receivables	–0–	$ 1,047
Average inventory	$ 6,452	16,787
Net cash provided by operating activities	1,237	7,580

Instructions

(a) For each company, compute the following ratios.

(1) Current.	(8) Return on assets.
(2) Receivables turnover.	(9) Return on common stockholders' equity.
(3) Average collection period.	(10) Debt to total assets.
(4) Inventory turnover.	(11) Times interest earned.
(5) Days in inventory.	(12) Current cash debt coverage.
(6) Profit margin.	(13) Cash return on sales.
(7) Asset turnover.	(14) Cash debt coverage.

(b) Compare the liquidity, solvency, and profitability of the two companies.

PROBLEMS: SET B*

Prepare vertical analysis and comment on profitability.
(SO 4, 5)

P13-1B   Here are comparative statement data for Jimmy Paige Company and Robert Plant Company, two competitors. All balance sheet data are as of December 31, 2002, and December 31, 2001.

---

*Follow the rounding procedures used in the chapter.

	Jimmy Paige Company		Robert Plant Company	
	2002	**2001**	**2002**	**2001**
Net sales	$350,000		$1,400,000	
Cost of goods sold	180,000		720,000	
Operating expenses	51,000		272,000	
Interest expense	3,000		10,000	
Income tax expense	11,000		65,000	
Current assets	130,000	$110,000	700,000	$650,000
Plant assets (net)	405,000	270,000	1,000,000	750,000
Current liabilities	60,000	52,000	250,000	275,000
Long-term liabilities	50,000	68,000	200,000	150,000
Common stock	360,000	210,000	950,000	700,000
Retained earnings	65,000	50,000	300,000	275,000

Instructions
(a) Prepare a vertical analysis of the 2002 income statement data for Paige Company and Plant Company.
(b) ▭▭▭▷ Comment on the relative profitability of the companies by computing the return on assets and the return on common stockholders' equity ratios for both companies.

P13-2B The comparative statements of Monster Magnet Company are presented here.   *Compute ratios from balance sheet and income statement.*
(SO 5)

MONSTER MAGNET COMPANY
Income Statements
For the Years Ended December 31

	2002	2001
Net sales	$780,000	$624,000
Cost of goods sold	440,000	405,600
Gross profit	340,000	218,400
Selling and administrative expense	143,880	149,760
Income from operations	196,120	68,640
Other expenses and losses		
Interest expense	9,920	7,200
Income before income taxes	186,200	61,440
Income tax expense	25,300	24,000
Net income	$160,900	$ 37,440

MONSTER MAGNET COMPANY
Balance Sheets
December 31

Assets	2002	2001
Current assets		
Cash	$ 23,100	$ 21,600
Short-term investments	34,800	33,000
Accounts receivable (net)	106,200	93,800
Inventory	122,400	64,000
Total current assets	286,500	212,400
Plant assets (net)	465,300	459,600
Total assets	$751,800	$672,000

	2002	2001
Liabilities and Stockholders' Equity		
Current liabilities		
Accounts payable	$184,200	$132,000
Income taxes payable	25,300	24,000
Total current liabilities	209,500	156,000
Bonds payable	132,000	120,000
Total liabilities	341,500	276,000
Stockholders' equity		
Common stock ($10 par)	140,000	150,000
Retained earnings	270,300	246,000
Total stockholders' equity	410,300	396,000
Total liabilities and stockholders' equity	$751,800	$672,000

On July 1, 2002, 1,000 shares were repurchased and canceled. All sales were on account. Net cash provided by operating activities was $36,000.

Instructions
Compute the following ratios for 2002.
(a) Earnings per share.
(b) Return on common stockholders' equity.
(c) Return on assets.
(d) Current.
(e) Acid-test.
(f) Receivables turnover.
(g) Average collection period.
(h) Inventory turnover.
(i) Days in inventory.
(j) Times interest earned.
(k) Asset turnover.
(l) Debt to total assets.
(m) Current cash debt coverage.
(n) Cash return on sales.
(o) Cash debt coverage.

Perform ratio analysis.
(SO 5)

P13-3B   These are condensed balance sheet and income statement data for Vicente Fernandez Corporation.

VICENTE FERNANDEZ CORPORATION
Balance Sheets
December 31

	2002	2001	2000
Cash	$ 40,000	$ 24,000	$ 20,000
Receivables (net)	120,000	45,000	48,000
Other current assets	80,000	75,000	62,000
Investments	90,000	70,000	50,000
Plant and equipment (net)	650,000	400,000	360,000
	$980,000	$614,000	$540,000
Current liabilities	$ 98,000	$ 75,000	$ 70,000
Long-term debt	297,000	75,000	65,000
Common stock, $10 par	400,000	340,000	300,000
Retained earnings	185,000	124,000	105,000
	$980,000	$614,000	$540,000

VICENTE FERNANDEZ CORPORATION
Income Statements
For the Years Ended December 31

	2002	2001
Sales	$800,000	$750,000
Less: Sales returns and allowances	40,000	50,000
Net sales	760,000	700,000
Cost of goods sold	420,000	400,000
Gross profit	340,000	300,000
Operating expenses (including income taxes)	194,000	237,000
Net income	$146,000	$ 63,000

Additional information:

1. The market price of Vicente Fernandez's common stock was $5.00, $3.50, and $2.30 for 2000, 2001, and 2002, respectively.
2. You must compute dividends paid. All dividends were paid in cash.
3. On July 1, 2001, 4,000 shares of common stock were issued, and on July 1, 2002, 6,000 shares were issued.

Instructions
(a) Compute the following ratios for 2001 and 2002.
　(1) Profit margin.　　(5) Price-earnings.
　(2) Gross profit rate.　(6) Payout.
　(3) Asset turnover.　　(7) Debt to total assets.
　(4) Earnings per share.
(b) ▭▭▭▭▷ Based on the ratios calculated, discuss briefly the improvement or lack thereof in the financial position and operating results from 2001 to 2002 of Vicente Fernandez Corporation.

P13-4B　Financial information for Dwight Yoakam Company is presented here.

Compute ratios; comment on overall liquidity and profitability.
(SO 5)

DWIGHT YOAKAM COMPANY
Balance Sheets
December 31

	2002	2001
Assets		
Cash	$ 50,000	$ 42,000
Short-term investments	80,000	50,000
Receivables (net)	100,000	87,000
Inventories	440,000	300,000
Prepaid expenses	25,000	31,000
Land	75,000	75,000
Building and equipment (net)	570,000	400,000
Total assets	$1,340,000	$985,000
Liabilities and Stockholders' Equity		
Notes payable	$ 125,000	$ 25,000
Accounts payable	160,000	90,000
Accrued liabilities	50,000	50,000
Bonds payable, due 2004	200,000	100,000
Common stock, $5 par	500,000	500,000
Retained earnings	305,000	220,000
Total liabilities and stockholders' equity	$1,340,000	$985,000

DWIGHT YOAKAM COMPANY
Income Statements
For the Years Ended December 31

	2002	2001
Sales	$1,000,000	$940,000
Cost of goods sold	650,000	635,000
Gross profit	350,000	305,000
Operating expenses	235,000	215,000
Net income	$ 115,000	$ 90,000

Additional information:

1. Inventory at the beginning of 2001 was $350,000.
2. Receivables at the beginning of 2001 were $80,000.
3. Total assets at the beginning of 2001 were $1,175,000.
4. No common stock transactions occurred during 2001 or 2002.
5. All sales were on account.

Instructions
(a) Indicate, by using ratios, the change in liquidity and profitability of Dwight Yoakam Company from 2001 to 2002. [*Note:* Not all profitability ratios can be computed nor can cash-basis ratios be computed.]
(b) Given below are three independent situations and a ratio that may be affected. For each situation, compute the affected ratio (1) as of December 31, 2002, and (2) as of December 31, 2003, after giving effect to the situation. Net income for 2003 was $125,000. Total assets on December 31, 2003, were $1,500,000.

Situation	Ratio
1. 65,000 shares of common stock were sold at par on July 1, 2003.	Returns on common stockholder's equity
2. All of the notes payable were paid in 2003.	Debt to total assets
3. The market price of common stock on December 31, 2003, was $6.25. The market price on December 31, 2002, was $5.	Price-earnings

Compute selected ratios, and compare liquidity, profitability, and solvency for two companies.
(SO 5)

P13-5B Selected financial data for **Bethlehem Steel** and **USX** are presented here (in millions).

	Bethlehem Steel Corporation	USX Corporation
Income Statement Data for Year		
Net sales	$4,477.8	$28,310
Cost of goods sold	3,883.2	20,712
Selling and administrative expenses	370.1	5,839
Interest expense	62.4	279
Other income (expense)	(18.0)	(491)
Income tax expense	24.0	315
Net income	$ 120.1	$ 674

	Bethlehem Steel Corporation	USX Corporation
Balance Sheet Data (End of Year)		
Current assets	$1,494.8	$ 4,206
Property, plant, and equipment (net)	2,655.7	12,929
Other assets	1,471.0	3,998
Total assets	$5,621.5	$21,133
Current liabilities	$ 985.2	$ 3,619
Long-term debt	3,160.6	11,112
Total stockholders' equity	1,475.7	6,402
Total liabilities and stockholders' equity	$5,621.5	$21,133
Beginning-of-Year Balances		
Total assets	$4,802.6	$17,284
Total stockholders' equity	1,201.1	5,397
Current liabilities	910.8	3,523
Total liabilities	3,601.5	11,887
Other Data		
Average net receivables	$ 307	$ 1,540
Average inventory	967	1,847
Net cash provided by operating activities	444	1,803

Instructions

(a) For each company, compute the following ratios.

(1) Current ratio.	(8) Return on assets.
(2) Receivables turnover.	(9) Return on common stockholders' equity.
(3) Average collection period.	(10) Debt to total assets.
(4) Inventory turnover.	(11) Times interest earned.
(5) Days in inventory.	(12) Current cash debt coverage.
(6) Profit margin.	(13) Cash return on sales.
(7) Asset turnover.	(14) Cash debt coverage.

(b) Compare the liquidity, solvency, and profitability of the two companies.

◆ **B R O A D E N I N G   Y O U R   P E R S P E C T I V E**

*F*INANCIAL REPORTING AND ANALYSIS

FINANCIAL REPORTING PROBLEM: *Tootsie Roll Industries, Inc.*

BYP13-1   Your parents are considering investing in **Tootsie Roll Industries** common stock. They ask you, as an accounting expert, to make an analysis of the company for them. Fortunately, excerpts from a recent annual report of Tootsie Roll are presented in Appendix A of this textbook.

Instructions

(a) Make a 5-year trend analysis, using 1994 as the base year, of (1) net revenues and (2) net earnings. Comment on the significance of the trend results.

(b) Compute for 1998 and 1997 the (1) debt to total assets ratio and (2) times interest earned ratio. How would you evaluate Tootsie Roll's long-term solvency?

(c) Compute for 1998 and 1997 the (1) profit margin ratio, (2) asset turnover ratio, (3) return on assets ratio, and (4) return on common stockholders' equity ratio. How would you evaluate Tootsie Roll's profitability? Total assets at December 31, 1996, were $391,456,000, and total stockholders' equity at December 31, 1996, was $312,881,000.

(d) What information outside the annual report may also be useful to your parents in making a decision about Tootsie Roll?

COMPARATIVE ANALYSIS PROBLEM: *Tootsie Roll vs. Hershey Foods*

BYP13-2 The financial statements of **Hershey Foods** are presented in Appendix B, following the financial statements for **Tootsie Roll Industries** in Appendix A.

Instructions
(a) Based on the information in the financial statements, determine each of the following for each company.
   (1) The percentage increase in net sales and in net income from 1997 to 1998.
   (2) The percentage increase in total assets and in total stockholders' equity from 1997 to 1998.
   (3) The earnings per share for 1998.
(b) What conclusions concerning the two companies can be drawn from these data?

*I*NTERPRETING FINANCIAL STATEMENTS

BYP13-3 **The Coca-Cola Company** and **PepsiCo, Inc.** provide refreshments to every corner of the world. Selected data from the 1998 consolidated financial statements for the Coca-Cola Company and for PepsiCo, Inc., are presented here (in millions).

	Coca-Cola	PepsiCo
Total current assets (including cash, accounts receivable, and short-term investments totaling $3,473 for Coke and $2,847 for Pepsi)	$6,380	$4,362
Total current liabilities	8,640	7,914
Net sales	18,813	22,348
Cost of goods sold	5,562	9,330
Net income	3,533	1,993
Average receivables for the year	1,653	2,302
Average inventories for the year	925	874
Average total assets	18,013	21,381
Average common stockholders' equity	7,839	6,669
Average current liabilities	8,010	6,086
Average total liabilities	10,225	14,712
Total assets	19,145	22,660
Total liabilities	10,742	16,259
Income taxes	1,665	270
Interest expense	277	395
Cash provided by operating activities	3,433	3,211

Instructions
(a) Compute the following liquidity ratios for 1998 for Coca-Cola and for PepsiCo, and comment on the relative liquidity of the two competitors.
   (1) Current ratio.   (5) Inventory turnover.
   (2) Acid-test.   (6) Days in inventory.
   (3) Receivables turnover.   (7) Current cash debt coverage.
   (4) Average collection period.
(b) Compute the following solvency ratios for the two companies, and comment on the relative solvency of the two competitors.
   (1) Debt to total assets ratio.   (3) Cash debt coverage ratio.
   (2) Times interest earned.
(c) Compute the following profitability ratios for the two companies, and comment on the relative profitability of the two competitors.
   (1) Profit margin.   (4) Return on assets.
   (2) Cash return on sales.   (5) Return on common stockholders' equity.
   (3) Asset turnover.

GROUP DECISION CASE

BYP13-4   You are a loan officer for Second State Bank of Port Washington. Ted Worth, president of T. Worth Corporation, has just left your office. He is interested in an 8-year loan to expand the company's operations. The borrowed funds would be used to purchase new equipment. As evidence of the company's debt-worthiness, Worth provided you with the following facts.

	2002	**2001**
Current ratio	3.1	2.1
Acid-test ratio	0.8	1.4
Asset turnover ratio	2.8	2.2
Cash debt coverage ratio	0.1	0.2
Net income	Up 32%	Down 8%
Earnings per share	$3.30	$2.50

Ted Worth is a very insistent (some would say pushy) man. When you told him that you would need additional information before making your decision, he acted offended, and said, "What more could you possibly want to know?" You responded that, at a minimum, you would need complete, audited financial statements.

Instructions
With the class divided into groups, answer the following.
(a) Explain why you would want the financial statements to be audited.
(b) Discuss the implications of the ratios provided for the lending decision you are to make. That is, does the information paint a favorable picture? Are these ratios relevant to the decision?
(c) List three other ratios that you would want to calculate for this company, and explain why you would use each.
(d) What are the limitations of ratio analysis for credit and investing decisions?

REAL-WORLD FOCUS

BYP13-5   The use of railroad transportation has changed dramatically around the world. Attitudes about railroads and railroad usage differ across countries. In England, the railroads were run by the government until recently. Five years ago, **Railtrack Group PLC** became a publicly traded company. The largest railroad company in the United States is **Burlington Northern Railroad Company**. The following data were taken from the 1998 financial statements of each company.

Financial Highlights	Railtrack Group (pounds in millions)		Burlington Northern (dollars in millions)	
	1998	**1997**	**1998**	**1997**
Cash and short-term investments	£ 380	£ 26	$ 95	$ –0–
Accounts receivable	434	402	676	632
Total current assets	909	521	1,357	1,197
Total assets	7,095	5,760	22,725	21,199
Current liabilities	1,128	1,209	2,175	2,089
Total liabilities	3,882	2,888	14,497	14,176
Total stockholders' equity	3,213	2,872	8,228	7,023
Sales	2,573		8,936	
Operating costs	2,102		6,781	
Interest expense	93		293	
Income tax expense	3		733	
Net income	425		1,206	
Cash provided by operations	988		2,107	

Instructions

(a) Calculate the following 1998 liquidity ratios and discuss the relative liquidity of the two companies.
   (1) Current ratio.   (3) Current cash debt coverage.
   (2) Acid-test.   (4) Receivables turnover.
(b) Calculate the following 1998 solvency ratios and discuss the relative solvency of the two companies.
   (1) Debt to total assets.   (3) Cash debt coverage.
   (2) Times interest earned.
(c) Calculate the following 1998 profitability ratios and discuss the relative profitability of the two companies.
   (1) Asset turnover.   (3) Return on assets.
   (2) Profit margin.   (4) Return on common stockholders' equity.
(d) What other issues must you consider when comparing these two companies?

EXPLORING THE WEB

BYP13-6 *Purpose:* To employ comparative data and industry data to evaluate a company's performance and financial position.

Address: **biz.yahoo.com/i**
        (or go to www.wiley.com/college/weygandt)

Steps:

(1) Identify two competing companies.
(2) Go to the above address.
(3) Type in the first company's name and choose **Search**.
(4) Choose **Profile**.
(5) Choose **Ratio Comparisons**.
(6) Print out the results.
(7) Repeat steps 3–6 for the competitor.

Instructions
Perform the following evaluations.
(a) Evaluate the company's liquidity relative to the industry averages and to the competitor that you chose.
(b) Evaluate the company's solvency relative to the industry averages and to the competitor that you chose.
(c) Evaluate the company's profitability relative to the industry averages and to the competitor that you chose.

COMMUNICATION ACTIVITY

BYP13-7 L. R. Stanton is the chief executive officer of Hi-Tech Electronics. Stanton is an expert engineer but a novice in accounting. Stanton asks you, as an accounting major, to explain (a) the bases for comparison in analyzing Hi-Tech's financial statements and (b) the limitations, if any, in financial statement analysis.

Instructions
Write a memo to L. R. Stanton that explains the basis for comparison and the limitations of financial statement analysis.

RESEARCH ASSIGNMENT

BYP13-8 The chapter stresses the importance of comparing an individual company's financial ratios to industry norms. Robert Morris Associates (RMA), a national association of bank loan and credit officers, publishes industry-specific financial data in its *Annual Statement Studies*. This publication includes vertical analysis financial statements and various ratios classified by four-digit SIC code. (*Note:* An alternative source is Dun & Bradstreet's *Industry Norms and Key Business Ratios.*)

Obtain the most recent edition of *Annual Statement Studies* and the most recent annual report of **Wal-Mart Stores, Inc.**

Instructions

(a) Prepare a vertical analysis balance sheet and income statement for Wal-Mart.
(b) Calculate those ratios for Wal-Mart that are covered by RMA. (*Note:* The specific ratio definitions used by RMA are described in the beginning of the book. Use ending values for balance sheet items.)
(c) What is Wal-Mart's SIC code? Use your answers from parts (a) and (b) to compare Wal-Mart to the appropriate current industry data. How does Wal-Mart compare to its competitors? (*Note:* RMA sorts current-year data by firm assets and sales, and presents 5 years of historical data on an aggregate basis.)
(d) How many sets of financial statements did RMA use in compiling the current industry data sorted by sales?

ETHICS CASE

BYP13-9 Vern Fairly, president of Fairly Industries, wishes to issue a press release to bolster his company's image and maybe even its stock price, which has been gradually falling. As controller, you have been asked to provide a list of 20 financial ratios along with some other operating statistics relative to Fairly Industries' first-quarter financials and operations.

Two days after you provide the ratios and data requested, you are asked by Roberta Sanchez, the public relations director of Fairly, to prove the accuracy of the financial and operating data contained in the press release written by the president and edited by Roberta. In the news release, the president highlights the sales increase of 25% over last year's first quarter and the positive change in the current ratio from 1.5:1 last year to 3:1 this year. He also emphasizes that production was up 50% over the prior year's first quarter. You note that the release contains only positive or improved ratios and none of the negative or deteriorated ratios. For instance, no mention is made that the debt to total assets ratio has increased from 35% to 55%, that inventories are up 89%, and that although the current ratio improved, the acid-test ratio fell from 1:1 to 0.5:1. Nor is there any mention that the reported profit for the quarter would have been a loss had not the estimated lives of Fairly's plant and machinery been increased by 30%. Roberta emphasized, "The Prez wants this release by early this afternoon."

Instructions

(a) Who are the stakeholders in this situation?
(b) Is there anything unethical in president Fairly's actions?
(c) Should you as controller remain silent? Does Sanchez have any responsibility?

Answers to Self-Study Questions

1. d   2. d   3. b   4. d   5. c   6. c   7. a   8. c   9. c
10. b   11. a   12. a

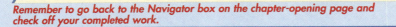
Remember to go back to the Navigator box on the chapter-opening page and check off your completed work.

Specimen Financial Statements:
Tootsie Roll Industries, Inc.

THE ANNUAL REPORT

Once each year a corporation communicates to its stockholders and other interested parties by issuing a complete set of audited financial statements. The
annual report, as this communication is called, summarizes the financial results of the company's operations for the year and its plans for the future. Many
annual reports are attractive, multicolored, glossy public relations ad pieces con-
taining pictures of corporate officers and directors as well as photos and descriptions of new products and new buildings. Yet the basic function of every
annual report is to report financial information, almost all of which is a product of the corporation's accounting system.

　　The content and organization of corporate annual reports have become fairly
standardized. Excluding the public relations part of the report (pictures, products, and propaganda), the following items are the traditional financial portions
of the annual report:

> Financial Highlights
> Letter to the Stockholders
> Management's Discussion and Analysis
> Financial Statements
> Notes to the Financial Statements
> Auditor's Report
> Supplementary Financial Information

　　In this appendix we illustrate current financial reporting with a comprehensive set of corporate financial statements that are prepared in accordance with
generally accepted accounting principles and audited by an international independent certified public accounting firm. We are grateful for permission to use
the actual financial statements and other accompanying financial information from
the annual report of a large, publicly held company, Tootsie Roll Industries, Inc.

FINANCIAL HIGHLIGHTS

The financial highlights section is usually presented inside the front cover or on
the first two pages of the annual report. This section generally reports the total
or per share amounts for five to ten financial items for the current year and one
or more previous years. Financial items from the income statement and the balance sheet that typically are presented are sales, income from continuing operations, net income, net income per share, dividends per common share, and the
amount of capital expenditures. The financial highlights section from **Tootsie
Roll Industries' Annual Report** is shown on page A-2. We have also included
Tootsie Roll's discussion of its corporate principles and corporate profile.

---

*The financial information herein is reprinted with permission from the Tootsie Roll Industries, Inc.
1998 Annual Report.

Financial Highlights

	December 31,	
	1998	1997
	(in thousands except per share data)	
Net Sales	$388,659	$375,594
Net Earnings.	67,526	60,682
Working Capital	175,155	153,355
Net Property, Plant and Equipment	83,024	78,364
Shareholders' Equity.	396,457	351,163
Average Shares Outstanding*.	48,051	48,294
Per Share Items*		
Net Earnings.	$1.41	$1.26
Shareholders' Equity	8.29	7.29
Cash Dividends Paid.	.20	.16

*Based on average shares outstanding adjusted for stock dividends and 2-for-1 stock split.

Corporate Principles

We believe that the differences among companies are attributable to the caliber of their people, and therefore we strive to attract and retain superior people for each job.

We believe that an open family atmosphere at work combined with professional management fosters cooperation and enables each individual to maximize his or her contribution to the company and realize the corresponding rewards.

We do not jeopardize long-term growth for immediate, short-term results.

We maintain a conservative financial posture in the deployment and management of our assets.

We run a trim operation and continually strive to eliminate waste, minimize cost and implement performance improvements.

We invest in the latest and most productive equipment to deliver the best quality product to our customers at the lowest cost.

We seek to outsource functions where appropriate and to vertically integrate operations where it is financially advantageous to do so.

We view our well known brands as prized assets to be aggressively advertised and promoted to each new generation of consumers.

Melvin J. Gordon, Chairman and Chief Executive Officer and Ellen R. Gordon, President and Chief Operating Officer.

Corporate Profile

Tootsie Roll Industries, Inc. has been engaged in the manufacture and sale of candy for 102 years. Our products are primarily sold under the familiar brand names, Tootsie Roll, Tootsie Roll Pops, Caramel Apple Pops, Child's Play, Charms, Blow Pop, Blue Razz, Cella's, Mason Dots, Mason Crows, Junior Mints, Charleston Chew, Sugar Daddy and Sugar Babies.

LETTER TO THE STOCKHOLDERS

Nearly every annual report contains a letter to the stockholders from the Chairman of the Board or the President (or both). This letter typically discusses the company's accomplishments during the past year and highlights significant events such as mergers and acquisitions, new products, operating achievements, business philosophy, changes in officers or directors, financing commitments, expansion plans, and future prospects. The letter to the stockholders signed by Melvin J. Gordon, Chairman of the Board and Chief Executive Officer, and Ellen R. Gordon, President and Chief Operating Officer, of Tootsie Roll Industries is shown below. The letter is followed by a discussion referred to as the "Operating Report" by Tootsie Roll.

To Our Shareholders

We are once again pleased to report another year of record operating performance for Tootsie Roll Industries. Sales in 1998 reached $389 million, a $13 million or 3.5% increase over 1997. This was our twenty-second consecutive year of record sales results.

Sales increases were attributable to another strong Halloween season and effective, ongoing promotional programs. Gains were seen in all major domestic brands and trade classes, as movement of our basic product lines continues to be strong at the retail level.

This growth in our base business was supplemented by strength in several new products and line extensions that have been introduced in the past few years. Domestic sales growth more than offset a decline in Mexico, where results were adversely affected by currency devaluations and increased local competitive pressure.

Net Income rose to $67 million, a $7 million or 11.3% increase over 1997. On a per share basis, net income was up by an even larger 11.9% due to share repurchases that were made throughout the year. As a percent of sales, our net income rose to 17.4% from 16.2% in the prior year.

Net income gains were due to increased sales, improved manufacturing productivity, lower costs for packaging and certain commodities, increased investment income

and ongoing efforts within the company to control expenses. 1998 represents the seventeenth consecutive year the company has achieved record earnings.

Our financial position has been further strengthened by these successful operating results. Cash and investments in marketable securities at year end increased over 1997. These financial assets place us in a position to respond to growth and investment opportunities as they arise. In this regard, we continue our pursuit of appropriate, strategic acquisitions.

Capital expenditures for the year were $15 million, representing capacity additions, efficiency improvements and infrastructure enhancements needed to support our growth into the new millennium.

Our thirty-fourth consecutive 3% stock dividend was distributed in April. Cash dividends, which have been paid for fifty-six consecutive years, were increased in July, the same month in which a two-for-one stock split was distributed.

During 1998 Tootsie Roll established a presence on the internet with the launch of "tootsie.com" The introduction of this interactive web site was immediately met with a positive response and received widespread press coverage. The company also received favorable coverage in Forbes magazine and in numerous other publications throughout the year.

We have taken appropriate steps to review our computer systems, ensuring that they are "Y2K compliant." We have begun testing to confirm that all systems will function in the new millennium and are confident that final testing will be completed by mid 1999.

We have also invested heavily in preparing our company to function in the next century. Since building niche brands is one of our primary goals, we have focused on increasing the market penetration of our well-known brands. Accordingly, we are encouraged by the continued growth of Tootsie Rolls, Tootsie Pops, Blow Pops, Junior Mints, Dots and other established products, as well as by Child's Play, Caramel Apple Pops, Super Blow Pops and other more recently introduced items.

To efficiently meet growing demand for these products, we have increased our production capacity and implemented the latest manufacturing technology, enabling us to produce the highest quality at the lowest cost. Consequently, sufficient blending, cooking, forming, cut and wrap and bagging capacity, as well as the infrastructure to support it, is either in place or on the drawing board to carry us into the next century.

Our distribution systems have been tailored to meet the evolving shipping patterns our customers require and tuned to handle each order with maximum efficiency. Through the use of advanced technology, we are able to precisely track inventory quantities to minimize out-of-stock situations. In 1998 our order fulfillment rate reached a record level.

Likewise, we have upgraded our EDP systems to handle the vast data requirements we foresee as both we and the companies we do business with move forward in the "information age." Our financial and accounting systems utilize state-of-the-art software and provide extensive capability for future growth.

These past investments, along with those that we will make in the years to come, are essential as we strive to continue providing good, branded values for our consumers in the new millennium and beyond.

We wish to thank our customers, suppliers, sales brokers and employees for their contributions to the success of the company in 1998 and years prior, and for helping to make Tootsie Roll Industries an attractive investment for our shareholders.

As we look forward to further profitable growth in the new millennium, we welcome the above mentioned constituencies to the business opportunities we anticipate there.

Melvin J. Gordon

Melvin J. Gordon
Chairman of the Board and Chief Executive Officer

Ellen R. Gordon

Ellen R. Gordon
President and Chief Operating Officer

"Tootsie Caramel Apple Pops—so good, only the stick will remain."

Operating Report

Marketing and Sales

Sales reached a new record high in 1998, driven by continued growth in our core brands. These increases resulted from successfully targeted promotions such as shipper displays, combo packs and bonus bags.

Sales growth was also realized from a shift to larger sized bags which reflect a continuing trend in the trade toward a higher "ring" or selling price per item. This trend meshes well with our products which continue to offer quality, branded confections that are attractive values.

Another trend that emerged recently is the popularity of multi-packs which feature popular bars or boxed goods in 5 and 10 count lay-down packs. Incremental sales were realized by launching snack-size Tootsie Roll and Charleston Chew bars and mini-boxes of Junior Mints and Dots in this new format. We also extended our popular Caramel Apple Pop to several new pack configurations, including a unique bulk display that incorporates a real wooden apple basket!

As is customary for our company, the third quarter was again our highest selling period due to Halloween and back-to-school programs. Halloween was led by continuing strength in our bagged goods, particularly in the larger sized assortments that have become well established consumer favorites during the past several years. We also experienced Halloween growth from the introduction of several new and larger pack sizes for existing items that we felt could become even more popular among trick-or-treaters.

New product growth included Wicked Red-berry Blow Pop, a mouth-watering strawberry-kiwi flavored Blow Pop in a bold, eye catching wrapper and Caramel-A-Lot, a blend of luscious caramel and chewy nougat wrapped in chocolaty goodness. In addition, several promising new items were developed for introduction in early 1999.

Advertising and Public Relations

Television was again the chief medium used to advertise our products to broad audiences of children and adults in 1998. Numerous placements in selected spot and cable markets featured our classic "How Many Licks?" theme, as well as two new commercials that were developed and introduced during the year.

The first of these new commercials, "Caramel Apple Pops," tempts consumers with the message that this remarkable pop is "so good only the stick will remain," while "Chocolate Attack" encourages mothers to quell their youngsters' chocolate cravings with delicious, low-fat Tootsie Rolls and Tootsie Pops. Both of these messages were economically delivered in ten and fifteen second formats on popular talk, game and adventure shows to maximize their reach.

Also in 1998 we launched the company's first web site on the internet. Both children and adults can now enhance their cyber travels by visiting "tootsie.com" to learn interesting facts about Tootsie Roll Industries, its history and its products in an enjoyable, user friendly environment. Whether curious about Clara Hirshfield (the original "Tootsie"), looking for our latest financial release or seeking an answer to the famous question "How many licks does it take to get to the Tootsie Roll center of a Tootsie Pop?," "tootsie.com" has something of interest for every Tootsie Roll fan.

The introduction of our web site was but one of the many positive mentions we received in the press and on television news programs last year. The company was also favorably reviewed in Forbes' Annual Report on American Industry.

We again received thousands of positive letters from our loyal consumers during the year. These serve as a constant reminder that each of the millions of Tootsie Rolls, Tootsie Pops and other popular confections we produce each day can make a life-long impression.

Manufacturing and Distribution

Continuing capital investments and operating improvements were made throughout the company in 1998 to support growth, increase efficiency or improve quality.

We added production capacity to meet growing demand for the products we make in Chicago, Illinois and Covington, Tennessee. We also reengineered several key processes at these plants to increase efficiency and reduce cost, and began the first of several infrastructure enhancements that are needed to support expanding production.

Also in support of our continued growth, we acquired land adjacent to our Covington, Tennessee plant and have commenced construction of a new regional distribution center there. This center will incorporate the automated inventory tracking systems that we have successfully implemented in Chicago, utilizing advanced technology to maximize control and minimize out of stock situations.

Purchasing

Markets for the key commodities and ingredients we use remained stable or declined slightly in 1998 as adverse economic conditions in many markets continued to dampen world-wide demand. Further, our ongoing hedging program and fixed price contracts helped to insulate us from those price fluctuations that did occur in spot markets.

The cost of the various packaging materials we use remained stable during the year. Also, leveraging the high volume of annual purchases we make of these items, competitive bidding was again successfully utilized to further control cost.

Information Technology

During 1998 we completed an extensive review of the information systems we utilize throughout the company and determined that the vast majority of these systems—indeed those most critical to our operations—are "Y2K" compliant by design. Our initial testing has confirmed this, and final testing is scheduled for completion by the middle of 1999.

Y2K issues were identified in our systems in Mexico and the necessary corrective programming changes have been written and implemented. Final testing of these changes is scheduled to be completed by mid year, as are the other minor program corrections that were identified in several secondary domestic systems.

We view information technology as an indispensable tool with which we can streamline an ever-expanding variety of functions and tasks. In this regard, during 1998 we completed the initial phases of automating a number of operations that had previously been handled manually. Completion of the final phases of these projects is scheduled for 1999, and we expect that these and other information technology applications will yield ongoing efficiencies.

International

Our Canadian subsidiary reported increased sales and profits in 1998, both due to growth in seasonal sales at Halloween and to distribution gains throughout the year. Also, the Super Blow Pop was introduced in that market during the year with promising results.

Our Mexican operations had a difficult year due to currency devaluations and increased competitive pressures on top of generally soft local market conditions for confectionery. On the positive side, the latest phase of our plant modernization program was completed there, which will increase productivity and enhance our competitive position in Mexico. These improvements will enable us to respond more quickly to local competition with efficiently produced, high quality products. Our Tutsi Pop still remains the local favorite.

Sales trends in other international markets were positive as we continue to export our well known items to many markets throughout the world.

"Oh-oh, another chocolate attack! Better reach for a Tootsie Roll or chocolatey center Tootsie Pop! Delicious and always low in fat."

MANAGEMENT DISCUSSION AND ANALYSIS

The management discussion and analysis (MD&A) section covers three financial aspects of a company: its results of operations, its ability to pay near-term obligations, and its ability to fund operations and expansion. Management must highlight favorable or unfavorable trends and identify significant events and uncertainties that affect these three factors. This discussion obviously involves a number of subjective estimates and opinions. The MD&A section of Tootsie Roll's annual report is presented below.

Management's Discussion and Analysis of Financial Condition and Results of Operations

(in thousands except per share, percentage and ratio figures)

NET SALES
Millions of dollars

$389
$376
$341
$313
$297

94 95 96 97 98

NET EARNINGS
Millions of dollars

$67.5
$60.7
$47.2
$40.4
$37.9

94 95 96 97 98

FINANCIAL REVIEW

This financial review discusses the company's financial condition, results of operations, liquidity and capital resources. It should be read in conjunction with the Consolidated Financial Statements and related footnotes that follow this discussion.

FINANCIAL CONDITION

The sound financial condition in which we entered 1998 was further strengthened by our record operating results for the year. Net earnings for the year increased by 11.3% to a record $67,526. Shareholders' equity increased by 12.9% to $396,457 and cash and investments increased by $41,154 to $223,172, the result of continued strong cash flow from operating activities.

Cash flow from operating activities was also used to fund capital expenditures of $14,878, share repurchases of $13,445 and cash dividends of $9,150. The cash dividend rate was increased by 31% during 1998, the fifty-sixth consecutive year in which cash dividends have been paid.

A 3% stock dividend was also distributed to shareholders during the year. This was the thirty-fourth consecutive year that a stock dividend has been distributed.

As a consequence of the successful operations of this past year, our financial position remains such that we can respond to future growth opportunities

that may arise with internally generated funds. In this regard, we continue to reinvest in our own operations as well as to pursue acquisitions that would complement those operations.

Our financial position in 1998, versus 1997, measured by commonly used financial ratios, is as follows: the current ratio rose from 3.9:1 to 4.3:1 due to increased cash and equivalents at the end of 1998. Current liabilities to net worth declined from 15.3% to 13.5% and debt to equity fell from 2.1% to 1.9%, both due to the increase in the company's net worth during the year.

These statistics reflect both the company's history of successful operations and its conservative financial posture.

RESULTS OF OPERATIONS

1998 vs. 1997

1998 represented the company's twenty-second consecutive year of record sales. Sales reached $388,659, an increase of 3.5% over 1997 sales of $375,594. Increases were seen in each quarter, and the third quarter, which was driven by another successful Halloween season, continued to be our largest selling period.

Sales throughout the year were favorably impacted by successful promotional programs. Increases were seen in all major trade classes and in all major domestic brands. Line extensions, new products and seasonal packs that have been introduced in recent years also contributed to sales gains.

Domestic sales growth was partially offset by declines in the sales of our Mexican subsidiary due to currency devaluations and difficult local market conditions. Sales in our Canadian operation increased due to distribution gains, seasonal sales growth at Halloween and a new product introduction. These increases were also partially offset by the effects of adverse currency translation.

Cost of goods sold, as a percentage of sales, decreased from 50.1% to 48.3%. This reflected favorable ingredient costs and increased operating efficiencies associated with higher production volumes, coupled with stable packaging and labor costs. Consequently, gross margin, which was $201,042 or 7.3% higher than in 1997, improved as a percentage of sales from 49.9% to 51.7%.

Gross margin as a percent of sales has historically been lower in the third and fourth quarters of the year due to the seasonal nature of our business and the product mix sold at that time of year. This occurred again in 1998.

Selling, marketing and administrative expenses, as a percent of sales were 25.0% in 1998, a decrease of .2% versus 1997. This improvement is due to effective expense control programs aimed at keeping costs in check. Earnings from operations were $101,265 or 26.1% of sales versus 24.0% in 1997, reflecting the combined effects of an increased gross margin percentage and lower operating costs as a percent of sales.

Other income decreased to $4,798, due to exchange losses from Mexico, partially offset by higher investment income. Inasmuch as most of this investment income is not subject to federal income taxes, the effective tax rate declined from 36.4% in 1997 to 36.3% in 1998.

Consolidated net earnings rose 11.9% to a new company record of $1.41 per share, or $67,526, from the previous record of $1.26, or $60,682, in 1997. This represents an improvement in earnings as a percent of sales to 17.4% and the seventeenth consecutive year of record earnings for the company.

"Comprehensive earnings" is a newly required disclosure whereby traditionally reported net earnings must be adjusted by items that are normally recorded directly to the equity accounts. By this measure, our 1998 earnings were $68,472 or 13.7% higher than in 1997.

1997 vs. 1996

1997 was our twenty-first consecutive year of record sales achievement. Sales of $375,594 were up 10.2% over 1996 sales of $340,909 and increases were seen in each quarter. The third quarter, driven by Halloween sales, continued to be our largest selling period. Halloween sales also carried over and drove a double digit sales increase in the fourth quarter.

Throughout the year, sales were favorably impacted by successful promotional programs as we continued to broaden distribution in mass merchandisers and other select trade classes with our core product offerings. Line extensions, new products and seasonal packs all contributed to added sales.

Sales growth occurred in our two most significant foreign operations as well. In Mexico, the introduction of a new assortment complemented the already strong business we have developed for the Christmas holiday season in that market.

Sales growth in our Canadian operation was attributable to further distribution gains in the mass merchandiser and grocery trade classes and to a successful new product introduction.

Cost of goods sold, as a percentage of sales, decreased from 52.4% to 50.1%. This improvement reflected lower costs for certain packaging and ingredients as well as higher production efficiencies associated with increased volumes in relation to fixed costs.

Gross margin dollars grew by 15.3% to $187,281, and increased as a percent of sales from 47.6% to 49.9%, due to the factors cited above. Gross margins in the third and fourth quarters continued to be somewhat lower due to the seasonal nature of our business and to the product mix sold in those quarters.

Selling, marketing and administrative

GROSS MARGIN
Millions of dollars

$141 $146 $162 $187 $201
94   95   96   97   98

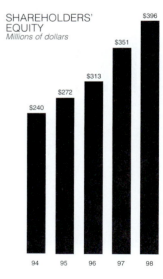

SHAREHOLDERS' EQUITY
Millions of dollars

$240 $272 $313 $351 $396
94   95   96   97   98

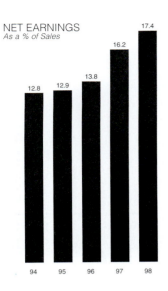

NET EARNINGS
As a % of Sales

12.8 12.9 13.8 16.2 17.4

94   95   96   97   98

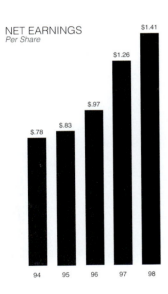

NET EARNINGS
Per Share

$.78 $.83 $.97 $1.26 $1.41

94   95   96   97   98

expenses, as a percent of sales, declined from 25.9% to 25.2%. This improvement was due to distribution and warehousing efficiencies and to effective expense control programs aimed at holding down costs. Earnings from operations increased by 25.9% to $90,087, or 24.0% of sales, as a result of favorable gross margins and operating expenses.

Other income increased by $1,708 to $5,274, primarily reflecting lower interest expense and higher interest income due to lower average borrowings and increased investments in marketable securities, respectively. As a majority of our interest income is not subject to federal income tax, the effective tax rate declined from 37.1% to 36.4%.

Consolidated net earnings rose to a new company record of $60,682. Earnings per share increased 30% to $1.26 from the previous record of $.97 reached in 1996. Our net earnings as a percent of sales increased to 16.2% from 13.8%. 1997 was the sixteenth consecutive year of record earnings achievement for the company.

Liquidity and Capital Resources

Cash flows from operating activities increased to $77,735 in 1998 from $68,176 in 1997 and $76,710 in 1996. The increase in 1998 is attributable to higher net earnings augmented by other receivables, inventory, deferred compensation and other liabilities and income taxes payable and deferred, partially offset by accounts receivable and accounts payable and accrued liabilities.

Cash flows from investing activities reflect net increases in marketable securities of $19,951, $23,087 and $42,573, as well as capital expenditures of $14,878, $8,611 and $9,791 in 1998, 1997 and 1996, respectively.

Cash flows from financing activities in 1998 reflect a short-term borrowing and the subsequent repayment thereof during the year as well as share repurchases of $13,445 and $14,401 in 1998 and 1997, respectively. Cash dividends of $9,150 were paid in 1998, the fifty-sixth in which we have paid cash dividends.

Year 2000 Conversion

The company recognizes the need to ensure that its operations will not be adversely impacted by software failures arising from calculations using the year 2000 date. Accordingly, we have established a process for evaluating and managing the risks and costs associated with this problem.

We have completed an internal review of our financial and operational systems and have begun final testing of these systems to ensure that they are Year 2000 compliant. Likewise, we have surveyed significant vendors and customers to determine the status of their systems with respect to this issue. We believe that the risks and costs of year 2000 compliance will be minimal for the systems we use, and do not expect this issue to have a material impact on the company or its operations.

The results of these operations and our financial condition are expressed in the following financial statements.

*F*INANCIAL STATEMENTS AND ACCOMPANYING NOTES

The standard set of financial statements consists of: (1) a comparative income statement for three years, (2) a comparative balance sheet for two years, (3) a comparative statement of cash flows for three years, (4) a statement of retained earnings (or stockholders' equity) for three years, and (5) a set of accompanying notes that are considered an integral part of the financial statements. The auditor's report, unless stated otherwise, covers the financial statements and the accompanying notes. The financial statements and accompanying notes plus some supplementary data and analyses for Tootsie Roll Industries follow.

CONSOLIDATED STATEMENT OF

Earnings, Comprehensive Earnings and Retained Earnings

TOOTSIE ROLL INDUSTRIES, INC. AND SUBSIDIARIES (in thousands except per share data)

	For the year ended December 31,		
	1998	1997	1996
Net sales	$388,659	$375,594	$340,909
Cost of goods sold	187,617	188,313	178,489
Gross margin	201,042	187,281	162,420
Selling, marketing and administrative expenses	97,071	94,488	88,182
Amortization of intangible assets	2,706	2,706	2,706
Earnings from operations	101,265	90,087	71,532
Other income, net	4,798	5,274	3,566
Earnings before income taxes	106,063	95,361	75,098
Provision for income taxes	38,537	34,679	27,891
Net earnings	$ 67,526	$ 60,682	$ 47,207
Net earnings	$ 67,526	$ 60,682	$ 47,207
Other comprehensive earnings, net of tax			
Unrealized gains (losses) on securities	976	(417)	
Foreign currency translation adjustments	(30)	(17)	(57)
Other comprehensive earnings	946	(434)	(57)
Comprehensive earnings	$ 68,472	$ 60,248	$ 47,150
Retained earnings at beginning of year	$159,124	$136,352	$121,477
Net earnings	67,526	60,682	47,207
Cash dividends ($.20, $.16 and $.13 per share)	(9,484)	(7,472)	(6,372)
Stock dividends	(52,514)	(30,438)	(25,960)
Retained earnings at end of year	$164,652	$159,124	$136,352
Earnings per share	$1.41	$1.26	$.97
Average common and class B common shares outstanding	48,051	48,294	48,442

(The accompanying notes are an integral part of these statements.)

CONSOLIDATED STATEMENT OF

Financial Position

TOOTSIE ROLL INDUSTRIES, INC. AND SUBSIDIARIES   (in thousands)

Assets   December 31,

	1998	1997
CURRENT ASSETS:		
Cash and cash equivalents	$ 80,744	$ 60,433
Investments	83,176	81,847
Accounts receivable trade, less allowances of $2,184 and $2,085	19,110	18,636
Other receivables	3,324	4,683
Inventories:		
Finished goods and work-in-process	21,395	22,938
Raw materials and supplies	15,125	13,721
Prepaid expenses	3,081	2,910
Deferred income taxes	2,584	1,793
Total current assets	228,539	206,961
PROPERTY, PLANT AND EQUIPMENT, at cost:		
Land	7,774	6,895
Buildings	22,226	22,100
Machinery and equipment	133,601	122,430
	163,601	151,425
Less—Accumulated depreciation	80,577	73,061
	83,024	78,364
OTHER ASSETS:		
Intangible assets, net of accumulated amortization of $20,791 and $18,085	87,843	90,549
Investments	59,252	39,738
Cash surrender value of life insurance and other assets	28,765	21,130
	175,860	151,417
	$487,423	$436,742

(The accompanying notes are an integral part of these statements.)

(in thousands except per share data)

Liabilities and Shareholders' Equity   December 31,

	1998	1997
CURRENT LIABILITIES:		
Accounts payable	$12,450	$ 11,624
Dividends payable	2,514	1,930
Accrued liabilities	31,297	32,793
Income taxes payable	7,123	7,259
Total current liabilities	53,384	53,606
NONCURRENT LIABILITIES:		
Deferred income taxes	9,014	8,650
Postretirement health care and life insurance benefits	6,145	5,904
Industrial development bonds	7,500	7,500
Deferred compensation and other liabilities	14,923	9,919
Total noncurrent liabilities	37,582	31,973
SHAREHOLDERS' EQUITY:		
Common stock, $.69-4/9 par value—		
50,000 shares authorized—		
32,439 and 15,851, respectively, issued	22,527	11,008
Class B common stock, $.69-4/9 par value—		
20,000 shares authorized—		
15,422 and 7,547, respectively, issued	10,710	5,241
Capital in excess of par value	210,064	187,259
Retained earnings, per accompanying statement	164,652	159,124
Accumulated other comprehensive earnings	(10,523)	(11,469)
Treasury stock (at cost)—		
25 shares and 0 shares, respectively	(973)	—
	396,457	351,163
	$487,423	$436,742

CONSOLIDATED STATEMENT OF
Cash Flows
TOOTSIE ROLL INDUSTRIES, INC. AND SUBSIDIARIES   (in thousands)

	For the year ended December 31,		
	1998	1997	1996
CASH FLOWS FROM OPERATING ACTIVITIES:			
Net earnings	$67,526	$60,682	$47,207
Adjustments to reconcile net earnings to net cash provided by operating activities:			
Depreciation and amortization	12,807	12,819	12,068
Loss on retirement of fixed assets	118	26	714
Changes in operating assets and liabilities:			
Accounts receivable	(915)	199	2,355
Other receivables	1,358	(2,526)	(41)
Inventories	(106)	(6,463)	1,879
Prepaid expenses and other assets	(7,723)	(6,622)	(4,253)
Accounts payable and accrued liabilities	(596)	9,624	9,362
Income taxes payable and deferred	(625)	(2,049)	3,718
Postretirement health care and life insurance benefits	241	269	250
Deferred compensation and other liabilities	5,004	1,932	3,460
Other	646	285	(9)
Net cash provided by operating activities	77,735	68,176	76,710
CASH FLOWS FROM INVESTING ACTIVITIES:			
Capital expenditures	(14,878)	(8,611)	(9,791)
Purchase of held to maturity securities	(259,112)	(68,982)	(47,221)
Maturity of held to maturity securities	240,195	27,473	16,523
Purchase of available for sale and trading securities	(217,799)	(304,910)	(35,883)
Sale and maturity of available for sale and trading securities	216,765	323,332	24,008
Net cash used in investing activities	(34,829)	(31,698)	(52,364)
CASH FLOWS FROM FINANCING ACTIVITIES:			
Issuance of notes payable	7,000	—	—
Repayments of notes payable	(7,000)	—	(20,000)
Treasury stock purchases	(973)	—	—
Shares repurchased and retired	(12,472)	(14,401)	—
Dividends paid in cash	(9,150)	(7,303)	(6,211)
Net cash used in financing activities	(22,595)	(21,704)	(26,211)
Increase (decrease) in cash and cash equivalents	20,311	14,774	(1,865)
Cash and cash equivalents at beginning of year	60,433	45,659	47,524
Cash and cash equivalents at end of year	$80,744	$60,433	$45,659
Supplemental cash flow information:			
Income taxes paid	$40,000	$36,716	$23,969
Interest paid	$ 803	$ 389	$ 1,015

(The accompanying notes are an integral part of these statements.)

Notes to Consolidated Financial Statements

TOOTSIE ROLL INDUSTRIES, INC. AND SUBSIDIARIES   *($ in thousands except per share data)*

NOTE 1—SIGNIFICANT ACCOUNTING POLICIES:

Basis of consolidation:

The consolidated financial statements include the accounts of Tootsie Roll Industries, Inc. and its wholly-owned subsidiaries (the company), which are primarily engaged in the manufacture and sale of candy products. All significant intercompany transactions have been eliminated.

The preparation of financial statements in conformity with generally accepted accounting principles requires management to make estimates and assumptions that affect the reported amounts of assets and liabilities and disclosure of contingent assets and liabilities at the date of the financial statements and the reported amounts of revenues and expenses during the reporting period. Actual results could differ from those estimates.

Revenue recognition:

Revenues are recognized when products are shipped. Accounts receivable are unsecured.

Cash and cash equivalents:

The company considers temporary cash investments with an original maturity of three months or less to be cash equivalents.

Investments:

Investments consist of various marketable securities with maturities of generally less than one year. In accordance with Statement of Financial Accounting Standards (SFAS) No. 115, "Accounting For Certain Investments in Debt and Equity Securities," the company's debt and equity securities are considered as either held to maturity, available for sale or trading. Held to maturity securities represent those securities that the company has both the positive intent and ability to hold to maturity and are carried at amortized cost. Available for sale securities represent those securities that do not meet the classification of held to maturity, are not actively traded and are carried at fair value. Unrealized gains and losses on these securities, where material, are excluded from earnings and are reported as a separate component of shareholders' equity, net of applicable taxes, until realized. Trading securities relate to deferred compensation arrangements and are carried at fair value.

Inventories:

Inventories are stated at cost, not in excess of market. The cost of domestic inventories ($31,307 and $30,530 at December 31, 1998 and 1997, respectively) has been determined by the last-in, first-out (LIFO) method. The excess of current cost over LIFO cost of inventories approximates $5,016 and $4,918 at December 31, 1998 and 1997, respectively. The cost of foreign inventories ($5,213 and $6,129 at December 31, 1998 and 1997, respectively) has been determined by the first-in, first-out (FIFO) method.

From time to time, the company enters into commodity futures and option contracts in order to fix the future price of certain key ingredients which may be subject to price volatility (primarily sugar and corn syrup). Gains or losses, if any, resulting from these contracts are considered as a component of the cost of the ingredients being hedged. At December 31, 1998 the company had open contracts to purchase approximately eighteen months of its expected sugar usage.

Property, plant and equipment:

Depreciation is computed for financial reporting purposes by use of both the straight-line and accelerated methods based on useful lives of 20 to 35 years for buildings and 12 to 20 years for machinery and equipment. For income tax purposes the company uses accelerated methods on all properties. Depreciation expense was $10,101, $9,947 and $9,839 in 1998, 1997 and 1996, respectively.

Carrying value of long-lived assets:

In the event that facts and circumstances indicate that the company's long-lived assets may be impaired, an evaluation of recoverability would be performed. Such an evaluation entails comparing the estimated future undiscounted cash flows associated with the asset to the asset's carrying amount to determine if a write down to market value or discounted cash flow value is required. The company considers that no circumstances exist that would require such an evaluation.

Postretirement health care and life insurance benefits:

The company provides certain postretirement health care and life insurance benefits. The cost of these postretirement benefits is accrued during employees' working careers.

Income taxes:

The company uses the liability method of computing deferred income taxes.

Intangible assets:

Intangible assets represent the excess of cost over the acquired net tangible assets of operating companies and is amortized on a straight-line basis over a 40 year period. The company assesses the recoverability of its intangible assets using undiscounted future cash flows.

Foreign currency translation:

Prior to January 1, 1997, management designated the local currency as the functional currency for the company's Mexican operations. Accordingly, the net effect of translating the Mexican operations' financial statements was reported in a separate component of shareholders' equity. During 1997, management determined that the Mexican economy was hyper-inflationary. Accordingly, the US dollar is now used as the functional currency, and translation gains and losses are included in the determination of 1997 and 1998 earnings.

Comprehensive earnings

Effective January 1, 1998, the company adopted SFAS No. 130, "Reporting Comprehensive Income." Accordingly, net income, foreign currency translation adjustments and unrealized gains/losses on marketable securities are presented in the accompanying Statement of Earnings, Comprehensive Earnings and Retained Earnings. The adoption of SFAS No. 130 had no impact on shareholders' equity and prior year financial statements have been reclassified to conform to its requirements.

Earnings per share:

On December 31, 1997, the company adopted SFAS No. 128, "Earnings per Share." A dual presentation of basic and diluted earnings per share is not required due to the lack of potentially dilutive securities under the company's simple capital structure. Therefore, all earnings per share amounts represent basic earnings per share.

NOTE 2—ACCRUED LIABILITIES:

Accrued liabilities are comprised of the following:

	December 31,	
	1998	1997
Compensation	**$ 8,433**	$ 6,114
Other employee benefits	**4,143**	5,490
Taxes, other than income	**2,460**	2,494
Advertising and promotions	**8,451**	6,939
Other	**7,810**	11,756
	$31,297	$32,793

NOTE 3—INCOME TAXES:

The domestic and foreign components of pretax income are as follows:

	1998	1997	1996
Domestic	$106,667	$93,318	$71,660
Foreign	(604)	2,043	3,438
	$106,063	$95,361	$75,098

The provision for income taxes is comprised of the following:

	1998	1997	1996
Current:			
Federal	$34,373	$29,764	$23,907
Foreign	618	626	375
State	4,286	3,836	3,167
	39,277	34,226	27,449
Deferred:			
Federal	(250)	738	(322)
Foreign	(479)	(368)	802
State	(11)	83	(38)
	(740)	453	442
	$38,537	$34,679	$27,891

Deferred income taxes are comprised of the following:

	December 31,	
	1998	1997
Workers' compensation	$ 413	$ 428
Reserve for uncollectible accounts	547	537
Other accrued expenses	1,137	1,107
VEBA funding	(478)	(387)
Other, net	965	108
Net current deferred income tax asset	$2,584	$1,793

	December 31,	
	1998	1997
Depreciation	$9,371	$8,930
Post retirement benefits	(2,132)	(2,045)
Deductible goodwill	5,176	4,390
Deferred compensation	(4,244)	(3,441)
DISC commissions	1,729	1,553
Foreign subsidiary tax loss carryforward	(1,428)	(1,470)
Other, net	542	733
Net long-term deferred income tax liability	$9,014	$8,650

At December 31, 1998, gross deferred tax assets and gross deferred tax liabilities are $13,465 and $19,895, respectively.

The effective income tax rate differs from the statutory rate as follows:

	1998	1997	1996
U.S. statutory rate	35.0%	35.0%	35.0%
State income taxes, net	2.6	2.7	2.8
Amortization of intangible assets	0.4	0.5	0.6
Other, net	(1.7)	(1.8)	(1.3)
Effective income tax rate	36.3%	36.4%	37.1%

The company has not provided for U.S. federal or foreign withholding taxes on $3,034 of foreign subsidiaries' undistributed earnings as of December 31, 1998 because such earnings are considered to be permanently reinvested. When excess cash has accumulated in the company's foreign subsidiaries and it is advantageous for tax or foreign exchange reasons, subsidiary earnings may be remitted, and income taxes will be provided on such amounts. It is not practicable to determine the amount of income taxes that would be payable upon remittance of the undistributed earnings.

NOTE 4—SHARE CAPITAL AND CAPITAL IN EXCESS OF PAR VALUE:

	Common Stock Shares (000's)	Amount	Class B Common Stock Shares (000's)	Amount	Treasury Stock Shares (000's)	Amount	Capital in excess of par value
Balance at January 1, 1996	15,109	$10,492	7,234	$ 5,024	—	$ —	$146,171
Issuance of 3% stock dividend	449	312	212	147	—	—	25,418
Conversion of Class B common shares to common shares	59	41	(59)	(41)	—	—	—
Balance at December 31, 1996	15,617	10,845	7,387	5,130	—	—	171,589
Issuance of 3% stock dividend	465	323	221	153	—	—	29,868
Conversion of Class B common shares to common shares	61	42	(61)	(42)	—	—	—
Purchase and retirement of common shares	(292)	(202)	—	—	—	—	(14,198)
Balance at December 31, 1997	15,851	11,008	7,547	5,241	—	—	187,259
Issuance of 3% stock dividend	473	329	225	156	—	—	51,780
Purchase of shares for the treasury	—	—	—	—	(20)	(973)	—
Issuance of 2-for-1 stock split	16,305	11,323	7,748	5,381	(5)	—	(16,704)
Conversion of Class B common shares to common shares	98	68	(98)	(68)	—	—	—
Purchase and retirement of common shares	(288)	(201)	—	—	—	—	(12,271)
Balance at December 31, 1998	32,439	$22,527	15,422	$10,710	(25)	$(973)	$210,064

The Class B Common Stock has essentially the same rights as Common Stock, except that each share of Class B Common Stock has ten votes per share (compared to one vote per share of Common Stock), is not traded on any exchange, is restricted as to transfer and is convertible on a share-for-share basis, at any time and at no cost to the holders, into shares of Common Stock which are traded on the New York Stock Exchange.

Average shares outstanding and all per share amounts included in the financial statements and notes thereto have been adjusted retroactively to reflect annual three percent stock dividends and the two-for-one stock split distributed in 1998.

NOTE 5—NOTES PAYABLE AND INDUSTRIAL DEVELOPMENT BONDS:

In 1993, the company entered into two 3-year term notes aggregating $20,000 the proceeds of which were used to purchase the company's Chicago manufacturing facility and headquarters. These term notes bore interest payable monthly at 3.55% and matured in September, 1996.

During 1992, the company entered into an industrial development bond agreement with the City of Covington, Tennessee. The bond proceeds of $7.5 million were used to finance the expansion of the company's existing facilities. Interest is payable at various times during the year based upon the interest calculation option (fixed, variable or floating) selected by the company. As of December 31, 1998 and 1997, interest was calculated under the floating option (3.7% and 3.8%, respectively) which requires monthly payments of interest. Principal on the bonds is due in its entirety in the year 2027.

In connection with the issuance of the bonds, the company entered into a letter of credit agreement with a bank for the amount of principal outstanding plus 48 days' accrued interest. The letter of credit, which expires in January 2000, carries an annual fee of 32½ basis points on the outstanding principal amount of the bonds.

NOTE 6—EMPLOYEE BENEFIT PLANS:

Pension plans:

The company sponsors defined contribution pension plans covering certain nonunion employees with over one year of credited service. The company's policy is to fund pension costs accrued based on compensation levels. Total pension expense for 1998, 1997 and 1996 approximated $1,951, $2,153 and $1,814, respectively. The company also maintains certain profit sharing and savings-investment plans. Company contributions in 1998, 1997 and 1996 to these plans were $582, $540 and $485, respectively.

The company also contributes to multi-employer defined benefit pension plans for its union employees. Such contributions aggregated $680, $609 and $436 in 1998, 1997 and 1996, respectively. The relative position of each employer associated with the multi-employer plans with respect to the actuarial present value of benefits and net plan assets is not determinable by the company.

Postretirement health care and life insurance benefit plans:

The company provides certain postretirement health care and life insurance benefits for corporate office and management employees. Employees become eligible for these benefits if they meet minimum age and service requirements and if they agree to contribute a portion of the cost. The company has the right to modify or terminate these benefits. The company does not fund postretirement health care and life insurance benefits in advance of payments for benefit claims.

The changes in the accumulated postretirement benefit obligation at December 31, 1998 and 1997 consist of the following:

	December 31,	
	1998	1997
Benefit obligation, beginning of year	$5,904	$5,636
Net periodic postretirement benefit cost	438	435
Benefits paid	(197)	(167)
Benefit obligation, end of year	$6,145	$5,904

Net periodic postretirement benefit cost included the following components:

	1998	1997	1996
Service cost—benefits attributed to service during the period	$258	$251	$263
Interest cost on the accumulated postretirement benefit obligation	279	285	277
Amortization of unrecognized net gain	(99)	(101)	(87)
Net periodic postretirement benefit cost	$438	$435	$453

For measurement purposes, an 8.5% annual rate of increase in the per capita cost of covered health care benefits was assumed for 1998; the rate was assumed to decrease gradually to 5.5% for 2004 and remain at that level thereafter. The health care cost trend rate assumption has a significant effect on the amounts reported. The weighted-average discount rate used in determining the accumulated postretirement benefit obligation was 6.25% and 6.75% at December 31, 1998 and 1997, respectively.

Increasing or decreasing the health care trend rates by one percentage point in each year would have the following effect:

	1% Increase	1% Decrease
Effect on postretirement benefit obligation	$716	$(580)
Effect on total of service and interest cost components	$98	$(77)

NOTE 7—OTHER INCOME, NET:

Other income (expense) is comprised of the following:

	1998	1997	1996
Interest income	$6,934	$5,764	$3,887
Interest expense	(756)	(483)	(1,498)
Dividend income	822	999	1,386
Foreign exchange losses	(2,140)	(447)	(50)
Royalty income	155	312	92
Miscellaneous, net	(217)	(871)	(251)
	$4,798	$5,274	$3,566

NOTE 8—COMMITMENTS:

During 1993 and 1994, the company entered into operating leases for certain manufacturing equipment which provided the company with the option to terminate the lease in 1996 and to purchase the equipment at its fair market value. The company exercised this option and purchased the equipment for $5,401 on January 2, 1996.

Rental expense aggregated $432, $477 and $439 in 1998, 1997 and 1996, respectively.

Future operating lease commitments are not significant.

NOTE 9—COMPREHENSIVE INCOME:

Components of accumulated other comprehensive earnings are shown as follows:

	Foreign Currency Items	Unrealized Gains (Losses) on Securities	Accumulated Other Comprehensive Earnings
Balance at December 31, 1995	$(10,978)	$ —	$(10,978)
Change during period	(57)	—	(57)
Balance at December 31, 1996	(11,035)	—	(11,035)
Change during period	(17)	(417)	(434)
Balance at December 31, 1997	(11,052)	(417)	(11,469)
Change during period	(30)	976	946
Balance at December 31, 1998	$(11,082)	$559	$(10,523)

The individual tax effects of each component of other comprehensive earnings for the year ended December 31, 1998 are shown as follows:

	Before Tax Amount	Tax (Expense) Benefit	Net-of-Tax Tax Amount
Foreign currency translation adjustment	$ (30)	$ —	$ (30)
Unrealized gains (losses) on securities:			
Unrealized holding gains (losses) arising during 1998	1,123	(262)	861
Less: reclassification adjustment for gains (losses) realized in earnings	182	(67)	115
Net unrealized gains	1,305	(329)	976
Other comprehensive earnings	$1,275	$(329)	$946

NOTE 10—DISCLOSURES ABOUT THE FAIR VALUE OF FINANCIAL INSTRUMENTS:

Carrying amount and fair value:

The carrying amount approximates fair value of cash and cash equivalents because of the short maturity of those instruments. The fair values of investments are estimated based on quoted market prices. The fair value of the company's industrial development bonds approximates their carrying value because they have a floating interest rate. The carrying amount and estimated fair values of the company's financial instruments are as follows:

	1998		1997	
	Carrying Amount	Fair Value	Carrying Amount	Fair Value
Cash and cash equivalents	$ 80,744	$ 80,744	$60,433	$60,433
Investments held to maturity	106,415	109,182	95,086	97,000
Investments available for sale	28,214	28,214	22,010	22,010
Investments in trading securities	7,799	7,799	4,489	4,489
Industrial development bonds	7,500	7,500	7,500	7,500

A summary of the aggregate fair value, gross unrealized gains, gross unrealized losses and amortized cost basis of the company's investment portfolio by major security type is as follows:

December 31, 1998

	Amortized Cost	Fair Value	Unrealized Gains	Unrealized Losses
Held to Maturity:				
Unit investment trusts of preferred stocks	$ 3,626	$ 5,978	$2,352	$ —
Tax-free commercial paper	8,250	8,250	—	—
Municipal bonds	96,828	97,266	438	—
Unit investment trusts of municipal bonds	979	956	—	(23)
US gov't/gov't agency obligations	—	—	—	—
Private export funding securities	4,982	4,982	—	—
	$114,665	$117,432	$2,790	$ (23)
Available for Sale:				
Municipal bonds	$ 39,397	$ 39,264	$ —	$ (133)
Mutual funds	3,007	4,028	1,021	—
	$ 42,404	$ 43,292	$1,021	$ (133)

December 31, 1997

	Amortized Cost	Fair Value	Unrealized Gains	Unrealized Losses
Held to Maturity:				
Unit investment trusts of preferred stocks	$ 4,724	$ 6,794	$2,070	$ —
Tax-free commercial paper	15,300	15,300	—	—
Municipal bonds	87,456	87,218	—	(238)
Unit investment trusts of municipal bonds	1,103	1,484	381	—
US gov't/gov't agency obligations	1,803	1,803	—	—
	$110,386	$112,599	$2,451	$ (238)
Available for Sale:				
Municipal bonds	$ 37,587	$ 37,484	$ —	$ (103)
Mutual funds	3,307	2,993	—	(314)
	$ 40,894	$ 40,477	$ —	$ (417)

Held to maturity securities of $8,250 and $15,300 and available for sale securities of $15,078 and $18,467 were included in cash and cash equivalents, and held to maturity securities greater than one year were $51,453 and $35,249 at December 31, 1998 and 1997, respectively. There were no securities with maturities greater than three years and gross realized gains and losses on the sale of available for sale securities in 1998 and 1997 were not significant.

NOTE 11—GEOGRAPHIC AREA AND SALES INFORMATION:

Summary of sales, net earnings and assets by geographic area

	1998			1997			1996		
	United States	Mexico and Canada	Consoli-dated	United States	Mexico and Canada	Consoli-dated	United States	Mexico and Canada	Consoli-dated
Sales to unaffiliated customers	$363,569	$25,090	$388,659	$346,487	$29,107	$375,594	$315,131	$25,778	$340,909
Sales between geographic areas ...	2,339	4,374		1,694	3,314		1,888	3,152	
	$365,908	$29,464		$348,181	$32,421		$317,019	$28,930	
Net earnings	$ 68,270	$ (744)	$ 67,526	$ 58,898	$ 1,784	$ 60,682	$ 44,946	$ 2,261	$ 47,207
Total assets	$467,265	$20,158	$487,423	$414,629	$22,113	$436,742	$373,925	$17,531	$391,456
Net assets	$379,106	$17,351	$396,457	$332,410	$18,753	$351,163	$298,565	$14,316	$312,881

Total assets are those assets associated with or used directly in the respective geographic area, excluding intercompany advances and investments.

Major customer

Revenues from a major customer aggregated approximately 17.2%, 15.9% and 16.2% of total net sales during the years ended December 31, 1998, 1997 and 1996, respectively.

AUDITOR'S REPORT

All publicly held corporations, as well as many other enterprises and organizations (both profit and not-for-profit, large and small), engage the services of independent certified public accountants for the purpose of obtaining an objective, expert report on their financial statements. Based on a comprehensive examination of the company's accounting system and records, and the financial statements, the outside CPA issues the auditor's report.

The standard auditor's report consists of three paragraphs: (1) an introductory paragraph, (2) a scope paragraph, and (3) the opinion paragraph. In the introductory paragraph, the auditor identifies who and what was audited and indicates the responsibilities of management and the auditor relative to the financial statements. In the scope paragraph the auditor states that the audit was conducted in accordance with generally accepted auditing standards and discusses the nature and limitations of the audit. In the opinion paragraph, the auditor expresses an informed opinion as to (1) the fairness of the financial statements and (2) their conformity with generally accepted accounting principles. The Report of PricewaterhouseCoopers LLP appearing in Tootsie Roll's Annual Report is shown below.

Report of Independent Accountants

To the Board of Directors and Shareholders of Tootsie Roll Industries, Inc.

In our opinion, the accompanying consolidated statement of financial position and the related consolidated statement of earnings, comprehensive earnings and retained earnings and of cash flows present fairly, in all material respects, the financial position of Tootsie Roll Industries, Inc. and its subsidiaries at December 31, 1998 and 1997, and the results of their operations and their cash flows for each of the three years in the period ended December 31, 1998, in conformity with generally accepted accounting principles. These financial statements are the responsibility of the Company's management; our responsibility is to express an opinion on these financial statements based on our audits. We conducted our audits of these statements in accordance with generally accepted auditing standards which require that we plan and perform the audit to obtain reasonable assurance about whether the financial statements are free of material misstatement. An audit includes examining, on a test basis, evidence supporting the amounts and disclosures in the financial statements, assessing the accounting principles used and significant estimates made by management, and evaluating the overall financial statement presentation. We believe that our audits provide a reasonable basis for the opinion expressed above.

PricewaterhouseCoopers LLP

Chicago, Illinois
February 9, 1999

SUPPLEMENTARY FINANCIAL INFORMATION

In addition to the financial statements and the accompanying notes, supplementary financial information is often presented. Tootsie Roll has provided quarterly financial data, stock performance information, and a five-year summary of earnings and financial highlights.

Quarterly Financial Data

TOOTSIE ROLL INDUSTRIES, INC. AND SUBSIDIARIES

(Thousands of dollars except per share data)

1998	First	Second	Third	Fourth	Total
Net sales	$69,701	$85,931	$144,230	$88,797	$388,659
Gross margin	36,966	45,133	73,251	45,692	201,042
Net earnings	11,217	13,910	27,216	15,183	67,526
Net earnings per share	.23	.29	.57	.32	1.41
1997					
Net sales	$66,258	$82,287	$140,645	$86,404	$375,594
Gross margin	33,323	41,382	69,746	42,830	187,281
Net earnings	9,751	12,507	24,695	13,729	60,682
Net earnings per share	.20	.26	.51	.29	1.26
1996					
Net sales	$63,265	$72,511	$128,658	$76,475	$340,909
Gross margin	30,687	35,292	60,415	36,026	162,420
Net earnings	8,118	9,327	19,143	10,619	47,207
Net earnings per share	.17	.19	.39	.22	.97

Net earnings per share is based upon average outstanding shares as adjusted for 3% stock dividends issued during the second quarter of each year and the 2-for-1 stock split effective July 13, 1998.

1998-1997 QUARTERLY SUMMARY OF TOOTSIE ROLL INDUSTRIES, INC. STOCK PRICE AND DIVIDENDS PER SHARE

STOCK PRICES*

	1998		1997	
	High	Low	High	Low
1st Qtr	38-13/32	29-27/32	23-3/8	18-7/8
2nd Qtr	40-3/4	34-31/32	24-15/16	22-1/4
3rd Qtr	47-1/4	33-3/4	25-7/16	22-7/8
4th Qtr	42-7/8	34-1/8	32-7/16	25-1/2

*NYSE—Composite Quotations adjusted for the 2-for-1 stock split effective July 13,1998
Estimated Number of shareholders at 12/31/98 9,500

DIVIDENDS**

	1998	1997
1st Qtr	$.0401	$.0344
2nd Qtr	$.0525	$.0402
3rd Qtr	$.0525	$.0402
4th Qtr	$.0525	$.0401

NOTE: In addition to the above cash dividends, a 3% stock dividend was issued on 4/22/98 and 4/22/97.

**Cash dividends are restated to reflect 3% stock dividends and the 2-for-1 stock split.

Five Year Summary of Earnings and Financial Highlights

TOOTSIE ROLL INDUSTRIES, INC. AND SUBSIDIARIES

(Thousands of dollars except per share, percentage and ratio figures)

(See Management's Comments starting on page A-6)

	1998	1997	1996	1995	1994
Sales and Earnings Data					
Net sales	$388,659	$375,594	$340,909	$312,660	$296,932
Gross margin	201,042	187,281	162,420	145,922	141,367
Interest expense	756	483	1,498	1,515	1,649
Provision for income taxes	38,537	34,679	27,891	23,670	23,236
Net earnings	67,526	60,682	47,207	40,368	37,931
% of sales	17.4%	16.2%	13.8%	12.9%	12.8%
% of shareholders' equity	17.0%	17.3%	15.1%	14.8%	15.8%
Per Common Share Data (1)					
Net sales	$ 8.09	$ 7.78	$ 7.04	$ 6.45	$ 6.13
Net earnings	1.41	1.26	.97	.83	.78
Shareholders' equity	8.29	7.29	6.46	5.62	4.96
Cash dividends declared	.20	.16	.13	.11	.09
Stock dividends	3%	3%	3%	3%	3%
Additional Financial Data					
Working capital	$175,155	$153,355	$153,329	$109,643	$ 92,626
Current ratio	4.3	3.9	4.2	3.0	4.5
Net cash provided by operating activities	77,735	68,176	76,710	50,851	40,495
Net cash used in (provided by) investing activities	34,829	31,698	52,364	14,544	(1,077)
Net cash used in financing activities	22,595	21,704	26,211	5,292	27,049
Property, plant & equipment additions	14,878	8,611	9,791	4,640	8,179
Net property, plant & equipment	83,024	78,364	81,687	81,999	85,648
Total assets	487,423	436,742	391,456	353,816	310,083
Long term debt	7,500	7,500	7,500	7,500	27,500
Shareholders' equity	396,457	351,163	312,881	272,186	240,461
Average shares outstanding (1)	48,051	48,294	48,442	48,442	48,442

(1) Adjusted for annual 3% stock dividends and the 2-for-1 stock splits effective July 13, 1998 and July 11, 1995.

Specimen Financial Statements: Hershey Foods Corporation

HERSHEY FOODS CORPORATION

CONSOLIDATED STATEMENTS OF INCOME

For the years ended December 31,	1998	1997	1996
In thousands of dollars except per share amounts			
Net Sales	**$ 4,435,615**	$ 4,302,236	$ 3,989,308
Costs and Expenses:			
Cost of sales	**2,625,057**	2,488,896	2,302,089
Selling, marketing and administrative	**1,167,895**	1,183,130	1,124,087
Loss on disposal of businesses	**—**	—	35,352
Total costs and expenses	**3,792,952**	3,672,026	3,461,528
Income before Interest and Income Taxes	**642,663**	630,210	527,780
Interest expense, net	**85,657**	76,255	48,043
Income before Income Taxes	**557,006**	553,955	479,737
Provision for income taxes	**216,118**	217,704	206,551
Net Income	**$ 340,888**	$ 336,251	$ 273,186
Net Income Per Share—Basic	**$ 2.38**	$ 2.25	$ 1.77
Net Income Per Share—Diluted	**$ 2.34**	$ 2.23	$ 1.75
Cash Dividends Paid Per Share:			
Common Stock	**$ .920**	$ .840	$ .760
Class B Common Stock	**.835**	.760	.685

The notes to consolidated financial statements are an integral part of these statements.

HERSHEY FOODS CORPORATION

CONSOLIDATED BALANCE SHEETS

December 31,	1998	1997
In thousands of dollars		
ASSETS		
Current Assets:		
Cash and cash equivalents	$ 39,024	$ 54,237
Accounts receivable—trade	451,324	360,831
Inventories	493,249	505,525
Deferred income taxes	58,505	84,024
Prepaid expenses and other	91,864	30,197
Total current assets	1,133,966	1,034,814
Property, Plant and Equipment, Net	1,648,058	1,648,237
Intangibles Resulting from Business Acquisitions	530,464	551,849
Other Assets	91,610	56,336
Total assets	$ 3,404,098	$ 3,291,236
LIABILITIES AND STOCKHOLDERS' EQUITY		
Current Liabilities:		
Accounts payable	$ 156,937	$ 146,932
Accrued liabilities	294,415	371,545
Accrued income taxes	17,475	19,692
Short-term debt	345,908	232,451
Current portion of long-term debt	89	25,095
Total current liabilities	814,824	795,715
Long-term Debt	879,103	1,029,136
Other Long-term Liabilities	346,769	346,500
Deferred Income Taxes	321,101	267,079
Total liabilities	2,361,797	2,438,430
Stockholders' Equity:		
Preferred Stock, shares issued: none in 1998 and 1997	—	—
Common Stock, shares issued: 149,502,964 in 1998 and 149,484,964 in 1997	149,503	149,485
Class B Common Stock, shares issued: 30,447,908 in 1998 and 30,465,908 in 1997	30,447	30,465
Additional paid-in capital	29,995	33,852
Unearned ESOP compensation	(25,548)	(28,741)
Retained earnings	2,189,693	1,977,849
Treasury—Common Stock shares, at cost: 36,804,157 in 1998 and 37,018,566 in 1997	(1,267,422)	(1,267,861)
Accumulated other comprehensive loss	(64,367)	(42,243)
Total stockholders' equity	1,042,301	852,806
Total liabilities and stockholders' equity	$ 3,404,098	$ 3,291,236

The notes to consolidated financial statements are an integral part of these balance sheets.

HERSHEY FOODS CORPORATION

CONSOLIDATED STATEMENTS OF CASH FLOWS

For the years ended December 31,	1998	1997	1996
In thousands of dollars			
Cash Flows Provided from (Used by)			
Operating Activities			
Net income	**$ 340,888**	$ 336,251	$ 273,186
Adjustments to reconcile net income to net cash provided from operations:			
Depreciation and amortization	**158,161**	152,750	133,476
Deferred income taxes	**82,241**	16,915	22,863
Loss on disposal of businesses	**—**	—	35,352
Changes in assets and liabilities, net of effects from business acquisitions and divestitures:			
Accounts receivable—trade	**(90,493)**	(68,479)	5,159
Inventories	**12,276**	(33,538)	(41,038)
Accounts payable	**10,005**	12,967	14,032
Other assets and liabilities	**(124,118)**	85,074	15,120
Other, net	**745**	4,018	5,593
Net Cash Provided from Operating Activities	**389,705**	505,958	463,743
Cash Flows Provided from (Used by)			
Investing Activities			
Capital additions	**(161,328)**	(172,939)	(159,433)
Capitalized software additions	**(42,859)**	(29,100)	—
Business acquisitions	**—**	—	(437,195)
Proceeds from divestitures	**—**	—	149,222
Other, net	**9,284**	21,368	9,333
Net Cash (Used by) Investing Activities	**(194,903)**	(180,671)	(438,073)
Cash Flows Provided from (Used by)			
Financing Activities			
Net change in short-term borrowings partially classified as long-term debt	**(36,543)**	(217,018)	210,929
Long-term borrowings	**—**	550,000	—
Repayment of long-term debt	**(25,187)**	(15,588)	(3,103)
Cash dividends paid	**(129,044)**	(121,546)	(114,763)
Exercise of stock options	**19,368**	14,397	22,049
Incentive plan transactions	**(22,458)**	(35,063)	(45,634)
Repurchase of Common Stock	**(16,151)**	(507,654)	(66,072)
Net Cash (Used by) Provided from Financing Activities	**(210,015)**	(332,472)	3,406
Increase (Decrease) in Cash and Cash Equivalents	**(15,213)**	(7,185)	29,076
Cash and Cash Equivalents as of January 1	**54,237**	61,422	32,346
Cash and Cash Equivalents as of December 31	**$ 39,024**	$ 54,237	$ 61,422
Interest Paid	**$ 89,001**	$ 64,937	$ 52,143
Income Taxes Paid	**123,970**	181,377	180,347

The notes to consolidated financial statements are an integral part of these statements.

HERSHEY FOODS CORPORATION

CONSOLIDATED STATEMENTS OF STOCKHOLDERS' EQUITY

In thousands of dollars

	Preferred Stock	Common Stock	Class B Common Stock	Additional Paid-in Capital	Unearned ESOP Compensation	Retained Earnings	Treasury Common Stock	Accumulated Other Comprehensive Loss	Total Stockholders' Equity
Balance as of January 1, 1996	$—	$ 74,734	$ 15,241	$ 47,732	$ (35,128)	$1,694,696	$ (685,076)	$ (29,240)	$ 1,082,959
Comprehensive income (loss)									
Net income						273,186			273,186
Other comprehensive income (loss):									
Foreign currency translation adjustments								(3,635)	(3,635)
Comprehensive income									269,551
Dividends:									
Common Stock, $.76 per share						(93,884)			(93,884)
Class B Common Stock, $.685 per share						(20,879)			(20,879)
Two-for-one stock split		74,736	15,239			(89,975)			—
Conversion of Class B Common Stock into Common Stock		2	(2)						—
Incentive plan transactions				(426)					(426)
Exercise of stock options				(5,391)			(8,547)		(13,938)
Employee stock ownership trust transactions				517	3,193				3,710
Repurchase of Common Stock							(66,072)		(66,072)
Balance as of December 31, 1996	—	149,472	30,478	42,432	(31,935)	1,763,144	(759,695)	(32,875)	1,161,021
Comprehensive income (loss)									
Net income						336,251			336,251
Other comprehensive income (loss):									
Foreign currency translation adjustments								(9,368)	(9,368)
Comprehensive income									326,883
Dividends:									
Common Stock, $.84 per share						(98,390)			(98,390)
Class B Common Stock, $.76 per share						(23,156)			(23,156)
Conversion of Class B Common Stock into Common Stock		13	(13)						—
Incentive plan transactions				(879)					(879)
Exercise of stock options				(8,200)			(512)		(8,712)
Employee stock ownership trust transactions				499	3,194				3,693
Repurchase of Common Stock							(507,654)		(507,654)
Balance as of December 31, 1997	—	149,485	30,465	33,852	(28,741)	1,977,849	(1,267,861)	(42,243)	852,806
Comprehensive income (loss)									
Net income						340,888			340,888
Other comprehensive income (loss):									
Foreign currency translation adjustments								(18,073)	(18,073)
Minimum pension liability adjustments, net of tax benefit								(4,051)	(4,051)
Comprehensive income									318,764
Dividends:									
Common Stock, $.92 per share						(103,616)			(103,616)
Class B Common Stock, $.835 per share						(25,428)			(25,428)
Conversion of Class B Common Stock into Common Stock		18	(18)						—
Incentive Plan transactions				(985)					(985)
Exercise of stock options				(3,375)			16,590		13,215
Employee stock ownership trust transactions				503	3,193				3,696
Repurchase of Common Stock							(16,151)		(16,151)
Balance as of December 31, 1998	$—	$149,503	$30,447	$29,995	$(25,548)	$2,189,693	$(1,267,422)	$(64,367)	$1,042,301

The notes to consolidated financial statements are an integral part of these statements.

Time Value of Money

After studying this appendix, you should be able to:

1. Distinguish between simple and compound interest.

2. Solve for future value of a single amount.

3. Solve for future value of an annuity.

4. Identify the variables fundamental to solving present value problems.

5. Solve for present value of a single amount.

6. Solve for present value of an annuity.

7. Compute the present values in capital budgeting situations.

Would you rather receive $1,000 today or a year from now? You should prefer to receive the $1,000 today because you can invest the $1,000 and earn interest on it. As a result, you will have more than $1,000 a year from now. What this example illustrates is the concept of the **time value of money**. Everyone prefers to receive money today rather than in the future because of the interest factor.

NATURE OF INTEREST

Interest is payment for the use of another person's money. It is the difference between the amount borrowed or invested (called the **principal**) and the amount repaid or collected. The amount of interest to be paid or collected is usually stated as a rate over a specific period of time. The rate of interest is generally stated as an annual rate.

The amount of interest involved in any financing transaction is based on three elements:

1. **Principal (p):** The original amount borrowed or invested.
2. **Interest Rate (i):** An annual percentage of the principal.
3. **Time (n):** The number of years that the principal is borrowed or invested.

SIMPLE INTEREST

Simple interest is computed on the principal amount only. It is the return on the principal for one period. Simple interest is usually expressed as shown in Illustration C-1.

Illustration C-1 Interest computation

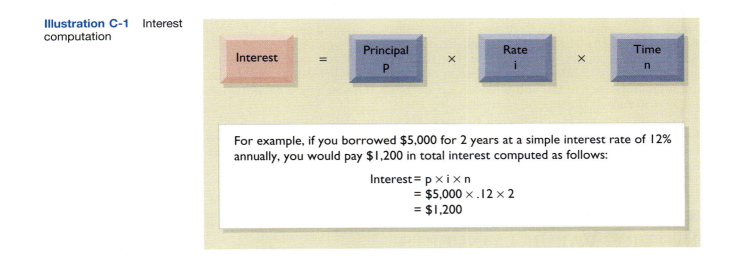

| Interest | = | Principal p | × | Rate i | × | Time n |

For example, if you borrowed $5,000 for 2 years at a simple interest rate of 12% annually, you would pay $1,200 in total interest computed as follows:

$$\text{Interest} = p \times i \times n$$
$$= \$5,000 \times .12 \times 2$$
$$= \$1,200$$

COMPOUND INTEREST

Compound interest is computed on principal **and** on any interest earned that has not been paid or withdrawn. It is the return on (or growth of) the principal for two or more time periods. Compounding computes interest not only on the principal but also on the interest earned to date on that principal, assuming the interest is left on deposit.

To illustrate the difference between simple and compound interest, assume that you deposit $1,000 in Bank One, where it will earn simple interest of 9 percent per year, and you deposit another $1,000 in CityCorp, where it will earn compound interest of 9 percent per year compounded annually. Also assume that in both cases you will not withdraw any interest until three years from the date of deposit. The computation of interest to be received and the accumulated year-end balances are indicated in Illustration C-2.

Illustration C-2 Simple vs. compound interest

Bank One				City Corp.		
Simple Interest Calculation	Simple Interest	Accumulated Year-end Balance		Compound Interest Calculation	Compound Interest	Accumulated Year-end Balance
Year 1 $1,000.00 × 9%	$ 90.00	$1,090.00		Year 1 $1,000.00 × 9%	$ 90.00	$1,090.00
Year 2 $1,000.00 × 9%	90.00	$1,180.00		Year 2 $1,090.00 × 9%	98.10	$1,188.10
Year 3 $1,000.00 × 9%	90.00	$1,270.00		Year 3 $1,188.10 × 9%	106.93	$1,295.03
	$ 270.00				$ 295.03	

$25.03 Difference

Note in the illustration above that simple interest uses the initial principal of $1,000 to compute the interest in all three years. Compound interest uses the accumulated balance (principal plus interest to date) at each year-end to compute interest in the succeeding year—which explains why your compound interest account is larger.

Obviously if you had a choice between investing your money at simple interest or at compound interest, you would choose compound interest, all other things—especially risk—being equal. In the example, compounding provides $25.03 of additional interest income. For practical purposes, compounding assumes that unpaid interest earned becomes a part of the principal, and the accumulated balance at the end of each year becomes the new principal on which interest is earned during the next year.

As can be seen in Illustration C-2, you should invest your money at City-Corp, which compounds interest annually. Compound interest is used in most business situations. Simple interest is generally applicable only to short-term situations of one year or less.

SECTION 1
FUTURE VALUE CONCEPTS

FUTURE VALUE OF A SINGLE AMOUNT

The **future value of a single amount** is the value at a future date of a given amount invested assuming compound interest. For example, in Illustration C-2, $1,295.03 is the future value of the $1,000 at the end of three years. The $1,295.03 could be determined more easily by using the following formula.

STUDY OBJECTIVE

2

Solve for future value of a single amount.

$$FV = p \times (1 + i)^n$$

where:

FV = future value of a single amount
p = principal (or present value)
i = interest rate for one period
n = number of periods

The $1,295.03 is computed as follows.

$$FV = p \times (1 + i)^n$$
$$= \$1,000 \times (1 + i)^3$$
$$= \$1,000 \times 1.29503$$
$$= \$1,295.03$$

The 1.29503 is computed by multiplying (1.09 × 1.09 × 1.09). The amounts in this example can be depicted in the following time diagram.

Illustration C-3 Time diagram

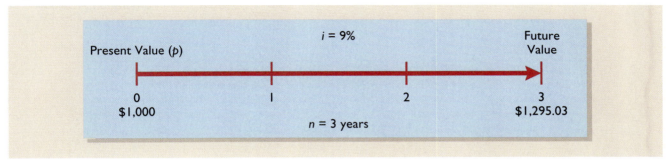

Another method that may be used to compute the future value of a single amount involves the use of a compound interest table. This table shows the future value of 1 for n periods. Table 1, shown below, is such a table.

TABLE 1 Future Value of 1

(n) Periods	4%	5%	6%	8%	9%	10%	11%	12%	15%
1	1.04000	1.05000	1.06000	1.08000	1.09000	1.10000	1.11000	1.12000	1.15000
2	1.08160	1.10250	1.12360	1.16640	1.18810	1.21000	1.23210	1.25440	1.32250
3	1.12486	1.15763	1.19102	1.25971	1.29503	1.33100	1.36763	1.40493	1.52088
4	1.16986	1.21551	1.26248	1.36049	1.41158	1.46410	1.51807	1.57352	1.74901
5	1.21665	1.27628	1.33823	1.46933	1.53862	1.61051	1.68506	1.76234	2.01136
6	1.26532	1.34010	1.41852	1.58687	1.67710	1.77156	1.87041	1.97382	2.31306
7	1.31593	1.40710	1.50363	1.71382	1.82804	1.94872	2.07616	2.21068	2.66002
8	1.36857	1.47746	1.59385	1.85093	1.99256	2.14359	2.30454	2.47596	3.05902
9	1.42331	1.55133	1.68948	1.99900	2.17189	2.35795	2.55803	2.77308	3.51788
10	1.48024	1.62889	1.79085	2.15892	2.36736	2.59374	2.83942	3.10585	4.04556
11	1.53945	1.71034	1.89830	2.33164	2.58043	2.85312	3.15176	3.47855	4.65239
12	1.60103	1.79586	2.01220	2.51817	2.81267	3.13843	3.49845	3.89598	5.35025
13	1.66507	1.88565	2.13293	2.71962	3.06581	3.45227	3.88328	4.36349	6.15279
14	1.73168	1.97993	2.26090	2.93719	3.34173	3.79750	4.31044	4.88711	7.07571
15	1.80094	2.07893	2.39656	3.17217	3.64248	4.17725	4.78459	5.47357	8.13706
16	1.87298	2.18287	2.54035	3.42594	3.97031	4.59497	5.31089	6.13039	9.35762
17	1.94790	2.29202	2.69277	3.70002	4.32763	5.05447	5.89509	6.86604	10.76126
18	2.02582	2.40662	2.85434	3.99602	4.71712	5.55992	6.54355	7.68997	12.37545
19	2.10685	2.52695	3.02560	4.31570	5.14166	6.11591	7.26334	8.61276	14.23177
20	2.19112	2.65330	3.20714	4.66096	5.60441	6.72750	8.06231	9.64629	16.36654

In Table 1, n is the number of compounding periods, the percentages are the periodic interest rates, and the five-digit decimal numbers in the respective columns are the future value of 1 factors. In using Table 1, the principal amount is multiplied by the future value factor for the specified number of periods and interest rate. For example, the future value factor for 2 periods at 9 percent is 1.18810. Multiplying this factor by $1,000 equals $1,188.10, which is the accumulated balance at the end of year 2 in the CityCorp example in Illustration C-2. The $1,295.03 accumulated balance at the end of the third year can be calculated from Table 1 by multiplying the future value factor for 3 periods (1.29503) by the $1,000.

The following demonstration problem illustrates how to use Table 1.

Illustration C-4   Demonstration Problem—Using Table 1 for FV of 1

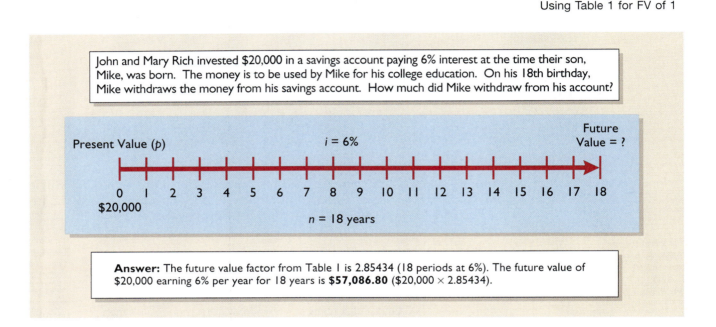

John and Mary Rich invested $20,000 in a savings account paying 6% interest at the time their son, Mike, was born. The money is to be used by Mike for his college education. On his 18th birthday, Mike withdraws the money from his savings account. How much did Mike withdraw from his account?

Answer: The future value factor from Table 1 is 2.85434 (18 periods at 6%). The future value of $20,000 earning 6% per year for 18 years is **$57,086.80** ($20,000 × 2.85434).

FUTURE VALUE OF AN ANNUITY

The preceding discussion involved the accumulation of only a single principal sum. Individuals and businesses frequently encounter situations in which a series of equal dollar amounts are to be paid or received periodically, such as loans or lease (rental) contracts. Such payments or receipts of equal dollar amounts are referred to as **annuities**. The **future value of an annuity** is the sum of all the payments (receipts) plus the accumulated compound interest on them. In computing the future value of an annuity, it is necessary to know (1) the interest rate, (2) the number of compounding periods, and (3) the amount of the periodic payments or receipts.

To illustrate the computation of the future value of an annuity, assume that you invest $2,000 at the end of each year for three years at 5 percent interest compounded annually. This situation is depicted in the time diagram in Illustration C-5.

STUDY OBJECTIVE
3
Solve for future value of an annuity.

Illustration C-5 Time diagram for a 3-year annuity

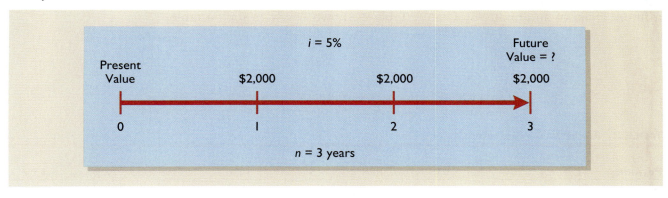

As can be seen in Illustration C-5, the $2,000 invested at the end of year 1 will earn interest for two years (years 2 and 3), and the $2,000 invested at the end of year 2 will earn interest for one year (year 3). However, the last $2,000 investment (made at the end of year 3) will not earn any interest. The future value of these periodic payments could be computed using the future value factors from Table 1 as shown in Illustration C-6.

Illustration C-6 Future value of periodic payments

Year Invested	Amount Invested	×	Future Value of 1 Factor at 5%	=	Future Value
1	$2,000	×	1.10250	=	$ 2,205
2	$2,000	×	1.05000	=	2,100
3	$2,000	×	1.00000	=	2,000
			3.15250		**$6,305**

The first $2,000 investment is multiplied by the future value factor for two periods (1.1025) because two years' interest will accumulate on it (in years 2 and 3). The second $2,000 investment will earn only one year's interest (in year 3) and therefore is multiplied by the future value factor for one year (1.0500). The final $2,000 investment is made at the end of the third year and will not earn any interest. Consequently, the future value of the last $2,000 invested is only $2,000 since it does not accumulate any interest.

This method of calculation is required when the periodic payments or receipts are not equal in each period. However, when the periodic payments (receipts) are the same in each period, the future value can be computed by using a future value of an annuity of 1 table. Table 2, shown below, is such a table.

TABLE 2 Future Value of an Annuity of 1

(n) Periods	4%	5%	6%	8%	9%	10%	11%	12%	15%
1	1.00000	1.00000	1.00000	1.00000	1.00000	1.00000	1.00000	1.00000	1.00000
2	2.04000	2.05000	2.06000	2.08000	2.09000	2.10000	2.11000	2.12000	2.15000
3	3.12160	3.15250	3.18360	3.24640	3.27810	3.31000	3.34210	3.37440	3.47250
4	4.24646	4.31013	4.37462	4.50611	4.57313	4.64100	4.70973	4.77933	4.99338
5	5.41632	5.52563	5.63709	5.86660	5.98471	6.10510	6.22780	6.35285	6.74238
6	6.63298	6.80191	6.97532	7.33592	7.52334	7.71561	7.91286	8.11519	8.75374
7	7.89829	8.14201	8.39384	8.92280	9.20044	9.48717	9.78327	10.08901	11.06680
8	9.21423	9.54911	9.89747	10.63663	11.02847	11.43589	11.85943	12.29969	13.72682
9	10.58280	11.02656	11.49132	12.48756	13.02104	13.57948	14.16397	14.77566	16.78584
10	12.00611	12.57789	13.18079	14.48656	15.19293	15.93743	16.72201	17.54874	20.30372
11	13.48635	14.20679	14.97164	16.64549	17.56029	18.53117	19.56143	20.65458	24.34928
12	15.02581	15.91713	16.86994	18.97713	20.14072	21.38428	22.71319	24.13313	29.00167
13	16.62684	17.71298	18.88214	21.49530	22.95339	24.52271	26.21164	28.02911	34.35192
14	18.29191	19.59863	21.01507	24.21492	26.01919	27.97498	30.09492	32.39260	40.50471
15	20.02359	21.57856	23.27597	27.15211	29.36092	31.77248	34.40536	37.27972	47.58041
16	21.82453	23.65749	25.67253	30.32428	33.00340	35.94973	39.18995	42.75328	55.71747
17	23.69751	25.84037	28.21288	33.75023	36.97351	40.54470	44.50084	48.88367	65.07509
18	25.64541	28.13238	30.90565	37.45024	41.30134	45.59917	50.39593	55.74972	75.83636
19	27.67123	30.53900	33.75999	41.44626	46.01846	51.15909	56.93949	63.43968	88.21181
20	29.77808	33.06595	36.78559	45.76196	51.16012	57.27500	64.20283	72.05244	102.44358

Table 2 shows the future value of 1 to be received periodically for a given number of periods. From Table 2 it can be seen that the future value of an annuity of 1 factor for 3 periods at 5 percent is 3.15250. The future value factor is the total of the three individual future value factors as shown in Illustration C-6. Multiplying this amount by the annual investment of $2,000 produces a future value of $6,305.

The demonstration problem in Illustration C-7 illustrates how to use Table 2.

**Illustration C-7   Demon-
stration Problem**—Using
Table 2 for FV of an
annuity of 1

Henning Printing Company knows that in four years it must replace one of its existing printing presses with a new one. To insure that some funds are available to replace the machine in four years, the company is depositing $25,000 in a savings account at the end of each of the next four years (4 deposits in total). The savings account will earn 6% interest compounded annually. How much will be in the savings account at the end of four years when the new printing press is to be purchased?

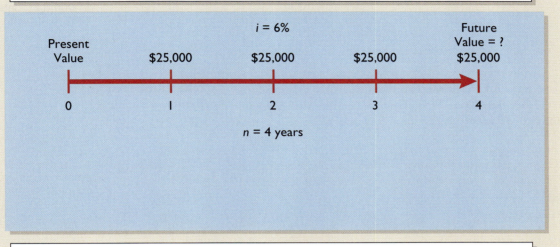

Answer: The future value factor from Table 2 is 4.37462 (4 periods at 6%). The future value of $25,000 invested at the end of each year for 4 years at 6% interest is **$109,365.50** ($25,000 × 4.37462).

PRESENT VALUE CONCEPTS

*P*RESENT VALUE VARIABLES

STUDY OBJECTIVE

4

Identify the variables fundamental to solving present
value problems.

The **present value**, like the future value, is based on three variables: (1) the dollar amount to be received (future amount), (2) the length of time until the amount is received (number of periods), and (3) the interest rate (the discount rate). The process of determining the present value is referred to as **discounting the future amount**.

In this textbook, present value computations are used in measuring several items. For example, capital budgeting and other investment proposals are evaluated using present value computations. All rate of return and internal rate of return computations involve present value techniques.

PRESENT VALUE OF A SINGLE AMOUNT

STUDY OBJECTIVE

5

Solve for present value of a single amount.

To illustrate present value concepts, assume that you are willing to invest a sum of money that will yield $1,000 at the end of one year. In other words, what amount would you need to invest today to have $1,000 one year from now? If you want a 10 percent rate of return, the investment or present value is $909.09 ($1,000 ÷ 1.10). The computation of this amount is shown in Illustration C-8.

$$\text{Present Value} = \text{Future Value} \div (1 + i)^1$$
$$PV = FV \div (1 + 10\%)^1$$
$$PV = \$1,000 \div 1.10$$
$$\mathbf{PV = \$909.09}$$

Illustration C-8 Present value computation— $1,000 discounted at 10% for 1 year

The future amount ($1,000), the discount rate (10 percent), and the number of periods (1) are known. The variables in this situation can be depicted in the following time diagram.

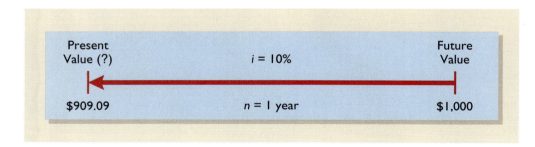

Illustration C-9 Finding present value if discounted for one period

If the single amount of $1,000 is to be received **in two years** and discounted at 10 percent [PV = $1,000 ÷ (1 + 10%)^2], its present value is $826.45 [($1,000 ÷ 1.10) ÷ 1.10], depicted as follows.

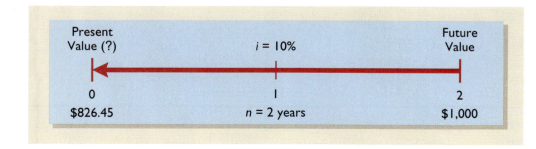

Illustration C-10 Finding present value if discounted for two periods

The present value of 1 may also be determined through tables that show the present value of 1 for n periods. In Table 3, n is the number of discounting periods involved. The percentages are the periodic interest rates or discount rates, and the five-digit decimal numbers in the respective columns are the present value of 1 factors.

TABLE 3   Present Value of 1

(*n*) Periods	4%	5%	6%	8%	9%	10%	11%	12%	15%
1	.96154	.95238	.94340	.92593	.91743	.90909	.90090	.89286	.86957
2	.92456	.90703	.89000	.85734	.84168	.82645	.81162	.79719	.75614
3	.88900	.86384	.83962	.79383	.77218	.75132	.73119	.71178	.65752
4	.85480	.82270	.79209	.73503	.70843	.68301	.65873	.63552	.57175
5	.82193	.78353	.74726	.68058	.64993	.62092	.59345	.56743	.49718
6	.79031	.74622	.70496	.63017	.59627	.56447	.53464	.50663	.43233
7	.75992	.71068	.66506	.58349	.54703	.51316	.48166	.45235	.37594
8	.73069	.67684	.62741	.54027	.50187	.46651	.43393	.40388	.32690
9	.70259	.64461	.59190	.50025	.46043	.42410	.39092	.36061	.28426
10	.67556	.61391	.55839	.46319	.42241	.38554	.35218	.32197	.24719
11	.64958	.58468	.52679	.42888	.38753	.35049	.31728	.28748	.21494
12	.62460	.55684	.49697	.39711	.35554	.31863	.28584	.25668	.18691
13	.60057	.53032	.46884	.36770	.32618	.28966	.25751	.22917	.16253
14	.57748	.50507	.44230	.34046	.29925	.26333	.23199	.20462	.14133
15	.55526	.48102	.41727	.31524	.27454	.23939	.20900	.18270	.12289
16	.53391	.45811	.39365	.29189	.25187	.21763	.18829	.16312	.10687
17	.51337	.43630	.37136	.27027	.23107	.19785	.16963	.14564	.09293
18	.49363	.41552	.35034	.25025	.21199	.17986	.15282	.13004	.08081
19	.47464	.39573	.33051	.23171	.19449	.16351	.13768	.11611	.07027
20	.45639	.37689	.31180	.21455	.17843	.14864	.12403	.10367	.06110

When Table 3 is used, the future value is multiplied by the present value factor specified at the intersection of the number of periods and the discount rate. For example, the present value factor for 1 period at a discount rate of 10 percent is .90909, which equals the $909.09 ($1,000 × .90909) computed in Illustration C-8. For 2 periods at a discount rate of 10 percent, the present value factor is .82645, which equals the $826.45 ($1,000 × .82645) computed previously.

Note that a higher discount rate produces a smaller present value. For example, using a 15 percent discount rate, the present value of $1,000 due one year from now is $869.57 versus $909.09 at 10 percent. It should also be recognized that the further removed from the present the future value is, the smaller the present value. For example, using the same discount rate of 10 percent, the present value of $1,000 due in **five** years is $620.92 versus $1,000 due in **one** year is $909.09.

The following two demonstration problems (Illustrations C-11, C-12) illustrate how to use Table 3.

Illustration C-11 **Demon-stration Problem**—Using Table 3 for PV of 1

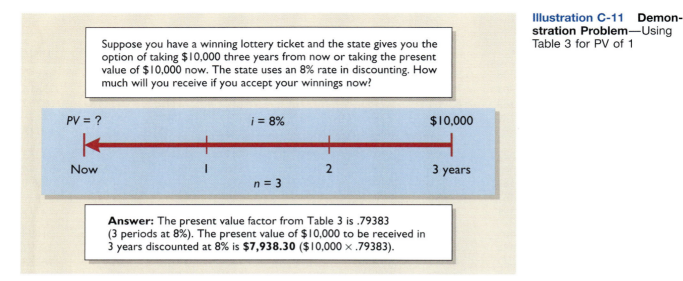

Suppose you have a winning lottery ticket and the state gives you the option of taking $10,000 three years from now or taking the present value of $10,000 now. The state uses an 8% rate in discounting. How much will you receive if you accept your winnings now?

PV = ?   i = 8% $10,000

Now   1   2   3 years

n = 3

Answer: The present value factor from Table 3 is .79383 (3 periods at 8%). The present value of $10,000 to be received in 3 years discounted at 8% is **$7,938.30** ($10,000 × .79383).

Illustration C-12 **Demon-stration Problem**—Using Table 3 for PV of 1

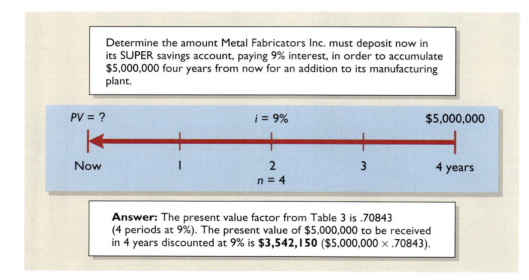

Determine the amount Metal Fabricators Inc. must deposit now in its SUPER savings account, paying 9% interest, in order to accumulate $5,000,000 four years from now for an addition to its manufacturing plant.

PV = ?   i = 9% $5,000,000

Now   1   2   3   4 years

n = 4

Answer: The present value factor from Table 3 is .70843 (4 periods at 9%). The present value of $5,000,000 to be received in 4 years discounted at 9% is **$3,542,150** ($5,000,000 × .70843).

PRESENT VALUE OF AN ANNUITY

The preceding discussion involved the discounting of only a single future amount. Businesses and individuals frequently engage in transactions in which a series of equal dollar amounts are to be received or paid periodically. Examples of a series of periodic receipts or payments are loan agreements, installment sales, mortgage notes, lease (rental) contracts, and pension obligations. These series of periodic receipts or payments are called **annuities**. In computing the **present value of an annuity**, it is necessary to know (1) the discount rate, (2) the number of discount periods, and (3) the amount of the periodic receipts or payments. To illustrate the computation of the present value of an annuity, assume that you will receive $1,000 cash annually for three years at a time when the discount rate is 10 percent. This situation is depicted in the time diagram in Illustration C-13.

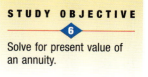

STUDY OBJECTIVE

6

Solve for present value of an annuity.

Illustration C-13 Time diagram for a 3-year annuity

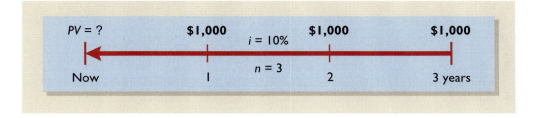

The present value in this situation may be computed as follows.

Illustration C-14 Present value of a series of future amounts computation

Future Amount	×	Present Value of 1 Factor at 10%	=	Present Value
$1,000 (One year away)	×	.90909	=	$ 909.09
1,000 (Two years away)	×	.82645	=	826.45
1,000 (Three years away)	×	.75132	=	751.32
		2.48686		**$2,486.86**

This method of calculation is required when the periodic cash flows are not uniform in each period. However, when the future receipts are the same in each period, there are two other ways to compute present value. First, the annual cash flow can be multiplied by the sum of the three present value factors. In the previous example, $1,000 × 2.48686 equals $2,486.86. Second, annuity tables may be used. As illustrated in Table 4 below, these tables show the present value of 1 to be received periodically for a given number of periods.

TABLE 4   Present Value of an Annuity of 1

(n) Periods	4%	5%	6%	8%	9%	10%	11%	12%	15%
1	.96154	.95238	.94340	.92593	.91743	.90909	.90090	.89286	.86957
2	1.88609	1.85941	1.83339	1.78326	1.75911	1.73554	1.71252	1.69005	1.62571
3	2.77509	2.72325	2.67301	2.57710	2.53130	2.48685	2.44371	2.40183	2.28323
4	3.62990	3.54595	3.46511	3.31213	3.23972	3.16986	3.10245	3.03735	2.85498
5	4.45182	4.32948	4.21236	3.99271	3.88965	3.79079	3.69590	3.60478	3.35216
6	5.24214	5.07569	4.91732	4.62288	4.48592	4.35526	4.23054	4.11141	3.78448
7	6.00205	5.78637	5.58238	5.20637	5.03295	4.86842	4.71220	4.56376	4.16042
8	6.73274	6.46321	6.20979	5.74664	5.53482	5.33493	5.14612	4.96764	4.48732
9	7.43533	7.10782	6.80169	6.24689	5.99525	5.75902	5.53705	5.32825	4.77158
10	8.11090	7.72173	7.36009	6.71008	6.41766	6.14457	5.88923	5.65022	5.01877
11	8.76048	8.30641	7.88687	7.13896	6.80519	6.49506	6.20652	5.93770	5.23371
12	9.38507	8.86325	8.38384	7.53608	7.16073	6.81369	6.49236	6.19437	5.42062
13	9.98565	9.39357	8.85268	7.90378	7.48690	7.10336	6.74987	6.42355	5.58315
14	10.56312	9.89864	9.29498	8.24424	7.78615	7.36669	6.98187	6.62817	5.72448
15	11.11839	10.37966	9.71225	8.55948	8.06069	7.60608	7.19087	6.81086	5.84737
16	11.65230	10.83777	10.10590	8.85137	8.31256	7.82371	7.37916	6.97399	5.95424
17	12.16567	11.27407	10.47726	9.12164	8.54363	8.02155	7.54879	7.11963	6.04716
18	12.65930	11.68959	10.82760	9.37189	8.75563	8.20141	7.70162	7.24967	6.12797
19	13.13394	12.08532	11.15812	9.60360	8.95012	8.36492	7.83929	7.36578	6.19823
20	13.59033	12.46221	11.46992	9.81815	9.12855	8.51356	7.96333	7.46944	6.25933

From Table 4 it can be seen that the present value of an annuity of 1 factor for 3 periods at 10 percent is 2.48685.[1] This present value factor is the total of the three individual present value factors as shown in Illustration C-14. Applying this amount to the annual cash flow of $1,000 produces a present value of $2,486.85.

The following demonstration problem (Illustration C-15) illustrates how to use Table 4.

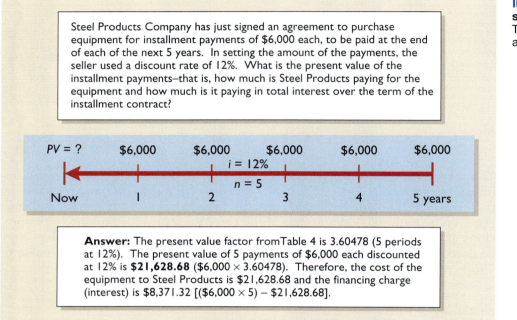

Steel Products Company has just signed an agreement to purchase equipment for installment payments of $6,000 each, to be paid at the end of each of the next 5 years. In setting the amount of the payments, the seller used a discount rate of 12%. What is the present value of the installment payments–that is, how much is Steel Products paying for the equipment and how much is it paying in total interest over the term of the installment contract?

PV = ? $6,000 $6,000 $6,000 $6,000 $6,000
$i = 12\%$
$n = 5$
Now   1   2   3   4   5 years

Answer: The present value factor from Table 4 is 3.60478 (5 periods at 12%). The present value of 5 payments of $6,000 each discounted at 12% is **$21,628.68** ($6,000 × 3.60478). Therefore, the cost of the equipment to Steel Products is $21,628.68 and the financing charge (interest) is $8,371.32 [($6,000 × 5) − $21,628.68].

Illustration C-15   Demonstration Problem—Using Table 4 for PV of an annuity of 1

TIME PERIODS AND DISCOUNTING

In the preceding calculations, the discounting has been done on an annual basis using an annual interest rate. Discounting may also be done over shorter periods of time such as monthly, quarterly, or semiannually. When the time frame is less than one year, it is necessary to convert the annual interest rate to the applicable time frame. Assume, for example, that the investor in Illustration C-14 received $500 **semiannually** for three years instead of $1,000 annually. In this case, the number of periods becomes 6 (3 × 2), the discount rate is 5 percent (10% ÷ 2), the present value factor from Table 4 is 5.07569, and the present value of the future cash flows is $2,537.85 (5.07569 × $500). This amount is slightly higher than the $2,486.86 computed in Illustration C-14 because interest is computed twice during the same year; therefore interest is earned on the first half year's interest.

---

[1]The difference of .00001 between 2.48686 and 2.48685 is due to rounding.

COMPUTING THE PRESENT VALUES IN A CAPITAL BUDGETING DECISION

STUDY OBJECTIVE

7

Compute the present values in capital budgeting situations.

The decision to make long-term capital investments is best evaluated using discounting techniques that recognize the time value of money, that is, the present value of the cash flows involved in a capital investment. The evaluation must reduce all cash inflows and outflows to a common comparable amount. That can be accomplished by either future valuing to some future date all the cash flows, or present valuing (discounting) to the present date all cash flows. While both are useful for evaluating the investment, the present value (discounting) technique is more appealing and universally used.

Nagel-Siebert Trucking Company, a cross-country freight carrier in Montgomery, Illinois, is considering adding another truck to its fleet because of a purchasing opportunity. Navistar Inc., Nagel-Siebert's primary supplier of overland rigs, is overstocked and offers to sell its biggest rig for $154,000 cash payable upon delivery. Nagel-Siebert knows that the rig will produce a net cash flow per year of $40,000 for five years (received at the end of each year), at which time it will be sold for an estimated salvage value of $35,000. Nagel-Siebert's discount rate in evaluating capital expenditures is 10 percent. Should Nagel-Siebert commit to the purchase of this rig?

The cash flows that must be discounted to present value by Nagel-Siebert are as follows.

Cash payable on delivery (now): $154,000.

Net cash flow from operating the rig: $40,000 for five years (at the end of each year).

Cash received from sale of rig at the end of five years: $35,000.

The time diagrams for the latter two cash flows are shown in Illustration C-16.

Illustration C-16   Time diagrams for Nagel-Siebert Trucking Company

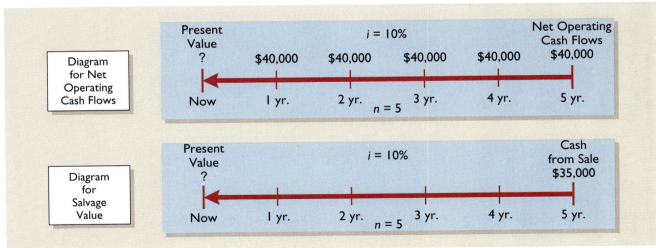

Notice from the diagrams that computing the present value of the net operating cash flows ($40,000 at the end of each year) is **discounting an annuity** (Table 4), while computing the present value of the $35,000 salvage value is **discounting a single sum** (Table 3).

The computation of these present values is shown in Illustration C-17.

Illustration C-17 Present value computations at 10 percent

Present Values Using a 10 Percent Discount Rate

Present value of net operating cash flows received annually over 5 years:	
$40,000 × PV of 1 received annually for 5 years at 10%	
$40,000 × 3.79079 =	$151,631.60
Present value of salvage value (cash) to be received in 5 years	
$35,000 × PV of 1 received in 5 years at 10%	
$35,000 × .62092 =	21,732.20
Present value of cash **inflows**	173,363.80
Present value cash **outflows** (purchase price due now at 10%):	
$154,000 × PV of 1 due now	
$154,000 × 1.00000 =	154,000.00
Net present value	**$ 19,363.80**

Because the present value of the cash receipts (inflows) of $173,363.80 ($151,631.60 + $21,732.20) exceeds the present value of the cash payments (outflows) of $154,000.00, the net present value of $19,363.80 is positive, and **the decision to invest should be accepted**.

Now assume that Nagel-Siebert uses a discount rate of 15 percent, not 10 percent, because it wants a greater return on its investments in capital assets. The cash receipts and cash payments by Nagel-Siebert are the same. The present values of these receipts and cash payments discounted at 15 percent are shown in Illustration C-18.

Illustration C-18 Present value computations at 15 percent

Present Values Using a 15 Percent Discount Rate

Present value of net operating cash flows received annually over 5 years at 15%:	
$40,000 × 3.35216	$134,086.40
Present value of salvage value (cash) to be received in 5 years at 15%	
$35,000 × .49718	17,401.30
Present value of cash **inflows**	$151,487.70
Present value of cash **outflows** (purchase price due now at 15%):	
$154,000 × 1.00000	154,000.00
Net present value	**$ (2,512.30)**

Because the present value of the cash payments (outflows) of $154,000 exceeds the present value of the cash receipts (inflows) of $151,487.70 ($134,086.40 + $17,401.30), the net present value of $2,512.30 is negative, and **the investment should be rejected**.

The above discussion relied on present value tables in solving present value problems. Electronic hand-held calculators may also be used to compute present values without the use of these tables. Some calculators, especially the "business" or "MBA" type calculators, have present value (PV) functions that allow you to calculate present values by merely identifying the proper amount, discount rate, periods, and pressing the PV key.

SUMMARY OF STUDY OBJECTIVES

1 *Distinguish between simple and compound interest.* Simple interest is computed on the principal only while compound interest is computed on the principal and any interest earned that has not been withdrawn.

2 *Solve for future value of a single amount.* Prepare a time diagram of the problem. Identify the principal amount, the number of compounding periods, and the interest rate. Using the future value of 1 table, multiply the principal amount by the future value factor specified at the intersection of the number of periods and the interest rate.

3 *Solve for future value of an annuity.* Prepare a time diagram of the problem. Identify the amount of the periodic payments, the number of compounding periods, and the interest rate. Using the future value of an annuity of 1 table, multiply the amount of the payments by the future value factor specified at the intersection of the number of periods and the interest rate.

4 *Identify the variables fundamental to solving present value problems.* The following three variables are fundamental to solving present value problems: (1) the future amount, (2) the number of periods, and (3) the interest rate (the discount rate).

5 *Solve for present value of a single amount.* Prepare a time diagram of the problem. Identify the future amount, the number of discounting periods, and the discount (interest) rate. Using the present value of 1 table, multiply the future amount by the present value factor specified at the intersection of the number of periods and the discount rate.

6 *Solve for present value of an annuity.* Prepare a time diagram of the problem. Identify the future amounts (annuities), the number of discounting periods, and the discount (interest) rate. Using the present value of an annuity of 1 table, multiply the amount of the annuity by the present value factor specified at the intersection of the number of periods and the interest rate.

7 *Compute the present values in capital budgeting situations.* Compute the present values of all cash inflows and all cash outflows related to the capital budgeting proposal (an investment-type decision). If the **net** present value is positive, accept the proposal (make the investment). If the **net** present value is negative, reject the proposal (do not make the investment).

GLOSSARY

Annuity A series of equal dollar amounts to be paid or received periodically. (p. C-5)

Compound interest The interest computed on the principal and any interest earned that has not been paid or received. (p. C-2)

Discounting the future amount(s) The process of determining present value. (p. C-8)

Future value of a single amount The value at a future date of a given amount invested assuming compound interest. (p. C-3)

Future value of an annuity The sum of all the payments or receipts plus the accumulated compound interest on them. (p. C-5)

Interest Payment for the use of another's money. (p. C-2)

Present value The value now of a given amount to be invested or received in the future assuming compound interest. (p. C-8)

Present value of an annuity A series of future receipts or payments discounted to their value now assuming compound interest. (p. C-11)

Principal The amount borrowed or invested. (p. C-2)

Simple interest The interest computed on the principal only. (p. C-2)

BRIEF EXERCISES (USE TABLES TO SOLVE EXERCISES)

Compute the future value of a single amount.
(SO 2)

BEC-1 Don Smith invested $5,000 at 6% annual interest, and left the money invested without withdrawing any of the interest for 10 years. At the end of the 10 years, Don withdrew the accumulated amount of money.
(a) What amount did Don withdraw assuming the investment earns simple interest?
(b) What amount did Don withdraw assuming the investment earns interest compounded annually?

BEC-2   For each of the following cases, indicate (a) to what interest rate columns and (b) to what number of periods you would refer in looking up the future value factor.

Use future value tables.
(SO 2, 3)

1. In Table 1 (future value of 1):

	Annual Rate	Number of Years Invested	Compounded
(a)	6%	5	Annually
(b)	5%	3	Semiannually

2. In Table 2 (future value of an annuity of 1):

	Annual Rate	Number of Years Invested	Compounded
(a)	5%	10	Annually
(b)	4%	6	Semiannually

BEC-3   Porter Company signed a lease for an office building for a period of 10 years. Under the lease agreement, a security deposit of $10,000 is made. The deposit will be returned at the expiration of the lease with interest compounded at 5% per year. What amount will Porter receive at the time the lease expires?

Compute the future value of a single amount.
(SO 2)

BEC-4   Gordon Company issued $1,000,000, 10-year bonds and agreed to make annual sinking fund deposits of $80,000. The deposits are made at the end of each year into an account paying 5% annual interest. What amount will be in the sinking fund at the end of 10 years?

Compute the future value of an annuity.
(SO 3)

BEC-5   David and Kathy Hatcher invested $5,000 in a savings account paying 6% annual interest when their daughter, Sue, was born. They also deposited $1,000 on each of her birthdays until she was 18 (including her 18th birthday). How much will be in the savings account on her 18th birthday (after the last deposit)?

Compute the future value of a single amount and of an annuity.
(SO 2, 3)

BEC-6   Ron Watson borrowed $20,000 on July 1, 1996. This amount plus accrued interest at 6% compounded annually is to be repaid on July 1, 2001. How much will Ron have to repay on July 1, 2001?

Compute the future value of a single amount.
(SO 2)

BEC-7   For each of the following cases, indicate (a) to what interest rate columns and (b) to what number of periods you would refer in looking up the discount rate.

Use present value tables.
(SO 5, 6)

1. In Table 3 (present value of 1):

	Annual Rate	Number of Years Involved	Discounts Per Year
(a)	12%	6	Annually
(b)	10%	15	Annually
(c)	8%	8	Semiannually

2. In Table 4 (present value of an annuity of 1):

	Annual Rate	Number of Years Involved	Number of Payments Involved	Frequency of Payments
(a)	12%	20	20	Annually
(b)	10%	5	5	Annually
(c)	8%	4	8	Semiannually

BEC-8   (a) What is the present value of $10,000 due 8 periods from now, discounted at 8%? (b) What is the present value of $10,000 to be received at the end of each of 6 periods, discounted at 9%?

Determine present values.
(SO 5, 6)

BEC-9   Smolinski Company is considering an investment which will return a lump sum of $500,000 five years from now. What amount should Smolinski Company pay for this investment to earn a 15% return?

Compute the present value of a single amount investment.
(SO 5)

Compute the present value of a single amount investment.
(SO 5)

BEC-10   Pizzeria Company earns 11% on an investment that will return $875,000 eight years from now. What is the amount Pizzeria should invest now to earn this rate of return?

Compute the present value of an annuity investment.
(SO 6)

BEC-11   Kilarny Company is considering investing in an annuity contract that will return $20,000 annually at the end of each year for 15 years. What amount should Kilarny Company pay for this investment if it earns a 6% return?

Compute the present value of an annuity investment.
(SO 6)

BEC-12   Zarita Enterprises earns 11% on an investment that pays back $110,000 at the end of each of the next four years. What is the amount Zarita Enterprises invested to earn the 11% rate of return?

Compute the present value of bonds.
(SO 5, 6)

BEC-13   Hernandez Railroad Co. is about to issue $100,000 of 10-year bonds paying a 12% interest rate, with interest payable semiannually. The discount rate for such securities is 10%. How much can Hernandez expect to receive for the sale of these bonds?

Compute the present value of bonds.
(SO 5, 6)

BEC-14   Assume the same information as BEC-13 except that the discount rate was 12% instead of 10%. In this case, how much can Hernandez expect to receive from the sale of these bonds?

Compute the present value of a note.
(SO 5, 6)

BEC-15   Caledonian Taco Company receives a $50,000, 6-year note bearing interest of 11% (paid annually) from a customer at a time when the discount rate is 12%. What is the present value of the note received by Caledonian?

Compute the present value of bonds.
(SO 5, 6)

BEC-16   Galway Bay Enterprises issued 10%, 8-year, $2,000,000 par value bonds that pay interest semiannually on October 1 and April 1. The bonds are dated April 1, 2002, and are issued on that date. The discount rate of interest for such bonds on April 1, 2002, is 12%. What cash proceeds did Galway Bay receive from issuance of the bonds?

Compute the present value of a machine for purposes of making a purchase decision.
(SO 7)

BEC-17   Barney Googal owns a garage and is contemplating purchasing a tire retreading machine for $16,280. After estimating costs and revenues, Barney projects a net cash flow from the retreading machine of $2,790 annually for 8 years. Barney hopes to earn a return of 11% on such investments. What is the present value of the retreading operation? Should Barney Googal purchase the retreading machine?

Compute the present value of a note.
(SO 5, 6)

BEC-18   Hung-Chao Yu Company issues a 10%, 6-year mortgage note on January 1, 2002 to obtain financing for new equipment. Land is used as collateral for the note. The terms provide for semiannual installment payments of $112,825. What were the cash proceeds received from the issuance of the note?

Compute the maximum price to pay for a machine.
(SO 7)

BEC-19   Ramos Company is considering purchasing equipment. The equipment will produce the following cash flows: Year 1, $30,000; Year 2, $40,000; Year 3, $50,000. Ramos requires a minimum rate of return of 15%. What is the maximum price Ramos should pay for this equipment?

Compute the interest rate on a single amount.
(SO 5)

BEC-20   Kerry Rodriquez invests $1,827 now and will receive $10,000 at the end of 15 years. What annual rate of interest will Kerry earn on her investment? (*Hint:* Use Table 3.)

Compute the number of periods of a single amount.
(SO 5)

BEC-21   Maloney Cork has been offered the opportunity of investing $24,719 now. The investment will earn 15% per year and will at the end of that time return Maloney $100,000. How many years must Maloney wait to receive $100,000? (*Hint:* Use Table 3.)

Compute the interest rate on an annuity.
(SO 6)

BEC-22   Annie Dublin purchased an investment of $11,469.92. From this investment, she will receive $1,000 annually for the next 20 years starting one year from now. What rate of interest will Annie's investment be earning for her? (*Hint:* Use Table 4.)

Compute the number of periods of an annuity.
(SO 6)

BEC-23   Andy Sanchez invests $8,851.37 now for a series of $1,000 annual returns beginning one year from now. Andy will earn a return of 8% on the initial investment. How many annual payments of $1,000 will Andy receive? (*Hint:* Use Table 4.)

Ethical Standards

*E*THICAL BEHAVIOR FOR PRACTITIONERS OF MANAGEMENT ACCOUNTING AND FINANCIAL MANAGEMENT

In today's modern world of business, individuals in management accounting and financial management constantly face ethical dilemmas. For example, if the accountant's immediate superior instructs the accountant to record the physical inventory at its original costs when it is obvious that the inventory has a reduced value due to obsolescence, what should the accountant do? To help make such a decision, here is a brief general discussion of ethics and the "Standards of Ethical Conduct for Practitioners of Management Accounting and Financial Management."

Ethics, in its broader sense, deals with human conduct in relation to what is morally good and bad, right and wrong. To determine whether a decision is good or bad, the decision maker must compare his/her options with some standard of perfection. This standard of perfection is not a statement of static position but requires the decision maker to assess the situation and the values of the parties affected by the decision. The decision maker must then estimate the outcome of the decision and be responsible for its results. Two good questions to ask when faced with an ethical dilemma are, "Will my actions be fair and just to all parties affected?" and "Would I be pleased to have my closest friends learn of my actions?"

Individuals in management accounting and financial management have a unique set of circumstances relating to their employment. To help them assess their situation, the Institute of Management Accountants has developed the following "Standards of Ethical Conduct for Practitioners of Management Accounting and Financial Management."

Issued with permission from the Institute of Management Accountants.

STANDARDS OF ETHICAL CONDUCT FOR PRACTITIONERS OF MANAGEMENT ACCOUNTING AND FINANCIAL MANAGEMENT

Practitioners of management accounting and financial management have an obligation to the public, their profession, the organization they serve, and themselves, to maintain the highest standards of ethical conduct. In recognition of this obligation, the Institute of Management Accountants has promulgated the following standards of ethical conduct for practitioners of management accounting and financial management. Adherence to these standards, both domestically and internationally, is integral to achieving the *Objectives of Management Accounting.* Practitioners of management accounting and financial management shall not commit acts contrary to these standards nor shall they condone the commission of such acts by others within their organizations.

COMPETENCE

Practitioners of management accounting and financial management have a responsibility to:

- Maintain an appropriate level of professional competence by ongoing development of their knowledge and skills.
- Perform their professional duties in accordance with relevant laws, regulations, and technical standards.
- Prepare complete and clear reports and recommendations after appropriate analyses of relevant and reliable information.

CONFIDENTIALITY

Practitioners of management accounting and financial management have a responsibility to:

- Refrain from disclosing confidential information acquired in the course of their work except when authorized, unless legally obligated to do so.
- Inform subordinates as appropriate regarding the confidentiality of information acquired in the course of their work and monitor their activities to assure the maintenance of that confidentiality.
- Refrain from using or appearing to use confidential information acquired in the course of their work for unethical or illegal advantage either personally or through third parties.

INTEGRITY

Practitioners of management accounting and financial management have a responsibility to:

- Avoid actual or apparent conflicts of interest and advise all appropriate parties of any potential conflict.
- Refrain from engaging in any activity that would prejudice their ability to carry out their duties ethically.

- Refuse any gift, favor, or hospitality that would influence or would appear to influence their actions.
- Refrain from either actively or passively subverting the attainment of the organization's legitimate and ethical objectives.
- Recognize and communicate professional limitations or other constraints that would preclude responsible judgment or successful performance of an activity.
- Communicate unfavorable as well as favorable information and professional judgments or opinions.
- Refrain from engaging in or supporting any activity that would discredit the profession.

OBJECTIVITY

Practitioners of management accounting and financial management have a responsibility to:

- Communicate information fairly and objectively.
- Disclose fully all relevant information that could reasonably be expected to influence an intended user's understanding of the reports, comments, and recommendations presented.

RESOLUTION OF ETHICAL CONFLICT

In applying the standards of ethical conduct, practitioners of management accounting and financial management may encounter problems in identifying unethical behavior or in resolving an ethical conflict. When faced with significant ethical issues, practitioners of management accounting and financial management should follow the established policies of the organization bearing on the resolution of such conflict. If these policies do not resolve the ethical conflict, such practitioners should consider the following courses of action.

- Discuss such problems with the immediate superior except when it appears that the superior is involved, in which case the problem should be presented initially to the next higher managerial level. If a satisfactory resolution cannot be achieved when the problem is initially presented, submit the issues to the next higher managerial level. If the immediate superior is the chief executive officer, or equivalent, the acceptable reviewing authority may be a group such as the audit committee, executive committee, board of directors, board of trustees, or owners. Contact with levels above the immediate superior should be initiated only with the superior's knowledge, assuming the superior is not involved. Except where legally prescribed, communication of such problems to authorities or individuals not employed or engaged by the organization is not considered appropriate.
- Clarify relevant ethical issues by confidential discussion with an objective advisor (e.g., IMA Ethics Counseling service) to obtain a better understanding of possible courses of action. Consult your own attorney as to legal obligations and rights concerning the ethical conflict.
- If the ethical conflict still exists after exhausting all levels of internal review, there may be no other recourse on significant matters than to resign from the organization and to submit an informative memorandum to an appropriate representative of the organization. After resignation, depending on the nature of the ethical conflict, it may also be appropriate to notify other parties.

CASES FOR

Management Decision Making

CASE	RELATED CHAPTER	OVERVIEW
CASE-1 *Card-Mart Swims in the Dot-com Sea: Job Order Costing*	**2** Job Order Cost Accounting	This case is the first in a series of four cases that presents a business situation in which a traditional retailer decides to employ Internet technology to expand its sales opportunities. It requires the student to employ traditional job order costing techniques and then requests an evaluation of the resulting product costs.
CASE-2 *Card-Mart Swims in the Dot-com Sea: Activity-Based Costing*	**4** Activity-Based Costing	This case focuses on decision-making benefits of activity-based costing relative to the traditional approach. It also offers an opportunity to discuss the cost/benefit trade-off between simple ABC systems versus refined systems, and the potential benefit of using capacity rather than expected sales when allocating fixed overhead costs.
CASE-3 *CardMart Swims in the Dot-com Sea: Capital Budgeting*	**10** Capital Budgeting	This case is set in an environment in which the company is searching for new opportunities for growth. It requires evaluation of a proposal based on initial estimates as well as sensitivity analysis. It also requires evaluation of the underlying assumptions used in the analysis.
CASE-4 *Card-Mart Swims in the Dot-com Sea: Transfer Pricing*	**11** Transfer Pricing	This case illustrates the importance of proper transfer pricing for decision making as well as performance evaluation. The student is required to evaluate profitability using two different transfer pricing approaches and comment on the terms of the proposed transfer pricing agreement.
CASE-5 *Richland Circular Club Pro Rodeo Roundup*	**5** Cost-Volume-Profit Relationships **6** Budgeting Basics **9** Incremental Analysis	This comprehensive case is designed to be used as a capstone activity at the end of the course. It deals with a not-for-profit service company. The case involves many managerial accounting issues that would be common for a start-up business.

CARD-MART Inc.

CARD-MART SWIMS IN THE DOT-COM SEA: JOB ORDER COSTING

Developed by Thomas L. Zeller, Loyola University Chicago and Paul D. Kimmel, University of Wisconsin–Milwaukee

THE BUSINESS SITUATION

Card-Mart Inc. has operated for many years as a nationally recognized retailer of greeting cards and small gift items. It has 1,500 stores throughout the United States located in high-traffic malls.

During the late 1990s, as the stock price of many other companies soared, Card-Mart's stock price remained flat. As a result of a heated 1998 shareholders' meeting, the president of Card-Mart, William Green, came under pressure from shareholders to grow Card-Mart's stock value. As a consequence of this pressure, in 1999 Mr. Green called for a formal analysis of the company's options with regard to business opportunities.

Location was the first issue considered in the analysis. Card-Mart stores are located in high-traffic malls where rental costs are high. The additional rental cost was justified, however, by the revenue that resulted from these highly visible locations. In recent years, though, the intense competition from other stores in the mall selling similar merchandise has become a disadvantage of the mall locations.

Mr. Green felt that to increase revenue in the mall locations, Card-Mart would need to attract new customers and sell more goods to repeat customers. In order to do this, the company would need to add a new product line. However, to keep costs down, the product line should be one that would not require much additional store space. In order to improve earnings, rather than just increase revenues, Card-Mart would have to carefully manage the costs of this new product line.

After careful consideration of many possible products, the company's management found a product that seemed to be a very good strategic fit for its existing products: high-quality unframed and framed prints. The critical element of this plan was that customers would pick out prints by viewing them on wide-screen computer monitors in each store. Orders would be processed and shipped from a central location. Thus, store size would not have to increase at all. To offer these products, Card-Mart established a new business unit called WallDécor.com. WallDécor is a "profit center"; that is, the manager of the new business unit is responsible for decisions affecting both revenues and costs.

WallDécor was designed to distribute unframed and framed print items to each Card-Mart store on a just-in-time (JIT) basis. The system works as follows: The WallDécor Web site allows customers to choose from several hundred prints. The print can be purchased in various forms: unframed, framed with a metal frame and no matting, or framed with a wood frame and matting. When a customer purchases an unframed print, it is packaged and shipped the same day from WallDécor. When a customer purchases a framed print, the print is framed at WallDécor and shipped within 48 hours.

Each Card-Mart store has a computer linked to WallDécor's Web server so Card-Mart customers can browse the many options to make a selection. Once a selection is made, the customer can complete the order immediately. Store employees are trained to help customers use the Web site and complete the purchase. The advantage to this approach is that each Card-Mart store, through the WallDécor Web site, can offer a wide variety of prints, yet the individual Card-Mart stores do not have to hold any inventory of prints or framing materials. About the only cost to the individual store is the computer and high-speed line connection to WallDécor. The advantage to the customer is the wide variety of unframed and framed print items that can be conveniently purchased and delivered to the home or business, or to a third party as a gift.

WallDécor uses a traditional job-order costing system. Operation of WallDécor would be substantially less complicated, and overhead costs would be substantially less, if it sold only unframed prints. Unframed prints require no additional processing, and they can be easily shipped in simple protective tubes. Framing and matting requires the company to have multiple matting colors and frame styles, which requires considerable warehouse space. It also requires skilled employees to assemble the products and more expensive packaging procedures. Manufacturing overhead is allocated to each unframed or framed print, based on the cost of the print. This overhead allocation approach is based on the assumption that more expensive prints will usually be framed and therefore more overhead costs should be assigned to these items. The predetermined overhead rate is the total expected manufacturing overhead divided by the total expected cost of prints. This method of allocation appeared reasonable to the accounting team and distribution floor manager. Direct labor costs for unframed prints consist of picking the prints off the shelf and packaging them for shipment. For framed prints, direct labor costs consist of picking the prints, framing, matting, and packaging.

The information in Illustration 1-1 on the next page for unframed and framed prints was collected by the accounting and production teams. The manufacturing overhead budget is presented in Illustration 1-2.

Instructions

Use the information in the case and your reading from Chapters 1 and 2 of the text to answer each of the following questions.

1. Define and explain the meaning of a predetermined manufacturing overhead rate that is applied in a job-order costing system.
2. What are the advantages and disadvantages to using the cost of each print as a manufacturing overhead cost driver?
3. Using the information below, compute and interpret the predetermined manufacturing overhead rate for WallDécor.

ILLUSTRATION 1-1
Information about prints
and framed items for
Card-Mart

	Unframed Print	Steel-Framed Print, No Matting	Wood-Framed Print, with Matting
Volume—expected units sold	75,000	15,000	7,000
Cost Elements			
Direct materials			
Print (expected average cost for each of the three categories)	$12	$16	$20
Frame and glass		$4	$6
Matting			$2
Direct labor			
Picking time	10 minutes	10 minutes	10 minutes
Picking labor rate/hour	$12	$12	$12
Matting and framing time		20 minutes	30 minutes
Matting and framing rate/hour		$18	$18

ILLUSTRATION 1-2
Manufacturing overhead
budget for Card-Mart

Manufacturing Overhead Budget	
Supervisory salaries	$100,000
Factory rent	75,000
Equipment rent (framing and matting equipment)	50,000
Utilities	20,000
Insurance	10,000
Information technology	50,000
Building maintenance	11,000
Equipment maintenance	4,000
Budgeted total print cost	$320,000

4. Compute the product cost for the following three items.
   (a) Michael Jordan unframed print (base cost of print $12).
   (b) Walter Payton print in steel frame, no mat (base cost of print $16).
   (c) Wrigley Field print in wood frame with mat (base cost of print $20).
5. (a) How much of the total overhead cost is expected to be allocated to unframed prints?
   (b) How much of the total overhead cost is expected to be allocated to steel framed prints?
   (c) How much of the total overhead cost is expected to be allocated to wood framed prints?
   (d) What percentage of the total overhead cost is expected to be allocated to unframed prints?
6. Do you think the amount of overhead allocated to the three product categories is reasonable? Relate your response to this question to your findings in previous questions.
7. Anticipate business problems that may result from allocating manufacturing overhead based on the cost of the prints.

CARD-MART SWIMS IN THE DOT-COM SEA: ACTIVITY-BASED COSTING

*Developed by Thomas L. Zeller, Loyola University Chicago
and Paul D. Kimmel, University of Wisconsin–Milwaukee*

THE BUSINESS SITUATION

*M*r. Green, president of Card-Mart, created the WallDécor unit of Card-Mart three years ago to increase the company's revenue and profits. Unfortunately, even though WallDécor's revenues have grown quickly, Card-Mart appears to be losing money on WallDécor. Mr. Green has hired you to provide consulting services to WallDécor's management. Your assignment is to make WallDécor a profitable business unit.

Your first step is to talk with the WallDécor work force. From your conversations with store managers you learn that the individual Card-Mart stores are very happy with the WallDécor arrangement. The stores are generating additional sales revenue from the sale of unframed and framed prints. They are especially enthusiastic about this revenue source because the online nature of the product enables them to generate revenue without the additional cost of carrying inventory. WallDécor sells unframed and framed prints to each store at product cost plus 20 percent. A 20 percent mark-up on products is a standard policy of all Card-Mart intercompany transactions. Each store is allowed to add an additional mark-up to the unframed and framed print items according to market pressures. That is, the selling price charged by each store for unframed and framed prints is determined by each store manager. This policy ensures competitive pricing in the respective store locations, an important business issue because of the intense mall competition.

While the store managers are generally happy with the WallDécor products, they have noted a significant difference in the sales performance of the unframed prints and the framed prints. They find it difficult to sell unframed prints at a competitive price. The price competition in the malls is very intense. On average, stores find that the profits on unframed prints are very low because the cost for unframed prints charged by WallDécor to the Card-Mart stores is only slightly below what competing stores charge their customers for unframed prints. As a result, the profit margin on unframed prints is very low, and the overall profit earned is small even, with the large volume of prints sold. In contrast, stores make a very good profit on framed prints and still beat the nearest competitor's price by about 15 percent. That is, the mall competitors cannot meet at a competitive price the quality of framed prints provided by the Card-Mart stores. As a result, store managers advertise the lowest prices in town for high-quality framed prints. One store manager referred to WallDécor's computer on the counter as a "cash machine" for framed prints and a "lemonade stand" for unframed prints.

In a conversation with the production manager you learned that she believes that the relative profitability of framed and unframed prints is distorted because of improper product costing. She feels that the costs provided by the company's traditional job-order costing system are inaccurate. From the very beginning, she has carefully managed production and distribution costs. She explains, "WallDécor is essentially giving away expensive framed prints, and it appears that it is charging the stores too much for unframed prints." In her office she shows you her own product costing system, which supports her point of view.

Your tour of the information technology (IT) department provided additional insight as to why WallDécor is having financial problems. You discovered that to keep the Web site running requires separate computer servers and several information technology professionals. Two separate activities are occurring in the technology area. First, purchasing professionals and IT professionals spend many hours managing thousands of prints and frame and matting materials. Their tasks include selecting the prints and the types of framing material to sell. They also must upload, manage, and download prints and framing material onto and off of the Web site. The IT staff tells you much of their time is spent with framing and matting material. Only a highly skilled IT professional can properly scan a print and load it up to the site so that it graphically represents what it will look like, properly matted and framed.

In addition, you discover that a different team of IT professionals is dedicated to optimizing the operating performance of the Web site. These costs are classified as manufacturing overhead because a substantial amount of work is required to keep the site integrated with purchasing and production and to safeguard WallDécor's assets online. Most time-consuming is the effort to develop and maintain the site so that customers can view the prints as they would appear either unframed or framed and matted.

A discussion with the IT professionals suggests that the time spent developing and maintaining the site for the unframed prints is considerably less than that required for the framed prints and in particular for the framed and matted prints. Developing and maintaining a site that can display the unframed prints is relatively straightforward. It becomes more complicated when the site must allow the customer to view every possible combination of print with every type of steel frame, and it becomes immensely more complicated when one considers all of the possible wood frames and different matting colors. Obviously, a very substantial portion of the IT professionals' time and resources is required to present the over 1,000 different framing and matting options.

Based on your preliminary findings, you have decided that the company's ability to measure and evaluate the profitability of individual products would be improved if the company employed an activity-based costing (ABC) system. As a first step in this effort, you compiled a list of costs, activities, and values. Your work consisted of taking the original manufacturing overhead cost

($320,000, provided in Case 1) and allocating the costs to activities. You identified four activities: picking prints; inventory selection and management (includes general management and overhead); Web-site optimization; and framing and matting cost (includes equipment, insurance, rent, and supervisor's salary).

The first activity is picking prints. The estimated overhead related to this activity is $24,250. The cost driver for this activity is the number of prints. It is expected that the total number of prints will be 97,000. This is the sum of 75,000 unframed, 15,000 steel-framed, and 7,000 wood-framed.

ILLUSTRATION 2-1
Information for activity 1

Activity	Cost Driver	Estimated Overhead	Expected Use of Cost Driver
Picking prints	Number of prints	$24,250	(75,000 + 15,000 + 7,000) = 97,000 prints

The second activity is inventory selection and management. The cost driver for this activity is the number of components per print item. An unframed print has one component, a steel-framed print has two components (the print and the frame), and a wood-framed print has three components (the print, the mat, and the frame). The total number of components is expected to be 126,000.

ILLUSTRATION 2-2
Information for activity 2

Activity	Cost Driver	Estimated Overhead	Expected Use of Cost Driver
Inventory selection and management	Number of components: Print (1) Print and frame (2) Print, mat, frame (3)	$63,000	Prints: 75,000 components Print and frame: 15,000 × 2 = 30,000 components Print, mat, and frame 7,000 × 3 = 21,000 components Total = 126,000 components

The third activity is Web-site optimization. The total overhead cost related to Web-site optimization is expected to be $125,000. It was difficult to identify a cost driver that directly related Web-site optimization to the products. In order to reflect the fact that the majority of the time spent on this activity related to framed prints, you first split the cost of Web-site optimization between unframed prints and framed prints. Based on your discussion with the IT professionals, you determined that they spend roughly one-fifth of their time developing and maintaining the site for unframed prints, and the other four-fifths of their time on framed prints, even though the number of framed prints sold is substantially less than the number of unframed prints. As a consequence, you allocated $25,000 of the overhead costs related to Web-site optimization to unframed prints and $100,000 to framed prints. You contemplated having three

categories (unframed, steel-framed, and wood-framed with matting), but chose not to add this additional refinement.

Once the $125,000 of the third activity was allocated across the two broad product categories, the number of prints at *operating capacity* was used as the cost driver. Note that operating capacity was used instead of expected units sold. The overhead costs related to Web-site optimization are relatively fixed because the employees are salaried. If a fixed cost is allocated using a value that varies from period to period (like expected sales), then the cost per unit will vary from period to period. When allocating fixed costs it is better to use a base that does not vary as much, such as operating capacity. The advantage of using operating capacity as the base is that it keeps the fixed costs per unit stable over time.

ILLUSTRATION 2-3
Information for activity 3

Activity	Cost Driver	Estimated Overhead	Expected Use of Cost Driver
Web-site optimization:			
Unframed	Number of prints at capacity	$ 25,000	Unframed prints—100,000 print capacity
Framed	Number of prints at capacity	$100,000	Framed and/or matted prints—25,000 print capacity (16,000 steel; 9,000 wood)

The final activity is framing and matting. The expected overhead costs related to framing and matting are $107,750. None of this overhead cost should be allocated to unframed prints. The costs related to framing and matting are relatively fixed because the costs relate to equipment and other costs that do not vary with sales volume. As a consequence, like Web-site optimization, you chose to base the cost driver on levels at operating *capacity*, rather than at the expected sales level. The cost driver is the number of components. Steel-framed prints have two components (the print and frame), and wood-framed prints have three components (the print, mat, and frame). The total components at operating capacity would be steel frame 32,000 or (16,000 × 2) and wood frame 27,000 or (9,000 × 3,000).

ILLUSTRATION 2-4
Information for activity 4

Activity	Cost Driver	Estimated Overhead	Expected Use of Cost Driver
Framing and matting cost (equipment, insurance, rent, and supervisory labor)	Total item components	$107,750	Print and frame: 16,000 × 2 = 32,000 components at capacity Print, mat, and frame: 9,000 × 3 = 27,000 components at capacity Total = 59,000 components

To summarize, the overhead costs and cost drivers used for each product are expected to be:

ILLUSTRATION 2-5
Summary of overhead
costs and cost drivers

Activity	Cost Driver	Unframed	Steel-Framed, No Matting	Wood-Framed, with Matting	Total	Overhead Cost
Picking prints	Number of prints	75,000	15,000	7,000	97,000	$ 24,250
Inventory selection and management	Number of components	75,000	30,000	21,000	126,000	63,000
Web-site optimization	Number of prints at capacity	100,000			100,000	25,000
			16,000	9,000	25,000	100,000
Framing and matting	Number of components at capacity	na	32,000	27,000	59,000	107,750
						$320,000

Instructions

Answer the following questions.

1. Identify two reasons why an activity-based costing system may be appropriate for WallDécor.

2. Compute the activity-based overhead rates for each of the four activities.

3. Compute the product cost for the following three items using ABC. (Review Case 1 for additional information that you will need to solve this problem.)
   (a) Michael Jordan unframed print (base cost of print $12)
   (b) Walter Payton print in steel frame, no mat (base cost of print $16)
   (c) Wrigley Field print in wood frame with mat (base cost of print $20)

4. In Case 1 for Card-Mart, the overhead allocations using a traditional volume-based approach were $3 for Michael Jordan, $4 for Walter Payton, and $5 for Wrigley Field. The total product costs from Case 1 were Michael Jordan $17, Walter Payton $32, and Wrigley Field $44. The overhead allocation rate for unframed prints, such as the unframed Michael Jordan print in question 3, decreased under ABC compared to the amount of overhead that was allocated under the traditional approach in Case 1. Why is this the case? What are the potential implications for the company?

5. Explain why the overhead cost related to Web-site optimization was first divided into two categories (unframed prints and framed prints) and then allocated based on number of prints.

6. When allocating the cost of Web-site optimization, the decision was made to initially allocate the cost across two categories (unframed prints and framed prints) rather than three categories (unframed prints, steel-framed prints, and wood-framed prints with matting). Discuss the pros and cons of splitting the cost between two categories rather than three.

7. Discuss the implications of using operating *capacity* as the cost driver rather than the expected units sold when allocating fixed overhead costs.

8. (a) Allocate the overhead to the three product categories (unframed prints, steel-framed prints, and wood-framed prints with matting), assuming that the estimate of the expected units sold is correct and the actual amount of overhead incurred equaled the estimated amount of $320,000.
   (b) Calculate the total amount of overhead allocated. Explain why the total overhead of $320,000 was not allocated, even though the estimate of sales was correct. What are the implications of this for management?

 CASE 2 ◆ ◆ ◆ ◆ ◆ ◆ ◆ ◆ ◆ ◆ ◆ ◆

CARD-MART SWIMS IN THE DOT-COM SEA: CAPITAL BUDGETING

*Developed by Thomas L. Zeller, Loyola University Chicago
and Paul D. Kimmel, University of Wisconsin–Milwaukee*

THE BUSINESS SITUATION

Card-Mart stores, as well as the WallDécor division, have enjoyed healthy profitability during the last two years. Although the profit margin on prints is often thin, the volume of print sales has been substantial enough to generate 15 percent of Card-Mart store profits. In addition, the increased customer traffic resulting from the prints has generated significant additional sales of related non-print products. As a result, the company's rate of return has exceeded the industry average during this two-year period. Card-Mart store managers likened the e-business leverage created by WallDécor to a "high-octane" fuel to supercharge the stores' profitability.

This high rate of return (ROI) was accomplished even though WallDécor's venture into e-business proved to cost more than originally budgeted. Why was it a profitable venture even though costs exceeded estimates? Card-Mart stores were able to generate a considerable volume of business for WallDécor. This helped spread the high e-business operating costs, many of which were fixed, across many unframed and framed prints. This experience taught top management that maintaining an e-business structure and making this business model successful are very expensive and require substantial sales as well as careful monitoring of costs.

WallDécor's success gained widespread industry recognition. The business press documented WallDécor's approach to using information technology to increase profitability. The company's CEO, William Green, has become a frequent luncheon speaker on the topic of how to use information technology to offer a great product mix to the customer and increase shareholder value. From the outside looking in, all appears to be going very well for Card-Mart stores and WallDécor.

However, the sun is not shining as brightly on the inside at Card-Mart. The mall stores that compete with Card-Mart have begun to offer prints at very competitive prices. Although Card-Mart stores enjoyed a selling price advantage for a few years, the competition eventually responded, and now the pressure on selling price is as intense as ever. The pressure on the stores is heightened by the fact that the company's recent success has led shareholders to expect the stores to generate an above-average rate of return. Mr. Green is very concerned about how the stores and WallDécor can continue on a path of continued growth.

Fortunately, more than a year ago, Mr. Green anticipated that competitors would eventually find a way to match the selling price of prints. As a consequence, he formed a committee to explore ways to employ technology to further reduce costs and to increase revenues and profitability. The committee is comprised of store managers and staff members from the information technology, marketing, finance, and accounting departments. Early in the group's discussion, the focus turned to the most expensive component of the existing business model—the large inventory of prints that WallDécor has in its centralized warehouse. In addition, WallDécor incurs substantial costs for shipping the prints from the centralized warehouse to customers across the country. Ordering and maintaining such a large inventory of prints consumes valuable resources.

One of the committee members suggested that the company should pursue a model that music stores have experimented with, where CDs are burned in the store from a master copy. This saves the music store the cost of maintaining a large inventory and increases its ability to expand its music offerings. It virtually guarantees that the store can always provide the CDs requested by customers.

Applying this idea to prints, the committee decided that each Card-Mart store could invest in an expensive color printer connected to its online ordering system. This printer would generate the new prints. WallDécor would have to pay a royalty on a per print basis. However, this approach does offer certain advantages. First, it would eliminate all ordering and inventory maintenance costs related to the prints. Second, shrinkage from lost and stolen prints would be reduced. Finally, by reducing the cost of prints for WallDécor, the cost of prints to Card-Mart stores would decrease, thus allowing the stores to sell prints at a lower price than competitors. The stores are very interested in this option because it enables them to maintain their current customers and to sell prints to an even wider set of customers at a potentially lower cost. A new set of customers means even greater related sales and profits.

As the accounting/finance expert on the team, you have been asked to perform a financial analysis of this proposal. The team has collected the information presented in Illustration 3-1.

Available Data	Amount
Cost of equipment (zero residual value)	$700,000
Cost of ink and paper supplies (purchase immediately)	100,000
Annual cash flow saving for WallDécor	150,000
Annual additional store cash flow from increased sales	100,000
Sale of ink and paper supplies at end of 5 years	50,000
Expected life of equipment	5 years
Cost of capital	12%

ILLUSTRATION 3-1
Information about the proposed capital investment project

CASE 3 ◆ ◆ ◆ ◆ ◆ ◆ ◆ ◆ ◆ ◆ ◆ ◆ Cases for Management Decision Making CASES-13

Instructions

Mr. Green has asked you to do the following as part of your analysis of the capital investment project.

1. Calculate the net present value using the numbers provided. Assume that annual cash flows occur at the end of the year.

2. Mr. Green is concerned that the original estimates may be too optimistic. He has suggested that you do a sensitivity analysis assuming all costs are 10% higher than expected and that all inflows are 10% less than expected.

3. Identify possible flaws in the numbers or assumptions used in the analysis, and identify the risk(s) associated with purchasing the equipment.

4. In a one-page memo, provide a recommendation based on the above analysis. Include in this memo: (a) a challenge to store and WallDécor management and (b) a suggestion on how Card-Mart stores could use the computer connection for related sales.

CARD-MART SWIMS IN THE DOT-COM SEA: TRANSFER PRICING ISSUES

Developed by Thomas L. Zeller, Loyola University Chicago and Paul D. Kimmel, University of Wisconsin–Milwaukee

THE BUSINESS SITUATION

*T*wo years ago, prior to a major capital-budgeting decision (Case-3), William Green, the president of Card-Mart, faced a challenging transfer pricing issue. He knew that Card-Mart store managers had heard about the ABC study (see Case-2) and that they knew a price increase for framed items would soon be on the way. In an effort to dissuade him from increasing the transfer price for framed prints, several store managers e-mailed him with detailed analyses showing how framed-print sales had given stores a strong competitive position and had increased revenues and profits. The store managers mentioned, however, that while they were opposed to an increase in the cost of framed prints, they were looking forward to a price decrease for unframed prints.

Management at WallDécor was very interested in changing the transfer pricing strategy. You had reported to them that setting the transfer price based on the product costs calculated by using traditional overhead allocation measures had been a major contributing factor to its non-optimal performance.

Here is a brief recap of what happened during your presentation to Mr. Green and the WallDécor managers. Mr. Green smiled during your presentation and graciously acknowledged your excellent activity-based costing (ABC) study and analysis. He even nodded with approval as you offered the following suggestions.

1. WallDécor should decrease the transfer price for high-volume, simple print items.
2. WallDécor should increase the transfer price for low-volume, complex framed print items.
3. Your analysis points to a transfer price that maintains the 20 percent markup over cost.

4. Adoption of these changes will provide WallDécor with an 11 percent return on investment (ROI), beating the required 10 percent expected by Card-Mart's board of directors.

5. Despite the objections of the store managers, the Card-Mart stores must accept the price changes.

Finishing your presentation, you asked the executive audience, "What questions do you have?" Mr. Green responded as follows.

"Your analysis appears sound. However, it focuses almost exclusively on WallDécor. It appears to tell us little about how to move forward and benefit the entire company, especially the Card-Mart retail stores. Let me explain.

I am concerned about how individual store customers will react to the price changes, assuming the price increase of framed-print items is passed along to the customer. Store managers will welcome a decrease in the transfer price of unframed prints. They have complained about the high cost of prints from the beginning. With a decrease in print cost, store managers will be able to compete against mall stores for print items at a competitive selling price. In addition, the increase in store traffic for prints should increase the sales revenue for related items, such as cards, wrapping paper, and more. These are all low-margin items, but with increased sales volume of prints and related products, revenues and profits should grow for each store.

Furthermore, store managers will be upset with the increase in the cost of framed prints. Framed prints have generated substantial revenues and profits for the stores. Increasing the cost of framed prints to the stores could create one of three problems: First, a store manager may elect to keep the selling price of framed-print items the same. The results of this would be no change in revenues, but profits would decline because of the increase in cost of framed prints.

Second, a store manager may elect to increase the selling price of the framed prints to offset the cost increase. In this case, sales of framed prints would surely decline and so would revenues and profits. In addition, stores would likely see a decline in related sales of other expensive, high-quality, high-margin items. This is because sales data indicate that customers who purchase high-quality, high-price framed prints also purchase high-quality, high-margin items such as watches, jewelry, and cosmetics.

Third, a store manager may elect to search the outside market for framed prints."

Mr. Green offered you the challenge of helping him bring change to the company's transfer prices so that both business units, Card-Mart stores and WallDécor, win. From his explanation, you could see and appreciate that setting the transfer price for unframed and framed prints impacts sale revenues and profits for related items and for the company overall. You immediately recognized the error in your presentation by simply providing a solution for WallDécor alone.

You drove home that night thinking about the challenge. You recognized the need and importance of anticipating the reaction of Card-Mart store customers to changes in the prices of unframed and framed prints. The next day, the marketing team provided you with the following average data.

- For every unframed print sold (assume one print per customer), that customer purchases related products resulting in $5 of additional profit.

- For every framed print sold (assume one print per customer), that customer purchases related products resulting in $8 of additional profit.
- Each Card-Mart store sets its own selling price for unframed and framed prints. Store managers need this type of flexibility to be responsive to competitive pressures. On average the following pricing for stores is as follows: unframed prints $21, steel-framed without matting $50, wood-framed with matting $70.

Instructions

Answer each of the following questions.

1. Prepare for class discussion what you think were the critical challenges for Mr. Green. Recognize that WallDécor is a profit center and each Card-Mart store is a profit center.

2. After lengthy and sometimes heated negotiations between WallDécor and the store managers, a new transfer price was determined that calls for the stores and WallDécor to split the profits on unframed prints 30/70 (30% to the store, 70% to WallDécor) and the profits on framed prints 50/50. The following additional terms were also agreed to:

   - "Profits" are defined as the store selling price less the ABC cost.
   - Stores do not share the profits from related products with WallDécor.
   - WallDécor will not seek to sell unframed and framed print items through anyone other than Card-Mart.
   - WallDécor will work to decrease costs.
   - Card-Mart stores will not seek suppliers of prints other than WallDécor.
   - Stores will keep the selling price of framed prints as before the change in transfer price. On average, stores will decrease the selling price of unframed prints to $19.50, with an expected increase in volume to 100,000 prints.

   Analyze how WallDécor and the stores benefited from this new agreement. In your analysis, first (a) compute the profits of the stores and WallDécor using traditional amounts related to pricing, cost, and a 20% mark-up on WallDécor costs. Next, (b) compute the profits of the stores and WallDécor using the ABC cost and negotiated transfer price approach. Finally, (c) explain your findings, linking the overall profits for stores and WallDécor.

   The following data apply to this analysis. (Round all calculations to three decimal places.)

	Unframed print	Steel-framed, no matting	Wood-framed, with matting
Average selling price by stores before transfer pricing study	$21	$50	$70
Average selling price by stores after transfer pricing study	$19.50	$50	$70
Volume at traditional selling price	75,000	15,000	7,500
Volume at new selling price	100,000	15,000	7,500
WallDécor cost (traditional)	$17	$32	$44
ABC cost	$15	$37.15	$50.48

3. Review the additional terms of the agreement listed in instruction 2, above. In each case, state whether the item is appropriate, unnecessary, ineffective, or potentially harmful to the overall company.

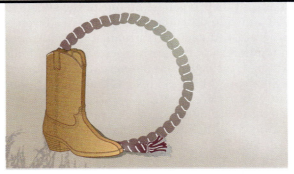

RICHLAND CIRCULAR CLUB PRO RODEO ROUNDUP

Developed by Jessica Frazier, Eastern Kentucky University and Patricia Mounce, Mississippi College

THE BUSINESS SITUATION

*W*hen Jacqueline Kaiser became president-elect of the Circular Club of Richland, Kentucky, she was asked to suggest a new fund-raising activity for the club. After a considerable amount of research, Jacqueline proposed that the Circular Club sponsor a professional rodeo. In her presentation to the club, Jacqueline said that she wanted a fund-raiser that would (1) continue to get better each year, (2) give back to the community, and (3) provide the club a presence in the community. Jacqueline's goal was to have an activity that would become an "annual community event" and that would break even the first year and raise $5,000 the following year. In addition, based on the experience of other communities, Jacqueline believed that a rodeo could grow in popularity so that the club would eventually earn an average of $20,000 annually.

A rodeo committee was formed. Jacqueline contacted the world's oldest and largest rodeo-sanctioning agency to apply to sponsor a professional rodeo. The sanctioning agency requires a rodeo to consist of the following five events: Bareback Riding, Bronco Riding, Steer Wrestling, Bull Riding, and Calf Roping. Because there were a number of team ropers in the area and because they wanted to include females in the competition, members of the rodeo committee added Team Roping and Women's Barrels. Prize money of $2,500 would be paid to winners in each of the seven events.

Members of the rodeo committee contracted with J Bar J Rodeo, a livestock contractor on the rodeo circuit, to provide bucking stock, fencing, and chutes. Realizing that costs associated with the rodeo were tremendous and that ticket sales would probably not be sufficient to cover the costs, the rodeo committee sent letters to local businesses soliciting contributions in exchange for various sponsorships. Exhibiting Sponsors would contribute $1,000 to exhibit their products or services, while Major Sponsors would contribute $600. Chute Sponsors would contribute $500 to have the name of their business on one of the six bucking chutes. For a contribution of $100, individuals would be included in a Friends of Rodeo list found in the rodeo programs. At each performance the rodeo announcer would repeatedly mention the names of the businesses and individuals at each level of sponsorship. In addition, large signs and banners with the names of the businesses of the Exhibiting Sponsors, Major Sponsors, and Chute Sponsors were to be displayed prominently in the arena.

A local youth group was contacted to provide concessions to the public and divide the profits with the Circular Club. The Richland Circular Club Pro Rodeo Roundup would be held on June 1, 2, and 3. The cost of an adult ticket was set at $8 in advance or $10 at the gate; the cost of a ticket for a child 12 or younger was set at $6 in advance or $8 at the gate. Tickets were not date-specific. Rather, one ticket would admit an individual to one performance of his or her choice—Friday, Saturday, or Sunday. The rodeo committee was able to secure a location through the county supervisor board at a nominal cost to the Circular Club. The arrangement allowed the use of the county fair grounds and arena for a one-week period. Several months prior to the rodeo, members of the rodeo committee had been assured that bleachers at the arena would hold 2,500 patrons. However, on Saturday night there were 1,663 in attendance and all seats were filled. Attendance was 898 Friday and 769 on Sunday.

The following revenue and expense figures relate to the first year of the rodeo.

Receipts		
Contributions from sponsors	$19,500	
Receipts from ticket sales	29,637	
Share of concession profits	1,513	
Sale of programs	600	
Total receipts		$51,250
Expenses		
Livestock contractor	26,000	
Prize money	17,500	
Contestant hospitality	3,315*	
Sponsor signs for arena	1,900	
Insurance	1,800	
Ticket printing	1,050	
Sanctioning fees	925	
Entertainment	900	
Judging fees	750	
Port-a-potties	716	
Rent	600	
Hay for horses and sand for arena	538	
Programs	500	
Western hats to first 500 children	450	
Hotel rooms for stock contractor	325	
Utilities	300	
Interest expense	251	
Miscellaneous fixed costs	105	
Total expenses		57,925
Net loss		$(6,675)

ILLUSTRATION 5-1
Revenue and expense data, year 1

*The club contracted with a local caterer to provide a tent and food for the contestants. The cost of the food was contingent on the number of contestants each evening. Information concerning the number of contestants and the costs incurred are as follows:

	Contestants	Total Cost
Friday	74	$1,003
Saturday	96	1,212
Sunday	83	1,100

On Wednesday after the rodeo, members of the rodeo committee met to discuss and critique the rodeo. John Art, CPA and President of the Circular Club, commented that the club did not lose money. Rather, John said, "The club made an investment in the rodeo."

Instructions

Answer each of the following questions.

1. Do you think it was necessary for Jacqueline Kaiser to stipulate that she wanted a fund-raiser that would (1) continue to get better each year, (2) give back to the community, and (3) provide the club a presence in the community? Why or why not?

2. What did John Art mean when he said the club had made an investment in the rodeo?

3. Is John's comment concerning the investment consistent with Jacqueline's idea that the club should have a fund-raiser that would (1) continue to get better each year, (2) give back to the community, and (3) provide the club a presence in the community? Why or why not?

4. What do you believe is the behavior of the rodeo expenditures in relation to ticket sales?

5. Determine the fixed and variable cost components of the catering costs using the high-low method.

6. Assume you are elected chair of the rodeo committee for next year. What steps would you suggest the committee take to make the rodeo profitable?

7. Jacqueline, John, and Abe Dobbins, the Fundraising Chairperson, are beginning to make plans for next year's rodeo. Jacqueline believes that by negotiating with local feed stores, innkeepers, and other business owners, costs can be cut dramatically. John agrees. After carefully analyzing costs, John has estimated that the fixed expenses can be pared to approximately $48,000. In addition, John has determined that variable costs are 4% of total gross receipts.

    After talking with business owners who attended the rodeo, Abe is confident that funds solicited from sponsors will increase. Abe is comfortable in budgeting revenue from sponsors at $20,125. The local youth group is unwilling to provide concessions to the audience unless they receive all of the profits. Not having the personnel to staff the concession booth, members of the Circular Club reluctantly agree to let the youth group have 100 percent of the profits from the concessions. In addition, members of the rodeo committee, recognizing that the net income from programs was only $100, decide not to sell rodeo programs next year. Compute the breakeven in dollars of ticket sales assuming Abe and John are correct in their assumptions.

8. Jacqueline has just learned that you are calculating breakeven in ticket sales. She is still convinced that the Club can make a profit using the assumptions in number 7 above.
    (a) Calculate the dollars of ticket sales needed in order to earn a target profit of $5,000.
    (b) Calculate the dollars of ticket sales needed in order to earn a target profit of $10,000.

9. Are the facilities at the fairgrounds adequate to handle crowds needed to generate ticket revenues calculated in number 8 above to earn a $5,000 profit? Show calculations to support your answers.

10. Prepare a budgeted income statement for next year using the estimated revenues from sponsors and other assumptions in number 7 above. In addition, use ticket sales based on the target profit of $10,000 estimated in 8(b). The cost of the livestock contractor, prize money, sanctioning fees, entertainment, judging fees, rent, and utilities will remain the same next year.

   Changes in expenses include the following: Members of the Club have decided to eliminate all costs related to contestant hospitality by soliciting a tent and food for the contestants and taking care of the "Contestant Hospitality Tent" themselves. The county has installed permanent restrooms at the arena, eliminating the need to rent port-a-potties. The rodeo committee intends to pursue arrangements to have hotel rooms, hay and sand, and children's hats provided at no charge in exchange for sponsorships. The cost of banners varies with the number of sponsors. Signs and More charged the Circular Club $130 for each Exhibiting Sponsor banner and $80 for each Major Sponsor banner. At this time there is no way to know whether additional sponsors will be Exhibiting Sponsors or Major Sponsors. Therefore, for budgeting purposes you should increase the cost of the banners by the percentage increase in sponsor contributions. (*Hint*: Round all calculations to three decimal places.) By checking prices, the Circular Club will be able to obtain insurance providing essentially the same amount of coverage as this year for only $600. For the first rodeo the Club ordered 10,000 tickets. Realizing the constraints on available seating, the Club is ordering only 5,000 tickets for next year, and therefore its costs are reduced 50%. The interest expense for next year will be $200, and miscellaneous fixed costs are to be budgeted at $100.

11. A few members in the Circular Club do not want to continue with the annual rodeo. However, Jacqueline is insistent that the Club must continue to conduct the rodeo as an annual fund-raiser. Jacqueline argues that she has spent hundreds of dollars on western boots, hats, and other items of clothing to wear to the rodeo. Are the expenses related to Jacqueline's purchases of rodeo clothing relevant costs? Why or why not?

12. Rather than hire the local catering company to cater the Contestant Hospitality Tent, members of the Circular Club are considering asking Shady's Bar-B-Q to cater the event in exchange for a $600 Major Sponsor spot. In addition, Eventions, a local party supply business, will be asked to donate a tent to use for the event. Eventions will also be given a $600 Major Sponsor spot. Several members of the Club are opposed to this consideration, arguing that the two Major Sponsor spots will take away from the money to be earned through other sponsors. Abe Dobbins has explained to the members that the Major Sponsor signs for the arena cost only $48 each. In addition, there is more than enough room to display two additional sponsor signs. What would you encourage the Club to do concerning the Contestant Hospitality Tent? Would your answer be different if the arena were limited in the number of additional signs that could be displayed? What kind of cost would we consider in this situation that would not be found on a financial statement?

PHOTO CREDITS

Chapter 1
Opener: Andrew Olney/Stone. Page 6: Premium Stock/CORBIS. Page 8: Paul A. Souders/CORBIS. Page 17 (top): Eric Kamp/Index Stock. Page 17 (bottom): Andrew Sacks/Stone. Page 18: Shaun Egan/Stone. Page 41: Courtesy Anchor Glass Container Corp.

Chapter 2
Opener: Karen Beard/Stone. Page 48: David Frazier/Stone. Page 52: James Porto/FPG International. Page 56: Ed Honowitz/Stone. Page 63: Robert Tinney/Corbis Stock Market. Page 65: Richard Pasley/Stock, Boston/ PNI. Page 85: Courtesy Parlex Corporation, Methuen, MA.

Chapter 3
Opener: John Burwell/FoodPix. Page 95: John Wilkinson/CORBIS. Page 106: James Leynse/SABA.

Chapter 4
Opener: Courtesy Super Donut. Page 148: Paul Chesley/Stone. Page 151: PhotoDisc. Page 153: David Madison/Stone. Page 159: Nick Vedros, Vedros & Associates/Stone.

Chapter 5
Opener: Dave Crosier/Stone. Page 190: Martin Schreiber/Stone. Page 199: CORBIS. Page 203: Cyberimage/Stone. Page 204: Yael/Retna. Page 207: Micheal Simpson/FPG International.

Chapter 6
Opener: ©2000 Artville, Inc. Page 231: Gary Conner/Index Stock. Page 237: Peter Zeray/Photonica. Page 238: Donald C. Johnson/Corbis Stock Market. Page 240: Ralph Mercer/Stone. Page 243: Larry Gilpin/Stone. Page 246: Paul Muns/Stock Illustration Source. Page 249: Mark Wiens/Stone. Page 266: Courtesy Network Computing Devices, Inc.

Chapter 7
Opener: ©EyeWire. Page 284: ©2000 Artville, Inc. Page 287: ©EyeWire. Page 318: Courtesy Computer Associates.

Chapter 8
Opener: Dick Luria/FPG International. Page 327: John Syoboda/FoodPix. Page 332: Michel Tchervkoff/The Image Bank. Page 335: Courtesy United Parcel Service. Page 340: Garry Gay/The Image Bank. Page 361: Courtesy Glassmaster Company, PO Box 788, Lexington, SC.

Chapter 9
Opener: Gary Gladstone/The Image Bank. Page 371: Ed Eckstein/CORBIS. Page 376: William Tautic/Corbis Stock Market. Page 380: PhotoDisc. Page 381: Mitch Kezar/Stone.

Chapter 10
Opener: Pat Lacroix/The Image Bank. Page 401: Chris Thomaidis/Stone. Page 413: Tim Jonke/The Image Bank. Page 416: Ken Ross/Liaison Agency, Inc.

Chapter 11
Opener: Don Bonsey/Stone. Page 437: Jac Depczyk/The Image Bank. Page 441: Anthony Marsland/Stone. Page 453: ©2000 Artville, Inc. Page 476: Courtesy Merck & Company Inc.

Chapter 12
Opener: John Lund/Stone. Page 483: Jonathan Elderfield/Liaison Agency, Inc. Page 486: Mark Richards/PhotoEdit. Page 515: Microsoft is a registered trademark of Microsoft Corporation. Page 516: D. Redfearn/The Image Bank. Page 521: Index Stock. Page 522: Courtesy Intel. Page 545: Courtesy Saint-Gobain.

Chapter 13
Opener: Mitchell Funk/The Image Bank. Pages 559, 561, 562, 565, 566, 582, and 583: Kellogg's logo is a registered trademark of Kellogg Company. Used with permission. Page 567: SuperStock. Page 569: Courtesy J.C. Penney. Page 571: Jay Ahrend/FoodPix. Page 573: Mark Wiens/Stone. Page 579: Courtesy Toys "R" Us.

COMPANY INDEX

SUBJECT INDEX